THE
JANUARY 6TH
REPORT

THE
JANUARY 6TH
REPORT

THE REPORT OF THE SELECT COMMITTEE
TO INVESTIGATE THE JANUARY 6TH ATTACK
ON THE UNITED STATES CAPITOL

WITH A FOREWORD BY
DARREN BEATTIE
FORMER SPEECHWRITER FOR PRESIDENT DONALD J. TRUMP

Skyhorse Publishing

Skyhorse Publishing books may be purchased in bulk at special discounts for sales promotion, corporate gifts, fund-raising, or educational purposes. Special editions can also be created to specifications. For details, contact the Special Sales Department, Skyhorse Publishing, 307 West 36th Street, 11th Floor, New York, NY 10018 or info@skyhorsepublishing.com.

Skyhorse® and Skyhorse Publishing® are registered trademarks of Skyhorse Publishing, Inc.®, a Delaware corporation.

Visit our website at www.skyhorsepublishing.com.

10 9 8 7 6 5 4 3 2 1

Library of Congress Cataloging-in-Publication Data is available on file.

Cover design by Brian Peterson

ISBN: 978-1-5107-7508-4
Ebook ISBN: 978-1-5107-7517-6

Printed in the United States of America

CONTENTS

THE JANUARY 6TH REPORT

FOREWORD TO THE JANUARY 6TH REPORT

BY DR. DARREN J. BEATTIE

January 6 is a date that will live in controversy. To many top Democrats, much of the legacy media, and even some establishment Republicans that "darkest of days" warrants a spot in the pantheon of great American tragedies—right alongside Pearl Harbor and September 11. Vice President Kamala Harris likened the so-called "assault on democracy" on January 6 to both of those attacks. Not to be outdone, President Biden described the January 6 "insurrection" as "the worst attack on Democracy since the Civil War." Former president George W. Bush commemorated the twentieth anniversary of 9/11 with a subtle comparison to January 6—a striking comparison also entertained by fellow Republican war hawks Liz Cheney and Lindsey Graham.

Much of Trump's base, meanwhile, embraces a radically different interpretation of the events of January 6. Though Congressman Andrew Clyde indelicately downplayed the January 6 rioters' intrusion into the Capitol as a "normal tourist visit," he nonetheless reflected the thinking of many Trump supporters in his view that "there were some rioters, and some who committed acts of vandalism . . . but to call it an insurrection is a bold-faced lie." Many share the view that among the modest percentage of rally-goers who committed violence or vandalism, many were not Trump supporters at all, and indeed may have been Antifa sympathizers. Still others, including the author of this foreword, advance the highly disturbing thesis that the federal government may have had a hand in allowing the riot to happen, and even in some cases may have actively instigated it.

These radically different interpretations of the events of January 6 reflect the extreme political polarization that helped to condition those events in the first place. And while there is surely hyperbole on both sides, the notion that the events of January 6 amount to "terrorism," much less "terrorism" of a variety comparable to September 11, is not only untenable, but also absurd and dangerous.

September 11 was the deadliest terrorist attack in history, claiming the lives of nearly three thousand victims and resulting in insurance losses of approximately $40 billion. This, of course, does not include the impact on the stock market, airline industry, or the immeasurable blood and treasure spent on the ensuing Afghanistan and Iraq Wars. The alleged "insurrection" of January 6, by contrast, directly resulted in four deaths, all of whom were Trump supporters, including the unarmed Ashli Babbitt, who was fatally shot in the neck by a Capitol Police officer. According to March 2021 estimate, the rioters who "stormed the Capitol" inflicted a grand total of $1.5 million in property damage—a fraction of the $1 billion damage caused by politically charged riots in the aftermath of George Floyd's death, much less September 11.

There is one crucial sense, however, in which the otherwise offensively stupid comparison between September 11 and January 6 is devastatingly appropriate. The War on Terror that President George W. Bush launched in response to the 9/11 attack didn't simply involve wars in Afghanistan and Iraq, it involved an unprecedented enlargement and reconfiguration of America's national security apparatus. The Patriot Act, the NSA's domestic surveillance campaign, and the creation of the mammoth Department of Homeland Security mark just a few highlights of the muscular post-9/11 national security state. Just as we associate 9/11 with the War on Terror, and specifically the war on "Radical Islamic Terror," so might we associate January 6 with the "Domestic War on Terror"—that is, the government's repurposing of the national security state domestically in order to silence, suppress, and crush the alleged national security threats emerging from the political right. This Domestic War on Terror kicked into high gear in the aftermath of Donald Trump's presidential victory in 2016. For better or worse, the national security state perceived not only Donald Trump, but the Trump phenomenon (the energies surrounding the emergence of Trump as a political force) as an existential threat and acted accordingly.

In early September 2021, *Politico* reported on a Department of Homeland Security memo identifying "white supremacy" as the number one terror threat America faces—ahead of not only the left-wing groups responsible for an extended summer of fire and violence while protesting the death of George Floyd (DHS did not even name Antifa as a threat), but also ahead of foreign terrorist groups. President Biden's attorney general Merrick Garland echoed FBI Director Christopher Wray in his assessment that racially motivated extremism of the "especially white" variety presents the premier "threat to democracy." President Biden himself took the occasion of his State of the Union speech to echo the alleged consensus of intelligence agencies that "the most lethal threat to the homeland today is white supremacist terrorism."

In another speech, Biden was quick to assert that the January 6 "deadly insurrection was about white supremacy." One or two out of the tens of thousands of people who attended the January 6 rally carried a Confederate flag. A Capitol Police officer alleged that rioters repeatedly called him the "n-word" after he revealed that he voted for Biden. In the mountains of video of January 6, no evidence has emerged that would support that officer's claims, and we can be pretty sure if there were such evidence the media would be happy to play it nonstop to add additional scandal to the so-called insurrection. Even the Proud Boys militia group, described in countless media headlines as "white supremacist," was run by an Afro-Cuban during January 6.

Ultimately, the lack of evidence of genuine white supremacy in relation to January 6 is immaterial. When Biden suggests that January 6 was motivated by white supremacy, he means "white supremacy" in the broad sense, in which partisan detractors and much of the media refer to anything adjacent to Donald Trump as white supremacist. This is the same sense in which Hillary Clinton described January 6 as a "tragically predictable result of white supremacist grievances aired by Donald Trump," and referred to the phrase "Make America Great Again" as a slogan favored by "white nationalists." It is in the context of this broader, politically weaponized conception of "white supremacy" that we can see how ominous it really is that major national security bureaucracies now target white supremacy as the number one security threat. The Domestic War on Terror then starts to look dangerously distant from a situation in which the nation's national security apparatus exists to protect Americans from foreign threats, and more like a situation in which the national security apparatus exists to suppress, demonize, and destroy one political faction of the nation on behalf of it rival.

Many on the right are frustrated with the seeming inordinate attention the medi and hostile Democrat politicians give to January 6 and would prefer to ignore it an move on. And if January 6 were treated as an isolated event, this attitude might hav some validity. Even if we grant that January 6 as a factual matter is far less significan than advertised, January 6 is powerfully intertwined narratively with a number of th most important themes of the past several years, from COVID, to the 2020 electior to the aforementioned reconfiguration and political weaponization of America national security apparatus. As the saying goes, many on the right may not be inter ested in January 6, but January 6 is interested in them. The right needs to understan and address January 6 if only for purposes of self-preservation in counteracting th dominant "domestic terrorist insurrection" narrative used as a pretext to portray ter of millions of Trump supporters as potential terror threats.

It is not just the right that should be interested in a proper understanding of Janu ary 6. The increasing political weaponization of the national security state is a tren that ought to concern all citizens, even those who at the moment are sufficientl apolitical or politically correct as to not be directly affected by it. Even those wh might despise Trump and his supporters would benefit from reassessing with an ope mind what they think they know about the events of January 6. Even if we grant th offensively absurd notion that it was an act of domestic terror comparable to 9/1 shouldn't the rioters at least be granted the same courtesy the *New York Tim* extended to the rioters protesting George Floyd's death in front of the White Hous The protestors set off fires that spread to the "Church of the Presidents," assaulte police officers, and stormed through the barricades of the Department of Treasur right next to the White House, forcing then-president Trump to retreat to a speci security bunker. The *Times* chastises Trump for painting such protestors with th broad brush of violent radicalism "without addressing the underlying conditions tha led such rioters to the streets."[1]

---

1 Peter Baker and Maggie Haberman, "As Protests and Violence Spill Over, Trump Shrinks Back," *New Yo Times*, May 31, 2020, https://www.nytimes.com/2020/05/31/us/politics/trump-protests-george-floyd.html.

No matter one's political perspective, there is much at stake in gaining an accurate understanding of the context, significance, and causes of the events of January 6. In theory, a well-functioning, objective investigative body like the January 6 Committee might even make sense toward gaining such understanding. Indeed, part of the purpose of this foreword is to sketch out the sorts of questions that such a body might want to investigate in order to get to the bottom of the events of January 6 and prevent anything similar from happening in the future.

Before exploring such questions, however, it will be useful to show that the current January 6 Committee is the absolute worst vehicle imaginable for investigating January 6. Far from serving as an objective fact-finding body, the January 6 Committee functioned as such an egregiously performative, partisan kangaroo display as to make propagandists in North Korea blush.

JANUARY 6 COMMITTEE: GENEALOGY OF A SHOW TRIAL

Established on July 1, 2021, via a party-line vote, the United States House Select Committee to Investigate the January 6 Attack on the United States Capitol (hereafter Committee) announced its purpose to "investigate and report on the facts, circumstances, and causes" of the "domestic terrorist attack" upon the United States Capitol Complex on January 6. As suggested above, an accurate understanding of the "facts, circumstances, and causes" of the events of January 6 should be of great interest to all Americans. Unfortunately, one would be hard pressed to conceive of an institution less suited to an unbiased, objective, and accurate investigation of January 6.

A quick glance at the profiles of those staffing the Committee is damning enough. The Committee of nine members of Congress consists of seven Democrats and two Republicans, all approved by arch-partisan Speaker of the House Nancy Pelosi, who was one of the driving forces behind the second impeachment of Donald Trump. The two Republicans on the committee, Liz Cheney and Adam Kinzinger, are stalwart Trump-detractors who arguably oppose Trump more than most of the Democrats on the Committee. Thus, the putatively (slightly) bipartisan Committee consists of seven anti-Trump Democrats who voted for Trump's impeachment and two anti-Trump Republicans who voted for Trump's impeachment (out of over two hundred House Republicans, only ten voted for impeachment). One of the Democrat

Committee members, Jamie Raskin, served as lead impeachment manager for the second impeachment of Donald Trump. Another member, Democrat congressman Adam Schiff, was one of the most aggressive promoters of the so-called Steele dossier that became the basis of the Russiagate conspiracy alleging that Donald Trump colluded with Russians during the 2016 campaign. The Steele dossier turned out to be a complete fabrication and the Russian source of the information was later charged with lying to the FBI.

Recall that the second impeachment against Trump charged the former president with "incitement of insurrection." It is hardly conceivable that those who not only supported impeachment (and conviction) for this charge, but played active leadership roles in the impeachment, could conduct a fresh and objective investigation into the "causes and circumstances of January 6." Impeachment wasn't even fast enough for some January 6 Committee members—Republican Adam Kinzinger was so eager to get rid of Trump that he was the first Republican to urge Mike Pence to invoke the 25th Amendment to declare Trump unfit for office and have him removed as president.

Just as noteworthy as the heavy presence in the Committee of those associated with impeachment efforts against Trump is the presence of officials with connections to the national security state. The aforementioned Adam Schiff is currently the head of the United States House Permanent Select Committee on Intelligence. Liz Cheney daughter of infamous war hawk and national security insider Dick Cheney, sits on the Armed Services Committee. The senior staff to the January 6 Committee includes a former CIA inspector general, a Homeland Security advisor to Chairman Bennie Thompson, and a career Department of Homeland Security official who has worked with the organization since its inception in the aftermath of September 11.

The most striking and unreported national security connection exists with the chairman of the January 6 Committee itself, Representative Bennie Thompson. Not only is Bennie Thompson the chair of the January 6 Committee, he also happens to be the chair of the Homeland Security Committee. In fact, this is Bennie Thompson's ninth term as chairman of the Homeland Security Committee. Essentially whenever Democrats run Congress Thompson is tapped to run the Homeland

Security Committee, which oversees all matters pertaining to the Department of Homeland Security.

In 2007, Thompson's first act as chair of the Homeland Security Committee was to sponsor a bill that granted sweeping new police powers to the DHS, using the pretext of 9/11. Given his favored position with both the Democrat establishment and with the national security state, there is perhaps no man better suited than Bennie Thompson to use his perch on the January 6 Committee to facilitate the weaponization of the DHS domestically against Trump supporters, using January 6 as a pretext (more on this later).

It is fair to say that our biographical tour of the January 6 Committee is sufficient to manage our expectations regarding the objectivity of its investigation. The Committee was never set up to present a good faith account of January 6, and so we won't waste our time with an extended point-by-point refutation of the Committee's arguments. Nonetheless, we will briefly cover some of the highlights of the Committee's farcical conduct.

The most striking (albeit not terribly surprising) aspect of the January 6 Committee is how relentlessly Trump-focused it is. Chairman Bennie Thompson kicked off the televised Committee hearing with the pronouncement that January 6 was the culmination of "an attempted coup . . . a sprawling multistep conspiracy aimed at overturning an election." Donald Trump was the "center of the conspiracy," who spurred on the mob to the Capitol in order to "subvert American democracy." Liz Cheney asserted that Trump "summoned the mob, assembled the mob, and lit the flame of attack" and carried out a sophisticated "seven-part plan to overturn the 2020 election and prevent the peaceful transition of power."

The actual evidence that President Trump did anything close to incitement is underwhelming, to put it generously. Many Trump detractors, including Liz Cheney, lean on specific phrases in Trump's January 6 speech, such as his exhortation to "fight like hell, and if you don't fight like hell, you're not going to have a country anymore." That such a routine piece of political rhetoric could be adduced as proof that Trump somehow "summoned" the mob or incited a riot against the Capitol gives us a sense of how maniacally desperate and ultimately ridiculous the case against

Trump really is. And this is leaving aside the fact that Trump explicitly urged his supporters to march to the Capitol "peacefully and patriotically." Nonetheless, the allegedly incriminating nature of the "fight like hell" phrase played a substantial role in the second impeachment of Donald Trump for inciting the Capitol riot.

Perhaps out of recognition that the incitement case against Trump is too weak on its own, the Committee alleges that Trump's "summoning the mob" on January 6 was the culmination of "a sophisticated seven-part plan to overturn the 2020 election and prevent the peaceful transition of power," in Liz Cheney's words. Other than the claim that Trump directly summoned the mob to the Capitol, the seven-point plan pertains to Trump's behavior days, weeks, and in some cases months before January 6, acting upon the so-called "Big Lie" that the 2020 election was stolen from him.

For all of the Committee's fixation on the term "Big Lie," the Committee presents precious little if any evidence that Donald Trump didn't genuinely believe that election fraud ultimately tipped the balance against him, causing him to lose the 2020 election to Joe Biden. The Committee's first televised hearing repeated ad nauseum a video clip of Trump's former attorney general Bill Barr referring to Trump's election fraud theories as "bullshit." Apart from Barr, the Committee referenced numerous Trump associates who claim to have told the former president that his election fraud theories were wrong. The simple fact that some of Trump's senior staffers may have disagreed with Trump on the election issue is hardly proof that Trump was persuaded by them, and that therefore Trump's efforts to "stop the steal" amounted to a deliberate lie and malicious attempt to prevent the legitimate and peaceful transition of power. Barr's additional remark that Trump was "completely detached from reality" when it came to the 2020 election unwittingly undermines the Committee's suggestion that Trump was lying about the matter.

It would take us too far afield to consider the election fraud allegations in detail or the merits. It is perhaps understandable that Trump wouldn't simply have been convinced by staffers who disagreed, no matter how senior. From the beginning, the Trump presidency was plagued with personnel who revealed themselves to be just as antagonistic toward Trump as his more conspicuous detractors—by the end of the first term even Trump was beginning to realize this. During the "lame duck" period of Trump's presidency, many staff members would be especially concerned with preserving whatever political capital they had left, and the way to do that would not have been going along with Trump's election fraud theories, irrespective of their truth or falsity. No doubt Trump also must have remembered Bill Barr's September 2020 interview on CNN, in which the former attorney general emphatically warned that mail-in voting was "playing with fire," and characterized implementing an unprecedented mail-in voting scheme, which "as a matter of logic is very open to fraud and coercion," as "reckless and dangerous," given how divided the country is and how important it is for the public to accept the legitimacy of the election. In light of this damning assessment by Attorney General Bill Barr (which, curiously, the Committee did not highlight), and the context of relentless political antagonism against Trump coming from just about every institution in the United States, one can perhaps understand why Trump would approach the 2020 election results with some degree of skepticism.

Many of the other charges against Trump have to do with actions he allegedly took with staffers and other political officials and institutions stemming from his conviction that a substantial degree of fraud occurred in 2020. For instance, the Committee made much of reports that President Trump considered replacing acting Attorney General Jeffrey Rosen with another Department of Justice staffer, Jeffrey Clark, who was more closely aligned with Trump's views on the election. Executive branch employees, including the acting attorney general, serve at the pleasure of the president. There is nothing ostensibly wrong about the president considering the appointment of someone more in line with his thinking to the position, just as DOJ staffers were within their rights when they threatened to resign should Trump go ahead with that replacement.

Another point of contention with the Committee is Trump's belief that Vice President Pence had the authority not to certify the election results, and that states could appoint "alternate slates" of electors who would be more favorable to Trump than Biden. Like the broader issue of voter fraud itself, it would be impossible and inadvisable to adjudicate the merits of the legal theories behind these strategies. It suffices to say that approaches such as the "alternate slates" strategy enjoyed the support of well-credentialed legal professionals, including University of Chicago–educated law professor John Eastman. There is no question that Trump believed the election was substantially compromised by fraud, and contemplated strategies to address this fraud that were procedurally available to him according to the advice of various legal professionals.

The spectacle of the televised portion of the January 6 Committee was still less convincing when it comes to the case against Trump. Some of the highlights include the so-called "bombshell" testimony of Cassidy Hutchinson, a former aide to then White House chief of staff Mark Meadows. Hutchinson reported that a Secret Service agent refused Trump's request to head to the Capitol after his January 6 speech whereupon Trump allegedly said, "I'm the f-ing President," lunged toward the Secret Service agent, and grabbed the steering wheel of the presidential limo.

A few things must be understood in relation to this remarkable testimony. Hutchinson did not claim to have witnessed this incredible display in person, but rather heard about it from a member of Trump's security detail. It is unclear why the January 6 Committee wouldn't prefer to have the alleged eyewitness to Trump's behavior testify, rather than rely on Hutchinson's secondhand testimony. Remarkably, both the alleged eyewitness, Secret Service agent Robert Engel, and the individual who Hutchinson claims told her the story, Tony Ornato, had given private depositions to the January 6 Committee. Indeed, why not have both testify to give their account of the events? At the very least, release the transcript of their depositions. The Committee's negligence in this regard makes more sense in light of multiple news reports citing Secret Service sources refuting Hutchinson's account of events, including Secret Service sources claiming that both Engel and Ornato denied Hutchinson claims and wanted the opportunity to testify to this. The Secret Service even tweeted a message indicating a desire and willingness to testify on the matter, though this message was apparently either declined or ignored.

Of course, the Hutchinson debacle would not have been possible if the January 6 Committee allowed for the cross-examination of its witnesses. Allowing cross-examination would severely undermine the credibility of many of the Committee's cherry-picked star witnesses, and therefore detract from the show-trial experience.

Cross-examination would have been especially instructive for January 6 hearing witness Stephen Ayres. Ayres is a self-described "family man" who allegedly attended Trump's speech on January 6 and ended up going inside the Capitol, for which he faces criminal charges. The January 6 Committee paraded Ayres before the public as someone who had been duped by Trump, who maliciously led Ayres to the Capitol with his lies about stolen election and other rhetoric. Ayres claims Trump's talk of a stolen election "made him very upset" and he "just needed to be down there" at the Capitol. He expressed anger at being duped by Trump's "big lie" regarding the stolen election, revealing that "it makes him mad" to think about Trump's election rhetoric "because I was hanging on every word."

In true show-trial fashion, the Committee made a big spectacle of Ayres's dramatic denunciation of his former belief that election fraud had taken place in 2020. Whereas he used to have "horse blinders" on thanks to Trump's lies, he has since "done his own research" and discovered the error of his ways. With great contrition and remorse, he assured the Committee that he no longer believed in the thought crime of election fraud. And indeed, to call the belief a thought crime is hardly an exaggeration—some January 6 defendants have actually received stiffer penalties as a result of their belief that the election was stolen.

The Committee does not bother to explain how Trump, who called on rally-goers to march peacefully to the capitol, could be responsible for Ayres's regrettable decision to go into the Capitol. Most importantly, the Committee did not reveal a potentially profound conflict of interest affecting Ayres's testimony. Indeed, Ayres had entered a cooperation deal with the government to "aid in the investigation of 1/6." Ayres's codefendant, who was being charged with non-violent offenses related to entering the Capitol, tragically committed suicide. It is hard to believe that Ayres's testimony before the Committee was entirely unaffected by the fact that he still awaited sentencing, and that the government reserved the right to change its sentencing guidelines based on his behavior.

This is just one of many examples of disturbing coordination, whether formal or informal, between the January 6 Committee and the Department of Justice. The Department of Justice announced its seditious conspiracy indictment against Proud

Boys members just days before the Committee's first and much-hyped televised hearing which heavily emphasized the Proud Boys' alleged role in the so-called attack on the Capitol. In a far more outrageous example of political intimidation, federal authorities raided the home of former senior Department of Justice official Jeffrey Clark, who claimed that they "put him in the streets in his pajamas and took his electronics." This political spectacle occurred just one day before a televised January 6 Committee hearing set to discuss Clark's alleged role in Trump's January 6 plot. As discussed above, Clark's great crime was that he was a senior DOJ official who happened to agree with the president that there was substantial election fraud, wanted to take steps to address the fraud, and who President Trump allegedly dared to consider naming as attorney general.

Thus, we see a pattern according to which the DOJ would time various actions against individuals to generate press coverage ahead of a January 6 Committee hearing concerning said individuals. Still more troubling, we see the January 6 Committee using its subpoena power to legally compromise political targets close to Trump. The Committee voted to recommend criminal charges against Jeffrey Clark for refusing to comply with its subpoena. Former White House chief strategist Steve Bannon was convicted of contempt of Congress for refusing to comply with the Committee's subpoena regarding privileged communications with former President Trump.

The notion that such a heavily politicized body as the Committee would have subpoena power to demand sensitive conversations between senior political officials and the President of the United States is indeed remarkable. The contempt of Congress charge applied to those refusing subpoenas is a very rare one, and convictions are rarer still. The fact that the Committee is pursuing such charges at all—and in the case of Steve Bannon, charges which may result in real jail time—underscores how aggressively and ruthlessly political the body really is.

From the standpoint of inappropriate political abuse on the part of the Committee, the most troubling of all is the pressure the Committee exerts both implicitly and explicitly on the Department of Justice to criminally prosecute Donald Trump. Despite the incredible hype, the Committee's kangaroo-style hearings were a disappointing ratings flop. But the Committee's lackluster performance in television ratings may not matter, depending on the Committee's success in persuading an audience of one—namely, Attorney General Merrick Garland. In fact, during a press conference, Garland took the ominous step of announcing that he was watching the Committee hearings and sternly assuring the public that "all of the January 6 prosecutors are watching the hearings as well." It would be one thing if the Committee were generally discounted as the highly tendentious political spectacle that it is. It is quite another when the head of the Department of Justice, which is overseeing January 6 criminal prosecutions, lends gravitas to the Committee by assuring the public that he and the January 6 prosecutors are watching the hearings closely. This, combined with the fact that the Department of Justice would time its actions against certain individuals to coincide with the January 6 Committee's televised hearings, ascribes a legal weight to the Committee which, as we have seen, lacks any of the balance and rigor that one would expect from a legal proceeding.

Given the Committee's inordinate and indeed maniacal focus on Trump, it is no surprise that one of the chief purposes of the Committee is to create pressure and pretext for the Department of Justice to criminally prosecute Donald Trump. Committee member Adam Kinzinger expressed his hope that the DOJ would move forward with prosecuting Trump. Many commentators have expressed the view that the Committee effectively tees up a ready-made criminal prosecution against Trump to the Department of Justice. One of the most vocal advocates of this position is former Obama official Norm Eisen, who, with Noah Bookbinder and Fred Wertheimer, penned an Opinion piece for CNN titled, "The January 6 Committee is methodically building a case for criminal conspiracy." Eisen advertised one of his many media appearances on this topic with the statement, "after two blockbuster hearings, everyone is asking if the January 6 Committee has enough evidence for a criminal prosecution to make criminal referrals" against Donald Trump—"I think yes," he added.

It is rather illuminating to consider the Committee's flimsy allegations against Trump for interfering with the peaceful transfer of power in light of the prospect of the DOJ's prosecution of Trump and the Committee's role in assisting that prosecution. One might be forgiven for entertaining the thought that Joe Biden's Department of Justice hanging the prospect of criminal prosecution over Joe Biden's 2024 presidential rival constitutes a far greater threat to the peaceful transfer of power and other basic democratic norms, especially given how tenuous, circumstantial, and contrived the criminal evidence against Trump really is.

The Committee's inordinate focus on Trump's role on January 6, together with the prospect of criminal prosecution for Trump, highlights why some would describe the Committee and associated efforts as a third impeachment of Trump. It certainly functions as a third impeachment insofar as it is clearly designed to neutralize Trump and his allies as a political force.

A brief look at the genealogy of the January 6 Committee's case against Trump shows that this description is no mere rhetorical flourish. Of all of the conflicts of interest pointing toward the hopelessly partisan nature of the Committee, perhaps none is so egregious as the seldom reported fact that the Committee's chairman, Bennie Thompson, was the lead plaintiff in a lawsuit against Donald Trump for the former president's alleged role in "inciting" an insurrection on January 6. The lawsuit named four defendants: Donald Trump, Rudy Giuliani, the Oath Keepers militia group, and the Proud Boys militia group. In his February 2021 complaint, Thompson alleges an elaborate theory whereby Trump and members of his inner circle coordinated with militia groups such as the Proud Boys and Oath Keepers to incite a crowd to attack the Capitol. The conspiracy theory Thompson alleges in his lawsuit—namely, that the storming of the Capitol was the foreseeable result of a "carefully coordinated campaign" by Trump to prevent the certification of the election—is strikingly similar to the foregone conclusion advanced by the January 6 Committee.

Bennie Thompson ultimately dropped the lawsuit when he was appointed to head the January 6 Committee in order to "avoid the appearance of conflict." One wonders how it wouldn't be a conflict of interest for someone who filed a personal lawsuit against Trump advancing a specific theory that Trump incited the January 6 insurrection to lead an allegedly objective Committee tasked with investigating January 6

Equally striking as the similarity of Thompson's lawsuit with the Committee's theory of the case are its similarities with the failed second impeachment of Donald Trump for inciting an insurrection on January 6. This is especially noteworthy considering that Thompson filed his lawsuit scarcely a month after the second failed impeachment attempt against Trump. In this context, it is difficult not to view Bennie

Thompson's lawsuit as an extension of the second impeachment of Trump, and therefore as a "missing link," as it were, between second impeachment of Trump and the Committee.

The case gets even more damning when we look into the details of Thompson's lawsuit. As mentioned above, Thompson filed his lawsuit against Trump, ready-made and complete with a theory of the case, scarcely a month after the failed second impeachment attempt against Trump. Given the timeline alone, it is hard to imagine that the planning for Thompson's lawsuit began too long after Trump's second impeachment, and at the very least there is little chance that it reflects a fresh reflection on January 6. It is also highly unlikely that Bennie Thompson himself somehow came up with the theory of the case presented in the lawsuit, and one wonders whether the lawsuit was undertaken primarily under Thompson's initiative or whether he was chosen as an optimal vehicle for the continuation of procedural legal attacks on Trump go all the way back to the first days of his election.

Taking a closer look at the Thompson lawsuit, we see that Thompson was joined by both the NAACP and a lawyer named Joseph Sellers, of the law firm Cohen Milstein Sellers & Toll. Sellers isn't just some random lawyer, and this wouldn't be the first time Sellers was involved in legal action to harass and hinder Trump. In fact, Sellers was counsel to one of the very first legal efforts against Trump, a lawsuit against Trump for his alleged violation of the emoluments clause. This absurd suit was predicated on the theory that foreign officials staying at Trump properties while visiting DC amounted to a violation of the Constitution's emoluments clause, which bans presidents from accepting gifts from foreign officials.

Joseph Sellers's emoluments clause lawsuit was organized by a group called Citizens for Responsibility and Ethics in Washington (CREW). CREW is a lawfare outfit that enjoyed favorable mention in Clinton operative David Brock's infamous memo (written before Trump took office) on how to knee-cap the Trump presidency with lawfare, censorship, and other tools. CREW was founded by Joseph Sellers's friend, former Obama ethics czar Norm Eisen—yes, the same Norm Eisen quoted a few paragraphs above as being one of the most aggressive proponents of the notion that the January 6 Committee has established the basis for an effective criminal prosecution of Trump. And when it comes to plots against Trump, few are more dedicated than Eisen. Apart from the fact that Eisen's organization CREW was ultimately responsible for no less than 180 lawsuits against the Trump administration, Eisen also drafted ten articles of impeachment against Trump before Trump ever made the call to Ukraine that became the subject of his first impeachment attempt (on which Eisen sat as special counsel). Similarly, the emoluments clause lawsuit against Trump in which Sellers joined Eisen as co-counsel was teed up and ready to go just days after Trump's inauguration. The timeline of these lawsuits against Trump suggests that they do not reflect good faith, considered reactions to Trump's behavior, but rather a preordained attack strategy to nullify the 2016 election and ensure that such an outcome can never happen again.

Thus, Joseph Sellers, the key lawyer spearheading Bennie Thompson's personal lawsuit against Trump for January 6, was a key participant going back to the earliest days of Trump's presidency in a coordinated effort to paralyze and subvert the Trump presidency with politicized and highly adversarial legal action. How could a January 6 Committee run by Bennie Thompson be anything but a politicized sham?

Just because the January 6 Committee is totally unsuited to fulfill its stated mission to investigate the events of January 6 and prevent a repeat of such events, does not mean that such an endeavor is not worthwhile. For the remainder of this foreword, we will explore some key points that a fair, objective, and unbiased Committee would explore in order to better understand what really happened on January 6.

JANUARY 6: "INTELLIGENCE FAILURE" OR INTELLIGENCE OPERATION?

With all the obsessive and politicized focus on Donald Trump, the Committee fail to adequately explore what is perhaps the most puzzling mystery of January 6— namely, the astonishing security failures that had to take place in order for the January 6 rally to transform into a riot, complete with a so-called "breach" of the Capitol. Given everything that was to transpire in Washington, DC on January 6, it would be bizarre enough if the Capitol had merely a routine level of security on that particular day. Any remotely substantive study of January 6 reveals that far from not having enhanced security, there seemed to be uniquely poor security on that day.

To begin with, it doesn't take a security professional to realize that January 6 would be a day that would warrant additional security in Washington, DC generally, and at the Capitol in particular. Congress was set to certify the results of a highly controversial election, about which President Trump was scheduled to speak on precisely the issue of controversy. In early November, Trump supporters conducted numerous "Stop the Steal" protests at various state Capitols, including Michigan, Arizona, New York, and Oregon, to name a few. Before the Stop the Steal protests at state capitols, there were numerous high-profile protests against COVID restrictions at various state capitols. The most notable of these was an April protest in which hundreds of protestors, some armed, entered the Michigan Capitol. It is important to note that all of these protests were entirely peaceful and legal—in Michigan, one is allowed to open-carry firearms, and the protestors were let into the Michigan state Capitol, subject to the appropriately comical condition that they had their temperatures checked for COVID. Granting the fact that such protests (in contrast to the Black Lives Matter protests of the summer) were peaceful and legal, they nonetheless would have reinforced the commonsense understanding that the US Capitol would require additional security on a day like January 6.

One would think that the above commonsense considerations would make it into the type of routine threat assessment that security agencies conduct before such events as protests and rallies. Not only did such considerations not make it into such threat assessments, these routine assessments curiously did not occur in preparation for January 6. Indeed, for whatever reason, the FBI failed to produce a joint intelligence bulletin ahead of January 6, and the Department of Homeland Security failed to produce a threat assessment. A source described to NPR the DHS's omission of a routine threat assessment as an "intelligence failure and . . . weird."[2] But like many things associated with January 6, it gets still weirder. The individual whose responsibility it was to produce such a threat assessment, Principal Deputy General Counsel Joseph Maher, is actually a senior staffer on the January 6 Committee, hired by none other than Liz Cheney! How odd that the Committee hires as a staffer someone it

---

2 Dina Temple-Raston, "Why Didn't the FBI and DHS Produce a Threat Report Ahead of The Capitol Insurrection?" *Morning Edition* NPR, January 13, 2021, https://www.npr.org/2021/01/13/956359496/why-didnt-the-fbi-and-dhs-produce-a-threat-report-ahead-of-the-capitol-insurrect.

should really have on the witness stand to explain in detail why no routine threat assessment for January 6 was written at the DHS. Perhaps Liz Cheney should be questioned as to why, of all people she could have hired on her staff for the January 6 Committee, she chose this individual. One would think Committee chairman Bennie Thompson would take a special interest in this, given that Bennie Thompson is the chairman of the Homeland Security Committee and Maher is a career DHS official, having joined at the organization's inception in 2002.

The FBI's failure to produce a joint intelligence bulletin ahead of January 6 is still more bizarre given the information we know that the Bureau had at its disposal. Numerous reports emerged of several quite specific warnings pertaining to January 6 from the FBI field office in Norfolk, VA. This so-called "Norfolk memo," issued on January 5, reportedly identified specific threats to members of Congress. "Be ready to fight. Congress needs to hear glass breaking, doors being kicked in . . . Go there ready for war," were some of the statements from an online thread mentioned in the FBI's memo. The memo, which was shared with the Capitol Police and DC Metro Police, also reportedly included maps of a tunnel system inside the Capitol complex. Another map depicted where caravans may have intended to depart from meeting points in South Carolina, Kentucky, and Pennsylvania, en route to DC.

The Norfolk memo exposed the FBI's original claim, advanced by assistant director of Washington Field Office Steven D'Antuono (more on him later), that the FBI lacked any intelligence suggesting there could be a need for additional security at the US Capitol on January 6. Once the Norfolk memo became known to the public, the FBI's position shifted to the claim that the memo did not provide sufficiently "digested" intelligence to be actionable. This claim is hard to believe, especially in light of other actions we know the FBI took in the days before January 6. According to an NBC report, senior FBI officials acknowledged that prior to Jan 6, the FBI had obtained "credible and actionable information about individuals who were planning on traveling"[3] to DC on January 6 with disruptive or violent intentions. The same

---

3 Ken Dilanian et al., "FBI, NYPD told Capitol Police about possibility of violence before riot, senior officials say," NBC News, January 10, 2021, https://www.nbcnews.com/news/crime-courts/fbi-nypd-told-capitol-police-about-possibility-violence-riot-senior-n1253646.

report revealed that the FBI took efforts "to discourage such individuals from going to DC."

It looks plausible that the FBI took steps to prevent certain pro-Trump media influencers from attending events on January 6 as well. On January 5, for instance, pro-Trump media personality Milo Yiannopoulos sent the following ominous message on social network Parler: "Just had a knock on the door. I won't be going to DC. Whatever operation they've got running to fuck with patriots, it's massive and they aren't playing around. Take care, everyone."

If the FBI was concerned enough about January 6 to dissuade certain people from going to DC, it was also concerned enough to attempt to recruit informants in the weeks leading up to January 6. Former Green Beret Jeremy Brown released a recording of an encounter he had with Department of Homeland Security agents in December of 2020. The DHS agents expressed unspecified concern about something that might transpire in January, and attempted to recruit Brown, who had recently joined the Oath Keepers militia group, to work as a confidential informant. The two DHS agents revealed to Brown that he was only one of nineteen individuals that they intended to approach, presumably to make similar proposals. If just two Tampa DHS agents approached nineteen people in Tampa alone, this suggests Brown's encounter was a part of a much more aggressive campaign to recruit informants in various militia groups leading up to January 6. We know from court documents that the vice president of the Oath Keepers militia group was an FBI informant, likely one of many embedded within the organization. In September of 2021, the *New York Times* confirmed that the FBI had at least two active informants embedded within the Proud Boys on January 6, suggesting, in the *Times*'s own description, that "federal law enforcement had a far greater visibility into the assault on the Capitol, even as it was taking place, than was previously known."[4] A more recent *New York Times* report conceded that the number of informants could be as many as eight. One of the Proud Boys informants was texting his FBI handler contemporaneously throughout the day,

---

4 Alan Feuer and Adam Goldman, "Among Those Who Marched Into the Capitol on Jan. 6: An F.B.I. Informant," *New York Times*, September 25, 2021, https://www.nytimes.com/2021/09/25/us/politics/capitol-riot-fbi-informant.html.

including during the initial breach of Capitol grounds and when he entered the Capitol building itself.

An interesting detail about this particular informant, who according to leaked documents, began a relationship with federal authorities back in July, is that he travelled to DC from Kansas City by way of Lexington, Kentucky. Recall that the Norfolk FBI field office memo mentioned Kentucky as one of the hubs from which caravans would transport potentially unruly rally participants to DC. This raises the question of whether the information regarding the Kentucky rally point came from the informant in question, and if so, whether this implies that information of other rally points in South Carolina and Pennsylvania suggests there were additional informants who arrived in DC from those hubs. In any case, the presence of informants is known to be far greater than that which was officially acknowledged by FBI director Christopher Wray. Indeed, it is very easy to underestimate the degree of federal infiltration especially into the most prominent militia groups associated with January 6—namely the Oath Keepers and Proud Boys. Both the founder of the Proud Boys, Enrique Tarrio, and senior Proud Boy member Joe Biggs, have been charged with seditious conspiracy and are known to have been FBI informants in the past, as a matter of public record.

If the January 6 Committee were serious about getting to the bottom of January 6, one would expect them to use their subpoena and investigative power to determine just how many informants were embedded within the militia groups whose members the Justice Department has since prosecuted for January 6–related crimes. It is one thing to be caught off guard, but at a certain level of informant penetration one has to start asking troubling questions as to why the FBI and other government agencies didn't act upon the information available to them.

Some of the Department of Justice's behavior in the days leading up to January 6 was so remarkable that it is astonishing that neither the January 6 Committee nor the national media has bothered to ask further questions. In January of 2022, William Arkin published a remarkable story[5] revealing that on January 3, heads of multiple

---

5 William M. Arkin, "Exclusive: Secret Commandos with Shoot-to-Kill Authority Were at the Capitol," *Newsweek*, January 3, 2022, https://www.newsweek.com/exclusive-secret-commandos-shoot-kill-authority -were-capitol-1661330.

elite government special operations teams met in Quantico, VA to prepare for "extreme possibilities" related to January 6. Unbeknownst to the Capitol Police, secret FBI and military commandos with "shoot to kill" authority had been deployed around the Capitol on January 6. The report reveals that these extraordinary forces operating in the shadows were deployed at the request of then acting attorney general Jeffrey Rosen—not at the request of any other agency. FBI tactical teams from this operation, among other things, responded to pipe bombs that were discovered at the Democratic National Committee and Republican National Committee buildings just a few blocks from the Capitol, while other agents were deployed around the Capitol to provide "selective security" to Congress and Capitol staff. The author finishes the piece with a burning question, which, again, any serious January 6 Committee would have investigated: "What was it that caused the Department of Justice to see January 6 as an extraordinary event" that would have justified the highly unusual activation of multiple elite commando units in DC and around the Capitol?

Perhaps the most puzzling example that contradicts the notion that authorities were simply caught off guard comes from the Washington, DC fusion center. The *Washington Post* covers a series of uncanny alarm bells sounded by Donell Harvin, who served as chief of Homeland Security and Intelligence and head of the Fusion Intelligence Center for Washington, DC. According to the *Post*,[6] Harvin saw increasing signs of violence expected on January 6 when Congress met to formalize the electoral vote. Harvin was reportedly so concerned that he took the extraordinary step of calling the DC Health Department and urging them to prepare for a mass casualty event—"empty your emergency rooms," he said, "and stock up your blood banks."

Still more striking than the severity of Harvin's warnings is their almost impossible specificity. The *Post* report reveals that Harvin's fusion center coordinated with counterpart fusion centers and the alarm bells were all ringing not only for a specific date, but a specific time—"the hour, the date, and the location of concern was the same: 1:00 p.m., US Capitol, January 6th." The specificity is truly remarkable given the fact

---

6 Reporting by Jacqueline Alemany et al., "The Attack: Before, During and After" *Washington Post*, October 31, 2021, https://www.washingtonpost.com/politics/interactive/2021/jan-6-insurrection-capitol/.

that the very first and decisive breach point of Capitol grounds, on the west side of the Capitol, occurred at exactly 12:53 p.m.

Amazingly, this specific prediction is not the most remarkable one that came from Donell Harvin's Washington, DC fusion center. The same report takes note of an aide to Harvin who arrived at a still more incredibly specific concern that he expressed at a December 30 planning session: "someone could plant an improvised explosive device near the Capitol . . . with law enforcement distracted, extremists might then band together and attack government buildings, maybe even the Capitol."

As it so happens, this is precisely what transpired. Indeed, on January 6 pipe bombs were discovered at the Republican National Committee building and the Democratic National Committee building, barely half a mile away from the Capitol. What's even more incredible is the timing of the pipe bombs' discovery. Indeed, according to news reports, the first pipe bomb was discovered fortuitously by a pedestrian doing her laundry at approximately 12:40 p.m. on January 6. Within fifteen minutes, authorities arrived on the scene and a second pipe bomb was discovered near the Democratic National Committee building. As mentioned above, the first and decisive breach of the Capitol grounds occurred on the west side of the Capitol at 12:53 p.m. Authorities including Capitol Police began responding to the pipe bomb at just the same time, almost to the exact minute, that the very first breach of the Capitol barriers took place. The timing was so perfectly aligned to the initial breach that the pipe bombs must have been placed for diversionary purposes. Former Capitol Police chief Steven Sund suggested that the location of the pipe bombs and timing of their discovery led him to believe that the pipe bombs were placed to divert resources away from the Capitol Police as the breach of Capitol barriers began.

And we see the exact same scenario entertained by Harvin's aide at the DC Fusion Intelligence Center, as reported by the *Washington Post*—namely, that "someone could plant an improvised explosive device near the Capitol . . . with law enforcement distracted, extremists might then band together and attack government buildings, maybe the Capitol." Furthermore, the timing of the pipe bombs' discovery matches precisely with the report that the DC fusion center was concerned specifically with 1:00 p.m. on January 6 at the Capitol. Just to put a fine point on it, the pedestrian who discovered the pipe bomb at the RNC building, less than a mile from the Capitol, discovered it at approximately 12:40 p.m., and reported that the timer on the bomb was set to twenty minutes, which would add up to exactly 1:00 p.m.!

One would think that such a remarkable set of coincidences would have prompted a genuine investigation into January 6 to interview the employees at the DC fusion center who reportedly made such remarkably accurate predictions regarding January 6.

But the story of the January 6 pipe bombs gets even stranger when we consider the significance of one critical detail which seems to have been completely overlooked: both of the pipe bombs were hooked up to mechanical one-hour kitchen timers. Given that the FBI's released footage depicts the pipe bomber planting bombs on the evening of January 5, this presents some challenging questions that remain woefully unaddressed and unexplored. Given that the pipe bomber used a mechanical timer with a one-hour limit, and he or she planted the bombs around 8:00 p.m. on January 5, there was no way that the pipe bomber could have intended for the bombs to go off on the sixth. Unless the pipe bombs simply had nothing to do with January 6, this would seem to suggest that the pipe bombs weren't meant to go off, but rather were intended as a diversionary tool, just as Capitol Police Chief Steven Sund speculated. But in order for the pipe bombs to function as the type of diversion that would facilitate the Capitol breach, they would have to be found pretty much exactly when they were found. If the pipe bombs were found earlier, this would cause a premature evacuation of congressional buildings and likely lead to enhanced security around the Capitol leading up to the certification proceedings. Considered in this light, the fact that the pipe bombs weren't discovered until within fifteen minutes of the first breach of Capitol barricades is remarkable to say the least.

Almost as remarkable (and convenient) as the fact that the RNC pipe bomb was discovered nearly contemporaneously with the initial breach of the Capitol, is that the pipe bomb planted at the DNC building was not discovered until after 1:00 p.m. In January of 2022, a full year after the Capitol riot, news reports revealed that Kamala Harris was actually at the DNC building on January 6, and was only evacuated at 1:15 p.m., after the RNC pipe bomb was discovered. Harris seemingly went to great lengths to conceal the fact that she was at the DNC on the morning of the 6, complicating several Department of Justice indictments which originally stipulated that Harris was inside the Capitol when in fact she was in the DNC building (such indictments had to be rewritten when Harris's true whereabouts became known). It is important to remember that as Vice President–elect, Kamala Harris was protected by the Secret Service on January 6. If Harris was in the DNC building from approximately 11:30 a.m. to 1:15 p.m. on January 6, this would mean that the Secret Service managed to miss the DNC pipe bomb on its initial sweep. That the Secret Service could miss the DNC pipe bomb in a sweep is so strange as to scarcely be believable—indeed, the pipe bomb was sitting right by a bench in front of the DNC building. If the Secret Service had discovered the bomb at 11:30 a.m. when Harris was going to enter the DNC, this could have led to an early evacuation of the Capitol building and enhanced security that would have prevented the January 6 rally from turning into a riot. Instead, the Secret Service managed to overlook the DNC pipe bomb at 11:30 a.m., only for a random passerby to discover the RNC pipe bomb within the exact time frame that it would have to be discovered to serve as a diversion that helped to enable the initial breach of the Capitol grounds.

That the DNC pipe bomb lay conspicuously at the foot of a park bench right outside of the entrance and parking garage to the DNC building for nearly seventeen hours before being discovered is indeed remarkable. No motorists, no pedestrians on the high foot traffic morning of January 6, nor the security guard who is stationed barely eight feet from where the pipe bomb was planted, and not the Secret Service of the United States—everyone managed to miss the pipe bomb. The strangeness of this is compounded significantly by certain suspicious and indeed damning facts about the surveillance footage from the DNC that the FBI released to the public. One shocking report released by *Revolver News* proved definitively that the FBI chose to withhold the footage that would have shown the DNC pipe bomber actually planting the bomb, thus confirming that it was indeed planted where and when they say it was. Stranger still, a follow-up report from *Revolver News* suggests a high probability that the FBI tampered with the parts of the footage it did release. Indeed, the frame rate on the released surveillance footage at the DNC was approximately 1.3 frames per second, a frame rate so low, and so far below even the lowest commercially available security cameras as to be unbelievable. For perspective, the security cameras at an average gas station and McDonalds typically have a frame rate of 15 frames per second. Is it believable that the DNC would have surveillance cameras with an order of magnitude worse than that of an average McDonalds? Even if we assumed that the DNC bought the cheapest surveillance camera available (a strange decision as we know they pay for a physical security guard in that exact spot) it wouldn't explain the 1.3 frame rate. As mentioned above, a frame rate that low is simply not commercially available—the lowest end is around 8. The latest major study conducted on operative surveillance cameras reflected that zero percent of such cameras in current operation have a frame rate of less than three frames per second! We won't speculate on why the frame rate of the DNC footage may have been tampered with beyond noting that such modifications would make it more difficult to identify the pipe bomber, his or her gait, and to determine whether the pipe bomber was in active communication with a third party over a cell phone. We leave it to the reader to determine why the FBI wouldn't want the public to know these things, and why, for that matter, the Democrats aren't demanding the FBI release the unedited footage of the pipe bomber allegedly planting an explosive device outside their national headquarters.

Although circumstantial, the evidence that many government agencies had much more visibility into January 6 than is commonly understood, together with the compound effect of multiple bizarre coincidences pertaining to the pipe bomb, at the very least warrants some fairly pointed investigation and questioning. At a certain point, the accumulated weight of evidence suggests the possibility of something more nefarious than the mere "intelligence failure" that FBI Director Wray attributes to the events of January 6. At a certain point, the evidence demands that we seriously entertain the notion that certain elements of the government had some reasonable foreknowledge of the events on January 6 and may not have taken basic steps to intervene for political reasons. As said above, January 6 has been incredibly useful to the regime as a pretext to reconfigure the national security apparatus domestically as a political weapon—a lot of money and power is invested in the regime's narrative of January 6.

The possibility of foul play on the part of elements of the government is an exceedingly tough pill to swallow, especially for conservatives who traditionally and by disposition are inclined to respect institutions of authority—particularly institutions such as the FBI. Of course, we could go back through decades of dirty tricks on the part of the FBI and other government agencies to help refine the intuitions of those who might think this isn't the sort of thing elements of the government are capable of. For our purposes, however, we need not go back any further than a few months before January 6, when an alleged plot on the part of Trump-inspired militiamen to kidnap Michigan governor Gretchen Whitmer took the country by storm.

The suspects in the Michigan kidnapping conspiracy allegedly plotted to kidnap the Michigan governor from her vacation home and leave her stranded out on a lake. The plotters also allegedly discussed blowing up a bridge to slow police response time, and separately discussed storming the Michigan State Capitol. Indeed, several of the arrested plotters had attended the protest at the Michigan State Capitol in April, in which authorities eventually allowed armed protestors inside the building so long as they agreed to a COVID temperature test.

When the Michigan kidnapping suspects were arrested in October, the media predictably had a frenzy. Just as the alleged "domestic terror" event of January 6 is used to demonize and silence any discussion of election fraud in 2020, so was the Michigan kidnapping plot used to demonize criticism of COVID lockdown policies. But given the curiously political timing of the Michigan kidnapping arrests in October 2020, just a month before the presidential election, it is perhaps no surprise that Trump was a primary target of blame. Many Democrat politicians, including Governor Whitmer herself, blamed Trump for inciting the alleged kidnapping plot against her. In just the same way that the media seized on Trump's January 6 speech remark "fight like hell" to blame him for January 6, the media seized on an anti-lockdown tweet Trump sent ("Liberate Michigan") for inspiring, emboldening, and inciting the kidnapping plot against Whitmer.

As time passed it became clear that there was incitement in the Whitmer kidnapping plot, but it didn't come from Trump—it came from the FBI itself. Indeed, out of the twenty or so alleged kidnapping plotters, a whopping twelve were either FBI informants or undercover FBI agents! Subsequent embarrassing revelations came out exposing just the sort of quality FBI agent that was assigned to this case. One of the lead agents in the Whitmer case, Richard Trask, was arrested in 2022 for assaulting his wife on the way back from a swinger's party. Another lead agent in the case, Jason Chambers, had to recuse himself when it was revealed that he was moonlighting in a private intelligence firm, whose Twitter account he sometimes operated to reveal sensitive details of the cases in which he was involved.

But the real scandal in the Michigan case is not simply the level of informant penetration into the plot, or the sordid activities of the agents on the case. The real scandal is that FBI informants played an active role in nearly every critical element of the so-called plot, to the point that it is severely doubtful whether there would have even been a plot if it hadn't been for the FBI and its informants. First, many of the alleged plotters met in the first place at a gathering in Ohio arranged by FBI informant Steve Robeson. In another instance, Robeson arranged a training exercise in Wisconsin, and a separate informant, Dan, drove the "plotters" to this training exercise, along with six thousand rounds of ammunition. Of course, the informant rented the car, paid for gas, and paid for lodging for the group, all on the FBI's tab.

One day in late August, Dan's FBI handler texted him, encouraging him to get the alleged "plotters" into a van on a surveillance mission of Whitmer's home—"I default to getting as many other guys as possible, so whatever works to maximize attendance" the FBI handler instructed Dan. Even the explosives expert who actively encouraged the plotters to purchase explosives from him was an undercover FBI agent, introduced to the plotters by FBI informant Dan. When the plotters were arrested, they were being driven to the explosives expert (undercover agent) by Dan, though they didn't bring the money the undercover agent requested to purchase the explosives. For his services as an informant, the FBI bought Dan a car and gave him twenty-four thousand dollars.

The behavior of the undercover FBI agents and informants was so egregious that the judge in the case approved an entrapment defense, which was ultimately successful. Given the hype surrounding the alleged threat of right-wing domestic terrorism, it is remarkable DOJ initially failed to obtain a single conviction in what was arguably the highest profile domestic terror case in recent history—a case which turned out to be a failed FBI entrapment operation. The embarrassment was so extreme that the DOJ retried two of the original Whitmer defendants, who were ultimately found guilty under extremely dubious and controversial circumstances.

Looking at the Michigan entrapment plot, we note some striking parallels to the January 6 case. First off, many of the alleged plotters were affiliated with the Three Percenters militia group, which also happens to be one of the three main militia groups imputed to January 6 (together with Proud Boys and Oath Keepers). In fact, longtime FBI informant Steve Robeson (mentioned above) was actually the head of Wisconsin's Three Percenters chapter and used this position to his advantage as an informant—a detail that might help to calibrate our intuitions regarding the questions raised earlier in this foreword regarding federal penetration of Oath Keepers and Proud Boys. Secondly, contrary to the colloquial understanding of the Michigan plot as a kidnapping plot, the alleged plotters also discussed storming the Michigan State Capitol and even apprehending the governor from the Capitol.

And thus, we see that the infamous Michigan case involved one of the three main militia groups imputed to January 6 and involved discussions of storming a state Capitol. And this plot was both heavily infiltrated by feds, to the point that twelve out of twenty alleged plotters were either informants or agents—and furthermore, that the informants did not just sit passively and allow the plot to unfold, but rather took proactive steps to encourage and materialize nearly every critical stage of its development. And for the final cherry on top of it all, the very day after the so-called Michigan plotters were arrested in October 2020, FBI Director Wray quietly promoted Steven D'Antuono, the head of the FBI Detroit Field Office who oversaw the Michigan entrapment operation, to the coveted position of assistant director of the Washington, DC Field Office—where he went on to oversee the January 6 investigation. Indeed, the FBI official in the initial FBI public service videos asking for the public's help in identifying the pipe bombers is none other than Steven D'Antuono! D'Antuono, the public face of the FBI's pipe bomb investigation, resigned from his coveted DC post just as quietly and mysteriously as he had been promoted to it. An FBI source told this author that it was simply "unheard of" for someone to resign from D'Antuono's perch at the Washington Field Office—a launching pad to the highest levels of leadership on the seventh floor of the FBI's Hoover building—after such a short period of time.

At the very least, the Michigan kidnapping case should count as yet another cause for suspicion regarding the uniquely poor security at the US Capitol on January 6. We know that the FBI was aggressively infiltrating (to put it charitably) the militia groups blamed for some of the more egregious behavior on January 6, and we know that the FBI should have been especially alert to vulnerabilities at the Capitol given that the alleged Michigan plotters spoke about doing the same thing at the Michigan State Capitol. But the Michigan case also suggests something darker than merely compounding the magnitude of the alleged intelligence failure on January 6, or even than the possibility that elements in the government knew something might happen on January 6 in advance but held back in order to exploit the event politically; indeed, the Michigan case suggests that elements of the government are very capable of and willing to take active steps in ensuring that the January 6 rally turned into a riot.

Perhaps the most damning such case of foul play involves the curious case of Ray Epps. Ray Epps is an individual who was caught on camera on January 5, the evening before the Capitol riot, urging people to go into the Capitol on the next day. In now iconic and seemingly ubiquitous video clips, the commanding figure of Ray Epps, sporting a bright red Trump hat, tells the crowd around him: "Tomorrow . . . I don't even like to say it because I'll be arrested. But I'll say it. Tomorrow—we need to go INTO the Capitol, INTO the Capitol." On a second occasion, to the same crowd, Epps repeats his seemingly rehearsed formulation: "I'm gonna put it out there. I'm probably going to go to jail for it OK . . . Tomorrow, we need to go INTO the Capitol." This suggestion was so outrageous, so outlandish, and so out of place that the crowd immediately assumed something was off, and started pointing at Mr. Epps and chanting in unison, "Fed, fed, fed, fed," upon which Epps clarified that he wanted the crowd to go into the Capitol "peacefully." The low buying temperature of the crowd did not phase Mr. Epps, however. Video footage shows Epps doggedly fixated on his mission. In one clip, Epps attempts to refocus a distracted crowd on the mission at hand, absurdly emphasizing that "our enemy is the Capitol!" as though the crowd should cultivate a hatred for neoclassical architecture.

Epps's determination carried on until January 6. On the morning of the sixth, before Trump's speech began, video footage depicts Epps near the Ellipse instructing the crowd to go to the Capitol after Trump's speech: "As soon as our president is done speaking, we are going to the Capitol, where our problems are. It's in that direction. Please spread the word." In another clip he can be seen directing the crowd similarly: "As soon as President Trump is finished speaking, we are going to the Capitol—it's in that direction. That's where our true problems lie." In at least three additional video clips, Epps is captured similarly instructing the crowd to go to the Capitol. In another noteworthy clip, we see Epps positioned at the west side of the Capitol right at the site of the initial breach. Just minutes before the breach, Epps can be heard instructing a man, "When we go in, leave this here. We don't need to get shot." The remark clearly reveals an understanding on Epps's part that the crowd would be going in, and in the quote, he apparently refers to a can of bear spray that he encourages an individual not to take with him. In another bit of footage, we see Epps right by the barricades to the Capitol grounds, whispering in an individual's ear. No more than two seconds after the whisper, that individual becomes one of the very first people to break down the barricades in the first and decisive breach of Capitol grounds on the west side of the Capitol.

Epps's behavior was so egregious that many in the media and in law enforcement took notice. He quickly became one of the primary targets of left-wing vigilante groups attempting to identify riot participants for the purposes of passing on the information to law enforcement. Ray Epps was depicted in a *New York Times* video documentary on January 6 as one of the handful of January 6 riot participants who intended to storm the capitol in advance. He was one of the first twenty individuals put on the FBI's most wanted list in relation to the events of January 6 and appeared on posters asking for the public's help in identifying him. Then a strange thing happened—the public did identify Epps in January, and Epps wasn't arrested. Over five months later, in mid-June 2021, investigative news outlet *Revolver News* published a piece that brought the possibility of federal involvement in January 6 to national attention. On June 17, a viral Twitter thread explored Epps's behavior in the context of being a "fed." Then, on July 1, the FBI quietly removed Epps from its most wanted list.

Congressman Thomas Massie brought up the strange case of Epps in an exchange with FBI officials. *Revolver News* ran two pieces on Epps that achieved national prominence. In the wake of this focus on Epps, Senator Ted Cruz brought up the case of Epps in his own questioning of FBI officials. The legacy media and other anti-Trump institutions began to take a very different posture toward Epps.

The January 6 Committee took the rare step of a public statement, announcing that the Committee had interviewed Epps and that Epps had informed them, "he was not employed by, working with or acting at the direction of any law enforcement agency on January 5th or January 6th, and that he has never been an informant with the FBI or other law enforcement agency." That's it! Nothing to see here folks! The only individual caught on camera repeatedly urging people into the Capitol as early as January 6, who was positioned right at the initial breach site of the Capitol whispering in people's ears seconds before the breech, denies involvement with law enforcement and that's good enough for us!

Of course, the Committee won't release the transcript of either of its two conversations with Epps, and those conversations did not take place under oath. There is also something noteworthy about the very specific and legalistic formulation of Epps's apparent denial and its repeated and specific denial of involvement with the FBI and "law enforcement." In a brief statement to the *Epoch Times*, Ray Epps's lawyer (himself a nine-year veteran of the Phoenix FBI field office) repeated this specific formulation: "unequivocally, he is not an FBI agent."[7] Epps's very specific denials of involvement with the FBI and law enforcement leave open a wide range of possibilities consistent with him not acting authentically and independently in his apparent mission to urge people into the Capitol. Indeed, just to name a couple possibilities, neither military intelligence nor the Department of Homeland Security classify as law enforcement agencies, and this is to say nothing of the possibility of working as a contractor or at an arm's length cut-out group of those agencies. Recall that the agents who tried to recruit Oath Keeper Green Beret Jeremy Brown as an informant ahead of January 6 represented themselves as belonging to DHS—not a law enforcement agency. The specificity

---

* *Epoch Times*, Twitter post, January 12, 2022, 4.55 p.m., https://twitter.com/epochtimes/status/14813842427 4189825

of Epps's lawyer's "unequivocal" denial that Epps belongs to the FBI contrasts suspiciously with his "not to my knowledge" response to *Epoch Times*'s question as to whether Epps was an asset for any government agency "law enforcement, intelligence, or otherwise."

The January 6 Committee wasn't alone in the damage control efforts regarding Ray Epps. Committee member Adam Kinzinger took to Twitter to admonish the "crazies" who dared to ask inconvenient questions: "he didn't enter the Capitol on January 6th, and was taken off the FBI most wanted list because he apparently didn't break any laws." It is true that Epps did not go into the Capitol, but utterly false that Epps didn't break any laws. At the very least, Epps is guilty of trespassing on Capitol grounds after the initial breach of the Capitol barricades on the west side of the Capitol. Jeremy Brown, Owen Shroyer, Mark Ibrahim, Couy Griffin, just to name a handful, have been charged with trespassing.

Judging on the basis of conspiracy standards applied to other criminal cases, it is very likely that Epps could have been charged with conspiracy as well. For instance, there is the above-mentioned exchange, just minutes before the initial breach of the Capitol, in which Epps tells another individual, "When we go in, leave this here . . . we don't want to get shot." Compare this to the exchange between George Tanios and Julius Khater, for which Tanios was charged with serious conspiracy charges to assault an officer with bear spray. When Khater said to Tanios, "give me that bear shit," Tanios replied, "hold on, not yet, not yet, it's still early." According to government documents, this exchange revealed that the two were "working in concert and had plan to use toxic spray against law enforcement." If this is the standard for a serious conspiracy charge, it is hard to see why Ray Epps's "when we go in" remark isn't as well. This is especially so since the individual Epps said this to was one of the most aggressive participants in January 6, who evidently played a role in both the west side and east side breach of the Capitol, and who went into the Capitol. This individual is also listed in court documents as having communicated with the Proud Boys in advance (some of whom were charged with seditious conspiracy), promising to bring "three of the baddest m-fers" he knows to the January 6 protest in DC.

Given the aggressive prosecutorial standards applied to countless other January defendants, and given Epps's egregious role as the only participant to have repeatedly urged crowds to go into the Capitol as early as the evening of January 5, it is bizarre indeed that Epps got off without being arrested. It is still more bizarre to see the January 6 Committee and Adam Kinzinger step in and attempt to stymie obvious and commonsense questions regarding Ray Epps. Perhaps the **most bizarre piece** of damage control of all comes courtesy of the *New York Times*, which treated Ray Epps to a full-length sympathetic puff piece.[8] Poor Ray Epps's life had become hell, the *Times* piece revealed, because of "conspiracy theorists" asking questions about Epps's bizarre behavior on January 5 and 6.

Let the strangeness of it all sink in—of all of the January 6 riot participants the *New York Times* could have written a puff piece on, they write a puff piece on the one individual caught on camera repeatedly urging crowds to go into the Capitol in advance. If the *Times* piece wanted to dispel so-called conspiracy theories regarding Epps, it could have reported on where Epps got the idea to urge people into the Capitol in the first place, and why he was so doggedly fixated on this mission even when the crowd dismissed him.

Some other aspects of the *Times* piece are still stranger. For instance, it describes Epps as a Trump supporter who went to DC on a last-minute whim with his son to hear Trump's speech on election fraud. Incredibly, the piece in question fails to address the fact that Epps didn't even attend Trump's speech—this alleged Trump supporter traveled all the way from Arizona to DC, ostensibly to hear Trump's speech with his son, which he didn't attend. Instead, he fixated on his mission to get people to the Capitol! How bizarre! And how unfortunate that the *Times*—ever eager, of course, to give air cover to genuine Trump supporters and January 6 rioters—fails to even address it!

Epps may be the most prominent suspicious figure related to January 6, but he is by no means the only one. A ground-breaking, detailed video analysis conducted by *Revolver News* revealed a number of curious operators whose actions proved decisive in allowing the January 6 rally to turn into a riot. Several curious individuals, including one known to researchers only as "FenceCutterBulwark," can be seen on camera

---

8 Alan Feuer, "New Evidence Undercuts Jan. 6 Instigator Conspiracy Theory," *New York Times*, May 5, 2022, https://www.nytimes.com/2022/05/05/us/jan-6-ray-epps-evidence.html.

calmly and methodically removing fencing around the Capitol. FenceCutterBulwark engaged in this activity long before Trump's speech was finished. As a result, the thousands of Trump supporters who walked to the Capitol after Trump finished speaking were walking into one of the greatest legal booby traps in American history. Indeed, the area cordoned off by fencing is not typically a restricted area, and with much of the fencing removed by the time Trump's speech was over, the attendees ended up unwittingly walking into a legally restricted area, technically committing a criminal offense. Although prosecutions for trespassing were rare, the government wielded tremendous leverage of selective prosecution in this regard, which it did use against some prominent Trump supporters such as *Infowars* host Owen Shroyer (Ray Epps, as mentioned above, was not selected for prosecution).

It was bad enough that the crowds arrived on the newly unfenced Capitol grounds, and thus were doomed to unwittingly trespass on Capitol grounds and congregate much closer to the Capitol than they likely would have had nefarious operators not methodically cut down fencing in advance. There were also operators with bullhorns authoritatively directing the crowd. One of the most egregious and mysterious actors is known to researchers only as "Scaffold Commander." He is so called because after doing his own part in methodically removing fencing (while Trump was still speaking), he managed to position himself on top of a tall, white scaffolding that was put in place for Joe Biden's inauguration. From this perch and with his bullhorn, he continuously intoned commands to the unsuspecting crowd below: "Don't just stand there! Keep moving forward!" Once the crowd had continuously moved forward and the first handful of rioters entered the Capitol building, NWScaffoldCommander altered his message: "Okay we're in! We're in! Come on! We gotta fill up the Capitol! Come on! Come now! We need help. We gotta fill up the Capitol! They got in."

For perspective, it's important to step into the shoes of January 6 rally-goers to see just how dominant and pervasive NWScaffoldCommander's influence was over the crowd's psychology the entire time.

Rally-goers could hear his confident and constant commands with total clarity all the way back at the entrance to the Capitol lawn. For new entrants arriving at the Capitol grounds (with fencing removed), NWScaffoldCommander's voice would be the first and loudest voice they heard. NWScaffoldCommander even mixed in damsel-in-distress type appeals so new arrivals would perceive that "moving forward" would be doing their part to rescue innocent Trump supporters who "need your help." From the perspective of a peaceful rally-goer, a loud, authoritative voice literally coming from "on high," pleading that people "need your help," and asking you to simply and lawfully "move forward," creates a strong suction effect to comply with authority.

Despite NWScaffoldCommander's pivotal, indeed decisive role in crowd control, he might as well not even exist as far as the FBI is concerned—he didn't even make it on a single most wanted list, a single "Be on the Lookout" list, and hasn't been arrested. It is unclear and dubious as to whether the Department of Justice has applied any of its panopticon surveillance powers to identifying this critical January 6 operative.

What's especially noteworthy is like Ray Epps, both NWScaffoldCommander and the aforementioned FenceCutterBulwark were positioned at the site of the initial breach of Capitol grounds before Trump finished speaking, and indeed before the Proud Boys even arrived at the breach site.

According to the regime-approved narrative of January 6, the riot really kicked off when the Proud Boys initiated the first breach of Capitol barricades on the west side of the Capitol. The fact that there were numerous riot participants who were pre-positioned at the initial breach point before the Proud Boys arrived, who each played a decisive role in allowing the rally to turn into a riot, is entirely absent from the false regime-approved narrative. Unlike the Proud Boys, however, who have received an avalanche of media attention, the suspicious actors in question remain undiscussed, underexplored, and unindicted. Unsurprisingly, the January 6 Committee has expressed zero interest in identifying these operators.

It would take us outside the scope of this foreword to delve further into the suspicious actors and circumstances of the January 6 riot. Suffice it to say at this point that these unexplored discrepancies relating to the inexplicable lack of security on January 6, coupled with a still more vigorously unexplored presence of unindicted agitators, explain how the January 6 rally was able to turn into a riot far better than any politically motivated and tortured attempt to blame Trump for incitement on account of a politically commonplace rhetorical exhortation to "fight like hell."

As much as the political theater and spectacle surrounding January 6 is to target Trump and his political allies, it is still more important to understand that the ultimate targets are Trump supporters themselves. There is perhaps no better demonstration of the media, Democrat, and national security state's eagerness to cast blame on Trump's supporters than its coverage of deceased Capitol Police officer Brian Sicknick. The *New York Times* headline "He Dreamed of Being a Police Officer, Then Was Killed by a Pro-Trump Mob" set the tone for a media frenzy of false reporting that Capitol Police officer Brian Sicknick was bludgeoned to death by the rabid pro-Trump mob with a fire extinguisher. President Joe Biden shamefully amplified this falsehood in a press conference (with Vladimir Putin no less), in which he suggested that Trump supporters "broke through a cordon, went into the Capitol, and killed a police officer without accountability."

When researchers in independent media (including the author of this foreword) showed that the fire extinguisher story was false, the media quietly pivoted to a new narrative that the Trump-loving mob actually killed Sicknick with bear spray. Independent media (principally this author) went on to show this second bear spray narrative to be false, and eventually the media was forced to concede that Sicknick died of natural causes. Despite this late correction, the damage had already been done and the false narrative of a murderous mob of Trump-supporting domestic terrorists was effectively seeded into the immediate aftermath of January 6.

Indeed, if a murderous mob of Trump supporters ruthlessly bludgeoned a Capitol Police officer to death, this would certainly reinforce the notion that Trump supporters are de facto or potential domestic terrorists, and in this key respect the national security apparatus ought to direct its resources and attentions to this potential national security threat just in the same way it directed its attentions to "radical Islamists" in the aftermath of 9/11. This national security suspicion extends to certain beliefs as well, including (perhaps especially) the belief that the 2020 presidential election tipped over to Biden on account of election fraud. The former Assistant Secretary for Counterterrorism and Threat Prevention at the Department of Homeland Security exemplifies this dangerous outlook best. In addition to suggesting that a second Trump term would pose a national security threat and catalyze mass resignations within the intelligence community, former DHS official Elizabeth Neumann spoke directly on the national security threat allegedly posed by American citizens who dare to believe hat the 2020 election was stolen. While she was generous enough not to characterize all 51 million Americans who have concerns about the 2020 election as domestic errorists, she implies that at least 250,000 of such "election denying" Americans pose a similar threat to American national security as ISIS sympathizers! It is also noteworthy that the context of Neumann's remarks was a recorded hearing for the Homeland Security Committee, chaired by none other than Bennie Thompson, of course!

Elizabeth Neumann's classification of 2020 election skeptics as similar to ISIS sympathizers helps us to understand some truly Orwellian developments as of late hat have come out of the Department of Homeland Security. For instance, the department set up a so-called "Disinformation Governance Board" for the purpose of targeting information the Department of Homeland Security doesn't like in unspecified ways. According to leaked government documents, one of the three types of information targeted for attack by the Department of Homeland Security's "Ministry of Truth" department is so-called "disinformation surrounding the validity of he 2020 election underpinning calls for violence on January 6."

Of course, instead of classifying Trump supporters and those skeptical of the 2020 election as domestic terrorists, the authorities could take reasonable steps to assure he public of the legitimacy of elections. In the end, we must agree with then attorney general Bill Barr's assessment that a massive, unprecedented mail-in voting scheme at time of such severe political polarization was playing with fire. Add to this fire the legitimate and well-earned distrust of American regime institutions on the part of many Trump supporters and you have a recipe for continued and intensified national strife. As mentioned above, Trump supporters had been bombarded ad infinitum with a narrative that Trump colluded with Russians to win the 2016 election, with the implication that not only was Trump's presidency illegitimate, but that Trump supporters posed something of a national security threat by virtue of their witting or unwitting proximity to the interests of a hostile foreign power. As it turns out, the Steele dossier, a key document underpinning the Trump-Russia story, was based on a lie.

Rather than work in good faith to restore the American people's trust in their institutions, the "regime" broadly undertook reclassification of essentially half of the country as domestic terrorists based on their political beliefs. Insofar as January 6

serves as a major pretext to accelerate the troubling political weaponization of th
American national security state, we are compelled to conclude that the false officia
narratives and political theater surrounding January 6 represent the true threat t
whatever is left of American democracy and must be challenged accordingly.

THE
JANUARY 6TH
REPORT

FINAL REPORT

Select Committee to Investigate the

January 6th

Attack on the United States Capitol

December 00, 2022
117th Congress Second Session
House Report 117–000

Union Calendar No. XXX

117th Congress
2d Session

HOUSE OF REPRESENTATIVES

Report
117-000

FINAL REPORT

OF THE

SELECT COMMITTEE TO INVESTIGATE THE JANUARY 6TH ATTACK ON THE UNITED STATES CAPITOL

December X, 2022
Committed to the Committee of the Whole House on the
State of the Union and ordered to be printed

U.S. GOVERNMENT PUBLISHING OFFICE
WASHINGTON : 2022

49-937

DAVID B. BUCKLEY *Staff Director*
KRISTIN L. AMERLING *Deputy Staff Director and Chief Counsel*
HOPE GOINS *Senior Counsel to the Chairman*
JOSEPH B. MAHER *Senior Counsel to the Vice Chair*
TIMOTHY J. HEAPHY *Chief Investigative Counsel*
JAMIE FLEET *Senior Advisor*
TIMOTHY R. MULVEY *Communications Director*
CANDYCE PHOENIX *Senior Counsel and Senior Advisor*
JOHN F. WOOD *Senior Investigative Counsel and Of Counsel to the Vice Chair*

KATHERINE B. ABRAMS, *Staff Associate*
TEMIDAYO AGANGA-WILLIAMS, *Senior Investigative Counsel*
ALEJANDRA APECECHEA, *Investigative Counsel*
LISA A. BIANCO, *Director of Member Services and Security Manager*
JEROME P. BJELOPERA, *Investigator*
BRYAN BONNER, *Investigative Counsel*
RICHARD R. BRUNO, *Senior Administrative Assistant*
MARCUS CHILDRESS, *Investigative Counsel*
JOHN MARCUS CLARK, *Security Director*
JACQUELINE N. COLVETT, *Digital Director*
HEATHER I. CONNELLY, *Professional Staff Member*
MEGHAN E. CONROY, *Investigator*
HEATHER L. CROWELL, *Printer Proofreader*
WILLIAM C. DANVERS, *Senior Researcher*
SOUMYALATHA O. DAYANANDA, *Senior Investigative Counsel*
STEPHEN W. DEVINE, *Senior Counsel*
LAWRENCE J. EAGLEBURGER, *Professional Staff Member*
KEVIN S. ELLIKER, *Investigative Counsel*
MARGARET E. EMAMZADEH, *Staff Associate*
SADALLAH A. FARAH, *Professional Staff Member*
DANIEL GEORGE, *Senior Investigative Counsel*
JACOB H. GLICK, *Investigative Counsel*
AARON S. GREENE, *Clerk*
MARC S. HARRIS, *Senior Investigative Counsel*
ALICE K. HAYES, *Clerk*
QUINCY T. HENDERSON, *Staff Assistant*
JENNA HOPKINS, *Professional Staff Member*
CAMISHA L. JOHNSON, *Professional Staff Member*

THOMAS E. JOSCELYN, *Senior Professional Staff Member*
REBECCA L. KNOOIHUIZEN, *Financial Investigator*
CASEY E. LUCIER, *Investigative Counsel*
DAMON M. MARX, *Professional Staff Member*
EVAN B. MAULDIN, *Chief Clerk*
YONATAN L. MOSKOWITZ, *Senior Counsel*
HANNAH G. MULDAVIN, *Deputy Communications Director*
JONATHAN D. MURRAY, *Professional Staff Member*
JACOB A. NELSON, *Professional Staff Member*
ELIZABETH OBRAND, *Staff Associate*
RAYMOND O'MARA, *Director of External Affairs*
ELYES OUECHTATI, *Technology Partner*
ROBIN M. PEGUERO, *Investigative Counsel*
SANDEEP A. PRASANNA, *Investigative Counsel*
BARRY PUMP, *Parliamentarian*
SEAN M. QUINN, *Investigative Counsel*
BRITTANY M. J. RECORD, *Senior Counsel*
DENVER RIGGLEMAN, *Senior Technical Advisor*
JOSHUA D. ROSELMAN, *Investigative Counsel*
JAMES N. SASSO, *Senior Investigative Counsel*
GRANT H. SAUNDERS, *Professional Staff Member*
SAMANTHA O. STILES, *Chief Administrative Officer*
SEAN P. TONOLLI, *Senior Investigative Counsel*
DAVID A. WEINBERG, *Senior Professional Staff Member*
AMANDA S. WICK, *Senior Investigative Counsel*
DARRIN L. WILLIAMS, JR., *Staff Assistant*
ZACHARY S. WOOD, *Clerk*

CONTRACTORS & CONSULTANTS

Rawaa Alobaidi
Melinda Arons
Steve Baker
Elizabeth Bisbee
David Canady
John Coughlin
Aaron Dietzen
Gina Ferrise
Angel Goldsborough
James Goldston
Polly Grube
L. Christine Healey
Danny Holladay
Percy Howard
Dean Jackson
Stephanie J. Jones
Hyatt Mamoun
Mary Marsh
Todd Mason
Ryan Mayers
Jeff McBride
Fred Muram
Alex Newhouse
John Norton
Orlando Pinder
Owen Pratt
Dan Pryzgoda
Brian Sasser
William Scherer
Driss Sekkat
Chris Stuart
Preston Sullivan
Brian Young

Innovative Driven

HOUSE OF REPRESENTATIVES,
SELECT COMMITTEE TO
INVESTIGATE THE
JANUARY 6TH ATTACK ON THE
UNITED STATES CAPITOL,
Washington, DC,
December 00, 2022.

Hon. CHERYL L. JOHNSON,
Clerk, U.S. House of Representatives,
Washington, DC.

DEAR MS. JOHNSON: By direction of the Select
Committee to Investigate the January 6th Attack on the
United States Capitol, I hereby transmit its final report
pursuant to section 4(a) of House Resolution 503, 117th
Congress.

         Sincerely,

BENNIE G. THOMPSON,
Chairman.

"THE LAST BEST HOPE OF EARTH"

"I do solemnly swear that I will support and defend the Constitution of the United States against all enemies, foreign and domestic; that I will bear true faith and allegiance to the same; that I take this obligation freely, without any mental reservation or purpose of evasion; and that I will well and faithfully discharge the duties of the office on which I am about to enter: So help me God."

All Members of the United States Congress take this sacred oath. On January 6, 2021, Democrats and Republicans agreed that we would fulfill this oath— and that we had an obligation to signal to the world that American Democracy would prevail.

In furtherance of fulfilling this duty, the Select Committee to Investigate the January 6th Attack on the United States Capitol was charged with investigating the facts, circumstances and causes that led to this domestic terror attack on the Capitol, the Congress and the Constitution.

We owe a debt of gratitude to Chairman Bennie Thompson, Vice Chair Liz Cheney, the patriotic Members of Congress and dedicated staff—who devoted themselves to this investigation, to uncovering the truth and to writing a report that is a "Roadmap for Justice."

The Select Committee to Investigate the January 6th Attack has succeeded in bringing clarity and demonstrating with painstaking detail the fragility of our Democracy. Above all, the work of the Select Committee underscores that our democratic institutions are only as strong as the commitment of those who are entrusted with their care.

As the Select Committee concludes its work, their words must be a clarion call to all Americans: to vigilantly guard our Democracy and to give our vote only to those dutiful in their defense of our Constitution.

Let us always honor our oath to, as Abraham Lincoln said, "nobly save, or meanly lose, the last best hope of earth." So help us God.

NANCY PELOSI
Speaker of the House

We were told to remove our lapel pins. At the start of every new Congress, House Members are presented with lapel pins. They are about the size of a quarter and carry a seal of a bald eagle.

On a routine day in the Capitol, there are thousands of tourists, advocates, and workers. Typically, the pins are an easy way to spot House Members.

However, on January 6, 2021, the pin that once was a badge of honor and distinction turned into a bullseye.

On that day, tear gas fogged the air as gunfire rang out, and a violent mob crashed against the sealed doors. Concerned for our safety, Capitol Police officers told us that our lapel pins would make us a target for rioters.

As the Capitol Police rushed Members of Congress and staff to safety, that simple and, in context, sensible warning stuck with me. On January 6, 2021, my colleagues and I came to work with the intent of fulfilling our oaths of office and constitutional duty to carry out the peaceful transfer of power. We were the people's representatives in the people's House doing the people's business. Sadly, on that day, the danger was too great for our work to continue and for us to remain in the Capitol. It was too dangerous to be identified as a representative of the American people.

I've been a Member of the House for nearly 30 years. In that time, there's not a day that goes by that I don't feel a profound sense of duty and responsibility to the men and women who sent me to Congress to be their voice. After all, I'm from a part of the country where, in my lifetime, Black people were excluded entirely from political processes. Jim Crow laws prevented my father from registering to vote, and tragically during his life, he never cast a vote.

For generations, the people in communities I represent have struggled to have their voices heard by their government. Therefore, I take my duties and responsibilities seriously, advocating for greater economic opportunity, robust infrastructure, better schools, and safer housing for my constituents.

However, that long struggle to overcome oppression and secure basic civil and human rights continues to be my highest priority. I am always mindful of the journey that brought me to Washington as a member of Congress to be the voice of the women and men of Mississippi. As a violent mob stormed the Capitol trying to take away people's votes, rioters carried the battle flag from a failed rebellion of confederate states. This moment resonated deeply with me because of my personal history. Additionally, I continually think about the ongoing struggle to ensure justice and equality for all Americans.

The Capitol building itself is a fixture in our country's history, of both good and bad. After all, this structure is among the most recognizable symbols of American democracy. The Capitol's shining dome, topped with the statue of goddess Freedom, was built partially by the labor of enslaved people in the 18th and 19th centuries. Dark chapters of America's history are written into the building's marble, sandstone, and mortar. And yet in the halls and chambers of this building, leaders of courage passed amendments to our Constitution and enacted the laws that banned slavery, guaranteed equal rights under the law, expanded the vote, promoted equality, and moved our country, and her people, forward. The Capitol Building itself is a symbol of our journey toward a more perfect union. It is a temple to our democracy.

Those great moments in our history have come when men and women put loyalty to our country and Constitution ahead of politics and party. They did the right thing. The work of the Select Committee certainly originates from the same tradition. Our bipartisan membership has moved politics to the side and focused on the facts, circumstances, and causes of January 6th.

When I think back to January 6th, after nearly a year and a half of investigation, I am frightened about the peril our democracy faced. Specifically, I think about what that mob was there to do: to block the peaceful transfer of power from one president to another based on a lie that the election was rigged and tainted with widespread fraud.

I also think about why the rioters were there, besieging the legislative branch of our government. The rioters were inside the halls of Congress because the head of the executive branch of our government, the then-President of the United States, told them to attack. Donald Trump summoned that mob to Washington, DC. Afterward, he sent them to the Capitol to try to prevent my colleagues and me from doing our Constitutional duty to certify the election. They put our very democracy to the test.

Trump's mob came dangerously close to succeeding. Courageous law enforcement officers put their lives on the line for hours while Trump sat in the White House, refusing to tell the rioters to go home, while watching the assault on our republic unfold live on television.

When it was clear the insurrection would fail, Trump finally called off the mob, telling them, "We love you." Afterward, Congress was able to return to this Capitol Building and finish the job of counting the Electoral College votes and certifying the election.

This is the key conclusion of the Select Committee, all nine of us, Republicans and Democrats alike.

But who knows what would have happened if Trump's mob had succeeded in stopping us from doing our job? Who knows what sort of constitutional grey zone our country would have slid into? Who would have been
left to correct that wrong?

As required by House Resolution 503, which established the Select
Committee, we've explored in great detail the facts, circumstances, and
causes of the attack. This report will provide new details that supplement
those findings the committee already presented during our hearings.

But there are some questions for which there are still no clear answers,
even if all the facts, circumstances, and causes are brought to bear. The
"What If?" questions. For the good of American democracy, those questions
must never again be put to the test. So, while it's important that this report
lays out what happened, it's just as important to focus on how to make sure
that January 6th was a one-time event—to identify the ongoing threats
that could lead us down that dangerous path again—with hopes and
humble prayers that the committee's work is carried on through corrective
action.

This report will provide greater detail about the multistep effort devised
and driven by Donald Trump to overturn the 2020 election and block the
transfer of power. Building on the information presented in our hearings
earlier this year, we will present new findings about Trump's pressure
campaign on officials from the local level all the way up to his Vice President, orchestrated and designed solely to throw out the will of the voters
and keep him in office past the end of his elected term.

As we've shown previously, this plan faltered at several points because
of the courage of officials (nearly all of them Republicans) who refused to
go along with it. Donald Trump appeared to believe that anyone who shared
his partisan affiliation would also share the same callous disregard for his
or her oath to uphold the rule of law. Fortunately, he was wrong.

The failure of Trump's plan was not assured. To the contrary, Trump's
plan was successful at several turns. When his scheme to stay in power
through political pressure hit roadblocks, he relentlessly pushed ahead with
a parallel plan: summoning a mob to gather in Washington, DC on January
6th, promising things "will be wild!"

That mob showed up. They were armed. They were angry. They believed
the "Big Lie" that the election had been stolen. And when Donald Trump
pointed them toward the Capitol and told them to "fight like hell," that's
exactly what they did.

Donald Trump lit that fire. But in the weeks beforehand, the kindling he
ultimately ignited was amassed in plain sight.

That's why as part of the Select Committee's investigation, we took a hard look at whether enough was done to mitigate that risk. Our investigative teams focused on the way intelligence was gathered, shared, and assessed. We probed preparations by law enforcement agencies and security responses on the day of the attack. We followed the money, to determine who paid for a number of events in the run-up to the attack and to gain a clearer understanding of the way the former President's campaign apparatus cashed in on the big lie. And we pulled back the curtain at certain major social media companies to determine if their policies and protocols were up to the challenge when the President spread a message of violence and his supporters began to plan and coordinate their descent on Washington.

The Select Committee's conclusion on these matters—particularly dealing with intelligence and law enforcement—is consistent with our broader findings about the causes of January 6th. Were agencies perfect in their preparations for January 6th and their responses as the violence unfolded? Of course not. Relevant oversight committees and watchdogs should continue to find efficiencies and improvements, some of which are laid out in Committee's recommendations.

But the shortfall of communications, intelligence and law enforcement around January 6th was much less about what they did or did not know. It was more about what they could not know. The President of the United States inciting a mob to march on the Capitol and impede the work of Congress is not a scenario our intelligence and law enforcement communities envisioned for this country. Prior to January 6th, it was unimaginable. Whatever weaknesses existed in the policies, procedures, or institutions, they were not to blame for what happened on that day.

And so, when I think about the ongoing threats—when I think about how to avoid having to confront those "What-Ifs?" in the future—my concerns are less with the mechanics of intelligence gathering and security posture, as important as those questions are. My concerns remain first and foremost with those who continue to seek power at the expense of American democracy.

What if those election officials had given in to Donald Trump's pressure? What if the Justice Department had gone along with Trump's scheme to declare the 2020 election fraudulent? What if the Vice President had tried to throw out electoral votes? What if the rioters bent on stopping the peaceful transfer of power hadn't been repelled?

To cast a vote in the United States of America is an act of both hope and faith. When you drop that ballot in the ballot box, you do so with the confidence that every person named on that ballot will hold up their end of the bargain. The person who wins must swear an oath and live up to it. The people who come up short must accept the ultimate results and abide by the will of the voters and the rule of law. This faith in our institutions and laws is what upholds our democracy.

If that faith is broken—if those who seek power accept only the results of elections that they win—then American democracy, only a few centuries old, comes tumbling down.

That's the danger.

What's the solution?

The Committee believes a good starting point is the set of recommendations we set forth in our report, pursuant to House Resolution 503. Driven by our investigative findings, these recommendations will help strengthen the guardrails of our democracy.

Beyond what we recommend, in my view and as I said during our hearings, the best way to prevent another January 6th is to ensure accountability for January 6th. Accountability at all levels.

I have confidence in our Department of Justice and institutions at the state and local level to ensure accountability under the law. As this report is released, we see those processes moving forward.

But preventing another January 6th will require a broader sort of accountability. Ultimately, the American people chart the course for our country's future. The American people decide whom to give the reins of power. If this Select Committee has accomplished one thing, I hope it has shed light on how dangerous it would be to empower anyone whose desire for authority comes before their commitment to American democracy and the Constitution.

I believe most Americans will turn their backs on those enemies of democracy.

But some will rally to the side of the election deniers, and when I think about who some of those people are, it troubles me deep inside. White supremacists. Violent extremists. Groups that subscribe to racism, anti-Semitism, and violent conspiracy theories; those who would march through the halls of the Capitol waving the Confederate battle flag.

These are people who want to take America backward, not toward some imagined prior greatness, but toward repression. These are people who want to roll back what we've accomplished. I believe that those who aligned with the scheme to overturn the election heeded Donald Trump's call to march on the Capitol because they thought taking up Donald Trump's cause was a way to advance their vile ambitions.

That is why I did not remove my lapel pin on January 6th.

Our country has come too far to allow a defeated President to turn himself into a successful tyrant by upending our democratic institutions, fomenting violence, and, as I saw it, opening the door to those in our country whose hatred and bigotry threaten equality and justice for all Americans.

We can never surrender to democracy's enemies. We can never allow America to be defined by forces of division and hatred. We can never go backward in the progress we have made through the sacrifice and dedication of true patriots. We can never and will never relent in our pursuit of a more perfect union, with liberty and justice for all Americans.

I pray that God continues to bless the United States of America.

BENNIE G. THOMPSON
Chairman

In April 1861, when Abraham Lincoln issued the first call for volunteers for the Union Army, my great-great grandfather, Samuel Fletcher Cheney, joined the 21st Ohio Volunteer Infantry. He fought through all four years of the Civil War, from Chickamauga to Stones River to Atlanta. He marched with his unit in the Grand Review of Troops up Pennsylvania Avenue in May 1865, past a reviewing stand where President Johnson and General Grant were seated.

Silas Canfield, the regimental historian of the 21st OVI, described the men in the unit this way:

> *Industry had taught them perseverance, and they had learned to turn aside for no obstacle. Their intelligence gave them a just appreciation of the value and advantage of free government, and the necessity of defending and maintaining it, and they enlisted prepared to accept all the necessary labors, fatigues, exposures, dangers, and even death for the unity of our Nation, and the perpetuity of our institutions.*[1]

I have found myself thinking often, especially since January 6th, of my great-great grandfather, and all those in every generation who have sacrificed so much for "the unity of our Nation and the perpetuity of our institutions."

At the heart of our Republic is the guarantee of the peaceful transfer of power. Members of Congress are reminded of this every day as we pass through the Capitol Rotunda. There, eight magnificent paintings detail the earliest days of our Republic. Four were painted by John Trumbull, including one depicting the moment in 1793 when George Washington resigned his commission, handing control of the Continental Army back to Congress. Trumbull called this, "one of the highest moral lessons ever given the world." With this noble act, George Washington established the indispensable example of the peaceful transfer of power in our nation.

Standing on the West Front of the Capitol in 1981, President Ronald Reagan described it this way:

> *To a few of us here today, this is a solemn and most momentous occasion, and yet in the history of our nation it is a commonplace occurrence. The orderly transfer of authority as called for in the Constitution routinely takes place, as it has for almost two centuries, and few of us stop to think how unique we really are. In the eyes of many in the world, this every-4-year ceremony we accept as normal is nothing less than a miracle.*

Every President in our history has defended this orderly transfer of authority, except one. January 6, 2021 was the first time one American President refused his Constitutional duty to transfer power peacefully to the next.

In our work over the last 18 months, the Select Committee has recognized our obligation to do everything we can to ensure this never happens again. At the outset of our investigation, we recognized that tens of millions of Americans had been persuaded by President Trump that the 2020 Presidential election was stolen by overwhelming fraud. We also knew this was flatly false, and that dozens of state and federal judges had addressed and resolved all manner of allegations about the election. Our legal system functioned as it should, but our President would not accept the outcome.

What most of the public did not know before our investigation is this: Donald Trump's own campaign officials told him early on that his claims of fraud were false. Donald Trump's senior Justice Department officials—each appointed by Donald Trump himself—investigated the allegations and told him repeatedly that his fraud claims were false. Donald Trump's White House lawyers also told him his fraud claims were false. From the beginning, Donald Trump's fraud allegations were concocted nonsense, designed to prey upon the patriotism of millions of men and women who love our country.

Most Americans also did not know exactly how Donald Trump, along with a handful of others, planned to defeat the transfer of Presidential power on January 6th. This was not a simple plan, but it was a corrupt one. This report lays that plan out in detail—a plan that ultimately had seven parts, anticipating that Vice President Pence, serving in his role as President of the Senate, would refuse to count official Biden electoral slates from multiple states. We understood from the beginning that explaining all the planning and machinations would be complex and would require many hours of public presentations and testimony. We also understood that our presentations needed to be organized into a series of hearings that presented the key evidence for the American public to watch live or streamed over a reasonable time period, rather than rely on second-hand accounts as reported by media organizations with their own editorial biases. We organized our hearings in segments to meet that goal. Tens of millions of Americans watched.

Among the most shameful findings from our hearings was this: President Trump sat in the dining room off the Oval Office watching the violent riot at the Capitol on television. For hours, he would not issue a public statement instructing his supporters to disperse and leave the Capitol, despite urgent pleas from his White House staff and dozens of others to do so. Members of his family, his White House lawyers, virtually all those around him knew that this simple act was critical. For hours, he would not do it. During this time, law enforcement agents were attacked and seriously injured, the Capitol was invaded, the electoral count was halted and the lives of those in the Capitol were put at risk. In addition to being unlawful, as described in this report, this was an utter moral failure—and a clear dereliction of duty. Evidence of this can be seen in the testimony of his White House Counsel and several other White House witnesses. No man who would behave that way at that moment in time can ever serve in any position of authority in our nation again. He is unfit for any office.

*　　*　　*　　*　　*

In presenting all of the information in our hearings, we decided that the vast majority of our witnesses needed to be Republicans. They were. We presented evidence from two former Trump Administration Attorneys General, a former White House Counsel, many former Trump-appointed White House, Justice Department, and Trump Campaign staff, a respected former conservative judge, the former Secretary of Labor, and many others.

Like our hearings, this report is designed to deliver our findings in detail in a format that is accessible for all Americans. We do so in an executive summary, while also providing immense detail for historians and others. We are also releasing transcripts and evidence for the public to review, consistent with a small number of security and privacy concerns. A section of this report also explains the legal conclusions we draw from the evidence, and our concerns about efforts to obstruct our investigation.

The Committee recognizes that this investigation is just a beginning; it is only an initial step in addressing President Trump's effort to remain in office illegally. Prosecutors are considering the implications of the conduct we describe in this report. As are voters. John Adams wrote in 1761, "The very ground of our liberties is the freedom of elections." Faith in our elections and the rule of law are paramount to our Republic. Election-deniers—those who refuse to accept lawful election results—purposely attack the rule of law and the foundation of our country.

As you read this report, please consider this: Vice President Pence, along with many of the appointed officials who surrounded Donald Trump, worked to defeat many of the worst parts of Trump's plan to overturn the election. This was not a certainty. It is comforting to assume that the institutions of our Republic will always withstand those who try to defeat our Constitution from within. But our institutions are only strong when those who hold office are faithful to our Constitution. We do not know what would have happened if the leadership of the Department of Justice declared, as Donald Trump requested, that the election was "corrupt," if Jeff Clark's letters to State Legislatures had been sent, if Pat Cipollone, Jeff Rosen, Richard Donoghue, Steve Engel and others were not serving as guardrails on Donald Trump's abuses.

Part of the tragedy of January 6th is the conduct of those who knew that what happened was profoundly wrong, but nevertheless tried to downplay it, minimize it or defend those responsible. That effort continues every day. Today, I am perhaps most disappointed in many of my fellow conservatives who know better, those who stood against the threats of communism and Islamic terrorism but concluded that it was easier to appease Donald Trump, or keep their heads down. I had hoped for more from them.

The late Charles Krauthammer wrote, "The lesson of our history is that the task of merely maintaining strong and sturdy the structures of a constitutional order is unending, the continuing and ceaseless work of every generation." This task is unending because democracy can be fragile and our institutions do not defend themselves.

The history of our time will show that the bravery of a handful of Americans, doing their duty, saved us from an even more grave Constitutional crisis. Elected officials, election workers, and public servants stood against Donald Trump's corrupt pressure. Many of our witnesses showed selfless patriotism and their words and courage will be remembered.

The brave men and women of the Capitol Police, Metropolitan Police and all the other law enforcement officers who fought to defend us that day undoubtedly saved lives and our democracy.

Finally, I wish to thank all who honorably contributed to the work of the Committee and to this Report. We accomplished much over a relatively short period of time, and many of you sacrificed for the good of your nation. You have helped make history and, I hope, helped right the ship.

LIZ CHENEY
Vice Chair

ENDNOTE

1.   Silas S. Canfield, *History of the 21st Regiment Ohio Volunteer Infantry in the War of the Rebellion* (Vrooman, Anderson & Bateman, printers, 1893), p. 10.

Contents . . . . Page

Contents.. Page

Contents . . . . Page

Contents.. Page

APPENDICES

On October 31, 2022, in a Federal courthouse in Washington, DC, Graydon Young testified against Stewart Rhodes and other members of the Oath Keepers militia group. The defendants had been charged with seditious conspiracy against the United States and other crimes related to the January 6, 2021, attack on Congress.[1]

In his testimony that day, Young explained to the jury how he and other Oath Keepers were provoked to travel to Washington by President Donald Trump's tweets and by Trump's false claims that the 2020 Presidential election was "stolen" from him.[2] And, in emotional testimony, Young acknowledged what he and others believed they were doing on January 6th: attacking Congress in the manner the French had attacked the Bastille at the outset of the French Revolution.[3] Reflecting on that day more than a year and half later, Young testified:

> Prosecutor: And so how do you feel about the fact that you were pushing towards a line of police officers?
>
> Young: Today I feel extremely ashamed and embarrassed. . . .
>
> Prosecutor: How did you feel at the time?
>
> Young: I felt like, again, we were continuing in some kind of historical event to achieve a goal.
>
> * * *
>
> Prosecutor: Looking back now almost two years later, what would that make you as someone who was coming to D.C. to fight against the government?
>
> Young: I guess I was [acting] like a traitor, somebody against my own government.[4]

Young's testimony was dramatic, but not unique. Many participants in the attack on the Capitol acknowledged that they had betrayed their own country:

- Reimler: "And I'm sorry to the people of this country for threatening the democracy that makes this country so great . . . My participation in the events that day were part of an attack on the rule of law."[5]
- Pert: "I know that the peaceful transition of power is to ensure the common good for our nation and that it is critical in protecting our country's security needs. I am truly sorry for my part and accept full responsibility for my actions."[6]
- Markofski: "My actions put me on the other side of the line from my

Protestors gather at the Capitol.

(Photo by Samuel Corum/Getty Images)

brothers in the Army. The wrong side. Had I lived in the area, I would have been called up to defend the Capitol and restore order . . . My actions brought dishonor to my beloved U.S. Army National Guard." [7]

- Witcher: "Every member—every male member of my family has served in the military, in the Marine Corps, and most have saw combat. And I cast a shadow and cast embarrassment upon my family name and that legacy." [8]
- Edwards: "I am ashamed to be for the first time in my 68 years, standing before a judge, having pleaded guilty to committing a crime, ashamed to be associated with an attack on the United States Capitol, a symbol of American democracy and greatness that means a great deal to me." [9]

Hundreds of other participants in the January 6th attack have pleaded guilty, been convicted, or await trial for crimes related to their actions that day. And, like Young, hundreds of others have acknowledged exactly what provoked them to travel to Washington, and to engage in violence. For example:

- Ronald Sandlin, who threatened police officers in the Capitol saying, "[y]ou're going to die," posted on December 23, 2020: "I'm going to be there to show support for our president and to do my part to stop the steal and stand behind Trump when he decides to cross the rubicon. If you are a patriot I believe it's your duty to be there. I see it as my civic responsibility." [10]

- Garret Miller, who brought a gun to the Capitol on January 6th, explained: "I was in Washington, D.C. on January 6, 2021, because I believed I was following the instructions of former President Trump and he was my president and the commander-in-chief. His statements also had me believing the election was stolen from him." [11]

- John Douglas Wright explained that he brought busloads of people to Washington, DC, on January 6th "because [Trump] called me there, and he laid out what is happening in our government." [12]

- Lewis Cantwell testified: If "the President of the United States . . . [is] out on TV telling the world that it was stolen, what else would I believe, as a patriotic American who voted for him and wants to continue to see the country thrive as I thought it was?" [13]

- Likewise, Stephen Ayres testified that "with everything the President was putting out" ahead of January 6th that "the election was rigged . . . the votes were wrong and stuff . . . it just got into my head." "The President [was] calling on us to come" to Washington, DC. [14] Ayres "was hanging on every word he [President Trump] was saying" [15] Ayres posted that "Civil War will ensue" if President Trump did not stay in power after January 6th. [16]

The Committee has compiled hundreds of similar statements from participants in the January 6th attack. [17]

House Resolution 503 instructed the Select Committee to "investigate and report upon the facts, circumstances, and causes relating to the January 6, 2021, domestic terrorist attack upon the United States Capitol Complex" and to "issue a final report" containing "findings, conclusions, and recommendations for corrective measures." The Select Committee has conducted nine public hearings, presenting testimony from more than 70 witnesses. In structuring our investigation and hearings, we began with President Trump's contentions that the election was stolen and took testimony from nearly all of the President's principal advisors on this topic. We focused on the rulings of more than 60 Federal and State courts rejecting President Trump's and his supporters' efforts to reverse the electoral outcome.

Despite the rulings of these courts, we understood that millions of Americans still lack the information necessary to understand and evaluate what President Trump has told them about the election. For that reason, our hearings featured a number of members of President Trump's inner circle refuting his fraud claims and testifying that the election was not in fact stolen. In all, the Committee displayed the testimony of more than four dozen Republicans—by far the majority of witnesses in our hearings—including two of President Trump's former Attorneys General, his former White House Counsel, numerous members of his White House staff, and the highest-ranking members of his 2020 election campaign, including his campaign manager and his campaign general counsel. Even key individuals who worked closely with President Trump to try to overturn the 2020 election on January 6th ultimately *admitted* that they lacked actual evidence sufficient to change the election result, and they *admitted* that what they were attempting was unlawful.[18]

This Report supplies an immense volume of information and testimony assembled through the Select Committee's investigation, including information obtained following litigation in Federal district and appellate courts, as well as in the U.S. Supreme Court. Based upon this assembled evidence, the Committee has reached a series of specific findings,[19] including the following:

1. Beginning election night and continuing through January 6th and thereafter, Donald Trump purposely disseminated false allegations of fraud related to the 2020 Presidential election in order to aid his effort to overturn the election and for purposes of soliciting contributions. These false claims provoked his supporters to violence on January 6th.

2. Knowing that he and his supporters had lost dozens of election lawsuits, and despite his own senior advisors refuting his election fraud claims and urging him to concede his election loss, Donald Trump refused to accept the lawful result of the 2020 election. Rather than honor his constitutional obligation to "take Care that the Laws be faithfully executed," President Trump instead plotted to overturn the election outcome.

3. Despite knowing that such an action would be illegal, and that no State had or would submit an altered electoral slate, Donald Trump corruptly pressured Vice President Mike Pence to refuse to count electoral votes during Congress's joint session on January 6th.

4. Donald Trump sought to corrupt the U.S. Department of Justice by attempting to enlist Department officials to make purposely false statements and thereby aid his effort to overturn the Presidential election. After that effort failed, Donald Trump offered the position of Acting Attorney General to Jeff Clark knowing that Clark intended to disseminate false information aimed at overturning the election.

5. Without any evidentiary basis and contrary to State and Federal law, Donald Trump unlawfully pressured State officials and legislators to change the results of the election in their States.

6. Donald Trump oversaw an effort to obtain and transmit false electoral certificates to Congress and the National Archives.

7. Donald Trump pressured Members of Congress to object to valid slates of electors from several States.

8. Donald Trump purposely verified false information filed in Federal court.

9. Based on false allegations that the election was stolen, Donald Trump summoned tens of thousands of supporters to Washington for January 6th. Although these supporters were angry and some were armed, Donald Trump instructed them to march to the Capitol on January 6th to "take back" their country.

10. Knowing that a violent attack on the Capitol was underway and knowing that his words would incite further violence, Donald Trump purposely sent a social media message publicly condemning Vice President Pence at 2:24 p.m. on January 6th.

11. Knowing that violence was underway at the Capitol, and despite his duty to ensure that the laws are faithfully executed, Donald Trump refused repeated requests over a multiple hour period that he instruct his violent supporters to disperse and leave the Capitol, and instead watched the violent attack unfold on television. This failure to act perpetuated the violence at the Capitol and obstructed Congress's proceeding to count electoral votes.

12. Each of these actions by Donald Trump was taken in support of a multi-part conspiracy to overturn the lawful results of the 2020 Presidential election.

13. The intelligence community and law enforcement agencies did successfully detect the planning for potential violence on January 6th, including planning specifically by the Proud Boys and Oath Keeper militia groups who ultimately led the attack on the Capitol. As January 6th approached, the intelligence specifically identified the potential for violence at the U.S. Capitol. This intelligence was shared within the executive branch, including with the Secret Service and the President's National Security Council.

14. Intelligence gathered in advance of January 6th did not support a conclusion that Antifa or other left-wing groups would likely engage in a violent counter-demonstration, or attack Trump supporters on January 6th. Indeed, intelligence from January 5th indicated that some left-wing groups were instructing their members to "stay at home" and not attend on January 6th.[20] Ultimately, none of these groups was involved to any material extent with the attack on the Capitol on January 6th.

15. Neither the intelligence community nor law enforcement obtained intelligence in advance of January 6th on the full extent of the ongoing planning by President Trump, John Eastman, Rudolph Giuliani and their associates to overturn the certified election results. Such agencies apparently did not (and potentially could not) anticipate the provocation President Trump would offer the crowd in his Ellipse speech, that President Trump would "spontaneously" instruct the crowd to march to the Capitol, that President Trump would exacerbate the violent riot by sending his 2:24 p.m. tweet condemning Vice President Pence, or the full scale of the violence and lawlessness that would ensue. Nor did law enforcement anticipate that President Trump would refuse to direct his supporters to leave the Capitol once violence began. No intelligence community advance analysis predicted exactly how President Trump would behave; no such analysis recognized the full scale and extent of the threat to the Capitol on January 6th.

16. Hundreds of Capitol and DC Metropolitan police officers performed their duties bravely on January 6th, and America owes those individuals immense gratitude for their courage in the defense of Congress and our Constitution. Without their bravery, January 6th would have been far worse. Although certain members of the Capitol Police leadership regarded their approach to January 6th as "all hands on deck," the Capitol Police leadership did not have sufficient assets in place to address the violent and lawless crowd.[21] Capitol Police leadership did not anticipate the scale of the violence that would ensue after President Trump instructed tens of thousands of his supporters in the Ellipse crowd to march to the Capitol, and then tweeted at 2:24 p.m. Although Chief Steven Sund raised the idea of National Guard support, the Capitol Police Board did not request Guard assistance prior to January 6th. The Metropolitan Police took an even more proactive approach to January 6th, and deployed roughly 800 officers, including responding to the emergency calls for help at the Capitol. Rioters still managed to break their line in certain locations, when the crowd surged forward in the immediate aftermath of Donald Trump's 2:24 p.m. tweet. The Department of Justice readied a group of Federal agents at Quantico and in the District of Columbia, anticipating that January 6th could become violent, and then deployed those agents once it became clear that police at the Capitol were overwhelmed. Agents from the Department of Homeland Security were also deployed to assist.

17. President Trump had authority and responsibility to direct deployment of the National Guard in the District of Columbia, but never gave

any order to deploy the National Guard on January 6th or on any other day. Nor did he instruct any Federal law enforcement agency to assist. Because the authority to deploy the National Guard had been delegated to the Department of Defense, the Secretary of Defense could, and ultimately did deploy the Guard. Although evidence identifies a likely miscommunication between members of the civilian leadership in the Department of Defense impacting the timing of deployment, the Committee has found no evidence that the Department of Defense intentionally delayed deployment of the National Guard. The Select Committee recognizes that some at the Department had genuine concerns, counseling caution, that President Trump might give an illegal order to use the military in support of his efforts to overturn the election.

* * *

This Report begins with a factual overview framing each of these conclusions and summarizing what our investigation found. That overview is in turn supported by eight chapters identifying the very specific evidence of each of the principal elements of President Trump's multi-part plan to overturn the election, along with evidence regarding intelligence gathered before January 6th and security shortfalls that day.

Although the Committee's hearings were viewed live by tens of millions of Americans and widely publicized in nearly every major news source,[22] the Committee also recognizes that other news outlets and commentators have actively discouraged viewers from watching, and that millions of other Americans have not yet seen the actual evidence addressed by this Report. Accordingly, the Committee is also releasing video summaries of relevant evidence on each major topic investigated.

This Report also examines the legal implications of Donald Trump and his co-conspirators' conduct and includes criminal referrals to the Department of Justice regarding President Trump and certain other individuals. The criminal referrals build upon three relevant rulings issued by a Federal district court and explain in detail how the facts found support further evaluation by the Department of Justice of specific criminal charges. To assist the public in understanding the nature and importance of this material, this Report also contains sections identifying how the Committee has evaluated the credibility of its witnesses and suggests that the Department of Justice further examine possible efforts to obstruct our investigation. We also note that more than 30 witnesses invoked their Fifth Amendment privilege against self-incrimination, others invoked Executive Privilege or categorically refused to appear (including Steve Bannon, who has since been convicted of contempt of Congress).

Finally, this report identifies a series of legislative recommendations, including the Presidential Election Reform Act, which has already passed the House of Representatives.

EXECUTIVE SUMMARY: OVERVIEW OF THE EVIDENCE DEVELOPED

In the Committee's hearings, we presented evidence of what ultimately became a multi-part plan to overturn the 2020 Presidential election. That evidence has led to an overriding and straight forward conclusion: the central cause of January 6th was one man, former President Donald Trump, whom many others followed. None of the events of January 6th would have happened without him.

THE BIG LIE

In the weeks before election day 2020, Donald Trump's campaign experts, including his campaign manager Bill Stepien, advised him that the election results would not be fully known on election night.[23] This was because certain States would not begin to count absentee and other mail-in votes until election day or after election-day polls had closed.[24] Because Republican voters tend to vote in greater numbers on election day and Democratic voters tend to vote in greater numbers in advance of election day, it was widely anticipated that Donald Trump could initially appear to have a lead, but that the continued counting of mail-in, absentee and other votes beginning election night would erode and could overcome that perceived lead.[25] Thus, as President Trump's campaign manager cautioned, understanding the results of the 2020 election would be a lengthy "process," and an initial appearance of a Trump lead could be a "red mirage." [26] This was not unique to the 2020 election; similar scenarios had played out in prior elections as well.[27]

Prior to the 2020 election, Donald Trump's campaign manager Bill Stepien, along with House Republican Leader Kevin McCarthy, urged President Trump to embrace mail-in voting as potentially beneficial to the Trump Campaign.[28] Presidential advisor and son-in-law Jared Kushner recounted others giving Donald Trump the same advice: "[M]ail in ballots could be a good thing for us if we looked at it correctly." [29] Multiple States, including Florida, had successfully utilized mail-in voting in prior elections, and in 2020.[30] Trump White House Counselor Hope Hicks testified: "I think he [President Trump] understood that a lot of people vote via absentee ballot in places like Florida and have for a long time and that it's worked fine." [31] Donald Trump won in numerous States that allowed no-excuse absentee voting in 2020, including Alaska, Florida, Idaho, Iowa, Kansas, Montana, North Carolina, North Dakota, Ohio, Oklahoma, South Dakota, and Wyoming.[32]

On election night 2020, the election returns were reported in almost exactly the way that Stepien and other Trump Campaign experts predicted, with the counting of mail-in and absentee ballots gradually diminishing President Trump's perceived lead. As the evening progressed, President Trump called in his campaign team to discuss the results. Stepien and other campaign experts advised him that the results of the election would not be known for some time, and that he could not truthfully declare victory.[33] "It was far too early to be making any calls like that. Ballots—ballots were still being counted. Ballots were still going to be counted for days."[34]

Campaign Senior Advisor Jason Miller told the Select Committee that he argued against declaring victory at that time as well, because "it was too early to say one way [or] the other" who had won.[35] Stepien advised Trump to say that "votes were still being counted. It's too early to tell, too early to call the race but, you know, we are proud of the race we run—we ran and we, you know, think we're—think we're in a good position" and would say more in the coming days.[36]

President Trump refused, and instead said this in his public remarks that evening: "This is a fraud on the American public. This is an embarrassment to our country. We were getting ready to win this election. Frankly, we did win this election. We did win this election . . . . We want all voting to stop."[37] And on the morning of November 5th, he tweeted "STOP THE COUNT!"[38] Halting the counting of votes at that point would have violated both State and Federal laws.[39]

According to testimony received by the Select Committee, the only advisor present who supported President Trump's inclination to declare victory was Rudolph Giuliani, who appeared to be inebriated.[40] President Trump's Attorney General, William Barr, who had earlier left the election night gathering, perceived the President's statement this way:

> [R]ight out of the box on election night, the President claimed that there was major fraud underway. I mean, this happened, as far as I could tell, before there was actually any potential of looking at evidence. He claimed there was major fraud. And it seemed to be based on the dynamic that, at the end of the evening, a lot of Democratic votes came in which changed the vote counts in certain States, and that seemed to be the basis for this broad claim that there was major fraud. And I didn't think much of that, because people had been talking for weeks and everyone understood for weeks that that was going to be what happened on election night . . . .[41]

President Trump's decision to declare victory falsely on election night and, unlawfully, to call for the vote counting to stop, was not a spontaneous decision. It was premeditated. The Committee has assembled a range of

President Trump declares victory in a speech at an election night party.
(Photo by Chip Somodevilla/Getty Images)

evidence of President Trump's preplanning for a false declaration of victory. This includes multiple written communications on October 31 and November 3, 2020, to the White House by Judicial Watch President Tom Fitton.[42] This evidence demonstrates that Fitton was in direct contact with President Trump and understood that President Trump would falsely declare victory on election night and call for vote counting to stop. The evidence also includes an audio recording of President Trump's advisor Steve Bannon, who said this on October 31, 2020, to a group of his associates from China:

> And what Trump's gonna do is just declare victory, right? He's gonna declare victory. But that doesn't mean he's a winner. He's just gonna say he's a winner . . . The Democrats—more of our people vote early that count. Theirs vote in mail. And so they're gonna have a natural disadvantage, and Trump's going to take advantage of it—that's our strategy. He's gonna declare himself a winner. So when you wake up Wednesday morning, it's going to be a firestorm . . . . Also, if Trump, if Trump is losing, by 10 or 11 o'clock at night, it's going to be even crazier. No, because he's gonna sit right there and say "They stole it. I'm directing the Attorney General to shut down all ballot places in all 50 states." It's

going to be, no, he's not going out easy. If Trump—if Biden's winning, Trump is going to do some crazy shit.[43]

Also in advance of the election, Roger Stone, another outside advisor to President Trump, made this statement:

I really do suspect it will still be up in the air. When that happens, the key thing to do is to claim victory. Possession is nine-tenths of the law. No, we won. Fuck you, Sorry. Over. We won. You're wrong. Fuck you.[44]

On election day, Vice President Pence's staff, including his Chief of Staff and Counsel, became concerned that President Trump might falsely claim victory that evening. The Vice President's Counsel, Greg Jacob, testified about their concern that the Vice President might be asked improperly to echo such a false statement.[45] Jacob drafted a memorandum with this specific recommendation: "[I]t is essential that the Vice President not be perceived by the public as having decided questions concerning disputed electoral votes prior to the full development of all relevant facts." [46]

Millions of Americans believed that President Trump was telling the truth on election night—that President Trump actually had proof the election was stolen and that the ongoing counting of votes was an act of fraud.

As votes were being counted in the days after the election, President Trump's senior campaign advisors informed him that his chances of success were almost zero.

Former Trump Campaign Manager Bill Stepien testified that he had come to this conclusion by November 7th, and told President Trump:

Committee Staff: What was your view on the state of the election at that point?

Stepien: You know, very, very, very bleak. You know, I—we told him—the group that went over there outlined, you know, my belief and chances for success at this point. And then we pegged that at, you know, 5, maybe 10 percent based on recounts that were—that, you know, either were automatically initiated or could be—could be initiated based on, you know, realistic legal challenges, not all the legal challenges that eventually were pursued. But, you know, it was—you know, my belief is that it was a very, very—5 to 10 percent is not a very good optimistic outlook.[47]

Trump Campaign Senior Advisor Jason Miller testified to the Committee about this exchange:

> Miller: I was in the Oval Office. And at some point in the conversation Matt Oczkowski, who was the lead data person, was brought on, and I remember he delivered to the President in pretty blunt terms that he was going to lose.

> Committee Staff: And that was based, Mr. Miller, on Matt and the data team's assessment of this sort of county-by-county, State-by-State results as reported?

> Miller: Correct.[48]

In one of the Select Committee's hearings, former Fox News political editor Chris Stirewalt was asked what the chance President Trump had of winning the election after November 7th, when the votes were tallied and every news organization had called the race for now-President Biden. His response: "None." [49]

As the Committee's hearings demonstrated, President Trump made a series of statements to White House staff and others during this time period indicating his understanding that he had lost.[50] President Trump also took consequential actions reflecting his understanding that he would be leaving office on January 20th. For example, President Trump personally signed a Memorandum and Order instructing his Department of Defense to withdraw all military forces from Somalia by December 31, 2020, and from Afghanistan by January 15, 2021.[51] General Keith Kellogg (ret.), who had been appointed by President Trump as Chief of Staff for the National Security Council and was Vice President Pence's National Security Advisor on January 6th, told the Select Committee that "[a]n immediate departure that that memo said would have been catastrophic. It's the same thing what President Biden went through. It would have been a debacle." [52]

In the weeks that followed the election, President Trump's campaign experts and his senior Justice Department officials were informing him and others in the White House that there was no genuine evidence of fraud sufficient to change the results of the election. For example, former Attorney General Barr testified:

> And I repeatedly told the President in no uncertain terms that I did not see evidence of fraud, you know, that would have affected the outcome of the election. And, frankly, a year and a half later, I haven't seen anything to change my mind on that.[53]

Former Trump Campaign lawyer Alex Cannon, who was asked to oversee incoming information about voter fraud and set up a voter fraud tip line, told the Select Committee about a pertinent call with White House Chief of Staff Mark Meadows in November 2020:

> Cannon: So I remember a call with Mr. Meadows where Mr. Meadows was asking me what I was finding and if I was finding anything. And I remember sharing with him that we weren't finding anything that would be sufficient to change the results in any of the key States.

> Committee Staff: When was that conversation?

> Cannon: Probably in November. Mid- to late November . . . .

> Committee Staff: And what was Mr. Meadows's reaction to that information?

> Cannon: I believe the words he used were: "So there is no there there?" [54]

President Trump's Campaign Manager Bill Stepien recalled that President Trump was being told "wild allegations" and that it was the Campaign's job to "track [the allegations] down":

> Committee Staff: You said that you were very confident that you were telling the President the truth in your dealings with [him]. And had your team been able to verify any of these allegations of fraud, would you have reported those to the President?

> Stepien: Sure.

> Committee Staff: Did you ever have to report that—

> Stepien: One of my frustrations would be that, you know, people would throw out, you know, these reports, these allegations, these things that they heard or saw in a State, and they'd tell President Trump. And, you know, it would be the campaign's job to track down the information, the facts. And, you know, President Trump, you know—if someone's saying, hey, you know, all these votes aren't counted or were miscounted, you know, if you're down in a State like Arizona, you liked hearing that. It would be our job to track it down and come up dry because the allegation didn't prove to be true. And we'd have to, you know, relay the news that, yeah, that tip that someone told you about those votes or that fraud or, you know, nothing came of it.

> That would be our job as, you know, the truth telling squad and, you know, not—not a fun job to be, you know, much—it's an easier job to

be telling the President about, you know, wild allegations. It's a harder job to be telling him on the back end that, yeah, that wasn't true.

Committee Staff: How did he react to those types of conversations where you [told] him that an allegation or another wasn't true?

Stepien: He was—he had—usually he had pretty clear eyes. Like, he understood, you know—you know, we told him where we thought the race was, and I think he was pretty realistic with our viewpoint, in agreement with our viewpoint of kind of the forecast and the uphill climb we thought he had.[55]

Trump Campaign Senior Advisor Jason Miller told the Committee that he informed President Trump "several" times that "specific to election day fraud and irregularities, there were not enough to overturn the election."[56]

Vice President Pence has also said publicly that he told President Trump there was no basis to allege that the election was stolen. When a reporter recently asked "Did you ever point blank say to the President [that] we lost this election?," Pence responded that "I did . . . Many times."[57] Pence has also explained:

There was never evidence of widespread fraud. I don't believe fraud changed the outcome of the election. But the President and the Campaign had every right to have those examined in court. But I told the President that, once those legal challenges played out, he should simply accept the outcome of the election and move on.[58]

The General Counsel of President Trump's campaign, Matthew Morgan, informed members of the White House staff, and likely many others, of the Campaign's conclusion that none of the allegations of fraud and irregularities could be sufficient to change the outcome of the election:

What was generally discussed on that topic was whether the fraud, maladministration, abuse, or irregularities, if aggregated and read most favorably to the campaign, would that be outcome determinative. And I think everyone's assessment in the room, at least amongst the staff, Marc Short, myself, and Greg Jacob, was that it was not sufficient to be outcome determinative.[59]

In a meeting on November 23rd, Barr told President Trump that the Justice Department was doing its duty by investigating every fraud allegation "if it's specific, credible, and could've affected the outcome," but that "they're just not meritorious. They're not panning out."[60]

Barr then told the Associated Press on December 1st that the Department had "not seen fraud on a scale that could have effected a different outcome in the election." [61] Next, he reiterated this point in private meetings with the President both that afternoon and on December 14th, as well as in his final press conference as Attorney General later that month.[62] The Department of Homeland Security had reached a similar determination two weeks earlier: "**There is no evidence that any voting system deleted or lost votes, changed votes, or was in any way compromised.**" [63]

In addition, multiple other high ranking Justice Department personnel appointed by President Trump also informed him repeatedly that the allegations were false. As January 6th drew closer, Acting Attorney General Rosen and Acting Deputy Attorney General Donoghue had calls with President Trump on almost a daily basis explaining in detail what the Department's investigations showed.[64] Acting Deputy Attorney General Richard Donoghue told the Select Committee that he and Acting Attorney General Rosen tried "to put it in very clear terms to the President. And I said something to the effect of 'Sir, we've done dozens of investigations, hundreds of interviews. The major allegations are not supported by the evidence developed. We've looked in Georgia, Pennsylvania, Michigan, Nevada. We're doing our job.'" [65] On December 31st, Donoghue recalls telling the President that "people keep telling you these things and they turn out not to be true." [66] And then on January 3rd, Donoghue reiterated this point with the President:

> [A]s in previous conservations, we would say to him, you know, "We checked that out, and there's nothing to it." [67]

Acting Attorney General Rosen testified before the Select Committee that "the common element" of all of his communications with President Trump was President Trump urging the Department to find widespread fraud that did not actually exist. None of the Department's investigations identified any genuine fraud sufficient to impact the election outcome:

> During my tenure as the Acting Attorney General, which began on December 24 of [2020], the Department of Justice maintained the position, publicly announced by former Attorney General William Barr, that the Department had been presented with no evidence of widespread voter fraud in a scale sufficient to change the outcome of the 2020 election.[68]

As President Trump was hearing from his campaign and his Justice Department that the allegations of widespread fraud were not supported by the evidence, his White House legal staff also reached the same conclusions, and agreed specifically with what Barr told President Trump. Both White House Counsel Pat Cipollone and White House Senior Advisor Eric Herschmann reinforced to President Trump that the Justice Department was doing its duty to investigate allegations of supposed voter fraud.[69]

Cipollone told the Select Committee that he "had seen no evidence of massive fraud in the election" and that he "forcefully" made this point "over and over again." For example, during a late-night group meeting with President Trump on December 18th, at which he and Herschmann urged Trump not to heed the advice of several election conspiracists at the meeting:

> Cipollone: They didn't think that we were, you know—they didn't think we believed this, you know, that there had been massive fraud in the election, and the reason they didn't think we believed it is because we didn't.

> Committee Staff: And you articulated that forcefully to them during the meeting?

> Cipollone: I did, yeah. I had seen no evidence of massive fraud in the election. . . . At some point, you have to deliver with the evidence. And I—again, I just to go back to what [Barr] said, he had not seen and I was not aware of any evidence of fraud to the extent that it would change the results of the election. That was made clear to them, okay, over and over again.[70]

Similarly, White House Attorney Eric Herschmann was also very clear about his views:

> [T]hey never proved the allegations that they were making, and they were trying to develop.[71]

In short, President Trump was informed over and over again, by his senior appointees, campaign experts and those who had served him for years, that his election fraud allegations were nonsense.

How did President Trump continue to make false allegations despite all of this unequivocal information? President Trump sought out those who were not scrupulous with the facts, and were willing to be dishonest. He found a new legal team to assert claims that his existing advisors and the Justice Department had specifically informed him were false. President Trump's new legal team, headed by Rudolph Giuliani, and their allies ultimately lost dozens of election lawsuits in Federal and State courts.

The testimony of Trump Campaign Manager Bill Stepien helps to put this series of events in perspective. Stepien described his interaction with Giuliani as an intentional "self-demotion," with Stepien stepping aside once it became clear that President Trump intended to spread falsehoods.

Stepien knew the President's new team was relying on unsupportable accusations, and he refused to be associated with their approach:

There were two groups of family. We called them kind of my team and Rudy's team. I didn't mind being characterized as being part of "team normal," as reporters, you know, kind of started to do around that point in time. [72]

Having worked for Republican campaigns for over two decades, Stepien said, "I think along the way I've built up a pretty good -- I hope a good reputation for being honest and professional, and I didn't think what was happening was necessarily honest or professional at that point in time." [73]

As Giuliani visited Campaign headquarters to discuss election litigation, the Trump Campaign's professional staff began to view him as unhinged.[74] In addition, multiple law firms previously engaged to work for the Trump Campaign decided that they could not participate in the strategy being instituted by Giuliani. They quit. Campaign General Counsel Matthew Morgan explained that he had conversations with "probably all of our counsel who [we]re signed up to assist on election day as they disengaged with the campaign." [75] The "general consensus was that the law firms were not comfortable making the arguments that Rudy Giuliani was making publicly." [76] When asked how many outside firms expressed this concern, Morgan recalled having "a similar conversation with most all of them." [77]

Stepien grew so wary of the new team that he locked Giuliani out of his office:

Committee Staff: Yeah. I'm getting the sense from listening to you here for a few hours that you sort of chose to pull back, that you were uncomfortable with what Mr. Giuliani and others were saying and doing and, therefore, you were purposefully stepping back from a day-to-day role as the leader of the campaign. Is that—I don't want to put words in your mouth. Is that accurate?

Stepien: That's accurate. That's accurate. You know, I had my assistant -- it was a big glass kind of wall office in our headquarters, and I had my assistant lock my door. I told her, don't let anyone in. You know, I'll be around when I need to be around. You know, tell me what I need to know. Tell me what's going on here, but, you know, you're going to see less of me.

And, you know, sure enough, you know, Mayor Giuliani tried to, you know, get in my office and ordered her to unlock the door, and she didn't do that, you know. She's, you know, smart about that. But your words are ones I agree with.[78]

Over the weeks that followed, dozens of judges across the country specifically rejected the allegations of fraud and irregularities being advanced by the Trump team and their allies. For example, courts described the arguments as "an amalgamation of theories, conjecture, and speculation," "allegations ... sorely wanting of relevant or reliable evidence," "strained legal arguments without merit," assertions that "did not prove by any standard of proof that any illegal votes were cast and counted," and even a "fundamental and obvious misreading of the Constitution." [79]

Reflecting back on this period, Trump Campaign Communications Director Tim Murtaugh texted colleagues in January 2021 about a news report that the New York State Bar was considering expelling Rudolph Giuliani over the Ellipse rally: "Why wouldn't they expel him based solely on the outrageous lies he told for 2 1/2 months?" [80]

This is exactly what ultimately came to pass. When suspending his license, a New York court said that Giuliani "communicated demonstrably false and misleading statements to courts, lawmakers and the public at large in his capacity as lawyer for former President Donald J. Trump and the Trump campaign in connection with Trump's failed effort at reelection in 2020." [81] The court added that "[t]he seriousness of [Giuliani's] uncontroverted misconduct cannot be overstated." [82]

Other Trump lawyers were sanctioned for making outlandish claims of election fraud without the evidence to back them up, including Sidney Powell, Lin Wood and seven other pro-Trump lawyers in a case that a Federal judge described as "a historic and profound abuse of the judicial process":

> It is one thing to take on the charge of vindicating rights associated with an allegedly fraudulent election. It is another to take on the charge of deceiving a federal court and the American people into believing that rights were infringed, without regard to whether any laws or rights were in fact violated. This is what happened here.[83]

A group of prominent Republicans have more recently issued a report— titled *Lost, Not Stolen*—examining "every count of every case brought in these six battleground states" by President Trump and his allies. The report concludes "that Donald Trump and his supporters had their day in court and failed to produce substantive evidence to make their case." [84] President Trump and his legal allies "failed because of a lack of evidence and not because of erroneous rulings or unfair judges . . . . In many cases, after making extravagant claims of wrongdoing, Trump's legal representatives showed up in court or state proceedings empty-handed, and then returned to their rallies and media campaigns to repeat the same unsupported claims." [85]

There is no reasonable basis for the allegation that these dozens of rulings by State and Federal courts were somehow politically motivated.[86] The outcome of these suits was uniform regardless of who appointed the judges.

One of the authors of *Lost, Not Stolen*, longtime Republican election lawyer Benjamin Ginsberg, testified before the Select Committee that "in no instance did a court find that the charges of fraud were real," without variation based on the judges involved.[87] Indeed, eleven of the judges who ruled against Donald Trump and his supporters were appointed by Donald Trump himself.

One of those Trump nominees, Judge Stephanos Bibas of the U.S. Court of Appeals for the Third Circuit, rejected an appeal by the Trump Campaign claiming that Pennsylvania officials "did not undertake any meaningful effort" to fight illegal absentee ballots and uneven treatment of voters across counties.[88] Judge Bibas wrote in his decision that "calling an election unfair does not make it so. Charges require specific allegations and then proof. We have neither here."[89] Another Trump nominee, Judge Brett Ludwig of the Eastern District of Wisconsin, ruled against President Trump's lawsuit alleging that the result was skewed by illegal procedures that governed drop boxes, ballot address information, and individuals who claimed "indefinitely confined" status to vote from home.[90] Judge Ludwig wrote in his decision, that "[t]his Court has allowed plaintiff the chance to make his case and he has lost on the merits" because the procedures used "do not remotely rise to the level" of breaking Wisconsin's election rules.[91]

Nor is it true that these rulings focused solely on standing, or procedural issues. As Ginsberg confirmed in his testimony to the Select Committee, President Trump's team "did have their day in court."[92] Indeed, he and his co-authors determined in their report that 30 of these post-election cases were dismissed by a judge after an evidentiary hearing had been held, and many of these judges explicitly indicated in their decisions that the evidence presented by the plaintiffs was wholly insufficient on the merits.[93]

Ultimately, even Rudolph Giuliani and his legal team acknowledged that they had no definitive evidence of election fraud sufficient to change the election outcome. For example, although Giuliani repeatedly had claimed in public that Dominion voting machines stole the election, he admitted during his Select Committee deposition that "I do not think the machines stole the election."[94] An attorney representing his lead investigator, Bernard Kerik, declared in a letter to the Select Committee that "it was impossible for Kerik and his team to determine conclusively whether there was widespread fraud or whether that widespread fraud would have altered the outcome of the election."[95] Kerik also emailed President Trump's chief of staff on December 28, 2020, writing: "We can do all the investigations we want later, but if the president plans on winning, it's the legislators that have to be moved and this will do just that."[96] Other Trump lawyers and supporters, Jenna Ellis, John Eastman, Phil Waldron, and Michael Flynn, all invoked their Fifth Amendment privilege against self-incrimination when

Rudolph Giuliani, Bernard Kerik, and other hold a press conference at Four Seasons Total Landscaping on November 7, 2020 falsely claiming Donald Trump had won the state of Pennsylvania.

(Photo by Chris McGrath/Getty Images)

asked by the Select Committee what supposed proof they uncovered that the election was stolen.[97] Not a single witness--nor any combination of witnesses--provided the Select Committee with evidence demonstrating that fraud occurred on a scale even remotely close to changing the outcome in any State.[98]

By mid-December 2020, Donald Trump had come to what most of his staff believed was the end of the line. The Supreme Court rejected a lawsuit he supported filed by the State of Texas in the Supreme Court, and Donald Trump had this exchange, according to Special Assistant to the President Cassidy Hutchinson:

> The President was fired up about the Supreme Court decision. And so I was standing next to [Chief of Staff Mark] Meadows, but I had stepped back . . . The President [was] just raging about the decision and how it's wrong, and why didn't we make more calls, and just this typical anger outburst at this decision . . . And the President said I think—so he had said something to the effect of, "I don't want people to know we lost, Mark. This is embarrassing. Figure it out. We need to figure it out. I don't want people to know that we lost."[99]

On December 14, 2020, the Electoral College met to cast and certify each State's electoral votes. By this time, many of President Trump's senior staff, and certain members of his family, were urging him to concede that he had lost.

Labor Secretary Gene Scalia told the Committee that he called President Trump around this time and gave him such feedback quite directly:

> [S]o, I had put a call in to the President—I might have called on the 13th; we spoke, I believe, on the 14th—in which I conveyed to him that I thought that it was time for him to acknowledge that President Biden had prevailed in the election . . . . But I communicated to the President that when that legal process is exhausted and when the electors have voted, that that's the point at which that outcome needs to be expected . . . . And I told him that I did believe, yes, that once those legal processes were run, if fraud had not been established that had affected the outcome of the election, that, unfortunately, I believed that what had to be done was concede the outcome.[100]

Deputy White House Press Secretary Judd Deere also told President Trump that he should concede. He recalled other staffers advising President Trump at some point to concede and that he "encouraged him to do it at least once after the electoral college met in mid-December." [101] White House Counsel Pat Cipollone also believed that President Trump should concede: "[I]f your question is did I believe he should concede the election at a point in time, yes, I did." [102]

Attorney General Barr told the Select Committee this: "And in my view, that [the December 14 electoral college vote] was the end of the matter. I didn't see—you know, I thought that this would lead inexorably to a new administration. I was not aware at that time of any theory, you know, why this could be reversed. And so I felt that the die was cast . . . ." [103]

Barr also told the Committee that he suggested several weeks earlier that the President's efforts in this regard needed to come to an end soon, in conversation with several White House officials after his meeting with Trump on November 23rd:

> [A]s I walked out of the Oval Office, Jared was there with Dan Scavino, who ran the President's social media and who I thought was a reasonable guy and believe is a reasonable guy. And I said, how long is he going to carry on with this 'stolen election' stuff? Where is this going to go?

> And by that time, Meadows had caught up with me and—leaving the office, and caught up to me and said that—he said, look, I think that he's becoming more realistic and knows that there's a limit to how far he can take this. And then Jared said, you know, yeah, we're working on this, we're working on it.[104]

Despite all that Donald Trump was being told, he continued to purposely and maliciously make false claims. To understand the very stark differences between what he was being told and what he said publicly and in fundraising solicitations, the Committee has assembled the following examples.

Then-Deputy Attorney General Jeffrey Rosen (12/15/20): "And so he said, 'Well, what about this? I saw it on the videotape, somebody delivering a suitcase of ballots.' And we said, 'It wasn't a suitcase. It was a bin. That's what they use when they're counting ballots. It's benign.'" [105]	*President Trump one week later (12/22/20):* "There is even security camera footage from Georgia that shows officials telling poll watchers to leave the room before pulling suitcases of ballots out from under the tables and continuing to count for hours." [106]
Acting Deputy Attorney General Richard Donoghue (12/27 & 12/31/20): "I told the President myself that several times, in several conversations, that these allegations about ballots being smuggled in in a suitcase and run through the machine several times, it was not true, that we looked at it, we looked at the video, we interviewed the witnesses, that it was not true . . . . I believe it was in the phone call on December 27th. It was also in a meeting in the Oval Office on December 31st." [107]	*President Trump later that week (1/2/21):* "[S]he stuffed the machine. She stuffed the ballot. Each ballot went three times, they were showing: Here's ballot number one. Here it is a second time, third time, next ballot." [108]
GA Sec. State Brad Raffensperger (1/2/21): "You're talking about the State Farm video. And I think it's extremely unfortunate that Rudy Giuliani or his people, they sliced and diced that video and took it out of context." . . . "[W]e did an audit of that and we proved conclusively that they were not scanned three times. . . . Yes, Mr. President, we'll send you the link from WSB." [Trump]: "I don't care about a link. I don't need it." [109]	*President Trump one day later (1/3/21):* "I spoke to Secretary of State Brad Raffensperger yesterday about Fulton County and voter fraud in Georgia. He was unwilling, or unable, to answer questions such as the 'ballots under table' scam, ballot destruction, out of state 'voters', dead voters, and more. He has no clue!" [110]

Attorney General Barr (12/1/20): "Then he raised the 'big vote dump,' as he called it, in Detroit. And, you know, he said, people saw boxes coming into the counting station at all hours of the morning and so forth.... I said, 'Mr. President, there are 630 precincts in Detroit, and unlike elsewhere in the State, they centralize the counting process, so they're not counted in each precinct, they're moved to counting stations, and so the normal process would involve boxes coming in at all different hours.' And I said, 'Did anyone point out to you—did all the people complaining about it point out to you, you actually did better in Detroit than you did last time? I mean, there's no indication of fraud in Detroit.'" [111]	*President Trump one day later (12/2/20):* "I'll tell you what's wrong, voter fraud. Here's an example. This is Michigan. At 6:31 in the morning, a vote dump of 149,772 votes came in unexpectedly. We were winning by a lot. That batch was received in horror. . . . In Detroit everybody saw the tremendous conflict . . . there were more votes than there were voters." [112]
Acting Deputy Attorney General Richard Donoghue (12/27/20): "The President then continued, there are 'more votes than voters...'. But I was aware of that allegation, and I said, you know, that was just a matter of them 'comparing the 2020 votes cast to 2016 registration numbers.' That is 'not a valid complaint.'" [113]	*President Trump ten days later (1/6/21):* "More votes than they had voters. And many other States also." [114]
Acting Deputy Attorney General Richard Donoghue (1/3/21): "[W]e would say to him, you know, 'We checked that out, and there's nothing to it. . . . And we would cite to certain allegations. And so—like such as Pennsylvania, right. 'No, there were not 250,000 more votes reported than were actually cast. That's not true.' So we would say things like that." [115]	*President Trump three days later (1/6/21):* "In Pennsylvania, you had 205,000 more votes than you had voters. And the number is actually much greater than that now. That was as of a week ago. And this is a mathematical impossibility unless you want to say it's a total fraud." [116]

GA Sec. State Brad Raffensperger (1/2/21): [Trump]: "[I]t's 4,502 who voted, but they weren't on the voter registration roll, which they had to be. You had 18,325 vacant address voters. The address was vacant, and they're not allowed to be counted. That's 18,325." . . . [Raffensperger]: "Well, Mr. President, the challenge that you have is the data you have is wrong." [117]	*President Trump two days later (1/4/21):* "4,502 illegal ballots were cast by individuals who do not appear on the state's voter rolls. Well, that's sort of strange. 18,325 illegal ballots were cast by individuals who registered to vote using an address listed as vacant according to the postal service." [118]
GA Sec. of State Brad Raffensperger (1/2/21): [Trump]: "So dead people voted, and I think the number is close to 5,000 people. And they went to obituaries. They went to all sorts of methods to come up with an accurate number, and a minimum is close to about 5,000 voters." . . . [Raffensperger]: "The actual number were two. Two. Two people that were dead that voted. So that's wrong." [119]	*President Trump four days later (1/6/21):* "[T]he number of fraudulent ballots that we've identified across the state is staggering. Over 10,300 ballots in Georgia were cast by individuals whose names and dates of birth match Georgia residents who died in 2020 and prior to the election." [120]
GA Sec. State General Counsel Ryan Germany (1/2/21): [Trump]: "You had out-of-state voters. They voted in Georgia, but they were from out of state, of 4,925." . . . [Germany]: "Every one we've been through are people that lived in Georgia, moved to a different state, but then moved back to Georgia legitimately." . . . "They moved back in years ago. This was not like something just before the election. So there's something about that data that, it's just not accurate." [121]	*President Trump four days later (1/6/21):* "And at least 15,000 ballots were cast by individuals who moved out of the state prior to November 3rd election. They say they moved right back." [122]

White House Press Secretary Kayleigh McEnany (n.d.): "[T]he one specific I remember referencing was I don't agree with the Dominion track." . . . "I specifically referenced waving him off of the Dominion theory earlier in my testimony." . . . [Q] "Are you saying you think he still continued to tweet that after you waved him off of it?" [A] "Yeah . . ." [123]	*President Trump:* Between mid-November and January 5, 2021, President Trump tweeted or retweeted conspiracy theories about Dominion nearly three dozen times. [124]
Trump Campaign Senior Advisor Jason Miller: "...the international allegations for Dominion were not valid." [Q] "Okay. Did anybody communicate that to the President?" [A]: "I know that that was—I know that was communicated. I know I communicated it" [125]	*President Trump:* "You have Dominion, which is very, very suspect to start off with. Nobody knows the ownership. People say the votes are counted in foreign countries and much worse..." [126]
Attorney General Barr (11/23/20): "I specifically raised the Dominion voting machines, which I found to be one of the most disturbing allegations—'disturbing' in the sense that I saw absolutely zero basis for the allegations . . . I told him that it was crazy stuff and they were wasting their time on that and it was doing great, great disservice to the country." [127]	*President Trump three days later (11/26/20):* "[T]hose machines are fixed, they're rigged. You can press Trump and the vote goes to Biden. . . . All you have to do is play with a chip, and they played with a chip, especially in Wayne County and Detroit." [128]
Attorney General Barr (12/1/20): "I explained, I said, look, if you have a machine and it counts 500 votes for Biden and 500 votes for Trump, and then you go back later and you have a—you will have the 1,000 pieces of paper put through that machine, and you can see if there's any discrepancy...there has been no discrepancy." [129]	*President Trump one day later (12/2/20):* "In one Michigan County, as an example, that used Dominion systems, they found that nearly 6,000 votes had been wrongly switched from Trump to Biden, and this is just the tip of the iceberg. This is what we caught. How many didn't we catch?" [130]

Attorney General Barr (12/14/20): "'I will, Mr. President. But there are a couple of things,' I responded. 'My understanding is that our experts have looked at the Antrim situation and are sure it was a human error that did not occur anywhere else. And, in any event, Antrim is doing a hand recount of the paper ballots, so we should know in a couple of days whether there is any real problem with the machines.'"[131]	*President Trump one day later (12/15/20):* "This is BIG NEWS. Dominion Voting Machines are a disaster all over the Country. Changed the results of a landslide election. Can't let this happen...."[132]
Then-Deputy Attorney General Jeffrey Rosen (12/15/20): "[O]ther people were telling him there was fraud, you know, corruption in the election. The voting machines were no good. And we were telling him that is inconsistent, by 'we,' I mean Richard Donoghue and myself, that that was not what we were seeing." ... "There was this open issue as to the Michigan report. And—I think it was Mr. Cuccinelli, not certain, but had indicated that there was a hand recount. And I think he said, 'That's the gold standard.'"[133]	*President Trump one day later (12/16/20):* "'Study: Dominion Machines shifted 2-3% of Trump Votes to Biden. Far more votes than needed to sway election.' Florida, Ohio, Texas and many other states were won by even greater margins than projected. Did just as well with Swing States, but bad things happened. @OANN"[134]
National Security Adviser Robert O'Brien (12/18/20): "I got a call from, I think, Molly Michael in outer oval, the President's assistant, and she said, 'I'm connecting you to the Oval' ... somebody asked me, was there—did I have any evidence of election fraud in the voting machines or foreign interference in our voting machines. And I said, no, we've looked into that and there's no evidence of it."[135]	*President Trump one day later (12/19/20):* "... There could also have been a hit on our ridiculous voting machines during the election, which is now obvious that I won big, making it an even more corrupted embarrassment for the USA. @DNI_Ratcliffe @SecPompeo"[136]

Acting Deputy AG Richard Donoghue (12/31/20):	President Trump two days later (1/2/21):
"We definitely talked about Antrim County again. That was sort of done at that point, because the hand recount had been done and all of that. But we cited back to that to say, you know, this is an example of what people are telling you and what's being filed in some of these court filings that are just not supported by the evidence." [137]	"Well, Brad. Not that there's not an issue, because we have a big issue with Dominion in other states and perhaps in yours. . . . in other states, we think we found tremendous corruption with Dominion machines, but we'll have to see." . . . "I won't give Dominion a pass because we found too many bad things." [138]
GA Sec. State Brad Raffensperger (1/2/21):	President Trump four days later (1/6/21):
"I don't believe that you're really questioning the Dominion machines. Because we did a hand re-tally, a 100 percent re-tally of all the ballots, and compared them to what the machines said and came up with virtually the same result. Then we did the recount, and we got virtually the same result." [139]	"In addition, there is the highly troubling matter of Dominion Voting Systems. In one Michigan county alone, 6,000 votes were switched from Trump to Biden and the same systems are used in the majority of states in our country." . . . "There is clear evidence that tens of thousands of votes were switched from President Trump to former Vice President Biden in several counties in Georgia." [140]

Evidence gathered by the Committee indicates that President Trump raised roughly one quarter of a billion dollars in fundraising efforts between the election and January 6th.[141] Those solicitations persistently claimed and referred to election fraud that did not exist. For example, the Trump Campaign, along with the Republican National Committee, sent millions of emails to their supporters, with messaging claiming that the election was "rigged," that their donations could stop Democrats from

Taped footage of William Barr speaking to the January 6th Select Committee is shown at one of its hearings.

(Photo by Mandel Ngan-Pool/Getty Images)

"trying to steal the election," and that Vice President Biden would be an "illegitimate president" if he took office.

Ultimately, Attorney General Barr suggested that the Department of Justice's investigations disproving President Trump's fraud claims may have prevented an even more serious series of events:

> [F]rankly, I think the fact that I put myself in the position that I could say that we had looked at this and didn't think there was fraud was really important to moving things forward. And I sort of shudder to think what the situation would have been if the position of the Department was, "We're not even looking at this until after Biden's in office." I'm not sure we would've had a transition at all.[142]

RATHER THAN CONCEDE, DONALD TRUMP CHOOSES TO OBSTRUCT THE JANUARY 6TH PROCEEDING

President Trump disregarded the rulings of the courts and rejected the findings and conclusions and advice from his Justice Department, his campaign experts, and his White House and Cabinet advisors. He chose instead to try to overturn the election on January 6th and took a series of very specific steps to attempt to achieve that result.

A central element of Donald Trump's plan to overturn the election relied upon Vice President Mike Pence. As Vice President, Pence served as the President of the Senate, the presiding officer for the joint session of Congress on January 6th. Beginning in December, and with greater frequency as January 6th approached, Trump repeatedly and unlawfully pressured Pence in private and public to prevent Congress from counting lawful electoral votes from several States.

To understand the plan President Trump devised with attorney and law professor John Eastman, it is necessary to understand the constitutional structure for selecting our President.

At the Constitutional Convention 233 years ago, the framers considered but rejected multiple proposals that Congress itself vote to select the President of the United States.[143] Indeed the Framers voiced very specific concerns with Congress selecting the President. They viewed it as important that the electors, chosen for the specific purpose of selecting the President, should make the determination rather than Congress:

> It was desireable, that the sense of the people should operate in the choice of the person to whom so important a trust was to be confided. This end will be answered by committing the right of making it, not to any pre-established body, but to men, chosen by the people for the special purpose, and at the particular conjuncture.[144]

The Framers understood that a thoughtful structure for the appointment of the President was necessary to avoid certain evils: "Nothing was more to be desired, than that every practicable obstacle should be opposed to cabal, intrigue and corruption."[145] They were careful to ensure that "those who from situation might be suspected of too great devotion to the president in office" "were not among those that chose the president."[146] For that reason, "[n]o senator, representative, or other person holding a place of trust or profit under the United States, can be of the number of the electors."[147]

Article II of our Constitution, as modified by the Twelfth Amendment, governs election of the President. Article II created the electoral college, providing that the States would select electors in the manner provided by State legislatures, and those electors would in turn vote for the President. Today, every State selects Presidential electors by popular vote, and each State's laws provide for procedures to resolve election disputes, including through lawsuits if necessary. After any election issues are resolved in State or Federal court, each State's government transmits a certificate of the ascertainment of the appointed electors to Congress and the National Archives.

The electoral college meets in mid-December to cast their votes, and all of these electoral votes are then ultimately counted by Congress on January 6th. The Vice President, as President of the Senate, presides over the joint session of Congress to count votes. The Twelfth Amendment provides this straight forward instruction: "The president of the Senate shall, in the presence of the Senate and House of Representatives, open all the certificates and the votes shall then be counted; The person having the greatest number of votes for President shall be the President..." The Vice President has only a ministerial role, opening the envelopes and ensuring that the votes are counted. Likewise, the Electoral Count Act of 1887 provides no substantive role for the Vice President in counting votes, reinforcing that he or she can only act in a ministerial fashion—the Vice President may not choose, for example, to decline to count particular votes. In most cases (*e.g.*, when one candidate has a majority of votes submitted by the States) Congress has only a ministerial role, as well. It simply counts electoral college votes provided by each State's governor. Congress is not a court and cannot overrule State and Federal court rulings in election challenges.

As January 6th approached, John Eastman and others devised a plan whereby Vice President Pence would, as the presiding officer, declare that certain electoral votes from certain States *could not* be counted at the joint session.[148] John Eastman knew before proposing this plan that it was not legal. Indeed, in a pre-election document discussing Congress's counting of electoral votes, Dr. Eastman specifically disagreed with a colleague's proposed argument that the Vice President had the power to choose which envelopes to "open" and which votes to "count." Dr. Eastman wrote:

> I don't agree with this. The 12th Amendment only says that the President of the Senate opens the ballots in the joint session then, in the passive voice, that the votes shall then be counted. 3 USC § 12 [of the Electoral Count Act] says merely that he is the presiding officer, and then it spells out specific procedures, presumptions, and default rules for which slates will be counted. Nowhere does it suggest that the president of the Senate gets to make the determination on his own. § 15 [of the Electoral Count Act] doesn't either.[149]

Despite recognizing prior to the 2020 election that the Vice President had no power to refuse to count certain electoral votes, Eastman nevertheless drafted memoranda two months later proposing that Pence could do exactly that on January 6th—refuse to count certified electoral votes from Arizona, Georgia, Michigan, Nevada, New Mexico, Pennsylvania and Wisconsin.[150]

Eastman's theory was related to other efforts overseen by President Trump (described in detail below, *see infra*) to create and transmit fake electoral slates to Congress and the National Archives, and to pressure States to change the election outcome and issue new electoral slates. Eastman supported these ideas despite writing two months earlier that:

> Article II [of the Constitution] says the electors are appointed "in such manner as the Legislature thereof may direct," but I don't think that entitles the Legislature to change the rules after the election and appoint a different slate of electors in a manner different than what was in place on election day. And 3 U.S.C. §15 [of the Electoral Count Act] gives dispositive weight to the slate of electors that was certified by the Governor in accord with 3 U.S.C. §5.[151]

Even after Eastman proposed the theories in his December and January memoranda, he acknowledged in conversations with Vice President Pence's counsel Greg Jacob that Pence could not lawfully do what his own memoranda proposed.[152] Eastman admitted that the U.S. Supreme Court would unanimously reject his legal theory. "He [Eastman] had acknowledged that he would lose 9-0 at the Supreme Court." [153] Moreover, Eastman acknowledged to Jacob that he didn't think Vice President Al Gore had that power in 2001, nor did he think Vice President Kamala Harris should have that power in 2025.[154]

In testimony before the Select Committee, Jacob described in detail why the Trump plan for Pence was illegal:

> [T]he Vice President's first instinct, when he heard this theory, was that there was no way that our Framers, who abhorred concentrated power, who had broken away from the tyranny of George III, would ever have put one person—particularly not a person who had a direct interest in the outcome because they were on the ticket for the election—in a role to have decisive impact on the outcome of the election. And our review of text, history, and, frankly, just common sense, all confirmed the Vice President's first instinct on that point. There is no justifiable basis to conclude that the Vice President has that kind of authority.[155]

This is how the Vice President later described his views in a public speech:

> I had no right to overturn the election. The Presidency belongs to the American people, and the American people alone. And frankly,

there is no idea more un-American than the notion that any one person could choose the American President. Under the Constitution, I had no right to change the outcome of our election.[156]

But as January 6th approached, President Trump nevertheless embraced the new Eastman theories, and attempted to implement them. In a series of meetings and calls, President Trump attempted to pressure Pence to intervene on January 6th to prevent Congress from counting multiple States' electoral votes for Joe Biden. At several points in the days before January 6th, President Trump was told directly that Vice President Pence could not legally do what Trump was asking. For example, at a January 4th meeting in the Oval Office, Eastman acknowledged that any variation of his proposal—whether rejecting electoral votes outright or delaying certification to send them back to the States—would violate several provisions of the Electoral Count Act. According to Greg Jacob:

> In the conversation in the Oval Office on the 4th, I had raised the fact that . . . [Eastman's] preferred course had issues with the Electoral Count Act, which he had acknowledged was the case, that there would be an inconsistency with the Electoral Count Act[ ][157]

Jacob recorded Eastman's admission in an internal memo he drafted for Vice President Pence on the evening of January 4th: "Professor Eastman acknowledges that his proposal violates several provisions of statutory law." [158] And, during a phone call with President Trump and Eastman on the evening of January 5, 2021, Eastman *again* acknowledged that his proposal also would violate several provisions of the Electoral Count Act.

> [W]e did have an in-depth discussion about [the Electoral Count Act] in the subsequent phone calls as I walked him through provision after provision on the recess and on the fact that . . . Congressmen and Senators are supposed to get to object and debate. And he acknowledged, one after another, that those provisions would—in order for us to send it back to the States, we couldn't do those things as well. We can't do a 10-day, send it back to the States, and honor an Electoral Count Act provision that says you can't recess for more than one day and, once you get to the 5th, you have to stay continuously in session.[159]

As Pence's Chief of Staff, Marc Short, testified that the Vice President also repeatedly informed President Trump that the Vice President's role on January 6th was only ministerial.

Committee Staff: But just to pick up on that, Mr. Short, was it your impression that the Vice President had directly conveyed his position on these issues to the President, not just to the world through a Dear Colleague Letter, but directly to President Trump?

Marc Short: Many times.

Committee Staff: And had been consistent in conveying his position to the President?

Short: Very consistent.[160]

As the situation grew increasingly acrimonious, Vice President Pence's private counsel Richard Cullen contacted former Fourth Circuit Judge Michael Luttig, a renowned conservative judge for whom Eastman had previously clerked, and asked Luttig to make a public statement. On January 5th, Luttig wrote the following on Twitter: "The only responsibility and power of the Vice President under the Constitution is to faithfully count the electoral college votes as they have been cast."[161] As Judge Luttig testified in the Committee's hearings, "there was no basis in the Constitution or laws of the United States at all for the theory espoused by Eastman—at all. None."[162] Judge Luttig completely rejected Eastman's "blueprint to overturn the 2020 election" as "constitutional mischief" and 'the most reckless, insidious, and calamitous failure[ ] in both legal and political judgment in American history."[163]

Contemporaneous written correspondence also confirms both that: (1) Eastman himself recognized Pence could not lawfully refuse to count electoral votes, and (2) President Trump also knew this. While sheltering in a loading dock with the Vice President during the violent January 6th attack, Greg Jacob asked Eastman in an email, "Did you advise the President that in your professional judgment the Vice President DOES NOT have the power to decide things unilaterally?" Eastman's response stated that the President had "been so advised," but then indicated that President Trump continued to pressure the Vice President to act illegally: "But you know him—once he gets something in his head, it is hard to get him to change course."[164]

To be absolutely clear, no White House lawyer believed Pence could lawfully refuse to count electoral votes. White House Counsel Pat Cipollone told the Select Committee this:

I thought that the Vice President did not have the authority to do what was being suggested under a proper reading of the law. I conveyed that, ok? I think I actually told somebody, you know, in the Vice President's—"Just blame me." You know this is—I'm not a politician, you know . . . but, you know, I just said, "I'm a lawyer. This is my legal opinion."[165]

Greg Jacob and Judge Michael Luttig testify at January 6th Select Committee hearing.
(Photo by House Creative Services)

Cipollone also testified that he was "sure [he] conveyed" his views.[166] Indeed, other testimony from Cipollone indicates that Trump knew of Cipollone's view and suggests that Trump purposely excluded Cipollone from the meeting with Pence and Pence's General Counsel on January 4th.[167] Indeed, at one point, Cipollone confronted Eastman in the hallway outside the Oval Office and expressed his disapproval of and anger with Eastman's position. According to Jason Miller, "Pat Cipollone thought the idea was nutty and had at one point confronted Eastman basically with the same sentiment" outside the Oval Office.[168] Pat Cipollone did not deny having an angry confrontation with Eastman outside of the Oval Office— though he said he didn't have a specific recollection, he had no reason to contradict what Jason Miller said and, moreover, said that Eastman was aware of his views.[169]

Likewise, Eric Herschmann, another White House lawyer, expressed the same understanding that Eastman's plan "obviously made no sense" and "had no practical ability to work."[170] Herschmann also recounted telling Eastman directly that his plan was "completely crazy":

> And I said to [Eastman], hold on a second, I want to understand what you're saying. You're saying you believe the Vice President, acting as President of the Senate, can be the sole decisionmaker as to, under your theory, who becomes the next President of the

United States? And he said, yes. And I said, are you out of your F'ing mind, right. And that was pretty blunt. I said, you're completely crazy.[171]

Deputy White House Counsel Pat Philbin also had the same understanding.[172] Indeed, as Herschmann testified, even Rudolph Giuliani doubted that Vice President Mike Pence had any legal ability to do what Eastman had proposed.[173]

Despite all this opposition from all White House lawyers, Trump nevertheless continued to exert immense pressure on Pence to refuse to count electoral votes.

The pressure began before the January 4th Oval Office meeting with Pence, Eastman, Jacob, Short and Trump, but became even more intense thereafter. On the evening of January 5, 2021, the New York Times published an article reporting that "Vice President Mike Pence told President Trump on Tuesday that he did not believe he had the power to block congressional certification of Joseph R. Biden, Jr.'s victory in the Presidential election despite President Trump's baseless insistence that he did."[174] This reporting was correct—both as to the Vice President's power and as to Vice President Pence having informed President Trump that he did not have the authority to change the outcome of the election. But in response to that story, late in the evening before the January 6th joint session, President Trump dictated to Jason Miller a statement falsely asserting, "The Vice President and I are in *total agreement* that the Vice President has the power to act."[175] This statement was released at President Trump's direction and was false.[176]

Thereafter, Trump continued to apply public pressure in a series of tweets. At 1:00 a.m. on January 6th, "[i]f Vice President @Mike_Pence comes through for us, we will win the Presidency. Many States want to decertify the mistake they made in certifying incorrect & even fraudulent numbers in a process NOT approved by their State Legislatures (which it must be). Mike can send it back!"[177] At 8:17 a.m. on January 6th, he tweeted again: "States want to correct their votes, which they now know were based on irregularities and fraud, plus corrupt process never received legislative approval. All Mike Pence has to do is send them back to the States, AND WE WIN. Do it Mike, this is a time for extreme courage!"[178]

President Trump tried to reach the Vice President early in the morning of January 6th, but the Vice President did not take the call. The President finally reached the Vice President later that morning, shouting from the Oval Office to his assistants to "get the Vice President on the phone."[179] After again telling the Vice President that he had "the legal authority to send [electoral votes] back to the respective states," President Trump grew very heated.[180] Witnesses in the Oval Office during this call told the Select

President Trump speaks with Vice President Pence over the phone in the Oval Office on the morning of January 6th.
(Photo provided to the Select Committee by the National Archives and Records Administration)

Committee that the President called Vice President Pence a "wimp," [181] told him it would be "a political career killer" to certify the lawful electoral votes electing President Biden,[182] and accused him of "not [being] tough enough to make the call." [183] As Ivanka Trump would recount to her chief of staff moments later, her father called the Vice President "the p-word" for refusing to overturn the election.[184]

In response, Vice President Pence again refused to take any action other than counting the lawfully certified electoral votes of the States. But President Trump was angry and undeterred. After the conclusion of this call, he edited his speech for the Ellipse to insert language to which his lawyers objected—targeting Vice President Pence directly.[185]

Earlier that morning, Eric Herschmann had tried to remove the reference to Vice President Pence from the speech. As he told speechwriter Stephen Miller, he "didn't concur with the legal analysis" that John Eastman had advanced and believed it "wouldn't advance the ball" to discuss it publicly.[186] But after the call with Vice President Pence, speechwriters were instructed to reinsert the line. Although the final written draft of his speech referred to Pence just once—a line President Trump didn't end up reading[187]—the President went off-script five different times to pressure the Vice President:

"I hope Mike is going to do the right thing. I hope so. Because if Mike Pence does the right thing, we win the election," Trump first told the crowd.[188]

"Mike Pence is going to have to come through for us," Trump later said, "and if he doesn't, that will be a, a sad day for our country because you're sworn to uphold our Constitution."[189]

Addressing Pence directly, Trump told the assembled crowd: "Mike Pence, I hope you're going to stand up for the good of our Constitution and for the good of our country." Trump said at another point, "And if you're not, I'm going to be very disappointed in you. I will tell you right now. I'm not hearing good stories."[190]

"So I hope Mike has the courage to do what he has to do. And I hope he doesn't listen to the RINOs and the stupid people that he's listening to," Trump said.[191]

These statements to the assembled crowd at the Ellipse had Trump's intended effect—they produced substantial anger against Pence. When Pence released a statement confirming that he would not act to prevent Congress from counting electoral votes, the crowd's reaction was harshly negative.

"I'm telling you what, I'm hearing that Pence—hearing the Pence just caved. No. Is that true? I didn't hear it. I'm hear — I'm hearing reports that Pence caved. No way. I'm telling you, if Pence caved, we're going to drag motherfuckers through the streets. You fucking politicians are going to get fucking drug through the streets."[192]

Pence voted against Trump. [Interviewer: "Ok. And that's when all this started?"] Yup. That's when we marched on the Capitol.[193]

"We just heard that Mike Pence is not going to reject any fraudulent electoral votes. [Other speaker: "Boo. You're a traitor!"] That's right. You've heard it here first. Mike Pence has betrayed the United States of America. [Other speaker: "Fuck you, Mike Pence!"] Mike Pence has betrayed this President and he has betrayed the people of the United States and we will never, ever forget." [Cheers][194]

"This woman cames [sic] up to the side of us and she says Pence folded. So it was kind of, like, Ok, well — in my mind I was thinking, well that's it. You know. Well, my son-in-law looks at me and he says I want to go in."[195]

"[Q] "What percentage of the crowd is going to the Capitol?" [A] [Oath Keeper Jessica Watkins]: "One hundred percent. It has, it has spread like wildfire that Pence has betrayed us, and everybody's marching on the Capitol. All million of us. it's insane."[196]

"Bring him out. Bring out Pence. Bring him out. Bring out Pence. Bring him out. Bring out Pence. Bring him out. Bring out Pence." [197]

"Hang Mike Pence. Hang Mike Pence. Hang Mike Pence. Hang Mike Pence. Hang Mike Pence." [198]

Once Trump returned to the White House, he was informed almost immediately that violence and lawlessness had broken out at the Capitol among his supporters.[199] At 2:24 p.m., President Trump applied yet further pressure to Pence (*see infra*), posting a tweet accusing Vice President Mike Pence of cowardice for not using his role as President of the Senate to change the outcome of the election: "Mike Pence didn't have the courage to do what should have been done to protect our Country and our Constitution, giving States a chance to certify a corrected set of facts, not the fraudulent or inaccurate ones which they were asked to previously certify. USA demands the truth!" [200] Almost immediately thereafter, the crowd around the Capitol surged, and more individuals joined the effort to confront police and break further into the building.

The sentiment expressed in President Trump's 2:24 p.m. tweet, already present in the crowd, only grew more powerful as the President's words spread. Timothy Hale-Cusanelli—a white supremacist who expressed Nazi sympathies—heard about the tweet while in the Crypt around 2:25 p.m., and he, according to the Department of Justice, "knew what that meant." Vice President Pence had decided not to keep President Trump in power.[201] Other rioters described what happened next as follows:

Once we found out Pence turned on us and that they had stolen the election, like officially, the crowd went crazy. I mean, it became a mob. We crossed the gate.[202]

Then we heard the news on [P]ence . . . And lost it . . . So we stormed.[203]

They're making an announcement right now saying if Pence betrays us you better get your mind right because we're storming that building.[204]

Minutes after the tweet—at 2:35 p.m.—rioters continued their surge and broke a security line of the DC Metropolitan Police Department, resulting in the first fighting withdrawal in the history of that force.[205]

President Trump issued this tweet after he had falsely claimed to the angry crowd that Vice President Mike Pence could "do the right thing" and ensure a second Trump term, after that angry crowd had turned into a violent mob assaulting the Capitol while chanting, "Hang Mike Pence!" [206] and after the U.S. Secret Service had evacuated the Vice President from the Senate floor.[207] One minute after the President's tweet, at 2:25 p.m., the Secret Service determined they could no longer protect the Vice President in his ceremonial office near the Senate Chamber, and evacuated the Vice President and his family to a secure location, missing the violent mob by a mere 40 feet.[208]

Further evidence presented at our hearing shows the violent reaction following President Trump's 2:24 p.m. tweet and the efforts to protect Vice President Pence in the time that followed.[209]

The day after the attack on the Capitol, Eastman called Eric Herschmann to talk about continuing litigation on behalf of the Trump Presidential Campaign in Georgia. Herschmann described his reaction to Eastman this way:

> And I said to him, are you out of your F'ing mind? Right? I said, because I only want to hear two words coming out of your mouth from now on: Orderly transition. I said, I don't want to hear any other F'ing words coming out of your mouth, no matter what, other than orderly transition. Repeat those words to me." [210]

Herschmann concluded the call by telling Eastman: "Now I'm going to give you the best free legal advice you're ever getting in your life. Get a great F'ing criminal defense lawyer, you're going to need it," and hanging up the phone.[211]

In the course of investigating this series of facts, the Select Committee subpoenaed Eastman's emails from his employer, Chapman University.[212] Eastman sued to prevent Chapman from producing the emails, arguing that the emails were attorney-client privileged. Federal District Court Judge David Carter reviewed Eastman's emails *in camera* to determine, among other things, whether the emails had to be produced because they likely furthered a crime committed by one of Eastman's clients or by Eastman himself. In addition to reviewing the emails themselves, Judge Carter reviewed substantial additional evidence presented by the Select Committee and by Eastman.

After reciting a series of factual findings regarding President Trump's multi-part plan to overturn the election, Judge Carter concluded that President Trump likely violated two criminal statutes: 18 U.S.C. § 1512(c) (corruptly obstructing, impeding or influencing Congress's official proceeding to count electoral votes); and 18 U.S.C. § 371 (conspiring to defraud the United States). The Court also concluded that John Eastman likely violated at least one of these criminal laws. As to §1512(c), Judge Carter explained:

> Taken together, this evidence demonstrates that President Trump likely knew the electoral count plan had no factual justification.
>
> The plan not only lacked factual basis but also legal justification. . . .

The illegality of the plan was obvious. Our nation was founded on the peaceful transition of power, epitomized by George Washington laying down his sword to make way for democratic elections. Ignoring this history, President Trump vigorously campaigned for the Vice President to single-handedly determine the results of the 2020 election. . . . Every American—and certainly the President of the United States—knows that in a democracy, leaders are elected, not installed. With a plan this "BOLD," President Trump knowingly tried to subvert this fundamental principle. Based on the evidence, the Court finds it more likely than not that President Trump corruptly attempted to obstruct the Joint Session of Congress on January 6, 2021.[213]

As to 18 U.S.C. § 371, Judge Carter identified evidence demonstrating that both President Trump and John Eastman knew their electoral count plan was illegal, and knew it could not "survive judicial scrutiny" in any of its iterations:

Dr. Eastman himself repeatedly recognized that his plan had no legal support. . . . Dr. Eastman likely acted deceitfully and dishonestly each time he pushed an outcome-driven plan that he knew was unsupported by the law.[214]

Finally, Judge Carter concluded:

Dr. Eastman and President Trump launched a campaign to overturn a democratic election, an action unprecedented in American history. Their campaign was not confined to the ivory tower—it was a coup in search of a legal theory. The plan spurred violent attacks on the seat of our nation's government, led to the deaths of several law enforcement officers, and deepened public distrust in our political process.[215]

Judge Luttig reached similar conclusions during his live hearing testimony: "I have written, as you said, Chairman Thompson, that, today, almost two years after that fateful day in January 2021, that, still, Donald Trump and his allies and supporters are a clear and present danger to American democracy."[216]

During the hearing, Judge Luttig took issue with certain of Greg Jacob's characterizations of the 12th Amendment's text, explaining that the applicable text was not ambiguous in any way. The Committee agrees with Judge Luttig: the application of the Twelfth Amendment's text is plain in this context; it does not authorize Congress to second-guess State and Federal courts and refuse to count State electoral votes based on concerns about fraud. *See infra.* Although Jacob did not discuss his position in great detail during the hearing, his private testimony gives more insight on his actual views:

> In my view, a lot has been said about the fact that the role of the Vice President in the electoral count on January 6th is purely ministerial, and that is a correct conclusion. But if you look at the constitutional text, the role of Congress is purely ministerial as well. You open the certificates and you count them. Those are the only things provided for in the Constitution.[217]

EFFORTS TO PRESSURE STATES TO CHANGE THE ELECTION OUTCOME, AND TO CREATE AND TRANSMIT FAKE ELECTION CERTIFICATES

Anticipating that the Eastman strategy for January 6th would be implemented, President Trump worked with a handful of others to prepare a series of false Trump electoral slates for seven States Biden actually won. President Trump personally conducted a teleconference with Eastman and Republican National Committee Chair Ronna McDaniel "a few days before December 14" and solicited the RNC's assistance with the scheme.[218] McDaniel agreed to provide that assistance.[219]

A series of contemporaneous documents demonstrate what President Trump and his allies, including attorney Kenneth Chesebro, were attempting to accomplish: they anticipated that the President of the Senate (which, under the Constitution, is the Vice President) could rely upon these false slates of electors on January 6th to justify refusing to count genuine electoral votes.[220]

The false slates were created by fake Republican electors on December 14th, at the same time the actual, certified electors in those States were meeting to cast their States' Electoral College votes for President Biden. By that point in time, election-related litigation was over in all or nearly all of the subject States, and Trump Campaign election lawyers realized that the fake slates could not be lawful or justifiable on any grounds. Justin Clark, the Trump Campaign Deputy Campaign Manager and Senior Counsel told the Select Committee that he "had real problems with the process."[221] Clark warned his colleagues, "unless we have litigation pending like in these States, like, I don't think this is appropriate or, you know, this isn't the right thing to do. I don't remember how I phrased it, but I got into a little bit of a back and forth and I think it was with Ken Chesebro, where I said, 'Alright, you know, you just get after it, like, I'm out.' "[222]

Matthew Morgan, the Trump Campaign General Counsel, told the Select Committee that without an official State certificate of ascertainment,[223] "the [fake] electors were, for lack of a better way of saying it, no good or not—not valid."[224]

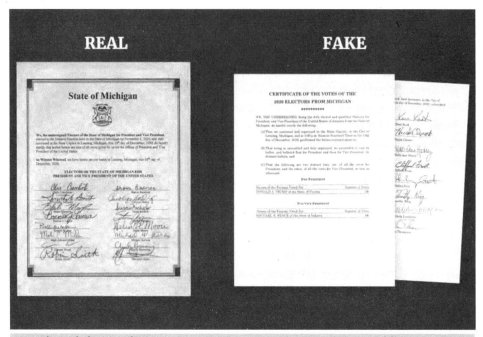

REAL   **FAKE**

Graphic depicting the difference between the real and the fake elector certificates.

The Office of White House Counsel also appears to have expressed concerns with this fake elector plan. In his interview by the Select Committee, White House Counsel Pat Cipollone acknowledged his view that by mid-December, the process was "done" and that his deputy, Pat Philbin, may have advised against the fake elector strategy.[225] In an informal Committee interview, Philbin described the fake elector scheme as one of the "bad theories" that were like "Whac-A-Mole" in the White House during this period.[226] Cipollone agreed with this characterization.[227]

In her testimony, Cassidy Hutchinson testified that she heard at least one member of the White House Counsel's Office say that the plan was not legal:

> Committee Staff: [T]o be clear, did you hear the White House Counsel's Office say that this plan to have alternate electors meet and cast votes for Donald Trump in States that he had lost was not legally sound?

> Hutchinson: Yes, sir.[228]

Multiple Republicans who were persuaded to sign the fake certificates also testified that they felt misled or betrayed, and would not have done so had they known that the fake votes would be used on January 6th without an intervening court ruling. One elector told the Select Committee that he thought his vote would be strictly contingent: "[I]t was a very consistent message that we were told throughout all of that, is this is the only reason why we're doing this, is to preserve the integrity of being able to have a challenge."[229]

The "Chairperson" of the Wisconsin fake electors, who was also at the time Chairman of the Wisconsin Republican Party, insisted in testimony to the Select Committee that he "was told that these would only count if a court ruled in our favor" and that he wouldn't have supported anyone using the Trump electors' votes without a court ruling.[230]

Despite the fact that all major election lawsuits thus far had failed, President Trump and his co-conspirators in this effort, including John Eastman and Kenneth Chesebro, pressed forward with the fake elector scheme. Ultimately, these false electoral slates, five of which purported to represent the "duly elected" electoral college votes of their States, were transmitted to Executive Branch officials at the National Archives, and to the Legislative Branch, including to the Office of the President of the Senate, Vice President Mike Pence.[231]

The fake electors followed Chesebro's step-by-step instructions for completing and mailing the fake certificates to multiple officials in the U.S. Government,[232] complete with registered mail stickers and return address labels identifying senders like the "Arizona Republican Party" and the "Georgia Republican Party."[233] The Wisconsin Republican Party's fake certificates apparently weren't properly delivered, however, so the Trump Campaign arranged to fly them to Washington just before the joint session on January 6th, and try to deliver them to the Vice President via Senator Ron Johnson and Representative Mike Kelly's offices.[234] Both Johnson and Kelly's offices attempted to do so, but Vice President Pence's aide refused the delivery.[235]

Despite pressure from President Trump, Vice President Pence and the Senate parliamentarian refused to recognize or count the unofficial fake electoral votes. Greg Jacob testified that he advised Vice President Pence on January 2nd that "none of the slates that had been sent in would qualify as an alternate slate" under the law and that the Senate Parliamentarian "was in agreement" with this conclusion.[236]

* * *

In addition to this plan to create and transmit fake electoral slates, Donald Trump was also personally and substantially involved in multiple efforts to pressure State election officials and State legislatures to alter official lawful election results. As U.S. District Judge Carter stated in his June 7, 2022, opinion:

Dr. Eastman's actions in these few weeks [in December 2020] indicate that his and President Trump's pressure campaign to stop the electoral count did not end with Vice President Pence—it targeted every tier of federal and state elected officials. Convincing state legislatures to certify competing electors was essential to stop the count and ensure President Trump's reelection.[237]

Judge Carter also explained that "Dr. Eastman and President Trump's plan to disrupt the Joint Session was fully formed and actionable as early as December 7, 2020."[238]

Chapter 2 of this report provides substantial detail on many of President Trump's specific efforts to apply pressure to State officials and legislators. We provide a few examples here:

During a January 2, 2021, call, President Trump pressured Georgia's Republican Secretary of State Brad Raffensperger to "find 11,780 votes." During that call, President Trump asserted conspiracy theories about the election that Department of Justice officials had already debunked. President Trump also made a thinly veiled threat to Raffensperger and his attorney about his failure to respond to President Trump's demands: "That's a criminal, that's a criminal offense . . . That's a big risk to you and to Ryan, your lawyer . . . I'm notifying you that you're letting it happen."[239]

Judge Carter drew these conclusions:

Mr. Raffensperger debunked the President's allegations "point by point" and explained that "the data you have is wrong;" however, President Trump still told him, "I just want to find 11,780 votes."[240]

* * *

President Trump's repeated pleas for Georgia Secretary of State Raffensperger clearly demonstrate that his justification was not to investigate fraud, but to win the election. . . . Taken together, this evidence demonstrates that President Trump likely knew the electoral count plan had no factual justification. The plan not only lacked factual basis but also legal justification.[241]

That call to Raffensperger came on the heels of President Trump's repeated attacks on Raffensperger, election workers, and other public servants about President Trump's loss in the election. A month earlier, the Georgia Secretary of State's Chief Operating Officer, Gabriel Sterling, had given this explicit public warning to President Trump and his team, a warning that the Select Committee has determined President Trump apparently saw and disregarded:[242]

[I]t has all gone too far. All of it. . . .

A 20-something tech in Gwinnett County today has death threats and a noose put out, saying he should be hung for treason because he was transferring a report on batches from an EMS to a county computer so he could read it.

It has to stop.

Mr. President, you have not condemned these actions or this language. Senators, you have not condemned this language or these actions. This has to stop. We need you to step up. And if you're going to take a position of leadership, show some.

My boss, Secretary Raffensperger—his address is out there. They have people doing caravans in front of their house, they've had people come onto their property. Tricia, his wife of 40 years, is getting sexualized threats through her cellphone.

It has to stop.

This is elections, this is the backbone of democracy, and all of you who have not said a damn word are complicit in this. It's too much....

What you don't have the ability to do—and you need to step up and say this—is stop inspiring people to commit potential acts of violence. Someone's going to get hurt. Someone's going to get shot. Someone's going to get killed.[243]

The stark warning was entirely appropriate, and prescient. In addition to the examples Sterling identified, President Trump and his team were also fixated on Georgia election workers Ruby Freeman and Wandrea "Shaye" Moss. He and Giuliani mentioned Freeman repeatedly in meetings with State legislators, at public rallies, and in the January 2nd call with Raffensperger. Referring to a video clip, Giuliani even accused Freeman and Moss of trading USB drives to affect votes "as if they [were] vials of heroin or cocaine."[244] This was completely bogus: it was not a USB drive; it was a ginger mint.[245]

After their contact information was published, Trump supporters sent hundreds of threats to the women and even showed up at Freeman's home.[246] As Freeman testified to the Select Committee, Trump and his followers' conduct had a profound impact on her life. She left her home based on advice from the FBI, and wouldn't move back for months.[247] And she explained, "I've lost my sense of security—all because a group of people, starting with Number 45 [Donald Trump] and his ally Rudy Giuliani, decided to scapegoat me and my daughter Shaye to push their own lies

Gabriel Sterling at a press conference on November 6, 2020 in Atlanta, Georgia.
(Photo by Jessica McGowan/Getty Images)

about how the Presidential election was stolen." [248] The treatment of Freeman and Moss was callous, inhumane, and inexcusable. Rudolph Giuliani and others with responsibility should be held accountable.

In Arizona, a primary target of President Trump's pressure, and ire, was House Speaker Russell "Rusty" Bowers, a longtime Republican who had served 17 years in the State legislature. Throughout November and December, Bowers spoke to President Trump, Giuliani, and members of Giuliani's legal team, in person or on the phone. During these calls, President Trump and others alleged that the results in Arizona were affected by fraud and asked that Bowers consider replacing Presidential electors for Biden with electors for President Trump.[249] Bowers demanded proof for the claims of fraud, but never got it. At one point, after Bowers pressed Giuliani on the claims of fraud, Giuliani responded, "we've got lots of theories, we just don't have the evidence." [250] Bowers explained to Giuliani: "You are asking me do something against my oath, and I will not break my oath." [251]

President Trump and his supporters' intimidation tactics affected Bowers, too. Bowers's personal cell phone and home address were doxed,[252] leading demonstrators to show up at his home and shout insults until police arrived. One protestor who showed up at his home was armed and believed to be a member of an extremist militia.[253] Another hired a truck with a defamatory and profane allegation that Bowers, a deeply religious man, was a pedophile, and drove it through Bowers's neighborhood.[254] This, again, is the conduct of thugs and criminals, each of whom should be held accountable.

In Michigan, President Trump focused on Republican Senate Majority Leader Mike Shirkey and Republican House Speaker Lee Chatfield. He invited them to the White House for a November 20, 2020, meeting during which President Trump and Giuliani, who joined by phone, went through a "litany" of false allegations about supposed fraud in Michigan's election.[255] Chatfield recalled President Trump's more generic directive for the group to "have some backbone and do the right thing," which he understood to mean overturning the election by naming Michigan's Electoral College electors for President Trump.[256] Shirkey told President Trump that he wouldn't do anything that would violate Michigan law,[257] and after the meeting ended, issued a joint statement with Chatfield: "We have not yet been made aware of any information that would change the outcome of the election in Michigan and as legislative leaders, we will follow the law and follow the normal process regarding Michigan's electors, just as we have said throughout this election." [258]

When President Trump couldn't convince Shirkey and Chatfield to change the outcome of the election in Michigan during that meeting or in calls after, he or his team maliciously tweeted out Shirkey's personal cell phone number and a number for Chatfield that turned out to be wrong.[259] Shirkey received nearly 4,000 text messages after that, and another private citizen reported being inundated with calls and texts intended for Chatfield.[260]

None of Donald Trump's efforts ultimately succeeded in changing the official results in any State. That these efforts had failed was apparent to Donald Trump and his co-conspirators well before January 6th. By January 6th, there was no evidence at all that a majority of any State legislature would even attempt to change its electoral votes.[261]

This past October, U.S. District Court Judge David Carter issued a further ruling relating to one of President Trump's lawsuits in Georgia. Judge Carter applied the crime-fraud exception to attorney-client privilege again, and identified potential criminal activity related to a knowingly false representation by Donald Trump to a Federal court. He wrote:

> The emails show that President Trump knew that the specific numbers of voter fraud were wrong but continued to tout those numbers, both in court and in public.[262]

Steven Engel, Jeffrey Rosen and Richard Donoghue at a Select Committee hearing on June 23, 2022.

(Photo by House Creative Services)

As John Eastman wrote in an email on December 31, 2020, President Trump was "made aware that some of the allegations (and evidence proffered by the experts)" in a verified State court complaint was "inaccurate." [263] Dr. Eastman noted that "with that knowledge" President Trump could not accurately verify a Federal court complaint that incorporated by reference the "inaccurate" State court complaint: "I have no doubt that an aggressive DA or US Atty someplace will go after both the President and his lawyers once all the dust settles on this." [264] Despite this specific warning, "President Trump and his attorneys ultimately filed the complaint with the same inaccurate numbers without rectifying, clarifying, or otherwise changing them." [265] And President Trump personally "signed a verification swearing under oath that the incorporated, inaccurate numbers 'are true and correct' or 'believed to be true and correct' to the best of his knowledge and belief." [266] The numbers were not correct, and President Trump and his legal team knew it.

EFFORTS TO CORRUPT THE DEPARTMENT OF JUSTICE

In the weeks after the 2020 election, Attorney General Barr advised President Trump that the Department of Justice had not seen any evidence to support Trump's theory that the election was stolen by fraud. Acting Attorney General Jeffrey Rosen and his Deputy repeatedly reinforced to President Trump that his claims of election fraud were false when they took over in mid-December. Also in mid-December 2020, Attorney General Barr announced his plans to resign. Between that time and January 6th, Trump spoke with Acting Attorney General Jeff Rosen and Acting Deputy Richard Donoghue repeatedly, attempting to persuade them and the Department of Justice to find factual support for his stolen election claims and thereby to assist his efforts to reverse election results.

As Rosen publicly testified, ". . . between December 23rd and January 3rd, the President either called me or met with me virtually every day, with one or two exceptions, like Christmas Day."[267] As discussed earlier, Justice Department investigations had demonstrated that the stolen election claims were false; both Rosen and Donoghue told President Trump this comprehensively and repeatedly.

One of those conversations occurred on December 27th, when President Trump called Rosen to go through a "stream of allegations" about the election.[268] Donoghue described that call as an "escalation of the earlier conversations" they had.[269] Initially, President Trump called Rosen directly. When Donoghue joined the call, he sought to "make it clear to the President [that] these allegations were simply not true."[270]

> So [the President] went through [the allegations]—in what for me was a 90-minute conversation or so, and what for the former Acting AG was a 2-hour conversation—as the President went through them I went piece by piece to say "no, that's false, that is not true," and to correct him really in a serial fashion as he moved from one theory to another.[271]

The President raised, among others, debunked claims about voting machines in Michigan, a truck driver who allegedly moved ballots from New York to Pennsylvania, and a purported election fraud at the State Farm Arena in Georgia.[272] None of the allegations were credible, and Rosen and Donoghue said so to the President.[273]

At one point during the December 27th call in which Donoghue refuted President Trump's fraud allegations, Donoghue recorded in handwritten notes a request President Trump made specifically to him and Acting Attorney General Rosen: "Just say the election was corrupt and leave the rest to me and the Republican Congressmen."[274] Donoghue explained: "[T]he Department had zero involvement in anyone's political strategy," and "he wanted us to say that it was corrupt."[275] "We told him we were not going to do that."[276] At the time, neither Rosen nor Donoghue knew the full extent to which Republican Congressmen, including Representative Scott Perry, were attempting to assist President Trump to overturn the election results.

The Committee's investigation has shown that Congressman Perry was working with one Department of Justice official, Jeffrey Clark, regarding the stolen election claims. Perry was working with Clark and with President Trump and Chief of Staff Mark Meadows with this goal: to enlist Clark to reverse the Department of Justice's findings regarding the election and help overturn the election outcome.[277]

After introducing Clark to the President, Perry sent multiple text messages to Meadows between December 26th and December 28th, pressing that Clark be elevated within the Department. Perry reminded Meadows that there are only "11 days to 1/6 . . . We gotta get going!," and, as the days went on, one asking, "Did you call Jeff Clark?" [278]

Acting Attorney General Rosen first learned about Clark's contact with President Trump in a call on Christmas Eve. On that call, President Trump mentioned Clark to Rosen, who was surprised to learn that Trump knew Clark and had met with him. Rosen later confronted Clark about the contact: "Jeff, anything going on that you think I should know about?" [279] Clark didn't "immediately volunteer" the fact that he had met with the President, but ultimately "acknowledged that he had been at a meeting with the President in the Oval Office, not alone, with other people." [280] Clark was "kind of defensive" and "somewhat apologetic," "casting it as that he had had a meeting with Congressman Perry from Pennsylvania and that, to his surprise, or, you know, he hadn't anticipated it, that they somehow wound up at a meeting in the Oval Office." [281] Clark's contact with President Trump violated both Justice Department and White House policies designed to prevent political pressure on the Department.[282]

While Clark initially appeared apologetic and assured Rosen that "[i]t won't happen again," [283] he nevertheless continued to work and meet secretly with President Trump and Congressman Perry. Less than five days after assuring Rosen that he would comply with the Department's White House contacts policy, Clark told Rosen and Donoghue that he had again violated that policy. Donoghue confronted him: "I reminded him that I was his boss and that I had directed him to do otherwise." [284]

Around the same time, Representative Perry called Acting Deputy Attorney General Donoghue, criticized the FBI, and suggested that the Department hadn't been doing its job. Perry told Donoghue that Clark "would do something about this." [285]

On December 28th, Clark worked with a Department employee named Kenneth Klukowski—a political appointee who had earlier worked with John Eastman—to produce a draft letter from the Justice Department to the

State legislature of Georgia.[286] That letter mirrored a number of the positions President Trump and Eastman were taking at the time.[287] (Although both Clark and Eastman refused to answer questions by asserting their Fifth Amendment right against self-incrimination, evidence shows that Clark and Eastman were in communication in this period leading up to January 6th.[288] The draft letter to Georgia was intended to be one of several Department letters to State legislatures in swing States that had voted for Biden.[289]

The letter read: "The Department of Justice is investigating various irregularities in the 2020 election for President of the United States."[290] Clark continued: "The Department will update you as we are able on investigatory progress, but at this time we have identified significant concerns that may have impacted the outcome of the election in multiple States, including the State of Georgia."[291] This was *affirmatively untrue.* The Department had conducted many investigations of election fraud allegations by that point, but it absolutely did not have "significant concerns" that fraud "may have impacted the outcome of the election" in any State. Jeff Clark knew this; Donoghue confirmed it again in an email responding to Clark's letter: "[W]e simply do not currently have a basis to make such a statement. Despite dramatic claims to the contrary, we have not seen the type of fraud that calls into question the reported (and certified) results of the election."[292]

The letter also explicitly recommended that Georgia's State legislature should call a special session to evaluate potential election fraud. "In light of these developments, the Department recommends that the Georgia General Assembly should convene in special session so that its legislators are in a special position to take additional testimony, receive new evidence, and deliberate on the matter consistent with its duties under the U.S. Constitution."[293]

Clark's draft letter also referenced the fake electors that President Trump and his campaign organized—arguing falsely that there were currently two competing slates of legitimate Presidential electors in Georgia:[294]

> The Department believes that in Georgia and several other States, both a slate of electors supporting Joseph R. Biden, Jr., and a separate slate of electors supporting Donald J. Trump, gathered on [December 14, 2020] at the proper location to cast their ballots, and that both sets of those ballots have been transmitted to Washington, D.C., to be opened by Vice President Pence.[295]

This, of course, was part of Donald Trump and John Eastman's plan for January 6th. This letter reflects an effort to use the Department of Justice to help overturn the election outcome in Georgia and elsewhere. Rosen and Donoghue reacted immediately to this draft letter:

"[T]here's no chance that I would sign this letter or anything remotely like this," Donoghue wrote.[296] The plan set forth by Clark was "not even within the realm of possibility,"[297] and Donoghue warned that if they sent Clark's letter, it "would be a grave step for the Department to take and it could have tremendous Constitutional, political and social ramifications for the country."[298]

As Richard Donoghue testified when describing his response to Clark's proposed letter:

> Well, I had to read both the email and the attached letter twice to make sure I really understood what he was proposing because it was so extreme to me I had a hard time getting my head around it initially.
>
> But I read it, and I did understand it for what he intended, and I had to sit down and sort of compose what I thought was an appropriate response . . . .
>
> In my response I explained a number of reasons this is not the Department's role to suggest or dictate to State legislatures how they should select their electors. But more importantly, this was not based on fact. This was actually contrary to the facts as developed by Department investigations over the last several weeks and months.
>
> So, I respond to that. And for the department to insert itself into the political process this way I think would have had grave consequences for the country. It may very well have spiraled us into a constitutional crisis.[299]

Rosen and Donoghue also met with Clark about the letter. Their conversation "was a very difficult and contentious" one, according to Donoghue.[300] "What you're proposing is nothing less than the United States Justice Department meddling in the outcome of a Presidential election," Donoghue admonished Clark, to which Clark indignantly responded, "I think a lot of people have meddled in this election."[301]

Both Rosen and Donoghue refused to sign the letter, and confronted Clark with the actual results of the Department's investigations.[302] They also permitted Clark access to a classified briefing from the Office of the Director of National Intelligence ("ODNI") showing Clark that allegations he made to Rosen and Donoghue about foreign interference with voting machines were not true. According to Rosen, the decision to give Clark the briefing at that point "was a difficult question because, if he's going to brief the President, I reluctantly think it's probably better that he's heard from Director Ratcliffe than that he not, even if—I don't think he should brief the President. But, at this point, he's telling me that this is happening whether I agree with it or not. So, so I let him have that briefing." [303]

After Clark received the ODNI briefing, "he acknowledged [to Donoghue] that there was nothing in that briefing that would have supported his earlier suspicion about foreign involvement." [304] While Clark then dropped his claims about foreign interference, he continued to press to send the letter to Georgia and other States, despite being told that the Department of Justice investigations had found no fraud sufficient to overturn the election outcome in Georgia or any other States. This was an intentional choice by Jeff Clark to contradict specific Department findings on election fraud, and purposely insert the Department into the Presidential election on President Trump's behalf and risk creating or exacerbating a constitutional crisis.

By this point, President Trump recognized that neither Rosen nor Donoghue would sign the letter or support his false election claims. President Trump and his team then communicated further with Clark and offered him the job of Acting Attorney General. On January 2nd, Clark told Rosen that he "would turn down the President's offer if [Rosen] reversed [his] position and signed the letter" that he and Klukowski had drafted. [305] The next day, Clark decided to accept and informed Rosen, who then called White House Counsel to seek a meeting directly with President Trump. As Rosen put it, "I wasn't going to accept being fired by my subordinate, so I wanted to talk to the President directly." [306]

On January 3rd, that meeting was convened. Although contemporaneous White House documents suggest that Clark had *already* been appointed as the Acting Attorney General, [307] all the participants in the meeting other than Clark and President Trump aggressively opposed Clark's appointment.

At that point, Rosen decided to "broaden the circle" and ask that his subordinates inform all the other Assistant Attorneys General (AAGs) what was afoot. [308] Rosen wanted to know how the AAGs would respond if Jeff Clark was installed as the Acting Attorney General. Pat Hovakimian, who worked for Rosen, then set up a conference call. The AAGs almost immediately agreed that they would resign if Rosen was removed from office. [309]

Rosen, Donoghue, and Steve Engel, the Assistant Attorney General for the Office of Legal Counsel, attended the meeting. White House lawyers Pat Cipollone, Eric Herschmann and Pat Philbin joined as well.

When the meeting started, Clark attempted to defend his appointment. Clark declared that this was the "last opportunity to sort of set things straight with this defective election," and he had the "intelligence," the "will," and "desire" to "pursue these matters in the way that the President thought most appropriate." [310] Everyone else present disagreed that Clark could conceivably accomplish these things.

White House Counsel Pat Cipollone threatened to resign as well, describing Clark's letter as a "murder-suicide pact." [311] Cipollone warned that the letter would "damage everyone who touches it" and no one should have anything to do with it.[312]

President Trump asked Donoghue and Engel what they would do if Clark took office. Both confirmed they would resign.[313] Steve Engel recalled that the President next asked if he would resign:

> At some point, [ ] I believe Rich Donoghue said that senior Department officials would all resign if Mr. Clark were put in, and the President turned to me and said, "Steve, you wouldn't resign, would you?" I said, "Well, Mr. President, I've been with you through four Attorneys General, including two Acting Attorneys General, and I just couldn't be part of this if Mr. Clark were here." And I said, "And I believe that the other senior Department officials would resign as well. And Mr. Clark would be here by himself with a hostile building, those folks who remained, and nothing would get done." [314]

Donoghue added that they would not be the only ones to resign. "You should understand that your entire Department leadership will resign," Donoghue recalled saying. This included every Assistant Attorney General. "Mr. President, these aren't bureaucratic leftovers from another administration," Donoghue reminded Trump, "You picked them. This is your leadership team." Donoghue added, "And what happens if, within 48 hours, we have hundreds of resignations from your Justice Department because of your actions? What does that say about your leadership?" [315] Steve Engel then reinforced Donoghue's point, saying that Clark would be leading a "graveyard."

Faced with mass resignations and recognizing that the "breakage" could be too severe, Donald Trump decided to rescind his offer to Clark and drop his plans to use the Justice Department to aid in his efforts to overturn the election outcome.[316] The President looked at Clark and said, "I appreciate your willingness to do it. I appreciate you being willing to suffer the abuse. But the reality is, you're not going to get anything done. These guys are going to quit. Everyone else is going to resign. It's going to be a disaster. The bureaucracy will eat you alive. And no matter how much you want to get things done in the next few weeks, you won't be able to get it done, and it's not going to be worth the breakage." [317]

* * *

Evidence gathered by the Committee also suggests that President Trump offered Sidney Powell the position of Special Counsel for election

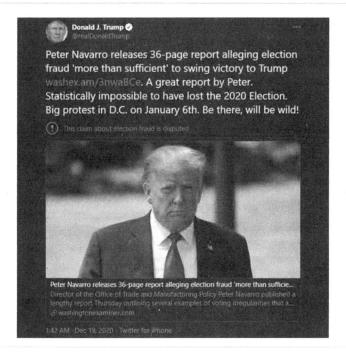

related matters during a highly charged White House meeting on December 18, 2020.[318] White House lawyers vehemently opposed Powell's appointment, and it also was not ultimately made formal.

SUMMONING A MOB TO WASHINGTON, AND KNOWING THEY WERE ANGRY AND ARMED, INSTRUCTING THEM TO MARCH TO THE CAPITOL

In the early morning hours of December 19th, shortly after the contentious December 18th White House meeting with Sidney Powell and others, Donald Trump sent a tweet urging his supporters to travel to Washington for January 6th. In that tweet, President Trump attached false allegations that the election was stolen and promised a "wild" time on January 6th.[319] This Twitter invitation was followed by over a dozen other instances in which he used Twitter to encourage supporters to rally for him in Washington, DC on January 6th.[320]

The Committee has assembled detailed material demonstrating the effects of these communications on members of far-right extremist groups, like the Proud Boys, Oath Keepers, Three Percenters, and others, and on individuals looking to respond to their president's call to action. President Trump's supporters believed the election was stolen because they listened to his words,[321] and they knew what he had called them to do; stop the certification of the electoral count.[322]

For example, one supporter, Charles Bradford Smith, noted on December 22, 2020, that "Trump is asking everyone to go" to Washington, DC on

January 6th "to fill the streets" on the "day Pence counts up the votes."[323] Derek Sulenta posted to Facebook on December 23, 2020, that "I'll be there Jan 6th to support the president no matter what happens" because "That's the day he called for patriots to show up."[324] By December 31, 2020, Robert Morss believed January 6th stood for the moment when "1776 Will Commence Again" because President Trump asked them to "Be there, Will be Wild."[325] Kenneth Grayson predicted what would eventually happen on January 6th, when on December 23, 2020, he wrote on Facebook that President Trump called people to Washington, DC through his December 19th tweet and then added "IF TRUMP TELLS US TO STORM THE FUKIN CAPITAL IMA DO THAT THEN!"[326] Some demonstrated their inspiration for January 6th by circulating flyers, which proclaimed "#OccupyCongress" over images of the United States Capitol.[327] Robert Gieswein, a Coloradan affiliated with Three Percenters who was among the first to breach the Capitol, said that he came to Washington, DC "to keep President Trump in."[328]

Chapter 8 of this report documents how the Proud Boys led the attack, penetrated the Capitol, and led hundreds of others inside. Multiple Proud Boys reacted immediately to President Trump's December 19th tweet and began their planning. Immediately, Proud Boys leaders reorganized their hierarchy, with Enrique Tarrio, Joseph Biggs, and Ethan Nordean messaging groups of Proud Boys about what to expect on January 6th.[329] Tarrio created a group chat known as the Ministry of Self-Defense for hand-selected Proud Boys whom he wanted to "organize and direct" plans for January 6th.[330] On social media, Tarrio referenced "revolt" and "[r]evolution," and conspicuously asked "What if we invade it?" on Telegram.[331] As of December 29, 2020, Tarrio told the group the events on January 6th would be "centered around the Capitol."[332]

At the time of publication of this report, prosecutions of certain Proud Boys are ongoing. To date, one Proud Boy has pled guilty to seditious conspiracy and other Proud Boys have pled guilty to other crimes, including conspiracy to obstruct Congress.[333] Jeremy Bertino, a Proud Boy who pled guilty to seditious conspiracy, admitted that he:

> understood from internal discussions among the Proud Boys that in the leadup to January 6, the willingness to resort to unlawful conduct increasingly included a willingness to use and promote violence to achieve political objectives.[334]

Moreover,

> Bertino believed that the 2020 election had been "stolen" and, as January 6, 2021, approached, believed that drastic measures,

including violence, were necessary to prevent Congress from certifying the Electoral College Vote on January 6, 2021. Bertino made his views in this regard known publicly, as well as in private discussions with MOSD leadership. Bertino understood from his discussions with MOSD leadership that they agreed that the election had been stolen, that the purpose of traveling to Washington, D.C., on January 6, 2021, was to stop the certification of the Electoral College Vote, and that the MOSD leaders were willing to do whatever it would take, including using force against police and others, to achieve that objective.[335]

As set out in Bertino's plea agreement, members of MOSD:

openly discussed plans for potential violence at the Capitol [. . . and] members of MOSD leadership were discussing the possibility of storming the Capitol. Bertino believed that storming the Capitol would achieve the group's goal of stopping Congress from certifying the Electoral College Vote. Bertino understood that storming the Capitol or its grounds would be illegal and would require using force against police or other government officials.[336]

Another Proud Boy who has pled guilty to conspiracy and assault charges, Charles Donohoe, understood that the Proud Boys planned to storm the Capitol. Donohoe, a Proud Boys local chapter leader from North Carolina:

was aware [as early as January 4, 2021] that members of MOSD leadership were discussing the possibility of storming the Capitol. Donohoe believed that storming the Capitol would achieve the group's goal of stopping the government from carrying out the transfer of presidential power.[337]

The Department of Justice has charged a number of Oath Keepers with seditious conspiracy. Specifically, the government alleges that "[a]fter the Presidential Election, Elmer Stewart Rhodes III conspired with his co-defendants, introduced below, and other co-conspirators, known and unknown to the Grand Jury, to oppose by force the lawful transfer of presidential power."[338] A jury agreed, convicting Stewart Rhodes and Kelly Meggs—the leader of the Florida Oath Keepers chapter—of seditious conspiracy. The jury also convicted Rhodes and Meggs, as well as fellow Oath Keepers Jessica Watkins, Kenneth Harrelson, and Thomas Caldwell,[339] of other serious felonies for their actions on January 6th.[340]

Meggs celebrated the December 19th tweet, sending an encrypted Signal message to Florida Oath Keepers that President Trump "wants us to make it WILD that's what he's saying. He called us all to the Capitol and wants us to make it wild!!! . . . Gentlemen we are heading to DC pack your shit!!"[341] Similarly, Oath Keeper Joshua James—who pleaded guilty to seditious conspiracy—told Oath Keepers that there was now a "NATIONAL CALL TO ACTION FOR DC JAN 6TH" following President Trump's words.[342]

Stewart Rhodes, the Oath Keepers' founder, felt that "the time for peaceful protest is over" after December 19th and, according to the government, "urged President Trump to use military force to stop the lawful transfer of presidential power, describing January 6, 2021, as "a hard constitutional deadline" to do so.[343] Rhodes created a "an invitation-only Signal group chat titled, 'DC OP: Jan 6 21'" on December 30, 2020, which he and other Oath Keepers, like Meggs and James, used to plan for January 6th, including by creating a "quick reaction force" of firearms to be stashed in Virginia.[344]

Multiple members of the Oath Keepers have pleaded guilty to seditious conspiracy. Brian Ulrich started planning for January 6th right after President Trump sent out his December 19th tweet. The Department of Justice summarized Ulrich's communications, as follows:

> Ulrich messaged the "Oath Keepers of Georgia" Signal group chat, "Trump acts now maybe a few hundred radicals die trying to burn down cities . . . Trump sits on his hands Biden wins . . . millions die resisting the death of the 1st and 2nd amendment." On December 20, 2020, an individual in the "Oath Keepers of Georgia" Signal group chat, who later traveled with Ulrich to Washington, D.C., and breached the Capitol grounds with Ulrich on January 6, 2021, messaged, "January 6th. The great reset. America or not."[345]

The Justice Department's Statement of Offense for Oath Keeper Joshua James provided these details:

> In advance of and on January 6, 2021, James and others agreed to take part in the plan developed by Rhodes to use any means necessary, up to and including the use of force, to stop the lawful transfer of presidential power. In the weeks leading up to January 6, 2021, Rhodes instructed James and other coconspirators to be prepared, if called upon, to report to the White House grounds to secure the perimeter and use lethal force if necessary against anyone who tried to remove President Trump from the White House, including the National Guard or other government actors who might be sent to remove President Trump as a result of the Presidential Election.[346]

The former President's call also galvanized Three Percenters to act. A group known as The Three Percenters Original sent a message to its members on December 16, 2020, noting they "stand ready and are standing by to answer the call from our President should the need arise" to combat the "pure evil that is conspiring to steal our country away from the american people" through the "2020 presidential election."[347] After President Trump's tweet, the group put out another letter instructing "any member who can attend . . . to participate" on January 6th because "[t]he President of the United States has put out a general call for the patriots of this Nation to gather" in Washington, DC.[348]

Other Three Percenter groups also responded. Alan Hostetter and Russell Taylor led a group of Three Percenters calling themselves the California Patriots–DC Brigade, who have been charged with conspiracy to obstruct Congress because they organized to fight to keep President Trump in power on January 6th after President Trump's December 19th tweet inspired them to come to Washington, DC.[349] On December 19th, Hostetter posted on Instagram:

> President Trump tweeted that all patriots should descend on Washington DC on Wednesday 1/6/2021. This is the date of the Joint Session of Congress in which they will either accept or reject the fake/phony/stolen electoral college votes.[350]

Between December 19th and January 6th, Hostetter, Taylor, and other members of the California Patriots–DC Brigade exchanged messages and posted to social media about bringing gear, including "weaponry," like "hatchet[s]," "bat[s]," or "[l]arge metal flashlights," and possibly "firearms," and, about being "ready and willing to fight" like it was "1776." Taylor even spoke in front of the Supreme Court on January 5, 2021, explaining that "[p]atriots" would "not return to our peaceful way of life until this election is made right . . . ."[351] On December 29, 2020, Taylor exclaimed "I personally want to be on the front steps and be one of the first ones to breach the doors!"[352]

Similarly, members of the Florida Guardians of Freedom, Three Percent sent around a flyer on December 24, 2020, saying they were "responding to the call from President Donald J. Trump to assist in the security, protection, and support of the people as we all protest the fraudulent election and re-establish liberty for our nation."[353] Their leader, Jeremy Liggett, posted a meme to Facebook stating that "3% Will Show In Record Numbers In DC"[354] and put out a "safety video" instructing people that they could bring "an expandable metal baton, a walking cane and a folding knife"[355] to Washington, DC on January 6th. Several have been arrested for participating in the violence around the tunnel on January 6th.[356]

When interviewed by the FBI on March 31, 2021, Danny Rodriguez—a Three Percenter from California who tased Officer Michael Fanone in the neck as rioters tried to break through a door on the west side of the Capitol—reflected on his decision to go to Washington, DC[357]:

Trump called us to D.C. .... and he's calling for help—I thought he was calling for help. I thought he was—I thought we were doing the right thing. .... [W]e thought we were going to hit it like a civil war. There was going to be a big battle. .... I thought that the main fight, the main battle, was going to be in D.C. because Trump called everyone there.[358]

These groups were not operating in silos. Meggs bragged on Facebook that following President Trump's December 19th tweet he had formed an alliance between the Oath Keepers, the Florida Three Percenters, and the Proud Boys "to work together to shut this shit down."[359] On December 19th, Meggs called Enrique Tarrio and they spoke for more than three minutes.[360] Three days later, Meggs messaged Liggett, echoing his excitement about the December 19th tweet and specifically referencing the seat of Congress: "He called us all to the Capitol and wants us to make it wild!!!"[361] Liggett said "I will have a ton of men with me" and Meggs replied that "we have made Contact [sic] with PB [Proud Boys] and they always have a big group. Force multiplier. .... I figure we could splinter off the main group of PB and come up behind them. Fucking crush them for good."[362] Aside from Meggs, Stewart Rhodes brought in at least one local militia leader[363] and Three Percenters into the Oath Keepers January 6th planning chats that came about following President Trump's tweet.[364]

Even on January 6th, rioters referenced the tweet. An unknown rioter was caught on video as they ascended the Capitol steps saying "He said it was gonna be wild. He didn't lie."[365] MPD body-worn cameras captured Cale Clayton around 3:15 p.m. as he taunted officers from under the scaffolding: "Your fucking president told us to be here. You should be on this side, right here, going with us. You are an American citizen. Your fucking President told you to do that. You too. You too. You. All of you guys. That Tweet was for you guys. For us. For you."[366]

As January 6th neared, intelligence emerged indicating that January 6th was likely to be violent, and specifically that the Capitol was a target. On January 3rd, an intelligence summary informed Department of Justice officials of plans to "occupy the Capitol" and "invade" the Capitol on January 6th. This summarized a "SITE Intelligence Group" report about the "online rhetoric focused on the 6 Jan event." Some of the reporting includes: "Calls to occupy federal buildings." "intimidating Congress and invading the capitol building." The email also quoted WUSA9 local reporting: "one of the websites used for organizing the event was encouraging attendees to bring guns."

Acting Deputy Attorney General Richard Donoghue testified:

And we knew that if you have tens of thousands of very upset people showing up in Washington, DC, that there was potential for violence.[368]

At the same time, a Defense Department official predicted on a White House National Security Council call that violence could be targeted at the Capitol on January 6th. According to Chairman of the Joint Chiefs of Staff Gen. Mark Milley:

> So during these calls, I—I only remember in hindsight because he was almost like clairvoyant. [Deputy Secretary of Defense David] Norquist says during one of these calls, the greatest threat is a direct assault on the Capitol. I'll never forget it.[369]

Likewise, documentation received by the Committee from the Secret Service demonstrates a growing number of warnings both that January 6th was likely to be violent, and specifically that the Capitol would likely be the target, including intelligence directly regarding the Proud Boys and Oath Keepers militia groups.

Even two weeks ahead of January 6th, the intelligence started to show what could happen. On December 22, 2020, the FBI received a screenshot of an online chat among Oath Keepers, seemingly referring to the State capitols besieged by protesters across the country earlier that year: "if they were going to go in, then they should have went all the way."[370] "There is only one way. It is not signs. It's not rallies. It's fucking bullets," one user replied.[371]

A public source emailed the Secret Service a document titled "Armed and Ready, Mr. President," on December 24th, which summarized online comments responding to President Trump's December 19th tweet.[372] Protestors should "start marching into the chambers," one user wrote.[373] Trump "can't exactly openly tell you to revolt," another replied. "This is the closest he'll ever get."[374] "I read [the President's tweet] as armed," someone said.[375] "[T]here is not enough cops in DC to stop what is coming," replied yet another.[376] "[B]e already in place when Congress tries to get to their meeting," the comments continued, and "make sure they know who to fear.'"[377] "[W]aiting for Trump to say the word," a person said, and "this is what Trump expects," exclaimed another.[378] Capitol Police's head of intelligence, Jack Donohue, got the same compilation from a former colleague at the New York Police Department on December 28, 2020.[379]

On December 26, 2020, the Secret Service received a tip about the Proud Boys detailing plans to have "a large enough group to march into DC armed [that] will outnumber the police so they can't be stopped."[380] "Their plan is to literally kill people," the informant stated. "Please please take this tip seriously . . . "[381] On December 29, 2020, Secret Service forwarded related warnings to Capitol Police that pro-Trump demonstrators were being urged to "occupy federal building[s]," including "march[ing] into the capital building and mak[ing] them quake in their shoes by our mere presence." [382]

Civilians also tipped off Capitol Police about people bringing weapons to besiege the Capitol. One tipster, who had "track[ed] online far right extremism for years," emailed Capitol Police warning "I've seen countless tweets from Trump supporters saying they will be armed," and "I[']ve also seen tweets from people organizing to 'storm the Capitol' on January 6th." [383]

On December 29, 2020, Secret Service forwarded related warnings to Capitol Police that pro-Trump demonstrators were being urged to "occupy federal building," including "march[ing] into the capital building and mak-[ing] them quake in their shoes by our mere presence." [384] Indeed, a Secret Service intelligence briefing on December 30th entitled "March for Trump," highlighted the President's "Will be wild!" tweet alongside hashtags #WeAreTheStorm, #1776Rebel, and #OccupyCapitols, writing "President Trump supporters have proposed a movement to occupy Capitol Hill." [385]

On January 1, 2021, a lieutenant in the intelligence branch at DC Police forwarded a civilian tip about "a website planning terroristic behavior on Jan 6th, during the rally" to Capitol Police intelligence. [386] "There are detailed plans to storm federal buildings," including "the capitol in DC on Jan 6th," the tipster reported, linking to thedonald.win. [387]

On January 2, 2021, the FBI discovered a social media posting that read, "This is not a rally and it's no longer a protest. This is a final stand . . . many are ready to die to take back #USA . . . . And don't be surprised if we take the #capital building." [388]

On January 3, 2021, a Parler user's post—under the name 1776(2.0) Minuteman— noting "after weds we are going to need a new congress" and "Jan 6 may actually be their [Members of Congress] last day in office" reached the FBI and Capitol Police. [389]

The FBI field office in Norfolk, Virginia issued an alert to law enforcement agencies on January 5th tiled "Potential for Violence in Washington, D.C. Area in Connection with Planned 'StopTheSteal' Protest on 6 January 2021," which noted:

> An online thread discussed specific calls for violence to include stating, "Be ready to fight. Congress needs to hear glass breaking, doors being kicked in, and blood . . . being spilled. Get violent . . . stop calling this a march, or rally, or a protest. Go there ready for war. We get our President or we die. NOTHING else will achieve this goal." [390]

In addition, the alert copied "perimeter maps [of the Capitol] and caravan pictures [that] were posted" on thedonald.win, particularly worrying that the "caravans . . . had the same colors as the sections of the perimeter" of the Capitol.[391] Secret Service also knew about caravans planning to come to DC to "Occupy the Capitol." [392]

That same day, representatives from DHS, FBI, DC's Homeland Security and Emergency Management Agency, Secret Service, DC Police, and Capitol Police shared a website, Red State Secession, which had a post titled "Why the Second American Revolution Starts Jan 6." A user asked visitors to post where they could find the home addresses of Democratic congressmen and "political enemies" and asked if "any of our enemies [will] be working in offices in DC that afternoon." [393] "What are their routes to and from the event?" the post continued.[394] "[T]he crowd will be looking for enemies." [395]

A Secret Service open-source unit flagged an account on thedonald.win that threatened to bring a sniper rifle to a rally on January 6th. The user also posted a picture of a handgun and rifle with the caption, "Sunday Gun Day Providing Overwatch January 6th Will be Wild." [396]

The Secret Service learned from the FBI on January 5th about right-wing groups establishing armed quick reaction forces in Virginia, where they could amass firearms illegal in DC[397] Trump supporters staged there waiting across the river "to respond to 'calls for help.'" [398] The Oath Keepers were such a group.[399]

President Trump's closest aides knew about the political power of sites like thedonald.win, which is where much of this violent rhetoric and planning happened. On December 30, 2020, Jason Miller—a Senior Adviser to and former spokesman for the former President—texted Chief of Staff Mark Meadows a link to the thedonald.win, adding "I got the base FIRED UP." [400] The link connected to a page with comments like "Gallows don't require electricity," "if the filthy commie maggots try to push their fraud through, there will be hell to pay," and Congress can certify Trump the winner or leave "in a bodybag." [401] Symbolic gallows were constructed on January 6th at the foot of the Capitol.[402]

After President Trump's signal, his supporters did not hide their plans for violence at the Capitol, and those threats made their way to national and local law enforcement agencies. As described in this report, the intelligence agencies did detect this planning, and they shared it with the White House and with the U.S. Secret Service.

Noose set up outside of the Capitol on January 6th.

Testimony from White House staff also suggests real concerns about the risk of violence as January 6th approached. Cassidy Hutchinson, for example, testified about a conversation she had with her boss, Mark Meadows, on January 2nd:

> I went into Mark's office, and he was still on his phone . . . . I said to Mark, "Rudy [Giuliani] said these things to me. What's going on here? Anything I should know about?"

> This was—he was, like, looking at his phone. He was like, "Oh, it's all about the rally on Wednesday. Isn't that what he was talking to you about?"

> I said, "Yeah. Yeah, sounds like we're going to the Capitol."

> He said, "Yeah. Are you talking with Tony?"

> "I'm having a conversation, sir."

> He said—still looking at his phone. I remember he was scrolling. He was like, "Yeah. You know, things might get real, real bad on the 6th."

> And I remember saying to him, "What do you mean?"

Mark Meadows walks along the South Lawn on October 30, 2020.
(Photo by Sarah Silbiger/Getty Images)

He was like, "I don't know. There's just going to be a lot of people here, and there's a lot of different ideas right now. I'm not really sure of everything that's going on. Let's just make sure we keep tabs on it." [403]

Hutchinson also testified about a conversation she had with Director of National Intelligence, Ratcliffe:

He had expressed to me that he was concerned that it could spiral out of control and potentially be dangerous, either for our democracy or the way that things were going for the 6th. [404]

Hope Hicks texted Trump Campaign spokesperson Hogan Gidley in the midst of the January 6th violence, explaining that she had "suggested . . . several times" on the preceding days (January 4th and January 5th) that President Trump publicly state that January 6th must remain peaceful and that he had refused her advice to do so. [405] Her recollection was that Herschmann earlier advised President Trump to make a preemptive public statement in advance of January 6th calling for no violence that day. [406] No such statement was made.

The District of Columbia Homeland Security office explicitly warned that groups were planning to "occupy the [Capitol] to halt the vote." [407]

[W]e got derogatory information from OSINT suggesting that some very, very violent individuals were organizing to come to DC, and not only were they organized to come to DC, but they were—these groups, these nonaligned groups were aligning. And so all the red flags went up at that point, you know, when you have armed militia, you know, collaborating with White supremacy groups, collaborating with conspiracy theory groups online all toward a common goal, you start seeing what we call in, you know, terrorism, a blended ideology, and that's a very, very bad sign. . . . [T]hen when they were clearly across—not just across one platform but across multiple platforms of these groups coordinating, not just like chatting, "Hey, how's it going, what's the weather like where you're at," but like, "what are you bringing, what are you wearing, you know, where do we meet up, do you have plans for the Capitol." That's operational—that's like preoperational intelligence, right, and that is something that's clearly alarming.[408]

Again, this type of intelligence was shared, including obvious warnings about potential violence prior to January 6th.[409] What was not shared, and was not fully understood by intelligence and law enforcement entities, is what role President Trump would play on January 6th in exacerbating the violence, and later refusing for multiple hours to instruct his supporters to stand down and leave the Capitol. No intelligence collection was apparently performed on President Trump's plans for January 6th, nor was there any analysis performed on what he might do to exacerbate potential violence. Certain Republican members of Congress who were working with Trump and the Giuliani team may have had insight on this particular risk, but none appear to have alerted the Capitol Police or any other law enforcement authority.

On January 2, 2021, Katrina Pierson wrote in an email to fellow rally organizers, "POTUS expectations are to have something intimate at the [E]llipse, and call on everyone to march to the Capitol."[410] And, on January 4, 2021, another rally organizer texted Mike Lindell, the MyPillow CEO, that President Trump would "unexpectedly" call on his supporters to march to the Capitol:

This stays only between us . . . . It can also not get out about the march because I will be in trouble with the national park service and all the agencies but POTUS is going to just call for it "unexpectedly."[411]

Testimony obtained by the Committee also indicates that President Trump was specifically aware that the crowd he had called to Washington was fired up and angry on the evening of January 5th. Judd Deere, a deputy

White House press secretary recalled a conversation with President Trump in the Oval Office on the evening of January 5th:

> Judd Deere: I said he should focus on policy accomplishments. I didn't mention the 2020 election.
>
> Committee Staff: Okay. What was his response?
>
> Deere: He acknowledged that and said, "We've had a lot," something along those lines, but didn't—he fairly quickly moved to how fired up the crowd is, or was going to be.
>
> Committee Staff: Okay. What did he say about it?
>
> Deere: Just that they were—they were fired up. They were angry. They feel like the election's been stolen, that the election was rigged, that—he went on and on about that for a little bit. [412]

Testimony indicated that President Trump was briefed on the risk of violence on the morning of the 6th before he left the White House. Cassidy Hutchinson provided this testimony:

> Vice Chair Cheney: So, Ms. Hutchinson, is it your understanding that Mr. Ornato told the President about weapons at the rally on the morning of January 6th?
>
> Hutchinson: That is what Mr. Ornato relayed to me. [413]

The head of President Trump's security detail, Bobby Engel, told the Select Committee that when he shared critical information with White House Deputy Chief of Staff Anthony Ornato, it was a means of conveying that information with the Oval Office: "So, when it came to passing information to Mr. Ornato, I—my assumption was that it would get to the chief [of staff, Mark Meadows], or that he was sharing the information with the chief. I don't—and the filtering process, or if the chief thinks it needs to get to the President, then he would share it with the President." [414] Also, Engel confirmed that if "information would come to my attention, whether it was a protective intelligence issue or a concern or—primarily, I would—I would make sure that the information got filtered up through the appropriate chain usually through Mr. Ornato. So if I received a report on something that was happening in the DC area, I'd either forward that information to Mr. Ornato, or call him about that information or communicate in some way." [415]

The Select Committee also queried Deputy Chief of Staff Ornato this November about what he generally would have done in this sort of situation, asking him the following: "Generally you receive information about things like the groups that are coming, the stuff that we talked earlier. You would bring that to Mr. Meadows and likely did here, although you don't have a specific recollection?" [416] Ornato responded: "That is correct, sir." [417] Ornato also explained to the Committee that "... in my normal daily functions, in my general functions as my job, I would've had a conversation with him about all the groups coming in and what was expected from the secret service." [418] As for the morning of January 6th itself, he had the following answer:

> Committee Staff: Do you remember talking to Chief of Staff Mark Meadows about any of your concerns about the threat landscape going into January 6th?
>
> Ornato: I don't recall; however, in my position I would've made sure he was tracking the demos, which he received a daily brief, Presidential briefing. So he most likely was getting all this in his daily brief as well. I wouldn't know what was in his intelligence brief that day, but I would've made sure that he was tracking these things and just mentioned, "Hey, are you tracking the demos?" If he gave me a "yeah", I don't recall it today, but I'm sure that was something that took place. [419]

Ornato had access to intelligence that suggested violence at the Capitol on January 6th, and it was his job to inform Meadows and President Trump of that. Although Ornato told us that he did not recall doing so, the Select Committee found multiple parts of Ornato's testimony questionable. The Select Committee finds it difficult to believe that neither Meadows nor Ornato told President Trump, as was their job, about the intelligence that was emerging as the January 6th rally approached.

Hours before the Ellipse rally on January 6th, the fact that the assembled crowd was prepared for potential violence was widely known. In addition to intelligence reports indicating potential violence at the Capitol, weapons and other prohibited items were being seized by police on the streets and by Secret Service at the magnetometers for the Ellipse speech. Secret Service confiscated a haul of weapons from the 28,000 spectators who did pass through the magnetometers: 242 cannisters of pepper spray, 269 knives or blades, 18 brass knuckles, 18 tasers, 6 pieces of body armor, 3 gas masks, 30 batons or blunt instruments, and 17 miscellaneous items like scissors, needles, or screwdrivers. [420] And thousands of others purposely remained outside the magnetometers, or left their packs outside. [421]

Others brought firearms. Three men in fatigues from Broward County, Florida brandished AR-15s in front of Metropolitan police officers on 14th Street and Independence Avenue on the morning of January 6th. [422] MPD advised over the radio that one individual was possibly armed with a "Glock" at 14th and Constitution Avenue, and another was possibly armed

President Trump looks backstage at the crowd gathered at the Ellipse.
(Photo provided to the Select Committee by the National Archives and Records Administration)

with a "rifle" at 15th and Constitution Avenue around 11:23 a.m.[423] The National Park Service detained an individual with a rifle between 12 and 1 p.m.[424] Almost all of this was known before Donald Trump took the stage at the Ellipse.

By the time President Trump was preparing to give his speech, he and his advisors knew enough to cancel the rally. And he certainly knew enough to cancel any plans for a march to the Capitol. According to testimony obtained by the Select Committee, President Trump knew that elements of the crowd were armed, and had prohibited items, and that many thousands would not pass through the magnetometers for that reason. Testimony indicates that the President had received an earlier security briefing, and testimony indicates that the Secret Service mentioned the prohibited items again as they drove President Trump to the Ellipse.

Cassidy Hutchinson was with the President backstage. Her contemporaneous text messages indicate that President Trump was "effing furious" about the fact that a large number of his supporters would not go through the magnetometers:

> Cassidy Hutchinson: But the crowd looks good from this vanish [sic] point. As long as we get the shot. He was fucking furious

Tony Ornato: He doesn't get it that the people on the monument side don't want to come in. They can see from there and don't want to come in. They can see from there and don't have to go through mags. With 30k magged inside.

Cassidy Hutchinson: That's what was relayed several times and in different iterations

Cassidy Hutchinson: Poor max got chewed out

Cassidy Hutchinson: He also kept mentioning [an off the record trip] to Capitol before he took the stage

Tony Ornato: Bobby will tell him no. It's not safe to do. No assets available to safely do it.[425]

And Hutchinson described what President Trump said as he prepared to take the stage:

When we were in the off-stage announce area tent behind the stage, he was very concerned about the shot. Meaning the photograph that we would get because the rally space wasn't full. One of the reasons, which I've previously stated, was because he wanted it to be full and for people to not feel excluded because they had come far to watch him at the rally. And he felt the mags were at fault for not letting everybody in, but another leading reason and likely the primary reasons is because he wanted it full and he was angry that we weren't letting people through the mags with weapons—what the Secret Service deemed as weapons, and are, are weapons. But when we were in the off-stage announce tent, I was a part of a conversation, I was in the vicinity of a conversation where I overheard the President say something to the effect of, "I don't F'ing care that they have weapons. They're not here to hurt me. Take the F'ing mags away. Let my people in. They can march to the Capitol from here. Let the people in. Take the F'ing mags away."[426]

The Secret Service special agent who drove the President after his speech told the Select Committee that Trump made a similar remark in the vehicle when his demand to go to the Capitol was refused—essentially that Trump did not believe his supporters posed a security risk to him personally.[427]

Minutes after the exchange that Hutchinson described—when President Trump took the stage—he pointedly expressed his concern about the thousands of attendees who would not enter the rally area and instructed Secret Service to allow that part of the crowd to enter anyway:

. . . I'd love to have if those tens of thousands of people would be allowed. The military, the secret service. And we want to thank you and the police law enforcement. Great. You're doing a great job. But I'd love it if they could be allowed to come up here with us. Is that possible? Can you just let [them] come up, please?[428]

Although President Trump and his advisors knew of the risk of violence, and knew specifically that elements of the crowd were angry and some were armed, from intelligence and law enforcement reports that morning, President Trump nevertheless went forward with the rally, and then specifically instructed the crowd to march to the Capitol: "Because you'll never take back our country with weakness. You have to show strength and you have to be strong. We have come to demand that Congress do the right thing and only count the electors who have been lawfully slated, lawfully slated."[429] Much of President Trump's speech was improvised. Even before his improvisation, during the review of President Trump's prepared remarks, White House lawyer Eric Herschmann specifically requested that "if there were any factual allegations, someone needed to independently validate or verify the statements."[430] And in the days just before January 6th, Herschmann "chewed out" John Eastman and told him he was "out of [his] F'ing mind" to argue that the Vice President could be the sole decision-maker as to who becomes the next President.[431] Herschmann told us, "I so berated him that I believed that theory would not go forward."[432] But President Trump made that very argument during his speech at the Ellipse and made many false statements. Herschmann attended that speech, but walked out during the middle of it.[433]

President Trump's speech to the crowd that day lasted more than an hour. The speech walked through dozens of known falsehoods about purported election fraud. And Trump again made false and malicious claims about Dominion voting systems.[434] As discussed earlier, he again pressured Mike Pence to refuse to count lawful electoral votes, going off script repeatedly, leading the crowd to believe falsely that Pence could and would alter the election outcome:

And I actually, I just spoke to Mike. I said: "Mike, that doesn't take courage. What takes courage is to do nothing. That takes courage." And then we're stuck with a president who lost the election by a lot and we have to live with that for four more years. We're just not going to let that happen . . . .

When you catch somebody in a fraud, you're allowed to go by very different rules.

So I hope Mike has the courage to do what he has to do. And I hope he doesn't listen to the RINOs and the stupid people that he's listening to." [435]

This characterization of Vice President Pence's decision had a direct impact on those who marched to and approached the Capitol, as illustrated by this testimony from a person convicted of crimes committed on January 6th:

So this woman came up to the side of us, and she, says, Pence folded. So it was kind of, like, okay. Well, in my mind I was thinking, "Well, that's it, you know." Well, my son-in-law looks at me, and he says, "I want to go in." [436]

Trump used the word "peacefully," written by speech writers, one time. But he delivered many other scripted and unscripted comments that conveyed a very different message:

Because you'll never take back our country with weakness. You have to show strength and you have to be strong. We have come to demand that Congress do the right thing and only count the electors who have been lawfully slated, lawfully slated. . . .

And we fight. We fight like hell. And if you don't fight like hell, you're not going to have a country anymore . . . . [437]

Trump also was not the only rally speaker to do these things. Giuliani, for instance, also said, "Let's have trial by combat." [438] Likewise, Eastman used his two minutes on the Ellipse stage to make a claim already known to be false—that corrupted voted machines stole the election. [439]

The best indication of the impact of President Trump's words, both during the Ellipse speech and beforehand, are the comments from those supporters who attended the Ellipse rally and their conduct immediately thereafter. Videoclips show several of the attendees on their way to the Capitol or shortly after they arrived:

I'm telling you what, I'm hearing that Pence—hearing the Pence just caved. No. Is that true? I didn't hear it. I'm hear—I'm hearing reports that Pence caved. No way. I'm telling you, if Pence caved, we're going to drag motherfuckers through the streets. You fucking politicians are going to get fucking drug through the streets. [440]

Yes. I guess the hope is that there's such a show of force here that Pence will decide do the right thing, according to Trump. [441]

Pence voted against Trump. [Interviewer: Ok. And that's when all this started?] Yup. That's when we marched on the Capitol. [442]

We just heard that Mike Pence is not going to reject any fraudulent electoral votes. [Other speaker: Boo. You're a traitor! Boo!] That's right. You've heard it here first. Mike Pence has betrayed the United States of America. [Other speaker: Boo! Fuck you, Mike Pence!] Mike Pence has betrayed this President and he has betrayed the people of the United States and we will never, ever forget. [Cheers][443]

[Q] What percentage of the crowd is going to the Capitol? [A] [Oath Keeper Jessica Watkins]: One hundred percent. It has, it has spread like wildfire that Pence has betrayed us, and everybody's marching on the Capitol. All million of us. It's insane. [444]

Another criminal defendant—charged with assaulting an officer with a flagpole and other crimes—explained in an interview why he went to the Capitol and fought:

Dale Huttle: We were not there illegally, we were invited there by the President himself. . . . Trump's backers had been told that the election had been stolen. . . .

Reporter Megan Hickey: But do you think he encouraged violence?

Dale Huttle: Well, I sat there, or stood there, with half a million people listening to his speech. And in that speech, both Giuliani and [Trump] said we were going to have to fight like hell to save our country. Now, whether it was a figure of speech or not—it wasn't taken that way.

Reporter Megan Hickey: You didn't take it as a figure of speech?

Dale Huttle: No.[445]

President Trump concluded his speech at 1:10 p.m.

Among other statements from the Ellipse podium, President Trump informed the crowd that he would be marching to the Capitol with them:

Now, it is up to Congress to confront this egregious assault on our democracy. And after this, we're going to walk down, **and I'll be there with you**, we're going to walk down, we're going to walk down. Anyone you want, but I think right here, **we're going to walk down to the Capitol**, and we're going to cheer on our brave senators and congressmen and women, and we're probably not going to be cheering so much for some of them.[446]

Hutchinson testified that she first became aware of President Trump's plans to attend Congress's session to count votes on or about January 2nd. She learned this from a conversation with Giuliani: "It's going to be great.

The President's going to be there. He's going to look powerful. He's—he's going to be with the members. He's going to be with the Senators." [447] Evidence also indicates that multiple members of the White House staff, including White House lawyers, were concerned about the President's apparent intentions to go to the Capitol. [448]

After he exited the stage, President Trump entered the Presidential SUV and forcefully expressed his intention that Bobby Engel, the head of his Secret Service detail, direct the motorcade to the Capitol. The Committee has now obtained evidence from several sources about a "furious interaction" in the SUV. The vast majority of witnesses who have testified before the Select Committee about this topic, including multiple members of the Secret Service, a member of the Metropolitan police, and national security and military officials in the White House, described President Trump's behavior as "irate," "furious," "insistent," "profane" and "heated." Hutchinson heard about the exchange second-hand and related what she heard in our June 28, 2022, hearing from Ornato (as did another witness, a White House employee with national security responsibilities, who shared that Ornato also recounted to him President Trump's "irate" behavior in the Presidential vehicle). Other members of the White House staff and Secret Service also heard about the exchange after the fact. The White House employee with national security responsibilities gave this testimony:

> Committee Staff: But it sounds like you recall some rumor or some discussion around the West Wing about the President's anger about being told that he couldn't go to the Capitol. Is that right?

> Employee: So Mr. Ornato said that he was angry that he couldn't go right away. In the days following that, I do remember, you know, again, hearing again how angry the President was when, you know, they were in the limo. But beyond specifics of that, that's pretty much the extent of the cooler talk. [449]

The Committee has regarded both Hutchinson and the corroborating testimony by the White House employee with national security responsibilities as earnest and has no reason to conclude that either had a reason to invent their accounts. A Secret Service agent who worked on one of the details in the White House and was present in the Ellipse motorcade had this comment:

> Committee Staff: Ms. Hutchinson has suggested to the committee that you sympathized with her after her testimony, and believed her account. Is that accurate?

> Special Agent: I have no—yeah, that's accurate. I have no reason—I mean, we—we became friends. We worked—I worked every day

with her for 6 months. Yeah, she became a friend of mine. We had a good working relationship. I have no reason—she's never done me wrong. She's never lied that I know of.[450]

The Committee's principal concern was that the President actually intended to participate personally in the January 6th efforts at the Capitol, leading the attempt to overturn the election either from inside the House Chamber, from a stage outside the Capitol, or otherwise. The Committee regarded those facts as important because they are relevant to President Trump's intent on January 6th. There is no question from all the evidence assembled that President Trump *did have that intent.*[451]

As it became clear that Donald Trump desired to travel to the Capitol on January 6th, a White House Security Official in the White House complex became very concerned about his intentions:

> To be completely honest, we were all in a state of shock. . . . it just—
> one, I think the actual physical feasibility of doing it, and then also
> we all knew what that implicated and what that meant, that this
> was no longer a rally, that this was going to move to something else
> if he physically walked to the Capitol. I—I don't know if you want to
> use the word "insurrection," "coup," whatever. We all knew that
> this would move from a normal, democratic, you know, public event
> into something else.[452]

President Trump continued to push to travel to the Capitol even after his return to the White House, despite knowing that a riot was underway. Kayleigh McEnany, the White House press secretary, spoke with President Trump about his desire to go to the Capitol after he returned to the White House from the Ellipse. "So to the best of my recollection, I recall him being—wanting to—saying that he wanted to physically walk and be a part of the march and then saying that he would ride the Beast if he needed to, ride in the Presidential limo."[453]

Later in the afternoon, Mark Meadows relayed to Cassidy Hutchinson that President Trump was still upset that he would not be able to go to the Capitol that day. As he told Hutchinson, "the President wasn't happy that Bobby [Engel] didn't pull it off for him and that Mark didn't work hard enough to get the movement on the books."[454]

187 MINUTES: TRUMP'S DERELICTION OF DUTY

Just after 1:00 p.m., Vice President Pence, serving as President of the Senate under Article I of the Constitution, gaveled the Congress into its Joint Session. President Trump was giving a speech at the Ellipse, which he concluded at 1:10 pm. For the next few hours, an attack on our Capitol occurred, perpetrated by Trump supporters many of whom were present at the Ellipse for President Trump's speech. More than 140 Capitol and Metropolitan police were injured, some very seriously.[455] A perimeter security line of Metropolitan Police intended to secure the Capitol against intrusion broke in the face of thousands of armed rioters—more than 2,000 of whom gained access to the interior of the Capitol building.[456] A woman who attempted to forcibly enter the Chamber of the House of Representatives through a broken window while the House was in session was shot and killed by police guarding the chamber. Vice President Pence and his family were at risk, as were those Secret Service professionals protecting him. Congressional proceedings were halted, and legislators were rushed to secure locations.

From the outset of the violence and for several hours that followed, people at the Capitol, people inside President Trump's Administration, elected officials of both parties, members of President Trump's family, and Fox News commentators sympathetic to President Trump all tried to contact him to urge him to do one singular thing—one thing that all of these people immediately understood was required: Instruct his supporters to stand down and disperse—to leave the Capitol.

As the evidence overwhelmingly demonstrates, President Trump specifically and repeatedly refused to do so—for multiple hours—while the mayhem ensued. Chapter 8 of this report explains in meticulous detail the horrific nature of the violence taking place, that was directed at law enforcement officers at the Capitol and that put the lives of American lawmakers at risk. Yet in spite of this, President Trump watched the violence on television from a dining room adjacent to the Oval Office, calling Senators to urge them to help him delay the electoral count, but refusing to supply the specific help that everyone knew was unequivocally required. As this report shows, when Trump finally did make such a statement at 4:17 p.m.—after hours of violence—the statement immediately had the expected effect; the rioters began to disperse immediately and leave the Capitol.[457]

To fully understand the President's behavior during those hours—now commonly known as the "187 minutes"—it is important to understand the context in which it occurred. As outlined in this report, by the afternoon of January 6th, virtually all of President Trump's efforts to overturn the outcome of the 2020 election had failed. Virtually all the lawsuits had already been lost. Vice President Mike Pence had refused Trump's pressure to stop the count of certain electoral votes. State officials and legislators had refused to reverse the election outcomes in every State where Trump and his team applied pressure. The Justice Department's investigations of alleged election fraud had all contradicted Trump's allegations.

The only factor working in Trump's favor that might succeed in materially delaying the counting of electoral votes for President-elect Biden was the violent crowd at the Capitol. And for much of the afternoon of January 6th, it appeared that the crowd had accomplished that purpose. Congressional leaders were advised by Capitol Police at one or more points during the attack that it would likely take several days before the Capitol could safely be reopened.[458]

By the time the President's speech concluded, the lawlessness at the United States Capitol had already begun, but the situation was about to get much worse.

By 1:25 p.m., President Trump was informed that the Capitol was under attack.

Minutes after arriving back at the White House, the President ran into a member of the White House staff and asked if they had watched his speech on television. "Sir, they cut it off because they're rioting down at the Capitol," the employee said. The President asked what they meant by that. "[T]hey're rioting down there at the Capitol," the employee repeated. "Oh really?" the President asked. "All right, let's go see."[459] A photograph taken by the White House photographer—the last one permitted until later in the day—captures the moment the President was made aware of the violent uprising at the Capitol.[460]

Not long thereafter, as thousands of Trump supporters from the Ellipse speech continued to arrive at the Capitol, the DC Metropolitan Police Department declared a riot at the Capitol at 1:49 p.m., the same time Capitol Police Chief Steven Sund informed the DC National Guard "that there was a dire emergency on Capitol Hill and requested the immediate assistance" of as many national guard troops as possible.[461]

No photographs exist of the President for the remainder of the afternoon until after 4 p.m. President Trump appears to have instructed that the White House photographer was not to take any photographs.[462] The Select Committee also was unable to locate any official records of President Trump's telephone calls that afternoon.[463] And the President's official Daily Diary contains no information for this afternoon between the hours of 1:19 p.m. and 4:03 p.m., at the height of the worst attack on the seat of the United States Congress in over two centuries.[464]

The Select Committee did, however, obtain records from non-official sources that contained data of some phone calls President Trump made that afternoon. Even though "he was placing lots of calls" that afternoon, according to his personal assistant,[465] the Select Committee was given no records of any calls from the President to security or law enforcement officials that afternoon, and that absence of data is consistent with testimony of witnesses who would have knowledge of any such calls, who said that he did not do so.[466] Based on testimony from President Trump's close aides, we know that President Trump remained in the Dining Room adjacent to the Oval Office for the rest of the afternoon until after 4:03 p.m.[467]

In fact, from cellular telephone records, it appears that at 1:39 p.m. and 2:03 p.m., after being informed of the riot at the Capitol, President Trump called his lawyer, Rudolph Giuliani. These calls lasted approximately four minutes and eight minutes, respectively.[468] And Press Secretary Kayleigh McEnany testified that President Trump also called a number of Senators.[469] The number or names of all such Members of Congress is unknown, although Senator Mike Lee (R–UT) received one such outgoing call from the President within the hour that followed.[470]

At 1:49 p.m., just as the DC Metropolitan Police officially declared a riot and the Capitol Police were calling for help from the National Guard to address the crisis, President Trump sent a tweet with a link to a recording of his speech at the Ellipse.[471]

At about that point, White House Counsel Pat Cipollone became aware of the Capitol riot. The Committee collected sworn testimony from several White House officials, each with similar accounts. The President's White House Counsel Pat Cipollone testified that he raced downstairs, and went to the Oval Office Dining Room as soon as he learned about the violence at the Capitol—likely just around or just after 2 p.m. Cipollone knew immediately that the President had to deliver a message to the rioters—asking them to leave the Capitol.

Here is how he described this series of events:

> . . . the first time I remember going downstairs was when people had breached the Capitol... But I went down with [Deputy White House Counsel] Pat [Philbin], and I remember we were both very upset about what was happening. And we both wanted, you know, action to be taken related to that . . . But we went down to the Oval Office, we went through the Oval office, and we went to the back where the President was. . . . I think he was already in the dining room . . . I can't talk about conversations [with the President]. I think I was pretty clear there needed to be an immediate and forceful response, statement, public statement, that people need to leave the Capitol now.[472]

Cipollone also left little doubt that virtually everyone among senior White House staff had the same view:

> There were a lot of people in the White House that day . . . Senior people who, you know, felt the same way that I did and who were working very hard to achieve that result. There were—I think

Ivanka was one of them. And Eric Herschmann was there, Pat Philbin was there, and a number of other people . . . . many people suggested it. . . . Many people felt the same way. I'm sure I had conversations with Mark [Meadows] about this during the course of the day and expressed my opinion very forcefully that this needs to be done.[473]

Likewise, senior staff cooperated to produce a message for the President on a notecard, which read:

ANYONE WHO ENTERED THE CAPITOL ~~ILLEGALLY~~ WITHOUT PROPER AUTHORITY SHOULD LEAVE IMMEDIATELY.[474]

The President declined to make the statement. Cipollone also made it clear that the advice they were giving to the President never changed throughout this three-hour period. Trump refused to do what was necessary.

Committee Staff: [I]t sounds like you from the very onset of violence at the Capitol right around 2 o'clock were pushing for a strong statement that people should leave the Capitol. Is that right?

Cipollone: I was, and others were as well.[475]

Cassidy Hutchinson, who worked closely with Mark Meadows and sat directly outside his office, confirmed this account and described several additional details:

I see Pat Cipollone barreling down the hallway towards our office. And he rushed right in, looked at me, said, "Is Mark in his office?" And I said, "Yes." And on a normal day he would've said, "Can I pop in," or, "Is he talking to anyone," or, "Is it an appropriate time for me to go chat with him," and myself or Eliza would go let him in or tell him no. But after I had said yes, he just looked at me and started shaking his head and went over, opened Mark's office door, stood there with the door propped open, and said something to the—Mark was still sitting on his phone. I remember, like, glancing in. He was still sitting on his phone.

And I remember Pat saying to him something to the effect of, "The rioters have gotten to the Capitol, Mark. We need to go down and see the President now." And Mark looked up at him and said, "He doesn't want to do anything, Pat." And Pat said something to the effect of—and very clearly said this to Mark—something to the effect of, "Mark, something needs to be done, or people are going to die and the blood's gonna be on your F'ing hands. This is getting out of control. I'm going down there.[476]

The Select Committee believes that the entire White House senior staff was in favor of a Presidential statement specifically instructing the violent rioters to leave. But President Trump refused. White House Counsel Pat Cipollone answered certain questions from the Select Committee on this subject as follows:

> Vice Chair Cheney: And when you talk about others on the staff thinking more should be done, or thinking that the President needed to tell people to go home, who would you put in that category?
>
> Cipollone: Well, I would put . . . Pat Philbin, Eric Herschmann. Overall, Mark Meadows, Ivanka. Once Jared got there, Jared. General Kellogg. I'm probably missing some, but those are—Kayleigh I think was there. But I don't—Dan Scavino.
>
> Vice Chair Cheney: And who on the staff did not want people to leave the Capitol?"
>
> Cipollone: On the staff?
>
> Vice Chair Cheney: In the White House?
>
> Cipollone: I can't think of anybody on that day who didn't want people to get out of the Capitol once the—particularly once the violence started. No. I mean—
>
> Mr. Schiff: What about the President?
>
> Vice Chair Cheney: Yeah.
>
> . . .
>
> [Consultation between Mr. Cipollone and his counsel.]
>
> Cipollone: Yeah. I can't reveal communications. But obviously I think, you know—yeah.[477]

The testimony of a White House employee with national security responsibilities also corroborated these facts. This employee testified about a conversation between Pat Cipollone and Eric Herschmann in which Herschmann indicated that the President did not want to do anything to halt the violence. That employee told the Select Committee that he overheard Herschmann saying something to the effect of "the President didn't want anything done."[478]

Deputy Press Secretary Judd Deere also testified to the Select Committee that as soon as it was clear that the Capitol's outer perimeter had been breached, he urged that the President make a statement telling the rioters to go home:

Committee Staff: And so what did you do at that point?

Judd Deere: If I recall, I went back up to [Press Secretary] Kayleigh [McEnany]'s office and indicated that we now likely needed to say something.

Committee Staff: Okay. And why did you think it was necessary to say something?

Deere: Well, I mean, it appears that individuals are storming the U.S. Capitol building. They also appear to be supporters of Donald Trump, who may have been in attendance at the rally. We're going to need to say something.

Committee Staff: And did you have a view as to what should be said by the White House?

Deere: If I recall, I told Kayleigh that I thought that we needed to encourage individuals to stop, to respect law enforcement, and to go home.... And it was—it was incumbent upon us to encourage those individuals, should they be supporters of ours, to stop.[479]

Testimony from both Deputy Press Secretary Matthews and White House Counsel Cipollone indicated that it would have been easy, and nearly instantaneous, for Trump to make a public statement insisting that the crowd disperse. As Matthews explained, he could have done so in under a minute:

... it would take probably less than 60 seconds from the Oval Office dining room over to the Press Briefing Room. And, for folks that might not know, the Briefing Room is the room that you see the White House Press Secretary do briefings from with the podium and the blue backdrop. And there is a camera that is on in there at all times. And so, if the President had wanted to make a statement and address the American people, he could have been on camera almost instantly.[480]

Cipollone also shared that assessment:

Committee Staff: Would it have been possible at any moment for the President to walk down to the podium in the briefing room and talk to the nation at any time between when you first gave him that advice at 2 o'clock and 4:17 when the video statement went out? Would that have been possible?

Cipollone: Would it have been possible?"

Committee Staff: Yes.

Cipollone: Yes, it would have been possible.[481]

At 2:13 p.m., rioters broke into the Capitol and flooded the building.[482]

As the violence began to escalate, many Trump supporters and others outside the White House began urgently seeking his intervention. Mark Meadows's phone was flooded with text messages. These are just some of them:

2:32 p.m. from Fox News anchor Laura Ingraham: "Hey Mark, The president needs to tell people in the Capitol to go home." [483]

2:35 p.m. from Mick Mulvaney: "Mark: he needs to stop this, now. Can I do anything to help?" [484]

2:46 p.m. from Rep. William Timmons (R–SC): "The president needs to stop this ASAP" [485]

2:53 p.m. from Donald Trump, Jr.: "He's got to condem [sic] this shit. Asap. The captiol [sic] police tweet is not enough." [486]

3:04 p.m. from Rep. Jeff Duncan (R–SC): "POTUS needs to calm this shit down" [487]

3:09 p.m. from former White House Chief of Staff Reince Priebus: "TELL THEM TO GO HOME !!!" [488]

3:13 p.m. from Alyssa Farah Griffin: "Potus has to come out firmly and tell protestors to dissipate. Someone is going to get killed." [489]

3:15 p.m. from Rep. Chip Roy (R–TX): "Fix this now." [490]

3:31 p.m. from Fox News anchor Sean Hannity: "Can he make a statement. I saw the tweet. Ask people to peacefully leave the capital [sic]" [491]

3:58 p.m. from Fox News anchor Brian Kilmeade: "Please get him on tv. Destroying every thing you guys have accomplished" [492]

Others on Capitol Hill appeared in the media, or otherwise appeared via internet. Representative Mike Gallagher (R–WI) issued a video appealing directly to the President:

Mr. President, you have got to stop this. You are the only person who can call this off. Call it off. The election is over. Call it off![493]

Some Members of Congress sent texts to President Trump's immediate staff or took to Twitter, where they knew the President spent time:

Sen. Bill Cassidy (R–LA) issued a tweet: @realDonaldTrump please appear on TV, condemn the violence and tell people to disband.[494]

Rep. Jaime Herrera Beutler (R–WA) sent a text to Mark Meadows: We need to hear from the president. On TV. I hate that Biden jumped him on it.[495]

Republican Leader Kevin McCarthy tried repeatedly to reach President Trump, and did at least once. He also reached out for help to multiple members of President Trump's family, including Ivanka Trump and Jared Kushner.[496] Kushner characterized Leader McCarthy's demeanor on the call as "scared":

Kushner: I could hear in his voice that he really was nervous, and so, obviously, I took that seriously. And, you know, I didn't know if I'd be able to have any impact, but I said, you know, it's better to at least try. And so I—like I said, I turned the shower off, threw on a suit, and, you know, and rushed into the White House as quickly as I could.

Committee Staff: Yeah. What did he ask you to do? When you say have an impact, what is it specifically that he needed your help with?

Kushner: I don't recall a specific ask, just anything you could do. Again, I got the sense that, you know, they were—they were—you know, they were scared.

Committee Staff: "They" meaning Leader McCarthy and people on the Hill because of the violence?

Kushner: That he was scared, yes.[497]

Kevin McCarthy told Fox News at 3:09 p.m. about his call with the President[498] and elaborated about its contents in a conversation with CBS News's Norah O'Donnell at around 3:30 p.m.:

O'Donnell: Have you spoken with the President and asked him to perhaps come to the Capitol and tell his supporters it's time to leave?

Leader McCarthy: I have spoken to the President. I asked him to talk to the nation and tell them to stop this. . . .

* * *

O'Donnell: The President invited tens of thousands of people to quote unquote stop the steal. I don't know if you heard his more-than-hour-long remarks or the remarks of his son, who was the wind-up. It was some heated stuff, Leader McCarthy. I just wonder whether someone is going to accurately call a spade a spade, and I am giving you the opportunity right now that your precious and beloved United States Capitol and our democracy is witnessing this. Call a spade a spade.

Leader McCarthy: I was very clear with the President when I called him. This has to stop. And he has to, he's gotta go to the American public and tell them to stop this.

* * *

O'Donnell: Leader McCarthy, the President of the United States has a briefing room steps from the Oval Office. It is, the cameras are hot 24/7, as you know. Why hasn't he walked down and said that, now?

Leader McCarthy: I conveyed to the President what I think is best to do, and I'm hopeful the President will do it.[499]

The Committee has evidence from multiple sources regarding the content of Kevin McCarthy's direct conversation with Donald Trump during the violence.

Rep. Jaime Herrera Beutler (R–WA), to whom McCarthy spoke soon after, relayed more of the conversation between McCarthy and President Trump:

And he said [to President Trump], "You have got to get on TV. You've got to get on Twitter. You've got to call these people off." You know what the President said to him? This is as it's happening. He said, "Well Kevin, these aren't my people. You know, these are Antifa. And Kevin responded and said, "No, they're your people. They literally just came through my office windows and my staff are running for cover. I mean they're running for their lives. You need to call them off." And the President's response to Kevin to me was chilling. He said, "Well Kevin, I guess they're just more upset about the election, you know, theft than you are".[500]

Rep. Herrera Beutler's account of the incident was also corroborated by former Acting White House Chief of Staff Mick Mulvaney, who testified that Leader McCarthy told him several days later that President Trump had said during their call: "Kevin, maybe these people are just more angry about this than you are. Maybe they're more upset."[501]

Mulvaney was also trying to reach administration officials to urge President Trump to instruct his supporters to leave the Capitol.[502] As were many elected officials in both parties, including Nancy Pelosi and Chuck Schumer, and several Republican Members of Congress.[503]

As already noted, Cipollone and others in the White House repeatedly urged President Trump to tell his supporters to leave the Capitol. Cipollone described his conversations with Meadows after they failed to convince President Trump to deliver the necessary message:

> Committee Staff: Do you remember any discussion with Mark Meadows with respect to his view that the President didn't want to do anything or was somehow resistant to wanting to say something along the lines that you suggested.
>
> Pat Cipollone: Not just—just to be clear, many people suggested it.
>
> Committee Staff: Yeah.
>
> Cipollone: Not just me. Many people felt the same way. I'm sure I had conversations with Mark about this during the course of the day and expressed my opinion very forcefully that this needs to be done.[504]

* * *

> Committee Staff: So your advice was tell people to leave the Capitol, and that took over 2 hours when there were subsequent statements made, tweets put forth, that in your view were insufficient. Did you continue, Mr. Cipollone, throughout the period of time up until 4:17, continue, you and others, to push for a stronger statement?
>
> Cipollone: Yes.[505]

* * *

> Committee Staff: . . . at the onset of the violence when you first notice on television or wherever that rioters have actually breached the Capitol, did you have a conversation with Mark Meadows in which Meadows indicated he doesn't want to do anything, "he" meaning the President?
>
> Cipollone: I don't—I had a conversation I'm sure with Mark Meadows, I'm sure with other people, of what I thought should be done. Did Mark say that to me? I don't have a recollection of him saying that to me, but he may have said something along the lines.[506]

At 2:16 p.m., security records indicate that the Vice President was "being pulled" to a safer location.[507]

In an interview with the Select Committee, a White House Security Official on duty at the White House explained his observations as he listened to Secret Service communications and made contemporaneous entries into a security log. In particular, he explained an entry he made at 2:24 p.m.:

> Committee Staff: Ok. That last entry on this page is: "Service at the Capitol does not sound good right now."

Official: Correct.

Committee Staff: What does that mean?

Official: The members of the VP detail at this time were starting to fear for their own lives. There were a lot of—there was a lot of yelling, a lot of—I don't know—a lot [of] very personal calls over the radio. So—it was disturbing. I don't like talking about it, but there were calls to say good-bye to family members, so on and so forth. It was getting—for whatever the reason was on the ground, the VP detail thought that this was about to get very ugly.

Committee Staff: And did you hear that over the radio?

Official: Correct.

. . .

Committee Staff: ... obviously, you've conveyed that's disturbing, but what prompted you to put it into an entry as it states there, "Service at the Capitol—"

Official: That they're running out of options, and they're getting nervous. It sounds like that we came very close to either Service having to use lethal options or worse. At that point, I don't know. Is the VP compromised? Is the detail—like, I don't know. Like, we didn't have visibility, but it doesn't—if they're screaming and saying things, like, say good-bye to the family, like, the floor needs to know this is going to a whole another level soon.[508]

Also at 2:24 p.m., knowing the riot was underway and that Vice President Pence was at the Capitol, President Trump sent this tweet:

> Mike Pence didn't have the courage to do what should have been done to protect our Country and our Constitution, giving States a chance to certify a corrected set of facts, not the fraudulent or inaccurate ones which they were asked to previously certify. USA demands the truth![509]

Evidence shows that the 2:24 p.m. tweet immediately precipitated further violence at the Capitol. Immediately after this tweet, the crowds both inside and outside of the Capitol building violently surged forward.[510] Outside the building, within ten minutes thousands of rioters overran the line on the west side of the Capitol that was being held by the Metropolitan Police Force's Civil Disturbance Unit, the first time in history of the DC Metro Police that such a security line had ever been broken.[511]

Virtually everyone on the White House staff the Select Committee interviewed condemned the 2:24 p.m. tweet in the strongest terms.

Police officers attempt to clear rioters inside the Capitol building.
(Photo by Brent Stirton/Getty Images)

Deputy National Security Adviser Matthew Pottinger told the Select Committee that the 2:24 p.m. tweet was so destructive that it convinced him to resign as soon as possible:

> One of my aides handed me a sheet of paper that contained the tweet that you just read. I read it and was quite disturbed by it. I was disturbed and worried to see that the President was attacking Vice President Pence for doing his constitutional duty.

> So the tweet looked to me like the opposite of what we really needed at that moment, which was a de-escalation. And that is why I had said earlier that it looked like fuel being poured on the fire.

> So that was the moment that I decided that I was going to resign, that that would be my last day at the White House. I simply didn't want to be associated with the events with the events that were unfolding at the Capitol.[512]

Deputy Press Secretary Sarah Matthews had a similar reaction:

> So it was obvious that the situation at the Capitol was violent and escalating quickly. And so I thought that the tweet about the Vice President was the last thing that was needed in that moment.

And I remember thinking that this was going to be bad for him to tweet this, because it was essentially him giving the green light to these people, telling them that what they were doing at the steps of the Capitol and entering the Capitol was okay, that they were justified in their anger.

And he shouldn't have been doing that. He should have been telling these people to go home and to leave and to condemn the violence that we were seeing.

And I am someone who has worked with him, you know, I worked on the campaign, traveled all around the country, going to countless rallies with him, and I have seen the impact that his words have on his supporters. They truly latch onto every word and every tweet that he says.

And so, I think that in that moment for him to tweet out the message about Mike Pence, it was him pouring gasoline on the fire and making it much worse.[513]

Deputy Press Secretary Judd Deere stated the following:

Committee Staff: What was your reaction when you saw that tweet?

Deere: Extremely unhelpful.

Committee Staff: Why?

Deere: It wasn't the message that we needed at that time. It wasn't going to—the scenes at the U.S. Capitol were only getting worse at that point. This was not going to help that.[514]

White House Counsel Pat Cipollone told the Select Committee, "I don't remember when exactly I heard about that tweet, but my reaction to it is that's a terrible tweet, and I disagreed with the sentiment. And I thought it was wrong."[515]

Likewise, Counselor to the President Hope Hicks texted a colleague that evening: "Attacking the VP? Wtf is wrong with him."[516]

At 2:26 p.m., Vice President Pence was again moved to a different location.[517]

President Trump had the TV on in the dining room.[518] At 2:38 p.m., Fox News was showing video of the chaos and attack, with tear gas filling the air in the Capitol Rotunda. And a newscaster reported, "[T]his is a very dangerous situation."[519] This is the context in which Trump sent the tweet.

Testimony obtained by the Committee indicates that President Trump knew about the rioters' anger at Vice President Pence and indicated something to the effect that the Vice President "deserves it." [520] As Cassidy Hutchinson explained:

> I remember Pat saying something to the effect of, "Mark, we need to do something more. They're literally calling for the Vice President to be f'ing hung." And Mark had responded something to the effect of, "You heard him, Pat. He thinks Mike deserves it. He doesn't think they're doing anything wrong." To which Pat said something, "[t]his is f'ing crazy, we need to be doing something more," briefly stepped into Mark's office, and when Mark had said something—when Mark had said something to the effect of, "He doesn't think they're doing anything wrong," knowing what I had heard briefly in the dining room coupled with Pat discussing the hanging Mike Pence chants in the lobby of our office and then Mark's response, I understood "they're" to be the rioters in the Capitol that were chanting for the Vice President to be hung. [521]

Although White House Counsel Pat Cipollone was limited in what he would discuss because of privilege concerns, he stated the following:

> Committee Staff: Do you remember any discussion at any point during the day about rioters at the Capitol chanting 'hang Mike Pence?'

> Cipollone: Yes. I remember—I remember hearing that—about that. Yes.

> Committee Staff: Yeah. And—

> Cipollone: I don't know if I observed that myself on TV. I don't remember.

> Committee Staff: I'm just curious, I understand the privilege line you've drawn, but do you remember what you can share with us about the discussion about those chants, the 'hang Mike Pence' chants?

> Cipollone: I could tell you my view of that.

> Committee Staff: Yeah. Please.

> Cipollone: My view of that is that is outrageous.

> Committee Staff: Uh-huh.

> Cipollone: And for anyone to suggest such a thing as the Vice President of the United States, for people in that crowd to be chanting

that I thought was terrible. I thought it was outrageous and wrong. And I expressed that very clearly to people.[522]

Almost immediately after the 2:24 p.m. tweet, Eric Herschmann went upstairs in the West Wing to try to enlist Ivanka Trump's assistance to persuade her father to do the right thing.[523] Ivanka rushed down to the Oval Office dining room. Although no one could convince President Trump to call for the violent rioters to leave the Capitol, Ivanka persuaded President Trump that a tweet could be issued to discourage violence against the police.

At 2:38 p.m., President Trump sent this tweet:

"Please support our Capitol Police and Law Enforcement. They are truly on the side of our Country. Stay peaceful!"[524]

While some in the meeting invoked executive privilege, or failed to recall the specifics, others told us what happened at that point. Sarah Matthews, the White House Deputy Press Secretary, had urged her boss, Kayleigh McEnany, to have the President make a stronger statement. But she informed us that President Trump resisted using the word "peaceful" in his message:

Committee Staff: Ms. Matthews, Ms. McEnany told us she came right back to the press office after meeting with the President about this particular tweet. What did she tell you about what happened in that dining room?

Sarah Matthews: When she got back, she told me that a tweet had been sent out. And I told her that I thought the tweet did not go far enough, that I thought there needed to be a call to action and he needed to condemn the violence. And we were in a room full of people, but people weren't paying attention. And so, she looked directly at me and in a hushed tone shared with me that the President did not want to include any sort of mention of peace in that tweet and that it took some convincing on their part, those who were in the room. And she said that there was a back and forth going over different phrases to find something that he was comfortable with. And it wasn't until Ivanka Trump suggested the phrase 'stay peaceful' that he finally agreed to include it.[525]

At 3:13 p.m., President Trump sent another tweet, but again declined to tell people to go home:

"I am asking for everyone at the U.S. Capitol to remain peaceful. No violence! Remember, WE are the Party of Law & Order—respect the Law and our great men and women in Blue. Thank you!"[526]

Almost everyone, including staff in the White House also found the President's 2:38 p.m. and 3:13 p.m. tweets to be insufficient because they did not instruct the rioters to leave the Capitol. As mentioned, President Trump's son, Donald Trump Jr., texted Meadows:

He's got to condem [sic] this shit. Asap. The captiol [sic] police tweet is not enough. [527]

Sean Hannity also texted Mark Meadows:

Can he make a statement. I saw the tweet. Ask people to peacefully leave the capital [sic]. [528]

None of these efforts resulted in President Trump immediately issuing the message that was needed. White House staff had these comments:

Pottinger: Yeah. It was insufficient. I think what—you could count me among those who was hoping to see an unequivocal strong statement clearing out the Capitol, telling people to stand down, leave, go home. I think that's what we were hoping for. [529]

. . .

Matthews: Yeah. So a conversation started in the press office after the President sent out those two tweets that I deemed were insufficient. . . . I thought that we should condemn the violence and condemn it unequivocally. And I thought that he needed to include a call to action and to tell these people to go home. [530]

And they were right. Evidence showed that neither of these tweets had any appreciable impact on the violent rioters. Unlike the video-message tweet that did not come until 4:17 finally instructing rioters to leave, neither the 2:38 nor the 3:13 tweets made any difference.

At some point after 3:05 p.m. that afternoon, President Trump's Chief of Staff—and President Trump himself—were informed that someone had been shot. [531] That person was Ashli Babbitt, who was fatally shot at 2:44 p.m. as she and other rioters tried to gain access to the House chamber. [532] There is no indication that this affected the President's state of mind that day, and we found no evidence that the President expressed any remorse that day.

Meanwhile, leaders in Congress—including Speaker Pelosi, Senator Schumer, Senator McConnell—and the Vice President, were taking action. They called the Secretary of Defense, the Attorney General, governors and officials in Virginia, Maryland, and the District of Columbia, begging for assistance. [533]

President-elect Biden also broadcast a video calling on President Trump to take action:

I call on President Trump to go on national television now to fulfill his oath and defend the Constitution and demand an end to this siege.[534]

President Trump could have done this, of course, anytime after he learned of the violence at the Capitol. At 4:17 p.m., 187 minutes after finishing his speech (and even longer after the attack began), President Trump finally broadcast a video message in which he asked those attacking the Capitol to leave:

I know your pain. I know you're hurt. We had an election that was stolen from us. It was a landslide election, and everyone knows it, especially the other side, but you have to go home now. We have to have peace.[535]

President Trump's Deputy Press Secretary, Sarah Matthews testified about her reaction to this video message:

[H]e told the people who we had just watched storm our nation's Capitol with the intent on overthrowing our democracy, violently attack police officers, and chant heinous things like, "Hang Mike Pence," "We love you. You're very special." As a spokesperson for him, I knew that I would be asked to defend that. And to me, his refusal to act and call off the mob that day and his refusal to condemn the violence was indefensible. And so, I knew that I would be resigning that evening.[536]

By this time, the National Guard and other additional law enforcement had begun to arrive in force and started to turn the tide of the violence. Many of those attackers in the Capitol saw or received word of President Trump's 4:17 p.m. message, and they understood this message as an instruction to leave:[537]

- Stephen Ayres testified in front of the Select Committee that: "Well, we were there. As soon as that come out, everybody started talking about it, and it seemed like it started to disperse, you know, some of the crowd. Obviously, you know, once we got back to the hotel room, we seen that it was still going on, but it definitely dispersed a lot of the crowd."[538]
- Jacob Chansley, also known as the QAnon-Shaman answered President Trump's directive: "I'm here delivering the President's message. Donald Trump has asked everybody to go home." Another responded to Chansley: "That's our order."[539]
- Other unknown individuals also listened to President Trump's message while outside the Capitol, and responded: "He says, go home. He says, go home." And "Yeah. Here. He said to go home."[540]

At 6:01 p.m., President Trump sent his last tweet of the day, not condemning the violence, but instead attempting to justify it:

These are the things and events that happen when a sacred election landslide victory is so unceremoniously & viciously stripped away from great patriots who have been badly & unfairly treated for so long. Go home with love & in peace. Remember this day forever![541]

Staff in President Trump's own White House and campaign had a strong reaction to this message:

Sarah Matthews: At that point I had already made the decision to resign and this tweet just further cemented my decision. I thought that January 6, 2021, was one of the darkest days in our Nation's history and President Trump was treating it as a celebratory occasion with that tweet. And so, it just further cemented my decision to resign.[542]

Tim Murtaugh: I don't think it's a patriotic act to attack the Capitol. But I have no idea how to characterize the people other than they trespassed, destroyed property, and assaulted the U.S. Capitol. I think calling them patriots is a, let's say, a stretch, to say the least. . . . I don't think it's a patriotic act to attack the U.S. Capitol.[543]

Pat Cipollone: [W]hat happened at the Capitol cannot be justified in any form or fashion. It was wrong, and it was tragic. And a lot—and it was a terrible day. It was a terrible day for this country.[544]

Greg Jacob: I thought it was inappropriate. . . . To my mind, it was a day that should live in infamy.[545]

At 6:27 p.m., President Trump retired to his residence for the night. As he did, he had one final comment to an employee who accompanied him to the residence. The one takeaway that the President expressed in that moment, following a horrific afternoon of violence and the worst attack against the U.S. Capitol building in over two centuries, was this: "Mike Pence let me down."[546]

President Trump's inner circle was still trying to delay the counting of electoral votes into the evening, even after the violence had been quelled. Rudolph Giuliani tried calling numerous Members of Congress in the hour before the joint session resumed, including Rep. Jim Jordan (R–OH) and Senators Marsha Blackburn (R–TN), Tommy Tuberville (R–AL), Bill Hagerty (R–TN), Lindsey Graham (R–SC), Josh Hawley (R–MO), and Ted Cruz (R–TX).[547] His voicemail intended for Senator Tuberville at 7:02 p.m. that evening eventually was made public:

A Trump sign with Vice President Mike Pence's name removed.
(Photo by Michael Ciaglo/Getty Images)

Guiliani: Sen. Tuberville? Or I should say Coach Tuberville. This is Rudy Guiliani, the President's lawyer. I'm calling you because I want to discuss with you how they're trying to rush this hearing and how we need you, our Republican friends, to try to just slow it down so we can get these legislatures to get more information to you.[548]

Reflecting on President Trump's conduct that day, Vice President Pence noted that President Trump "had made no effort to contact me in the midst of the rioting or any point afterward."[549] He wrote that President Trump's "reckless words had endangered my family and all those serving at the Capitol."[550]

President Trump did not contact a single top national security official during the day. Not at the Pentagon, nor at the Department of Homeland Security, the Department of Justice, the F.B.I., the Capitol Police Department, or the D.C. Mayor's office.[551] As Vice President Pence has confirmed, President Trump didn't even try to reach his own Vice President to make sure that Pence was safe.[552] President Trump did not order any of his staff to facilitate a law enforcement response of any sort.[553] His Chairman of the Joint Chiefs of Staff—who is by statute the primary military advisor to the President—had this reaction:

General Milley: You know, you're the Commander in Chief. You've got an assault going on on the Capitol of the United States of America. And there's nothing? No call? Nothing? Zero?[554]

General Milley did, however, receive a call from President Trump's Chief of Staff Mark Meadows that day. Here is how he described that call:

He said, "We have to kill the narrative that the Vice President is making all the decisions. We need to establish the narrative, you know, that the President is still in charge and that things are steady or stable," or words to that effect. I immediately interpreted that as politics, politics, politics. Red flag for me, personally. No action. But I remember it distinctly. And I don't do political narratives.[555]

Some have suggested that President Trump gave an order to have 10,000 troops ready for January 6th.[556] The Select Committee found no evidence of this. In fact, President Trump's Acting Secretary of Defense Christopher Miller directly refuted this when he testified under oath:

Committee Staff: To be crystal clear, there was no direct order from President Trump to put 10,000 troops to be on the ready for January 6th, correct?

Miller: No. Yeah. That's correct. There was no direct—there was no order from the President.[557]

Later, on the evening of January 6th, President Trump's former campaign manager, Brad Parscale, texted Katrina Pierson, one of President Trump's rally organizers, that the events of the day were the result of a "sitting president asking for civil war" and that "This week I feel guilty for helping him win" now that ". . . a woman is dead." Pierson answered: "You do realize this was going to happen." Parscale replied: "Yeah. If I was Trump and knew my rhetoric killed someone." "It wasn't the rhetoric," Pierson suggested. But Parscale insisted: "Yes it was." [558]

THE IMMEDIATE AFTERMATH OF JANUARY 6TH

In days following January 6th, President Trump's family and staff attempted repeatedly to persuade him not to repeat his election fraud allegations, to concede defeat, and to allow the transition to President Biden to proceed. Trump did make two video recordings, which initially appeared contrite. But evidence suggests that these statements were designed at least in part to ward off other potential consequences of January 6th, such as invocation of the 25th Amendment or impeachment.

In fact, Minority Leader Kevin McCarthy indicated after the attack, in a discussion with House Republican leaders, that he would ask President Trump to resign:

Rep. Cheney: I guess there's a question when we were talking about the 25th Amendment resolution, and you asked what would happen after he's gone? Is there any chance? Are you hearing that he might resign? Is there any reason to think that might happen?

Leader McCarthy: I've had a few discussions. My gut tells me no. I'm seriously thinking of having that discussion with him tonight. I haven't talked to him in a couple of days. From what I know of him, I mean, you guys all know him too, do you think he'd ever back away? But what I think I'm going to do is I'm going to call him. This is what I think. We know [the 25th Amendment resolution] will pass the House. I think there's a chance it will pass the Senate, even when he's gone. And I think there's a lot of different ramifications for that. . . . Again, the only discussion I would have with him is that I think this will pass, and it would be my recommendation you should resign.[559]

Before January 6th, Fox News personality Sean Hannity warned that January 6th could be disastrous:

Dec. 31, 2020 text from Sean Hannity to Mark Meadows: "We can't lose the entire WH counsels office. I do NOT see January 6 happening the way he is being told. After the 6 th [sic]. He should announce will lead the nationwide effort to reform voting integrity. Go to Fl and watch Joe mess up daily. Stay engaged. When he speaks people will listen." [560]

January 5, 2021 texts from Sean Hannity to Mark Meadows:

"Im very worried about the next 48 hours"

"Pence pressure. WH counsel will leave."

"Sorry, I can't talk right now."

"On with boss"[561]

A member of the Republican Freedom caucus also warned, on December 31, 2020, and on January 1, 2021:

The President should call everyone off. It's the only path. If we substitute the will of states through electors with a vote by Congress every 4 years . . . we have destroyed the electoral college . . . Respectfully.[562] If POTUS allows this to occur . . . we're driving a stake in the heart of the federal republic . . . [563]

After January 6th, Hannity worked to persuade President Trump to stop talking about election fraud, proposed that Trump pardon Hunter Biden, and discussed attending the Inauguration:

1. No more stolen election talk.
2. Yes, impeachment and 25th amendment are real, and many people will quit.
3. He was intrigued by the Pardon idea!! (Hunter)
4. Resistant but listened to Pence thoughts, to make it right.
5. Seemed to like attending Inauguration talk.[564]

Ultimately, President Trump took little of the advice from Hannity and his White House staff. A few days later, Hannity wrote again to Meadows and Jim Jordan:

Guys, we have a clear path to land the plane in 9 days. He can't mention the election again. Ever. I did not have a good call with him today. And worse, I'm not sure what is left to do or say, and I don t like not knowing if it's truly understood. Ideas?[565]

Likewise, despite her many contrary public statements, Republican Congresswoman Marjorie Taylor Greene privately texted her concerns on January 6th about a continuing and real threat of violence.

Mark I was just told there is an active shooter on the first floor of the Capitol Please tell the President to calm people This isn't the way to solve anything[566]

Donald Trump was impeached on January 13th. In a speech that day, Republican Leader Kevin McCarthy made this statement from the House floor, but voted against impeachment:

The President bears responsibility for Wednesday's attack on Congress by mob rioters. He should have immediately denounced the mob when he saw what was unfolding. These facts require immediate action by President Trump, accept his share of responsibility, quell the brewing unrest and ensure President-elect Biden is able to successfully begin his term. The President's immediate action also deserves congressional action, which is why I think a fact-finding commission and a censure resolution would be prudent.[567]

Later, McCarthy told members of the House Republican conference that Trump had acknowledged that he was at least partially responsible for the January 6th attack.

Kevin McCarthy speaks at a press conference at the Capitol building on August 27, 2021.
(Photo by Anna Moneymaker/Getty Images)

I asked him personally today, does he hold responsibility for what happened? Does he feel bad about what happened? He told me he does have some responsibility for what happened. And he need to acknowledge that.[568]

Since January 6th, President Trump has continued to claim falsely that the 2020 Presidential election was stolen. Not only that, he has urged other politicians to push this argument as well. Representative Mo Brooks has issued a public statement appearing to represent Trump's private views and intentions:

President Trump asked me to rescind the 2020 elections, immediately remove Joe Biden from the White House, immediately put President Trump back in the White House, and hold a new special election for the presidency.[569]

REFERRALS TO THE U.S. DEPARTMENT OF JUSTICE SPECIAL COUNSEL AND HOUSE ETHICS COMMITTEE

The Committee's work has produced a substantial body of new information. We know far more about the President's plans and actions to overturn the election than almost all Members of Congress did when President Trump was impeached on January 13, 2021, or when he was tried by the Senate in February of that year. Fifty-seven of 100 Senators voted to convict President Trump at that time, and more than 20 others condemned the President's conduct and said they were voting against conviction because the President's term had already expired.[570] At the time, the Republican Leader of the U.S. Senate said this about Donald Trump: "A mob was assaulting the Capitol in his name. These criminals were carrying his banners, hanging his flags, and screaming their loyalty to him. It was obvious that only President Trump could end this. He was the only one who could."[571] House Republican Leader Kevin McCarthy, who spoke directly with President Trump during the violence of January 6th, expressed similar views both in private and in public. Privately, Leader McCarthy stated: "But let me be very clear to you and I have been very clear to the President. He bears responsibility for his words and actions. No if, ands or buts."[572] In public, Leader McCarthy concluded: "The President bears responsibility for Wednesday's attack on Congress by mob rioters."[573]

Today we know that the planning to overturn the election on January 6th was substantially more extensive, and involved many other players, and many other efforts over a longer time period. Indeed, the violent attack and invasion of the Capitol, and what provoked it, are only a part of the story.

From the outset of its hearings, the Committee has explained that President Trump and a number of other individuals made a series of very specific plans, ultimately with multiple separate elements, but all with one overriding objective: to corruptly obstruct, impede, or influence the counting of electoral votes on January 6th, and thereby overturn the lawful results of the election. The underlying and fundamental feature of that planning was the effort to get one man, Vice President Mike Pence, to assert and then exercise unprecedented and lawless powers to unilaterally alter the actual election outcome on January 6th. Evidence obtained by the Committee demonstrates that John Eastman, who worked with President Trump to put that and other elements of the plan in place, knew even before the 2020 Presidential election that Vice President Pence could not lawfully refuse to count official, certified electoral slates submitted by the Governors of the States.[574] Testimony and contemporaneous documentary evidence also indicate that President Trump knew that the plan was unlawful before January 6th.[575] When the Vice President's counsel wrote to Eastman on January 6th to ask whether the latter had informed the President that the Vice President did not have authority to decide the election unilaterally, Eastman responded: "He's been so advised," and added, "[b]ut you know him—once he gets something in his head, it is hard to get him to change course."[576]

Many of the other elements of President Trump's plans were specifically designed to create a set of circumstances on January 6th to assist President Trump in overturning the lawful election outcome during Congress's joint session that day. For example, President Trump pressured State legislatures to adopt new electoral slates that Vice President Pence could, unlawfully, count. Trump solicited State officials to "find" a sufficient number of votes to alter the final count, and instructed the Department of Justice to "just say that the election was was [sic] corrupt + leave the rest to me and the R[epublican] Congressmen."[577] President Trump offered the job of Acting Attorney General to Jeffrey Clark. As our evidence has unequivocally demonstrated, Clark intended to use that position to send a series of letters from the Department of Justice to multiple States falsely asserting that the Department had found fraud and urging those States to convene their legislatures to alter their official electoral slates.[578] And President Trump, with the help of the Republican National Committee and others, oversaw an effort to create and transmit to Government officials a series of intentionally false electoral slates for Vice President Pence to utilize on January 6th to alter or delay the count of lawful votes.[579]

Of course, other elements of the plan complemented these efforts too. As this Report documents, President Trump was advised by his own experts and the Justice Department that his election fraud allegations were false, and he knew he had lost virtually all the legal challenges to the election, but he nevertheless engaged in a successful but fraudulent effort to persuade tens of millions of Americans that the election was stolen from him. This effort was designed to convince Americans that President Trump's actions to overturn the election were justified. President Trump then urged his supporters to travel to Washington on January 6th to apply pressure to Congress to halt the count and change the election outcome, explaining to those who were coming to Washington that they needed to "take back" their country and "stop the steal."[580]

It is helpful in understanding these facts to focus on specific moments in time when President Trump made corrupt, dishonest, and unlawful choices to pursue his plans. For example, by December 14th when the electoral college met and certified Joe Biden's victory, President Trump knew that he had failed in all the relevant litigation; he had been advised by his own experts and the Justice Department that his election fraud claims were false; and he had been told by numerous advisors that he had lost and should concede. But despite his duty as President to take care that the laws are faithfully executed, he chose instead to ignore all of the judicial rulings and the facts before him and push forward to overturn the election. Likewise, in the days and hours before the violence of January 6th, President Trump knew that no State had issued any changed electoral slate. Indeed, neither President Trump nor his co-conspirators had any evidence that any majority of any State legislature was willing to do so. President Trump also knew that Vice President Pence could not lawfully refuse to count legitimate votes. Despite all of these facts, President Trump nevertheless proceeded to instruct Vice President Pence to execute a plan he already knew was illegal. And then knowing that a violent riot was underway, President Trump breached his oath of office; our Commander in Chief refused for hours to take the one simple step that his advisors were begging him to take—to instruct his supporters to disperse, stand down, and leave the Capitol. Instead, fully understanding what had unfolded at the Capitol, President Trump exacerbated the violence with a tweet attacking Vice President Pence.[581] Any rational person who had watched the events that day knew that President Trump's 2:24 p.m. tweet would lead to further violence. It did. And, at almost exactly the same time, President Trump continued to lobby Congress to delay the electoral count.

As the evidence demonstrates, the rioters at the Capitol had invaded the building and halted the electoral count. They did not begin to relent until President Trump finally issued a video statement instructing his supporters to leave the Capitol at 4:17 p.m., which had an immediate and helpful effect: rioters began to disperse[582]—but not before the Capitol was invaded, the election count was halted, feces were smeared in the Capitol, the Vice President and his family and many others were put in danger, and more than 140 law enforcement officers were attacked and seriously injured by mob rioters. Even if it were true that President Trump genuinely believed the election was stolen, *this is no defense*. No President can ignore the courts and purposely violate the law no matter what supposed "justification" he or she presents.

These conclusions are not the Committee's alone. In the course of its investigation, the Committee had occasion to present evidence to Federal District Court Judge David Carter, who weighed that evidence against submissions from President Trump's lawyer, John Eastman. Judge Carter considered this evidence in the context of a discovery dispute—specifically whether the Committee could obtain certain of Eastman's documents pursuant to the "crime-fraud" exception to the attorney-client privilege. That exception provides that otherwise privileged documents may lose their privilege if they were part of an effort to commit a crime or a fraud, in this case by President Trump. Judge Carter set out his factual findings, discussing multiple elements of President Trump's multi-part plan to overturn the election,[583] and then addressed whether the evidence, including Eastman's email communications, demonstrated that Trump and Eastman committed crimes. "Based on the evidence," Judge Carter explained, "the Court finds it more likely than not that President Trump corruptly attempted to obstruct the Joint Session of Congress on January 6, 2021," and "more likely than not that President Trump and Dr. Eastman dishonestly conspired to obstruct the Joint Session of Congress on January 6th."[584] Judge Carter also concluded that President Trump's and Eastman's "pressure campaign to stop the electoral count did not end with Vice President Pence—it targeted every tier of federal and state elected officials"[585] and was "a coup in search of a legal theory."[586] "The plan spurred violent attacks on the seat of our nation's government," Judge Carter wrote, and it threatened to "permanently end[] the peaceful transition of power. . . ."[587]

The U.S. Department of Justice has been investigating and prosecuting persons who invaded the Capitol, engaged in violence, and planned violence on that day. The Department has charged more than 900 individuals, and nearly 500 have already been convicted or pleaded guilty as we write.[588] As the Committee's investigation progressed through its hearings, public reporting emerged suggesting that the Department of Justice had also begun to investigate several others specifically involved in the events being examined by the Committee. Such reports indicated that search warrants had been issued, based on findings of probable cause, for the cell phones of John Eastman, Jeffrey Clark, and Representative Scott Perry.[589] Other reports suggested that the Department had empaneled one or more grand juries and was pursuing a ruling compelling several of this Committee's witnesses, including Pat Cipollone and Greg Jacob, to give testimony on topics for which President Trump had apparently asserted executive privilege. Recent reporting suggests that a Federal district court judge has now rejected President Trump's executive privilege claims in that context.[590]

Criminal referrals from a congressional committee are often made in circumstances where prosecutors are not yet known to be pursuing some of the same facts and evidence. That is not the case here. During the course of our investigation, both the U.S. Department of Justice and at least one local prosecutor's office (Fulton County, Georgia) have been actively conducting criminal investigations concurrently with this congressional investigation.[591] In fact, the U.S. Department of Justice has recently taken the extraordinary step of appointing a Special Counsel to investigate the former President's conduct.[592]

The Committee recognizes that the Department of Justice and other prosecutorial authorities may be in a position to utilize investigative tools, including search warrants and grand juries, superior to the means the Committee has for obtaining relevant information and testimony. Indeed, both the Department of Justice and the Fulton County District Attorney may now have access to witness testimony and records that have been unavailable to the Committee, including testimony from President Trump's Chief of Staff Mark Meadows, and others who either asserted privileges or invoked their Fifth Amendment rights.[593] The Department may also be able to access, via grand jury subpoena or otherwise, the testimony of Republican Leader Kevin McCarthy, Representative Scott Perry, Representative Jim Jordan and others, each of whom appears to have had materially relevant communications with Donald Trump or others in the White House but who failed to comply with the Select Committee's subpoenas.

Taking all of these facts into account, and based on the breadth of the evidence it has accumulated, the Committee makes the following criminal referrals to the Department of Justice's Special Counsel.

I. Obstruction of an Official Proceeding (18 U.S.C. § 1512(c))

Section 1512(c)(2) of Title 18 of the United States Code makes it a crime to "corruptly" "obstruct[], influence[], or impede[] any official proceeding, or attempt[] to do so." [594] Sufficient evidence exists of one or more potential violations of this statute for a criminal referral of President Trump and others.[595]

First, there should be no question that Congress's joint session to count electoral votes on January 6th was an "official proceeding" under section 1512(c). Many Federal judges have already reached that specific conclusion.[596]

Second, there should be no doubt that President Trump knew that his actions were likely to "obstruct, influence or impede" that proceeding. Based on the evidence developed, President Trump was attempting to prevent or delay the counting of lawful certified electoral college votes from multiple States.[597] President Trump was directly and personally involved in this effort, personally pressuring Vice President Pence relentlessly as the joint session on January 6th approached.[598]

Third, President Trump acted with a "corrupt" purpose. Vice President Pence, Greg Jacob, and others repeatedly told the President that the Vice President had no unilateral authority to prevent certification of the election.[599] Indeed, in an email exchange during the violence of January 6th, Eastman admitted that President Trump had been "advised" that Vice President Pence could not lawfully refuse to count votes under the Electoral Count Act, but "once he gets something in his head, it's hard to get him to change course." [600] In addition, President Trump knew that he had lost dozens of State and Federal lawsuits, and that the Justice Department, his campaign and his other advisors concluded that there was insufficient fraud to alter the outcome. President Trump also knew that no majority of any State legislature had taken or manifested any intention to take any official action that could change a State's electoral college votes.[601] But President Trump pushed forward anyway. As Judge Carter explained, "[b]ecause

President Trump likely knew that the plan to disrupt the electoral count was wrongful, his mindset exceeds the threshold for acting 'corruptly' under § 1512(c)." [602]

Sufficient evidence exists of one or more potential violations of 18 U.S.C. § 1512(c) for a criminal referral of President Trump based solely on his plan to get Vice President Pence to prevent certification of the election at the joint session of Congress. Those facts standing alone are sufficient. But such a charge under that statute can also be based on the plan to create and transmit to the executive and legislative branches fraudulent electoral slates, which were ultimately intended to facilitate an unlawful action by Vice President Pence, to refuse to count legitimate, certified electoral votes during Congress's official January 6th proceeding.[603] Additionally, evidence developed about the many other elements of President Trump's plans to overturn the election, including soliciting State legislatures, State officials, and others to alter official electoral outcomes, provides further evidence that President Trump was attempting through multiple means to corruptly obstruct, impede, or influence the counting of electoral votes on January 6th. This is also true of President Trump's personal directive to the Department of Justice to "just say that the election was was [sic] corrupt + leave the rest to me and the R[epublican] Congressmen." [604]

We also stress in particular the draft letter to the Georgia legislature authored by Jeffrey Clark and another Trump political appointee at the Department of Justice. The draft letter embraces many of the same theories that John Eastman and others were asserting in President Trump's effort to lobby State legislatures. White House Counsel Pat Cipollone described that letter as "a murder-suicide pact," and other White House and Justice Department officials offered similar descriptions.[605] As described herein, that draft letter was intended to help persuade a State legislature to change its certified slate of electoral college electors based on false allegations of fraud, so Vice President Pence could unilaterally and unlawfully decide to count a different slate on January 6th.[606] The letter was transparently false, improper, and illegal. President Trump had multiple communications with Clark in the days before January 6th, and there is no basis to doubt that President Trump offered Clark the position of Acting Attorney General knowing that Clark would send the letter and others like it.[607]

Of course, President Trump is also responsible for recruiting tens of thousands of his supporters to Washington for January 6th, and knowing they were angry and some were armed, instructing them to march to the Capitol and "fight like hell." [608] And then, while knowing a violent riot was underway, he refused for multiple hours to take the single step his advisors and supporters were begging him to take to halt the violence: to make a public statement instructing his supporters to disperse and leave the Capitol.[609] Through action and inaction, President Trump corruptly obstructed, delayed, and impeded the vote count.

In addition, the Committee believes sufficient evidence exists for a criminal referral of John Eastman and certain other Trump associates under 18 U.S.C. §1512(c). The evidence shows that Eastman knew in advance of the 2020 election that Vice President Pence could not refuse to count electoral votes on January 6th.[610] In the days before January 6th, Eastman was warned repeatedly that his plan was illegal and "completely crazy," and would "cause riots in the streets." [611] Nonetheless, Eastman continued to assist President Trump's pressure campaign in public and in private, including in meetings with the Vice President and in his own speech at the Ellipse on January 6th. And even as the violence was playing out at the Capitol, Eastman admitted in writing that his plan violated the law but pressed for Pence to do it anyway.[612] In the immediate aftermath of January 6th, White House lawyer Eric Herschmann told Eastman that he should "[g]et a great F'ing criminal defense lawyer, you're going to need it." [613] Others working with Eastman likely share in Eastman's culpability. For example, Kenneth Chesebro was a central player in the scheme to submit fake electors to the Congress and the National Archives.

The Committee notes that multiple Republican Members of Congress, including Representative Scott Perry, likely have material facts regarding President Trump's plans to overturn the election. For example, many Members of Congress attended a White House meeting on December 21, 2020, in which the plan to have the Vice President affect the outcome of the election was disclosed and discussed. Evidence indicates that certain of those Members unsuccessfully sought Presidential pardons from President Trump after January 6th,[614] as did Eastman,[615] revealing their own clear consciousness of guilt.

II. Conspiracy to Defraud the United States (18 U.S.C. § 371)

Section 371 of Title 18 of the U.S. Code provides that "[i]f two or more persons conspire either to commit any offense against the United States, or to defraud the United States, or any agency thereof in any manner or for any purpose, and one or more of such persons do any act to effect the object of the conspiracy, each shall be fined under this title or imprisoned not more than five years, or both." The Committee believes sufficient evidence exists for a criminal referral of President Trump and others under this statute.[616]

First, President Trump entered into an agreement with individuals to obstruct a lawful function of the government (the certification of the election). The evidence of this element overlaps greatly with the evidence of the section 1512(c)(2) violations, so we will not repeat it at length here. President Trump engaged in a multi-part plan described in this Report to obstruct a lawful certification of the election. Judge Carter focused his opinions largely on John Eastman's role, as Eastman's documents were at issue in that case, concluding that "the evidence shows that an agreement to enact the electoral count plan likely existed between President Trump and Eastman." [617] But President Trump entered into agreements—whether formal or informal[618]—with several other individuals who assisted with the multi-part plan. With regard to the Department of Justice, Jeffrey Clark stands out as a participant in the conspiracy, as the evidence suggests that Clark entered into an agreement with President Trump that if appointed Acting Attorney General, he would send a letter to State officials falsely stating that the Department of Justice believed that State legislatures had a sufficient factual basis to convene to select new electors. This was false—the Department of Justice had reached the conclusion that there was no factual basis to contend that the election was stolen. Again, as with section 1512(c), the conspiracy under section 371 appears to have also included other individuals such as Chesebro, Rudolph Giuliani, and Mark Meadows, but this Committee does not attempt to determine all of the participants of the conspiracy, many of whom refused to answer this Committee's questions.

Second, there are several bases for finding that the conspirators used "deceitful or dishonest means." For example, President Trump repeatedly lied about the election, after he had been told by his advisors that there was no evidence of fraud sufficient to change the results of the election.[619] In addition, the plot to get the Vice President to unilaterally prevent certification of the election was manifestly (and admittedly) illegal, as discussed above. Eastman and others told President Trump that it would violate the Electoral Count Act if the Vice President unilaterally rejected electors. Thus Judge Carter once again had little trouble finding that the intent requirement ("deceitful or dishonest means") was met, stating that "President Trump continuing to push that plan despite being aware of its illegality constituted obstruction by 'dishonest' means under § 371." [620] Judge Carter rejected the notion that Eastman's plan—which the President adopted and actualized—was a "good faith interpretation" of the law, finding instead that it was "a partisan distortion of the democratic process." [621] Similarly, both President Trump and Clark had been told repeatedly that the Department of Justice had found no evidence of significant fraud in any of its investigations, but they nonetheless pushed the Department of Justice to send a letter to State officials stating that the Department had found such fraud. And Georgia Secretary of State Brad Raffensperger and others made clear to President Trump that they had no authority to "find" him 11,780 votes, but the President relentlessly insisted that they do exactly that, even to the point of suggesting there could be criminal consequences if they refused.[622]

Third, there were numerous overt acts in furtherance of the agreement, including each of the parts of the President's effort to overturn the election. As Judge Carter concluded, President Trump and Eastman participated in "numerous overt acts in furtherance of their shared plan." [623] These included, but certainly were not limited to, direct pleas to the Vice President to reject electors or delay certification, including in Oval Office meetings and the President's vulgar comments to the Vice President on the morning of January 6th. Judge Carter also addressed evidence that President Trump knowingly made false representations to a court. Judge Carter concluded that Eastman's emails showed "that President Trump knew that the specific numbers of voter fraud" cited in a complaint on behalf of President Trump "were wrong but continued to tout those numbers, both in court and to the public." Judge Carter found that the emails in question were related to and in furtherance of a conspiracy to defraud the United States.[624]

In finding that President Trump, Eastman, and others engaged in conspiracy to defraud the United States under section 371, Judge Carter relied on the documents at issue (largely consisting of Eastman's own emails) and evidence presented to the court by this Committee. This Committee's investigation has progressed significantly since Judge Carter issued his first crime-fraud ruling in March 2022. The evidence found by this Committee and discussed in detail in this Report further documents that the conspiracy to defraud the United States under section 371 extended far beyond the effort to pressure the Vice President to prevent certification of the election. The Committee believes there is sufficient evidence for a criminal referral of the multi-part plan described in this Report under section 371, as the very purpose of the plan was to prevent the lawful certification of Joe Biden's election as President.

III. Conspiracy to Make a False Statement (18 U.S.C. §§ 371, 1001)

President Trump, through others acting at his behest, submitted slates of fake electors to Congress and the National Archives. Section 1001 of Title 18 of the United States Code applies, in relevant part, to "whoever, in any matter within the jurisdiction of the executive, legislative, or judicial branch of the Government of the United States, knowingly and willfully—

(1) falsifies, conceals, or covers up by any trick, scheme, or device a material fact;

(2) makes any materially false, fictitious, or fraudulent statement or representation; or

(3) makes or uses any false writing or document knowing the same to contain any materially false, fictitious, or fraudulent statement or entry."

According to the Department of Justice, whether a false statement is criminal under section 1001 "depends on whether there is an affirmative response to each of the following questions:

1. Was the act or statement material?
2. Was the act within the jurisdiction of a department or agency of the United States?
3. Was the act done knowingly and willfully?" [625]

In addition, and as explained above, 18 U.S.C. § 371 makes it a crime to conspire to "commit any offense against the United States." [626]

The evidence suggests President Trump conspired with others to submit slates of fake electors to Congress and the National Archives. Sufficient evidence exists of a violation of 18 U.S.C. §§ 371 and 1001 for a criminal referral of President Trump and others.

As explained earlier and in Chapter 3 of this Report, the certifications signed by Trump electors in multiple States were patently false. Vice President Biden won each of those States, and the relevant State authorities had so certified. It can hardly be disputed that the false slates of electors were material, as nothing can be more material to the joint session of Congress to certify the election than the question of which candidate won which States. Indeed, evidence obtained by the Committee suggests that those attempting to submit certain of the electoral votes regarded the need to provide that material to Vice President Pence as urgent.[627]

There should be no question that section 1001 applies here. The false electoral slates were provided both to the executive branch (the National Archives) and the legislative branch.[628] The statute applies to "any matter within the jurisdiction of the executive, legislative, or judicial branch of the Government of the United States." [629] It is well established that false statements to Congress can constitute violations of section 1001.[630]

Finally, the false statement was made knowingly and willfully. There is some evidence suggesting that some signatories of the fake certificates believed that the certificates were contingent, to be used only in the event that President Trump prevailed in litigation challenging the election results in their States. That may be relevant to the question whether those electors knowingly and willfully signed a false statement at the time they signed the certificates. But it is of no moment to President Trump's conduct, as President Trump (including acting through co-conspirators such as John Eastman and Kenneth Chesebro) relied on the existence of those fake electors as a basis for asserting that the Vice President could reject or delay certification of the Biden electors. In fact, as explained earlier and in Chapter 5 of this Report, Eastman's memorandum setting out a six-step plan for overturning the election on January 6th begins by stating that "7 states have transmitted dual slates of electors to the President of the Senate."

The remaining question is who engaged in this conspiracy to make the false statement to Congress under section 1001. The evidence is clear that President Trump personally participated in a scheme to have the Trump electors meet, cast votes, and send their votes to the joint session of Congress in several States that Vice President Biden won, and then his supporters relied on the existence of these fake electors as part of their effort to obstruct the joint session. Republican National Committee (RNC) Chairwoman Ronna McDaniel testified before this Committee that President Trump and Eastman directly requested that the RNC organize the effort to have these fake (i.e., Trump) electors meet and cast their votes.[631] Thus, the Committee believes that sufficient evidence exists for a criminal referral of President Trump for illegally engaging in a conspiracy to violate section 1001; the evidence indicates that he entered into an agreement with Eastman and others to make the false statement (the fake electoral certificates), by deceitful or dishonest means, and at least one member of the conspiracy engaged in at least one overt act in furtherance of the conspiracy (e.g., President Trump and Eastman's call to Ronna McDaniel).

IV. "Incite," "Assist" or "Aid and Comfort" an Insurrection (18 U.S.C. § 2383)

Section 2383 of Title 18 of the United States Code applies to anyone who "incites, sets on foot, assists, or engages in any rebellion or insurrection against the authority of the United States or the laws thereof, or gives aid or comfort thereto."[632] The Committee recognizes that section 2383 does not require evidence of an "agreement" between President Trump and the violent rioters to establish a violation of that provision; instead, the President need only have incited, assisted, or aided and comforted those engaged in violence or other lawless activity in an effort to prevent the peaceful transition of the Presidency under our Constitution. A Federal court has already concluded that President Trump's statements during his Ellipse speech were "plausibly words of incitement not protected by the First Amendment."[633] Moreover, President Trump was impeached for "Incitement of Insurrection," and a majority of the Senate voted to convict, with many more suggesting they might have voted to convict had President Trump still been in office at the time.[634]

As explained throughout this Report and in this Committee's hearings, President Trump was directly responsible for summoning what became a violent mob to Washington, DC, urging them to march to the Capitol, and then further provoking the already violent and lawless crowd with his 2:24 p.m. tweet about the Vice President. Even though President Trump had repeatedly been told that Vice President Pence had no legal authority to stop the certification of the election, he asserted in his speech on January 6th that if the Vice President "comes through for us" that he could deliver victory to Trump: "[I]f Mike Pence does the right thing, we win the election." This created a desperate and false expectation in President Trump's mob that ended up putting the Vice President and his entourage and many others at the Capitol in physical danger. When President Trump tweeted at 2:24 p.m., he knew violence was underway. His tweet exacerbated that violence.[635]

During the ensuing riot, the President refused to condemn the violence or encourage the crowd to disperse despite repeated pleas from his staff and family that he do so. The Committee has evidence from multiple sources establishing these facts, including testimony from former White House Counsel Pat Cipollone. Although Cipollone's testimony did not disclose a number of direct communications with President Trump in light of concerns about executive privilege, the Department now appears to have obtained a ruling that Cipollone can testify before a grand jury about these communications. Based on the information it has obtained, the Committee believes that Cipollone and others can provide direct testimony establishing that President Trump refused repeatedly, for multiple hours, to make a public statement directing his violent and lawless supporters to leave the Capitol. President Trump did not want his supporters (who had effectively halted the vote counting) to disperse. Evidence obtained by the Committee also indicates that President Trump did not want to provide security assistance to the Capitol during that violent period.[636] This appalling behavior by our Commander in Chief occurred despite his affirmative constitutional duty to act to ensure that the laws are faithfully executed.[637]

The Committee believes that sufficient evidence exists for a criminal referral of President Trump for "assist[ing]" or "ai[ding] and comfort[ing]" those at the Capitol who engaged in a violent attack on the United States. The Committee has developed significant evidence that President Trump intended to disrupt the peaceful transition of power and believes that the Department of Justice can likely elicit testimony relevant to an investigation under section 2383.

For example, Chief of Staff Mark Meadows told White House Counsel Pat Cipollone that the President "doesn't want to do anything" to stop the violence.[638] Worse, at 2:24 p.m., the President inflamed and exacerbated the mob violence by sending a tweet stating that the Vice President "didn't have the courage to do what should have been done." [639] The President threw gasoline on the fire despite knowing that there was a violent riot underway at the Capitol. Indeed, video and audio footage from the attack shows that many of the rioters specifically mentioned Vice President

Pence.[640] And immediately after President Trump sent his tweet, the violence escalated. Between 2:25 p.m. and 2:28 p.m., rioters breached the East Rotunda doors, other rioters breached the police line in the Capitol Crypt, Vice President Pence had to be evacuated from his Senate office, and Leader McCarthy was evacuated from his Capitol office.[641]

Evidence developed in the Committee's investigation showed that the President, when told that the crowd was chanting "Hang Mike Pence," responded that perhaps the Vice President deserved to be hanged.[642] And President Trump rebuffed pleas from Leader McCarthy to ask that his supporters leave the Capitol stating, "Well, Kevin, I guess these people are more upset about the election than you are." After hours of deadly riot, President Trump eventually released a videotaped statement encouraging the crowd to disperse, though openly professing his "love" for the members of the mob and empathizing with their frustration at the "stolen" election. President Trump has since expressed a desire to pardon those involved in the attack.[643]

Both the purpose and the effect of the President's actions were to mobilize a large crowd to descend on the Capitol. Several defendants in pending criminal cases identified the President's allegations about the "stolen election" as the key motivation for their activities at the Capitol. Many of them specifically cited the President's tweets asking his supporters to come to Washington, DC, on January 6th. For example, one defendant who later pleaded guilty to threatening House Speaker Nancy Pelosi texted a family member on January 6th to say: "[Trump] wants heads and I'm going to deliver." [644] Another defendant released a statement through his attorney stating: "I was in Washington, DC on January 6, 2021, because I believed I was following the instructions of former President Trump and he was my President and the commander-in-chief. His statements also had me believing the election was stolen from him." [645]

As the violence began to subside and law enforcement continued to secure the Capitol, President Trump tweeted again, at 6:01 pm to justify the actions of the rioters: "These are the things and events that happen," he wrote, when his so-called victory was "so unceremoniously & viciously stripped away...." [646] When he wrote those words, he knew exactly what he was doing. Before President Trump issued the tweet, a White House staffer cautioned him that the statement would imply that he "had something to do with the events that happened at the Capitol"—but he tweeted it anyway.[647] The final words of that tweet leave little doubt about President Trump's sentiments toward those who invaded the Capitol: "Remember this day forever!" [648]

V. Other Conspiracy Statutes (18 U.S.C. §§ 372 and 2384)

Depending on evidence developed by the Department of Justice, the President's actions with the knowledge of the risk of violence could also constitute a violation of 18 U.S.C. § 372 and § 2384, both of which require proof of a conspiracy. Section 372 prohibits a conspiracy between two or more persons "to prevent, by force, intimidation, or threat, any person from accepting or holding any office, trust, or place of confidence under the United States, or from discharging any duties thereof, or to induce by like means any officer of the United States to leave the place, where his duties as an officer are required to be performed, or to injure him in the discharge of his official duties." [649] Oath Keepers Kelly Meggs, Kenneth Harrelson, and Jessica Watkins were convicted of violating 18 U.S.C. § 372 in connection with the January 6th attack on the Capitol.[650] The Committee believes that former Chief of Staff Mark Meadows (who refused to testify and was held in contempt of Congress) could have specific evidence relevant to such charges, as may witnesses who invoked their Fifth Amendment rights against self-incrimination before this Committee.

Section 2384, the seditious conspiracy statute, prohibits "conspir[acy] to overthrow, put down, or to destroy by force the Government of the United States . . . or to oppose by force the authority thereof, or by force to prevent, hinder or delay the execution of any law of the United States . . . ." [651] A jury has already determined beyond a reasonable doubt that a conspiracy existed under section 2384, as the leader of the Oath Keepers and at least one other individual were convicted of seditious conspiracy under section 2384 for their actions related to the attack on the Capitol.[652] A trial regarding a series of other "Proud Boy" defendants may also address similar issues.[653]

The Department of Justice, through its investigative tools that exceed those of this Committee, may have evidence sufficient to prosecute President Trump under sections 372 and 2384. Accordingly, we believe sufficient evidence exists for a criminal referral of President Trump under these two statutes.

VI. The Committee's Concerns Regarding Possible Obstruction of its Investigation

The Committee has substantial concerns regarding potential efforts to obstruct its investigation, including by certain counsel (some paid by groups connected to the former President) who may have advised clients to provide false or misleading testimony to the Committee.[654] Such actions could violate 18 U.S.C. §§ 1505, 1512. The Committee is aware that both the U.S. Department of Justice and the Fulton County District Attorney's Office have already obtained information relevant to these matters, including from the Committee directly. We urge the Department of Justice to examine the facts to discern whether prosecution is warranted. The Committee's broad concerns regarding obstruction and witness credibility are addressed in the Executive Summary to this Report.

VII. ACCOUNTABILITY FOR THOSE WHO PLOTTED UNLAWFULLY TO OVERTURN THE ELECTION IS CRITICAL.

To date, the Justice Department has pursued prosecution of hundreds of individuals who planned and participated in the January 6th invasion of and attack on our Capitol. But the Department has not yet charged individuals who engaged in the broader plan to overturn the election through the means discussed in this Report. The Committee has concluded that it is critical to hold those individuals accountable as well, including those who worked with President Trump to create and effectuate these plans.

In his speech from the Ellipse on January 6th, President Trump recited a host of election fraud allegations he knew to be false, and then told tens of thousands of his angry supporters this:

> And fraud breaks up everything, doesn't it? When you catch some-body in a fraud, you're allowed to go by very different rules. So I hope Mike has the courage to do what he has to do. And I hope he doesn't listen to the RINOs and the stupid people that he's listening to. [655]

The meaning of President Trump's comments was sufficiently clear then, but he recently gave America an even more detailed understanding of his state of mind. Trump wrote that allegations of "massive fraud" related to the 2020 election "allow[] for the termination of all rules, regulations and articles, even those found in the Constitution." [656] And President Trump considered pardoning those involved in the attack and has since expressed a desire to pardon them—and even give them an apology—if he returns to the Oval Office.[657]

In the Committee's judgment, based on all the evidence developed, President Trump believed then, and continues to believe now, that he is above the law, not bound by our Constitution and its explicit checks on Presidential authority. This recent Trump statement only heightens our concern about accountability. If President Trump and the associates who assisted him in an effort to overturn the lawful outcome of the 2020 election are not ultimately held accountable under the law, their behavior may become a precedent, and invitation to danger, for future elections. A failure to hold them accountable now may ultimately lead to future unlawful efforts to overturn our elections, thereby threatening the security and viability of our Republic.

VIII. REFERRAL OF MEMBERS TO THE HOUSE ETHICS COMMITTEE FOR FAILURE TO COMPLY WITH SUBPOENAS

During the course of the Select Committee's investigation of President Trump's efforts to subvert the election, the Committee learned that various Members of Congress had information relevant to the investigation. Accordingly, the Committee wrote letters to a number of Members involved in that activity inviting them to participate voluntarily in the Select Committee's investigation. None of the members was willing to provide information, which forced the Select Committee to consider alternative means of securing evidence about the conduct of these Members and the information they might have. On May 12, 2022, the Select Committee subpoenaed several members of Congress—including House Minority Leader Kevin McCarthy, Representative Jim Jordan, Representative Scott Perry, and Representative Andy Biggs—to obtain information related to the Committee's investigation.

This was a significant step, but it was one that was warranted by the certain volume of information these Members possessed that was relevant to the Select Committee's investigation, as well as the centrality of their efforts to President Trump's multi-part plan to remain in power.

Representative McCarthy, among other things, had multiple communications with President Trump, Vice President Pence, and others on and related to January 6th. For example, during the attack on the Capitol, Representative McCarthy urgently requested that the former President issue a statement calling off the rioters, to which President Trump responded by "push[ing] back" and said: "Well, Kevin, I guess these people are more upset about the election than you are." [658] And, after the attack, Representative McCarthy spoke on the House floor and said that, "[t]here is absolutely no evidence" that Antifa caused the attack on the Capitol and instead called on President Trump to "accept his share of responsibility" for the violence.[659] As noted above, Representative McCarthy privately confided in colleagues that President Trump accepted some responsibility for the attack on the Capitol.[660]

Representative Jordan was a significant player in President Trump's efforts. He participated in numerous post-election meetings in which senior White House officials, Rudolph Giuliani, and others, discussed strategies for challenging the election, chief among them claims that the election had been tainted by fraud. On January 2, 2021, Representative Jordan led a conference call in which he, President Trump, and other Members of Congress discussed strategies for delaying the January 6th joint session. During that call, the group also discussed issuing social media posts encouraging President Trump's supporters to "march to the Capitol" on the 6th.[661] An hour and a half later, President Trump and Representative

Jordan spoke by phone for 18 minutes.[662] The day before January 6th, Representative Jordan texted Mark Meadows, passing along advice that Vice President Pence should "call out all the electoral votes that he believes are unconstitutional as no electoral votes at all." [663] He spoke with President Trump by phone at least twice on January 6th, though he has provided inconsistent public statements about how many times they spoke and what they discussed.[664] He also received five calls from Rudolph Giuliani that evening, and the two connected at least twice, at 7:33 p.m. and 7:49 p.m.[665] During that time, Giuliani has testified, he was attempting to reach Members of Congress after the joint session resumed to encourage them to continue objecting to Joe Biden's electoral votes.[666] And, in the days following January 6th, Representative Jordan spoke with White House staff about the prospect of Presidential pardons for Members of Congress.[667]

Like Representative Jordan, Representative Perry was also involved in early post-election messaging strategy. Both Representative Jordan and Representative Perry were involved in discussions with White House officials about Vice President Pence's role on January 6th as early as November 2020.[668] Representative Perry was present for conversations in which the White House Counsel's Office informed him and others that President Trump's efforts to submit fake electoral votes were not legally sound.[669] But perhaps most pivotally, he was involved in President Trump's efforts to install Jeffrey Clark as the Acting Attorney General in December 2020 and January 2021. Beginning in early December 2020, Representative Perry suggested Clark as a candidate to Mark Meadows,[670] then introduced Clark to President Trump.[671] In the days before January 6th, Representative Perry advocated for President Trump to speak at the Capitol during the joint session, speaking to Mark Meadows on at least one occasion about it.[672] He was also a participant in the January 2, 2021, call in which Representative Jordan, President Trump, and others discussed issuing social media posts to encourage Trump supporters to march to the Capitol on January 6th.[673] After January 6th, Representative Perry reached out to White House staff asking to receive a Presidential pardon.[674]

Representative Biggs was involved in numerous elements of President Trump's efforts to contest the election results. As early as November 6, 2020, Representative Biggs texted Mark Meadows, urging him to "encourage the state legislatures to appoint [electors]." [675] In the following days, Representative Biggs told Meadows not to let President Trump concede his loss.[676] Between then and January 6th, Representative Biggs coordinated with Arizona State Representative Mark Finchem to gather signatures from Arizona lawmakers endorsing fake Trump electors.[677] He also contacted fake Trump electors in at least one State seeking evidence related to voter fraud.[678]

To date, none of the subpoenaed Members has complied with either voluntary or compulsory requests for participation.

Representative McCarthy initially responded to the Select Committee's subpoena in two letters on May 27 and May 30, 2022, in which he objected to the Select Committee's composition and validity of the subpoena and offered to submit written interrogatories in lieu of deposition testimony. Although the Select Committee did not release Representative McCarthy from his subpoena obligations, Representative McCarthy failed to appear for his scheduled deposition on May 31, 2022. The Select Committee responded to Representative McCarthy's letters this same day, rejecting his proposal to participate via written interrogatories and compelling his appearance for deposition testimony no later than June 11, 2022. Although Representative McCarthy again responded via letter on June 9, 2022, he did not appear for deposition testimony on or before the specified June 11, 2022, deadline.

Representative Jordan also responded to the Select Committee's subpoena just before his scheduled deposition in a letter on May 25, 2022, containing a variety of objections. Representative Jordan also requested material from the Select Committee, including all materials referencing him in the Select Committee's possession and all internal legal analysis related to the constitutionality of Member subpoenas. Although the Select Committee did not release Representative Jordan from his subpoena obligations, Representative Jordan failed to appear for his scheduled deposition on May 27, 2022. On May 31, 2022, the Select Committee responded to the substance of Representative Jordan's May 25th letter and indicated that Representative Jordan should appear for deposition testimony no later than June 11, 2022. On June 9, 2022, Representative Jordan again wrote to reiterate the points from his May 25th letter. That same day, Representative Jordan sent out a fundraising email with the subject line: "I'VE BEEN SUBPOENED." [679] Representative Jordan did not appear before the Select Committee on or before the June 11, 2022, deadline.

Representative Perry likewise responded to the Select Committee's subpoena on May 24, 2022, in a letter, "declin[ing] to appear for deposition" and requesting that the subpoena be "immediately withdrawn." [680] Although the Select Committee did not release Representative Perry from his subpoena obligations, Representative Perry failed to appear on May 26, 2022, for his scheduled deposition. Representative Perry sent a second letter to the Select Committee on May 31, 2022, with additional objections. That same day, the Select Committee responded to Representative Perry's letters and stated that he should appear before the Select Committee no later than June 11, 2022, for deposition testimony. Representative Perry responded via letter on June 10, 2022, maintaining his objections. He did not appear before the June 11, 2022, deadline.

Representative Biggs issued a press release on the day the Select Committee issued its subpoena, calling the subpoena "illegitimate" and "pure political theater." The day before his scheduled deposition, Representative Biggs sent a letter to the Select Committee with a series of objections and an invocation of Speech or Debate immunity. Although the Select Committee did not release Representative Biggs from his subpoena obligations, Representative Biggs did not appear for his scheduled deposition on May 26, 2022. On May 31, 2022, the Select Committee responded to the substance of Representative Biggs' May 25th letter and indicated that Representative Biggs should appear for deposition testimony no later than June 11, 2022. Although Representative Biggs responded with another letter on June 9th, he did not appear before the June 11, 2022, deadline.

Despite the Select Committee's repeated attempts to obtain information from these Members and the issuance of subpoenas, each has refused to cooperate and failed to comply with a lawfully issued subpoena. Accordingly, the Select Committee is referring their failure to comply with the subpoenas issued to them to the Ethics Committee for further action. To be clear, this referral is only for failure to comply with lawfully issued subpoenas.

The Rules of the House of Representatives make clear that their willful noncompliance violates multiple standards of conduct and subjects them to discipline. Willful non-compliance with compulsory congressional committee subpoenas by House Members violates the spirit and letter of House rule XXIII, clause 1, which requires House Members to conduct themselves "at all times in a manner that shall reflect creditably on the House." As a previous version of the House Ethics Manual explained, this catchall provision encompasses "'flagrant' violations of the law that reflect on 'Congress as a whole,' and that might otherwise go unpunished." [681] The subpoenaed House Members' refusal to comply with their subpoena obligations satisfies these criteria. A House Member's willful failure to comply with a congressional subpoena also reflects discredit on Congress. If left unpunished, such behavior undermines Congress's longstanding power to investigate in support of its lawmaking authority and suggests that Members of Congress may disregard legal obligations that apply to ordinary citizens.

For these reasons, the Select Committee refers Leader McCarthy and Representatives Jordan, Perry, and Biggs for sanction by the House Ethics Committee for failure to comply with subpoenas. The Committee also believes that each of these individuals, along with other Members who attended the December 21st planning meeting with President Trump at the

White House,[682] should be questioned in a public forum about their advance knowledge of and role in President Trump's plan to prevent the peaceful transition of power.

EFFORTS TO AVOID TESTIFYING, EVIDENCE OF OBSTRUCTION, AND ASSESSMENTS OF WITNESS CREDIBILITY

More than 30 witnesses before the Select Committee exercised their Fifth Amendment privilege against self-incrimination and refused on that basis to provide testimony. They included individuals central to the investigation, such as John Eastman, Jeffrey Clark, Roger Stone, Michael Flynn, Kenneth Chesebro, and others.[683] The law allows a civil litigant to rely upon an "adverse inference" when a witness invokes the Fifth Amendment. "[T]he Fifth Amendment does not forbid adverse inferences against parties to civil actions . . .."[684] The Committee has not chosen to rely on any such inference in this Report or in its hearings.

We do note that certain witness assertions of the Fifth Amendment were particularly troubling, including this:

Vice Chair Cheney: General Flynn, do you believe the violence on January 6th was justified?

Counsel for the Witness: Can I get clarification, is that a moral question or are you asking a legal question?

Vice Chair Cheney: I'm asking both.

General Flynn: The Fifth.

Vice Chair Cheney: Do you believe the violence on January 6th was justified morally?

General Flynn: Take the Fifth.

Vice Chair Cheney: Do you believe the violence on January 6th was justified legally?

General Flynn: Fifth.

Vice Chair Cheney: General Flynn, do you believe in the peaceful transition of power in the United States of America?

General Flynn: The Fifth.[685]

President Trump refused to comply with the Committee's subpoena, and also filed suit to block the National Archives from supplying the Committee with White House records. The Committee litigated the National Archives case in Federal District Court, in the Federal Appellate Court for the District of Columbia, and before the Supreme Court. The Select Committee was successful in this litigation. The opinion of the D.C. Circuit explained:

> On January 6, 2021, a mob professing support for then-President Trump violently attacked the United States Capitol in an effort to prevent a Joint Session of Congress from certifying the electoral college votes designating Joseph R. Biden the 46th President of the United States. The rampage left multiple people dead, injured more than 140 people, and inflicted millions of dollars in damage to the Capitol. Then-Vice President Pence, Senators, and Representatives were all forced to halt their constitutional duties and flee the House and Senate chambers for safety.[686]

> Benjamin Franklin said, at the founding, that we have "[a] Republic"—"if [we] can keep it." The events of January 6th exposed the fragility of those democratic institutions and traditions that we had perhaps come to take for granted. In response, the President of the United States and Congress have each made the judgment that access to this subset of presidential communication records is necessary to address a matter of great constitutional moment for the Republic. Former President Trump has given this court no legal reason to cast aside President Biden's assessment of the Executive Branch interests at stake, or to create a separation of powers conflict that the Political Branches have avoided.[687]

Several other witnesses have also avoided testifying in whole or in part by asserting Executive Privilege or Absolute Immunity from any obligation to appear before Congress. For example, the President's Chief of Staff Mark Meadows invoked both, and categorically refused to testify, even about text messages he provided to the Committee. The House of Representatives voted to hold him in criminal contempt.[688] Although the Justice Department has taken the position in litigation that a former high level White House staffer for a former President is not entitled to absolute immunity,[689] and that any interests in the confidentiality of his communications with President Trump and others are overcome in this case, the Justice Department declined to prosecute Meadows for criminal contempt. The reasons for Justice's refusal to do so are not apparent to the Committee.[690] Commentators have speculated that Meadows may be cooperating in the Justice Department's January 6th investigation.[691] The same may be true for Daniel Scavino, President Trump's White House Deputy Chief of Staff for Communications and Director of Social Media, whom the House also voted to hold in contempt.[692]

Steve Bannon also chose not to cooperate with the Committee, and the Justice Department prosecuted him for contempt of Congress.[693] Bannon has been sentenced and is currently appealing his conviction. Peter Navarro, another White House Staffer who refused to testify, is currently awaiting his criminal trial.[694]

Although the Committee issued letters and subpoenas to seven Republican members of Congress who have unique knowledge of certain developments on or in relation to January 6th, none agreed to participate in the investigation; none considered themselves obligated to comply with the subpoenas. A number of these same individuals were aware well in advance of January 6th of the plotting by Donald Trump, John Eastman, and others to overturn the election, and certain of them had an active role in that activity.[695] None seem to have alerted law enforcement of this activity, or of the known risk of violence. On January 5th, after promoting unfounded objections to election results, Rep. Debbie Lesko appears to have recognized the danger in a call with her colleagues:

> I also ask leadership to come up with a safety plan for Members [of Congress]. . . . We also have, quite honestly, Trump supporters who actually believe that we are going to overturn the election, and when that doesn't happen—most likely will not happen—they are going to go nuts.[696]

During our hearings, the Committee presented the testimony of numerous White House witnesses who testified about efforts by certain Republican Members of Congress to obtain Presidential pardons for their conduct in connection with January 6th.[697] Cassidy Hutchinson provided extensive detail in this regard:

> Vice Chair Cheney: And are you aware of any members of Congress seeking pardons?
>
> Hutchinson: I guess Mr. Gaetz and Mr. Brooks, I know, have both advocated for there'd be a blanket pardon for members involved in that meeting, and a — a handful of other members that weren't at the December 21st meeting as the presumptive pardons. Mr. Gaetz was personally pushing for a pardon, and he was doing so since early December.
>
> I'm not sure why Mr. Gaetz would reach out to me to ask if he could have a meeting with Mr. Meadows about receiving a presidential pardon.
>
> Vice Chair Cheney: Did they all contact you?
>
> Hutchinson: Not all of them, but several of them did.

Vice Chair Cheney: So, you mentioned Mr. Gaetz, Mr. Brooks.

Hutchinson: Mr. Biggs did. Mr. Jordan talked about Congressional pardons, but he never asked me for one. It was more for an update on whether the White House was going to pardon members of Congress. Mr. Gohmert asked for one as well. Mr. Perry asked for a pardon, too. I'm sorry.

Vice Chair Cheney: Mr. Perry? Did he talk to you directly?

Hutchinson: Yes, he did.

Vice Chair Cheney: Did Marjorie Taylor Greene contact you?

Hutchinson: No, she didn't contact me about it. I heard that she had asked White House Counsel's Office for a pardon from Mr. Philbin, but I didn't frequently communicate with Ms. Greene.[698]

Many of these details were also corroborated by other sources. President Personnel Director Johnny McEntee confirmed that he was personally asked for a pardon by Representative Matt Gaetz (R-FL).[699] Eric Herschmann recalled that Representative Gaetz ". . . asked for a very, very broad pardon. . . . And I said Nixon's pardon was never nearly that broad." [700] When asked about reporting that Representatives Mo Brooks and Andy Biggs also requested pardons, Herschmann did not reject either possibility out of hand, instead answering: "It's possible that Representative Brooks or Biggs, but I don't remember." [701] The National Archives produced to the Select Committee an email from Representative Mo Brooks to the President's executive assistant stating that "President Trump asked me to send you this letter" and "... pursuant to a request from Matt Gaetz" that recommended blanket Presidential pardons to every Member of Congress who objected to the electoral college votes on January 6th.[702]

These requests for pardons suggest that the Members identified above were conscious of the potential legal jeopardy arising from their conduct. As noted *infra* 136, the Committee has referred a number of these individuals to the House Ethics Committee for their failure to comply with subpoenas, and believes that they each owe the American people their direct and unvarnished testimony.

The Select Committee has also received a range of evidence suggesting specific efforts to obstruct the Committee's investigation. Much of this evidence is already known by the Department of Justice and by other prosecutorial authorities. For example:

1. The Committee received testimony from a witness about her decision to terminate a lawyer who was receiving payments for the representation from a group allied with President Trump. Among other concerns expressed by the witness:

- The lawyer had advised the witness that the witness could, in certain circumstances, tell the Committee that she did not recall facts when she actually did recall them.
- During a break in the Select Committee's interview, the witness expressed concerns to her lawyer that an aspect of her testimony was not truthful. The lawyer did not advise her to clarify the specific testimony that the witness believed was not complete and accurate, and instead conveyed that, "They don't know what you know, [witness]. They don't know that you can recall some of these things. So you saying 'I don't recall' is an entirely acceptable response to this."
- The lawyer instructed the client about a particular issue that would cast a bad light on President Trump: "No, no, no, no, no. We don't want to go there. We don't want to talk about that."
- The lawyer refused directions from the client not to share her testimony before the Committee with other lawyers representing other witnesses. The lawyer shared such information over the client's objection.
- The lawyer refused directions from the client not to share information regarding her testimony with at least one and possibly more than one member of the press. The lawyer shared the information with the press over her objection.
- The lawyer did not disclose who was paying for the lawyers' representation of the client, despite questions from the client seeking that information, and told her, "we're not telling people where funding is coming from right now."
- The client was offered potential employment that would make her "financially very comfortable" as the date of her testimony approached by entities apparently linked to Donald Trump and his associates. Such offers were withdrawn or did not materialize as reports of the content of her testimony circulated. The client believed this was an effort to impact her testimony.

Further details regarding these instances will be available to the public when transcripts are released.

2. Similarly, the witness testified that multiple persons affiliated with President Trump contacted her in advance of the witness's testimony and made the following statements:

What they said to me is, as long as I continue to be a team player, they know that I am on the right team. I am doing the right thing. I am protecting who I need to protect. You know, I will continue to stay in good graces in Trump World. And they have reminded me a couple of times that Trump does read transcripts and just keep that in mind as I proceed through my interviews with the committee.

Here is another sample in a different context. This is a call received by one of our witnesses:

[A person] let me know you have your deposition tomorrow. He wants me to let you know he's thinking about you. He knows you're a team player, you're loyal, and you're going do the right thing when you go in for your deposition.[703]

3. The Select Committee is aware of multiple efforts by President Trump to contact Select Committee witnesses. The Department of Justice is aware of at least one of those circumstances.

4. Rather than relying on representation by Secret Service lawyers at no cost, a small number of Secret Service agents engaged private counsel for their interviews before the Committee.[704] During one such witness's transcribed interview, a retained private counsel was observed writing notes to the witness regarding the content of the witness's testimony while the questioning was underway. The witness's counsel admitted on the record that he had done so.[705]

Recently, published accounts of the Justice Department's Mar-a-Lago investigation suggest that the Department is investigating the conduct of counsel for certain witnesses whose fees are being paid by President Trump's Save America Political Action Committee.[706] The public report implies the Department is concerned that such individuals are seeking to influence the testimony of the witnesses they represent.[707] This Committee also has these concerns, including that lawyers who are receiving such payments have specific incentives to defend President Trump rather than zealously represent their own clients. The Department of Justice and the Fulton County District Attorney have been provided with certain information related to this topic.

The Select Committee recognizes of course that most of the testimony we have gathered was given more than a year after January 6th. Recollections are not perfect, and the Committee expects that different accounts of the same events will naturally vary. Indeed, the lack of any inconsistencies in witness accounts would itself be suspicious. And many witnesses may simply recall different things than others.

Many of the witnesses before this Committee had nothing at all to gain from their testimony, gave straightforward responses to the questions posted, and made no effort to downplay, deflect, or rationalize. Trump Administration Justice Department officials such as Attorney General Barr,

Acting Attorney General Rosen, and Acting Deputy Attorney General Dono-ghue are good examples. Multiple members of President Trump's White House staff were also suitably forthcoming, including Sarah Matthews, Matthew Pottinger, Greg Jacob, and Pat Philbin, as were multiple career White House, military and agency personnel whose names the Committee agreed not to disclose publicly; as were former Secretary of Labor Eugene Scalia, Bill Stepien, and certain other members of the Trump Campaign. The Committee very much appreciates the earnestness and bravery of Cassidy Hutchinson, Rusty Bowers, Shaye Moss, Ruby Freeman, Brad Raffensperger, Gabriel Sterling, Al Schmidt, and many others who provided important live testimony during the Committees hearings.[708]

The Committee, along with our nation, offers particular thanks to Offi-cers Caroline Edwards, Michael Fanone, Harry Dunn, Aquilino Gonell, and Daniel Hodges, along with hundreds of other members of law enforcement who defended the Capitol on that fateful day, all of whom should be com-mended for their bravery and sacrifice. We especially thank the families of Officer Brian Sicknick, Howard Liebengood and Jeffrey Smith, whose loss can never be repaid.

The Committee very much appreciates the invaluable testimony of Gen-eral Milley and other members of our military, Judge J. Michael Luttig, and the important contributions of Benjamin Ginsberg and Chris Stirewalt. This, of course is only a partial list, and the Committee is indebted to many others, as well.

The Committee believes that White House Counsel Pat Cipollone gave a particularly important account of the events of January 6th, as did White House lawyer, Eric Herschmann. For multiple months, Cipollone resisted giving any testimony at all, asserting concerns about executive privilege and other issues, until after the Committee's hearing with Hutchinson. When he did testify, Cipollone corroborated key elements of testimony given by several White House staff, including Hutchinson—most impor-tantly, regarding what happened in the White House during the violence of January 6th—but also frankly recognized the limits on what he could say due to privilege: "Again, I'm not going to get into either my legal advice on matters, and the other thing I don't want to do is, again, other witnesses have their own recollections of things." Cipollone also told the Committee that, to the extent that other witnesses recall communications attributable to White House counsel that he does not, the communications might have been with his deputy Pat Philbin, or with Eric Herschmann, who had strong feelings and was particularly animated about certain issues.[709]

Of course, that is not to say that all witnesses were entirely frank or forthcoming. Other witnesses, including certain witnesses from the Trump White House, displayed a lack of full recollection of certain issues, or were not otherwise as frank or direct as Cipollone. We cite two examples here, both relating to testimony played during the hearings.

Kayleigh McEnany was President Trump's Press Secretary on January 6th. Her deposition was taken early in the investigation. McEnany seemed to acknowledge that President Trump: (1) should have instructed his violent supporters to leave the Capitol earlier than he ultimately did on January 6th;[710] (2) should have respected the rulings of the courts;[711] and (3) was wrong to publicly allege that Dominion voting machines stole the election.[712] But a segment of McEnany's testimony seemed evasive, as if she was testifying from pre-prepared talking points. In multiple instances, McEnany's testimony did not seem nearly as forthright as that of her press office staff, who testified about what McEnany said.

For example, McEnany disputed suggestions that President Trump was resistant to condemning the violence and urging the crowd at the Capitol to act peacefully when they crafted his tweet at 2:38 p.m. on January 6th.[713] Yet one of her deputies, Sarah Matthews, told the Select Committee that McEnany informed her otherwise: that McEnany and other advisors in the dining room with President Trump persuaded him to send the tweet, but that "... she said that he did not want to put that in and that they went through different phrasing of that, of the mention of peace, in order to get him to agree to include it, and that it was Ivanka Trump who came up with 'stay peaceful' and that he agreed to that phrasing to include in the tweet, but he was initially resistant to mentioning peace of any sort." [714] When the Select Committee asked "Did Ms. McEnany describe in any way how resistant the President was to including something about being peaceful," Matthews answered: "Just that he didn't want to include it, but they got him to agree on the phrasing 'stay peaceful.'" [715]

The Committee invites the public to compare McEnany's testimony with the testimony of Pat Cipollone, Sarah Matthews, Judd Deere, and others.

Ivanka Trump is another example. Among other things, Ivanka Trump acknowledged to the Committee that: (1) she agreed with Attorney General Barr's statements that there was no evidence of sufficient fraud to overturn the election; (2) the President and others are bound by the rulings of the courts and the rule of law; (3) President Trump pressured Vice President Pence on the morning of January 6th regarding his authorities at the joint session of Congress that day to count electoral votes; and (4) President Trump watched the violence on television as it was occurring.[716] But again, Ivanka Trump was not as forthcoming as Cipollone and others about President Trump's conduct.

Indeed, Ivanka Trump's Chief of Staff Julie Radford had a more specific recollection of Ivanka Trump's actions and statements. For example, Ivanka

Trump had the following exchange with the Committee about her attendance at her father's speech on January 6th that was at odds with what the
Committee learned from Radford:

> Committee Staff: It's been reported that you ultimately decided to
> attend the rally because you hoped that you would calm the Presi-
> dent and keep the event on an even keel. Is that accurate?
>
> Ivanka Trump: No. I don't know who said that or where that came
> from.[717]

However, this is what Radford said about her boss's decision:

> Committee Staff: What did she share with you about why it was
> concerning that her father was upset or agitated after that call with
> Vice President Pence in relation to the Ellipse rally? Why did that
> matter? Why did he have to be calmed down, I should say.
>
> Radford: Well, she shared that he had called the Vice President a
> not—an expletive word. I think that bothered her. And I think she
> could tell based on the conversations and what was going on in the
> office that he was angry and upset and people were providing mis-
> information. And she felt like she might be able to help calm the
> situation down, at least before he went on stage.
>
> Committee Staff: And the word that she relayed to you that the
> President called the Vice President—apologize for being impolite—
> but do you remember what she said her father called him?
>
> Radford: The "P" word.[718]

When the Committee asked Ivanka Trump whether there were "[a]ny
particular words that you recall your father using during the conversation"
that morning with Vice President Pence, she answered simply: "No." [719]

In several circumstances, the Committee has found that less senior
White House aides had significantly better recollection of events than
senior staff purported to have.

The Select Committee also has concerns regarding certain other witnesses, including those who still rely for their income or employment on
organizations linked to President Trump, such as the America First Policy
Institute. Certain witnesses and lawyers were unnecessarily combative,
answered hundreds of questions with variants of "I do not recall" in circumstances where that answer seemed unbelievable, appeared to testify
from lawyer-written talking points rather than their own recollections,
provided highly questionable rationalizations or otherwise resisted telling
the truth. The public can ultimately make its own assessment of these

issues when it reviews the Committee transcripts and can compare the accounts of different witnesses and the conduct of counsel.

One particular concern arose from what the Committee realized early on were a number of intentional falsehoods in former White House Chief of Staff Mark Meadows's December 7, 2021 book, *The Chief's Chief.* [720] Here is one of several examples: Meadows wrote, "When he got offstage, President Trump let me know that he had been speaking metaphorically about going to the Capitol." [721] Meadows goes on in his book to claim that it "was clear the whole time" President Trump didn't intend to go to the Capitol.[722] This appeared to be an intentional effort to conceal the facts. Multiple witnesses directly contradicted Meadows's account about President Trump's desire to travel to the Capitol, including Kayleigh McEnany, Cassidy Hutchinson, multiple Secret Service agents, a White House employee with national security responsibilities and other staff in the White House, a member of the Metropolitan Police and others. This and several other statements in the Meadows book were false, and the Select Committee was concerned that multiple witnesses might attempt to repeat elements of these false accounts, as if they were the party line. Most witnesses did not, but a few did.

President Trump's desire to travel to the Capitol was particularly important for the Committee to evaluate because it bears on President Trump's intent on January 6th. One witness account suggests that President Trump even wished to participate in the electoral vote count from the House floor, standing with Republican Congressmen, perhaps in an effort to apply further pressure to Vice President Mike Pence and others.[723]

Mark Meadows's former Deputy Chief of Staff for Operations Anthony Ornato gave testimony consistent with the false account in Meadows book. In particular, Ornato told the Committee that he was not aware of a genuine push by the President to go to the Capitol, suggesting instead that "it was one of those hypotheticals from the good idea fairy . . . [b]ecause it's ridiculous to think that a President of the United States can travel especially with, you know, people around just on the street up to the Capitol and peacefully protest outside the Capitol...." [724] He told the Select Committee that the only conversation he had about the possibility of the President traveling to the Capitol was in a single meeting officials from the President's advance team,[725] and his understanding is that this idea "wasn't from the President." [726] Two witnesses before the Committee, including a White House employee with national security responsibilities and Hutchinson, testified that Ornato related an account of President Trump's "irate" behavior when he was told in the Presidential SUV on January 6th that he would not be driven to the Capitol.[727] Both accounts recall Ornato doing so from his office in the White House, with another member of the Secret Service present.[728] Multiple other witness accounts indicate that the President genuinely was "irate," "heated," "angry," and "insistent" in the Presidential vehicle.[729] But Ornato professed that he did not recall either communication, and that he had no knowledge at all about the President's anger.[730]

Likewise, despite a significant and increasing volume of intelligence information in the days before January 6th showing that violence at the Capitol was indeed possible or likely, and despite other intelligence and law enforcement agencies similar conclusions,[731] Ornato claimed never to have reviewed or had any knowledge of that specific information[732] He testified that he was only aware of warnings that opposing groups might "clash on the Washington Monument" and that is what he "would have briefed to [Chief of Staff] Meadows."[733] The Committee has significant concerns about the credibility of this testimony, including because it was Ornato's responsibility to be aware of this information and convey it to decision-makers.[734] The Committee will release Ornato's November Transcript so the public can review his testimony on these topics.

SUMMARY: CREATION OF THE SELECT COMMITTEE; PURPOSES.

In the week after January 6th, House Republican Leader Kevin McCarthy initially supported legislation to create a bipartisan commission to investigate the January 6th attack on the United States Capitol, stating that "the President bears responsibility for Wednesday's attack on Congress by mob rioters" and calling for creation of a "fact-finding commission."[735] Leader McCarthy repeated his support for a bipartisan commission during a press conference on January 21st: "The only way you will be able to answer these questions is through a bipartisan commission."[736]

On February 15th, House Speaker Nancy Pelosi announced in a letter to the House Democratic Caucus her intent to establish the type of independent commission McCarthy had supported, to "investigate and report on the facts and causes relating to the January 6, 2021 domestic terrorist attack upon the United States Capitol Complex."[737] A few days thereafter, Leader McCarthy provided the Speaker a wish list that mirrored "suggestions from the Co-Chairs of the 9/11 Commission" that he and House Republicans hoped would be included in the House's legislation to establish the Commission.[738]

In particular, Leader McCarthy requested an equal ratio of Democratic and Republican nominations, equal subpoena power for the Democratic Chair and Republican Vice Chair of the Commission, and the exclusion of predetermined findings or outcomes that the Commission itself would produce. Closing his letter, Leader McCarthy quoted the 9/11 Commission

Co-Chairs, writing that a "bipartisan independent investigation will earn credibility with the American public." [739] He again repeated his confidence in achieving that goal.[740] In April 2021, Speaker Pelosi agreed to make the number of Republican and Democratic Members of the Commission equal, and to provide both parties with an equal say in subpoenas, as McCarthy had requested.[741]

In May 2021, House Homeland Security Committee Chairman Bennie G. Thompson began to negotiate more of the details for the Commission with his Republican counterpart, Ranking Member John Katko.[742] On May 14th, Chairman Thompson announced that he and Ranking Member Katko had reached an agreement on legislation to "form a bipartisan, independent Commission to investigate the January 6th domestic terrorism attack on the United States Capitol and recommend changes to further protect the Capitol, the citadel of our democracy." [743]

On May 18th, the day before the House's consideration of the Thompson-Katko agreement, Leader McCarthy released a statement in opposition to the legislation.[744] Speaker Pelosi responded to that statement, saying: "Leader McCarthy won't take yes for an answer." [745] The Speaker referred to Leader McCarthy's February 22nd letter where "he made three requests to be addressed in Democrats' discussion draft." [746] She noted that "every single one was granted by Democrats, yet he still says no." [747]

In the days that followed, Republican Ranking Member Katko defended the bipartisan nature of the bill to create the Commission:

> As I have called for since the days just after the attack, an independent, 9/11-style review is critical for removing the politics around January 6 and focusing solely on the facts and circumstances of the security breach at the Capitol, as well as other instances of violence relevant to such a review. Make no mistake about it, Mr. Thompson and I know this is about facts. It's not partisan politics. We would have never gotten to this point if it was about partisan politics.[748]

That evening, the House passed the legislation to establish a National Commission to Investigate the January 6th Attack on the United States Capitol Complex in a bipartisan fashion, with 35 Republicans joining 217 Democrats voting in favor and 175 Republicans voting against.[749] In the days thereafter, however, only six Senate Republicans joined Senate Democrats in supporting the legislation, killing the bill in the Senate.[750]

On June 24th, Speaker Pelosi announced her intent to create a House select committee to investigate the attack.[751] On June 25th, Leader McCarthy met with DC Metropolitan Police Officer Michael Fanone, who was seriously injured on January 6th.[752] Officer Fanone pressed Leader McCarthy "for a commitment not to put obstructionists and the wrong people in that position."[753]

On June 30th, the House voted on H. Res. 503 to establish a 13-Member Select Committee to Investigate the January 6th Attack on the United States Capitol by a vote of 222 Yeas and 190 Nays with just two Republicans supporting the measure: Representative Liz Cheney and Representative Adam Kinzinger.[754] On July 1st, Speaker Pelosi named eight initial Members to the Select Committee, including one Republican: Representative Cheney.[755]

On July 17th, Leader McCarthy proposed his selection of five members:

Representative Jim Jordan, Ranking Member of the House Judiciary Committee;

Representative Kelly Armstrong of North Dakota; House Energy and Commerce Committee;

Representative Troy Nehls, House Transportation & Infrastructure and Veterans' Affairs Committees.

Representative Jim Banks, Armed Services, Veterans' Affairs and Education and Labor Committees;

Representative Rodney Davis, Ranking Member of the Committee on House Administration.[756]

Jordan was personally involved in the acts and circumstances of January 6th, and would be one of the targets of the investigation. By that point, Banks had made public statements indicating that he had already reached his own conclusions and had no intention of cooperating in any objective investigation of January 6th, proclaiming, for example, that the Select Committee was created ". . . solely to malign conservatives and to justify the Left's authoritarian agenda."[757]

On July 21st, Speaker Nancy Pelosi exercised her power under H. Res. 503 not to approve the appointments of Representatives Jordan or Banks, expressing "concern about statements made and actions taken by these Members" and "the impact their appointments may have on the integrity of the investigation."[758] However, she also stated that she had informed Leader McCarthy ". . . that I was prepared to appoint Representatives Rodney Davis, Kelly Armstrong and Troy Nehls, and requested that he recommend two other Members."[759]

In response, Leader McCarthy elected to remove all five of his Republican appointments, refusing to allow Representatives Armstrong, Davis and Nehls to participate on the Select Committee.[760] On July 26, 2021, Speaker Pelosi then appointed Republican Representative Adam Kinzinger.[761] In resisting the Committee's subpoenas, certain litigants attempted to argue that the Commission's Select Committee's composition violated House Rules or H. Res. 503, but those arguments failed in court.[762]

SELECT COMMITTEE WITNESSES WERE ALMOST ENTIRELY REPUBLICAN

In its ten hearings or business meetings, the Select Committee called live testimony or played video for several dozen witnesses, the vast majority of whom were Republicans. A full list is set forth below.

Republicans:

- **John McEntee** (served as Director of the White House Presidential Personnel Office in Trump Administration)
- **Judd Deere** (served as Deputy Assistant to the President and White House Deputy Press Secretary in the Trump Administration)
- **Jared Kushner** (served as a Senior Advisor to President Donald Trump)
- **Pat Cipollone** (served as White House Counsel for President Donald Trump)
- **Eric Herschmann** (served as a Senior Advisor to President Donald Trump)
- **Kayleigh McEnany** (served as White House Press Secretary in Trump Administration)
- **Derek Lyons** (served as White House Staff Secretary and Counselor to the President in the Trump Administration)
- **Cassidy Hutchinson** (served as Assistant to Chief of Staff Mark Meadows in the Trump Administration)
- **Matt Pottinger** (served as Deputy National Security Advisor in the Trump Administration)
- **Ben Williamson** (served as Senior Advisor to Chief of Staff Mark Meadows)
- **Sarah Matthews** (served as Deputy Press Secretary in the Trump Administration)
- **William Barr** (served as Attorney General in the Trump Administration)
- **Mike Pompeo** (served as Director of the Central Intelligence Agency and Secretary of State in the Trump Administration)
- **Ivanka Trump** (served as a Senior Advisor and Director of the Office of Economic Initiatives and Entrepreneurship in the Trump Administration)
- **Donald Trump Jr.** (eldest child of Donald Trump)
- **Molly Michael** (served as Deputy Assistant to the President and Executive Assistant to the President)
- **Tim Murtaugh** (served as Director of Communications for the Trump 2020 Presidential campaign)

- **Richard Donoghue** (served as Acting Deputy Attorney General in the Trump Administration)
- **Jeffrey Rosen** (served as Acting Attorney General in the Trump Administration)
- **Steven Engel** (served as Assistant Attorney General for the Office of Legal Counsel in the Trump Administration)
- **Marc Short** (served as Chief of Staff to Vice President Mike Pence)
- **Greg Jacob** (served as Counsel to Vice President Mike Pence)
- **Keith Kellogg** (served as National Security Advisor to Vice President Mike Pence)
- **Chris Hodgson** (served as Director of Legislative Affairs for Vice President Mike Pence)
- **Douglas Macgregor** (served as advisor to the Secretary of Defense in the Trump Administration)
- **Jason Miller** (served as spokesman for the Donald Trump 2016 Presidential Campaign and was a Senior Adviser to the Trump 2020 Presidential Campaign)
- **Alex Cannon** (Counsel for the Trump 2020 Presidential Campaign)
- **Bill Stepien** (served as the Campaign Manager for the Trump 2020 Presidential Campaign and was the White House Director of Political Affairs in the Trump Administration from 2017 to 2018)
- **Rudolph Giuliani** (an attorney for Donald Trump)
- **John Eastman** (an attorney for Donald Trump)
- **Michael Flynn** (served as National Security Advisor in the Trump Administration)
- **Eugene Scalia** (served as the Secretary of Labor in the Trump Administration)
- **Matthew Morgan** (General Counsel for the Trump 2020 Presidential Campaign)
- **Sidney Powell** (an attorney and advisor to Donald Trump)
- **Jeffrey Clark** (served as Acting Assistant Attorney General for the Civil Division in the Trump Administration)
- **Cleta Mitchell** (an attorney working with the Trump 2020 Presidential Campaign)
- **Ronna Romney McDaniel** (Chair of the Republican National Committee)
- **Justin Clark** (served as Deputy Campaign Manager for the Trump 2020 Presidential Campaign)
- **Robert Sinners** (Georgia State Director of Election Day Operations for the Trump 2020 Presidential Campaign)
- **Andrew Hitt** (Wisconsin Republican Party Chair)
- **Laura Cox** (Michigan Republican Party Chair)

- **Mike Shirkey** (Majority Leader, Michigan State Senate)
- **Bryan Cutler** (Speaker, Pennsylvania House of Representatives)
- **Rusty Bowers** (Speaker, Arizona House of Representatives)
- **Brad Raffensperger** (Georgia Secretary of State)
- **Gabriel Sterling** (Georgia Secretary of State, Chief Operating Officer)
- **BJay Pak** (served as United States Attorney for the Northern District of Georgia in the Trump Administration)
- **Al Schmidt** (City Commissioner of Philadelphia)
- **Chris Stirewalt** (Fox News Political Editor)
- **Benjamin Ginsberg** (Election Attorney)
- **J. Michael Luttig** (Retired judge for the U.S. Court of Appeals for the Fourth Circuit and informal advisor to Vice President Mike Pence)
- **Katrina Pierson** (served as a liaison for the White House and organizers at Donald Trump's "Save America" rally on January 6)
- **Nicholas Luna** (served as Personal Aide to President Trump)
- **Stephen Miller** (served as Senior Advisor to President Trump)
- **Vincent Haley** (served as Deputy Assistant to the President and Advisor for Policy, Strategy and Speechwriting in the Trump Administration)
- **Julie Radford** (Chief of Staff to Ivanka Trump in the Trump Administration)
- **Mick Mulvaney** (former Acting Chief of Staff and Special Envoy for Northern Ireland in the Trump Administration)
- **Elaine Chao** (Secretary of Transportation in the Trump Administration)
- **Roger Stone** (Trump associate)

Democrats:

- **Jocelyn Benson** (Michigan Secretary of State)

Other:

- **U.S. Capitol Police Officer Harry Dunn**
- **DC Metropolitan Police Officer Michael Fanone**
- **U.S. Capitol Police Sgt. Aquilino Gonell**
- **DC Metropolitan Police Officer Daniel Hodges**
- **General Mark Milley** (Chairman of the Joint Chiefs of Staff)
- **U.S. Capitol Police Officer Caroline Edwards**
- **Nick Quested** (award-winning British filmmaker)
- **Robert Schornack** (sentenced to 36 months' probation)
- **Eric Barber** (charged with theft and unlawful demonstration in the Capitol)
- **John Wright** (awaiting trial for felony civil disorder and other charges)
- **George Meza** (Proud Boy)

- **Daniel Herendeen** (sentenced to 36 months' probation for role in Capitol attack)
- **Matthew Walter** (Proud Boy)
- **Wandrea ArShaye "Shaye" Moss** (Georgia election worker)
- **Ruby Freeman** (Georgia election worker)
- **Anika Collier Navaroli** (former Twitter employee)
- **White House Security Official**
- **Jim Watkins** (Founder and owner, 8kun)
- **Jody Williams** (former owner of TheDonald.win)
- **Dr. Donell Harvin** (Chief of Homeland Security and Intelligence for the government of the District of Columbia)
- **Kellye SoRelle** (attorney for Oath Keepers)
- **Shealah Craighead** (White House Photographer)
- **Jason Van Tatenhove** (former Oath Keepers spokesperson)
- **Stephen Ayres** (plead guilty to disorderly and disruptive conduct related to Capitol attack)
- **Sgt. Mark Robinson** (Ret.) (Metropolitan Police Department)
- **Janet Buhler** (plead guilty to charges related to the Capitol attack)

ENDNOTES

1. A few weeks later, Rhodes and his associate Kelly Meggs were found guilty of seditious conspiracy, and other Oath Keepers were found guilty on numerous charges for obstructing the electoral count. Trial Transcript at 10502-508, *United States v. Rhodes et al.*, No. 1:22-cr-15 (D.D.C. Nov. 29, 2022); Alan Feuer and Zach Montague, "Oath Keepers Leader Convicted of Sedition in Landmark Jan. 6 Case," *New York Times*, (Nov. 29, 2022), available at https://www.nytimes.com/2022/11/29/us/politics/oath-keepers-trial-verdict-jan-6.html.

2. Trial Transcript at 5698, 5759, *United States v. Rhodes et al.*, No. 1:22-cr-15 (D.D.C. Oct. 31, 2022).

3. Trial Transcript at 5775, *United States v. Rhodes et al.*, No. 1:22-cr-15 (D.D.C. Oct. 31, 2022) ("for me at the time, it meant I felt it was like a Bastille type moment in history where in the French Revolution it was that big turning point moment where the population made their presence felt. I thought it was going to be a similar type of event for us").

4. Trial Transcript at 5783, 5866, *United States v. Rhodes et al.*, No. 1:22-cr-15 (D.D.C. Oct. 31, 2022).

5. Sentencing Transcript at 15-17, *United States v. Reimler*, No. 1:21-cr-239 (D.D.C. Jan. 11, 2022), ECF No. 37.

6. Sentencing Transcript at 33, *United States v. Pert*, No. 1:21-cr-139 (D.D.C. Feb. 11, 2022), ECF No. 64.

7. Sentencing Memorandum by Abram Markofski, Exhibit B, *United States v. Markofski*, No. 1:21-cr-344 (D.D.C. Dec. 2, 2021), ECF No. 44-2.

8. Sentencing Transcript at 49, *United States v. Witcher*, No. 1:21-cr-235 (D.D.C. Feb. 24, 2022), ECF No. 53.

9. Sentencing Transcript at 19–20, *United States v. Edwards*, No. 1:21-cr-366 (D.D.C. Jan. 21, 2022), ECF No. 33. *See also*, Sentencing Memorandum by Brandon Nelson, Exhibit B, *United States v. Nelson*, No. 1:21-cr-344 (D.D.C. Dec. 6, 2021), ECF No. 51-2; Sentencing Transcript at 65–66, *United States v. Griffith*, No. 1:21-cr-204 (D.D.C. Oct. 30, 2021), ECF No. 137; Sentencing

Transcript at 45, *United States v. Schornak*, 1:21-cr-278 (D.D.C. May 11, 2022), ECF No. 90; Sentencing Transcript at 35, *United States v. Wilkerson*, No. 1:21-cr-302 (D.D.C. Nov. 22, 2021), ECF No. 31; Select Committee to Investigate the January 6th Attack on the United States Capitol, Transcribed Interview of Eric Barber, (Mar. 16, 2022), pp. 50–51.

10. Statement of Facts at 5, *United States v. Sandlin*, No. 1:21-cr-88 (D.D.C. Jan. 20, 2021), ECF No. 1-1; Ryan J. Reily (@ryanjreily), Twitter Oct. 1, 2022 3:33 p.m. ET, available at https://twitter.com/ryanjreilly/status/1576295667412017157; Ryan J. Reily (@ryanjreily), Twitter, Oct. 1, 2022 3:40 p.m. ET, available at https://twitter.com/ryanjreilly/status/1576296016512692225; Government's Sentencing Memorandum at 2, 16, *United States v. Sandlin*, No. 1:21-cr-88 (D.D.C. Dec. 2, 2022), ECF No. 92.

11. Government's Opposition to Defendant's Motion to Revoke Magistrate Judge's Detention Order at 4, *United States v. Miller*, No. 1:21-cr-119 (D.D.C. Mar. 29, 2021), ECF No 16; Dan Mangan, "Capitol Rioter Garret Miller Says He Was Following Trump's Orders, Apologizes to AOC for Threat," CNBC, (Jan. 25, 2021), available at https://www.cnbc.com/2021/01/25/capitol-riots-garret-miller-says-he-was-following-trumps-orders-apologizes-to-aoc.html.

12. Select Committee to Investigate the January 6th Attack on the United States Capitol, Transcribed Interview of John Douglas Wright, (Mar. 31, 2022), pp. 22, 63.

13. Select Committee to Investigate the January 6th Attack on the United States Capitol, Transcribed Interview of Lewis Cantwell, (Apr. 26, 2022), p. 54.

14. Select Committee to Investigate the January 6th Attack on the United States Capitol, Transcribed Interview of Stephen Ayres, (June 22, 2022), p. 8.

15. Select Committee to Investigate the January 6th Attack on the United States Capitol, *Hearing on the January 6th Investigation*, 117th Cong., 2d sess., (July 12, 2022), available at https://www.govinfo.gov/committee/house-january6th.

16. Affidavit at 8, *United States v. Ayres*, No. 1:21-cr-156 (D.D.C. Jan. 22, 2021), ECF No. 5-1.

17. *See infra*, Chapter 6. See also Documents on file with the Select Committee to Investigate the January 6th Attack on the United States Capitol (Select Committee Chart Compiling Defendant Statements). The Select Committee Chart Compiling Defendant Statements identifies hundreds of examples of such testimony. Select Committee staff tracked cases filed by the Department of Justice against defendants who committed crimes related to the attack on the United States Capitol. Through Department of Justice criminal filings, through public reporting, through social media research, and through court hearings, staff collected a range of statements by these defendants about why they came to Washington, DC, on January 6th. Almost always, it was because President Trump had called upon them to support his big lie. Those defendants also discussed plans for violence at the Capitol, against law enforcement, against other American citizens, and against elected officials in the days leading up to January 6th. In the days immediately following the attack, defendants also bragged about their conduct. Some defendants later reflected on their actions at sentencing. The Select Committee Chart Compiling Defendant Statements is not meant to be comprehensive or polished; it is a small sampling of the tremendous work the Department of Justice has done tracking down and prosecuting criminal activity during the attempted insurrection.
Moreover, the trial of multiple members of the Proud Boys on seditious conspiracy and other charges is set to begin on December 19, 2022, and may provide additional information directly relevant to this topic. See Court Calendar: December 9, 2022–December 31, 2022, United States District Court for the District of Columbia, available at https://media.dcd.uscourts.gov/datepicker/index.html (last accessed Dec. 9, 2022); Alan Feuer, "Outcome in Oath Keepers Trial Could Hold Lessons for Coming Jan. 6 Cases," New York Times, (Nov. 30, 2022), available at https://www.nytimes.com/2022/11/30/us/politics/oath-keepers-stewart-rhodes.html.

18. Documents on file with the Select Committee to Investigate the January 6th Attack on the United States Capitol (National Archives Production), 076P-R000001890_00001 (December 28, 2020, email from Bernard Kerik to Mark Meadows explaining that "[w]e can do all the investigations we want later"); Documents on file with the Select Committee to Investigate

the January 6th Attack on the United States Capitol (National Archives Production), 076P-R000005090_0001 (January. 6, 2021, email from John Eastman to Gregory Jacob acknowledging that President Trump had "been so advised" that Vice President Pence "DOES NOT have the power to decide things unilaterally"); Select Committee to Investigate the January 6th Attack on the United States Capitol, *Hearing on the January 6th Investigation*, 117th Cong., 2d sess., (June 21, 2022), available at https://www.govinfo.gov/committee/house-january6th (Russell "Rusty" Bowers testimony recalling Rudolph Giuliani stating that "[w]e've got lots of theories; we just don't have the evidence"); *see also* Select Committee to Investigate the January 6th Attack on the United States Capitol, Transcribed Interview of Eric Herschmann (Apr. 6, 2022), p. 128 ("Whether Rudy was at this stage of his life in the same abilities to manage things at this level or not, I mean, obviously, I think Bernie Kerik publicly said it, they never proved the allegations that they were making, and they were trying to develop.") *Note*: Some documents cited in this report show timestamps based on a time zone other than Eastern Time—such as Greenwich Mean Time—because that is how they were produced to the Committee.

19. The Committee notes that a number of these findings are similar to those Federal Judge David Carter reached after reviewing the evidence presented by the Committee. Order Re Privilege of Documents Dated January 4-7, 2021 at 31-40, *Eastman v. Thompson et al.*, 594 F. Supp. 3d 1156 (C.D. Cal. Mar. 28, 2022) (No. 8:22-cv-99-DOC-DFM); Order Re Privilege of 599 Documents Dated November 3, 2020 - January 20, 2021 at 23-24, *Eastman v. Thompson et al.*, No. 8:22-cv-99 (C.D. Cal. June 7, 2022), ECF No. 356; Order Re Privilege of Remaining Documents at 13-17, *Eastman v. Thompson et al.*, No. 8:22-cv-99 (C.D. Cal. Oct. 19, 2022), ECF No. 372.

20. *See* Documents on file with the Select Committee to Investigate the January 6th Attack on the United States Capitol (Secret Service Production), CTRL0000091086 (United States Secret Service: Protective Intelligence Division communication noting left wing groups telling members to "stay at home" on January 6th).

21. Committee on House Administration, *Oversight of the United States Capitol Police and Preparations for and Response to the Attack of January 6th: Part I*, 117th Cong., 1st sess., (Apr. 21, 2021), available at https://cha.house.gov/committee-activity/hearings/oversight-united-states-capitol-police-and-preparations-and-response; Committee on House Administration, *Oversight of the United States Capitol Police and Preparations for and Response to the Attack of January 6th: Part II*, 117th Cong., 1st sess.,, (May 10, 2021), available at https://cha.house.gov/committee-activity/hearings/oversight-january-6th-attack-united-states-capitol-police-threat; Committee on House Administration, *Oversight of the January 6th Attack: Review of the Architect of the Capitol's Emergency Preparedness*, 117th Cong., 1st sess., (May 12, 2021), available at https://cha.house.gov/committee-activity/hearings/oversight-january-6th-attack-review-architect-capitol-s-emergency; Committee on House Administration, *Reforming the Capitol Police and Improving Accountability for the Capitol Police Board*, 117th Cong., 1st sess., (May 19, 2021), available at https://cha.house.gov/committee-activity/hearings/reforming-capitol-police-and-improving-accountability-capitol-police; Committee on House Administration, *Oversight of the January 6th Attack: United States Capitol Police Containment Emergency Response Team and First Responders Unit*, 117th Cong., 1st sess., (June 15, 2021), available at https://cha.house.gov/committee-activity/hearings/oversight-january-6th-attack-united-states-capitol-police-containment; Committee on House Administration, *Oversight of the January 6th Capitol Attack: Ongoing Review of the United States Capitol Police Inspector General Flash Reports*, 117th Cong., 2d sess., (Feb. 17, 2022), available at https://cha.house.gov/committee-activity/hearings/oversight-january-6th-capitol-attack-ongoing-review-united-states.

22. John Koblin, "At Least 20 Million Watched Jan. 6 Hearing," *New York Times*, (June 10, 2022), available at https://www.nytimes.com/2022/06/10/business/media/jan-6-hearing-ratings.html. Their findings were also widely noted by major media outlets, including conservative ones. "Editorial: What the Jan. 6 Hearings Accomplished," *Wall Street Journal*, (Oct. 14, 2022), available at https://www.wsj.com/articles/what-the-jan-6-inquiry-accomplished-donald-trump-liz-cheney-subpoena-congress-11665699321; "Editorial: The Jan. 6 Hearings are Over. Time to Vote.," *Washington Post*, (Oct. 13, 2022), available at

https://www.washingtonpost.com/opinions/2022/10/13/jan-6-hearings-are-over-time-vote/; "Editorial: The President Who Stood Still on Jan. 6," *Wall Street Journal*, (July 22, 2022), available at https://www.wsj.com/articles/the-president-who-stood-still-donald-trump-jan-6-committee-mike-pence-capitol-riot-11658528548; "Editorial: 'We All have a Duty to Ensure that What Happened on Jan. 6 Never Happens Again'," *New York Times*, (June 10, 2022), available at https://www.nytimes.com/2022/06/10/opinion/january-6-hearing-trump.html; "Editorial: Trump's Silence on Jan. 6 is Damning," *New York Post*, (July 22, 2022), available at https://nypost.com/2022/07/22/trumps-jan-6-silence-renders-him-unworthy-for-2024-reelection/

23. Select Committee to Investigate the January 6th Attack on the United States Capitol, Transcribed Interview of William Stepien, (Feb. 10, 2022), p. 45 ("And I told him it was going to be a process. It was going to be, you know—you know, we're going to have to wait and see how this turned out. So I, just like I did in 2016, I did the same thing in 2020.").

24. "When States Can Begin Processing and Counting Absentee/Mail-In Ballots, 2020," Ballotpedia (accessed on Dec. 5, 2022), available at https://ballotpedia.org/When_states_can_begin_processing_and_counting_absentee/mail-in_ballots,_2020.

25. *See* Select Committee to Investigate the January 6th Attack on the United States Capitol, *Hearing on the January 6th Investigation*, 117th Cong., 2d sess., (June 13, 2022), available at https://www.govinfo.gov/committee/house-january6th.

26. Select Committee to Investigate the January 6th Attack on the United States Capitol, Transcribed Interview of William Stepien, (Feb. 10, 2022), p. 45; Select Committee to Investigate the January 6th Attack on the United States Capitol, *Hearing on the January 6th Investigation*, 117th Cong., 2d sess., (June 13, 2022), available at https://www.govinfo.gov/committee/house-january6th.

27. Select Committee to Investigate the January 6th Attack on the United States Capitol, *Hearing on the January 6th Investigation*, 117th Cong., 2d sess., (June 13, 2022), available at https://www.govinfo.gov/committee/house-january6th.

28. Select Committee to Investigate the January 6th Attack on the United States Capitol, Transcribed Interview of William Stepien, (Feb. 10, 2022), p. 36.

29. Select Committee to Investigate the January 6th Attack on the United States Capitol, Transcribed Interview of Jared Kushner, (Mar. 31, 2022), p. 21.

30. John J. Martin, *Mail-in Ballots and Constraints on Federal Power under the Electors Clause*, 107 Va. L. Rev. Online 84, 86 (Apr. 2021) (noting that 45 States and DC permitted voters to request a mail-in ballot or automatically receive one in the 2020 election); Nathanial Rakich and Jasmine Mithani, "What Absentee Voting Looked Like In All 50 States," FiveThirtyEight, (Feb. 9, 2021), available at https://fivethirtyeight.com/features/what-absentee-voting-looked-like-in-all-50-states/; Lisa Danetz, "Mail Ballot Security Features: A Primer," Brennan Center for Justice, (Oct. 16, 2020), available at https://www.brennancenter.org/our-work/research-reports/mail-ballot-security-features-primer.

31. Select Committee to Investigate the January 6th Attack on the United States Capitol, Transcribed Interview of Hope Hicks, (Oct. 25, 2022), p. 24.

32. He also won in Utah, which mailed absentee ballots to all active voters, and won one or more electoral votes in both Maine and Nebraska, which allowed no-excuse absentee voting and assign their electoral votes proportionally. *See* "Table 1: States with No-Excuse Absentee Voting," National Conference of State Legislatures, (July 12, 2022), available at http://web.archive.org/web/20201004185006/https://www.ncsl.org/research/elections-and-campaigns/vopp-table-1-states-with-no-excuse-absentee-voting.aspx (archived); "Voting Outside the Polling Place: Absentee, All-Mail and Other Voting at Home Options," National Conference of State Legislatures, (Sep. 24, 2020), available at http://web.archive.org/web/20201103175057/https://www.ncsl.org/research/elections-and-campaigns/absentee-and-early-voting.aspx (archived); Federal Election Commission, "Federal Elections 2020 – Election Results for the U.S. President, the U.S. Senate and the U.S. House of Representatives," (Oct. 2022), p. 12, available at https://www.fec.gov/resources/cms-content/documents/federalelections2020.pdf.

33. *See, e.g.*, Select Committee to Investigate the January 6th Attack on the United States Capitol, Transcribed Interview of William Stepien, (Feb. 10, 2022), p. 66; Select Committee to Investigate the January 6th Attack on the United States Capitol, Deposition of Jason Miller, (Feb. 3, 2022), pp. 75-76.

34. Select Committee to Investigate the January 6th Attack on the United States Capitol, Transcribed Interview of William Stepien, (Feb. 10, 2022), pp. 54, 66.

35. Select Committee to Investigate the January 6th Attack on the United States Capitol, Deposition of Jason Miller, (Feb. 3, 2022), pp. 74-77.

36. Select Committee to Investigate the January 6th Attack on the United States Capitol, Transcribed Interview of William Stepien, (Feb. 10, 2022), pp. 60-61.

37. "Donald Trump 2020 Election Night Speech Transcript," Rev, (Nov. 4, 2020), available at https://www.rev.com/blog/transcripts/donald-trump-2020-election-night-speech-transcript.

38. Donald J. Trump (@realDonaldTrump), Twitter, Nov. 5, 2020 9:12 a.m. ET, available at http://web.archive.org/web/20201105170250/https://twitter.com/realdonaldtrump/status/1324353932022480896 (archived). *Note:* Citations in this report that refer to an archived tweet may list a timestamp that is several hours earlier or later than the one shown on the suggested webpage because tweets are archived from various time zones.

39. *See, e.g.*, 52 U.S.C. § 10307; Ariz. Rev. Stat. § 16-1010.

40. Select Committee to Investigate the January 6th Attack on the United States Capitol, Deposition of Jason Miller, (Feb. 3, 2022), pp. 77-78.

41. Select Committee to Investigate the January 6th Attack on the United States Capitol, Transcribed Interview of William Barr, (June 2, 2022), p. 8.

42. Documents on file with the Select Committee to Investigate the January 6th Attack on the United States Capitol (National Archives Production), 076P-R000010020_0001 (November 3, 2020, email exchange between Tom Fitton and Molly Michael copying proposed election day victory statement).

43. Dan Friedman, "Leaked Audio: Before Election Day, Bannon Said Trump Planned to Falsely Claim Victory," *Mother Jones*, (July 12, 2022), available at https://www.motherjones.com/politics/2022/07/leaked-audio-steve-bannon-trump-2020-election-declare-victory. We note that Mr. Bannon refused to testify and has been convicted of criminal contempt by a jury of his peers. "Stephen K. Bannon Sentenced to Four Months in Prison on Two counts of Contempt of Congress," Department of Justice, (Oct. 21, 2022), available at https://www.justice.gov/usao-dc/pr/stephen-k-bannon-sentenced-four-months-prison-two-counts-contempt-congress.

44. At his interview, Stone invoked his Fifth Amendment right not to incriminate himself in response to over 70 questions, including questions regarding his direct communications with Donald Trump and his role in January 6th. Select Committee to Investigate the January 6th Attack on the United States Capitol, Deposition of Roger Stone (Dec. 17, 2021). *See also* Documents on file with the Select Committee to Investigate the January 6th Attack on the United States Capitol (Christoffer Guldbrandsen Production), Video file 201101_1 (November 1, 2020, footage of Roger Stone speaking to associates).

45. Select Committee to Investigate the January 6th Attack on the United States Capitol, Deposition of Greg Jacob, (Feb. 1, 2022), pp. 12-13.

46. Documents on file with the Select Committee to Investigate the January 6th Attack on the United States Capitol (National Archives Production), 79VP-R000011578_0001, 079VP-R000011579_0001, 079VP-R000011579_0002 (November 3, 2020, email and memorandum from Gregory Jacob to Marc Short regarding electoral vote count).

47. Select Committee to Investigate the January 6th Attack on the United States Capitol, Transcribed Interview of William Stepien, (Feb. 10, 2022), pp. 117-18.

48. Select Committee to Investigate the January 6th Attack on the United States Capitol, Deposition of Jason Miller, (Feb. 3, 2022), p. 91.

49. Select Committee to Investigate the January 6th Attack on the United States Capitol, *Hearing on the January 6th Investigation*, 117th Cong., 2d sess., (June 13, 2022), available at https://www.govinfo.gov/committee/house-january6th.

50. *See, e.g.*, Select Committee to Investigate the January 6th Attack on the United States Capitol, Transcribed Interview of General Mark A. Milley, (Nov. 17, 2021), p. 121; Select Committee to Investigate the January 6th Attack on the United States Capitol, Transcribed Interview of Alyssa Farah Griffin, (Apr. 15, 2022), p. 62; Select Committee to Investigate the January 6th Attack on the United States Capitol, Continued Interview of Cassidy Hutchinson, (Sep. 14, 2022), p. 113; Select Committee to Investigate the January 6th Attack on the United States Capitol, Transcribed Interview of Kellyanne Conway, (Nov. 28, 2022), pp. 79-84.

51. *See* Select Committee to Investigate the January 6th Attack on the United States Capitol, Deposition of Keith Kellogg, Jr., (Dec. 14, 2021), pp. 212-21; Select Committee to Investigate the January 6th Attack on the United States Capitol, Transcribed Interview of General Mark A. Milley, (Nov. 17, 2021), pp. 108-10; Select Committee to Investigate the January 6th Attack on the United States Capitol, Deposition of John McEntee, (Mar. 28, 2022), pp. 44, 46, 48-51; Select Committee to Investigate the January 6th Attack on the United States Capitol, Transcribed Interview of Douglas Macgregor, (June 7, 2022), pp. 27-41.

52. Select Committee to Investigate the January 6th Attack on the United States Capitol, Deposition of Keith Kellogg, Jr., (Dec. 14, 2021), p. 215.

53. Select Committee to Investigate the January 6th Attack on the United States Capitol, Transcribed Interview of William Barr, (June 2, 2022), p. 6.

54. Select Committee to Investigate the January 6th Attack on the United States Capitol, Transcribed Interview of Alex Cannon, (Apr. 13, 2022), pp. 22, 33-34.

55. Select Committee to Investigate the January 6th Attack on the United States Capitol, Transcribed Interview of William Stepien, (Feb. 10, 2022), pp. 111-12.

56. Select Committee to Investigate the January 6th Attack on the United States Capitol, Deposition of Jason Miller, (Feb. 3, 2022), p. 119.

57. ABC News, "Pence Opens Up with David Muir on Jan. 6: Exclusive," YouTube, at 2:13, Nov. 14, 2022, available at https://youtu.be/-AAyKAoPFQs?t=133.

58. "CNN Townhall: Former Vice President Mike Pence," CNN, (Nov. 16, 2022), available at https://transcripts.cnn.com/show/se/date/2022-11-16/segment/01.

59. Select Committee to Investigate the January 6th Attack on the United States Capitol, Transcribed Interview of Matthew Morgan, (Apr. 25, 2022), p. 118.

60. *Select Committee to Investigate the January 6th Attack on the United States Capitol, Transcribed Interview of William Barr, (June 2, 2022), p. 18.*

61. Michael Balsamo, "Disputing Trump, Barr Says No Widespread Election Fraud," Associated Press, (Dec. 1, 2020, updated June 28, 2022), available at https://apnews.com/article/barr-no-widespread-election-fraud-b1f1488796c9a98c4b1a9061a6c7f49d.

62. Select Committee to Investigate the January 6th Attack on the United States Capitol, Transcribed Interview of William Barr, (June 2, 2022), pp. 24-30; "Bill Barr Press Conference Transcript: No Special Counsels Needed to Investigate Election or Hunter Biden," Rev, (Dec. 21, 2020), available at https://www.rev.com/blog/transcripts/bill-barr-press-conference-transcript-no-special-counsels-needed-to-investigate-election-or-hunter-biden.

63. "Joint Statement from Elections Infrastructure Government Coordinating Council & the Election Infrastructure Sector Coordinating Executive Committees," Cybersecurity and Infrastructure Security Agency, (Nov. 12, 2020), available at https://www.cisa.gov/news/2020/11/12/joint-statement-elections-infrastructure-government-coordinating-council-election (emphasis in original).

64. Select Committee to Investigate the January 6th Attack on the United States Capitol, *Hearing on the January 6th Investigation*, 117th Cong., 2d sess., (June 23, 2022), available at https://www.govinfo.gov/committee/house-january6th.

65. Select Committee to Investigate the January 6th Attack on the United States Capitol, Transcribed Interview of Richard Peter Donoghue, (Oct. 21, 2021), pp. 59-60.

66. Select Committee to Investigate the January 6th Attack on the United States Capitol, Transcribed Interview of Richard Peter Donoghue, (Oct. 21, 2021), pp. 108-09.

67. Senate Committee on the Judiciary, Transcribed Interview of Richard Donoghue, (Aug. 6, 2021), p. 156, available at https://www.judiciary.senate.gov/imo/media/doc/Donoghue%20Transcript.pdf.

68. Select Committee to Investigate the January 6th Attack on the United States Capitol, Transcribed Interview of Jeffrey Rosen, (Oct. 13, 2021), pp. 18-19.

69. Select Committee to Investigate the January 6th Attack on the United States Capitol, Transcribed Interview of Pasquale Anthony "Pat" Cipollone, (July 8, 2022), pp. 50, 123; Select Committee to Investigate the January 6th Attack on the United States Capitol, Transcribed Interview of Eric Herschmann, (Apr. 6, 2022), pp. 168-69, 184, 187.

70. Select Committee to Investigate the January 6th Attack on the United States Capitol, Transcribed Interview of Pasquale Anthony "Pat" Cipollone, (July 8, 2022), p. 50.

71. Select Committee to Investigate the January 6th Attack on the United States Capitol, Transcribed Interview of Eric Herschmann, (April 6, 2022), p. 128.

72. Select Committee to Investigate the January 6th Attack on the United States Capitol, Transcribed Interview of William Stepien, (Feb. 10, 2022), pp. 172-73.

73. Select Committee to Investigate the January 6th Attack on the United States Capitol, Transcribed Interview of William Stepien, (Feb. 10, 2022), p. 174.

74. Select Committee to Investigate the January 6th Attack on the United States Capitol, Transcribed Interview of Justin Clark, (May 17, 2022), pp. 63-70; Select Committee to Investigate the January 6th Attack on the United States Capitol, Transcribed Interview of Matthew Morgan, (Apr. 25, 2022), pp. 57-62; Select Committee to Investigate the January 6th Attack on the United States Capitol, Transcribed Interview of Timothy Murtaugh, (May 19, 2022), pp, 66-68; Select Committee to Investigate the January 6th Attack on the United States Capitol, Transcribed Interview of Alex Cannon, (Apr. 19, 2022), pp. 37-38; Documents on file with the Select Committee to Investigate the January 6th Attack on the United States Capitol (Tim Murtaugh production), XXM-0021349 (text chain with Giuliani, Ellis, Epshteyn, Ryan, Bobb, and Herschmann).

75. Select Committee to Investigate the January 6th Attack on the United States Capitol, Transcribed Interview of Matthew Morgan, (Apr. 25, 2022), p. 58.

76. Select Committee to Investigate the January 6th Attack on the United States Capitol, Transcribed Interview of Matthew Morgan, (Apr. 25, 2022), p. 58.

77. Select Committee to Investigate the January 6th Attack on the United States Capitol, Transcribed Interview of Matthew Morgan, (Apr. 25, 2022), p. 58.

78. Select Committee to Investigate the January 6th Attack on the United States Capitol, Transcribed Interview of William Stepien, (Feb. 10, 2022), p. 173.

79. *King v. Whitmer*, 505 F. Supp. 3d 720, 738 (E.D. Mich. 2020), also available at https://electioncases.osu.edu/wp-content/uploads/2020/11/King-v-Whitmer-Doc62.pdf; *Bowyer v. Ducey*, 506 F. Supp. 3d 699, 706 (D. Ariz. 2020), also available at https://storage.courtlistener.com/recap/gov.uscourts.azd.1255923/gov.uscourts.azd.1255923.84.0_2.pdf; *Donald J. Trump for President v. Boockvar*, 502 F. Supp. 3d 899, 906 (M.D. Pa. 2020), also available at https://storage.courtlistener.com/recap/gov.uscourts.pamd.127057/gov.uscourts.pamd.127057.202.0_1.pdf; *Law v. Whitmer*, No. 10 OC 00163 1B, 2020 Nev. Unpub. LEXIS 1160, at *1, 29-31, 33, 48-49, 52, 54 (Nev. Dec. 8, 2020), available at https://casetext.com/case/law-v-whitmer-1 (attaching and affirming lower

court decision), also available at https://election.conservative.org/files/2020/12/20-OC-00163-Order-Granting-Motion-to-Dismiss-Statement-of-Contest.pdf; *Wisconsin Voters Alliance v. Pence*, 514 F. Supp. 3d 117, 119 (D.D.C. 2021), also available at https://electioncases.osu.edu/wp-content/uploads/2020/12/WVA-v-Pence-Doc10.pdf.

80. Documents on file with the Select Committee to Investigate the January 6th Attack on the United States Capitol (Zach Parkinson Production), Parkinson0620 (text message between Tim Murtaugh, Zach Parkinson, and "Matt").

81. *In the Matter of Rudolph W. Giuliani*, No. 2021-00506, slip op at *2, 22 (N.Y. App. Div. May 3, 2021), available at https://int.nyt.com/data/documenttools/giuliani-law-license-suspension/1ae5ad6007c0ebfa/full.pdf.

82. *In the Matter of Rudolph W. Giuliani*, No. 2021-00506, slip op at *2, 22 (N.Y. App. Div. May 3, 2021), available at https://int.nyt.com/data/documenttools/giuliani-law-license-suspension/1ae5ad6007c0ebfa/full.pdf.

83. Opinion and Order at 1, *King v. Whitmer*, 505 F. Supp. 3d 720 (E.D. Mich. Aug. 25, 2020) (No. 20-13134), ECF No. 172.

84. Senator John Danforth, Benjamin Ginsberg, The Honorable Thomas B. Griffith, et al., *Lost, Not Stolen: The Conservative Case that Trump Lost and Biden Won the 2020 Presidential Election*, (July 2022), p. 3, available at https://lostnotstolen.org/download/378/.

85. Senator John Danforth, Benjamin Ginsberg, The Honorable Thomas B. Griffith, et al., *Lost, Not Stolen: The Conservative Case that Trump Lost and Biden Won the 2020 Presidential Election*, (July 2022), pp. 3-4, available at https://lostnotstolen.org/download/378/. We also note this: The authors of *Lost, Not Stolen* also conclude that one of the pieces of supposed evidence that President Trump and his allies have pointed to since January 6, 2021, to try to bolster their allegations that the 2020 election was stolen shows nothing of the sort. *Lost, Not Stolen* explains that Dinesh D'Souza's "2000 Mules" tries to establish widespread voter fraud in the 2020 election using phone-tracking data. "Yet the film, heartily endorsed by Trump at its Mar-a-Lago premiere, has subsequently been thoroughly debunked in analysis. What the film claims to portray is simply not supported by the evidence invoked by the film." *Id.*, at 6. Likewise, former Attorney General Bill Barr told the Select Committee: ". . . I haven't seen anything since the election that changes my mind [that fraud determined the outcome] including, the 2000 Mules movie." Select Committee to Investigate the January 6th Attack on the United States Capitol, Transcribed Interview of William Barr, (June 2, 2022), p. 37. He called its cell phone tracking data "singularly unimpressive" because ". . . in a big city like Atlanta or wherever, just by definition you're going to find many hundreds of them have passed by and spent time in the vicinity of these boxes" for submitting ballots, and to argue that those people must be "mules" delivering fraudulent ballots was "just indefensible." *Id.*, at 37–38.

86. White House Senior Advisor Eric Herschmann told the Committee that when he disputed allegations of election fraud in a December 18th Oval Office meeting, Sidney Powell fired back that "the judges are corrupt. And I was like, every one? Every single case that you've done in the country you guys lost every one of them is corrupt, even the ones we appointed?" Select Committee to Investigate the January 6th Attack on the United States Capitol, Transcribed Interview of Eric Herschmann, (Apr. 6, 2022), p. 171.

87. Select Committee to Investigate the January 6th Attack on the United States Capitol, *Hearing on the January 6th Investigation*, 117th Cong., 2d sess., (June 13, 2022), at 1:53:10-1:53:20, available at https://january6th.house.gov/legislation/hearings/06132022-select-committee-hearing.

88. Verified Complaint for Declaratory and Injunctive Relief at 46-47, *Donald J. Trump for President, Inc. v. Boockvar*, No. 4:20-cv-02078 (M.D. Pa. Nov. 9, 2020), available at https://cdn.donaldjtrump.com/public-files/press_assets/2020-11-09-complaint-as-filed.pdf.

89. Opinion at 2, 3, 16, *Donald J. Trump for President, Inc. v. Boockvar*, No. 20-3371 (3d Cir. Nov. 27, 2020), available at https://electioncases.osu.edu/wp-content/uploads/2020/11/Donald-J.-Trump-for-President-v-Boockvar-3rd-Cir-Doc91.pdf.

90. Complaint for Expedited Declaratory and Injunctive Relief Pursuant to Article II of the United States Constitution, *Trump v. Wisconsin Elections Commission*, No. 2:20-cv-01785 (E.D. Wis. Dec. 2, 2020), available at https://electioncases.osu.edu/wp-content/uploads/2020/12/Trump-v-WEC-Doc1.pdf.

91. *Trump v. Wisconsin Elections Commission*, 506 F. Supp. 3d 620, 21, 22 (E.D. Wis. 2020), available at https://electioncases.osu.edu/wp-content/uploads/2020/12/Trump-v-WEC-Doc134.pdf.

92. Select Committee to Investigate the January 6th Attack on the United States Capitol, *Hearing on the January 6th Investigation*, 117th Cong., 2d sess., (June 13, 2022), at 1:52:45 to 1:53:20, available at https://january6th.house.gov/legislation/hearings/06132022-select-committee-hearing.

93. The authors determined that thirty cases were dismissed by a judge after an evidentiary hearing had been held, compared to twenty cases that were dismissed by a judge beforehand, while the remaining fourteen were withdrawn voluntarily by plaintiffs. *See* Senator John Danforth, Benjamin Ginsberg, The Honorable Thomas B. Griffith, et al, *Lost, Not Stolen: The Conservative Case that Trump Lost and Biden Won the 2020 Presidential Election*, (July 2022), p. 3, available at https://lostnotstolen.org/download/378/.

94. Select Committee to Investigate the January 6th Attack on the United States Capitol, Deposition of Rudolph Giuliani, (May 20, 2022), p. 111.

95. Letter from Timothy C. Parlatore to Chairman Bennie G. Thompson on "Re: Subpoena to Bernard B. Kerik," (Dec. 31, 2021).

96. Documents on file with the Select Committee to Investigate the January 6th Attack on the United States Capitol (National Archives Production), 076P-R000004125_0001 (December 28, 2020, email from Kerik to Meadows).

97. When our courts weigh evidence to determine facts, they often infer that disputed facts do not favor a witness who refuses to testify by invoking his Fifth Amendment right against incriminating himself. *See Baxter v. Palmigiano*, 425 U.S. 308, 318 (1976) (the Fifth Amendment allows for "adverse inferences against parties to civil actions when they refuse to testify to probative evidence offered against them").

98. Nor was there such evidence of widespread fraud in any of the documents produced in response to Select Committee subpoenas issued to the proponents of the claims, including Rudy Giuliani and his team members and investigators Bernard Kerik and Christina Bobb, or other proponents of election fraud claims such as Pennsylvania Senator Doug Mastriano, Arizona legislator Mark Finchem, disbarred attorney Phill Kline, and attorneys Sidney Powell, Cleta Mitchell, and John Eastman. Not one of them provided evidence raising genuine questions about the election outcome. In short, it was a big scam.

99. Select Committee to Investigate the January 6th Attack on the United States Capitol, *Business Meeting on the January 6th Investigation*, 117th Cong., 2d sess., (Oct. 19, 2022), at 56:30 to 58:10, available at https://january6th.house.gov/legislation/hearings/101322-select-committee-hearing.

100. Select Committee to Investigate the January 6th Attack on the United States Capitol, Transcribed Interview of Eugene Scalia (June 30, 2022), pp. 11-13. Then-Secretary Scalia also sent a memorandum to President Trump on January 8, 2021. In that memorandum, he requested that the President "convene an immediate meeting of the Cabinet." He told the President that he was "concerned by certain statements you made since the election . . . of further actions you may be considering," and he "concluded that [his] responsibilities as a Cabinet Secretary obligate[d] [him] to take further steps to address those concerns." The Select Committee will make this memorandum available to the public. Documents on file with the Select Committee to Investigate the January 6th Attack on the United States Capitol (Department of Labor Production), CTRL0000087637, (January 8, 2021, Memorandum for The President of the United States from Secretary of Labor Eugene Scalia, regarding Request for Cabinet Meeting).

101. Select Committee to Investigate the January 6th Attack on the United States Capitol, Deposition of Judson Deere, (Mar. 3, 2022), pp. 23-25.

102. Select Committee to Investigate the January 6th Attack on the United States Capitol, Transcribed Interview of Pasquale Anthony "Pat" Cipollone (July 8, 2022), p. 12.

103. Select Committee to Investigate the January 6th Attack on the United States Capitol, Transcribed Interview of William Barr, (June 3, 2022), p. 62.

104. Select Committee to Investigate the January 6th Attack on the United States Capitol, Transcribed Interview of William Barr, (June 3, 2022), pp. 19-20.

105. Senate Committee on the Judiciary, Transcribed Interview of Jeffrey Rosen, (Aug. 7, 2021), pp. 30-31, available at https://www.judiciary.senate.gov/imo/media/doc/Rosen%20Transcript.pdf; Select Committee to Investigate the January 6th Attack on the United States Capitol, Transcribed Interview of Jeffrey Rosen, (Oct. 13, 2021), pp. 14-15 (in which Rosen confirms the general accuracy of the transcription of his Senate testimony and then is asked and agrees to the following question: [Committee staff]: "And we are going to – the select committee is going to essentially incorporate those transcripts as part of our record and rely upon your testimony there for our purposes going forward, as long as you're comfortable with that?" [Rosen]: "Yes.")

106. "Donald Trump Vlog: Contesting Election Results – December 22, 2020," Factba.se, at 9:11-9:25 (Dec. 22, 2020), available at https://factba.se/transcript/donald-trump-vlog-contesting-election-results-december-22-2020.

107. Select Committee to Investigate the January 6th Attack on the United States Capitol, Transcribed Interview of Richard Peter Donoghue, (Oct. 1, 2021), p. 43.

108. Brad Raffensperger, Integrity Counts (New York: Simon & Schuster, 2021), p. 191 (reproducing the call transcript); Amy Gardner and Paulina Firozi, "Here's the Full Transcript and Audio of the Call Between Trump and Raffensperger," Washington Post, (Jan. 5, 2021), available at https://www.washingtonpost.com/politics/trump-raffensperger-call-transcript-georgia-vote/2021/01/03/2768e0cc-4ddd-11eb-83e3-322644d82356_story.html

109. Brad Raffensperger, Integrity Counts (New York: Simon & Schuster, 2021), p. 191 (reproducing the call transcript); Amy Gardner and Paulina Firozi, "Here's the Full Transcript and Audio of the Call Between Trump and Raffensperger," Washington Post, (Jan. 5, 2021), available at https://www.washingtonpost.com/politics/trump-raffensperger-call-transcript-georgia-vote/2021/01/03/2768e0cc-4ddd-11eb-83e3-322644d82356_story.html

110. Donald J. Trump (@realDonaldTrump), Twitter, Jan. 3, 2021 8:57 a.m. ET, available at http://web.archive.org/web/20210103135742/https://twitter.com/realdonaldtrump/status/1345731043861659650 (archived).

111. Select Committee to Investigate the January 6th Attack on the United States Capitol, Transcribed Interview of William Barr, (June 2, 2022), pp. 25-26.

112. "Donald Trump Speech on Election Fraud Claims Transcript December 2," Rev, at 15:12-15:44, (Dec. 2, 2020), available at https://www.rev.com/blog/transcripts/donald-trump-speech-on-election-fraud-claims-transcript-december-2.

113. Select Committee to Investigate the January 6th Attack on the United States Capitol, Transcribed Interview of Richard Peter Donoghue, (Oct. 1, 2021), p. 64.

114. PBS NewsHour, "WATCH LIVE: Trump Speaks as Congress Prepares to Count Electoral College Votes in Biden Win," YouTube, at 1:42:58-1:43:02, Jan. 6, 2021, available at https://youtu.be/pa9sT4efsqY?t=6178.

115. Senate Committee on the Judiciary, Interview of Richard Donoghue, (Aug. 6, 2021), p. 156, available at https://www.judiciary.senate.gov/imo/media/doc/Donoghue%20Transcript.pdf.

116. PBS NewsHour, "WATCH LIVE: Trump Speaks as Congress Prepares to Count Electoral College Votes in Biden Win," YouTube, at 1:15:19-1:15:39, Jan. 6, 2021, available at https://youtu.be/pa9sT4efsqY?t=4519.

117. Brad Raffensperger, Integrity Counts (New York: Simon & Schuster, 2021), p. 191 (reproducing the call transcript); Amy Gardner and Paulina Firozi, "Here's the Full Transcript and Audio of the Call Between Trump and Raffensperger," *Washington Post*, (Jan. 5, 2021), available at https://www.washingtonpost.com/politics/trump-raffensperger-call-transcript-georgia-vote/2021/01/03/2768e0cc-4ddd-11eb-83e3-322644d82356_story.html

118. "Donald Trump Rally Speech Transcript Dalton, Georgia: Senate Runoff Election," Rev, at 51:38-52:01, (Jan. 4, 2021), available at https://www.rev.com/blog/transcripts/donald-trump-rally-speech-transcript-dalton-georgia-senate-runoff-election.

119. Brad Raffensperger, *Integrity Counts* (New York: Simon & Schuster, 2021), p. 191 (reproducing the call transcript); Amy Gardner and Paulina Firozi, "Here's the Full Transcript and Audio of the Call Between Trump and Raffensperger," *Washington Post*, (Jan. 5, 2021), available at https://www.washingtonpost.com/politics/trump-raffensperger-call-transcript-georgia-vote/2021/01/03/2768e0cc-4ddd-11eb-83e3-322644d82356_story.html

120. PBS NewsHour, "WATCH LIVE: Trump Speaks as Congress Prepares to Count Electoral College Votes in Biden Win," YouTube, at 1:32:25-1:32:43, Jan. 6, 2021, available at https://youtu.be/pa9sT4efsqY?t=5545.

121. Brad Raffensperger, *Integrity Counts* (New York: Simon & Schuster, 2021), p. 191 (reproducing the call transcript); Amy Gardner and Paulina Firozi, "Here's the Full Transcript and Audio of the Call Between Trump and Raffensperger," *Washington Post*, (Jan. 5, 2021), available at https://www.washingtonpost.com/politics/trump-raffensperger-call-transcript-georgia-vote/2021/01/03/2768e0cc-4ddd-11eb-83e3-322644d82356_story.html

122. PBS NewsHour, "WATCH LIVE: Trump Speaks as Congress Prepares to Count Electoral College Votes in Biden Win," YouTube, at 1:33:35-1:33:44, Jan. 6, 2021, available at https://youtu.be/pa9sT4efsqY?t=5615.

123. Select Committee to Investigate the January 6th Attack on the United States Capitol, Deposition of Kayleigh McEnany, (Jan. 12, 2022), pp. 143, 290-91.

124. Search results for "dominion", Trump Twitter Archive v2, (accessed Sep. 20, 2022), https://www.thetrumparchive.com/?searchbox=%22dominion%22&results=1.

125. Select Committee to Investigate the January 6th Attack on the United States Capitol, Deposition of Jason Miller (Feb. 3, 2022), pp. 117, 133.

126. "Donald Trump Thanksgiving Call to Troops Transcript 2020: Addresses Possibility of Conceding Election," Rev, at 23:35-23:46, (Nov. 26, 2020), available at https://www.rev.com/blog/transcripts/donald-trump-thanksgiving-call-to-troops-transcript-2020-addresses-possibility-of-conceding-election.

127. Select Committee to Investigate the January 6th Attack on the United States Capitol, Transcribed Interview of William Barr, (Jun. 2, 2022), p. 19.

128. "Donald Trump Thanksgiving Call to Troops Transcript 2020: Addresses Possibility of Conceding Election," Rev, at 24:16-24:35 (Nov. 26, 2020), available at https://www.rev.com/blog/transcripts/donald-trump-thanksgiving-call-to-troops-transcript-2020-addresses-possibility-of-conceding-election.

129. Select Committee to Investigate the January 6th Attack on the United States Capitol, Transcribed Interview of William Barr, (Jun. 2, 2022), p. 27.

130. "Donald Trump Speech on Election Fraud Claims Transcript December 2," Rev, at 10:46-11:06, (Dec. 2, 2020), available at https://www.rev.com/blog/transcripts/donald-trump-speech-on-election-fraud-claims-transcript-december-2.

131. William P. Barr, *One Damn Thing After Another: Memoirs of an Attorney General*, (New York: HarperCollins, 2022), at p. 554.

132. Donald J. Trump (@realDonaldTrump), Twitter, Nov. 15, 2020 12:21 a.m. ET, available at https://media-cdn.factba.se/realdonaldtrump-twitter/1338715842931023873.jpg (archived).

133. Senate Committee on the Judiciary, Transcribed Interview of Jeffrey Rosen, (Aug. 7, 2021), pp. 25, 31, available at https://www.judiciary.senate.gov/imo/media/doc/Rosen%20Transcript.pdf.

134. Donald J. Trump (@realDonaldTrump), Twitter, Dec. 16, 2020 1:09 a.m. ET, available at https://media-cdn.factba.se/realdonaldtrump-twitter/1339090279429775363.jpg (archived).

135. Select Committee to Investigate the January 6th Attack on the United States Capitol, Transcribed Interview of Robert O'Brien, (Aug. 23, 2022), pp. 164-65.

136. Donald J. Trump (@realDonaldTrump), Twitter, Dec. 19, 2020 11:30 a.m. ET, available at https://media-cdn.factba.se/realdonaldtrump-twitter/1340333619299147781.jpg (archived).

137. Select Committee to Investigate the January 6th Attack on the United States Capitol, Transcribed Interview of Richard Peter Donoghue, (Oct. 1, 2021), p. 109.

138. Brad Raffensperger, *Integrity Counts* (New York: Simon & Schuster, 2021), p. 191 (reproducing the call transcript); Amy Gardner and Paulina Firozi, "Here's the Full Transcript and Audio of the Call Between Trump and Raffensperger," *Washington Post*, (Jan. 5, 2021), available at https://www.washingtonpost.com/politics/trump-raffensperger-call-transcript-georgia-vote/2021/01/03/2768e0cc-4ddd-11eb-83e3-322644d82356_story.html

139. Brad Raffensperger, Integrity Counts (New York: Simon & Schuster, 2021), p. 191 (reproducing the call transcript); Amy Gardner and Paulina Firozi, "Here's the Full Transcript and Audio of the Call Between Trump and Raffensperger," *Washington Post*, (Jan. 5, 2021), available at https://www.washingtonpost.com/politics/trump-raffensperger-call-transcript-georgia-vote/2021/01/03/2768e0cc-4ddd-11eb-83e3-322644d82356_story.html

140. PBS NewsHour, "WATCH LIVE: Trump Speaks as Congress Prepares to Count Electoral College Votes in Biden Win," YouTube, at 1:39:09 to 1:39:27 and 1:40:51 to 1:41:01, Jan. 6, 2021, available at https://youtu.be/pa9sT4efsqY?t=5949.

141. Select Committee to Investigate the January 6th Attack on the United States Capitol, *Hearing on the January 6th Investigation*, 117th Cong., 2d sess., (June 13, 2022), available at https://www.govinfo.gov/committee/house-january6th

142. Select Committee to Investigate the January 6th Attack on the United States Capitol, Transcribed Interview of William Barr, (June 2, 2022), p. 15.

143. The framers specifically considered and rejected two constitutional plans that would have given Congress the power to select the Executive. Under both the Virginia and New Jersey Plans, the national executive would have been chosen by the national legislature. *See* Curtis A. Bradley & Martin S. Flaherty, *Executive Power Essentialism and Foreign Affairs*, 102 Mich. L. Rev. 545, 592, 595 (2004); *see also* 1 The Records of the Federal Convention of 1787, at 21, 244 (Max Farrand ed., 1911) (introducing Virginia and New Jersey Plans), available at https://oll.libertyfund.org/title/farrand-the-records-of-the-federal-convention-of-1787-vol-1; James Madison, *Notes of the Constitutional Convention* (Sep. 4, 1787) (Gov. Morris warning of "the danger of intrigue & faction" if Congress selected the President), available at https://www.consource.org/document/james-madisons-notes-of-the-constitutional-convention-1787-9-4/.

144. The Federalist No. 68, at 458 (Alexander Hamilton) (Jacob E. Cooke ed., 1961).

145. The Federalist No. 68, at 459 (Alexander Hamilton) (Jacob E. Cooke ed., 1961).

146. The Federalist No. 68, at 459 (Alexander Hamilton) (Jacob E. Cooke ed., 1961).

147. The Federalist No. 68, at 459 (Alexander Hamilton) (Jacob E. Cooke ed., 1961). *See also* U.S. Const. art. II, § 1, cl. 2 ("but no Senator or Representative, or Person holding an Office of Trust or Profit under the United States, shall be appointed an Elector").

148. Documents on file with the Select Committee to Investigate the January 6th Attack on the United States Capitol (Chapman University Production), Chapman052976 (Eastman Jan 6 scenario dual slates of electors memo); Documents on file with the Select Committee to Investigate the January 6th Attack on the United States Capitol (Chapman University Production), CTRL0000923171 (Eastman Jan. 6 scenario conduct by elected officials memo).

149. Documents on file with the Select Committee to Investigate the January 6th Attack on the United States Capitol (Chapman University Production), Chapman003228 (Eastman memo to President Trump).

150. *See Eastman v. Thompson et al.* at 6-8, 594 F. Supp. 3d 1156, (C.D. Cal. Mar. 28, 2022) (No. 8:22-cv-99-DOC-DFM).

151. Documents on file with the Select Committee to Investigate the January 6th Attack on the United States Capitol (Chapman University Production), Chapman003228 (Eastman memo to President Trump).

152. Select Committee to Investigate the January 6th Attack on the United States Capitol, Deposition of Greg Jacob (Feb. 1, 2022), p. 118.

153. Select Committee to Investigate the January 6th Attack on the United States Capitol, Deposition of Greg Jacob (Feb. 1, 2022), pp. 110, 117.

154. Select Committee to Investigate the January 6th Attack on the United States Capitol, Deposition of Greg Jacob (Feb. 1, 2022), pp. 109-10; Select Committee to Investigate the January 6th Attack on the United States Capitol, *Hearing on the January 6th Investigation*, 117th Cong., 2d sess., (June 16, 2022), available at https://www.govinfo.gov/committee/house-january6th.

155. Select Committee to Investigate the January 6th Attack on the United States Capitol, *Hearing on the January 6th Investigation*, 117th Cong., 2d sess., (June 16), available at https://www.govinfo.gov/committee/house-january6th.

156. "Former Vice President Pence Remarks at Federalist Society Conference," C-SPAN (Feb. 4, 2022), available at https://www.c-span.org/video/?517647-2/vice-president-pence-remarks-federalist-society-conference.

157. Select Committee to Investigate the January 6th Attack on the United States Capitol, Deposition of Greg Jacob, (Feb. 1, 2022), p. 122.

158. Document on file with the Select Committee (National Archives Production), VP-R0000107 (January 5, 2021, Greg Jacob memo to Vice President); *see also* Select Committee to Investigate the January 6th Attack on the United States Capitol, Deposition of Greg Jacob, (Feb. 1, 2022), pp. 127-28 (discussing memorandum).

159. Select Committee to Investigate the January 6th Attack on the United States Capitol, Deposition of Greg Jacob, (Feb. 1, 2022), pp. 122-23.

160. Select Committee to Investigate the January 6th Attack on the United States Capitol, Deposition of Marc Short, (Jan. 26, 2022), pp. 26-27.

161. Judge Luttig (@judgeluttig), Twitter, Jan. 5, 2021 9:53 a.m. ET available at https://twitter.com/judgeluttig/status/1346469787329646592.

162. Select Committee to Investigate the January 6th Attack on the United States Capitol, *Hearing on the January 6th Investigation*, 117th Cong., 2d sess., (June 16, 2022), available at https://www.govinfo.gov/committee/house-january6th.

163. Select Committee to Investigate the January 6th Attack on the United States Capitol, *Hearing on the January 6th Investigation*, 117th Cong., 2d sess., (June 16, 2022), available at https://www.govinfo.gov/committee/house-january6th.

164. Documents on file with the Select Committee, (Chapman University Production), Chapman005442 (Eastman emails with Greg Jacob).

165. Select Committee to Investigate the January 6th Attack on the United States Capitol, Transcribed Interview of Pasquale Anthony "Pat" Cipollone, (July 8, 2022), p. 88.

166. Select Committee to Investigate the January 6th Attack on the United States Capitol, Transcribed Interview of Pasquale Anthony "Pat" Cipollone, (July 8, 2022), p. 85.

167. Select Committee to Investigate the January 6th Attack on the United States Capitol, Transcribed Interview of Pasquale Anthony "Pat" Cipollone, (July 8, 2022), pp. 85-86.

168. Select Committee to Investigate the January 6th Attack on the United States Capitol, Deposition of Jason Miller, (Feb. 3, 2022), p. 157.

169. Select Committee to Investigate the January 6th Attack on the United States Capitol, Transcribed Interview of Pasquale Anthony "Pat" Cipollone, (July 8, 2022), pp. 86-87.

170. Select Committee to Investigate the January 6th Attack on the United States Capitol, Transcribed Interview of Eric Herschmann, (Apr. 6, 2022), p. 34.

171. Select Committee to Investigate the January 6th Attack on the United States Capitol, Transcribed Interview of Eric Herschmann, (Apr. 6, 2022), p. 26.

172. Select Committee to Investigate the January 6th Attack on the United States Capitol, Transcribed Interview of Pasquale Anthony "Pat" Cipollone, (July 8, 2022), p. 85.

173. Select Committee to Investigate the January 6th Attack on the United States Capitol, Transcribed Interview of Eric Herschmann, (Apr. 6, 2022), p. 40.

174. Maggie Haberman and Annie Karni, "Pence Said to Have Told Trump He Lacks Power to Change Election Result," *New York Times*, (Jan. 5, 2021), available at https://www.nytimes.com/2021/01/05/us/politics/pence-trump-election-results.html.

175. Meredith Lee (@meredithllee), Twitter, Jan. 5, 2021 9:58 p.m. ET, available at https://twitter.com/meredithllee/status/1346652403605647367; Select Committee to Investigate the January 6th Attack on the United States Capitol, Deposition of Jason Miller, (Feb. 3, 2022), p. 174-76; Greg Jacob testified that the President's statement was "categorically untrue." Select Committee to Investigate the January 6th Attack on the United States Capitol, *Hearing on the January 6th Investigation*, 117th Cong., 2d sess., (June 16, 2022), available at https://www.govinfo.gov/committee/house-january6th; Marc Short testified that the statement was "incorrect" and "false." Select Committee to Investigate the January 6th Attack on the United States Capitol, Deposition of Marc Short, (Jan. 26, 2022), p. 224; Chris Hodgson testified that it was not an accurate statement. Select Committee to Investigate the January 6th Attack on the United States Capitol, Deposition of Chris Hodgson, (Mar. 30, 2022), pp. 184-85.

176. Select Committee to Investigate the January 6th Attack on the United States Capitol, Deposition of Jason Miller, (Feb. 3, 2022), pp. 175-77 (acknowledging that Miller normally would have called the Vice President's office before issuing a public statement describing the Vice President's views but stating "I don't think that ultimately -- don't know if it ultimately would have changed anything as the President was very adamant that this is where they both were" and acknowledging that "the way this [statement] came out was the way that [Trump] wanted [it] to.").

177. Donald J. Trump (@realDonaldTrump), Twitter, Jan. 6, 2021 1:00 a.m. ET, available at http://web.archive.org/web/20210106072109/https://twitter.com/realDonaldTrump/status/1346698217304584192 (archived).

178. Donald J. Trump (@realDonaldTrump), Twitter, Jan. 6, 2021 8:17 a.m. ET, available at http://web.archive.org/web/20210106175200/https://twitter.com/realDonaldTrump/status/1346808075626426371 (archived).

179. Select Committee to Investigate the January 6th Attack on the United States Capitol, Transcribed Interview of Eric Herschmann, (Apr. 6, 2022), p. 47; Select Committee to Investigate the January 6th Attack on the United States Capitol, Deposition of Nicholas Luna, (Mar. 21, 2022), p. 126.

180. Select Committee to Investigate the January 6th Attack on the United States Capitol, Deposition of General Keith Kellogg, Jr., (Dec. 14, 2021), p. 90; *See also,* Select Committee to Investigate the January 6th Attack on the United States Capitol, Transcribed Interview of Donald John Trump Jr., (May 3, 2022), p. 84; Select Committee to Investigate the January 6th Attack on the United States Capitol, Transcribed Interview of Eric Herschmann, (Apr. 6, 2022), p. 49; Select Committee to Investigate the January 6th Attack on the United States Capitol, Transcribed Interview of White House Employee, (June 10, 2022), pp. 21-22. The Select Committee is not revealing the identity of this witness to guard against the risk of retaliation.

181. Select Committee to Investigate the January 6th Attack on the United States Capitol, Deposition of Nicholas Luna, (Mar. 21, 2022), p. 127.

182. Select Committee to Investigate the January 6th Attack on the United States Capitol, Transcribed Interview of White House Employee (June 10, 2022), p. 20. The Select Committee is not revealing the identity of this witness to guard against the risk of retaliation.

183. Select Committee to Investigate the January 6th Attack on the United States Capitol, Deposition of General Keith Kellogg, Jr., (Dec. 14, 2021), p. 92.

184. Select Committee to Investigate the January 6th Attack on the United States Capitol, Transcribed Interview of Julie Radford, (May 24, 2022), p. 19. *See also* Peter Baker, Maggie Haberman, and Annie Karni, "Pence Reached His Limit with Trump. It Wasn't Pretty," *New York Times*, (Jan. 12, 2021), available at https://www.nytimes.com/2021/01/12/us/politics/mike-pence-trump.html; Jonathan Karl, *Betrayal: The Final Act of the Trump Show*, (New York: Dutton, 2021), at pp. 273-74.

185. At 11:33 a.m., Stephen Miller's assistant, Robert Gabriel, emailed the speechwriting team with the line: "REINSERT THE MIKE PENCE LINES." Documents on file with the Select Committee to Investigate the January 6th Attack on the United States Capitol (National Archives Production), 076P-R000007531_0001 (January 6, 2021, Robert Gabriel email to Trump speechwriting team at 11:33 a.m.).

186. Select Committee to Investigate the January 6th Attack on the United States Capitol, Deposition of Stephen Miller (Apr. 14, 2022), p. 153.

187. Document on file with the Select Committee (Ross Worthington Production), RW_0002341-2351 (S. Miller Jan. 6 Speech Edits Native File), pp. 2-3.

188. "Transcript of Trump's Speech at Rally Before US Capitol Riot," *Associated Press*, (Jan. 13, 2021), available at https://apnews.com/article/election-2020-joe-biden-donald-trump-capitol-siege-media-e79eb5164613d6718e9f4502eb471f27; Documents on file with the Select Committee to Investigate the January 6th Attack on the United States Capitol (Ross Worthington Production), CTRL0000924249, (changes in speech between draft and as delivered), pp. 2, 5, 12, 16, 22.

189. "Transcript of Trump's Speech at Rally Before US Capitol Riot," *Associated Press*, (Jan. 13, 2021), available at https://apnews.com/article/election-2020-joe-biden-donald-trump-capitol-siege-media-e79eb5164613d6718e9f4502eb471f27.

190. "Transcript of Trump's Speech at Rally Before US Capitol Riot," *Associated Press*, (Jan. 13, 2021), available at https://apnews.com/article/election-2020-joe-biden-donald-trump-capitol-siege-media-e79eb5164613d6718e9f4502eb471f27.

191. "Transcript of Trump's Speech at Rally Before US Capitol Riot," *Associated Press*, (Jan. 13, 2021), available at https://apnews.com/article/election-2020-joe-biden-donald-trump-capitol-siege-media-e79eb5164613d6718e9f4502eb471f27.

192. Select Committee to Investigate the January 6th Attack on the United States Capitol, *Hearing on the January 6th Investigation*, 117th Cong., 2d sess., (June 16, 2022), at 0:14:11-0:14:29, available at https://youtu.be/vBjUWVKuDj0?t=851.

193. Select Committee to Investigate the January 6th Attack on the United States Capitol, *Hearing on the January 6th Investigation*, 117th Cong., 2d sess., (June 16, 2022), at 2:07:02-2:07:07, available at https://youtu.be/vBjUWVKuDj0?t=7609.

194. Select Committee to Investigate the January 6th Attack on the United States Capitol, *Hearing on the January 6th Investigation*, 117th Cong., 2d sess., (June 16, 2022), at 2:07:02-2:07:07, available at https://youtu.be/vBjUWVKuDj0?t=7609.

195. Select Committee to Investigate the January 6th Attack on the United States Capitol, *Hearing on the January 6th Investigation*, 117th Cong., 2d sess., (July 21, 2022), at 1:00:46-1:01:12, available at https://youtu.be/pbRVqWbHGuo?t=3645.

196. Select Committee to Investigate the January 6th Attack on the United States Capitol, *Hearing on the January 6th Investigation*, 117th Cong., 2d sess., (July 21, 2022), at 1:01:13-1:01:26, available at https://youtu.be/pbRVqWbHGuo?t=3645.

197. Select Committee to Investigate the January 6th Attack on the United States Capitol, *Hearing on the January 6th Investigation*, 117th Cong., 2d sess., (June 16, 2022), at 0:14:37-0:14:46, available at https://youtu.be/vBjUWVKuDj0?t=851.

198. Select Committee to Investigate the January 6th Attack on the United States Capitol, *Hearing on the January 6th Investigation*, 117th Cong., 2d sess., (June 16, 2022), at 0:14:47-0:14:55, available at https://youtu.be/vBjUWVKuDj0?t=851.

199. Select Committee to Investigate the January 6th Attack on the United States Capitol, Transcribed Interview of White House Employee, (June 10, 2022), pp. 26-27 (establishing time as 1:21 p.m. based on time stamp of a photograph recognized and described).

200. Donald J. Trump (@realDonaldTrump), Twitter, Jan. 6, 2021 2:24 p.m. ET, available at https://web.archive.org/web/20210106192450/https://twitter.com/realdonaldtrump/status/1346900434540240897 (archived).

201. Government's Sentencing Memorandum at 32-33, *United States v. Cusanelli*, No. 1:21-cr-37 (D.D.C. Sept. 15, 2022), ECF No. 110.

202. *See* Affidavit in Support of Criminal Complaint and Arrest Warrant at 5, *United States v. Black*, No. 1:21-cr-127 (D.D.C. Jan. 13, 2021), ECF No. 1-1, available at https://www.justice.gov/opa/page/file/1354806/download.

203. Indictment at 9, *United States v. Neefe*, No. 1:21-cr-567 (D.D.C. Sept. 8, 2021), ECF No. 1, available at https://www.justice.gov/usao-dc/case-multi-defendant/file/1432686/download.

204. Affidavit in Support of Criminal Complaint and Arrest Warrant at 8, *United States v. Evans*, No. 1:21-cr-337 (D.D.C. Jan. 8, 2021), ECF No. 1-1, available at https://www.justice.gov/usao-dc/press-release/file/1351946/download.

205. Select Committee to Investigate the January 6th Attack on the United States Capitol, *Business Meeting on the January 6th Investigation*, 117th Cong., 2d sess., (Oct. 13, 2022), at 2:26:06-2:26:26, available at https://youtu.be/IQvuBoLBuC0?t=8766; Sentencing Transcript at 19, United States v. Yo*ung, No. 1:21-cr-291* (D.D.C. Sept. 27, 2022), ECF No. 170 (testifying for a victim impact statement, Officer Michael Fanone said: "At approximately 1435 hours, with rapidly mounting injuries and most of the MPD less than lethal munitions expended, the defending officers were forced to conduct a fighting withdrawal back towards the United States Capitol Building entrance. This is the first fighting withdrawal in the history of the Metropolitan Police Department").

206. *See* Transcript of Trump's Speech at Rally Before US Capitol Riot," *Associated Press*, (Jan. 13, 2021), available at https://apnews.com/article/election-2020-joe-biden-donald-trump-capitol-siege-media-e79eb5164613d6718e9f4502eb471f27.

207. United States Secret Service Radio Tango Frequency at 14:16.

208. United States Secret Service Radio Tango Frequency at 14:25; *see also* Spencer S. Hsu, "Pence Spent Jan. 6 at Underground Senate Loading Dock, Secret Service Confirms," *Washington Post*, (Mar. 21, 2022), available at https://www.washingtonpost.com/dc-md-va/2022/03/21/couy-griffin-cowboys-trump-jan6/.

209. Select Committee to Investigate the January 6th Attack on the United States Capitol, *Hearing on the January 6th Investigation*, 117th Cong., 2d sess., (June 16, 2022), at 2:11:22-2:13:55, available at https://youtu.be/vBjUWVKuDj0?t=7882.

210. Select Committee to Investigate the January 6th Attack on the United States Capitol, Transcribed Interview of Eric Herschmann, (Apr. 6, 2022), pp. 43-44.

211. Select Committee to Investigate the January 6th Attack on the United States Capitol, Transcribed Interview of Eric Herschmann, (Apr. 6, 2022), p. 44.

212. Complaint, Exhibit 2 (Select Committee to Investigate the January 6th Attack on the United States Capitol subpoena to Chapman University, dated Jan. 21, 2022), *Eastman v. Thompson et al. et al.*, No. 8:22-cv-99, (C.D. Cal. Jan. 20, 2022) ECF No. 1-2.

213. Order Re Privilege of Documents Dated January 4-7, 2021 at 51-52, Eastman v. Thompson et al., 594 F. Supp. 3d 1156, (C.D. Cal. Mar. 28, 2022) (No. 8:22-cv-99-DOC-DFM).

214. Order Re Privilege of Documents Dated January 4-7, 2021 at 56-57, Eastman v. Thompson et al., 594 F. Supp. 3d 1156 (C.D. Cal. Mar. 28, 2022) (No. 8:22-cv-99-DOC-DFM).

215. Order Re Privilege of Documents Dated January 4-7, 2021 at 63-64, Eastman v. Thompson et al., 594 F. Supp. 3d 1156 (C.D. Cal. Mar. 28, 2022) (No. 8:22-cv-99-DOC-DFM).

216. Select Committee to Investigate the January 6th Attack on the United States Capitol, *Hearing on the January 6th Investigation*, 117th Cong., 2d sess., (June 16, 2022), available at https://www.govinfo.gov/committee/house-january6th.

217. Select Committee to Investigate the January 6th Attack on the United States Capitol, Deposition of Greg Jacob, (Feb. 1, 2022), p. 223.

218. Select Committee to Investigate the January 6th Attack on the U.S. Capitol, Transcribed Interview of Ronna Romney McDaniel, (June 1, 2022), pp. 7-8.

219. Select Committee to Investigate the January 6th Attack on the U.S. Capitol, Transcribed Interview of Ronna Romney McDaniel, (June 1, 2022), pp. 9-11.

220. On December 13th, Chesebro memorialized the strategy in an email he sent Rudy Giuliani with the subject line: "PRIVILEGED AND CONFIDENTIAL – Brief notes on 'President of the Senate strategy." Documents on file with the Select Committee to Investigate the January 6th Attack on the United States Capitol (Chapman UniversityProduction), Chapman004708 (Dec. 13, 2020, Kenneth Chesebro email to Rudy Giuliani). Chesebro argued that the Trump team could use the fake slates of electors to complicate the joint session on January 6th if the President of the Senate "firmly t[ook] the position that he, and he alone, is charged with the constitutional responsibility not just to open the votes, but to count them— including making judgments about what to do if thereare conflicting votes." *Id.* In the weeks that followed, Chesebro and John Eastman would build upon that framework and write two memos asserting that Joe Biden's certification could be derailed on January 6th if Vice President Pence acted as the "ultimate arbiter" when opening the real and fake Electoral College votes during the joint session of Congress. Documents on file with the Select Committee to Investigate the January 6th Attack on the United States Capitol (Chapman University Production), Chapman053476 (December 23, 2020, Eastman memo titled "PRIVILEGED AND CONFIDENTIAL – Dec 23 memo on Jan 6 scenario.docx"); *see also* Documents on file with the Select Committee to Investigate the January 6th Attack on the United States Capitol (Chapman University Production), Chapman061863 (January 1, 2021, Chesebro email to Eastman).

221. Select Committee to Investigate the January 6th Attack on the U.S. Capitol, Transcribed Interview of Justin Clark, (May 17, 2022), pp. 114, 116.

222. Select Committee to Investigate the January 6th Attack on the U.S. Capitol, Transcribed Interview of Justin Clark, (May 17, 2022), pp. 116.

223. The "certificate of ascertainment" is a State executive's official documentation announcing the official electors appointed pursuant to State law. *See* 3 U.S.C. § 6.

224. Select Committee to Investigate the January 6th Attack on the U.S. Capitol, Transcribed Interview of Matthew Morgan, (Apr. 25, 2022), p. 70.

225. Select Committee to Investigate the January 6th Attack on the U.S. Capitol, Transcribed Interview of Pasquale Anthony "Pat" Cipollone (July 8, 2022), pp. 70-72.

226. Select Committee to Investigate the January 6th Attack on the U.S. Capitol, Informal Interview of Patrick Philbin (Apr. 13, 2022).

227. Select Committee to Investigate the January 6th Attack on the U.S. Capitol, Transcribed Interview of Pasquale Anthony "Pat" Cipollone (July 8, 2022), p. 75.

228. Select Committee to Investigate the January 6th Attack on the United States Capitol, Continued Interview of Cassidy Hutchinson, (Mar. 7, 2022), p. 64.

229. Select Committee to Investigate the January 6th Attack on the United States Capitol, Deposition of Shawn Still, (Feb. 25, 2022), p. 24.

230. Select Committee to Investigate the January 6th Attack on the United States Capitol, Deposition of Andrew Hitt, (Feb. 28, 2022), pp. 50–51.

231. The National Archives produced copies of the seven slates of electoral votes they received from Trump electors in States that President Trump lost. *See* Documents on file with the Select Committee to Investigate the January 6th Attack on the United States Capitol (National Archives Production), CTRL0000037568, CTRL0000037944, CTRL0000037945, CTRL0000037946, CTRL0000037947, CTRL0000037948, CTRL0000037949 (December 14, 2020, memoranda from slates of purported electors in Arizona, Georgia, Michigan, New Mexico, Nevada, Pennsylvania, and Wisconsin); Documents on file with the Select Committee to Investigate the January 6th Attack on the United States Capitol (National Archives Production), VP-R0000323_0001 (Senate Parliamentarian office tracking receipt and attaching copies of the seven slates); *See also* Documents on file with the Select Committee to Investigate the January 6th Attack on the United States Capitol (Robert Sinners Production), CTRL0000083893 (Trump campaign staffers emailing regarding submission); Documents on file with the Select Committee to Investigate the January 6th Attack on the United States Capitol (Bill Stepien Production), WS 00096 – WS 00097 (Trump campaign staffers emailing regarding submission).

232. Documents on file with the Select Committee to Investigate the January 6th Attack on the United States Capitol (David Shafer Production), 108751.0001 000004 (December 10, 2020, Kenneth Chesebro email to David Shafer).

233. Documents on file with the Select Committee to Investigate the January 6th Attack on the United States Capitol (National Archives Production), CTRL0000037944 (December 14, 2020, certificate and mailing envelope from Georgia); Documents on file with the Select Committee to Investigate the January 6th Attack on the United States Capitol (National Archives Production), CTRL0000037941 (December 14, 2020, certificate and mailing envelope from Arizona), Documents on file with the Select Committee to Investigate the January 6th Attack on the United States Capitol (National Archives Production), CTRL0000037945 (December 14, 2020, certificate and mailing envelope from Michigan).

234. Documents on file with the Select Committee to Investigate the January 6th Attack on the United States Capitol (Andrew Hitt Production), Hitt000080 (January 4, 2021, Hitt text message with Mark Jefferson); Documents on file with the Select Committee to Investigate the January 6th Attack on the United States Capitol (Angela McCallum Production), McCallum_01_001576 - McCallum_01_001577 (January 5, 2021, McCallum text messages with G. Michael Brown); Documents on file with the Select Committee to Investigate the January 6th Attack on the United States Capitol (Chris Hodgson Production) CTRL0000056548_00007 (January 6, 2021, Hodgson text messages with Matt Stroia); Documents on file with the Select Committee to Investigate the January 6th Attack on the United States Capitol (Chris Hodgson Production), CTRL0000056548_00035 (January 6, 2021, text messages from Senator Johnson's Chief of Staff, Sean Riley, to Chris Hodgson around 12:37 p.m.).

235. Select Committee to Investigate the January 6th Attack on the United States Capitol, Deposition of Chris Hodgson (Mar. 30, 2022), pp. 206–07; Documents on file with the Select Committee to Investigate the January 6th Attack on the United States Capitol (Chris Hodgson Production) CTRL0000056548_00007 (January 6, 2021, text message from Rep. Kelly's Chief of Staff, Matt Stroia, to Chris Hodgson at 8:41 a.m.), CTRL0000056548_00035 (January 6, 2021, text messages from Senator Johnson's Chief of Staff, Sean Riley, to Chris Hodgson around 12:37 p.m.); Jason Lennon, "Johnson Says Involvement with 1/6 Fake Electors Plan Only 'Lasted Seconds'," *Newsweek*, (Aug. 21, 2022), available at https://www.newsweek.com/johnson-says-involvement-1-6-fake-electors-plan-only-lasted-seconds-1735486.

236. Select Committee to Investigate the January 6th Attack on the United States Capitol, Deposition of Greg Jacob, (Feb. 1, 2022), pp. 52–54.

237. Order Re Privilege of 599 Documents Dated November 3, 2020 - January 20, 2021 at 6, *Eastman v. Thompson et al.*, No. 8:22-cv-99 (C.D. Cal June 7, 2022), ECF No. 356.

238. Order Re Privilege of 599 Documents Dated November 3, 2020 - January 20, 2021 at 20, *Eastman v. Thompson et al.*., No. 8:22-cv-99 (C.D. Cal June 7, 2022), ECF No. 356.

239. Brad Raffensperger, *Integrity Counts* (New York: Simon & Schuster, 2021), p. 191 (reproducing the call transcript); Amy Gardner and Paulina Firozi, "Here's the Full Transcript and Audio of the Call Between Trump and Raffensperger," *Washington Post*, (Jan. 5, 2021), available at https://www.washingtonpost.com/politics/trump-raffensperger-call-transcript-georgia-vote/2021/01/03/2768e0cc-4ddd-11eb-83e3-322644d82356_story.html.

240. Order Re Privilege of Documents Dated January 4-7, 2021 at 5, *Eastman v. Thompson et al.*, 594 F. Supp. 3d 1156 (C.D. Cal. Mar. 28, 2022) (No. 8:22-cv-99-DOC-DFM), also available at https://www.cacd.uscourts.gov/sites/default/files/documents/Dkt%20260%2C%20Order%20RE%20Privilege%20of%20Jan.%204-7%2C%202021%20Documents_0.pdf. .

241. Order Re Privilege of Documents Dated January 4-7, 2021 at 35, *Eastman v. Thompson et al.*, 594 F. Supp. 3d 1156 (C.D. Cal. Mar. 28, 2022) (No. 8:22-cv-99-DOC-DFM), also available at https://www.cacd.uscourts.gov/sites/default/files/documents/Dkt%20260%2C%20Order%20RE%20Privilege%20of%20Jan.%204-7%2C%202021%20Documents_0.pdf.

242. After a journalist tweeted a video clip of key remarks from Gabriel Sterling's warning addressed to President Trump, President Trump responded by quote-tweeting that post, along with a comment that doubled down on demonizing Georgia election workers in spite of Sterling's stark and detailed warning. *See* Donald J. Trump (@realDonaldTrump), Twitter, Dec. 1, 2020 10:27 p.m. ET, available at http://web.archive.org/web/20201203173245/https://mobile.twitter.com/realDonaldTrump/status/1333975991518187521 (archived) ("Rigged Election. Show signatures and envelopes. Expose the massive voter fraud in Georgia. What is Secretary of State and @BrianKempGA afraid of. They know what we'll find!!! [linking to] twitter.com/BrendanKeefe/status/1333884246277189633"); Brendan Keefe (@BrendanKeefe), Twitter, Dec. 1, 2020 4:22 p.m. ET, available at https://twitter.com/BrendanKeefe/status/1333884246277189633 (""It. Has. All. Gone. Too. Far," says @GabrielSterling with Georgia Sec of State after a Dominion tech's life was threatened with a noose. "Mr. President, you have not condemned these actions or this language….all of you who have not said a damn word are complicit in this."" with embedded video of Gabriel Sterling's remarks); Select Committee to Investigate the January 6th Attack on the United States Capitol, *Hearing on the January 6th Investigation*, 117th Cong., 2d sess., (June 21, 2022), available at https://www.govinfo.gov/committee/house-january6th.

243. Stephen Fowler, "'Someone's Going to Get Killed': Election Official Blasts GOP Silence on Threats," GPB News, (Dec. 1, 2020, updated Dec. 2, 2020), available at https://www.gpb.org/news/2020/12/01/someones-going-get-killed-election-official-blasts-gop-silence-on-threats.

244. House Governmental Affairs Committee, Georgia House of Representatives, Public Hearing (Dec. 10, 2020), YouTube, at 1:55:10-1:59:10, available at https://youtu.be/9EfgETUKfsl?t=6910.

245. Select Committee to Investigate the January 6th Attack on the United States Capitol, *Hearing on the January 6th Investigation*, 117th Cong., 2d sess., (June 21, 2022), at 2:25:45 to 2:26:00, available at https://youtu.be/xa43_z_82Og?t=8745.

246. Jason Szep and Linda So, "A Reuters Special Report: Trump Campaign Demonized Two Georgia Election Workers – and Death Threats Followed," *Reuters* (Dec. 1, 2021), available at https://www.reuters.com/investigates/special-report/usa-election-threats-georgia/.

247. Amended Complaint at 52, *Freeman v. Giuliani*, No. 21-cv-03354-BAH (D.D.C. filed May 10, 2022), ECF No. 22, available at https://www.courtlistener.com/docket/61642105/22/freeman-v-herring-networks-inc.

248. Select Committee to Investigate the January 6th Attack on the United States Capitol, Transcribed Interview of Ruby Freeman, (May 31, 2022), pp. 7-8.

249. Select Committee to Investigate the January 6th Attack on the United States Capitol, *Hearing on the January 6th Investigation*, 117th Cong., 2d sess., (June 21, 2022), at 41:30-46:35, available at https://www.youtube.com/watch?v=xa43_z_82Og; Yvonne Wingett Sanchez and Ronald J. Hansen, "White House Phone Calls, Baseless Fraud Charges: The Origins of the Arizona Election Review," *Arizona Republic*, (Nov. 17, 2021), available at https://www.azcentral.com/in-depth/news/politics/elections/2021/11/17/arizona-audit-trump-allies-pushed-to-undermine-2020-election/6045151001/; Yvonne Wingett Sanchez and Ronald J. Hansen, "'Asked to do Something Huge': An Audacious Pitch to Reserve Arizona's Election Results," *Arizona Republic*, (Nov. 18, 2021, updated Dec. 2, 2021), available at https://www.azcentral.com/in-depth/news/politics/elections/2021/11/18/arizona-audit-rudy-giuliani-failed-effort-replace-electors/6349795001/.

250. Select Committee to Investigate the January 6th Attack on the United States Capitol, *Hearing on the January 6th Investigation*, 117th Cong., 2d sess., (June 21, 2022), at 53:00-53:40, available at https://www.youtube.com/watch?v=xa43_z_82Og.

251. Select Committee to Investigate the January 6th Attack on the United States Capitol, *Hearing on the January 6th Investigation*, 117th Cong., 2d sess., (June 21, 2022), at 41:30-46:35, available at https://www.youtube.com/watch?v=xa43_z_82Og.

252. Dennis Welch (@dennis_welch), Twitter, Dec. 8, 2020 11:23 p.m. ET, available at https://twitter.com/dennis_welch/status/1336526978640302080 (retweeting people who were posting Bowers's personal information); Dennis Welch (@dennis_welch), Twitter, Dec. 8, 2020 11:28 p.m. ET, available at https://twitter.com/dennis_welch/status/1336528029791604737.

253. Select Committee to Investigate the January 6th Attack on the U.S. Capitol, Transcribed Interview of Russel "Rusty" Bowers, (June 19, 2022), pp. 50-52; Kelly Weill, "Arizona GOP Civil War Somehow Keeps Getting Weirder," *Daily Beast*, (Dec. 11, 2020), available at https://www.thedailybeast.com/arizona-republican-party-civil-war-somehow-keeps-getting-weirder; Yvonne Wingett Sanchez and Ronald J. Hansen, "'Asked to do Something Huge': An Audacious Pitch to Reserve Arizona's Election Results," *Arizona Republic*, (Nov. 18, 2021, updated Dec. 2, 2021), available at https://www.azcentral.com/in-depth/news/politics/elections/2021/11/18/arizona-audit-rudy-giuliani-failed-effort-replace-electors/6349795001/.

254. Select Committee to Investigate the January 6th Attack on the United States Capitol, *Hearing on the January 6th Investigation*, 117th Cong., 2d sess., (June 21, 2022), available at https://www.govinfo.gov/committee/house-january6th.

255. Select Committee to Investigate the January 6th Attack on the United States Capitol, Transcribed Interview of Michael Shirkey, (June 8, 2022), pp. 16-22.

256. Select Committee to Investigate the January 6th Attack on the United States Capitol, Informal Interview of Lee Chatfield, (Oct. 15, 2021).

257. Select Committee to Investigate the January 6th Attack on the United States Capitol, Transcribed Interview of Michael Shirkey, (June 8, 2022), p. 57.

258. "Legislative Leaders Meet with President Trump," State Senator Mike Shirkey, (Nov. 20, 2020), available at https://www.senatormikeshirkey.com/legislative-leaders-meet-with-president-trump/.

259. Team Trump (Text TRUMP to 88022) (@TeamTrump), Twitter, Jan. 3, 2021 9:00 a.m. ET, available at http://web.archive.org/web/20210103170109/https://twitter.com/TeamTrump/status/1345776940196659201 (archived); Beth LeBlanc, "Trump Campaign Lists Lawmakers' Cells, Misdirects Calls for Chatfield to Former Petoskey Resident," *Detroit News*, (Jan. 4, 2021), available at https://www.detroitnews.com/story/news/politics/2021/01/04/trump-campaign-lists-michigan-lawmakers-cell-numbers-misdirects-private-citizen/4130279001/; Jaclyn Peiser, "Trump Shared the Wrong Number for a Michigan Lawmaker: A 28-Year-Old Has Gotten Thousands of Angry Calls," *Washington Post*, (Jan. 5, 2021), available at https://www.washingtonpost.com/nation/2021/01/05/michigan-trump-wrong-number-chatfield/.

260. Select Committee to Investigate the January 6th Attack on the United States Capitol, Transcribed Interview of Michael Shirkey, (June 8, 2022), p. 52; Aaron Parseghian, "Former Michigan Resident Slammed with Calls After Trump Campaign Mistakenly Posts Number on Social Media," Fox 17 West Michigan, (Jan. 4, 2021), available at https://www.fox17online.com/news/politics/former-michigan-resident-slammed-with-calls-after-trump-campaign-mistakenly-posts-number-on-social-media.

261. Nor would any State legislature have had such authority.

262. Order Re Privilege of Remaining Documents at 16-17, *Eastman v. Thompson et al..*, No. 8:22-cv-99 (C.D. Cal Oct. 19, 2022), ECF No. 372, available at https://www.cacd.uscourts.gov/sites/default/files/documents/Dkt.%20372%2C%20Order%20Re%20Privilege%20of%20Remaining%20Documents.pdf.

263. Documents on file with the Select Committee to Investigate the January 6th Attack on the United States Capitol (Chapman University Production), Chapman060742, (December 31, 2020, from John Eastman to Alex Kaufman and Kurt Hilbert)

264. Documents on file with the Select Committee to Investigate the January 6th Attack on the United States Capitol (Chapman University Production), Chapman060742, (December 31, 2020, from John Eastman to Alex Kaufman and Kurt Hilbert).

265. Order Re Privilege of Remaining Documents at 17, *Eastman v. Thompson et al.*, No. 8:22-cv-99 (C.D. Cal Oct. 19, 2022), ECF No. 372, available at https://www.cacd.uscourts.gov/sites/default/files/documents/Dkt.%20372%2C%20Order%20Re%20Privilege%20of%20Remaining%20Documents.pdf..

266. Order Re Privilege of Remaining Documents at 17, *Eastman v. Thompson et al.*, No. 8:22-cv-099 (C.D. Cal Oct. 19, 2022), ECF No. 372, available at https://www.cacd.uscourts.gov/sites/default/files/documents/Dkt.%20372%2C%20Order%20Re%20Privilege%20of%20Remaining%20Documents.pdf.

267. Select Committee to Investigate the January 6th Attack on the United States Capitol, *Hearing on the January 6th Investigation*, 117th Cong., 2d sess., (June 23, 2022), available at https://www.govinfo.gov/committee/house-january6th.

268. Select Committee to Investigate the January 6th Attack on the United States Capitol, Transcribed Interview of Richard Peter Donoghue, (Oct. 1, 2021), p. 53.

269. Select Committee to Investigate the January 6th Attack on the United States Capitol, Transcribed Interview of Richard Peter Donoghue, (Oct. 1, 2021), pp. 47-48, 53; Select Committee to Investigate the January 6th Attack on the United States Capitol, *Hearing on the January 6th Investigation*, 117th Cong., 2d sess., (June 23, 2022), available at https://www.govinfo.gov/committee/house-january6th.

270. Select Committee to Investigate the January 6th Attack on the United States Capitol, *Hearing on the January 6th Investigation*, 117th Cong., 2d sess., (June 23, 2022), available at https://www.govinfo.gov/committee/house-january6th.

271. Select Committee to Investigate the January 6th Attack on the United States Capitol, *Hearing on the January 6th Investigation*, 117th Cong., 2d sess., (June 23, 2022), available at https://www.govinfo.gov/committee/house-january6th.

272. Select Committee to Investigate the January 6th Attack on the United States Capitol, *Hearing on the January 6th Investigation*, 117th Cong., 2d sess., (June 23, 2022), available at https://www.govinfo.gov/committee/house-january6th.

273. Select Committee to Investigate the January 6th Attack on the United States Capitol, *Hearing on the January 6th Investigation*, 117th Cong., 2d sess., (June 23, 2022), available at https://www.govinfo.gov/committee/house-january6th .

274. Select Committee to Investigate the January 6th Attack on the United States Capitol, Transcribed Interview of Richard Peter Donoghue, (Oct. 1, 2021), p. 58; Documents on file with the Select Committee to Investigate the January 6th Attack on the United States Capitol (Department of Justice Production), HCOR-Pre-Certification-Events-07282021-000738, HCOR-Pre-Certification-Events-07282021-000739 (December 27, 2020, handwritten notes from Richard Donoghue about call with President Trump).

275. Select Committee to Investigate the January 6th Attack on the United States Capitol, Transcribed Interview of Richard Peter Donoghue, (Oct. 1, 2021), p. 59.

276. Select Committee to Investigate the January 6th Attack on the United States Capitol, Transcribed Interview of Richard Peter Donoghue, (Oct. 1, 2021), p. 59.

277. Documents on file with the Select Committee to Investigate the January 6th Attack on the United States Capitol (Mark Meadows Production), MM014099 (December 26, 2020, message from Representative Perry to Meadows stating: "Mark, just checking in as time continues to count down. 11 days to 1/6 and 25 days to inauguration. We gotta get going!"), MM014100 (December 26, 2020, message from Representative Perry to Meadows stating: "Mark, you should call Jeff. I just got off the phone with him and he explained to me why the principal deputy won't work especially with the FBI. They will view it as as [sic] not having the authority to enforce what needs to be done."), MM014101 (Dec. 26, 2020 Message from Meadows to Rep. Perry stating: "I got it. I think I understand. Let me work on the deputy position"), MM014102 (Dec. 26, 2020 Message from Rep. Perry to Meadows stating: "Roger. Just sent you something on Signal"), MM014162 (December 27, 2020, message from Rep. Perry to Meadows stating: "Can you call me when you get a chance? I just want to talk to you for a few moments before I return the presidents [sic] call as requested."), MM014178 (December 28, 2020, message from Rep. Perry to Meadows stating: "Did you call Jeff Clark?"), MM014208 (December 29, 2020, message from Representative Perry to Meadows stating: "Mark, I sent you a note on signal"), MM014586 (January 2, 2021, message from Representative Perry to Meadows stating: "Please call me the instant you get off the phone with Jeff."). President Trump, Mark Meadows, and Representative Perry refused to testify before the Select Committee, and Jeffrey Clark asserted his Fifth Amendment rights in refusing to answer questions from the Select Committee. "Thompson & Cheney Statement on Donald Trump's Defiance of Select Committee Subpoena," Select Committee to Investigate the January 6th Attack on the United States Capitol, (Nov. 14, 2022), available at https://january6th.house.gov/news/press-releases/thompson-cheney-statement-donald-trump-s-defiance-select-committee-subpoena; Luke Broadwater, "Trump Sues to Block Subpoena from Jan. 6 Committee," *New York Times*, (Nov. 11, 2022), available at https://www.nytimes.com/2022/11/11/us/politics/trump-subpoena-jan-6-committee.html; H. Rept. 117-216, Resolution Recommending that the House of Representatives Find Mark Randall Meadows in Contempt of Congress for Refusal to Comply with a Subpoena Duly Issued by the Select Committee to Investigate the January 6th Attack on the United States Capitol, 117th Cong., 1st Sess. (2021), available at https://www.congress.gov/117/crpt/hrpt216/CRPT-117hrpt216.pdf; Letter from John P. Rowley III to the Honorable Bennie G. Thompson, re: Subpoena to Representative Scott Perry, May 24, 2022, available at https://keystonenewsroom.com/wp-content/uploads/sites/6/2022/05/575876667-Rep-perry-Ltr-SelectComm.pdf; Select Committee to Investigate the January 6th Attack on the United States Capitol, Deposition of Jeffrey Clark, (Nov. 5, 2021); Select Committee to Investigate the January 6th Attack on the United States Capitol, Continued Deposition of Jeffrey Clark, (Feb. 2, 2022). See also Jonathan Tamari and Chris Brennan, "Pa. Congressman Scott Perry Acknowledges Introducing Trump to Lawyer at the Center of Election Plot," *Philadelphia Inquirer*, (Jan. 25, 2021), available at https://www.inquirer.com/politics/pennsylvania/scott-perry-trump-georgia-election-results-20210125.html .

278. Documents on file with the Select Committee to Investigate the January 6th Attack on the United States Capitol (Mark Meadows Production), MM014099-014103, MM014178.

279. Select Committee to Investigate the January 6th Attack on the United States Capitol, Transcribed Interview of Jeffrey Rosen, (Oct. 13, 2021), pp. 54-55.

280. Select Committee to Investigate the January 6th Attack at the United States Capitol, Transcribed Interview of Jeffrey Rosen, (Oct. 13, 2021), p. 55.

281. Select Committee to Investigate the January 6th Attack at the United States Capitol, Transcribed Interview of Jeffrey Rosen, (Oct. 13, 2021), p. 56.

282. Select Committee to Investigate the January 6th Attack on the United States Capitol, Transcribed Interview of Richard Peter Donoghue, (Oct. 1, 2021), p. 114; Documents on file with the Select Committee to Investigate the January 6th Attack on the United States Capitol (Department of Justice Production), HCOR-Pre-CertificationEvents-07262021-000681 (Department of Justice policy), HCOR-Pre-CertificationEvents-07262021-000685 (White House policy).

283. Select Committee to Investigate the January 6th Attack at the United States Capitol, Transcribed Interview of Jeffrey Rosen, (Oct. 13, 2021), p. 56.

284. Select Committee to Investigate the January 6th Attack on the United States Capitol, Transcribed Interview of Richard Peter Donoghue, (Oct. 1, 2021), p. 82.

285. Select Committee to Investigate the January 6th Attack on the United States Capitol, Transcribed Interview of Richard Peter Donoghue, (Oct. 1, 2021), pp. 72-73; Documents on file with the Select Committee to Investigate the January 6th Attack on the United States Capitol (Department of Justice Production), HCOR-Pre-CertificationEvents-07262021-000698, (December 27, 2020, handwritten notes from Richard Donoghue about call with Congressman Perry).

286. Select Committee to Investigate the January 6th Attack on the United States Capitol, Deposition of Kenneth Klukowski, (Dec. 15, 2021), pp. 15-17, 64-80, 179-191; Documents on file with the Select Committee to Investigate the January 6th Attack on the United States Capitol (Department of Justice Production), HCOR-Pre-CertificationEvents-07262021-000697, HCOR-Pre-CertificationEvents-07262021-000698 (email with draft letter attached to December 28, 2020, email from Jeffrey Clark to Jeffrey Rosen and Richard Donoghue).

287. Select Committee to Investigate the January 6th Attack on the United States Capitol, Deposition of Kenneth Klukowski, (Dec. 15, 2021), pp. 184-88; Documents on file with the Select Committee to Investigate the January 6th Attack on the United States Capitol (Department of Justice Production), HCOR-Pre-CertificationEvents-07262021-000697, HCOR-Pre-CertificationEvents-07262021-000698 (email with draft letter attached to Dec. 28 email from Jeffrey Clark to Jeffrey Rosen and Richard Donoghue). As further discussed in Chapter 4 of this report, Klukowski, a lawyer, joined DOJ's Civil Division with just weeks remaining in President Trump's term and helped Clark on issues related to the 2020 election, despite the fact that "election-related matters are not part of the Civil portfolio." Select Committee to Investigate the January 6th Attack on the United States Capitol, Deposition of Kenneth Klukowski (Dec. 15, 2021), p. 66-67. Although Klukowski told the Select Committee that the Trump Campaign was his client before joining DOJ, *id.* at p. 190, and despite the fact that he had sent John Eastman draft talking points titled "TRUMP RE-ELECTION" that encouraged Republican State legislatures to "summon" new Electoral College electors for the 2020 election less than a week before starting at DOJ, Klukowski nevertheless helped Clark draft the December 28th letter described in this Report that, if sent, would have encouraged one or more State legislatures to take actions that could have changed the outcome of the 2020 election. *See* Documents on file with the Select Committee to Investigate the January 6th Attack on the United States Capitol (Chapman University Production), Chapman028219, Chapman028220 (December 9, 2020, email from Klukowski to Eastman with attached memo). The Select Committee has concerns about whether Klukowski's actions at DOJ, and his continued contacts with those working for, or to benefit, the Trump Campaign, may have presented a conflict of interest to the detriment of DOJ's mission. In addition, the Select Committee has concerns about many of the "privilege" claims Klukowski used to withhold information responsive to his subpoena, as well as concerns about some of his testimony, including his testimony about contacts with, among others,

John Eastman. The Committee has learned that their communications included at least four known calls between December 22, 2020, and January 2, 2021. Documents on file with the Select Committee to Investigate the January 6th Attack on the United States Capitol (Verizon Production, July 1, 2022) (showing that Klukowski called Eastman on 12/22 at 7:38 a.m. EST for 22.8 min, that Klukowski called Eastman on 12/22 at 7:09 p.m. EST for 6.4 min, that Eastman called Klukowski on 12/30 at 9:11 p.m. EST for 31.9 min, and that Klukowski called Eastman on 1/02 at 6:59 p.m. EST for 6.4 min).

288. Documents on file with the Select Committee to Investigate the January 6th Attack on the United States Capitol (Chapman University Production), Chapman061893 (Jan. 1, 2021, emails between Jeffrey Clark and John Eastman); see Documents on file with the Select Committee to Investigate the January 6th Attack on the United States Capitol (Verizon Production, July 1, 2022) (showing five calls between John Eastman and Jeffrey Clark from January 1, 2021, through January 8, 2021).

289. Documents on file with the Select Committee to Investigate the January 6th Attack on the United States Capitol (Department of Justice Production), HCOR-Pre-CertificationEvents-07262021-000697 (Dec. 28 email from Jeffrey Clark to Jeffrey Rosen and Richard Donoghue titled "Two Urgent Action Items") ("The concept is to send it to the Governor, Speaker, and President pro temp of each relevant state..."); Select Committee to Investigate the January 6th Attack on the United States Capitol, Deposition of Kenneth Klukowski, (Dec. 15, 2021), pp. 68-69, 79.

290. Documents on file with the Select Committee to Investigate the January 6th Attack on the United States Capitol (Department of Justice Production), HCOR-Pre-CertificationEvents-07262021-000697 (draft letter attached to December 28, 2020, email from Jeffrey Clark to Jeffrey Rosen and Richard Donoghue).

291. Documents on file with the Select Committee to Investigate the January 6th Attack on the United States Capitol (Department of Justice Production), HCOR-Pre-CertificationEvents-07262021-000697 (draft letter attached to December 28, 2020, email from Jeffrey Clark to Jeffrey Rosen and Richard Donoghue).

292. Documents on file with the Select Committee to Investigate the January 6th Attack on the United States Capitol (Department of Justice Production), HCOR-Pre-CertificationEvents-07262021-000703.

293. Documents on file with the Select Committee to Investigate the January 6th Attack on the United States Capitol (Department of Justice Production), HCOR-Pre-CertificationEvents-07262021-000697 (draft letter attached to December 28, 2020, email from Jeffrey Clark to Jeffrey Rosen and Richard Donoghue).

294. Documents on file with the Select Committee to Investigate the January 6th Attack on the United States Capitol (Department of Justice Production), HCOR-Pre-CertificationEvents-07262021-000697 (draft letter attached to December 28, 2020, email from Jeffrey Clark to Jeffrey Rosen and Richard Donoghue).

295. Documents on file with the Select Committee to Investigate the January 6th Attack on the United States Capitol (Department of Justice Production), HCOR-Pre-CertificationEvents-07262021-000697 (draft letter attached to December 28, 2020, email from Jeffrey Clark to Jeffrey Rosen and Richard Donoghue).

296. Documents on file with the Select Committee to Investigate the January 6th Attack on the United States Capitol (Department of Justice Production), HCOR-Pre-CertificationEvents-06032021-000200 (January 2, 2021, email from Jeffrey Rosen to Richard Donoghue titled "RE: Two Urgent Action Items").

297. Documents on file with the Select Committee to Investigate the January 6th Attack on the United States Capitol (Department of Justice Production), HCOR-Pre-CertificationEvents-06032021-000200 (January 2, 2021, email from Jeffrey Rosen to Richard Donoghue titled "RE: Two Urgent Action Items").

298.   Documents on file with the Select Committee to Investigate the January 6th Attack on the United States Capitol (Department of Justice Production), HCOR-Pre-CertificationEvents-06032021-000200 (January 2, 2021, email from Jeffrey Rosen to Richard Donoghue titled "RE: Two Urgent Action Items").

299.   Select Committee to Investigate the January 6th Attack on the United States Capitol, *Hearing on the January 6th Investigation*, 117th Cong., 2d sess., (June 23, 2022), available at https://www.govinfo.gov/committee/house-january6th.

300.   Select Committee to Investigate the January 6th Attack on the United States Capitol, Transcribed Interview of Richard Peter Donoghue, (Oct. 1, 2021), p. 82.

301.   Select Committee to Investigate the January 6th Attack on the United States Capitol, Transcribed Interview of Richard Peter Donoghue, (Oct. 1, 2021), p. 82.

302.   Select Committee to Investigate the January 6th Attack on the United States Capitol, *Hearing on the January 6th Investigation*, 117th Cong., 2d sess., (June 23, 2022), available at https://www.govinfo.gov/committee/house-january6th; Select Committee to Investigate the January 6th Attack on the United States Capitol, Transcribed Interview of Richard Peter Donoghue, (Oct. 1, 2021), pp. 79-82; Documents on file with the Select Committee to Investigate the January 6th Attack on the United States Capitol (Department of Justice Production), HCOR-Pre-CertificationEvents-07262021-000703 (December 28, 2020, email from Richard Donoghue to Jeffrey Clark, cc'ing Jeffrey Rosen re: Two Urgent Action Items in which Donoghue writes: "there is no chance that I would sign this letter or anything remotely like this.").

303.   Select Committee to Investigate the January 6th Attack at the United States Capitol, Transcribed Interview of Jeffrey Rosen, (Oct. 13, 2021), p. 73; Documents on file with the Select Committee to Investigate the January 6th Attack on the United States Capitol (Department of Justice Production), HCOR-Pre-CertificationEvents-07262021-000703 (December 28, 2020, email from Richard Donoghue to Jeffrey Clark, cc'ing Jeffrey Rosen re: Two Urgent Action Items in which Donoghue writes: "there is no chance that I would sign this letter or anything remotely like this."); Senate Committee on the Judiciary, Interview of Richard Donoghue, (August 6, 2021), at p. 99, available at https://www.judiciary.senate.gov/imo/media/doc/Donoghue%20Transcript.pdf.

304.   Select Committee to Investigate the January 6th Attack on the United States Capitol, Transcribed Interview of Richard Peter Donoghue, (Oct. 1, 2021), p. 113.

305.   Select Committee to Investigate the January 6th Attack on the United States Capitol, *Hearing on the January 6th Investigation*, 117th Cong., 2d sess., (June 23, 2022), available at https://www.govinfo.gov/committee/house-january6th.

306.   Select Committee to Investigate the January 6th Attack on the United States Capitol, *Hearing on the January 6th Investigation*, 117th Cong., 2d sess., (June 23, 2022), available at https://www.govinfo.gov/committee/house-january6th.

307.   Documents on file with the Select Committee to Investigate the January 6th Attack on the United States Capitol (National Archives Production), CTRL0000083040 (January 3, 2021, White House Presidential Call Log).

308.   Select Committee to Investigate the January 6th Attack on the United States Capitol, Transcribed Interview of Richard Peter Donoghue, (Oct. 1, 2021), p. 119.

309.   Select Committee to Investigate the January 6th Attack on the United States Capitol, Transcribed Interview of Richard Peter Donoghue, (Oct. 1, 2021), p. 119-20. ("And so it was unanimous; everyone was going to resign if Jeff Rosen was removed from the seat." The only exception was John Demers, the Assistant Attorney General for the National Security Division. Donoghue encouraged Demers to stay on because he didn't want to further jeopardize national security.)

310.   Select Committee to Investigate the January 6th Attack on the United States Capitol, Transcribed Interview of Richard Peter Donoghue, (Oct. 1, 2021), p. 124.

311. Select Committee to Investigate the January 6th Attack on the United States Capitol, Transcribed Interview of Richard Peter Donoghue, (Oct. 1, 2021), pp. 126-28; Select Committee to Investigate the January 6th Attack on the United States Capitol, Transcribed Interview of Pasquale Anthony "Pat" Cipollone, (July 8, 2022), p. 120.

312. Select Committee to Investigate the January 6th Attack on the United States Capitol, Transcribed Interview of Richard Peter Donoghue, (Oct. 1, 2021), p. 126.

313. Select Committee to Investigate the January 6th Attack on the United States Capitol, Transcribed Interview of Richard Peter Donoghue, (Oct. 1, 2021), p. 125.

314. Select Committee to Investigate the January 6th Attack on the United States Capitol, Transcribed Interview of Steven A. Engel, (Jan. 13, 2022), p. 64.

315. Select Committee to Investigate the January 6th Attack on the United States Capitol, Transcribed Interview of Richard Peter Donoghue, (Oct. 1, 2021), p. 125.

316. Select Committee to Investigate the January 6th Attack on the United States Capitol, Transcribed Interview of Richard Peter Donoghue, (Oct. 1, 2021), pp. 131-132.

317. Select Committee to Investigate the January 6th Attack on the United States Capitol, Transcribed Interview of Richard Peter Donoghue, (Oct. 1, 2021), pp. 131-32.

318. Select Committee to Investigate the January 6th Attack on the United States Capitol, Deposition of Sidney Powell, (May 7, 2022), pp. 75, 84.

319. Donald J. Trump (@realDonaldTrump), Twitter, Dec. 19, 2020 1:42 a.m. ET, available at http://web.archive.org/web/20201219064257/https://twitter.com/realDonaldTrump/status/1340185773220515840 (archived).

320. Donald J. Trump (@realDonaldTrump), Twitter, Dec. 26, 2020 8:14 a.m. ET, available at https://twitter.com/realDonaldTrump/status/1342821189077622792; Donald J. Trump (@realDonaldTrump), Twitter, Dec. 27, 2020 5:51 p.m. ET, available at https://twitter.com/realDonaldTrump/status/1343328708963299338; Donald J. Trump (@realDonaldTrump), Twitter, Dec. 30, 2020 2:06 p.m. ET, available at https://twitter.com/realDonaldTrump/status/1344359312878149634; Donald J. Trump (@realDonaldTrump), Twitter, Jan. 1, 2021 12:52 p.m. ET, available at https://www.thetrumparchive.com/?searchbox=%22RT+%40KylieJaneKremer%22 (archived) (retweeting @KylieJaneKremer, Dec. 19, 2020 3:50 p.m. ET, available at https://twitter.com/KylieJaneKremer/status/1340399063875895296)); Donald J. Trump (@realDonaldTrump), Twitter, Jan. 1, 2021 2:53 p.m. ET, available at https://twitter.com/realDonaldTrump/status/1345095714687377418; Donald J. Trump (@realDonaldTrump), Twitter, Jan. 1, 2021 3:34 p.m. ET, available at https://twitter.com/realDonaldTrump/status/1345106078141394944; Donald J. Trump (@realDonaldTrump), Twitter, Jan. 1, 2021 6:38 p.m. ET, available at https://twitter.com/realDonaldTrump/status/1345152408591204352; Donald J. Trump (@realDonaldTrump), Twitter, Jan. 2, 2021 9:04 p.m. ET, available at https://twitter.com/realDonaldTrump/status/1345551634907209730; Donald J. Trump (@realDonaldTrump), Twitter, Jan. 3, 2021 1:29 a.m. ET, available at https://www.thetrumparchive.com/?searchbox=%22RT+%40realDonaldTrump%3A+https%3A%2F%2Ft.co%2FnslWcFwkCj%22 (archived) (retweeting Donald J. Trump (@realDonaldTrump), Jan. 2, 2021 9:04 p.m. ET, available at https://twitter.com/realDonaldTrump/status/1345551634907209730)); Donald J. Trump (@realDonaldTrump), Twitter, Jan. 3, 2021 10:15 a.m. ET, available at https://www.thetrumparchive.com/?searchbox=%22RT+%40JenLawrence21%22 (archived) (retweeting Jennifer Lynn Lawrence (@JenLawrence21)), Jan. 3, 2021 12:17 a.m. ET, available at https://twitter.com/JenLawrence21/status/1345600194826686464); Donald J. Trump (@realDonaldTrump), Twitter, Jan. 3, 2021 10:17 a.m. ET, available at https://www.thetrumparchive.com/?searchbox=%22RT+%40CodeMonkeyZ+if%22 (archived) (retweeting Ron Watkins (@CodeMonkeyZ) Jan. 2, 2021 9:14 p.m. ET, available at http://web.archive.org/web/20210103151826/https://twitter.com/CodeMonkeyZ/status/1345599512560078849 (archived)); Donald J. Trump, (@realDonaldTrump), Twitter, Jan. 3,

2021 10:24 a.m. ET, available at https://www.thetrumparchive.com/?searchbox= %22RT+%40realMikeLindell%22 (archived) (retweeting Mike Lindell (@realMikeLindell), Jan. 2, 2021 5:47 p.m. ET, available at http://web.archive.org/web/20210103152421/https:// twitter.com/realMikeLindell/status/1345547185836978176 (archived)); Donald J. Trump (@realDonaldTrump), Twitter, Jan. 3, 2021 10:27 a.m. ET, available at https://twitter.com/ realDonaldTrump/status/1345753534168506370; Donald J. Trump (@realDonaldTrump), Twitter, Jan. 3, 2021 10:28 a.m. ET, available at https://www.thetrumparchive.com/?searchbox= %22RT+%40AmyKremer+we%22 (archived) (retweeting Amy Kremer (@AmyKremer), Jan. 2, 2021 2:58 p.m. ET, available at https://twitter.com/AmyKremer/status/ 1345459488107749386); Donald J. Trump (@realDonaldTrump), Twitter, Jan. 4, 2021 9:46 a.m. ET, available at https://www.thetrumparchive.com/?searchbox= %22RT+%40realDonaldTrump+I+will+be+there.+Historic+day%21%22 (retweeting Donald J. Trump (@realDonaldTrump), Jan. 3, 2021 10:27 a.m. ET, available at https://twitter.com/ realDonaldTrump/status/1345753534168506370); Donald J. Trump (@realDonaldTrump), Twitter, Jan. 5, 2021 10:27 a.m. ET, available at https://twitter.com/realDonaldTrump/ status/1346478482105069568; Donald J. Trump (@realDonaldTrump), Twitter, Jan. 5, 2021 5:43 p.m. ET, available at https://twitter.com/realDonaldTrump/status/ 1346588064026685443.

321. *See, e.g.*, Sentencing Memorandum of Daniel Johnson at 5, *United States v. Johnson*, No. 1:21-cr-407 (D.D.C. May 25, 2022), ECF No. 56 ("Mr. Johnson believed what he read on the internet and heard from the President himself - that the election had been stolen."); Select Committee to Investigate the January 6th Attack on the United States Capitol, Transcribed Interview of Zac Martin, (Mar. 9, 2022), p. 20 (answering that he believed President Trump wanted "patriots to show up in Washington, DC on January 6th" because "we felt like our rights were being taken away from us" given the election results).

322. *See, e.g.*, Trial Transcript at 4106-08, *United States v. Rhodes et al.*, No. 1:22-cr-15 (D.D.C. Oct. 18, 2022) (Oath Keeper Jason Dolan testified that the Oath Keepers came to Washington, DC "to stop the certification of the election. ... [b]y any means necessary. That's why we brought our firearms."); Motion to Suppress, Exhibit A at 34, 85-86, *United States v. Rodriguez*, No. 1:21-cr-246 (D.D.C. Oct. 15, 2021), ECF No. 38-1 ("Trump called us. Trump called us to DC ... and he's calling for help -- I thought he was calling for help. I thought he was -- I thought we were doing the right thing."); Statement of Facts at 2, *United States v. Martin*, No. 1:21-cr-394 (D.D.C. Apr. 20, 2021) ("MARTIN reported that he decided to travel to Washington, D.C. after reading then-President Donald Trump's tweets regarding the election being stolen and a protest on January 6, 2021, flying to D.C. on January 5, 2021, and attending the rallies on January 6, 2021, and then heading to the U.S. Capitol where he entered along with a crowd of other individuals."); Statement of Facts at 9-10, *United States v. Denney*, No. 1:22-cr-70 (D.D.C. Dec. 7, 2021) ("So Trump has called this himself. For everyone to come. It's the day the electoral college is suppose [sic] to be certified by congress to officially elect Biden."); Select Committee to Investigate the January 6thth Attack on the United States Capitol, Transcribed Interview of Dustin Thompson (Nov. 16, 2022), pp. 34, 44, 70-71 (noting that he went to the Capitol at President Trump's direction and that he "figured [stopping the certification of the vote] was [President Trump's] plan"; *see also*, Documents on file with the Select Committee to Investigate the January 6th Attack on the United States Capitol (Select Committee Chart Compiling Defendant Statements).

323. Indictment at 6, *United States v. Smith*, No. 1:21-cr-567 (D.D.C. Sept. 9, 2021), ECF No. 1.

324. Statement of Facts at 3, *United States v. Sulenta*, No. 1:22-mj-00129-ZMF (D.D.C. June 6, 2022), ECF No. 1-1.

325. Stipulated Statement of Facts at 7, *United States v. Morss*, No. 1:21-cr-40 (D.D.C. August 23, 2022), ECF No. 430.

326. Statement of Facts at 9, *United States v. Grayson*, No. 1:21-cr-224 (D.D.C. Jan. 25, 2021), ECF No. 1-1.

327. Statement of Facts at 11, *United States v. Denney*, No. 1:21-mj-00686-RMM-ZMF (D.D.C. Dec. 7, 2021), ECF No. 1-1.

328. Gieswein denies that he was a Three Percenter as of January 6, 2021, even though he affiliated with an apparent Three Percenter group at previous times. *See* Gieswein's Motion for Hearing & Revocation of Detention Order at 2-3, 18-19, 25, *United States v. Gieswein*, No. 1:21-cr-24 (D.D.C. June 8, 2021), ECF No. 18. When the FBI arrested Gieswein, the criminal complaint noted that he "appears to be affiliated with the radical militia group known as the Three Percenters." Criminal Complaint at 5, *United States v. Gieswein*, No. 1:21-cr-24 (D.D.C. Jan. 16, 2021), available at https://www.justice.gov/opa/page/file/1360831/download. *See also* Adam Rawnsley (@arawnsley), Twitter, Jan. 17, 2021 9:13 p.m. ET, available at https://twitter.com/arawnsley/status/1350989535954530315 (highlighting photos of Gieswein flashing a Three Percenter symbol).

329. Second Superseding Indictment at 9-10, *United States v. Nordean et al.*, No. 1:21-cr-175 (D.D.C. March 7, 2022), ECF No. 305.

330. Statement of Offense at 5, *United States v. Bertino*, No. 1:22-cr-329 (D.D.C. Oct. 6, 2022), ECF No. 5; Third Superseding Indictment at 6, *United States v. Nordean, et al.*, No. 1:21-cr-175 (D.D.C. June 6, 2022), ECF No. 380; Statement of Offense at 3, *United States v. Donohoe*, No. 1:21-cr-175 (D.D.C. Apr. 8, 2022), ECF No. 336.

331. Third Superseding Indictment at 13, *United States v. Nordean, et al.*, No. 1:21-cr-175 (D.D.C. June 6, 2022), ECF No. 380; Georgia Wells, Rebecca Ballhaus, and Keach Hagey, "Proud Boys, Seizing Trump's Call to Washington, Helped Lead Capitol Attack," *Wall Street Journal*, (Jan.17, 2021), available at https://www.wsj.com/articles/proud-boys-seizing-trumps-call-to-washington-helped-lead-capitol-attack-11610911596.

332. Documents on file with the Select Committee to Investigate the January 6th Attack on the United States Capitol (Jay Thaxton Production), CTRL0000070865, (December 29, 2020, Telegram chat at 11:09 a.m. from Enrique Tarrio under the name "HEIKA NOBLELEAD.").

333. "Former Leader of Proud Boys Pleads Guilty to Seditious Conspiracy for Efforts to Stop Transfer of Power Following 2020 Presidential Election," Department of Justice, (Oct. 6, 2022), available at https://www.justice.gov/opa/pr/former-leader-proud-boys-pleads-guilty-seditious-conspiracy-efforts-stop-transfer-power; "Leader of North Carolina Chapter of Proud Boys Pleads Guilty to Conspiracy and Assault Charges in Jan. 6 Capitol Breach," Department of Justice, (Apr. 8, 2022), available at https://www.justice.gov/opa/pr/leader-north-carolina-chapter-proud-boys-pleads-guilty-conspiracy-and-assault-charges-jan-6.

334. Statement of Offense at 2, *United States v. Bertino*, No. 1:22-cr-329 (D.D.C. Oct. 6, 2022), ECF No. 5.

335. Statement of Offense at 4, *United States v. Bertino*, No. 1:22-cr-329 (D.D.C. Oct. 6, 2022), ECF No. 5.

336. Statement of Offense at 4-5, *United States v. Bertino*, No. 1:22-cr-329 (D.D.C. Oct. 6, 2022), ECF No. 5.

337. Statement of Offense at 4, *United States v. Donohoe*, No. 1:21-cr-175 (D.D.C. Apr. 8, 2022), ECF No. 336. Indeed, Proud Boys leaders Biggs and Nordean told MOSD on January 5th about a plan they had discussed with Tarrio for January 6th. Although Biggs and Nordean did not share the plan's precise details, Proud Boys like Bertino and Donohoe nonetheless understood the "objective in Washington, D.C., on January 6, 2021, was to obstruct, impede, or interfere with the certification of the Electoral College vote, including by force if necessary," and that the Proud Boys "would accomplish this through the use of force and violence, which could include storming the Capitol through police lines and barricades if necessary." Statement of Offense at 8, *United States v. Bertino*, No. 1:22-cr-329 (D.D.C. Oct. 6, 2022), ECF No. 5; Statement of Offense at 6, *United States v. Donohoe*, No. 1:21-cr-175 (D.D.C. Apr. 8, 2022), ECF No. 336.

338. Superseding Indictment at 2-3, *United States v. Rhodes et al*, No. 1:22-cr-15 (D.D.C. June 22, 2022), ECF No. 167.

339. Caldwell testified that he was not an Oath Keeper. *See* Trial Transcript at 8778-79, *United States v. Rhodes et al.*, No. 1:22-cr-15 (D.D.C. Nov. 15, 2022); Hannah Rabinowitz and Holmes Lybrand, "Capitol Riot Defendant Calls Himself a 'Little Bit of a Goof' Regarding Pelosi and Pence Comments," CNN, (Nov. 15, 2022), available at https://www.cnn.com/2022/11/15/

politics/thomas-caldwell-testifies-oath-keeper-trial. Because the government tried Caldwell in a conspiracy case with known Oath Keepers, the Select Committee has referred to him as an Oath Keeper.

340. See Trial Transcript at 10502-08, *United States v. Rhodes et al.*, No. 1:22-cr-15 (D.D.C. Nov. 29, 2022).

341. Trial Exhibit 6860 (1.S.656.9328 - 9396), *United States v. Rhodes*, No. 1:22-cr-15 (D.D.C. Oct. 13, 2022).

342. Superseding Indictment at 13, *United States v. Rhodes, III, et al.*, No. 22-cr-15 (D.D.C. June 22, 2022), ECF No 167.

343. Superseding Indictment at 13-14, *United States v. Rhodes, et al.*, No. 1:22-cr-15 (D.D.C. June 22, 2022), ECF No. 167.

344. Superseding Indictment at 15-17, *United States v. Rhodes, et al.*, No. 22-cr-15 (D.D.C. June 22, 2022), ECF No 167.

345. Statement of Offense at 5, *United States v. Ulrich*, No. 1:22-cr-15 (D.D.C. Apr. 29, 2022), ECF No. 117.

346. Statement of Offense at 5, *United States v. James*, No. 1:22-cr-15 (D.D.C. Mar. 2, 2022), ECF No. 60.

347. "TTPO Stance on Election Fraud," The Three Percenters - Original, available at https://archive.ph/YemCC#selection-289.0-289.29 (archived).

348. Statement of Facts at 7-8, *United States v. Buxton*, No. 1:21-cr-739 (D.D.C. Dec. 8, 2021), ECF No. 1-1; Post: "Oath Keepers claim to stand for the constitution yet will not call up its 30k membership to attend the 6th. I thought you guys stood for the constitution? It's your only job as an organization...now or never boys," Patriots.win, Dec. 29, 2020, available at https://patriots.win/p/11RO2hdyR2/x/c/4DrwV8RcV1s.

349. Indictment at 1, 7, *United States v. Hostetter et al.*, No. 1:21-cr-392 (D.D.C. June 9, 2021), ECF No. 1.

350. Indictment at 7, *United States v. Hostetter et al.*, No. 1:21-cr-392 (D.D.C. June 9, 2021), ECF No. 1.

351. Indictment at 8-13, *United States v. Hostetter et al.*, No. 1:21-cr-392 (D.D.C. June 9, 2021), ECF No. 1.

352. Indictment at 9, *United States v. Hostetter et al.*, No. 1:21-cr-392 (D.D.C. June 9, 2021), ECF No. 1.

353. Statement of Facts at 4, *United States v. Cole et al.*, No. 1:22-mj-184, (D.D.C. Aug. 29, 2022), ECF No. 5-1.

354. Statement of Facts at 5, *United States v. Cole et al.*, No. 1:22-mj-184, (D.D.C. Aug. 29, 2022), ECF No. 5-1. When the Select Committee asked about this post to the leader of the Florida Guardians of Freedom, Liggett downplayed any significance or any knowledge about other Three Percenter groups that might "show in record numbers." Select Committee to Investigate the January 6th Attack on the United States Capitol, Deposition of Jeremy Liggett, (May 17, 2022), pp. 51-52.

355. Statement of Facts at 5-6, *United States v. Cole et al.*, No. 1:22-mj-184, (D.D.C. Aug. 29, 2022), ECF No. 5-1; #SeditionHunters (@SeditionHunters), Twitter, June 7, 2021 2:11 p.m. ET, available at https://twitter.com/SeditionHunters/status/1401965056980627458.

356. Statement of Facts at 15-17, *United States v. Cole et al.*, No. 1:22-mj-184, (D.D.C. Aug. 29, 2022), ECF No. 5-1. The "tunnel" is actually a flight of stairs leading to a doorway from which the President emerges on Inauguration Day to take the oath of office. When the inauguration stage is present, the stairs leading to the doorway are converted into a "10-foot-wide, slightly sloped, short tunnel that was approximately 15 feet long." Government's Sentencing Memorandum at 5-6, *United States v. Young*, No. 1:21-cr-291-3 (D.D.C. Sept. 13, 2022), ECF No. 140. For other examples of how extremist groups responded to President Trump's call to action, *see* Chapter 6.

357. Indictment at 11, *United States v. Rodriguez et al.*, No. 1:21-cr-246 (D.D.C. Nov. 19, 2021), ECF No. 65; Motion to Suppress, Exhibit A at 70, *United States v. Rodriguez*, No. 1:21-cr-246 (D.D.C. Oct. 15, 2021), ECF No. 38-1.

358. Motion to Suppress, Exhibit A at 34, 85-86, *United States v. Rodriguez*, No. 1:21-cr-246 (D.D.C. Oct. 15, 2021), ECF No. 38-1.

359. Government's Opposition to Defendant's Renewed Request for Pretrial Release at 7, *United States v. Meggs*, No. 1:21-cr-28 (D.D.C Mar. 23, 2021), ECF No. 98.

360. Documents on file with the Select Committee to Investigate the January 6th Attack on the United States Capitol (Documents on file with the Select Committee to Investigate the January 6th Attack on the United States Capitol (Google Voice Production, Feb. 25, 2022).

361. Trial Exhibit 6868 (2000.T.420), *United States v. Rhodes et al.*, No. 1:22-cr-15 (D.D.C. Oct. 13, 2022).

362. Trial Exhibit 6868 (2000.T.420), *United States v. Rhodes et al.*, No. 1:22-cr-15 (D.D.C. Oct. 13, 2022).

363. Trial Exhibit 9221, *United States v. Rhodes et al.*, No.1:22-cr-15 (D.D.C. Nov. 9, 2022).

364. Motion for Bond, Exhibit 1 at 125-26, *United States v. Vallejo*, No. 1:22-cr-15 (D.D.C. Apr. 18, 2022), ECF No. 102-1 (Collection of redacted text messages, labeled as Exhibit 8, showing Rhodes adding "a CA Oath Keeper who is in with a four man team, followed by that person announcing his identifiable radio frequency) Ryan J. Reilly, "New Evidence Reveals Coordination Between Oath Keepers, Three Percenters on Jan. 6," NBC News, (May 28, 2022), available at https://www.nbcnews.com/politics/justice-department/new-evidence-reveals-coordination-oath-keepers-three-percenters-jan-6-rcna30355 (noting how public source investigators linked the identifiable radio frequency to Derek Kinnison, who is one of the California Three Percenters indicted on conspiracy charges for their conduct on January 6th. *See* Indictment, *United States v. Hostetter et al.*, No. 1:21-cr-392 (D.D.C. June 9, 2021), ECF No. 1).

365. Documents on file with the Select Committee to Investigate the January 6th Attack on the United States Capitol (Department of Justice Production), CTRL 0000010471, at 7:01 (January 6, 2021, video footage recorded by Samuel Montoya at the U.S. Capitol).

366. Documents on file with the Select Committee to Investigate the January 6th Attack on the United States Capitol, (District of Columbia Production), Axon Body 3 X6039BKH5 13.53.47 20210106-FELONYRIOT-FIRSTSTSE, at 15:28:13 (MPD body camera footage); Statement of Facts at 3, *United States v. Cale*, No. 1:22-cr-139 (D.D.C. Mar. 28, 2022), ECF No. 1-1.

367. Documents on file with the Select Committee to Investigate the January 6th Attack on the United States Capitol (Department of Justice Production), HCOR-Jan6-07222021-000603.

368. Select Committee to Investigate the January 6th Attack on the United States Capitol, Transcribed Interview of Richard Peter Donoghue, (Oct. 1, 2021), p. 143.

369. Select Committee to Investigate the January 6th Attack on the United States Capitol, Transcribed Interview of General Mark A. Milley, (Nov. 17, 2021), p. 199.

370. Documents on file with the Select Committee to Investigate the January 6th Attack on the United States Capitol (Mary McCord Production), CTRL0000930476 (December 22, 2020, email to the FBI noting troubling Oath Keepers chats),

371. Documents on file with the Select Committee to Investigate the January 6th Attack on the United States Capitol (Mary McCord Production), CTRL0000930476 (December 22, 2020, email to the FBI noting troubling Oath Keepers chats),

372. Documents on file with the Select Committee to Investigate the January 6th Attack on the United States Capitol (Secret Service Production), USSS0000038637, (December 25, 2020, email chain from PIOC on January 6th intelligence).

373. Documents on file with the Select Committee to Investigate the January 6th Attack on the United States Capitol (Secret Service Production), USSS0000038637, (December 25, 2020, email chain from PIOC on January 6th intelligence).

374. Documents on file with the Select Committee to Investigate the January 6th Attack on the United States Capitol (Secret Service Production), USSS0000038637, (December 25, 2020, email chain from PIOC on January 6th intelligence).

375. Documents on file with the Select Committee to Investigate the January 6th Attack on the United States Capitol (Secret Service Production), USSS0000038637, (December 25, 2020, email chain from PIOC on January 6th intelligence).

376. Documents on file with the Select Committee to Investigate the January 6th Attack on the United States Capitol (Secret Service Production), USSS0000038637, (December 25, 2020, email chain from PIOC on January 6th intelligence).

377. Documents on file with the Select Committee to Investigate the January 6th Attack on the United States Capitol (Secret Service Production), USSS0000038637, (December 25, 2020, email chain from PIOC on January 6th intelligence).

378. Documents on file with the Select Committee to Investigate the January 6th Attack on the United States Capitol (Secret Service Production), USSS0000038637, (December 25, 2020, email chain from PIOC on January 6th intelligence).

379. Documents on file with the Select Committee to Investigate the January 6th Attack on the United States Capitol (Capitol Police Production), CTRL0000000080 (December 28, 2020, email to John Donohue re: (LES) Armed and Ready SITE.pdf.); Select Committee to Investigate the January 6th Attack on the United States Capitol, Transcribed Interview of Jack Donohue, (Jan. 31, 2022), p. 8; Select Committee to Investigate the January 6th Attack on the United States Capitol, Informal Interview of Jack Donohue, (Jan. 7, 2022).

380. Documents on file with the Select Committee to Investigate the January 6th Attack on the United States Capitol (Secret Service Production), USSS0000067420 (December 26, 2020, email to PIOC regarding possible Proud Boys plan for January 6, 2021).

381. Documents on file with the Select Committee to Investigate the January 6th Attack on the United States Capitol (Secret Service Production), USSS0000067420 (December 26, 2020, email to PIOC regarding possible Proud Boys plan for January 6, 2021).

382. Documents on file with the Select Committee to Investigate the January 6th Attack on the United States Capitol (Capitol Police Production), CTRL0000001473 (December 29, 2020, email from PIOC-ONDUTY to THREAT ASSESSMENT re: FW: [EXTERNAL EMAIL] - Neo-Nazi Calls on D.C. Pro-Trump Protesters to Occupy Federal Building.).

383. Documents on file with the Select Committee to Investigate the January 6th Attack on the United States Capitol (Capitol Police Production), CTRL0000000087 (December 28, 2020, email re: 1/6 warning.).

384. Documents on file with the Select Committee to Investigate the January 6th Attack on the United States Capitol (Capitol Police Production), CTRL0000001473 (December 29, 2020, email from PIOC-ONDUTY@USSS.DHS.GOV to THREATS@uscp.gov titled "FW: [EXTERNAL EMAIL] - Neo-Nazi Calls on D.C. Pro-Trump Protesters to Occupy Federal Building.").

385. Documents on file with the Select Committee to Investigate the January 6th Attack on the United States Capitol (Secret Service Production), CTRL0000101135.0001, pp. 1, 3 (December 30, 2020, Protective Intelligence Brief titled "Wild Protest").

386. *See* Documents on file with the Select Committee to Investigate the January 6th Attack on the United States Capitol (Capitol Police Production), CTRL0000001527 (Email titled "Fwd: MPD MMS Text Tip.").

387. *See* Documents on file with the Select Committee to Investigate the January 6th Attack on the United States Capitol (Capitol Police Production), CTRL0000001527 (Email titled "Fwd: MPD MMS Text Tip.").

388. Documents on file with the Select Committee to Investigate the January 6th Attack on the United States Capitol, (Parler Production) PARLER_00000013 (January 2, 2021, email from Parler to the FBI re: Another to check out, attaching Parler posts).

389. Documents on file with the Select Committee to Investigate the January 6th Attack on the United States Capitol (Capitol Police Production), CTRL0000001487 (January 2, 2021, email to Capitol Police and Department of Justice with screenshots of Parler posts); Documents on file with the Select Committee to Investigate the January 6th Attack on the United States Capitol (Capitol Police Production), CTRL0000000116, CTRL0000000116.0001 (January 4, 2021, email from U.S. Capitol Police re: Comments of concern for Jan 6 rally, collecting Parler posts).

390. Documents on file with the Select Committee to Investigate the January 6th Attack on the United States Capitol (Capitol Police Production), CTRL0000001532.0001, p.2 (January 5, 2021, FBI Situational Information Report).

391. Documents on file with the Select Committee to Investigate the January 6th Attack on the United States Capitol (Capitol Police Production), CTRL0000001532.0001, p.2 (January 5, 2021, FBI Situational Information Report).

392. Documents on file with the Select Committee to Investigate the January 6th Attack on the United States Capitol (Secret Service Production), CTRL0000293417 (December 30, 2020, email to OSU-ALL titled "Discovery of Event Website- MAGA Drag the Interstate & Occupy the Capitol").

393. Documents on file with the Select Committee to Investigate the January 6th Attack on the United States Capitol (Capitol Police Production), CTRL0000000083, CTRL0000000083.0001 (January 5, 2021, email re: (U//FOUO//LES) OSINT Post of Concern.).

394. Documents on file with the Select Committee to Investigate the January 6th Attack on the United States Capitol (Capitol Police Production), CTRL0000000083, CTRL0000000083.0001 (January 5, 2021, email al re: (U//FOUO//LES) OSINT Post of Concern.).

395. Documents on file with the Select Committee to Investigate the January 6th Attack on the United States Capitol (Capitol Police Production), CTRL0000000083, CTRL0000000083.0001 (January 5, 2021, email Deleted for privacy concerns. et. al re: (U//FOUO//LES) OSINT Post of Concern.).

396. Documents on file with the Select Committee to Investigate the January 6th Attack on the United States Capitol (Secret Service Production), USSS0000066986, USSS0000066986.0001 (January 5, 2021, Secret Service email noting social media user threatening to bring a firearm to Washington, D.C. on January 6th).

397. Documents on file with the Select Committee to Investigate the January 6th Attack on the United States Capitol (Department of Interior Production), DOI_46000114_00000238, DOI_46000114_00000239 (January 5, 2021, Situational Information Report Federal Bureau of Investigation. "Potential for Violence in Washington, D.C. Area in Connection with Planned 'StopTheSteal' Protest on 6 January 2021.").

398. See Documents on file with the Select Committee to Investigate the January 6th Attack on the United States Capitol (Department of Interior Production), DOI_46000114_00000238, DOI_46000114_00000239 (January 5, 2021, Situational Information Report Federal Bureau of Investigation. "Potential for Violence in Washington, D.C. Area in Connection with Planned 'StopTheSteal' Protest on 6 January 2021.").

399. Trial Exhibit 6923 (1.S.159.817, 955), United States v. Rhodes et al., No. 22-cr-15 (D.D.C. Oct. 14, 2022) (Rhodes sent an encrypted message to Oath Keeper leadership on January 5, 2021, stating: "We will have several well equipped QRFs outside DC. And there are many, many others, from other groups, who will be watching and waiting on the outside in case of worst case scenarios.").

400. Documents on file with the Select Committee to Investigate the January 6th Attack on the United States Capitol (Mark Meadows Production), MM014441-MM01442 (December 30, 2020, 6:05 p.m. ET text from Jason Miller to Mark Meadows).

401. Select Committee to Investigate the January 6th Attack on the United States Capitol, Deposition of Jason Miller, (Feb. 3, 2022), Exhibit 45, pp. 4, 13. Miller claimed he had no idea about the comments and would have "flag[ged]" them for "Secret Service" had he seen

them. Select Committee to Investigate the January 6th Attack on the United States Capitol, Deposition of Jason Miller, (Feb. 3, 2022), pp. 210-12.

402. On his way to the Capitol, Proud Boy David Nicholas Dempsey stopped on the National Mall in front of an erected gallows, fitted with a noose, to tell the world what he hoped would happen: "Them worthless shitholes like Jerry Nadler, fuckin Pelosi … They don't need a jail cell. They need to hang from these motherfuckers [pointing to gallows]. They need to get the point across that the time for peace is over. … For four, or five years really, they've been fucking demonizing us, belittling us, … doing everything they can to stop what this is, and people are sick of that shit …. Hopefully one day soon we really have someone hanging from one of these motherfuckers … ." Statement of Facts at 2-3, *United States v. Dempsey*, No. 1:21-cr-566 (D.D.C. Aug. 25, 2021); #SeditionHunters (@SeditionHunters), Twitter, Mar. 11, 2021 8:12 p.m. ET, available at https://twitter.com/SeditionHunters/status/1370180789770588163.

403. Select Committee to Investigate the January 6th Attack on the United States Capitol, Continued Interview of Cassidy Hutchinson, (June 20, 2022), p. 49.

404. Select Committee to Investigate the January 6th Attack on the United States Capitol, Continued Interview of Cassidy Hutchinson, (May 17, 2022), p. 92.

405. Documents on file with the Select Committee to Investigate the January 6th Attack on the United States Capitol (Hope Hicks Production), SC_HH_035, SC_HH_036 (January 6, 2021, text messages with Hogan Gidley).

406. Select Committee to Investigate the January 6th Attack on the United States Capitol, Transcribed Interview of Hope Hicks, (Oct. 25, 2022), pp. 109-10.

407. Documents on file with the Select Committee to Investigate the January 6th Attack on the United States Capitol (Homeland Security and Emergency Management Agency, DC Production), CTRL0000926794 (Talking points put together by Dr. Christopher Rodriguez, Director of HSEMA, for a briefing with Mayor Muriel Bowers on December 30, 2020).

408. Select Committee to Investigate the January 6th Attack on the United States Capitol, *Hearing on the January 6th Investigation*, 117th Cong., 2d sess., (July 12, 2022), available at https://www.govinfo.gov/committee/house-january6th; Select Committee to Investigate the January 6th Attack on the United States Capitol, Transcribed Interview of Donnell Harvin, (Jan. 24, 2022), pp. 22-23.

409. Given the timing of receipt of much of this intelligence immediately in advance of January 6th, it is unclear that any comprehensive intelligence community analytical product could have been reasonably expected. But it is clear that the information itself was communicated.

410. Documents on file with the Select Committee to Investigate the January 6th Attack on the United States Capitol (Caroline Wren Production), REVU_000181 (January 2, 2021, email from Katrina Pierson to Caroline Wren and Taylor Budowich re: 1/6 Speaker Schedule).

411. Documents on file with the Select Committee to Investigate the January 6th Attack on the United States Capitol (Kylie Kremer Production), KKremer5449; Select Committee to Investigate the January 6th Attack on the United States Capitol, *Hearing on the January 6th Investigation*, 117th Cong., 2d sess., (July 12, 2022), available at https://www.govinfo.gov/committee/house-january6th.

412. Select Committee to Investigate the January 6th Attack on the United States Capitol, Deposition of Judson P. Deere, (Mar. 3, 2022), pp. 83, 86.

413. Select Committee to Investigate the January 6th Attack on the United States Capitol, *Hearing on the January 6th Investigation*, 117th Cong., 2d sess., (June 28, 2022), available at https://www.govinfo.gov/committee/house-january6th.

414. Select Committee to Investigate the January 6th Attack on the United States Capitol, Transcribed Interview of Robert "Bobby" Engel, (Nov. 17, 2022), p. 64.

415. Select Committee to Investigate the January 6th Attack on the United States Capitol, Continued Interview of Robert Engel, (Nov. 17, 2022), p. 21.

416. Select Committee to Investigate the January 6th Attack on the United States Capitol, Continued Interview of Anthony Ornato, (Nov. 29, 2022), p. 152.

417. Select Committee to Investigate the January 6th Attack on the United States Capitol, Continued Interview of Anthony Ornato, (Nov. 29, 2022), p. 152.

418. Select Committee to Investigate the January 6th Attack on the United States Capitol, Continued Interview of Anthony Ornato, (Nov. 29, 2022), p. 152.

419. Select Committee to Investigate the January 6th Attack on the United States Capitol, Continued Interview of Anthony Ornato, (Mar. 29, 2022), p. 16.

420. Documents on file with the Select Committee to Investigate the January 6th Attack on the United States Capitol (Capitol Police Production), CTRL0000086772, p. 4 (November 18, 2021, document titled: United States Secret Service - Coordinated Response to a Request for Information from the Select Committee to Investigate the January 6th Attack on the United States Capitol).

421. Documents on file with the Select Committee to Investigate the January 6th Attack on the United States Capitol (Nick Quested Production), Video file ML_DC_20210106_Sony_FS7-GC_1935.mov; Documents on file with the Select Committee to Investigate the January 6th Attack on the United States Capitol (Secret Service Production), CTRL0000882478 (Summary of updates from January 6, 2021); Select Committee to Investigate the January 6th Attack on the United States Capitol, Transcribed Interview of Dustin Thompson, (Nov. 16, 2022), pp. 30-31 ("I was seeing these, like, piles of backpacks and flagpoles [outside the magnetometers]. And some people were watching that for other people. And I just -- there were lots of piles all over the place of stuff like that.").

422. Tom Jackman, Rachel Weiner, and Spencer S. Hsu, "Evidence of Firearms in Jan. 6 Crowd Grows as Arrests and Trials Mount," *Washington Post*, (July 8, 2022), https://www.washingtonpost.com/dc-md-va/2022/07/08/jan6-defendants-guns/.

423. Documents on file with the Select Committee to Investigate the January 6th Attack on the United States Capitol (Secret Service Production), CTRL0000882478 (summary of radio traffic on January 6, 2021).

424. Documents on file with the Select Committee to Investigate the January 6th Attack on the United States Capitol (District of Columbia Production), MPD 73-78 (District of Columbia, Metropolitan Police Department, Transcript of Radio Calls, January 6, 2021); Documents on file with the Select Committee to Investigate the January 6th Attack on the United States Capitol (District of Columbia Production), CTRL0000070375, at 3:40 (District of Columbia, Metropolitan Police Department, audio file of radio traffic from January 6, 2021, from 12:00 - 13:00).

425. Documents on file with the Select Committee to Investigate the January 6th Attack on the United States Capitol (Cassidy Hutchinson Production), CH-CTRL0000000069.

426. Select Committee to Investigate the January 6th Attack on the United States Capitol, *Hearing on the January 6th Investigation*, 117th Cong., 2d sess., (June 28, 2022), available at https://www.govinfo.gov/committee/house-january6th.

427. Select Committee to Investigate the January 6th Attack on the United States Capitol, Transcribed Interview of United States Secret Service Employee, (Nov. 7, 2022), p. 77 ("The most--the thing that sticks out most was he kept asking why we couldn't go, why we couldn't go, and that he wasn't concerned about the people that were there or referenced them being Trump people or Trump supporters.").

428. "Transcript of Trump's Speech at Rally before US Capitol Riot," *Associated Press*, (Jan. 13, 2021), available at https://apnews.com/article/election-2020-joe-biden-donald-trump-capitol-siege-media-e79eb5164613d6718e9f4502eb471f27.

429. "Transcript of Trump's Speech at Rally before US Capitol Riot," *Associated Press*, (Jan. 13, 2021), available at https://apnews.com/article/election-2020-joe-biden-donald-trump-capitol-siege-media-e79eb5164613d6718e9f4502eb471f27.

430. Select Committee to Investigate the January 6th Attack on the United States Capitol, Transcribed Interview of Eric Herschmann, (Apr. 6, 2022), pp. 20-21.

431. Select Committee to Investigate the January 6th Attack on the United States Capitol, Transcribed Interview of Eric Herschmann, (Apr. 6, 2022), pp. 24, 26.

432. Select Committee to Investigate the January 6th Attack on the United States Capitol, Transcribed Interview of Eric Herschmann, (Apr. 6, 2022), pp. 26.

433. Select Committee to Investigate the January 6th Attack on the United States Capitol, Transcribed Interview of Eric Herschmann, (Apr. 6, 2022), pp. 23.

434. *See* "Donald Trump Speech 'Save America' Rally Transcript January 6," Rev, (Jan. 6, 2021), at 1:00:00 – 1:02:31, available at https://www.rev.com/blog/transcripts/donald-trump-speech-save-america-rally-transcript-january-6 (timestamping the speech).

435. "Transcript of Trump's Speech at Rally before US Capitol Riot," *Associated Press*, (Jan. 13, 2021), available at https://apnews.com/article/election-2020-joe-biden-donald-trump-capitol-siege-media-e79eb5164613d6718e9f4502eb471f27.

436. Select Committee to Investigate the January 6th Attack on the United States Capitol, *Hearing on the January 6th Investigation*, 117th Cong., 2d sess., (July 21, 2022), at 1:00:45-1:01:12, available at https://youtu.be/pbRVqWbHGuo?t=3645; Select Committee to Investigate the January 6th Attack on the United States Capitol, Transcribed Interview of Janet West Buhler, (Feb. 28, 2022), p. 40.

437. "Transcript of Trump's Speech at Rally before US Capitol Riot," *Associated Press*, (Jan. 13, 2021), available at https://apnews.com/article/election-2020-joe-biden-donald-trump-capitol-siege-media-e79eb5164613d6718e9f4502eb471f27.

438. "Transcript of Trump's Speech at Rally before US Capitol Riot," *Associated Press*, (Jan. 13, 2021), available at https://apnews.com/article/election-2020-joe-biden-donald-trump-capitol-siege-media-e79eb5164613d6718e9f4502eb471f27.

439. "Transcript of Trump's Speech at Rally before US Capitol Riot," *Associated Press*, (Jan. 13, 2021), available at https://apnews.com/article/election-2020-joe-biden-donald-trump-capitol-siege-media-e79eb5164613d6718e9f4502eb471f27.

440. Select Committee to Investigate the January 6th Attack on the United States Capitol, *Hearing on the January 6th Investigation*, 117th Cong., 2d sess., (June 16, 2022), at 0:14:11-0:15:00, available at https://youtu.be/vBjUWVKuDj0?t=851; Hearing on Motion to Modify Conditions of Release, Exhibit 07 at 7:43 - 8:00, *United States v. Nichols*, No. 1:21-cr-117 (D.D.C. Dec. 20, 2021).

441. Unframe of Mind, "Unframe of Mind in DC #stopthesteal Rally," YouTube, at 9:40 – 9:47, Jan. 6, 2021, available at https://www.youtube.com/watch?v=OFbvpBu_7ws&t=579s; Select Committee to Investigate the January 6th Attack on the United States Capitol, *Hearing on the January 6th Investigation*, 117th Cong., 2d sess., (June 16, 2022), at, at 0:14:11-0:15:00, available at https://youtu.be/vBjUWVKuDj0?t=851.

442. Walter Masterson, "Live from the Trump Rally in Washington, D.C.," YouTube, at 17:32 – 17:50, Jan. 11, 2021, available at https://www.youtube.com/watch?v=OFbvpBu_7ws&t=579s; Select Committee to Investigate the January 6th Attack on the United States Capitol, *Hearing on the January 6th Investigation*, 117th Cong., 2d sess., (June 16, 2022), at, at 2:07:02-2:07:07, available at https://youtu.be/vBjUWVKuDj0?t=7609.

443. Select Committee to Investigate the January 6th Attack on the United States Capitol, *Hearing on the January 6th Investigation*, 117th Cong., 2d sess., (June 16, 2022) at, at 2:07:13-2:07:47, available at https://youtu.be/vBjUWVKuDj0?t=7609.

444. Select Committee to Investigate the January 6th Attack on the United States Capitol, *Hearing on the January 6th Investigation*, 117th Cong., 2d sess., (July 21, 2022), at 1:00:45-1:01:12, available at https://youtu.be/pbRVqWbHGuo?t=3645; On the Media, "Jessica Watkins on 'Stop the Steal J6' Zello Channel (Unedited)," Soundcloud, at 4:00-4:18, available at https://soundcloud.com/user-403747081/jessica-watkins-on-stop-the-steal-j6-zello-channel-unedited .

445. For a video of the interview, *see* "Crown Point, Indiana Man Charged in Jan. 6 Capitol Riot Says He Has 'No Regrets'," CBS Chicago, Nov. 29, 2022, available at https://www.cbsnews.com/chicago/video/crown-point-indiana-man-charged-in-jan-6-capitol-riot-says-he-has-no-regrets/#x.

446. "Transcript of Trump's Speech at Rally before US Capitol Riot," *Associated Press*, (Jan. 13, 2021), available at https://apnews.com/article/election-2020-joe-biden-donald-trump-capitol-siege-media-e79eb5164613d6718e9f4502eb471f27 (emphasis added).

447. Select Committee to Investigate the January 6th Attack on the United States Capitol, *Hearing on the January 6th Investigation*, 117th Cong., 2d sess., (June 28, 2022), available at https://www.govinfo.gov/committee/house-january6th; Select Committee to Investigate the January 6th Attack on the United States Capitol, Continued Interview of Cassidy Hutchinson, (June 20, 2022), p. 49.

448. Select Committee to Investigate the January 6th Attack on the United States Capitol, Transcribed Interview of Pasquale Anthony "Pat" Cipollone, (July 8, 2022), p. 131 ("I just didn't think it would be, you know, a good idea for the President to go up to the Capitol."). While Cipollone did not specifically recall talking with Cassidy Hutchinson about this topic, he informed the Select Committee that he was sure that he did express his view to some people. *Id.* Hutchinson believes it was Pat Cipollone, but also testified that it may have been a different lawyer. *See* Select Committee to Investigate the January 6th Attack on the United States Capitol, Transcribed Interview of Cassidy Hutchinson, (Feb. 23, 2022), pp. 113-16.

449. For security reasons, the Select Committee is not releasing the name of this employee. Select Committee to Investigate the January 6th Attack on the United States Capitol, Transcribed Interview of White House employee with national security responsibilities, (July 19, 2022) at p. 73. *See also* Chapter 7, which discusses this topic in greater detail.

450. Select Committee to Investigate the January 6th Attack on the United States Capitol, Transcribed Interview of United States Secret Service Agent, (Nov. 21, 2022), pp. 22-23. The Select Committee has agreed to keep confidential the identity of this witness due to their sensitive national security responsibilities.

451. A book written by Chief of Staff Mark Meadows in December 2021 made the categorical claim that the President never intended to travel to the Capitol that day. *See* Mark Meadows, *The Chief's Chief* (St. Petersburg, FL: All Seasons Press, 2021), p. 250. The Committee's evidence demonstrates that Meadows's claim is categorically false. Because the Meadows book conflicted sharply with information that was being received by the Select Committee, the Committee became increasingly wary that other witnesses might intentionally conceal what happened. That appeared to be the case with Ornato. Ornato does not recall that he conveyed the information to Cassidy Hutchinson regarding the SUV, and also does not recall that he conveyed similar information to a White House employee with national security responsibilities who testified that Ornato recalled a similar account to him. The Committee is skeptical of Ornato's account.

452. Select Committee to Investigate the January 6th Attack on the United States Capitol, Transcribed Interview of White House Security Official, (July 11, 2022), p. 45. The Select Committee has agreed to keep confidential the identity of this witness due to their sensitive national security responsibilities.

453. Select Committee to Investigate the January 6th Attack on the United States Capitol, Deposition of Kayleigh McEnany, (Jan. 12, 2022), p. 159.

454. Select Committee to Investigate the January 6th Attack on the United States Capitol, Continued Interview of Cassidy Hutchinson, (June 20, 2022), p. 8.

455. Government's Sentencing Memorandum at 2-9, *United States v. Young*, No. 1:21-cr-291 (D.D.C. Sept. 13, 2022), ECF No. 140; 167 Cong. Rec. S619 (daily ed. Feb. 10, 2021), available at https://www.congress.gov/117/crec/2021/02/10/CREC-2021-02-10-pt1-PgS615-4.pdf; Michael S. Schmidt and Luke Broadwater, "Officers' Injuries, Including Concussions, Show Scope of Violence at Capitol Riot," *New York Times*, (Feb. 11, 2021), available at https://www.nytimes.com/2021/02/11/us/politics/capitol-riot-police-officer-injuries.html.

456. *See* Sentencing Transcript at 35, *United States v. Griffith*, No. 1:21-cr-204 (D.D.C. Oct. 30, 2021), ECF No. 137; Kyle Cheney and Josh Gerstein, "Where Jan. 6 Prosecutions Stand, 18 Months after the Attack," *Politico*, (July 7, 2022), available at https://www.politico.com/news/2022/07/07/jan-6-prosecutions-months-later-00044354.

457. Select Committee to Investigate the January 6th Attack on the United States Capitol, *Hearing on the January 6th Investigation*, 117th Cong., 2d sess., (July 12, 2022), at 2:36:58-2:37:30, 2:44:00-2:45:05, available at https://www.youtube.com/watch?v=rrUa0hfG6Lo ("[W]hen President Trump put his tweet out, we literally left right after that come out . . . As soon as that come out, everybody started talking about it . . . it definitely dispersed a lot of the crowd. . . . We left."); Select Committee to Investigate the January 6th Attack on the United States Capitol, *Hearing on the January 6th Investigation*, 117th Cong., 2d sess., (July 21, 2022), at 1:58:00, available at https://www.youtube.com/watch?v=pbRVqWbHGuo ("I'm here delivering the President's message. Donald Trump has asked everybody to go home. ... That's our order.").

458. Select Committee to Investigate the January 6th Attack on the United States Capitol, *Hearing on the January 6th Investigation*, 117th Cong., 2d sess., (July 21, 2022), at 1:50:59-1:52:19, available at https://youtu.be/pbRVqWbHGuo?t=6659; Select Committee to Investigate the January 6th Attack on the United States Capitol, *Business Meeting on the January 6th Investigation*, 117th Cong., 2d sess., (Oct. 13, 2022), at 2:15:45-2:17:12, available at https://youtu.be/IQvuBoLBuC0?t=8145; CBS News, "Former Vice President Mike Pence on 'Face the Nation with Margaret Brennan' | Full Interview," YouTube, at 16:23-19:01, Nov. 21, 2022, available at https://youtu.be/U9GbkPhG1Lo?t=983; Select Committee to Investigate the January 6th Attack on the United States Capitol, Transcribed Interview of Steven Andrew Sund, (Apr. 20, 2022), p. 173.

459. Select Committee to Investigate the January 6th Attack on the United States Capitol, Transcribed Interview of White House Employee, (June 10, 2022), p. 27. The Select Committee is not revealing the identity of this witness to guard against the risk of retaliation; *See* "Donald Trump Speech 'Save America' Rally Transcript January 6," Rev, (Jan. 6, 2021), available at https://www.rev.com/blog/transcripts/donald-trump-speech-save-america-rally-transcript-january-6 (timestamping the speech).

460. Documents on file with the Select Committee to Investigate the January 6th Attack on the United States Capitol (National Archives Production), Photo file 40a8_hi_j0087_0bea; Select Committee to Investigate the January 6th Attack on the United States Capitol, *Hearing on the January 6th Investigation*, 117th Cong., 2d sess., (July 21, 2022), at 34:18, available at https://youtu.be/pbRVqWbHGuo?t=2058.

461. Washington Post, "D.C. Police requested backup at least 17 times in 78 minutes during Capitol riot | Visual Forensics," YouTube, at 7:58 to 8:45, Apr. 15, 2021, available at https://youtu.be/rsQTY9083r8?t=478; Senate Committee on Homeland Security and Governmental Affairs and Senate Committee on Rules and Administration, Public Hearing, (Mar. 3, 2021), Written Testimony of William J. Walker, Commanding General District of Columbia National Guard, p. 3, available at https://www.hsgac.senate.gov/imo/media/doc/Testimony-Walker-2021-03-03.pdf.

462. Select Committee to Investigate the January 6th Attack on the United States Capitol, Transcribed Interview of Shealah Craighead, (June 8, 2022), pp. 42, 46.

463. Documents on file with the Select Committee to Investigate the January 6th Attack on the United States Capitol (National Archives Production), P-R000261; Select Committee to Investigate the January 6th Attack on the United States Capitol, *Hearing on the January 6th Investigation*, 117th Cong., 2d sess., (July 21, 2022), available at https://www.govinfo.gov/committee/house-january6th

464. Documents on file with the Select Committee to Investigate the January 6th Attack on the United States Capitol (National Archives Production), P-R000257; Select Committee to Investigate the January 6th Attack on the United States Capitol, *Hearing on the January 6th Investigation*, 117th Cong., 2d sess., (July 21, 2022), available at https://www.govinfo.gov/committee/house-january6th

465. Select Committee to Investigate the January 6th Attack on the United States Capitol, Deposition of Molly Michael, (Mar. 24, 2022), p. 138.

466. Select Committee to Investigate the January 6th Attack on the United States Capitol, Transcribed Interview of Pasquale Anthony "Pat" Cipollone, (Jul. 8, 2022), p. 174; Select Committee to Investigate the January 6th Attack on the United States Capitol, Deposition of Keith Kellogg Jr., (Dec. 14, 2021), pp. 126–27; Select Committee to Investigate the January 6th Attack on the United States Capitol, Deposition of Nicholas Luna, (Mar. 21, 2022), pp. 151-52; Select Committee to Investigate the January 6th Attack on the United States Capitol, Transcribed Interview of Christopher Charles Miller, (Jan. 14, 2022), pp. 124-26; Select Committee to Investigate the January 6th Attack on the United States Capitol, Transcribed Interview of General Mark A. Milley, (Nov. 17, 2021), pp. 80-82; Select Committee to Investigate the January 6th Attack on the United States Capitol, *Hearing on the January 6th Investigation*, 117th Cong., 2d sess., (June 23, 2022), available at https://www.govinfo.gov/committee/house-january6th; Select Committee to Investigate the January 6th Attack on the United States Capitol, Transcribed Interview of Richard Peter Donoghue, (Oct. 1, 2021), pp. 186-90.

467. Select Committee to Investigate the January 6th Attack on the United States Capitol, Deposition of Molly Michael, (Mar. 24, 2022), pp. 127, 129, 131-32, 137, 141, 143-44, 148-49, 159.

468. Documents on file with the Select Committee to Investigate the January 6th Attack on the United States Capitol (AT&T Production, Feb. 9, 2022).

469. Select Committee to Investigate the January 6th Attack on the United States Capitol, Deposition of Kayleigh McEnany, (Jan. 12, 2022), pp. 163-64; Select Committee to Investigate the January 6th Attack on the United States Capitol, *Hearing on the January 6th Investigation*, 117th Cong., 2d sess., (July 21, 2022), available at https://www.govinfo.gov/committee/house-january6th.

470. Senator Lee wrote to a reporter that he received a call from the President moments after the Senate halted its proceedings and that the President claimed he had dialed Sen. Tommy Tuberville (R-AL), so Lee let Tuberville talk to the President on his phone for 5 or 10 minutes until they were ordered to evacuate. Bryan Schott, "What Sen. Mike Lee Told Me about Trump's Call the Day of the Capitol Riot," *Salt Lake Tribune*, (Feb. 10, 2021, updated Feb. 11, 2021), available at https://www.sltrib.com/news/politics/2021/02/11/what-sen-mike-lee-told-me/; *see also* Kyle Cheney, "Tuberville Says He Informed Trump of Pence's Evacuation before Rioters Reached Senate," *Politico*, (Feb. 11, 2021), available at https://www.politico.com/news/2021/02/11/tuberville-pences-evacuation-trump-impeachment-468572.

471. 167 Cong. Rec. S634 (daily ed. Feb. 10, 2021), available at https://www.congress.gov/117/crec/2021/02/10/CREC-2021-02-10-pt1-PgS615-4.pdf; Donald J. Trump (@realDonaldTrump), Twitter, Jan. 6, 2021 1:49 p.m. ET, available at http://web.archive.org/web/20210107235835/https://twitter.com/realDonaldTrump/status/1346891760174329859 (archived).

472. Select Committee to Investigate the January 6th Attack on the United States Capitol, Transcribed Interview of Pasquale Anthony "Pat" Cipollone, (July 8, 2022), pp. 149-50.

473. Select Committee to Investigate the January 6th Attack on the United States Capitol, Transcribed Interview of Pasquale Anthony "Pat" Cipollone, (July 8, 2022), pp. 150-51.

474. Select Committee to Investigate the January 6th Attack on the United States Capitol, *Hearing on the January 6th Investigation*, 117th Cong., 2d sess., (June 28, 2022), at 1:39:03-1:40:42, available at https://youtu.be/HeQNV-aQ_jU?t=5943. Two witnesses recall writing this note: Cassidy Hutchinson and Eric Herschmann, although Hutchinson recalls that Herschmann was responsible for the revision made to the note. The Committee's review of Hutchinson's handwriting was consistent with the script of the note. Select Committee to Investigate the January 6th Attack on the United States Capitol, Transcribed Interview of Cassidy Hutchinson, (Feb. 23, 2022), p. 167; Select Committee to Investigate the January 6th Attack on the United States Capitol, Transcribed Interview of Eric Herschmann (Apr. 6, 2022), pp. 67-68. Who wrote the note is not material to the Select Committee—the important point is that it was prepared for the President.

475. Select Committee to Investigate the January 6th Attack on the United States Capitol, Transcribed Interview of Pasquale Anthony "Pat" Cipollone, (July 8, 2022), p. 162.

476. Select Committee to Investigate the January 6th Attack on the United States Capitol, *Hearing on the January 6th Investigation*, 117th Cong., 2d sess., (June 28, 2022), at 1:27:52-1:28:53, available at https://youtu.be/HeQNV-aQ_jU?t=5272; Select Committee to Investigate the January 6th Attack on the United States Capitol, Continued Interview of Cassidy Hutchinson, (June 20, 2022), pp. 25-26.

477. Select Committee to Investigate the January 6th Attack on the United States Capitol, Transcribed Interview of Pasquale Anthony "Pat" Cipollone, (July 8, 2022), p. 161; Select Committee to Investigate the January 6th Attack on the United States Capitol, *Hearing on the January 6th Investigation*, 117th Cong., 2d sess., (July 21, 2022), at 1:29:30 - 1:31:51, available at https://www.youtube.com/watch?v=pbRVqWbHGuo.

478. Select Committee to Investigate the January 6th Attack on the United States Capitol, Transcribed Interview of White House employee with national security responsibilities, (July 19, 2022), pp. 12-15, 98-99; Select Committee to Investigate the January 6th Attack on the United States Capitol, *Hearing on the January 6th Investigation*, 117th Cong., 2d sess., (July 21, 2022), at 38:02-38:44, available at https://youtu.be/pbRVqWbHGuo?t=2283.

479. Select Committee to Investigate the January 6th Attack on the United States Capitol, Deposition of Judson P. Deere, (Mar. 3, 2022), pp. 108-09.

480. Select Committee to Investigate the January 6th Attack on the United States Capitol, *Hearing on the January 6th Investigation*, 117th Cong., 2d sess., (July 21, 2022), available at https://www.govinfo.gov/committee/house-january6th.

481. Select Committee to Investigate the January 6th Attack on the United States Capitol, Transcribed Interview of Pasquale Anthony "Pat" Cipollone, (July 8, 2022), p. 163.

482. Third Superseding Indictment at 21, *United States v. Nordean et al.*, No. 1:21-cr-175 (D.D.C. June 6, 2022), ECF No. 380 (noting that Dominic Pezzola "used [a] riot shield … to break a window of the Capitol" at "2:13 p.m." and that "[t]he first members of the mob entered the Capitol through this broken window."); 167 Cong. Rec. S634 (daily ed. Feb. 10, 2021), available at https://www.congress.gov/117/crec/2021/02/10/CREC-2021-02-10-pt1-PgS615-4.pdf.

483. Documents on file with the Select Committee to Investigate the January 6th Attack on the United States Capitol (Mark Meadows Production), MM014907.

484. Documents on file with the Select Committee to Investigate the January 6th Attack on the United States Capitol (Mark Meadows Production), MM014912.

485. Documents on file with the Select Committee to Investigate the January 6th Attack on the United States Capitol (Mark Meadows Production), MM014919.

486. Documents on file with the Select Committee to Investigate the January 6th Attack on the United States Capitol (Mark Meadows Production), MM014925.

487. Documents on file with the Select Committee to Investigate the January 6th Attack on the United States Capitol (Mark Meadows Production), MM014933.

488. Documents on file with the Select Committee to Investigate the January 6th Attack on the United States Capitol (Mark Meadows Production), MM014935.

489. Documents on file with the Select Committee to Investigate the January 6th Attack on the United States Capitol (Mark Meadows Production), MM014937.

490. Documents on file with the Select Committee to Investigate the January 6th Attack on the United States Capitol (Mark Meadows Production), MM014939.

491. Documents on file with the Select Committee to Investigate the January 6th Attack on the United States Capitol (Mark Meadows Production), MM014944.

492. Documents on file with the Select Committee to Investigate the January 6th Attack on the United States Capitol (Mark Meadows Production), MM014961.

493. Select Committee to Investigate the January 6th Attack on the United States Capitol, *Hearing on the January 6th Investigation*, 117th Cong., 2d sess., (July 21, 2022), available at https://www.govinfo.gov/committee/house-january6th.

494. U.S. Senator Bill Cassidy, M.D. (@SenBillCassidy), Twitter, Jan. 6, 2021 4:03 p.m. ET, available at https://twitter.com/SenBillCassidy/status/1346925444189327361.

495. Documents on file with the Select Committee to Investigate the January 6th Attack on the United States Capitol (Mark Meadows Production), MM014971.

496. Select Committee to Investigate the January 6th Attack on the United States Capitol, Transcribed Interview of Jared Kushner, (Mar. 31, 2022), pp. 149-50; Select Committee to Investigate the January 6th Attack on the United States Capitol, Transcribed Interview of Julie Radford, (May 25, 2022), p. 37.

497. Select Committee to Investigate the January 6th Attack on the United States Capitol, Transcribed Interview of Jared Kushner, (Mar. 31, 2022), pp. 145, 150.

498. Leader McCarthy spoke on the air to Fox News starting at 3:05 p.m. ET and told the network that "I've already talked to the President. I called him. I think we need to make a statement, make sure that we can calm individuals down." Fox News (FoxNews), "LISTEN: Rep. Kevin McCarthy on protesters storming Capitol," Facebook, at 3:27-3:40, Jan. 6, 2021 (uploaded to Facebook at 3:35 p.m. ET), available at https://www.facebook.com/FoxNews/videos/listen-rep-kevin-mccarthy-on-protesters-storming-capitol/232725075039919/.

499. CBS News, "Live coverage: Protesters Swarm Capitol, Abruptly Halting Electoral Vote Count," YouTube, at 3:29:02-3:29:15, 3:29:43-3:30:03, 3:31:28-3:32:07, 3:33:52-3:34:12, Jan. 6, 2021, available at https://youtu.be/3Fsf4aWudJk?t=12542.

500. Rep. Herrera Beutler Describes Efforts to Get Trump to Intervene in Stopping Jan. 6 riot," WTHR (Feb. 13, 2021), at 1:20 - 1:50, available at https://www.wthr.com/video/news/nation-world/capitol-riot-herrera-beutler-trump-mccarthy-call/507-477fa84f-1277-444a-aad6-716c5ec9f66f.

501. Select Committee to Investigate the January 6th Attack on the United States Capitol, Transcribed Interview of John Michael "Mick" Mulvaney, (July 28, 2022), p. 43. CNN's Jamie Gangel related that she also confirmed the account with multiple other sources, reporting that "I've spoken to multiple Republican Members of the House who have knowledge of that call, who tell us that after Trump tried to say to Kevin, 'these are not my people, it's Antifa,' Kevin McCarthy said to Trump, 'no, it's not Antifa. These are your people'.... We're also told by several other Republican Members that Kevin McCarthy wasn't shy about this heated exchange with Trump, that he wanted his Members to know about it." CNN, "New Details Emerge in McCarthy's Call with Trump on January 6," YouTube, at 0:25 - 1:50, Feb. 12, 2021, available at https://www.youtube.com/watch?v=Gy1FPNluoOE.

502. Committee to Investigate the January 6th Attack on the United States Capitol, Transcribed Interview of John Michael "Mick" Mulvaney, (July 28, 2022), pp. 10-12 (describing calls and text messages to Dan Scavino and Mark Meadows).

503. *See, e.g.,* Documents on file with the Select Committee to Investigate the January 6th Attack on the United States Capitol (HBO Productions), Video file Reel_204I - All Clips Compilation.mp4 at 5:32-5:55 (January 6, 2021 footage from HBO of Nancy Pelosi and Chuck Schumer on phone call with Jeffrey Rosen); Documents on file with the Select Committee to Investigate the January 6th Attack on the United States Capitol (Mark Meadows Production), MM014906 (January 6, 2021 text message from Marjorie Taylor Greene to Mark Meadows), MM014919 (January 6, 2021 text message from William Timmons to Mark Meadows), MM014939 (January 6, 2021 text message from Chip Roy to Mark Meadows).

504. Select Committee to Investigate the January 6th Attack on the United States Capitol, Transcribed Interview of Pasquale Anthony "Pat" Cipollone, (July 8, 2022), p. 151.

505. Select Committee to Investigate the January 6th Attack on the United States Capitol, Transcribed Interview of Pasquale Anthony "Pat" Cipollone, (July 8, 2022), p. 162.

506. Select Committee to Investigate the January 6th Attack on the United States Capitol, Transcribed Interview of Pasquale Anthony "Pat" Cipollone, (July 8, 2022), p. 152.

507. Select Committee to Investigate the January 6th Attack on the United States Capitol, *Hearing on the January 6th Investigation*, 117th Cong., 2d sess., (July 21, 2022), at 0:57:48 - 0:58:19, available at https://youtu.be/pbRVqWbHGuo?t=3468.

508. Select Committee to Investigate the January 6th Attack on the United States Capitol, Transcribed Interview of White House Security Official, (July 11, 2022), pp. 81-83; Select Committee to Investigate the January 6th Attack on the United States Capitol, *Hearing on the January 6th Investigation*, 117th Cong., 2d sess., (July 21, 2022), available at https://www.govinfo.gov/committee/house-january6th. The Select Committee is not revealing the identity of this witness because of national security concerns as well as to guard against the risk of retaliation.

509. Donald J. Trump (@realDonaldTrump), Twitter, Jan. 6, 2021 2:24 p.m. ET, available at https://media-cdn.factba.se/realdonaldtrump-twitter/1346900434540240897.jpg (archived).

510. Select Committee to Investigate the January 6th Attack on the United States Capitol, *Hearing on the January 6th Investigation*, 117th Cong., 2d sess., (June 16, 2022), at 2:11:22-2:13:55, available at https://youtu.be/vBjUWVKuDj0?t=7882.

511. Select Committee to Investigate the January 6th Attack on the United States Capitol, *Hearing on the January 6th Investigation*, 117th Cong., 2d sess., (June 16, 2022), at 2:26:06-2:26:26, available at https://youtu.be/IQvuBoLBuC0?t=8766; Sentencing Transcript at 19, *United States v. Young*, No. 1:21-cr-291 (D.D.C. Sept. 27, 2022), ECF No. 170 (testifying for a victim impact statement, Officer Michael Fanone said: "At approximately 1435 hours, with rapidly mounting injuries and most of the MPD less than lethal munitions expended, the defending officers were forced to conduct a fighting withdrawal back towards the United States Capitol Building entrance. This is the first fighting withdrawal in the history of the Metropolitan Police Department.").

512. Select Committee to Investigate the January 6th Attack on the United States Capitol, *Hearing on the January 6th Investigation*, 117th Cong., 2d sess., (July 21, 2022), available at https://www.govinfo.gov/committee/house-january6th.

513. Select Committee to Investigate the January 6th Attack on the United States Capitol, *Hearing on the January 6th Investigation*, 117th Cong., 2d sess., (July 21, 2022), available at https://www.govinfo.gov/committee/house-january6th.

514. Select Committee to Investigate the January 6th Attack on the United States Capitol, Deposition of Judson P. Deere, (Mar. 3, 2022), p. 113.

515. Select Committee to Investigate the January 6th Attack on the United States Capitol, Transcribed Interview of Pasquale Anthony "Pat" Cipollone, (July 8, 2022), p. 160.

516. Documents on file with the Select Committee to Investigate the January 6th Attack on the United States Capitol (Hope Hicks Production), SC_HH_043-044 (January 6, 2021, text message from Hope Hicks to Julie Radford at 7:18 p.m.).

517. 167 Cong. Rec. S635 (daily ed. Feb. 10, 2021), available at https://www.congress.gov/117/crec/2021/02/10/CREC-2021-02-10-pt1-PgS615-4.pdf; Spencer S. Hsu, "Pence Spent Jan. 6 at Underground Senate Loading Dock, Secret Service Confirms," *Washington Post*, (Mar. 21, 2022), available at https://www.washingtonpost.com/dc-md-va/2022/03/21/couy-griffin-cowboys-trump-jan6/.

518. Select Committee to Investigate the January 6th Attack on the United States Capitol, Deposition of Molly Michael, (Mar. 24, 2022), p. 137.

519. Select Committee to Investigate the January 6th Attack on the United States Capitol, *Hearing on the January 6th Investigation*, 117th Cong., 2d sess., (July 21, 2022), available at https://www.govinfo.gov/committee/house-january6th.

520. Select Committee to Investigate the January 6th Attack on the United States Capitol, Continued Interview of Cassidy Hutchinson, (June 20, 2022), p. 27.

521. Select Committee to Investigate the January 6th Attack on the United States Capitol, *Hearing on the January 6th Investigation*, 117th Cong., 2d sess., (June 28, 2022), at 1:31:25 –

1:32:22, available at https://youtu.be/HeQNV-aQ_jU?t=5359; Select Committee to Investigate the January 6th Attack on the United States Capitol, Continued Interview of Cassidy Hutchinson, (June 20, 2022), pp. 27-28.

522. Select Committee to Investigate the January 6th Attack on the United States Capitol, Transcribed Interview of Pasquale Anthony "Pat" Cipollone, (July 8, 2022), p. 182.

523. Select Committee to Investigate the January 6th Attack on the United States Capitol, Transcribed Interview of Eric Herschmann, (Apr. 6, 2022), pp. 68-69, 71.

524. Donald J. Trump (@realDonaldTrump), Twitter, Jan. 6, 2021 2:38 p.m. ET, available at https://media-cdn.factba.se/realdonaldtrump-twitter/1346904110969315332.jpg (archived).

525. Select Committee to Investigate the January 6th Attack on the United States Capitol, *Hearing on the January 6th Investigation*, 117th Cong., 2d sess., (July 21, 2022), available at https://www.govinfo.gov/committee/house-january6th.

526. Donald J. Trump (@realDonaldTrump), Twitter, Jan. 6, 2021 3:13 p.m. ET, available at https://media-cdn.factba.se/realdonaldtrump-twitter/1346912780700577792.jpg (archived).

527. Documents on file with the Select Committee to Investigate the January 6th Attack on the United States Capitol (Mark Meadows Production), MM014925.

528. Documents on file with the Select Committee to Investigate the January 6th Attack on the United States Capitol (Mark Meadows Production), MM014944.

529. Select Committee to Investigate the January 6th Attack on the United States Capitol, *Hearing on the January 6th Investigation*, 117th Cong., 2d sess., (July 21, 2022), available at https://www.govinfo.gov/committee/house-january6th.

530. Select Committee to Investigate the January 6th Attack on the United States Capitol, *Hearing on the January 6th Investigation*, 117th Cong., 2d sess., (July 21, 2022), available at https://www.govinfo.gov/committee/house-january6th].

531. Documents on file with the Select Committee to Investigate the January 6th Attack on the United States Capitol (National Archives Production), 076P-R000004112_0001 (January 6, 2021 email at 3:05 p.m. notifying Beau Harrison of Ashli Babbitt shooting); Select Committee to Investigate the January 6th Attack on the United States Capitol, Transcribed Interview of William Beau Harrison (Aug. 18, 2022), pp. 73–76 (describing writing note and passing it to Mark Meadows or Tony Ornato); Documents on file with the Select Committee to Investigate the January 6th Attack on the United States Capitol (National Archives Production), P-R000241 (January 6, 2021 pocket card written by Beau Harrison with the message, "1x CIVILIAN GUNSHOT WOUND TO CHEST @ DOOR OF HOUSE CHABER [sic]"); Select Committee to Investigate the January 6th Attack on the United States Capitol, Transcribed Interview of White House Employee, (June 10, 2022), pp. 46–47 ("I remember seeing that [note] in front of [President Trump], yeah."). The Select Committee is not revealing the identity of this witness to guard against the risk of retaliation. *See also* Select Committee to Investigate the January 6th Attack on the United States Capitol, Transcribed Interview of Anthony Ornato, (January 28, 2022), p. 115; Select Committee to Investigate the January 6th Attack on the United States Capitol, Transcribed Interview of Eric Herschmann, (Apr. 6, 2022), p. 87 (recalling announcing during the afternoon that a Trump supporter had been killed).

532. "Department of Justice Closes Investigation into the Death of Ashli Babbitt," Department of Justice, (Apr. 14, 2021), available at https://www.justice.gov/usao-dc/pr/department-justice-closes-investigation-death-ashli-babbitt.

533. Select Committee to Investigate the January 6th Attack on the United States Capitol, *Hearing on the January 6th Investigation*, 117th Cong., 2d sess., (July 21, 2022), available at https://www.govinfo.gov/committee/house-january6th; Select Committee to Investigate the January 6th Attack on the United States Capitol, *Business Meeting on the January 6th Investigation*, 117th Cong., 2d sess., (Oct. 13, 2022), available at https://www.govinfo.gov/committee/house-january6th; ABC News, "Mike Pence Opens Up with David Muir on Jan. 6: Exclusive," YouTube, at 9:27-10:00, Nov. 14, 2022, available at https://youtu.be/-AAyKAoPFQs?t=567; Select Committee to Investigate the January 6th Attack on the United

States Capitol, Transcribed Interview of General Mark A. Milley (Nov. 17, 2021), pp. 80-81; Select Committee to Investigate the January 6th Attack on the United States Capitol, Transcribed Interview of Christopher Charles Miller (Jan. 14, 2022), pp. 124-25; Select Committee to Investigate the January 6th Attack on the United States Capitol, Transcribed Interview of Jeffrey Rosen, (Oct. 13, 2021), pp. 172-73, 182-84; Select Committee to Investigate the January 6th Attack on the United States Capitol, Transcribed Interview of Richard Peter Donoghue, (Oct. 1, 2021), p. 186.

534. NBC News, "Biden Condemns Chaos at the Capitol as 'Insurrection,'" YouTube, Jan. 6, 2021, available at https://www.youtube.com/watch?v=FBCWTqJT7M4; Select Committee to Investigate the January 6th Attack on the United States Capitol, *Hearing on the January 6th Investigation*, 117th Cong., 2d sess., (July 21, 2022), available at https://www.govinfo.gov/committee/house-january6th.

535. "Trump Video Telling Protesters at Capitol Building to Go Home: Transcript," Rev, (Jan. 6, 2021), available at https://www.rev.com/blog/transcripts/trump-video-telling-protesters-at-capitol-building-to-go-home-transcript.

536. Select Committee to Investigate the January 6th Attack on the United States Capitol, *Hearing on the January 6th Investigation*, 117th Cong., 2d sess., (July 21, 2022), available at https://www.govinfo.gov/committee/house-january6th.

537. Select Committee to Investigate the January 6th Attack on the United States Capitol, *Hearing on the January 6th Investigation*, 117th Cong., 2d sess., (July 21, 2022), available at https://www.govinfo.gov/committee/house-january6th

538. Select Committee to Investigate the January 6th Attack on the United States Capitol, *Hearing on the January 6th Investigation*, 117th Cong., 2d sess., (July 12, 2022), at 2:36:58-2:37:30, 2:44:00-2:45:05, available at https://www.youtube.com/watch?v=rrUa0hfG6Lo ("[W]hen President Trump put his tweet out, we literally left right after that come out . . . As soon as that come out, everybody started talking about it . . . it definitely dispersed a lot of the crowd. . . . We left.").

539. Select Committee to Investigate the January 6th Attack on the United States Capitol, *Hearing on the January 6th Investigation*, 117th Cong., 2d sess., (July 12, 2022), at 1:58:00, available at https://www.youtube.com/watch?v=pbRVqWbHGuo.

540. Select Committee to Investigate the January 6th Attack on the United States Capitol, *Hearing on the January 6th Investigation*, 117th Cong., 2d sess., (July 12, 2022), at 1:58:00, available at https://www.youtube.com/watch?v=pbRVqWbHGuo.

541. Donald J. Trump (@realDonaldTrump), Twitter, Jan. 6, 2021 at 6:01 p.m. ET, available at http://web.archive.org/web/20210106232133/https://twitter.com/realdonaldtrump/status/1346954970910707712 (archived).

542. Select Committee to Investigate the January 6th Attack on the United States Capitol, *Hearing on the January 6th Investigation*, 117th Cong., 2d sess., (July 21, 2022), available at https://www.govinfo.gov/committee/house-january6th.

543. Select Committee to Investigate the January 6th Attack on the United States Capitol, Transcribed Interview of Timothy Murtaugh, (May 19, 2022), p. 175; Select Committee to Investigate the January 6th Attack on the United States Capitol, *Hearing on the January 6th Investigation*, 117th Cong., 2d sess., (July 21, 2022), available at https://www.govinfo.gov/committee/house-january6th.

544. Select Committee to Investigate the January 6th Attack on the United States Capitol, Transcribed Interview of Pasquale Anthony "Pat" Cipollone, (July 8, 2022), p. 194; Select Committee to Investigate the January 6th Attack on the United States Capitol, *Hearing on the January 6th Investigation*, 117th Cong., 2d sess., (July 21, 2022), available at https://www.govinfo.gov/committee/house-january6th.

545. Select Committee to Investigate the January 6th Attack on the United States Capitol, Deposition of Greg Jacob, (Feb. 1, 2022), p. 192.

546. Select Committee to Investigate the January 6th Attack on the United States Capitol, Transcribed Interview of White House Employee, (June 10, 2022), p. 53. The Select Committee is not revealing the identity of this witness to guard against the risk of retaliation.

547. Documents on file with the Select Committee to Investigate the January 6th Attack on the United States Capitol, (Rudolph Giuliani Production, Mar. 11, 2022); Documents on file with the Select Committee to Investigate the January 6th Attack on the United States Capitol, (AT&T Production, Feb. 9, 2022).

548. Select Committee to Investigate the January 6th Attack on the United States Capitol, Deposition of Rudolph Giuliani, (May 20, 2022), pp. 205-07; Sunlen Serfaty, Devan Cole, and Alex Rogers, "As Riot Raged at Capitol, Trump Tried to Call Senators to Overturn Election," CNN, (Jan. 8, 2021), available at https://www.cnn.com/2021/01/08/politics/mike-lee-tommy-tuberville-trump-misdialed-capitol-riot; Documents on file with the Select Committee to Investigate the January 6th Attack on the United States Capitol, (Rudolph Giuliani Production, Mar. 11, 2022); Documents on file with the Select Committee to Investigate the January 6th Attack on the United States Capitol, (AT&T Production, Feb. 9, 2022).

549. Mike Pence, *So Help Me God* (New York: Simon & Schuster, 2022), p. 475.

550. Mike Pence, *So Help Me God* (New York: Simon & Schuster, 2022), p. 474.

551. Select Committee to Investigate the January 6th Attack on the United States Capitol, Transcribed Interview of Steven Andrew Sund, (Apr. 20, 2022), pp. 170-71; Select Committee to Investigate the January 6th Attack on the United States Capitol, Transcribed Interview of Pasquale Anthony "Pat" Cipollone, (Jul. 8, 2022), p. 174; Select Committee to Investigate the January 6th Attack on the United States Capitol, Deposition of Keith Kellogg Jr., (Dec. 14, 2021), pp. 126–27; Select Committee to Investigate the January 6th Attack on the United States Capitol, Deposition of Nicholas Luna, (Mar. 21, 2022), pp. 151-52; Select Committee to Investigate the January 6th Attack on the United States Capitol, Transcribed Interview of Christopher Charles Miller, (Jan. 14, 2022), pp. 124-26; Select Committee to Investigate the January 6th Attack on the United States Capitol, Transcribed Interview of General Mark A. Milley, (Nov. 17, 2021), pp. 80-82; Select Committee to Investigate the January 6th Attack on the United States Capitol, Transcribed Interview of Richard Peter Donoghue, (Oct. 1, 2021), pp. 186-89; Select Committee to Investigate the January 6th Attack on the United States Capitol, Transcribed Interview of Muriel Bowser, (Jan. 12, 2022), pp. 21-22.

552. ABC News, "Pence Opens Up with David Muir on Jan. 6: Exclusive," YouTube, at 10:45-11:02, Nov. 14, 2022, available at https://www.youtube.com/watch?v=-AAyKAoPFQs.

553. Select Committee to Investigate the January 6th Attack on the United States Capitol, Transcribed Interview of Steven Andrew Sund, (Apr. 20, 2022), pp. 170-71; Select Committee to Investigate the January 6th Attack on the United States Capitol, Transcribed Interview of Pasquale Anthony "Pat" Cipollone, (Jul. 8, 2022), p. 174; Select Committee to Investigate the January 6th Attack on the United States Capitol, Deposition of Keith Kellogg Jr., (Dec. 14, 2021), pp. 126–27; Select Committee to Investigate the January 6th Attack on the United States Capitol, Deposition of Nicholas Luna, (Mar. 21, 2022), pp. 151-52; Select Committee to Investigate the January 6th Attack on the United States Capitol, Transcribed Interview of Christopher Charles Miller, (Jan. 14, 2022), pp. 124-26; Select Committee to Investigate the January 6th Attack on the United States Capitol, Transcribed Interview of General Mark A. Milley, (Nov. 17, 2021), pp. 80-82; Select Committee to Investigate the January 6th Attack on the United States Capitol, Transcribed Interview of Richard Peter Donoghue, (Oct. 1, 2021), pp. 186-89; Select Committee to Investigate the January 6th Attack on the United States Capitol, Transcribed Interview of Muriel Bowser, (Jan. 12, 2022), pp. 21-22.

554. Select Committee to Investigate the January 6th Attack on the United States Capitol, Transcribed Interview of General Mark A. Milley (Nov. 17, 2021), pp. 17, 268.

555. Select Committee to Investigate the January 6th Attack on the United States Capitol, Transcribed Interview of General Mark A. Milley (Nov. 17, 2021), p. 296; Select Committee to Investigate the January 6th Attack on the United States Capitol, *Hearing on the January 6th Investigation*, 117th Cong., 2d sess., (July 21, 2022), available at https://www.govinfo.gov/committee/house-january6th.

556. Glenn Kessler, "Trump Falsely Claims He 'Requested' 10,000 Troops Rejected by Pelosi," *Washington Post*, (Mar. 2, 2021), available at https://www.washingtonpost.com/politics/2021/03/02/trump-falsely-claims-he-requested-10000-troops-rejected-by-pelosi/; "Mark Meadows: Biden Administration Policies Put 'America Last'," Fox News, (Feb. 7, 2021), available at https://www.foxnews.com/transcript/mark-meadows-biden-administration-policies-put-america-last.

557. Select Committee to Investigate the January 6th Attack on the United States Capitol, Transcribed Interview of Christopher Charles Miller (Jan. 14, 2022), pp. 100-01. On January 4, 2021, Max Miller and Katrina Pierson exchanged text messages discussing their planning activities for the 6th. In those messages, Max Miller stated: "Just glad we killed the national guard and a procession" and that "... chief [Mark Meadows] already had said no for days!". Documents on file with the Select Committee to Investigate the January 6th Attack on the United States Capitol (Max Miller Production), Miller Production 0001 (January 4, 2021, text messages between Max Miller and Katrina Pierson).

558. Select Committee to Investigate the January 6th Attack on the United States Capitol, *Hearing on the January 6th Investigation*, 117th Cong., 2d sess., (July 12, 2022), at 2:22:45-2:23:22, available at https://youtu.be/rrUa0hfG6Lo?t=8565; Documents on file with the Select Committee to Investigate the January 6th Attack on the United States Capitol (Katrina Pierson Production), KPierson0717-719.

559. "House Republican Leader Kevin McCarthy on Asking President Trump for his Resignation," ed. Alex Burns and Jonathan Martin, ThisWillNotPass.com, (Jan. 8, 2021), available at https://www.thiswillnotpass.com/bookresources.

560. Documents on file with the Select Committee to Investigate the January 6th Attack on the United States Capitol (Mark Meadows Production), MM014456.

561. Documents on file with the Select Committee to Investigate the January 6th Attack on the United States Capitol (Mark Meadows Production), MM014858 - MM014861.

562. Documents on file with the Select Committee to Investigate the January 6th Attack on the United States Capitol (Mark Meadows Production), MM014467 (December 31, 2020, text message from telephone number assigned to Carrah Jo Roy, wife of Rep. Chip Roy. to Mark Meadows). The Select Committee believes that Rep. Chip Roy sent this message.

563. Documents on file with the Select Committee to Investigate the January 6th Attack on the United States Capitol (Mark Meadows Production), MM014503 (January 1, 2021, text message from telephone number assigned to Carrah Jo Roy, wife of Rep. Chip Roy. to Mark Meadows). The Select Committee believes that Rep. Chip Roy sent this message.

564. Documents on file with the Select Committee to Investigate the January 6th Attack on the United States Capitol (Kayleigh McEnany Production), CTRL0000925383, p. 3 (January 7, 2021, text message from Sean Hannity to Kayleigh McEnany)

565. Documents on file with the Select Committee to Investigate the January 6th Attack on the United States Capitol (Mark Meadows Production), MM015209 (January 10, 2021, text message Sean Hannity to Mark Meadows and Jim Jordan).

566. Documents on file with the Select Committee to Investigate the January 6th Attack on the United States Capitol (Mark Meadows Production), MM014906.

567. "U.S. House Impeaches President Trump for Second Time, 232-197," C-SPAN, at 4:14:56 - 4:15:31, Jan. 13, 2021, available at https://www.c-span.org/video/?507879-101/house-impeaches-president-trump-time-232-197&live=.

568. "Republican Leader Kevin McCarthy says Pres. Trump Admitted He Bears Some Responsibility for the January 6 Insurrection at the U.S. Capitol," ed. Alex Burns and Jonathan Martin, ThisWillNotPass.com, (Jan. 11, 2021), available at https://www.thiswillnotpass.com/bookresources.

569. "Statement by Mo Brooks," Mo Brooks for U.S. Senate, available at https://mobrooks.com/statement-by-mo-brooks/; Joe Walsh, "GOP Rep. Mo Brooks Claims Trump Asked Him to Reinstate Trump Presidency," *Forbes*, (Mar. 23, 2022), available at https://www.forbes.com/

sites/joewalsh/2022/03/23/gop-rep-mo-brooks-claims-trump-asked-him-to-reinstate-trump-presidency/?sh=7264e1d91edd (noting that Rep. Mo Brooks issued this statement on Wednesday, March 23, 2022).

570. *See* Ryan Goodman and Josh Asabor, "In Their Own Words: The 43 Republicans' Explanations of Their Votes Not to Convict Trump in Impeachment Trial," Just Security, (Feb. 15, 2021), *available at* https://www.justsecurity.org/74725/in-their-own-words-the-43-republicans-explanations-of-their-votes-not-to-convict-trump-in-impeachment-trial/.

571. C-SPAN, "Senate Minority Leader Mitch McConnell Remarks Following Senate Impeachment Vote," YouTube, at 5:10 – 5:46, (Feb. 13, 2021), available at https://www.youtube.com/watch?v=yxRMoqNnfvw.

572. "Republican Leader Kevin McCarthy Says Pres. Trump Admitted He Bears Some Responsibility for the January 6 Insurrection at the U.S. Capitol," Alex Burns and Jonathan Martin, eds., ThisWillNotPass.com, (Jan. 11, 2021), available at https://www.thiswillnotpass.com/bookresources; Melanie Zanona, "New Audio Reveals McCarthy said Trump Admitted Bearing Some Responsibility for Capitol Attack," CNN, (April 22, 2022), available at https://www.cnn.com/2022/04/22/politics/trump-january-6-responsibility-book/index.html. Leader McCarthy also relayed this conversation with President Trump to his Republican colleagues: "I asked him [Trump] personally today, does he hold responsibility for what happened. And he needs to acknowledge that." *Id.* The Committee believes that House Republican Leader McCarthy's testimony would be material to any criminal investigation of Donald Trump, not just to probe this apparent Trump acknowledgement of culpability, but also because Leader McCarthy spoke directly to Donald Trump and others who were in the White House on January 6th and unsuccessfully pleaded for the President's immediate assistance to halt the violence. Leader McCarthy did not comply with the Select Committee's subpoena.

573. "U.S. House Impeaches President Trump for Second Time, 232-197," C-SPAN, at 4:14:56 - 4:15:31, (Jan. 13, 2021), available at https://www.c-span.org/video/?507879-101/house-impeaches-president-trump-time-232-197&live=; 167 Cong. Rec. H172 (daily ed. Jan. 13, 2021), available at https://www.congress.gov/117/crec/2021/01/13/CREC-2021-01-13-pt1-PgH165.pdf.

574. *See supra*, Executive Summary.

575. *See supra*, Executive Summary.

576. Documents on file with the Select Committee (National Archives Production), VP-R0000156_0001 (January 6, 2021, email chain between John Eastman and Greg Jacob re: Pennsylvania letter).

577. Documents on file with Select Committee (Department of Justice Production), HCOR-Pre-Certification-Events-07282021-000738—HCOR-Pre-Certification-Events-07282021-000739 (December 27, 2020, handwritten notes from Richard Donoghue).

578. *See supra*, Executive Summary. The State legislatures lacked authority to change the lawful outcome of the State elections at that point. Nevertheless Eastman, Trump, and others nevertheless pushed for such action.

579. *See supra*, Executive Summary.

580. *See Supra*, Executive Summary; Donald J. Trump (@realDonaldTrump), Twitter, Dec. 19, 2020 1:42 a.m. ET, available at http://web.archive.org/web/20201219064257/https://twitter.com/realDonaldTrump/status/1340185773220515840 (archived); *see also, e.g.,* Donald J. Trump (@realDonaldTrump), Twitter, Dec. 26, 2020 8:14 a.m. ET, available at https://twitter.com/realDonaldTrump/status/1342821189077622792; Donald J. Trump (@realDonaldTrump), Twitter, Dec. 27, 2020 5:51 p.m. ET, available at https://twitter.com/realDonaldTrump/status/1343328708963299338; Donald J. Trump (@realDonaldTrump), Twitter, Dec. 30, 2020 2:06 p.m. ET, available at https://twitter.com/realDonaldTrump/status/1344359312878149634; Donald J. Trump (@realDonaldTrump), Twitter, Jan. 1, 2021 12:52 p.m. ET, available at https://www.thetrumparchive.com/?searchbox=%22RT+%40KylieJaneKremer%22 (retweeting @KylieJaneKremer, Dec. 19, 2020 3:50 p.m. ET, available at https://twitter.com/KylieJaneKremer/status/1340399063875895296); Donald J. Trump (@realDonaldTrump),

Twitter, Jan. 1, 2021 2:53 p.m. ET, available at https://twitter.com/realDonaldTrump/status/ 1345095714687377418; Donald J. Trump (@realDonaldTrump), Twitter, Jan. 1, 2021 3:34 p.m. ET, available at https://twitter.com/realDonaldTrump/status/1345106078141394944; Donald J. Trump (@realDonaldTrump), Twitter, Jan. 1, 2021 6:38 p.m. ET, available at https:// twitter.com/realDonaldTrump/status/1345152408591204352; Donald J. Trump (@realDonaldTrump), Twitter, Jan. 2, 2021 9:04 p.m. ET, available at https://twitter.com/ realDonaldTrump/status/1345551634907209730; Donald J. Trump (@realDonaldTrump), Twitter, Jan. 3, 2021 1:29 a.m. ET, available at https://www.thetrumparchive.com/ ?searchbox=%22RT+%40realDonaldTrump%3A+https%3A%2F%2Ft.co%2FnslWcFwkCj%22 (retweeting Donald J. Trump (@realDonaldTrump), Jan. 2, 2021 9:04 p.m. ET, available at https://twitter.com/realDonaldTrump/status/1345551634907209730); Donald J. Trump (@realDonaldTrump), Twitter, Jan. 3, 2021 10:15 a.m. ET, available at https:// www.thetrumparchive.com/?searchbox=%22RT+%40JenLawrence21%22 (retweeting Jennifer Lynn Lawrence (@JenLawrence21), Jan. 3, 2021 12:17 a.m. ET, available at https:// twitter.com/JenLawrence21/status/1345600194826686464); Donald J. Trump (@realDonaldTrump), Twitter, Jan. 3, 2021 10:17 a.m. ET, available at https:// www.thetrumparchive.com/?searchbox=%22RT+%40CodeMonkeyZ+if%22 (retweeting Ron Watkins (@CodeMonkeyZ) Jan. 2, 2021 9:14 p.m. ET, available at http://web.archive.org/ web/20210103151826/https://twitter.com/CodeMonkeyZ/status/1345599512560078849 (archived)); Donald J. Trump, (@realDonaldTrump), Twitter, Jan. 3, 2021 10:24 a.m. ET, available at https://www.thetrumparchive.com/?searchbox=%22RT+%40realMikeLindell%22 (retweeting Mike Lindell (@realMikeLindell), Jan. 2, 2021 5:47 p.m. ET, available at http:// web.archive.org/web/20210103152421/https://twitter.com/realMikeLindell/status/ 1345547185836978176 (archived)); Donald J. Trump (@realDonaldTrump), Twitter, Jan. 3, 2021 10:27 a.m. ET, available at https://twitter.com/realDonaldTrump/status/ 1345753534168506370; Donald J. Trump (@realDonaldTrump), Twitter, Jan. 3, 2021 10:28 a.m. ET, available at https://www.thetrumparchive.com/?searchbox= %22RT+%40AmyKremer+we%22 (retweeting Amy Kremer (@AmyKremer), Jan. 2, 2021 2:58 p.m. ET, available at https://twitter.com/AmyKremer/status/1345459488107749386); Donald J. Trump (@realDonaldTrump), Twitter, Jan. 4, 2021 9:46 a.m. ET, available at https:// www.thetrumparchive.com/?searchbox= %22RT+%40realDonaldTrump+I+will+be+there.+Historic+day%21%22 (retweeting Donald J. Trump (@realDonaldTrump), Jan. 3, 2021 10:27 a.m. ET, available at https://twitter.com/ realDonaldTrump/status/1345753534168506370); Donald J. Trump (@realDonaldTrump), Twitter, Jan. 5, 2021 10:27 a.m. ET, available at https://twitter.com/realDonaldTrump/ status/1346478482105069568; Donald J. Trump (@realDonaldTrump), Twitter, Jan. 5, 2021 5:43 p.m. ET, available at https://twitter.com/realDonaldTrump/status/ 1346588064026685443.

581. Donald J. Trump (@realDonldTrump), Twitter, Jan. 6, 2021 2:24 p.m. ET, available at https:// www.thetrumparchive.com/?searchbox=%22mike+pence+%22&results=1 (archived) ("Mike Pence didn't have the courage to do what should have been done to protect our Country and our Constitution, giving States a chance to certify a corrected set of facts, not the fraudulent or inaccurate ones which they were asked to previously certify. USA demands the truth!"); USA Today Graphics (@usatgraphics), Twitter, Jan. 7, 2021 9:56 p.m. ET, available at https://twitter.com/usatgraphics/status/1347376642956603392 (screenshotting the since-deleted tweet).

582. "Trump Video Telling Protesters at Capitol Building to Go Home: Transcript," Rev, (Jan. 6, 2021), available at https://www.rev.com/blog/transcripts/trump-video-telling-protesters-at-capitol-building-to-go-home-transcript; Select Committee to Investigate the January 6th Attack on the United States Capitol, *Hearing on the January 6th Investigation*, 117th Cong., 2d sess., (July 12, 2022), at 2:36:58-2:37:30 and 2:44:00-2:45:05, available at https:// www.youtube.com/watch?v=rrUa0hfG6Lo ("[W]hen President Trump put his tweet out, we literally left right after that come out . . . As soon as that come out, everybody started talking about it . . . it definitely dispersed a lot of the crowd. . . . We left.").

583. Order Re Privilege of Documents Dated January 4-7, 2021 at 3-16, *Eastman v. Thompson et al.*, 594 F. Supp. 3d 1156, (C.D. Cal. March 28, 2022) (No. 8:22-cv-99-DOC-DFM).

584. Order Re Privilege of Documents Dated January 4-7, 2021 at 53–53, 58, *Eastman v. Thompson et al.*, 594 F. Supp. 3d 1156, (C.D. Cal. March 28, 2022) (No. 8:22-cv-99-DOC-DFM) (referring to two Federal criminal statutes).

585. Order Re Privilege of 599 Documents Dated November 3, 2020 – January 20, 2021 at 24, *Eastman v. Thompson et al.*, No. 8:22-cv-99-DOC-DFM, (C.D. Cal. June 7, 2022), ECF No. 24.

586. Order Re Privilege of Documents Dated January 4-7, 2021 at 63–64, *Eastman v. Thompson et al.*, 594 F. Supp. 3d 1156, (C.D. Cal. March 28, 2022) (No. 8:22-cv-99-DOC-DFM).

587. Order Re Privilege of Documents Dated January 4-7, 2021 at 64, *Eastman v. Thompson et al.*, 594 F. Supp. 3d 1156, (C.D. Cal. March 28, 2022) (No. 8:22-cv-99-DOC-DFM).

588. *See* "23 Months Since the January 6th Attack on the Capitol," Department of Justice, (Dec. 8, 2022), available at https://www.justice.gov/usao-dc/23-months-january-6-attack-capitol.

589. Kyle Cheney, "Rep. Scott Perry Suing to Block DOJ Access to His Cell Phone," Politico, (Aug. 24, 2022), available at https://www.politico.com/news/2022/08/24/rep-scott-perry-suing-to-block-doj-access-to-his-cell-phone-00053486; Betsy Woodruff Swan, Josh Gerstein, and Kyle Cheney, "DOJ Searches Home of Former Official Who Aided Alleged Pro-Trump 'Coup'," Politico, (June 23, 2022), available at https://www.politico.com/news/2022/06/23/law-enforcement-trump-official-coup-00041767.

590. *See, e.g.*, Sarah Murray, Evan Perez, and Katelyn Polantz, "Federal Judge Orders Former Top Lawyers in Trump's White House to Testify in Criminal Grand Jury Probe," CNN, (Dec. 1, 2022), available at https://www.cnn.com/2022/12/01/politics/cipollone-philbin-trump-lawyers-testify.

591. Sara Murray and Jason Morris, "Fulton County Prosecutor Investigating Trump Aims for Indictments as Soon as December," CNN, (Oct. 6, 2022), available at https://www.cnn.com/2022/10/06/politics/fani-willis-georgia-prosecutor-trump-indictments-december/index.html.

592. The Special Counsel is to oversee the Department's ongoing investigation "into whether any person or entity unlawfully interfered with the transfer of power following the 2020 Presidential election or the certification of the Electoral College vote held on or about January 6, 2021." "Appointment of a Special Counsel," Department of Justice, (Nov. 18, 2022), available at https://www.justice.gov/opa/pr/appointment-special-counsel-0. In addition, the Special Counsel is to oversee the Department's "ongoing investigation involving classified documents and other Presidential records, as well as the possible obstruction of that investigation. . . ." *Id.*

593. The House of Representatives held Meadows in contempt for refusing to testify before the Committee, 167 Cong. Rec. H7814-7815 (daily ed. Dec. 14, 2021), but DOJ declined to prosecute him. *See* Josh Gerstein, Kyle Cheny, and Nicholas Wu, "DOJ Declines to Charge Meadows, Scavino with Contempt of Congress for Defying Jan. 6 Committee," *Politico*, (June 3, 2022), available at https://www.politico.com/news/2022/06/03/doj-declines-to-charge-meadows-scavino-with-contempt-of-congress-for-defying-jan-6-committee-00037230.

594. 18 U.S.C. § 1512(c)(2).

595. According to DOJ, "[a] conviction under Section 1512(c)(2) requires proof that": (1) "the natural and probable effect of the defendant's actions were to obstruct [influence or impede] the official proceeding;" (2) "that [defendant] knew that his actions were likely to obstruct [influence or impede] that proceeding;" and (3) "that he acted with the wrongful or improper purpose of delaying or stopping the official proceeding." *United States v. Andries*, No. 21-93 (RC), 2022 U.S. Dist. LEXIS 44794 at *37 n.8 (D.D.C. Mar. 14, 2022) (quoting Government's Response to Defendant's Second Supplemental Brief at 6); *see United States v. Aguilar*, 515 U.S. 593, 616 (1995) (Scalia, J., concurring in part, dissenting in part) (describing the "longstanding and well-accepted meaning" of "corruptly" as denoting "an act done with an intent to give some advantage inconsistent with official duty and the rights of others" (quoting *United States v. Ogle*, 613 F.2d 233, 238 (10th Cir. 1979))).

596. *See, e.g.*, *United States v. Gillespie*, No. 22-CR-60 (BAH), 2022 U.S. Dist. LEXIS 214833, at *7-8 (D.D.C. Nov. 29, 2022); *United States v. Seefried*, No. 1:21-cr-287 (TNM), 2022 U.S. Dist. LEXIS

196980, at *2-3 (D.D.C. Oct. 29, 2022); *United States v. Miller*, 589 F. Supp. 3d 60, 67 (D.D.C. 2022), *reconsideration denied*, No. 1:21-CR-119 (CJN), 589 F. Supp. 3d 60 (D.D.C. May 27, 2022); *United States v. Puma*, No. 1:21-CR-454 (PLF), 2022 U.S. Dist. LEXIS 48875, at *10 (D.D.C. Mar. 19, 2022); *United States v. McHugh*, 583 F. Supp. 3d 1, 14-15 (D.D.C. 2022). *See also* T. Kanefield, "January 6 Defendants Are Raising a Creative Defense. It Isn't Working," *Washington Post*, (Feb. 15, 2022), available at https://www.washingtonpost.com/outlook/2022/02/15/jan-6-official-proceeding/.

597. *See supra*, Executive Summary.

598. *See supra*, Executive Summary.

599. *See supra*, Executive Summary.

600. Documents on file with the Select Committee (National Archives Production), VP-R0000156_0001 (January 6, 2021, email chain between John Eastman and Greg Jacob re: Pennsylvania letter). One judge on the U.S. District Court for the District of Columbia, in the course of concluding that section 1512(c) is not void for vagueness, interpreted the "corruptly" element as meaning "contrary to law, statute, or established rule." *United States v. Sandlin*, 575 F. Supp. 3d. 15–16, (D.D.C. 2021). As explained above, President Trump attempted to cause the Vice President to violate the Electoral Count Act, and even Dr. Eastman advised President Trump that the proposed course of action would violate the Act. We believe this satisfies the "corruptly" element of the offense under the *Sandlin* opinion.

601. Indeed, it would not have been legally possible for a State to have done so in the days before January 6th.

602. Order Re Privilege of Documents Dated January 4-7, 2021 at 49-50, *Eastman v. Thompson et al.*, 594 F. Supp. 3d 1156, (C.D. Cal. March 28, 2022) (No. 8:22-cv-99-DOC-DFM).

603. *See supra*, Executive Summary.

604. Documents on file with Select Committee (Department of Justice Production), HCOR-Pre-Certification-Events-07282021-000738 - COR-Pre-Certification-Events-07282021-000739 (December 27, 2020, handwritten notes from Richard Donoghue).

605. *See supra*, Executive Summary.

606. *See supra*, Executive Summary.

607. *See supra*, Executive Summary. Jeffrey Clark invoked his Fifth Amendment privilege against self-incrimination in response to questions regarding this letter. As already noted, the political appointee who assisted in drafting the letter was hired at the Justice Department on December 15, 2020, but had worked on behalf of President Trump on election challenges in the weeks beforehand (including, apparently, while simultaneously serving as Special Counsel for the White House Office of Management and Budget).

608. *See supra*, Executive Summary.

609. *See supra*, Executive Summary.

610. *See supra*, Executive Summary.

611. Select Committee to Investigate the January 6th Attack on the United States Capitol, Transcribed Interview of Eric Herschmann, (Apr. 6, 2022), p. 26.

612. Documents on file with the Select Committee (National Archives Production), VP-R0000156_0001 (January 6, 2021, email chain between John Eastman and Greg Jacob re: Pennsylvania letter).

613. Select Committee to Investigate the January 6th Attack on the United States Capitol, Transcribed Interview of Eric Herschmann, (Apr. 6, 2022), p. 44. Although Eastman invoked his Fifth Amendment rights as a reason not to answer any of this Committee's substantive questions during his deposition, he has recently suggested in public that he only wished to delay the count of votes by multiple days. As the evidence developed by this Committee demonstrates, Eastman knew that such an effort to delay the count would also be illegal. *See* Select Committee to Investigate the January 6th Attack on the United States Capitol,

Hearing on the January 6th Investigation, 117th Cong., 2d sess., (June 16, 2022), at 1:32:00-1:35:13, available at https://www.youtube.com/watch?v=vBjUWVKuDj0 ("[D]id Dr. Eastman seem to admit that both of these theories suffered from similar legal flaws? [T]his new theory, as I was pointing out to him, or the procedural theory, still violates several provisions of the Electoral Count Act, as he acknowledged.... So, he acknowledged in those conversations that the underlying legal theory was the same...."). In addition, neither Eastman nor any other co-conspirator had information establishing that any delay in counting votes would or could have changed the outcome of the election in any State.

614. *See supra*, Executive Summary. We also note that these Republican Members of Congress, who had more knowledge of Trump's planning for January 6th than any other Members of Congress, were also likely in a far superior position than any other Members to warn the Capitol Police of the risks of violence at the Capitol on January 6th.

615. *See* Select Committee to Investigate the January 6th Attack on the U.S. Capitol, *Hearing on the January 6th Investigation*, 117th Cong., 2d sess., (June 16, 2022), at 2:29:50, available at https://www.youtube.com/watch?v=vBjUWVKuDj0 ("I've decided that I should be on the pardon list, if that is still in the works.").

616. The elements of a section 371 conspiracy to defraud the United States are: (1) at least two people entered into an agreement to obstruct a lawful function of the government, (2) by deceitful or dishonest means, and (3) a member of the conspiracy engaged in at least one overt act in furtherance of the agreement. Order Re Privilege of Documents Dated January 4-7, 2021 at 53, *Eastman v. Thompson et al.*, 594 F. Supp. 3d 1156, (C.D. Cal. Mar. 28, 2022) (No. 8:22-cv-99-DOC-DFM). Put similarly, to prove a violation section 371's "defraud" provision, the Government must prove that the defendant: (1) agreed with at least one other person to defraud the United States, (2) knowingly participated in the conspiracy with the intent to defraud the United States, and (3) that at least one overt act was taken in furtherance of the conspiracy. *See United States v. Dean*, 55 F.3d 640, 647 (D.C. Cir. 1995) (citing *United States v. Treadwell*, 760 F.2d 327, 333 (D.C. Cir. 1985)); *see also United States v. Mellen*, 158, 393 F.3d 175, 181 (D.C. Cir. 2004). An individual "defrauds" the Government for purposes of section 371 if he "interfere[s] with or obstruct[s] one of its lawful governmental functions by deceit, craft or trickery, or at least by means that are dishonest." *Hammerschmidt v. United States*, 265 U.S. 182, 188 (1924); *see also United States v. Haldeman*, 559 F.2d 31, 122 n.255 (D.C. Cir. 1976) (upholding jury verdict on instruction defining "defrauding the United States" as: "depriv[ing] the Government of its right to have the officials of its departments and agencies transact their official business honestly and impartially, free from corruption, fraud, improper and undue influence, dishonesty and obstruction").

617. Order Re Privilege of Documents Dated January 4-7, 2021 at 54-55, *Eastman v. Thompson et al.*, 594 F. Supp. 3d 1156, (C.D. Cal. Mar. 28, 2022) (No. 8:22-cv-99-DOC-DFM).

618. *See* Order Re Privilege of Documents Dated January 4-7, 2021 at 53, *Eastman v. Thompson et al.*, 594 F. Supp. 3d 1156, (C.D. Cal. Mar. 28, 2022) (No. 8:22-cv-99-DOC-DFM). ("An 'agreement' between co-conspirators need not be express and can be inferred from the conspirators' conduct.").

619. *See infra*, Chapter 1.

620. Order Re Privilege of Documents Dated January 4-7, 2021 at 55, *Eastman v. Thompson et al.*, 594 F. Supp. 3d 1156, (C.D. Cal. Mar. 28, 2022) (No. 8:22-cv-99-DOC-DFM).

621. Order Re Privilege of Documents Dated January 4-7, 2021 at 57, *Eastman v. Thompson et al.*, 594 F. Supp. 3d 1156, (C.D. Cal. Mar. 28, 2022) (No. 8:22-cv-99-DOC-DFM).

622. *See infra*, Chapter 2. President Trump's call with Secretary Raffensperger may have violated several provisions of both Federal and Georgia law. We do not attempt to catalogue all the possible violations here.

623. Order Re Privilege of Documents Dated January 4-7, 2021 at 57, *Eastman v. Thompson et al.*, 594 F. Supp. 3d 1156, (C.D. Cal. Mar. 28, 2022) (No. 8:22-cv-99-DOC-DFM).

624. Order Re Privilege of Documents Dated January 4-7, 2021 at 59, *Eastman v. Thompson et al.*, 594 F. Supp. 3d 1156, (C.D. Cal. Mar. 28, 2022) (No. 8:22-cv-99-DOC-DFM).

625. "908. ELEMENTS OF 18 U.S.C. § 1001," Department of Justice, (last accessed on Dec. 13, 2022), available at https://www.justice.gov/archives/jm/criminal-resource-manual-908-elements-18-usc-1001.

626. The elements of a section 371 conspiracy are discussed above.

627. As explained in Chapter 5, staffers for Rep. Mike Kelly (R-PA) and Sen. Ron Johnson (R-WI) reached out to Vice President Pence's director of legislative affairs, apparently seeking to deliver fake certificates on January 6. Documents on file with the Select Committee to Investigate the January 6th Attack on the United States Capitol (Chris Hodgson Production), 00012 (January 6, 2021, text message from Rep. Kelly's Chief of Staff, Matt Stroia, to Chris Hodgson on January at 8:41 a.m.), 00058 (January 6, 2021, text messages from Senator Johnson's Chief of Staff, Sean Riley, to Chris Hodgson around 12:37 p.m.).

628. *See infra,* Chapter 3.

629. 18 U.S.C. § 1001 (emphasis added).

630. *See, e.g., United States v. Bowser,* 964 F.3d 26, 31 (D.C. Cir. 2020), *cert. denied,* 141 S. Ct. 1390 (2021) ("[T]he False Statements Act applies to 'any investigation or review, conducted pursuant to the authority of any committee, subcommittee, commission *or office of the Congress.*' 18 U.S.C. § 1001(c)(2) (emphasis added)."); *United States v. Stone,* 394 F. Supp. 3d 1, 10 (D.D.C. 2019).

631. *See* Select Committee to Investigate the January 6th Attack on the United States Capitol, *Business Meeting on the January 6th Investigation,* 117th Cong., 2d sess., (Oct. 13, 2022), at 1:14:59-1:15:22 available at https://www.youtube.com/watch?v=IQvuBoLBuC0 ("[President Trump] turned the call over to Mr. Eastman, who then proceeded to talk about the importance of the RNC helping the campaign gather these contingent electors, in case any of the legal challenges that were ongoing changed the result of any of the states.").

632. 18 U.S.C. § 2383.

633. *Thompson v. Trump,* 590 F. Supp. 3d 46, 115 (D.D.C. 2022), appeal pending, No. 22-5069 (D.C. Cir. Mar. 18, 2022).

634. *See* Ryan Goodman and Josh Asabor, "In Their Own Words: The 43 Republicans' Explanations of Their Votes Not to Convict Trump in Impeachment Trial," Just Security, (Feb. 15, 2021), available at https://www.justsecurity.org/74725/in-their-own-words-the-43-republicans-explanations-of-their-votes-not-to-convict-trump-in-impeachment-trial/.

635. *See supra,* Executive Summary.

636. *See supra,* Executive Summary. The evidence suggests that the Vice President and certain members of President Trump's staff urged DOD to deploy the National Guard notwithstanding the President's wishes.

637. A prominent U.S. professor of criminal law has opined that President Trump can be held criminally responsible under section 2383 for his failure to act, when he had a duty to act given his constitutional obligation under Article II section 3 of the Constitution to "take Care that the Laws be faithfully executed." *See* Albert W. Alschuler, "Trump and the Insurrection Act: The Legal Framework," Just Security, (Aug. 16, 2022), available at https://www.justsecurity.org/82696/trump-and-the-insurrection-act-the-true-legal-framework/. Professor Albert Alschuler, the Julius Kreeger Professor Emeritus at the University of Chicago Law School, taught criminal law for over 50 years at many of our Nation's leading law schools. He has published a number of analytical pieces applying the "assists" and "aid and comfort" clauses of that provisions (which he analogizes to "aiding and abetting" accomplice liability) to the evidence presented at the Committee's hearings. In any event, as described above, President Trump *did* act, including through his 2:24 p.m. tweet about the Vice President that inflamed the crowd attacking the Capitol.

638. Select Committee to Investigate the January 6th Attack on the United States Capitol, Continued Interview of Cassidy Hutchinson, (June 20, 2022) p. 26.

639. Select Committee to Investigate the January 6th Attack on the United States Capitol, *Hearing on the January 6th Investigation,* 117th Cong., 2d sess., (July 21, 2022), at 1:02:53, available at https://www.youtube.com/watch?v=pbRVqWbHGuo; Donald J. Trump

(@realDonaldTrump), Twitter, Jan. 6, 2021 2:24 p.m. ET, available at https://
www.thetrumparchive.com/?searchbox=
"didn't+have+the+courage+to+do+what+should+have+been+done" (archived).

640. See *infra*, Chapter 8.

641. *See supra*, Executive Summary

642. Select Committee to Investigate the January 6th Attack on the United States Capitol, Continued Interview of Cassidy Hutchinson, (June 20, 2022), p. 27.

643. *See* Mariana Alfaro, "Trump Vows Pardons, Government Apology to Capitol Rioters if
Elected," *Washington Post*, (Sept. 1, 2022), available at https://www.washingtonpost.com/
national-security/2022/09/01/trump-jan-6-rioters-pardon/.

644. Jordan Fischer, Eric Flack, and Stephanie Wilson, "Georgia Man Who Wanted to 'Remove
Some Craniums' on January 6 Sentenced to More than 2 Years in Prison," WUSA9, (Dec. 14,
2021), available at https://perma.cc/RSY2-J3RU.

645. Dan Mangan, "Capitol Rioter Garret Miller Says He Was Following Trump's Orders, Apologizes to AOC for Threat," CNBC, (Jan. 25, 2021), available at https://www.cnbc.com/2021/01/
25/capitol-riots-garret-miller-says-he-was-following-trumps-orders-apologizes-to-
aoc.html.

646. Donald J. Trump (@realDonaldTrump), Twitter, Jan. 6, 2021 6:01 p.m. ET, available at
https://www.thetrumparchive.com/?searchbox=%22these+are+the+things+and+events%22
(archived).

647. Select Committee to Investigate the January 6th Attack on the United States Capitol, Deposition of Nicholas Luna, (Mar. 21, 2022), pp. 166–67.

648. Donald J. Trump (@realDonaldTrump), Twitter, Jan. 6, 2021 6:01 p.m. ET, available at
https://www.thetrumparchive.com/?searchbox=%22these+are+the+things+and+events%22
(archived).

649. 18 U.S.C. § 372.

650. *See* "Leader of Oath Keepers and Oath Keepers Member Found Guilty of Seditious Conspiracy and Other Charges Related to U.S. Capitol Breach," Department of Justice, (Nov. 29,
2022), available at https://www.justice.gov/opa/pr/leader-oath-keepers-and-oath-
keepers-member-found-guilty-seditious-conspiracy-and-other.

651. 18 U.S.C. § 2384. To establish a violation of section 2384, the government must establish (1)
a conspiracy, (2) to overthrow, put down, or destroy by force the Government of the United
States, or to levy war against them, or to oppose by force the authority thereof, or by force
to prevent, hinder or delay the execution of any law of the United States, or by force
to seize, take, or possess any property of the United States contrary to the authority
thereof. *See United States v. Khan*, 461 F.3d 477, 487 (4th Cir. 2006).

652. "Leader of Oath Keepers and Oath Keepers Member Found Guilty of Seditious Conspiracy
and Other Charges Related to U.S. Capitol Breach," Department of Justice, (Nov. 29, 2022),
available at https://www.justice.gov/opa/pr/leader-oath-keepers-and-oath-keepers-
member-found-guilty-seditious-conspiracy-and-other.

653. "Leader of Proud Boys and Four Other Members Indicted in Federal Court for Seditious
Conspiracy and Other Offenses Related to U.S. Capitol Breach," Department of Justice,
(June 6, 2022), available at https://www.justice.gov/opa/pr/leader-proud-boys-and-four-
other-members-indicted-federal-court-seditious-conspiracy-and.

654. *See supra*, Executive Summary.

655. Brian Naylor, "Read Trump's Jan. 6 Speech, A Key Part of Impeachment Trial," NPR, (Feb. 10,
2021), available at https://www.npr.org/2021/02/10/966396848/read-trumps-jan-6-speech-
a-key-part-of-impeachment-trial.

656. Kristen Holmes, "Trump Calls for the Termination of the Constitution in Truth Social Post,"
CNN, (Dec. 4, 2022), available at https://www.cnn.com/2022/12/03/politics/trump-
constitution-truth-social/index.html.

657. *See* Mariana Alfaro, "Trump Vows Pardons, Government Apology to Capitol Rioters if Elected," *Washington Post,* (Sept. 1, 2022), available at https://www.washingtonpost.com/national-security/2022/09/01/trump-jan-6-rioters-pardon/.

658. *See infra,* Chapter 7.

659. 167 Cong. Rec. H171-72 (daily ed. Jan. 13, 2021).

660. *See supra,* Executive Summary.

661. Select Committee to Investigate the January 6th Attack on the United States Capitol, Continued Interview of Cassidy Hutchinson, (June 20, 2022), pp. 84-87.

662. Documents on file with the Select Committee to Investigate the January 6th Attack on the United States Capitol (National Archives Production), 076P-R000008962_0009 (January 2, 2021, White House Presidential Call Log).

663. Documents on file with the Select Committee to Investigate the January 6th Attack on the United States Capitol (Mark Meadows Production), MM014864 (January 5, 2021, text message from Rep. Jim Jordan to Mark Meadows describing the Vice President's actions on January 6th).

664. *See* Documents on file with the Select Committee to Investigate the January 6th Attack on the United States Capitol (National Archives Production), P-R000255-259 (January 6, 2021, Presidential Daily Diary); Felicia Somnez, "Rep. Jim Jordan Tells House Panel He Can't Recall How Many Times He Spoke with Trump on Jan. 6," *Washington Post,* (Oct. 20, 2021), available at https://www.washingtonpost.com/politics/jordan-trump-calls-capitol-attack/2021/10/20/1a570d0e-31c7-11ec-9241-aad8e48f01ff_story.html.

665. Documents on file with the Select Committee to Investigate the January 6th Attack on the United States Capitol, (AT&T Production, Feb. 9, 2022).

666. Select Committee to Investigate the January 6th Attack on the United States Capitol, Deposition of Rudolph Giuliani, (May 20, 2022), pp. 205-07.

667. Select Committee to Investigate the January 6th Attack on the United States Capitol, Continued Interview of Cassidy Hutchinson, (May 17, 2022), p. 106.

668. Select Committee to Investigate the January 6th Attack on the United States Capitol, Transcribed Interview of Cassidy Hutchinson, (Feb. 23, 2022), pp. 72-73.

669. Select Committee to Investigate the January 6th Attack on the United States Capitol, Continued Interview of Cassidy Hutchinson, (Mar. 7, 2022), pp. 66-67.

670. Select Committee to Investigate the January 6th Attack on the United States Capitol, Continued Interview of Cassidy Hutchinson, (June 20, 2022), pp. 62-64.

671. *See* Sarah Lynch and David Shepardson, "Watchdog to Probe if Justice Dept. Officials Improperly Tried to Alter 2020 Election," *Reuters,* (Jan. 25, 2021), available at https://www.reuters.com/article/us-usa-trump-justice/watchdog-to-probe-if-justice-dept-officials-improperly-tried-to-alter-2020-election-idUSKBN29U21E ("'Throughout the past four years, I worked with Assistant Attorney General Clark on various legislative matters. When President Trump asked if I would make an introduction, I obliged,' Perry said in a statement.").

672. Select Committee to Investigate the January 6th Attack on the United States Capitol, Continued Interview of Cassidy Hutchinson, (June 20, 2022), p. 48.

673. Select Committee to Investigate the January 6th Attack on the United States Capitol, Transcribed Interview of Cassidy Hutchinson, (Feb. 23, 2022), p. 45.

674. Select Committee to Investigate the January 6th Attack on the United States Capitol, Continued Interview of Cassidy Hutchinson, (May 17, 2022), pp. 106-07.

675. Documents on file with the Select Committee to Investigate the January 6th Attack on the United States Capitol (Mark Meadows Production), MM011449.

676. Documents on file with the Select Committee to Investigate the January 6th Attack on the United States Capitol (Mark Meadows Production), MM011506, (November 2020 text messages from Rep. Andy Biggs to Mark Meadows).

677. Josh Kelety, "Congressman Andy Biggs Coordinated Efforts with Mark Finchem before Capitol Riot," *Phoenix New Times*, (Feb. 18, 2021), available at https://www.phoenixnewtimes.com/news/congressman-andy-biggs-coordinated-with-mark-finchem-before-capitol-riot-11532527.

678. Documents on file with the Select Committee to Investigate the January 6th Attack on the United States Capitol (Jim DeGraffenreid Production), DEGRAFFENREID 000554 (December 18, 2020, text messages between James DeGraffenreid, a Nevada fake elector for Trump, and another remarking that "Andy Biggs ... has reached out to NV to ask about our evidence").

679. Audrey Fahlberg, "January 6 Hearings Become Fundraising Fodder," *The Dispatch*, (July 7, 2022), available at https://thedispatch.com/p/january-6-hearings-become-fundraising; Archive of Political Emails, Jim Jordan, "The January 6th Committee Is After Me," June 9, 2022 12:41 p.m., available at https://politicalemails.org/messages/686023.

680. John Rowley III to the Honorable Bennie G. Thompson re: "Subpoena to Representative Scott Perry," (May 24, 2022), available at https://www.documentcloud.org/documents/22061774-scott-perry-j6-response.

681. Committee on Standards of Official Conduct, *House Ethics Manual*, p. 13 (2008).

682. Documents on file with the Select Committee to Investigate the January 6th Attack on the United States Capitol (National Archives Production), 076P-R001080 (December 21, 2020, WAVES records showing Representatives Babin, Biggs, Brooks, Gaetz, Gohmert, Gosar, Taylor Greene, Harris, Hice, Jordan, and Perry entering the White House).

683. *See* Select Committee to Investigate the January 6th Attack on the United States Capitol, Deposition of John Eastman, (Dec. 9, 2021); Select Committee to Investigate the January 6th Attack on the United States Capitol, Deposition of Roger Stone, (Dec. 17, 2021); Select Committee to Investigate the January 6th Attack on the United States Capitol, Deposition of Jeffrey Clark, (Feb. 2, 2022); Select Committee to Investigate the January 6th Attack on the United States Capitol, Deposition of Michael Flynn, (Mar. 10, 2022).

684. *Latif v. Obama*, 677 F.3d 1175, 1193 (D.C. Cir. 2012) (quoting *Mitchell v. United States*, 526 U.S. 314, 328 (1999)). Justice Scalia not only agreed with this principle, but he also reasoned that the Fifth Amendment does not prevent an adverse inference in even criminal cases. This is because the text of that Amendment does not require such a rule and applying an adverse inference to a refusal to testify is exactly in keeping with "normal evidentiary inferences." *See Mitchell*, 526 U.S. at 332 (Scalia, J., dissenting). Justice Thomas agreed with Justice Scalia. *See id.* at 341-42 (Thomas, J., dissenting).

685. Select Committee to Investigate the January 6th Attack on the United States Capitol, Deposition of Michael Flynn, (Mar. 10, 2022), p. 82.

686. *Trump v. Thompson*, 20 F.4th 10, 15-16 (D.C. Cir. 2021), *cert. denied*, 142 S.Ct. 1350 (2022).

687. *Trump v. Thompson*, 20 F.4th 10, 89 (D.C. Cir. 2021) (citation omitted), *cert. denied*, 142 S.Ct. 1350 (2022). Former President Trump also asked the United State Supreme Court to block the Select Committee from accessing his documents. The Supreme Court denied that request stating, "Because the Court of Appeals concluded that President Trump's claims would have failed even if he were the incumbent, his status as a former President necessarily made no difference to the court's decision." *Trump v. Thompson*, 142 S.Ct. 680, 680 (2022) (citation omitted).

688. H. Res. 851, 117th Cong., (2021); H. Rept. 117-216, Resolution Recommending that the House of Representatives Find Mark Randall Meadows in Contempt of Congress for Refusal to Comply with a Subpoena Duly Issued by the Select Committee to Investigate the January 6th Attack on the United States Capitol, 117th Cong., 1st Sess. (2021), available at https://www.congress.gov/117/crpt/hrpt216/CRPT-117hrpt216.pdf.

689. Statement of Interest of the United States at 9-10, *Meadows v. Pelosi et al.*, No. 1:21-cv-03217 (CJN) (D.D.C. July 15, 2022), ECF No. 42.

690. "Thompson & Cheney Statement on Justice Department Decisions on Contempt Referrals," Select Committee to Investigate the January 6th Attack on the United States Capitol, (June

3, 2022), available at https://january6th.house.gov/news/press-releases/thompson-cheney-statement-justice-department-decisions-contempt-referrals.

691.   Dennis Aftergut, "Why the DOJ Did Not Indict Mark Meadows (and What It Should Do Next)," NBC News, (June 7, 2022), available at https://www.nbcnews.com/think/opinion/trump-lackey-mark-meadows-escaped-january-6-prosecution-peter-navarro-rcna32319.

692.   H. Res. 1037, 117th Cong., (2022); H. Rept. 117-284, Resolution Recommending that the House of Representatives Find Peter K. Navarro and Daniel Scavino, Jr., in Contempt of Congress for Refusal to Comply with a Subpoena Duly Issued by the Select Committee to Investigate the January 6th Attack on the United States Capitol, 117th Cong., 2d Sess. (2022), available at https://www.congress.gov/117/crpt/hrpt284/CRPT-117hrpt284.pdf. In particular, Scavino may have further information on President Trump's advance knowledge from social media posts of the rioters' plans to invade the Capitol. See *supra* __.

693.   H. Res. 730, 117th Cong., (2021); H. Rept. 117-152, Resolution Recommending that the House of Representatives Find Stephen K. Bannon in Contempt of Congress for Refusal to Comply with a Subpoena Duly Issued by the Select Committee to Investigate the January 6th Attack on the United States Capitol, 117th Cong., 1st Sess. (2021), available at https://www.congress.gov/117/crpt/hrpt152/CRPT-117hrpt152.pdf.

694.   H. Res. 1037, 117th Cong., (2022); "Peter Navarro Indicted for Contempt of Congress," Department of Justice, (June 3, 2022), available at https://www.justice.gov/usao-dc/pr/peter-navarro-indicted-contempt-congress; H. Rept. 117-284, Resolution Recommending that the House of Representatives Find Peter K. Navarro and Daniel Scavino, Jr., in Contempt of Congress for Refusal to Comply with a Subpoena Duly Issued by the Select Committee to Investigate the January 6th Attack on the United States Capitol, 117th Cong., 2d Sess. (2022), available at https://www.congress.gov/117/crpt/hrpt284/CRPT-117hrpt284.pdf.

695.   See *infra* 136.

696.   Select Committee to Investigate the January 6th Attack on the United States Capitol, *Hearing on the January 6th Investigation*, 117th Cong., 2d sess., (July 12, 2022), at 2;14:00-2:14:50, available at https://youtu.be/rrUa0hfG6Lo.

697.   Select Committee to Investigate the January 6th Attack on the United States Capitol, Deposition of John McEntee, (Mar. 28, 2022), pp. 153-55; Select Committee to Investigate the January 6th Attack on the United States Capitol, Transcribed Interview of Eric Herschmann, (Apr. 6, 2022), pp. 129-35; Select Committee to Investigate the January 6th Attack on the United States Capitol, Transcribed Interview of Pasquale Anthony "Pat" Cipollone, (July 8, 2022), pp. 176-77; Select Committee to Investigate the January 6th Attack on the United States Capitol, Continued Interview of Cassidy Hutchinson, (May 17, 2022), pp. 104-06.

698.   Select Committee to Investigate the January 6th Attack on the United States Capitol, *Hearing on the January 6th Investigation*, 117th Cong., 2d sess., (June 23, 2022), at 2:22:05-2:23:41, available at https://www.youtube.com/live/Z4535-VW-bY?feature=share&t=8525.

699.   Select Committee to Investigate the January 6th Attack on the United States Capitol, Deposition of John McEntee, (Mar. 28, 2022), pp. 153-55; Select Committee to Investigate the January 6th Attack on the United States Capitol, *Hearing on the January 6th Investigation*, 117th Cong., 2d sess., (June 23, 2022), at 2:23:41-2:24:42, available at https://www.youtube.com/watch?v=Z4535-VW-bY&t=8620s.

700.   Select Committee to Investigate the January 6th Attack on the United States Capitol, Transcribed Interview of Eric Herschmann, (Apr. 6, 2022), pp. 129-35, esp. pp. 130-131; Select Committee to Investigate the January 6th Attack on the United States Capitol, *Hearing on the January 6th Investigation*, 117th Cong., 2d sess., (June 23, 2022), at 2:21:26-2:22:04, available at https://www.youtube.com/live/Z4535-VW-bY?feature=share&t=8486.

701.   Select Committee to Investigate the January 6th Attack on the United States Capitol, Transcribed Interview of Eric Herschmann, (Apr. 6, 2022), p. 133.

702.   Documents on file with the Select Committee to Investigate the January 6th Attack on the United States Capitol (National Archives Production), 076P-R000005854_0001 (January 11, 2021, email from Molly Michael to Rep. Mo Brooks, confirming receipt of email from Brooks

recommending pardons, including for "Every Congressman and Senator who voted to reject the electoral college vote submissions of Arizona and Pennsylvania"); Select Committee to Investigate the January 6th Attack on the United States Capitol, *Hearing on the January 6th Investigation*, 117th Cong., 2d sess., (June 23, 2022), at 2:20:52-2:21:12, available at https://www.youtube.com/live/Z4535-VW-bY?feature=share&t=8452.

703. Select Committee to Investigate the January 6th Attack on the United States Capitol, *Hearing on the January 6th Investigation*, 117th Cong., 2d sess., (June 28, 2022), available at https://www.govinfo.gov/committee/house-january6th.

704. The Committee has enormous respect for the U.S. Secret Service and recognized that the testimony regarding their work is sensitive for law enforcement, protectee security, and national security reasons. *See, e.g.*, Select Committee to Investigate the January 6th Attack on the United States Capitol, Transcribed Interview of USSS Employee "Driver", (Nov. 7, 2022), p. 4 (the Select Committee is not releasing the name of this individual); Select Committee to Investigate the January 6th Attack on the United States Capitol, Continued Interview of Anthony Ornato, (Nov. 28, 2022), p. 4; Select Committee to Investigate the January 6th Attack on the United States Capitol, Transcribed Interview of USSS Employee, (Nov. 21, 2022), p. 4; Select Committee to Investigate the January 6th Attack on the United States Capitol, Transcribed Interview of USSS Employee, (Nov. 18, 2022), p. 4 Select Committee to Investigate the January 6th Attack on the United States Capitol, Transcribed Interview of Robert Engel, (Nov. 17, 2022), p. 4.

705. Select Committee to Investigate the January 6th Attack on the United States Capitol, Transcribed Interview of USSS Employee, (Nov. 7, 2022), pp. 4, 86-87.

706. *See, e.g.*, Devlin Barrett, Jacqueline Alemany, Josh Dawsey, and Rosalind S. Heldeman, "The Justice Dept.'s Jan. 6 Investigation Is Looking at ... Everything," *Washington Post*, (Sept. 16, 2022), available at https://www.washingtonpost.com/national-security/2022/09/15/trump-january-6-subpoenas-meadows/; Josh Dawsey and Isaac Arnsdorf, "Prosecutors Seek Details from Trump's PAC in Expanding Jan. 6 Probe," *Washington Post*, (Sept. 8, 2022), available at https://www.washingtonpost.com/national-security/2022/09/08/trump-subpoenas-pac-jan-6/.

707. *See* Devlin Barrett, Josh Dawsey, and Isaac Stanley-Becker, "Trump's Committee Paying for Lawyers of Key Mar-a-Lago Witnesses," *Washington Post*, (Dec. 5, 2022), available at https://www.washingtonpost.com/national-security/2022/12/05/trump-witnesses-legal-bills-pac/.

708. The Committee sat for dozens of hours with Hutchinson and concluded that she is brave and earnest, and understood the intense backlash that would inevitably result from those who were enlisted to defend President Trump's behavior. [See *infra*, Chapter 7]. The thuggish behavior from President Trump's team, including efforts to intimidate described elsewhere in this report (*see e.g.* Chapter 3), gave rise to many concerns about Hutchinson's security, both in advance of and since her public testimony. (We note that multiple members of the Committee were regularly receiving threats of violence during this period.) Accordingly, the Committee attempted to take appropriate measures to help ensure her safety in advance of her testimony, including measures designed to minimize the risk of leaks that might put her safety at risk.

709. *See, e.g.*, Select Committee to Investigate the January 6th Attack on the United States Capitol, Transcribed Interview of Pasquale Anthony "Pat" Cipollone, (July 8, 2022), pp. 71-72 (noting that another witness reference may have been to Pat Philbin).

710. Select Committee to Investigate the January 6th Attack on the United States Capitol, Deposition of Kayleigh McEnany, (Jan. 12, 2022), pp. 264-65.

711. Select Committee to Investigate the January 6th Attack on the United States Capitol, Deposition of Kayleigh McEnany, (Jan. 12, 2022), pp. 52-57, 70-74, 282-88.

712. Select Committee to Investigate the January 6th Attack on the United States Capitol, Deposition of Kayleigh McEnany, (Jan. 12, 2022), pp. 142-45, 288-92. *See also* Select Committee to Investigate the January 6th Attack on the United States Capitol, Transcribed Interview of Sarah Matthews, (Feb. 8, 2022), pp. 12-15.

713. Select Committee to Investigate the January 6th Attack on the United States Capitol, Deposition of Kayleigh McEnany, (Jan. 12, 2022), pp. 183-86.

714. Select Committee to Investigate the January 6th Attack on the United States Capitol, Transcribed Interview of Sarah Matthews, (Feb. 8, 2022), pp. 39-41.

715. Select Committee to Investigate the January 6th Attack on the United States Capitol, Transcribed Interview of Sarah Matthews, (Feb. 8, 2022), p. 41.

716. Select Committee to Investigate the January 6th Attack on the United States Capitol, Transcribed Interview of Ivanka Trump, (Apr. 5, 2022), pp. 38-39, 120, 205, 210, 213-14.

717. Select Committee to Investigate the January 6th Attack on the United States Capitol, Transcribed Interview of Ivanka Trump, (Apr. 5, 2022), p. 27.

718. Select Committee to Investigate the January 6th Attack on the United States Capitol, Transcribed Interview of Julie Radford, (May 24, 2022), p. 19.

719. Select Committee to Investigate the January 6th Attack on the United States Capitol, Transcribed Interview of Ivanka Trump, (Apr. 5, 2022), p. 40.

720. Mark Meadows, *The Chief's Chief* (Ft. Lauderdale, FL: All Seasons Press, 2021).

721. Mark Meadows, *The Chief's Chief* (Ft. Lauderdale, FL: All Seasons Press, 2021), p. 259.

722. Mark Meadows, *The Chief's Chief* (Ft. Lauderdale, FL: All Seasons Press, 2021), p. 259.

723. Select Committee to Investigate the January 6th Attack on the United States Capitol, Continued Interview of Cassidy Hutchinson, (June 20, 2022), pp. 47-49.

724. Select Committee to Investigate the January 6th Attack on the United States Capitol, Transcribed Interview of Anthony Ornato, (Jan.y 28, 2022), pp. 76-77.

725. Select Committee to Investigate the January 6th Attack on the United States Capitol, Continued Interview of Anthony Ornato, (Mar. 29, 2022), pp. 46-47. Ornato was interviewed at length by the Select Committee in November 2022, after the Secret Service produced nearly a million new internal documents in August and September of this year.

726. Select Committee to Investigate the January 6th Attack on the United States Capitol, Continued Interview of Anthony Ornato, (Nov. 29, 2022), p. 92; *see also* Select Committee to Investigate the January 6th Attack on the United States Capitol, Continued Interview of Anthony Ornato, (Mar. 29, 2022), pp. 45-46 (stating that he had not heard about President Trump's instruction to others to ask Ornato about going to the Capitol).

727. Select Committee to Investigate the January 6th Attack on the United States Capitol, Interview of White House employee with national security responsibilities, (July 19, 2022), pp. 69-70; Select Committee to Investigate the January 6th Attack on the United States Capitol, Continued Interview of Cassidy Hutchinson, (June 20, 2022), pp. 4-6.

728. Select Committee to Investigate the January 6th Attack on the United States Capitol, Interview of White House employee with national security responsibilities, (July 19, 2022), pp. 69-70; Select Committee to Investigate the January 6th Attack on the United States Capitol, Continued Interview of Cassidy Hutchinson, (June 20, 2022), pp. 4-6.

729. Select Committee to Investigate the January 6th Attack on the United States Capitol, Transcribed Interview of White House employee with national security responsibilities, (July 19, 2022), pp. 69-70; Select Committee to Investigate the January 6th Attack on the United States Capitol, Continued Interview of Cassidy Hutchinson, (June 20, 2022), pp. 4-7; Select Committee to Investigate the January 6th Attack on the United States Capitol, Transcribed Interview of USSS Employee "Driver", (Nov. 7, 2022), pp. 77-80, 92-93; Select Committee to Investigate the January 6th Attack on the United States Capitol, Transcribed Interview of Mark Robinson, (July 7, 2022), pp. 17-18.

730. Select Committee to Investigate the January 6th Attack on the United States Capitol, Continued Interview of Anthony Ornato, (Nov. 29, 2022), pp. 104-105, 131-32, 135-36. *See also* Chapter 7.

731. *See, e.g.*, Select Committee to Investigate the January 6th Attack on the United States Capitol, Transcribed Interview of General Mark A. Milley, (Nov. 17, 2021), p. 199 (describing

another senior intelligence official worrying, ahead of January 6th, about violence at the Capitol); Select Committee to Investigate the January 6th Attack on the United States Capitol, Transcribed Interview of Donnell Harvin, (Jan. 24, 2022), pp. 22-23 (former Chief of Homeland Security and Intelligence for the District of Columbia describing the threat scene ahead of January 6th); Documents on file with the Select Committee to Investigate the January 6th Attack on the United States Capitol (Capitol Police Production), CTRL0000001532.0001, p.2 (January 5, 2021, FBI Situational Information Report).

732. Select Committee to Investigate the January 6th Attack on the United States Capitol, Continued Interview of Anthony Ornato, (Nov. 29, 2022), pp. 54-56.

733. Select Committee to Investigate the January 6th Attack on the United States Capitol, Continued Interview of Anthony Ornato, (Nov. 29, 2022), pp. 55-56.

734. See *supra* pp. 81-83. *See also* Select Committee to Investigate the January 6th Attack on the United States Capitol, Continued Interview of Anthony Ornato, (Nov. 29, 2022), p. 13 (Ornato confirming that one of his responsibilities was briefing the chief of staff and, through the chief of staff at times, the President on security-related issues).

735. "U.S. House of Representatives Debate on Impeachment of President Trump," C-SPAN, at 1:03:53 - 1:13:42, Jan. 13, 2021, available at https://www.c-span.org/video/?507879-4/debate-impeachment-president-trump; Tyler Moyer, "McCarthy: "President Bears Responsibility for Wednesday's Attack"," *Bakersfield Now*, (Jan. 13, 2021), available at https://bakersfieldnow.com/news/local/mccarthy-president-bears-responsibility-for-wednesdays-attack.

736. "House Minority Leader Weekly Briefing." C-SPAN, at 7:30 - 8:44, Jan. 21, 2021, available at https://www.c-span.org/video/?508185-1/minority-leader-mccarthy-backs-gop-conference-chair-liz-cheney; Rudy Talaka, "GOP Leader McCarthy Calls for Bipartisan Commission to Investigate Allegations of Members Helping Rioters," Mediaite, (Jan. 21, 2021), available at https://www.mediaite.com/news/gop-leader-mccarthy-calls-for-bipartisan-commission-to-investigate-allegations-of-members-helping-rioters/; "Rep. McCarthy Calls for Bipartisan Commission to Probe Capitol Riot," Newsmax, (Jan. 22, 2021), available at https://www.newsmax.com/politics/kevin-mccarthy-capitol-riot-boebert-probe/2021/01/21/id/1006648/.

737. Clare Foran, Ryan Nobles, and Annie Grayer, "Pelosi Announces Plans for '9/11-Type Commission' to Investigate Capitol Attack," CNN, (Feb. 15, 2021), available at https://www.cnn.com/2021/02/15/politics/pelosi-capitol-attack-commission/index.html.

738. "Letter to The Honorable Speaker Nancy Pelosi," House Republican Leader Kevin McCarthy, (Feb. 22, 2021), available at https://www.speaker.gov/sites/speaker.house.gov/files/Sharp%20MX-4141_20210518_081238.pdf.

739. "Letter to The Honorable Speaker Nancy Pelosi," House Republican Leader Kevin McCarthy, (Feb. 22, 2021), available at https://www.speaker.gov/sites/speaker.house.gov/files/Sharp%20MX-4141_20210518_081238.pdf.

740. "Letter to The Honorable Speaker Nancy Pelosi," House Republican Leader Kevin McCarthy, (Feb. 22, 2021), available at https://www.speaker.gov/sites/speaker.house.gov/files/Sharp%20MX-4141_20210518_081238.pdf.

741. Ryan Nobles, Annie Grayer, and Jeremy Herb, "Pelosi Concedes to Even Partisan Split on 1/6 Commission in Effort to Jumpstart Talks," CNN, (Apr. 20, 2021), available at https://www.cnn.com/2021/04/20/politics/nancy-pelosi-january-6-commission-talks/index.html; Ryan Nobles and Daniella Diaz, "Pelosi Makes Concession on Subpoenas for 9/11 Style Commission to Investigate Insurrection," CNN, (Apr. 22, 2021), available at https://www.cnn.com/2021/04/22/politics/nancy-pelosi-911-style-commission-insurrection-subpoenas/index.html.

742. John Bresnahan, Anna Palmer, and Jake Sherman, "Pelosi Taps Top Dem to Negotiate on Jan. 6 Commission," *Punchbowl News*, (May 11, 2021), available at https://punchbowl.news/archive/punchbowl-news-am-5-11/.

743. "Chairman Thompson Announces Bipartisan Agreement with Ranking Member Katko to Create Commission to Investigate the January 6 Attack on the Capitol," House Committee on Homeland Security, (May 14, 2021), available at https://homeland.house.gov/news/press-releases/chairman-thompson-announces-bipartisan-agreement-with-ranking-member-katko-to-create-commission-to-investigate-the-january-6-attack-on-the-capitol.

744. "McCarthy Statement on January 6 Commission Legislation," House Republican Leader Kevin McCarthy, (May 18, 2021), available at https://www.republicanleader.gov/mccarthy-statement-on-january-6-commission-legislation/.

745. "Pelosi Statement on McCarthy Opposition to January 6th Commission," Speaker of the House Nancy Pelosi, (May 18, 2021), available at https://www.speaker.gov/newsroom/51821.

746. "Pelosi Statement on McCarthy Opposition to January 6th Commission," Speaker of the House Nancy Pelosi, (May 18, 2021), available at https://www.speaker.gov/newsroom/51821; "Letter to The Honorable Speaker Nancy Pelosi," House Republican Leader Kevin McCarthy, (Feb. 22, 2021), available at https://www.speaker.gov/sites/speaker.house.gov/files/Sharp%20MX-4141_20210518_081238.pdf.

747. "Pelosi Statement on McCarthy Opposition to January 6th Commission," Speaker of the House Nancy Pelosi, (May 18, 2021), available at https://www.speaker.gov/newsroom/51821.

748. "U.S. House of Representatives House Session," C-SPAN, at 4:12:23-4:12:55, May 19, 2021, available at https://www.c-span.org/video/?511820-2/houses-passes-bill-create-january-6-commission-252-175.

749. "Roll Call 154 | Bill Number: H. R. 3233," Clerk of the U.S. House of Representatives, (May 19, 2021), available at https://clerk.house.gov/Votes/2021154?Page=1&Date=05%2F19%2F2021.

750. "Roll Call Vote 117th Congress - 1st Session," Question: On the Cloture Motion (Motion to Invoke Cloture Re: Motion to Proceed to H.R. 3233), H.R. 3233 - 117th Congress (2021): National Commission to Investigate the January 6 Attack on the United States Capitol Complex Act, H.R.3233, 117th Cong. (2021), available at https://www.senate.gov/legislative/LIS/roll_call_votes/vote1171/vote_117_1_00218.htm.

751. "House Speaker Nancy Pelosi Announces Select Committee on the January 6th Insurrection," C-SPAN, at 4:44-5:26, June 24, 2021, available at https://www.youtube.com/watch?v=guCcy9tUfn8.

752. Manu Raju and Clare Foran, "Officer Injured in Capitol Riot asks McCarthy to Denounce GOP January 6 Conspiracies," CNN, (June 25, 2021), available at https://www.cnn.com/2021/06/25/politics/michael-fanone-kevin-mccarthy-meeting/index.html.

753. Manu Raju and Clare Foran, "Officer Injured in Capitol Riot asks McCarthy to Denounce GOP January 6 Conspiracies," CNN, (June 25, 2021), available at https://www.cnn.com/2021/06/25/politics/michael-fanone-kevin-mccarthy-meeting/index.html.

754. "Roll Call 197 | Bill Number: H. Res. 503," Clerk of the U.S. House of Representatives, (June 30, 2021), available at https://clerk.house.gov/Votes/2021197.

755. "Pelosi Names Members to Select Committee to Investigate January 6th Attack on the U.S. Capitol," House Speaker Nancy Pelosi, (July 1, 2021), available at https://www.speaker.gov/newsroom/7121-0.

756. "McCarthy Names House Republicans to Serve on Select Committees," House Republican Leader Kevin McCarthy, (July 19, 2021), available at https://www.republicanleader.gov/mccarthy-names-house-republicans-to-serve-on-select-committees/.

757. "McCarthy Taps Banks to Lead Republicans on Jan 6 Committee," Congressman Jim Banks, (Jul. 19, 2021), available at https://banks.house.gov/news/documentsingle.aspx?DocumentID=1921.

758. "Pelosi Statement on Republican Recommendations to Serve on the Select Committee to Investigate the January 6th Attack on the U.S. Capitol," Speaker of the House Nancy Pelosi, (Jul. 21, 2021), available at https://www.speaker.gov/newsroom/72121-2.

759. "Pelosi Statement on Republican Recommendations to Serve on the Select Committee to Investigate the January 6th Attack on the U.S. Capitol," Speaker of the House Nancy Pelosi, (Jul. 21, 2021), available at https://www.speaker.gov/newsroom/72121-2.

760. "McCarthy Statement about Pelosi's Abuse of Power on January 6th Select Committee," Republican Leader Kevin McCarthy, (July 21, 2021), available at https://republicanleader.house.gov/mccarthy-statement-about-pelosis-abuse-of-power-on-january-6th-select-committee/; "McCarthy Pulls Republicans from Jan. 6 Select Committee after Pelosi Rejects Picks," Axios, (July 21, 2021), available at https://www.axios.com/2021/07/21/pelosi-jim-jordan-banks-select-committee.

761. "Pelosi Announces Appointment of Congressman Adam Kinzinger to Select Committee to Investigate the January 6th Attack on the U.S. Capitol," House Speaker Nancy Pelosi, (July 25, 2021), available at https://www.speaker.gov/newsroom/72521; 167 Cong. Rec. H3885 (daily ed. July 26, 2021).

762. See, e.g., Eastman v. Thompson et al., No. 8:22-cv-99-DOC-DFM, 2022 U.S. Dist. LEXIS 25546, at *12-14 (C.D. Cal. Jan. 25, 2022); Memorandum Opinion, Republican National Committee v. Nancy Pelosi et al.. https://storage.courtlistener.com/recap/gov.uscourts.dcd.241102/gov.uscourts.dcd.241102.33.0.pdf.

1

THE BIG LIE

Late on election night 2020, President Donald J. Trump addressed the nation from the East Room of the White House. When Trump spoke, at 2:21 a.m. on November 4th, the President's re-election was very much in doubt. Fox News, a conservative media outlet, had correctly called Arizona for former Vice President Joseph R. Biden. Every Republican presidential candidate since 1996 had won Arizona. If the President lost the State, and in the days ahead it became clear that he had, then his campaign was in trouble. But as the votes continued to be counted, President Trump's apparent early lead in other key States—States he needed to win—steadily shrank. Soon, he would not be in the lead at all—he'd be losing.

So, the President of the United States did something he had planned to do long before election day: he lied.

"This is a fraud on the American public. This is an embarrassment to our country," President Trump said. "We were getting ready to win this election," the President continued. "Frankly, we did win this election. We did win this election." Trump claimed, without offering any evidence, that a "major fraud" was occurring "in our nation." [1]

Neither of President Trump's claims were true. He had no basis for claiming victory or that fraud was taking place. Millions of votes still had not been counted. The States were simply tabulating the ballots cast by the American people. Trump's own campaign advisors told him to wait—that it was far too early to declare victory.

As the evening progressed, President Trump called in his campaign team to discuss the results. Trump Campaign Manager William Stepien and other campaign experts advised him that the results of the election would not be known for some time, and that he could not truthfully declare victory. Stepien was of the view that, because ballots were going to be counted for days, "it was far too early to be making any proclamation [about having won the election]." Stepien told President Trump that his recommendation was to say, "votes are still being counted. It's...too early to call the race." [2]

Jason Miller, another senior Trump Campaign advisor, told the Select Committee that he argued in conversations with Stepien and others that night against declaring victory at the time as well, because "it was too early to say one way [or] the other" who had won. Miller recalled recommending that "we should not go and declare victory until we had a better sense of the numbers." [3]

According to testimony received by the Committee, the only advisor present who supported President Trump's inclination to declare victory was Rudy Giuliani, who, according to Miller, was "definitely intoxicated" that evening. [4]

President Trump's decision to declare victory falsely on election night and, unlawfully, to call for the vote counting to stop, was not a spontaneous decision. It was premeditated. The Committee has assembled a range of evidence of President Trump's preplanning for a false declaration of victory. This includes multiple written communications on October 31st and November 3, 2020, to the White House by Judicial Watch President Tom Fitton. [5] This evidence demonstrates that Fitton was in direct contact with President Trump and understood that he would falsely declare victory on election night and call for vote counting to stop. The evidence also includes an audio recording of President Trump's advisor Steve Bannon, who said this on October 31, 2020, to a group of his associates from China:

> And what Trump's going to do is just declare victory, right? He's gonna declare victory. But that doesn't mean he's the winner. He's just gonna say he's a winner....The Democrats, more of our people vote early that count. Their vote in mail. And so they're gonna have a natural disadvantage, and Trump's going to take advantage of it. That's our strategy. He's gonna declare himself a winner. So when you wake up Wednesday morning, it's going to be a firestorm....Also, if Trump, if Trump is losing, by ten or eleven o'clock at night, it's going to be even crazier. No, because he's gonna sit right there and say 'They stole it. I'm directing the Attorney General to shut down all ballot places in all 50 states. It's going to be, no, he's not going out easy. If Trump—if Biden's winning, Trump is going to do some crazy shit. [6]

Also in advance of the election, Roger Stone, another outside advisor to President Trump, made this statement:

I really do suspect it will still be up in the air. When that happens, the key thing to do is to claim victory. Possession is 9/10s of the law. No, we won. Fuck you, Sorry. Over. We won. You're wrong. Fuck you.[7]

In the days after the election, the President's own campaign team told him he had lost and there was no evidence of significant fraud. When his campaign staff wouldn't tell him what he wanted to hear, President Trump replaced them with what Attorney General William Barr described as a "clown car" of individuals willing to promote various conspiracy theories.[8]

But Donald Trump was no passive consumer of these lies. He actively propagated them. Time and again President Trump was informed that his election fraud claims were not true. He chose to spread them anyway. He did so even after they were legally tested and rejected in dozens of lawsuits. Not even the electoral college's certification of former Vice President Biden's victory on December 14, 2020, stopped the President from lying. Throughout, the Big Lie remained central to President Trump's efforts to block the peaceful transfer of power on January 6, 2021.

1.1 THE BIG LIE REFLECTED DELIBERATE EXPLOITATION OF THE "RED MIRAGE"

President Trump's "Big Lie" on election night was based on simple differences in how Americans vote. In 2020, it was well-known that Democrats were much more likely to vote via mail-in ballots than in person in 2020. On the other hand, Republicans generally preferred to vote in person on election day.[9] In key swing States with tight margins between the candidates, the election day votes would favor President Trump and disproportionately be counted first. Mail-in ballots, which would favor former Vice President Biden, would disproportionately be counted later. In some States it would take days to process the remaining mail-in ballots.

The timing of how votes are counted created the potential for what is known as a "Red Mirage"—or an illusion of a Republican (Red) victory in the early stages of vote counting. President Trump would appear to be in the lead on election night, but this was not the whole picture. Many mail-in votes for former Vice President Biden would not be counted on election day. Therefore, the actual winner would likely not be known on election night.

The "Red Mirage" phenomenon was widely known prior to the 2020 presidential election. Chris Stirewalt was the head of the Fox News elections desk that correctly called Arizona for Biden. Stirewalt and his team tried to warn viewers of the Red Mirage. He testified that over the past 40 or 50 years, "Americans have increasingly chosen to vote by mail or early or absentee," and that "Democrats prefer that method of voting more than

Photo by House Creative Services

Republicans do." [10] In nearly "every election," Stirewalt elaborated, "Republicans win Election Day and Democrats win the early vote, and then you wait and start counting." It "[h]appens every time." [11]

President Trump's campaign team made sure the President was briefed on the timing of vote tallying. Stepien, his campaign manager, told the Select Committee that President Trump was reminded on election day that large numbers of mail-in ballots would still remain to be counted over the coming days. [12] Stepien added that he personally reminded the President that while early returns may be favorable, the counting would continue: "I recounted back to 2016 when I had a very similar conversation with him on election day...I recounted back to that conversation with him in which I said, just like I said in 2016 was going to be a long night, I told him in 2020 that, you know, it was going to be a process again, as, you know, the early returns are going to be positive. Then we're going to, you know, be watching the returns of ballots as, you know, they rolled in thereafter." [13]

Ordinarily, the "Red Mirage" anomaly does not create problems in the election process because candidates wait for the votes to be tallied before declaring victory or conceding. As Stirewalt emphasized, prior to President Trump, "no candidate had ever tried to avail themselves of this quirk in the election counting system." [14]

President Trump, however, made a different choice. In an extraordinary breach of the American democratic process, he decided to exploit the potential for confusion about the staggered timing of vote counting to deceive the American public about the election results. He and his allies foreshadowed this decision in their statements in the months leading up to the November 2020 election.

1.2 TRUMP'S PRE-ELECTION PLANS TO DECLARE VICTORY

On Halloween, advisor Steve Bannon, who had served four years earlier as Donald Trump's 2016 campaign manager, laid out the election night plan. "What Trump's gonna do is just declare victory. Right? He's gonna declare victory. But that doesn't mean he's a winner," Bannon told a private audience. "He's just gonna *say* he's a winner."[15]

Bannon explained that the Democrats "[would] have a natural disadvantage" on election night, because more Democrats would vote by mail than Republicans and it would take time to count the mail-in ballots. This would give President Trump the illusion of a lead. "And Trump's going to take advantage of it," Bannon said. "That's our strategy. He's gonna declare himself a winner."[16]

In an interview on Fox News the morning of the election, Bannon insisted that President Trump needed to address the nation that night, to "provide the narrative engine for how we go forward."[17] During an episode of his podcast later that same day, Bannon clarified what he meant: President Trump is "going to claim victory. Right? He's going to claim victory."[18]

Tom Fitton drafted a victory statement for the President to read on election night.[19] On October 31st, he emailed the statement to President Trump's assistant, Molly Michael, and social media guru, Dan Scavino. Fitton wrote that election day, November 3rd, was the "deadline by which voters in states across the country *must* choose a president." Fitton argued that counting ballots that arrived after election day would be part of an effort by "partisans" to "overturn" the election results.[20]

Of course, that claim wasn't true—mail-in ballots are regularly processed after election day. Regardless, Fitton encouraged the President to pre-emptively declare victory. "We had an election today—and I won," Fitton wrote for President Trump.[21] Early in the evening on election day, Fitton emailed Michael again to say he had "[j]ust talked to him [President Trump] about the draft [statement]."[22] Later that evening, before President Trump made his election night remarks, Michael replied that she was "…redelivering to him [President Trump] now."[23]

October 31, 2020

He's just gonna say he's a winner.

Photo by Alex Wong/Getty Images

Roger Stone, President Trump's longtime political confidante, told several associates just prior to the election that Trump needed to declare victory—especially if the race wasn't called on election day. "Let's just hope we are celebrating" on election night, Stone said. "I really do suspect it will still be up in the air. When that happens, the key thing to do is claim victory." Stone elaborated with colorful language. "Possession is nine-tenths of the law. No, we won. Fuck you. Sorry. Over. We won. You're wrong. Fuck you." [24]

Indeed, published reports echoed these warnings about President Trump's election strategy. Two days before the election, Jonathan Swan of *Axios* reported that President Trump "has told confidants he'll declare victory on Tuesday night if it looks like he's 'ahead.'" [25] Swan added that "Trump's team is preparing to falsely claim that mail-in ballots counted after Nov. 3—a legitimate count expected to favor Democrats—are evidence of election fraud." [26] If the vote tally swung against Trump after election night in States such as Pennsylvania, then the Trump team would claim the Democrats had "stolen" the election.[27] Fox News election analysis Chris Stirewalt testified that he and his team "had gone to pains" to inform viewers that early votes would favor Republicans but the lead would be illusory "because the Trump campaign and the President had made it clear that they were going to try to exploit this anomaly."[28] Others warned that President Trump could exploit the Red Mirage as well.[29]

1.3 TRUMP'S PRE-ELECTION EFFORTS TO DELEGITIMIZE THE ELECTION PROCESS

President Trump also paved the way for his false election-night declaration of victory by blanketing voters with a blizzard of lies and statements delegitimizing mail-in voting in the middle of a deadly pandemic and consistently questioning the security of ballots. President Trump used the president's bully pulpit, including his heavily-trafficked Twitter feed, to tell one lie after another.

The Select Committee found dozens of instances in which President Trump claimed that mail-in voting would produce a "rigged" election. Trump repeatedly denounced mail-in voting on Twitter, during interviews, and even during the presidential debate. Here is a small sample of President Trump's attempts to delegitimize mail-in balloting.

On April 7, 2020, President Trump claimed:

Mail ballots are a very dangerous thing for this country, because they're cheaters. They go and collect them. They're fraudulent in many cases.... These mailed ballots come in. The mailed ballots are corrupt, in my opinion. And they collect them, and they get people to go in and sign them. And then they—they're forgeries in many cases. It's a horrible thing.[30]

The following day, April 8, President Trump tweeted:

Republicans should fight very hard when it comes to statewide mail-in voting. Democrats are clamoring for it. Tremendous potential for voter fraud, and for whatever reason, doesn't work out well for Republicans. @foxandfriends[31]

On May 24, President Trump tweeted:

The United States cannot have all Mail In Ballots. It will be the greatest Rigged Election in history. People grab them from mailboxes, print thousands of forgeries and "force" people to sign. Also, forge names. Some absentee OK, when necessary. Trying to use Covid for this Scam![32]

On September 17, President Trump falsely alleged that mail-in ballots were ripe for foreign interference:

@TrueTheVote There is a group of people (largely Radical Left Democrats) that want ELECTION MAYHEM. States must end this CRAZY mass

sending of Ballots. Also, a GIFT to foreign interference into our elec-
tion!!! Stop it now, before it is too late.[33]

Before the election, as President Trump campaigned against mail-in voting, Bill Stepien sought an intercession. Along with House Minority Leader Kevin McCarthy, Stepien attempted to convince the President that mail-in voting was "not...a bad thing for his campaign."[34] They argued that President Trump's decision to discourage mail-in voting, while "urging [his] voters to vote only on election day leaves a lot to chance" and would fail to take advantage of a superior grassroots operation that could encourage Trump voters to return their ballots.[35] President Trump did not heed their warning. He continued to demonize mail-in voting. The Red Mirage was a key part of his "Big Lie."

Ominously, President Trump consistently refused to commit to accepting the outcome of the election. During an interview on Fox News in July, Chris Wallace asked: "Can you give a direct answer [if] you will accept the election?" President Trump responded: "I have to see. Look, you—I have to see. No, I'm not going to just say yes. I'm not going to say no, and I didn't last time either."[36]

On September 23, 2020, a reporter asked President Trump if he would commit to a "peaceful transferal of power after the election." The President refused, saying, "we're going to have to see what happens."[37] The President claimed, "the ballots are disaster," adding that if he could "get rid of the ballots...we'll have a very peaceful—there won't be a transfer, frankly; there'll be a continuation."[38] That is, according to President Trump, there would be a "continuation" of his presidency.

The following day, September 24, another reporter followed up by asking if the election would be legitimate only if President Trump won. The President again suggested there was something suspect about mail-in ballots, adding that he was "not sure" the election could be an honest one.[39]

1.4 PRESIDENT TRUMP'S LAUNCH OF THE BIG LIE

Consistent with the pre-election narrative planted by President Trump, within hours of polls closing, President Trump began pushing the claim that late-reported vote tallies were illegitimate.[40] Even though he had been reminded by his Campaign Manager that very day that a large number of mail-in ballots would not be counted for several hours or days,[41] President Trump claimed that Democrats were going to "find...ballots at four o'clock in the morning and add them to the list."[42] He also suggested that Democrats were continuing to vote after the polls had closed.[43]

Indeed, this is exactly what Steve Bannon described when he said President Trump would "take advantage" of the Democrats' "natural disadvantage" on election night.[44]

In the ensuing days and weeks, President Trump often referred to "dumps" of votes that were injected into the counting process.[45] His supporters latched onto these false claims.[46] There were no "dumps" of votes—just tallies of absentee ballots as they were reported by jurisdictions throughout the country in a fully transparent process.[47] These batches of ballots included votes for both Trump and Biden. The late-reported votes favored the former Vice President, just as President Trump's campaign advisors said they would, particularly in primarily Democratic cities.[48]

Attorney General Bill Barr recognized immediately that the "Red Mirage" was the basis for President Trump's erroneous claim of fraud. "[R]ight out of the box on election night, the President claimed that there was major fraud underway," Barr said. "I mean, this happened, as far as I could tell, before there was actually any potential of looking at evidence."[49] President Trump's claim "seemed to be based on the dynamic that, at the end of the evening, a lot of Democratic votes came in which changed the vote counts in certain states, and that seemed to be the basis for this broad claim that there was major fraud."[50]

President Trump knew about the Red Mirage. He chose to lie about it repeatedly—even after being directly informed that his claims were false. This was often the case in the post-election period. The President consciously disregarded facts that did not support his Big Lie.

1.5 POST-ELECTION: PRESIDENT TRUMP REPLACES HIS CAMPAIGN TEAM

President Trump's campaign leadership, including Bill Stepien (the campaign's manager) and Justin Clark (the campaign's deputy manager), supported President Trump, and were willing to pursue recounts and other standard post-election litigation, but they were not willing to promote baseless conspiracy theories.[51] Stepien and others characterized this group as "Team Normal."[52]

Less than two weeks after the election, President Trump pushed "Team Normal" aside because its members didn't tell him what he wanted to hear. In their place, Trump promoted Rudy Giuliani and his associates, men and women who spread baseless and extreme claims of election fraud. Giuliani, the former mayor of New York City, recruited several investigators and lawyers to assist him.[53] Giuliani's team included Jenna Ellis, Bernard Kerik, Boris Epshteyn, Katherine Friess, and Christina Bobb.[54] Ellis functioned as

Giuliani's deputy on the new Trump Campaign legal team.[55] Kerik, the former commissioner of the New York Police Department and a pardoned felon, served as Giuliani's chief investigator.[56] Other attorneys who collaborated with Giuliani's legal team included Sidney Powell, Cleta Mitchell, and John Eastman. As discussed elsewhere in this report, Eastman became a key player in President Trump's efforts to overturn the election.

1.6   PRESIDENT TRUMP'S CAMPAIGN TEAM TOLD HIM HE LOST THE ELECTION AND THERE WAS NO SIGNIFICANT FRAUD

President Trump's campaign team quickly realized that none of the significant fraud claims were real. Bill Stepien testified that, as of November 5th, the Trump Campaign had not found any proof of fraudulent activity. There were "allegations and reports," but "nothing hard [and] fast" that drew the results of the election into question.[57]

The Trump Campaign continued to investigate claims of fraud into the second week after the election. According to Stepien, as people shared "wild allegations" with the President, the campaign team was forced to review the facts and then serve as a "truth telling squad" to the President regarding why the claims "didn't prove to be true." [58] For example, Stepien recalled someone alleging that thousands of illegal votes had been cast in Arizona. That wasn't true. The votes had been submitted by overseas voters (such as military deployed or stationed abroad) who were obviously eligible to participate in the election.[59]

Alex Cannon was a lawyer for the Trump Campaign and previously worked for the Trump Organization. After the election, Cannon was tasked with looking into allegations of voter fraud in the 2020 election—including the claim that thousands of ineligible votes had been cast in Arizona.[60] Cannon recalled that Vice President Pence asked him what he was finding. "And I said that I didn't believe we were finding it, or I was not personally finding anything sufficient to alter the results of the election," Cannon responded. Vice President Pence thanked him.[61]

Cannon reported his assessment to Mark Meadows, the White House Chief of Staff, as well. In mid to late-November 2020, Meadows asked Cannon what his investigation had turned up. "And I remember sharing with him that we weren't finding anything that would be sufficient to change the results in any of the key states," Cannon told Meadows. "So there is no there, there?" Meadows replied.[62]

Jason Miller, a senior advisor to the Trump Campaign, pushed claims of election fraud in public. In private, however, Miller says that he told President Trump a different story, informing him numerous times that there was not enough election fraud to have changed the election:

> Miller: My understanding is that I think there are still very valid questions and concerns with the rules that were changed under the guise of COVID, but, specific to election day fraud and irregularities, there were not enough to overturn the election.

> Committee Staff: And did you give your opinion on that to the President?

> Miller: Yes.

> Committee Staff: What was his reaction when you told him that?

> Miller: "You haven't seen or heard"—I'm paraphrasing, but—"you haven't seen or heard all the different concerns and questions that have been raised."

> Committee Staff: How many times did you have this conversation with the President?

> Miller: Several. I couldn't put a specific number on it, though.

> Committee Staff: But more than one?

> Miller: Correct.[63]

Matthew Morgan, the Trump Campaign's top lawyer, came to a similar conclusion. Nearly two months after the election, on January 2nd, Morgan met with the Vice President's staff. According to Morgan, the consensus in the room was that even if all the claims of fraud and irregularities were "aggregated and read most favorably to the campaign...it was not sufficient to be outcome determinative." [64]

As far as the Trump Campaign's professional leadership was concerned, there was no evidence that the election had been "stolen" from President Trump. To the contrary, they had seen ample evidence that President Trump simply lost—and told the President so.

On November 6th, Jared Kushner arranged for the senior campaign staff to brief President Trump in the Oval Office on the state of the race.[65] Since election day, Matt Oczkowski, the Campaign's leading data expert, had tracked voting returns in the swing States to analyze the campaign's odds of success.[66] Miller texted such updates on data from key States to Meadows.[67] The Trump Campaign's data did not add up to victory. Oczkowski "delivered to the President in pretty blunt terms that he was going to lose"

Photo by Alex Wong/Getty Images

the election.[68] There were not enough outstanding votes in the battle-ground States for President Trump to overcome Biden's lead. President Trump disagreed and insisted that he would still prevail through legal challenges.[69]

But the data did not lie.

On November 7th, the *Associated Press* called Pennsylvania and the overall presidential election for former Vice President Biden.[70] At that point, a small team of the President's campaign advisors including Stepien met with the President and told him that his path to victory was virtually non-existent.[71] The campaign team conveyed to the President that his chance of success was only "5, maybe 10 percent," which Stepien explained to the Committee was a "very, very, very bleak" assessment.[72]

In retrospect, the campaign's estimate of a 5 to 10 percent chance of winning, as of November 7th, was far *too optimistic.* In one of the most favorable possible scenarios, for example, President Trump and his team would need to win recounts in Arizona and Georgia, while also prevailing in litigation challenging absentee or vote by mail ballots in Wisconsin, or possibly Michigan or Pennsylvania.[73] But the election wasn't even close enough to trigger automatic recounts in Arizona or Georgia.

The narrowest margin of total votes between the two candidates was in Arizona, where former Vice President Biden won by more than 10,000 votes. This may seem like a small number of votes, but it was more than enough to avoid an automatic recount. As Benjamin Ginsberg, a longtime Republican elections lawyer, explained to the Select Committee, "the 2020 election was not close." [74] Previous campaigns had successfully challenged vote differentials in the hundreds—not thousands—of votes.[75] Ginsberg explained, "you just don't make up those sorts of numbers in recounts." [76] Georgia performed a hand recount of all the ballots anyway, confirming within weeks of the election that Biden had won the State.[77] Also, by January 6th, Arizona and New Mexico had conducted statutory post-election audits of voting machines or randomly-selected, representative samples of ballots at the State- or county-level that affirmed the accuracy of their election results.[78]

Chris Stirewalt, who led the elections desk at Fox News at the time, concurred with Ginsberg's analysis. Asked what President Trump's odds of victory were as of November 7th, Stirewalt replied: "None." [79]

Meanwhile, the Trump Campaign continued to crunch the numbers. On the morning of November 12th, Oczkowski circulated among top campaign advisors a presentation describing what happened in each of the battleground States the campaign was monitoring.[80] This analysis by the data team examined the turnout and margins on a county-by-county basis in a dozen States while also analyzing demographic changes that impacted the results.[81] Among the States were Arizona, Georgia, Michigan, Pennsylvania, Nevada, and Wisconsin.[82] Oczkowski's team determined that President Trump lost each of those six States because Biden had performed better than President Trump in certain areas like population centers or suburbs.[83] Yet, in the weeks that followed, President Trump and his new legal team— the "clown car"—went to great lengths to challenge the results of the election in these six states, spreading multiple conspiracy theories.

The voting data told a clear story: President Trump lost. But, regardless of the facts, the President had no intention of conceding defeat.

On election night, President Trump and Rudy Giuliani agreed that the President should just declare victory—even though he had no basis for doing so. Giuliani also told the Select Committee that President Trump asked him on November 4th to take over his campaign's legal operation.[84] Giuliani thought the only way that it would work would be for the President to call the existing campaign team to announce Giuliani's takeover because, in Giuliani's words, "they are going to be extraordinarily resentful, because they don't like me already, and I don't trust them." [85] He said that the President agreed.[86]

Although Giuliani wouldn't assume leadership of the Campaign's legal operations until mid-November, the former New York City mayor quickly began to butt heads with "Team Normal."

On November 6th, Giuliani and his team met with the Trump Campaign's leadership at its headquarters in Arlington, Virginia.[87]

"Team Normal" was not impressed. Stepien told the Select Committee the campaign team was concerned that Giuliani would be a distraction to them and to President Trump.[88] When Giuliani suggested traveling to Pennsylvania to assist in the campaign's efforts, the campaign team "didn't dissuade him from doing so." [89] After just 10 to 15 minutes in the conference room, Stepien and other staffers left the meeting.[90]

That same day, President Trump discussed the Campaign's legal strategy in the Oval Office with Giuliani, Clark, and Matt Morgan, the Trump Campaign's General Counsel.[91] Prior to the election, Morgan was responsible for the Campaign's litigation strategy.[92] Morgan and his team filed lawsuits challenging the changes States made to voting practices during the coronavirus pandemic.[93] Morgan also studied previous elections to determine the types of cases that were likely to succeed.[94] Clark described how the Campaign's original legal strategy was based on his general theory for election cases: "to look at what do you think, what do you know, and what can you prove" and then determine which cases to file from there.[95]

Giuliani had other ideas and advocated to President Trump that he be put in charge of the Campaign's legal operation so that he could pursue his preferred strategy.[96] "Mr. Giuliani didn't seem bound by those cases or by those precedents. He felt he could press forward on anything that he thought was wrong with the election and bring a strategy around that," Morgan explained.[97] "Rudy was just chasing ghosts," Clark said.[98] Morgan and Clark excused themselves from the meeting because it "was going nowhere." [99]

The next day, November 7th, Giuliani held a press conference at Four Seasons Total Landscaping in Philadelphia, Pennsylvania. He immediately began making outlandish claims, arguing that the Democrats had conspired to steal the election. "As you know from the very beginning, mail-in ballots were a source of some degree of skepticism, if not a lot of skepticism, as being innately prone to fraud," Giuliani said. "Those mail-in ballots could have been written the day before by the Democratic Party hacks that were all over the Convention Center." [100] Giuliani offered no evidence to support his shocking and baseless allegation. Echoes of President Trump's relentless campaign against mail-in balloting, and his decision to exploit the Red Mirage, were easy to hear.

Photo by Chris McGrath/Getty Images

On November 10th, Giuliani and Kerik met with President Trump in the Oval Office to discuss their investigation into voter fraud. White House Counsel Pat Cipollone and White House Senior Advisor Eric Herschmann were also in attendance. After Giuliani's presentation, President Trump asked Cipollone whether he had spoken to Attorney General Barr about the allegations of fraud.[101] One day before, Barr had issued a memorandum outlining a shift in DOJ policy that allowed Federal prosecutors to investigate claims of voting irregularities without waiting for the results to be certified.[102] President Trump's question was an early indication that he was going to pressure the DOJ to endorse his phony fraud claims.

Days later, Giuliani and Justin Clark engaged in a screaming match during a meeting in the Oval Office.[103] Giuliani was urging President Trump to file a lawsuit in Georgia, but Clark pointed out that a hand recount was already being conducted and argued it was better to wait.[104] Giuliani told President Trump that Clark was lying to him.[105] A formal changing of the guard would follow.

On November 14th, President Trump announced on Twitter that Giuliani was now the head of his campaign's legal team.[106] "Team Normal" saw drastic changes to their roles on the newly-structured campaign team—some self-imposed—and many outside law firms that had signed up to support the campaign's legal efforts disengaged completely.[107]

"I didn't think what was happening was necessarily honest or professional at that point in time," Stepien explained. "This wasn't a fight that I was comfortable with," he added.[108]

On the day the leadership change was announced, Giuliani participated in a "surrogate" briefing to coordinate messaging by Trump loyalists during their media appearances.[109] Giuliani announced that the messaging strategy should be "to go hard on Dominion/Smartmatic, bringing up Chavez and Maduro." [110] Giuliani claimed that additional lawsuits would soon be filed "to invalidate upwards of 1M ballots." [111]

Consistent with the messaging advanced by the new campaign team, President Trump in mid-November remained dug-in, still refusing to concede defeat. President Trump continued to insist that he was cheated out of victory, endorsing one wild conspiracy theory after another to deny the simple fact that he lost.

1.7 PRESIDENT TRUMP HAD HIS DAY IN COURT

"We've proven" the election was stolen, but "no judge, including the Supreme Court of the United States, has had the courage to allow it to be heard." [112] That was how President Trump described efforts to overturn the election in court one day before the electoral college met on December 14, 2020. That was false.

Judges across the nation *did* evaluate President Trump's claims that the election was stolen. As longtime Republican election attorney Benjamin Ginsberg testified before the Select Committee, the President's camp "did have their day in court," it's just that "in no instance did a court find that the charges of fraud were real." [113] In total, the Trump Campaign and allies of President Trump filed 62 separate lawsuits between November 4, 2020, and January 6, 2021, calling into question or seeking to overturn the election results.[114] Out of 62 cases, only one case resulted in a victory for the President Trump or his allies, which affected relatively few votes, did not vindicate any underlying claims of fraud, and would not have changed the outcome in Pennsylvania.[115] Thirty of the cases were dismissed by a judge *after* a hearing on the merits.[116]

In every State in which claims were brought, one or more judges specifically explained as part of their dismissal orders that they had evaluated the plaintiffs' allegations or supposed proof of widespread election fraud or other irregularities, and found the claims to be entirely unconvincing. In

62 CASES

9 states and D.C. are the sites of case filings between November 4, 2020 and January 6, 2021

61 losses, 1 win

22 judges appointed by Republican presidents oversaw cases

10 Trump appointed judges

3 All three Trump appointed Supreme Court justices rejected the fraud claims

Arizona, for example, the plaintiffs in *Bowyer v. Ducey* alleged that the election was tainted by the introduction of "hundreds of thousands of illegal, ineligible, duplicate or purely fictitious ballots."[117] A Federal judge dismissed their suit, finding it "void of plausible allegations" and "sorely wanting of relevant or reliable evidence."[118] Likewise, in *Ward v. Jackson*, an Arizona State-court judge dismissed a lawsuit by the State GOP chair following a two-day trial, finding no evidence of misconduct, fraud, or illegal votes.[119] This ruling was unanimously upheld by the State supreme court, where all seven justices were appointed by GOP governors.[120]

In Georgia, a State court dismissed *Boland v. Raffensperger*, which alleged that tens of thousands of illegal ballots were cast by out-of-State voters or with invalid signature matches.[121] The judge found that "the Complaint's factual allegations ... rest on speculation rather than duly pled facts" and "do not support ... a conclusion that sufficient illegal votes were cast to change or place in doubt the result of the election."[122] The judge who issued this decision had been appointed by a Republican governor, as had seven of the eight justices of the State supreme court who upheld her ruling.[123] Likewise, a Federal judge denied relief to the plaintiff in *Wood v. Raffensperger*, which alleged that new procedures for checking absentee ballot signatures spoiled the result by making it harder to reject illegal ballots, finding "no basis in fact or law to grant him the relief he seeks."[124]

The judge wrote that "[t]his argument is belied by the record" because absentee ballots were actually rejected for signature issues at the same rate as in 2018.[125]

In Michigan, a Federal judge found in *King v. Whitmer* that the plaintiffs' claims of "massive election fraud" were based on "nothing but speculation and conjecture that votes for President Trump were destroyed, discarded or switched to votes for Vice President Biden...."[126] Similarly, a State-court judge rejected plaintiffs' claims in two cases brought against Detroit and the surrounding county that accused them of systematic fraud in how absentee ballots were counted; the judge found that one group of plaintiffs "...offered no evidence to support their assertions,"[127] and that the other group's "interpretation of events is incorrect" and "decidedly contradicted" by "highly-respected" election experts.[128]

In Nevada, a State-court judge rejected a litany of claims of systematic election fraud in *Law v. Whitmer*, ruling that plaintiffs "did not prove under any standard of proof that illegal votes were cast and counted, or legal votes were not counted at all, due to voter fraud" or "for any other improper or illegal reason."[129] The ruling was unanimously upheld by the Nevada Supreme Court.[130]

In Pennsylvania, a Federal judge dismissed *Donald Trump for President v. Boockvar*, finding that the Trump Campaign had presented nothing but "strained legal arguments without merit and speculative accusations unpled in the operative complaint and unsupported by evidence."[131] The dismissal was upheld by the United States Court of Appeals for the Third Circuit, which held: "[C]alling an election unfair does not make it so. Charges require specific allegations and then proof. We have neither here."[132] That opinion was authored by another Trump appointee.[133]

Lastly, in Wisconsin, another judge dismissed a lawsuit accusing the Wisconsin Elections Commission of "constitutional violations" that "likely tainted more than 50,000 ballots."[134] The judge ruled: "This Court has allowed plaintiff the chance to make his case and he has lost on the merits," failing to show that the outcome was affected by Commission rules about drop boxes, ballot addresses, or individuals who claimed "indefinitely confined" status to vote from home.[135] The ruling was upheld by a three-judge panel of the United States Court of Appeals for the Seventh Circuit, all of whom were Republican appointees, including one appointed by President Trump himself.[136]

In all, the judges who heard these post-election cases included 22 Federal judges appointed by Republican presidents.[137]

President Trump and his lawyers were well-aware that courts were consistently rejecting his claims. During a December 18th meeting in the

Oval Office with President Trump, Sidney Powell and others, White House Senior Advisor Eric Herschmann pointed out that President Trump's lawyers had their opportunity to prove their case in court, and failed. Powell fired back that "the judges are corrupt." Herschmann responded: "Every one? Every single case that you've done in the country you guys lost, every one of them is corrupt, even the ones we appointed?"[138]

President Trump was faced with another choice after having his day in court. He could accept that there was no real evidence of voter fraud, or he could continue to amplify conspiracy theories and lies. He chose the latter.

1.8 PRESIDENT TRUMP REPEATEDLY PROMOTED CONSPIRACY THEORIES

Instead of accepting his defeat, President Trump attempted to justify his Big Lie with a series of increasingly preposterous claims. The President was not simply led astray by those around him. The opposite was true. He actively promoted conspiracy theories and false election fraud claims even after being informed they were baseless. Millions of President Trump's supporters believed the election was stolen from him. Many of them still do, but President Trump knew the truth and chose to lie about it.

The power of the President's bully pulpit should not be underestimated, especially in the digital age.[139] President Trump's relentless lying sowed seeds of distrust in America's election system. Researchers who studied this election-denial phenomenon have noted: "President Trump didn't just prime his audience to be receptive to false narratives of election fraud—he inspired them to produce those narratives and then echoed those false claims back to them."[140] Social media played a prominent role in amplifying erroneous claims of election fraud. Shortly after election day, the "Stop the Steal" campaign, discussed more fully in Chapter 6, went viral. "Stop the Steal" influencers echoed President Trump's premature declaration of victory, asserting that he won the election, the Democrats stole it from him, and it was the responsibility of American "patriots" to combat this supposed injustice.[141]

This resulted in what Attorney General Barr has described as an "avalanche" of false claims, as President Trump's supporters attempted to justify his "Big Lie."[142] The post-election allegations of fraud or other malfeasance were "completely bogus," "silly" and "usually based on complete misinformation," Barr explained.[143] Nonetheless, many of President Trump's supporters wanted to believe them. The stolen election narrative has proven to be remarkably durable precisely because it is a matter of belief—not evidence, or reason. Each time a claim was debunked, more

Photo by Michael Ciaglo/Getty Images

claims emerged in its place. Barr later complained that this dynamic forced him and others to play "whack-a-mole." [144]

The United States Department of Justice, under Barr's leadership and then Acting Attorney General Jeffrey Rosen, was forced to knock down one lie after another. As discussed in Chapter 4, Barr took unprecedented steps to investigate the "avalanche" of lies. Claims of election fraud were referred to United States Attorney's offices and the FBI for investigation. Deputy Attorney General Richard Donoghue tracked dozens of investigations. None of them were found to have merit. [145] The top officials in President Trump's Justice Department personally told the President that the claims he was promoting were false. But that did not matter to the President. As Barr told the Select Committee, President Trump never showed any "indication of interest in what the actual facts were." [146]

For example, on December 27th, Rosen and Donoghue spent approximately two hours on the phone with President Trump. They debunked a litany of claims regarding the election, explaining that each had been investigated and found to be baseless. [147] According to Donoghue, President Trump "had this arsenal of allegations that he wanted to rely on." Donoghue thought it was necessary to explain to the President "based on actual investigations, actual witness interviews, actual reviews of documents, that these allegations simply had no merit." Donoghue wanted "to cut through the noise" and be "very blunt" with the President, making it clear "these allegations were simply not true."[148]

During their December 27th conversation with President Trump, Rosen and Donoghue rebutted false claims regarding: suitcases of ballots in Georgia, Dominion's voting machines in Antrim County, a truckload of ballots in Pennsylvania, ballots being scanned multiple times, people voting more than once, dead people voting, Native Americans being paid to vote, and more votes than voters in particular jurisdictions.[149] As the officials debunked each claim, President Trump "would just roll on to another one."[150] Donoghue told President Trump that Federal law enforcement officials had conducted dozens of investigations and hundreds of interviews, and they had concluded that the major allegations were not supported by the evidence developed.[151] Donoghue and Rosen told President Trump "flat out" that "much of the information he [was] getting [was] false and/or just not supported by the evidence."[152] President Trump responded: "You guys may not be following the internet the way I do."[153]

The Department of Justice was not alone in trying to contain the President's conspiracy-mongering. President Trump's lies were often debunked in real-time by State authorities, judges, experts, journalists, Federal officials, and even members of his own legal team. As discussed above, the President's campaign team found that there was no significant fraud in the election. So, the President pushed them aside. The courts rejected nearly every claim brought by the President's legal team. Even though courts rejected the claims as speculative, unsupported and meritless, President Trump, Rudy Giuliani, and others continued to assert them as truth to Trump's followers in speeches, tweets, and podcasts.[154]

The burden of refuting the false claims made by President Trump and his surrogates often fell on State and local officials. For example, in Michigan, the Secretary of State's office posted thorough and prompt responses to the claims of election fraud on a "Fact Check" page on its website.[155] In Georgia, the Secretary of State's office issued news releases and held frequent press conferences in the weeks following the election to respond to claims of fraud.[156] County clerks in the contested States also spoke out publicly to refute allegations. Even as the President undermined the public's confidence in how votes are cast and counted, these clerks assured voters that their elections were secure and they could have confidence in the results.[157] Outside experts also publicly denounced and dismantled the claims being raised and amplified by President Trump. This was done in the context of litigation, congressional hearings, and press releases.[158] President Trump simply ignored these authoritative sources and continued to promote false claims that had been soundly discredited.

Below, the Select Committee presents two case studies demonstrating how President Trump and his surrogates lied in the face of overwhelming evidence. The first case study deals with Dominion Voting Systems. President Trump repeatedly claimed that Dominion's software "switched votes" and "rigged" the election well after the leaders of campaign and Justice Department officials told him that these claims were baseless. The President's smear of Dominion was central to his "Big Lie."

The second case study examines video footage recorded in Fulton County on election night. President Trump and his representatives concocted a fictional narrative based on a deceptively edited version of the footage. After these two case studies, the Select Committee examines a variety of other claims the President repeatedly made. Once again, these claims had no basis in truth.

DOMINION VOTING SYSTEMS

Between election day and January 6th, President Trump repeatedly spread conspiracy theories about Dominion voting machines. The President tweeted or retweeted false claims about Dominion more than 30 times.[159] He also repeatedly lied about the company's software during his post-election speeches and interviews.[160] President Trump's own campaign staff, administration officials, and State officials, all told him the claims had no merit. Hand recounts confirmed the fidelity of the machines. But none of this overwhelming evidence mattered. President Trump demonstrated a conscious disregard for the facts and continued to maliciously smear Dominion.

President Trump's allies began spreading false claims regarding Dominion within days of the election. On November 8th, the day after networks called the election for Joe Biden, Sidney Powell claimed on Fox News that Dominion machines "were flipping votes in the computer system or adding votes that did not exist."[161] On November 12th, Rudy Giuliani appeared on Fox News to claim that Dominion was connected to Venezuelan dictator Hugo Chavez and its software was created "in order to fix elections."[162] The same day, President Trump retweeted a "REPORT" claiming that Dominion had "DELETED 2.7 MILLION TRUMP VOTES NATIONWIDE" and switched hundreds of thousands of votes in key swing states.[163]

By that time, the Trump Campaign team had looked into allegations regarding Dominion and its software and concluded that the claims were false. An internal campaign memo, dated November 12, said that Dominion's software "did not lead to improper vote counts" and cited reports concluding that, among other things, Dominion machines "Did Not Affect The Final Vote Count."[164] The memo also addressed various claims of foreign influence regarding Dominion.[165] Jason Miller told the Select Committee that by November 12th he had told President Trump the results of the analysis of the Dominion claims by the campaign's internal research team, specifically telling him "that the international allegations for Dominion were not valid."[166] Emails and text messages show that this same analysis was shared with Mark Meadows, President Trump's chief of staff.[167] White House Press Secretary Kayleigh McEnany told the Select Committee that she found herself "waving [President Trump] off of the Dominion theory," encouraging him to use more "fact-driven" arguments.[168] But it was to no avail.

Even though members of the Trump Campaign team reported that the result of the election was not compromised by any problems with Dominion machines, the President continued to assail Dominion on Twitter in the days that followed, for example retweeting a false claim that Dominion's machines were "engineered by China, Venezuela, [and] Cuba" and claiming that Dominion had "[r]igged" the election.[169]

Officials in the Trump administration also worked to debunk the false rumors about vote manipulation. The United States Department of Homeland Security's Cybersecurity & Infrastructure Security Agency (CISA) released a joint statement of election security officials on November 12, reassuring voters that the election was "the most secure in American history." CISA emphasized: "There is no evidence that any voting system deleted or lost votes, changed votes, or was in any way compromised."[170]

This was another decision point for the President. He could choose to endorse the findings of his administration's own cyber security experts, or he could continue to promote baseless fictions about Dominion. President Trump chose the lies. The President and his supporters never did produce any evidence showing that Dominion's machines affected the results of the election. But President Trump was undeterred by the facts. Indeed, the President and his supporters seized upon a simple human error in a small Michigan county as their initial pretense for these allegations as well as to keep the Dominion conspiracy theory alive.

During the early-morning hours of November 4th, Sheryl Guy, a clerk in Antrim County, Michigan, reported the *unofficial* results of the vote count.[171] Guy's online report was odd. It showed that former Vice President Biden had somehow won Antrim, a county that is majority-Republican and President Trump was expected to easily win. Trump's supporters quickly pointed to Biden's improbable win as evidence that Dominion had tampered with the votes.[172] That wasn't true. Guy had made a mistake in updating the election counting software after a late addition of a local candidate to the ballot in some of the county's precincts, which caused her unofficial counts to be off when she tallied the votes reported by the various precincts.[173] Guy, a Republican, was informed of the odd result and began to investigate immediately. The result was corrected, and President Trump won Antrim just as was expected.[174]

Within days, local and State officials in Michigan explained to the public what had happened. On November 7th, the Michigan Secretary of State's office issued a detailed description of Guy's error and assured the public that the *official* results were not impacted.[175] The Michigan Senate's Committee on Oversight, led by Republican Senator Ed McBroom, conducted its own comprehensive review of the claims related to Antrim County and confirmed that the initial reporting error was entirely attributable to an honest mistake by the county clerk.[176]

The mix-up in Antrim County was quickly corrected. A human erred— not the voting machines. But President Trump used it as a pretext to continue lying about Dominion.

On November 12th, the same day CISA released its statement on election security, President Trump asked Tim Walberg, a Republican Congressman from Michigan, to "check with key leadership in Michigan's Legislature as to how supportive they could be in regards to pushing back on election irregularities and potential fraud." [177] That night, President Trump asked his Acting Secretary of Homeland Security, Chad Wolf, to look into allegations of election irregularities in Michigan.[178] The next day, President Trump's assistant sent Wolf a letter from Michigan State legislators raising claims about the election, including an incorrect claim that flawed Dominion software had caused votes to be counted for the wrong candidate.[179]

Administration officials quickly knocked down the Dominion claim. Wolf forwarded the allegations to the leadership of CISA, including CISA Director Christopher Krebs.[180] Krebs provided Wolf with a press release from the Michigan Secretary of State that debunked the false claim about Antrim County and Dominion's software in detail.[181] Wolf shared an update about the information he received from Krebs with White House Chief of Staff Mark Meadows.[182]

On November 17th, Krebs tweeted out a statement issued by the nation's leading election scientists that dismissed claims that election systems had been manipulated as either "unsubstantiated" or "technically incoherent." [183] President Trump fired Krebs that same day.[184] President Trump claimed the statement released by Krebs was "highly inaccurate, in that there were massive improprieties and fraud." [185] The President had no evidence for his claim.

On November 19th, Rudy Giuliani, Sidney Powell, and Jenna Ellis held a press conference at the Republican National Committee (RNC) headquarters in Washington, DC. Powell asserted that there was "massive influence of communist money through Venezuela, Cuba, and likely China in the interference with our elections here in the United States."[186] She pointed a finger at Dominion, claiming its software was "created in Venezuela at the direction of Hugo Chavez to make sure he never lost an election," and Giuliani echoed her claims.[187]

Hope Hicks told the Select Committee how that press conference was received in the White House. The day after the press conference, President Trump spoke by phone with Sidney Powell from the Oval Office. During the call, Powell repeated the same claims of foreign interference in the election she had made at the press conference. While she was speaking, the President muted his speakerphone and laughed at Powell, telling the others in the room, "This does sound crazy, doesn't it?"[188]

A few days later, the Trump Campaign issued a statement claiming Powell was not part of the Trump Campaign's legal team.[189] But Powell's outlandish claims were no different from those President Trump was making himself. On November 19th, the same day as Powell's appearance at the RNC, President Trump tweeted and retweeted a link to a segment on One America News Network (OAN) that was captioned, "Dominion-izing the Vote."[190] The segment claimed that Dominion had switched votes from Trump to Biden. OAN featured a supposed cyber expert, Ron Watkins, a key figure in the QAnon conspiracy movement.[191] On his own Twitter account, Watkins celebrated and thanked his supporters just minutes after President Trump tweeted the clip, and President Trump went on to share the clip again several times in the days that followed.[192]

Officials inside the Trump administration continued to debunk the Dominion conspiracy theory, including during in-person meetings with President Trump. Attorney General Bill Barr met with President Trump face-to-face on three occasions after the election.[193] Barr told the Select Committee, "every time I was with the President, I raised the machines as sort of Exhibit A of how irresponsible this was."[194] During the first of these meetings, on November 23rd, Barr explained to the President that the conspiracy theory about Dominion's voting machines had "zero basis," and was "one of the most disturbing allegations." Barr stressed that this was "crazy stuff" and was poisoning Americans' confidence in the voting system for no reason. This "complete nonsense" was "doing [a] great, great disservice to the country," Barr said.[195]

President Trump ignored Barr's grave concerns. On November 29th, President Trump was interviewed by Fox News' Maria Bartiromo. It was the

President's first interview since he lost his bid for reelection. He claimed the election was "rigged" and rife with "theft" and "a total fraud."[196] He repeated various conspiracy theories, leading with the claim that Dominion's voting machines had "glitches," which he alleged moved "thousands of votes from my account to Biden's account."[197] He claimed that there had been "big, massive dumps" of votes—a reference to the Red Mirage.[198] He rambled off various other, spurious allegations, including that dead people voted in significant numbers.[199] None of it was true.

On December 1st, Attorney General Barr met again with President Trump and told him that "the stuff his people were shoveling out to the public was bullshit."[200] Attorney General Barr specifically told President Trump that the claims about Dominion voting machines were "idiotic claims."[201] President Trump was still not dissuaded from continuing the lie. The day after his meeting with the Attorney General, President Trump released a video in which he repeated several claims of election fraud, including a claim that "votes had been wrongly switched from Trump to Biden" using Dominion voting machines.[202]

By early-December, courts had assessed and rejected claims that Dominion machines were manipulated to affect the outcome of the 2020 election. In Michigan, a Federal judge found that claims, including those related to fraud due to the use of Dominion voting machines, were based on "nothing but speculation and conjecture that votes were destroyed, discarded or switched...."[203] In Arizona, a Federal judge dismissed claims that Dominion machines had deleted, switched, or changed votes.[204] But President Trump and his supporters refused to accept denunciations of the fabricated Dominion claims.

Through December, President Trump and his legal team tried to echo the Dominion conspiracy theory by claiming to have found evidence that votes were switched in Antrim County. The clerk's unintentional error was fixed weeks earlier and there was no evidence showing that Dominion had altered the vote tally in Antrim, or anywhere else.[205] But President Trump's legal team used a case challenging a local marijuana ordinance that had passed by one vote to gain access to Dominion's voting machines. An Antrim County judge issued an order granting the plaintiff's experts access to the county's computer, Dominion voting machines, thumb drives and memory cards.[206] Although the purpose of the order was to allow the plaintiff to seek evidence related to his ordinance challenge, it soon became clear that President Trump's legal team was behind the effort.[207]

An organization named Allied Security Operations Group ("ASOG"), led by Russell Ramsland, conducted an analysis of Antrim County's voting machines and related systems. On December 13th, ASOG released a report on its findings. The inspection yielded no evidence of vote manipulation. Still, the report included an unsubstantiated assertion that the Dominion voting machines used in Antrim County and throughout Michigan were "purposefully designed with inherent error to create systemic fraud and influence election results" and that a malicious algorithm was used to manipulate the results of the 2020 election.[208] Documents obtained by the Select Committee show that President Trump and Vice President Mike Pence were briefed on ASOG's findings by Giuliani's team.[209] On December 14th, President Trump widely disseminated the ASOG report and accompanying talking points prepared by Giuliani's team.[210] He also trumpeted the report on Twitter, writing on December 14th: "WOW. This report shows massive fraud. Election changing result!"[211]

During a meeting with Attorney General Bill Barr that day, President Trump claimed the ASOG report was "absolute proof that the Dominion machines were rigged" and meant he was "going to have a second term."[212] Barr told the Select Committee that he believed the ASOG report was "very amateurish," its authors lacked "any real qualifications," and it failed to provide any supporting information for its sweeping conclusions about Dominion.[213] Barr told President Trump he would look into the report, but that the DOJ already had a good idea of what happened in Antrim County and it was human error, not a problem with the machines.[214] In any event, Barr promised President Trump they would have a definitive answer within a couple of days because a hand recount was being conducted.[215]

In the ensuing days, as Barr predicted, the ASOG report was swiftly and soundly criticized by experts within and outside the Trump Administration, including the Department of Justice and the Department of Homeland Security.[216] The initial analysis of election security experts at the Department of Homeland Security was that the ASOG report was "false and misleading" and "demonstrates a callous misunderstanding of the actual current voting certification process."[217] Subsequent analyses of the ASOG report and the underlying data from Antrim County were even more critical.[218] These thorough assessments of the Antrim County data and the ASOG report demonstrate that virtually every one of the claims that President Trump and his surrogates made about the report was false.[219] ASOG's inspection did not reveal any malicious software or algorithms or any other evidence that the voting machines had been compromised.[220]

Most importantly, as Attorney General Barr had promised President Trump, within days of the release of the ASOG report, a full hand recount of every ballot cast in Antrim County confirmed the results reported by the Dominion machines and refuted ASOG's assertion that an algorithm has manipulated the vote count.[221] Giuliani's chief investigator, Bernie Kerik, acknowledged that his team was not able to find any proof that a Dominion voting machine improperly switched, deleted, or injected votes during the 2020 election.[222]

President Trump was not swayed by these basic facts. The President continued to promote the ASOG report, hounding DOJ to investigate the matter further. He returned to ASOG's claims during a December 27th call with Acting Attorney General Rosen and Acting Deputy Attorney General Donoghue, citing the report's claimed error rate of 68 percent in Antrim County. Donoghue pointed out to the President that the difference between the computer and hand count was only one vote and that he "cannot and should not be relying on" ASOG's fraudulent claim, because it was simply "not true."[223]

President Trump's fixation on Dominion's voting machines and the baseless theory that the machines had manipulated votes led to a concerted effort to gain access to voting machines in States where President Trump was claiming election fraud. On the evening of December 18th, Powell, Lt. Gen. Michael Flynn (ret.) and Patrick Byrne met with the President at the White House. Over several hours, they argued that President Trump had the authority, under a 2018 executive order, to seize voting machines. Several administration officials joined the meeting and forcefully rejected this extreme proposal.[224] Multiple lawyers in the White House, including Eric Herschmann, Derek Lyons, and White House Counsel Pat Cipollone "pushed back strongly" against the idea of seizing voting machines. Cipollone told the Select Committee it was a "horrible idea," which had "no legal basis,"[225] and he emphasized that he had "seen no evidence of massive fraud in the election."[226] White House advisor Eric Herschmann similarly told the Select Committee that he "never saw any evidence whatsoever" to sustain the allegations against Dominion.[227] National Security Adviser Robert O'Brien phoned into the December 18th meeting and was asked if he had seen "any evidence of election fraud in the voting machines or foreign interference in our voting machines." O'Brien responded that his team had "looked into that, and there's no evidence of it."[228]

Around the same time, President Trump, Mark Meadows, and Rudy Giuliani were repeatedly asking the leadership of DHS whether the agency had authority to seize voting machines, and they were repeatedly told that DHS has no such unilateral authority.[229] Giuliani and Powell were also engaged in efforts to access voting machines in multiple States with the assistance of sympathetic local election officials.[230] Those efforts turned up no evidence of any vote manipulation by any Dominion machine, but President Trump continued to press this bogus claim.

On January 2, 2021, President Trump had a lengthy phone call with Georgia Secretary of State Brad Raffensperger. The President repeatedly brought up Dominion's voting machines, alleging that they were at the heart of a conspiracy against him.[231] Raffensperger was incredulous. "I don't believe that you're really questioning the Dominion machines," Raffensperger said. "Because we did a hand re-tally, a 100 percent re-tally of all the ballots, and compared them to what the machines said and came up with virtually the same result. Then we did the recount, and we got virtually the same result."[232] In other words, the story in Georgia was the same as the story in Antrim County, Michigan: Officials performed a hand recount to put to rest any allegations that Dominion's machines had manipulated the vote. But once again, President Trump consciously disregarded these basic facts and persisted with his lies.

During a January 4, 2021, speech in Dalton, Georgia, President Trump chose to ignore Secretary Raffensperger's straightforward observations. The President rhetorically attacked Dominion once again, claiming that a "crime" had been "committed in this state" and it was "immeasurable."[233] The President called for an "immediate forensic audit of an appropriate sampling of Dominion's voting machines and related equipment."[234] His allegations were both false and nonsensical. Georgia had already performed a statewide hand recount of all ballots.

President Trump and his allies have never provided any evidence showing that Dominion's voting software altered votes in the 2020 presidential election. In fact, some of the most vocal proponents of the Dominion claims harbored their own misgivings about the claims they were making in public. For example, Rudy Giuliani repeatedly claimed in public that Dominion voting machines stole the election, and that foreign countries had interfered in the election, but the evidence uncovered by the Select Committee reveals that he did not believe either of those things to be true. Giuliani testified that he did not believe that voting machines stole the election.[235] He also acknowledged that he had seen no evidence that foreign countries had interfered in the election or manipulated votes.[236]

This testimony is consistent with his lead investigator Bernie Kerik's acknowledgment that he had not come across proof that voting machines were used to switch, delete, or inject votes improperly.[237] Christina Bobb, an attorney who worked with Giuliani, similarly could not point to any evidence of wrongdoing by Dominion.[238] Even Sidney Powell, perhaps the most committed proponent of the Dominion falsehoods, was unable to provide the Select Committee with any evidence or expert report that demonstrated that the 2020 election outcome in any State had been altered through manipulation of voting machines.[239] And Powell defended herself in a defamation suit brought by Dominion by claiming that "no reasonable person would conclude that her statements were truly statements of fact." [240]

By January 6, 2021, President Trump's claims regarding Dominion had been debunked time and again. The President knew, or should have known, that he had no basis for alleging that Dominion's voting machines had cost him the election.

THE STATE FARM ARENA VIDEO

President Trump also recklessly promoted allegations that video footage from a ballot counting center in Fulton County, Georgia, was proof of major election fraud. He was repeatedly informed that these allegations were false, but he pressed them anyway.

On December 3rd, Rudy Giuliani presented State legislators with selectively edited footage of ballots being counted on Election Night at Fulton County's State Farm Arena.[241] Giuliani misrepresented the video as "a smoking gun" proving election fraud.[242] The President repeatedly claimed that he would have won Georgia, if not for a supposed conspiracy that unfolded on election night. President Trump and some of his supporters alleged that political operatives faked a water main rupture to expel Republican poll watchers.[243] These same operatives then supposedly took illegal ballots from suitcases hidden under tables and added those ballots to the official count multiple times over by scanning them more than once.[244] Not one of these allegations was true.

In a speech on December 5th, President Trump made the false claim about the State Farm Arena and claimed that "if you just take the crime of what those Democrat workers were doing...[t]hat's 10 times more than I need to win this state." [245] During a December 22nd speech, he played the same deceptive footage presented by Giuliani several weeks earlier.[246] President Trump also repeatedly scapegoated one of these Fulton County election workers during his January 2nd phone call with Georgia's Secretary of State, repeatedly referencing her by name and calling her "a professional vote scammer and hustler." [247] It was a malicious smear.

President Trump was directly notified *at least* four different times that the allegations he was making were false. On December 15th, then–Deputy Attorney General Jeffrey Rosen told him: "It wasn't a suitcase. It was a bin. That's what they use when they're counting ballots. It's benign." [248] Rosen's deputy, Richard Donoghue, also debunked this claim, including on a phone call on December 27th and in a meeting in the Oval Office on December 31st: "I told the President myself...several times, in several conversations, that these allegations about ballots being smuggled in in a suitcase and run through the machines several times, it was not true, that we had looked at it, we looked at the video, we interviewed the witnesses, and it was not true." [249]

Likewise, Georgia Secretary of State Brad Raffensperger told President Trump that his allegations about the video were false. During his January 2nd call with the President, Raffensperger explained that Giuliani's team "sliced and diced that video and took it out of context" and that "the events that transpired are nowhere near what was projected" once one looks at more complete footage.[250] Raffensperger also explained to the President that his team "did an audit of that, and we proved conclusively that they were not scanned three times." [251] Yet, when Raffensperger said he would send President Trump a link to the television segment, the President refused: "I don't care about the link. I don't need it." [252]

The actual evidence contradicted all of President Trump's claims about what the Fulton County video depicted. For example, the chief investigator for Raffensperger's office explained in a December 6th court filing that "there were no mystery ballots that were brought in from an unknown location and hidden under tables...." [253] As the investigator noted, the security footage showed there was nothing under the table when it was brought into the room. Hours later, with reporters and observers present, the "video shows ballots that had already been opened but not counted placed in the boxes, sealed up, [and] stored under the table." [254] This finding was affirmed by the FBI, DOJ, and the Georgia Bureau of Investigation, which interviewed witnesses and reviewed the full video footage and machine data from the site.[255]

The ballots in question were not double counted. This was confirmed by a full hand recount in November, as well as a subsequent review by investigators.[256] They found that although one of the workers was shown in the video scanning certain batches multiple times, this was for a valid reason: her scanner kept jamming. The investigators confirmed from scanner logs, as well as the footage, that she only hit the "accept" button once per batch.[257] Investigators also found that staff likely did not tell the observers to leave, let alone forcefully eject them from the facility.[258]

Despite this conclusive evidence and testimony, President Trump continued to point to the Fulton County video as evidence of a grand conspiracy. On January 5th, for instance, President Trump's executive assistant emailed a document "from POTUS" to Senator Josh Hawley (R-MO), Senator Ted Cruz (R-TX), and Representative Jim Jordan (R-OH) that cited "Suitcase Gate" among the "worst fraud incidents" in Georgia.[259]

During his January 6th speech, President Trump told the crowd that "in Fulton County, Republican poll watchers were ejected, in some cases, physically from the room under the false pretense of a pipe burst." The President continued:

> ...then election officials pull boxes, Democrats, and suitcases of ballots out from under a table. You all saw it on television, totally fraudulent. And illegally scanned them for nearly two hours, totally unsupervised. Tens of thousands of votes. This act coincided with a mysterious vote dump of up to 100,000 votes for Joe Biden, almost none for Donald Trump.[260]

No part of President Trump's story was true. He had already been informed that it was false.

In June 2021, when Giuliani's law license was revoked by a New York State appellate court, the court's ruling cited his statements about supposed suitcases of ballots in Georgia as one of its reasons for doing so. "If, as respondent claims, he reviewed the entire video, he could not have reasonably reached a conclusion that illegal votes were being counted," the court's ruling reads.[261]

President Trump's conspiracy-mongering endangered innocent public servants around the country, including in Fulton County. For example, during a December 10, 2020, appearance in Georgia, Giuliani falsely accused Ruby Freeman and Shaye Moss, two Black public servants shown in the Fulton County video, of "surreptitiously passing around USB ports as if they're vials of heroin or cocaine."[262] In fact, Moss had been given a ginger mint by her mother, Freeman.[263] As described in Chapter 2, baseless accusations like these forever changed the lives of election workers like Freeman and Moss. All in service of President Trump's Big Lie.

THE FAKE BALLOT MYTH

The Trump Campaign's distortion of the State Farm Arena video is just one example of the "fake ballots" lie. President Trump frequently claimed that "fake ballots" for Biden were injected into the vote-counting process. To hear the President tell it, there were truckloads of ballots delivered in the middle of the night to vote-counting centers and millions more votes were cast than there were registered voters. Judges, Trump administration officials, State authorities, and independent election experts found each iteration of the "fake ballot" claim to be just that: fake. The Trump Campaign and its surrogates brought nine cases that raised some version of a "fake ballots" claim. Every one of those cases was promptly dismissed.[264] For example, in *Costantino v. City of Detroit*, a Michigan court ruled that the plaintiff's claims regarding forged, backdated and double-counted votes in

Detroit were "incorrect and not credible" and "rife with speculation and guess-work about sinister motives." [265]

Many of the fake ballot claims were publicly raised and repeated by President Trump, but never included in any lawsuit. For example, a truck driver for the U.S. Postal Service claimed that he delivered hundreds of thousands of completed ballots from Bethpage, New York to Lancaster, Pennsylvania.[266] President Trump repeated this allegation numerous times.[267] The DOJ and FBI interviewed the relevant witnesses, including the truck driver, and reviewed the loading manifests. They determined that the allegation was not true.[268] Both Attorney General Barr and his successor, Jeffrey Rosen, told President Trump this claim was false. But that didn't stop the President from repeating it.

Another alleged "truckload of ballots" was supposedly delivered to the Detroit counting center at 4:30 a.m. on election night. This truck allegedly carried 100,000 ballots in garbage cans, wastepaper bins, cardboard boxes, and shopping baskets.[269] A widely circulated video purportedly showed an unmarked van dropping off ballots, which were then wheeled into the counting center on a wagon.[270] In fact, the only ballot delivery in Detroit after midnight on election night was an official delivery of 16,000 ballots, stacked in 45 well-organized trays of approximately 350 ballots each.[271] The wagon depicted in the video contained camera equipment being pulled by a reporter.[272] The claim of 100,000 fake ballots being smuggled into the counting center in the middle of the night is even more ridiculous in light of the fact that only 174,384 absent voter ballots were recorded in the City of Detroit in the 2020 election.[273] The addition of 100,000 fake ballots to approximately 74,000 legitimate ballots would certainly have been obvious to election officials.[274]

President Trump also repeatedly claimed that more votes were cast than there were registered voters in certain States, cities, or precincts. It was easy to fact-check these allegations and demonstrate they were false.

For example, in Pennsylvania, approximately nine million people were registered to vote and approximately 6.8 million votes were cast in the 2020 presidential election.[275] Nevertheless, President Trump and his allies made numerous "more votes than voters" claims in Pennsylvania. Citing 2020 mail-in voting data tweeted by Pennsylvania State Senator Doug Mastriano, President Trump claimed that 1.1 million ballots had been "created" and counted improperly.[276] In fact, there was no discrepancy in the actual numbers—Mastriano erroneously compared the 2.6 million mail-in ballots cast *in the November general* election to the 1.5 million ballots that were returned *in the June primary* election.[277]

President Trump also promoted a false claim by a different Pennsylvania legislator that Pennsylvania had 205,000 more votes than voters.[278] This claim was based on a flawed comparison by State Representative Frank Ryan of the votes recorded by State election authorities as having been cast and those reflected in a separate State registry.[279] In fact, the discrepancy was a result of some counties not yet uploading their official results to the registry.[280] In late-December 2020, Acting Deputy Attorney General Donoghue told President Trump that this allegation was baseless.[281] President Trump kept repeating it anyway.[282]

The President and his surrogates made similar false claims concerning excess votes in Michigan. Many of those claims originated with a grossly inaccurate affidavit submitted by Russell Ramsland, the person behind the "very amateurish" and "false and misleading" ASOG report regarding Dominion voting machines in Antrim County.[283] Ramsland claimed in a similar affidavit filed in Federal court in Georgia that 3,276 precincts in Michigan had turnout of between 84% and 350%, with 19 precincts reporting turnout in excess of 100%.[284] Ramsland's affidavit was widely ridiculed, in part, because he relied on data for dozens of precincts that are located in Minnesota, not Michigan.[285] Even after he corrected his affidavit to remove the Minnesota townships, his Michigan data remained wildly off-base.[286]

THE "MULTIPLE COUNTING OF BALLOTS" FICTION

The President and his surrogates repeatedly claimed that ballots for former Vice President Biden were counted multiple times.[287] These claims originated when some noticed election officials re-running stacks of ballots through counting machines. But the allegation is based on a fundamental misunderstanding of the vote-counting process—it is routine and appropriate for election officials to re-scan ballots if they are not properly scanned and tabulated in the initial effort. In *Costantino v. City of Detroit*, the court rejected the "incorrect and not credible" affidavits speculating that ballots were run through scanners and counted multiple times in favor of the "more accurate and persuasive explanation of activity" put forward by the "highly-respected" election official with 40 years of experience.[288]

As with other misguided claims of election fraud, the claim that ballots were counted multiple times disregards the safeguards in the voting process. In particular, as noted above, it would certainly have been apparent in the canvassing process if hundreds of ballots were counted multiple times in Detroit because the total number of ballots would greatly exceed the number of voters who voted. But that was not the case.

THE IMAGINARY "DEAD" AND "INELIGIBLE" VOTERS

In addition to their false claims regarding fake ballots, President Trump and his surrogates also relentlessly asserted that tens of thousands of ballots were cast by dead or otherwise ineligible voters. For example, President Trump and Giuliani frequently alleged that more than 66,000 unregistered juveniles voted in Georgia.[289] In fact, no underage people voted in Georgia.[290] Giuliani offered several different made-up figures of the number of non-citizens who supposedly voted in Arizona, but provided no evidence to substantiate his claims.[291] In fact, Arizona requires every new voter to provide proof of citizenship in order to register to vote—or to complete a Federal voter registration form that requires the individual to sign an attestation to citizenship status under penalty of perjury—and no person can vote without being registered.[292] By mid-November, Trump Campaign staff determined this allegation that thousands of non-citizens voted in Arizona was based on "highly unreliable" information, and it is one of the false claims that led to Giuliani losing his New York law license.[293] These "ineligible" voters did not exist.

Nor were thousands of votes cast in the names of dead Americans.

During his January 2nd, call with Georgia Secretary of State Raffensperger, the President claimed that "close to about 5,000 [dead] voters" cast ballots in the election. Raffensperger quickly informed the President this wasn't true.[294] But the "dead voter" lie wasn't limited to Georgia. President Trump wanted Americans to believe that "dead voters" contributed to his defeat in several battleground States.[295]

But even the Trump Campaign and its lawyers recognized early on that the claims regarding "dead voters" were grossly exaggerated, to say the least. By early November, Trump lawyers discovered that many people listed by the campaign as having died were actually alive and well.[296] In early December, Eric Herschmann advised Chief of Staff Meadows by text message that the Trump legal team had determined that the claim of more than 10,000 dead people voting in Georgia was not accurate.[297] The ensuing exchange makes clear that both men knew that Giuliani's claims were absurd:

> Herschmann: Just an FYI. Alex Cannon and his team verified that the 10k+ supposed dead people voting in GA is not accurate

> Meadows: I didn't hear that claim. It is not accurate. I think I found 22 if I remember correctly. Two of them died just days before the general

> Herschmann: It was alleged in Rudy's hearing today. Your number is much closer to what we can prove. I think it's 12

Meadows: My son found 12 obituaries and 6 other possibles depending on the Voter roll acuracy [sic]

Herschmann: That sounds more like it. Maybe he can help Rudy find the other 10k ??

Meadows: lol [298]

Shortly thereafter, a Georgia court dismissed the claim that there were tens of thousands of votes cast by ineligible voters, noting the claims "rest on speculation rather than duly pled facts." [299]

The Trump Campaign's own expert on the supposed "dead voters" admitted that the Campaign lacked the necessary data to make any conclusions about whether any (or how many) votes were cast in the name of a deceased person. [300] State officials *did* have such data, however, and were able to conduct the type of matching analysis required. These State authorities determined that there were only a handful of cases in which people voted on behalf of deceased individuals. [301]

Even in those cases where the person who voted actually did die, President Trump's lawyers knew that the vast majority of the voters included on their list of dead voters actually cast their votes before they passed. [302] In early-January 2021, just days before January 6th, Republican Senator Lindsey Graham asked several Trump lawyers to provide evidence to support the Campaign's claims regarding dead voters. [303] As Giuliani's team investigated, they concluded that they could not find evidence of dead voters anywhere near the number that Giuliani and President Trump were claiming publicly. After noting the shortcomings in their evidence, Katherine Friess, a lawyer working with the Giuliani legal team, warned that Senator Graham would "push back" on their evidence. [304] As predicted by Friess, Senator Graham was not impressed by the information provided by Giuliani's team. In his speech on the Senate floor on January 6th, Graham explained why he would not object to the certification of electoral votes. Senator Graham referred to the failure of the Trump attorneys to provide the evidence he requested:

> They said there's 66,000 people in Georgia under 18 voted. How many people believe that? I asked, 'Give me 10.' Hadn't had one. They said 8,000 felons in prison in Arizona voted. Give me 10. Hadn't gotten one. Does that say there's—There's problems in every election. I don't buy this. Enough's enough. We've got to end it. [305]

Documents obtained by the Select Committee reveal that President Trump and his lawyers knew that the claims being made in court about dead or ineligible voters in Georgia were inaccurate, and the lawyers were concerned that if the President vouched for those claims in another court pleading he might be criminally prosecuted. On December 31st, as the lawyers rushed to file a Federal lawsuit in Georgia, some of the lawyers raised concerns about the President signing a "verification" under oath that the allegations regarding voter fraud in Georgia, including claims regarding dead people voting, were true. As Eastman noted in an email to his colleagues on December 31st:

> Although the President signed a verification [regarding the Georgia claims] back on Dec. 1, he has since been made aware that some of the allegations (and evidence proffered by the experts) has been inaccurate. For him to sign a new verification with that knowledge... would not be accurate. And I have no doubt that an aggressive DA or US Atty someplace will go after both the President and his lawyers once all the dust settles on this.[306]

Despite these concerns, President Trump and his attorneys filed a complaint that incorporated the same inaccurate numbers, and President Trump signed a verification swearing under oath that the inaccurate numbers were "true and correct" or "believed to be true and correct" to the best of his knowledge and belief.[307] A Federal judge reviewing the relevant emails and pleadings recently concluded:

> The emails show that President Trump knew that the specific numbers of voter fraud were wrong but continued to tout those numbers, both in court and to the public. The Court finds that these emails are sufficiently related to and in furtherance of a conspiracy to defraud the United States.[308]

1.9 PRESIDENT TRUMP'S JANUARY 6TH SPEECH

At noon on January 6, 2021, President Trump addressed thousands of his supporters at a rally just south of the White House. The election had been decided two months earlier. The courts found there was no evidence of significant fraud. The States certified their votes by mid-December. It was over—President Trump lost. But that's not what the President told those in attendance. He delivered an incendiary speech from beginning to end, arguing that nothing less than the fate of America was at stake.

"Our country has had enough," President Trump said. "We will not take it anymore and that's what this is all about." [309] He claimed that his followers had descended on Washington to "save our democracy" and "stop the

steal." [310] He refused, once again, to concede. And he proclaimed that "[t]oday I will lay out just some of the evidence proving that we won this election and we won it by a landslide." [311]

For months, President Trump had relentlessly promoted his Big Lie.[312] He and his associates manufactured one tale after another to justify it. For more than an hour on January 6th, the President wove these conspiracy theories and lies together.[313]

By the Select Committee's assessment, there were more than 100 times during his speech in which President Trump falsely claimed that either the election had been stolen from him, or falsely claimed that votes had been compromised by some specific act of fraud or major procedural violations. That day, President Trump repeated many of the same lies he had told for months—even after being informed that many of these claims were false. He lied about Dominion voting machines in Michigan, suitcases of ballots in Georgia, more votes than voters in Pennsylvania, votes cast by non-citizens in Arizona, and dozens of other false claims of election fraud.[314] None of those claims were true.

As explained in the chapters that follow, the Big Lie was central to President Trump's plan to stay in power. He used the Big Lie to pressure

State and local officials to undo the will of the people. His campaign convened fake electors on the baseless pretense that former Vice President Biden won several States due to fraud or other malfeasance. The President tried to subvert the Department of Justice by browbeating its leadership to endorse his election lies. And when the DOJ's senior personnel did not acquiesce, President Trump sought to install a loyalist who would.

When all those efforts failed, President Trump betrayed his own Vice President. He pressured Vice President Pence to obstruct the joint session of Congress on January 6th, falsely claiming that he had the power to refuse to count certain electoral votes. President Trump knew this was illegal but attempted to justify it with lies about the election.

On December 19, 2020, President Trump summoned a mob to Washington, DC on the same day that Congress was set to certify former Vice President Biden's victory by claiming the election was stolen and promising a "wild" protest.[315]

And the bogus stolen election claim was the focus of President Trump's speech on January 6th. The litany of lies he told riled up a mob that would march to the U.S. Capitol to intimidate Vice President Pence and Members of Congress.

"And we fight. We fight like hell. And if you don't fight like hell, you're not going to have a country anymore," President Trump told the crowd.[316] He incited them with these words just after praising his own election night lie—the Big Lie.

President Trump told his followers to "fight" to "save" their country from a bogus specter of supposed election fraud.[317] And many of them did.

ENDNOTES

1. "Donald Trump 2020 Election Night Speech Transcript," Rev, (Nov. 4, 2020), available at https://www.rev.com/blog/transcripts/donald-trump-2020-election-night-speech-transcript.

2. Select Committee to Investigate the January 6th Attack on the United States Capitol, Transcribed Interview of William Stepien, (Feb. 10, 2022), pp. 54, 60.

3. Select Committee to Investigate the January 6th Attack on the United States Capitol, Deposition of Jason Miller, (Feb. 3, 2022), pp. 74-75.

4. Select Committee to Investigate the January 6th Attack on the United States Capitol, Deposition of Jason Miller, (Feb. 3, 2022), pp. 75, 78.

5. Documents on file with the Select Committee to Investigate the January 6th Attack on the United States Capitol (National Archives Production), 076P-R000010020_0001 (Email chain between Tom Fitton and Molly Michael, starting on October 31, 2020, and ending on November 3, 2020, discussing a draft victory statement for President Trump).

6. We note that Bannon refused to testify and has been convicted of criminal contempt by a jury of his peers. See "Stephen K. Bannon Sentenced to Four Months in Prison on Two Counts of Contempt of Congress," Department of Justice, (Oct. 21, 2022), available at

https://www.justice.gov/usao-dc/pr/stephen-k-bannon-sentenced-four-months-prison-two-counts-contempt-congress; Dan Friedman, "Leaked Audio: Before Election Day, Bannon Said Trump Planned to Falsely Claim Victory," Mother Jones, (July 12, 2022), available at https://www.motherjones.com/politics/2022/07/leaked-audio-steve-bannon-trump-2020-election-declare-victory/.

7.   At his interview, Stone invoked his Fifth Amendment Right not to incriminate himself, including to questions regarding his direct communications with Donald Trump and his role on January 6th. Select Committee to Investigate the January 6th Attack on the United States Capitol, *Business Meeting on the January 6th Investigation*, 117th Cong., 2d sess., (Oct. 13, 2022), at 39:15 - 39:33 available at https://www.youtube.com/watch?v=IQvuBoLBuC0.

8.   Select Committee to Investigate the January 6th Attack on the United States Capitol, Transcribed Interview of William Barr, (June 2, 2022), p. 27.

9.   Jennifer Agiesta and Marshall Cohen, "CNN Poll: Questions about Accuracy of Vote Counting Rise as Most Want to Vote before Election Day," CNN, (Aug. 18, 2020), available at https://www.cnn.com/2020/08/18/politics/cnn-poll-trump-biden-election-security-mail-in-voting/index.html; Mark Murray, "Biden Leads Trump by 10 points in Final Pre-Election NBC News/WSJ poll," NBC News, (Nov. 1, 2020, updated Nov. 2, 2020), available at https://www.nbcnews.com/politics/meet-the-press/biden-leads-trump-10-points-final-pre-election-nbc-news-n1245667.

10.   Select Committee to Investigate the January 6th Attack on the United States Capitol, *Hearing on the January 6th Investigation*, 117th Cong., 2d sess., (June 13, 2022), available at https://www.govinfo.gov/committee/house-january6th.

11.   Select Committee to Investigate the January 6th Attack on the United States Capitol, *Hearing on the January 6th Investigation*, 117th Cong., 2d sess., (June 13, 2022), available at https://www.govinfo.gov/committee/house-january6th.

12.   Select Committee to Investigate the January 6th Attack on the United States Capitol, Transcribed Interview of William Stepien, (Feb. 10, 2022), p. 44.

13.   Select Committee to Investigate the January 6th Attack on the United States Capitol, Transcribed Interview of William Stepien, (Feb. 10, 2022), pp. 44-45.

14.   Select Committee to Investigate the January 6th Attack on the United States Capitol, *Hearing on the January 6th Investigation*, 117th Cong., 2d sess., (June 13, 2022), available at https://www.govinfo.gov/committee/house-january6th.

15.   Dan Friedman, "Leaked Audio: Before Election Day, Bannon Said Trump Planned to Falsely Claim Victory," Mother Jones, (July 12, 2022), available at https://www.motherjones.com/politics/2022/07/leaked-audio-steve-bannon-trump-2020-election-declare-victory/. During our October 13 hearing, Robert Costa tweeted: "CBS News has confirmed that Oct. 31, 2020, was a key date in the pre-election maneuvers by Trump. Set off alarm with WH counsel and Herschmann, among others. I've seen texts from that night from some aides and they knew it was no joke; declaring victory was Trump's plan. Period." Maggie Haberman retweeted Costa, writing: "Trump told a conference call of a bunch of lawyers and informal advisers working for him earlier that month that he was going to go up and say he won, first reported by @jonathanvswan." Robert Costa (@costareports), Twitter, Oct. 13, 2022 1:29 p.m. ET, available at https://twitter.com/costareports/status/1580611586674151424?lang=en; *see also* Maggie Haberman (@maggieNYT), Twitter, Oct. 13, 2022 1:35 p.m. ET, available at https://twitter.com/maggienyt/status/1580613143637635072 ("Trump told a conference call of a bunch of lawyers and informal advisers working for him earlier that month that he was going to go up and say he won, first reported by @jonathanvswan").

16.   Dan Friedman, "Leaked Audio: Before Election Day, Bannon Said Trump Planned to Falsely Claim Victory," Mother Jones, (July 12, 2022), available at https://www.motherjones.com/politics/2022/07/leaked-audio-steve-bannon-trump-2020-election-declare-victory/.

17. Fox Business, "Steve Bannon: Trump Won't Allow the Election to Be Stolen," YouTube, at 3:24, Nov. 3, 2020, available at https://www.youtube.com/watch?v=PDdxoyAUqoo.

18. "Steve Bannon: Donald Trump Will Claim Victory 'Right Before the 11 O'clock News'," Media Matters, (Nov. 3, 2020), available at https://www.mediamatters.org/steve-bannon/steve-bannon-donald-trump-will-claim-victory-right-11-oclock-news-0.

19. Documents on file with the Select Committee to Investigate the January 6th Attack on the United States Capitol (National Archives Production), 076P-R000010020_0001 (Email chain between Tom Fitton and Molly Michael, starting on October 31, 2020, and ending on November 3, 2020, discussing a draft victory statement for President Trump).

20. Documents on file with the Select Committee to Investigate the January 6th Attack on the United States Capitol (National Archives Production), 076P-R000010020_0001 (Email chain between Tom Fitton and Molly Michael, starting on October 31, 2020, and ending on November 3, 2020, discussing a draft victory statement for President Trump).

21. Documents on file with the Select Committee to Investigate the January 6th Attack on the United States Capitol (National Archives Production), 076P-R000010020_0001 (Email chain between Tom Fitton and Molly Michael, starting on October 31, 2020, and ending on November 3, 2020, discussing a draft victory statement for President Trump).

22. Documents on file with the Select Committee to Investigate the January 6th Attack on the United States Capitol (National Archives Production), 076P-R000010020_0001 (Email chain between Tom Fitton and Molly Michael, starting on October 31, 2020, and ending on November 3, 2020, discussing a draft victory statement for President Trump).

23. Documents on file with the Select Committee to Investigate the January 6th Attack on the United States Capitol (National Archives Production), 076P-R000010020_0001 (Email chain between Tom Fitton and Molly Michael, starting on October 31, 2020, and ending on November 3, 2020, discussing a draft victory statement for President Trump).

24. Select Committee to Investigate the January 6th Attack on the United States Capitol, *Business Meeting on the January 6th Investigation*, 117th Cong., 2d sess., (Oct. 13, 2022), at 38:18 - 39:32, available at https://www.youtube.com/watch?v=IQvuBoLBuC0.

25. Jonathan Swan, "Trump Plans to Declare Premature Victory If He Appears on Election Night," *Axios*, (Nov. 1, 2020), available at https://www.axios.com/2020/11/01/trump-claim-election-victory-ballots.

26. Jonathan Swan, "Trump Plans to Declare Premature Victory If He Appears on Election Night," *Axios*, (Nov. 1, 2020), available at https://www.axios.com/2020/11/01/trump-claim-election-victory-ballots.

27. Jonathan Swan, "Trump Plans to Declare Premature Victory If He Appears on Election Night," *Axios*, (Nov. 1, 2020), available at https://www.axios.com/2020/11/01/trump-claim-election-victory-ballots.

28. Select Committee to Investigate the January 6th Attack on the United States Capitol, *Hearing on the January 6th Investigation*, 117th Cong., 2d sess., (June 13, 2022), available at https://www.govinfo.gov/committee/house-january6th.

29. Months prior to the election, Josh Mendelsohn, the CEO of Hawkfish, a Democratic data and analytics firm, warned that President Trump would try to take advantage of the Red Mirage. *See* Margaret Talev, "Exclusive: Dem Group Warns of Apparent Trump Election Day Landslide," *Axios*, (Sept. 1, 2020), available at https://www.axios.com/2020/09/01/bloomberg-group-trump-election-night-scenarios. For other accounts warning that election night would see a Red Mirage, *see* Marshall Cohen, "Deciphering the 'Red Mirage,' the 'Blue Shift,' and the Uncertainty Surrounding Election Results This November," CNN, (Sept. 1, 2020), available at https://www.cnn.com/2020/09/01/politics/2020-election-count-red-mirage-blue-shift/index.html; Darragh Roche, "Trump Is Heading for a 'Red Mirage' Win on Election Night, Bloomberg-Funded Data Firm Says," *Newsweek*, (Sept. 1, 2020), available at https://www.newsweek.com/trump-phantom-win-election-1528948; Tom McCarthy, "'Red

Mirage': The 'Insidious' Scenario If Trump Declares Victory," *The Guardian*, (Oct. 31, 2020), available at https://www.theguardian.com/us-news/2020/oct/31/red-mirage-trump-election-scenario-victory.

30. "Remarks by President Trump, Vice President Pence, and Members of the Coronavirus Task Force in Press Briefing," White House, April 7, 2020, available at https://trumpwhitehouse.archives.gov/briefings-statements/remarks-president-trump-vice-president-pence-members-coronavirus-task-force-press-briefing-april-7-2020/.

31. Donald J. Trump (@realDonaldTrump), Twitter, Apr. 8, 2020 8:20 a.m. ET, available at http://web.archive.org/web/20201201162757/https://twitter.com/realDonaldTrump/status/1247861952736526336 (archived).

32. Donald J. Trump (@realDonaldTrump), Twitter, May 24, 2020 10:08 a.m. ET, available at http://web.archive.org/web/20200701075716/https://twitter.com/realDonaldTrump/status/1264558926021959680 (archived).

33. Donald J. Trump (@realDonaldTrump), Twitter, Sept. 17, 2020 7:56 a.m. ET, available at http://web.archive.org/web/20201115164217/https://twitter.com/realDonaldTrump/status/1306562791894122504 (archived).

34. Select Committee to Investigate the January 6th Attack on the United States Capitol, Transcribed Interview of William Stepien, (Feb. 10, 2022), p. 36; Documents on file with the Select Committee to Investigate the January 6th Attack on the United States Capitol, (National Archives Production), 076P-R000010941_0001-2, 076P-R000010940_0001-6 (July 23, 2020, emails regarding scheduling a meeting for the President with McCarthy, Stepien, and others).

35. Select Committee to Investigate the January 6th Attack on the United States Capitol, Transcribed Interview of William Stepien, (Feb. 10, 2022), p. 36.

36. Fox News, "President Trump Goes One-on-One with Chris Wallace," YouTube, July 19, 2020, available at https://www.youtube.com/watch?v=W6XdpDOH1JA; Pat Ward (@WardDPatrick), Twitter, July 19, 2020 10:15 a.m. ET, available at https://twitter.com/WardDPatrick/status/1284854318575878144.

37. "Remarks by President Trump in Press Briefing," White House, Sept. 23, 2020, available at https://trumpwhitehouse.archives.gov/briefings-statements/remarks-president-trump-press-briefing-092420/.

38. "Remarks by President Trump in Press Briefing," White House, Sept. 23, 2020, available at https://trumpwhitehouse.archives.gov/briefings-statements/remarks-president-trump-press-briefing-092420/.

39. Barbara Sprunt, "Trump Questions Election Again after White House Walked Back His Earlier Remarks," NPR, (Sept. 24, 2020), available at https://www.npr.org/2020/09/24/916440816/republican-leaders-reject-trump-hedging-on-transfer-of-power-amid-war-over-confi.

40. Donald J. Trump (@realDonaldTrump), Twitter, Nov. 4, 2020 12:49 a.m. ET, available at http://web.archive.org/web/20201105044240/https://twitter.com/realDonaldTrump/status/1323864823680126977 (archived); Donald J. Trump (@realDonaldTrump), Twitter, Nov. 4, 2020 10:04 a.m. ET, available at http://web.archive.org/web/20201104153504/https://twitter.com/realDonaldTrump/status/1324004491612618752 (archived).

41. Select Committee to Investigate the January 6th Attack on the United States Capitol, Transcribed Interview of William Stepien, (Feb. 10, 2022), pp. 44-45.

42. "Donald Trump 2020 Election Night Speech Transcript," Rev, (Nov. 4, 2020), available at https://www.rev.com/blog/transcripts/donald-trump-2020-election-night-speech-transcript.

43. *See* "Donald Trump 2020 Election Night Speech Transcript," Rev, (Nov. 4, 2020), available at https://www.rev.com/blog/transcripts/donald-trump-2020-election-night-speech-transcript; Donald J. Trump (@realDonaldTrump), Twitter, Nov. 4, 2020 12:49 a.m. ET, available at http://web.archive.org/web/20201104060648/https://twitter.com/realDonaldTrump/status/1323864823680126977 (archived).

44. Dan Friedman, "Leaked Audio: Before Election Day, Bannon Said Trump Planned to Falsely Claim Victory," Mother Jones, (July 12, 2022), available at https://www.motherjones.com/politics/2022/07/leaked-audio-steve-bannon-trump-2020-election-declare-victory/.

45. Factba.se, "Interview: Maria Bartiromo Interviews Donald Trump on Fox News - November 29, 2020," Vimeo, Nov. 29, 2020, at esp. 1:42-3:35, available at https://vimeo.com/485180163; Donald J. Trump (@realDonaldTrump), Twitter, Nov. 4, 2020 10:17 a.m. ET, available at https://media-cdn.factba.se/realdonaldtrump-twitter/1324007806694023169.jpg (archived); Donald J. Trump (@realDonaldTrump), Twitter, Nov. 4, 2020 10:04 a.m. ET, available at https://media-cdn.factba.se/realdonaldtrump-twitter/1324004491612618752.jpg (archived); Donald J. Trump (@realDonaldTrump), Twitter, Nov. 18, 2020 8:22 p.m. ET, available at https://media-cdn.factba.se/realdonaldtrump-twitter/1329233502139715586.jpg (archived); Donald J. Trump (@realDonaldTrump), Twitter, Nov. 19, 2020 8:49 p.m. ET, available at https://media-cdn.factba.se/realdonaldtrump-twitter/1329602736053252107.jpg (archived).

46. For example, one widely shared post claimed that, in the early-morning hours of November 4, hundreds of thousands of mail in ballots were "found" in Wisconsin, Michigan, and Pennsylvania, and all of the ballots were for Biden. Nick Adams (@NickAdamsinUSA), Twitter, Nov. 4, 2020 4:48 p.m., available at https://web.archive.org/web/20201110150437/https://twitter.com/NickAdamsinUSA/status/1324151663641448448 (archived).

47. In many metropolitan areas, absentee ballots are counted in centralized locations and reported in batches. For example, the ballots that were supposedly "found" in Wisconsin were absentee ballots reported by Milwaukee County when that county completed its tally. Of the approximately 181,000 votes reported between 3:26 and 3:44 a.m., Biden received approximately 83% of the votes and Trump received approximately 17%. *See* Eric Litke and Madeline Heim, "Fact check: Wisconsin Did Not 'Find' 100K Ballots around 4 a.m. the Morning after the Election, or Take Break from Counting Votes," *Milwaukee Journal Sentinel*, (Nov. 4, 2020), available at https://www.jsonline.com/story/news/politics/elections/2020/11/04/wisconsin-didnt-find-ballots-stop-count-voter-fraud-claims-untrue-politifact/6165435002/. In Michigan, no ballots were "found" between 3:30-5:00 a.m. Rather, approximately 200,000 votes were reported by Wayne County shortly after 6:00 a.m., the vast majority of which were for Biden. *See* Geoffrey Skelley, "Live Bog: 2020 Election Results Coverage: Michigan's Morning Update," FiveThirtyEight, (Nov. 4, 2020), available at https://fivethirtyeight.com/live-blog/2020-election-results-coverage/#294294. Overall, Biden won 68% of the vote in Wayne County, to 30% for Trump. However, among absentee voters, Biden won 75% to Trump's 23%. *See* "November 3, 2020 - General Election Results," Charter County of Wayne, Michigan, available at https://www.waynecounty.com/elected/clerk/november-3-2020-general-election-results.aspx.

48. Select Committee to Investigate the January 6th Attack on the United States Capitol, Transcribed Interview of William Stepien, (Feb. 10, 2022), p. 45; *See also* John Curiel, Charles Stewart III, and Jack Williams, *One Shift, Two Shifts, Red Shift, Blue Shifts: Reported Election Returns in the 2020 Election*, MIT Election Data and Science Lab, (July 9, 2021), p. 40, available at https://electionlab.mit.edu/sites/default/files/2021-07/curiel_stewart_williams_blue_shift_esra_final.pdf, (detailed analysis of timed reporting data shows that "smaller and more rural counties, which favored Trump, could report their ballots before the counties with hundreds of precincts and hundreds of thousands of voters").

49. Select Committee to Investigate the January 6th Attack on the United States Capitol, Transcribed Interview of William Barr, (June 2, 2022), p. 8.

50. Select Committee to Investigate the January 6th Attack on the United States Capitol, Transcribed Interview of William Barr, (June 2, 2022), p. 8.

51. Select Committee to Investigate the January 6th Attack on the United States Capitol, Transcribed Interview of William Stepien, (Feb. 10, 2022), p. 119, 124-26, 174.

52. Select Committee to Investigate the January 6th Attack on the United States Capitol, Transcribed Interview of William Stepien, (Feb. 10, 2022), p. 174.

53. Select Committee to Investigate the January 6th Attack on the United States Capitol, Deposition of Rudy Giuliani, (May 20, 2022), pp. 22–23.

54. Select Committee to Investigate the January 6th Attack on the United States Capitol, Deposition of Rudy Giuliani, (May 20, 2022), pp. 23, 26.

55. Select Committee to Investigate the January 6th Attack on the United States Capitol, Deposition of Rudy Giuliani, (May 20, 2022), p. 35 (describing Ellis as "a co-counsel" and "my number two person" so "generally, if you got an opinion from Jenna, it would be just like getting an opinion from me").

56. Select Committee to Investigate the January 6th Attack on the United States Capitol, Transcribed Interview of Bernard Kerik, (Jan. 13, 2022), pp. 10, 15–18.

57. Select Committee to Investigate the January 6th Attack on the United States Capitol, Transcribed Interview of William Stepien, (Feb. 10, 2022), p. 92.

58. Select Committee to Investigate the January 6th Attack on the United States Capitol, Transcribed Interview of William Stepien, (Feb. 10, 2022), pp. 111–112.

59. Select Committee to Investigate the January 6th Attack on the United States Capitol, Transcribed Interview of William Stepien, (Feb. 10, 2022), p. 134; Documents on file with the Select Committee to Investigate the January 6th Attack on the United States Capitol, (Mark Meadows Production), MM007288, (November 13, 2020, email from Bill Stepien to Mark Meadows, Justin Clark, and Jason Miller titled "Fwd: AZ Federal ID Voters").

60. Select Committee to Investigate the January 6th Attack on the United States Capitol, Transcribed Interview of Alex Cannon, (Apr. 13, 2022), pp. 19–23.

61. Select Committee to Investigate the January 6th Attack on the United States Capitol, Transcribed Interview of Alex Cannon, (Apr. 13, 2022), pp. 38–39.

62. Select Committee to Investigate the January 6th Attack on the United States Capitol, Transcribed Interview of Alex Cannon, (Apr. 13, 2022), pp. 33-34.

63. Select Committee to Investigate the January 6th Attack on the United States Capitol, Deposition of Jason Miller (Feb. 3, 2022), p. 119.

64. Select Committee to Investigate the January 6th Attack on the United States Capitol, Transcribed Interview of Matthew Morgan, (Apr. 25, 2022), pp. 117–18.

65. Select Committee to Investigate the January 6th Attack on the United States Capitol, Transcribed Interview of William Stepien, (Feb. 10, 2022), pp. 112–13.

66. Select Committee to Investigate the January 6th Attack on the United States Capitol, Deposition of Jason Miller (Feb. 3, 2022), p. 88–91.

67. Documents on file with the Select Committee to Investigate the January 6th Attack on the United States Capitol (Mark Meadows Production), MM010951-52 (November 3, 2020, Jason Miller text message to Mark Meadows at 10:27 pm); Documents on file with the Select Committee to Investigate the January 6th Attack on the United States Capitol (Mark Meadows Production), MM010972 (November 3, 2020, Jason Miller group text message to Mark Meadows and David Bossie at 11:53 pm); Documents on file with the Select Committee to Investigate the January 6th Attack on the United States Capitol (Mark Meadows Production), MM011343 (November 6, 2020, Jason Miller group text message to Mark Meadows, Ivanka Trump, Bill Stepien, Hope Hicks, Dan Scavino, and Jared Kushner at 11:10 am).

68. Select Committee to Investigate the January 6th Attack on the United States Capitol, Deposition of Jason Miller (Feb. 3, 2022), p. 91.

69. Select Committee to Investigate the January 6th Attack on the United States Capitol, Deposition of Jason Miller (Feb. 3, 2022), p. 91.

70. Select Committee to Investigate the January 6th Attack on the United States Capitol, Transcribed Interview of William Stepien, (Feb. 10, 2022), pp. 115–17; Brian Slodysko, "Explainer: Why AP Called Pennsylvania for Biden," Associated Press (Nov. 7, 2020), available at https://apnews.com/article/ap-called-pennsylvania-joe-biden-why-f7dba7b31bd21ec2819a7ac9d2b028d3.

71. Select Committee to Investigate the January 6th Attack on the United States Capitol, Transcribed Interview of William Stepien, (Feb. 10, 2022), pp. 115–20.

72. Select Committee to Investigate the January 6th Attack on the United States Capitol, Transcribed Interview of William Stepien, (Feb. 10, 2022), p. 118.

73. Select Committee to Investigate the January 6th Attack on the United States Capitol, Transcribed Interview of William Stepien, (Feb. 10, 2022), p. 119.

74. Select Committee to Investigate the January 6th Attack on the United States Capitol, *Hearing on the January 6th Investigation*, 117th Cong., 2d sess., (June 13, 2022), available at https://www.govinfo.gov/committee/house-january6th.

75. Select Committee to Investigate the January 6th Attack on the United States Capitol, *Hearing on the January 6th Investigation*, 117th Cong., 2d sess., (June 13, 2022), available at https://www.govinfo.gov/committee/house-january6th.; Federal Election Commission, "Federal Elections 2020 – Election Results for the U.S. President, the U.S. Senate and the U.S. House of Representatives," Oct. 2022, p. 12, available at https://www.fec.gov/resources/cms-content/documents/federalelections2020.pdf.

76. Select Committee to Investigate the January 6th Attack on the United States Capitol, *Hearing on the January 6th Investigation*, 117th Cong., 2d sess., (June 13, 2022), available at https://www.govinfo.gov/committee/house-january6th.

77. "Risk-Limiting Audit Report – Georgia Presidential Contest, November 2020," Georgia Secretary of State, (Nov. 19, 2020), available at https://sos.ga.gov/sites/default/files/2022-02/11.19_.20_risk_limiting_audit_report_memo_1.pdf.

78. *See* "Summary of Hand Count Audits – 2020 General Election," Arizona Secretary of State, (Nov. 17, 2020), available at https://azsos.gov/2020-general-election-hand-count-results; "Agreed Upon Procedures Report – Evaluation of the Accuracy of Voting Machine Tabulators Used for the 2020 General Elections Held on November 3, 2020 (Voting System Check)," New Mexico Secretary of State, (Dec. 15, 2020), available at https://api.realfile.rtsclients.com/PublicFiles/ee3072ab0d43456cb15a51f7d82c77a2/f740346c-7b6b-4479-acd6-068829382307/2020%20Post%20Election%20Voting%20System%20Check%20Audit%20Results.pdf. Similar audits conducted by Michigan, Pennsylvania, and Wisconsin also affirmed the results in those states, but their results are excluded from this list because in those instances their audit results were not available until after January 6th. Shortly after the election, Nevada also conducted some post-election checks that supported the validity of the results there too, including testing a sample of the voting machines to make sure votes were accurately recorded. Deposition of Joseph Gloria at 33, *Law v. Whitmer*, No. A-22-858609-W (Nev. Ct., Clark Cty. Dec. 1, 2020), p. 33, available at https://www.democracydocket.com/wp-content/uploads/2022/09/2022.10.31-NV-Poll-Worker-Response-to-Application-for-Mandamus-STAMPED.pdf; Rex Briggs, "Trump Supporters Asked me to Look into Voter Fraud in Nevada; What I found Debunked What They were Alleging," *Nevada Independent*, (Dec. 22, 2020), available at https://thenevadaindependent.com/article/trump-supporters-asked-me-to-look-into-voter-fraud-in-nevada-what-i-found-debunked-what-they-were-alleging.

79. Select Committee to Investigate the January 6th Attack on the United States Capitol, *Hearing on the January 6th Investigation*, 117th Cong., 2d sess., (June 13, 2022), available at https://www.govinfo.gov/committee/house-january6th.

80. Documents on file with the Select Committee to Investigate the January 6th Attack on the United States Capitol (Jared Kushner Production), JK_00115, JK00117-132 (November 12, 2020, email from Matt Oczkowski, and attached analysis of battleground states).

81. Documents on file with the Select Committee to Investigate the January 6th Attack on the United States Capitol (Jared Kushner Production), JK_00115, JK_00117-132 (November 12, 2020, email from Matt Oczkowski, and attached analysis of battleground states).

82. Documents on file with the Select Committee to Investigate the January 6th Attack on the United States Capitol (Jared Kushner Production), JK_00115, JK_00117-132 (November 12, 2020, email from Matt Oczkowski, and attached analysis of battleground states).

83. Documents on file with the Select Committee to Investigate the January 6th Attack on the United States Capitol (Jared Kushner Production), JK_00115, JK_00117-132 (November 12, 2020, email from Matt Oczkowski, and attached analysis of battleground states).

84. Select Committee to Investigate the January 6th Attack on the United States Capitol, Deposition of Rudolph Giuliani (May 20, 2022), pp. 22-23.

85. Select Committee to Investigate the January 6th Attack on the United States Capitol, Deposition of Rudolph Giuliani (May 20, 2022), pp. 22-23.

86. Select Committee to Investigate the January 6th Attack on the United States Capitol, Deposition of Rudolph Giuliani (May 20, 2022), pp. 22-23.

87. Select Committee to Investigate the January 6th Attack on the United States Capitol, Transcribed Interview of William Stepien, (Feb. 10, 2022), pp. 106-107. Sidney Powell and Jenna Ellis accompanied Giuliani. The campaign was represented by Jared Kushner, Bill Stepien, David Bossie (a former senior official on President Trump's 2016 campaign), Derek Lyons, and Justin Clark. *See* Select Committee to Investigate the January 6th Attack on the United States Capitol, Transcribed Interview of Jared Kushner, (Mar. 31, 2022), pp. 50-51; Select Committee to Investigate the January 6th Attack on the United States Capitol, Transcribed Interview of Derek Lyons, (Mar. 17, 2022), pp. 64-65. Eric Herschmann also arrived at the campaign headquarters as the meeting was underway. *See* Select Committee to Investigate the January 6th Attack on the United States Capitol, Transcribed Interview of Eric Herschmann, (Mar. 17, 2022), pp. 160-61.

88. Select Committee to Investigate the January 6th Attack on the United States Capitol, Transcribed Interview of William Stepien, (Feb. 10, 2022), p. 109.

89. Select Committee to Investigate the January 6th Attack on the United States Capitol, Transcribed Interview of William Stepien, (Feb. 10, 2022), p. 109.

90. Select Committee to Investigate the January 6th Attack on the United States Capitol, Transcribed Interview of William Stepien, (Feb. 10, 2022), p. 107.

91. Select Committee to Investigate the January 6th Attack on the United States Capitol, Transcribed Interview of Justin Clark, (May 17, 2022), p. 63; Select Committee to Investigate the January 6th Attack on the United States Capitol, Transcribed Interview of Matthew Morgan, (Apr. 25, 2022), pp. 34-35.

92. Select Committee to Investigate the January 6th Attack on the United States Capitol, Transcribed Interview of Matthew Morgan, (Apr. 25, 2022), pp. 14-16.

93. Select Committee to Investigate the January 6th Attack on the United States Capitol, Transcribed Interview of Matthew Morgan, (Apr. 25, 2022), p. 14-16.

94. Select Committee to Investigate the January 6th Attack on the United States Capitol, Transcribed Interview of Matthew Morgan, (Apr. 25, 2022), p. 41.

95. Select Committee to Investigate the January 6th Attack on the United States Capitol, Transcribed Interview of Justin Clark, (May 17, 2022), p. 63.

96. Select Committee to Investigate the January 6th Attack on the United States Capitol, Transcribed Interview of Matthew Morgan, (Apr. 25, 2022), pp. 34-35, 41-42.

97. Select Committee to Investigate the January 6th Attack on the United States Capitol, Transcribed Interview of Matthew Morgan, (Apr. 25, 2022), p. 41.

98. Select Committee to Investigate the January 6th Attack on the United States Capitol, Transcribed Interview of Justin Clark, (May 17, 2022), p. 63.

99. Select Committee to Investigate the January 6th Attack on the United States Capitol, Transcribed Interview of Justin Clark, (May 17, 2022), p. 63.

100. "Rudy Giuliani Trump Campaign Philadelphia Press Conference at Four Seasons Total Landscaping," Rev, (Nov. 7, 2020), available at https://www.rev.com/blog/transcripts/rudy-giuliani-trump-campaign-philadelphia-press-conference-november-7.

101. Select Committee to Investigate the January 6th Attack on the United States Capitol, Transcribed Interview of Bernard Kerik, (Jan. 13, 2022), pp. 30-32.

102. "Memorandum from Attorney General William Barr on Post-Voting Election Irregularity Inquiries to the United States Attorneys, to the Assistant Attorneys General for the Criminal Division, Civil Rights Division, and National Security Division, and to the Director of the Federal Bureau of Investigation," Department of Justice, (Nov. 9, 2020), available at https://www.documentcloud.org/documents/20403358-william-barr-election-memo-november-9. Longstanding DOJ policy had been not to conduct such investigations prior to certification to avoid impacting election results. *See Federal Prosecution of Election Offenses*, 8th ed. Department of Justice, December 2017, at 84, available at https://www.justice.gov/criminal/file/1029066/download.

103. Select Committee to Investigate the January 6th Attack on the United States Capitol, Transcribed Interview of Justin Clark, (May 17, 2022), pp. 66-67; Mike Pence, *So Help Me God*, (New York: Simon & Schuster, 2022), at pp. 431-432.

104. Select Committee to Investigate the January 6th Attack on the United States Capitol, Transcribed Interview of Justin Clark, (May 17, 2022), pp. 66-67.

105. Select Committee to Investigate the January 6th Attack on the United States Capitol, Transcribed Interview of Justin Clark, (May 17, 2022), p. 67; Mike Pence, *So Help Me God*, (New York: Simon & Schuster, 2022), at pp. 431.

106. *See* Donald J. Trump (@realDonaldTrump), Twitter, Nov. 15, 2020 7:11 p.m. ET, available at http://web.archive.org/web/20201117115935/https://twitter.com/realDonaldTrump/status/1327811527123103746 (archived).

107. Select Committee to Investigate the January 6th Attack on the United States Capitol, Transcribed Interview of Matthew Morgan, (Apr. 25, 2022), pp. 37-38.

108. Select Committee to Investigate the January 6th Attack on the United States Capitol, Transcribed Interview of William Stepien, (Feb. 10, 2022), pp. 174-175.

109. Documents on file with the Select Committee to Investigate the January 6th Attack on the United States Capitol, (Mark Meadows Production), MM007112 (Nov. 14, 2020 email from Jason Miller to Bill Stepien, Justin Clark, David Bossie, Mark Meadows, and Jared Kushner describing Rudy Giuliani's surrogate briefing).

110. Documents on file with the Select Committee to Investigate the January 6th Attack on the United States Capitol, (Mark Meadows Production), MM007112 (Nov. 14, 2020 email from Jason Miller to Bill Stepien, Justin Clark, David Bossie, Mark Meadows, and Jared Kushner describing Rudy Giuliani's surrogate briefing).

111. Documents on file with the Select Committee to Investigate the January 6th Attack on the United States Capitol, (Mark Meadows Production), MM007112 (Nov. 14, 2020 email from Jason Miller to Bill Stepien, Justin Clark, David Bossie, Mark Meadows, and Jared Kushner describing Rudy Giuliani's surrogate briefing).

112. Factba.se, "Interview: Brian Kilmeade of Fox News Interviews Donald Trump - December 13, 2020," Vimeo, at 7:47, Dec. 13, 2020, available at https://vimeo.com/490517184.

113. Select Committee to Investigate the January 6th Attack on the United States Capitol, *Hearing on the January 6th Investigation*, 117th Cong., 2d sess., (June 13, 2022), available at https://www.govinfo.gov/committee/house-january6th.

114. Select Committee staff analyzed the lawsuits. *See also*, Brendan Williams, *Did President Trump's 2020 Election Litigation Kill Rule 11?*, 30 Pub. Interest L. J. 181, 189 (2021), available at https://www.bu.edu/pilj/files/2021/06/Williams.pdf.

115. The only case that involved a victory for the campaign was the Pennsylvania case of *Trump v. Boockvar*. In that case, the court found that the Pennsylvania Secretary of State could not extend the deadline for voters to cure their failure to provide proper identification for absentee ballots. This decision affected just a few thousand votes, which were not included in any tallies. *Trump v. Boockvar*, No. 602 MD 2020 (Pa. Commw. Ct. Nov. 12, 2020), available at https://www.democracydocket.com/wp-content/uploads/2020/11/602-MD-20-1.pdf.

116. *See* John Danforth, Benjamin Ginsberg, Thomas B. Griffith, et al., *Lost, Not Stolen: The Conservative Case that Trump Lost and Biden Won the 2020 Presidential Election*, (July 2022), p. 3, available at https://lostnotstolen.org/download/378/.

117. Complaint at 2, *Bowyer v. Ducey*, 506 F. Supp. 3d 699 (D. Ariz. Dec. 2, 2020) (No. 2:20-cv-02321), ECF No. 1.

118. *Bowyer v. Ducey*, 506 F. Supp. 3d 699, 706, 723 (D. Ariz. 2020).

119. Minute Entry and Order at 6-9, *Ward v. Jackson*, No. CV2020-015285 (Az. Sup. Ct. Dec. 4, 2020).

120. See *Ward v. Jackson*, No. CV-20-0343-AP, 2020 Ariz. LEXIS 313, at *6 (Ariz. 2020), also available at https://www.clerkofcourt.maricopa.gov/home/showpublisheddocument/1984/637437053596970000; Howard Fischer, "State Supreme Court rejects GOP bid to void election," *Arizona Capitol Times*, (Dec. 8, 2020), available at https://azcapitoltimes.com/news/2020/12/08/federal-judge-hears-arguments-in-election-challenge/; "Meet the Justices," Arizona Judicial Branch, (Dec. 8, 2020), available at http://web.archive.org/web/20201208032900/https://www.azcourts.gov/meetthejustices/ (archived); "Brutinel Elected as Next Arizona Supreme Court Chief Justice," *Associated Press*, (Nov. 20, 2018), available at https://apnews.com/article/27b725d44d384e2cb7a0e491ac82fe7f; Bob Christie, "Ducey Names 2 to New Arizona Supreme Court Seats," *Associated Press*, (Nov. 28, 2016), available at https://apnews.com/article/26fc7f154b0e4b4fb358987941ded8d0; "Arizona Governor Appoints New Supreme Court Justice," *Associated Press*, (Apr. 26, 2019), available at https://apnews.com/article/4ce4bf1d79724c03b1d4cf36f4b97cf1; Jonathan J. Cooper, "Ducey Appoints Montgomery to Arizona Supreme Court," *Associated Press*, (Sep. 4, 2019), available at https://apnews.com/article/bac43d42185c4b8bb9e8c465a59792c8.

121. Complaint at 1-2, *Boland v. Raffensperger*, No. 2020CV343018 (Ga. Super. Ct. Nov. 30, 2020), available at https://electioncases.osu.edu/wp-content/uploads/2020/11/Boland-v-Raffensperger-Complaint.pdf.

122. Final Order at 5-6, *Boland v. Raffensperger*, No. No. 2020CV343018 (Ga. Super. Ct. Dec. 8, 2020), available at https://electioncases.osu.edu/wp-content/uploads/2020/11/Boland-v-Raffensperger-Order-Dismissing-Complaint.pdf.

123. Order Denying Appeal, *Boland v. Raffensperger*, No. S21M0565 (Ga. Dec. 14, 2020), available at https://electioncases.osu.edu/wp-content/uploads/2020/11/Boland-v-Raffensperger-GA-SC-Order-Denying-Appeal.pdf; Jonathan Ringel, "Deal Picks Krause, Richardson for Fulton Superior," Law.com, (Dec. 28, 2018), available at https://www.law.com/dailyreportonline/2018/12/28/deal-picks-krause-richardson-for-fulton-superior/; "Chief Justice Harold D. Melton," Supreme Court of Georgia, (Oct. 16, 2020), available at http://web.archive.org/web/20201016174745/https://www.gasupreme.us/court-information/biographies/justice-harold-d-melton/ (archived); "Presiding Justice David E. Nahmias," Supreme Court of Georgia, (Nov. 20, 2020), available at http://web.archive.org/web/20201120204518/https://www.gasupreme.us/court-information/biographies/justice-david-e-nahmias/ (archived); "Chief Justice Michael P. Boggs," Supreme Court of Georgia, (last accessed Dec. 3, 2022), available at https://www.gasupreme.us/court-information/biographies/justice-michael-p-boggs/; "Presiding Justice Nels S.D. Peterson," Supreme Court of Georgia, (last accessed Dec. 3, 2022), available at https://www.gasupreme.us/court-information/biographies/justice-nels-s-d-peterson/; "Justice Sarah Hawkins Warren," Supreme Court of Georgia, (last accessed Dec. 3, 2022), available at https://www.gasupreme.us/court-information/biographies/justice-sarah-hawkins-warren/; "Justice Charles J. Bethel," Supreme Court of Georgia, (last accessed Dec. 3, 2022), available at

https://www.gasupreme.us/court-information/biographies/justice-charles-j-bethel/; "Justice Carla Wong McMillian," Supreme Court of Georgia, (last accessed Dec. 3, 2022), available at https://www.gasupreme.us/court-information/biographies/justice-carla-wong-mcmillian/.

124. *Wood v. Raffensperger*, 501 F. Supp. 3d 1310, 1317, 1327, 1331 (N.D. Ga. 2020).

125. *Wood v. Raffensperger*, 501 F. Supp. 3d 1310, 1327 (N.D. Ga. 2020).

126. Complaint for Declaratory, Emergency, and Permanent Injunctive Relief, *King v. Whitmer*, Case No. 2:20-cv-13134-LVP-RSW, (E.D. Mich. Nov. 25, 2020), ECF No. 1; *King v. Whitmer*, 505 F. Supp. 3d 720, 738 (E.D. Mich. 2020). In a subsequent decision, the judge called the case "a historic and profound abuse of the judicial process" and sanctioned the attorneys who filed the lawsuit *King v. Whitmer*, 556 F. Supp. 3d 680, 688-89 (E.D. Mich. 2021).

127. Opinion and Order at 1, 4, *Stoddard v. City Election Commission*, No. 20-014604-CZ, (Mich. Cty. Cir. Ct. Nov. 6, 2020), available at https://www.michigan.gov/-/media/Project/Websites/AG/releases/2020/november/Stoddard_et_al_v_City_Election_Commission_et_al_-_11-06-2020.pdf?rev=2fa32f93caa94365a1ee8c1c492a4e75.

128. Opinion and Order at 12-13, *Costantino v. Detroit*, No. 20-014780-AW, (Mich. Cty. Cir. Ct. Nov. 13, 2020), available at https://electioncases.osu.edu/wp-content/uploads/2020/11/Costantino-v-Detroit-Opinion-and-Order.pdf.

129. *Law v. Whitmer*, No. 10 OC 00163 1B, 2020 Nev. Unpub. LEXIS 1160, at *1, 29-31, 33, 48-49, 52, 54 (Nev. Dec. 8, 2020), available at https://casetext.com/case/law-v-whitmer-1 (attaching and affirming lower court decision).

130. *Law v. Whitmer*, No. 10 OC 00163 1B, 2020 Nev. Unpub. LEXIS 1160, at *3-4 (Nev. Dec. 8, 2020), available at https://casetext.com/case/law-v-whitmer-1 (attaching and affirming lower court decision).

131. *Donald J. Trump for President v. Boockvar*, 502 F. Supp. 3d 899, 906 (M.D. Pa. 2020).

132. *Donald J. Trump for President v. Boockvar*, 803 Fed. App'x. 377, 381 (M.D. Pa. 2020).

133. "Eleven Nominations Sent to the Senate Today," Trump White House Archives, (June 19, 2017), available at https://trumpwhitehouse.archives.gov/presidential-actions/eleven-nominations-sent-senate-today-3/.

134. Complaint at 72, *Trump v. Wisconsin Election Commission*, 506 F. Supp. 3d 620 (E.D. Wis. 2020) (No. 2:20-cv-01785), ECF No. 1; *Trump v. Wisconsin Election Commission*, 506 F. Supp. 3d 620, 625 (E.D. Wis. 2020) (dismissing case with prejudice).

135. *Trump v. Wisconsin Election Commission*, 506 F. Supp. 3d 620, 637-39 (E.D. Wis. 2020).

136. *Trump v. Wisconsin Election Commission*, 983 F.3d 919, 922 (7th Cir. 2020); Bill Glauber, "Federal Appeals Court Turns Down Donald Trump Push to Overturn Election Results in Wisconsin," *Milwaukee Journal Sentinel*, (Dec. 24, 2020), available at https://www.jsonline.com/story/news/politics/elections/2020/12/24/federal-appeals-court-rejects-trump-bid-overturn-wisconsin-results/4043650001/.

137. Select Committee to Investigate the January 6th Attack on the United States Capitol, *Hearing on the January 6th Investigation*, 117th Cong., 2d sess., (June 23, 2022), available at https://www.govinfo.gov/committee/house-january6th.

138. Select Committee to Investigate the January 6th Attack on the United States Capitol, Transcribed Interview of Eric Herschmann, (Apr. 6, 2022), pp. 170-71.

139. For example, Select Committee data analysts found that certain legacy media networks played a role in promoting false claims of voter fraud and other election conspiracies. *See* Staff Memorandum from Select Committee to Investigate the January 6th Attack on the United States Capitol Data Analysts, "Legacy Media Analysis," (Dec. 3, 2022).

140. Center for an Informed Public, Digital Forensic Research Lab, Graphika, & Stanford Internet Observatory, *The Long Fuse: Misinformation and the 2020 Election*, (Jun. 15, 2021), p. 173, available at https://stacks.stanford.edu/file/druid:tr171zs0069/EIP-Final-Report.pdf.

141. Center for an Informed Public, Digital Forensic Research Lab, Graphika, & Stanford Internet Observatory, *The Long Fuse: Misinformation and the 2020 Election*, (Jun. 15, 2021), p. 82, available at https://stacks.stanford.edu/file/druid:tr171zs0069/EIP-Final-Report.pdf.

142. Select Committee to Investigate the January 6th Attack on the United States Capitol, Transcribed Interview of William Barr, (June 2, 2022), p. 9.

143. Select Committee to Investigate the January 6th Attack on the United States Capitol, Transcribed Interview of William Barr, (June 2, 2022), p. 10.

144. Select Committee to Investigate the January 6th Attack on the United States Capitol, Transcribed Interview of William Barr, (June 2, 2022), p. 9; Select Committee to Investigate the January 6th Attack on the United States Capitol, Transcribed Interview of Richard Peter Donoghue, (Oct. 1, 2021), p. 67.

145. Select Committee to Investigate the January 6th Attack on the United States Capitol, Transcribed Interview of Richard Peter Donoghue, (Oct. 1, 2021) pp. 59-60.

146. Select Committee to Investigate the January 6th Attack on the United States Capitol, Transcribed Interview of William Barr, (June 2, 2022), pp. 36-37.

147. Select Committee to Investigate the January 6th Attack on the United States Capitol, *Hearing on the January 6th Investigation*, 117th Cong., 2d sess., (June 23, 2022), available at https://www.govinfo.gov/committee/house-january6th.

148. Select Committee to Investigate the January 6th Attack on the United States Capitol, *Hearing on the January 6th Investigation*, 117th Cong., 2d sess., (June 23, 2022), available at https://www.govinfo.gov/committee/house-january6th; *see also* Select Committee to Investigate the January 6th Attack on the United States Capitol, Transcribed Interview of Jeffrey Rosen, (Oct. 13, 2022), p. 60.

149. Select Committee to Investigate the January 6th Attack on the United States Capitol, Transcribed Interview of Richard Peter Donoghue, (Oct. 1, 2021), pp. 60-61, 63-64.

150. Select Committee to Investigate the January 6th Attack on the United States Capitol, Transcribed Interview of Richard Peter Donoghue, (Oct. 1, 2021), pp. 53, 67.

151. Select Committee to Investigate the January 6th Attack on the United States Capitol, Transcribed Interview of Richard Peter Donoghue, (Oct. 1, 2021), pp. 59-60.

152. Select Committee to Investigate the January 6th Attack on the United States Capitol, Transcribed Interview of Richard Peter Donoghue, (Oct. 1, 2021), pp. 61-62.

153. Select Committee to Investigate the January 6th Attack on the United States Capitol, Transcribed Interview of Richard Peter Donoghue, (Oct. 1, 2021), pp. 54-55.

154. *See, e.g.*, "Transcript of Trump's Speech at Rally Before US Capitol Riot," *Associated Press*, (Jan. 13, 2021), available at https://apnews.com/article/election-2020-joe-biden-donald-trump-capitol-siege-media-e79eb5164613d6718e9f4502eb471f27; *Law v. Whitmer*, No. 10 OC 00163 1B, 2020 Nev. Unpub. LEXIS 1160, at *3-4 (Nev. Dec. 8, 2020), available at https://casetext.com/case/law-v-whitmer-1 (attaching and affirming lower court decision); *Donald J. Trump for President v. Boockvar*, 502 F. Supp. 3d 899, 906 (M.D. Pa. 2020); *Wood v. Raffensperger*, 501 F. Supp. 3d 1310, 1317, 1327, 1331 (N.D. Ga. 2020); Donald J. Trump (@realDonaldTrump), Twitter, Dec. 26, 6:23 a.m. ET, available at http://web.archive.org/web/20201228020228/https://twitter.com/realDonaldTrump/status/1342974373632876545 (archived); Rudy Giuliani's Common Sense, "WATCH this BEFORE January 6th | Rudy Giuliani's Common Sense | Ep. 100," Rumble, at 29:30, available at https://rumble.com/embed/vcrv8j/?pub=4.

155. "Fact Checks," Michigan Department of State, (last accessed on Dec. 3, 2022), available at https://www.michigan.gov/sos/faqs/elections-and-campaign-finance/fact-checks.

156. *See, e.g.,* "Secretary of State's Office Debunks Ware County Voting Machine Story," Georgia Secretary of State, (Dec. 7, 2020), available at https://sos.ga.gov/news/secretary-states-office-debunks-ware-county-voting-machine-story; "News Conference on Georgia Vote Count," C-SPAN, Nov. 9, 2020, available at https://www.c-span.org/video/?477943-1/news-conference-georgia-vote-count; "Georgia Election Security," C-SPAN, Jan. 4, 2021, available at https://www.c-span.org/video/?507710-1/georgia-election-official-refutes-president-trumps-voter-fraud-allegations.

157. *See, e.g.,* PBS NewsHour, "WATCH: Wisconsin Elections Commission Gives Vote Counting Update," YouTube, Nov. 4, 2020, available at https://www.youtube.com/watch?v=Yg5liyyrObc.

158. *See, e.g.,* Declaration of Charles Stewart III, *Trump v. Raffensperger,* No. 2020CV33255 (Ga. Super. Ct. filed Dec. 14, 2020) (expert declaration of political scientist at MIT); *Examining Irregularities in the 2020 Election Before the S. Comm. on Homeland Security and Governmental Affairs,* 116th Cong. (Dec. 16, 2020) (statement of Chris Krebs, former Director of the Cybersecurity and Infrastructure Security Agency); "Scientists Say No Credible Evidence of Computer Fraud in the 2020 Election Outcome, But Policymakers Must Work with Experts to Improve Confidence," Matt Blaze's Exhaustive Search, (Nov. 16, 2020), available at https://www.mattblaze.org/blog/election-letter/.

159. Search results for "Dominion," Trump Twitter Archive V2, (last accessed Dec. 12, 2022), available at https://www.thetrumparchive.com/?searchbox=%22dominion%22.

160. *See, e.g.,* "Remarks by President Trump During Thanksgiving Video Teleconference with Members of the Military," Trump White House archives, (Nov. 27, 2020), available at https://trumpwhitehouse.archives.gov/briefings-statements/remarks-president-trump-thanksgiving-video-teleconference-members-military/; Factba.se, "Interview: Maria Bartiromo Interviews Donald Trump on Fox News – November 29, 2020," Vimeo, Nov. 29, 2020, available at https://factba.se/trump/transcript/donald-trump-interview-fox-news-sunday-morning-futures-maria-bartiromo-november-29-2020; "Donald Trump Speech on Election Fraud Claims Transcript December 2," Rev, (Dec. 2, 2020), available at https://www.rev.com/blog/transcripts/donald-trump-speech-on-election-fraud-claims-transcript-december-2; Factba.se, "Donald Trump Vlog: Contesting Election Results – December 22, 2020," (Dec. 22, 2020), available at https://factba.se/transcript/donald-trump-vlog-contesting-election-results-december-22-2020; "Donald Trump Rally Speech Transcript Dalton, Georgia: Senate Runoff Election," Rev, (Jan. 4, 2021), available at https://www.rev.com/blog/transcripts/donald-trump-rally-speech-transcript-dalton-georgia-senate-runoff-election; "Transcript of Trump's Speech at Rally Before US Capitol Riot," *Associated Press,* (Jan. 13, 2021), available at https://apnews.com/article/election-2020-joe-biden-donald-trump-capitol-siege-media-e79eb5164613d6718e9f4502eb471f27.

161. J.M. Rieger, "The False Claims from Fox News and Trump Allies Cited in Dominion's $1.6 Billion Lawsuit," *Washington Post,* (Mar. 26, 2021), available at https://www.washingtonpost.com/politics/2021/03/26/fox-trump-election-dominion/.

162. Elahe Izadi and Sarah Ellison, "Fox News Has Dropped 'Lou Dobbs Tonight,' Promoter of Trump's False Election Fraud Claims," *Washington Post,* (Feb. 5, 2021), available at https://www.washingtonpost.com/media/2021/02/05/lou-dobbs-canceled-fox/; 60 Minutes, "Dominion Voting Systems and the Baseless Conspiracy Theories about the 2020 Election | 60 Minutes," YouTube, at 2:12 – 3:20, (Oct. 23, 2022), at 2:12-2:51, available at https://youtu.be/492jILlPtlA?t=132.

163. Donald J. Trump (@realDonaldTrump), Twitter, Nov. 12, 2020 11:34 a.m. ET, available at http://web.archive.org/web/20201112163413/https://twitter.com/realDonaldTrump/status/1326926226888544256 (archived).

164. Documents on file with the Select Committee to Investigate the January 6th Attack on the United States Capitol (Zach Parkinson Production), Parkinson0388-0407 (Internal Trump Campaign memo dated November 12, 2020); Select Committee to Investigate the January 6th Attack on the United States Capitol, Deposition of Andrew Zachary "Zach" Parkinson, (May 18, 2022), pp. 46-47.

165. Documents on file with the Select Committee to Investigate the January 6th Attack on the United States Capitol (Zach Parkinson Production), Parkinson0388-0407 (Internal Trump Campaign memo dated November 12, 2020).

166. Select Committee to Investigate the January 6th Attack on the United States Capitol, Deposition of Jason Miller, (Feb. 3, 2022), pp. 117, 133.

167. Documents on file with the Select Committee to Investigate the January 6th Attack on the United States Capitol (Mark Meadows Production), MM007666, MM007669 (November 12, 2020, email and attachment from Jason Miller to Mark Meadows transmitting abridged and full internal Trump Campaign memo); Documents on file with the Select Committee to Investigate the January 6th Attack on the United States Capitol (Mark Meadows Production), MM011902, MM011974 (Nov. 12 and 13, 2020 text messages from Jason Miller to Mark Meadows discussing the investigation into Dominion and the lack of evidence of foreign interference).

168. Select Committee to Investigate the January 6th Attack on the United States Capitol, Deposition of Kayleigh McEnany, (Jan. 12, 2022), pp. 143, 291.

169. Donald J. Trump (@realDonaldTrump), Twitter, Nov. 16, 2020 8:22 a.m. ET, available at https://www.thetrumparchive.com/?results=1&searchbox=%22engineered+by+china%22 (archived); Donald J. Trump (@realDonaldTrump), Twitter, Nov. 16, 2020 8:26 a.m. ET, available at http://web.archive.org/web/20201116132750/https://twitter.com/realdonaldtrump/status/1328328547598000130 (archived).

170. "Joint Statement from Elections Infrastructure Government Coordinating Council & the Election Infrastructure Sector Coordinating Executive Committees," Department of Homeland Security's Cybersecurity & Infrastructure Security Agency, (Nov. 12, 2020), available at https://www.cisa.gov/news/2020/11/12/joint-statement-elections-infrastructure-government-coordinating-council-election.

171. Mark Bowden and Matthew Teague, "How a County Clerk in Michigan Found Herself at the Center of Trump's Attempt to Overthrow the Election," *Time*, (Dec. 15, 2021), available at https://time.com/6128812/the-steal-antrim-county-michigan/; Emma Brown, Aaron C. Davis, Jon Swaine, and Josh Dawsey, "The Making of a Myth," *Washington Post*, (May 9, 2021), available at https://www.washingtonpost.com/investigations/interactive/2021/trump-election-fraud-texas-businessman-ramsland-asog/.

172. Steven Nelson, "Michigan Republicans Claim Software Issue Undercounted Trump Votes," *New York Post*, (Nov. 6, 2020), available at https://nypost.com/2020/11/06/michigan-gop-claims-software-issue-undercounted-trump-votes/.

173. "Isolated User Error in Antrim County Does Not Affect Election Results, Has No Impact on Other Counties or States," Michigan Secretary of State, (Nov. 7, 2020), available at https://www.michigan.gov/-/media/Project/Websites/sos/30lawens/Antrim_Fact_Check.pdf?rev=7a929e4d262e4532bbe574a3b82ddbcf; "Hand Audit of All Presidential Election Votes in Antrim County Confirms Previously Certified Results, Voting Machines Were Accurate," Michigan Secretary of State, (Dec. 17, 2020), available at https://www.michigan.gov/sos/resources/news/2020/12/17/hand-audit-of-all-presidential-election-votes-in-antrim-county-confirms-previously-certified-result; J. Alex Halderman, *Analysis of the Antrim County, Michigan November 2020 Election Incident*, (Mar. 26, 2021), pp. 17-27, available at https://www.michigan.gov/-/media/Project/Websites/sos/30lawens/Antrim.pdf?rev=fbfe881cdc0043a9bb80b783d1bb5fe9; Michigan Senate Oversight Committee, *Report on the November 2020 Election in Michigan*, (June 23, 2021), pp. 14-19, 36-55, available at https://misenategopcdn.s3.us-east-1.amazonaws.com/99/doccuments/20210623/SMPO_2020ElectionReport_2.pdf.

174. Michigan Senate Oversight Committee, *Report on the November 2020 Election in Michigan*, (June 23, 2021), pp. 14-15, available at https://misenategopcdn.s3.us-east-1.amazonaws.com/99/doccuments/20210623/SMPO_2020ElectionReport_2.pdf.

175. "Isolated User Error in Antrim County Does Not Affect Election Results, Has No Impact on Other Counties or States," Michigan Secretary of State website, (Nov. 7, 2020), available at

https://www.michigan.gov/-/media/Project/Websites/sos/30lawens/
Antrim_Fact_Check.pdf?rev=7a929e4d262e4532bbe574a3b82ddbcf.

176.   Michigan Senate Oversight Committee, *Report on the November 2020 Election in Michigan*,
       (June 23, 2021), pp. 14-19, available at https://misenategopcdn.s3.us-east-
       1.amazonaws.com/99/doccuments/20210623/SMPO_2020ElectionReport_2.pdf.

177.   Documents on file with the Select Committee to Investigate the January 6th Attack on the
       United States Capitol (National Archives Production), 076P-R000010292_0001 (November 12,
       2020, email from Tim Walberg to Molly Michel re: Additional Presidential Phone call follow
       up).

178.   Select Committee to Investigate the January 6th Attack on the United States Capitol, Tran-
       scribed Interview of Chad Wolf, (Jan. 21, 2022), pp. 70-74; Documents on file with the Select
       Committee to Investigate the January 6th Attack on the United States Capitol, (Department
       of Homeland Security Production), CTRL0000033284, (Nov. 13, 2020, email from Molly
       Michael to Chad Wolf titled "Re: Michigan Letter").

179.   Select Committee to Investigate the January 6th Attack on the United States Capitol, Tran-
       scribed Interview of Chad Wolf, (Jan. 21, 2022), pp. 72-74; Documents on file with the Select
       Committee to Investigate the January 6th Attack on the United States Capitol, (Department
       of Homeland Security Production), CTRL0000033284, (Nov. 13, 2020, email from Molly
       Michael to Chad Wolf titled "Re: Michigan Letter"); Select Committee to Investigate the
       January 6th Attack on the United States Capitol, Transcribed Interview of Chad Wolf, (Jan.
       21, 2022), Exhibit 44, CTRL0000926977 (Nov. 13, 2020 letter to Michigan Secretary of State
       Jocelyn Benson from Michigan State Senators Lana Theis and Tom Barrett).

180.   Select Committee to Investigate the January 6th Attack on the United States Capitol, Tran-
       scribed Interview of Chad Wolf, (Jan. 21, 2022), pp. 74-77 Select Committee to Investigate
       the January 6th Attack on the United States Capitol, Transcribed Interview of Chad Wolf
       (Jan. 21, 2022), Exhibit 45, CTRL0000926978, (Nov. 16, 2020 email from Christopher Krebs
       responding to Chad Wolf, Matthew Travis, and Brandon Wales entitled "RE: Allegations").

181.   Select Committee to Investigate the January 6th Attack on the United States Capitol, Tran-
       scribed Interview of Chad Wolf, (Jan. 21, 2022), pp. 74-77; Select Committee to Investigate
       the January 6th Attack on the United States Capitol, Transcribed Interview of Chad Wolf
       (Jan. 21, 2022), Exhibit 45, CTRL0000926978, (Nov. 16, 2020 email from Christopher Krebs to
       Chad Wolf, Matthew Travis, and Brandon Wales entitled "RE: Allegations"); "Isolated User
       Error in Antrim County Does Not Affect Election Results, Has No Impact on Other Counties
       or States," Michigan Secretary of State, (Nov. 7, 2020), available at https://
       www.michigan.gov/-/media/Project/Websites/sos/30lawens/Antrim_Fact_Check.pdf?rev=
       7a929e4d262e4532bbe574a3b82ddbcf.

182.   Select Committee to Investigate the January 6th Attack on the United States Capitol, Tran-
       scribed Interview of Chad Wolf, (Jan. 21, 2022), pp. 78-80. Even as the acting Secretary of
       DHS was providing Meadows information he received from his Director of CISA debunking
       the Dominion claims, the acting Assistant Secretary of DHS, Ken Cuccinelli, was providing
       back channel information to Meadows in a possible effort to promote the false Dominion
       claims. *See* Documents on file with the Select Committee to Investigate the January 6th
       Attack on the United States Capitol (National Archives Production), TEXT0000072,
       TEXT0000073, (Nov. 12, 2020 text messages from Ken Cuccinelli to Mark Meadows) (Cuc-
       cinelli: "I have the dominion list of everywhere the machines are deployed that we know
       of. [I]t is pretty extensive. It is in my DHS email account. Where do you want me to send
       it?" Meadows then provided Cuccinelli with his personal email address.)

183.   Chris Krebs #Protect2020 (@CISAKrebs), Twitter, Nov. 17, 2020 11:45 a.m. ET, available at
       https://twitter.com/CISAKrebs/status/1328741106624901120.

184.   Documents on file with the Select Committee to Investigate the January 6th Attack on the
       United States Capitol (National Archives Production), 076P-R000010360_0001, 076P-
       R000010361_0001, (November 17, 2020 email and attached letter to Christopher Krebs from
       White House Office of Presidential Personnel, stating respectively that "the President has

terminated your appointment" and that "Pursuant to the direction of the President, your appointment… is hereby terminated, effective immediately").

185. Donald J. Trump (@realDonaldTrump), Twitter, Nov. 17, 2020 7:07 p.m. ET, available at http://web.archive.org/web/20201118040513/https://twitter.com/realdonaldtrump/status/1328852352787484677 (archived); Donald J. Trump (@realDonaldTrump), Twitter, Nov. 17, 2020 7:07 p.m. ET, available at http://web.archive.org/web/20201118040930/https://twitter.com/realDonaldTrump/status/1328852354049957888 (archived).

186. "Rudy Giuliani Trump Campaign Press Conference Transcript November 19: Election Fraud Claims," Rev, (Nov. 19, 2020), available at https://www.rev.com/blog/transcripts/rudy-giuliani-trump-campaign-press-conference-transcript-november-19-election-fraud-claims.

187. "Rudy Giuliani Trump Campaign Press Conference Transcript November 19: Election Fraud Claims," Rev, (Nov. 19, 2020), available at https://www.rev.com/blog/transcripts/rudy-giuliani-trump-campaign-press-conference-transcript-november-19-election-fraud-claims.

188. Select Committee to Investigate the January 6th Attack on the United States Capitol, Transcribed Interview of Hope Hicks, (Oct. 25, 2022), pp. 88-91. *See also* Tucker Carlson: "Time for Sidney Powell to Show Us Her Evidence: We Asked the Trump Campaign Attorney for Proof of her Bombshell Claims. She Gave Us Nothing," Fox News, (Nov. 19, 2020), available at https://www.foxnews.com/opinion/tucker-carlson-rudy-giuliani-sidney-powell-election-fraud.

189. Jenna Ellis (@JennaEllisEsq), Twitter, Nov. 22, 2020, 5:23 p.m. ET, available at https://twitter.com/JennaEllisEsq/status/1330638034619035655.

190. Donald J. Trump, (@realDonaldTrump), Twitter, Nov. 19, 2020 12:41 a.m. ET and 3:47 p.m. ET, available at https://www.thetrumparchive.com/?searchbox=%22dominion-izing%22 (archived).

191. One America News Network, "Cyber Analyst on Dominion Voting: Shocking Vulnerabilities," YouTube, at 0:41-1:14, 1:37-2:23, 2:42-3:36, Nov. 15, 2020, available at https://www.youtube.com/watch?v=eKcPoCNW8AA.

192. Ron Watkins, (@codemonkeyz), Twitter, Nov. 19, 2020 12:45 a.m. ET, available at http://web.archive.org/web/20201121092200/https://twitter.com/CodeMonkeyZ/status/1329299640848584710 (archived); Ron Watkins, (@codemonkeyz), Twitter, Nov. 19, 2020 12:46 a.m. ET, available at http://web.archive.org/web/20201201175413/https://twitter.com/CodeMonkeyZ/status/1329300069623820289 (archived); Donald J. Trump, Twitter, Nov. 21, 2020 11:30 p.m. ET, Nov. 21, 2020, 11:31 p.m. ET, Nov. 21, 2020, 11:32 p.m. ET, Nov. 22, 2020, 3:35 p.m. ET, available at https://www.thetrumparchive.com/?searchbox=%22dominion-izing%22&dates=%5B%222020-11-20%22%2C%222020-11-24%22%5D (archived).

193. Barr met with President Trump between election day and January 6th on November 23, December 1, and December 14. *See* Select Committee to Investigate the January 6th Attack on the United States Capitol, Transcribed Interview of William Barr, (Jun. 2, 2022), pp. 16, 22, 28.

194. Select Committee to Investigate the January 6th Attack on the United States Capitol, Transcribed Interview of William Barr, (Jun. 2, 2022), pp. 25, 27, 50; William Barr, *One Damn Thing After Another: Memoirs of an Attorney General*, (New York: HarperCollins, 2022), at pp. 539, 554.

195. Select Committee to Investigate the January 6th Attack on the United States Capitol, Transcribed Interview of William Barr, (Jun. 2, 2022), p. 19.

196. Factba.se, "Interview: Maria Bartiromo Interviews Donald Trump on Fox News - November 29, 2020," Vimeo, Nov. 29, 2020, at. 1:00-1:43, 3:23-4:36, available at https://vimeo.com/485180163.

197. Factba.se, "Interview: Maria Bartiromo Interviews Donald Trump on Fox News - November 29, 2020," Vimeo, at 1:00-1:43, Nov. 29, 2020, available at https://vimeo.com/485180163.

198. Factba.se, "Interview: Maria Bartiromo Interviews Donald Trump on Fox News - November 29, 2020," Vimeo, at 1:50-2:40, Nov. 29, 2020, available at https://vimeo.com/485180163.

199. Factba.se, "Interview: Maria Bartiromo Interviews Donald Trump on Fox News - November 29, 2020," Vimeo, at 3:50-4:24, 22:40-23:52, 24:26-24:50, Nov. 29, 2020, available at https://vimeo.com/485180163.

200. Select Committee to Investigate the January 6th Attack on the United States Capitol, Transcribed Interview of William Barr, (Jun. 2, 2022), pp. 22, 25-26.

201. Select Committee to Investigate the January 6th Attack on the United States Capitol, Transcribed Interview of William Barr, (Jun. 2, 2022), pp. 22, 25-26.

202. "Donald Trump Speech on Election Fraud Claims Transcript December 2," Rev, (Dec. 2, 2020), available at https://www.rev.com/blog/transcripts/donald-trump-speech-on-election-fraud-claims-transcript-december-2.

203. *King v. Whitmer*, 505 F. Supp. 3d 720, 738 (E.D. Mich. 2020)

204. *Bowyer v. Ducey*, 506 F. Supp. 3d 699, 723 (D. Ariz. 2020) (finding the complaint "void of plausible allegations that Dominion voting machines were hacked or compromised in Arizona during the 2020 General Election").

205. "Isolated User Error in Antrim County Does Not Affect Election Results, Has No Impact on Other Counties or States," Michigan Secretary of State, (Nov. 7, 2020), available at https://www.michigan.gov/-/media/Project/Websites/sos/30lawens/Antrim_Fact_Check.pdf?rev=7a929e4d262e4532bbe574a3b82ddbcf.

206. Decision and Order Granting Plaintiff's Motion for an Ex Parte Temporary Restraining Order, Show Cause Order and Preliminary Injunction, No. 2020009238CZ (Mich. Cty. Cir. Ct. Dec. 4, 2020).

207. Rudy W. Giuliani (@RudyGiuliani), Twitter, Dec. 4, 2020 7:12 p.m. ET, available at https://twitter.com/RudyGiuliani/status/1335014224532221952?s=20&t=20AZkk4gS2DeBo6q6QR-mw; Ronn Blitzer, "Trump Legal Team Celebrates after Michigan Judge Allows Probe of Dominion Voting Machines," Fox News, (Dec. 6, 2020), available at https://www.foxnews.com/politics/trump-legal-team-michigan-antrim-county-judge-order-dominion-machines; Select Committee to Investigate the January 6th Attack on the United States Capitol, Transcribed Interview of Bernard Kerik, (Jan. 13, 2022), pp. 19, 147.

208. Documents on file with the Select Committee to Investigate the January 6th Attack on the United States Capitol (National Archives Production), 076P-R000001368_00001, pp. 1, 6 (Allied Security Operations Group Antrim Michigan Forensics Report, dated Dec. 13, 2020).

209. Documents on file with the Select Committee to Investigate the January 6th Attack on the United States Capitol (National Archives Production), 076P-R00001254_00001 (December 14, 2020, email from Joanna Miller to Peter Navarro attaching the ASOG Report and noting that "POTUS and VPOTUS are briefed").

210. *See, e.g.*, Documents on file with the Select Committee to Investigate the January 6th Attack on the United States Capitol (Department of Justice Production), HouseSelect-Jan6-PartII-01132022-000798(December 14, 2020, email from Molly Michael re: From POTUS asking the AG to look at ASOG report); Documents on file with the Select Committee to Investigate the January 6th Attack on the United States Capitol (National Archives Production), 076P-R000001337_00001(December 14, 2020, email from Molly Michael to Acting Attorney General Jeffrey Rosen re: From POTUS attaching ASOG report); Documents on file with the Select Committee to Investigate the January 6th Attack on the United States Capitol (National Archives Production), 076P-R000001367_00001(December 14, 2020, email from Molly Michael to Michigan Senate Majority Leader Mike Shirkey re: From POTUS attaching ASOG report); Documents on file with the Select Committee to Investigate the January 6th Attack on the United States Capitol (National Archives Production) 076P-R000001361_00001(December 14, 2020, email from Molly Michael to Senator Kelly Loeffler re: From POTUS attaching ASOG report); Documents on file with the Select Committee to Investigate the January 6th Attack

on the United States Capitol (National Archives Production), 076P-R000001358_00001(December 14, 2020, email from Molly Michael to Arizona Governor Doug Ducey re: From POTUS attaching ASOG report); Documents on file with the Select Committee to Investigate the January 6th Attack on the United States Capitol (National Archives Production), 076P-R000001370_00001 (December 14, 2020, email from Molly Michael to Republican Party Chairwoman Ronna McDaniel re: From POTUS attaching ASOG report); Documents on file with the Select Committee to Investigate the January 6th Attack on the United States Capitol (National Archives Production), 076P-R000001378_00001 (December 14, 2020, email from Molly Michael to Pennsylvania State Senator Doug Mastriano re: From POTUS attaching ASOG report).

211.   Donald J. Trump (@realDonaldTrump), Twitter, Dec. 14, 2020 2:59 p.m. ET, available at http://web.archive.org/web/20201214214435/https://twitter.com/realdonaldtrump/status/1338574268154646528 (archived).

212.   Select Committee to Investigate the January 6th Attack on the United States Capitol, Transcribed Interview of William Barr, (Jun. 2, 2022), pp. 28-29.

213.   Select Committee to Investigate the January 6th Attack on the United States Capitol, Transcribed Interview of William Barr, (Jun. 2, 2022), p. 29.

214.   Select Committee to Investigate the January 6th Attack on the United States Capitol, Transcribed Interview of William Barr, (Jun. 2, 2022), pp. 29-30.

215.   Select Committee to Investigate the January 6th Attack on the United States Capitol, Transcribed Interview of William Barr, (Jun. 2, 2022), pp. 29-30.

216.   See, e.g., Select Committee to Investigate the January 6th Attack on the United States Capitol, Transcribed Interview of William Barr, (Jun. 2, 2022), pp. 29-30.

217.   See Documents on file with the Select Committee to Investigate the January 6th Attack on the United States Capitol (Department of Homeland Security Production) CTRL0000915111, CTRL0000915117-CTRL0000915118 (draft analyses of ASOG report). Notably, the final version of this review, which had been requested by the Attorney General, was edited by senior DHS officials to remove the language most critical of ASOG before being sent to the Department of Justice by Acting Assistant Secretary Ken Cuccinelli. See Documents on file with the Select Committee to Investigate the January 6th Attack on the United States Capitol (Department of Homeland Security Production) CTRL0000915120 (emails circulating draft analyses), CTRL0000926941 (noting report was "currently in the Secretary's office"); Documents on file with the Select Committee to Investigate the January 6th Attack on the United States Capitol (Department of Justice Production) HCOR-Pre-CertificationEvents-07262021-000687-HCOR-Pre-CertificationEvents-07262021-000688 (email and report provided to Donoghue by Cuccinelli); Select Committee to Investigate the January 6th Attack on the United States Capitol, Transcribed Interview of Richard Peter Donoghue, (Oct. 1, 2021), pp. 29-31.

218.   See Michigan Senate Oversight Committee, Report on the November 2020 Election in Michigan, (June 23, 2021), p. 16, available at https://misenategopcdn.s3.us-east-1.amazonaws.com/99/doccuments/20210623/SMPO_2020ElectionReport_2.pdf; J. Alex Halderman, Analysis of the Antrim County, Michigan November 2020 Election Incident," (Mar. 26, 2021), available at https://www.michigan.gov//media/Project/Websites/sos/30lawens/Antrim.pdf?rev=fbfe881cdc0043a9bb80b783d1bb5fe9.

219.   For example, President Trump and others frequently cited ASOG's finding that the Dominion machines had a "68% error rate," but that conclusion was based on a complete misunderstanding of the scanner log files reviewed by ASOG. Their report also claimed that, due to these perceived "errors," a "staggering number of votes" were determined through an adjudication process that allowed for manipulation of votes, but no adjudication software was installed on the Dominion machines. J. Alex Halderman, Analysis of the Antrim County, Michigan November 2020 Election Incident, (Mar. 26, 2021), pp. 40-41, available at https://www.michigan.gov/-/media/Project/Websites/sos/30lawens/Antrim.pdf?rev=fbfe881cdc0043a9bb80b783d1bb5fe9.

220. Halderman concluded that "I am not aware of any credible evidence that any security problem was ever exploited against Antrim County's election system. As my analysis shows, the anomalies that occurred in the November 2020 results are fully explained by human error." J. Alex Halderman, *Analysis of the Antrim County, Michigan November 2020 Election Incident*, (Mar. 26, 2021), p. 46, available at https://www.michigan.gov/-/media/Project/Websites/sos/30lawens/Antrim.pdf?rev=fbfe881cdc0043a9bb80b783d1bb5fe9.

221. "Audits of the November 3, 2020 General Election," Michigan Secretary of State, (April 21, 2021), p. 32, available at https://www.michigan.gov/-/media/Project/Websites/sos/30lawens/BOE_2020_Post_Election_Audit_Report_04_21_21.pdf?rev=a3c7ee8c06984864870c540a266177f2.; "Hand Count Calculation Sheet (Office: President of the United States, County: Antrim)," Michigan Secretary of State, available at https://www.michigan.gov/-/media/Project/Websites/sos/30lawens/AntrimCounty_Presidential_Race_Full_Hand_Count_November2020.pdf?rev=0bf12f08c33444c59bd145fbcfbb3e40.

222. Select Committee to Investigate the January 6th Attack on the United States Capitol, Transcribed Interview of Bernard Kerik, (Jan. 13, 2022), p. 182.

223. Select Committee to Investigate the January 6th Attack on the United States Capitol, *Hearing on the January 6th Investigation*, 117th Cong., 2d sess., (June 23, 2022), available at https://www.govinfo.gov/committee/house-january6th.

224. Select Committee to Investigate the January 6th Attack on the United States Capitol, Transcribed Interview of Derek Lyons, (Mar. 17, 2022), pp. 21-22, 99; Select Committee to Investigate the January 6th Attack on the United States Capitol, Transcribed Interview of Pasquale Anthony "Pat" Cipollone, (Jul. 8, 2022), pp. 44-50.

225. Select Committee to Investigate the January 6th Attack on the United States Capitol, Transcribed Interview of Pasquale Anthony "Pat" Cipollone, (Jul. 8, 2022), pp. 42-43.

226. Select Committee to Investigate the January 6th Attack on the United States Capitol, Transcribed Interview of Pasquale Anthony "Pat" Cipollone, (Jul. 8, 2022), p. 50.

227. Select Committee to Investigate the January 6th Attack on the United States Capitol, Transcribed Interview of Eric Herschmann, (Apr. 6, 2022), p. 129.

228. Select Committee to Investigate the January 6th Attack on the United States Capitol, Transcribed Interview of Robert O'Brien, (Aug. 23, 2022), pp. 163-65.

229. Select Committee to Investigate the January 6th Attack on the United States Capitol, Transcribed Interview of Chad Wolf, (Jan. 21, 2022), pp. 97-98, 102-103; Select Committee to Investigate the January 6th Attack on the United States Capitol, Transcribed Interview of Ken Cuccinelli, (Dec. 7, 2021), pp. 49-54.

230. Select Committee to Investigate the January 6th Attack on the United States Capitol, Deposition of Rudolph Giuliani (May 20, 2022), pp. 157-59; Select Committee to Investigate the January 6th Attack on the United States Capitol, Deposition of Sidney Powell, (May 7, 2022), pp. 102-03; Documents on file with the Select Committee to Investigate the January 6th Attack on the United States Capitol, (Jenna Ellis Production), J.007465Ellis, J.007467Ellis (December 28-29, 2020, emails with Katherine Freiss, Doug Mastriano, Christina Bobb, Giuliani, and others about accessing voting machines); Emma Brown and Jon Swaine, "Inside the Secretive Effort by Trump Allies to Access Voting Machines," *Washington Post*, (Oct. 28, 2022), available at https://www.washingtonpost.com/investigations/2022/10/28/coffee-county-georgia-voting-trump/.

231. Brad Raffensperger, *Integrity Counts* (New York: Simon & Schuster, 2021), p. 191 (reproducing the call transcript);Amy Gardner and Paulina Firozi, "Here's the Full Transcript and Audio of the Call Between Trump and Raffensperger," *Washington Post*, (Jan. 5, 2021), available at https://www.washingtonpost.com/politics/trump-raffensperger-call-transcript-georgia-vote/2021/01/03/2768e0cc-4ddd-11eb-83e3-322644d82356_story.html.

232. Brad Raffensperger, *Integrity Counts* (New York: Simon & Schuster, 2021), p. 191 (reproducing the call transcript); Amy Gardner and Paulina Firozi, "Here's the Full Transcript and

Audio of the Call Between Trump and Raffensperger," *Washington Post*, (Jan. 5, 2021), available at https://www.washingtonpost.com/politics/trump-raffensperger-call-transcript-georgia-vote/2021/01/03/2768e0cc-4ddd-11eb-83e3-322644d82356_story.html.

233. "Donald Trump Rally Speech Transcript Dalton, Georgia: Senate Runoff Election," Rev, (Jan. 4, 2021), available at https://www.rev.com/blog/transcripts/donald-trump-rally-speech-transcript-dalton-georgia-senate-runoff-election.

234. "Donald Trump Rally Speech Transcript Dalton, Georgia: Senate Runoff Election," Rev, (Jan. 4, 2021), available at https://www.rev.com/blog/transcripts/donald-trump-rally-speech-transcript-dalton-georgia-senate-runoff-election.

235. Select Committee to Investigate the January 6th Attack on the United States Capitol, Deposition of Rudolph Giuliani, (May 20, 2022), p. 111.

236. Select Committee to Investigate the January 6th Attack on the United States Capitol, Deposition of Rudolph Giuliani, (May 20, 2022), p. 166.

237. Select Committee to Investigate the January 6th Attack on the United States Capitol, Transcribed Interview of Bernard Kerik (Jan. 13, 2022), p. 182. Kerik also emailed President Trump's chief of staff, Mark Meadows, on December 28, 2020, writing: "We can do all the investigations we want later, but if the president plans on winning, it's the legislators that have to be moved, and this will do just that." Document on file with the Select Committee (National Archives Production) 076P-R000004125_0001.

238. Select Committee to Investigate the January 6th Attack on the United States Capitol, Transcribed Interview of Christina Bobb, (Apr. 21, 2022), p. 46.

239. Select Committee to Investigate the January 6th Attack on the United States Capitol, Deposition of Sidney Powell, (May 7, 2022), pp. 89-96.

240. Defendant's Motion to Dismiss at 27-28, *U.S. Dominion, Inc. v. Powell*, No. 1:21-cv-00040 (D.D.C. filed Mar. 22, 2021), ECF No. 22-2.

241. Justin Gray, "Georgia Election Officials Show Frame-by-Frame What Happened in Fulton Surveillance Video," WSB-TV, (Dec. 4, 2020), https://www.wsbtv.com/news/politics/georgia-election-officials-show-frame-by-frame-what-really-happened-fulton-surveillance-video/T5M3PYIBYFHFFOD3CIB2ULDVDE/.

242. 11Alive, "Second Georgia Senate election hearing," YouTube, at 5:31:50-5:32:45, Dec. 3, 2020, available at https://www.youtube.com/watch?v=hRCXUNOwOjw.

243. *See, e.g.*, Donald J. Trump, (@realDonaldtrump), Twitter, Dec. 14, 2020 8:57 a.m. ET, available at http://web.archive.org/web/20201217181730/https://twitter.com/realDonaldTrump/status/1338483200046354434; Brad Raffensperger, *Integrity Counts* (New York: Simon & Schuster, 2021), p. 191 (reproducing the call transcript); Amy Gardner and Paulina Firozi, "Here's the Full Transcript and Audio of the Call Between Trump and Raffensperger," *Washington Post*, (Jan. 5, 2021), available at https://www.washingtonpost.com/politics/trump-raffensperger-call-transcript-georgia-vote/2021/01/03/2768e0cc-4ddd-11eb-83e3-322644d82356_story.html.

244. Brad Raffensperger, *Integrity Counts* (New York: Simon & Schuster, 2021), p. 191 (reproducing the call transcript); Amy Gardner and Paulina Firozi, "Here's the Full Transcript and Audio of the Call Between Trump and Raffensperger," *Washington Post*, (Jan. 5, 2021), available at https://www.washingtonpost.com/politics/trump-raffensperger-call-transcript-georgia-vote/2021/01/03/2768e0cc-4ddd-11eb-83e3-322644d82356_story.html.

245. Ryan Taylor, "Donald Trump Georgia Rally Transcript Before Senate Runoff Elections December 5," Rev, (Dec. 5, 2020), available at https://www.rev.com/blog/transcripts/donald-trump-georgia-rally-transcript-before-senate-runoff-elections-december-5.

246. "Donald Trump Vlog: Contesting Election Results—December 22, 2020," Factba.se, (Dec. 22, 2020), at 9:11 – 9:31, available at https://factba.se/transcript/donald-trump-vlog-contesting-election-results-december-22-2020.

247. Ryan Taylor, "Donald Trump Georgia Phone Call Transcript with Sec. of State Brad Raffensperger: Says He Wants to 'Find' Votes," Rev, (Jan. 4, 2021), available at https://www.rev.com/blog/transcripts/donald-trump-georgia-phone-call-transcript-brad-raffensperger-recording.

248. U.S. Senate Committee on the Judiciary, Transcribed Interview of Jeffrey Rosen, (Aug. 7, 2021), pp. 30-31, available at https://www.judiciary.senate.gov/imo/media/doc/Rosen%20Transcript.pdf.

249. Select Committee to Investigate the January 6th Attack on the United States Capitol, Transcribed Interview of Richard Peter Donoghue, (Oct. 1, 2021), pp. 42-43.

250. Brad Raffensperger, Integrity Counts (New York: Simon & Schuster, 2021), p. 191 (reproducing the call transcript); Amy Gardner and Paulina Firozi, "Here's the Full Transcript and Audio of the Call Between Trump and Raffensperger," Washington Post, (Jan. 5, 2021), available at https://www.washingtonpost.com/politics/trump-raffensperger-call-transcript-georgia-vote/2021/01/03/2768e0cc-4ddd-11eb-83e3-322644d82356_story.html.

251. Brad Raffensperger, Integrity Counts (New York: Simon & Schuster, 2021), p. 191 (reproducing the call transcript); Amy Gardner and Paulina Firozi, "Here's the Full Transcript and Audio of the Call Between Trump and Raffensperger," Washington Post, (Jan. 5, 2021), available at https://www.washingtonpost.com/politics/trump-raffensperger-call-transcript-georgia-vote/2021/01/03/2768e0cc-4ddd-11eb-83e3-322644d82356_story.html.

252. Brad Raffensperger, Integrity Counts (New York: Simon & Schuster, 2021), p. 191 (reproducing the call transcript); Amy Gardner and Paulina Firozi, "Here's the Full Transcript and Audio of the Call Between Trump and Raffensperger," Washington Post, (Jan. 5, 2021), available at https://www.washingtonpost.com/politics/trump-raffensperger-call-transcript-georgia-vote/2021/01/03/2768e0cc-4ddd-11eb-83e3-322644d82356_story.html.

253. Declaration of Frances Watson at 1-3, Pearson v. Kemp, 831 F. App'x. 467 (N.D. Ga. 2020) (No. 1:20-cv-04809), ECF No. 72-1.

254. Declaration of Frances Watson at 1-3, Pearson v. Kemp, 831 F. App'x. 467 (N.D. Ga. 2020) (No. 1:20-cv-04809), ECF No. 72-1.

255. U.S. Senate Judiciary Committee, Transcribed Interview of Byung J. "BJay" Pak, (Aug. 11, 2021), pp. 14-25, available at https://www.judiciary.senate.gov/imo/media/doc/Pak%20Transcript.pdf; Response of the Georgia Secretary of State to the Court's Order of September 20, 2021 at 4-6, Favorito v. Wan, No. 2020CV343938 (Ga. Super. Ct. filed Oct. 12, 2021).

256. "Georgia Election Officials Briefing Transcript December 7: Will Recertify Election Results Today," Rev, (December 7, 2020), available at https://www.rev.com/blog/transcripts/georgia-election-officials-briefing-transcript-december-7-will-recertify-election-results-today; Response of the Georgia Secretary of State to the Court's Order of September 20, 2021 at 4-6, Favorito v. Wan, No. 2020CV343938 (Ga. Super. Ct. filed Oct. 12, 2021).

257. "Georgia Election Officials Briefing Transcript December 7: Will Recertify Election Results Today," Rev, (December 7, 2020), available at https://www.rev.com/blog/transcripts/georgia-election-officials-briefing-transcript-december-7-will-recertify-election-results-today; Response of the Georgia Secretary of State to the Court's Order of September 20, 2021, at 4-6 and Exhibit A: Videotaped Deposition of James P. Callaway (Deputy Chief Investigator of the Office of the Secretary of State) at 29-35, Favorito v. Wan, No. 2020CV343938 (Ga. Super. Ct. filed Oct. 12, 2021) available at, https://s3.documentcloud.org/documents/21084096/favorito-sos-brief-in-response-to-order-of-92021-with-exs-a-and-b.pdf.

258. Declaration of Frances Watson at 2-3, Pearson v. Kemp, 831 F. App'x. 467 (N.D. Ga. 2020) (No. 1:20-cv-04809), ECF No. 72-1; U.S. Senate Judiciary Committee, Transcribed Interview of Byung J. "BJay" Pak, (August 11, 2021), pp. 14-25, available at https://www.judiciary.senate.gov/imo/media/doc/Pak%20Transcript.pdf.

259. Documents on file with the Select Committee to Investigate the January 6th Attack on the United States Capitol, (National Archives Production), 076P-R000004670_0001-0013, 076P-R000004888_0001-0013, 076P-R000004948_0001-0013 (January 5, 2021, emails from Molly Michael re: "from POTUS" to Senators Josh Hawley and Ted Cruz and to Representative Jim Jordan attaching Background Briefing on 2020 Fraud).

260. "Transcript of Trump's Speech at Rally Before US Capitol Riot," *Associated Press*, (Jan. 13, 2021), available at https://apnews.com/article/election-2020-joe-biden-donald-trump-capitol-siege-media-e79eb5164613d6718e9f4502eb471f27.

261. *In the Matter of Rudolph W. Giuliani*, No. 2021-00506, slip op at *2, 22 (N.Y. App. Div. May 3, 2021), available at https://int.nyt.com/data/documenttools/giuliani-law-license-suspension/1ae5ad6007c0ebfa/full.pdf.

262. GA House Mobile Streaming, Governmental Affairs 12.10.20, Vimeo – Livestream, at 2:09:03 to - 2:13:10, available at https://livestream.com/accounts/25225474/events/9117221/videos/214677184.

263. Select Committee to Investigate the January 6th Attack on the United States Capitol, *Hearing on the January 6th Investigation*, 117th Cong., 2d sess., (June 21, 2022), available at https://www.govinfo.gov/committee/house-january6th.

264. *See* John Danforth, Benjamin Ginsberg, Thomas B. Griffith, et al., "Lost, Not Stolen: The Conservative Case that Trump Lost and Biden Won the 2020 Presidential Election," (July 2022), p. 3, available at https://lostnotstolen.org/download/378/.

265. Opinion and Order at *6, 13, *Costantino v. Detroit*, No. 20-014780-AW (Mich. Cty. Cir. Ct. filed Nov. 13, 2020), available at https://electioncases.osu.edu/wp-content/uploads/2020/11/Costantino-v-Detroit-Opinion-and-Order.pdf.

266. Complaint, Exhibit 2: Affidavit of Jesse Richard Morgan at 2, 10, *Mecalfe v. Wolf*, 2020 Pa. Commw. LEXIS 794 (Pa. Commw. Ct. 2020) (No. 636 MD 2020), available at https://www.pacourts.us/Storage/media/pdfs/20210603/212420-file-10836.pdf.

267. *See, e.g.*, Donald J. Trump (@realdonaldtrump), Twitter, Dec. 1, 2020 2:31 p.m. ET, available at http://web.archive.org/web/20201202014959/https://twitter.com/realdonaldtrump/status/1333856259662077954 (archived); Donald J. Trump (@realdonaldtrump), Twitter, Dec. 1, 2020 3:49 p.m. ET, available at http://web.archive.org/web/20201201221335/https://twitter.com/realDonaldTrump/status/1333875814585282567 (archived); Donald J. Trump (@realdonaldtrump), Twitter, Dec 2, 2020 6:42 p.m. ET, available at http://web.archive.org/web/20201203024425/https://twitter.com/realDonaldTrump/status/1334327204847775744 (archived).

268. Select Committee to Investigate the January 6th Attack on the United States Capitol, Transcribed Interview of Richard Peter Donoghue, (Oct. 1, 2021), p. 60; Select Committee to Investigate the January 6th Attack on the United States Capitol, Transcribed Interview of William Barr, (Jun. 2, 2022), pp. 45-46.

269. FOX News, "Sean Hannity," Nov. 19, 2020, available at https://archive.org/details/FOXNEWSW_20201120_060000_Hannity?start/1983.1.end/2077.5.

270. Brandon Waltens, "VIDEO: Wagons, Suitcases, and Coolers Roll into Detroit Voting Center at 4 AM [UPDATED]," *Texas Scorecard*, (Nov. 4, 2020), available at https://texasscorecard.com/federal/video-wagons-suitcases-and-coolers-roll-into-detroit-voting-center-at-4-am/; "Rudy Giuliani Trump Campaign Press Conference Transcript November 19: Election Fraud Claims," Rev, (Nov. 19, 2020), at 22:29-26:53, available at https://www.rev.com/blog/transcripts/rudy-giuliani-trump-campaign-press-conference-transcript-november-19-election-fraud-claims.

271. Affidavit of Christopher Thomas ¶ 18, *Texas v. Pennsylvania*, 592 U.S. ____ (2020) (describing ballot delivery), available at https://www.supremecourt.gov/DocketPDF/22/22O155/163387/20201210145418055_22O155%20MI%20APP.pdf; *see also* Opinion and Order at *6, 13, *Costantino v. Detroit*, No. 20-014780-AW (Mich. Cty. Cir. Ct. filed Nov. 13, 2020), available at

https://electioncases.osu.edu/wp-content/uploads/2020/11/Costantino-v-Detroit-Opinion-and-Order.pdf (relying on Christopher Thomas' affidavit to deny a petition for various relief related to allegations that the November 3, 2020 election in Michigan was fraudulent).

272. "How a WXYZ Wagon Sparked False Election Fraud Claims in Detroit," WXYZ, (Nov. 5, 2020), available at https://www.wxyz.com/news/how-a-wxyz-wagon-sparked-false-election-fraud-claims-in-detroit.

273. "Election Summary Report," City of Detroit, (Nov. 19, 2020), available at https://detroitmi.gov/document/november-3-2020-general-election-official-results.

274. A canvassing process in every State verifies that the number of voters indicated as having voted matches the number of ballots cast. If, as claimed, tens of thousands of illegitimate ballots were counted at the TCF Center in Detroit, the total number of ballots counted would be substantially higher than the total number of voters who voted, but in Detroit slightly fewer ballots were counted than voters who were listed as having voted. The net number of ballots for the City of Detroit counting boards was 21 more names than ballots, out of approximately 174,000 absentee votes cast. Michigan Secretary of State, "Audits of the November 3, 2020 General Election," (Apr. 21, 2021), p. 20, available at https://www.michigan.gov/-/media/Project/Websites/sos/30lawens/BOE_2020_Post_Election_Audit_Report_04_21_21.pdf?rev=a3c7ee8c06984864870c540a266177f2.

275. Approximately 4.2 million ballots were cast in-person on election day and 2.6 million mail and absentee ballots were cast. See "Pennsylvania's Election Stats," Pennsylvania Department of State, (accessed Dec. 4, 2022), available at https://www.dos.pa.gov/VotingElections/BEST/Pages/BEST-Election-Stats.aspx;"Official Returns – 2020 Presidential Election," Pennsylvania Department of State, (accessed Dec. 4, 2022), available at https://www.electionreturns.pa.gov/General/SummaryResults?ElectionID=83&ElectionType=G&IsActive=0.

276. Donald J. Trump, (@realDonaldTrump), Twitter, Nov. 28, 2020 12:09 a.m. ET, available at http://web.archive.org/web/20201128080915/https://twitter.com/realDonaldTrump/status/1332552283553476608 (archived), retweeting Senator Doug Mastriano (@SenMastriano), Twitter, Nov. 27, 2020, 1:59 p.m. ET, available at https://twitter.com/SenMastriano/status/1332398733401591808.

277. Jessica Calefati, "Fact-Checking False Claims about Pennsylvania's Presidential Election by Trump and His Allies," Philadelphia Inquirer, (Dec. 7, 2020), available at https://www.inquirer.com/politics/election/pennsylvania-election-results-trump-fraud-fact-check-20201206.html.

278. Donald J. Trump (@realDonaldTrump), Twitter, Dec. 28, 2020, 4:00 p.m. ET, available at http://web.archive.org/web/20201228211304/https://twitter.com/realdonaldtrump/status/1343663159085834248 (archived); Donald J. Trump (@realDonaldTrump), Twitter, Dec. 29, 2020, 8:59 a.m. ET, available at http://web.archive.org/web/20201229205204/https://twitter.com/realDonaldTrump/status/1343919651336712199 (archived); Donald J. Trump (@realDonaldTrump), Twitter, Dec. 29, 2020, 5:55 p.m. ET, available at http://web.archive.org/web/20201229225512/https://twitter.com/realdonaldtrump/status/1344054358418345985. Note that timestamps in archived tweets may reflect a time zone different from that where the tweet originated.

279. See Pennsylvania House Republican Caucus, "PA Lawmakers: Numbers Don't Add Up, Certification of Presidential Results Premature and In Error," (Dec. 28, 2020), available at https://www.pahousegop.com/News/18754/Latest-News/PA-Lawmakers-Numbers-Don%E2%80%99t-Add-Up,-Certification-of-Presidential-Results-Premature-and-In-Error. Representative Ryan also promoted the groundless claim of an unexplained discrepancy of 400,000 mail-in ballots in the state's database, which was based entirely on his ignorance of the fact that the database in question accounts for mail-in ballots and absentee ballots separately. Senate Committee on Homeland Security & Governmental Affairs, Examining Irregularities in the 2020 Election, (Dec. 16, 2020), Written Testimony of Pennsylvania State

Representative Frank Ryan, available at https://www.hsgac.senate.gov/imo/media/doc/Testimony-Ryan-2020-12-16.pdf; Senate Committee on Homeland Security & Governmental Affairs, Examining Irregularities in the 2020 Election, (Dec. 16, 2020), Letter Submitted by Pennsylvania Secretary of the Commonwealth Kathy Boockvar, available at https://www.dos.pa.gov/about-us/Documents/statements/2020-12-16-Senator-Johnson-and-Peters.pdf.

280. "Dept. of State: Republicans' Election Claims Are 'Repeatedly Debunked Conspiracy Theories'," WJAC-TV, (Dec. 29, 2020), available at https://wjactv.com/news/local/dept-of-state-republicans-election-claims-are-repeatedly-debunked-conspiracy-theories.

281. Senate Committee on the Judiciary, Transcribed Interview of Richard Donoghue, (Aug. 6, 2021), p. 156, available at https://www.judiciary.senate.gov/imo/media/doc/Donoghue%20Transcript.pdf.

282. See "Donald Trump Rally Speech Transcript Dalton, Georgia: Senate Runoff Election," Rev, (Jan. 4, 2021), at 58:09, available at https://www.rev.com/blog/transcripts/donald-trump-rally-speech-transcript-dalton-georgia-senate-runoff-election; "Transcript of Trump's Speech at Rally Before US Capitol Riot," *Associated Press* (January 13, 2021), available at https://apnews.com/article/election-2020-joe-biden-donald-trump-capitol-siege-media-e79eb5164613d6718e9f4502eb471f27.

283. Select Committee to Investigate the January 6th Attack on the United States Capitol, Transcribed Interview of William Barr, (Jun. 2, 2022), p. 29; Affidavit of Russell James Ramsland, Jr., 556 F. Supp. 3d. 680, 724 (E.D. Mich. 2021), ECF 6-24, available at https://www.courtlistener.com/docket/18693929/6/24/king-v-whitmer/. Ramsland submitted a similar affidavit in a case in Georgia. *See* Affidavit of Russell Ramsland, *Wood v. Raffensperger*, 501 F. Supp. 3d 1310 (N.D. Ga. 2020), ECF No. 7-1.

284. Affidavit of Russell Ramsland, *Wood v. Raffensperger*, 501 F. Supp. 3d 1310 (N.D. Ga. 2020), ECF No. 7-1.

285. Aaron Blake, "The Trump Campaign's Much-Hyped Affidavit Features a Big, Glaring Error," *Washington Post*, (Nov. 20, 2020), available at https://www.washingtonpost.com/politics/2020/11/20/trump-campaigns-much-hyped-affidavit-features-big-glaring-error/.

286. For example, Ramsland claimed 781.91% turnout in North Muskegon (actual turnout: 77.78%); 460.51% turnout in Zeeland Charter Township (actual turnout: 80.11%); and 139.29% turnout in Detroit (actual turnout: 50.88%). *See King v. Whitmer*, 556 F. Supp. 3d. 680, 724 (E.D. Mich. 2021); Michigan Senate Oversight Committee, *Report on the November 2020 Election in Michigan*, (June 23, 2021), available at https://misenategopcdn.s3.us-east-1.amazonaws.com/99/doccuments/20210623/SMPO_2020ElectionReport_2.pdf.

287. *See, e.g.,* "Transcript of Trump's Speech at Rally Before US Capitol Riot," *Associated Press*, (Jan. 13, 2021), available athttps://apnews.com/article/election-2020-joe-biden-donald-trump-capitol-siege-media-e79eb5164613d6718e9f4502eb471f27; "Donald Trump Speech on Election Fraud Claims Transcript December 2" Rev (Dec. 2, 2020), available at https://www.rev.com/blog/transcripts/donald-trump-speech-on-election-fraud-claims-transcript-december-2; Donald J. Trump (@realDonaldTrump), Twitter, Dec. 3, 2020, 4:11 p.m. ET, available at http://web.archive.org/web/20201203211154/https://twitter.com/realdonaldtrump/status/1334606278388277253 (archived); "Trump Lawyers Rudy Giuliani & Jenna Ellis Testify Before Michigan House Oversight Committee: Full Transcript," Rev, (Dec. 3, 2020), at 26:13, available at https://www.rev.com/blog/transcripts/trump-lawyers-rudy-giuliani-jenna-ellis-testify-before-michigan-house-oversight-committee-transcript; Affidavit of Mellissa A. Carone, *King v. Whitmer*, 505 F. Supp. 3d 720 (E.D. Mich. 2020), ECF No. 1-5, available at https://www.courtlistener.com/docket/18693929/1/5/king-v-whitmer/.

288. *See, e.g.,* Opinion and Order at *3, 12-13, *Costantino v. Detroit*, No. 20-014780-AW (Mich. Cty. Cir. Ct. filed Nov. 13, 2020), available at https://electioncases.osu.edu/wp-content/uploads/2020/11/Costantino-v-Detroit-Opinion-and-Order.pdf; Affidavit of Christopher Thomas ¶¶ 2-18, *Texas v. Pennsylvania*, 592 U.S. ____ (2020) (describing his experience and

the process for tabulating votes), available at https://www.supremecourt.gov/DocketPDF/22/22O155/163387/20201210145418055_22O155%20MI%20APP.pdf.

289. *See, e.g.,* "Transcript of Trump's Speech at Rally Before US Capitol Riot," *Associated Press* (January 13, 2021), available at https://apnews.com/article/election-2020-joe-biden-donald-trump-capitol-siege-media-e79eb5164613d6718e9f4502eb471f27; Rudy Giuliani's Common Sense, "I CAN'T SAY THIS On National Television | Rudy Giuliani | Ep. 98," Rumble, at 13:10 – 13:25, Dec. 30, 2020, available at https://rumble.com/vex72l-i-cant-say-this-on-national-television-rudy-giuliani-ep.-98.html.

290. Right Side Broadcasting Network, "LIVE: Georgia House Hearing on Election Fraud, Brad Raffensperger to Participate 12/23/20," YouTube, at 27:28, 43:02-43:28, Dec. 23, 2020, available at https://www.youtube.com/watch?v=R4cuakECmuA&t=2582s (Testimony of Ryan Germany, counsel to Georgia Secretary of State, before Georgia legislature stating: "The total number of underage people who voted is zero. We were able to look at everyone who voted and look at their birthdate in the voter registration system, and I think there was four people who requested a ballot before they turned 18, and they all turned 18 prior to November 3rd, which means they're allowed to vote.").

291. *See, e.g.* Bannon's War Room, "Episode 980 – The Border Tipping Point … Peter Navarro on the Stolen Election and Desperation in Del Rio," Rumble, May 27, 2021, available at https://rumble.com/vhpam3-episode-980the-border-tipping-pointpeter-navarro-on-the-stolen-election-and.html; Bannon's War Room, "Episode 979 – The HQ of the Runaway Train … Rachel Maddow's Anna Karenina Moment," Rumble, May 27, 2021, available at https://rumble.com/vhp8yn-episode-979-the-hq-of-the-runaway-train-rachel-maddows-anna-karenina-moment.html; Right Side Broadcasting Network, "LIVE: Arizona State Legislature Holds Public Hearing on 2020 Election," YouTube, at 2:06:33-2:07:02, Nov. 30, 2020, available at https://www.youtube.com/watch?v=rri6flxaXww.

292. "Proof of Citizenship Requirements," Arizona Secretary of State, (accessed Dec. 4, 2022), available at https://azsos.gov/elections/voting-election/proof-citizenship-requirements. In 2013, the Supreme Court struck down Arizona's "evidence-of-citizenship" requirement as applied to federal elections. *See Arizona v. Inter Tribal Council of Arizona, Inc.,* 570 U.S. 1, 4, 19 (2013). Arizona law allows voters to register as "federal only" voters without proof of citizenship, but those voters must provide a driver's license or Social Security Number, which is then checked by election officials against immigration records before the person is added to voter registration rolls. Daniel González, "Are Undocumented Immigrants Voting Illegally in Arizona?," *Arizona Republic,* (Oct. 27, 2016), available at https://www.azcentral.com/story/news/politics/elections/2016/10/27/voter-fraud-undocumented-immigrants-voting-illegally-arizona-donald-trump/91703916/.

293. Documents on file with the Select Committee to Investigate the January 6th Attack on the United States Capitol, (Mark Meadows Production), MM007288, (November 13, 2020, email from Bill Stepien to Mark Meadows, Justin Clark, and Jason Miller re: AZ Federal ID Voters); In the Matter of Rudolph W. Giuliani, No. 2021-00506, slip op at *23-25 (N.Y. App. Div. May 3, 2021), available at https://int.nyt.com/data/documenttools/giuliani-law-license-suspension/1ae5ad6007c0ebfa/full.pdf.

294. Brad Raffensperger, *Integrity Counts* (New York: Simon & Schuster, 2021), p. 191 (reproducing the call transcript); Amy Gardner and Paulina Firozi, "Here's the Full Transcript and Audio of the Call Between Trump and Raffensperger," Washington Post, (Jan. 5, 2021), available at https://www.washingtonpost.com/politics/trump-raffensperger-call-transcript-georgia-vote/2021/01/03/2768e0cc-4ddd-11eb-83e3-322644d82356_story.html.

295. For example, the President alleged in his January 6th speech that large numbers of ballots were cast on behalf of dead people not just in Georgia but also in Michigan, Nevada, and Pennsylvania. "Transcript of Trump's Speech at Rally Before US Capitol Riot," Associated Press (January 13, 2021), https://apnews.com/article/election-2020-joe-biden-donald-trump-capitol-siege-media-e79eb5164613d6718e9f4502eb471f27; *See also* Rudy Giuliani's Common Sense, "I CAN'T SAY THIS On National Television | Rudy Giuliani | Ep. 98," Rumble,

at 15:10-15:46, (Dec. 30, 2020, reposted Mar. 22, 2021), available at https://rumble.com/vex72l-i-cant-say-this-on-national-television-rudy-giuliani-ep.-98.html (making similar claims).

296. Documents on file with the Select Committee to Investigate the January 6th Attack on the United States Capitol, (Alex Cannon Production) AC-0013946, (November 12, 2020, email from Alex Cannon to Matt Wolking, Zach Parkinson, Tim Murtaugh, Ali Pardo, Matthew Morgan, and Andrew Clark titled "Re: dead voters"); Documents on file with the Select Committee to Investigate the January 6th Attack on the United States Capitol, (Tim Murtaugh Production) XXM-0009451 (November 8, 2020, email from Jason Miller to Zach Parkinson, Tim Murtaugh, and Matt Wolking re: PA Death Data stating that quality control checks will "significantly decrease[]" the number of "possible dead voters"), XXM-0009467 (November 8, 2020, email from Jason Miller to Zach Parkinson, Tim Murtaugh, and Matt Wolking re: GA Dead Voters), XXM-0009566 (November 9, 2020 email from Zach Parkinson to Jason Miller, Tim Murtaugh, and Matt Wolking re PA Death Data noting there "may be errors" with their data about people who were dead voters); Mark Niesse, "Alleged 'Dead' Georgia Voters Found Alive and Well after 2020 Election," *Atlanta Journal-Constitution*, (Dec. 27, 2021), available at https://www.ajc.com/politics/alleged-dead-georgia-voters-found-alive-and-well-after-2020-election/DAL3VY7NFNHL5OREMHD7QECOCA/.

297. Documents on file with the Select Committee to Investigate the January 6th Attack on the United States Capitol, (National Archives Production), TEXT0000198, (December 3, 2020, text message from Eric Herschmann to Mark Meadows).

298. Documents on file with the Select Committee to Investigate the January 6th Attack on the United States Capitol, (National Archives Production), TEXT0000198-203, (December 3, 2020, text messages between Eric Herschmann and Mark Meadows).

299. Final Order at 5-6, *Boland v. Raffensperger*, No.2020CV343018 (Ga. Super. Ct. filed Dec. 14 2020), available at https://electioncases.osu.edu/wp-content/uploads/2020/11/Boland-v-Raffensperger-Order-Dismissing-Complaint.pdf.

300. The expert, Bryan Geels, based his claims on a comparison of public voter information to public death records. *See* Documents on file with the Select Committee to Investigate the January 6th Attack on the U.S. Capitol (Christina Bobb Production), BOBB_CONG_00000683-84, 692-93, 706-07 (Affidavit of Bryan Geels dated Dec. 1, 2020, in *Trump v. Barron*, a case filed by the Trump Campaign in a Georgia Superior Court in Fulton County). However, the records reviewed included only name and year of birth for each individual listed. *Id.* at ¶ 28. Based on this limited information, it was impossible for Geels (or anyone else) to conclude that the person with a particular name and birth year was the same person listed in public death records with that name and birth year. *See id.*, at ¶ 50 (only the Secretary of State has the information to conduct a full analysis of this issue); *see also* Declaration of Charles Stewart III at 22, *Trump v. Raffensperger*, No. 2020CV33255 (Ga. Super. Ct. filed Dec. 14, 2020).

301. In Georgia, the Secretary of State found four cases where people voted in the names of deceased individuals. Mark Niesse, "Alleged 'Dead' Georgia Voters Found Alive and Well after 2020 Election," *Atlanta Journal-Constitution*, (Dec. 27, 2021), available at https://www.ajc.com/politics/alleged-dead-georgia-voters-found-alive-and-well-after-2020-election/DAL3VY7NFNHL5OREMHD7QECOCA/; In Arizona, the Attorney General recently concluded its investigation into claims of supposed dead voters in the 2020 election and found only one instance in which a vote was cast on behalf of a person who died prior to the election. Mark Brnovich, Arizona Attorney General to The Honorable Karen Fann, Arizona Senate President, (Aug. 1, 2022), available at https://www.azag.gov/sites/default/files/2022-08/Letter%20to%20Fann%20-%20EIU%20Update%2080122.pdf. In Michigan, the Senate Oversight Committee found only two instances in which votes were cast in the names of dead people: one was a clerical error (poll worker attributed vote to deceased father of person with same name residing at same address) and the other was a woman who died four days before the election but had sent in her absentee ballot before her death. Michigan Senate Oversight Committee, *Report on the November 2020 Election in*

Michigan, (June 23, 2021), available at https://misenategopcdn.s3.us-east-1.amazonaws.com/99/doccuments/20210623/SMPO_2020ElectionReport_2.pdf.

302. In an email obtained by the Select Committee, Katherine Friess, a lawyer who worked closely with Giuliani, shared this information with Giuliani and noted, "I don't think this makes a particularly strong case." Documents on file with the Select Committee to Investigate the January 6th Attack on the U.S. Capitol (Christina Bobb Production), BOBB-_CONG_00000621 (January 4, 2021, email from Katherine Friess re: Chairman Graham dead votes memo for your consideration).

303. Documents on file with the Select Committee to Investigate the January 6th Attack on the U.S. Capitol (Cleta Mitchell Production), CM00026036 (January 5, 2021 email from Cleta Mitchell to Richard Perry re: GA Data request by Senator Graham); Documents on file with the Select Committee to Investigate the January 6th Attack on the U.S. Capitol (Christina Bobb Production), BOBB_CONG_00000621 (January 4, 2021, email from Katherine Friess re: Chairman Graham dead votes memo for your consideration); Select Committee to Investigate the January 6th Attack on the United States Capitol, Transcribed Interview of Christina Bobb, (Apr. 21, 2022), pp. 141-42.

304. Documents on file with the Select Committee to Investigate the January 6th Attack on the U.S. Capitol (Christina Bobb Production), BOBB_CONG_00000621 (January 4, 2021, email from Katherine Friess re: Chairman Graham dead votes memo for your consideration).

305. ABC News, "Lindsey Graham Delivers Remarks on Capitol Breach," YouTube, at 3:05-3:30, Jan. 6, 2021, available at https://www.youtube.com/watch?v=JKHkYlRm_XM.

306. Documents on file with the Select Committee to Investigate the January 6th Attack on the United States Capitol, (Chapman University Production), Chapman060742, (Dec. 31, 2020 email from John Eastman to Alex Kaufman and Kurth Hibert); *see also* Documents on file with the Select Committee to Investigate the January 6th Attack on the United States Capitol, (National Archives Production), 076P-R000008384_0001 (December 31, 2020, email from Eric Herschmann to Cleta Mitchell and cc'ed to Mark Meadows and Molly Michael in which Herschmann wrote: "I was concerned about the President signing a verification about facts that may not be sustainable upon detailed scrutiny.").

307. Order Re Privilege of Remaining Documents at 17, *Eastman v. Thompson*, No. 8:22-cv-99-DOC_DFM, (Oct. 19, 2022), ECF no. 372, available at https://www.courtlistener.com/docket/62613089/372/john-c-eastman-v-bennie-g-thompson/.

308. Order Re Privilege of Remaining Documents at 17, *Eastman v. Thompson*, Case 8:22-cv-00099-DOC_DFM, (Oct. 19, 2022), ECF no. 372, available at https://www.courtlistener.com/docket/62613089/372/john-c-eastman-v-bennie-g-thompson/.

309. "Transcript of Trump's Speech at Rally Before US Capitol Riot," *Associated Press*, (Jan. 13, 2021), https://apnews.com/article/election-2020-joe-biden-donald-trump-capitol-siege-media-e79eb5164613d6718e9f4502eb471f27.

310. "Transcript of Trump's Speech at Rally Before US Capitol Riot," *Associated Press*, (Jan. 13, 2021), https://apnews.com/article/election-2020-joe-biden-donald-trump-capitol-siege-media-e79eb5164613d6718e9f4502eb471f27.

311. "Transcript of Trump's Speech at Rally Before US Capitol Riot," *Associated Press*, (Jan. 13, 2021), https://apnews.com/article/election-2020-joe-biden-donald-trump-capitol-siege-media-e79eb5164613d6718e9f4502eb471f27.

312. *See* "Donald Trump 2020 Election Night Speech Transcript," Rev, (Nov. 4, 2020), available at https://www.rev.com/blog/transcripts/donald-trump-2020-election-night-speech-transcript.

313. *See* "Donald Trump Speech 'Save America' Rally Transcript January 6," Rev, (Jan. 6, 2021), available at https://www.rev.com/blog/transcripts/donald-trump-speech-save-america-rally-transcript-january-6.

314. "Transcript of Trump's Speech at Rally Before US Capitol Riot," *Associated Press*, (Jan. 13,

2021), https://apnews.com/article/election-2020-joe-biden-donald-trump-capitol-siege-media-e79eb5164613d6718e9f4502eb471f27.

315. Donald J. Trump (@realDonaldTrump), Twitter, Dec. 19, 2020, 1:42 a.m. ET, available at https://www.thetrumparchive.com/?searchbox=%22wild+protest%22 (archived).

316. "Transcript of Trump's Speech at Rally Before US Capitol Riot," *Associated Press*, (Jan. 13, 2021), https://apnews.com/article/election-2020-joe-biden-donald-trump-capitol-siege-media-e79eb5164613d6718e9f4502eb471f27.

317. "Transcript of Trump's Speech at Rally Before US Capitol Riot," *Associated Press*, (Jan. 13, 2021), https://apnews.com/article/election-2020-joe-biden-donald-trump-capitol-siege-media-e79eb5164613d6718e9f4502eb471f27.

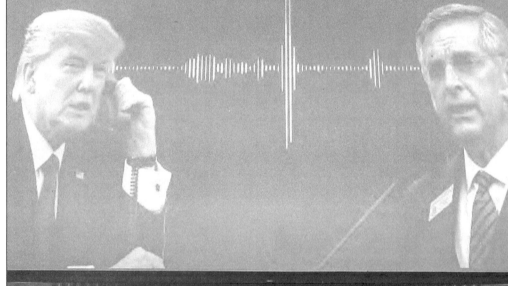

January 2, 2021

Look, we need only 11,000 votes.

2

"I JUST WANT TO FIND 11,780 VOTES"

In a now infamous telephone call on January 2, 2021, President Trump pressured Georgia Secretary of State Brad Raffensperger for more than an hour. The President confronted him with multiple conspiracy theories about the election—none of which were true. Raffensperger and other Georgia officials debunked these allegations, one after another, during their call. Under Raffensperger's leadership, Georgia had, by that time, already conducted a statewide hand recount of all ballots. That recount and other post-election reviews proved that there was no widespread fraud, and that voting machines didn't alter the outcome of the election.[1] This should have put President Trump's allegations to rest. But, undeterred by the facts, the President badgered Raffensperger to overturn the Georgia results.

President Trump insisted that "the ballots are corrupt" and someone was "shredding" them.[2] He issued a thinly veiled threat, telling Raffensperger, "it is more illegal for you than it is for them because you know what they did and you're not reporting it."[3] Of course, the Georgia officials weren't doing anything "illegal," and there was nothing to "report." Even so, President Trump suggested that both Raffensperger and his general counsel, Ryan Germany, could face criminal jeopardy.[4] "That's a criminal, that's a criminal offense. And you can't let that happen," the President said.[5] "That's a big risk to you and to Ryan, your lawyer . . . I'm notifying you that you're letting it happen."[6]

And then the President made his demand. "So look. All I want to do is this. I just want to find 11,780 votes, which is one more than we have," President Trump told Raffensperger.[7]

It was a stunning moment. The President of the United States was asking a State's chief election officer to "find" enough votes to declare him the winner of an election he lost.

Raffensperger saw the President's warning to him on January 2nd as a threat. "I felt then—and I still believe today—that this was a threat," Raffensperger wrote in his book.[8] And this threat was multifaceted: first, the President "notifying" Raffensperger and his team of criminal activity could be understood as directing the law-enforcement power of the Federal Government against them. While Raffensperger did not know for certain whether President Trump was threatening such an investigation, he knew Trump had "positional power" as President and appeared to be promising to "make [my] life miserable."[9]

But the threat was also of a more insidious kind. As Raffensperger wrote in his book: "Others obviously thought [it was a threat], too, because some of Trump's more radical followers have responded as if it was their duty to carry out this threat."[10] Raffensperger's deputy held a press conference and publicly warned all Americans, including President Trump, that President Trump's rhetoric endangered innocent officials and private citizens, and fueled death threats against Georgia election workers, sexualized threats directed towards Raffensperger's wife, and harassment at the homes of Georgia election officials.[11] The January 2nd call promised more of the same. The upshot of President Trump's message to Raffensperger was: do what I ask, or you will pay.

President Trump's phone call with Secretary Raffensperger received widespread coverage after it was leaked. But Georgia was not the only State targeted by President Trump and his allies. The call was one element of a larger and more comprehensive effort—much of it unseen by and unknown to the general public—to overturn the votes cast by millions of American citizens across several States.

As Chapter 1 explained, the root of this effort was the "Big Lie": President Trump and his allies publicly claiming that the election was rife with fraud that could have changed the result, even though the President's own advisors, and the Department of Justice, told the President time and time again that this was not the case.[12] But in parallel with this strategy, President Trump and his allies zeroed in on key battleground States the President had lost, leaning on Republican State officials to overrule voters, disregard valid vote counts, and deliver the States' electoral votes to the losing candidate. Had this scheme worked, President Trump could have, for the first time in American history, subverted the results of a lawful election to stay in power. His was a deeply anti-democratic plan: to co-opt State legislatures—through appeals to debunked theories of election fraud, or pure partisan politics—to replace Biden electors with Trump electors, so President Trump would win the electoral vote count in the joint session of Congress on January 6th.

Had enough State officials gone along with President Trump's plot, his attempt to stay in power might have worked. It is fortunate that a critical mass of honorable officials withstood President Trump's pressure to participate in this scheme. They and others who stood up to him closed off avenues for thwarting the election so that, by noon on January 6th, President Trump was left with one desperate, final gambit for holding on to power: sending his armed, angry supporters to the U.S. Capitol.

2.1 THE ELECTORAL COLLEGE, AND PRESIDENT TRUMP'S ATTEMPT TO SUBVERT IT

When Americans vote for a presidential candidate on election day, they are actually casting votes for that candidate's proposed presidential electors to participate in the electoral college. After a State certifies its election results and announces a winner, it also issues a "certificate of ascertainment," which contains the names of the duly chosen electoral college electors. The electors whose names appear as having received the most votes on the certificate of ascertainment will go on to participate in the electoral college, while a losing candidate's proposed electors have no role to play and no standing to participate in the electoral college. This happens after every Presidential election, in each of the fifty States and the District of Columbia.

This process comes from a clause in the U.S. Constitution that gives States the power to choose electoral college electors according to State law.[13] That clause says that each State "shall appoint" electoral college electors "in such [m]anner as the Legislature thereof may direct." All 50 States have decreed that electors will be selected by popular vote.

Tuesday, November 3rd, was the day established by Federal law as election day in 2020. Each State's rules had been set—and courts had weighed in when certain rules were challenged. Polls opened around the country and votes came in, whether in person or via the mail, according to each State's laws.

Over 154 million voters cast votes according to the rules in place on election day.[14] President Trump lost. He and his supporters went to court, filing long-shot legal challenges to the election, but they failed in courts around the country, before judges appointed by executives of both parties (including President Trump himself), and, for those judges who were elected, that are members of both parties.

Rather than abiding by the rule of law and accepting the courts' rulings, President Trump and his advisors tried every which way to reverse the outcome at the State level. They pressured local and State elections officials to stop counting votes once it became clear that former Vice President Joseph Biden would prevail in the final count. They pressured Governors, secretaries of State, and local officials not to certify the popular vote in several swing States that former Vice-President Biden had won. And, when that did not work, they pressured State legislators to disregard the vote counts and instead appoint Trump electors to vote in the electoral college.

This fundamentally anti-democratic effort was premised on the incorrect theory that, because the Constitution assigns to State legislatures the role of directing how electoral college electors are chosen (which every State legislature had done *before* the election, giving that power to the people at the ballot boxes) then the State legislatures could simply choose Trump/Pence electors *after* seeing the election results. In effect, President Trump and his advisors pushed for the rules to be changed after the election—even if it meant disenfranchising millions of Americans.

2.2 THE PLAN EMERGES

More than a month before the Presidential election, the media reported that the Trump Campaign was already developing a fallback plan that would focus on overturning certain election results at the State level. An article published on September 23, 2020, in *The Atlantic* explained, "[a]ccording to sources in the Republican Party at the State and national levels, the Trump Campaign is discussing contingency plans to bypass election results and appoint loyal electors in battleground States where Republicans hold the legislative majority." [15] Ominously, the same reporting predicted, almost exactly, what would later come to pass: "With a justification based on claims of rampant fraud, Trump would ask State legislators to set aside the popular vote and exercise their power to choose a slate of electors directly." [16]

Numerous senior Trump Campaign advisors—including Campaign Manager William Stepien, Deputy Campaign Manager and Senior Counsel Justin Clark, and President Trump's lead attorney Rudolph Giuliani—all told the Select Committee that there was, indeed, a State-focused "strategy" or "track" to challenge the outcome of the election, which included pressing State legislators to challenge results in key States and to appoint new electoral college electors. [17]

"You know, in the days after election day, later in that first week, bleeding into the second, as our numbers and data looked bleaker, internally we knew that," Stepien told the Select Committee. [18] "As the AP [Associated Press] called the race, I think some surrounding the President were looking for different avenues to pursue." That's when Stepien remembered the concept first coming up. [19]

Those around President Trump were pushing this idea, and pushing it hard.

Just two days after the election, President Trump's son, Donald Trump, Jr., forwarded to White House Chief of Staff Mark Meadows a suggestion that "State Assemblies can step in and vote to put forward the electoral slate[,] Republicans control Pennsylvania, Wisconsin, Michigan, North Carolina, etc. we get Trump electors" and so "we either have a vote WE control and WE win OR it gets kicked to Congress 6 January . . ."[20] Chief of Staff Meadows responded: "Working on this for pa, ga and nc already."[21]

Within one week after the election, Meadows had also sent or received several other similar messages:

"The state legislature can take over the electoral process"—Mark Meadows's text to Georgia State Senator Marty Harbin.[22]

"Agreed"—Mark Meadows's text to a different sender, who suggested that the Trump Administration "should get that out there" if they were "seriously considering the state legislature strategy."[23]

"I will tell him"—Mark Meadows's text to a sender who suggested President Trump "[s]tart building momentum for the state legislatures."[24]

"I love it"—Mark Meadows's text to Representative Andy Biggs, who relayed what he acknowledged as a "highly controversial" idea to have "Republican legislature's (sic)" "appoint a look doors (sic) [electors]."[25]

". . . Why can't the states of GA NC PENN and other R controlled state houses declare this is BS (where conflicts and election not called that night) and just send their own electors . . . I wonder if POTUS knows this . . ."—former Secretary of Energy Rick Perry to Mark Meadows.[26]

Another White House official exploring such a plan less than a week after the election was Vince Haley, Deputy Assistant to the President for Policy, Strategy and Speechwriting. He suggested:

". . . Imagine if every red state legislature slated zero electors. It would reveal that we are a red country. To do this we would have to jack this to the nth degree as a battle of tribes . . . ."[27]

Haley pushed this strategy in several texts and emails, including to Assistant to the President and Director of Presidential Personnel Johnny McEntee,[28] an individual Haley characterized as "a very trusted lieutenant" for President Trump, "a direct conveyor to Boss with ideas," and "[a]t his side almost all the time."[29]

For Haley, however, purported election fraud was a way to justify President Trump-friendly legislatures changing the outcome of the election, but there were other reasons for doing so, too. Election fraud was "only one rationale for slating Trump electors," Haley told McEntee, and "[w]e should baldly assert" that State legislators "have the constitutional right to substitute their judgment for a certified majority of their constituents" if that prevents socialism.[30] Haley added, "[i]ndependent of the fraud—or really along with that argument—Harrisburg [Pennsylvania], Madison [Wisconsin], and Lansing [Michigan] do not have to sit idly by and submit themselves to rule by Beijing and Paris," proposing that radio hosts "rally the grassroots to apply pressure to the weak kneed legislators in those states . . ."[31]

McEntee replied "Yes!" and then: "Let's find the contact info for all these people now."[32] Hours later, Haley sent him names and—in most cases—cell phone numbers for top GOP legislators in six States, suggesting ". . . for POTUS to invite them down for a WH meeting . . ."[33] The President would later call several named in that message, including Rusty Bowers and Karen Fann in Arizona; Lee Chatfield and Mike Shirkey in Michigan; and Jake Corman in Pennsylvania.[34]

Others weighed in with the President about a State-focused plan, too. Some were already looking ahead to January 6th.

On November 8th, former Speaker of the House Newt Gingrich met President Trump at the White House.[35] Two days later, he sent a follow-up note to the President's executive assistant titled "please give to POTUS[,] newt."[36] It suggested that "[t]he only way Trump loses is rigged system" and added that President Trump could encourage "GOP legislatures elect not to send in electors," forcing a House vote by State delegations on January 6th that Gingrich expected President Trump would win.[37] Meadows replied: "Thanks Speaker."[38]

Newsmax CEO Christopher Ruddy had President Trump's ear and reportedly spoke with him by phone at least four times before December.[39] He forwarded a memo to other close advisors of the President recommending that the Trump team persuade one or more Republican-led chambers in Arizona, Georgia, Michigan, Pennsylvania, Wisconsin, and even Minnesota to "pick a separate competitive State slate of Electors," which the memo predicted might turn January 6th into "a cat-fight in Congress wherein VP Pence is Presiding."[40]

Attorney and conservative activist Cleta Mitchell was recruited by Mark Meadows immediately after the election to assist the Trump Campaign's legal work.[41] By November 5th, she emailed Dr. John Eastman of Chapman University,[42] who would later play an outsized role pushing a theory about

Photo by Alex Wong/Getty Images

what Vice President Pence could or couldn't do during the January 6th joint session of Congress that is detailed in Chapter 5 of this Report. In her email, Mitchell asked Eastman to write a memo justifying an idea that State legislators "reclaim" the power to pick electors and asked, rhetorically, "Am I crazy?"[43] Dr. Eastman wrote the memo, entitled "The Constitutional Authority of State Legislatures to Choose Electors," and sent it along for sharing "widely."[44]

According to the Office of Presidential Scheduling, President Trump was scheduled to meet in the Oval Office on November 10th with Morgan Warstler and John Robison, Texas entrepreneurs close to former Governor Rick Perry.[45] The next day, Warstler tweeted that he "[w]as in Oval yesterday,"[46] and months later wrote that "I told whole Trump team in Oval" that "State legislatures can choose the electors-no matter what current state law OR state courts say."[47]

After this apparent meeting, John Robison sent the White House an email entitled "URGENT follow up to our Tuesday Meeting with POTUS," that he asked be printed out for the President to "explain the move forward plan for what was discussed."[48] The email stated that "[President Trump] liked the plan we presented to use a parallel path of state legislators," and the attached memo proposed hundreds of briefings for State lawmakers by

President Trump's surrogates and members of the Freedom Caucus.[49] The email envisioned President Trump hosting "4+ MONSTER RALLY-TRIALS" with "[t]ens of thousands of Trump voters staring up at the GOP state legislators from their districts who ALONE control which slate of electors their state will submit," a proposal that seemed to foreshadow the State hearings that Rudolph Giuliani and President Trump championed less than a month later.[50]

Deputy White House Chief of Staff Dan Scavino called Robison's message "Bat. Shit. Crazy," but the President's executive assistant, who was asked to print it for the President, wrote "Printed," and may have shared it with the President anyway.[51]

By then, President Trump was engaged. According to Stepien, his Campaign Manager, the State-focused strategy came up in a November 11th meeting among close advisors as "something to consider."[52] At that point, the election had been called, but the President "was very interested in keeping pathways to victory open, so [Stepien] believe[d] [the President] found the concept intriguing."[53] Then, the plan "just started happening" even though it was something Stepien, "honestly, kind of dismissed at hand," characterizing it as one "of the crazy, crazier ideas that w[as] thrown out, in and around that time."[54]

But not everyone was convinced. On November 19th, the prior Republican Presidential nominee, Senator Mitt Romney (R-UT), issued a harsh public condemnation of President Trump's open and notorious efforts to overturn the election:

> Having failed to make even a plausible case of widespread fraud or conspiracy before a court of law, the President has now resorted to overt pressure on state and local officials to subvert the will of the people and overturn the election. It is difficult to imagine a worse, more undemocratic action by a sitting American President.[55]

Senator Romney was right to identify and decry President Trump's actions. And yet, in hindsight, it is clear that the effort to pressure State and local officials by the Trump team was only just getting started.

2.3 OUTREACH AND IMPLEMENTATION OF THE PLAN

Just one day after the State-focused plan came up in the Oval Office with the President and his top lieutenants, President Trump started taking concrete steps aimed at State legislators. And in the weeks that followed, the

President spearheaded outreach aimed at numerous officials in States he lost but that had GOP-led legislatures, including in Michigan, Pennsylvania, Georgia, and Arizona.

The Select Committee estimates that in the two months between the November election and the January 6th insurrection, President Trump or his inner circle engaged in at least 200 apparent acts of public or private outreach, pressure, or condemnation, targeting either State legislators or State or local election administrators, to overturn State election results. This included at least:

- 68 meetings, attempted or connected phone calls, or text messages, each aimed at one or more State or local officials;
- 18 instances of prominent public remarks, with language targeting one or more such officials;[56] and
- 125 social media posts by President Trump or senior aides targeting one or more such officials, either explicitly or implicitly, and mostly from his own account.[57]

Furthermore, these efforts by President Trump's team also involved two other initiatives that tried to enlist support from large numbers of State legislators all at once:

- The Trump Campaign contacted, or attempted to contact, nearly 200 State legislators from battleground States between November 30, 2020 and December 3, 2020, to solicit backing for possible Statehouse resolutions to overturn the election. At least some messages said they were "on behalf of the president." [58]
- Nearly 300 State legislators from battleground States reportedly participated in a private briefing with President Trump, Rudolph Giuliani, John Eastman, and others on January 2nd. The President reportedly urged them to exercise what he called "the real power" to choose electoral votes before January 6th, because, as President Trump said on the call, "I don't think the country is going to take it." [59]

It may be impossible to document each and every meeting, phone call, text message, or other contact that President Trump and his allies had with State and local officials in various battleground States. What follows is a summary that focuses on four States and that demonstrates the lengths to which President Trump would go in order to stay in power based on lies—the Big Lie—about the election.

PRESIDENT TRUMP'S EARLY PRESSURE ON PUBLIC SERVANTS

To carry out his plan, President Trump, Rudolph Giuliani, and other surrogates of President Trump publicly and privately sought assistance from State and local officials whom they assumed would help as Republicans on the same team with the "same goal." [60] Some helped. Others didn't.

On November 12th, U.S. Representative Tim Walberg (R–MI) sent an email to President Trump's Executive Assistant Molly Michael, describing a request he had received earlier that day:

> During my conversation with the President this morning he asked me to check with key leadership in Michigan's Legislature as to how supportive they could be in regards to pushing back on election irregularities and potential fraud. He wanted me to gauge their willingness to talk with him about efforts to bring about transparency and integrity in Michigan's election and report back to him.[61]

Representative Walberg added that he had already acted on this request: "I've had conversations with [Michigan] Speaker Lee Chatfield, Senate Majority Leader Mike Shirkey, and Senate President Pro Tempore Aric Nesbitt. They all assured me they would look forward to speaking with the President to report on their continuing efforts" related to overseeing the election "and receiving any suggestions from President Trump." [62] The President would soon host Chatfield, Shirkey, Nesbitt, and four other Michigan State lawmakers at the White House.[63]

In Arizona, on November 13, 2020, the day after officials finished counting ballots cast in Maricopa County, Chairwoman Kelli Ward, of the Arizona Republican Party, texted Mark Meadows that she had "[j]ust talked to POTUS" and that "[h]e may call the Chairman of the Maricopa Board of Supervisors," Clint Hickman.[64] Ward also left a message for Hickman that said, "I just talked to President Trump, and he would like me to talk to you and also see if he needs to give you a call to discuss what's happening on the ground in Maricopa. Give me a call back when you can." [65] According to Hickman, Ward was unusually active after the election, even for a party chair, and was the first person to pressure him. One of her first messages to Hickman before trying to connect him with President Trump was: "We need you to stop the counting." [66]

In Georgia, the President initially took a more public approach. After the Associated Press called the race there on November 12th, President Trump tweeted harsh criticisms of Governor Brian Kemp and Secretary of State Brad Raffensperger.[67] Often these tweets called for them to take specific actions that would have shifted the election results in his favor, such as rejecting a court settlement (which he referred to as a consent decree) that dictated the procedures for verifying signatures on absentee ballots. And he was relentless.

In November alone, President Trump tweeted that Raffensperger was "a so-called Republican (RINO)" and asked "Where is @BrianKempGA," [68] before suggesting that "They knew they were going to cheat." [69] He called to "Break the unconstitutional Consent Decree!" [70] and urged stricter signature matches with a demand to "Get it done! @BrianKempGA." [71] He called Kemp "hapless" and asked why he wouldn't use emergency powers to overrule Raffensperger on the signature-verification procedures, declaring that "Georgia Republicans are angry." [72] President Trump also retweeted posts asking, "Who needs Democrats when you have Republicans like Brian Kemp," and "why bother voting for Republicans if what you get is Ducey and Kemp?" [73]

Pennsylvania was an early, but not unique, example of how President Trump's State-pressure campaign affected the lives of the public servants running this country's elections.

On November 7th, Rudy Giuliani headlined a Philadelphia press conference in front of a landscaping business called Four Seasons Total Landscaping, near a crematorium and down the street from a sex shop.[74]

Standing in front of former New York Police Commissioner and recently-pardoned convicted felon, Bernard Kerik, Giuliani gave opening remarks and handed the podium over to his first supposed eyewitness to election fraud, who turned out to be a convicted sex offender.[75] Giuliani claimed "at least 600,000 ballots are in question" in Pennsylvania and falsely suggested that large numbers of ballots in the State had been cast for dead people, including boxer Joe Frazier and actor Will Smith's father.[76]

Within days, Republican Philadelphia City Commissioner Al Schmidt and others publicly debunked Giuliani's specific allegations of election fraud, including the claims about dead people voting in Pennsylvania elections.[77] In reaction, President Trump tweeted on the morning of November 11th that "[a] guy named Al Schmidt, a Philadelphia Commissioner and so-called Republican (RINO), is being used big time by the Fake News Media to explain how honest things were with respect to the Election in Philadelphia. He refuses to look at a mountain of corruption & dishonesty. We win!" [78]

That statement targeting Schmidt led to a deluge of threatening and harassing phone calls and emails by people who heard President Trump and falsely held out hope that Schmidt or someone else could overturn the results of Pennsylvania's election.[79]

As a public official, Schmidt was no stranger to threats. But being targeted by the President of the United States was different. In Schmidt's public testimony to the Select Committee, he described why. "[P]rior to that the threats were pretty general in nature. 'Corrupt election officials in Philadelphia are going to get what's coming to them'" and other similar threats.[80] "After the President tweeted at me by name, calling me out the way that he did," Schmidt explained, "the threats became much more specific, much more graphic, and included not just me by name but included members of my family by name, their ages, our address, pictures of our home. Just every bit of detail that you could imagine." [81]

As the President continued to push the Big Lie and vilify public officials, such threats multiplied.

EFFORTS TO PREVENT STATE AND LOCAL OFFICIALS FROM CERTIFYING THE ELECTION
Some of President Trump's early outreach was part of an effort to prevent State and local officials from certifying his loss. One example comes from Michigan, and the other from Arizona.

Wayne County, Michigan, includes Detroit and its surrounding areas. On November 17th, the county's Board of Canvassers met to certify election results, a process the Michigan Supreme Court described over a century ago as ministerial and clerical.[82]

The meeting started at 6:00 p.m. and lasted over three hours.[83] Its two Republican members, Board Chair Monica Palmer and Board Member William Hartmann, first voted to block the certification of the election.[84] After a brief break, Palmer and Hartmann returned, changed their votes, and certified the election results.[85] Just over twenty minutes later, Palmer and Hartmann received a call from President Trump and RNC Chair Ronna McDaniel.[86]

Palmer claimed that the call "was not pressure." Rather, she said, "[i]t was genuine concern for my safety" and "there were general comments about different States, but we really didn't discuss the details of the certification." [87]

The Select Committee doesn't know exactly what President Trump privately said on that phone call.[88] By the next evening, however, Palmer and Hartmann had each issued signed affidavits reassuming their earlier position that Wayne County's results should not be certified.[89] Palmer's affidavit even declared that "I rescind my prior vote," though rescinding wasn't possible and her statement had no legal effect.[90] And, President Trump apparently knew before it was public that Hartmann and Palmer would try to change their votes; almost eight hours *before* either of these affidavits were publicly released, President Trump tweeted that these "two harassed patriot Canvassers refuse to sign the papers!" [91]

Republicans in Arizona experienced similar treatment. In the most populous and electorally significant county in Arizona, Maricopa County's Board of Supervisors met on November 20th to certify the county's election results. Their Board, made up of four Republicans and one Democrat, carefully reviewed the official canvass, asked questions for approximately two hours, then unanimously voted to certify the results.[92]

Earlier that day, Kelli Ward contacted two of the board's members, Jack Sellers and Bill Gates, and asked them to delay the certification on the basis of supposed improprieties.[93] According to Sellers and Gates, however, Arizona law required certification that day and they had no information (neither then, nor ever) to doubt the county's election results.[94]

When Arizona certified its 2020 statewide election results on November 30th, it fell to Governor Doug Ducey, a Republican, to sign the certification. While on camera during the signing ceremony, Governor Ducey's phone played a ringtone for the song "Hail to the Chief," which he immediately silenced.[95]

The Governor later confirmed it had been President Trump calling and that he returned the President's call shortly afterwards, but declined to say what the two discussed other than saying that President Trump did not ask him to withhold certification.[96] The Select Committee does not know whether that is true, but that evening President Trump blasted Ducey on Twitter, accusing him of "rushing to put a Democrat in office," and warning that "Republicans will long remember!"[97] The President also retweeted posts bashing Ducey and his Georgia counterpart Brian Kemp, which asked "Who needs Democrats when you have Republicans like Brian Kemp and Doug Ducey?", "why bother voting for Republicans if what you get is Ducey and Kemp?", and "Brian Kemp: 'My state ran the most corrupt election in American history.' Doug Ducey: 'Hold my beer.'"[98] President Trump even commented "TRUE!" when retweeting a post that "Gov Ducey has betrayed the people of Arizona."[99]

Governor Ducey pushed back, writing on Twitter that, "I've been pretty outspoken about Arizona's election system, and bragged about it quite a bit, including in the Oval Office . . . In Arizona, we have some of the strongest election laws in the country . . . The problems that exist in other states simply don't apply here."[100] Governor Ducey explained the law for certifying elections in Arizona and pointed out that the certification now triggered a "5-day window for any elector to bring a credible challenge to the election results in court. If you want to contest the results, now is the time. Bring your challenges."[101] And, Governor Ducey referenced his oath of office:

Photo by Samuel Corum/Getty Images

"That's the law. I've sworn an oath to uphold it, and I take my responsibility seriously."[102] President Trump and his allies never brought a credible challenge and, instead, lost every case they brought challenging the results in Arizona.

EFFORTS TO REPLACE ELECTORAL COLLEGE ELECTORS AND OVERTURN THE ELECTION
Once counties and States certified the election, or when it was nearly certain that they would, President Trump and his team's focus largely shifted. President Trump and his team encouraged State legislators to meet in special sessions, if necessary, and choose electoral college electors who would vote for the Trump/Pence ticket. Ultimately, no State legislature took that step, but it was the basis for pressuring State officials from November through January 6, 2021.

MEETINGS WITH STATE LEGISLATORS—THE "HEARINGS"
The concept of State legislators appointing their own electors featured prominently in a series of hastily arranged official and unofficial "hearings" with State legislators that the Trump team announced on November 24, 2020.[103]

On November 25th, President Trump called in to an unofficial meeting with legislators in Gettysburg, Pennsylvania.[104] The meeting was set up to appear like an official hearing, but it was not. It took place in a hotel ball-room, and those presenting arguments or purported evidence, like Giuliani, Jenna Ellis, and others, were not placed under oath.[105] According to President *Pro Tempore* of the Pennsylvania Senate Jake Corman, he had initially been asked by State Senator Doug Mastriano to hold a hearing about the election. Corman responded that any formal hearing should be official, with sworn testimony, and open to both parties.[106] That was not what Senator Mastriano ultimately convened.

President Trump had originally made plans to attend the Pennsylvania gathering in person, but he cancelled after several advisors tested positive for COVID-19.[107] When President Trump called in and spoke to those gathered in the hotel ballroom, his false claims were met with cheers, and he made his purpose clear: "this election has to be turned around . . . Why wouldn't they overturn an election? Certainly overturn it in your State . . . We have to turn the election over." [108]

President Trump made the ask and Giuliani told the legislators how to carry it out. Giuliani told the assembled legislators that it was their "power" and "responsibility" to pick Pennsylvania's presidential electors and that "[they] have to convince the rest of [their] members, Republican and Democrat, they owe that to the people of" Pennsylvania.[109] Jenna Ellis told them that although Pennsylvania law dictates that electors are chosen by popular vote, "[y]ou can take that power back at any time. You don't need a court to tell you that." [110]

President Trump invited some of the lawmakers to come meet him at the White House that evening and, according to Giuliani, it was "a large group" that went.[111] Special Assistant to the President Cassidy Hutchinson's text messages with Kerik included the guest list and descriptions of the vehicles that would need access to the White House grounds.[112] Pennsylvania State Senator Doug Mastriano drove one car, a hired driver drove a van with most of the State legislators, and Kerik drove an SUV with attorney Katherine Friess and election-conspiracy proponent Phil Waldron.[113] Hutchinson estimated that at least 29 visitors traveled from Pennsylvania to the White House that day, and she explained that their conversation with the President touched on holding a special session of the State legislature to appoint Trump electors.[114]

Just a few days later, on November 30, 2020, President Trump also called into another one of Giuliani and Jenna Ellis's hotel "hearings," this time in Arizona. Several Arizona State lawmakers hosted the meeting at a Hyatt Regency in Phoenix after they did not receive permission to organize an official hearing at the State Capitol.[115] Before the hearing started, State GOP Representative Mark Finchem "promised information to show that the state's 11 electoral votes should not go to Democrat Joe Biden," and argued that "the U.S. Constitution empowers lawmakers to decide, on their own, whether the election was valid and, if not, to select the electors of their choice." [116]

Giuliani told the assembled legislators that the officials certifying Arizona's election results "have made no effort to find out" if the results of the election were accurate, "which seems to me gives the state legislature a perfect reason to take over the conduct of this election because it's being conducted irresponsibly and unfairly." [117] Likewise, Jenna Ellis said that it was "not just the choice, but the actual duty and obligation of the legislature to step in and to make sure that you don't certify false results." [118] During a recess, she also took to Twitter, writing, "[t]he certification of Arizona's FALSE results is unethical and knowingly participating in the corruption that has disenfranchised AZ voters. BUT, this in no way impacts the state legislature's ability to take back the proper selection of delegates." [119]

When it was President Trump's turn to address this handful of lawmakers over the phone, he called them "legends for taking this on," and used the opportunity to criticize Governor Ducey: "you'll have to figure out what's that all about with Ducey. He couldn't [certify] fast enough" and "Arizona will not forget what Ducey just did. We're not gonna forget." [120] That night Giuliani joined President Trump in criticizing Governor Ducey, while at the same time making baseless allegations about voting machines in Arizona and calling for a special legislative session to change the outcome of the election: "Governor Ducey of Arizona refuses to meet with me. He doesn't want to explain that he selected a foreign corrupt Voting Machine company to count the vote. I understand his reluctance, but [sic] just call a special session. Let's find out how crooked your election really was?" [121]

Michigan was next. Giuliani's team announced that the Michigan legislature would hold a hearing on December 1st, but the relevant committee chair excluded Giuliani because it was only open to witnesses "with first hand knowledge." [122] That chairman, Michigan State Senator Edward McBroom (R-Vulcan), had already held Senate Oversight hearings by then in an actual effort to evaluate claims of fraud in the 2020 election, which ultimately resulted in a comprehensive report that concluded that the Republican-led committee "found no evidence of widespread or systematic fraud" in Michigan's election. [123]

Michigan's House Oversight Committee, however, did allow Giuliani to testify in a hearing on December 2nd. Before the hearing, Giuliani joined the State's GOP chairwoman to give what was billed as a legal briefing. In the online presentation, Giuliani told the audience there's "nothing wrong with putting pressure on your state legislators"[124] to pick new electors and that "you have got to get them to remember that their oath to the Constitution sometimes requires being criticized. Sometimes it even requires being threatened."[125]

When Giuliani appeared for the hearing in Michigan, he was not placed under oath, used his time to refer to Michigan's election as a "con job," and urged legislators to "have the courage to say that certification that was done by your state is a complete phony."[126] The information presented was baseless—and sometimes racist—conspiracy theories. One witness brought to criticize Michigan's voter verification even said: "I think Chinese all look alike. So how would you tell? If some Chow shows up, you can be anybody and you can vote."[127] And, as he had promised in the legal briefing the day before, Giuliani then called on the legislators to do what the Trump Campaign had reportedly been discussing since before election day. He said that the State legislature could still singlehandedly decide the election result "anytime you want to. Anytime. You can take it back tonight. You can take it back the day before the electors go down to Washington."[128] Jenna Ellis also participated, insisting "no honest person can hear these citizens of your own state today . . . and can let this proceed. What the Constitution obligates you to do is to take back your plenary power."[129]

Finally, Georgia. There, Giuliani and others appeared in multiple hearings, the first of which was held on December 3, 2020. In that hearing, Giuliani was direct and called on Georgia legislators to overturn the election results—"you are the final arbiter of who the electors should be"—based on the false premise that "there is more than ample evidence to conclude that this election was a sham."[130] Then, at a separate hearing on December 10th, he told State legislators that Georgia's Governor, Lieutenant Governor, and secretary of State were engaged in a "cover up" of "a crime in plain sight," and that it fell to "the state legislature [ ] to vindicate the honor of the state."[131] And, Giuliani used yet another appearance, on December 30th, to call the 2020 election "the most crooked election, the most manipulated election in American history," and implore the Republican legislators to hold a special session to vote on appointing new electors, something he said that they could do "right up until the last moment" before January 6th.[132]

More perniciously, Giuliani also used these hearings to advance conspiracy theories that falsely accused Fulton County election workers of rigging Georgia's election results. His delegation to the December 3rd hearing played clips of election-night surveillance footage from the State Farm

Arena that showed election workers scanning ballots, sometimes after partisan poll watchers had gone home.[133] Although the poll watchers should have been there the entire time while election workers counted the votes, there was nothing nefarious about the circumstances and no question about the end result. In fact, the FBI, Department of Justice, and Georgia Bureau of Investigation would determine that these ballots were legitimate ballots, that observers were not illegally ejected, and that the ballots were scanned and counted properly, contrary to claims by President Trump and his attorneys.[134] And yet Giuliani baselessly declared at the December 3rd hearing that, to him, the video was a "powerful smoking gun" proving that "those votes are not legitimate votes."[135]

But Giuliani's claims took a more ominous turn during the December 10th hearing. There, he publicly named two of the election workers shown in the video, Ruby Freeman and her daughter, Wandrea ArShaye "Shaye" Moss, and accused them of vote-tampering and engaging in criminal conduct.[136] He seized on a clip of Freeman passing Moss a ginger mint, claiming that the two women, both Black, were smuggling USB drives "as if they're vials of heroin or cocaine." He also suggested that Freeman and Moss should be jailed and that they deserved to have their homes searched.[137] Not only were Giuliani's claims about Freeman and Moss reckless, racist, and false, they had real-world consequences that turned both women's lives upside down. And further heightening the personal impact of these baseless attacks, President Trump supported, and even repeated, them, as described later.

In the end, the hearings were widely panned. In Michigan alone, current and former Republican lawmakers publicly questioned the hearings and implored President Trump and his team to stop. U.S. Representative Paul Mitchell (R-Mich.) implored on Twitter "Please JUST STOP!" and "wondered why Republican leaders allowed testimony he said was 'driving the party into this ditch.'"[138] Similarly, former Michigan lawmaker Martin Howrylak (R-Oakland) said that he was "embarrassed" by the hearing, and former Michigan Senator Ken Sikkema (R-Grand Rapids) said that "the way the committee was run was atrocious."[139] Later, the President promoted a tweet calling a Democratic lawmaker a "#pos" for speaking out at the Michigan hearing.[140] Months later, Giuliani's license to practice law in New York was suspended for, among other reasons, the "false claims" he made on various dates, including during the hearings in Michigan, Pennsylvania, Arizona, and Georgia.[141]

THE TRUMP CAMPAIGN'S BARRAGE OF PHONE CALLS TO STATE LEGISLATORS

Not only was replacing electors a theme during the official and unofficial State hearings, it was also a critical component of President Trump's plan both before and after the hearings took place.

In fact, while the hearings were happening, the Trump Campaign set up an operation to contact hundreds of State legislators and ask them to support an effort to appoint electoral college electors for the Trump/Pence ticket in States that President Trump had lost.

On the same day as Giuliani's hearing in Michigan, Trump Campaign staff contacted dozens of Republicans in Michigan's State legislature. A Trump Campaign supervisor sent text messages to his team, directing them to reach out to lawmakers "to explain the process for legislative redress and tell them how to send representative[s] to th[e] electoral college."[142] He added: "We're gonna be lobbyists. Woot."[143]

According to a Campaign staffer's spreadsheet produced to the Select Committee, the Trump Campaign apparently tried contacting over 190 Republican State legislators in Arizona, Georgia, and Michigan, alone.[144]

One voicemail left as part of this initiative was leaked to the press on December 1, 2020. In it, a Trump Campaign staffer said, "I did want to personally reach out to you on behalf of the President."[145] Her main point came later in the message: "we want to know when there is a resolution in the House to appoint electors for Trump if the President can count on you to join in support."[146] Another message from this effort that reached reporters made the same ask and claimed that, "[a]fter a roundtable with the President, he asked us to reach out to you individually" to whip support for a "joint resolution from the State House and Senate" that would "allow Michigan to send electors for Donald J. Trump to the Electoral College and save our country."[147]

Soon after the voicemail leaked, the Campaign staffer who left this voicemail got a text message from one of her supervisors, who wrote: "Honest to god I'm so proud of this" because "[t]hey unwittingly just got your message out there."[148] He elaborated: "you used the awesome power of the presidency to scare a state rep into getting a statewide newspaper to deliver your talking points."[149]

OUTREACH BY PRESIDENT TRUMP AND SENIOR AIDES

While Campaign aides blanketed State officials with these calls, some State officials received more personalized outreach directly from President Trump, Giuliani, and their allies throughout the post-election period about this issue.

Michigan. As discussed earlier, Rep. Walberg reached out to State legislators in Michigan at the President's request in mid-November, including Senate Majority Leader Mike Shirkey and House Speaker Lee Chatfield. By November 18th, President Trump called Chatfield and Shirkey to invite them to what would become a meeting for a group of Michigan lawmakers in the Oval Office.[150] Although President Trump didn't tell Shirkey what the meeting would be about, the President was focused on the election and asked Shirkey what he and others were doing to investigate election fraud.[151] The meeting happened on November 20th.[152]

In Shirkey's words, there "wasn't a mystery" about why the group was at the White House once the meeting started.[153] When the President mentioned several baseless claims of election fraud in Wayne County, Shirkey told the President that he had lost the election and that it had nothing to do with Wayne County, where he had actually performed better than he had in 2016.[154]

From the President's body language, Shirkey concluded that wasn't what he wanted to hear. But the meeting continued, and the President dialed in Giuliani, who delivered a "long monologue," reciting a "litany" of allegations about supposed fraud that was short on substance.[155] Shirkey challenged Giuliani, asking "when are you going to . . . file a lawsuit in Michigan," which he said Giuliani did not answer.[156] Although Shirkey says he did not recall the President making any precise "ask," Chatfield recalled President Trump's more generic directive for the group to "have some backbone and do the right thing."[157] Chatfield understood that to mean they should investigate claims of fraud and overturn the election by naming electors for President Trump.[158] Shirkey told the President that he was not going to do anything that would violate Michigan law.[159]

After the meeting ended, Shirkey and Chatfield issued a joint statement: "We have not yet been made aware of any information that would change the outcome of the election in Michigan and as legislative leaders, we will follow the law and follow the normal process regarding Michigan's electors, just as we have said throughout this election."[160]

That was not the end, however. Chatfield and Shirkey received numerous calls from the President in the weeks following the election. Chatfield told the Select Committee that he received approximately five to ten phone calls from President Trump after the election, during which the President would usually ask him about various allegations of voter fraud.[161] Chatfield said that he repeatedly looked into the President's claims but never found anything persuasive that could have changed the outcome of the election.[162]

President Trump's calls were not enough, so he turned to the public. On January 3, 2021, the Trump Campaign posted a tweet that urged supporters

Photo by Rey Del Rio/Getty Images

to "Contact Speaker Lee Chatfield & Senate Majority Leader Mike Shirkey" to "Demand [a] vote on decertification." [163] Why President Trump thought the Michigan legislature would convene to decertify the election in a matter of hours when it had refused to do so since early November is not clear. But that didn't stop the President from making things personal. The President's January 3rd tweet included Shirkey's personal cellphone number as well as a number for Chatfield that turned out to be wrong. As a result, Shirkey said he received nearly 4,000 text messages, and another private citizen reported being inundated with calls and texts intended for Chatfield.[164]

Pennsylvania. On November 21st, Mark Meadows texted a number apparently belonging to Representative Scott Perry (R–PA) and asked: "Can you send me the number for the speaker and the leader of the PA Legislature. POTUS wants to chat with them." [165] Hours later, Meadows received a response of "Yes sir." [166] At the time, the leader of the Pennsylvania Senate was Jake Corman and the Speaker of the Pennsylvania House was Bryan Cutler.

Corman told the Select Committee that he received a call on Thanksgiving Day 2020 from Giuliani, urging him to call the legislature into a special session to replace Biden electors with Trump electors.[167] This idea wasn't new to Corman. President Trump and his allies had gone public about their intentions before then, including during the Pennsylvania hotel hearing, but Corman had braced himself for this even before the election. Before election day in 2020, a reporter from *The Atlantic* interviewed Corman and other prominent Republicans in Pennsylvania about the possibility that President Trump would try to circumvent the popular vote in swing States by asking the legislatures to appoint Trump/Pence electors. After the article, Corman drafted an op-ed, making it clear that the Pennsylvania legislature did not have the legal authority to appoint Trump/Pence electors in contravention of the popular vote, a position that he would generally maintain through the 2020 Presidential election cycle.[168]

During that call, Giuliani first tried "pumping [Corman] up as a patriot" before asking the Senator to call the Pennsylvania legislature into a special session. Corman told Giuliani that he did not have the authority to do that, a position with which his own lawyers agreed.[169] Giuliani's reply was that Corman must have bad lawyers. Corman said he offered to connect Giuliani with his legal team. His legal team spoke with Giuliani and a lawyer working with him, Jenna Ellis, the following day, reiterating their view that such a move by the legislature would be illegal.[170] That same day, or possibly the next, Giuliani and Ellis called him back to renew their request for a special legislative session and to demean Corman's attorneys, calling them "terrible," "bad," and "wrong."[171] Corman, however, held his ground and ended the call.[172]

While packing to return to Pennsylvania from his Thanksgiving visit to Florida, Corman says he received a call from an unknown number with a Washington, DC area code, which he let go to voicemail.[173] It turned out to be a White House operator calling on behalf of President Trump.[174]

Corman called back and spoke to President Trump, who insisted that he had won the election in Pennsylvania and said something to the effect of, "Jake, this is a big issue. We need your help."[175] Corman told the President that he couldn't do what the Trump team was asking; President Trump replied, "I'm not sure your attorneys are very good."[176] Corman wanted to end the call and offered to have his lawyers speak again with President Trump's, but they never had another call with the President's lawyers.[177]

Pennsylvania House Speaker Bryan Cutler was another main target for the President's team. He received voicemails in late November for four days in a row from Giuliani and/or Jenna Ellis, which he provided to the Select Committee.[178] Cutler explained that he did not feel comfortable talking with the President's team in case he ended up having to preside over a legislative session about the election, and he had his attorneys relay that to the President's team.[179] Giuliani received the message but continued to call Speaker Cutler nonetheless.[180]

In the first of these voicemails, on November 26th, Giuliani asked to "get together, quietly" to discuss "the amount of fraud that went on in your State," and said that Giuliani and Ellis had also just spoken to Pennsylvania House Majority Leader Kerry Benninghoff.[181] On November 27th, Ellis called and said in a second voicemail that they had just talked to Pennsylvania House Member Russ Diamond and were "very grateful" to the State's legislature "for doing your Article II duty."[182] On November 28th, Giuliani left a third voicemail and claimed to have "something important" that "really changes things," and said that "the president wanted me to make sure I got it to you."[183] And then on November 29th, Giuliani left a fourth message and said, "I understand that you don't want to talk to me now" but still sought "the courtesy of being able to talk to you as the president's lawyer" and a "fellow Republican" because "you're certifying what is a blatantly false statement . . . I can't imagine how that's in your interests or in the interests of our party."[184]

Giuliani and Ellis didn't get through, but the President did. "[I]f we wanted to do something, what were the options[?]" the President asked Cutler.[185] Cutler explained to President Trump that he could file a legal challenge contesting the election, and asked the President why his team had never requested a statewide recount.[186] Cutler was also clear about the "constitutional peculiarities" of Pennsylvania, where the State constitution specifically prohibits retroactive changes to how electors are chosen.[187]

Practically, President Trump's call achieved nothing. The President wasn't getting what he wanted in his calls to leaders in Pennsylvania: a special session of the legislature to appoint Trump/Pence electors.

Seemingly undeterred, President Trump invited several leaders of the Pennsylvania legislature to the White House for Christmas gatherings.[188] Senator Corman decided not to go, although Speaker Cutler did. President Trump spoke with Cutler on December 3rd, while Cutler, his chief of staff, and their wives were at that White House Christmas tour.[189] The issue of overturning the results of Pennsylvania's election came up again, as did the possibility of a special session of the State legislature to appoint Trump electors.[190] Cutler told the President that the State legislature could not reconvene without an order from the Governor and a petition from a super-majority of legislators, neither of which was likely to happen.[191] Cutler also told the President that they could not appoint new electors without a court order. In Cutler's opinion, President Trump "seemed to understand. And that was—that was clear."[192] The President's apparent understanding, however, did not result in any meaningful changes to his public rhetoric.

On December 3rd, the same day that Cutler met with President Trump, Cutler, Corman, House Majority Leader Benninghoff, and Senate Majority

Leader Kim Ward issued a three-page single-spaced joint statement asserting, in no uncertain terms, that Pennsylvania's General Assembly "lacks
the authority . . . to overturn the popular vote and appoint our own slate of
electors," since "[d]oing so would violate our Election Code and Constitution, particularly a provision that prohibits us from changing the rules for
election contests of the President after the election." [193] In response, President Trump retweeted a December 4th post by Bernard Kerik, which tagged
all four of these State legislators with the hashtag "Traitors," and declared
that "These are the four cowardice[sic] Pennsylvania legislators that intend
to allow the Democrat machine to #StealtheVote! #Cowards #Liars #Trai-
tors." [194]

But five days later, President Trump publicly thanked Cutler for signing
onto a December 4th letter that encouraged Members of Congress from
Pennsylvania to object to their State's electoral votes on January 6th. The
President tweeted: "Thank you to Speaker Cutler and all others in Pennsylvania and elsewhere who fully understand what went on in the 2020 election. It's called total corruption!" [195] When the Select Committee asked
Cutler about this apparent change in his position, he said that he signed on
to this letter not because of concerns that fraud or corruption meant the
results of the election Pennsylvania were wrong, but rather because of concerns about "programmatic changes or areas for improvement" related to
the election.[196] In fact, Cutler reiterated to the Committee that he "was not
personally aware of" any widespread election fraud that would have
changed the result of the election.[197]

The pressure facing State legislators during this period was significant.
On December 9th, the *New York Times* quoted Pennsylvania's Senate Majority Leader Kim Ward, revealing that she too had received a call from President Trump in which he pushed his election fraud narrative.[198] Ward told
the *Times* that she hadn't been given enough time to sign the same December 4th letter that Cutler did, but commented that if she had taken a stand
against it, "I'd get my house bombed tonight." [199]

Arizona. In late November, Arizona House Speaker Russell "Rusty" Bowers,
a longtime Republican who served 17 years in the State legislature, received
a call from President Trump and Giuliani.[200] Giuliani alleged that Arizona's
election results were skewed by illicit ballots, cast by non-citizens or on
behalf of dead people.[201] Bowers demanded proof for these audacious
claims on the call and President Trump told Giuliani to comply, but the evidence never came.[202] The point of the call, however, was different. Like in
Michigan and Pennsylvania, President Trump and his allies were working
the phones to get something. They wanted Bowers to hold a public hearing

Photo by House Creative Services

with the ultimate aim of replacing Presidential electors for former Vice President Joe Biden with electors for President Trump.[203]

Bowers had never heard of anything like that before, and Giuliani acknowledged that it had never been done. Where President Trump and Giuliani saw a potential opportunity, however, Bowers saw a fundamental problem.

As Bowers explained it, what they wanted him to do was "counter to my oath when I swore to the Constitution to uphold it." [204] And he said that to the President and Giuliani: "you are asking me to do something against my oath, and I will not break my oath." [205] Giuliani replied: "aren't we all Republicans here? I mean, I would think you would listen a little more open to my suggestions, that we're all Republicans." [206]

The pressure didn't stop with that call. On December 1st, Giuliani and Ellis got an audience with some of the most powerful Republican lawmakers in Arizona, including Bowers, Senate President Karen Fann, Senate President Pro Tempore Vince Leach, House Majority Leader and Senator-Elect Warren Petersen, Senate Majority Whip Sonny Borrelli, Senator Michelle Ugenti-Rita, and others.[207] The Select Committee was unable to get Giuliani and Ellis' perspective on this outreach because Giuliani claimed that his communications with Bowers—who was not his client nor part of his legal team—were "privileged," while Ellis invoked her Fifth Amendment rights against self-incrimination.[208]

Bowers, on the other hand, told the Select Committee that Giuliani and Ellis asked the lawmakers to deliver Arizona's electors for President Trump, despite the certified popular vote count.[209] To bolster their request, Giuliani and Ellis raised numerous allegations of election fraud at the meeting, though they never produced evidence in support of their claims. In live testimony before the Committee, Bowers recalled Giuliani saying in this meeting that "we've got lots of theories, we just don't have the evidence." [210] At the time, Bowers didn't know whether it was a gaffe or an example of Giuliani not thinking through what he had just said.[211] In any event, Bowers said he and others in his group made particular note of that comment.[212] And it was borne out; Bowers testified that "No one provided me, ever, such evidence." [213]

In late December, in another phone call with President Trump, Bowers reiterated that he would not do anything illegal for him.[214] Afterward, John Eastman joined the chorus of Trump allies attempting to change his mind. In a call on January 4th that included the Speaker's chief counsel as well as Arizona House Majority Leader-Elect Ben Toma, Eastman urged Bowers to hold a vote to decertify Arizona's Presidential electors.[215] When Bowers told Eastman he couldn't unilaterally reconvene the legislature, Eastman urged him to "just do it and let the court sort it out." [216] Bowers refused and the Arizona legislature took no such action.

Many of President Trump's efforts in Arizona focused on State officials, but his team also continued to reach out to the Board of Supervisors for Maricopa County even after it certified the election. One focus was voting machines. According to the *Arizona Republic*, Giuliani left a voicemail in mid- to late-December for Board Member Steve Chucri that "I see we're gonna get a chance to take a good look at those machines . . . give me a call as soon as you get a chance. The president also wanted me to pass on a few things to you, too." [217] On December 4th, Giuliani also left a message for the Board's Chairman Clint Hickman: "I was very happy to see that there's gonna be a forensic audit of the machines. And I really wanted to talk to you about it a bit. The President wanted me to give you a call. All right? Thank you. Give me a call back." [218] Hickman chose not to call back.[219]

Then, on Christmas Eve, Giuliani left voicemails for Board Members Bill Gates and Jack Sellers, asking them to call him back. In his message for Gates, Giuliani said:

> It's Giuliani, President Trump's lawyer. If you get a chance, would you please give me a call? I have a few things I'd like to talk over with you. Maybe we can get this thing fixed up. You know, I really

think it's a shame that Republicans sort of are both in this, kind of, situation. And I think there may be a nice way to resolve this for everybody.[220]

In his message for Sellers, Giuliani said "I'd like to see if there is a way that we can resolve this so that it comes out well for everyone. We're all Republicans, I think we all have the same goal. Let's see if . . . we can get this done outside of the court." [221] Like Hickman, neither Gates nor Sellers returned Giuliani's calls.[222]

So President Trump made the call himself. On December 31st, Board Chair Clint Hickman received a voicemail from the White House switchboard, asking him to call back for President Trump. Hickman said that he did not return the call, in part because the county was still facing litigation over the election.[223] Another call from the White House came through on January 3rd with a request that Hickman call back for the President. But, by then, the President's call with Georgia Secretary of State Brad Raffensperger, described below, had leaked, and Hickman "didn't want to walk into that space." [224]

Georgia. On December 5th, President Trump traveled to Georgia to headline a rally and mobilize voters in advance of a January Senate runoff. But the President's day started with a morning call to Governor Brian Kemp during which they discussed reconvening the legislature in a special session.[225] After the call, Kemp took to Twitter. He acknowledged that he had spoken to the President and that he told the President that he supported the idea of, and had already called for, a signature audit in Georgia.[226] President Trump responded later that night by complaining that Georgia had not yet done a signature-verification audit and instead insisted that the Governor should "[a]t least immediately ask for a Special Session of the Legislature." [227] The following day, Governor Kemp and Lieutenant Governor Geoff Duncan issued a definitive statement rejecting President Trump and his allies' calls to overturn the results in Georgia:

> While we understand four members of the Georgia Senate are requesting the convening of a special session of the General Assembly, doing this in order to select a separate slate of presidential electors is not an option that is allowed under state or federal law.
>
> State law is clear: the legislature could only direct an alternative method for choosing presidential electors if the election was not able to be held on the date set by federal law. In the 1960s, the General Assembly decided that Georgia's presidential electors will be determined by the winner of the State's popular vote. Any attempt

by the legislature to retroactively change that process for the
November 3rd election would be unconstitutional and immediately
enjoined by the courts, resulting in a long legal dispute and no
short-term resolution.[228]

President Trump responded by directing his ire at Georgia officials and,
throughout the month of December, President Trump grew even more
relentless in his social media attacks against Kemp than he had been the
previous month. He retweeted attorney Lin Wood calling on Georgians to
call and urge the FBI to focus more on election fraud and "[t]ell them to
also investigate @BrianKempGA @GeoffDuncanGA & @GaSecofState."[229]
And he retweeted another post by Lin Wood that depicted Governor Kemp
and Secretary Raffensperger wearing masks digitally altered to show the
Chinese flag, and warned that they "will soon be going to jail."[230] Even
without his many retweets, President Trump posted an average of about
one tweet per day in December 2020 either criticizing Governor Kemp or
pressuring him explicitly or implicitly to take actions to help overturn the
election.[231]

President Trump seemed consumed with his plans to overturn the election and, based on documents obtained by the Select Committee, it appears
that the President received input from many outside donors or advisors
who had access to his staff's email addresses. On December 7th, a Trump
donor named Bill White emailed senior Trump advisors, including Dan
Scavino and Rudolph Giuliani, to say that he "[j]ust spoke to [Georgia
State] Senator [William Burton] Jones [who] asked if Potus can R[e]T[weet]
this now pls," along with a tweet by Senator Jones that read: "Georgia
Patriot Call to Action…call your state Senate & House Reps & ask them to
sign the petition for a special session."[232] President Trump and Giuliani
each retweeted Senator Jones's tweet an hour later.[233]

Bill White also emailed Molly Michael, Dan Scavino, and Giuliani, on
December 8th with information that he said "POTUS asked me last night"
to send right away.[234] He recommended a Presidential tweet criticizing
Georgia's Lt. Gov. Duncan as well as tweets to put pressure on Senate
Majority Leader Mike Dugan and Senate President Pro Tempore Butch
Miller.[235] He wrote that President Trump would be calling Dugan and Miller
"to ask them to call special session and strategize with them why they are
keeping this from happening."[236] Dugan later confirmed that he had
received a call from President Trump's office but that the two of them were
not able to connect.[237] And the following day, Steve Bannon revealed on his
podcast that President Trump spoke to Georgia House Speaker Ralston and
Speaker Pro Tempore Jan Jones.[238] Speaker Ralston confirmed that he spoke

to President Trump on December 7th about the election, during which he told the President that Georgia law made a special legislative session "very much an uphill battle." [239]

2.4 AN OUTRIGHT REQUEST FOR VICTORY

Beyond asking State officials to not certify, to decertify, or to appoint Trump electors for consideration during the joint session, President Trump and some of his closest advisors inserted themselves directly into the counting of ballots and asked, outright, for enough votes to win.

White House Chief of Staff Mark Meadows did this. Not only did he place calls on behalf of the President to election officials in Georgia, Meadows traveled there to personally visit election officials and volunteers, coordinated with Members of Congress, and even suggested that the President send election workers Trump memorabilia like presidential challenge coins and autographed MAGA hats, a suggestion that his assistant Cassidy Hutchinson thought could be problematic and, ultimately, did not act on. [240]

When Meadows made a visit on short notice to examine the audit of absentee ballots in Cobb County, Georgia, he spoke to Deputy Secretary of State Jordan Fuchs and Frances Watson, the Secretary of State's chief investigator. Ultimately, Meadows connected Watson with the President, who claimed that he had won the election and pressed her to say that he had won. The Select Committee obtained a copy of their recorded call, which is detailed below.

The President told Watson that he had "won Georgia . . . by a lot," told her, "you have the most important job in the country right now," and suggested, "when the right answer comes out you'll be praised." [241] Four days later, Meadows texted Deputy Secretary of State Fuchs, in which he asked, "[i]s there a way to speed up Fulton county signature verification in order to have results before Jan 6 if the trump campaign assist[s] financially." [242] Fuchs wrote in response that she "Will answer ASAP." [243]

Meadows also played a central role in the lead up to the President's January 2, 2021, call with Georgia Secretary of State Brad Raffensperger. In fact, it was Meadows who originally sent text messages to Raffensperger and requested to speak: On November 19th, he texted "Mr Secretary. Mark Meadows here. If you could give me a brief call at your convenience. Thank you". [244] And on December 5th, Meadows texted, "mr Secretary. Can you call the White House switchboard at [phone number]. For a call. Your voice-mail is full." [245] Then, on December 11th, Meadows texted, "Thanks so much" to a number that apparently belongs to United States Representative

Photo by House Creative Services

Jody Hice (R–GA) after Rep. Hice told him that he had just made a state-ment "regarding a recall on Raffensperger. If this is something Potus wants to know and help push. . . ."[246]

All of that led to the remarkable January 2nd call between President Trump and his advisors on one side, and Secretary of State Brad Raffens-perger and his advisors on the other. By January 2nd, the President had tried to speak by phone with Raffensperger at least 18 times.[247] Raffensper-ger, for his part, had avoided talking to the President because of ongoing litigation with the President's Campaign.[248] Despite Raffensperger's reluc-tance, the two spoke, with their respective lawyers on the line. During the call, President Trump went through his litany of false election-fraud claims and then asked Raffensperger to deliver him a second term by "finding" just enough votes to ensure victory. The President said, "I just want to find 11,780 votes, which is one more than we have because we won the State."[249] He reiterated it several different ways: "fellas, I need 11,000 votes. Give me a break. You know, we have that in spades already. Or we can keep going, but that's not fair to the voters of Georgia because they're going to see what happened."[250]

When it was clear that Raffensperger and his advisors would not agree to the President's request, the President ramped up the pressure by accusing them of committing crimes: "the ballots are corrupt. And you are going to find that they are—which is totally illegal—it is more illegal for you than it is for them because, you know, what they did and you're not reporting it. That's a criminal, that's a criminal offense. And you can't let that happen. That's a big risk to you and to Ryan, your lawyer . . . I'm notifying you that you're letting it happen."[251]

The President would stop at nothing to win Georgia. Separate from asking Raffensperger to alter, without justification, the election results in Georgia, he also attacked election workers. In that call, President Trump mentioned Ruby Freeman's name 18 times, referred to her daughter Shaye Moss several of those times, and accused them of crimes.[252] Raffensperger and his aides rebutted President Trump's false claims of fraud on the call and explained why they were wrong, but they did not deliver the one thing President Trump wanted most: the 11,780 votes he asked for.[253]

The next day, President Trump tweeted about his phone call with Raffensperger, falsely claiming that "[Secretary Raffensperger] was unwilling, or unable, to answer questions such as the 'ballots under table' scam. . . . He has no clue!"[254] He added that Raffensperger, Governor Kemp, and Lt. Governor Duncan "are a disgrace" and "have done less than nothing" about rampant political corruption.[255]

Even though Raffensperger and his team repeatedly told the President why his specific allegations of election fraud in Georgia were wrong,[256] President Trump met the next day with the top leadership of the Justice Department in an effort to convince them to send a letter falsely claiming that the Department had "identified significant concerns" affecting the election results in Georgia and calling on Governor Kemp, Speaker Ralston, and Senate President Pro Tempore Miller to convene a special session.[257] It was only after a showdown in the Oval Office, described in Chapter 4 during which the White House Counsel and others threatened to resign that President Trump decided against replacing Department of Justice leadership and issuing that letter.

2.5 SOME OFFICIALS EAGERLY ASSISTED PRESIDENT TRUMP WITH HIS PLANS

While many State officials resisted President Trump's demands, some eagerly joined the President's efforts.

President Trump routinely coordinated with Pennsylvania State Senator Doug Mastriano, whose request led to the November 25, 2020, hotel "hearing" in Gettysburg, and who traveled to Washington to meet with the

Photo by Spencer Platt/Getty Images

President afterward.[258] Senator Mastriano, who would later charter and pay for buses to Washington for the President's "Stop the Steal" rally on January 6th and was near the Capitol during the attack, quickly rose to favor with the President.[259]

On November 30th, President Trump called Mastriano, interrupting him during a radio interview and telling listeners that "Doug is the absolute hero" and people are "really angry in Pennsylvania."[260]

On December 5th, Senator Mastriano sent an email to President Trump's executive assistant, Molly Michael, with a Supreme Court Amicus Brief for the President that the pair "discussed yesterday," related to a case brought by Representative Mike Kelly (R–PA) against his own State, which the Supreme Court rejected just a few days later.[261]

On December 14th, President Trump's executive assistant sent Mastriano an email "From POTUS" with talking points promoting a conspiracy theory about election machines.[262]

And on December 21st, Mastriano sent another email for President Trump, in which he wrote: "Dear Mr. President—attached please find the 'killer letter' on the Pennsylvania election that we discussed last night" that "I only just completed."[263] This letter recapped the Gettysburg hotel hearing on November 25th, and claimed that "there is rampant election fraud in Pennsylvania that must be investigated, remedied and recti-fied."[264] President Trump sent that letter to John Eastman, Acting Attorney General Jeffrey Rosen, Acting Deputy Attorney General Richard Donoghue, Rush Limbaugh, former Florida Attorney General Pam Bondi, Lou Dobbs, and others.[265]

As January 6th approached, Senator Mastriano's involvement in attempts to overturn the election only grew. On December 23rd, he led a second group of Pennsylvania State senators for a meeting with President Trump in the Oval Office, which Giuliani claimed "swayed about 20" of them.[266] Neither Speaker Cutler nor Senate President Corman participated.

Mastriano also sent emails indicating that he spoke with President Trump on December 27th, 28th, and 30th, along with files that President Trump had requested or that he had promised to him.[267] One of these was a pair of letters from State senators asking U.S. Senate Majority Leader Mitch McConnell and House Minority Leader Kevin McCarthy to reject Pennsylvania's electoral votes on January 6th.[268] President Trump's executive assistant notified the White House's Director of Legislative Affairs that "[t]he President would like the below attached letters to be sent to Mitch and Kevin and all GOP house and senate members," but was told in reply, "[g]iven the political nature of the letters, would you mind sending them?"[269]

On January 5th, President Trump spoke again with Mastriano and then notified the White House operator that Mastriano "will be calling in for the Vice President" soon.[270] That evening Senator Mastriano sent two more emails for the President. One was a letter addressed to Vice President Pence on behalf of nearly 100 legislators from various States; the other was a letter directed to McConnell and McCarthy from Pennsylvania lawmakers, this time asking Congress to postpone acting on the 6th.[271] President Trump tweeted the letter that night, captioning it "BIG NEWS IN PENNSYLVANIA!" and, after midnight, he retweeted that "Pennsylvania is going to Trump. The legislators have spoken."[272] As described elsewhere in this report, that letter, and letters like it, were used in the effort to convince Vice President Pence that he could and should affect the outcome of the joint session of Congress on January 6th.

The Select Committee subpoenaed Senator Mastriano to testify about these interactions with President Trump and his advisors, among other matters. Unlike numerous other witnesses who complied with subpoenas and provided deposition testimony to the Select Committee, Mastriano did not; he logged in to a virtual deposition at the appointed time but logged out before answering any substantive questions or even taking the oath to the tell the truth.[273]

The President apparently got what he wanted in State officials like Senator Mastriano, but not those who dared question or outright reject his anti-democratic efforts to overturn the election. In some cases, those who questioned him made the President and his advisors dig in and push harder. On January 1st, Campaign Senior Advisor Jason Miller asked for a "blast text and Twitter blast out" that would urge President Trump's supporters to "Contact House Speaker Bryan Cutler & Senate President Pro Tem Jake Corman!" to "Demand a vote on certification."[274] Senior Campaign attorneys, however, replied that this might violate Pennsylvania's "very stringent" lobbying laws and get them prosecuted or fined.[275] Instead, they agreed on a similar call to action aimed at Arizona Governor Doug Ducey and Arizona House Speaker Rusty Bowers rather than Speaker Cutler and President *Pro Tempore* Corman in Pennsylvania.[276]

2.6 THE FINAL OUTREACH TO STATE LEGISLATORS

The efforts to overturn the election through State legislatures continued throughout the final two weeks before the joint session of Congress on January 6th. Based on actual events and documents obtained by the Select Committee, President Trump's Campaign team, outside advisors, and motivated volunteers generally acted in accord with what was written down in a "Strategic Communications Plan" when engaging with, and sometimes demonizing, State officials. Activities that occurred thereafter were in accord with the plan.

The "Plan" was explained in a document that was presented to the White House.[277] The plan contemplated pressuring Republican legislators both in Congress and in six key swing States. The document itself purports to be the product of the "GIULIANI PRESIDENTIAL LEGAL DEFENSE TEAM" and declared that "We Have 10 Days to Execute This Plan & Certify President Trump!"[278]

Kerik told the Select Committee that pieces of the plan had been in place for some period of time before the document was actually created, and that he thought that the "catalyst" for actually memorializing the plan was the approaching deadline of January 6th.[279] In fact, the 10-day plan to help "certify president Trump" had been the subject of "continual discussions" for "6 weeks" and was "being discussed every day at some point prior to the 10 days that we're talking about. So it was a continuous thing that went on."[280]

Ultimately, the Giuliani team shared the Strategic Communications Plan and urged its implementation. Kerik sent the plan to Mark Meadows via email on December 28th with this note, in part:

There is only one thing that's going to move the needle and force the legislators to do what their [sic] constitutionally obligated to do, and that is apply pressure . . . . We can do all the investigations we want later, but if the president plans on winning, it's the legislators that have to be moved, and this will do just that. We're just running out of time.[281]

Neither Giuliani nor Kerik told the Select Committee that they recalled officially implementing the plan, and Giuliani said that he thought Meadows even rejected it, but there is no doubt that President Trump's team took certain actions consistent with it.[282]

The document described its goal as a "[n]ationwide communications outreach campaign to educate the public on the fraud numbers, and inspire citizens to call upon legislators and Members of Congress to disregard the fraudulent vote count and certify the duly-elected President Trump."[283] The "FOCUS of CAMPAIGN" was "SWING STATE REPUBLICAN SENATORS" in Arizona, Georgia, Michigan, Nevada, Pennsylvania, and Wisconsin, "REPULBICAN [sic] MEMBERS OF THE HOUSE" and "REPUBLICAN MEMBERS OF THE SENATE."[284] Among the steps that it recommended were "RALLIES AND PROTESTS" in six key swing States, including protests at "Governor's Mansions," "Lt. Governor's home[s]," "Secretary of State's homes," and "weak Members' homes."[285]

Although the plan did not mention specific individuals by name, an apparently related document produced to the Select Committee by Giuliani did, naming State legislative leaders as "TARGETS" under a header of "KEY TARGET STATE POINTS," including Arizona House Speaker Rusty Bowers, Arizona Senate President Karen Fann (incorrectly described as the State Senate's majority leader), Georgia House Speaker David Ralston, Georgia Senate Majority Leader Mike Dugan, Georgia Senate President Pro Tempore Butch Miller as a possible back up, Michigan House Speaker Lee Chatfield, Michigan Senate Majority leader Mike Shirkey, Pennsylvania House Speaker Brian Cutler, Pennsylvania House Majority Leader Kerry Benninghoff, Pennsylvania Senate President Pro Tempore Jake Corman, Pennsylvania Senate Majority Leader Kim Ward, Wisconsin State Assembly Speaker Robin Vos, and Wisconsin Senate Majority Leader Scott Fitzgerald.[286]

Consistent with these proposals, Giuliani appeared as a guest on Steve Bannon's podcast on New Year's Eve and told him that "we have a weak element to our party . . . a cowardly element"[287] and, "[n]ow I think every Republican knows—maybe this is worse—this election was stolen. Now the question is: can they live up to their oath of office? . . . We gotta start working on the leadership."[288] Giuliani also described President Trump's objective in this effort: "For the president, the way forward is really it's in the hands of the leaders of those legislatures and the Members of Congress, and what our people can do is let them know what they think, and that they're not gonna get away with pushing this aside. That the consequences of turning your back on a massive voter fraud are gonna be dire for them, and historically these people are gonna become enemies of the country."[289]

A key component of this plan was to call out Republican officials who rejected President Trump and his team's efforts or claims of fraud. Kerik and numerous other members of the Campaign's legal team did just that. On December 27th, Kerik suggested that Senator Pat Toomey (R-PA) was "corrupt" and said that "for any Pennsylvania official to certify their vote, it's malfeasance and criminal."[290] That was entirely consistent with Kerik's past tweets about the election, one of which apparently called public officials "who betrayed" President Trump "spineless disloyal maggots."[291] It wasn't just rhetoric, however, because, as described below, people showed up outside certain officials' home—sometimes menacingly—and, of course, showed up at the Capitol on January 6th.

The pressure in those final days did not stop with the types of activities outlined in the Strategic Communications Plan. January 2, 2021, was a busy day for a Saturday at the Trump White House. That was the day President Trump called on Georgia Secretary of State Raffensperger to find enough votes for victory in Georgia and participated in a call with Lindsay Graham and Members of the Freedom Caucus to plan for the joint session on January 6th.[292]

It was also the day that the President joined in a virtual briefing for nearly 300 Republican legislators from swing States.[293] The event was hosted by a short-lived organization called "Got Freedom?" that listed Jenna Ellis among its leadership team,[294] and included Giuliani, John Eastman, and Peter Navarro as the program's "featured speakers."[295] A press release by Got Freedom? said that the meeting was hosted by Phillip Kline, a former attorney general of Kansas, who was disbarred in 2013.[296] It indicated that purported proof of voter fraud "should serve as an important resource for state legislators as they make calls for state legislatures to meet to investigate the election and consider decertifying their state election results."[297]

According to the *Washington Examiner*, when President Trump joined the call he told the participants: "You know that we won the election, and you were also given false numbers to certify." It quoted him saying "[y]ou are the real power" because "[y]ou're more important than the courts. You're more important than anything because the courts keep referring to you, and you're the ones that are going to make the decision." When asked about that quote, specifically, Giuliani, who was on the call, said he didn't recall the exact words that the President used but told the Select Committee "that would be the sum or substance of what he had been saying and what he believed." [298] During the call, the President reportedly "referenced the planned protests in Washington" just days later on January 6th, and told the group "I don't think the country is going to take it." [299]

When reporting on the call, the *Washington Examiner* also provided details about what Giuliani told the assembled State legislators. Consistent with his team's "Strategic Communications Plan," Giuliani said, "[w]e need you to put excessive pressure on your leadership where the real weakness and cowardice is mostly located," and the report quoted Navarro telling them that "Your job, I believe, is to take action, action, action." [300] That evening, Navarro stated on *Fox News* that "these legislators—they are hot, they're angry, they want action," and "we explained exactly how the Democrat Party as a matter of strategy stole this election from Donald J. Trump." [301]

Organizers from Got Freedom? sent a follow-up email that evening to participants on behalf of Phill Kline, in which they described the event as "an important briefing for legislators who hold the power to decertify the results of their state elections." [302] It emphasized the following:

> As elected officials in the House and Senate of your respective States, Professor Eastman laid out the Constitutional imperatives for you:
> • Assert your plenary power
> • Demand that your laws be followed as written
> • Decertify tainted results unless and until your laws are followed
> • Insist on enough time to properly meet, investigate, and properly certify results to ensure that all lawful votes (but only lawful votes) are counted.[303]

The email also recommended that they ". . . sign on to a joint letter from state legislators to Vice President Mike Pence to demand that he call for a 12-day delay on ratifying the election . . ." on January 6th.[304] The letter ultimately garnered more than 100 signatures by State legislators from Arizona, Georgia, Michigan, Pennsylvania, and Wisconsin.[305] Doug Mastriano forwarded a copy of the letter via email to President Trump's executive assistant, and the National Archives produced to the Select Committee a printed version with a stamp at the top indicating, "THE PRESIDENT HAS SEEN." [306]

But this plan would fail to sway its intended audience. As discussed in Chapter 5, the Vice President rejected this and numerous other attempts to convince him to act unlawfully on January 6th. The election had been decided and certified by the States. It was the Vice President and Congress's job to open and count the legitimate electoral college votes.

And in the early morning hours of January 7th, after a day unlike any seen in American history, when a mob of angry insurrectionists attempted to violently upend a Presidential election, the Vice President and Members of Congress, shaken but steady, delayed but resolute, regrouped and reconvened and did their Constitutional duty to certify Joseph R. Biden as the next President of the United States.

President Trump's plot to pressure State legislators to overturn the vote of the electoral college failed—but only barely. Even so, the consequences of President Trump's efforts to overturn State election results were significant.

2.7 THE HARM CAUSED BY DEMONIZING PUBLIC SERVANTS

Many of the people who refused to be pushed into manipulating election results—governors, secretaries of State, State legislators, State and local election officials, and frontline election workers just doing their jobs—found themselves subjected to public demonization and subsequent spamming, doxing, harassment, intimidation, and violent threats. Some of the threats were sexualized or racist in nature and targeted family members. President Trump never discouraged or condemned these tactics, and in fact he was an active participant in directing his supporters, through tweets and speeches, to apply pressure to public servants who would not comply.

President Trump and his team were not above using incendiary rhetoric or threats to achieve their goal of overturning the election. Giuliani said so before the purported hearing in Michigan in December. Recall that he told an online audience, there's "nothin' wrong with putting pressure on your state legislators" [307] and "you have got to get them to remember that their oath to the Constitution sometimes requires being criticized. Sometimes it even requires being threatened." [308]

That pressure came privately and publicly in the post-election period.

Privately, for example, President Trump called Michigan Senate Majority Leader Mike Shirkey three times after their White House meeting: November 21st, November 25th, and December 14th. [309] Shirkey did not recall many specifics of those calls and claimed he did not remember the President applying any specific pressure. [310] The day after one of those calls, however, Shirkey tweeted that "our election process MUST be free of intimidation and threats," and "it's inappropriate for anyone to exert pressure on them." [311] From this and other public statements, it is clear that Shirkey was sensitive to outside forces pressuring people with roles in the election. In fact, the same day that the electoral college met and voted former Vice President Joe Biden as the winner of the 2020 Presidential election, Shirkey received another call from President Trump and issued another public statement. Shirkey's statement that day, December 14, 2020, read: "Michigan's Democratic slate of electors should be able to proceed with their duty, free from threats of violence and intimidation" and "[i]t is our responsibility as leaders to follow the law . . . ."[312]

Publicly, President Trump used both Twitter posts and paid social media and cable television ads to advance his pressure campaign.

In Arizona, for example, President Trump used social media to both praise and criticize legislators. When Speaker Bowers and Senate President Karen Fann requested an audit of Maricopa County's election software and equipment, President Trump publicly commended them, retweeting a press release about their announcement and commenting: "Thank you to Senate President Karen Fann and House Speaker Russell Bowers—and all, for what you are doing in Arizona. A fast check of signatures will easily give us the state."[313] But just days later, President Trump assailed Bowers for opposing a special session to appoint new electors. He retweeted a post by Campaign lawyer Christina Bobb that accused Bowers of "intentionally misleading the people of Arizona" and that included a demand by Stop-the-Steal organizer Ali Alexander for 50,000 phone calls to Rusty Bowers "[r]ight the heck now" to threaten him with a primary challenge.[314]

And, as his efforts to change the outcome of the election continued to meet resistance, President Trump personally approved a series of advertisements that the Campaign ran on cable television and social media in several important States. One advertisement in Arizona called for pressure on Governor Ducey in particular, alleging, "The evidence is overwhelming. Call Governor Ducey and your legislators. Demand they inspect the machines and hear the evidence."[315] Another claimed that "illegal aliens voted, and here in Arizona Trump votes were discarded. It's an outrage. Call Governor Ducey and your legislators at 602–542–4331. Demand they inspect the machines and hear the evidence. Call Governor Ducey, at 602–542–4331. Stand up for President Trump. Call today. Paid for by Donald J. Trump for President, Inc."[316]

Several days earlier, Trump Campaign Senior Advisor Jason Miller had explained the intention for this round of advertisements in an email. He wrote that, "the President and Mayor Giuliani want to get back up on TV ASAP, and Jared [Kushner] has approved in budgetary concept, so here's the gameplan" in order to "motivate the GOP base to put pressure on the Republican Governors of Georgia and Arizona and the Republican-controlled State legislatures in Wisconsin and Michigan to hear evidence of voter fraud before January 6th." [317] Miller anticipated a budget of $5 million and asked for the messaging to follow an earlier round of advertisements, "but the endings need to be changed to include phone numbers and directions to call the local Governor or state legislature." [318] On December 22nd, Jason Miller texted Jared Kushner that "POTUS has approved the buy." [319]

References to anger and fighting were featured in some of the President's remarks during that period. After the Georgia Secretary of State's Chief Operating Officer, Gabriel Sterling, made an impassioned public plea and accurately warned that someone would die as a result of the threatening election-related rhetoric that President Trump failed to condemn, President Trump dismissively tweeted in response: "Rigged Election. Show signatures and envelopes. Expose the massive voter fraud in Georgia. What is Secretary of State and @BrianKempGA afraid of. They know what we'll find!!!" [320] The President also tweeted that, between Governor Ducey in Arizona and Governor Kemp in Georgia, "the Democrat Party could not be happier" because these Republicans "fight harder against us than do the Radical Left" and were singlehandedly responsible for losing him both States, something that "Republicans will NEVER forget[.]" [321] Regarding Kemp, he asked "What's wrong with this guy? What is he hiding?" [322] and he alleged that "RINOs" Governor Kemp, Lieutenant Governor Geoff Duncan, and Secretary Raffensperger "will be solely responsible" for Senators Loeffler and Perdue losing their senate runoff because they "[w]on't call a Special Session or check for Signature Verification! People are ANGRY!" [323]

President Trump's spoken remarks were not much different. After the President wrapped up a November 26th public phone call to wish U.S. service members a happy Thanksgiving, he answered a reporter's question about election integrity in Georgia by lashing out at Secretary Raffensperger in particular. President Trump made several baseless claims of election fraud in Georgia, declared that Raffensperger himself appeared to be complicit, and labeled the Georgia Secretary of State "an enemy of the people." [324]

President Trump and his team's practice of naming and viciously criticizing people had real consequences. Philadelphia City Commissioner Al Schmidt's story, recounted earlier, is just one of many examples. And the consequences weren't just limited to high-profile public figures. Schmidt's deputy, for example, Seth Bluestein faced threats after being demonized by a surrogate for President Trump, and many of the threats he received were anti-Semitic in nature. He received a Facebook message telling him that "EVERYONE WITH A GUN IS GOING TO BE AT YOUR HOUSE- AMERICANS LOOK AT THE NAME- ANOTHER JEW CAUGHT UP IN UNITED STATES

VOTER FRAUD."[325] Bluestein got a security detail at his home, and the experience gave his three-year-old daughter nightmares.[326]

Similarly, after President Trump promoted online accusations that Arizona House Speaker Rusty Bowers had been "intentionally misleading the people of Arizona . . ."[327] Bowers's personal cell phone and home address were published,[328] leading demonstrators to congregate at his home, honk horns and shout insults until police arrived.[329] Bowers told the Select Committee this was the first of at least nine protests at his home, sometimes with protesters shouting into bullhorns and calling him a pedophile.[330] One protestor who showed up at his home was armed and believed to be a member of an extremist militia.[331]

Sadly, those were not isolated incidents. Stories similar to Schmidt's and Bowers' proliferated after President Trump's loss in the election. Examples from each of the States discussed in this chapter are documented below, but this list is by no means exhaustive:

- *Arizona:* After Secretary of State Katie Hobbs's home address and son's phone number were publicly released, demonstrators congregated outside her home chanting "we are watching you."[332] A social media user at the time recommended: "Let's burn her house down and kill her family and teach these fraudsters a lesson."[333] Secretary Hobbs has continued to receive threats since then, reporting over 100 threats to the FBI in mid-2022, including a September 2021 voicemail message that "you should be hunted" and "will never be safe in Arizona again."[334]
- *Arizona:* Maricopa County Recorder Adrian Fontes testified before Congress that his family had "go-bags" packed in case they needed to evacuate and that, because of the threats, he had moved his children "out of the family home at least once for three days in the wake of serious threats to [his] family's safety."[335]
- *Arizona:* Paul Boyer, a Republican State senator, had to evacuate his family, get police protection, and change his phone number after he voted against jailing Maricopa's County Supervisors over election disputes.[336]
- *Arizona:* On January 5, 2021, a comment on a blog suggested some members of the Maricopa County Board of Supervisors "have earned a good old fashioned neck tie party" as "punishment for Treason."[337] According to Board member Clint Hickman, "the threats never abated."[338] And on January 6th, police convinced Hickman and his family to leave their home.[339]
- *Michigan:* Secretary of State Jocelyn Benson and her family were driven out of their home for several days after dozens of protestors with

bullhorns and firearms congregated outside "shouting obscenities and graphic threats into bullhorns"[340] while she spent time with her son and got him ready for bed.[341] Secretary Benson said that she only feels safe "sometimes" as a result of continuing threats.[342]

- *Michigan:* Several members of the Wayne County Board of Canvassers received threats, as did Aaron Van Langevelde, a Republican member of the State Board of Canvassers.[343] Van Langevelde was bombarded with communications and people began showing up at his family's home, forcing police to ensure his and his family's safety and escort him across the State after he voted to certify Michigan's election.[344]

- *Michigan:* Detroit City Clerk Janice Winfrey, a Democrat, and Rochester Hills City Clerk Tina Barton, a Republican, were both targeted. Barton had never before received a death threat in over a decade of work as an election official but, as a result of the 2020 Presidential election, was subject to "a torrent of threats and harassment," such as an anonymous caller who "repeatedly threatened to kill her and her family."[345] Winfrey was confronted outside her home by a man who indicated he had been surveilling her and that "You are going to pay dearly for your actions in this election!"[346] She started carrying a firearm because death threats against her continued.[347]

- *Michigan:* Michigan House Speaker Lee Chatfield confirmed that "I and my family have received numerous threats, along with members on both sides of the aisle."[348] This included the top Democrat on Michigan's House Oversight Committee, Rep. Cynthia Johnson, who was threatened with lynching after she challenged the witnesses that Giuliani offered to her committee.[349] One caller who allegedly threatened to kill Rep. Johnson and wipe out her family in December 2020 called the Capitol again on the morning of January 7, 2021, and said that "everyone better get out of the building because it'll fucking explode."[350]

- *Pennsylvania:* Secretary of the Commonwealth Kathy Boockvar said she received so many threats "I didn't feel comfortable walking the dog on the street."[351] This included a message in November 2020 threatening to murder her in her home at night, forcing her and her husband to flee for a week.[352] Another voicemail she received after certifying Pennsylvania's election results threatened: "You crooked f***ing bitch. You're done."[353]

- *Pennsylvania:* House Speaker Bryan Cutler told the Select Committee there were at least three protests outside either his district office or his home, and that his then-15-year-old son was home by himself for the first one.[354] Senate Jake Corman's spokesperson revealed in December 2020 that he, too, was being subjected to violent threats,[355] something

Senate Majority Leader Kim Ward also received.[356]

- *Pennsylvania:* Philadelphia City Commissioner Omar Sabir, spent several nights evacuated from his home and continued to receive death threats a year after the 2020 election, reflecting that, "I feel anxiety every time I walk outside of the house."[357] Commissioner Lisa Deeley, another City Commission colleague, also received death threats and said she suffers occasional anxiety attacks as a result.[358]

- *Georgia:* After Georgia Secretary of State Brad Raffensperger's email and phone number were published, he said that he and his wife received frequent hostile messages, some of which "typically came in sexualized attacks."[359] As a result, the Secretary's wife cancelled visits from their grandchildren out of fear for the kids' safety.[360] That was not an overreaction as that came after police found self-identified members of the Oath Keepers outside their home and after someone broke into their daughter-in-law's house.[361]

- *Georgia:* On January 5, 2021, Governor Kemp and Secretary Raffensperger were reportedly named in a Craigslist post encouraging people to "put an end to the lives of these traitors."[362]

- *Georgia:* Fulton County Elections Director Richard Barron was named and depicted on screen in the video President Trump played at his December 5th rally. He said that this incident led to a spike in death threats targeted at election workers, including himself.[363] His team's registration chief, Ralph Jones, received death threats following the election including one calling him a "n[igger] who should be shot," and another threatening "to kill him by dragging his body around with a truck."[364]

- *Georgia:* Election offices in ten Georgia counties received emailed threats of bombings that would "make the Boston bombings look like child's play" and that the "death and destruction" would continue "[u]ntil Trump is guaranteed to be POTUS...."[365]

One of the most striking examples of the terror that President Trump and his allies caused came in Georgia, where election workers Ruby Freeman and Shaye Moss, mother and daughter, were besieged by incessant, terrifying harassment and threats that often evoked racial violence and lynching, instigated and incited by the President of the United States.

As described earlier, in a State legislative hearing in Georgia, Giuliani publicly—and baselessly—accused Freeman and Moss of engaging in criminal conduct. He showed a video of Freeman passing Moss a ginger mint before claiming that the two women, both Black, were smuggling USB drives "as if they're vials of heroin or cocaine."[366]

Photo by Kevin Dietsch/Getty Images

President Trump seemed fixated on Freeman and Moss, too. He played surveillance video showing them inside the State Farm Arena at a December 5th rally in Georgia,[367] and mentioned Freeman by name 18 times during the January 2nd call to Secretary of State Raffensperger in which he asked the Secretary to simply "find" enough votes to ensure victory.[368]

Freeman's and Moss's lives were forever changed. After their contact information was published, they were besieged by the President's supporters. In early December 2020, Freeman "told police she had received hundreds of threats at her home."[369] Moss's son also started receiving threatening phone calls, including one stating he "should hang alongside [his] nigger momma."[370]

In the wake of President Trump's December 5, 2020, rally, Freeman called 911 because strangers had come to her home trying to lure her out, sending threatening emails and text messages.[371] She pleaded with the 911 dispatcher for help after hearing loud banging on her door just before 10 p.m. "Lord Jesus, where's the police?" she asked the dispatcher. "I don't know who keeps coming to my door." "Please help me!"[372]

Ultimately, Freeman fled from her own home based on advice from the FBI.[373] She would not move back for months.[374]

In her testimony to the Select Committee, Freeman recounted how she had received "hundreds of racist, threatening, horrible calls and messages" and that now "[t]here is nowhere I feel safe—nowhere." [375] But it's not just a sense of security that the President and his followers took from Freeman. She told the Select Committee that she also lost her name and reputation:

> My name is Ruby Freeman. I've always believed it when God says that he'll make your name great, but this is not the way it was supposed to be. I could have never imagined the events that followed the Presidential election in 2020. For my entire professional life, I was Lady Ruby. My community in Georgia where I was born and lived my whole life knew me as Lady Ruby. . . . Now I won't even introduce myself by my name anymore. I get nervous when I bump into someone I know in the grocery store who says my name. I'm worried about who's listening. I get nervous when I have to give my name for food orders. I'm always concerned of who's around me. I've lost my name, and I've lost my reputation.
>
> I've lost my sense of security—all because a group of people, starting with Number 45 and his ally Rudy Giuliani, decided to scapegoat me and my daughter Shaye to push their own lies about how the presidential election was stolen.[376]

Freeman's sense of dread is well-founded. According to Federal prosecutors, a member of the Oath Keepers militia convicted of multiple offenses for his role in the January 6th insurrection had a document in his residence with the words "DEATH LIST" written across the top.[377]

His death list contained just two names: Ruby Freeman and Shaye Moss.[378]

ENDNOTES

1. *See, e.g.,* Stephen Fowler, "Risk-Limiting Audit Confirms Biden Won Georgia," GPB, (Nov. 19, 2020), available at https://www.gpb.org/news/2020/11/19/risk-limiting-audit-confirms-biden-won-georgia; Addie Haney, "Georgia Election Recount Results: Breaking Down Final Numbers," 11Alive, (Dec. 7, 2020), available at https://www.11alive.com/article/news/politics/elections/georgia-election-recount-results-final-numbers/85-cbaacd70-f7e0-40ae-8dfa-3bf18f318645.

2. Brad Raffensperger, *Integrity Counts* (New York: Simon & Schuster, 2021), p. 191 (reproducing the call transcript); Amy Gardner and Paulina Firozi, "Here's the Full Transcript and Audio of the Call Between Trump and Raffensperger," *Washington Post* (Jan. 5, 2021), available at https://www.washingtonpost.com/politics/trump-raffensperger-call-transcript-georgia-vote/2021/01/03/2768e0cc-4ddd-11eb-83e3-322644d82356_story.html.

3. Brad Raffensperger, *Integrity Counts* (New York: Simon & Schuster, 2021), p. 191 (reproducing the call transcript); Amy Gardner and Paulina Firozi, "Here's the Full Transcript and

Audio of the Call Between Trump and Raffensperger," *Washington Post* (Jan. 5, 2021), available at https://www.washingtonpost.com/politics/trump-raffensperger-call-transcript-georgia-vote/2021/01/03/2768e0cc-4ddd-11eb-83e3-322644d82356_story.html.

4. Brad Raffensperger, *Integrity Counts* (New York: Simon & Schuster, 2021), p. 191 (reproducing the call transcript); Amy Gardner and Paulina Firozi, "Here's the Full Transcript and Audio of the Call Between Trump and Raffensperger," *Washington Post* (Jan. 5, 2021), available at https://www.washingtonpost.com/politics/trump-raffensperger-call-transcript-georgia-vote/2021/01/03/2768e0cc-4ddd-11eb-83e3-322644d82356_story.html.

5. Brad Raffensperger, *Integrity Counts* (New York: Simon & Schuster, 2021), p. 191 (reproducing the call transcript); Amy Gardner and Paulina Firozi, "Here's the Full Transcript and Audio of the Call Between Trump and Raffensperger," *Washington Post* (Jan. 5, 2021), available at https://www.washingtonpost.com/politics/trump-raffensperger-call-transcript-georgia-vote/2021/01/03/2768e0cc-4ddd-11eb-83e3-322644d82356_story.html.

6. Brad Raffensperger, *Integrity Counts* (New York: Simon & Schuster, 2021), p. 191 (reproducing the call transcript); Amy Gardner and Paulina Firozi, "Here's the Full Transcript and Audio of the Call Between Trump and Raffensperger," *Washington Post* (Jan. 5, 2021), available at https://www.washingtonpost.com/politics/trump-raffensperger-call-transcript-georgia-vote/2021/01/03/2768e0cc-4ddd-11eb-83e3-322644d82356_story.html.

7. Brad Raffensperger, *Integrity Counts* (New York: Simon & Schuster, 2021), p. 191 (reproducing the call transcript); Amy Gardner and Paulina Firozi, "Here's the Full Transcript and Audio of the Call Between Trump and Raffensperger," *Washington Post* (Jan. 5, 2021), available at https://www.washingtonpost.com/politics/trump-raffensperger-call-transcript-georgia-vote/2021/01/03/2768e0cc-4ddd-11eb-83e3-322644d82356_story.html.

8. Brad Raffensperger, *Integrity Counts*, (New York: Simon & Schuster, 2021), at p. 194.

9. Select Committee to Investigate the January 6th Attack on the United States Capitol, Transcribed Interview of Brad Raffensperger, (Nov. 22, 2021), pp. 121-122, 126-27.

10. Brad Raffensperger, *Integrity Counts*, (New York: Simon & Schuster, 2021), at p. 194.

11. The Georgia Secretary of State's Chief Operating Officer, Gabriel Sterling, gave an impassioned public statement that included these points. "Georgia Election Official Gabriel Sterling: 'Someone's Going to Get Killed' Transcript," Rev, (Dec. 1, 2020), available at https://www.rev.com/blog/transcripts/georgia-election-official-gabriel-sterling-someones-going-to-get-killed-transcript. Shortly thereafter, President Trump fired back on Twitter in the form of a quote-tweet of a journalist's post that included the full footage of these parts of Sterling's remarks. Donald J. Trump (@realDonaldTrump), Twitter, Dec. 1, 2020 10:27 p.m. ET, available at http://web.archive.org/web/20201203173245/https://mobile.twitter.com/realDonaldTrump/status/1333975991518187521 (quoting Brendan Keefe (@BrendanKeefe), Twitter, Dec. 1, 2020 4:22 p.m. ET, available at https://twitter.com/BrendanKeefe/status/1333884246277189633).

12. See Chapter 1.

13. U.S. Const. art. II, §1, cl. 2 ("Each State shall appoint, in such Manner as the Legislature thereof may direct, a Number of Electors, equal to the whole Number of Senators and Representatives to which the State may be entitled in the Congress: but no Senator or Representative, or Person holding an Office of Trust or Profit under the United States, shall be appointed an Elector.").

14. *See* "Census Bureau Releases 2020 Presidential Election Voting Report," United States Census Bureau, (Feb. 17, 2022), available at https://www.census.gov/newsroom/press-releases/2022/2020-presidential-election-voting-report.html.

15. Barton Gellman, "The Election That Could Break America," *Atlantic*, (Sept. 23, 2020) available at https://www.theatlantic.com/magazine/archive/2020/11/what-if-trump-refuses-concede/616424/.

16. Barton Gellman, "The Election That Could Break America," *Atlantic*, (Sept. 23, 2020) available at https://www.theatlantic.com/magazine/archive/2020/11/what-if-trump-refuses-concede/616424/.

17. Select Committee to Investigate the January 6th Attack on the United States Capitol, Transcribed Interview of William Stepien, (Feb. 10, 2022), pp. 145-46, 148-53, 158; Select Committee to Investigate the January 6th Attack on the United States Capitol, Transcribed Interview of Justin Clark, (May 17, 2022), pp. 96, 98; Select Committee to Investigate the January 6th Attack on the United States Capitol, Deposition of Rudolph Giuliani, (May 20, 2022), p. 42. Although certain Select Committee witnesses confirmed the existence of this state-focused strategy, none testified that they knew about the strategy before the election.

18. Select Committee to Investigate the January 6th Attack on the United States Capitol, Transcribed Interview of William Stepien, (Feb. 10, 2022), pp. 145-46.

19. Select Committee to Investigate the January 6th Attack on the United States Capitol, Transcribed Interview of William Stepien, (Feb. 10, 2022), pp. 145-46.

20. Documents on file with the Select Committee to Investigate the January 6th Attack on the United States Capitol (Mark Meadows Production), MM011213. Donald Trump Jr. publicly urged State legislators to help the same day. He called on Twitter for his father to "go to total war over this election" and retweeted a post by Fox News host Mark Levin urging Republican State legislatures to "GET READY TO DO YOUR CONSTITUTIONAL DUTY" by exercising "THE FINAL SAY OVER THE CHOOSING OF ELECTORS." David Knowles, "As Vote Count Swings Toward Biden, Trump's Backers Hit the Caps-Lock Key on Twitter," *Yahoo! News*, (Nov. 5, 2020), available at https://www.yahoo.com/video/as-vote-count-swings-toward-biden-trump-backers-hit-the-caps-lock-on-twitter-223931950.html.

21. Documents on file with the Select Committee to Investigate the January 6th Attack on the United States Capitol (Mark Meadows Production), MM011318 (November 6, 2020, text message from Mark Meadows to Donald J. Trump, Jr.).

22. Documents on file with the Select Committee to Investigate the January 6th Attack on the United States Capitol (Mark Meadows Production), MM011296 (November 5, 2020, text message from Mark Meadows to Marty Harbin).

23. Documents on file with the Select Committee to Investigate the January 6th Attack on the United States Capitol (Mark Meadows Production), MM011686, MM011687 (November 9, 2020, text messages between Mark Meadows and Russell Vought).

24. Documents on file with the Select Committee to Investigate the January 6th Attack on the United States Capitol (Mark Meadows Production), MM011560, MM011563 (November 7, 2020, text messages between Mark Meadows and Rep. Warren Davidson).

25. Documents on file with the Select Committee to Investigate the January 6th Attack on the United States Capitol (Mark Meadows Production), MM011449, MM011451 (November 6, 2020, text messages between Mark Meadows and Rep. Andy Biggs).

26. Documents on file with the Select Committee to Investigate the January 6th Attack on the United States Capitol (Mark Meadows Production), MM011087 (November 4, 2020, text message from Rick Perry to Mark Meadows).

27. Documents on file with the Select Committee to Investigate the January 6th Attack on the United States Capitol (Vincent Haley Production), VMH-00004070, p. 44; *see also* Documents on file with the Select Committee to Investigate the January 6th Attack on the United States Capitol (Vincent Haley Production), VMH-00003041.

28. Documents on file with the Select Committee to Investigate the January 6th Attack on the United States Capitol (Vincent Haley Production), VMH-00003543 (November 5, 2020, email from Vincent Haley to Johnny McEntee and Dan Huff re: State legislature plenary power under Constitution to state electoral college electors); Documents on file with the Select Committee to Investigate the January 6th Attack on the United States Capitol (Vincent Haley Production), VMH-00003559 (November 5, 2020, email from Vincent Haley to Johnny

McEntee and Dan Huff re: more notes on state legislature strategy); Documents on file with the Select Committee to Investigate the January 6th Attack on the United States Capitol (National Archives Production), 076P-R000010233_0001 (November 6, 2020, email chain between Vincent Haley, Johnny McEntee, and Daniel Huff re: Contact Info of key leaders in key States); Documents on file with the Select Committee to Investigate the January 6th Attack on the United States Capitol (National Archives Production), 076P-R000010198_0001 (November 6, 2020, email from Vincent Haley to Johnny McEntee and Daniel Huff re: Horowitz: How Republican-controlled state legislatures can rectify election fraud committed by courts and governors - TheBlaze); Documents on file with the Select Committee to Investigate the January 6th Attack on the United States Capitol (National Archives Production), 076P-R000010225_0001-10226_0001 (November 6, 2020, email from Vincent Haley to Johnny McEntee and Daniel Huff re: Contact info of key leaders in key States and attaching contact info); Documents on file with the Select Committee to Investigate the January 6th Attack on the United States Capitol (Vincent Haley Production), VMH-00004070, 4103-04, 4111-12, 4124-25 (various text messages between Vincent Haley, Johnny McEntee, and Daniel Huff discussing the state legislature plan).

29. Documents on file with the Select Committee to Investigate the January 6th Attack on the United States Capitol (Vincent Haley Production), VMH-00003009 (November 8, 2020, email chain between Vincent Haley and Newt Gingrich re: More of my exchange with John); Documents on file with the Select Committee to Investigate the January 6th Attack on the United States Capitol (Vincent Haley Production), VMH-00004103 (November 6, 2020, text message from Vincent Haley to Randy Evans).

30. Documents on file with the Select Committee to Investigate the January 6th Attack on the United States Capitol (Vincent Haley Production), VMH-00002107 (November 5, 2020, email chain between Vincent Haley, Daniel Huff, and Jonny McEntee re: more notes on the state legislature strategy).

31. Documents on file with the Select Committee to Investigate the January 6th Attack on the United States Capitol (Vincent Haley Production), VMH-00004103 (November 6, 2020, text message from Vincent Haley to Johnny McEntee).

32. Documents on file with the Select Committee to Investigate the January 6th Attack on the United States Capitol (Vincent Haley Production), VMH-00004104 (November 6, 2020, text message from Vincent Haley to Johnny McEntee).

33. Documents on file with the Select Committee to Investigate the January 6th Attack on the United States Capitol (National Archives Production), 076P-R000010225_0001 - 076P-R000010226_0001 (November 6, 2020, email from Vincent Haley to Johnny McEntee and Daniel Huff re: Contact info of key leaders in key States and attaching contact info); Documents on file with the Select Committee to Investigate the January 6th Attack on the United States Capitol (National Archives Production), 076P-R000010233_0001 (November 6, 2020, email chain between Vincent Haley, Johnny McEntee, and Daniel Huff re: Contact Info of key leaders in key States).

34. Documents on file with the Select Committee to Investigate the January 6th Attack on the United States Capitol (National Archives Production), 076P-R000010225_0001 - 076P-R000010226_0001 (November 6, 2020, email from Vincent Haley to Johnny McEntee and Daniel Huff re: Contact info of key leaders in key States and attaching contact info).

35. Documents on file with the Select Committee to Investigate the January 6th Attack on the United States Capitol (Vincent Haley Production), VMH-00004122-VMH-00004123 (November 8, 2020, text messages between Vincent Haley and Johnny McEntee).

36. Documents on file with the Select Committee to Investigate the January 6th Attack on the United States Capitol (National Archives Production), 076P-R000010533_0001 (November 10, 2020, email from Newt Gingrich to Molly Michael re: Only two options—please give to POTUS newt).

37. Documents on file with the Select Committee to Investigate the January 6th Attack on the United States Capitol (National Archives Production), 076P-R000010533_0001 (November 10, 2020, email from Newt Gingrich to Molly Michael re: Only two options—please give to POTUS newt).

38. Documents on file with the Select Committee to Investigate the January 6th Attack on the United States Capitol (National Archives Production), 076P-R000010586_0001 (November 10, 2020, email from Mark Meadows to Newt Gingrich re: Only two options—please give to POTUS newt).

39. Solange Reyner, "Newsmax CEO Ruddy: Trump 'Very Concerned' That Dems Will Steal Election," Newsmax, (Nov. 4, 2020), available at https://www.newsmax.com/newsmax-tv/chris-ruddy-2020-elections-democrats-white-house/2020/11/04/id/995386/; Christopher Ruddy (@ChrisRuddyNMX), Twitter, Nov. 12, 2020 4:43 p.m. ET, available at https://twitter.com/ChrisRuddyNMX/status/1327004111154319360; "Digest of Other White House Announcements (Administration of Donald J. Trump, 2020)," Government Publishing Office, p. 114, available at https://www.govinfo.gov/content/pkg/DCPD-2020DIGEST/pdf/DCPD-2020DIGEST.pdf; Michael M. Grynbaum and John Koblin, "Newsmax, Once a Right-Wing Also-Ran, Is Rising, and Trump Approves," New York Times, (Nov. 22, 2020), available at https://www.nytimes.com/2020/11/22/business/media/newsmax-trump-fox-news.html; Cordelia Lynch, "Trump Ally on President's Next Move after Thanksgiving Phone Call," Sky News, (Dec. 4, 2020), available at https://news.sky.com/story/trump-ally-on-presidents-next-move-after-thanksgiving-phone-call-12150612; Documents on file with the Select Committee to Investigate the January 6th Attack on the United States Capitol (National Archives Production), 076P-R000009409_0001 (December 2, 2020, email from John McLaughlin to Molly Michael re: Newsmax National Poll).

40. Documents on file with the Select Committee to Investigate the January 6th Attack on the United States Capitol (Mark Meadows Production), MM008861-MM008865 (November 7, 2020, email from John McLaughlin to Mark Meadows and Newt Gingrich re: "Gerald Brant's birthday party/ my Nov 7, 2020 memo on ON 'ELECTORAL L COUNT ACT OF 1887' AND REPUBLICAN PATHWAYS: [sic]," and attaching memo forwarded by Christopher Ruddy).

41. Select Committee to Investigate the January 6th Attack on the United States Capitol, Deposition of Cleta Mitchell, (May 18, 2022), pp. 14-15; Jeremy Herb and Sunlen Serfaty, "How GOP Lawyer Cleta Mitchell Joined Trump's 'Team Deplorables' Advancing His False Election Fraud Claims," CNN, (Oct. 13, 2021), available at https://www.cnn.com/2021/10/13/politics/trump-mitchell-georgia-election/index.html.

42. Select Committee to Investigate the January 6th Attack on the United States Capitol, Deposition of Cleta Mitchell, (May 18, 2022), pp. 74-75.

43. Documents on file with the Select Committee to Investigate the January 6th Attack on the United States Capitol (Chapman University Production), Chapman006671.

44. Documents on file with the Select Committee to Investigate the January 6th Attack on the United States Capitol (Chapman University Production), Chapman007670-Chapman007671, Chapman008087 (November 9, 2020, email chain between John Eastman, Lisa Nelson, Rep. Seth Grove, and Cleta Mitchell re: Connections for today! and attaching memo).

45. Documents on file with the Select Committee to Investigate the January 6th Attack on the United States Capitol (National Archives Production),076P-R000010584_0001 (November 10, 2020, email chain scheduling an external meeting with President Trump).

46. Break Up DC (@BreakItUp3), Twitter, Nov. 11, 2020, available at http://web.archive.org/web/20201111104529/https://twitter.com/BreakItUp3/status/1326475581005950976 ("Was in Oval yesterday. You are right."). For attribution of the account to Warstler, see The RSnake Show, "S01E10 - Morgan Warstler," YouTube, at 1:43:00 - 1:44:00, Apr. 20, 2022, available at https://www.youtube.com/watch?v=k-ojD3QAYfo; Break Up DC (@BreakItUp3), Twitter, June 16, 2022, available at http://web.archive.org/web/20220616124842/https://twitter.com/BreakItUp3/status/1537414050510000128 ("NO it is not. I went to the Oval right after election and spent an hour with Trump sitting at Resolute desk. I explain it all here: https://

youtu.be/k-ojD3QAYfo?t=2724 . . . Hint: the electoral count act is unconstitutional—there is only one slate of electors- whatever the state leg says").

47. Break Up DC (@BreakItUp3), Twitter, June 15, 2022 7:40 p.m. ET, available at http:// web.archive.org/web/20220615234134/https://twitter.com/BreakItUp3/status/ 1537218579225268225 (archived) ("She literally was advocating what I told whole Trump team in Oval- it's a fact - state legislatures can choose the electors- no matter what current state law OR state courts say . . . just ratify it amongst themselves That's WHY they call it a plenary power ever since Bush v. Gore.").

48. Documents on file with the Select Committee to Investigate the January 6th Attack on the United States Capitol (National Archives Production), 076P-R000008528_0001 - 076P-R000008530_0001.

49. Documents on file with the Select Committee to Investigate the January 6th Attack on the United States Capitol (National Archives Production), 076P-R000008528_0001-076P-R000008528_0003, 076P-R000008530_0001 - 076P-R000008530_0002.

50. Documents on file with the Select Committee to Investigate the January 6th Attack on the United States Capitol (National Archives Production), 076P-R000008528_0001 - 076P-R000008528_0003, 076P-R000008530_0001 - 076P-R000008530_0002.

51. Documents on file with the Select Committee to Investigate the January 6th Attack on the United States Capitol (National Archives Production), 076P-R000008531_0001, 076P-R000008257_0001.

52. Select Committee to Investigate the January 6th Attack on the United States Capitol, Transcribed Interview of William Stepien, (Feb. 10, 2022), pp. 151-52.

53. Select Committee to Investigate the January 6th Attack on the United States Capitol, Transcribed Interview of William Stepien, (Feb. 10, 2022), p. 153. This fits with several major news reports at the time. The *New York Times* reported that President Trump went into the meeting on the 11th with "something he wanted to discuss with his advisors," and "press[ed] them on whether Republican legislatures could pick pro-Trump electors in a handful of key states and deliver him the electoral votes he needs." Maggie Haberman, "Trump Floats Improbable Survival Scenarios as He Ponders His Future," *New York Times*, (Nov. 12, 2020, updated Nov. 23, 2020), available at https://www.nytimes.com/2020/11/12/ us/politics/trump-future.html. Similarly, late on November 11th, the *Washington Post* reported that President Trump had "raised the idea of pressuring state legislators to pick electors favorable to him," and the *Wall Street Journal* also called the option of state legislatures picking new electors "one potential strategy" discussed by his legal team. Philip Rucker, Josh Dawsey & Ashley Parker, "Trump Insists He'll Win, But Aides Say He Has No Real Plan to Overturn Results and Talks of 2024 Run," *Washington Post*, (Nov. 11, 2020), available at https://www.washingtonpost.com/politics/trump-election-results-strategy/ 2020/11/11/a32e2cba-244a-11eb-952e-0c475972cfc0_story.html; Rebecca Ballhaus, "What Is Trump's Legal Strategy? Try to Block Certification of Biden Victory in States," *Wall Street Journal*, (Nov. 11, 2020), available at https://www.wsj.com/articles/what-is-trumps-legal-strategy-try-to-block-certification-of-biden-victory-in-states-11605138852.

54. Select Committee to Investigate the January 6th Attack on the United States Capitol, Transcribed Interview of William Stepien, (Feb. 10, 2022), p. 148-49.

55. Senator Mitt Romney (@MittRomney), Twitter, Nov. 19, 2020 10:36 p.m. ET, available at https://twitter.com/MittRomney/status/1329629701447573504.

56. This figure is almost certainly a significant undercount, since it only includes public remarks by President Trump, public testimony, or the most noteworthy interviews conducted by one of his subordinates, but it does not include a review of every single remark targeting State or local officials during this period by those presidential subordinates.

57. This figure is also almost certainly an undercount, since it only includes those posts by President Trump's campaign or advisors when they covered new ground that was substantially different from social media posts that were already made by President Trump. Also, many of these posts were replicated across multiple platforms.

58. Jonathan Oosting, "Trump Campaign Lobbies Michigan Lawmakers to Ignore Vote, Give Him Electors," *Bridge Michigan*, (Dec. 2, 2020), available at https://www.bridgemi.com/michigan-government/trump-campaign-lobbies-michigan-lawmakers-ignore-vote-give-him-electors; MIRS Monday Podcast, "Call to Legislator From Someone Claiming to be with Trump Campaign (12/1/2020)," PodBean, Dec. 1, 2020, available at https://www.podbean.com/media/share/pb-iqskx-f3cfc6; Documents on file with the Select Committee to Investigate the January 6th Attack on the United States Capitol (Angela McCallum Production), McCallum_01_001570, (Undated Basic Script for calls to Representatives/Senators).

59. Paul Bedard, "Exclusive: Trump Urges State Legislators to Reject Electoral Votes, 'You Are the Real Power,'" *Washington Examiner*, (Jan. 3, 2021), available at https://www.washingtonexaminer.com/washington-secrets/exclusive-trump-urges-state-legislators-to-reject-electoral-votes-you-are-the-real-power.

60. Documents on file with the Select Committee to Investigate the January 6th Attack on the United States Capitol (Maricopa County Board of Supervisors Production), CTRL0000020072 (December 24, 2020, copy of voice message and a transcription) pp. 1–2); *see also* Yvonne Wingett Sanchez and Ronald J. Hansen, "'Asked to Do Something Huge': An Audacious Pitch to Reverse Arizona's Election Results," *AZ Central*, (Dec. 2, 2021), available at https://www.azcentral.com/in-depth/news/politics/elections/2021/11/18/arizona-audit-rudy-giuliani-failed-effort-replace-electors/6349795001/.

61. Documents on file with the Select Committee to Investigate the January 6th Attack on the United States Capitol (National Archives Production), 076P-R000010292_0001 (November 12, 2020, email from Rep. Tim Walberg to Molly Michael).

62. Documents on file with the Select Committee to Investigate the January 6th Attack on the United States Capitol (National Archives Production), 076P-R000010292_0001 (November 12, 2020, email from Rep. Tim Walberg to Molly Michael). The day after Representative Walberg's call with the President, President Trump's assistant forwarded to the Acting Secretary of the Department of Homeland Security a letter signed by two other Michigan legislators outlining claims of supposed election fraud. Documents on file with the Select Committee to Investigate the January 6th Attack on the United States Capitol, (Department of Homeland Security production), CTRL0000033284, (Nov. 13, 2020 email from Molly Michael to Chad Wolf titled "Re: Michigan Letter"); Documents on file with the Select Committee to Investigate the January 6th Attack on the United States Capitol, (no production listed, Ex. 44 from Chad Wolf interview), CTRL0000926977 (Nov. 13, 2020 letter to Michigan Secretary of State Jocelyn Benson from Michigan State Senators Lana Theis and Tom Barrett).

63. "Administration of Donald J. Trump, 2020, Digest of Other White House Announcements," Government Publishing Office, (Dec. 31, 2020), p. 115, available at https://www.govinfo.gov/content/pkg/DCPD-2020DIGEST/pdf/DCPD-2020DIGEST.pdf; Annie Grayer, Jeremy Herb & Kevin Liptak, "Trump Courts Michigan GOP Leaders in Bid to Overturn Election He Lost," CNN, (Nov. 19, 2020), available at https://www.cnn.com/2020/11/19/politics/gop-michigan-results-trump/.

64. Documents on file with the Select Committee to Investigate the January 6th Attack on the United States Capitol (Mark Meadows Production), MM012007 (text from Kelli Ward to Meadows).

65. Brahm Resnik, "'Stop the Counting': Records Show Trump and Allies Pressured Top Maricopa County Officials Over Election Results," 12News, (July 7, 2021), available at https://www.12news.com/article/news/politics/stop-the-counting-records-show-trump-and-allies-pressured-top-maricopa-county-officials-over-election-results/75-61a93e63-36c4-4137-b65e-d3f8bde846a7.

66. Select Committee to Investigation the January 6th Attack on the United States Capitol, Informal Interview with Clint Hickman, (Nov. 17, 2021); Documents on file with the Select Committee to Investigate the January 6th Attack on the United States Capitol (Maricopa County Board of Supervisors Production), CTRL0000020004.

67. Brian Slodysko, "EXPLAINER: Why AP called Georgia for Biden," *Associated Press*, (Nov. 13, 2020), available at https://apnews.com/article/why-ap-called-georgia-for-joe-biden-29c1fb0502efde50fdccb5e2c3611017.

68. Donald J. Trump (@realDonaldTrump), Twitter, Nov. 13, 2020 7:50 p.m. ET, available at https://media-cdn.factba.se/realdonaldtrump-twitter/1327413534901350400.jpg (archived).

69. Donald J. Trump (@realDonaldTrump), Twitter, Nov. 14, 2020 9:29 a.m. ET, available at https://media-cdn.factba.se/realdonaldtrump-twitter/1327619653020110850.jpg (archived).

70. Donald J. Trump (@realDonaldTrump), Twitter, Nov. 16, 2020 9:04 a.m. ET, available at https://media-cdn.factba.se/realdonaldtrump-twitter/1328338211284616193.jpg (archived).

71. Donald J. Trump (@realDonaldTrump), Twitter, Nov. 19, 2020 1:46 p.m. ET, available at https://media-cdn.factba.se/realdonaldtrump-twitter/1329420741553643522.jpg (archived).

72. Donald J. Trump (@realDonaldTrump), Twitter, Nov. 30, 2020 1:59 p.m. ET, available at https://media-cdn.factba.se/realdonaldtrump-twitter/1333410419554344964.jpg (archived).

73. President Donald J. Trump, "Tweets of November 30, 2020," The American Presidency Project, available at https://www.presidency.ucsb.edu/documents/tweets-november-30-2020; *see also* Fox 10 Staff, "Tweet mocking Arizona Gov. Doug Ducey and Georgia Gov. Brian Kemp Now on Billboard," Fox 10 News, (Dec. 9, 2020), available at https://www.fox10phoenix.com/news/tweet-mocking-arizona-gov-doug-ducey-and-georgia-gov-brian-kemp-now-on-billboard.

74. Miles Bryan, "From Obscure To Sold Out: The Story Of Four Seasons Total Landscaping In Just 4 Days," NPR, (Nov. 11, 2020), available at https://www.npr.org/2020/11/11/933635970/from-obscure-to-sold-out-the-story-of-four-seasons-total-landscaping-in-just-4-d.

75. Matt Friedman, "Man Featured at Giuliani Press Conference is a Convicted Sex Offender," *Politico*, (Nov. 9, 2020), available at https://www.politico.com/states/new-jersey/story/2020/11/09/man-featured-at-giuliani-press-conference-is-a-sex-offender-1335241.

76. McKenzie Sadeghi, "Fact Check: No Evidence Vote Was Cast in Joe Frazier's Name," *USA Today*, (Nov. 14, 2020), available at https://www.usatoday.com/story/news/factcheck/2020/11/14/fact-check-no-evidence-late-joe-frazier-voted-2020-election/6283956002/; Ledyard King and John Fritze, "Trump Attorney Rudy Giuliani Says Trump Won't Concede, Revives Baseless Claims of Voter Fraud," *USA Today*, (Nov. 7, 2020) available at https://www.usatoday.com/story/news/politics/elections/2020/11/07/joe-biden-victory-president-trump-claims-election-far-over/6202892002/.

77. Veronica Stracqualursi, "Republican Election Official in Philadelphia Says He's Seen No Evidence of Widespread Fraud," CNN, (Nov. 11, 2020), available at https://www.cnn.com/2020/11/11/politics/philadelphia-city-commissioner-2020-election-cnntv/index.html.

78. Donald Trump (@realDonaldTrump), Twitter, Nov. 11, 2020 9:03 a.m. ET, available at https://media-cdn.factba.se/realdonaldtrump-twitter/1326525851752656898.jpg (archived).

79. Select Committee to Investigate the January 6th Attack on the United States Capitol, *Hearing on the January 6th Investigation*, 117th Cong., 2d sess., (June 13, 2022), at 1:47:00 to 1:48:00, available at https://www.youtube.com/watch?v=pr5QUInmGI8.

80. Select Committee to Investigate the January 6th Attack on the United States Capitol, *Hearing on the January 6th Investigation*, 117th Cong., 2d sess., (June 13, 2022), at 1:47:00 to 1:48:00, available at https://www.youtube.com/watch?v=pr5QUInmGI8.

81. Select Committee to Investigate the January 6th Attack on the United States Capitol, *Hearing on the January 6th Investigation*, 117th Cong., 2d sess., (June 13, 2022), at 1:47:00 to 1:48:00, available at https://www.youtube.com/watch?v=pr5QUInmGI8.

82. *See McQuade v. Furgason*, 91 Mich. 438 (1892). The various Boards of Canvassers in Michigan know that the certification process is clerical because they are so instructed in the official "Michigan Boards of County Canvassers Manual." *See* "Procedures and Duties of the

Boards of County Canvassers," State of Michigan, (July 2022), pp. 18-19, available at https://www.michigan.gov/-/media/Project/Websites/sos/02lehman/BCC_Manual.pdf?rev=7270a5ddcefa465b8ab8b95930ef5890.

83. "Minutes of Meeting Wayne County Board of Canvassers," Wayne County Board of Canvassers, (Nov. 17, 2020), p. 1, available at https://www.waynecounty.com/elected/clerk/board-of-canvassers.aspx.

84. "Minutes of Meeting Wayne County Board of Canvassers," Wayne County Board of Canvassers, (Nov. 17, 2020), pp. 1-5, available at https://www.waynecounty.com/elected/clerk/board-of-canvassers.aspx.

85. "Minutes of Meeting Wayne County Board of Canvassers," Wayne County Board of Canvassers, (Nov. 17, 2020), p. 5, available at https://www.waynecounty.com/elected/clerk/board-of-canvassers.aspx.

86. Select Committee to Investigate the January 6th Attack on the United States Capitol, Informal Interview of Monica Palmer, (Sept. 28, 2021); Select Committee to Investigate the January 6th Attack on the United States Capitol, Informal Interview of Ronna Romney McDaniel, (Mar. 9, 2022); Phone records for Monica Palmer show calls from Ronna McDaniel at 9:53 PM and 10:04 PM. *See* Documents on file with the Select Committee to Investigate the January 6th Attack on the United States Capitol (Verizon Production, Feb. 9, 2022).

87. Annie Grayer, Jeremy Herb, and Kevin Liptak, "Trump Courts Michigan GOP Leaders in Bid to Overturn Election He Lost," CNN, (Nov. 19, 2020), https://www.cnn.com/2020/11/19/politics/gop-michigan-results-trump/.

88. Select Committee to Investigate the January 6th Attack on the United States Capitol, Informal Interview of Monica Palmer, (Sept. 28, 2021). Palmer told the Select Committee that she could not recall the exact words that President Trump used on the call, and she claimed that she could not even recall whether the President raised issues related to the election.

89. Kendall Karson, Katherine Faulders, and Will Steakin, "Republican Canvassers Ask to 'Rescind' Their Votes Certifying Michigan Election Results," ABC News, (Nov. 19, 2020), available at https://abcnews.go.com/US/wayne-county-republican-canvassers-rescind-votes-certifying-election/story?id=74290114; Krystle Holleman and Spencer Soicher, "Pair of Wayne Co. Board of Canvassers Members File Affidavits to Rescind Certification of Election Results," WILX10, (Nov. 19, 2020), available at https://www.wilx.com/2020/11/19/pair-of-wayne-county-board-of-canvassers-members-file-affidavits-to-rescind-certification-of-election-results/; Paul Egan, "GOP Members of Wayne County Board of Canvassers Say They Want to Rescind Votes to Certify," *Detroit Free Press*, (Nov. 19, 2020), available at https://www.freep.com/story/news/politics/elections/2020/11/19/wayne-county-board-of-canvassers-monica-palmer-william-hartmann/3775242001/.

90. Kendall Karson, Katherine Faulders, and Will Steakin, "Republican Canvassers Ask to 'Rescind' Their Votes Certifying Michigan Election Results," ABC News, (Nov. 19, 2020), available at https://abcnews.go.com/US/wayne-county-republican-canvassers-rescind-votes-certifying-election/story?id=74290114; Krystle Holleman and Spencer Soicher, "Pair of Wayne Co. Board of Canvassers Members File Affidavits to Rescind Certification of Election Results," WILX10, (Nov. 19, 2020), available at https://www.wilx.com/2020/11/19/pair-of-wayne-county-board-of-canvassers-members-file-affidavits-to-rescind-certification-of-election-results/; Paul Egan, "GOP Members of Wayne County Board of Canvassers Say They Want to Rescind Votes to Certify," *Detroit Free Press*, (Nov. 19, 2020), available at https://www.freep.com/story/news/politics/elections/2020/11/19/wayne-county-board-of-canvassers-monica-palmer-william-hartmann/3775242001/.

91. Donald Trump (@realDonaldTrump), Twitter, Nov. 18, 2020 10:38 a.m. ET, available at https://media-cdn.factba.se/realdonaldtrump-twitter/1329086548093014022.jpg (archived).

92. Select Committee to Investigate the January 6th Attack on the United States Capitol, Informal Interview of Jack Sellers and Bill Gates, (Oct. 6, 2021).

93. Select Committee to Investigate the January 6th Attack on the United States Capitol, Informal Interview of Jack Sellers and Bill Gates, (Oct. 6, 2021).

94. Select Committee to Investigate the January 6th Attack on the United States Capitol, Informal Interview of Jack Sellers and Bill Gates, (Oct. 6, 2021).

95. Jonathan J. Cooper, "Arizona Governor Silences Trump's Call, Certifies Election," *Associated Press*, (Dec. 2, 2020), available at https://apnews.com/article/election-2020-donald-trump-arizona-elections-doug-ducey-e2b8b0de5b809efcc9b1ad5d279023f4.

96. Jonathan J. Cooper, "Arizona Governor Silences Trump's Call, Certifies Election," *Associated Press*, (Dec. 2, 2020), available at https://apnews.com/article/election-2020-donald-trump-arizona-elections-doug-ducey-e2b8b0de5b809efcc9b1ad5d279023f4.

97. Donald Trump (@realDonaldTrump), Twitter, Nov. 30, 2020 3:39 p.m. ET, available at http://web.archive.org/web/20201201024920mp_/https:/twitter.com/realDonaldTrump/status/1333556242984431616 (archived).

98. President Donald J. Trump, "Tweets of November 30, 2020," The American Presidency Project, available at https://www.presidency.ucsb.edu/documents/tweets-november-30-2020; "Tweet Mocking Arizona Gov. Doug Ducey and Georgia Gov. Brian Kemp Now on Billboard," Fox 10 News, (Dec. 9, 2020), available at https://www.fox10phoenix.com/news/tweet-mocking-arizona-gov-doug-ducey-and-georgia-gov-brian-kemp-now-on-billboard.

99. Donald Trump (@realDonaldTrump), Twitter, Nov. 30, 2020 3:40 p.m. ET, available at http://web.archive.org/web/20201201022358/https:/twitter.com/realDonaldTrump/status/1333556458575818754 (archived).

100. Doug Ducey (@DougDucey), Twitter, Nov. 30, 2020 9:48 p.m. ET, available at https://twitter.com/dougducey/status/1333603735855976450.

101. Doug Ducey (@DougDucey), Twitter, Nov. 30, 2020 9:48 p.m. ET, available at https://twitter.com/dougducey/status/1333603735855976450.

102. Doug Ducey (@DougDucey), Twitter, Nov. 30, 2020 9:48 p.m. ET, available at https://twitter.com/dougducey/status/1333603735855976450.

103. "Pennsylvania, Arizona, Michigan Legislatures to Hold Public Hearings on 2020 Election,"" Donald J. Trump for President, (Nov. 24, 2020), available at http://web.archive.org/web/20201130045430/https://www.donaldjtrump.com/media/pennsylvania-arizona-michigan-legislatures-to-hold-public-hearings-on-2020-election/.

104. "Donald Trump Remarks Transcript: Pennsylvania Republican Hearing on 2020 Election," Rev, (Nov. 25, 2020), available at https://www.rev.com/blog/transcripts/donald-trump-remarks-transcript-pennsylvania-republican-hearing-on-2020-election.

105. Teresa Boeckel and J.D. Prose, "Pa. GOP Lawmakers Host Giuliani to Hear Election Concerns. Trump Visits Via Cell Phone," *York Daily Record*, (Nov. 25, 2020), available at https://www.ydr.com/story/news/politics/2020/11/25/pa-gop-lawmakers-host-rudy-giuliani-hear-election-concerns/6420319002/.

106. Select Committee to Investigate the January 6th Attack on the United States Capitol, Informal Interview of Jake Corman, (Jan. 25, 2022).

107. *See* Documents on file with the Select Committee to Investigate the January 6th Attack on the United States Capitol (National Archives Production), 076P-R000008474_0001 (November 25, 2020, email from Jared Small confirming that Trump will not be present in Gettysburg); Philip Rucker, Ashley Parker, Josh Dawsey, and Amy Gardner, "20 Days of Fantasy and Failure: Inside Trump's Quest to Overturn the Election," *Washington Post*, (Nov. 28, 2020), available at https://www.washingtonpost.com/politics/trump-election-overturn/2020/11/28/34f45226-2f47-11eb-96c2-aac3f162215d_story.html; Alayna Treene and Rebecca Falconer, "Trump Cancels Pennsylvania Trip for GOP Hearing on Voter Fraud Claims," *Axios*, (Nov. 25, 2020) available at https://www.axios.com/2020/11/25/trump-pennsylvania-gop-hearing-voter-fraud-claims. Apparently, White House Chief of Staff Mark Meadows also contemplated going to Pennsylvania for the hearing when the President couldn't attend.

Text messages between Cassidy Hutchinson and Meadows's Secret Service detail say, "U heard how mark is motorcading to gburg right[,] and potus isn't anymore." Documents on file with the Select Committee to Investigate the January 6th Attack on the United States Capitol (Cassidy Hutchinson production), CH-CTRL0000000080 (Nov. 25, 2020).

108. "Donald Trump Remarks Transcript: Pennsylvania Republican Hearing on 2020 Election," Rev, (Nov. 25, 2020), available at https://www.rev.com/blog/transcripts/donald-trump-remarks-transcript-pennsylvania-republican-hearing-on-2020-election.

109. "Pennsylvania Senate Republican Lawmaker Hearing Transcript on 2020 Election," Rev, (Nov. 26, 2020), available at https://www.rev.com/blog/transcripts/pennsylvania-senate-republican-lawmaker-hearing-transcript-on-2020-election.

110. "Pennsylvania Senate Republican Lawmaker Hearing Transcript on 2020 Election," Rev, (Nov. 26, 2020), available at https://www.rev.com/blog/transcripts/pennsylvania-senate-republican-lawmaker-hearing-transcript-on-2020-election.

111. Select Committee to Investigate the January 6th Attack on the United States Capitol, Deposition of Rudolph Giuliani, (May 20, 2022), pp. 65–66; Select Committee to Investigate the January 6th Attack on the United States Capitol, Deposition of Molly Michael, (Mar. 24, 2022), pp. 59–60, 62; "Administration of Donald J. Trump, 2020, Digest of Other White House Announcements," Government Publishing Office, (Dec. 31, 2020), p. 116, https://www.govinfo.gov/content/pkg/DCPD-2020DIGEST/pdf/DCPD-2020DIGEST.pdf.

112. Documents on file with the Select Committee to Investigate the January 6th Attack on the United States Capitol (Cassidy Hutchinson production), CH-CTRL0000000062 (Nov. 25, 2020, Cassidy Hutchinson's text messages with Bernie Kerik).

113. Documents on file with the Select Committee to Investigate the January 6th Attack on the United States Capitol (Cassidy Hutchinson production), CH-CTRL0000000062 (Nov. 25, 2020, Cassidy Hutchinson's text messages with Bernie Kerik).

114. Select Committee to Investigate the January 6th Attack on the United States Capitol, Continued Interview of Cassidy Hutchinson (Mar. 7, 2022), pp. 87, 91–92.

115. Howard Fischer, "GOP Officials Still Fighting Arizona's Vote Tally on Very Day Biden's Win Will Be Certified," Tuscon.com, (Nov. 30, 2020), available at https://tucson.com/news/local/gop-officials-still-fighting-arizonas-vote-tally-on-very-day-bidens-win-will-be-certified/article_021fbb5c-673f-549a-9cbb-900178c17079.html.

116. Howard Fischer, "GOP Officials Still Fighting Arizona's Vote Tally on Very Day Biden's Win Will Be Certified," Tuscon.com, (Nov. 30, 2020), available at https://tucson.com/news/local/gop-officials-still-fighting-arizonas-vote-tally-on-very-day-bidens-win-will-be-certified/article_021fbb5c-673f-549a-9cbb-900178c17079.html.

117. Right Side Broadcasting Network, "LIVE: Arizona State Legislature Holds Public Hearing on 2020 Election," YouTube, at 2:08:56, Nov. 30, 2020, available at https://www.youtube.com/watch?v=rri6flxaXww&t=7738s.

118. Right Side Broadcasting Network, "LIVE: Arizona State Legislature Holds Public Hearing on 2020 Election," YouTube, at 1:21:02, Nov. 30, 2020, available at https://www.youtube.com/watch?v=rri6flxaXww&t=4862s.

119. Jenna Ellis (@JennaEllisEsq), Twitter, Nov. 30, 2020 3:04 p.m. ET, available at https://twitter.com/jennaellisesq/status/1333502306176835588.

120. "Remarks: Donald Trump Calls in to Meeting of Arizona GOP Lawmakers on Election," Factbase, (Nov. 30, 2020), available at https://factba.se/transcript/donald-trump-remarks-arizona-gop-meeting-election-november-30-2020.

121. Rudy Giuliani (@RudyGiuliani), Twitter, Nov. 30, 2020 11:17 p.m. ET, available at https://twitter.com/RudyGiuliani/status/1333626364805533696.

122. "Pennsylvania, Arizona, Michigan Legislatures to Hold Public Hearings on 2020 Election," Donald J. Trump, (Nov. 24, 2020), available at http://web.archive.org/web/20201130045430/

https://www.donaldjtrump.com/media/pennsylvania-arizona-michigan-legislatures-to-hold-public-hearings-on-2020-election/; Jonathan Oosting (@jonathanoosting), Twitter, Nov. 24, 2020 5:35 p.m. ET, available at https://twitter.com/jonathanoosting/status/1331365885123178499; Jonathan Oosting (@jonathanoosting), Twitter, Nov. 30, 2020 3:42 p.m. ET, available at https://twitter.com/jonathanoosting/status/1333511772448370689.

123. See "Report on the November 2020 Election in Michigan," Michigan Senate Oversight Committee, (June 21, 2020), available at https://misenategopcdn.s3.us-east-1.amazonaws.com/99/doccuments/20210623/SMPO_2020ElectionReport_2.pdf.

124. Wood TV8, "Giuliani and Laura Cox Hold 'Legal Briefing' Before Giving Testimony Wednesday Evening," Facebook Watch, at 10:30-10:45, Dec. 2, 2020, available at https://www.facebook.com/woodtv/videos/rudy-giuliani-and-laura-cox-hold-legal-briefing-before-giving-testimony-wednesda/1996033023872394/.

125. Wood TV8, "Giuliani and Laura Cox Hold 'Legal Briefing' Before Giving Testimony Wednesday Evening," Facebook Watch, at 13:05-13:20, Dec. 2, 2020, available at https://www.facebook.com/woodtv/videos/rudy-giuliani-and-laura-cox-hold-legal-briefing-before-giving-testimony-wednesda/1996033023872394/.

126. Michigan House Oversight Committee, Public Hearing, (Dec. 12, 2020), at 4:03:13-4:04:22, 4:05:59-4:07:09, available at https://www.rev.com/tc-editor/shared/QQodU0TgHNW4ACZmBtqq6EbotJVTGos3UifEuLQA8ygjV7GrDDAeGJ6hdps86h_ywJAatI_KepUqEeZnloKHBiByyMI.

127. Edward-Isaac Dovere (@IsaacDovere), Twitter, Dec. 3, 2020 7:56 a.m. ET, available at https://twitter.com/IsaacDovere/status/1334481562193317888.

128. Michigan House Oversight Committee, Public Hearing, (Dec. 12, 2020), at 4:09:04, available at https://www.rev.com/tc-editor/shared/QQodU0TgHNW4ACZmBtqq6EbotJVTGos3UifEuLQA8ygjV7GrDDAeGJ6hdps86h_ywJAatI_KepUqEeZnloKHBiByyMI.

129. Michigan House Oversight Committee, Public Hearing, (Dec. 12, 2020), at 4:35:15, available at https://www.rev.com/tc-editor/shared/QQodU0TgHNW4ACZmBtqq6EbotJVTGos3UifEuLQA8ygjV7GrDDAeGJ6hdps86h_ywJAatI_KepUqEeZnloKHBiByyMI.

130. 11Alive, "Second Georgia Senate Election Hearing," YouTube, at 1:56:30 to 1:57:15, 5:29:20-5:32:45, Dec. 3, 2020, available at https://www.youtube.com/watch?v=hRCXUNOwOjw.

131. GA House Mobile Streaming, "Governmental Affairs 12.10.20," Vimeo – Livestream, at 1:51:55-1:52:55, available at https://livestream.com/accounts/25225474/events/9117221/videos/214677184.

132. Global TV Online, "#LIVE: Georgia State Senate Holds Meeting on 2020 Election . . . ," You-Tube, at 3:08:00 to 3:09:30, 3:20:15 to 3:21:2, Dec. 30, 2020, available at https://youtu.be/D5c034r0RlU?t=12016.

133. 11Alive, "Second Georgia Senate Election Hearing," YouTube, at 0:33:30-0:58:00, December 3, 2020, available at https://www.youtube.com/watch?v=hRCXUNOwOjw.

134. Select Committee to Investigate the January 6th Attack on the United States Capitol, Transcribed Interview of Byung J. Pak, (May 19, 2022), pp. 10-23; United States Senate Judiciary Committee, Interview of Jeffrey Rosen, (August 7, 2021), pp. 30-31, available at https://www.judiciary.senate.gov/rosen-transcript-final; Declaration of Frances Watson at 1-3, Pearson v. Kemp, No. 1:20-cv-04809 (N.D. Ga., Dec. 6, 2020), ECF No. 72-1, available at https://www.documentcloud.org/documents/20420664-frances-watson-affidavit; Response of the Georgia Secretary of State to the Court's Order of September 20, 2021 at 5-7, 41-47, 53, 55, Favorito v. Wan, No. 2020CV343938 (Fulton County Sup. Ct., Ga., October 12, 2021), available at https://s3.documentcloud.org/documents/21084096/favorito-sos-brief-in-response-to-order-of-92021-with-exs-a-and-b.pdf; William P. Barr, One Damn Thing After Another: Memoirs of an Attorney General (Harper Collins, 2022), at pp. 541-42; "Georgia Election Officials Briefing Transcript December 7: Will Recertify Election Results Today,"

Rev, (December 7, 2020), available at https://www.rev.com/blog/transcripts/georgia-election-officials-briefing-transcript-december-7-will-recertify-election-results-today.

135. 11Alive, "Second Georgia Senate Election Hearing," YouTube, at 5:31:50-5:32:10, Dec. 3, 2020, available at https://www.youtube.com/watch?v=hRCXUNOwOjw.

136. GA House Mobile Streaming, "Governmental Affairs 12.10.20," Vimeo – Livestream, at 2:09:00-2:13:00, available at https://livestream.com/accounts/25225474/events/9117221/videos/214677184.

137. GA House Mobile Streaming, "Governmental Affairs 12.10.20," Vimeo – Livestream, at 2:09:00-2:13:00, available at https://livestream.com/accounts/25225474/events/9117221/videos/214677184.

138. Mike Wilkinson, "The Rudy Giuliani 'Circus' Has Left Lansing. The Reviews Are Bad," *Bridge Michigan*, (Dec. 3, 2020), available at https://www.bridgemi.com/michigan-government/rudy-giuliani-circus-has-left-lansing-reviews-are-bad.

139. Mike Wilkinson, "The Rudy Giuliani 'Circus' Has Left Lansing. The Reviews Are Bad," *Bridge Michigan*, (Dec. 3, 2020), available at https://www.bridgemi.com/michigan-government/rudy-giuliani-circus-has-left-lansing-reviews-are-bad.

140. Donald J. Trump (@realDonaldTrump), Twitter, Dec. 6, 2020 6:01 a.m. ET, https://media-cdn.factba.se/realdonaldtrump-twitter/1335464302766149632.jpg (archived)..

141. *In the Matter of Rudolph W. Giuliani*, No. 2021-00506, slip op at *2, 32 (N.Y. App. Div. May 3, 2021), available at https://int.nyt.com/data/documenttools/giuliani-law-license-suspension/1ae5ad6007c0ebfa/full.pdf.

142. Documents on file with the Select Committee to Investigate the January 6th Attack on the United States Capitol (Angela McCallum Production), McCallum_01_001501 (November 30, 2021, Michael Brown text message to group at 2:47 a.m.).

143. Documents on file with the Select Committee to Investigate the January 6th Attack on the United States Capitol (Angela McCallum Production), McCallum_01_001501 (November 30, 2021, Michael Brown text message to group at 2:47 a.m.).

144. Documents on file with the Select Committee to Investigate the January 6th Attack on the United States Capitol (Angela McCallum Production), McCallum_01_001528 - 1564 (Trump Campaign spreadsheet).

145. Mirs Monday Podcast, "Call to Legislator from Someone Claiming to Be With Trump Campaign (12/1/20)," *Podbean.com*, at 0:08, (Dec. 1, 2020), available at https://www.podbean.com/media/share/pb-iqskx-f3cfc6.

146. Mirs Monday Podcast, "Call to Legislator from Someone Claiming to Be With Trump Campaign (12/1/20)," *Podbean.com*, at 1:32, (Dec. 1, 2020), available at https://www.podbean.com/media/share/pb-iqskx-f3cfc6.

147. Jonathan Oosting, "Trump Campaign Lobbies Michigan Lawmakers to Ignore Vote, Give Him Electors," *Bridge Michigan*, (Dec. 2, 2020), available at https://www.bridgemi.com/michigan-government/trump-campaign-lobbies-michigan-lawmakers-ignore-vote-give-him-electors.

148. Documents on file with the Select Committee to Investigate the January 6th Attack on the United States Capitol (Angela McCallum production), McCallum_01_001523 (text messages with Michael Brown).

149. Documents on file with the Select Committee to Investigate the January 6th Attack on the United States Capitol (Angela McCallum production), McCallum_01_001523 (text messages with Michael Brown).

150. Select Committee to Investigate the January 6th Attack on the United States Capitol, Transcribed Interview of Michael Shirkey, (June 8, 2022), pp. 8-10; Senator Mike Shirkey (@SenMikeShirkey), Twitter, Nov. 20, 2020 6:13 p.m. ET, available at https://twitter.com/SenMikeShirkey/status/1329925843053899780.

151. Select Committee to Investigate the January 6th Attack on the United States Capitol, Transcribed Interview of Michael Shirkey, (June 8, 2022), p. 10.

152. "Administration of Donald J. Trump, 2020, Digest of Other White House Announcements," Government Publishing Office, (December 31, 2020), p. 115, available at https://www.govinfo.gov/content/pkg/DCPD-2020DIGEST/pdf/DCPD-2020DIGEST.pdf.

153. Select Committee to Investigate the January 6th Attack on the United States Capitol, Transcribed Interview of Michael Shirkey, (June 8, 2022), p. 16.

154. Select Committee to Investigate the January 6th Attack on the United States Capitol, Transcribed Interview of Michael Shirkey, (June 8, 2022), pp. 16-18.

155. Select Committee to Investigate the January 6th Attack on the United States Capitol, Transcribed Interview of Michael Shirkey, (June 8, 2022), pp. 21-22.

156. Select Committee to Investigate the January 6th Attack on the United States Capitol, Transcribed Interview of Michael Shirkey, (June 8, 2022), p. 22.

157. Select Committee to Investigate the January 6th Attack on the United States Capitol, Informal Interview of Lee Chatfield (Oct. 15, 2021). Leader Shirkey did not remember any specific "ask" from the President during the Oval Office meeting. Select Committee to Investigate the January 6th Attack on the United States Capitol, Transcribed Interview of Michael Shirkey, (June 8, 2022), p. 16 ("One thing I do remember is that he never, ever, to the best of my recollection, ever made a specific ask. It was always just general topics[.]").

158. Select Committee to Investigate the January 6th Attack on the United States Capitol, Informal Interview of Lee Chatfield (Oct. 15, 2021).

159. Select Committee to Investigate the January 6th Attack on the United States Capitol, Transcribed Interview of Michael Shirkey, (June 8, 2022), p. 57.

160. "Legislative Leaders Meet with President Trump," State Senator Mike Shirkey, (Nov. 20, 2020), available at https://www.senatormikeshirkey.com/legislative-leaders-meet-with-president-trump/.

161. Select Committee to Investigate the January 6th Attack on the United States Capitol, Informal Interview of Lee Chatfield, (Oct. 15, 2021).

162. Select Committee to Investigate the January 6th Attack on the United States Capitol, Informal Interview of Lee Chatfield, (Oct. 15, 2021).

163. Team Trump (Text TRUMP to 88022) (@TeamTrump), Twitter, Jan. 3, 2021 9:00 a.m. ET, available at http://web.archive.org/web/20210103170109/https://twitter.com/TeamTrump/status/1345776940196659201 (archived).

164. Select Committee to Investigate the January 6th Attack on the United States Capitol, Transcribed Interview of Michael Shirkey, (June 8, 2022), p. 52; Aaron Parseghian, "Former Michigan Resident Slammed with Calls after Trump Campaign Mistakenly Posts Number on Social Media," Fox 17 West Michigan, (Jan. 4, 2021), available at https://www.fox17online.com/news/politics/former-michigan-resident-slammed-with-calls-after-trump-campaign-mistakenly-posts-number-on-social-media.

165. Documents on file with the Select Committee to Investigate the January 6th Attack on the United States Capitol (Mark Meadows Production), MM012414 (text to Rep. Scott Perry from Meadows).

166. Documents on file with the Select Committee to Investigate the January 6th Attack on the United States Capitol (Mark Meadows Production), MM012445 (text to Meadows from Rep. Scott Perry).

167. Select Committee to Investigate the January 6th Attack on the United States Capitol, Informal Interview of Jake Corman, (Jan. 25, 2022); Jake Corman and Kerry Benninghoff, "Pa. Lawmakers Have No Role to Play in Deciding Presidential Election," *Centre Daily Times*, (Oct. 19, 2020), available at https://www.centredaily.com/opinion/article246527648.html.

168. Barton Gellman, "The Election That Could Break America," *The Atlantic*, (Sept. 23, 2020), available at https://www.theatlantic.com/magazine/archive/2020/11/what-if-trump-refuses-concede/616424/; Select Committee to Investigate the January 6th Attack on the United States Capitol, Informal Interview of Jake Corman, (Jan. 25, 2022); see Jake Corman, "Pa. Lawmakers Have No Role to Play in Deciding Presidential Election," *Centre Daily Times*, (Oct. 19, 2020) available at https://www.centredaily.com/opinion/article246527648.html. Senator Corman and other Pennsylvania lawmakers sent a letter to Congress in January that mentioned "numerous unlawful violations" of State law and asked that Congress "delay certification of the electoral college." Documents on file with the Select Committee to Investigate the January 6th Attack on the United States Capitol (National Archives Production), 076P-R000002160_00001. In his informal interview with the Select Committee, however, Senator Corman acknowledged that he signed the letter due to pressure he was receiving after the election, but explained that he believed fraud and these types of issues should be adjudicated in the courtroom, not the legislature, and, in any event, he said that he was never presented with credible evidence of voter fraud. *See* Select Committee to Investigate the January 6th Attack on the United States Capitol, Informal Interview of Jake Corman, (Jan. 25, 2022).

169. Select Committee to Investigate the January 6th Attack on the United States Capitol, Informal Interview of Jake Corman, (Jan. 25, 2022).

170. Select Committee to Investigate the January 6th Attack on the United States Capitol, Informal Interview of Jake Corman, (Jan. 25, 2022).

171. Select Committee to Investigate the January 6th Attack on the United States Capitol, Informal Interview of Jake Corman, (Jan. 25, 2022).

172. Select Committee to Investigate the January 6th Attack on the United States Capitol, Informal Interview of Jake Corman, (Jan. 25, 2022).

173. Select Committee to Investigate the January 6th Attack on the United States Capitol, Informal Interview of Jake Corman, (Jan. 25, 2022).

174. Select Committee to Investigate the January 6th Attack on the United States Capitol, Informal Interview of Jake Corman, (Jan. 25, 2022).

175. Select Committee to Investigate the January 6th Attack on the United States Capitol, Informal Interview of Jake Corman, (Jan. 25, 2022).

176. Select Committee to Investigate the January 6th Attack on the United States Capitol, Informal Interview of Jake Corman, (Jan. 25, 2022).

177. Select Committee to Investigate the January 6th Attack on the United States Capitol, Informal Interview of Jake Corman, (Jan. 25, 2022).

178. Documents on file with the Select Committee to Investigate the January 6th Attack on the United States Capitol (Bryan Cutler Production), B_CUTLER_0000131-0000134 (Giuliani and Ellis voicemails).

179. Select Committee to Investigate the January 6th Attack on the U.S. Capitol, Transcribed Interview of Bryan Cutler, (May 31, 2022), p. 21.

180. Select Committee to Investigate the January 6th Attack on the U.S. Capitol, Transcribed Interview of Bryan Cutler, (May 31, 2022), p. 21.

181. Documents on file with the Select Committee to Investigate the January 6th Attack on the United States Capitol (Bryan Cutler Production), B_CUTLER_0000131 (Giuliani and Ellis voicemail).

182. Documents on file with the Select Committee to Investigate the January 6th Attack on the United States Capitol (Bryan Cutler Production), B_CUTLER_0000132 (Jenna Ellis voicemail).

183. Documents on file with the Select Committee to Investigate the January 6th Attack on the United States Capitol (Bryan Cutler Production), B_CUTLER_0000133 (Giuliani voicemail).

184. Documents on file with the Select Committee to Investigate the January 6th Attack on the United States Capitol (Bryan Cutler Production), B_CUTLER_0000134 (Giuliani voicemail).

185. Select Committee to Investigate the January 6th Attack on the U.S. Capitol, Transcribed Interview of Bryan Cutler, (May 31, 2022), pp. 42-44, 46-47. The *New York Times* reported that Speaker Cutler spoke with President Trump twice by phone, Cutler told the Select Committee that this claim was incorrect and that he only spoke with the President by phone once, followed by their second conversation on December 3rd, which was in person. *See* Trip Gabriel, "Trump Asked Pennsylvania House Speaker about Overturning His Loss," *New York Times*, (Dec. 8, 2020), available at https://www.nytimes.com/2020/12/08/us/politics/trump-pennsylvania-house-speaker.html; *see also* Amy Gardner, Josh Dawsey and Rachael Bade, "Trump Asks Pennsylvania House Speaker for Help Overturning Election Results, Personally Intervening in a Third State," *Washington Post*, (Dec. 8, 2020), available at https://www.washingtonpost.com/politics/trump-pennsylvania-speaker-call/2020/12/07/d65fe8c4-38bf-11eb-98c4-25dc9f4987e8_story.html.

186. Select Committee to Investigate the January 6th Attack on the U.S. Capitol, Transcribed Interview of Bryan Cutler, (May 31, 2022), pp. 43-44.

187. Select Committee to Investigate the January 6th Attack on the U.S. Capitol, Transcribed Interview of Bryan Cutler, (May 31, 2022), pp. 26-27, 44.

188. Select Committee to Investigate the January 6th Attack on the U.S. Capitol, Transcribed Interview of Bryan Cutler, (May 31, 2022), pp. 49-57; Select Committee to Investigate the January 6th Attack on the United States Capitol, Informal Interview of Jake Corman, (Jan. 25, 2022).

189. Select Committee to Investigate the January 6th Attack on the U.S. Capitol, Transcribed Interview of Bryan Cutler, (May 31, 2022), p. 50.

190. Select Committee to Investigate the January 6th Attack on the U.S. Capitol, Transcribed Interview of Bryan Cutler, (May 31, 2022), pp. 50-55.

191. Select Committee to Investigate the January 6th Attack on the U.S. Capitol, Transcribed Interview of Bryan Cutler, (May 31, 2022), pp. 54-55.

192. Select Committee to Investigate the January 6th Attack on the U.S. Capitol, Transcribed Interview of Bryan Cutler, (May 31, 2022), pp. 56-57.

193. "Statement on Election Reform," Pennsylvania Senate GOP (Dec 3, 2020, accessed July 14, 2022), available at https://www.pasenategop.com/wp-content/uploads/2020/12/election-reform-120320.pdf.

194. Donald J. Trump (@realDonaldTrump), Twitter, Dec. 6, 2020 12:56 a.m. ET, available at https://media-cdn.factba.se/realdonaldtrump-twitter/1335463148137164802.jpg (archived).

195. Donald J. Trump (@realDonaldTrump), Twitter, Dec. 8, 2020 2:51 p.m. ET, available at https://media-cdn.factba.se/realdonaldtrump-twitter/1336322408970559495.jpg (archived); "Letter to Pennsylvania's Congressional Delegation," Pennsylvania State GOP, (Dec. 4, 2020, last accessed July 14, 2022), available at http://www.pahousegop.com/Display/SiteFiles/1/2020/120420CongressElection2020B.pdf.

196. Select Committee to Investigate the January 6th Attack on the U.S. Capitol, Transcribed Interview of Bryan Cutler, (May 31, 2022), pp. 60-61.

197. Select Committee to Investigate the January 6th Attack on the U.S. Capitol, Transcribed Interview of Bryan Cutler, (May 31, 2022), p. 61.

198. Trip Gabriel, "Even in Defeat, Trump Tightens Grip on State G.O.P. Lawmakers," *New York Times*, (Dec. 9, 2020), available at https://www.nytimes.com/2020/12/09/us/politics/trump-pennsylvania-electoral-college.html.

199. Trip Gabriel, "Even in Defeat, Trump Tightens Grip on State G.O.P. Lawmakers," *New York Times*, (Dec. 9, 2020), available at https://www.nytimes.com/2020/12/09/us/politics/trump-pennsylvania-electoral-college.html.

200. Select Committee to Investigate the January 6th Attack on the United States Capitol, *Hearing on the January 6th Investigation*, 117th Cong., 2d sess., (June 21, 2022), at 41:30-46:35, available at https://www.youtube.com/watch?v=xa43_z_82Og; Yvonne Wingett Sanchez and

Ronald J. Hansen, "White House Phone Calls, Baseless Fraud Charges: The Origins of the Arizona Election Review," *AZ Central*, (Nov. 17, 2021), available at https://www.azcentral.com/in-depth/news/politics/elections/2021/11/17/arizona-audit-trump-allies-pushed-to-undermine-2020-election/6045151001/.

201. Select Committee to Investigate the January 6th Attack on the United States Capitol, *Hearing on the January 6th Investigation*, 117th Cong., 2d sess., (June 21, 2022), at 41:30-46:35, available at https://www.youtube.com/watch?v=xa43_z_82Og; Yvonne Wingett Sanchez and Ronald J. Hansen, "White House Phone Calls, Baseless Fraud Charges: The Origins of the Arizona Election Review," *AZ Central*, (Nov. 17, 2021), available at https://www.azcentral.com/in-depth/news/politics/elections/2021/11/17/arizona-audit-trump-allies-pushed-to-undermine-2020-election/6045151001/.

202. Select Committee to Investigate the January 6th Attack on the United States Capitol, *Hearing on the January 6th Investigation*, 117th Cong., 2d sess., (June 21, 2022), at 41:30-46:35, available at https://www.youtube.com/watch?v=xa43_z_82Og; Yvonne Wingett Sanchez and Ronald J. Hansen, "White House Phone Calls, Baseless Fraud Charges: The Origins of the Arizona Election Review," *AZ Central*, (Nov. 17, 2021), available at https://www.azcentral.com/in-depth/news/politics/elections/2021/11/17/arizona-audit-trump-allies-pushed-to-undermine-2020-election/6045151001/.

203. Select Committee to Investigate the January 6th Attack on the United States Capitol, *Hearing on the January 6th Investigation*, 117th Cong., 2d sess., (June 21, 2022), at 41:30-46:35, available at https://www.youtube.com/watch?v=xa43_z_82Og; Yvonne Wingett Sanchez and Ronald J. Hansen, "White House Phone Calls, Baseless Fraud Charges: The Origins of the Arizona Election Review," *AZ Central*, (Nov. 17, 2021), available at https://www.azcentral.com/in-depth/news/politics/elections/2021/11/17/arizona-audit-trump-allies-pushed-to-undermine-2020-election/6045151001/.

204. Select Committee to Investigate the January 6th Attack on the United States Capitol, *Hearing on the January 6th Investigation*, 117th Cong., 2d sess., (June 21, 2022), at 41:30-46:35, available at https://www.youtube.com/watch?v=xa43_z_82Og.

205. Select Committee to Investigate the January 6th Attack on the United States Capitol, *Hearing on the January 6th Investigation*, 117th Cong., 2d sess., (June 21, 2022), at 41:30-46:35, available at https://www.youtube.com/watch?v=xa43_z_82Og.

206. Select Committee to Investigate the January 6th Attack on the United States Capitol, *Hearing on the January 6th Investigation*, 117th Cong., 2d sess., (June 21, 2022), at 41:30-46:35, available at https://www.youtube.com/watch?v=xa43_z_82Og. In his testimony to the Select Committee, Speaker Bowers said this appeal to party loyalty occurred in that call or in a later meeting, and that the President brought it up "more than once."

207. Dillon Rosenblatt and Julia Shumway, "Giuliani COVID-19 Diagnosis Closes Arizona Legislature," *Arizona Capitol Times*, (Dec. 6, 2020), available at https://azcapitoltimes.com/news/2020/12/06/giuliani-covid-19-diagnosis-closes-arizona-legislature/; Select Committee to Investigate the January 6th Attack on the United States Capitol, Informal Interview of Arizona House Speaker Rusty Bowers, (Nov. 17, 2021); Vince Leach (@VinceLeach), Twitter, Dec. 1, 2020 11:28 p.m. ET, available at https://twitter.com/VinceLeach/status/1333991317500727298. Speaker Bowers told the Committee that Giuliani and Ellis were accompanied by Katherine Friess, J. Philip Waldron, Bernard Kerik, and others. *See* Select Committee to Investigate the January 6th Attack on the United States Capitol, Informal Interview of Arizona House Speaker Rusty Bowers, (Nov. 17, 2021).

208. Select Committee to Investigate the January 6th Attack on the United States Capitol, Deposition of Rudolph Giuliani, (May 20, 2022), pp. 58-59; Select Committee to Investigate the January 6th Attack on the United States Capitol, Deposition of Jenna Ellis, (Mar. 8, 2022), pp. 50-51.

209. "Select Committee to Investigate the January 6th Attack on the U.S. Capitol, Transcribed Interview of Russel "Rusty" Bowers, (June 19, 2022), pp. 35-36; Select Committee to Investigate the January 6th Attack on the United States Capitol, Informal Interview of Arizona

House Speaker Rusty Bowers, (Nov. 17, 2021); "Speaker Bowers Addresses Calls for the Legislature to Overturn 2020 Certified Election Results," Arizona State Legislature, (Dec. 4, 2020), available at https://www.azleg.gov/press/house/54LEG/2R/201204STATEMENT.pdf

210.   Select Committee to Investigate the January 6th Attack on the United States Capitol, *Hearing on the January 6th Investigation*, 117th Cong., 2d sess., (June 21, 2022), at 53:00-53:40, available at https://www.youtube.com/watch?v=xa43_z_82Og.

211.   Select Committee to Investigate the January 6th Attack on the United States Capitol, *Hearing on the January 6th Investigation*, 117th Cong., 2d sess., (June 21, 2022), at 53:00-53:40, available at https://www.youtube.com/watch?v=xa43_z_82Og.

212.   Select Committee to Investigate the January 6th Attack on the United States Capitol, *Hearing on the January 6th Investigation*, 117th Cong., 2d sess., (June 21, 2022), at 53:00-53:40, available at https://www.youtube.com/watch?v=xa43_z_82Og.

213.   Select Committee to Investigate the January 6th Attack on the United States Capitol, *Hearing on the January 6th Investigation*, 117th Cong., 2d sess., (June 21, 2022), at 53:00-53:40, available at https://www.youtube.com/watch?v=xa43_z_82Og.

214.   Select Committee to Investigate the January 6th Attack on the United States Capitol, *Hearing on the January 6th Investigation*, 117th Cong., 2d sess., (June 21, 2022), at 56:00-59:50, available at https://www.youtube.com/watch?v=xa43_z_82Og; Select Committee to Investigate the January 6th Attack on the United States Capitol, Transcribed Interview of Russell Bowers, (June 19, 2022), pp. 39-41.

215.   Select Committee to Investigate the January 6th Attack on the United States Capitol, *Hearing on the January 6th Investigation*, 117th Cong., 2d sess., (June 21, 2022), at 56:00-59:50, available at https://www.youtube.com/watch?v=xa43_z_82Og.

216.   Select Committee to Investigate the January 6th Attack on the United States Capitol, *Hearing on the January 6th Investigation*, 117th Cong., 2d sess., (June 21, 2022), at 56:00-59:50, available at https://www.youtube.com/watch?v=xa43_z_82Og.

217.   "Trump Allies Leave Voicemail Messages for Maricopa County Supervisors," *AZ Central*, (July 2, 2021), available at https://www.azcentral.com/videos/news/politics/elections/2021/07/02/trump-allies-left-voicemail-messages-maricopa-county-supervisors-election-and-contested-results/7837919002/.

218.   "Trump Allies Leave Voicemail Messages for Maricopa County Supervisors," *AZ Central*, (July 2, 2021), available at https://www.azcentral.com/videos/news/politics/elections/2021/07/02/trump-allies-left-voicemail-messages-maricopa-county-supervisors-election-and-contested-results/7837919002/.

219.   *See* Select Committee to Investigate the January 6th Attack on the United States Capitol, Informal Interview of Clint Hickman, (Nov. 17, 2021); *see also* Yvonne Wingett Sanchez, "'We Need You to Stop the Counting': Records Detail Intense Efforts by Trump Allies to Pressure Maricopa County Supervisors," *AZ Central* (July 2, 2021), available at https://www.azcentral.com/story/news/politics/elections/2021/07/02/records-show-trump-allies-kelli-ward-rudy-giuliani-pressed-county-officials-over-election-results/7813304002/.

220.   Yvonne Wingett Sanchez, "'Fighting for Democracy Here': Election Audit Pits Maricopa County Republicans vs. Arizona GOP," *AZ Central*, (May 23, 2021) available at https://www.azcentral.com/story/news/politics/elections/2021/05/23/election-audit-pits-maricopa-county-republicans-against-arizona-gop-senators/5186141001/; *see also* "Trump allies leave voicemail messages for Maricopa County supervisors," *AZ Central*, (July 2, 2021), available at https://www.azcentral.com/videos/news/politics/elections/2021/07/02/trump-allies-left-voicemail-messages-maricopa-county-supervisors-election-and-contested-results/7837919002/.

221.   Documents on file with the Select Committee to Investigate the January 6th Attack on the United States Capitol (Maricopa County Board of Supervisors Production), CTRL0000020072, pp. 1-2 (December 24, 2020, copy of voice message and a transcription); *see also* Yvonne Wingett Sanchez and Ronald J. Hansen, "'Asked to Do Something Huge': An Audacious Pitch

to Reverse Arizona's Election Results," *AZ Central*, (Dec. 2, 2021), available at https://www.azcentral.com/in-depth/news/politics/elections/2021/11/18/arizona-audit-rudy-giuliani-failed-effort-replace-electors/6349795001/.

222. Select Committee to Investigate the January 6th Attack on the United States Capitol, Informal Interview of Jack Sellers and Bill Gates, (Oct. 6, 2021).

223. Yvonne Wingett Sanchez, "'We Need You to Stop the Counting': Records Detail Intense Efforts by Trump Allies to Pressure Maricopa County Supervisors," *AZ Central*, (July 2, 2021), available at https://www.azcentral.com/story/news/politics/elections/2021/07/02/records-show-trump-allies-kelli-ward-rudy-giuliani-pressed-county-officials-over-election-results/7813304002/.

224. Yvonne Wingett Sanchez, "'We Need You to Stop the Counting': Records Detail Intense Efforts by Trump Allies to Pressure Maricopa County Supervisors," *AZ Central*, (July 2, 2021), available at https://www.azcentral.com/story/news/politics/elections/2021/07/02/records-show-trump-allies-kelli-ward-rudy-giuliani-pressed-county-officials-over-election-results/7813304002/.

225. Document on file with the Select Committee to Investigate the January 6th Attack on the United States Capitol (Bill Stepien Production), WS00104-105 (December 5, 2021, email from Joshua Findlay to Matthew Morgan, Justin Clark, and Bill Stepien at 11:44 pm).

226. Brian Kemp (@BrianKempGA), Twitter, Dec. 5, 2020 12:44 p.m., available at https://twitter.com/briankempga/status/1335278871630008324.

227. Donald J. Trump (@realDonaldTrump), Twitter, Dec. 5, 2020 9:35 pm ET, available at https://media-cdn.factba.se/realdonaldtrump-twitter/1335336916582084614.jpg (archived). As detailed later in this report, the call for special sessions of legislatures in various States, including Georgia, never gained traction and, when all else failed, became a focus for two Department of Justice lawyers.

228. Office of Governor Brian P. Kemp, "Gov. Kemp, Lt. Gov. Duncan Issue Statement on Request for Special Session of General Assembly," MadMimi.com, (Dec. 6, 2020), available at https://madmimi.com/p/50e7a11?pact=1301484-161142215-11561983238-b09ac0db7ff3f3c8bd594d6a33e7f63d0cf4c135.

229. Donald J. Trump (@realDonaldTrump), Twitter, Dec. 8, 2020 3:07 p.m., available at http://web.archive.org/web/20201208200907/https://twitter.com/realdonaldtrump/status/1336401919422640128 (archived) (retweeting Lin Wood (@LLinWood), Twitter, Dec. 8, 2020, 11:22 a.m., available at http://web.archive.org/web/20201208200908/https://twitter.com/LLinWood/status/1336390712380813313 (archived)).

230. Brett Samuels, "Trump Retweets Lawyer Who Said Republican Officials in Georgia Are 'Going to Jail'," *The Hill*, (Dec. 15, 2020), available at https://thehill.com/homenews/campaign/530250-trump-retweets-lawyer-who-says-republican-officials-in-georgia-are-going-to/.

231. Search results for "'The Republican Governor of Georgia refuses' | 'As badly as we were treated in Georgia' | kemp | @briankempga," from November 30 to December 31, 2020, Trump Twitter Archive V2, (last accessed December 12, 2022), available at https://www.thetrumparchive.com/?searchbox=%22%5C%22The+Republican+Governor+of+Georgia+refuses%5C%22+%7C+%5C%22As+badly+as+we+were+treated+in+Georgia%5C%22+%7C+kemp+%7C+%40briankempga%22&dates=%5B%222020-11-30%22%2C%222020-12-30%22%5D&results=1.

232. Document on file with the Select Committee to Investigate the January 6th Attack on the United States Capitol (National Archives Production), 076P-R000007750_0001, (December 7, 2020 email from Bill White to Dan Scavino and others) including screenshot of Burt Jones (@burtjonesforga), Twitter, Dec. 7, 2020 11:26 a.m., available at https://twitter.com/burtjonesforga/status/1335984150789173248), available at https://twitter.com/burtjonesforga/status/1335984150789173248.

233. Donald J. Trump (@realDonaldTrump), Twitter, Dec. 7, 2020 1:29 p.m. ET, available at
     https://factba.se/biden/topic/twitter?q=burtjonesforga&f= (archived); Rudy W. Giuliani
     (@RudyGiuliani), Twitter, Dec. 7, 2020 12:25 p.m., available at https://twitter.com/
     RudyGiuliani/status/1335998988101804035.

234. Documents on file with the Select Committee to Investigate the January 6th Attack on the
     United States Capitol (National Archives Production), 076P-R000007693_00001.

235. Documents on file with the Select Committee to Investigate the January 6th Attack on the
     United States Capitol (National Archives Production), 076P-R000007693_00001.

236. Documents on file with the Select Committee to Investigate the January 6th Attack on the
     United States Capitol (National Archives Production), 076P-R000007693_00001.

237. David Wickert and Greg Bluestein, "Inside the Campaign to Undermine Georgia's Election
     (Part I)," *Atlanta Journal-Constitution*, (Dec. 30, 2021), available at https://www.ajc.com/
     politics/election/georgia-2020-election-what-happened/.

238. Shepherd's Sling, "Steven K. Bannon - War Room Pandemic - Ep. #568/569 (Full 2hrs Pod-
     cast)," BitChute, at 16:50 - 18:00, Dec. 8, 2020, available at https://www.bitchute.com/
     video/KyK4QPP7Ngyt/; John Fredericks (@jfradioshow), Twitter, Dec. 7, 2020 5:30 p.m. ET,
     available at https://twitter.com/jfradioshow/status/1336075668090654724; Jim Hoft,
     "Developing: President Trump Speaks with Georgia House Speaker David Ralston and
     Speaker Pro-Tem Jan Jones on Endorsing Special Session," *Gateway Pundit*, (Dec. 7, 2020),
     available at https://www.thegatewaypundit.com/2020/12/developing-president-trump-
     speaks-georgia-house-speaker-david-ralston-speaker-pro-tem-jan-jones-endorsing-
     special-session/.

239. FYNTV FetchYourNews, "#BKP Has a Live Call-In with David Ralston," YouTube, at 2:30 - 3:12
     (Dec. 8, 2020), available at http://web.archive.org/web/20201224164814/https://
     www.youtube.com/watch?v=ZdN5vNOl6F4&gl=US&hl=en (archived); Julie Carr, "Georgia
     Speaker of the House David Ralston Joins BKP Politics to Discuss His Call with President
     Trump and a Legal Path Forward," *Tennessee Star*, (Dec. 20, 2020), available at https://
     tennesseestar.com/2020/12/20/georgia-speaker-of-the-house-david-ralston-joins-bkp-
     politics-to-discuss-his-call-with-president-trump-and-a-legal-path-forward/.

240. Select Committee to Investigate the January 6th Attack on the United States Capitol, Con-
     tinued Interview of Cassidy Hutchinson, (Mar. 7, 2022), pp. 162-67.

241. Documents on file with the Select Committee to Investigate the January 6th Attack on the
     United States Capitol (Georgia Secretary of State Production), GA SOS ORR (21-344) 005651
     (Dec. 23, 2020 call between President Trump and Frances Watson); Select Committee to
     Investigate the January 6th Attack on the U.S. Capitol, Informal Interview with Frances Wat-
     son (Dec. 15, 2021); *see also* "Georgia Secretary of State Recording of Trump Phone Call to
     Election Investigator," American Oversight (Mar. 10, 2021), available at https://
     www.americanoversight.org/document/georgia-secretary-of-state-recording-of-trump-
     phone-call-to-election-investigator.

242. Documents on file with the Select Committee to Investigate the January 6th Attack on the
     United States Capitol (Mark Meadows Production), MM014152 (December 27, 2020 text mes-
     sage at 5:18 p.m. from Mark Meadows to Jordan Fuchs).

243. Documents on file with the Select Committee to Investigate the January 6th Attack on the
     United States Capitol (Mark Meadows Production), MM014153 (December 27, 2020 text mes-
     sage at 5:20 p.m. from Jordan Fuchs to Mark Meadows).

244. Documents on file with the Select Committee to Investigate the January 6th Attack on the
     United States Capitol (Mark Meadows Production), MM012317 (November 19, 2020 text mes-
     sage at 9:56 a.m. from Mark Meadows to Brad Raffensperger).

245. Documents on file with the Select Committee to Investigate the January 6th Attack on the
     United States Capitol (Mark Meadows Production), MM013362.

246. Documents on file with the Select Committee to Investigate the January 6th Attack on the United States Capitol (Mark Meadows Production), MM013632-33; see also Newsmax (@newsmax), Twitter, Dec. 11, 2020 9:45 p.m. ET, available at https://twitter.com/newsmax/status/1337589238078922752.

247. Philip Rucker, Ashley Parker, Josh Dawsey, and Seung Min Kim, "Trump Sabotaging GOP on His Way Out of Office with Push to Overturn Election," *Washington Post*, (Jan. 4, 2021), available at https://www.washingtonpost.com/politics/trump-sabotage-republicans/2021/01/04/df5d301e-4eb1-11eb-83e3-322644d82356_story.html.

248. "Georgia Sec. of State Discusses Phone Call with Trump About Election Results," Good Morning America, at 1:40 to 2:20, (Jan. 4, 2021), available at https://www.goodmorningamerica.com/news/video/georgia-sec-state-discusses-phone-call-trump-election-75032599.

249. Brad Raffensperger, Integrity Counts (New York: Simon & Schuster, 2021), p. 191 (reproducing the call transcript); Amy Gardner and Paulina Firozi, "Here's the Full Transcript and Audio of the Call Between Trump and Raffensperger," *Washington Post*, (Jan. 5, 2021), available at https://www.washingtonpost.com/politics/trump-raffensperger-call-transcript-georgia-vote/2021/01/03/2768e0cc-4ddd-11eb-83e3-322644d82356_story.html.

250. Amy Gardner and Paulina Firozi, "Here's the Full Transcript and Audio of the Call Between Trump and Raffensperger," *Washington Post*, (Jan. 5, 2021), available at https://www.washingtonpost.com/politics/trump-raffensperger-call-transcript-georgia-vote/2021/01/03/2768e0cc-4ddd-11eb-83e3-322644d82356_story.html.

251. Amy Gardner and Paulina Firozi, "Here's the Full Transcript and Audio of the Call Between Trump and Raffensperger," *Washington Post*, (Jan. 5, 2021), available at https://www.washingtonpost.com/politics/trump-raffensperger-call-transcript-georgia-vote/2021/01/03/2768e0cc-4ddd-11eb-83e3-322644d82356_story.html.

252. Brad Raffensperger, Integrity Counts (New York: Simon & Schuster, 2021), p. 191 (reproducing the call transcript); Amy Gardner and Paulina Firozi, "Here's the Full Transcript and Audio of the Call Between Trump and Raffensperger," *Washington Post*, (Jan. 5, 2021), available at https://www.washingtonpost.com/politics/trump-raffensperger-call-transcript-georgia-vote/2021/01/03/2768e0cc-4ddd-11eb-83e3-322644d82356_story.html (the Washington Post redacted Freeman's name and instead used "[name]" in the transcript); "Donald Trump Georgia Phone Call Transcript with Sec. of State Brad Raffensperger: Says He Wants to 'Find' Votes," Rev, (Jan. 4, 2021), available at https://www.rev.com/blog/transcripts/donald-trump-georgia-phone-call-transcript-brad-raffensperger-recording.

253. Amy Gardner and Paulina Firozi, "Here's the Full Transcript and Audio of the Call Between Trump and Raffensperger," *Washington Post*, (Jan. 5, 2021), available at https://www.washingtonpost.com/politics/trump-raffensperger-call-transcript-georgia-vote/2021/01/03/2768e0cc-4ddd-11eb-83e3-322644d82356_story.html.

254. Donald J. Trump (@realDonaldTrump), Twitter, Jan. 3, 2021 8:57 a.m. ET, available at https://media-cdn.factba.se/realdonaldtrump-twitter/1345731043861659650.jpg (archived). The archived image is in universal time.

255. Donald J. Trump (@realDonaldTrump), Twitter, Jan. 3, 2021 8:29 a.m. ET, available at https://media-cdn.factba.se/realdonaldtrump-twitter/1345723944654024706.jpg, (archived).

256. Select Committee to Investigate the January 6th Attack on the United States Capitol, *Hearing on the January 6th Investigation*, 117th Cong., 2d sess., (June 21, 2022), available at https://www.govinfo.gov/committee/house-january6th.

257. *See, e.g.*, Select Committee to Investigate the January 6th Attack on the United States Capitol, Transcribed Interview of Richard Donoghue, (Oct. 1, 2021), pp. 117-32; Documents on file with the Select Committee to Investigate the January 6th Attack on the United States Capitol (Department of Justice Production), HCOR-Pre-CertificationEvents-07262021-000698–000702 (Draft letter written by Jeffrey Clark).

258.   "Senate Committee to Discuss Election Issues in Pennsylvania," Pennsylvania Senate GOP website (Nov. 24, 2020, last accessed on July 15, 2022), available at https://www.pasenategop.com/blog/senate-committee-to-discuss-election-issues-in-pennsylvania/; Select Committee to Investigate the January 6th Attack on the United States Capitol, Deposition of Rudolph Giuliani, (May 20, 2022), pp. 65-66. https://www.pasenategop.com/blog/senate-committee-to-discuss-election-issues-in-pennsylvania/.

259.   Jeremy Roebuck and Andrew Seidman, "Pa. GOP lawmaker Doug Mastriano says he left the Capitol area before the riot. New videos say otherwise," *Philadelphia Inquirer*, (May 25, 2021), available at https://www.inquirer.com/news/doug-mastriano-capitol-riot-pennslyvania-video-20210525.html.

260.   Eric Metaxas, "Interview: Eric Metaxas Interviews Donald Trump with Douglas Mastriano," Factba.se Archive, (Nov. 30, 2020), available at https://factba.se/transcript/donald-trump-interview-eric-metaxas-douglas-mastriano-november-30-2020; Senator Doug Mastriano (@SenMastriano), Twitter, Nov. 30, 2020 5:56 p.m. ET, available at https://twitter.com/senmastriano/status/1333545380965986307.

261.   Documents on file with the Select Committee to Investigate the January 6th Attack on the United States Capitol (National Archives Production), 076P-R000008230_0001, 076P-R000008231_0001 (email and attachment from Mastriano to Molly Michael); *see also Kelly v. Pennsylvania*, 141 S. Ct. 950 (2020) (order denying application for injunctive relief presented to Justice Alito and denying referral to the full Court).

262.   Documents on file with the Select Committee to Investigate the January 6th Attack on the United States Capitol (National Archives Production), 076P-R000001378_00001, 076P-R000001379_00001.

263.   Documents on file with the Select Committee to Investigate the January 6th Attack on the United States Capitol (National Archives Production), 076P-R000003771_0001, 076P-R000003772_0001 (Dec. 21, 2020, email from Doug Mastriano to Molly Michael titled "Letter Requested by the President").

264.   Documents on file with the Select Committee to Investigate the January 6th Attack on the United States Capitol (National Archives Production), 076P-R000003771_0001, 076P-R000003772_0001 (Dec. 21, 2020, email from Doug Mastriano to Molly Michael titled "Letter requested by the President").

265.   *See, e.g.,* Documents on file with the Select Committee to Investigate the January 6th Attack on the United States Capitol (National Archives Production), 076P-R000003748_0001, 076P-R000003749_0001, (Dec. 29, 2020, Doug Mastriano email to Molly Michael titled "Pennsylvania letter for AG Donoghue regarding election"; Documents on file with the Select Committee to Investigate the January 6th Attack on the United States Capitol, (National Archives Production), 076P-R000003753_0001, 076P-R000003754_0001, (Dec. 22, 2020, Molly Michael email to Rush Limbaugh titled "From POTUS"); Documents on file with the Select Committee to Investigate the January 6th Attack on the United States Capitol, (National Archives Production) 076P-R000003761_0001, 076P-R000003762_0001, (Dec. 22, 2020, Molly Michael email to Pam Bondi titled "From POTUS"); Documents on file with the Select Committee to Investigate the January 6th Attack on the United States Capitol, (National Archives Production) 076P-R000003766_0001, (Dec. 21, 2020, Molly Michael email to Lou Dobbs titled "2 attachments from POTUS"); Documents on file with the Select Committee to Investigate the January 6th Attack on the United States Capitol, (National Archives Production), 076P-R000008968_0001, (Jan. 1, 2021, Molly Michael email to Kevin McCarthy titled "From POTUS"); Documents on file with the Select Committee to Investigate the January 6th Attack on the United States Capitol, (National Archive Production) 076P-R000003759_0001, (Dec. 22, 2020, Molly Michael email to John Eastman, Justin Clark, and Michael Farris titled "From POTUS"); Documents on file with the Select Committee to Investigate the January 6th Attack on the United States Capitol, (National Archives Production) 076P-R000003763_0001, (December 21, 2020, email from Molly Michael to Christopher Michel re: From POTUS).

266. Charlotte Cuthbertson, "Trump 'Resolved, Determined' about Election, Says Pennsylvania Senator," *Epoch Times* (Dec. 24, 2020), available at https://www.theepochtimes.com/trump-resolved-determined-about-election-says-pennsylvania-senator_3632138.html; Marc Levy & Mark Scolforo, "White House Invites GOP Lawmakers in Pennsylvania to Lunch," *Associated Press*, (Dec. 23, 2020), available at https://apnews.com/article/donald-trump-pennsylvania-coronavirus-pandemic-c5b7f43af7794f01f6d339b7258b915a; Jan Murphy, "Pa. Senators Head to White House for Pre-Holiday Lunch with President Trump," *Penn Live – Patriot-News*, (Dec. 23, 2020), available at https://www.pennlive.com/news/2020/12/pa-senators-head-to-white-house-for-pre-holiday-lunch-with-president-trump.html; "Ep 608- Pandemic: Merry Christmas Eve Special Hour 1 (w/ Mayor Giuliani, Dr. Peter K. Navarro, Major Sgt. Scotty Neil, Former Navy Seal Tej Gill, Christopher Flannery)," War Room Podcast (Dec. 24, 2020), 25:17 to 25:25, available at https://warroom.org/2020/12/24/ep-608-pandemic-merry-christmas-eve-special-hour-1-w-dr-peter-k-navarro-major-sgt-scotty-neil-former-navy-seal-tej-gill-christopher-flannery/. Charlotte Cuthbertson, "Trump 'Resolved, Determined' about Election, Says Pennsylvania Senator," *Epoch Times* (Dec. 24, 2020), available at https://www.theepochtimes.com/trump-resolved-determined-about-election-says-pennsylvania-senator_3632138.html; Marc Levy & Mark Scolforo, "White House Invites GOP Lawmakers in Pennsylvania to Lunch," *Associated Press* (Dec. 23, 2020), available at https://apnews.com/article/donald-trump-pennsylvania-coronavirus-pandemic-c5b7f43af7794f01f6d339b7258b915a; Jan Murphy, "Pa. Senators Head to White House for Pre-Holiday Lunch with President Trump," *Penn Live – Patriot-News* (Dec. 23, 2020), available at https://www.pennlive.com/news/2020/12/pa-senators-head-to-white-house-for-pre-holiday-lunch-with-president-trump.html; "Ep 608- Pandemic: Merry Christmas Eve Special Hour 1 (w/ Mayor Giuliani, Dr. Peter K. Navarro, Major Sgt. Scotty Neil, Former Navy Seal Tej Gill, Christopher Flannery)", War Room Podcast (Dec.https://warroom.org/2020/12/24/ep-608-pandemic-merry-christmas-eve-special-hour-1-w-dr-peter-k-navarro-major-sgt-scotty-neil-former-navy-seal-tej-gill-christopher-flannery/.

267. *See, e.g.,* Documents on file with the Select Committee to Investigate the January 6th Attack on the United States Capitol (National Archives Production), 076P-R000008298_0001 (December 28, 2020, email from Molly Michael to Mark Meadows forwarding Senator Doug Mastriano info for the president), 076P-R000007593_0001 (December 28, 2020, email from Molly Michael to Scott Toland forwarding Senator Doug Mastriano info for the president), 076P-R000003748_0001, 076P-R000003749_0001 (December 29, 2020, email and attachments from Doug Mastriano to Molly Michael re: Pennsylvania letter for AG Donoghue regarding election), , 076P-R000003745_0001, 076P-R000003746_0001, 076P-R000003747_0001 (December 31, 2020, email from Doug Mastriano to Molly Michael re: Letters requested by President Trump and attachments).

268. *See* Documents on file with the Select Committee to Investigate the January 6th Attack on the United States Capitol (National Archives Production), 076P-R000003745_0001, 076P-R000003746_0001, 076P-R000003747_0001 (December 31, 2020, email from Doug Mastriano to Molly Michael re: Letters requested by President Trump and attachments).

269. Documents on file with the Select Committee to Investigate the January 6th Attack on the United States Capitol (National Archives Production), 076P-R000003732_0001(Email from Molly Michael to Amy Swonger, passing along information from Mastriano, 076P-R000008399_0001 (Email from Amy Swonger to Molly Michael responding)). According to the White House's Director of the Office of Legislative Affairs, Amy Swonger, the President repeatedly asked for her to distribute political materials after the election, which led her to seek advice from the White House Counsel's Office because fulfilling the President's request would likely violate the Hatch Act. *See* Select Committee to Investigate the January 6th Attack on the United States Capitol, Transcribed Interview of Amy Swonger, (Oct. 28, 2022), pp. 52-53.

270. Documents on file with the Select Committee to Investigate the January 6th Attack on the United States Capitol (National Archives Production), 076P-R000007439_0001 (White House switchboard call log from Jan. 5, 2022).

271. Documents on file with the Select Committee to Investigate the January 6th Attack on the United States Capitol (National Archives Production), 076P-R000004788_0001, 076P-R000004789_0001-0066 (January 5, 2021, email from Mastriano attaching letter for Vice President Pence signed by Pennsylvania legislators), 076P-R000004957_0001 (Molly Michael acknowledging receipt), 076P-R000005084_0001 (Molly Michael passing the letter along to Marc Short), 076P-R000007338_0001 (acknowledgment that the letter was printed for POTUS), 076P-R000004687_0001, 076P-R000004688_0001 (January 5, 2021, email and attached letter to Molly Michael re: Caucus Letter to Sen. McConnell and Rep. McCarthy).

272. Donald J. Trump (@realDonaldTrump), Twitter, Jan. 5, 2021 9:59 p.m. ET, available at https://www.thetrumparchive.com/?results=1&dates=%5B%222021-01-04%22%2C%222021-01-06%22%5D&searchbox=%22BIG+NEWS+IN+PENNSYLVANIA%21+https%3A%2F%2Ft.co%2F7JqTWYUgOr%22 (archived); Donald J. Trump (@realDonaldTrump), Twitter, Jan. 6, 2021 12:46 a.m. ET, available at https://www.thetrumparchive.com/?results=1&searchbox=%22pennsylvania+is+going+to+trump.+The+legislators%22 (archived).

273. Select Committee to Investigate the January 6th Attack on the United States Capitol, Deposition of Douglas Mastriano, (August 9, 2022), pp. 10-11.

274. Documents on file with the Select Committee to Investigate the January 6th Attack on the United States Capitol (Alex Cannon Production), AC-0000150 - 153(emails with Jason Miller re: emails to PA/AZ).

275. Documents on file with the Select Committee to Investigate the January 6th Attack on the United States Capitol (Alex Cannon Production), AC-0000150 - 153 (emails with Jason Miller re: emails to PA/AZ).

276. Documents on file with the Select Committee to Investigate the January 6th Attack on the United States Capitol (Alex Cannon Production), AC-0000150 - 153 (emails with Jason Miller re: emails to PA/AZ).

277. Select Committee to Investigate the January 6th Attack on the United States Capitol, Deposition of Rudolph Giuliani, (May 20, 2022), pp. 225-26; Select Committee to Investigate the January 6th Attack on the United States Capitol, Interview of Christina Bobb, (Apr. 21, 2022), pp. 128-34.

278. Documents on file with the Select Committee to Investigate the January 6th Attack on the United States Capitol (National Archives Production), 076P-R000001891_00001.

279. Select Committee to Investigate the January 6th Attack on the United States Capitol, Transcribed Interview of Bernard Kerik, (Jan. 13, 2022), pp. 138-39.

280. Select Committee to Investigate the January 6th Attack on the United States Capitol, Transcribed Interview of Bernard Kerik, (Jan. 13, 2022), pp. 136-37.

281. Documents on file with the Select Committee to Investigate the January 6th Attack on the United States Capitol (National Archives Production), 076P-R000001890_00001, 076P-R000001891_00001 (December 28, 2020, email with attachment from Bernard Kerik to Mark Meadows re: GIULIANI TEAM STRATEGIC COMMUNICATIONS PLAN - v1.pdf).

282. Select Committee to Investigate the January 6th Attack on the United States Capitol, Deposition of Rudolph Giuliani, (May 20, 2022), pp. 225-27; Select Committee to Investigate the January 6th Attack on the United States Capitol, Interview of Bernard Kerik, (Jan. 13, 2022), pp. 139-140.

283. Documents on file with the Select Committee to Investigate the January 6th Attack on the United States Capitol (National Archives Production), 076P-R000001891_00001.

284. Documents on file with the Select Committee to Investigate the January 6th Attack on the United States Capitol (National Archives Production), 076P-R000001891_00001.

285. Documents on file with the Select Committee to Investigate the January 6th Attack on the United States Capitol (National Archives Production), 076P-R000001891_00001.

286. Documents on file with the Select Committee to Investigate the January 6th Attack on the United States Capitol (Rudy Giuliani Production), RGGLOBAL_DOM_00008525.

287. Shepherd's Sling, "Steve Bannon's War Room, Episode 623," BitChute, at 13:20 - 13:29, Dec. 31, 2020, available at https://www.bitchute.com/video/KyK4QPP7Ngyt/.

288. Shepherd's Sling, "Steve Bannon's War Room, Episode 623," BitChute, at 17:07 - 18:17, Dec. 31, 2020, available at https://www.bitchute.com/video/KyK4QPP7Ngyt/.

289. Shepherd's Sling, "Steve Bannon's War Room, Episode 623," BitChute, at 24:49 - 25:14, Dec. 31, 2020, available at https://www.bitchute.com/video/KyK4QPP7Ngyt/.

290. Bernard B. Kerik (@BernardKerik), Twitter, Dec. 27, 2020 11:53 a.m. ET, available at https://twitter.com/bernardkerik/status/1343238609768501253.

291. Bernard B. Kerik (@BernardKerik), Twitter, Dec. 13, 2020 1:05 a.m. ET, available at https://twitter.com/bernardkerik/status/1338001989846888448.

292. Select Committee to Investigate the January 6th Attack on the United States Capitol, Transcribed Interview of Cassidy Hutchinson, (Feb. 23, 2022), pp. 43-45; Select Committee to Investigate the January 6th Attack on the United States Capitol, Continued Interview of Cassidy Hutchinson (Mar. 7, 2022), pp. 184-85; Select Committee to Investigate the January 6th Attack on the United States Capitol, Continued Interview of Cassidy Hutchinson (May 17, 2022), p. 74.

293. Documents on file with the Select Committee to Investigate the January 6th Attack on the United States Capitol (National Archives Production),076P-R000008962_0006 (January 2, 2021, White House Switchboard records); "Election Integrity Group Meets with Legislators from Contested States," *Cision PR Newswire*, (Jan. 2, 2021), available https://www.prnewswire.com/news-releases/election-integrity-group-meets-with-legislators-from-contested-states-301199902.html; Daniel Chaitin, "Navarro: Six-Person Team Briefed Hundreds of State Lawmakers, Showed 'Receipts' of 'Stolen' Election," *Washington Examiner*, (Jan. 2, 2021, updated Jan. 3, 2021), available at https://www.washingtonexaminer.com/news/navarro-6-person-team-briefed-hundreds-of-state-lawmakers-showed-receipts-of-stolen-election.

294. Team, Got Freedom?, available at http://web.archive.org/web/20201202221908/https:/got-freedom.org/team/ (archived).

295. Documents on file with the Select Committee to Investigate the January 6th Attack on the United States Capitol (Ed McBroom Production), M11-12 (January 2, 2021, email from Jillian Anderson, signed by Phil Kline re: BRIEFING FOLLOW UP: ELECTION 2020 | GOT FREEDOM?); "Election Integrity Group Meets with Legislators from Contested States," *Cision PR Newswire*, (Jan. 2, 2021), available https://www.prnewswire.com/news-releases/election-integrity-group-meets-with-legislators-from-contested-states-301199902.html.

296. Documents on file with the Select Committee to Investigate the January 6th Attack on the United States Capitol (Ed McBroom Production), M11-12 (January 2, 2021, email from Jillian Anderson, signed by Phil Kline re: BRIEFING FOLLOW UP: ELECTION 2020 | GOT FREEDOM?); "Election Integrity Group Meets with Legislators from Contested States," *Cision PR Newswire*, (Jan. 2, 2021), available https://www.prnewswire.com/news-releases/election-integrity-group-meets-with-legislators-from-contested-states-301199902.html.

297. "Election Integrity Group Meets with Legislators from Contested States," *Cision PR Newswire*, (Jan. 2, 2021), available https://www.prnewswire.com/news-releases/election-integrity-group-meets-with-legislators-from-contested-states-301199902.html.

298. Paul Bedard, "Exclusive: Trump Urges State Legislators to Reject Electoral Votes, 'You Are the Real Power'," *Washington Examiner*, (Jan. 3, 2021), available at https://www.washingtonexaminer.com/washington-secrets/exclusive-trump-urges-state-legislators-to-reject-electoral-votes-you-are-the-real-power; Select Committee to Investigate the January 6th Attack on the United States Capitol, Deposition of Rudolph Giuliani, (May 20, 2022), pp. 99-100.

299. Paul Bedard, "Exclusive: Trump Urges State Legislators to Reject Electoral Votes, 'You Are the Real Power'," *Washington Examiner*, (Jan. 3, 2021), available at https://www.washingtonexaminer.com/washington-secrets/exclusive-trump-urges-state-legislators-to-reject-electoral-votes-you-are-the-real-power.

300. Paul Bedard, "Exclusive: Trump Urges State Legislators to Reject Electoral Votes, 'You Are the Real Power'," *Washington Examiner*, (Jan. 3, 2021), available at https://www.washingtonexaminer.com/washington-secrets/exclusive-trump-urges-state-legislators-to-reject-electoral-votes-you-are-the-real-power.

301. Daniel Chaitan, "Navarro: Six-Person Team Briefed Hundreds of State Lawmakers Showed 'Receipts' of 'Stolen' Election," *Washington Exam*iner, (Jan. 2, 2021), available at https://www.washingtonexaminer.com/news/navarro-6-person-team-briefed-hundreds-of-state-lawmakers-showed-receipts-of-stolen-election. The Select Committee attempted to ask Navarro about his participation in the call and other topics, but he ignored the Select Committee's subpoena and has been indicted by the Department of Justice.

302. Documents on file with the Select Committee to Investigate the January 6th Attack on the United States Capitol (Ed McBroom Production), M11-12 (January 2, 2021, email from Jillian Anderson, signed by Phil Kline re: BRIEFING FOLLOW UP: ELECTION 2020 | GOT FREEDOM?).

303. Documents on file with the Select Committee to Investigate the January 6th Attack on the United States Capitol (Ed McBroom Production), M11-12 (January 2, 2021, email from Jillian Anderson, signed by Phil Kline re: BRIEFING FOLLOW UP: ELECTION 2020 | GOT FREEDOM?)(quoted text bolded and italicized in original)

304. Documents on file with the Select Committee to Investigate the January 6th Attack on the United States Capitol (Ed McBroom Production), M11-12 (January 2, 2021, email from Jillian Anderson, signed by Phil Kline re: BRIEFING FOLLOW UP: ELECTION 2020 | GOT FREEDOM?).

305. Melanie Conklin, "These 15 State Legislators Asked Pence Not to Certify Election Results," *Wisconsin Examiner*, (Jan. 14, 2021), available at https://wisconsinexaminer.com/2021/01/14/these-15-state-legislators-asked-pence-not-to-certify-election-results/.

306. Documents on file with the Select Committee to Investigate the January 6th Attack on the United States Capitol (National Archives Production Production), 076P-R000005084_0001 (January 5, 2021, email from Doug Mastriano to Molly Michael re: Final letter to VP Pence, attaching the letter signed); Documents on file with the Select Committee to Investigate the January 6th Attack on the United States Capitol (National Archives Production Production), 076P-R000008735_0001 (January 5, 2021, letter to Vice President Pence signed by state legislators with "The President Has Seen" stamp).

307. Wood TV8, "Giuliani and Laura Cox Hold 'Legal Briefing' Before Giving Testimony Wednesday Evening," Facebook Watch, at 10:30-10:45, Dec. 2, 2020, available at https://www.facebook.com/woodtv/videos/rudy-giuliani-and-laura-cox-hold-legal-briefing-before-giving-testimony-wednesda/1996033023872394/.

308. Wood TV8, "Giuliani and Laura Cox Hold 'Legal Briefing' Before Giving Testimony Wednesday Evening," Facebook Watch, at 13:05-13:20, Dec. 2, 2020, available at https://www.facebook.com/woodtv/videos/rudy-giuliani-and-laura-cox-hold-legal-briefing-before-giving-testimony-wednesda/1996033023872394/.

309. Select Committee to Investigate the January 6th Attack on the United States Capitol, Transcribed Interview of Michael Shirkey, (June 8, 2022), pp. 33, 37, & 47-48. Documents on file with the Select Committee to Investigate the January 6th Attack on the United States Capitol, (AT&T Production, Feb. 9, 2022).

310. Select Committee to Investigate the January 6th Attack on the United States Capitol, Transcribed Interview of Michael Shirkey, (June 8, 2022), pp. 33-38.

311. Senator Mike Shirkey (@SenMikeShirkey), Twitter, Nov. 22, 2020 10:47 a.m. ET, available at https://twitter.com/SenMikeShirkey/status/1330538438723063815.

312. "Shirkey Issues Statement Regarding Election," Michigan Senate GOP, (from text, December 14, 2020), available at https://www.misenategop.com/shirkey-issues-statement-regarding-election/.

313. Donald Trump (@realDonaldTrump), Twitter, Dec. 4, 2020 2:49 p.m. ET, available at http://web.archive.org/web/20201211204139/https:/twitter.com/realDonaldTrump/status/1334993249082236931 (archived).

314. Donald J. Trump (@realDonaldTrump) RT of Christina Bobb (@christina_bobb) QT of Ali #StopTheSteal Alexander (@ali), Twitter, Dec. 6, 2020 12:53 a.m. ET, available at https://media-cdn.factba.se/realdonaldtrump-twitter/1335462365370994689.jpg (archived); "Tweets of December 6, 2020," The American Presidency Project at University of California Santa Barbara, https://www.presidency.ucsb.edu/documents/tweets-december-6-2020.

315. Team Trump, Facebook, Dec. 24, 2020 1:52 p.m., available at https://www.facebook.com/officialteamtrump/videos/arizona-contact-governor-ducey-and-your-legislators-todaydemand-they-hear-the-ev/303213471090533/.

316. Team Trump, Facebook, Dec. 26, 2020 5:36 p.m., available at https://www.facebook.com/officialteamtrump/videos/arizona-contact-governor-ducey-and-your-legislators-today/3496886293698026/.

317. Documents on file with the Select Committee to Investigate the January 6th Attack on the United States Capitol (Jamestown Associates Production), JTA000074-81 (Dec. 20, 2020, email chain from Jason Miller).

318. Documents on file with the Select Committee to Investigate the January 6th Attack on the United States Capitol (Jamestown Associates Production), JTA000074-81 (Dec. 20, 2020, email chain from Jason Miller).

319. Documents on file with the Select Committee to Investigate the January 6th Attack on the United States Capitol (Jared Kushner Production), JK_00423-436 (Dec. 22, 2020, text messages between Jason Miller and Jared Kushner, pp. 10-13).

320. Donald J. Trump (@realDonaldTrump), Twitter, , Dec. 1, 2020 10:27 p.m. ET, available at http://web.archive.org/web/20201203173245/https://mobile.twitter.com/realDonaldTrump/status/1333975991518187521 (archived).

321. Donald J. Trump (@realDonaldTrump), Twitter, Dec. 5, 2020 10:33 p.m. ET, available at https://media-cdn.factba.se/realdonaldtrump-twitter/1335351633459310593.jpg (archived).

322. Donald J. Trump (@realDonaldTrump), Twitter, Dec. 7, 2020 3:37 p.m. UTC, available at https://media-cdn.factba.se/realdonaldtrump-twitter/1335971721262796801.jpg (archived).

323. Donald J. Trump (@realDonaldTrump), Twitter, Dec. 7, 2020 7:50 p.m. ET, available at https://media-cdn.factba.se/realdonaldtrump-twitter/1336110929856040960.jpg (archived).

324. Donald Trump Thanksgiving Call to Troops Transcript 2020: Addresses Possibility of Conceding Election, Rev, (Nov. 26, 2020), available at https://www.rev.com/blog/transcripts/donald-trump-thanksgiving-call-to-troops-transcript-2020-addresses-possibility-of-conceding-election.

325. Linda So and Jason Szep, "Campaign of Fear: U.S. Election Workers Get Little Help from Law Enforcement as Terror Threats Mount," Reuters, (Sept. 8, 2021), available at https://www.reuters.com/investigates/special-report/usa-election-threats-law-enforcement/.

326. Fredreka Schouten, "Personal Threats, Election Lies and Punishing New Laws Rattle Election Officials, Raising Fears of a Mass Exodus," CNN, (July 21, 2021), available at https://www.cnn.com/2021/07/21/politics/election-officials-exodus/index.html.

327. Donald J. Trump (@realDonaldTrump) RT of Christina Bobb (@christina_bobb) QT of Ali #StopTheSteal Alexander (@ali), Twitter, Dec. 6, 2020 12:53 a.m. ET, available at https://media-cdn.factba.se/realdonaldtrump-twitter/1335462365370994689.jpg (archive); Donald J. Trump (@realDonaldTrump), Twitter, Dec. 6, 2020 12:53 a.m. ET, available at https://www.thetrumparchive.com/?searchbox=%22rusty+bowers%22&dates=%5B%222020-11-29%22%2C%222020-12-29%22%5D&results=1 (archived) (retweeting Christina Bobb).

328. Dennis Welch (@dennis_welch), Twitter, Dec. 8, 2020 11:23 p.m. ET, available at https://
     twitter.com/dennis_welch/status/1336526978640302080 (retweeting people who were post-
     ing Bowers's personal information); Dennis Welch (@dennis_welch), Twitter, Dec. 8, 2020
     11:28 p.m. ET, available at https://twitter.com/dennis_welch/status/1336528029791604737.

329. Select Committee to Investigate the January 6th Attack on the U.S. Capitol, Transcribed
     Interview with Russel "Rusty" Bowers (June 19, 2022), pp. 50-52; Kelly Weill, "Arizona GOP
     Civil War Somehow Keeps Getting Weirder," *Daily Beast*, (Dec. 11, 2020), available at
     https://www.thedailybeast.com/arizona-republican-party-civil-war-somehow-keeps-
     getting-weirder; Yvonne Wingett Sanchez and Ronald J. Hansen, "'Asked to do Something
     Huge': An Audacious Pitch to Reserve Arizona's Election Results," *Arizona Republic*, (Nov. 18,
     2021, updated Dec. 2, 2021), available at https://www.azcentral.com/in-depth/news/
     politics/elections/2021/11/18/arizona-audit-rudy-giuliani-failed-effort-replace-electors/
     6349795001/.

330. Select Committee to Investigate the January 6th Attack on the U.S. Capitol, Transcribed
     Interview with Russel "Rusty" Bowers (June 19, 2022), pp. 50-52.

331. House Select Committee to Investigate the January 6th Attack on the U.S. Capitol, Tran-
     scribed Interview with Russel "Rusty" Bowers (June 19, 2022), pp. 50-52.

332. Brahm Resnik, "VIDEO: Group chants 'We are watching you' outside Arizona Secretary of
     State Katie Hobbs' home," KPNX 12 News, (Nov. 18, 2020), available at https://
     www.12news.com/article/news/politics/video-group-chants-we-are-watching-you-outside-
     arizona-secretary-of-state-katie-hobbs-home/75-a569ae35-3b62-424e-88f8-f03ca8b89458;
     "Arizona Sec. of State Says She Hays Received Threats of Violence Following Election," Fox
     10 Phoenix, (Nov. 18, 2020, updated Nov. 19, 2020), available at https://
     www.fox10phoenix.com/news/arizona-sec-of-state-says-she-has-received-threats-of-
     violence-following-election; Brahm Resnik, "Arizona Law Enforcement Investigating Social
     Media Threat against Top Elections Official," KPNX 12 News, (Nov. 18, 2020), available at
     https://www.12news.com/article/news/local/arizona/arizona-law-enforcement-
     investigating-social-media-threat-against-top-elections-official/75-486474ea-11c9-47ad-
     a325-8bbed6e3e231.

333. "Arizona Sec. of State Says She Hays Received Threats of Violence Following Election," Fox
     10 Phoenix, (Nov. 18, 2020, updated Nov. 19, 2020), available at https://
     www.fox10phoenix.com/news/arizona-sec-of-state-says-she-has-received-threats-of-
     violence-following-election; Brahm Resnik, "Arizona Law Enforcement Investigating Social
     Media Threat against Top Elections Official," KPNX 12 News, (Nov. 18, 2020), available at
     https://www.12news.com/article/news/local/arizona/arizona-law-enforcement-
     investigating-social-media-threat-against-top-elections-official/75-486474ea-11c9-47ad-
     a325-8bbed6e3e231.

334. Isaac Dovere and Jeremy Herb, "'It's Absolutely Getting Worse': Secretaries of State Tar-
     geted by Trump Election Lies Live in Fear for their Safety and are Desperate for Protec-
     tion," CNN, (Oct. 26, 2021), available at https://www.cnn.com/2021/10/26/politics/
     secretaries-of-state-personal-threats-trump-election-lies/index.html; Michael Wines and
     Eliza Fawcett, "Violent Threats to Election Workers are Common. Prosecutions are Not,"
     New York Times, (June 27, 2022, updated July 1, 2022), available at https://
     www.nytimes.com/2022/06/27/us/election-workers-safety.html.

335. Committee on House Administration, Election Subversion: A Growing Threat to Election
     Integrity, Statement of Adrian Fontes Maricopa County Recorder (2016-2020), at *1, 6 (July
     28, 2020), available at https://docs.house.gov/meetings/HA/HA00/20210728/113971/HHRG-
     117-HA00-Wstate-FontesA-20210728.pdf.

336. Bob Christie, "Months after Biden Win, Arizona Officials Still Face Threats," *Associated
     Press*, (Feb. 12, 2021), available at https://apnews.com/article/joe-biden-donald-trump-
     arizona-phoenix-elections-2bd2306acb2ae89c0ef37182fbb415b7.

337. Nicole Valdes, "Online Death Threats Target Maricopa County Board of Supervisors," ABC 15 Arizona, (Jan. 8, 2021, updated Jan. 9, 2021), available at https://www.abc15.com/news/state/enough-is-enough-online-death-threats-target-maricopa-county-board-of-supervisors.

338. *Washington Post*, "The Arizona election official who faced death threats for telling the truth," YouTube, at 0:21, Nov. 2, 2021, available at https://www.youtube.com/watch?v=6gAc47ivjYk.

339. Genesis Sandoval, "Hickman: A Year after 2020 Elections, Threats, Abuse Still Coming In," *Cronkite News Arizona PBS*, (Nov. 2, 2021), available at https://cronkitenews.azpbs.org/2021/11/02/hickman-a-year-after-2020-elections-threats-abuse-still-coming-in/.

340. United States Senate Committee on the Judiciary, Hearing on Protecting our Democracy's Frontline Workers (Aug. 3, 2022), Written testimony by Jocelyn Benson, available at https://www.judiciary.senate.gov/imo/media/doc/Testimony%20-%20Benson.pdf; Michigan Department of State, "Statement from Secretary of State Jocelyn Benson Concerning Threats against Her and Her Family," (Dec. 6, 2020), available at https://www.michigan.gov/sos/Resources/News/2020/12/06/statement-from-secretary-of-state-jocelyn-benson-concerning-threats-against-her-and-her-family; Select Committee to Investigate the January 6th Attack on the United States Capitol, Transcribed Interview of Jocelyn Benson, (June 2, 2022), pp. 35-39.

341. Michigan Department of State, "Statement from Secretary of State Jocelyn Benson Concerning Threats against Her and Her Family, (Dec. 6, 2020), available at https://www.michigan.gov/sos/Resources/News/2020/12/06/statement-from-secretary-of-state-jocelyn-benson-concerning-threats-against-her-and-her-family; Select Committee to Investigate the January 6th Attack on the United States Capitol, Transcribed Interview of Jocelyn Benson (June 2, 2022), pp. 35-39.

342. Isaac Dovere and Jeremy Herb, "'It's Absolutely Getting Worse': Secretaries of State Targeted by Trump Election Lies Live in Fear for their Safety and are Desperate for Protection," CNN, (Oct. 26, 2021), available at https://www.cnn.com/2021/10/26/politics/secretaries-of-state-personal-threats-trump-election-lies/index.html.

343. Select Committee to Investigate the January 6th Attack on the United States Capitol, Informal Interview of Aaron Van Langevelde and Adrianne Van Langevelde, (Oct. 21, 2021); Tim Alberta, "The Inside Story of Michigan's Fake Voter Fraud Scandal," *Politico*, (Nov. 24, 2020), available at https://www.politico.com/news/magazine/2020/11/24/michigan-election-trump-voter-fraud-democracy-440475; Rod Meloni and Natasha Dado, "Michigan AG Launches Investigation into Threats against Canvassers," *Click on Detroit*, (Nov. 24, 2020), available at https://www.clickondetroit.com/news/local/2020/11/24/michigan-ag-launches-investigation-into-threats-against-canvassers/.

344. Select Committee to Investigate the January 6th Attack on the United States Capitol, Informal Interview of Aaron Van Langevelde, (Oct. 21, 2021).

345. Trey Grayson, Matthew Masterson, Orion Danjuma, and Ben Berwick, "State and Local Solutions Are Integral to Protect Election Officials and Democracy," Just Security, (Feb. 9, 2022), available at https://www.justsecurity.org/80142/state-and-local-solutions-are-integral-to-protect-election-officials-and-democracy/; Stanford Internet Observatory, "Tina Barton – Aftermath – Death Threats," YouTube, (Sept. 20, 2021), available at https://www.youtube.com/watch?v=Xi5Y7bwvy-Y.

346. Melissa Nann Burke and George Hunter, "'I Feel Afraid': Detroit Clerk Winfrey Testifies to U.S. House Panel on Death Threats She Received," *Detroit News*, (July 28, 2021), available at https://www.detroitnews.com/story/news/politics/2021/07/28/winfrey-testifies-before-house-panel-threats-election-workers/5400419001/.

347. Linda So and Jason Szep, "Campaign of Fear: U.S. Election Workers Get Little Help from Law Enforcement as Terror Threats Mount," *Reuters*, (Sept. 8, 2021), available at https://www.reuters.com/investigates/special-report/usa-election-threats-law-enforcement/.

348. Dave Boucher, "Black Michigan Lawmaker Posts Voicemails Saying She Should be Lynched," *Detroit Free Press*, (Dec. 6, 2020), available at https://www.freep.com/story/news/politics/elections/2020/12/06/michigan-lawmaker-posts-voicemails-saying-she-should-lynched/3849695001/.

349. Dave Boucher, "Black Michigan Lawmaker Posts Voicemails Saying She Should be Lynched," *Detroit Free Press*, (Dec. 6, 2020), available at https://www.freep.com/story/news/politics/elections/2020/12/06/michigan-lawmaker-posts-voicemails-saying-she-should-lynched/3849695001/.

350. Kayla Clarke, "Man faces felony charges for bomb threat at Michigan Capitol Building, threats against state representative," *Click on Detroit*, (Jan. 8, 2021), available at https://www.clickondetroit.com/news/local/2021/01/08/man-faces-felony-charges-for-bomb-threat-at-michigan-capitol-building-threats-against-state-representative/ (linking to affidavit).

351. Isaac Dovere and Jeremy Herb, "'It's Absolutely Getting Worse': Secretaries of State Targeted by Trump Election Lies Live in Fear for their Safety and are Desperate for Protection," CNN, (Oct. 26, 2021), available at https://www.cnn.com/2021/10/26/politics/secretaries-of-state-personal-threats-trump-election-lies/index.html; *see also* Select Committee to Investigate the January 6thAttack on the United States Capitol, Informal Interview of Kathy Boockvar, (Dec. 22, 2021).

352. Linda So and Jason Szep, "Campaign of Fear: U.S. Election Workers Get Little Help from Law Enforcement as Terror Threats Mount," *Reuters*, (Sept. 8, 2021), available at https://www.reuters.com/investigates/special-report/usa-election-threats-law-enforcement/.

353. Isaac Dovere and Jeremy Herb, "'It's Absolutely Getting Worse': Secretaries of State Targeted by Trump Election Lies Live in Fear for their Safety and are Desperate for Protection," CNN, (Oct. 26, 2021), available at https://www.cnn.com/2021/10/26/politics/secretaries-of-state-personal-threats-trump-election-lies/index.html.

354. Select Committee to Investigate the January 6th Attack on the United States Capitol, Transcribed Interview of Bryan Cutler, (May 31, 2022), pp. 83-84.

355. Geoff Rushton, "Police Investigating Threat Made During State College Borough Council Meeting," *StateCollege.com*, (Dec. 8, 2020), available at https://www.statecollege.com/police-investigating-threat-made-during-state-college-borough-council-meeting/.

356. Jan Murphy, "Meet Pa. Senate GOP Leader Kim Ward, the First Woman to Hold That Post: 'I Have To Do a Good Job', *PennLive.com*, (Jan. 26, 2021), https://www.pennlive.com/news/2021/01/meet-pa-senate-gop-leader-kim-ward-the-first-woman-to-hold-that-post-i-have-to-do-a-good-job.html.

357. Matt Petrillo, "'We're Coming after You': Philadelphia Elections Officials Still Receiving Death Threats Following 2020 Presidential Election," CBS Philly 3, (Nov. 1, 2021), available at https://philadelphia.cbslocal.com/2021/11/01/philadelphia-election-officials-death-threat-donald-trump-joe-biden/; Linda So and Jason Szep, "Campaign of Fear: U.S. Election Workers Get Little Help from Law Enforcement as Terror Threats Mount," *Reuters*, (Sept. 8, 2021), available at https://www.reuters.com/investigates/special-report/usa-election-threats-law-enforcement/.

358. Linda So and Jason Szep, "Special Report: Terrorized U.S. Election Workers Get Little Help from Law Enforcement," *Reuters*, (Sept. 8, 2021), available at https://www.reuters.com/legal/government/terrorized-us-election-workers-get-little-help-law-enforcement-2021-09-08/.

359. Select Committee to Investigate the January 6th Attack on the United States Capitol, *Hearing on the January 6th Investigation*, 117th Cong., 2d sess., (June 21, 2022), at 2:10:00 to 2:11:00, available at https://www.youtube.com/watch?v=xa43_z_82Og.

360. Linda So, "Special Report: Trump-Inspired Death Threats are Terrorizing Election Workers," *Reuters*, (June 11, 2021), available at https://www.reuters.com/article/us-usa-trump-georgia-threats-special-rep/special-report-trump-inspired-death-threats-are-terrorizing-election-workers-idUSKCN2DN14M.

361. Select Committee to Investigate the January 6th Attack on the United States Capitol, *Hearing on the January 6th Investigation*, 117th Cong., 2d sess., (June 21, 2022), at 2:10:00 to 2:11:00, available at https://www.youtube.com/watch?v=xa43_z_82Og; Linda So, "Special Report: Trump-Inspired Death Threats are Terrorizing Election Workers," *Reuters*, (June 11, 2021), available at https://www.reuters.com/article/us-usa-trump-georgia-threats-special-rep/special-report-trump-inspired-death-threats-are-terrorizing-election-workers-idUSKCN2DN14M.

362. Jeff Pegues and Robert Legare, "Texas Man Charged with Making Election-Related Threats to Georgia Government Officials," CBS News, (Jan. 21, 2022), available at https://www.cbsnews.com/news/chad-christopher-stark-charged-election-related-threats-georgia-government-officials/.

363. Linda So, "Special Report: Trump-Inspired Death Threats are Terrorizing Election Workers," *Reuters*, (June 11, 2021), available at https://www.reuters.com/article/us-usa-trump-georgia-threats-special-rep/special-report-trump-inspired-death-threats-are-terrorizing-election-workers-idUSKCN2DN14M.

364. Linda So, "Special Report: Trump-Inspired Death Threats are Terrorizing Election Workers," *Reuters*, (June 11, 2021), available at https://www.reuters.com/article/us-usa-trump-georgia-threats-special-rep/special-report-trump-inspired-death-threats-are-terrorizing-election-workers-idUSKCN2DN14M.

365. Linda So, "Special Report: Trump-Inspired Death Threats are Terrorizing Election Workers," *Reuters* (June 11, 2021), available at https://www.reuters.com/article/us-usa-trump-georgia-threats-special-rep/special-report-trump-inspired-death-threats-are-terrorizing-election-workers-idUSKCN2DN14M.

366. GA House Mobile Streaming, "Governmental Affairs 12.10.20," Vimeo – Livestream, at 2:09:00-2:13:00, available at https://livestream.com/accounts/25225474/events/9117221/videos/214677184; Select Committee to Investigate the January 6th Attack on the United States Capitol, *Hearing on the January 6th investigation*, 117th Cong., 2d sess., (June 21, 2022), at 2:25:45 to 2:26:00, available at https://youtu.be/xa43_z_82Og?t=8745.

367. Donald Trump Georgia Rally Transcript Before Senate Runoff Elections December 5," Rev, (Dec. 5, 2020), available at https://www.rev.com/blog/transcripts/donald-trump-georgia-rally-transcript-before-senate-runoff-elections-december-5; Jason Szep and Linda So, "A Reuters Special Report: Trump Campaign Demonized Two Georgia Election Workers – and Death Threats Followed," *Reuters*, (Dec. 1, 2021), available at https://www.reuters.com/investigates/special-report/usa-election-threats-georgia/.

368. Brad Raffensperger, Integrity Counts (New York: Simon & Schuster, 2021), p. 191 (reproducing the call transcript); Amy Gardner and Paulina Firozi,Amy Gardner and Paulina Firozi, "Here's the Full Transcript and Audio of the Call Between Trump and Raffensperger," *Washington Post*, (Jan. 5, 2021), available at https://www.washingtonpost.com/politics/trump-raffensperger-call-transcript-georgia-vote/2021/01/03/2768e0cc-4ddd-11eb-83e3-322644d82356_story.html (the Washington Post redacted Freeman's name and instead used "[name]" in the transcript); "Donald Trump Georgia Phone Call Transcript with Sec. of State Brad Raffensperger: Says He Wants to 'Find' Votes," Rev, (Jan. 4, 2021), available at https://www.rev.com/blog/transcripts/donald-trump-georgia-phone-call-transcript-brad-raffensperger-recording.

369. Jason Szep and Linda So, "A Reuters Special Report: Trump Campaign Demonized Two Georgia Election Workers – and Death Threats Followed," *Reuters*, (Dec. 1, 2021), available at https://www.reuters.com/investigates/special-report/usa-election-threats-georgia/.

370. *Freeman v. Giuliani*, No. 21-cv-03354-BAH (D.D.C. filed May 10, 2022), ECF No. 22 (Amended Complaint at 52), available at https://www.courtlistener.com/docket/61642105/22/freeman-v-herring-networks-inc.

371. Jason Szep and Linda So, "A Reuters Special Report: Trump Campaign Demonized Two Georgia Election Workers – and Death Threats Followed," *Reuters*, (Dec. 1, 2021), available at https://www.reuters.com/investigates/special-report/usa-election-threats-georgia/.

372. Jason Szep and Linda So, "A Reuters Special Report: Trump Campaign Demonized Two Georgia Election Workers – and Death Threats Followed," *Reuters*, (Dec. 1, 2021), available at https://www.reuters.com/investigates/special-report/usa-election-threats-georgia/.   .

373. Amended Complaint at 52, *Freeman v. Giuliani*, No. 21-cv-03354-BAH (D.D.C. filed May 10, 2022), ECF No. 22, available at https://www.courtlistener.com/docket/61642105/22/freeman-v-herring-networks-inc.

374. Amended Complaint at 52, *Freeman v. Giuliani*, No. 21-cv-03354-BAH (D.D.C. filed May 10, 2022), ECF No. 22, available at https://www.courtlistener.com/docket/61642105/22/freeman-v-herring-networks-inc.

375. Select Committee to Investigate the January 6th Attack on the United States Capitol, Transcribed Interview of Ruby Freeman, (May 31, 2022), pp. 7-8.

376. Select Committee to Investigate the January 6th Attack on the United States Capitol, Transcribed Interview of Ruby Freeman, (May 31, 2022), pp. 7-8.

377. Government's Motion Regarding Anticipated Trial Evidence and Notice Pursuant to Federal Rule of Evidence 404(b) at 1-2, 24-26, *United States v. Rhodes, et al.*, No. 1:22-cr-15 (D.D.C. July 8, 2022), ECF No. 187; Brandi Buchman (@Brandi_Buchman), Twitter, Oct. 6, 2022 7:27 a.m. ET, available at https://twitter.com/Brandi_Buchman/status/1577983997711421441.

378. Hannah Rabinowitz and Holmes Lybrand, "Judge Says Oath Keepers Jury Won't See 'Death List'," CNN (Oct. 6, 2022), https://www.cnn.com/2022/10/06/politics/judge-says-oath-keepers-jury-wont-see-death-list-trial-day-3.

Georgia Electors cast their Electoral College votes at the Georgia State Capitol on December 14, 2020.

Photo by Jessica McGowan/Getty Images

3

FAKE ELECTORS AND THE "THE PRESIDENT OF THE SENATE STRATEGY"

On the morning of January 6th, in his speech at the Ellipse, President Trump exhorted his thousands of assembled supporters to march to the U.S. Capitol, explaining that "[w]e have come to demand that Congress do the right thing and only count the electors who have been lawfully slated, lawfully slated." [1] This was no off-the-cuff remark; it was the culmination of a carefully planned scheme many weeks in the making. This plea by the President turned the truth on its head. There was only one legitimate slate of electors from the battleground States of Arizona, Georgia, Michigan, Nevada, New Mexico, Pennsylvania, and Wisconsin, and Trump wanted them rejected. This scheme involved lawyers, such as Kenneth Chesebro and Rudy Giuliani, as well as Mark Meadows. It also was aided at key points by Chairwoman of the Republican National Committee Ronna McDaniel, Members of Congress, and Republican leaders across seven States—some of whom did not know exactly what they were being asked to do. President Trump oversaw it himself.

President Trump and his allies prepared their own fake slates of electoral college electors in seven States that President Trump lost: Arizona, Georgia, Michigan, Nevada, New Mexico, Pennsylvania, and Wisconsin. And on December 14, 2020—the date when true, certified electors were meeting to cast their electoral votes for the candidate who had won the popular vote in each of those States—these fake electors also met, ostensibly casting electoral votes for President Trump, the candidate who had lost.

There was no legitimate reason for Trump electors to meet, vote, and produce fake slates on December 14th in States that former Vice President Biden won. Instead, this effort was aimed directly at the President of the Senate (which, under the Constitution, is the Vice President) in his role at the joint session of Congress on January 6th. President Trump and his advisors wanted Vice President Pence to disregard real electoral college votes for former Vice President Biden, in favor of these fake competing electoral slates.

But there never were real, competing slates of electors. By the time the fake Trump electors met on December 14th, appropriate government officials in each of the seven States had already certified their State's official election results for former Vice President Biden. No court had issued an order reversing or calling into question those results, and most election-related litigation was over. And as detailed in Chapter 2, despite the illicit efforts of President Trump and his allies, no State legislature had agreed to the President's request to reverse the result of the election by appointing a different slate of electors.

Given all of this, these groups of Trump backers who called themselves Presidential electors were never actually electors, and the votes they purported to cast on December 14th were not valid. They were fake. They had no legal standing, and their fake votes could not have been used by Vice President Pence to disregard the real votes of electors chosen by the voters.

By January 6th, President Trump had been discouraged by his top lawyers from following through on this plan. The Trump Campaign's senior staff attorneys had concerns,[2] and several days before the joint session, the Acting Attorney General and the Deputy Attorney General blocked the sending of a letter indicating that there were "competing slates" of electors, including "in Georgia and several other States."[3] But this reasoning did nothing to change President Trump's rhetoric or plan. He continued to assert that there were "competing" or "dual" slates of electors to create an opportunity to stay in office on January 6th.[4]

These lawyers were right: President Trump's plan was illegal. In his June 7, 2022, opinion, Federal District Judge David Carter wrote that this initiative to "certify alternate slates of electors for President Trump" constituted a "critical objective of the January 6 plan."[5] This followed Judge Carter's earlier determination in March that "[t]he illegality of the plan was obvious," and "[e]very American—and certainly the President of the United States—knows that in a democracy, leaders are elected, not installed. With a plan this 'BOLD,' President Trump knowingly tried to subvert this fundamental principle. Based on the evidence the Court finds it more likely than not that President Trump corruptly attempted to obstruct the Joint Session of Congress on January 6, 2021."[6]

The fake elector effort was an unlawful, unprecedented and destructive break from the electoral college process that our country has used to select its President for generations.[7] It led directly to the violence that occurred on January 6th. To address the damage that it caused, it is important to understand how it transpired.

3.1 LAYING THE GROUNDWORK FOR THE FAKE ELECTOR PLAN: THE CHESEBRO MEMOS

The fake elector plan emerged from a series of legal memoranda written by an outside legal advisor to the Trump Campaign: Kenneth Chesebro. Although John Eastman would have a more prominent role in advising President Trump in the days immediately before January 6th, Chesebro—an attorney based in Boston and New York recruited to assist the Trump Campaign as a volunteer legal advisor—was central to the creation of the plan.[8] Memos by Chesebro on November 18th, December 9th, and December 13th, as discussed below, laid the plan's foundation.

Chesebro's first memo on November 18th suggested that the Trump Campaign could gain a few extra weeks for litigation to challenge Wisconsin's election results, so long as a Wisconsin slate of Republican nominees to the electoral college met on December 14th to cast placeholder electoral college votes on a contingent basis.[9] This memo acknowledged that "[i]t may seem odd that the electors pledged to Trump and Pence might meet and cast their votes on December 14 even if, at that juncture, the Trump-Pence ticket is behind in the vote count, and no certificate of election has been issued in favor of Trump and Pence."[10] However, Chesebro argued that if such a slate of alternate electors gathered to cast electoral votes on a contingent basis, this would preserve the Trump Campaign's options so "a court decision (or, perhaps, a state legislative determination) rendered after December 14 in favor of the Trump-Pence slate of electors should be timely."[11]

On December 9th, Chesebro penned a second memo, which suggested another purpose for fake electoral college votes on January 6th. It stated that unauthorized Trump electors in these States could be retroactively recognized "by a court, the state legislature, *or Congress*."[12] Under this theory, there would be no need for a court to decide that the election had been decided in error; instead, Congress itself could choose among dueling slates of purported electoral votes—and thereby decide the Presidential election—even though Article II of the Constitution grants that power to the electoral college via the States.[13]

Chesebro's contemporaneous communications make clear that the goal was having Congress act on the fake electoral votes. He emailed an organizer of the fake electors in Nevada that "the purpose of having the electoral votes sent in to Congress is to provide the opportunity to debate the election irregularities in Congress, and to keep alive the possibility that the votes could be flipped to Trump..."[14] And a legal advisor to the Arizona GOP reportedly described being told by Chesebro around this time that their supposed electors "would just be sending in 'fake' electoral votes to Pence so that 'someone' in Congress can make an objection when they start counting votes, and start arguing that the 'fake' votes should be counted."[15]

Many of the States contested by the Trump team had laws that specified requirements for electors to validly cast and transmit their votes—and the December 9, 2020, memo recognized that some of these criteria would be difficult, if not impossible, for the fake electors to fulfill. (As described later, most were not fulfilled.) For example, Nevada State law required that the secretary of state preside when Presidential electors meet,[16] and Nevada Secretary of State Barbara Cegavske, a Republican, had already signed a certificate ascertaining the Biden/Harris electors as the authorized, winning slate.[17] Several States also had rules requiring electors to cast their votes in the State capitol building, or rules governing the process for approving substitutes if any original proposed electors from the November ballot were unavailable. As a result, Chesebro's December 9, 2020, memo advised the Trump Campaign to abide by such rules, when possible, but also recognized that these slates could be "slightly problematic in Michigan," "somewhat dicey in Georgia and Pennsylvania," and "very problematic in Nevada."[18]

On December 13th, the fake elector scheme became even clearer in an email sent by Chesebro to Giuliani. His message was entitled "Brief notes on 'President of the Senate' strategy." It addressed how the fake electors meeting the next day, December 14th, could be exploited during the joint session of Congress on January 6th by the President of the Senate—a role that the Constitution grants to the Vice President of the United States.[19] Chesebro argued that, on January 6th, the President of the Senate could:

> ...firmly take the position that he, and he alone, is charged with the constitutional responsibility not just to open the votes, but to count them—including making judgments about what to do if there are conflicting votes...[20]

Chesebro's email suggested that the President of the Senate (which under the Constitution, is the Vice President) could toss out former Vice President Biden's actual electoral votes for any State where the Trump Campaign organized fake electors, simply "because there are two slates of votes." [21] Of course, there were never two slates of electoral votes, so this premise itself was fundamentally wrong. But he was arguing that even if votes by fake electors were never retroactively ratified under State law, their mere submission to Congress would be enough to allow the presiding officer to disregard valid votes for former Vice President Biden. [22] Chesebro suggested this might result in a second term for President Trump, or, at minimum, it would force a debate about purported election fraud—neither of which was a lawful, legitimate reason to organize and convene fake electors. [23]

As discussed below and in Chapter 5, John Eastman worked with Chesebro as January 6th approached and wrote two additional memos that built upon, and extended, the plan to use the fake electoral votes during the joint session. [24]

3.2   PRESIDENT TRUMP AND THE CAMPAIGN ADOPT THE FAKE ELECTOR SCHEME

In early December, the highest levels of the Trump Campaign took note of Chesebro's fake elector plan and began to operationalize it. On December 6th, White House Chief of Staff Mark Meadows forwarded a copy of Chesebro's November 18, 2020, memo to Trump Campaign Senior Advisor Jason Miller writing, "Let's have a discussion about this tomorrow." [25] Miller replied that he just engaged with reporters on the subject, to which Meadows wrote: "If you are on it then never mind the meeting. *We just need to have someone coordinating the electors for states.*" [26] Miller clarified that he had only been "working the PR angle" and they should still meet, to which Meadows answered: "Got it." [27] Later that week, Miller sent Meadows a spreadsheet that the Trump Campaign had compiled. [28] It listed contact information for nearly all of the 79 GOP nominees to the electoral college on the November ballot for Arizona, Georgia, Michigan, Nevada, Pennsylvania, and Wisconsin. [29] And on December 8th, Meadows received a text message from a former State legislator in Louisiana recommending that the proposed "Trump electors from AR [sic] MI GA PA WI NV all meet next Monday at their state capitols[,] [c]all themselves to order, elect officers, and cast their votes for the President.... Then they certify their votes and transmit that certificate to Washington." [30] Meadows replied: "We are." [31]

Cassidy Hutchinson, a Special Assistant to the President and an assistant to Chief of Staff Mark Meadows, confirmed Meadows's significant involvement in the plan. Hutchinson told the Select Committee that Meadows followed the progress of the fake elector effort closely and that she "remember[ed] him frequently having calls, meetings, and outreach with individuals and this just being a prominent topic of discussion in our office." When asked how many of his calls or meetings it came up in, she estimated "[d]ozens." [32]

The evidence indicates that by December 7th or 8th, President Trump had decided to pursue the fake elector plan and was driving it. Trump Campaign Associate General Counsel Joshua Findlay was tasked by the campaign's general counsel, Matthew Morgan, around December 7th or 8th with exploring the feasibility of assembling unrecognized slates of Trump electors in a handful of the States that President Trump had lost.[33] Findlay told the Select Committee "it was my understanding that the President made this decision...." [34] As recounted by Findlay, Morgan conveyed that the client—President Trump—directed the campaign lawyers to "look into electors in these potential litigation States[.]" [35]

President Trump personally called RNC Chairwoman Ronna Romney McDaniel days before December 14th to enlist the RNC's assistance in the scheme.[36] President Trump opened the call by introducing McDaniel to John Eastman, who described "the importance of the RNC helping the campaign to gather these contingent electors in case any of the legal challenges that were ongoing changed the results in any of the States." [37] According to McDaniel, she called President Trump back soon after the call ended, letting him know that she agreed to his request and that some RNC staffers were already assisting.[38]

On December 13th and 14th, President Trump worked with Rudolph Giuliani on the plan's implementation. On the 13th, Miller texted some of his colleagues to check in about the fake elector meetings scheduled for the following day. He let them know that Giuliani had told him "POTUS was aware" that they would be filing litigation in four States just "to keep the effort going"—which the Select Committee believes was to create a pretext to claim that it was still possible for the fake electors to be authorized retroactively.[39] (In subsequent litigation, a Federal district court found that President Trump "filed certain lawsuits not to obtain legal relief, but to disrupt or delay the January 6th congressional proceedings through the courts." [40]) The next day, Miller sent an email asking whether they were going to issue a press release about electors, and he was told the "Mayor [is] going to discuss with POTUS." [41]

3.3 THE CAMPAIGN LEGAL TEAM BOWS OUT, AND GIULIANI STEPS IN

Not everyone on the campaign was eager to pursue the fake elector plan. On December 11th, the U.S. Supreme Court rejected a high-profile lawsuit filed by the State of Texas challenging the election results in Pennsylvania,

Ronna McDaniel at the Republican National Convention on August 24, 2020.
(Photo by Chip Somodevilla/Getty Images)

Georgia, Michigan, and Wisconsin.[42] After that decision, the Trump Campaign's senior legal staffers said that they reduced their involvement in the fake elector effort, apparently because there was no longer a feasible scenario in which a court would determine that President Trump actually won

Rudy Giuliani speaks inside the Republican National Committee Headquarters in November about various lawsuits related to the 2020 election.

(Photo by Drew Angerer/Getty Images)

any of the States he contested.[43] Justin Clark, who oversaw the Trump Campaign's general counsel's office, said that he basically conveyed, "I'm out," and encouraged his colleagues on the legal team to do the same.[44] Findlay told the Select Committee that "we backed out of this thing," and Morgan, his boss, said he had Findlay pass off responsibility for the electors as "my way of taking that responsibility to zero."[45]

Clark told the Select Committee that "it never sat right with me that there was no...contingency whereby these votes would count."[46] "I had real problems with the process," Clark said, because "it morphed into something I didn't agree with."[47] In his view, the fake electors were "not necessarily duly nominated electors" despite being presented as such.[48] He said he believed he warned his colleagues that "unless we have litigation pending like in these States, like I don't think this is appropriate or, you know, this isn't the right thing to do."[49]

Morgan told the Select Committee that he saw no value in pushing slates of purported electors if they were not authorized by a State government's certificate of ascertainment. As he put it, "[M]y view was, as long as you didn't have a certificate of ascertainment, then the electors were, for lack of a better way of saying it, no good or not—not valid." [50] Findlay confirmed that Morgan told him after the Supreme Court ruling on December 11th that "there's not really anything left for us to do on this project" and that "it doesn't seem like a good idea for us to be involved in it." [51]

Campaign lawyers were not the only ones who doubted the legality of the fake elector plan. The Office of White House Counsel appears to have expressed concerns about it as well. In his testimony to the Select Committee, White House Counsel Pat Cipollone acknowledged his view that by mid-December, the electoral process was "done." Cipollone told the Select Committee that the White House Counsel's office "probably" had discussions about the electors plan and that his Deputy, Pat Philbin, would have been involved in evaluating the electors issue. [52] In an informal Committee interview, Philbin described the fake elector scheme as one of the "bad theories" that were like "Whac-A-Mole" in the White House during this period. [53] Mr. Cipollone agreed with this characterization. [54]

In her testimony, Cassidy Hutchinson testified that she heard at least one member of the White House Counsel's Office say that the plan was not legal:

> Committee Staff: ... to be clear, did you hear the White House Counsel's Office say that this plan to have alternate electors meet and cast votes for Donald Trump in States that he had lost was not legally sound?
>
> Hutchinson: Yes, sir. [55]

She also recalled a meeting that took place in or before mid-December during which this view was relayed to Giuliani and members of his team by lawyers in the White House Counsel's Office. [56]

By December 11th, Findlay emailed his main points of contact in six battleground States to say "[t]hank you for your work on the presidential elector project" and, in order to pass off his responsibilities, let them know that "Rudy's team has designated Kenneth Chesebro as the point person for the legal documents" going forward. [57]

While the campaign's core legal team stepped back from the fake elector effort on December 11th, it nonetheless went forward because "Rudy was in charge of [it]" and "[t]his is what he wanted to do," according to Findlay. [58] When Findlay was asked if this decision to let the effort proceed under Giuliani's direction "was coming from your client, the President," Findlay responded: "Yes, I believe so. I mean, he had made it clear that Rudy was in charge of this and that Rudy was executing what he wanted." [59] Findlay also recalled being told that Chesebro's elector memos had become "the justification for why Rudy and Ken were going to keep going forward with this stuff." [60] He explained that Giuliani "really bought into Ken's theory on this," and that the two of them "were kind of the main ones driving this" from that point forward.[61] Clark told the Select Committee that "...my understanding of who was driving the process...was Mayor Giuliani and his team." [62] On December 10th, when Kenneth Chesebro emailed one of the State party officials involved in organizing the fake elector effort in Nevada, he reported that "I spoke this evening with Mayor Guiliani [sic], who is focused on doing everything possible to ensure that that [sic] all the Trump-Pence electors vote on Dec. 14." [63]

In the days that followed this handoff, Chesebro would draft and distribute documents intended for use in the Trump team's fake elector ceremonies that were then shared with key contacts in Arizona,[64] Georgia,[65] Michigan,[66] Nevada,[67] New Mexico,[68] Pennsylvania,[69] and Wisconsin.[70] He also gave some of the groups step-by-step logistical guidance, such as when and where they should convene, how many copies each person would need to sign, and to send their fake votes to Congress via registered mail.[71] "Pretty Simple!" he commented in some of these emails.[72]

A campaign operative named Michael Roman was also tapped for a major operational role in the fake elector effort. When Findlay sent his email handing off certain responsibilities for the initiative, he also wrote that Giuliani's team had designated Roman "as the lead for executing the voting on Monday" December 14th.[73] Roman was the Trump Campaign's Director of Election Day Operations (EDO), with team members who specialized in political outreach and mobilization in battleground States where the Trump team now urgently needed the fake electors to meet on December 14th.

With help from his EDO staff, as well as Giuliani's team and RNC staffers working alongside the Campaign as part of the Trump Victory Committee, Roman ran an improvised "Electors Whip Operation." [74] For example, Roman sent an email on December 12th directing an aide to create "a tracker for the electors" with tabs for Arizona, Georgia, Michigan, Nevada, Pennsylvania, and Wisconsin, listing contact information, whether they had been contacted, whether they agreed to attend on December 14th, and names of "[s]ubstitute electors" to replace any reticent or unavailable participants as needed.[75] Roman referred to others on this email as the "WHIP TEAM" and directed them to fill out the spreadsheet, to update him on "what you have and what you need," and to plan on a call that evening.[76]

In the days that followed, this group focused on tracking which Republicans previously named as President Trump's nominees to the electoral college would be willing to show up for fake elector ceremonies, finding adequate substitutes for those who refused to attend, and actually coordinating the unrecognized elector signing ceremonies in seven States on December 14th.[77] In all seven States, these efforts to mobilize fake electors benefitted from support from the RNC, as well as the State Republican parties.[78] However, it was the Trump team who drove the process from start to finish, as one of the fake electors and later co-chair of the Michigan Republican party, Meshawn Maddock, told an audience in January 2022: "We fought to seat the electors. The Trump campaign asked us to do that."[79]

3.4 SOME OF THE PROPOSED FAKE ELECTORS EXPRESS CONCERNS ABOUT THE PLAN

The Trump team's fake elector plan raised concerns not just for several senior officials but also for some of the Republican activists being recruited to be the fake electors. Findlay told the Select Committee that "there were definitely electors in probably most of the States that had concerns about this process."[80] After being tasked with reaching out to the potential fake electors, Findlay notified his colleagues on December 10th that "a lot of questions are arising" from them.[81] He also noted that an RNC staffer seconded to the Trump Victory Committee "requested a call with the PA electors and/or leadership to address concerns," which "may be necessary to get people to appear."[82]

The Republican Party of Pennsylvania's general counsel relayed several specific concerns to the Trump Campaign via email on December 13th. Warning that "[w]e're all getting call [sic] from concerned Electors," he elaborated as follows:

> I'm told that on the call with the Electors they were told that the Ballot form would be conditioned upon ultimate certification by the Governor, indemnification by the campaign if someone gets sued or worse, (charged with something by the AG or someone else), and the receipt by the Electors of a legal opinion by a national firm and certified to be accurate by a Pa. lawyer.

> What was sent was a "memo" by Chesebro not addressed to the Electors, and no certification by a Pa. lawyer. To make it worse, Chesebro describes the Pa. plan as "dicey". And there's no indication by anyone with authority that there's any indemnification authorized by the campaign.[83]

Pennsylvania GOP Chairman Lawrence Tabas informed the Select Committee that his State's fake electors never were indemnified by the Trump Campaign.[84]

When Wisconsin Republican Party Chairman Andrew Hitt was notified in late November that "the campaign wants to [sic] list of electors," he texted his executive director that "I am def concerned about their inquiry" and that "I hope they are not planning on asking us to do anything like try and say we are only the proper electors."[85] On December 12th, after Hitt received a message about a phone call with Giuliani to discuss the fake elector issue, he texted a colleague: "These guys are up to no good and its [sic] gonna fail miserably."[86] Despite such concerns, Hitt and many other fake electors participated anyway.[87]

Even so, 14 of the original Republicans who had been listed as electoral college nominees on the November ballot bowed out when the fake Trump electors gathered in December.[88] Former Michigan Secretary of State Terri Lynn Land declined to attend, which the State's GOP chair, Laura Cox, told the Select Committee was because "I think she just said she was uncomfortable with the whole thing" and that she "has her own beliefs."[89] A senior advisor for the Pennsylvania GOP said that Chairman Tabas "did not serve as an elector because Joe Biden won the election and it was Biden's electors that were certified."[90] Former U.S. Representative Tom Marino (R-PA) said he backed out because "I'm a constitutionalist," and "as a former prosecutor, when the attorney general says that he's not finding anything there, that's good enough for me."[91] The other eleven dropouts included a Georgia State lawmaker, a former State party chair from New Mexico, two former State party chairs from Pennsylvania, and Pennsylvania's RNC national committeewoman.[92]

Other participants asserted that they would have had much greater concerns if the Trump team had been more forthcoming about how the fake electoral votes would be used.[93] The Trump Campaign's director of election day operations in Georgia told the Select Committee that "I absolutely would not have" wanted to participate in organizing the Trump team's fake electors in Georgia "had I known that the three main lawyers for the campaign that I'd spoken to in the past and were leading up were not on board."[94] He said he felt "angry" because "no one really cared if—if people were potentially putting themselves in jeopardy" by doing this, and "we were just...useful idiots or rubes at that point."[95]

3.5 ON DECEMBER 14TH, THE FAKE ELECTORS MEET AND VOTE

On December 14th, using instructions provided by Chesebro, the fake Trump electors gathered and participated in signing ceremonies in all seven States. In five of these States—Arizona, Georgia, Michigan, Nevada, and Wisconsin—the certificates they signed used the language that falsely

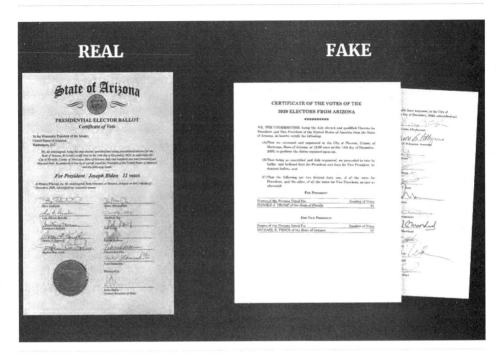

declared themselves to be "the duly elected and qualified Electors" from their State.[96] This declaration was false because none of the signatories had been granted that official status by their State government in the form of a certificate of ascertainment.

The paperwork signed by the fake Trump electors in two other States contained partial caveats. In New Mexico, the document they signed made clear that they were participating "on the understanding that it might later be determined that we are the duly elected and qualified Electors...."[97] In Pennsylvania, the document they signed indicated that they were participating "on the understanding that if, as a result of a final non-appealable Court Order or other proceeding prescribed by law, we are ultimately recognized as being the duly elected and qualified Electors...."[98]

All seven of these invalid sets of electoral votes were then transmitted to Washington, DC. Roman's team member in Georgia, for example, sent him an email on the afternoon of December 14th that affirmed the following: "All votes cast, paperwork complete, being mailed now. Ran pretty smoothly."[99] Likewise, Findlay updated Campaign Manager Bill Stepien and his bosses on the legal team that the Trump team's slate in Georgia was not able to satisfy all provisions of State law but still "voted as legally as possible under the circumstances" before transmitting their fake votes to Washington, DC, by mail.[100]

On the evening of December 14th, RNC Chairwoman McDaniel provided an update for President Trump on the status of the fake elector effort. She forwarded President Trump's executive assistant an "Elector Recap" email, which conveyed that "President Trump's electors voted" not just in "the states that he won" but also in six "contested states" (specifically, Arizona, Georgia, Michigan, Nevada, Pennsylvania, and Wisconsin).[101] Minutes later, President Trump's executive assistant replied: "It's in front of him!"[102]

The Trump team and the fake electors also engaged in acts of subterfuge to carry out their plans on December 14th. For instance, a campaign staffer notified the Georgia participants via email that he "must ask for your complete discretion."[103] He explained that their efforts required "complete secrecy," and told them to arrive at the State capitol building and "please state to the guards that you are attending a meeting with either Senator Brandon Beach or Senator Burt Jones."[104] Indeed, Greg Bluestein of the *Atlanta Journal-Constitution* reported that he tried to enter this group's meeting room but "[a] guy at the door called it an 'education meeting' and scrambled when I tried to walk in."[105]

Former Michigan GOP Chair Laura Cox told the Select Committee that an attorney who "said he was working with the President's Campaign" informed her that the Michigan slate for President Trump was "planning to meet in the capit[o]l and hide overnight so that they could fulfill the role of casting their vote in, per law, in the Michigan chambers."[106] She said that she "told him in no uncertain terms that that was insane and inappropriate," and that she warned Michigan's senate majority leader as a precaution.[107] Instead, the group of fake electors in Michigan signed their paperwork in the State GOP headquarters, where staff told them not to bring phones inside.[108]

3.6 THE FALLOUT FROM THE FAKE ELECTOR PLAN

In spite of the Trump Campaign's efforts to give the fake electors' votes the sheen of authenticity, they failed. The U.S. Senate Parliamentarian noted in correspondence by January 3rd that materials from the Trump team's supposed electors in Arizona, Georgia, Nevada, New Mexico, and Pennsylvania had "no seal of the state" and "no evidence votes were delivered by the executive of the state for signature by electors,"[109] and, as a result, these materials failed to meet requirements of federal law. Similarly, the Senate Parliamentarian noted that the Trump team's slates from Georgia, New Mexico, and Pennsylvania appeared to violate another statute which requires the approval of the Governor for the substitution of electors.[110]

Meanwhile, the documents from Michigan and Wisconsin did not even arrive to Congress on time, so they also had missed the required statutory deadline.[111]

Several of the Trump team's fake electoral slates also failed to follow State rules specifying where they were required to meet. In Georgia and Wisconsin, State lawmakers or their staff appear to have helped participants gather inside their State capitols.[112] But in Michigan, the fake Trump electors were blocked from entering the State capitol building.[113] Despite this, they still signed documents attesting that they "convened and organized in the State Capitol, in the City of Lansing, Michigan, and at 2:00 p.m. . . . performed the duties enjoined upon us." [114] That document had been signed earlier in the day off-site, and one of the signatories even told the Committee she didn't join their march to the State capitol building because she "didn't see a need to go." [115]

If the entire premise of the fake votes was not enough, these infirmities also meant that they had no legal relevance. In no way could they ever have been used by the Vice President to disregard the real votes of electors chosen by the voters.

In the weeks between December 14th and January 6th, President Trump's team continued to embrace the idea that the fake electoral votes had a purpose. Although Giuliani and White House speechwriter Stephen Miller made public comments on December 14th suggesting that the uncertified Trump votes were merely contingent, that pretense was dropped in short order.[116]

For example, on December 17th, White House Press Secretary Kayleigh McEnany said on Fox News that in numerous States "there has been an alternate slate of electors voted upon that Congress will decide in January." [117] On December 21st, President Trump and Vice President Pence each joined parts of a White House meeting in which Members of Congress from the Freedom Caucus encouraged the Vice President to reject Biden electors from one or more of the seven contested States.[118] And days later, Eastman cited the existence of the fake votes in an email to Boris Epshteyn, a member of the Giuliani legal team, writing, "[t]he fact that we have multiple slates of electors demonstrate[s] the uncertainty of either. That should be enough." [119]

As discussed further in Chapter 5, that email contained Eastman's 2-page memo proposing a strategy for January 6th based on the incorrect legal theory that Vice President Pence could assert some authority as President of the Senate to prevent or delay the election of former Vice President Biden during the joint session. Eastman's memo relied on the fake votes, which the memo featured in the very first line: "7 states have transmitted dual slates of electors."[120] When Eastman submitted his memo to Epshteyn, he also copied Chesebro, who had edited the memo and called it "[r]eally awesome."[121]

By that point, Chesebro and Eastman were coordinating their arguments about the fake-elector votes and how they should be used. On January 1, 2021, Chesebro sent an email to Eastman and Epshteyn that recommended that Vice President Pence derail the joint session of Congress. In it, he raised the idea of Vice President Pence declaring "that there are two competing slates of electoral votes" in several States, and taking the position that only he, or possibly Congress, could "resolve any disputes concerning them."[122]

Two days later, Eastman completed his second major memo advising President Trump and his team on strategies for January 6th, again arguing that there were "dual slates of electors from 7 states," and calling for Vice President Pence to assert power to act "[a]s the ultimate arbiter" to take steps that could overturn the election, either by sending the election back to State legislatures to reassess or by rejecting Biden's certified electoral votes from States in which there were also fake Trump electors.[123]

By early January, most of the fake elector votes had arrived in Washington, except those from Michigan and Wisconsin.[124] Undeterred, the Trump team arranged to fly them to Washington and hand deliver them to Congress for the Vice President himself. "Freaking trump idiots want someone to fly original elector papers to the senate President..." Wisconsin Republican Party official Mark Jefferson wrote to Party Chairman Hitt on January 4th.[125] Hitt responded, "Ok I see I have a missed call from [Mike] Roman and a text from someone else. Did you talk to them already? This is just nuts...."[126]

The next day, Trump Campaign Deputy Director for Election Day Operations G. Michael Brown sent a text message to other campaign staff suggesting that he was the person who delivered the fake votes to Congress.[127] After sending the group a photo of his face with the Capitol in the background, Brown said, "This has got to be the cover a book I write one day" and "I should probably buy [Mike] [R]oman a tie or something for sending me on this one. Hasn't been done since 1876 and it was only 3 states that did it."[128] The reference to 1876 alludes to a controversy during that election about certain States' electoral college votes.[129]

President Trump and his Campaign apparently had assistance from allies on Capitol Hill for this effort, including Senator Ron Johnson, his chief of staff, and the chief of staff to Representative Mike Kelly, although Senator Johnson has said that "[his] involvement in that attempt to

Senator Ron Johnson, February 12, 2021.

(Photo by Samuel Corum/Getty Images)

deliver" fake elector paperwork "spanned the course of a couple seconds."[130] On the morning of January 6th, Representative Kelly's then-chief of staff texted an aide to the Vice President, Chris Hodgson, about hand-delivering the fake elector votes to the Vice President's team before the joint session, a message that Hodgson ignored: "Just following up-any chance you or someone from your team can meet to take the Michigan and Wisconsin packets."[131]

According to the office of Senator Ron Johnson, Representative Kelly's chief of staff then had a phone call with Senator Johnson's chief of staff at 11:58 a.m. "about how Kelly's office could get us the electors [sic] because they had it."[132] Shortly after 11:30 a.m., the Trump Campaign's lead attorney in Wisconsin had texted Senator Johnson expressing a "[n]eed to get a document on Wisconsin electors to you [for] the VP immediately. Is there a staff person I can talk to immediately."[133] Senator Johnson then put his chief of staff in touch with the campaign to handle the issue.[134]

Shortly afterwards, Senator Johnson's chief of staff texted Hodgson: "[Sen.] Johnson needs to hand something to VPOTUS please advise."[135] When Hodgson asked what it was, the response he got was, "Alternate slate of electors for MI and WI because archivist didn't receive them."[136] Hodgson did not mince words: "Do not give that to him [the Vice President].

Senator Mike Lee, April 28, 2016.

(Photo by Leigh Vogel/Getty Images)

He's about to walk over to preside over the joint session, those were supposed to come in through the mail."[137]

Those fake electoral votes, which the Trump team tried for weeks to
manufacture and deliver, never made it to the Vice President. But they
would have been invalid even if they did arrive on time. The Trump team's
activities were based on the false pretense that these fake electoral votes
had a decisive role to play at the joint session of Congress. And yet any such
role that they could have played would have helped unlawfully obstruct an
official proceeding that determines how our Nation carries out the peaceful
transfer of power between Presidents.

Indeed, as the joint session approached, Senator Mike Lee had
expressed grave concerns about the fake elector effort in a series of text
messages to one of the Trump team's senior legal advisors. Although Senator Lee had spent a month encouraging the idea of having State legislatures
endorse competing electors for Trump, he grew alarmed as it became clear
that the Trump team wanted the fake electors' votes to be considered on
January 6th even without authorization from any State government body.[138]

On December 30th, Senator Lee texted Trump advisor Cleta Mitchell
that January 6th was "a dangerous idea," including "for the republic
itself."[139] He explained that, "I don't think we have any valid basis for

objecting to the electors" because "it cannot be true that we can object to any state's presidential electors simply because we don't think they handled their election well or suspect illegal activity."[140] Senator Lee even questioned her about the plan's dangerous long-term consequences: "[w]ill you please explain to me how this doesn't create a slippery slope problem for all future presidential elections?"[141]

ENDNOTES

1. "Transcript of Trump's Speech at Rally before US Capitol Riot," *Associated Press*, (Jan. 13, 2021), available at https://apnews.com/article/election-2020-joe-biden-donald-trump-capitol-siege-media-e79eb5164613d6718e9f4502eb471f27.

2. Documents on file with the Select Committee to Investigate the January 6th Attack on the United States Capitol, (Tim Murtaugh Production), XXM-0021349 (December 13, 2020, and December 14, 2020, text messages between Tim Murtaugh, Justin Clark, Jason Miller, and Eric Herschmann); Select Committee to Investigate the January 6th Attack on the United States Capitol, Transcribed Interview of Justin Clark, (May 17, 2022), p. 116; Select Committee to Investigate the January 6th Attack on the United States Capitol, Transcribed Interview of Matthew Morgan, (Apr. 25, 2022), pp. 70–72; Select Committee to Investigate the January 6th Attack on the United States Capitol, Transcribed Interview of Joshua Findlay, (May 25, 2022), pp. 38–43.

3. *See* Chapter 4; Senate Committee on the Judiciary Majority Staff Report, *Subverting Justice: How the Former President and His Allies Pressured DOJ to Overturn the 2020 Election*, (Oct. 7, 2021), pp. 20–39, 188, and Key Document H at pp. 185–191, available at https://www.judiciary.senate.gov/imo/media/doc/Interim%20Staff%20Report%20FINAL.pdf.

4. Documents on file with the Select Committee to Investigate the January 6th Attack on the United States Capitol (Chapman University Production), Chapman053475, Chapman053476 (December 23, 2020, email titled "PRIVILEGED AND CONFIDENTIAL—Dec 23 memo on Jan 6 scenario.docx" from John Eastman to Boris Epshteyn and Kenneth Chesebro, with attached memo titled "January 6 scenario"); Documents on file with the Select Committee to Investigate the January 6th Attack on the United States Capitol (Public Source), CTRL0000923050 (Jan. 3, 2021, John Eastman 6-page memo); John C. Eastman, "Privileged and Confidential-Jan 6 Scenario," (Jan. 3, 2021), available at https://www.scribd.com/document/528776994/Privileged-and-Confidential-Jan-3-Memo-on-Jan-6-Scenario; John C. Eastman, "Trying to Prevent Illegal Conduct from Deciding an Election is Not Endorsing a 'Coup'," American Greatness, (Sep. 30, 2021), available at https://amgreatness.com/2021/09/30/trying-to-prevent-illegal-conduct-from-deciding-an-election-is-not-endorsing-a-coup/ (embedded). *See also* Chapter 5.

5. Order Re Privilege of 599 Documents Dated November 3, 2020–January 20, 2021 at 23, *Eastman v. Thompson*, No. 8:22-cv-99 (C.D. Cal. June 7, 2022), ECF No. 356, available at https://storage.courtlistener.com/recap/gov.uscourts.cacd.841840/gov.uscourts.cacd.841840.356.0_1.pdf.

6. Order re Privilege of Documents Dated January 4–7, 2021 at 36, *Eastman v. Thompson*, 594 F. Supp. 3d 1156, (C.D. Cal. Mar. 28, 2022) (No. 8:22-cv-99-DOC-DFM), available at https://storage.courtlistener.com/recap/gov.uscourts.cacd.841840/gov.uscourts.cacd.841840.260.0_10.pdf.

7. The Trump team tried to justify its fake-elector scheme based in part on the 1960 Kennedy-Nixon election. At that time, following a close vote in Hawaii, Republican and Democratic electors each met and cast purported electoral college votes on the same day because there was ongoing litigation and a pending recount. Circumstances in 2020 were different, however, in part because there were no pending recounts. Kenneth Chesebro

reportedly recognized this difference in an email copied to Rudolph Giuliani that acknowledged certain concerns about their efforts could be "valid," because, as he put it, "in the Hawaii 1960 incident, when the Kennedy electors voted[,] there was a pending recount." Maggie Haberman and Luke Broadwater, "Arizona Officials Warned Fake Electors Plan Could 'Appear Treasonous'," *New York Times*, (Aug. 2, 2022), available at https://www.nytimes.com/2022/08/02/us/politics/arizona-trump-fake-electors.html.

8. David Thomas, "Lawyer Group Says Trump Attorney Broke Ethics Rules in Fake Elector Plan," *Reuters*, (Oct. 12, 2022), available at https://www.reuters.com/legal/legalindustry/lawyer-group-says-trump-attorney-broke-ethics-rules-fake-elector-plan-2022-10-12/; Select Committee to Investigate the January 6th Attack on the United States Capitol, *Hearing on the January 6th Investigation*, 117th Cong., 2d sess., (June 16, 2022), available at https://www.govinfo.gov/committee/house-january6th.

9. Documents on file with the Select Committee to Investigate the January 6th Attack on the United States Capitol (Chapman University Production), Chapman025125 (November 18, 2020, memo from Kenneth Chesebro titled "The Real Deadline for Settling a State's Electoral Votes"); Documents on file with the Select Committee to Investigate the January 6th Attack on the United States Capitol (Chapman University Production), Chapman025124 (December 7, 2020, email from Kenneth Chesebro with attachment "2020-11-20 Chesebro memo on real deadline2.pdf"); Documents on file with the Select Committee to Investigate the January 6th Attack on the United States Capitol (Joshua Findlay production), JF037 (November 18, 2020, memo from Kenneth Chesebro titled "The Real Deadline for Settling a State's Electoral Votes"). *See also* Alan Feuer, Maggie Haberman, and Luke Broadwater, "Memos Show Roots of Trump's Focus on Jan. 6 and Alternate Electors," *New York Times*, (Feb. 2, 2022), available at https://www.nytimes.com/2022/02/02/us/politics/trump-jan-6-memos.html.

10. Documents on file with the Select Committee to Investigate the January 6th Attack on the United States Capitol (Chapman University Production), Chapman025125 (November 18, 2020, memo from Kenneth Chesebro titled "The Real Deadline for Settling a State's Electoral Votes"); Documents on file with the Select Committee to Investigate the January 6th Attack on the United States Capitol (Chapman University Production), Chapman025124 (December 7, 2020, email from Kenneth Chesebro with attachment "2020-11-20 Chesebro memo on real deadline2.pdf"); Documents on file with the Select Committee to Investigate the January 6th Attack on the United States Capitol (Joshua Findlay Production), JF037 (Nov. 18, 2020, memo from Kenneth Chesebro titled "The Real Deadline for Settling a State's Electoral Votes"). *See also* Alan Feuer, Maggie Haberman, and Luke Broadwater, "Memos Show Roots of Trump's Focus on Jan. 6 and Alternate Electors," *New York Times*, (Feb. 2, 2022), available at https://www.nytimes.com/2022/02/02/us/politics/trump-jan-6-memos.html.

11. Documents on file with the Select Committee to Investigate the January 6th Attack on the United States Capitol (Chapman University Production), Chapman025125, (November 18, 2020, memo from Kenneth Chesebro titled "The Real Deadline for Settling a State's Electoral Votes") (underlining in original); Documents on file with the Select Committee to Investigate the January 6th Attack on the United States Capitol (Chapman University Production), Chapman025124, (December 7, 2020, email from Kenneth Chesebro with attachment "2020-11-20 Chesebro memo on real deadline2.pdf"); Documents on file with the Select Committee to Investigate the January 6th Attack on the United States Capitol (Joshua Findlay Production), CTRL0000082463_00009, (November 18, 2020, memo from Kenneth Chesebro titled "The Real Deadline for Settling a State's Electoral Votes"); Alan Feuer, Maggie Haberman, and Luke Broadwater, "Memos Show Roots of Trump's Focus on Jan. 6 and Alternate Electors," *New York Times*, (Feb. 2, 2022), available at https://www.nytimes.com/2022/02/02/us/politics/trump-jan-6-memos.html.

12. Emphasis added. Documents on file with the Select Committee to Investigate the January 6th Attack on the United States Capitol (Joshua Findlay Production), JF044, (December 9, 2020, memo from Kenneth Chesebro titled "Statutory Requirements for December 14 Electoral Votes"); Alan Feuer, Maggie Haberman, and Luke Broadwater, "Memos Show Roots of

Trump's Focus on Jan. 6 and Alternate Electors," *New York Times*, (Feb. 2, 2022), available at https://www.nytimes.com/2022/02/02/us/politics/trump-jan-6-memos.html.

13. U.S. Const., art. II, §. 1, cl. 2: ("Each State shall appoint, in such Manner as the Legislature thereof may direct, a Number of Electors, equal to the whole Number of Senators and Representatives to which the State may be entitled in the Congress: but no Senator or Representative, or Person holding an Office of Trust or Profit under the United States, shall be appointed an Elector.").

14. Documents on file with the Select Committee to Investigate the January 6th Attack on the United States Capitol (James DeGraffenreid Production), DEGRAFFENREID 000778, (December 11, 2020, email from Jim DeGraffenreid to Kenneth Chesebro with subject "URGENT—Trump-Pence campaign asked me to contact you to coordinate Dec. 14 voting by Nevada electors").

15. Maggie Haberman and Luke Broadwater, "'Kind of Wild/Creative': Emails Shed Light on Trump Fake Electors Plan," *New York Times*, (July 26, 2022), available at https://www.nytimes.com/2022/07/26/us/politics/trump-fake-electors-emails.html (emphasis in original). Although this alleged email described by the *New York Times* was not produced to the Select Committee, it matches certain information in a privilege log provided to the Select Committee by its reported sender. This includes the same reported sender (Jack Wilenchik), direct recipient (Boris Epshteyn), seven cc'ed recipients in the same order (Christina Bobb, Lee Miller, Dennis Wilenchik, Aaron Green, Josh Offenhartz, Christine Ferreira, and Victoria Stevens), title ("RE: [EXTERNAL]FW: petition for Cert and Motion for Expedited Consideration"), and date (12/8/2020), with only a negligible one-minute discrepancy in the time sent (4:27 p.m. versus 4:26 p.m.). *See* Documents on file with the Select Committee to Investigate the January 6th Attack on the United States Capitol, (Jack Wilenchik Production), CTRL0000922311, line 9 (Sept. 7, 2022, Jack Wilenchik Production 09_07_2022—PrivLog UPDATED).

16. "Nevada Revised Statutes," Title 24—Elections, Chapter 298—Presidential Electors and Elections, Nevada State Legislature, available at https://www.leg.state.nv.us/nrs/nrs-298.html#NRS298Sec065.

17. "Nevada Certificate of Ascertainment 2020," National Archives and Records Administration, (Dec. 2, 2020, also later updated Dec. 10, 2020), available at https://www.archives.gov/files/electoral-college/2020/ascertainment-nevada.pdf.

18. Documents on file with the Select Committee to Investigate the January 6th Attack on the United States Capitol (Joshua Findlay Production), JF044 (December 9, 2020, memo from Kenneth Chesebro titled "Statutory Requirements for December 14 Electoral Votes"). Where it wouldn't be possible to comply with State law, as in Nevada, Chesebro advised the so-called electors to proceed anyway, writing: "[T]hese technical aspects of state law are unlikely to matter much in the end." Documents on file with the Select Committee to Investigate the January 6th Attack on the United States Capitol (James DeGraffenreid Production), DEGRAFFENREID 000778, (December 11, 2020, email from Jim DeGraffenreid to Kenneth Chesebro with subject "URGENT—Trump-Pence campaign asked me to contact you to coordinate Dec. 14 voting by Nevada electors").

19. Documents on file with the Select Committee to Investigate the January 6th Attack on the United States Capitol (Chapman University Production), Chapman004708 (January 4, 2021, email from Kenneth Chesebro to John Eastman titled "Fwd: Draft 2, with edits", which includes in the chain a Dec. 13, 2020, email from Kenneth Chesebro to Rudy Giuliani titled "PRIVILEGED AND CONFIDENTIAL—Brief Notes on "President of the Senate" strategy").

20. Documents on file with the Select Committee to Investigate the January 6th Attack on the United States Capitol (Chapman University Production), Chapman004708 (January 4, 2021, email from Kenneth Chesebro to John Eastman titled "Fwd: Draft 2, with edits", which includes in the chain a Dec. 13, 2020, email from Kenneth Chesebro to Rudy Giuliani titled "PRIVILEGED AND CONFIDENTIAL—Brief Notes on "President of the Senate" strategy").

21. Documents on file with the Select Committee to Investigate the January 6th Attack on the United States Capitol (Chapman University Production), Chapman004708 (January 4, 2021, email from Kenneth Chesebro to John Eastman titled "Fwd: Draft 2, with edits", which includes in the chain a Dec. 13, 2020, email from Kenneth Chesebro to Rudy Giuliani titled "PRIVILEGED AND CONFIDENTIAL—Brief Notes on "President of the Senate" strategy").

22. Documents on file with the Select Committee to Investigate the January 6th Attack on the United States Capitol (Chapman University Production), Chapman004708 (January 4, 2021, email from Kenneth Chesebro to John Eastman titled "Fwd: Draft 2, with edits", which includes in the chain a Dec. 13, 2020, email from Kenneth Chesebro to Rudy Giuliani titled "PRIVILEGED AND CONFIDENTIAL—Brief Notes on "President of the Senate" strategy"). In his email, Mr. Chesebro argues that the President of the Senate should open "two envelopes" from the contested States including Arizona, "announce[ ] that he cannot and will not . . . count any electoral votes from [the contested State] because there are two slates of votes," and refuse to count them unless the election is "rerun," the courts engage in "adequate judicial review," or the State's legislature "appoint[s] electors." From this language, it is clear that Mr. Chesebro contemplated the fake votes being used in Congress without a court or State government adopting, ratifying, or otherwise selecting them as the proper electoral college votes from a contested State. To be fair, Chesebro concludes this email by telling Giuliani that "[m]any more points would need to be analyzed in making a complete argument that the President of the Senate possesses the sole power to count electoral votes, and anything to the contrary in the Electoral Count Act is unconstitutional." Despite that caution, the very next sentence advocates for a vigorous assertion of that power: "But at minimum this seems a defensible interpretation of the Twelfth Amendment, and one that ought to be asserted, vigorously, by whoever has the role of President of the Senate."

23. Documents on file with the Select Committee to Investigate the January 6th Attack on the United States Capitol (Chapman University Production), Chapman004708 (January 4, 2021, email from Kenneth Chesebro to John Eastman titled "Fwd: Draft 2, with edits", which includes in the chain a Dec. 13, 2020, email from Kenneth Chesebro to Rudy Giuliani titled "PRIVILEGED AND CONFIDENTIAL—Brief Notes on "President of the Senate" strategy").

24. Documents on file with the Select Committee to Investigate the January 6th Attack on the United States Capitol (Chapman University Production), Chapman053475, Chapman053476, (Dec. 23, 2020 email titled "PRIVILEGED AND CONFIDENTIAL—Dec 23 memo on Jan 6 scenario.docx" from John Eastman to Boris Epshteyn and Kenneth Chesebro, with attached memo titled "January 6 scenario"); Documents on file with the Select Committee to Investigate the January 6th Attack on the United States Capitol (Public Source), CTRL0000923050 (Jan. 3, 2021, John Eastman 6-page memo); John C. Eastman, "Privileged and Confidential–Jan 6 Scenario," (Jan. 3, 2021), available at https://www.scribd.com/ document/528776994/Privileged-and-Confidential-Jan-3-Memo-on-Jan-6-Scenario and embedded at John C. Eastman, "Trying to Prevent Illegal Conduct from Deciding an Election is Not Endorsing a 'Coup'," American Greatness (Sep. 30, 2021), available at https:// amgreatness.com/2021/09/30/trying-to-prevent-illegal-conduct-from-deciding-an-election-is-not-endorsing-a-coup/.

25. Documents on file with the Select Committee to Investigate the January 6th Attack on the United States Capitol (Mark Meadows Production), MM003771.

26. Documents on file with the Select Committee to Investigate the January 6th Attack on the United States Capitol (Mark Meadows Production), MM003771 (emphasis added).

27. Documents on file with the Select Committee to Investigate the January 6th Attack on the United States Capitol (Mark Meadows Production), MM003769.

28. Documents on file with the Select Committee to Investigate the January 6th Attack on the United States Capitol (Mark Meadows Production), MM010783, MM010784.

29. Documents on file with the Select Committee to Investigate the January 6th Attack on the United States Capitol (Mark Meadows Production), MM010783, MM010784.

30. Documents on file with the Select Committee to Investigate the January 6th Attack on the United States Capitol (Mark Meadows Production), MM013515.

31. Documents on file with the Select Committee to Investigate the January 6th Attack on the United States Capitol (Mark Meadows Production), MM013516.

32. Select Committee to Investigate the January 6th Attack on the United States Capitol, Continued Interview of Cassidy Hutchinson, (Mar. 7, 2022), pp. 54–55.

33. Select Committee to Investigate the January 6th Attack on the United States Capitol, Transcribed Interview of Joshua Findlay, (May 25, 2022), pp. 27–28.

34. Select Committee to Investigate the January 6th Attack on the United States Capitol, Transcribed Interview of Joshua Findlay, (May 25, 2022), p. 29.

35. Select Committee to Investigate the January 6th Attack on the United States Capitol, Transcribed Interview of Joshua Findlay, (May 25, 2022), pp. 86–87.

36. Select Committee to Investigate the January 6th Attack on the United States Capitol, Transcribed Interview of Ronna Romney McDaniel, (June 1, 2022), pp. 7–8. Ms. McDaniel didn't recall the exact date of the call, but thought it was at least "a few days before December 14th" and may have been sometime before the Supreme Court rejected the case *Texas v. Pennsylvania* on December 11th.

37. Select Committee to Investigate the January 6th Attack on the United States Capitol, Transcribed Interview of Ronna Romney McDaniel, (June 1, 2022), pp. 8–9.

38. Select Committee to Investigate the January 6th Attack on the United States Capitol, Transcribed Interview of Ronna Romney McDaniel, (June 1, 2022), pp. 9–13. McDaniel asserted to the Select Committee that even after December 14th she was under the impression that the seven slates of fake electors were strictly contingent in nature pending authorization by a court of law, and that she relayed this to several concerned Republican officials in the contested States. *See id.*, at 18. However, there is also no indication that she took action to condemn or block the misuse of these contingent elector slates by January 6th.

39. Documents on file with the Select Committee to Investigate the January 6th Attack on the United States Capitol (Tim Murtaugh Production), XXM-0021349, (December 13, 2020, text message from Jason Miller to Justin Clark and Eric Herschmann). For instance, on December 11th, Chesebro wrote to a lawyer working on litigation efforts in Arizona, asking him to file a petition that would keep the litigation alive through the 14th: "[C]an you get the cert. petition on file by Monday? Reason is that Kelli Ward & Kelly Townsend just spoke to the Mayor about the campaign's request that all electors vote Monday in all contested states. Ward and Townsend are concerned it could appear **treasonous** for the AZ electors to vote on Monday if there is no pending court proceeding that might, eventually, lead to the electors being ratified as the legitimate ones. Which is a valid point . . . ." Maggie Haberman and Luke Broadwater, "Arizona Officials Warned Fake Electors Plan Could 'Appear Treasonous,'" *The New York Times*, (Aug. 2, 2022), available at https://www.nytimes.com/2022/08/02/us/politics/arizona-trump-fake-electors.html (emphasis in original).

40. Order re Privilege of Remaining Documents at 15, *Eastman v. Thompson et al.*, No. 8:22-cv-99-DOC-DFM (C.D. Cal. Oct. 19, 2022), ECF No. 372.

41. Documents on file with the Select Committee to Investigate the January 6th Attack on the United States Capitol (Tim Murtaugh Production), XXM-0019417 (December 14, 2020, emails between Jason Miller and Boris Epshteyn).

42. Order Dismissing Bill of Complaint and Denying Certiorari, Texas v. Pennsylvania, 592 U.S. ___, (Dec. 11, 2020) (No. 155, Orig.), available at https://www.supremecourt.gov/orders/courtorders/121120zr_p860.pdf.

43. *See, e.g.*, Select Committee to Investigate the January 6th Attack on the United States Capitol, Transcribed Interview of Joshua Findlay, (May 25, 2022), pp. 87–88.

44. Select Committee to Investigate the January 6th Attack on the United States Capitol, Transcribed Interview of Justin Clark, (May 17, 2022), p. 116.

45. Select Committee to Investigate the January 6th Attack on the United States Capitol, Transcribed Interview of Joshua Findlay, (May 25, 2022), p. 69; Select Committee to Investigate the January 6th Attack on the United States Capitol, Transcribed Interview of Matthew Morgan, (Apr. 25, 2022), p. 74.

46. Select Committee to Investigate the January 6th Attack on the United States Capitol, Transcribed Interview of Justin Clark, (May 17, 2022), p. 118.

47. Select Committee to Investigate the January 6th Attack on the United States Capitol, Transcribed Interview of Justin Clark, (May 17, 2022), p. 114.

48. Select Committee to Investigate the January 6th Attack on the United States Capitol, Transcribed Interview of Justin Clark, (May 17, 2022), pp. 114, 116.

49. Select Committee to Investigate the January 6th Attack on the United States Capitol, Transcribed Interview of Justin Clark, (May 17, 2022), pp. 116, 118. However, Justin Clark's message in an email dated December 24th seems to potentially contradict his suggestions that the campaign legal team fully backed out: "In terms of political judgements on January 6 I know . . . that plans are being discussed and executed: alternate slates have been submitted, votes are being whipped, all of the arguments are in place and a not insignificant ad b[u]y was made highlighting the issues in the election." Documents on file with the Select Committee to Investigate the January 6th Attack on the United States Capitol (William Stepien Production), WS 00036.

50. Select Committee to Investigate the January 6th Attack on the United States Capitol, Transcribed Interview of Matthew Morgan, (Apr. 25, 2022), p. 70.

51. Select Committee to Investigate the January 6th Attack on the United States Capitol, Transcribed Interview of Joshua Findlay, (May 25, 2022), pp. 39–40.

52. Select Committee to Investigate the January 6th Attack on the United States Capitol, Transcribed Interview of Pasquale Anthony "Pat" Cipollone, (July 8, 2022), pp. 69–70, 73.

53. Select Committee to Investigate the January 6th Attack on the United States Capitol, Informal Interview of Patrick Philbin, (Apr. 13, 2022).

54. Select Committee to Investigate the January 6th Attack on the United States Capitol, Transcribed Interview of Pasquale Anthony "Pat" Cipollone, (July 8, 2022), pp. 75–76.

55. Select Committee to Investigate the January 6th Attack on the United States Capitol, Continued Interview of Cassidy Hutchinson, (Mar. 7, 2022), p. 64–65. (Hutchinson later clarified that she recalled hearing that from Pat Cipollone and, potentially, also Pat Philbin.)

56. Select Committee to Investigate the January 6th Attack on the United States Capitol, Continued Interview of Cassidy Hutchinson, (Mar. 7, 2022), pp. 64–65.

57. Documents on file with the Select Committee to Investigate the January 6th Attack on the United States Capitol (Joshua Findlay Production), JF052.

58. Select Committee to Investigate the January 6th Attack on the United States Capitol, Transcribed Interview of Joshua Findlay, (May 25, 2022), pp. 87–88.

59. Select Committee to Investigate the January 6th Attack on the United States Capitol, Transcribed Interview of Joshua Findlay, (May 25, 2022), pp. 87–88.

60. Select Committee to Investigate the January 6th Attack on the United States Capitol, Transcribed Interview of Joshua Findlay, (May 25, 2022), p. 44.

61. Select Committee to Investigate the January 6th Attack on the United States Capitol, Transcribed Interview of Joshua Findlay, (May 25, 2022), p. 30.

62. Select Committee to Investigate the January 6th Attack on the United States Capitol, Transcribed Interview of Justin Clark, (May 17, 2022), p. 125.

63. Documents on file with the Select Committee to Investigate the January 6th Attack on the United States Capitol (James DeGraffenreid Production), CTRL0000044010_00031 (Dec. 10, 2020 email from Kenneth Chesebro to James DeGraffenreid and others).

64. Documents on file with the Select Committee to Investigate the January 6th Attack on the United States Capitol (Joshua Findlay Production), JF051, JF054.

65. Documents on file with the Select Committee to investigate the January 6th Attack on the United States Capitol (David Shafer Production), 108751.0001_000004, 108751.0001_000019, 108751.0001_000020, 108751.0001_000021, 108751.0001_000024.

66. Documents on file with the Select Committee to Investigate the January 6th Attack on the United States Capitol (Joshua Findlay Production), JF049.

67. Documents on file with the Select Committee to Investigate the January 6th Attack on the United States Capitol (James DeGraffenreid Production), DEGRAFFENREID 000786; Documents on file with the Select Committee to investigate the January 6th Attack on the United States Capitol (Michael McDonald Production), MCDONALD 000789.

68. Documents on file with the Select Committee to Investigate the January 6th Attack on the United States Capitol (Joshua Findlay Production), JF061.

69. Documents on file with the Select Committee to Investigate the January 6th Attack on the United States Capitol (Lawrence Tabas Production), CTRL0000061077.

70. Documents on file with the Select Committee to Investigate the January 6th Attack on the United States Capitol (Andrew Hitt Production), Hitt000011.

71. Documents on file with the Select Committee to Investigate the January 6th Attack on the United States Capitol (Andrew Hitt Production), Hitt000011.

72. Documents on file with the Select Committee to Investigate the January 6th Attack on the United States Capitol (Andrew Hitt Production), Hitt000011; Documents on file with the Select Committee to Investigate the January 6th Attack on the United States Capitol (David Shafer Production), 108751.0001 000004; Documents on file with the Select Committee to Investigate the January 6th Attack on the United States Capitol (Lawrence Tabas Production), CTRL0000061077; Documents on file with the Select Committee to Investigate the January 6th Attack on the United States Capitol (James DeGraffenreid Production), DEGRAFFENREID 000786; Documents on file with the Select Committee to Investigate the January 6th Attack on the United States Capitol (Kenneth Chesebro Production), KC_Elector_Correspondence_000211, KC_Elector_Correspondence_000215.

73. Documents on file with the Select Committee to Investigate the January 6th Attack on the United States Capitol (Joshua Findlay Production), JF052.

74. Documents on file with the Select Committee to Investigate the January 6th Attack on the United States Capitol (Robert Sinners Production), CTRL0000083897, CTRL0000083898.

75. Documents on file with the Select Committee to Investigate the January 6th Attack on the United States Capitol (Robert Sinners Production), CTRL0000083897.

76. Documents on file with the Select Committee to Investigate the January 6th Attack on the United States Capitol (Robert Sinners Production), CTRL0000083897. Members of this team appear to have included Trump Victory Committee or Trump Campaign EDO State or regional directors for relevant States, including Arizona and New Mexico (Thomas Lane), Georgia (Robert Sinners), Michigan (Shawn Flynn), Nevada (Jesse Law and Valerie McConahay), Pennsylvania (James Fitzpatrick), and Wisconsin (Ryan Terrill, who had originally worked on North Carolina issues but later shifted to Wisconsin), as well as Mr. Roman's deputy (G. Michael Brown). *See* Documents on file with the Select Committee to Investigate the January 6th Attack on the United States Capitol (Laura Cox Production), Laura Cox 000339; Documents on file with the Select Committee to Investigate the January 6th Attack on the United States Capitol (Rudy Giuliani Production), RGGLOBAL_DOM_00001373; Documents on file with the Select Committee to Investigate the January 6th Attack on the United States Capitol (Tim Murtaugh Production) XXM-0010338, XXM-0008776, XXM-0011867; Richard Ruelas, "Trump Campaign Official Subpoenaed by FBI Appears to Be at Meeting of Fake Arizona Electors," *Arizona Republic*, (June 23, 2022), available at https://www.azcentral.com/story/news/politics/arizona/2022/06/23/fbi-subpoenas-thomas-lane-trump-campaign-arizona/7708133001/; Jonathan Oosting, "Trump Fake Elector Probe into

2020 Race Expands with Michigan Subpoenas," *Bridge Michigan*, (June 23, 2022), available at https://www.bridgemi.com/michigan-government/trump-fake-elector-probe-2020-race-expands-michigan-subpoenas; Zach Montellaro and Holly Otterbein, "Trump Calls for Poll Watchers. Election Officials Call for Calm," *Politico*, (Sept. 30, 2020), available at https://www.politico.com/news/2020/09/30/trump-poll-watchers-election-423996; Luke Broadwater, "Jan. 6 Inquiry Subpoenas 6 Tied to False Pro-Trump Elector Effort," *New York Times*, (Feb. 15, 2022), available at https://www.nytimes.com/2022/02/15/us/politics/jan-6-subpoenas-trump.html.

77. Documents on file with the Select Committee to Investigate the January 6th Attack on the United States Capitol (Robert Sinners Production), CTRL0000083898.

78. David Shafer (@DavidShafer), Twitter, Dec. 14, 2020 12:51 p.m. ET, available at https://twitter.com/DavidShafer/status/1338542161932021762; David Shafer (@DavidShafer), Twitter, Dec. 14, 2020 1:07 p.m. ET, available at https://twitter.com/DavidShafer/status/1338546066346676224; "Republican Electors Cast Procedural Vote, Seek to Preserve Trump Campaign Legal Challenge," Pennsylvania Republican Party website, (Dec. 14, 2020), available at https://pagop.org/2020/12/14/republican-electors-cast-procedural-vote/; "Statement on Republican Electors Meeting," Republican Party of Wisconsin, (Dec. 14, 2020), available at https://wisgop.org/republican-electors-2020/; Republican Party of Arizona (@AZGOP), Twitter, Dec. 14, 2020 5:13 p.m. ET, available at https://twitter.com/AZGOP/status/1338608056985239554.

79. Marshall Cohen, Zachary Cohen, and Dan Merica, "Trump Campaign Officials, Led by Rudy Giuliani, Oversaw Fake Electors Plot in 7 States," CNN, (Jan. 20, 2022), available at https://www.cnn.com/2022/01/20/politics/trump-campaign-officials-rudy-giuliani-fake-electors/index.html.

80. Select Committee to Investigate the January 6th Attack on the United States Capitol, Transcribed Interview of Joshua Findlay, (May 25, 2022), p. 58.

81. Documents on file with the Select Committee to Investigate the January 6th Attack on the United States Capitol (Tim Murtaugh Production), XXM-0016071 (December 10, 2020, email from Joshua Findlay to Nick Trainer and Matt Morgan re: Presidential Elector Issues).

82. Documents on file with the Select Committee to Investigate the January 6th Attack on the United States Capitol (Tim Murtaugh Production), XXM-0016071 (December 10, 2020, email from Joshua Findlay to Nick Trainer and Matt Morgan re: Presidential Elector Issues); Select Committee to Investigate the January 6th Attack on the United States Capitol, Transcribed Interview of Joshua Findlay, (May 25, 2022), pp. 55–59; Michael C. Bender, "Republicans Hire Nine Regional Directors for Trump 2020 Election," *Wall Street Journal*, (May 8, 2019), available at https://www.wsj.com/articles/trump-campaign-hires-nine-regional-directors-for-2020-election-11557355628.

83. Documents on file with the Select Committee to Investigate the January 6th Attack on the United States Capitol (Lawrence Tabas Production), CTRL0000061085 (December 13, 2020, email chain between Thomas King III and James Fitzpatrick re: Pa. Electors).

84. Select Committee to Investigate the January 6th Attack on the United States Capitol, Informal Interview of Lawrence Tabas, (Apr. 11, 2022).

85. Documents on file with the Select Committee to Investigate the January 6th Attack on the United States Capitol (Andrew Hitt Production), Hitt000076 (December 4, 2020, Text messages between Andrew Hitt and Mark Jefferson); Select Committee to Investigate the January 6th Attack on the United States Capitol, Deposition of Andrew Hitt, (Feb. 28, 2022), p. 8.

86. Documents on file with the Select Committee to Investigate the January 6th Attack on the United States Capitol (Andrew Hitt Production), Hitt000083 (December 12, 2020, Text messages between Andrew Hitt and Mark Jefferson).

87. Documents on file with the Select Committee to Investigate the January 6th Attack on the United States Capitol (National Archives Production), CTRL0000037949 (December 14, 2020, memorandum from purported electors in Wisconsin).

88. Kira Lerner, "UPDATED Trump's Fake Electors: Here's the Full List," *News from the States*, (June 29, 2022), available at https://www.newsfromthestates.com/article/updated-trumps-fake-electors-heres-full-list; Documents on file with the Select Committee to Investigate the January 6th Attack on the United States Capitol (National Archives Production), CTRL0000037568, CTRL0000037944, CTRL0000037945, CTRL0000037946, CTRL0000037947, CTRL0000037948, CTRL0000037949 (December 14, 2020, memoranda from slates of purported electors in Arizona, Georgia, Michigan, New Mexico, Nevada, Pennsylvania, and Wisconsin).

89. Select Committee to Investigate the January 6th Attack on the United States Capitol, Deposition of Laura Cox, (May 3, 2022), pp. 77–78.

90. Beth Reinhard, Amy Gardner, Josh Dawsey, Emma Brown, and Rosalind S. Helderman, "As Giuliani Coordinated Plan for Trump Electoral Votes in States Biden Won, Some Electors Balked," *Washington Post*, (Jan. 20, 2022), available at https://www.washingtonpost.com/investigations/electors-giuliani-trump-electoral-college/2022/01/20/687e3698-7587-11ec-8b0a-bcfab800c430_story.html.

91. Beth Reinhard, Amy Gardner, Josh Dawsey, Emma Brown, and Rosalind S. Helderman, "As Giuliani Coordinated Plan for Trump Electoral Votes in States Biden Won, Some Electors Balked," *Washington Post*, (Jan. 20, 2022), available at https://www.washingtonpost.com/investigations/electors-giuliani-trump-electoral-college/2022/01/20/687e3698-7587-11ec-8b0a-bcfab800c430_story.html.

92. Kira Lerner, "UPDATED Trump's fake electors: Here's the full list," *News from the States*, (June 29, 2022), available at https://www.newsfromthestates.com/article/updated-trumps-fake-electors-heres-full-list.

93. *See, e.g.*, Select Committee to Investigate the January 6th Attack on the United States Capitol, Deposition of Andrew Hitt, (Feb. 28, 2022), pp. 50–51.

94. Select Committee to Investigate the January 6th Attack on the United States Capitol, Transcribed Interview of Robert Sinners, (June 15, 2022), pp. 18–19.

95. Select Committee to Investigate the January 6th Attack on the United States Capitol, Transcribed Interview of Robert Sinners, (June 15, 2022), pp. 37–38.

96. Documents on file with the Select Committee to Investigate the January 6th Attack on the United States Capitol (National Archives Production), CTRL0000037568, CTRL0000037944, CTRL0000037945 CTRL0000037946, CTRL0000037947, CTRL0000037948, CTRL0000037949 (December 14, 2020, memoranda from slates of purported electors in Arizona, Georgia, Michigan, Nevada, and Wisconsin).

97. Documents on file with the Select Committee to Investigate the January 6th Attack on the United States Capitol (National Archives Production), CTRL0000037946 (December 14, 2020, memorandum from purported electors in New Mexico).

98. Documents on file with the Select Committee to Investigate the January 6th Attack on the United States Capitol (National Archives Production), CTRL0000037948 (December 14, 2020, memorandum from purported electors in Pennsylvania).

99. Documents on file with the Select Committee to Investigate the January 6th Attack on the United States Capitol (Robert Sinners Production), CTRL0000083893 (December 14, 2020, email chain from Robert Sinners to Mike Roman and others re: Whip Update).

100. Documents on file with the Select Committee to Investigate the January 6th Attack on the United States Capitol (William Stepien Production), WS 00095, WS 00096 (December 14, 2020, email from Joshua Findlay to Matt Morgan, Justin Clark, and cc'ing Bill Stepien re: Georgia Update).

101. Documents on file with the Select Committee to Investigate the January 6th Attack on the United States Capitol (National Archives Production), 076P-R000009527_0001, (December 14, 2020, forwarded email from Ronna McDaniel to Molly Michael with the subject line: "FWD: Electors Recap—Final").

102. Documents on file with the Select Committee to Investigate the January 6th Attack on the United States Capitol (National Archives Production), 076P-R000009527_0001, (December 14, 2020, forwarded email from Ronna McDaniel to Molly Michael with the subject line: "FWD: Electors Recap—Final").

103. Documents on file with the Select Committee to Investigate the January 6th Attack on the United States Capitol (Shawn Still Production), CTRL0000042623_00018 (December 13, 2020, email from Shawn Still to Dana Pagan subject: "Fwd: Information on Duties of Presidential Electors—Monday, December 14th").

104. Documents on file with the Select Committee to Investigate the January 6th Attack on the United States Capitol (Shawn Still Production), CTRL0000042623_00018 (December 13, 2020, email from Shawn Still to Dana Pagan subject: "Fwd: Information on Duties of Presidential Electors—Monday, December 14th").

105. Greg Bluestein (@bluestein), Twitter, Dec. 14, 2020 11:32 a.m. ET, available at https://twitter.com/bluestein/status/1338522299360800771; Select Committee to Investigate the January 6th Attack on the United States Capitol, Deposition of Shawn Still, (Feb. 25, 2022), pp. 41–48; Michael Isikoff and Daniel Klaidman, "Exclusive: Fulton County DA Sends 'Target' Letters to Trump Allies in Georgia Investigation," *Yahoo! News*, (July 15, 2022), available at https://news.yahoo.com/exclusive-fulton-county-da-sends-target-letters-to-trump-allies-in-georgia-investigation-152517469.html.

106. Select Committee to Investigate the January 6th Attack on the United States Capitol, Deposition of Laura Cox, (May 3, 2022), pp. 53–54.

107. Select Committee to Investigate the January 6th Attack on the United States Capitol, Deposition of Laura Cox, (May 3, 2022), pp. 53–54.

108. Select Committee to Investigate the January 6th Attack on the United States Capitol, Deposition of Mayra Rodriguez, (Feb. 22, 2022), pp. 14–18.

109. Documents on file with the Select Committee to Investigate the January 6th Attack on the United States Capitol (National Archives Production), VP-R0000417_0001, VP-R0000418_0001 (January 3, 2021, email from Elizabeth MacDonough, subject "RE: COV tracker" with attachment); Documents on file with the Select Committee to Investigate the January 6th Attack on the United States Capitol (Chris Hodgson Production), 00094 (Attachment to email from Elizabeth MacDonough, subject "RE: COV tracker").

110. Documents on file with the Select Committee to Investigate the January 6th Attack on the United States Capitol (National Archives Production), VP-R0000417_0001, VP-R0000418_0001 (January 3, 2021, email from Elizabeth MacDonough, subject "RE: COV tracker" with attachment); Documents on file with the Select Committee to Investigate the January 6th Attack on the United States Capitol (Chris Hodgson Production), 00094 (Attachment to email from Elizabeth MacDonough, subject "RE: COV tracker").

111. Select Committee to Investigate the January 6th Attack on the United States Capitol, Deposition of Chris Hodgson, (Mar. 30, 2022), pp. 144–45, 206–07.

112. In Wisconsin they were able to enter with apparent help from the chief of staff for then majority leader of the Wisconsin State Senate, Scott Fitzgerald, who now represents Wisconsin in the U.S. House of Representatives. In Georgia, a freelance reporter who has testified to the Fulton County grand jury claims to have found that the room in which the fake electors met was reserved by the office of Georgia House Speaker David Ralston, which is consistent with what Georgia GOP Chairman David Shafer told the Select Committee. *See* "Open Records Regarding Wisconsin's Fake Electors Suggest Congressman Scott Fitzgerald Played Significant Role in Trying to Overturn a Free and Fair Election," Office of Wisconsin State Senator Chris Larson, (Jan. 25, 2022), available at https://legis.wisconsin.gov/senate/07/Larson/media/2056/1-25-22-fitzgerald-electors-pr.pdf; Letter from Cyrus Anderson, Deputy Sergeant at Arms, Wisconsin State Senate to State Sen. Chris Larson, attaching documents, Jan. 24, 2022, available at https://legis.wisconsin.gov/senate/07/Larson/media/2052/12-14-20-open-records-request-results-short.pdf; Select Committee to Investigate the January 6th Attack on the United States Capitol, Deposition of David Shafer, (Feb.

25, 2022), pp. 93–94, 106; Michael Isikoff and Daniel Kladman, "Exclusive: Fulton County DA Sends 'Target' Letters to Trump Allies in Georgia Investigation," *Yahoo! News*, (July 15, 2022), available at https://news.yahoo.com/exclusive-fulton-county-da-sends-target-letters-to-trump-allies-in-georgia-investigation-152517469.html; George Chidi, "Bearing Witness," The Atlanta Objective with George Chidi, (June 29, 2022), available at https://theatlantaobjective.substack.com/p/bearing-witness; Documents on file with the Select Committee to Investigate the January 6th Attack on the United States Capitol (Shawn Still Production), 108755.0001_000009 (December 13, 2020, email from Shawn Still to Dana Pagan re: "Fwd: Information of Duties of Presidential Electors—Monday Dec. 14th").

113. Daniel Villareal, "Michigan Republicans Tried to Submit Fake Electoral Votes to Capitol," *Newsweek*, (Dec. 15, 2020), available at https://www.newsweek.com/michigan-republicans-tried-submit-fake-electoral-votes-capitol-1555028.

114. Documents on file with the Select Committee to Investigate the January 6th Attack on the United States Capitol (National Archives Production), CTRL0000037945, p. 2 (December 14, 2020, memorandum of purported Michigan electors for Donald J. Trump).

115. Select Committee to Investigate the January 6th Attack on the United States Capitol, Deposition of Mayra Rodriguez, (Feb. 22, 2022), pp. 18, 21; Laina G. Stebbins, "Feds Serve Subpoenas to Pro-Trump Fake Electors in Michigan," *Michigan Advance* (June 23, 2022), available at https://michiganadvance.com/blog/feds-serve-subpoenas-to-pro-trump-fake-electors-in-michigan/.

116. Brett Samuels, "Stephen Miller: 'Alternate' Electors Will Keep Trump Election Challenge Alive," *The Hill*, (Dec. 14, 2020), available at https://thehill.com/homenews/campaign/530092-stephen-miller-alternate-electors-will-keep-trump-challenge-alive-post/; Steve Bannon's War Room Radio, "STEVE BANNON'S WAR ROOM RADIO SPECIAL EPISODE582," *BitChute*, (aired on Dec. 14, 2020, reposted on BitChute Aug. 22, 2021), at 10:30–13:00, available at https://www.bitchute.com/video/v889V3Thxgcj/.

117. Mike Wereschagin, "Pa. Republicans' Hedged Language May Have Saved Them from Prosecution over Electoral Vote Scheme," *Lancaster Online*, (Jan. 17, 2022), available at https://lancasteronline.com/news/politics/pa-republicans-hedged-language-may-have-saved-them-from-prosecution-over-electoral-vote-scheme/article_849d4f7e-7589-11ec-8881-6383a823557d.html.

118. Select Committee to Investigate the January 6th Attack on the United States Capitol, Continued Interview of Cassidy Hutchinson, (Mar. 7, 2022), pp. 143–48.

119. Documents on file with the Select Committee to Investigate the January 6th Attack on the United States Capitol (Chapman University Production), Chapman053475 (December 23, 2020, John Eastman email to Boris Epshteyn and Ken Chesebro).

120. Documents on file with the Select Committee to Investigate the January 6th Attack on the United States Capitol (Chapman University Production), Chapman053476 (Word Document, "PRIVILEGED AND CONFIDENTIAL January 6 Scenario," attached in Dec. 23, 2020, John Eastman email to Boris Epshteyn and Ken Chesebro).

121. Documents on file with the Select Committee to Investigate the January 6th Attack on the United States Capitol (Chapman University Production), Chapman053475 (December 23, 2020, John Eastman email to Boris Epshteyn and Ken Chesebro).

122. Documents on file with the Select Committee to Investigate the January 6th Attack on the United States Capitol (Chapman University Production), Chapman061863 (January 1, 2021, Kenneth Chesebro email to John Eastman and Boris Epshteyn at 10:26 p.m.).

123. Both of Dr. Eastman's memos described here are discussed at length in the chapter addressing President Trump's pressure on the Vice President. *See* Chapter 5. *See also* Documents on file with the Select Committee to Investigate the January 6th Attack on the United States Capitol (Chapman University Production), Chapman053475, Chapman053476, (Dec. 23, 2020 email titled "PRIVILEGED AND CONFIDENTIAL—Dec 23 memo on Jan 6 scenario.docx" from John Eastman to Boris Epshteyn and Kenneth Chesebro, with attached memo titled "January 6 scenario"); Documents on file with the Select Committee

to Investigate the January 6th Attack on the United States Capitol (Public Source), CTRL0000923050 (Jan. 3, 2021, John Eastman 6-page memo); John C. Eastman, "Privileged and Confidential–Jan 6 Scenario," (Jan. 3, 2021), available at https://www.scribd.com/document/528776994/Privileged-and-Confidential-Jan-3-Memo-on-Jan-6-Scenario and embedded at John C. Eastman, "Trying to Prevent Illegal Conduct from Deciding an Election is Not Endorsing a 'Coup'," American Greatness (Sep. 30, 2021), available at https://amgreatness.com/2021/09/30/trying-to-prevent-illegal-conduct-from-deciding-an-election-is-not-endorsing-a-coup/

124. Documents on file with the Select Committee to Investigate the January 6th Attack on the United States Capitol (National Archives Production), VP-R0000417_0001, VP-R0000418_0001 (January 3, 2021 email and attachment from Senate Parliamentarian to Office of the Vice President); Documents on file with the Select Committee to Investigate the January 6th Attack on the United States Capitol (Chris Hodgson Production) 00094 (additional copy of same attachment sent from Senate Parliamentarian to Office of the Vice President).

125. Documents on file with the Select Committee to Investigate the January 6th Attack on the United States Capitol (Andrew Hitt Production), Hitt000089 (January 4, 2021, Andrew Hitt text message to Mark Jefferson at 9:02 p.m.).

126. Documents on file with the Select Committee to Investigate the January 6th Attack on the United States Capitol (Andrew Hitt Production), Hitt000089 (January 4, 2021, Andrew Hitt text message to Mark Jefferson at 9:02 p.m.).

127. Documents on file with the Select Committee to Investigate the January 6th Attack on the United States Capitol (Angela McCallum Production), McCallum_01_001576, McCallum_01_001577 (Michael Brown text message to Angela McCallum at undetermined time); Select Committee to Investigate the January 6th Attack on the United States Capitol, Deposition of Angela McCallum (Dec. 8, 2021), p. 122.

128. Documents on file with the Select Committee to Investigate the January 6th Attack on the United States Capitol (Angela McCallum Production), McCallum_01_001576, McCallum_01_001577 (Michael Brown text message to Angela McCallum at undetermined time); Select Committee to Investigate the January 6th Attack on the United States Capitol, Deposition of Angela McCallum (Dec. 8, 2021), p. 122.

129. The Select Committee does not know where Brown delivered the fake votes. The Select Committee attempted to contact Brown multiple ways, including by subpoena, but servers could not locate him and he never responded to outreach. The Select Committee served Mike Roman with a subpoena, but he asserted his Fifth Amendment rights and did not answer any substantive questions about the fake-elector scheme. What the Select Committee has determined, however, is that Brown likely delivered the fake electoral eollege votes to at least one of President Trump's allies in Congress. *See* Select Committee to Investigate the January 6th Attack on the United States Capitol, Deposition of Michael Roman, (Aug. 10, 2022), p. 40.

130. Jason Lemon, "Johnson Says Involvement With 1/6 Fake Electors Plan Only 'Lasted Seconds'," *Newsweek*, (Aug. 21, 2022), available at https://www.newsweek.com/johnson-says-involvement-1-6-fake-electors-plan-only-lasted-seconds-1735486; Documents on file with the Select Committee to Investigate the January 6th Attack on the United States Capitol (Chris Hodgson Production), CTRL0000056548_00007 (January 6, 2021, text message at 8:41 a.m. ET from Matt Stroia to Chris Hodgson); Documents on file with the Select Committee to Investigate the January 6th Attack on the United States Capitol (Chris Hodgson Production), CTRL0000056548_000035 (Jan. 6, 2021, text message around 12:37 p.m. ET from Sean Riley to Chris Hodgson) ("Johnson needs to hand something to VPOTUS please advise . . . Alternate slate of electors for MI and WI because archivist didn't receive them . . .").

131. Documents on file with the Select Committee to Investigate the January 6th Attack on the United States Capitol (Chris Hodgson Production), CTRL0000056548_00007 (January 6, 2021, Matt Stroia text message to Chris Hodgson at 8:41 a.m. ET).

132. Lawrence Andrea, "Pennsylvania Congressman Concludes Internal Investigation with Few Answers After Ron Johnson's Claims About False Electors," *Milwaukee Journal Sentinel*, (July 14, 2022), available at https://www.jsonline.com/story/news/politics/2022/07/14/few-answers-mike-kellys-probe-into-false-electors-ron-johnson-pennsylvania-wisconsin/10059776002/.

133. "The Vicki McKenna Show—Keep and Bear Arms," iHeart Radio, June 23, 2022, at 9:30–15:00, available at https://www.iheart.com/podcast/139-vicki-mckenna-27246267/episode/the-vicki-mckenna-show-keep-98666092/?position=570&embed=true; John Solomon, "Jan. 6 Panel's Ron Johnson Narrative Exposes Ills of One-Sided Hearing," *Just The News*, (June 23, 2022), available at https://justthenews.com/government/jan-6-panels-ron-johnson-narrative-exposes-ills-one-sided-hearing (linking to image of text message available at https://justthenews.com/sites/default/files/2022-06/TroupisJohnson1.pdf).

134. "The Vicki McKenna Show—Keep and Bear Arms," iHeart Radio, June 23, 2022, at 9:30–15:00, available at https://www.iheart.com/podcast/139-vicki-mckenna-27246267/episode/the-vicki-mckenna-show-keep-98666092/?position=570&embed=true; John Solomon, "Jan. 6 Panel's Ron Johnson Narrative Exposes Ills of One-Sided Hearing," *Just The News*, (June 23, 2022), available at https://justthenews.com/government/jan-6-panels-ron-johnson-narrative-exposes-ills-one-sided-hearing (linking to image of text message available at https://justthenews.com/sites/default/files/2022-06/JohnsonTroupis2Redacted.pdf).

135. Documents on file with the Select Committee to Investigate the January 6th Attack on the United States Capitol (Chris Hodgson Production), CTRL0000056548_00035 (January 6, 2021, Sean Riley text message to Chris Hodgson at 12:37 p.m. ET).

136. Documents on file with the Select Committee to Investigate the January 6th Attack on the United States Capitol (Chris Hodgson Production), CTRL0000056548_00035 (January 6, 2021, Sean Riley text message to Chris Hodgson at 12:37 p.m. ET).

137. Documents on file with the Select Committee to Investigate the January 6th Attack on the United States Capitol (Chris Hodgson Production), CTRL0000056548_00035 (January 6, 2021, Sean Riley text message to Chris Hodgson at 12:37 p.m. ET).

138. Documents on file with the Select Committee to Investigate the January 6th Attack on the United States Capitol (Mark Meadows Production), MM013494, MM014589, MM014592, MM014595, MM014598, MM014722 (Mark Meadows text messages with Sen. Mike Lee on December 8, 2020, January 3, 2021, and January 4, 2021); Documents on file with the Select Committee to Investigate the January 6th Attack on the United States Capitol (Cleta Mitchell Production), CM00015452, CM00015477 (Cleta Mitchell text messages with Sen. Mike Lee on December 9, 2020 and December 30, 2020).

139. Documents on file with the Select Committee to Investigate the January 6th Attack on the United States Capitol (Cleta Mitchell Production), CM00015477.

140. Documents on file with the Select Committee to Investigate the January 6th Attack on the United States Capitol (Cleta Mitchell Production), CM00015477.

141. Documents on file with the Select Committee to Investigate the January 6th Attack on the United States Capitol (Cleta Mitchell Production), CM00015477.

4

"JUST CALL IT CORRUPT AND LEAVE THE REST TO ME"

4.1 THE DOJ FOUND NO SIGNIFICANT EVIDENCE OF FRAUD

U.S. Attorney General William Barr knew there would be trouble before all the votes had been counted. "So, right out of the box on election night, the President claimed that there was major fraud underway," Barr explained. "I mean, this happened, as far as I could tell, before there was actually any potential of looking at evidence."[1] President Trump was quick to claim, "there was major fraud" based solely on the phenomenon known as the "Red Mirage."[2]

As explained elsewhere in this report, Democrats were more inclined to vote via mail-in ballot during the 2020 Presidential election than Republicans, who were more likely to vote in-person on election day. This was widely known, and partly a result of, President Trump's own public statements criticizing mail-in balloting. It also created a gap in the timing of how votes were tallied. The early vote tally favored Republicans on election night because the mail-in ballots, which skewed toward Democrats, were not yet fully counted. This occurred not just in 2020, but also in previous elections.[3] The President knew of this phenomenon but exploited it on election night, nonetheless, as he and his allies had planned to do.[4]

President Trump exploited this timing gap and used it as "the basis for this broad claim that there was major fraud," Barr said.[5] But the Attorney General "didn't think much of that." People "had been talking for weeks and everyone understood for weeks that that was going to be what happened on election night," Barr explained.[6] Cities with Democratic majorities in the battleground States wouldn't have their votes fully counted until "the end of the cycle," with "a lot of Democratic votes coming in at the end."[7] This was not some well-guarded secret, as "everyone understood that the dynamic of election night in many States would be whether or not the Democratic votes at the end of the day would overcome the election day votes." [8]

Within days of the election, the President made an "avalanche" of fraud allegations. It "was like playing Whac-A-Mole," Barr explained, "because something would come out one day and the next day it would be another issue." [9] Barr told his "staff very soon after the election" that he "didn't think the President would ever admit that he lost the election, and he would blame it on fraud, and then he would blame the actions and evidence on the Department of Justice." [10]

Barr soon took steps to investigate claims of fraud in the 2020 Presidential election, even in the absence of evidence. The Department of Justice's (DOJ) longstanding policy had been to avoid any substantive investigations until after the election's results were certified. [11] As the country's premier Federal law enforcement agency, DOJ is justifiably concerned that its substantial power can influence the outcome of an election, and it has enacted policies to mitigate this possibility. [12]

On November 7, 2020, the media declared former Vice President Biden the winner of the Presidential election. Two days later, on November 9th, Attorney General Barr authorized wider investigations into claims of election fraud. [13] Barr instructed DOJ and FBI personnel "to pursue substantial allegations of voting and vote tabulation irregularities prior to the certification of elections in your jurisdictions in certain cases." [14] Barr noted that nothing in his memo "should be taken as any indication that the Department has concluded that voting irregularities have impacted the outcome of any election." [15]

4.2 NOVEMBER 23, 2020: BARR CHALLENGES PRESIDENT TRUMP'S ELECTION LIES

As Barr predicted, the President did call on him for information about alleged election fraud. Trump challenged him with a blizzard of conspiracy theories in three face-to-face meetings after the election. The first such meeting occurred on November 23, 2020.

On November 23rd, the Attorney General spoke with White House Counsel Pat Cipollone, who said that it was important for him come to the White House and speak to President Trump. [16] Barr had not seen the President since before the election in late October, and the White House counsel believed that it was important that the Attorney General explain what the Department of Justice was doing related to claims of election fraud. [17]

"The President said there had been major fraud and that, as soon as the facts were out, the results of the election would be reversed," Barr recalled.

U.S. Attorney General William Barr at the Department of Justice on December 21, 2020.
(Photo by Michael Reynolds-Pool/Getty Images)

Trump continued "for quite a while," and Barr was "expecting" what came next.[18] President Trump alleged that "the Department of Justice doesn't think it has a role looking into these fraud claims."[19] Barr anticipated this line of attack because the President's counsel, Rudolph Giuliani, was making all sorts of wild, unsubstantiated claims.[20] And Giuliani wanted to blame DOJ for the fact that no one had come up with any real evidence of fraud.[21] Of course, by the time of this meeting, U.S. Attorneys' Offices had been explicitly authorized to investigate substantial claims for 2 weeks and had yet to find any evidence of significant voter fraud.[22]

Barr explained to the President why he was wrong. DOJ, was willing to investigate any "specific and credible allegations of fraud."[23] The fact of the matter was that the claims being made were "just not meritorious" and were "not panning out."[24] Barr emphasized to the President that DOJ "doesn't take sides in elections" and "is not an extension of your legal team."[25]

During the November 23rd meeting, Barr also challenged one of President Trump's central lies. He "specifically raised the Dominion voting machines, which I found to be one of the most disturbing allegations."[26] "Disturbing," Barr explained, because there was "absolutely zero basis for the allegations," which were being "made in such a sensational way that they obviously were influencing a lot of people, members of the public." [27] Americans were being deceived into thinking "that there was this systematic corruption in the system and that their votes didn't count and that these machines, controlled by somebody else, were actually determining it, which was complete nonsense." [28] Barr stressed to the President that this was "crazy stuff," arguing that not only was the conspiracy theory a waste of time, but it was also "doing [a] great, great disservice to the country." [29]

As Attorney General Barr left the meeting, he talked with Mark Meadows, the White House Chief of Staff, and Jared Kushner, President Trump's son-in-law.[30] "I think he's become more realistic and knows that there's a limit to how far he can take this," Meadows said, according to Barr.[31] Kushner reassured Barr, "we're working on this, we're working on it." [32] Barr was hopeful that the President was beginning to accept reality.[33] The opposite happened.

"I felt that things continued to deteriorate between the 23rd and the weekend of the 29th," Barr recalled.[34] Barr was concerned because President Trump began meeting with delegations of State legislators, and it appeared to him that "there was maneuvering going on." [35] Barr had "no problem" with challenging an election "through the appropriate process," but "worried" that he "didn't have any visibility into what was going on" and that the "President was digging in." [36]

4.3 DECEMBER 1, 2020: PRESIDENT TRUMP IS IRATE AFTER BARR SAYS THERE IS NO SIGNIFICANT FRAUD

Attorney General Barr had been clear that DOJ was investigating claims of fraud. The Department simply was not turning up any real evidence of malfeasance, and certainly nothing that would overturn the election. Just as Barr feared, the President turned on DOJ anyway.

On November 29, 2020, Fox News's Maria Bartiromo interviewed President Trump. It was his first TV interview since he lost his bid for reelection. The President claimed the election was "rigged" and rife with "fraud." [37] President Trump repeated various conspiracy theories, leading with the claim that Dominion's voting machines had "glitches," which moved "thousands of votes from my account to Biden's account." [38] President Trump pointed to "dumps of votes," a reference to the batches of mail-in ballots that had been tabulated later in the counting process.[39] He rambled off various other, spurious allegations, including that dead people voted in significant numbers.[40]

"This is total fraud," the President said.[41] "And how the FBI and Department of Justice—I don't know—maybe they're involved, but how people are getting away with this stuff—it's unbelievable. This election was rigged. This election was a total fraud." [42]

"Where is the DOJ and the FBI in all of this, Mr. President?" Bartiromo asked.[43] "You have laid out some serious charges here. Shouldn't this be something that the FBI is investigating? Are they? Is the DOJ investigating?" Bartiromo asked incredulously.[44]

"Missing in action," the President replied, "can't tell you where they are." [45] He conceded that when he asked if DOJ and FBI were investigating, "everyone says yes, they're looking at it." [46] But he didn't leave it there. "You would think if you're in the FBI or Department of Justice, this is, this is the biggest thing you could be looking at," President Trump said. "Where are they? I've not seen anything. I mean, just keep moving along. They go onto the next President." [47] He claimed the FBI was not even investigating Dominion, adding that votes processed in its machines "are counted in foreign countries." [48]

None of this was true. Just 6 days earlier, Attorney General Barr had explained to President Trump how DOJ and FBI were investigating fraud claims. Barr also made it a point to emphasize that the Dominion claims were nonsense. The President simply lied. The "crazy stuff," as Barr put it, was all Trump could cite.

Attorney General Barr then decided to speak out. He invited Michael Balsamo, an *Associated Press (AP)* reporter, to lunch on December 1st. Barr told the journalist that "to date, we have not seen fraud on a scale that could have effected a different outcome in the election." [49]

That made the President irate.

Later that evening, Attorney General Barr met with President Trump at the White House. It was their second face-to-face meeting after the November election.[50] At first, President Trump didn't even look at Attorney General Barr.[51] The President "was as mad as I've ever seen him, and he was trying to control himself," Barr said.[52] The President finally "shoved a newspaper" with the *AP* quote in Barr's face.[53]

"Well, this is, you know, killing me. You didn't have to say this. You must've said this because you hate Trump—you hate Trump," Barr remembered him saying.[54] "No, I don't hate you, Mr. President," Barr replied. "You know, I came in at a low time in your administration. I've tried to help your administration. I certainly don't hate you." [55]

President Trump peppered him with unsupported conspiracy theories.[56] Because he had authorized DOJ and FBI to investigate fraud claims, Attorney General Barr was familiar with the conspiracy theories raised by the President. The "big ones" he investigated included claims such as: Dominion voting machines switched votes, votes had been "dumped at the end of the night in Milwaukee and Detroit," non-residents voted in Nevada, the number of ballots counted in Pennsylvania exceeded the number of votes cast, as well as a story about a truck driver supposedly driving thousands of pre-filled ballots from New York to Pennsylvania, among others.[57] Under Attorney General Barr, DOJ would also investigate a false claim that a video feed in Fulton County captured multiple runs of ballots for former Vice President Biden. As explained in detail in Chapter 1 of this report, there was no truth to any of these allegations, but that didn't stop President Trump from repeatedly citing these fictional accounts.

"And I told him that the stuff that his people were shoveling out to the public was bullshit, I mean, that the claims of fraud were bullshit," Barr recalled about the December 1st meeting.[58] "And, you know, he was indignant about that. And I reiterated that they wasted a whole month of these claims on the Dominion voting machines and they were idiotic claims." [59]

President Trump repeated that there had been a "big vote dump" in Detroit.[60] But Attorney General Barr quickly parried this claim.[61] There was nothing suspicious in how the votes flowed into a central location, Barr explained, because that is how votes are always counted in Wayne County.[62] Moreover, Barr pointed out that the President performed *better* in Detroit in 2020 than he had in 2016. "I mean, there's no indication of fraud in Detroit," Barr said.[63] Barr explained that the "thing about the truck driver is complete, you know, nonsense." [64] DOJ and FBI had investigated the matter, including by interviewing the relevant witnesses.[65] There was no truck filled with ballots.

Nothing that Attorney General Barr said during that meeting could satisfy President Trump. So, the President shifted the focus to Barr. He complained that the Attorney General hadn't indicted former FBI Director James Comey and that U.S. Attorney John Durham's investigation into the origins of the FBI's Crossfire Hurricane investigation hadn't made more progress.[66] "Look, I know that you're dissatisfied with me," Barr said, "and I'm glad to offer my resignation." [67] President Trump pounded the table in front of him with his fist and said, "Accepted." [68]

White House lawyers Pat Cipollone and Eric Herschmann tracked Barr down in the parking lot after he left.[69] They convinced Barr to stay in the administration.[70] But his days as Attorney General were numbered. President Trump was not going to stop spreading conspiracy theories. Nor would the President cease in his effort to co-opt DOJ for his own corrupt political purposes.

President Trump released a video on Facebook the very next day.[71] He repeated many of the same lies, including the conspiracy theory about Dominion voting machines switching votes. The President also offered charts, falsely claiming that fraudulent "vote dumps" had swung the election against him.[72] Among the examples he cited was the supposed "vote dump" in Detroit, Michigan.[73] In fact, Barr had already debunked this and other claims.

On December 3, 2020, Rudolph Giuliani appeared before the Georgia Senate Government Oversight Committee to allege that massive cheating had occurred during the election.[74] Giuliani offered a video recorded on election night at the State Farm Arena in Atlanta, Georgia, as a key piece of evidence.[75] Giuliani alleged that the video showed a secret suitcase of ballots being double- and triple-counted after Republican poll watchers had been inappropriately dismissed.[76] The video was selectively edited and showed nothing of the sort. The Georgia Secretary of State's Office investigated and immediately debunked the claim, finding that the secret suitcase was just a secure box and nothing nefarious had occurred.[77] President Trump, Giuliani and others continued to push the lie anyway.

On December 4th, Attorney General Barr asked Byung J. ("BJay") Pak, who was then the U.S. Attorney for the Northern District of Georgia, to independently investigate the State Farm claim. Barr told Pak that this was a "priority," because "he was going to go to the White House for a meeting" and the "issue might come up." Barr asked Pak to "try to substantiate the allegation made by Mr. Giuliani." [78]

Pak watched the video from State Farm Arena and asked the FBI to investigate the matter further. Pak told the Select Committee that FBI agents "interviewed the individuals" shown in the video who were supposedly "double, triple counting" the ballots, and "determined that nothing irregular happened in the counting and the allegations made by Mr. Giuliani were false." [79] And, as noted above, the supposed "suitcase" was a secure storage container used to store ballots. With this evidence in hand, Pak told Attorney General Barr that there was no substance to the allegations.[80]

4.4 DECEMBER 14, 2020: BARR SUBMITS HIS RESIGNATION

Finally, Attorney General Barr had had enough. He submitted his resignation on December 14, 2020.[81] During an interview with the Select Committee, former Attorney General Barr reflected on his face-to-face encounters with President Trump in November and December 2020:

> And, in that context, I made clear I did not agree with the idea of saying the election was stolen and putting out this stuff which I told the President was bullshit. And, you know, I didn't want to be part of it. And that's one of the reasons that went into me deciding to leave when I did.

Former Acting Attorney General Jeffrey Rosen testifies before the Select Committee on June 23, 2022.

(Photo by House Creative Services)

I observed, I think it was on December 1st, that—you know, I believe you can't live in a world where the incumbent administration stays in power based on its view, unsupported by specific evidence, that the election—that there was fraud in the election.[82]

Around mid-day on December 14th, Attorney General Barr met with President Trump and Meadows in the Oval Office to discuss his resignation.[83] When he arrived, and even before Barr could mention his resignation, President Trump began speaking at length about the recently released Allied Security Operations Group (ASOG) report on Dominion voting machines in Antrim County, Michigan.[84] While the Attorney General had been briefed on the allegations in Antrim County and did not find them credible, he promised the President that he would have DOJ investigate them.[85] The Attorney General then told President Trump that he had come for a separate reason and wished to speak to the President privately, so Meadows left.[86]

Barr told President Trump that it was clear the President was dissatisfied with him as Attorney General and that he had decided to resign.[87] President Trump accepted his resignation and asked Barr who would replace him; Attorney General Barr recommended Jeffrey A. Rosen as Acting Attorney General and Richard Donoghue as his deputy.[88] Although President Trump called Donoghue to discuss the possibility of appointing him Acting Attorney General, Donoghue advised that normal procedures be followed and Rosen be named Acting Attorney General.[89] President Trump followed this advice, and upon Barr's departure, Rosen became Acting Attorney General while Donoghue would function as his deputy.

4.5 ACTING ATTORNEY GENERAL JEFFREY ROSEN AND ACTING DEPUTY ATTORNEY GENERAL RICHARD DONOGHUE HOLD THE LINE

Barr felt that he was leaving the Department in the hands of two trusted lieutenants. But President Trump immediately began to pressure Rosen and Donoghue, just as he had Barr.

On December 14, 2020, the day Barr resigned, Molly Michael, Special Assistant to the President and Oval Office Coordinator, sent an email to Acting Attorney General Jeffrey Rosen. The email had two documents attached, both of which were labeled "From POTUS."[90] The first was a set of talking points focused on false allegations of voter fraud in Antrim County, Michigan. The second document was the same ASOG report the President had given Barr.[91]

The next day, President Trump held a meeting in the White House with Acting Attorney General Rosen, Acting Deputy Attorney Donoghue, Cipollone, Meadows, Acting Deputy Secretary of Homeland Security Ken Cuccinelli, and Acting General Counsel of the Department of Homeland Security Chad Mizelle.[92] Barr did not attend, even though he was not scheduled to leave DOJ until the following week. The timing of the meeting was notable, as the previous day the electoral college had met and cast their votes in favor of former Vice President Biden.

During testimony before the Select Committee, Donoghue explained that the December 15th, meeting "was largely focused on" the ASOG report.[93] According to Donoghue, the President "was adamant that the report must be accurate, that it proved that the election was defective, that he in fact won the election, and the [D]epartment should be using that report to basically tell the American people that the results were not trustworthy."[94] President Trump discussed "other theories as well," including erroneous allegations of voter fraud in Georgia and Pennsylvania, but "the bulk of that conversation on December 15th focused on Antrim County, Michigan."[95] President Trump asked why DOJ wasn't "doing more to look at this" and whether the Department was "going to do its job."[96]

Former Acting Deputy Attorney General Richard Donoghue testifies before the Select Committee on June 23, 2022.

(Photo by House Creative Services)

The Department of Justice *was* doing its job. In fact, Attorney General Barr had ordered unprecedented investigations into the many specious claims of voter fraud. The President simply didn't want to hear the truth— that DOJ found that not one of the bogus claims was true. As explained in Chapter 1, the original vote totals in Antrim County were the result of a human error that had since been corrected, not the result of any problem with Dominion machines or software. There was no evidence of fraud.

4.6 PRESIDENT TRUMP IS INTRODUCED TO JEFFREY CLARK

On December 21, 2020, 11 House Republicans met with President Trump at the White House to discuss their plans for objecting to the certification of the electoral college vote on January 6th.[97] After the meeting, Mark Meadows tweeted: "Several members of Congress just finished a meeting in the Oval Office with @realDonaldTrump preparing to fight back against mounting evidence of voter fraud. Stay tuned."[98] Among those in attendance was Congressman Scott Perry, a Republican from Pennsylvania.[99]

By the next day, Representative Perry had introduced a little-known DOJ official named Jeffrey Clark to the President.[100] At the time, Clark was

Former Assistant Attorney General Jeffrey Clark appears on a screen during a Select Committee hearing on June 23, 2022.

(Photo by Mandel Ngan-Pool/Getty Images)

the Acting Head of the Civil Division and Head of the Environmental and Natural Resources Division at the Department of Justice.[101] Clark had no experience in, or responsibilities related to, investigating allegations of election fraud.

President Trump called Acting Attorney General Rosen "virtually every day" between December 23rd and January 3rd.[102] The President usually discussed his "dissatisfaction" with DOJ, claiming the Department was not doing enough to investigate election fraud.[103] On Christmas Eve, Trump brought up Jeffrey Clark's name. Rosen found it "peculiar," telling the Select Committee: "I was quizzical as to how does the President even know Mr. Clark?"[104]

Rosen then spoke directly with Clark on December 26th.[105] Clark revealed that he had met with the President in the Oval Office several days prior.[106] Clark had told the President that if he were to change the leadership at the Department of Justice, "then the Department might be able to do more" to support the President's claims that the election had been stolen from him.[107]

In his discussion with Acting Attorney General Rosen, Clark was "defensive" and "apologetic," claiming that the meeting with President

Trump was "inadvertent and it would not happen again, and that if anyone asked him to go to such a meeting, he would notify Rich Donoghue and me [Rosen]." [108] Of course, Clark had good reasons to be defensive. His meeting with President Trump and Representative Perry on December 22nd was a clear violation of Department policy, which limits interactions between the White House and the Department's staff. As Steven Engel, former Assistant Attorney General for the Office of Legal Counsel, explained to the Select Committee, "it's critical that the Department of Justice conducts its criminal investigations free from either the reality or any appearance of political interference." [109] For that reason, the Department has longstanding polices in place, across administrations, to "keep these communications as infrequent and at the highest levels as possible, just to make sure that people who are less careful about it, who don't really understand these implications, such as Mr. Clark, don't run afoul of the of those contact policies." [110] Rosen added that only the Attorney General or Deputy Attorney General "can have conversations about criminal matters with the White House," or they can "authorize" someone from within DOJ to do so.[111] Clark had no such authorization.

Representative Perry continued to advocate on Clark's behalf. The Congressman texted Meadows on December 26th, writing: "Mark, just checking in as time continues to count down. 11 days to 1/6 and 25 days to inauguration. We gotta get going!" [112] Representative Perry followed up: "Mark, you should call Jeff. I just got off the phone with him and he explained to me why the principal deputy [position] won't work especially with the FBI. They will view it as not having the authority to enforce what needs to be done." [113] Meadows responded: "I got it. I think I understand. Let me work on the deputy position." [114] Representative Perry then sent additional texts: "Roger. Just sent you something on Signal", "Just sent you an updated file", and "Did you call Jeff Clark?" [115]

4.7 DECEMBER 27TH PHONE CALL

On December 27, 2020, President Trump called Acting Attorney General Rosen once again. At some point during the lengthy call, Rosen asked that Acting Deputy Attorney General Donoghue be conferenced in.[116] According to Donoghue's contemporaneous notes, Trump referenced three Republican politicians, all of whom had supported the President's election lies and the "Stop the Steal" campaign.[117] One was Representative Scott Perry. Another was Doug Mastriano, a State senator from Pennsylvania who would later be on the grounds of the U.S. Capitol during the January 6th attack.[118] President Trump also referenced Representative Jim Jordan from Ohio, praising him as a "fighter."[119] Representatives Perry and Jordan had often teamed up to spread lies about the election. The two spoke at a "Stop the Steal" rally in front of the Pennsylvania State capitol in Harrisburg, just days after the November election.[120] The pair also pressed their conspiratorial case during interviews with friendly media outlets.[121]

President Trump made a "stream of allegations" during the December 27th call.[122] As reflected in his notes, Donoghue considered the call to be an "escalation of the earlier conversations," with the President becoming more adamant that "we weren't doing our job."[123] President Trump trafficked in "conspiracy theories" he had heard from others, and Donoghue sought to "make it clear to the President these allegations were simply not true."[124] Donoghue sought to "correct" President Trump "in a serial fashion as he moved from one theory to another."[125]

The President returned to the discredited ASOG report, which former Attorney General Barr had already dismissed as complete nonsense. ASOG had claimed—based on no evidence—that the Dominion voting machines in Antrim County, Michigan had suffered from a 68 percent error rate. As noted above and in Chapter 1, that was not close to being true.

Bipartisan election officials in Antrim County completed a hand recount of all machine-processed ballots on December 17, 2020, which should have ended the lies about Dominion's voting machines.[126] The net difference between the machine count and the hand recount was only 12 out of 15,718 total votes.[127] The machines counted just one vote more for former Vice President Biden than was tallied during the hand recount.[128] Donoghue informed the President that he "cannot and should not be relying on" ASOG's claim, because it was "simply not true."[129] This did not stop the President from later repeating the debunked allegation multiple times, including during his January 6th speech at the Ellipse.[130]

Acting Deputy Attorney General Donoghue debunked a "series" of other conspiracy theories offered by President Trump during the December 27th call as well. One story involved a truck driver "who claimed to have moved an entire tractor trailer of ballots from New York to Pennsylvania."[131] There was no truth to the story. The FBI "interviewed witnesses at the front end and the back end of" the truck's transit route, "looked at loading manifests," questioned the truck driver, and concluded that there were no ballots in the truck.[132]

President Trump then returned to the conspiracy theory about voting in Detroit. Former Attorney General Barr had already debunked the claim that a massive number of illegal votes had been dumped during the middle of the night, but the President would not let it go. President Trump alleged that someone "threw the poll watchers out," and "you don't even need to look at the illegal aliens voting—don't need to. It's so obvious." [133] The President complained that the "FBI will always say there's nothing there," because while the Special Agents ("the line guys") supported him, the Bureau's leadership supposedly did not. [134] This was inconsistent with Donoghue's view. [135] But President Trump complained that he had "made some bad decisions on leadership" at the FBI. [136]

President Trump also "wanted to talk a great deal about Georgia, [and] the State Farm Arena video," claiming it was "fraud staring you right in the face." [137] President Trump smeared Ruby Freeman, a Georgia election worker who was merely doing her job, as a "Huckster" and an "Election scammer." [138] President Trump said the "networks," meaning the television networks, had "magnified the tape and saw them running them [ballots] through repeatedly." [139] The President repeated the lie that Democrats had "[c]losed the facility and then came back with hidden ballots under the table." [140] He suggested that both Rosen and Donoghue "go to Fulton County and do a signature verification." They would "see how illegal it is" and "find tens of thousands" of illegal ballots. [141]

President Trump "kept fixating" on the supposed suitcase in the video. [142] But Acting Deputy Attorney General Donoghue debunked the President's obsession. "There is no suitcase," Donoghue made clear. [143] Donoghue explained that the DOJ had looked at the video and interviewed multiple witnesses. The "suitcase" was an official lock box filled with genuine votes. [144] And election workers simply did not scan ballots for former Vice President Biden multiple times. [145] All of this was recorded by security cameras. [146]

In response to what President Trump was saying during the conversation, Rosen and Donoghue tried to make clear that the claims the President made weren't supported by the evidence. "You guys must not be following the internet the way I do," the President remarked. [147] But President Trump was not finished peddling wild conspiracy theories.

The President pushed the claim that Pennsylvania had reported 205,000 more votes than there were voters in the state. [148] "We'll look at whether we have more ballots in Pennsylvania than registered voters," Acting Attorney General Rosen replied, according to Donoghue. They "[s]hould be able to check that out quickly." [149] But Rosen wanted President Trump to "understand that the DOJ can't and won't snap its fingers and change the outcome of the election. It doesn't work that way." [150]

"I don't expect you to do that," President Trump responded. "Just say the election was corrupt and leave the rest to me and the Republican Congressmen." [151]

Donoghue explained this "is an exact quote from the President." [152]

"We have an obligation to tell people that this was an illegal, corrupt election," President Trump told the DOJ team at another point in the call.[153] President Trump insisted this was DOJ's "obligation," even though Rosen and Donoghue kept telling him there was no evidence of fraud sufficient to overturn the outcome of the election. "We are doing our job," Donoghue informed the President. "Much of the info you're getting is false."[154]

The call on December 27th was contentious for additional reasons. President Trump did not want to accept that the Department of Justice was not an arm of his election campaign. He wanted to know why the Department did not assist in his campaign's civil suits against States. There was a simple answer: There was no evidence to support the campaign's claims of fraud.[155]

Donoghue and Rosen also "tried to explain to the President on this occasion and on several other occasions that the Justice Department has a very important, very specific, but very limited role in these elections."[156] The States "run their elections" and DOJ is not "quality control for the States."[157] DOJ has "a mission that relates to criminal conduct in relation to federal elections" and also has "related civil rights responsibilities."[158] But DOJ cannot simply intervene to alter the outcome of an election or support a civil suit.[159]

When President Trump made these demands on December 27th, it was already crystal clear that the Department of Justice had found no evidence of systemic fraud.[160] The Department simply had no reason to assert that the 2020 Presidential contest was "an illegal corrupt election."[161]

"People tell me Jeff Clark is great" and that "I should put him in," President Trump said on the call. "People want me to replace the DOJ leadership."[162] Donoghue responded "[S]ir, that's fine, you should have the leadership you want, but understand, changing the leadership in the Department won't change anything."[163]

The President did not really care what facts had been uncovered by the Department of Justice. President Trump just wanted the Department to say the election was corrupt, so he and the Republican Congressmen could exploit the statement in the days to come, including on January 6th. And when Rosen and Donoghue resisted the President's entreaties, he openly mused about replacing Rosen with someone who would do the President's bidding.

4.8 CONGRESSMAN SCOTT PERRY CALLS DONOGHUE

Toward the end of the December 27th call, President Trump asked Donoghue for his cell number.[164] Later that day, Representative Perry called

Representative Scott Perry, November 14, 2022.
(Photo by Anna Moneymaker/Getty Images)

Donoghue to press the President's case.[165] Representative Perry was one of President Trump's key congressional allies in the effort to overturn the election's results. Representative Perry was an early supporter of the "Stop the Steal" campaign and, as noted above, addressed the crowd at one such event outside the Pennsylvania State capitol in Harrisburg on November 5, 2020.[166] Representative Perry was also one of 27 Republican Congressmen who signed a letter requesting that President Trump "direct Attorney General Barr to appoint a Special Counsel to investigate irregularities in the 2020 election." The letter was dated December 9, 2020—more than 1 week after Barr told the press there was no evidence of significant fraud.[167] There was no reason to think that a Special Counsel was warranted. Representative Perry and the other congressmen advocated for one to be appointed anyway.

Representative Perry attended the December 21st Oval Office meeting along with at least 10 other congressional Republicans to discuss the strategy for objecting to the electoral college votes on January 6th. Along with 125 other Republican Members of Congress. Representative Perry also supported Texas's lawsuit against Pennsylvania and three other states.[168] That is, Representative Perry supported Texas's effort to nullify the certified electoral college vote from four states, including his own home state.

Donoghue took notes during his conversation with Representative Perry and provided those notes to the Select Committee.[169] The notes reflect that when Representative Perry called Donoghue on December 27th, Representative Perry explained that President Trump asked him to call and that he, Representative Perry, did not think DOJ had been doing its job on the election.[170] Representative Perry brought up other, unrelated matters and argued that the "FBI doesn't always do the right thing in all instances."[171] Representative Perry also brought up Jeff Clark. He said he liked him and thought that Clark "would do something about this," meaning the election fraud allegations.[172]

On the evening of December 27th, Representative Perry emailed Donoghue a set of documents alleging significant voting fraud had occurred in Pennsylvania.[173] One document asserted that election authorities had counted 205,000 more votes than had been cast.[174] Representative Perry also shared this same claim on Twitter the following day.[175] President Trump kept raising the same claim. Sometimes there was an alleged discrepancy of 205,000 votes, other times it was supposedly 250,000 votes.[176] Either way, it was not true.

Acting Deputy Attorney General Donoghue forwarded Representative Perry's email to Scott Brady, who was the U.S. Attorney for the Western District of Pennsylvania at the time.[177] As Brady soon discovered, there was no discrepancy.[178] President Trump's supporters came up with the claim by comparing the Pennsylvania Secretary of State's website, which reported the total number of votes as 5.25 million, to a separate State election registry, which showed only 5 million votes cast.[179] The problem was simple: Pennsylvania's election site had not been updated.[180] The totals for four counties had not yet been reported on the election site. Once those votes were counted on the site, the totals matched. This was simply not an example of fraud, as President Trump, Representative Perry and others would have it.

4.9 DECEMBER 28, 2020: THE CLARK LETTER

On December 28, 2020, Clark sent a 5-page draft letter to Donoghue and Rosen.[181] The letter was addressed to three Georgia State officials: Governor Brian Kemp, Speaker of the House David Ralston, and President *Pro Tempore* of the Senate Butch Miller. It contained places for Rosen and Donoghue to affix their signatures, which they steadfastly refused to do.[182] The letter, if signed and sent, may very well have provoked a constitutional crisis.[183]

The letter was attached to an email from Clark, in which he requested authorization to attend a classified briefing by the Office of the Director of

National Intelligence (ODNI) "led by DNI Ratcliffe on foreign election inter-ference issues."[184] ODNI did not find any foreign interference in the voting process or counting,[185] but Clark apparently believed some of the con-spiracy theories that had been floated. Specifically, Clark claimed that "hackers have evidence (in the public domain) that a Dominion machine accessed the internet through a smart thermostat with a net connection trail leading back to China." Clark added: "ODNI may have additional clas-sified evidence."[186] This crackpot claim had been shared by other Trump officials and associates as well.[187] Ultimately, after Clark received the ODNI briefing, "he acknowledged [to Donoghue] that there was nothing in that briefing that would have supported his earlier suspicion about foreign involvement."[188]

Clark intended to send the letter to officials in Georgia and several other contested States that President Trump needed to flip if he was going to overturn the election results. "The Department of Justice is investigating various irregularities in the 2020 election for President of the United States," Clark wrote.[189] Clark continued: "The Department will update you as we are able on investigatory progress, but at this time we have identified significant concerns that may have impacted the outcome of the election in multiple States, including the State of Georgia."[190]

Clark continued by arguing that Georgia's State legislature should call a special session. "In light of these developments, the Department recom-mends that the Georgia General Assembly should convene in special session so that its legislators are in a special position to take additional testimony, receive new evidence, and deliberate on the matter consistent with its duties under the U.S. Constitution," Clark wrote.[191] Clark referenced the fake electors that the President and his campaign organized and argued that there were two competing slates of electors, both of which were legiti-mate.[192] "The Department believes that in Georgia and several other States, both a slate of electors supporting Joseph R. Biden, Jr., and a separate slate of electors supporting Donald J. Trump, gathered on [December 14, 2020] at the proper location to cast their ballots, and that both sets of those ballots have been transmitted to Washington, D.C., to be opened by Vice President Pence," Clark wrote.[193]

The letter was a lie. Senior DOJ officials—Barr, Rosen and Donoghue—had repeatedly stated the opposite. They found no evidence of fraud that would have impacted the election's results—none. But since mid-November, the Trump Campaign's legal team under Giuliani attempted to execute its dual-track strategy of both filing lawsuits and convincing state legislatures in contested states to appoint separate slates of Presidential electors for President Trump.[194] By late December, however, the dual-track approach had largely failed, and no legislatures had sent a second lawful slate of electors for Trump to Congress. Clearly, President Trump and his campaign team could not get the job done. So, the President and those around him sought to use the hefty imprimatur of the U.S. Department of Justice to achieve the same thing. No doubt, a letter coming from the Department of Justice is different from a meandering call from Giuliani or one of his associates. And, because it was December 28th and there was little more than a week until the January 6th joint session of Congress, President Trump needed more, and soon. Clark's letter, which laid out a plan that was almost identical to what President Trump and his team had pressured State officials to carry out virtually since election day, could have been just what President Trump needed.

Several examples demonstrate the parallels between President Trump's and Rudolph Giuliani's approach to overturning the election in November and December, and what Clark proposed in this letter. First, the letter sought to have the Georgia State legislature convene a special session to focus on allegations of fraud in the election.[195] Giuliani and his team had been making calls to State legislatures and telling them in both official and unofficial State legislature committee hearings that State legislatures should convene in special sessions.[196] They also argued that State legislatures had the authority to convene a special session themselves, despite limitations in State law requiring such a session to be convened by the governor.[197] Clark included the same argument in his draft letter.[198]

Additionally, the draft letter recommended that the Georgia legislature consider choosing the alternate—fake—slate of electoral college electors that sent fake electoral college votes to Congress and Vice President Pence.[199] Having State legislatures choose Trump electors in States where President Trump lost was one of the Trump team's early goals immediately after the election, but it didn't work.[200] When no State legislature appointed its own set of electors before December 14th, the Trump Campaign arranged for electors to meet in contested States anyway and cast fake electoral college votes.[201] This letter, with the Department of Justice seal at the top, was just one more way that President Trump and those close to him could pressure State officials to send competing electoral college votes to Congress for consideration during the joint session, despite former Vice President Biden's certified victory in each of the contested States.

Despite the similarities between the requests in Clark's proposed letter and the requests that President Trump and his team made to State officials for nearly 2 months, the extent to which Clark directly coordinated his actions with the Trump Campaign and its outside advisors is unclear. Clark asserted his Fifth Amendment rights and various other privileges to avoid

answering the Select Committee's questions about these and other topics.[202] When Giuliani was asked during his Select Committee deposition
whether he remembered discussing DOJ issuing a letter like Clark's, Giuliani refused to answer because it implicated attorney-client privilege with
President Trump, but when asked if he recalled ever recommending that
Clark be given election-related responsibilities at DOJ, Giuliani said, "I do
recall saying to people that somebody should be put in charge of the Justice
Department who isn't frightened of what's going to be done to their reputation, because the Justice Department was filled with people like that."[203]
And the investigation has also revealed that Clark and John Eastman were
in communication throughout this period.[204]

One person who had worked with Eastman and others in his circle was a
lawyer installed to work with Clark at the Department of Justice in mid-
December—the final weeks of the Trump administration—named Ken Klukowski.[205] Klukowski was a Trump administration political appointee
serving as a senior counsel under Clark in DOJ's Civil Division.[206] After
serving as a lawyer in the Office and Management and Budget (OMB) for
more than a year and volunteering as a lawyer for the Trump Campaign
after election day, Klukowski only joined the Department when the administration's personnel staff "expedite[d]" his appointment because the
White House's Presidential Personnel Office "want[ed] him in soon."[207]

On the morning of December 28th, Clark asked Klukowski to draft the
Georgia letter for him.[208] Clark dictated the substantive key points of the
letter to Klukowski and told him exactly what to include.[209] After several
meetings with Clark throughout the day to update him on progress, Klukowski turned in his assignment and gave the letter to Clark, which Clark
sent along to Acting Attorney General Rosen and Acting Deputy Attorney
General Donoghue, as described above.[210]

Donoghue quickly responded to Clark's email, stating "there is no
chance that I would sign this letter or anything remotely like this."[211] The
plan set forth by Clark was "not even within the realm of possibility."[212]
Donoghue warned that if they sent Clark's letter, it "would be a grave step
for the Department to take and it could have tremendous Constitutional,
political and social ramifications for the country."[213] Contrary to President
Trump's and Clark's wild claims about the election, Donoghue stressed that
DOJ's ongoing investigations related to matters of such a "small scale that
they simply would not impact the outcome of the Presidential Election."[214]
Clark's assertion to the contrary was baseless.

Donoghue and Rosen reaffirmed their strong opposition to the draft
letter in a "contentious" meeting with Clark on December 28th.[215] "What
you are doing is nothing less than the United States Justice Department

meddling in the outcome of a presidential election," Donoghue admonished Clark, to which Clark indignantly responded, "I think a lot of people have meddled in this election." [216]

Under questioning by Rosen and Donoghue, Clark eventually also revealed that he had been in a meeting in the Oval Office with President Trump. Donoghue demanded to know, "Why the hell are we hearing your name from the President of the United States and a Congressman?" [217] When Clark was reminded that meeting the President without authorization or informing his superiors was a clear violation of the White House contacts policy, he retorted, "It's a policy, there's a lot more at stake here than a policy." [218] In fact, the contacts policy was designed for situations just like this where political figures might try to influence criminal investigations or legal actions taken by the Department of Justice, as President Trump attempting to do. [219]

In the days that followed, Clark called witnesses, got a briefing from ODNI and pursued his own investigations. Acting Deputy Attorney General Donoghue was "shocked" to learn that Clark did not cease his efforts even after learning there was "no foreign interference." [220] Instead of adhering to the facts, Clark "doubled down." During a follow-up meeting on January 2nd, Clark acknowledged he had received the ODNI briefing, and he acknowledged that there was nothing in the briefing that would have supported his earlier suspicion about foreign involvement, but he nevertheless "spewed out some of these theories, some of which we'd heard from the President, but others which were floating around the internet and media, and just kept insisting that the Department needed to act and needed to send those letters." [221]

4.10 DECEMBER 29TH MEETING

The next day, Rosen, Donoghue, and Engel had a meeting with Mark Meadows, Pat Cipollone, and Cipollone's deputy, Pat Philbin, in the White House Chief of Staff's office. [222] While the meeting dealt primarily with the Presidential transition, the group discussed a draft civil complaint modeled after *Texas v. Pennsylvania* that the President wanted the Department of Justice to file challenging the results of the Presidential election, tentatively called *United States v. Pennsylvania*. [223] The DOJ officials said that they had not had time to thoroughly review the proposed suit, but initially indicated that it appeared to be flawed and did not seem "viable" for DOJ to file. [224] Meadows suggested that the DOJ leadership meet with William Olson and Kurt Olsen,

the two attorneys affiliated with the Trump Campaign that had been working on the proposed suit, and added that Eastman and a retired judge from
North Carolina named Mark Martin both had views about the lawsuit.[225]

In this meeting, Meadows also raised a new and outrageous allegation
of election fraud: that an Italian company had been involved in changing
votes in the Presidential election.[226] According to Meadows, there was a
man, whom Donoghue later learned was in an Italian prison, who claimed
to have information supporting the allegation and that CIA officers stationed in Rome were either aware of the plot to interfere in the election or
had participated in it.[227] Donoghue described how it was apparent that
Meadows was not clear on the specifics of the allegation but passed them
along to DOJ to investigate, nonetheless.[228] Following the meeting Donoghue provided the information to the FBI, which quickly determined that
the allegations were not credible.[229] Meadows and other senior officials in
the Trump administration, however, pressed DOJ to investigate every allegation of fraud regardless of how absurd or specious.

In the days after the December 29th meeting with Meadows, the senior
DOJ officials more closely examined the proposed *United States v. Pennsylvania* lawsuit and determined that DOJ could not file it.[230] Engel was principally tasked with examining the veracity of the suit and summarized his
analysis in a series of talking points that he provided to Donoghue on
December 31st.[231] Engel concluded that for multiple reasons, the proposed
lawsuit lacked merit. First, the U.S. Government did not have standing to
challenge how a State administered its election.[232] Such a challenge could
only be brought by President Trump as a candidate and his campaign, or,
possibly, an aggrieved electoral college elector.[233] Second, there was no
identified precedent in the history of the Supreme Court establishing that
such a lawsuit could be filed by the U.S. Government.[234] Third, by late
December, States had already certified the results of their elections and the
electoral college had met, so suing States by this point would not impact
the results of the election.[235] Finally, unlike *Texas v. Pennsylvania*, which
was one State suing another State, this lawsuit would not automatically be
heard by the Supreme Court, so it should have been filed in a Federal district court months prior—if at all—to have any possibility of impacting the
outcome of the election.[236]

When asked about it during his interview with the Select Committee,
Engel described *United States v. Pennsylvania* as "a meritless lawsuit" and
said, "there was never a question" about whether "the Department was
going to file" it.[237] As senior DOJ officials had already explained to President Trump multiple times in November and December 2020, the Department of Justice was strictly limited in what election-related actions it could

Steven Engel testifies before the Select Committee on June 23, 2022.
(Photo by House Creative Services)

take. It could not oversee States' actions in administering their elections, and it could not support litigation filed by President Trump's campaign.[238] Nonetheless, President Trump continued to push DOJ to file this lawsuit over the following days and essentially act as an arm of his political campaign.

4.11 ROSEN'S DECEMBER 30TH CALL WITH PRESIDENT TRUMP

Even after the December 29th meeting, President Trump and those working on his behalf still wanted DOJ leadership to file *United States* v. *Pennsylvania*. On December 30th, Acting Attorney General Rosen had a phone call with President Trump that included a discussion about the lawsuit.[239] During the call, Rosen clearly explained to the President that DOJ could not file the lawsuit.[240] Rosen said, "This doesn't work. There's multiple problems with it. And the Department of Justice is not going to be able to do it." [241] According to Rosen, President Trump accepted what he said without argument.[242] Yet President Trump and his allies continued pressuring the Department to file the lawsuit.

4.12 DECEMBER 31ST MEETING

On December 31st, 2020, President Trump suddenly returned to Washington, DC, from Florida, where he had been celebrating Christmas. Shortly after Air Force One landed, Rosen and Donoghue were summoned to the Oval Office once again. They met with the President that afternoon. President Trump "was a little more agitated than he had been in the meeting on the 15th," according to Donoghue.[243] The President remained "adamant that the election has been stolen, that he won, that the American people were being harmed by fraud, and that he believed the Justice Department should be doing something about it."[244]

The President once again raised the prospect of naming Clark the Acting Attorney General.[245] Donoghue and Rosen repeated what they had told the President previously—that he "should have the leaders that" he wanted, "but it's really not going to change anything."[246]

President Trump again asked why DOJ would not file a complaint with the Supreme Court, alleging that the election was fraudulent. Rosen and Donoghue explained, once more, that the DOJ did not have standing.[247] DOJ represents the Federal government, not the American people. President Trump was incredulous and became "very animated."[248] The President kept repeating the same questions, "How is that possible? How can that possibly be?"[249]

President Trump also floated the prospect of naming a special counsel, suggesting Ken Cuccinelli from the Department of Homeland Security as a possible candidate.[250] "This sounds like the kind of thing that would warrant appointment of a special counsel," Donoghue recalled the President saying.[251] The President did not order the DOJ to name a special counsel, but he was clearly still thinking about it. Donoghue and Rosen "didn't say a lot" in response, but simply pointed out that there was no evidence to support the many individual allegations that had been made, so there was "no evidence that would warrant appointing a special counsel."[252]

President Trump again raised the Antrim County, Michigan allegations.[253] As mentioned above, bipartisan election officials in Antrim County completed a hand recount of all ballots on December 17th.[254] This should have resolved the matter once and for all. There was simply no evidence that Dominion's machines had manipulated the result. But President Trump would not accept this reality.

During the December 31st meeting, the President also raised the prospect of seizing the voting machines. "Why don't you guys seize machines?" he asked.[255] "You guys should seize machines because there will be evidence," Donoghue recalled President Trump saying.[256] Rosen pushed back, saying the DOJ had no basis to seize voting machines from the States. They needed a search warrant, but there was no evidence to justify one.[257] Rosen explained to President Trump again that the DOJ has no responsibility for oversight, as the States conduct the elections. Rosen added that to the extent that any Federal agency is involved, it is the Department of Homeland Security, which ensures "software selection and quality control."[258] At that point, the President called Ken Cuccinelli.[259] Donoghue recalled the President saying something along the lines of, "Ken, the Acting Attorney General is telling me it's your job to seize machines."[260] Rosen had said nothing of the sort, but Cuccinelli quickly shot down the President's line of inquiry, making it clear that the Department of Homeland Security had no such authority.[261] White House Counsel Pat Cipollone was also in attendance and supported the DOJ leadership throughout the meeting.[262]

When Rosen spoke to Clark by phone on December 31st or January 1st, Clark revealed that he had spoken to the President again, despite previously promising Rosen and Donoghue that he would inform them of any other contact that he received from the White House.[263] Clark told Rosen that President Trump had offered Clark the position of Acting Attorney General and asked him to respond by Monday, January 4th. Clark, however, said that he needed to do some "due diligence" related to claims of election fraud before deciding whether he would accept the President's offer.[264]

4.13 JANUARY 2, 2021: ROSEN AND DONOGHUE CONFRONT CLARK AGAIN

On Saturday, January 2nd, Rosen and Donoghue attempted, once again, to persuade Clark to stand down. The two reiterated that Clark should stop meeting with the President.[265] Donoghue reprimanded Clark, emphasizing that he was the boss and that Clark's ongoing contacts with the President were a violation of DOJ's White House contact policy.[266] Clark acknowledged that he had been briefed by the ODNI, as he had requested, and "that there was nothing in that briefing that would have supported his earlier suspicion about foreign involvement."[267] Nevertheless, Clark still wanted to send his letter to Georgia and other contested States alleging voter fraud.[268]

During the conversation, Clark confirmed President Trump had offered him the position of Acting Attorney General.[269] Clark told Rosen that he would decline the offer—if Rosen and Donoghue signed his dishonest letter to officials in Georgia.[270] The two refused once again, making it clear "that there was no way we were going to sign that letter."[271] Rosen reiterated his decision in an email on the night of January 2nd, writing: "I confirmed again today that I am not prepared to sign such a letter."[272]

That same day, President Trump attempted to coerce Georgia Secretary of State Brad Raffensperger into manufacturing enough votes to steal the election in that State. That call is discussed in Chapter 2 of this report. But one part of it deserves mention here. During that same call, President Trump brought up BJay Pak, whom President Trump had appointed as the U.S. Attorney for the Northern District of Georgia. President Trump referred to Pak as "your never-Trumper U.S. attorney there." [273] The implication was that Pak was not doing enough to validate President Trump's fictitious claims of voter fraud. President Trump's mention of Pak proved to be ominous.

4.14 JANUARY 3, 2021: CLARK INFORMS DOJ LEADERSHIP THAT HE WILL ACCEPT PRESIDENT TRUMP'S OFFER

On January 3rd, Clark informed Rosen that he had decided to accept the President's offer to serve as the Acting Attorney General. Clark offered Rosen the position of his deputy.[274] Rosen thought that Clark's offer was "preposterous" and "nonsensical." [275] Rosen told the Select Committee that "there was no universe where I was going to do that to stay on and support someone else doing things that were not consistent with what I thought should be done." [276] Donoghue believed it was a done deal, and Clark would become the head of DOJ. But Pat Cipollone told Rosen that it was "not a done deal and that we should fight this out at the White House." [277]

White House call logs from January 3rd show that President Trump and Clark spoke four times that day starting at 6:59 a.m.[278] The first three calls of the day, two in the morning and one in the early afternoon, show that the President spoke with "Mr. Jeffrey Clark." [279] The final call between the two of them, from 4:19 to 4:22 p.m., however, shows that President Trump spoke to "Acting Attorney General Jeffrey Clark," suggesting that Clark had, in fact, accepted the President's offer.[280]

Acting Attorney General Rosen told the Select Committee that he would have felt comfortable being replaced by either Donoghue or Engel, but he did not "want for the Department of Justice to be put in a posture where it would be doing things that were not consistent with the truth, were not consistent with its own appropriate role, or were not consistent with the Constitution." [281]

As a result, Rosen took four immediate steps to try and prevent Clark's ascension to Attorney General. First, he called Meadows and asked him to set up a meeting for that evening with President Trump.[282] Second, he

Select Committee graphic

spoke to Cipollone, who told Rosen that Clark's appointment was not inevitable and that he would also be at the meeting that evening to support Rosen and Donoghue.[283] Third, Rosen called Engel and asked him to come to DOJ headquarters so he could attend the White House meeting.[284] Finally, Rosen asked Donoghue and another senior Department attorney named Patrick Hovakimian to convene a meeting of the rest of the Department's leadership to describe the situation to them and hear how they would react to Clark's appointment.[285]

Hovakimian set up a conference call. Although some of the Assistant Attorneys General were not able to participate in the call, all of those who did agreed that they would resign if Rosen were removed from office.[286] Pat Hovakimian drafted a resignation letter that read:

> This evening, after Acting Attorney General Jeff Rosen over the course of the last week repeatedly refused the President's direct instructions to utilize the Department of Justice's law enforcement powers for improper ends, the President removed Jeff from the Department. PADAG Rich Donoghue and I resign from the Department, effectively immediately.[287]

Hovakimian never sent the letter because the threat of mass resignations dissuaded President Trump from replacing Rosen. Regardless, the letter stated a plain truth: President Trump was trying to use DOJ for his own "improper ends."

THE JANUARY 3, 2021, OVAL OFFICE MEETING

At Rosen's request, White House Chief of Staff Mark Meadows arranged a meeting with the President at 6:15 p.m. that evening.[288]

We should pause to reflect on the timing and purpose of the meeting. Congress was set to meet in a joint session in less than 72 hours. The States had already certified their electors. Former Vice President Biden was going to be certified as the winner of the 2020 Presidential election. There was no material dispute over Biden's victory. Trump and his lawyers had not produced any evidence of significant fraud. Instead, they presented one nonsensical conspiracy theory after another. The DOJ and FBI were forced to debunk these claims—and they did.

None of this stopped President Trump's effort to subvert DOJ. Quite the opposite. The President pushed forward with a plan to install Jeff Clark as the Acting Attorney General, apparently to attempt to interfere with the certification of the electoral college vote on January 6th. It is for this reason Rosen requested an emergency meeting on January 3rd.

Before heading into the Oval Office, Rosen and Donoghue discussed the possible leadership change with Cipollone and Pat Philbin. "They were completely opposed to it," Donoghue explained.[289] In fact, no one who attended the Oval Office meeting supported the leadership change—other than Jeff Clark.[290] Donoghue didn't initially join the meeting, but the President soon called him in.[291]

During the meeting, Clark attempted to defend the last-minute move to make him Acting Attorney General. Clark said he would "conduct real investigations that would, in his view, uncover widespread fraud."[292] Clark declared that this was the "last opportunity to sort of set things straight with this defective election," and he had the "intelligence," the "will," and "desire" to "pursue these matters in the way that the President thought most appropriate."[293] Everyone else quickly disagreed.[294]

President Trump asked Donoghue and Engel what they would do, and both confirmed they would resign.[295] Donoghue added that theirs would not be the only resignations. "You should understand that your entire Department leadership will resign," Donoghue recalled saying.[296] This included every Assistant Attorney General. "Mr. President, these aren't bureaucratic leftovers from another administration," Donoghue continued.[297] "You picked them. This is your leadership team. You sent every one of them to the Senate; you got them confirmed."[298] Donoghue argued that the President would look bad in the wake of the mass resignations. "What is that going to say about you, when we all walk out at the same time?"[299] Donoghue recalled asking the President. "And what happens if, within 48 hours, we have hundreds of resignations from your Justice Department because of your actions? What does that say about your leadership?"[300] Steve Engel reinforced Donoghue's point, saying that Clark would be leading a "grave-yard."[301]

White House Counsel Pat Cipollone threatened to resign as well, describing Clark's letter as a "murder-suicide pact."[302] Cipollone warned that the letter would "damage everyone who touches it" and no one should have anything to do with it.[303]

Some of the participants in the meeting argued that Clark was the wrong person for the job of Attorney General. Clark attempted to defend his credentials, arguing that he had been involved in complicated civil and environmental litigation.[304] "That's right. You're an environmental law-yer," Donoghue fired back.[305] "How about you go back to your office, and we'll call you when there's an oil spill."[306]

The meeting lasted approximately 3 hours.[307] Only toward the end of the contentious affair did President Trump decide to reverse his earlier decision to make Clark the Acting Assistant Attorney General. Donoghue recalled President Trump addressing Clark along the following lines:

> I appreciate your willingness to do it. I appreciate you being willing to suffer the abuse. But the reality is, you're not going to get any-thing done. These guys are going to quit. Everyone else is going to resign. It's going to be a disaster. The bureaucracy will eat you alive. And no matter how you want to get things done in the next few weeks, you won't be able to get it done, and it's not going to be worth the breakage.[308]

Clark tried to change President Trump's mind, saying "history is call-ing, this our opportunity" and "we can get this done."[309] But the President was clearly rattled by the threat of mass defections and reiterated that the change would not happen. President Trump then wondered what would happen to Clark, and if Donoghue was going to fire him. Donoghue explained that only the President had that authority. That was the end of the matter. "And we all got up and walked out of the Oval Office," Dono-ghue recalled.[310]

But for one DOJ employee, the matter was not entirely settled. During the January 3rd meeting in the Oval Office, President Trump complained bitterly about BJay Pak, the U.S. Attorney for the Northern District of Geor-gia.[311] Barr had tasked Pak with investigating the State Farm Arena video in early December 2020. Like the FBI and Georgia State officials, Pak con-cluded that nothing nefarious had occurred. President Trump was dissatis-fied.[312]

"No wonder nothing's been found in Atlanta, because the U.S. attorney there is a Never Trumper," Donoghue recalled the President saying.[313]

Donoghue objected, saying Pak had "been doing his job." [314] But the President insisted, pointing out that Pak criticized him years earlier. "This guy is a Never Trumper," the President reiterated. [315] "He should never have been in my administration to begin with. How did this guy end up in my administration?" [316] The President threatened to fire Pak. [317] When Donoghue pointed out that Pak was already planning to resign the next day, a Monday, President Trump insisted that it be Pak's last day on the job. [318] Pak later confirmed to Donoghue that he would be leaving the next day. [319]

President Trump asked if those in attendance at the Oval Office meeting knew Bobby Christine, who was the U.S. Attorney for the Southern District of Georgia. [320] Even though Pak had a first assistant, who was next in line for Pak's job upon his resignation, President Trump wanted Christine to take the role. [321] Christine did take over for Pak, but he did not find any evidence of fraud either. It was Donoghue's impression that Christine "concluded that the election matters…were handled appropriately." [322]

Later in the evening of January 3rd, President Trump called Donoghue to pass along yet another conspiracy theory. [323] The President had heard that an ICE agent outside of Atlanta was in custody of a truck filled with shredded ballots. [324] Donoghue explained that ICE agents are part of the Department of Homeland Security, so the matter would be under that Department's purview. President Trump asked Donoghue to inform Ken Cuccinelli. [325] That story—like all the others—turned out to be fiction when DOJ investigators evaluated the claim. The truck *was* carrying shredded ballots, but they were from a *previous* election. The old ballots had been shredded to make room for storing ballots from the 2020 election. [326]

4.15 PRESIDENT TRUMP'S UNPRECEDENTED ATTEMPT TO SUBVERT THE DOJ

The most senior DOJ officials at the end of President Trump's term stopped him from co-opting America's leading law enforcement agency for his own corrupt purposes. Recall that Attorney General Barr commented "you can't live in a world where the incumbent administration stays in power based on its view, unsupported by specific evidence, that the election—that there was fraud in the election. [327]

Richard Donoghue concluded that Jeffrey Clark's letter "may very well have spiraled us into a constitutional crisis." [328]

Jeffrey Rosen summed up his short time as the Acting Attorney General like this:

[D]uring my tenure, we appointed no special prosecutors, we sent no letters to States or State legislators disputing the election outcome; we made no public statements saying the election was corrupt and should be overturned; we initiated no Supreme Court actions, nor filed or joined any other lawsuits calling into question the legitimacy of our election and institutions.[329]

President Trump attempted to get DOJ to do each of those things.

ENDNOTES

1. Select Committee to Investigate the January 6th Attack on the United States Capitol, Transcribed Interview of William Barr, (June 2, 2022), p. 8. The Select Committee recognizes and appreciates the investigation conducted by the Senate Committee on the Judiciary and the report it issued about this Chapter's topic. *See* Senate Committee on the Judiciary, 117th Cong. 1st sess., *Subverting Justice: How the Former President and His Allies Pressured DOJ to Overturn the 2020 Election*, (Oct. 7, 2021), available at https://www.judiciary.senate.gov/imo/media/doc/Interim%20Staff%20Report%20FINAL.pdf.

2. Select Committee to Investigate the January 6th Attack on the United States Capitol, Transcribed Interview of William Barr, (June 2, 2022), p. 8; *See* Margaret Talev, "Exclusive: Dem Group Warns of Apparent Trump Election Day Landslide," *Axios*, (Sept. 1, 2020), available at https://www.axios.com/2020/09/01/bloomberg-group-trump-election-night-scenarios.

3. *See* Chapter 1.

4. *See* Chapter 1.

5. Select Committee to Investigate the January 6th Attack on the United States Capitol, Transcribed Interview of William Barr, (June 2, 2022), pp. 8-9.

6. Select Committee to Investigate the January 6th Attack on the United States Capitol, Transcribed Interview of William Barr, (June 2, 2022), pp. 8-9.

7. Select Committee to Investigate the January 6th Attack on the United States Capitol, Transcribed Interview of William Barr, (June 2, 2022), pp. 8-9.

8. Select Committee to Investigate the January 6th Attack on the United States Capitol, Transcribed Interview of William Barr, (June 2, 2022), pp. 8-9.

9. Select Committee to Investigate the January 6th Attack on the United States Capitol, Transcribed Interview of William Barr, (June 2, 2022), p. 9.

10. Select Committee to Investigate the January 6th Attack on the United States Capitol, Transcribed Interview of William Barr, (June 2, 2022), p. 23.

11. Richard C. Pilger, ed., "Federal Prosecution of Election Offenses: Eighth Edition," Department of Justice (December 2017), p. 84, available at https://www.justice.gov/criminal/file/1029066/download.

12. Richard C. Pilger, ed., "Federal Prosecution of Election Offenses: Eighth Edition," Department of Justice (December 2017), p. 84 available at https://www.justice.gov/criminal/file/1029066/download. The DOJ further advises that "federal law enforcement personnel should carefully evaluate whether an investigative step under consideration has the potential to affect the election itself." The department's concern is that "[s]tarting a public criminal investigation of alleged election fraud before the election to which the allegations pertain has been concluded runs the obvious risk of chilling legitimate voting and campaign activities." Moreover, "[i]t also runs the significant risk of interjecting the investigation itself as an issue, both in the campaign and in the adjudication of any ensuing election contest." *Id.*

13. Documents on file with the Select Committee to Investigate the January 6th Attack on the United States Capitol (Department of Justice Production), HouseSelect-Jan6-PartII-01132022-000616-617 (November 9, 2020, memorandum from Attorney General Barr).

14. Documents on file with the Select Committee to Investigate the January 6th Attack on the United States Capitol (Department of Justice Production), HouseSelect-Jan6-PartII-01132022-000616-617 (November 9, 2020, memorandum from Attorney General Barr).

15. Documents on file with the Select Committee to Investigate the January 6th Attack on the United States Capitol (Department of Justice Production), HouseSelect-Jan6-PartII-01132022-000616-617 (November 9, 2020, memorandum from Attorney General Barr).

16. Select Committee to Investigate the January 6th Attack on the United States Capitol, Transcribed Interview of William Barr, (June 2, 2022), p. 18.

17. Select Committee to Investigate the January 6th Attack on the United States Capitol, Transcribed Interview of William Barr, (June 2, 2022), p. 18.

18. Select Committee to Investigate the January 6th Attack on the United States Capitol, Transcribed Interview of William Barr, (June 2, 2022), p. 18.

19. Select Committee to Investigate the January 6th Attack on the United States Capitol, Transcribed Interview of William Barr, (June 2, 2022), p. 18.

20. Select Committee to Investigate the January 6th Attack on the United States Capitol, Transcribed Interview of William Barr, (June 2, 2022), p. 18.

21. Select Committee to Investigate the January 6th Attack on the United States Capitol, Transcribed Interview of William Barr, (June 2, 2022), p. 18.

22. Select Committee to Investigate the January 6th Attack on the United States Capitol, Transcribed Interview of William Barr, (June 2, 2022), pp. 18-19.

23. Select Committee to Investigate the January 6th Attack on the United States Capitol, Transcribed Interview of William Barr, (June 2, 2022), p. 18.

24. Select Committee to Investigate the January 6th Attack on the United States Capitol, Transcribed Interview of William Barr, (June 2, 2022), p. 18.

25. Select Committee to Investigate the January 6th Attack on the United States Capitol, Transcribed Interview of William Barr, (June 2, 2022), p. 18.

26. Select Committee to Investigate the January 6th Attack on the United States Capitol, Transcribed Interview of William Barr, (June 2, 2022), p. 19.

27. Select Committee to Investigate the January 6th Attack on the United States Capitol, Transcribed Interview of William Barr, (June 2, 2022), p. 19.

28. Select Committee to Investigate the January 6th Attack on the United States Capitol, Transcribed Interview of William Barr, (June 2, 2022), p. 19.

29. Select Committee to Investigate the January 6th Attack on the United States Capitol, Transcribed Interview of William Barr, (June 2, 2022), p. 19.

30. Select Committee to Investigate the January 6th Attack on the United States Capitol, Transcribed Interview of William Barr, (June 2, 2022), p. 19

31. Select Committee to Investigate the January 6th Attack on the United States Capitol, Transcribed Interview of William Barr, (June 2, 2022), p. 19.

32. Select Committee to Investigate the January 6th Attack on the United States Capitol, Transcribed Interview of William Barr, (June 2, 2022), pp. 19-20.

33. Select Committee to Investigate the January 6th Attack on the United States Capitol, Transcribed Interview of William Barr, (June 2, 2022), p. 20.

34. Select Committee to Investigate the January 6th Attack on the United States Capitol, Transcribed Interview of William Barr, (June 2, 2022), p. 22.

35. Select Committee to Investigate the January 6th Attack on the United States Capitol, Transcribed Interview of William Barr, (June 2, 2022), pp. 22-23.

36. Select Committee to Investigate the January 6th Attack on the United States Capitol, Transcribed Interview of William Barr, (June 2, 2022), pp. 22-23.

37. Factba.se, "Interview: Maria Bartiromo Interviews Donald Trump on Fox News - November 29, 2020," Vimeo, Nov. 29, 2020, available at https://vimeo.com/485180163; Fox News, "Trump Asks, 'Where's Durham?' During First Interview Since the Election," YouTube, Nov. 29, 2020, available at https://www.youtube.com/watch?v=szStcNBIL68; see also Alexis Benveniste, "Fox News' Maria Bartiromo Gave Trump His First TV Interview Since the Election. It Was Filled with Lies," CNN (Nov. 29, 2020), available at https://www.cnn.com/2020/11/29/media/bartiromo-trump-interview.

38. Factba.se, "Interview: Maria Bartiromo Interviews Donald Trump on Fox News - November 29, 2020," Vimeo, Nov. 29, 2020, available at https://vimeo.com/485180163; Fox News, "Trump Asks, 'Where's Durham?' During First Interview Since the Election," YouTube, Nov. 29, 2020, available at https://www.youtube.com/watch?v=szStcNBIL68; see also Alexis Benveniste, "Fox News' Maria Bartiromo Gave Trump His First TV Interview Since the Election. It Was Filled with Lies," CNN (Nov. 29, 2020), available at https://www.cnn.com/2020/11/29/media/bartiromo-trump-interview.

39. Factba.se, "Interview: Maria Bartiromo Interviews Donald Trump on Fox News - November 29, 2020," Vimeo, Nov. 29, 2020, available at https://vimeo.com/485180163; Fox News, "Trump Asks, 'Where's Durham?' During First Interview Since the Election," YouTube, Nov. 29, 2020, available at https://www.youtube.com/watch?v=szStcNBIL68; see also Alexis Benveniste, "Fox News' Maria Bartiromo Gave Trump His First TV Interview Since the Election. It Was Filled with Lies," CNN (Nov. 29, 2020), available at https://www.cnn.com/2020/11/29/media/bartiromo-trump-interview.

40. Factba.se, "Interview: Maria Bartiromo Interviews Donald Trump on Fox News - November 29, 2020," Vimeo, Nov. 29, 2020, available at https://vimeo.com/485180163; Fox News, "Trump Asks, 'Where's Durham?' During First Interview Since the Election," YouTube, Nov. 29, 2020, available at https://www.youtube.com/watch?v=szStcNBIL68; see also Alexis Benveniste, "Fox News' Maria Bartiromo Gave Trump His First TV Interview Since the Election. It Was Filled with Lies," CNN (Nov. 29, 2020), available at https://www.cnn.com/2020/11/29/media/bartiromo-trump-interview.

41. Factba.se, "Interview: Maria Bartiromo Interviews Donald Trump on Fox News - November 29, 2020," Vimeo, at 4:20, Nov. 29, 2020, available at https://vimeo.com/485180163; Fox News, "Trump Asks, 'Where's Durham?' During First Interview Since the Election," YouTube, Nov. 29, 2020, available at https://www.youtube.com/watch?v=szStcNBIL68; see also Alexis Benveniste, "Fox News' Maria Bartiromo Gave Trump His First TV Interview Since the Election. It Was Filled with Lies," CNN (Nov. 29, 2020), available at https://www.cnn.com/2020/11/29/media/bartiromo-trump interview.

42. "Interview: Maria Bartiromo Interviews Donald Trump on Fox News - November 29, 2020," Vimeo, at 4:25, Nov. 29, 2020, available at https://vimeo.com/485180163; Fox News, "Trump Asks, 'Where's Durham?' During First Interview Since the Election," YouTube, Nov. 29, 2020, available at https://www.youtube.com/watch?v=szStcNBIL68; see also Alexis Benveniste, "Fox News' Maria Bartiromo Gave Trump His First TV Interview Since the Election. It Was Filled with Lies," CNN (Nov. 29, 2020), available at https://www.cnn.com/2020/11/29/media/bartiromo-trump-interview.

43. Factba.se, "Interview: Maria Bartiromo Interviews Donald Trump on Fox News - November 29, 2020," Vimeo, Nov. 29, 2020, available at https://vimeo.com/485180163; Fox News, "Trump Asks, 'Where's Durham?' During First Interview Since the Election," YouTube, Nov. 29, 2020, available at https://www.youtube.com/watch?v=szStcNBIL68; see also Alexis Benveniste, "Fox News' Maria Bartiromo Gave Trump His First TV Interview Since the Election. It Was Filled with Lies," CNN (Nov. 29, 2020), available at https://www.cnn.com/2020/11/29/media/bartiromo-trump-interview.

44. Factba.se, "Interview: Maria Bartiromo Interviews Donald Trump on Fox News - November 29, 2020," Vimeo, Nov. 29, 2020, available at https://vimeo.com/485180163; Fox News, "Trump Asks, 'Where's Durham?' During First Interview Since the Election," YouTube, Nov.

29, 2020, available at https://www.youtube.com/watch?v=szStcNBIL68; *see also* Alexis Ben-veniste, "Fox News' Maria Bartiromo Gave Trump His First TV Interview Since the Election. It Was Filled with Lies," CNN (Nov. 29, 2020), available at https://www.cnn.com/2020/11/29/media/bartiromo-trump-interview.

45.   Factba.se, "Interview: Maria Bartiromo Interviews Donald Trump on Fox News - November 29, 2020," Vimeo, Nov. 29, 2020, available at https://vimeo.com/485180163; Fox News, "Trump Asks, 'Where's Durham?' During First Interview Since the Election," YouTube, Nov. 29, 2020, available at https://www.youtube.com/watch?v=szStcNBIL68; *see also* Alexis Ben-veniste, "Fox News' Maria Bartiromo Gave Trump His First TV Interview Since the Election. It Was Filled with Lies," CNN (Nov. 29, 2020), available at https://www.cnn.com/2020/11/29/media/bartiromo-trump-interview.

46.   Factba.se, "Interview: Maria Bartiromo Interviews Donald Trump on Fox News - November 29, 2020," Vimeo, Nov. 29, 2020, available at https://vimeo.com/485180163; Fox News, "Trump Asks, 'Where's Durham?' During First Interview Since the Election," YouTube, Nov. 29, 2020, available at https://www.youtube.com/watch?v=szStcNBIL68; *see also* Alexis Ben-veniste, "Fox News' Maria Bartiromo Gave Trump His First TV Interview Since the Election. It Was Filled with Lies," CNN (Nov. 29, 2020), available at https://www.cnn.com/2020/11/29/media/bartiromo-trump-interview.

47.   Factba.se, "Interview: Maria Bartiromo Interviews Donald Trump on Fox News - November 29, 2020," Vimeo, Nov. 29, 2020, available at https://vimeo.com/485180163; Fox News, "Trump Asks, 'Where's Durham?' During First Interview Since the Election," YouTube, Nov. 29, 2020, available at https://www.youtube.com/watch?v=szStcNBIL68; *see also* Alexis Ben-veniste, "Fox News' Maria Bartiromo Gave Trump His First TV Interview Since the Election. It Was Filled with Lies," CNN (Nov. 29, 2020), available at https://www.cnn.com/2020/11/29/media/bartiromo-trump-interview.

48.   Fox News, "Trump Asks, 'Where's Durham?' During First Interview Since the Election," You-Tube, Nov. 29, 2020, available at https://www.youtube.com/watch?v=szStcNBIL68; "Inter-view: Maria Bartiromo Interviews Donald Trump on Fox News - November 29, 2020," Vimeo, Nov. 29, 2020, available at ; Fox News, "Trump Asks, 'Where's Durham?' During First Inter-view Since the Election," YouTube, Nov. 29, 2020, available at https://www.youtube.com/watch?v=szStcNBIL68; *see also* Alexis Benveniste, "Fox News' Maria Bartiromo Gave Trump His First TV Interview Since the Election. It Was Filled with Lies," CNN (Nov. 29, 2020), avail-able at https://www.cnn.com/2020/11/29/media/bartiromo-trump-interview. https://vimeo.com/485180163; *see also* Alexis Benveniste, "Fox News' Maria Bartiromo Gave Trump His First TV Interview Since the Election. It Was Filled with Lies," CNN (Nov. 29, 2020), avail-able at https://www.cnn.com/2020/11/29/media/bartiromo-trump-interview.

49.   Michael Balsamo, "Disputing Trump, Barr Says No Widespread Election Fraud," *Associated Press*, (Dec. 1, 2020, updated June 28, 2022), available at https://apnews.com/article/barr-no-widespread-election-fraud-b1f1488796c9a98c4b1a9061a6c7f49d.

50.   Select Committee to Investigate the January 6th Attack on the United States Capitol, Tran-scribed Interview of William Barr, (June 2, 2022), pp. 23-24. Also attending the meeting were Pat Cipollone (Chief White House Counsel to the President), Pat Philbin (Deputy White House Counsel to the President), Eric Herschmann, and Barr's chief of staff, Will Levi. *Id.*

51.   Select Committee to Investigate the January 6th Attack on the United States Capitol, Tran-scribed Interview of William Barr, (June 2, 2022), pp. 23-24.

52.   Select Committee to Investigate the January 6th Attack on the United States Capitol, Tran-scribed Interview of William Barr, (June 2, 2022), pp. 23-24.

53.   Select Committee to Investigate the January 6th Attack on the United States Capitol, Tran-scribed Interview of William Barr, (June 2, 2022), pp. 23-24.

54.   Select Committee to Investigate the January 6th Attack on the United States Capitol, Tran-scribed Interview of William Barr, (June 2, 2022), pp. 23-24.

55.   Select Committee to Investigate the January 6th Attack on the United States Capitol, Tran-scribed Interview of William Barr, (June 2, 2022), pp. 24-25.

56. Select Committee to Investigate the January 6th Attack on the United States Capitol, Transcribed Interview of William Barr, (June 2, 2022), pp. 25-26.

57. Select Committee to Investigate the January 6th Attack on the United States Capitol, Transcribed Interview of William Barr, (June 2, 2022), pp. 11, 25-26.

58. Select Committee to Investigate the January 6th Attack on the United States Capitol, Transcribed Interview of William Barr, (June 2, 2022), p. 25.

59. Select Committee to Investigate the January 6th Attack on the United States Capitol, Transcribed Interview of William Barr, (June 2, 2022), p. 25.

60. Select Committee to Investigate the January 6th Attack on the United States Capitol, Transcribed Interview of William Barr, (June 2, 2022), p. 25.

61. Select Committee to Investigate the January 6th Attack on the United States Capitol, Transcribed Interview of William Barr, (June 2, 2022), p. 25.

62. Select Committee to Investigate the January 6th Attack on the United States Capitol, Transcribed Interview of William Barr, (June 2, 2022), p. 25.

63. Select Committee to Investigate the January 6th Attack on the United States Capitol, Transcribed Interview of William Barr, (June 2, 2022), pp. 25-26.

64. Select Committee to Investigate the January 6th Attack on the United States Capitol, Transcribed Interview of William Barr, (June 2, 2022), pp. 25-26.

65. Select Committee to Investigate the January 6th Attack on the United States Capitol, Transcribed Interview of William Barr, (June 2, 2022), p. 26.

66. Select Committee to Investigate the January 6th Attack on the United States Capitol, Transcribed Interview of William Barr, (June 2, 2022), p. 26.

67. Select Committee to Investigate the January 6th Attack on the United States Capitol, Transcribed Interview of William Barr, (June 2, 2022), p. 26.

68. Select Committee to Investigate the January 6th Attack on the United States Capitol, Transcribed Interview of William Barr, (June 2, 2022), p. 26.

69. Select Committee to Investigate the January 6th Attack on the United States Capitol, Transcribed Interview of William Barr, (June 2, 2022), p. 26.

70. Select Committee to Investigate the January 6th Attack on the United States Capitol, Transcribed Interview of William Barr, (June 2, 2022), pp. 26-28.

71. "Campaign 2020: President Trump Statement on 2020 Election Results," C-SPAN, Dec. 2, 2020, available at https://www.c-span.org/video/?506975-1/president-trump-statement-2020-election-results; "Donald Trump Speech on Election Fraud Claims Transcript December 2," Rev, (Dec. 2, 2020), available at https://www.rev.com/blog/transcripts/donald-trump-speech-on-election-fraud-claims-transcript-december-2.

72. "Campaign 2020: President Trump Statement on 2020 Election Results," C-SPAN, Dec. 2, 2020, available at https://www.c-span.org/video/?506975-1/president-trump-statement-2020-election-results; "Donald Trump Speech on Election Fraud Claims Transcript December 2," Rev, (Dec. 2, 2020), available at https://www.rev.com/blog/transcripts/donald-trump-speech-on-election-fraud-claims-transcript-december-2.

73. "Campaign 2020: President Trump Statement on 2020 Election Results," C-SPAN, Dec. 2, 2020, available at https://www.c-span.org/video/?506975-1/president-trump-statement-2020-election-results; "Donald Trump Speech on Election Fraud Claims Transcript December 2," Rev, (Dec. 2, 2020), available at https://www.rev.com/blog/transcripts/donald-trump-speech-on-election-fraud-claims-transcript-december-2. Trump said: "Here's an example. This is Michigan. At 6:31 in the morning, a vote dump of 149,772 votes came in unexpectedly. We were winning by a lot. That batch was received in horror. We have a company that's very suspect. Its name is Dominion. With the turn of a dial or the change of a chip, you can press a button for Trump and the vote goes to Biden. What kind of a system is this?" Id.

74. 11Alive, "Second Georgia Senate Election Hearing," YouTube, at 1:56:30 - 1:57:15, 5:29:20 - 5:32:45, Dec. 3, 2020, available at https://www.youtube.com/watch?v=hRCXUNOwOjw.

75. 11Alive, "Second Georgia Senate Election Hearing," YouTube, at 1:56:30 - 1:57:15, 5:29:20 - 5:32:45, Dec. 3, 2020, available at https://www.youtube.com/watch?v=hRCXUNOwOjw.

76. 11Alive, "Second Georgia Senate Election Hearing," YouTube, at 0:33:30 - 0:58:00, Dec. 3, 2020, available at https://www.youtube.com/watch?v=hRCXUNOwOjw. The Trump campaign also shared the video online. Donald J Trump, "Video from GA Shows Suitcases Filled with Ballots Pulled from Under a Table AFTER Poll Workers Left," YouTube, Dec. 3, 2020, available at https://www.youtube.com/watch?v=nVP_60Hm4P8.

77. Gabriel Sterling (@GabrielSterling), Twitter, Dec. 4, 2020 6:41 a.m. ET, available at https://twitter.com/GabrielSterling/status/1334825233610633217?ref_src=twsrc%5Etfw%7Ctwcamp%5Etweetembed%7Ctwterm%5E1334825233610633217%7Ctwgr%5E%7Ctwcon%5Es1_&ref_url=https%3A%2F%2Fwww.gpb.org%2Fnews%2F2020%2F12%2F04%2Ffact-checking-rudy-giulianis-grandiose-georgia-election-fraud-claim. At the time, Gabe Sterling was the Chief Operating Officer in the Georgia Secretary of State's Office.

78. Select Committee to Investigate the January 6th Attack on the United States Capitol, *Hearing on the January 6th Investigation*, 117th Cong., 2d sess., (June 13, 2022), available at https://www.govinfo.gov/committee/house-january6th.

79. Select Committee to Investigate the January 6th Attack on the United States Capitol, *Hearing on the January 6th Investigation*, 117th Cong., 2d sess., (June 13, 2022), available at https://www.govinfo.gov/committee/house-january6th.

80. Select Committee to Investigate the January 6th Attack on the United States Capitol, Transcribed Interview of Byung Jin Pak, (May 19, 2022), p. 19.

81. "Read William Barr's Resignation Letter to President Trump," *Washington Post*, (Dec. 14, 2020), available at https://www.washingtonpost.com/context/read-william-barr-s-resignation-letter-to-president-trump/2b0820cb-3890-498a-bd46-c1b248049c70/?itid=lk_inline_manual_4.

82. Select Committee to Investigate the January 6th Attack on the United States Capitol, Transcribed Interview of William Barr, (June 2, 2022), pp. 65-66.

83. Select Committee to Investigate the January 6th Attack on the United States Capitol, Transcribed Interview of William Barr, (June 2, 2022), p. 28.

84. Select Committee to Investigate the January 6th Attack on the United States Capitol, Transcribed Interview of William Barr, (June 2, 2022), p. 28.

85. Select Committee to Investigate the January 6th Attack on the United States Capitol, Transcribed Interview of William Barr, (June 2, 2022), pp. 28-30.

86. Select Committee to Investigate the January 6th Attack on the United States Capitol, Transcribed Interview of William Barr, (June 2, 2022), p. 30.

87. Select Committee to Investigate the January 6th Attack on the United States Capitol, Transcribed Interview of William Barr, (June 2, 2022), p. 32.

88. Select Committee to Investigate the January 6th Attack on the United States Capitol, Transcribed Interview of William Barr, (June 2, 2022), p. 32.

89. Select Committee to Investigate the January 6th Attack on the United States Capitol, Transcribed Interview of Richard Peter Donoghue, (Oct. 1, 2021), pp. 39-40.

90. Documents on file with the Select Committee to Investigate the January 6th Attack on the United States Capitol (Department of Justice Production), HCOR-Pre-CertificationEvents-06032021-000425, HCOR-Pre-CertificationEvents-06032021-000426, HCOR-Pre-CertificationEvents-06032021-000429 (December 14, 2020, email from Molly Michael to Jeffrey Rosen subject "From POTUS" with two attachments).

91. Documents on file with the Select Committee to Investigate the January 6th Attack on the United States Capitol (Department of Justice Production), HCOR-Pre-CertificationEvents-06032021-000425, HCOR-Pre-CertificationEvents-06032021-000426, HCOR-Pre-CertificationEvents-06032021-000429 (December 14, 2020, email from Molly Michael to Jeffrey Rosen subject "From POTUS" with two attachments).

92. Select Committee to Investigate the January 6th Attack on the United States Capitol, Transcribed Interview of Richard Peter Donoghue, (Oct. 1, 2021), pp. 32-33.

93. Select Committee to Investigate the January 6th Attack on the United States Capitol, *Hearing on the January 6th Investigation*, 117th Cong., 2d sess., (June 23, 2022), available at https://www.govinfo.gov/committee/house-january6th.

94. Select Committee to Investigate the January 6th Attack on the United States Capitol, *Hearing on the January 6th Investigation*, 117th Cong., 2d sess., (June 23, 2022), available at https://www.govinfo.gov/committee/house-january6th.

95. Select Committee to Investigate the January 6th Attack on the United States Capitol, *Hearing on the January 6th Investigation*, 117th Cong., 2d sess., (June 23, 2022), available at https://www.govinfo.gov/committee/house-january6th.

96. U.S. Senate Committee on the Judiciary, Transcribed Interview of Jeffrey Rosen, (Aug. 7, 2021), at p. 34, available at https://www.judiciary.senate.gov/imo/media/doc/Rosen%20Transcript.pdf.

97. Documents on file with the Select Committee to Investigate the January 6th Attack on the United States Capitol (National Archives Production), 076P-R001080 (December 21, 2020, WAVES visitor records).

98. Mark Meadows (@MarkMeadows), Twitter, Dec. 21, 2020 6:03 pm, available at https://twitter.com/MarkMeadows/status/1341157317451124745.

99. Documents on file with the Select Committee to Investigate the January 6th Attack on the United States Capitol (National Archives Production), 076P-R001080 (WAVES visitor records for December 21, 2020).

100. Select Committee to Investigate the January 6th Attack on the United States Capitol, Deposition of Molly Michael, (March 24, 2022), pp. 205-06; Documents on file with the Select Committee to Investigate the January 6th Attack on the United States Capitol (National Archives Production), 076P-R000009364_0001 (December 21 and 22, 2020 email chain between Molly Michael and Jeffrey Clark discussing a December 22, 2020 meeting at the White House); Documents on file with the Select Committee to Investigate the January 6th Attack on the United States Capitol (National Archives Production), 076P-R000009365_0001 (December 22, 2020 email from Molly Michael to staff regarding a meeting at 6 p.m. in the Yellow Oval with Jeffrey Clark and another guest); Jonathan Tamari & Chris Brennan, "Pa. Congressman Scott Perry Acknowledges Introducing Trump to Lawyer at the Center of Election Plot," *Philadelphia Inquirer*, (Jan. 25, 2021), available at https://www.inquirer.com/politics/pennsylvania/scott-perry-trump-georgia-election-results-20210125.html.

101. Select Committee to Investigate the January 6th Attack on the United States Capitol, Transcribed Interview of Jeffrey Rosen, (Oct. 13, 2021), pp. 52-53.

102. Select Committee to Investigate the January 6th Attack on the United States Capitol, *Hearing on the January 6th Investigation*, 117th Cong., 2d sess., (June 23, 2022), available at https://www.govinfo.gov/committee/house-january6th.

103. Select Committee to Investigate the January 6th Attack on the United States Capitol, *Hearing on the January 6th Investigation*, 117th Cong., 2d sess., (June 23, 2022), available at https://www.govinfo.gov/committee/house-january6th.

104. Select Committee to Investigate the January 6th Attack on the United States Capitol, *Hearing on the January 6th Investigation*, 117th Cong., 117th sess., (June 23, 2022), available at https://www.govinfo.gov/committee/house-january6th.

105. Select Committee to Investigate the January 6th Attack on the United States Capitol, Transcribed Interview of Jeffrey Rosen, (Oct. 13, 2021), pp. 55-56, 78.

106. Select Committee to Investigate the January 6th Attack on the United States Capitol, Transcribed Interview of Jeffrey Rosen, (Oct. 13, 2021), pp. 55-56.

107. Select Committee to Investigate the January 6th Attack on the United States Capitol, Deposition of Kenneth Klukowski, (Dec. 15, 2021), pp. 53-55.

108. Select Committee to Investigate the January 6th Attack on the United States Capitol, *Hearing on the January 6th Investigation*, 117th Cong., 2d sess., (June 23, 2022), available at https://www.govinfo.gov/committee/house-january6th.

109. Select Committee to Investigate the January 6th Attack on the United States Capitol, *Hearing on the January 6th Investigation*, 117th Cong., 2d sess., (June 23, 2022), available at https://www.govinfo.gov/committee/house-january6th.

110. Select Committee to Investigate the January 6th Attack on the United States Capitol, *Hearing on the January 6th Investigation*, 117th Cong., 2d sess., (June 23, 2022), available at https://www.govinfo.gov/committee/house-january6th.

111. Select Committee to Investigate the January 6th Attack on the United States Capitol, *Hearing on the January 6th Investigation*, 117th Cong., 2d sess., (June 23, 2022), available at https://www.govinfo.gov/committee/house-january6th ; Documents on file with the Select Committee to Investigate the January 6th Attack on the United States Capitol (Department of Justice Production), HCOR-Pre-CertificationEvents-07262021-000681 (May 11, 2009, memorandum laying out the policy for "Communications with the White House and Congress").

112. Documents on file with the Select Committee to Investigate the January 6th Attack on the United States Capitol (Mark Meadows Production), MM014099 (December 26, 2020, text message from Rep. Perry to Mark Meadows).

113. Documents on file with the Select Committee to Investigate the January 6th Attack on the United States Capitol (Mark Meadows Production), MM0140100 (December 26, 2020, text message from Rep. Perry to Mark Meadows).

114. Documents on file with the Select Committee to Investigate the January 6th Attack on the United States Capitol (Mark Meadows Production), MM014101 (December 26, 2020, text message from Mark Meadows to Rep. Perry).

115. Documents on file with the Select Committee to Investigate the January 6th Attack on the United States Capitol (Mark Meadows Production), MM014102-014103, MM014178.

116. Select Committee to Investigate the January 6th Attack on the United States Capitol, Transcribed Interview of Richard Peter Donoghue, (Oct. 1, 2021), pp. 47-48.

117. Documents on file with the Select Committee to Investigate the January 6th Attack on the United States Capitol (Department of Justice Production), HCOR-Pre-Certification-Events-07282021-000735.

118. Documents on file with the Select Committee to Investigate the January 6th Attack on the United States Capitol (Department of Justice Production), HCOR-Pre-Certification-Events-07282021-000735; Ryan Deto, "Sen. Mastriano and Former State Rep. Saccone among Trump Supporters who Occupied U.S. Capitol," *Pittsburgh City Paper*, (Jan. 6, 2021), available at https://www.pghcitypaper.com/pittsburgh/sen-mastriano-and-former-state-rep-saccone-among-trump-supporters-who-occupied-us-capitol/Content?oid=18690728; Erin Bamer, "Mastriano Defends Protest Appearance; Other GOP Lawmakers Say Little," York Dispatch, (Jan. 7, 2021), available at https://www.yorkdispatch.com/story/news/2021/01/07/mastriano-at-no-point-did-he-storm-us-capitol/6579049002/.

119. Select Committee to Investigate the January 6th Attack on the United States Capitol, Transcribed Interview of Richard Peter Donoghue, (Oct. 1, 2021), pp. 47-50; *see also* Documents on file with the Select Committee to Investigate the January 6th Attack on the United States Capitol (Department of Justice Production), HCOR-Pre-Certification-Events-07282021-000735.

120. Dan Geiter, "Rally to 'Stop the Steal' of the 2020 Election" *PennLive*, (Nov. 5, 2020) available at https://www.pennlive.com/galleries/J3FJ24LCKVCT5OW3U2TJ6BV4RE/.

121. *See, e.g.,* Scott Perry for Congress, "#StopTheSteal," Facebook, November 6, 2020, available at https://www.facebook.com/watch/?v=406418637058079.

122. Select Committee to Investigate the January 6th Attack on the United States Capitol, Transcribed Interview of Richard Peter Donoghue, (Oct. 1, 2021), pp. 47-48, 53.

123. Select Committee to Investigate the January 6th Attack on the United States Capitol, *Hearing on the January 6th Investigation*, 117th Cong., 2d sess., (June 23, 2022), available at https://www.govinfo.gov/committee/house-january6thSelect; Documents on file with the Select Committee to Investigate the January 6th Attack on the United States Capitol (Department of Justice Production), HCOR-Pre-Certification-Events-07282021-000739 (December 27, 2020, handwritten notes from Richard Donoghue about call with President Trump).

124. Select Committee to Investigate the January 6th Attack on the United States Capitol, *Hearing on the January 6th Investigation*, 117th Cong., 2d sess., (June 23, 2022), available at https://www.govinfo.gov/committee/house-january6thSelect; Documents on file with the Select Committee to Investigate the January 6th Attack on the United States Capitol (Department of Justice Production), HCOR-Pre-Certification-Events-07282021-000739 (December 27, 2020, handwritten notes from Richard Donoghue about call with President Trump).

125. Select Committee to Investigate the January 6th Attack on the United States Capitol, *Hearing on the January 6th Investigation*, 117th Cong., 2d sess., (June 23, 2022), available at https://www.govinfo.gov/committee/house-january6thSelect; Documents on file with the Select Committee to Investigate the January 6th Attack on the United States Capitol (Department of Justice Production), HCOR-Pre-Certification-Events-07282021-000739 (December 27, 2020, handwritten notes from Richard Donoghue about call with President Trump).

126. "Hand Audit of All Presidential Election Votes in Antrim County Confirms Previously Certified Results, Voting Machines Were Accurate," Michigan Secretary of State, (Dec. 17, 2020), available at https://www.michigan.gov/sos/resources/news/2020/12/17/hand-audit-of-all-presidential-election-votes-in-antrim-county-confirms-previously-certified-result.

127. "Hand Audit of All Presidential Election Votes in Antrim County Confirms Previously Certified Results, Voting Machines Were Accurate," Michigan Secretary of State, (Dec. 17, 2020), available at https://www.michigan.gov/sos/resources/news/2020/12/17/hand-audit-of-all-presidential-election-votes-in-antrim-county-confirms-previously-certified-result.

128. "Hand Audit of All Presidential Election Votes in Antrim County Confirms Previously Certified Results, Voting Machines Were Accurate," Michigan Secretary of State, (Dec. 17, 2020), available at https://www.michigan.gov/sos/resources/news/2020/12/17/hand-audit-of-all-presidential-election-votes-in-antrim-county-confirms-previously-certified-result.

129. Select Committee to Investigate the January 6th Attack on the United States Capitol, *Hearing on the January 6th Investigation*, 117th Cong., 2d sess., (June 23, 2022), available at https://www.govinfo.gov/committee/house-january6thSelect; Select Committee to Investigate the January 6th Attack on the United States Capitol, Transcribed Interview of Richard Peter Donoghue, (Oct. 1, 2021), p. 60; Documents on file with the Select Committee to Investigate the January 6th Attack on the United States Capitol (Department of Justice Production), HCOR-Pre-Certification-Events-07282021-000739 (December 27, 2020, handwritten notes from Richard Donoghue about call with President Trump).

130. Select Committee to Investigate the January 6th Attack on the United States Capitol, *Hearing on the January 6th Investigation*, 117th Cong., 2d sess., (June 23, 2022), available at https://www.govinfo.gov/committee/house-january6th?path=/browsecommittee/chamber/house/committee/january6th.

131. Select Committee to Investigate the January 6th Attack on the United States Capitol, *Hearing on the January 6th Investigation*, 117th Cong., 2d sess., (June 23, 2022), available at

https://www.govinfo.gov/committee/house-january6thSelect; Select Committee to Investigate the January 6th Attack on the United States Capitol, Transcribed Interview of Richard Peter Donoghue, (Oct. 1, 2021), p. 60.

132.   Select Committee to Investigate the January 6th Attack on the United States Capitol, *Hearing on the January 6th Investigation*, 117th Cong., 2d sess., (June 23, 2022), available at https://www.govinfo.gov/committee/house-january6thSelect; Select Committee to Investigate the January 6th Attack on the United States Capitol, Transcribed Interview of Richard Peter Donoghue, (Oct. 1, 2021), p. 60; Documents on file with the Select Committee to Investigate the January 6th Attack on the United States Capitol (Department of Justice Production), HCOR-Pre-Certification-Events-07282021-000739 (December 27, 2020, handwritten notes from Richard Donoghue about call with President Trump).

133.   Select Committee to Investigate the January 6th Attack on the United States Capitol, Transcribed Interview of Richard Peter Donoghue, (Oct. 1, 2021), p. 55; Documents on file with the Select Committee to Investigate the January 6th Attack on the United States Capitol (Department of Justice Production), HCOR-Pre-Certification-Events-07282021-000737 (December 27, 2020, handwritten notes from Richard Donoghue about call with President Trump).

134.   Select Committee to Investigate the January 6th Attack on the United States Capitol, Transcribed Interview of Richard Peter Donoghue, (Oct. 1, 2021), p. 55; Documents on file with the Select Committee to Investigate the January 6th Attack on the United States Capitol (Department of Justice Production), HCOR-Pre-Certification-Events-07282021-000737 (December 27, 2020, handwritten notes from Richard Donoghue about call with President Trump).

135.   Select Committee to Investigate the January 6th Attack on the United States Capitol, Transcribed Interview of Richard Peter Donoghue, (Oct. 1, 2021), p. 55.

136.   Select Committee to Investigate the January 6th Attack on the United States Capitol, Transcribed Interview of Richard Peter Donoghue, (Oct. 1, 2021), pp. 55-56; Documents on file with the Select Committee to Investigate the January 6th Attack on the United States Capitol (Department of Justice Production), HCOR-Pre-Certification-Events-07282021-000739 (December 27, 2020, handwritten notes from Richard Donoghue about call with President Trump).

137.   Select Committee to Investigate the January 6th Attack on the United States Capitol, *Hearing on the January 6th Investigation*, 117th Cong., 2d sess., (June 23, 2022), available at https://www.govinfo.gov/committee/house-january6thSelect.

138.   Select Committee to Investigate the January 6th Attack on the United States Capitol, Transcribed Interview of Richard Peter Donoghue, (Oct. 1, 2021), p. 54; Documents on file with the Select Committee to Investigate the January 6th Attack on the United States Capitol (Department of Justice Production), HCOR-Pre-Certification-Events-07282021-000739 (December 27, 2020, handwritten notes from Richard Donoghue about call with President Trump).

139.   Select Committee to Investigate the January 6th Attack on the United States Capitol, Transcribed Interview of Richard Peter Donoghue, (Oct. 1, 2021), p. 54; Documents on file with the Select Committee to Investigate the January 6th Attack on the United States Capitol (Department of Justice Production), HCOR-Pre-Certification-Events-07282021-000739 (December 27, 2020, handwritten notes from Richard Donoghue about call with President Trump).

140.   Select Committee to Investigate the January 6th Attack on the United States Capitol, Transcribed Interview of Richard Peter Donoghue, (Oct. 1, 2021), p. 54; Documents on file with the Select Committee to Investigate the January 6th Attack on the United States Capitol (Department of Justice Production), HCOR-Pre-Certification-Events-07282021-000739 (December 27, 2020, handwritten notes from Richard Donoghue about call with President Trump).

141. Select Committee to Investigate the January 6th Attack on the United States Capitol, Transcribed Interview of Richard Peter Donoghue, (Oct. 1, 2021), p. 64; Documents on file with the Select Committee to Investigate the January 6th Attack on the United States Capitol (Department of Justice Production), HCOR-Pre-Certification-Events-07282021-000741 (December 27, 2020, handwritten notes from Richard Donoghue about call with President Trump).

142. Select Committee to Investigate the January 6th Attack on the United States Capitol, Transcribed Interview of Richard Peter Donoghue, (Oct. 1, 2021), p. 60.

143. Select Committee to Investigate the January 6th Attack on the United States Capitol, Transcribed Interview of Richard Peter Donoghue, (Oct. 1, 2021), p. 60.

144. Select Committee to Investigate the January 6th Attack on the United States Capitol, Transcribed Interview of Richard Peter Donoghue, (Oct. 1, 2021), pp. 60-61.

145. Select Committee to Investigate the January 6th Attack on the United States Capitol, Transcribed Interview of Richard Peter Donoghue, (Oct. 1, 2021), pp. 60-61.

146. Select Committee to Investigate the January 6th Attack on the United States Capitol, Transcribed Interview of Richard Peter Donoghue, (Oct. 1, 2021), pp. 60-61.

147. Select Committee to Investigate the January 6th Attack on the United States Capitol, Transcribed Interview of Richard Peter Donoghue, (Oct. 1, 2021), pp. 54-55; Documents on file with the Select Committee to Investigate the January 6th Attack on the United States Capitol (Department of Justice Production), HCOR-Pre-Certification-Events-07282021-000737 (December 27, 2020, handwritten notes from Richard Donoghue about call with President Trump).

148. Select Committee to Investigate the January 6th Attack on the United States Capitol, Transcribed Interview of Richard Peter Donoghue, (Oct. 1, 2021), pp. 54, 58; Documents on file with the Select Committee to Investigate the January 6th Attack on the United States Capitol (Department of Justice Production), HCOR-Pre-Certification-Events-07282021-000737, HCOR-Pre-Certification-Events-07282021-000738 (December 27, 2020, handwritten notes from Richard Donoghue about call with President Trump).

149. Select Committee to Investigate the January 6th Attack on the United States Capitol, Transcribed Interview of Richard Peter Donoghue, (Oct. 1, 2021), pp. 54, 58; Documents on file with the Select Committee to Investigate the January 6th Attack on the United States Capitol (Department of Justice Production), HCOR-Pre-Certification-Events-07282021-000737, HCOR-Pre-Certification-Events-07282021-000738 (December 27, 2020, handwritten notes from Richard Donoghue about call with President Trump).

150. Select Committee to Investigate the January 6th Attack on the United States Capitol, Transcribed Interview of Richard Peter Donoghue, (Oct. 1, 2021), pp. 54, 58; Documents on file with the Select Committee to Investigate the January 6th Attack on the United States Capitol (Department of Justice Production), HCOR-Pre-Certification-Events-07282021-000737, HCOR-Pre-Certification-Events-07282021-000738 (December 27, 2020, handwritten notes from Richard Donoghue about call with President Trump).

151. Select Committee to Investigate the January 6th Attack on the United States Capitol, Transcribed Interview of Richard Peter Donoghue, (Oct. 1, 2021), p. 58; Documents on file with the Select Committee to Investigate the January 6th Attack on the United States Capitol (Department of Justice Production), HCOR-Pre-Certification-Events-07282021-000738, HCOR-Pre-Certification-Events-07282021-000739 (December 27, 2020, handwritten notes from Richard Donoghue about call with President Trump).

152. Select Committee to Investigate the January 6th Attack on the United States Capitol, Transcribed Interview of Richard Peter Donoghue, (Oct. 1, 2021), p. 58. Trump also mentioned the possibility of the DOJ saying the "election is corrupt or suspect or not reliable" during a public press conference. "We told him we were not going to do that," Donoghue explained. *Id.* at p. 59.

153. Select Committee to Investigate the January 6th Attack on the United States Capitol, Transcribed Interview of Richard Peter Donoghue, (Oct. 1, 2021), p. 62; Documents on file with the Select Committee to Investigate the January 6th Attack on the United States Capitol (Department of Justice Production), HCOR-Pre-Certification-Events-07282021-000740 (December 27, 2020, handwritten notes from Richard Donoghue about call with President Trump).

154. Select Committee to Investigate the January 6th Attack on the United States Capitol, Transcribed Interview of Richard Peter Donoghue, (Oct. 1, 2021), p. 60; Documents on file with the Select Committee to Investigate the January 6th Attack on the United States Capitol (Department of Justice Production), HCOR-Pre-Certification-Events-07282021-000739, HCOR-Pre-Certification-Events-07282021-000740 (December 27, 2020, handwritten notes from Richard Donoghue about call with President Trump).

155. Select Committee to Investigate the January 6th Attack on the United States Capitol, Transcribed Interview of Richard Peter Donoghue, (Oct. 1, 2021), p. 61.

156. Select Committee to Investigate the January 6th Attack on the United States Capitol, *Hearing on the January 6th Investigation*, 117th Cong., 2d sess., (June 23, 2022), available at https://www.govinfo.gov/committee/house-january6thSelect.

157. Select Committee to Investigate the January 6th Attack on the United States Capitol, *Hearing on the January 6th Investigation*, 117th Cong., 2d sess., (June 23, 2022), available at https://www.govinfo.gov/committee/house-january6thSelect.

158. Select Committee to Investigate the January 6th Attack on the United States Capitol, *Hearing on the January 6th Investigation*, 117th Cong., 2d sess., (June 23, 2022), available at https://www.govinfo.gov/committee/house-january6thSelect.

159. Select Committee to Investigate the January 6th Attack on the United States Capitol, *Hearing on the January 6th Investigation*, 117th Cong., 2d sess., (June 23, 2022), available at https://www.govinfo.gov/committee/house-january6thSelect.

160. Donoghue testified before the Select Committee: "There were isolated instances of fraud. None of them came close to calling into question the outcome of the election in any individual state." Select Committee to Investigate the January 6th Attack on the United States Capitol, *Hearing on the January 6th Investigation*, 117th Cong., 2d sess., (June 23, 2022), available at https://www.govinfo.gov/committee/house-january6thSelect.

161. Select Committee to Investigate the January 6th Attack on the United States Capitol, Transcribed Interview of Richard Peter Donoghue, (Oct. 1, 2021), p. 62; Documents on file with the Select Committee to Investigate the January 6th Attack on the United States Capitol (Department of Justice Production), HCOR-Pre-Certification-Events-07282021-000740 (December 27, 2020, handwritten notes from Richard Donoghue about call with President Trump).

162. Select Committee to Investigate the January 6th Attack on the United States Capitol, Transcribed Interview of Richard Peter Donoghue, (Oct. 1, 2021), p. 62.

163. Select Committee to Investigate the January 6th Attack on the United States Capitol, Transcribed Interview of Richard Peter Donoghue, (Oct. 1, 2021), p. 62.

164. Select Committee to Investigate the January 6th Attack on the United States Capitol, Transcribed Interview of Richard Peter Donoghue, (Oct. 1, 2021), p. 65.

165. Select Committee to Investigate the January 6th Attack on the United States Capitol, Transcribed Interview of Richard Peter Donoghue, (Oct. 1, 2021), pp. 72-75.

166. Dan Gleiter, "Rally to 'Stop the Steal' of the 2020 Election," *Penn Live*, (Nov. 5, 2020), available at https://www.pennlive.com/galleries/J3FJ24LCKVCT5OW3U2TJ6BV4RE/.

167. Letter from the Office of Rep. Lance Gooden and Signed by 26 other Members of Congress to the President of the United States, Dec. 9, 2020, available at https://www.politico.com/f/?id=00000176-4701-d52c-ad7e-d7fdbfe50000.

168. Motion for Leave to File Amicus Brief by U.S. Representative Mike Johnson and 125 other Members, *Texas v. Pennsylvania*, 592 U.S. ____ (Dec. 10, 2020) (No. 155, Orig.), available at https://www.supremecourt.gov/DocketPDF/22/220155/163550/20201211132250339_Texas%20v.%20Pennsylvania%20Amicus%20Brief%20of%20126%20Representatives%20--%20corrected.pdf.

169. Select Committee to Investigate the January 6th Attack on the United States Capitol, Transcribed Interview of Richard Peter Donoghue, (Oct. 1, 2021), pp. 72-73; Documents on file with the Select Committee to Investigate the January 6th Attack on the United States Capitol (Department of Justice Production), HCOR-Pre-CertificationEvents-07262021-000705, HCOR-Pre-CertificationEvents-07262021-000706, (Dec. 27, 2020, handwritten notes). Donoghue's handwritten notes from the call are dated Dec. 28, 2020, but he confirmed the call took place on Dec. 27.

170. Select Committee to Investigate the January 6th Attack on the United States Capitol, Transcribed Interview of Richard Peter Donoghue, (Oct. 1, 2021), pp. 72-73; Documents on file with the Select Committee to Investigate the January 6th Attack on the United States Capitol (Department of Justice Production), HCOR-Pre-CertificationEvents-07262021-000705, HCOR-Pre-CertificationEvents-07262021-000706, (Dec. 27, 2020, handwritten notes).

171. Select Committee to Investigate the January 6th Attack on the United States Capitol, Transcribed Interview of Richard Peter Donoghue, (Oct. 1, 2021), pp. 72-73; Documents on file with the Select Committee to Investigate the January 6th Attack on the United States Capitol (Department of Justice Production), HCOR-Pre-CertificationEvents-07262021-000705, HCOR-Pre-CertificationEvents-07262021-000705, (Dec. 27, 2020, handwritten notes).

172. Select Committee to Investigate the January 6th Attack on the United States Capitol, Transcribed Interview of Richard Peter Donoghue, (Oct. 1, 2021), p. 73; Documents on file with the Select Committee to Investigate the January 6th Attack on the United States Capitol (Department of Justice Production), HCOR-Pre-CertificationEvents-07262021-000705, HCOR-Pre-CertificationEvents-07262021-000706, (Dec. 27, 2020, handwritten notes).

173. Documents on file with the Select Committee to Investigate the January 6th Attack on the United States Capitol (Department of Justice Production), HCOR-Pre-CertificationEvents-06032021-000001 - HCOR-Pre-CertificationEvents-06032021-000018.

174. Documents on file with the Select Committee to Investigate the January 6th Attack on the United States Capitol (Department of Justice Production), HCOR-Pre-CertificationEvents-06032021-000008.

175. RepScottPerry (@RepScotPerry), Twitter, Dec. 28, 2020 6:01 p.m. ET, available at https://twitter.com/RepScottPerry/status/1343693703664308225.

176. *See* Chapter 1.

177. Select Committee to Investigate the January 6th Attack on the United States Capitol, Transcribed Interview of Richard Peter Donoghue, (Oct. 1, 2021), pp. 74-75.

178. Select Committee to Investigate the January 6th Attack on the United States Capitol, Transcribed Interview of Richard Peter Donoghue, (Oct. 1, 2021), pp. 75-76.

179. Select Committee to Investigate the January 6th Attack on the United States Capitol, Transcribed Interview of Richard Peter Donoghue, (Oct. 1, 2021), pp. 75-76.

180. Select Committee to Investigate the January 6th Attack on the United States Capitol, Transcribed Interview of Richard Peter Donoghue, (Oct. 1, 2021), pp. 75-76.

181. Documents on file with the Select Committee to Investigate the January 6th Attack on the United States Capitol (Department of Justice Production), HCOR-Pre-CertificationEvents-07262021-000697 – HCOR-Pre-CertificationEvents-07262021-000702.

182. Documents on file with the Select Committee to Investigate the January 6th Attack on the United States Capitol (Department of Justice Production), HCOR-Pre-CertificationEvents-07262021-000697 – HCOR-Pre-CertificationEvents-07262021-000702.; Documents on file with the Select Committee to Investigate the January 6th Attack on the United States Capitol

(Department of Justice Production), HCOR-Pre-CertificationEvents-06032021-000200 (December 28, 2020, email from Richard Donoghue to Jeffrey Clark, cc'ing Jeffrey Rosen, including Rosen's reply to Donoghue; Select Committee to Investigate the January 6th Attack on the United States Capitol, *Hearing on the January 6th Investigation*, 117th Cong., 2d sess., (June 23, 2022), available at https://www.govinfo.gov/committee/house-january6th.

183.   Select Committee to Investigate the January 6th Attack on the United States Capitol, *Hearing on the January 6th Investigation*, 117th Cong., 2d sess., (June 23, 2022), available at https://www.govinfo.gov/committee/house-january6th.

184.   Documents on file with the Select Committee to Investigate the January 6th Attack on the United States Capitol (Department of Justice Production), HCOR-Pre-CertificationEvents-07262021-000697 – HCOR-Pre-CertificationEvents-07262021-000702.

185.   *See* National Intelligence Council, *Intelligence Community Assessment: Foreign Threats to the 2020 US Federal Elections*, (Mar. 10, 2021), available at https://www.dni.gov/index.php/newsroom/reports-publications/reports-publications-2021/item/2192-intelligence-community-assessment-on-foreign-threats-to-the-2020-u-s-federal-elections (declassified version of a January 7, 2021, report to President Trump, senior Executive Branch officials, and Congressional leadership). The report concluded, among other things, "We have no indications that any foreign actor attempted to alter any technical aspect of the voting process in the 2020 US elections, including voter registration, casting ballots, vote tabulation, or reporting results."

186.   Documents on file with the Select Committee to Investigate the January 6th Attack on the United States Capitol (Department of Justice Production), HCOR-Pre-CertificationEvents-07262021-000697 – HCOR-Pre-CertificationEvents-07262021-000702.

187.   Zachary Cohen & Sara Murray, "New Details Shed Light on Ways Mark Meadows Pushed Federal Agencies to Pursue Dubious Election Claims," CNN, (Dec. 2, 2021), available at https://www.cnn.com/2021/12/02/politics/mark-meadows-election-fraud-liaison/index.html; Select Committee to Investigate the January 6th Attack on the United States Capitol, Transcribed Interview of Eric Herschmann, (Apr. 6, 2022) at pp. 168-69.

188.   Select Committee to Investigate the January 6th Attack on the United States Capitol, Transcribed Interview of Richard Peter Donoghue, (Oct. 1, 2021), p. 113.

189.   Documents on file with the Select Committee to Investigate the January 6th Attack on the United States Capitol (Department of Justice Production), HCOR-Pre-CertificationEvents-07262021-000697 – HCOR-Pre-CertificationEvents-07262021-000702.

190.   Documents on file with the Select Committee to Investigate the January 6th Attack on the United States Capitol (Department of Justice Production), HCOR-Pre-CertificationEvents-07262021-000697 – HCOR-Pre-CertificationEvents-07262021-000702.

191.   Documents on file with the Select Committee to Investigate the January 6th Attack on the United States Capitol (Department of Justice Production), HCOR-Pre-CertificationEvents-07262021-000697 – HCOR-Pre-CertificationEvents-07262021-000702.

192.   Documents on file with the Select Committee to Investigate the January 6th Attack on the United States Capitol (Department of Justice Production), HCOR-Pre-CertificationEvents-07262021-000697 – HCOR-Pre-CertificationEvents-07262021-000702.

193.   Documents on file with the Select Committee to Investigate the January 6th Attack on the United States Capitol (Department of Justice Production), HCOR-Pre-CertificationEvents-07262021-000697 – HCOR-Pre-CertificationEvents-07262021-000702.

194.   *See* Chapters 2 and 3 regarding the Trump Campaign's efforts to overturn the results of the election in contested states and have fake Electoral College electors submit fake votes to Congress.

195.   Documents on file with the Select Committee to Investigate the January 6th Attack on the United States Capitol (Department of Justice Production), HCOR-Pre-CertificationEvents-07262021-000697 – HCOR-Pre-CertificationEvents-07262021-000702.

196. *See* Chapter 2 for additional information on these hearings.

197. *See* Chapter 2; *see also* Ga. Const., art. V, § 2, ¶ VII.

198. Documents on file with the Select Committee to Investigate the January 6th Attack on the United States Capitol (Department of Justice Production), HCOR-Pre-CertificationEvents-07262021-000697 – HCOR-Pre-CertificationEvents-07262021-000702.

199. Documents on file with the Select Committee to Investigate the January 6th Attack on the United States Capitol (Department of Justice Production), HCOR-Pre-CertificationEvents-07262021-000698 – HCOR-Pre-CertificationEvents-07262021-000702.

200. *See* Chapter 2.

201. *See* Chapter 3.

202. Select Committee to Investigate the January 6th Attack on the United States Capitol, Deposition of Jeffrey Clark, (Feb 2, 2022), pp. 24-27.

203. Select Committee to Investigate the January 6th Attack on the United States Capitol, Deposition of Rudolph Giuliani, (May 20, 2022), pp. 101-03.

204. Documents on file with the Select Committee to Investigate the January 6th Attack on the United States Capitol (Chapman production), Chapman061893 (January 1, 2021, emails between Jeffrey Clark and John Eastman); *see* Documents on file with the Select Committee to Investigate the January 6th Attack on the United States Capitol (Verizon Production, July 1, 2022) (showing five calls between John Eastman and Jeffrey Clark from January 1, 2021, through January 8, 2021)

205. *See, e.g.,* Select Committee to Investigate the January 6th Attack on the United States Capitol, Deposition of Kenneth Klukowski (Dec. 15, 2021), p. 182. The Select Committee questioned, and sought documents from, Klukowski about his interactions with Eastman and others related to the 2020 election and the January 6th joint session of Congress. Klukowski, however, objected to certain questions, and withheld a number of relevant communications, on the basis of attorney-client privilege, work product, or the First Amendment, including communications that he had with Eastman. For example, on December 9th, before Klukowski joined the Department of Justice, he sent an email to Eastman with an attachment of draft talking points arguing that state legislators in states where Biden won could disregard the election results and appoint electors for Trump. *See* Documents on file with the Select Committee to Investigate the January 6th Attack on the United States Capitol (Chapman University Production), Chapman028219, Chapman028220 (December 9, 2020, email from Klukowski to Eastman, attaching memo). Those same talking points were circulated the same day among Ken Blackwell, Ed Meese, John Eastman, Jason Miller, Alan Dershowitz, and Chief of Staff Mark Meadows with Blackwell's comment, "A constitutional road map to victory and DJT's reelection! It's a matter of political will and courage to do the right thing." *See* Documents on file with the Select Committee to Investigate the January 6th Attack on the United States Capitol (Chapman University Production), Chapman027943, Chapman027944 (Klukowski was not included on the email from Blackwell, but his talking points were attached). During his deposition with the Select Committee, Klukowski said that the document containing the talking points looked like a document he had drafted, but asserted attorney-client privilege when asked certain questions asked about the document. *See* Select Committee to Investigate the January 6th Attack on the United States Capitol, Continued Deposition of Kenneth Klukowski, (June 10, 2022), pp. 27-29. The Select Committee also obtained from a source other than Klukowski an email sent to him, Eastman, Rep. Louis Gohmert's Chief of Staff, and others on December 28th with the subject line "VP Briefing on 1/6/21 Meeting" and a message from Edward Corrigan that said, "I believe the VP and his staff would benefit greatly from a briefing by John and Ken" but cautioned to "make sure we don't overexpose Ken given his new position." *See* Documents on file with the Select Committee to Investigate the January 6th Attack on the United States Capitol (Chapman University Production), Chapman056164 (December 28, 2020, email to Klukowski and others). Klukowski said he never participated in such a briefing, but Eastman did in the days leading up to January 6th and encouraged

the Vice President to prevent or delay the certification of the presidential election during the joint session of Congress. *See* Select Committee to Investigate the January 6th Attack on the United States Capitol, Deposition of Kenneth Klukowski, (June 10, 2022), pp. 50-57; *see also* Chapter 5 about Eastman and his communications with the Vice President. As described here, Klukowski drafted the letter for Clark that included discussions about state legislatures, Electoral College electors, and the joint session of Congress.

206. Select Committee to Investigate the January 6th Attack on the United States Capitol, Deposition of Kenneth Klukowski (Dec. 15, 2021), p. 17.

207. Select Committee to Investigate the January 6th Attack on the United States Capitol, Deposition of Kenneth Klukowski, (Dec. 15, 2021), p. 23; Documents on file with the Select Committee to Investigate the January 6th Attack on the United States Capitol (Department of Justice Production), HouseSelect-Jan6-PartII-12142021-000104. Klukowski's first day on the job was December 15th. When asked why he would be willing to start a job on December 15th that would end by January 20th, Klukowski said that he had been trying to get to the Department of Justice for several months, he was "hopeful" that he could "get as many medals on my chest as possible during that short period of time," and "given that it was going to cross the New Year's dateline, [he] figured [his] resume would say Department of Justice 2020 and 2021," enabling him to get into an interview for future jobs before a future employer "would find out how few of days in each of those calendar years we were actually talking about." Select Committee to Investigate the January 6th Attack on the United States Capitol, Deposition of Kenneth Klukowski, (Dec. 15, 2021), pp. 30, 41.

208. Select Committee to Investigate the January 6th Attack on the United States Capitol, Deposition of Kenneth Klukowski, (Dec. 15, 2021), pp. 65-66.

209. Select Committee to Investigate the January 6th Attack on the United States Capitol, Deposition of Kenneth Klukowski, (Dec. 15, 2021), pp. 71-73.

210. Select Committee to Investigate the January 6th Attack on the United States Capitol, Deposition of Kenneth Klukowski, (Dec. 15, 2021), pp. 66, 75-76.

211. Documents on file with the Select Committee to Investigate the January 6th Attack on the United States Capitol (Department of Justice Production), HCOR-Pre-CertificationEvents-06032021-000200 (December 28, 2020, email from Richard Donoghue to Jeffrey Clark, cc'ing Jeffrey Rosen, including Rosen's reply to Donoghue).

212. Documents on file with the Select Committee to Investigate the January 6th Attack on the United States Capitol (Department of Justice Production), HCOR-Pre-CertificationEvents-06032021-000200 (December 28, 2020, email from Richard Donoghue to Jeffrey Clark, cc'ing Jeffrey Rosen, including Rosen's reply to Donoghue).

213. Documents on file with the Select Committee to Investigate the January 6th Attack on the United States Capitol (Department of Justice Production), HCOR-Pre-CertificationEvents-06032021-000200 (December 28, 2020, email from Richard Donoghue to Jeffrey Clark, cc'ing Jeffrey Rosen, including Rosen's reply to Donoghue).

214. Documents on file with the Select Committee to Investigate the January 6th Attack on the United States Capitol (Department of Justice Production), HCOR-Pre-CertificationEvents-06032021-000200 (December 28, 2020, email from Richard Donoghue to Jeffrey Clark, cc'ing Jeffrey Rosen, including Rosen's reply to Donoghue).

215. Select Committee to Investigate the January 6th Attack on the United States Capitol, Transcribed Interview of Richard Peter Donoghue, (Oct. 1, 2021), pp. 81-82.

216. Select Committee to Investigate the January 6th Attack on the United States Capitol, Transcribed Interview of Richard Peter Donoghue, (Oct. 1, 2021), p. 82.

217. Select Committee to Investigate the January 6th Attack on the United States Capitol, Transcribed Interview of Richard Peter Donoghue, (Oct. 1, 2021), p. 83.

218. Select Committee to Investigate the January 6th Attack on the United States Capitol, Transcribed Interview of Richard Peter Donoghue, (Oct. 1, 2021), p. 82.

219. Documents on file with the Select Committee to Investigate the January 6th Attack on the United States Capitol (Department of Justice Production), HCOR-Pre-CertificationEvents-07262021-000681 (Department of Justice policy), HCOR-Pre-CertificationEvents-07262021-000685 (White House policy).

220. Select Committee to Investigate the January 6th Attack on the United States Capitol, *Hearing on the January 6th Investigation*, 117th Cong., 2d sess., (June 23, 2022), available at https://www.govinfo.gov/committee/house-january6th.

221. Select Committee to Investigate the January 6th Attack on the United States Capitol, *Hearing on the January 6th Investigation*, 117th Cong., 2d sess., (June 23, 2022), available at https://www.govinfo.gov/committee/house-january6th.

222. Select Committee to Investigate the January 6th Attack on the United States Capitol, Transcribed Interview of Steven Engel, (Jan. 13, 2022), pp. 27-28.

223. Select Committee to Investigate the January 6th Attack on the United States Capitol, Transcribed Interview of Richard Peter Donoghue, (Oct. 1, 2021), pp. 86-87; Select Committee to Investigate the January 6th Attack on the United States Capitol, Transcribed Interview of Jeffrey Rosen, (Oct. 13, 2021), pp. 79-80, 91-92, 132-33.

224. Select Committee to Investigate the January 6th Attack on the United States Capitol, Transcribed Interview of Jeffrey Rosen, (Oct. 13, 2021), pp. 91-93, 132-33.

225. Select Committee to Investigate the January 6th Attack on the United States Capitol, Transcribed Interview of Richard Peter Donoghue, (Oct. 1, 2021), p. 87; Select Committee to Investigate the January 6th Attack on the United States Capitol, Transcribed Interview of Jeffrey Rosen, (Oct. 13, 2021), pp. 91-93, 132-33.

226. Select Committee to Investigate the January 6th Attack on the United States Capitol, Transcribed Interview of Richard Peter Donoghue, (Oct. 1, 2021), pp. 88-89; Documents on file with the Select Committee to Investigate the January 6th Attack on the United States Capitol (Department of Justice Production), HCOR-Pre-CertificationEvents-06032021-000678 (January 1, 2021, email from Mark Meadows to Jeffrey Rosen with link to YouTube video); Brad Johnson, "Rome, Satellites, Servers: an Update," YouTube, available at https://web.archive.org/web/20210102201919/https://www.youtube.com/watch?v=YwtbK5XXAMk&feature=youtu.be (archived) (showing the conspiracy Meadows asked DOJ to investigate).

227. Select Committee to Investigate the January 6th Attack on the United States Capitol, Transcribed Interview of Richard Peter Donoghue, (Oct. 1, 2021), pp. 88-90.

228. Select Committee to Investigate the January 6th Attack on the United States Capitol, Transcribed Interview of Richard Peter Donoghue, (Oct. 1, 2021), p. 89.

229. Select Committee to Investigate the January 6th Attack on the United States Capitol, Transcribed Interview of Richard Peter Donoghue, (Oct. 1, 2021), pp. 90-91.

230. Select Committee to Investigate the January 6th Attack on the United States Capitol, Transcribed Interview of Richard Peter Donoghue, (Oct. 1, 2021), pp. 87, 91-92; Documents on file with the Select Committee to Investigate the January 6th Attack on the United States Capitol (Department of Justice Production), HCOR-Pre-CertificationEvents-07262021-000708 (December 31, 2020, email from Steven Engel to Richard Donoghue attaching "U.S. v. Penn OJ suit").

231. Documents on file with the Select Committee to Investigate the January 6th Attack on the United States Capitol (Department of Justice Production), HCOR-Pre-CertificationEvents-07262021-000708 - HCOR-Pre-CertificationEvents-07262021-000709 (December 31, 2020, email from Steven Engel to Richard Donoghue attaching "U.S. v. Penn OJ suit" re: one pager, with document titled "Evaluation of Potential Original-Jurisdiction Suit in the Supreme Court"); Select Committee to Investigate the January 6th Attack on the United States Capitol, Transcribed Interview of Richard Peter Donoghue, (Oct. 1, 2021), pp. 91-92.

232. Documents on file with the Select Committee to Investigate the January 6th Attack on the United States Capitol (Department of Justice Production), HCOR-Pre-CertificationEvents-07262021-000709 (Document titled "Evaluation of Potential Original-Jurisdiction Suit in the Supreme Court").

233. Documents on file with the Select Committee to Investigate the January 6th Attack on the United States Capitol (Department of Justice Production), HCOR-Pre-CertificationEvents-07262021-000709 (Document titled "Evaluation of Potential Original-Jurisdiction Suit in the Supreme Court").

234. Documents on file with the Select Committee to Investigate the January 6th Attack on the United States Capitol (Department of Justice Production), HCOR-Pre-CertificationEvents-07262021-000709 (Document titled "Evaluation of Potential Original-Jurisdiction Suit in the Supreme Court").

235. Documents on file with the Select Committee to Investigate the January 6th Attack on the United States Capitol (Department of Justice Production), HCOR-Pre-Certificationevents-07262021-000709 (Document titled "Evaluation of Potential Original-Jurisdiction Suit in the Supreme Court").

236. Documents on file with the Select Committee to Investigate the January 6th Attack on the United States Capitol (Department of Justice Production), HCOR-Pre-Certificationevents-07262021-000709 (Document titled "Evaluation of Potential Original-Jurisdiction Suit in the Supreme Court"). The memo cites *United States v. Texas* although it likely refers to the case filed by Texas and rejected by the Supreme Court, *Texas v. Pennsylvania. See* Order Dismissing Bill of Complaint and Denying Certiorari, *Texas v. Pennsylvania*, 592 U.S. ___, (Dec. 11, 2020) (No. 155, Orig.), available at https://www.supremecourt.gov/orders/courtorders/121120zr_p860.pdf.

237. Select Committee to Investigate the January 6th Attack on the United States Capitol, Transcribed Interview of Steven Engel, (Jan. 13, 2022), p. 33.

238. Select Committee to Investigate the January 6th Attack on the United States Capitol, Transcribed Interview of Richard Peter Donoghue, (Oct. 1, 2021), pp. 87, 91-92 (noting the Department's limited authority relative to *United States v. Pennsylvania*); Select Committee to Investigate the January 6th Attack on the United States Capitol, *Hearing on the January 6th Investigation*, 117th Cong., 2d sess., (June 23, 2022), available at https://www.govinfo.gov/committee/house-january6th (summarizing the many times Department officials told the President about the limited authority to take actions related to the election).

239. Select Committee to Investigate the January 6th Attack on the United States Capitol, Transcribed Interview of Jeffrey Rosen, (Oct. 13, 2021), pp. 96-97.

240. Select Committee to Investigate the January 6th Attack on the United States Capitol, Transcribed Interview of Jeffrey Rosen, (Oct. 13, 2021), pp. 96-97.

241. Select Committee to Investigate the January 6th Attack on the United States Capitol, Transcribed Interview of Jeffrey Rosen, (Oct. 13, 2021), pp. 96-97.

242. Select Committee to Investigate the January 6th Attack on the United States Capitol, Transcribed Interview of Jeffrey Rosen, (Oct. 13, 2021), pp. 96-97.

243. Select Committee to Investigate the January 6th Attack on the United States Capitol, Transcribed Interview of Richard Peter Donoghue, (Oct. 1, 2021), p. 106.

244. Select Committee to Investigate the January 6th Attack on the United States Capitol, Transcribed Interview of Richard Peter Donoghue, (Oct. 1, 2021), p. 106.

245. Select Committee to Investigate the January 6th Attack on the United States Capitol, Transcribed Interview of Richard Peter Donoghue, (Oct. 1, 2021), p. 107.

246. Select Committee to Investigate the January 6th Attack on the United States Capitol, Transcribed Interview of Richard Peter Donoghue, (Oct. 1, 2021), p. 107.

247. Select Committee to Investigate the January 6th Attack on the United States Capitol, Transcribed Interview of Richard Peter Donoghue, (Oct. 1, 2021), pp. 107-08.

248. Select Committee to Investigate the January 6th Attack on the United States Capitol, Transcribed Interview of Richard Peter Donoghue, (Oct. 1, 2021), p. 108.

249. Select Committee to Investigate the January 6th Attack on the United States Capitol, Transcribed Interview of Richard Peter Donoghue, (Oct. 1, 2021), p. 108.

250. Select Committee to Investigate the January 6th Attack on the United States Capitol, Transcribed Interview of Richard Peter Donoghue, (Oct. 1, 2021), p. 108.

251. Select Committee to Investigate the January 6th Attack on the United States Capitol, Transcribed Interview of Richard Peter Donoghue, (Oct. 1, 2021), p. 108.

252. Select Committee to Investigate the January 6th Attack on the United States Capitol, Transcribed Interview of Richard Peter Donoghue, (Oct. 1, 2021), pp. 108-09.

253. Select Committee to Investigate the January 6th Attack on the United States Capitol, Transcribed Interview of Richard Peter Donoghue, (Oct. 1, 2021), pp. 108-09.

254. "Hand Audit of All Presidential Election Votes in Antrim County Confirms Previously Certified Results, Voting Machines Were Accurate," Michigan Secretary of State, (Dec. 17, 2020), available at https://www.michigan.gov/sos/resources/news/2020/12/17/hand-audit-of-all-presidential-election-votes-in-antrim-county-confirms-previously-certified-result.

255. Select Committee to Investigate the January 6th Attack on the United States Capitol, Transcribed Interview of Richard Peter Donoghue, (Oct. 1, 2021), p. 109.

256. Select Committee to Investigate the January 6th Attack on the United States Capitol, Transcribed Interview of Richard Peter Donoghue, (Oct. 1, 2021), p. 109.

257. Select Committee to Investigate the January 6th Attack on the United States Capitol, Transcribed Interview of Richard Peter Donoghue, (Oct. 1, 2021), p. 109.

258. Select Committee to Investigate the January 6th Attack on the United States Capitol, Transcribed Interview of Richard Peter Donoghue, (Oct. 1, 2021), pp. 109-10.

259. Select Committee to Investigate the January 6th Attack on the United States Capitol, Transcribed Interview of Richard Peter Donoghue, (Oct. 1, 2021), p. 110.

260. Select Committee to Investigate the January 6th Attack on the United States Capitol, Transcribed Interview of Richard Peter Donoghue, (Oct. 1, 2021), p. 110.

261. Select Committee to Investigate the January 6th Attack on the United States Capitol, Transcribed Interview of Richard Peter Donoghue, (Oct. 1, 2021), pp. 109-10.

262. Select Committee to Investigate the January 6th Attack on the United States Capitol, Transcribed Interview of Richard Peter Donoghue, (Oct. 1, 2021), pp. 109-11.

263. Select Committee to Investigate the January 6th Attack on the United States Capitol, Hearing on the January 6th Investigation, 117th Cong., 2d sess., (June 23, 2022), available at https://www.govinfo.gov/committee/house-january6th; Select Committee to Investigate the January 6th Attack on the United States Capitol, Transcribed Interview of Jeffrey Rosen, (Oct. 13, 2021), pp. 72-73.

264. Select Committee to Investigate the January 6th Attack on the United States Capitol, Hearing on the January 6th Investigation, 117th Cong., 2d sess., (June 23, 2022), available at https://www.govinfo.gov/committee/house-january6th; Select Committee to Investigate the January 6th Attack on the United States Capitol, Transcribed Interview of Jeffrey Rosen, (Oct. 13, 2021), pp. 72-73.

265. Select Committee to Investigate the January 6th Attack on the United States Capitol, Transcribed Interview of Richard Peter Donoghue, (Oct. 1, 2021), p. 114.

266. Select Committee to Investigate the January 6th Attack on the United States Capitol, Transcribed Interview of Richard Peter Donoghue, (Oct. 1, 2021), pp. 113-14.

267. Select Committee to Investigate the January 6th Attack on the United States Capitol, Transcribed Interview of Richard Peter Donoghue, (Oct. 1, 2021), p. 113.

268. Select Committee to Investigate the January 6th Attack on the United States Capitol, Transcribed Interview of Richard Peter Donoghue, (Oct. 1, 2021), p. 113.

269. Select Committee to Investigate the January 6th Attack on the United States Capitol, Transcribed Interview of Richard Peter Donoghue, (Oct. 1, 2021), pp. 111-15.

270. Rosen confirmed this during testimony before the Select Committee. "ADAM KINZINGER: So in that meeting did Mr. Clark say he would turn down the President's offer if you reversed your position and signed the letter? JEFFREY A. ROSEN: Yes." Select Committee to Investigate the January 6th Attack on the United States Capitol, *Hearing on the January 6th Investigation*, 117th Cong., 2d sess., (June 23, 2022), available at https://www.govinfo.gov/committee/house-january6th

271. Select Committee to Investigate the January 6th Attack on the United States Capitol, *Hearing on the January 6th Investigation*, 117th Cong., 2d sess., (June 23, 2022), available at https://www.govinfo.gov/committee/house-january6th.

272. Documents on file with the Select Committee to Investigate the January 6th Attack on the United States Capitol (Department of Justice Production), HCOR-Pre-CertificationEvents-06032021-000200 (January 2, 2021, email from Jeffrey Rosen to Richard Donoghue re: Two Urgent Action Items).

273. Brad Raffensperger, *Integrity Counts* (New York: Simon & Schuster, 2021), p. 191 (reproducing the call transcript); Amy Gardner and Paulina Firozi, "Here's the Full Transcript and Audio of the Call between Trump and Raffensperger," *Washington Post*, (Jan. 5, 2021), available at https://www.washingtonpost.com/politics/trump-raffensperger-call-transcript-georgia-vote/2021/01/03/2768e0cc-4ddd-11eb-83e3-322644d82356_story.html.

274. Select Committee to Investigate the January 6th Attack on the United States Capitol, Transcribed Interview of Richard Peter Donoghue, (Oct. 1, 2021), pp. 117-18; Select Committee to Investigate the January 6th Attack on the United States Capitol, *Hearing on the January 6th Investigation*, 117th Cong., 2d sess., (June 23, 2022), available at https://www.govinfo.gov/committee/house-january6th.

275. Select Committee to Investigate the January 6th Attack on the United States Capitol, Transcribed Interview of Richard Peter Donoghue, (Oct. 1, 2021), pp. 117-18; Select Committee to Investigate the January 6th Attack on the United States Capitol, *Hearing on the January 6th Investigation*, 117th Cong., 2d sess., (June 23, 2022), available at https://www.govinfo.gov/committee/house-january6th.

276. Select Committee to Investigate the January 6th Attack on the United States Capitol, Transcribed Interview of Richard Peter Donoghue, (Oct. 1, 2021), pp. 117-18; Select Committee to Investigate the January 6th Attack on the United States Capitol, *Hearing on the January 6th Investigation*, 117th Cong., 2d sess., (June 23, 2022), available at https://www.govinfo.gov/committee/house-january6th.

277. Select Committee to Investigate the January 6th Attack on the United States Capitol, Transcribed Interview of Richard Peter Donoghue, (Oct. 1, 2021), p. 118.

278. Documents on file with the Select Committee to Investigate the January 6th Attack on the United States Capitol (National Archives Production), 076P-R000007891_0001 - 076P-R000007891_0009 (January 3, 2021, White House Presidential Call Log).

279. Documents on file with the Select Committee to Investigate the January 6th Attack on the United States Capitol (National Archives Production), 076P-R000007891_0001 - 076P-R000007891_0009 (January 3, 2021, White House Presidential Call Log).

280. Documents on file with the Select Committee to Investigate the January 6th Attack on the United States Capitol (National Archives Production), 076P-R000007891_0001 – 076P-R000007891_0009 (January 3, 2021, White House Presidential Call Log).

281. Select Committee to Investigate the January 6th Attack on the United States Capitol, *Hearing on the January 6th Investigation*, 117th Cong., 2d sess., (June 23, 2022), available at https://www.govinfo.gov/committee/house-january6th.

282. Select Committee to Investigate the January 6th Attack on the United States Capitol, *Hearing on the January 6th Investigation*, 117th Cong., 2d sess., (June 23, 2022), available at https://www.govinfo.gov/committee/house-january6th.

283. Select Committee to Investigate the January 6th Attack on the United States Capitol, Transcribed Interview of Richard Peter Donoghue, (Oct. 1, 2021), p. 118; Select Committee to Investigate the January 6th Attack on the United States Capitol, *Hearing on the January 6th Investigation*, 117th Cong., 2d sess., (June 23, 2022), available at https://www.govinfo.gov/committee/house-january6th.

284. Select Committee to Investigate the January 6th Attack on the United States Capitol, *Hearing on the January 6th Investigation*, 117th Cong., 2d sess., (June 23, 2022), available at https://www.govinfo.gov/committee/house-january6th.

285. Select Committee to Investigate the January 6th Attack on the United States Capitol, *Hearing on the January 6th Investigation*, 117th Cong., 2d sess., (June 23, 2022), available at https://www.govinfo.gov/committee/house-january6th.

286. Select Committee to Investigate the January 6th Attack on the United States Capitol, *Hearing on the January 6th Investigation*, 117th Cong., 2d sess., (June 23, 2022), available at https://www.govinfo.gov/committee/house-january6th ("And so it was unanimous; everyone was going to resign if Jeff Rosen was removed from the seat," Donoghue explained). The only exception was John Demers, the Assistant Attorney General for the National Security Division. Donohue encouraged Demers to stay on because he didn't want to further jeopardize national security. *See* Select Committee to Investigate the January 6th Attack on the United States Capitol, Transcribed Interview of Richard Peter Donoghue, (Oct. 1, 2021), pp. 119-20.

287. Documents on file with the Select Committee to Investigate the January 6th Attack on the United States Capitol (Department of Justice Production), HCOR-Pre-CertificationEvents-07262021-000729 (January 3, 2021, Resignation Letter by Patrick Hovakimian).

288. Select Committee to Investigate the January 6th Attack on the United States Capitol, Transcribed Interview of Richard Peter Donoghue, (Oct. 1, 2021), pp. 121-22; Select Committee to Investigate the January 6th Attack on the United States Capitol, *Hearing on the January 6th Investigation*, 117th Cong., 2d sess., (June 23, 2022), available at https://www.govinfo.gov/committee/house-january6th.

289. Select Committee to Investigate the January 6th Attack on the United States Capitol, Transcribed Interview of Richard Peter Donoghue, (Oct. 1, 2021), p. 122.

290. Select Committee to Investigate the January 6th Attack on the United States Capitol, Transcribed Interview of Richard Peter Donoghue, (Oct. 1, 2021), p. 127. "It was definitely a consensus. We were all on the same page except for Jeff Clark," Donoghue said. *Id.* The Oval Office meeting attendees include Jeffrey Rosen, Richard Donoghue, Pat Cipollone, Pat Philbin, Eric Herschmann, Steve Engel, Jeff Clark and President Trump. *See id.,* at 123.

291. Select Committee to Investigate the January 6th Attack on the United States Capitol, Transcribed Interview of Richard Peter Donoghue, (Oct. 1, 2021), p. 122.

292. Select Committee to Investigate the January 6th Attack on the United States Capitol, Transcribed Interview of Richard Peter Donoghue, (Oct. 1, 2021), p. 124.

293. Select Committee to Investigate the January 6th Attack on the United States Capitol, Transcribed Interview of Richard Peter Donoghue, (Oct. 1, 2021), p. 124.

294. Select Committee to Investigate the January 6th Attack on the United States Capitol, Transcribed Interview of Richard Peter Donoghue, (Oct. 1, 2021), pp. 124-25.

295. Select Committee to Investigate the January 6th Attack on the United States Capitol, Transcribed Interview of Richard Peter Donoghue, (Oct. 1, 2021), p. 125.

296. Select Committee to Investigate the January 6th Attack on the United States Capitol, Transcribed Interview of Richard Peter Donoghue, (Oct. 1, 2021), p. 125.

297. Select Committee to Investigate the January 6th Attack on the United States Capitol, Transcribed Interview of Richard Peter Donoghue, (Oct. 1, 2021), p. 125.

298. Select Committee to Investigate the January 6th Attack on the United States Capitol, Transcribed Interview of Richard Peter Donoghue, (Oct. 1, 2021), p. 125.

299. Select Committee to Investigate the January 6th Attack on the United States Capitol, Transcribed Interview of Richard Peter Donoghue, (Oct. 1, 2021), p. 125.

300. Select Committee to Investigate the January 6th Attack on the United States Capitol, Transcribed Interview of Richard Peter Donoghue, (Oct. 1, 2021), p. 125.

301. Select Committee to Investigate the January 6th Attack on the United States Capitol, Transcribed Interview of Richard Peter Donoghue, (Oct. 1, 2021), p. 125.

302. Select Committee to Investigate the January 6th Attack on the United States Capitol, Transcribed Interview of Richard Peter Donoghue, (Oct. 1, 2021), p. 126.

303. Select Committee to Investigate the January 6th Attack on the United States Capitol, Transcribed Interview of Richard Peter Donoghue, (Oct. 1, 2021), pp. 126-27.

304. Select Committee to Investigate the January 6th Attack on the United States Capitol, Transcribed Interview of Richard Peter Donoghue, (Oct. 1, 2021), p. 126.

305. Select Committee to Investigate the January 6th Attack on the United States Capitol, Transcribed Interview of Richard Peter Donoghue, (Oct. 1, 2021), p. 126.

306. Select Committee to Investigate the January 6th Attack on the United States Capitol, Transcribed Interview of Richard Peter Donoghue, (Oct. 1, 2021), p. 126.

307. Select Committee to Investigate the January 6th Attack on the United States Capitol, Transcribed Interview of Richard Peter Donoghue, (Oct. 1, 2021), p. 133.

308. Select Committee to Investigate the January 6th Attack on the United States Capitol, Transcribed Interview of Richard Peter Donoghue, (Oct. 1, 2021), pp. 131-32.

309. Select Committee to Investigate the January 6th Attack on the United States Capitol, Transcribed Interview of Richard Peter Donoghue, (Oct. 1, 2021), p. 132.

310. Select Committee to Investigate the January 6th Attack on the United States Capitol, Transcribed Interview of Richard Peter Donoghue, (Oct. 1, 2021), p. 132.

311. Select Committee to Investigate the January 6th Attack on the United States Capitol, Transcribed Interview of Richard Peter Donoghue, (Oct. 1, 2021), pp. 129-31.

312. Select Committee to Investigate the January 6th Attack on the United States Capitol, Transcribed Interview of Byung Jin Pak, (May 19, 2022), pp. 11-19.

313. Select Committee to Investigate the January 6th Attack on the United States Capitol, Transcribed Interview of Richard Peter Donoghue, (Oct. 1, 2021), p. 129.

314. Select Committee to Investigate the January 6th Attack on the United States Capitol, Transcribed Interview of Richard Peter Donoghue, (Oct. 1, 2021), p. 129.

315. Select Committee to Investigate the January 6th Attack on the United States Capitol, Transcribed Interview of Richard Peter Donoghue, (Oct. 1, 2021), p. 129.

316. Select Committee to Investigate the January 6th Attack on the United States Capitol, Transcribed Interview of Richard Peter Donoghue, (Oct. 1, 2021), p. 129.

317. Select Committee to Investigate the January 6th Attack on the United States Capitol, Transcribed Interview of Richard Peter Donoghue, (Oct. 1, 2021), p. 129.

318. Select Committee to Investigate the January 6th Attack on the United States Capitol, Transcribed Interview of Richard Peter Donoghue, (Oct. 1, 2021), p. 129-30.

319. Select Committee to Investigate the January 6th Attack on the United States Capitol, Transcribed Interview of Richard Peter Donoghue, (Oct. 1, 2021), pp. 134-35.

320. Select Committee to Investigate the January 6th Attack on the United States Capitol, Transcribed Interview of Richard Peter Donoghue, (Oct. 1, 2021), p. 130.

321. Select Committee to Investigate the January 6th Attack on the United States Capitol, Transcribed Interview of Richard Peter Donoghue, (Oct. 1, 2021), p. 130.

322. Select Committee to Investigate the January 6th Attack on the United States Capitol, Transcribed Interview of Richard Peter Donoghue, (Oct. 1, 2021), pp. 135-36.

323. Select Committee to Investigate the January 6th Attack on the United States Capitol, Transcribed Interview of Richard Peter Donoghue, (Oct. 1, 2021), pp. 133-34.

324. Select Committee to Investigate the January 6th Attack on the United States Capitol, Transcribed Interview of Richard Peter Donoghue, (Oct. 1, 2021), pp. 133-34.

325. Select Committee to Investigate the January 6th Attack on the United States Capitol, Transcribed Interview of Richard Peter Donoghue, (Oct. 1, 2021), p. 134.

326. Select Committee to Investigate the January 6th Attack on the United States Capitol, Transcribed Interview of Richard Peter Donoghue, (Oct. 1, 2021), pp. 134-37.

327. Select Committee to Investigate the January 6th Attack on the United States Capitol, Transcribed Interview of William Barr, (June 2, 2022), p. 66.

328. Select Committee to Investigate the January 6th Attack on the United States Capitol, *Hearing on the January 6th Investigation*, 117th Cong., 2d sess., (June 23, 2022), available at https://www.govinfo.gov/committee/house-january6th.

329. Select Committee to Investigate the January 6th Attack on the United States Capitol, Transcribed Interview of Jeffrey Rosen, (Oct. 13, 2021), pp. 8-9.

5

"A COUP IN SEARCH OF A LEGAL THEORY"

On the morning of January 6, 2021, Vice President Michael R. Pence gathered his staff to pray. Vice President Pence and his closest advisors knew the day ahead "would be a challenging one."[1] They asked God for "guidance and wisdom" in the hours to come.[2] No Republican had been more loyal to President Donald J. Trump throughout his turbulent presidency than Vice President Pence. The Vice President rarely, if ever, criticized his boss. But as January 6th approached, President Trump turned on his own Vice President.

President Trump was desperate. As described in the previous chapters, the President was searching for a way to stay in power. He had lost the election to former Vice President Biden. He had run out of legal options to overturn the election weeks earlier, when his lawyers lost nearly every court challenge they filed.

The President pursued other means as well. President Trump and his lawyers tried to convince State and local officials to overturn the election, but they met resistance. Those same officials would not break the law or violate their oath to the Constitution. President Trump and his associates tried to convince State legislatures to replace the legitimate electors won by former Vice President Biden with Trump electors. The Trump Campaign even convened their own fake electors who submitted false electoral votes to Washington. But those efforts failed, too.

President Trump also attempted to use the Department of Justice (DOJ) for his own corrupt political purposes. President Trump offered the job of Acting Attorney General to a loyalist. He wanted this same DOJ official, Jeffrey Clark, to send a letter to several States suggesting that they should certify the fake electors convened by the Trump Campaign. President Trump's effort to subvert the DOJ came to a head on January 3rd, when the Department's senior personnel and lawyers in the White House Counsel's Office threatened mass resignations if Clark was installed.

At that point, theories about a role the Vice President could play at the joint session had been circulating in certain corners of the internet and among Trump-supporting attorneys.[3] President Trump focused his attention on the man who had loyally served by his side for four years.

On January 4, 2021, President Trump summoned Vice President Pence to a meeting in the Oval Office with John Eastman, a law professor representing President Trump in litigation challenging the election result. Eastman argued, on President Trump's behalf, that the Vice President could take matters into his own hands during the joint session on January 6th. Eastman offered Vice President Pence two options. First, the Vice President could unilaterally reject the certified electors from several States won by former Vice President Biden, thereby handing the presidency to President Trump. Or, according to Eastman, Vice President Pence could delay the joint session to give State legislatures the opportunity to certify new electors loyal to the President. Eastman admitted, in front of the president, that both options violated the Electoral Count Act of 1887, the statute that sets forth the process for counting and disputing electoral votes during the joint session.[4] Eastman admitted as much in a subsequent conversation with the Vice President's staff as well.[5]

Therefore, President Trump knew, or should have known, that this scheme was illegal—in fact, it violated the Electoral Count Act and the U.S. Constitution. President Trump repeatedly demanded that Vice President Pence go through with it anyway.

Vice President Pence rejected President Trump's demands "many times" on January 4th and in the days that followed.[6] Vice President Pence correctly pointed out that he had no power to take any action other than counting the certified electoral votes. America's founders could not possibly have contemplated a scenario in which the Vice President could unilaterally reject electoral votes and decide the outcome of a Presidential election. However, instead of backing down, President Trump ratcheted up the pressure even further, relentlessly harassing Vice President Pence both in public and in private.

President Trump used his bully pulpit, at rallies and on Twitter, to lie to his supporters. President Trump told them that Vice President Pence had the power to deliver another 4 years in the White House. It was not true. President Trump's campaign of coercion became so intense that Marc Short, Vice President Pence's Chief of Staff, alerted the head of the Vice President's Secret Service detail to the impending danger. On January 5th, Short warned that as the "disagreements" between President Trump and Vice President Pence "became more public, that the president would lash out in some way."[7]

Indeed, President Trump did. And those around him recognized that his lashing out at the Vice President could have disastrous consequences. On the morning of January 6th, an agent in the Secret Service's intelligence division was alerted to online chatter "regarding the VP being a dead man walking if he doesn't do the right thing." [8] A few minutes later, another agent made a comment that turned out to be an ominous prediction: "I saw several other alerts saying they will storm the [C]apitol if he [the Vice President] doesn't do the right thing etc." [9]

During his speech at the Ellipse on January 6th, President Trump repeatedly pointed his finger at Vice President Pence. President Trump insisted that "if Mike Pence does the right thing, we win the election." [10] President Trump added: "And Mike Pence is going to have to come through for us, and if he doesn't, that will be a, a sad day for our country because you're sworn to uphold our Constitution." [11]

President Trump's scheme required Vice President Pence to *break* his oath to the Constitution, not uphold it. By the time President Trump spoke at the Ellipse, he also knew that Vice President Pence had no intention of overturning the election.

President Trump then sent a mob to the U.S. Capitol. He did so even after being informed by the Secret Service that people in the crowd possessed weapons. He wanted his supporters to intimidate Vice President Pence and any other Republican who refused his demands. The President told the crowd assembled before him to march down Pennsylvania Avenue, to "our Republicans, the weak ones" at the U.S. Capitol, "to try and give them the kind of pride and boldness that they need to take back our country." [12]

The mob overran the U.S. Capitol in short order. At 2:24 p.m., while the attack was well underway, President Trump tweeted:

> *Mike Pence didn't have the courage to do what should have been done to protect our Country and our Constitution, giving States a chance to certify a corrected set of facts, not the fraudulent or inaccurate ones which they were asked to previously certify. USA demands the truth!* [13]

Again, the opposite was true. Vice President Pence showed courage on January 6th. The Vice President refused to be intimidated by President Trump's mob, even as chants of "Hang Mike Pence!" echoed throughout the halls of the U.S. Capitol and a makeshift gallows was constructed on the Capitol grounds.[14]

It is no mystery why the mob turned on Vice President Pence. President Trump told his supporters that the election was stolen, and that Vice President Pence had the power, but lacked the courage, to fix it. None of this was true.

President Trump and Vice President Pence have both reflected on the events of January 6th in the months since then. Vice President Pence has described President Trump's demands as "un-American."[15] President Trump has since insisted that Vice President Pence "could have overturned the Election!"[16] Asked about the calls to hang the Vice President, President Trump said it was "common sense."[17]

In early 2022, U.S. District Judge David Carter evaluated the Trump-Eastman scheme to pressure the Vice President. Judge Carter described it as "a campaign to overturn a democratic election, an action unprecedented in American history."[18] It was "a coup in search of a legal theory," Judge Carter found, that likely violated at least two Federal laws.[19] The Trump-Eastman scheme was not a feature of the U.S. Constitution, as President Trump told his supporters. Instead, it "would have permanently ended the peaceful transition of power, undermining American democracy and the Constitution."[20]

And it all began because President Trump refused to accept the result of the election, expressed through the votes of 81 million Americans.

5.1   PRESIDENT TRUMP AND HIS ALLIES EMBARK ON A DESPERATE GAMBIT TO BLOCK CERTIFICATION OF THE 2020 PRESIDENTIAL ELECTION.

THE INTELLECTUAL FRAMEWORK FOR THE THEORY THAT THE VICE PRESIDENT COULD CHANGE THE OUTCOME OF THE ELECTION AT THE JOINT SESSION EMERGED FROM DISCUSSIONS AMONG THE LAWYERS WORKING WITH THE TRUMP CAMPAIGN AFTER THE 2020 ELECTION.

When the electoral college met to cast votes for the certified winner in each State on December 14, 2020, any possibility of President Trump reversing his defeat came to an end. The contest was decided well before then, but December 14th marked what should have been the formal end of the Trump campaign. Former Vice President Biden had won the election and his victory was cemented by the States' electoral votes. Instead of bowing to this reality, some pro-Trump lawyers had already begun scheming ways to deny the inevitable. Over the course of the post-election period, as their other plans each failed, the importance of January 6th and the need to pressure Vice President Pence increased. These same lawyers concluded that the Vice President could help President Trump subvert the election on January 6th, but they would need Vice President Pence to set aside history and the law to do so. They'd need him to violate the Electoral Count Act of 1887 ("the ECA"). The ECA had governed the joint session for 130 years, but it was an inconvenient barrier for President Trump's plan to stay in office.

KENNETH CHESEBRO ARTICULATED A "PRESIDENT OF THE SENATE" STRATEGY IN EARLY DECEMBER, WHEN THE TRUMP CAMPAIGN WAS CONVENING "ALTERNATE" ELECTORS IN KEY STATES PRESIDENT TRUMP LOST.

On December 13, 2020, Kenneth Chesebro, a pro-Trump lawyer, sent a memo to Rudolph Giuliani, the President's lead outside counsel, upon request from Trump Campaign official Boris Epshteyn.[21] Chesebro laid out a "'President of the Senate' strategy," arguing that the "President of the Senate" ("he, and he alone") is charged with "making judgments about what to do if there are conflicting votes."[22] Chesebro argued that when the joint session met on January 6th, the President of the Senate should not count Arizona's electoral college votes for former Vice President Biden, "[b]ecause there are two slates of votes."[23] Of course, there were not two legitimate "slates of votes" from Arizona. There were the official electors, certified by the State, and a group of fake electors convened by the Trump campaign.

Chesebro's memo set President Trump's pressure campaign on a course to target the Vice President on January 6.[24] Judge Carter found that the "draft memo pushed a strategy that knowingly violated the Electoral Count Act" and "is both intimately related to and clearly advanced the plan to obstruct the Joint Session of Congress on January 6, 2021."[25] That plan was also advanced by John Eastman.[26]

ON DECEMBER 23, JOHN EASTMAN DRAFTED THE FIRST OF HIS TWO "JANUARY 6TH SCENARIO" MEMOS, ARTICULATING THE ARGUMENT THAT UNDER THE CONSTITUTION THE VICE PRESIDENT IS THE "ULTIMATE ARBITER."

On December 23, 2020, Eastman wrote a two-page memo summarizing ways to ensure that "President Trump is re-elected."[27] Eastman suggested that Vice President Pence could refuse to count the electoral college votes from seven States: Arizona, Georgia, Michigan, Nevada, New Mexico, Pennsylvania, and Wisconsin. According to Eastman, Vice President Pence could simply reject these States' electoral college votes. At that point, President Trump would have 232 electoral college votes compared to former Vice President Biden's 222. This was sufficient, in Eastman's view, to guarantee President Trump's victory, because he would have a majority of the electoral college votes. "Pence then gavels President Trump as re-elected," Eastman wrote.

Eastman considered the possibility that Democrats in Congress would object, stating the plain truth that 270 electoral college votes are necessary to win. In that event, according to Eastman, the election could be sent to the House of Representatives.[28] The Republican-majority of delegations in the House would then re-elect Trump as president. Eastman concluded: "The main thing here is that Pence should do this without asking for

permission—either from a vote of the joint session or from the Court....
The fact is that the Constitution assigns this power to the Vice President as
the ultimate arbiter. We should take all of our actions with that in mind."[29]

From the start, President Trump was looped in on Eastman's proposal.
The same day Eastman started preparing the memo, he sent an email to
President Trump's assistant Molly Michael, at 1:32 p.m.: "Is the President
available for a very quick call today at some point? Just want to update him
on our overall strategic thinking."[30] Only five minutes later, Eastman
received a call from the White House switchboard; according to his phone
records, the conversation lasted for almost 23 minutes.[31]

EASTMAN CHANGED HIS EVALUATION OF THE 12TH AMENDMENT, AND THE ROLE OF THE VICE PRESIDENT, AFTER PRESIDENT TRUMP LOST THE ELECTION.

In Eastman's theory, which was the foundation of President Trump's January 6th plot, the Vice President of the United States is the "ultimate arbiter" and could unilaterally decide the victor of the 2020 Presidential
election.[32] However, just before the 2020 presidential election, Eastman had
acknowledged in writing that the Vice President had no such expansive
power.

In the course of a lengthy exchange of ideas and emails throughout the
pre- and post-election period with an individual named Bruce Colbert,
Eastman provided comments on a letter Colbert was drafting to President
Trump.[33] The draft letter purported to provide recommendations of "crucial legal actions" for the Trump Campaign to take "to help secure your
election victory as President of the United States."[34] One of the draft letter's recommendations was that "the President of the Senate decides
authoritatively what 'certificates' from the states to 'open.'" In response,
Eastman wrote on October 17, 2020, "I don't agree with this" and continued, "[t]he 12th Amendment only says that the President of the Senate
opens the ballots in the joint session and then, in the passive voice, that the
votes shall then be counted. 3 USC § 12 says merely that he is the presiding
officer, and then it spells out specific procedures, presumptions, and
default rules for which slates will be counted. *Nowhere does it suggest that
the President of the Senate gets to make the determination on his own. §15
doesn't, either.*"[35]

By the first week of December, Eastman's correspondence with this
same individual illustrates that he was open to advocating for the very
point he had rejected before the election—that is, that "the 12th Amendment confers dispositive authority on the President of the Senate to decide
which slate to count."[36] And on December 5, 2020, Eastman wrote to Colbert, "I have spoken directly with folks at the top of the chain of command
on this. They are now aware of the issues."[37]

The emails also signaled another idea that Eastman would continue to repeat in the coming weeks: that the Vice President could act without getting permission from a court. Specifically, he argued that they could take the position that the Vice President's authority was a "non-justiciable political question"—in other words, that Vice President Pence could just act, and no court would have jurisdiction to rule on the issue.[38] As Eastman's emails later in the month make clear, he thought there was an important reason to keep this issue out of the courts—they would rule that the theory was unlawful.

EASTMAN'S "JANUARY 6 SCENARIO" CLEARLY REQUIRED THE VICE PRESIDENT TO VIOLATE THE ELECTORAL COUNT ACT, THE FEDERAL LAW GOVERNING THE CERTIFICATION OF PRESIDENTIAL ELECTIONS.

There are other parts of Eastman's two-page December 23rd memo worthy of attention. Eastman wrote that Vice President Pence could recuse himself from presiding over the joint session of Congress on January 6th. In that event, the session would be overseen by the Senate President *Pro Tempore*, Senator Charles Grassley. Eastman was clearly arguing that Vice President Pence (or Senator Grassley) *should violate the Electoral Count Act.* "When he gets to Arizona, he announces that he has multiple slates of electors, and so is going to defer decision on that until finishing the other States," Eastman wrote.[39] "This would be the first break with the procedure set out in the Act."[40] This "break" with "procedure" that Eastman's memo was openly advocating for was in other words the Vice President breaking the law. When Chesebro read Eastman's memo, he commented favorably, declaring it "[r]eally awesome."[41]

At this point, Eastman continued, Congress would likely follow the "process" set forth in the Electoral Count Act, and "the two houses [would] break into their separate chambers" for debate.[42] But Eastman advised "we should not allow the Electoral Count Act constraint on debate to control" and the Trump team "should demand normal rules (which includes the filibuster)."[43] Eastman thought this would create a "stalemate," giving "the state legislatures more time to weigh in to formally support the alternate slate of electors, if they had not already done so."[44] As discussed previously in this report, at the time he drafted this memo—and throughout the post-election period—Eastman, Giuliani, President Trump and others were simultaneously working to replace certified electors for former Vice President Biden in certain States. Eastman, Giuliani, and President Trump all pressured State legislators to name their own separate electors or to certify the campaign's fake electors.

EASTMAN'S THEORY WAS—IN THE WORDS OF PRESIDENT TRUMP'S SENIOR WHITE HOUSE AND CAMPAIGN OFFICIALS—"INSANE," "CRAZY," "NUTTY" AND IT WOULD NEVER PRACTICALLY WORK.

Eric Herschmann, an attorney working for President Trump in the White House, met with Eastman to discuss his memo. Herschmann thought Eastman's plan was "crazy." Herschmann summarized the conversation to the Select Committee:

> And I said to him, hold on a second, I want to understand what you're saying. You're saying you believe the Vice President, acting as President of the Senate, can be the sole decisionmaker as to, under your theory, who becomes the next President of the United States? And he said, yes. And I said, are you out of your F'ing mind, right? And that was pretty blunt. I said, you're completely crazy. You're going to turn around and tell 78 plus million people in this country that your theory is, this is how you're going to invalidate their votes because you think the election was stolen? I said, they're not going to tolerate that. I said, you're going to cause riots in the streets. And he said words to the effect of there's been violence in this history of our country to protect the democracy or to protect the [R]epublic.[45]

As recounted by Herschmann, Eastman was shockingly unconcerned with the prospect of violence should Vice President Pence follow his and President Trump's recommended course.

Herschmann asked a straightforward question—if the States wanted to recertify their electors, then why weren't they doing it themselves? "Why aren't they already coming into session and saying, we want to change the [S]tates, and why do you need the VP to go down this path[?]"[46] Eastman had no response. In addition to being "crazy," Herschmann "didn't think there was any chance in the world" that Eastman's plan "could work."[47]

Herschmann pressed Eastman further, asking if he had "any precedent at all for the VP or anyone acting in the capacity as the President of the Senate declaring some statute invalid."[48] Eastman replied "no," but argued that "these are unprecedented times."[49] Herschmann was unimpressed, calling this a "ridiculous" answer.[50]

White House Counsel Pasquale Anthony "Pat" Cipollone thought the Eastman plan was "nutty."[51] Trump Campaign official Jason Miller testified that the Campaign's General Counsel, Matt Morgan, and Deputy Campaign Manager, Justin Clark, thought Eastman was "crazy," understood that there was "no validity to [his theory] in any way, shape, or form," and shared their views with "anyone who would listen."[52]

THE VICE PRESIDENT'S CONCLUSION THAT HE DID NOT HAVE THE ABILITY TO AFFECT THE OUTCOME OF THE ELECTION

Vice President Pence's counsel, Greg Jacob, was simultaneously researching the role of the Vice President during the joint session. The Office of the Vice President produced a preliminary staff memo on the subject on October 26, 2020.[53] Jacob then discussed the matter with Marc Short on election day or the day before.

This wasn't the first time Jacob would be required to write a memo about the Vice President's role in the electoral process. Before the election, Short explained to him that some in the White House were encouraging President Trump to prematurely declare victory on election night.[54] Of course, that is exactly what President Trump did. Jacob and Short wanted to avoid the Vice President getting drawn in to any such declarations, and Jacob pointed to his role in presiding over the counting of the electoral votes on January 6th as a reason not to. Jacob sent a memo to Short on election day reflecting this advice.[55]

Then, on December 7, 2020, the Lincoln Project aired a provocative ad taunting President Trump, saying that Vice President Pence "Will Put the Nail in Your Political Coffin" during the joint session on January 6th.[56] This prompted a discussion between Jacob and Vice President Pence.[57] Jacob authored another memo, dated December 8, 2020.[58] Jacob continued researching the Vice President's role during the joint session into early January. Jacob told the Select Committee that his view of the matter was not fully formed until then.[59]

Jacob did extensive research on and historical analysis of both the Electoral Count Act of 1887 and the 12th Amendment to the U.S. Constitution.[60] The 12th Amendment contains a single relevant line: "The President of the Senate shall, in the Presence of the Senate and House of Representatives, open all the Certificates, and the Votes shall then be counted." [61] Though Jacob concluded that this line was "inartfully drafted," it said nothing about resolving disputes over electoral votes.[62]

Jacob concluded that the Vice President must adhere to the Electoral Count Act.[63] The ECA has been followed for 130 years and "every single time that there has been any objection to electors, it has been resolved in accordance with the Electoral Count Act procedures," Jacob testified.[64] After reviewing the history and relevant cases, Jacob found that "[t]here is no justifiable basis to conclude that the Vice President has that kind of authority" to affect the outcome of the presidential election.[65] Jacob stated that his "review of text, history, and, frankly, just common sense" all confirmed that the Vice President had no such power.[66]

Greg Jacob testifies before the Select Committee on June 16, 2022.

Photo by House Creative Services

PRESIDENT TRUMP'S ALLIES FILED LAWSUITS SEEKING A COURT ORDER DIRECTING VICE PRESIDENT PENCE NOT TO COUNT CERTAIN ELECTORAL VOTES.

One of President Trump's congressional allies, Representative Louie Gohmert (R–TX), pushed a version of Eastman's theory in the courts. On December 27, 2020, Representative Gohmert and several of the Trump Campaign's fake electors for the State of Arizona (including Republican Party Chair Kelli Ward) filed suit against Vice President Pence in the U.S. District Court for the Eastern District of Texas.[67] As Ward explained to Marc Short in a phone call the day the suit was filed, President Trump was aware of the lawsuit and had signed off on it: "We wouldn't have done that without the president telling us it was okay," she told him.[68]

In the suit, the Plaintiffs alleged that there were "competing slates" of electors from five States.[69] They asked the court to rule that portions of the Electoral Count Act of 1887 were unconstitutional and that "the Twelfth Amendment contains the exclusive dispute resolution mechanisms" for determining an objection raised by a Member of Congress to the electors submitted by any State.[70] Essentially, Representative Gohmert was asking the court to tell Vice President Pence that he was prohibited from following the procedures set forth in the Electoral Count Act. Much like Eastman's

Representative Louie Gohmert outside the Capitol on March 17, 2021.
(Photo by Chip Somodevilla/Getty Images)

theory, the *Gohmert* plaintiffs asserted that the Vice President has the "exclusive authority and sole discretion" to determine which electoral votes to count.[71]

Although the *Gohmert* suit was premised on the same theory Eastman advocated, Eastman did not agree with the decision to file suit. Eastman argued that filing a suit against the Vice President had "close[ ] to zero" chance of succeeding, and there was a "very high" risk that the court would issue an opinion stating that "Pence has no authority to reject the Biden-certified ballots."[72] As highlighted by Judge Carter, Eastman's theory was that Vice President Pence should take this action "without asking for permission" from Congress or the courts.[73] Another attorney, Bill Olson, stated that getting a judicial determination "that Pence is constrained by [the Electoral Count Act]" could "completely tank the January 6 strategy."[74] Those who were advocating to press on with the Eastman scheme did not want to bring it before a Federal judge because of the high risk that a court's determination that the scheme was illegal would stop the plan to overturn the election dead in its tracks.

Eastman himself pushed this cavalier attitude towards the courts and compliance with the law during a call with Arizona House Speaker Rusty

John McEntee, February 28, 2020.

(Photo by Alex Wong/Getty Images)

Bowers on January 4th. During this call, just two days before the joint session, Eastman pressed Speaker Bowers to bring the Arizona House into session to certify Trump electors or decertify the Biden electors.[75] Speaker Bowers responded as he had previously responded to similar entreaties by Giuliani and President Trump: by explaining that doing so would require him to violate his oaths to the U.S. and Arizona Constitutions and that he "wasn't going to take such an action."[76] Undeterred, Eastman still pushed Speaker Bowers to "just do it and let the courts sort it through."[77]

Ultimately, Representative Gohmert's legal gambit failed; a U.S. district judge dismissed the case quickly.[78] The judge's ruling was upheld by the Supreme Court, which rejected Gohmert's appeal without further consideration.[79]

OTHER INDIVIDUALS ADVISING PRESIDENT TRUMP AND HIS CAMPAIGN ALSO ADVOCATED FOR A ROLE FOR THE VICE PRESIDENT AT THE JOINT SESSION.

Other individuals inside and outside the White House also advanced versions of the theory that the Vice President had agency in the joint session. The issue of Vice President Pence's role came up during a December meeting in the Oval Office. Either President Trump or his chief of staff, Mark Meadows, tasked John McEntee, the director of the Presidential Personnel Office, with researching the matter further.[80] Though McEntee was one of President Trump's close advisors, he was not a lawyer and had no relevant experience. Yet, he wrote a one-page memo claiming that "the VP has substantial discretion to address issues with the electoral process."[81]

This wasn't the only one-page analysis drafted by McEntee before January 6th.[82] He later proposed a "middle path" in which he envisioned the Vice President accepting *only half* the electoral votes from six disputed States (specifically, Wisconsin, Michigan, Pennsylvania, Georgia, Arizona and Nevada).[83] McEntee portrayed this as a way to avoid "disenfranchis-[ing]" States while still achieving the desired result: delivering a second term to President Trump. McEntee conveyed this memo to the President with a cover note reading, "This is probably our only realistic option because it would give Pence an out."[84] McEntee told the Select Committee that this judgment was based on his assessment that "it was, like, pretty obvious [the Vice President] wasn't going to just reject...the electors or whatever was being asked of him at that time."[85]

Another advocate of a plan for the Vice President to play a role in the joint session was Jenna Ellis, a lawyer working for the Trump Campaign. She argued in two memos that Vice President Pence had the power to delay the counting of certified electoral votes. In the first memo, addressed to President Trump and dated December 31, 2020, Ellis advised that Vice President Pence should "not open any of the votes" from six States that "currently have electoral delegates in dispute."[86] Ellis asserted that this "dispute" provided "sufficient rational and legal basis to question whether the [S]tate law and Constitution was followed." Ellis proposed a delay of ten days, as the Vice President and Congress awaited a "response from the [S]tate legislatures, which would then need to meet in an emergency electoral session." If any of the State legislatures "fails to provide a timely response, no electoral votes can be opened and counted from that [S]tate." Ellis claimed that Vice President Pence would not be "exercising discretion nor establishing new precedent," but instead "simply asking for clarification from the constitutionally appointed authority."[87]

Ellis sent the substance of this memorandum in an email to Fox News host Jeanine Pirro on January 1, 2021, under the subject line "Constitutional

Jenna Ellis on December 2, 2020 in Lansing, Michigan.

(Photo by Rey Del Rio/Getty Images)

option." [88] And, on January 4, 2021, she sent the same substance to Fox News contributor John Solomon under the subject line "Pence option." [89]

Ellis addressed a second memo, dated January 5, 2021, to Jay Sekulow, an outside attorney who represented President Trump during his first impeachment proceedings and in other litigation.[90] Ellis again claimed that Vice President Pence had the power to delay the certification of the vote. Ellis recommended that the Vice President should, when he arrived at the first contested State (Arizona), "simply stop the count" on the basis that the States had not made a "final determination of ascertainment of electors." "The [S]tates would therefore have to act." [91]

Sekulow clearly disagreed. "Some have speculated that the Vice President could simply say, 'I'm not going to accept these electors,' that he has the authority to do that under the Constitution," Sekulow said during an episode of his radio show.[92] "I actually don't think that's what the Constitution has in mind." Sekulow added that the Vice President serves a merely "ministerial, procedural function." [93]

In addition, Herschmann discussed this memo with Sekulow. They agreed that Ellis did not have the "qualifications or the experience to be giving advice on this" or to be "litigating the challenges" that President

Trump's team was filing in court.[94] Herschmann did not think that Sekulow shared the memo with the President.[95]

5.2 PRESIDENT TRUMP AND HIS ALLIES EXERT INTENSE PUBLIC AND PRIVATE PRESSURE ON THE VICE PRESIDENT IN ADVANCE OF THE JOINT SESSION OF CONGRESS ON JANUARY 6TH

JANUARY 2, 2021: THE VICE PRESIDENT MEETS WITH HIS ADVISORS, CEMENTING HIS INTENDED PATH FOR THE JOINT SESSION.

On January 2, 2021, Vice President Pence met with his counsel Greg Jacob, Chief of Staff Marc Short, and Matt Morgan to discuss the joint session.[96] Morgan was the Trump Campaign's General Counsel and had previously served as counsel to Vice President Pence. At this point, the Vice President already had a clear understanding of what his role would be in the electoral count.[97] Vice President Pence was concerned that most people did not understand how the certification of the electoral votes worked. So Jacob began drafting a statement for the Vice President to issue on January 6th. The statement was intended to provide a "civic education" on the joint session, explaining to the American people his actions, including why the Vice President "didn't have the authorities that others had suggested that he might." [98]

The men discussed the various points of pressure being applied to the Vice President, including Eastman's theories, the *Gohmert* suit, Ellis's arguments, as well as how the electoral count process should work. They also discussed allegations of irregularities and maladministration of the election, concluding that none of the allegations raised was sufficient to reverse President Trump's defeat.[99]

While Vice President Pence recognized Congress's authority under the Electoral Count Act to raise objections to the certification, neither he nor his staff were aware of any evidence of fraud that would have had a material effect on the outcome of the election in any State.[100] Because of President Trump's repetition of election fraud allegations, Jacob and the Vice President's staff conducted their own evaluation of these claims. Jacob asked Morgan to send the campaign's best evidence of election "fraud, maladministration, irregularities, [and] abuses in the system." [101] The Vice President's legal staff memorialized the review they conducted of these materials in a memo to Vice President Pence, which concluded: "most allegations of substantive voter fraud—defined to mean the casting of illegal ballots in violation of prevailing election laws—are either relatively small in number, or cannot be verified." [102]

Vice President Pence also discussed the Trump Campaign's fake electors with his advisors. Both Jacob and Morgan assured Vice President Pence that there were not dual slates of electors. The electors organized by the Trump Campaign were not valid.[103] Morgan had already written a memo on the topic in December, concluding that the "alternate" electors—that is, fake— lacked a certificate of ascertainment issued by the State.[104] Without such an ascertainment, the Trump Campaign's fake electors had no standing during the joint session. Jacob had also prepared a "flow chart" memo outlining each of the legal provisions implicated in the joint session on January 6th.[105] Jacob advised Vice President Pence that "none of the slates that had been sent in would qualify as an alternate slate within the meaning of the Electoral Count Act."[106] Vice President Pence was still worried that the fake elector issue was sowing confusion, so he wanted his statement on January 6th to be as transparent as possible.[107]

That same day, January 2nd, Marc Short released a brief statement on behalf of the Vice President. "Vice President Pence shares the concerns of millions of Americans about voter fraud and irregularities in the last election," the statement read. "The vice president welcomes the efforts of members of the House and Senate to use the authority they have under the law to raise objections and bring forward evidence before the Congress and the American people on January 6th."[108] Short testified that the statement was consistent with the Vice President's view that he did not have the power to reject electors.[109] Short issued this statement because of the "swirl" regarding the question of "where [Vice President Pence] stood."[110]

Steve Bannon's podcast, *War Room: Pandemic*, was one of the primary sources of this swirl.

JANUARY 2, 2021: EASTMAN AND BANNON QUESTION THE "COURAGE AND SPINE" OF VICE PRESIDENT PENCE.

Steve Bannon's podcast, *War Room: Pandemic*, was one of the primary sources of this swirl. Eastman was a guest on a January 2nd episode of Bannon's show. Much of their conversation focused on Vice President Pence, and the belief that he had the power to overturn the election.

"[W]e are entering into one of the most, um, important constitutional crisis [sic] the country's ever had," Bannon said.[111] Bannon complained that Vice President Pence had "spit the bit," meaning he had given up on efforts to keep President Trump in power.[112] Eastman claimed that the election had been "illegally conducted," and so the certified votes now "devolved back to the [S]tate legislature[s], and the only other place where it devolved back to is to Congress and particularly the Vice President, who will sit in presiding over a Joint Session of Congress beginning on January 6 to count the ballots."[113] Eastman claimed that the Vice President (and Congress) had the power to reject the certified electors from several States out-of-hand. "[T]hey've got multiple slates of ballots from seven states," Eastman said. "And they've gotta decide [ ] which is the valid slate to count...I think they have that authority to make that determination on their own." [114]

Bannon claimed the Vice President of the United States is "hardwired in," and an "actual decisionmaker." [115] The Vice President's role is not "ministerial," Bannon declared. [116] Eastman agreed. [117] "Are we to assume that this is going to be a climactic battle that's going to take place this week about the very question of the constitutionality of the Electoral Count Act of 1887?" Bannon asked. [118]

Eastman replied, "I think a lot of that depends on the courage and the spine of the individuals involved." Bannon asked Eastman if he meant Vice President Mike Pence. "Yes," Eastman answered. [119]

JANUARY 3, 2021: EASTMAN DRAFTS ANOTHER "JANUARY 6 SCENARIO" MEMO "WAR GAMING" THE WAYS THAT VICE PRESIDENT PENCE COULD CHANGE THE OUTCOME OF THE ELECTION.

The next day, January 3, 2021, Eastman drafted a six-page memo that imagined several scenarios for January 6th, only some of which led to President Trump's victory. [120] In a section titled, "War Gaming the Alternatives," Eastman set forth the ways he thought President Trump could remain in power. [121] Importantly, Eastman concluded that President Trump could remain president if—and only if—Vice President Pence followed Eastman's illegal advice and determined which electoral college ballots were "valid." [122] In another scenario, Eastman imagined that President Trump may somehow win re-election in January 2021 if Vice President Pence remanded the electoral votes to State legislatures, such that they could have ten days to investigate President Trump's baseless claims of fraud. In that case, Eastman allowed that former Vice President Biden may still win, should the State legislatures determine that the evidence was "insufficient to alter the results of the election." [123]

Eastman Knew that there Were No Valid "Alternate" Slates, But He Nonetheless Predicated His Advice to the Vice President and President on this Claim. In his six-page memo, consistent with the earlier two-page memo, Eastman states that "the Trump electors" met and transmitted votes, finding that "[t]here are thus dual slates of electors from 7 [S]tates." [124] Even since January 6th, Eastman has continued to affirm and defend his assertion that there were dual slates of electors, writing: "Trump electors from seven [S]tates in which election challenges were still pending met (albeit of their own accord) on the date designated by Congress, cast their votes, and transmitted those votes to Congress." [125]

Eastman used these slates as a premise for his argument that the result of the election was disputed. However, Eastman acknowledged on multiple occasions—both before and after January 6th—that these "dual slates" had no legal significance. In an email sent on December 19, 2020, Eastman wrote that the seven Trump/Pence slates of electors "will be dead on arrival in Congress" "unless those electors get a certification from their State Legislators."[126] Of course, this certification never came and there was no basis for any action on the "dual slates."[127]

Nevertheless, on December 23, 2020, Eastman used the existence of these slates as a justification for the Vice President to act, in an email to Boris Epshteyn, a Trump Campaign lawyer. "The fact that we have multiple slates of electors demonstrates the uncertainty of either. That should be enough."[128]

Again after January 6th, Eastman acknowledged in an email that the fake electors' documents were invalid and irrelevant.[129] "Alas," he said, "[T]hey had no authority" because "[n]o legislature certified them."[130]

Eastman concluded his memo by asserting that his plan was "BOLD, Certainly," but he attempted to justify it, arguing that "this Election was Stolen by a strategic Democrat plan to systematically flout existing election laws for partisan advantage; we're no longer playing by Queensbury Rules, therefore."[131]

Eastman repeated what he wrote in his earlier, shorter memo, claiming that Vice President Pence should act "without asking for permission—either from a vote of the joint session or from the Court."[132] Eastman claimed "that the Constitution assigns this power to the Vice President as the ultimate arbiter."[133] Eastman ended on an especially hyperbolic note. If the election's results were not upended, "then the sovereign people no longer control the direction of their government, and we will have ceased to be a self-governing people. The stakes could not be higher."[134]

January 4, 2021: President Trump and Eastman Meet with Pence and His Staff in the Oval Office.

Eastman Argues in an Oval Office Meeting that the Vice President can Reject Electoral Votes or that He Can Delay the Certification, Sending the Electoral Votes Back to the States. Late in the afternoon of January 4, 2021, President Trump summoned Vice President Pence to the Oval Office for a showdown.[135] President Trump and Eastman sought to convince the Vice President that he had the power to refuse to count the certified electors from several States won by former Vice President Biden.

Short and Jacob attended with the Vice President.[136] Trump's chief of staff, Mark Meadows, was only briefly present, leaving as the meeting started.[137]

The White House Counsel is Excluded from the Meeting. One key lawyer was conspicuously absent: Pat Cipollone, the White House Counsel. Cipollone and his deputy, Pat Philbin, were shooting down a series of "terrible" proposals at the time.[138] Philbin told the Select Committee that he considered resigning every day from approximately November 15 until the end of the administration.[139] Philbin had researched the Vice President's role in the January 6th joint session and concluded that Vice President Pence had no power to affect the outcome.[140] Cipollone agreed and informed Short and Jacob that this was the opinion of White House Counsel's Office.[141]

Mark Meadows invited Cipollone to speak with Eastman prior to the Oval Office meeting.[142] Cipollone told Eastman that his scheme was "not something that is consistent with the appropriate reading of the law."[143] After delivering this assessment directly to Eastman in Meadows' office, Cipollone walked to the Oval Office with the intent to attend the meeting. However, by the time the Vice President and his staff arrived, Cipollone was gone.[144]

Cipollone declined to testify as to what he told President Trump or why he did not attend the Oval Office meeting, but he was clear that he didn't end up attending the meeting because of something that happened after he walked into the Oval Office.[145] Whatever happened, Cipollone maintained, was protected by executive privilege, suggesting that he was asked to leave by the President.[146] What is clear, however, is that Cipollone had already shared his view directly with Meadows and Eastman, i.e., that the proposal President Trump and Eastman were about to advocate to the Vice President was illegal.[147]

During this Oval Office Meeting, Eastman Admits that Both Paths are Based on the Same Legal Theory and Concedes His Plan Violates the Electoral Count Act. During the Oval Office meeting, Eastman claimed that there were two legally viable options.[148] First, Vice President Pence could reject outright the certified electors submitted by several States, and second, he could suspend the joint session and send the "disputed" electoral votes back to the States.[149] Eastman advised that the Vice President had the "raw authority to determine objections himself," according to Jacob.[150] However, by the end of the meeting Eastman was emphasizing the second option that he argued would be "more politically palatable" than the "more aggressive" option of the Vice President rejecting electoral votes outright.[151] If Vice President Pence did not want to reject the electors, Eastman claimed, then the Vice President could send the certified electoral votes back to the States for further deliberation.

Eastman later conceded that both actions were based on the same underlying legal theory of the Vice President's power.[152] Eastman also

January 6th Committee Interview

Well, again,
I was the White House Counsel.

Pat Cipollone
Former White House Counsel

Pat Cipollone is seen on a screen during a Select Committee hearing on July 12, 2022.
(Photo by Sarah Silbiger-Pool/Getty Images)

admitted—during this meeting with the President and Vice President—that his proposal violated the Electoral Count Act.[153] Moreover, Eastman eventually acknowledged that the concept of the Vice President unilaterally rejecting electors was not supported by precedent and that the Supreme Court would never endorse it.[154]

Jacob recorded his reflections on the January 4th meeting in a contemporaneous memo to the Vice President.[155] Jacob's memo confirms that Eastman admitted that his proposal violated the law in the presence of President Trump.

First, Jacob wrote, Eastman acknowledged that "his proposal violates several provisions of statutory law"—namely, the Electoral Count Act of 1887.[156] Jacob's memo explains that the Electoral Count Act calls for all vote certificates to be "acted upon," and any objections to a State's certificates be "finally disposed of." However, as Jacob wrote, Eastman was proposing instead that "no action be taken" on the certificates from the States Eastman asserted were "contested." And, according to the Electoral Count Act, the Vice President (as President of the Senate) is to "call for objections." But Eastman did not want the Vice President to "call for objections" for these States. As Jacob noted, this would have deprived Congress of the ability under the Act to make, debate, and vote on objections.[157]

Additionally, the Electoral Count Act contains a provision that requires any "competing slates of electors" to be "submitted to the Senate and House for debate and disposition." As Jacob noted, Eastman conceded that the "alternate" (fake) electors' votes were not proper. But Eastman's proposal still would have refused to count the real electors' votes from those States and instead referred both the real and fake electors' votes to State legislatures "for disposition." Finally, in order for State legislatures to take action to determine which of the slates should be counted, Eastman's proposal called for "an extended recess of the joint session." But this too would have violated the Electoral Count Act, which provides only for very short delays.[158]

There was another foundational problem with Eastman's plan. There were no legitimate "competing" or "alternate" slates of electors. President Trump, Eastman and others had manufactured the conditions they needed in order to claim that the election result was "disputed" by convening fake electors who sent fake documents to Washington before January 6th. And their efforts to convince State legislatures to certify Trump electors had already failed.

Jacob noted in his memo that in the Oval Office meeting, Eastman conceded "no legislature has appointed or certified any alternate slate of electors" and that the purported "alternate slates" (fake electors) were illegitimate without what Jacob described as "the imprimatur of approval by a State legislature."[159] Moreover, Eastman acknowledged that "no Republican-controlled legislative majority in any disputed States has expressed an intention to designate an alternate slate of electors." [160] In other words, Eastman acknowledged that the fake votes were invalid, that no State legislature had approved them, and no State legislature *would* approve them.[161] But President Trump and Eastman still pressed this unlawful scheme on the Vice President. Although Eastman started the January 4th Oval Office meeting maintaining that Vice President Pence had unilateral authority to reject electors, by the end of the meeting he conceded that he would "not recommend that the Vice President assert that he has the authority unilaterally to decide which of the competing slates of electors should be counted." [162]

Jacob ended his memo with a scathing summary. "If the Vice President implemented Professor Eastman's proposal, he would likely lose in court," Jacob wrote. "In a best-case scenario in which the courts refused to get involved, the Vice President would likely find himself in an isolated standoff against both houses of Congress, as well as most or all of the applicable State legislatures, with no neutral arbiter to break the impasse." [163]

Following the Oval Office meeting, during the evening of January 4, 2021, Jacob invited Eastman to send along "any written materials on electoral vote counting issues," including a law review article by Laurence Tribe that Eastman had cited in the Oval Office meeting that day, for Jacob to review on the Vice President's behalf.[164] Jacob reviewed everything that Eastman submitted; nothing changed the analysis he had already done for the Vice President, indeed much of it did not even support Eastman's own arguments.[165]

The Vice President was Not Persuaded by Eastman's Theory and Remained Convinced That His Role at the Joint Session would be Merely Ceremonial. Pence did not relent on January 4th, or at any point during the harrowing two days that followed. "[F]rom my very first conversation with the Vice President on the subject, his immediate instinct was that there is no way that one person could be entrusted by the Framers to exercise that authority," Jacob testified. "And never once did I see him budge from that view, and the legal advice that I provided him merely reinforced it. So, everything that he said or did during [the January 4th meeting in the Oval Office] was consistent with his first instincts on this question." [166]

JANUARY 4, 2021: PRESIDENT TRUMP PUBLICLY PRESSURES THE VICE PRESIDENT DURING A RALLY SPEECH IN GEORGIA.
President Trump did not relent either. His instinct was to increase public pressure on Vice President Pence, despite the Vice President's consistent message to President Trump about the limits of his authority. That evening, during a Senate campaign rally in Dalton, Georgia, President Trump made it

seem as if the Presidential election hadn't already been decided and projected his unhinged ambitions onto his opponents.[167] President Trump claimed that "there's nothing the radical Democrats will not do to get power that they so desperately crave," including "the outright stealing of elections, like they're trying to do with us."[168]

"We're not going to let it happen," President Trump said, adding, "I hope Mike Pence comes through for us, I have to tell you." President Trump called Vice President Pence a "great vice president," a "great guy," as well as a "wonderful" and "smart man." But he alluded to the Vice President's role, "he's going to have a lot to say about it," and added an ominous note. "Of course, if he doesn't come through, I won't like him quite as much," President Trump said.[169]

JANUARY 5, 2021: EASTMAN PRESSURES PENCE'S STAFF IN A PRIVATE MEETING WHILE PRESIDENT TRUMP TWEETS.

In a Reversal of Where the Oval Office Meeting Ended the Day Before, Eastman Argues that Pence Should Reject Electors Outright. Eastman met with Jacob and Short again the following day.[170] During the Oval Office meeting the Vice President had made clear that he would not unilaterally reject electors, and, by pivoting to recommend the Vice President send the electors back to the States, Eastman seemed to recognize this. But the following morning, Eastman returned to pressing for the more "aggressive" path.[171]

Jacob recorded Eastman's request on January 5, 2021, in a handwritten note: "Requesting VP reject."[172] Jacob later summarized Eastman's remarks as follows: "I'm here asking you to reject the electors."[173] This overnight reversal surprised Jacob because Eastman was returning to the more aggressive position he had seemed to abandon in the Oval Office meeting the day before.[174] President Trump's tweets that morning may explain Eastman's reversal. While Eastman was meeting with the Vice President's staff, his client, President Trump, was pressing the argument publicly.

At 11:06 a.m. on the morning of January 5th, President Trump tweeted: "The Vice President has the power to reject fraudulently chosen electors." As his tweet made clear, President Trump would not be persuaded by reason—or the law. The President made this public statement despite the Vice President's clear and consistent rejection of this theory including during an in-person meeting the day before. During that same meeting, Eastman conceded that this "aggressive" path of rejecting electors was not advisable.

Herschmann briefly participated in the January 5th meeting, seeing it as "an opportunity... to just chew [Eastman] out."[175] Herschmann had already pushed back "brutal[ly]" on Eastman's theory regarding the Vice

President. In this conversation, he emphasized the need to fact check dubious claims of election fraud.[176] Herschmann told Eastman that "someone better make sure" that the allegations Eastman provided to members of Congress were accurate before they objected to the certification of the vote the next day.[177] "[N]othing should come out of someone's mouth that [isn't] independently verified and [ ] reliable."[178]

At the End of the Morning Meeting, Eastman Concedes to Pence's Counsel That His Theory Has No Historical Support. Jacob then had his own "Socratic" debate with Eastman over the legal merits of his position. According to Jacob, Eastman conceded much ground by the end of the session. Eastman "all but admitted that it [his plan] didn't work."[179]

For example, Eastman had previously claimed to have found historical support in the actions of John Adams and Thomas Jefferson, who both presided over the counting of electoral votes when they were Vice President. Not so. Jacob told the Select Committee that Eastman conceded in private that the cases of Jefferson and Adams did not serve "as examples for the proposition that he was trying to support of a Vice Presidential assertion of authority to decide disputes[,] because no dispute was raised in either case during the joint session." Jacob added: "And, moreover, there was no [question] as to the outcomes in those States."[180]

Eastman conceded that there was no historical support for the role that he and President Trump were pushing Vice President Pence to play. No Vice President—before or after the adoption of the Electoral Count Act—had ever exercised such authority. This included then-Vice President Richard Nixon's handling of the electoral votes of Hawaii following the 1960 election. Though Eastman and other Trump lawyers used this Hawaii example to justify the theory that the Vice President could unilaterally choose which electors to count, Eastman admitted to Jacob that Vice President Nixon had not in fact done what Eastman was recommending Vice President Pence do.[181]

Eastman also admitted that he would not grant the expansive powers he advocated for Vice President Pence to any other Vice President. Eastman did not think that Vice President Kamala Harris should have such power in 2025, nor did he think that Vice President Al Gore should have had such authority in 2001.[182] He also acknowledged that his theory would lose 9-0 at the Supreme Court.[183]

According to Jacob, Eastman "acknowledged by the end that, first of all, no reasonable person would actually want that clause [of the 12th Amendment] read that way because if indeed it did mean that the Vice President

Judge J. Michael Luttig testifies before the Select Committee on June 16, 2022.
Photo by House Creative Services

had such authority, you could never have a party switch thereafter." If politicians followed Eastman's advice, "[y]ou would just have the same party win continuously if indeed a Vice President had the authority to just declare the winner of every State."[184]

The Vice President's office was unmoved by Eastman's specious reasoning. As he left Marc Short's office, Eastman was thinking of his client's reaction. "They're going to be really disappointed that I wasn't able to persuade you," Eastman said.[185]

Former Republican Officials with Executive, Legislative, and Judicial Experience All Agreed with Vice President Pence's Conclusion about His Limited Role at the Joint Session. As President Trump's pressure campaign intensified, the Vice President's outside counsel, Richard Cullen, turned for support to John Michael Luttig, a conservative former judge of the U.S. Court of Appeals for the Fourth Circuit.[186] Eastman had clerked for Luttig—a man with impeccable legal and conservative credentials—more than two decades prior. Luttig rejected Eastman's so-called legal analysis of the Vice President's role in no uncertain terms. In a series of tweets, posted at 9:53 a.m. on January 5th, Luttig set forth his legal conclusions.

"The only responsibility and power of the Vice President under the Constitution is to faithfully count the electoral college votes as they have been cast," Judge Luttig wrote. "The Constitution does not empower the Vice President to alter in any way the votes that have been cast, either by rejecting certain of them or otherwise."[187]

Confusion in the media about where the Vice President stood on this issue prompted former Speaker of the House Paul Ryan to reach out to the Vice President to share his belief that the Vice President had no unilateral authority.[188] Short also spoke with former Speaker Ryan and as he testified to the Select Committee, "I said to him, Mr. Speaker, you know Mike…you know he recognizes that. And we sort of laughed about it, and he said, I get it."[189]

The Vice President also consulted with former Vice President Dan Quayle, who reinforced and affirmed Vice President Pence's consistent understanding of his role.[190]

JANUARY 5, 2021: PRESIDENT TRUMP AGAIN PRESSURES VICE PRESIDENT PENCE IN A ONE-ON-ONE MEETING AT THE WHITE HOUSE AND ANOTHER PHONE CALL WITH EASTMAN.

President Trump demanded to see Vice President Pence again that same day. Vice President Pence had canceled a planned lunch with President Trump, intending to work on the statement he planned to issue on January 6th to explain publicly why he wouldn't bow to the President's pressure.[191] But Pence couldn't avoid Trump. Vice President Pence had to delay a Coronavirus Task Force meeting later that same day when he was called to the Oval Office to meet with the President.[192]

The two men met alone, without staff present. While we have not developed direct evidence of what was discussed during this one-on-one meeting between the President and Vice President, it did not change the fundamental disagreement between them about the limits of the Vice President's authority during the joint session. Jacob said the Vice President left the meeting "determined."[193] Vice President Pence did tell Marc Short what transpired during the meeting, but Short refused to tell the Select Committee what was said.[194] Short described Vice President Pence's demeanor as "steady."[195] Short testified that the below excerpt from the book *Peril* may have been sensationalized but was generally consistent with Short's understanding of the discussion:

> "If these people say you have the power, wouldn't you want to?" Trump asked.
>
> "I wouldn't want any one person to have that authority," Pence said.

"But wouldn't it almost be cool to have that power?" Trump asked.

"No," Pence said. "Look, I've read this, and I don't see a way to do it. We've exhausted every option. I've done everything I could and then some to find a way around this. It's simply not possible. My interpretation is: No....

"No, no, no!" Trump shouted. "You don't understand, Mike. You can do this. I don't want to be your friend anymore if you don't do this."[196]

Later that day, Jacob and Short were both present for a call between President Trump and Vice President Pence.[197] Eastman and at least one other lawyer were with President Trump on the call as well.[198]

Eastman recognized that Vice President Pence was not going to change his mind on rejecting electors outright, but he still asked if the Vice President would consider sending the electors back to the States.[199] "I don't see it," Vice President Pence responded, "but my counsel will hear out whatever Mr. Eastman has to say."[200]

Jacob received other calls from Eastman on January 5th.[201] Jacob told the Select Committee that he had a detailed discussion with Eastman concerning the ways his proposal would violate the Electoral Count Act.[202] Eastman resorted to a ridiculous argument—comparing their current situation to the crisis that faced President Abraham Lincoln during the Civil War. Eastman invoked President Lincoln's suspension of the writ of habeas corpus.[203] He also told Jacob to "stay tuned" because "we" were trying to get some letters from State legislators indicating that they were interested in the Vice President sending the electors back to the States.[204]

JANUARY 5, 2021: AN ACCURATE NEW YORK TIMES ARTICLE ABOUT THE VICE PRESIDENT PROMPTS A FALSE STATEMENT IN RESPONSE BY PRESIDENT TRUMP.
On the evening of January 5th, *The New York Times* published an article titled, "Pence Said to Have Told Trump He Lacks Power to Change Election Result."[205] The *Times* reported on the tension brewing within the White House, citing "people briefed on the conversation" between President Trump and Vice President Pence that had taken place in the Oval Office the previous day. "Vice President Mike Pence told President Trump on Tuesday [January 4th] that he did not believe he had the power to block congressional certification of Joseph R. Biden, Jr.'s victory in the presidential election despite Mr. Trump's baseless insistence that he did," the *Times* reported.[206]

The *Times'* report was published at approximately 7:36 that evening.[207] Jason Miller called President Trump to make sure he had seen it.[208] President Trump spoke to Miller at least twice, once at 8:18 p.m. and a second time at 9:22 p.m.[209] Immediately after concluding his second call with Jason

Miller, President Trump asked to speak to the Vice President; President Trump and Vice President Pence spoke from 9:33 to 9:41 p.m.[210] President Trump also spoke with Steve Bannon and Eastman, among others.[211]

At 9:58 p.m. on January 5th, President Trump issued a statement that he had dictated to Jason Miller disputing the *Times'* account.[212] President Trump lied—repeatedly—in his short statement.[213] The President claimed the article was "fake news." It wasn't. President Trump claimed he and Vice President Pence were "in total agreement that the Vice President has the power to act." They weren't. President Trump claimed the election "was illegal." It wasn't. President Trump then laid out Vice President Pence's options for the next day, summarizing Eastman's theory:

> Our Vice President has several options under the U.S. Constitution. He can decertify the results or send them back to the [S]tates for change and certification. He can also decertify the illegal and corrupt results and send them to the House of Representatives for the one vote for one [S]tate tabulation.[214]

This was also a blatant attempt to mischaracterize the Vice President's position in the hope that public opinion would somehow sway the resolute Vice President. President Trump knew full well at the time that he and Vice President Pence were *not* "in total agreement." The Vice President's counsel, Greg Jacob, was shocked by the statement.[215] "[T]he Vice President was not in agreement that the Vice President had the power to take the actions that were being asked of him that day," Jacob later told the Select Committee.[216] Marc Short was furious as well and called Jason Miller to forcefully "express [his] displeasure that a statement could have gone out that misrepresented the Vice President's viewpoint without consultation." [217]

The Vice President was "obviously irritated that a statement putting words in his mouth" was issued by the President and considered issuing his own statement contradicting President Trump's.[218] Ultimately, Pence and Short concluded that it was not worthwhile since it was already late in the evening and they expected the question to be resolved by Vice President Pence's "Dear Colleague" letter the next day.[219]

JANUARY 5, 2021: BANNON PUBLICLY AMPLIFIES THE PRESSURE ON VICE PRESIDENT PENCE.

While President Trump misrepresented the Vice President's agreement with Eastman's theory, his on-again, off-again political advisor, Steve Bannon, pressed President Trump's campaign against Vice President Pence in public. Bannon echoed the public pressure on Pence that the President continued to propagate by talking about his purported authority. The Select Committee learned from phone records that Bannon spoke to President Trump at least twice on January 5th.[220]

During a January 5, 2021, episode of *War Room: Pandemic*, Bannon and his guests openly berated Vice President Pence. Bannon cited an erroneous news report claiming that Senator Grassley would preside over the certification of the electoral college vote—instead of Vice President Pence.[221] Bannon's cohost, Raheem Kassam, took credit for the public pressure placed on Vice President Pence. "I want to remind people who has been sitting here, saying 'Light Pence Up' for the last couple of weeks. Right? That would be Raheem Kassam." They then discussed President Trump's speech in Georgia the previous evening. "I think the President of the United States took your advice last night, wrote a line in there," Bannon said. To which Kasseem responded: "...and yours...hold the line."

Jack Posobiec, an alt-right personality with a large Twitter following, chimed in quoting a member of their audience as saying that "Pence will betray Donald Trump."[222] In response, Bannon stated: "Call the play. Run the play."[223]

The "play" was Bannon's version of the "Green Bay Sweep"—a plan to subvert the transfer of power on January 6th named for a brutally effective power running play developed in the National Football League (NFL) in the 1960's. Steve Bannon's political version of the sweep was intended to undermine the legitimate results of the 2020 presidential election.

One account of Bannon's "Green Bay Sweep" comes from Peter Navarro, Director of the White House Office of Trade and Manufacturing Policy. Navarro refused to cooperate with the Select Committee and was subsequently indicted for contempt of Congress. Although he doesn't fully explain in his book, *In Trump Time: A Journal of America's Plague Year*, how Bannon's sweep was intended to work, Navarro writes that Vice President Pence was envisioned as the "quarterback" who would "assert his constitutional power" to delay certification.[224] Navarro writes that his own role was to "carefully document the fraud and myriad election irregularities," while Bannon's "role was to figure out how to use this information—what he called the 'receipts.'"[225]

Navarro's account helps explain why Trump and his loyalists became so fixated on Vice President Pence. They saw Vice President Pence as their last hope for keeping President Trump in office. Navarro writes of Pence's supposed "betrayal."[226] In a telling sentence, Navarro likens Vice President Pence to Brutus, a Roman politician and the most famous assassin of Julius Caesar. Navarro writes:

On this cold, momentous day, I shiver as I think to myself, "January 6 will be either Mike Pence's finest hour or the traitorous 'Et tu, Brute?' end of both his and Donald Trump's political careers." [227]

The goal of these Trump allies was clear: to overturn the election result.[228] Statements by participants in this effort indicate there were several different endgame strategies in mind. One was to get the Vice President to unilaterally reject the Electoral College votes of Arizona, Georgia, Pennsylvania, and other States, then simply declare that Trump had won a majority of the electors actually submitted. The other major possibility was to reject or "return" the Electoral College votes of these States and then declare there was no majority in the Electoral College process, thereby triggering a so-called contingent election under the 12th Amendment.[229] This would have meant that the House of Representatives had chosen the president not on the basis of one-member-one-vote, but on the basis of one-State-one-vote, pursuant to the 12th Amendment. Donald Trump's strategists emphasized repeatedly that the GOP had a 27-to-22 margin in control of the States' Congressional delegations, with Pennsylvania being tied at 9-to-9, therefore presumably a non-factor.

5.3 PRESIDENT TRUMP AND HIS ALLIES CONTINUE TO PRESSURE THE VICE PRESIDENT ON JANUARY 6TH, THREATENING HIS LIFE AND OUR DEMOCRACY.

JANUARY 6, 2021: PRESIDENT TRUMP CONTINUED TO FALSELY ASSERT IN MULTIPLE TWEETS POSTED THE MORNING OF JANUARY 6TH THAT THE VICE PRESIDENT HAD A ROLE TO PLAY IN THE OUTCOME OF THE ELECTION.
Despite the public pressure initiated by the President and amplified by Bannon, Navarro and others, there was no ambiguity in the Vice President's decision. By January 6th, President Trump had been told multiple times that Vice President Pence was not going to reject the certified electors from any State. Nor was Vice President Pence going to move for a delay and send the electors back to the States. Either move would have been illegal, requiring Vice President Pence to break the law, violating his oath to the U.S. Constitution. Pence made his decision clear "[m]any times" to President Trump, and he was "very consistent" in rejecting the President's demands.[230] President Trump continued to publicly pressure the Vice President anyway.

At 1:00 a.m. on January 6th, President Trump tweeted:

If Vice President @Mike_Pence comes through for us, we will win the Presidency. Many States want to decertify the mistake they made in certifying incorrect & even fraudulent numbers in a process NOT approved by their State Legislatures (which it must be). Mike can send it back![231]

Later that morning, at 8:17 a.m., President Trump tweeted again:

States want to correct their votes, which they now know were based on irregularities and fraud, plus corrupt process never received legislative approval. All Mike Pence has to do is send them back to the States, AND WE WIN. Do it Mike, this is a time for extreme courage![232]

And, at 8:22 a.m., President Trump tweeted again, making a pitch for Congress to choose him, as if people's votes on election day and the electoral college didn't matter:

THE REPUBLICAN PARTY AND, MORE IMPORTANTLY, OUR COUNTRY, NEEDS THE PRESIDENCY MORE THAN EVER BEFORE—THE POWER OF THE VETO. STAY STRONG![233]

President Trump's tweets made it clear that he thought the Republican State legislatures would simply deliver him victory. President Trump emphasized this point, writing twice that if Vice President Pence gave in, "we win." However, there was no sign of a change in the Vice President's position. A moment of truth was looming.

January 6, 2021: President Trump Has a "[H]eated" Conversation with Vice President Pence Before his Rally on the Ellipse. President Trump tried to reach Vice President Pence by phone early that morning.[234] He finally talked to his Vice President at approximately 11:20 a.m.[235] The exchange quickly became contentious.

Eric Herschmann, a lawyer in the White House Counsel's Office, overheard the conversation. Members of President Trump's family and other White House officials were present as well.[236] Herschmann recalled that "it started off as a calmer tone, everything, and then it became heated."[237] Ivanka Trump also described the call as "pretty heated."[238] Ivanka Trump elaborated: "It was a different tone than I'd heard him take with the Vice President before."[239] Ivanka Trump told her Chief of Staff, Julie Radford, that "her dad had just had an upsetting conversation with the Vice President."[240] President Trump had even called Vice President Pence the "P Word."[241]

Nick Luna, President Trump's personal assistant (commonly known as the "body man"), was also in the Oval Office during the conversation. Luna told the Select Committee that President Trump called Vice President Pence

President Trump on the phone in the Oval Office.
Photo provided to the Select Committee by the National Archives and Records Administration.

a "wimp" on the call, with President Trump adding that he "made the wrong decision" in choosing Pence as his running mate.[242]

Keith Kellogg, Vice President Pence's National Security Advisor, also heard the conversation. President Trump "told the Vice President that, you know, he has legal authority to send these folks [the electors] back to the respective States," Kellogg told the Select Committee.[243] President Trump insisted that Vice President Pence had the "constitutional authority to" reject certain electoral college votes.[244] When Vice President Pence would not budge, President Trump told him "you're not tough enough to make the call."[245]

But Vice President Pence would not be bullied. The Vice President, who was at his residence at the time, had been meeting with Greg Jacob to finalize the statement he would be releasing later that day. When the President called, Pence stepped away to answer the phone. According to Jacob, when Pence returned, he did not say anything about the call—but he looked "steely, determined, [and] grim," as he reentered the room.[246]

c. January 6, 2021: Trump, Eastman and Giuliani Continue to Pressure Vice President Pence at the Ellipse Rally. Despite the Vice President's unwavering stance, the President and his outside counsel continued to turn up the heat of public pressure.

At President Trump's urging, thousands had gathered on the morning of January 6th to hear the President and others speak at a rally held at the Ellipse, a park just south of the White House. Before President Trump spoke, Eastman took the stage alongside Giuliani. Both would further amplify the President's public pressure on the Vice President, but when Giuliani spoke on the Ellipse, he already knew that what Eastman had outlined would never practically happen.

At 9:31 a.m. that morning, Giuliani called Eric Herschmann "out of the blue" to ask him for his view and analysis of the practical implications of Eastman's theory.[247] According to Herschmann, after an "intellectual discussion about...the VP's role," Giuliani agreed that the "practical implication of [what Eastman had proposed] would be almost impossible."[248] Immediately after this 5½ minute conversation with Herschmann, Giuliani had two calls with the White House, at 9:41 a.m. and 9:53 a.m.[249]

Giuliani recognized Eastman who joined him on stage, claiming that he was "one of the preeminent constitutional scholars in the United States."[250]

Giuliani said Vice President Pence could either "decide on the validity of these crooked ballots, or he can send it back to the legislat[ures], give them five to 10 days to finally finish the work."[251] He added that that they had "letters from five legislat[ures] begging us to do that."[252] This was not true. At most, what Giuliani, Eastman and other allies of President Trump had managed to procure were letters from individual State legislators or groups of State legislators. None of the letters came from a majority of any State's legislative chamber, let alone a majority of an entire State legislature.[253]

For instance, a letter that Eastman described to Jacob as a "[m]ajor new development" on the evening of January 5th contained the signatures of 21 members of the Pennsylvania Senate.[254] Eastman claimed that it "now looks like PA Legislature will vote to recertify its electors if Vice President Pence implements the plan we discussed," but the letter asked only for a "delay" in certification to "allow for due process."[255] The Select Committee learned from the most senior Pennsylvania Senate Republican that he signed the letter because of pressure he was feeling due to the voluminous post-election outreach from President Trump, Trump allies, and the public.[256] And, he only agreed to sign a letter directed to Congressional leaders—not the Vice President—after raising in a conversation with Vice President Pence's brother, Congressman Greg Pence, his desire to avoid pressuring the Vice President.[257]

Moreover, as Jacob explained, "what any of the State legislatures said they did or did not want to do had no impact on the legal analysis of what the Vice President's authorities were."[258] There was simply no legal path to send any votes back to the States on January 6th.

On the stage at the President's rally on the Ellipse, Giuliani repeated a conspiracy theory about the "crooked Dominion machines...deliberately" changing votes via an algorithm.[259] He explained that the 10-day delay in the certification would be used "to see the machines that are crooked" and "to find criminality there"—demonstrating that his repeated assertions of a stolen election were not based on any real proof, or even evidence, of actual widespread fraud or criminality.[260]

"Let's have trial by combat," Giuliani told the crowd.[261]

Eastman came to the microphone following Giuliani, and he proceeded to repeat proven falsehoods regarding voting machines. He then issued his "demand":

> And all we are demanding of Vice President Pence is this afternoon, at 1:00, he let the legislatures of the state look into this so we get to the bottom of it, and the American people know whether we have control of the direction of our government, or not. We no longer live in a self-governing republic if we can't get the answer to this question. This is bigger than President Trump. It is a very essence of our republican form of government, and it has to be done. And anybody that is not willing to stand up to do it, does not deserve to be in the office. It is that simple.[262]

Eastman told the assembled crowd that nothing less than the fate of the American Republic was in Vice President Pence's hands.

President Trump Directs the Angry Mob at the Capitol to Pressure Vice President Pence.

When President Trump later took the stage at the Ellipse, he heaped praise on Giuliani and Eastman. "He's got guts, unlike a lot of people in the Republican Party," President Trump said of Giuliani. "He's got guts. He fights, he fights."[263] President Trump described Eastman as "one of the most brilliant lawyers in the country."[264] President Trump claimed that Eastman had looked at the election and said, "What an absolute disgrace that this can be happening to our Constitution."[265] Trump falsely argued that the keys to the election were in Vice President Pence's hands, saying:

And he [Eastman] looked at Mike Pence, and I hope Mike is going to do the right thing. I hope so. I hope so. Because if Mike Pence does the right thing, we win the election.... [T]his is from the number one, or certainly one of the top, Constitutional lawyers in our country. He has the absolute right to do it.[266]

President Trump repeatedly lied, claiming that several States wanted to overturn former Vice President Biden's victory:

States want to revote. The States got defrauded. They were given false information. They voted on it. Now they want to recertify. They want it back. All Vice President Pence has to do is send it back to the States to recertify and we become president and you are the happiest people.[267]

Contrary to the statement President Trump dictated the night before, he all but admitted that Vice President Pence did not agree with him:

And I actually, I just spoke to Mike. I said: "Mike, that doesn't take courage. What takes courage is to do nothing. That takes courage." And then we're stuck with a president who lost the election by a lot and we have to live with that for four more years. We're just not going to let that happen.[268]

Later in his speech at the Ellipse, President Trump repeated:

So, I hope Mike has the courage to do what he has to do. And I hope he doesn't listen to the RINOs and the stupid people that he's listening to.[269]

This was nothing less than a direct appeal to the large angry crowd to pressure Vice President Mike Pence to change his settled and oft-repeated conclusion about the limits of his authority. It was a shocking attempt to use public opinion to change the Vice President's position. President Trump launched a mob toward the Capitol with the false hope that there was a scenario in which Vice President Pence would do what Eastman and President Trump had asked him to do, preventing the transfer of authority to President-elect Biden.

VICE PRESIDENT PENCE FULFILLED HIS DUTY ON JANUARY 6TH

The Vice President Waited to Release His Statement Out of Deference to President Trump, Who Was Still Speaking on the Ellipse, and Ultimately Released It Just Minutes Before the Joint Session Convened at 1:00 p.m. President Trump's speech began late and ran long. He didn't finish speaking until approximately 1:10 p.m.—after the joint session had begun at 1:00 p.m. Minutes before he gaveled the joint session into order, Vice President Mike Pence released the "Dear Colleague" letter he had been working on for days with his staff.[270] There was never any ambiguity in Vice President Pence's understanding of his role and authority, but he wanted to make it clear for everyone to see. "This may be the most important thing I ever say," Vice President Pence remarked.[271]

"Today it will be my duty to preside when the Congress convenes in Joint Session to count the votes of the Electoral College, and I will do so to the best of my ability," Vice President Pence wrote. Vice President Pence explained that his "role as presiding officer is largely ceremonial" and dismissed the arguments that he could take unilateral action as contrary to his oath to support and defend the Constitution:

> As a student of history who loves the Constitution and reveres its Framers, I do not believe that the Founders of our country intended to invest the Vice President with unilateral authority to decide which electoral votes should be counted during the Joint Session of Congress, and no Vice President in American history has ever asserted such authority. Instead, Vice Presidents presiding over Joint Sessions have uniformly followed the Electoral Count Act, conducting the proceedings in an orderly manner even where the count resulted in the defeat of their party or their own candidacy.[272]

Vice President Pence Adheres to the U.S. Constitution and Complies with the Law Governing the Certification of the Presidential Election. When Vice President Pence gaveled the opening of the joint session, he knew that many of his Republican colleagues planned to challenge the election's results based on fictitious claims of fraud. The Vice President took steps to ensure that those objections adhered to the process set forth in the Electoral Count Act.

Every four years, on January 6th, vice presidents read from a script that remains essentially unchanged. Eastman's theory of the Vice President's power and the Trump Campaign's scheme to convene and submit the slates of "alternate" (fake) electors motivated Vice President Pence and his advisors to alter the script and to make sure they were prepared to respond to any unexpected actions in the joint session.[273]

Vice President Pence met with the Senate Parliamentarian on January 3rd to discuss the joint session and revised the joint session scripts in consultation with her office.[274] Vice President Pence and the Parliamentarian agreed that the Vice President's role is ministerial.[275]

The Vice President knew that the fake slates of electors organized by the Trump Campaign were not certified by the States and thus were not valid; he revised the script for the joint session to be transparent with the American people about what the Vice President would—and wouldn't—be doing during the joint session.[276]

Vice President Pence during the Joint Session of Congress.
(Photo by Win McNamee/Getty Images)

One of the most noticeable and important changes to the script was directed specifically at thwarting the fake electors scheme. The Vice President knew, informed by the research and analysis of his staff, that absent certification of the electoral votes by a State authority, the purported "alternate" slates were "not consequential" and would play no role in the certification of the Presidential election at the joint session.[277] The Senate Parliamentarian confirmed this understanding.[278]

For decades, Vice Presidents read a similar simple passage concerning the ascertainment of the vote. Most recently, Vice President Joseph Biden read this passage aloud in 2017, as did his most recent predecessors:

> After ascertainment has been had that the certificates are authentic and correct in form, the tellers will count and make a list of the votes cast by the electors of the several States.

On January 6, 2021, Vice President Pence read from a revised script (emphasis added):

> After ascertaining that the certificates are regular in form and authentic, tellers will announce the votes cast by the electors for each state, beginning with Alabama, which the parliamentarians

advise me is the only certificate of vote from that State and purports to be a return from the State that has annexed to it a certificate from an authority of that State purporting to appoint or ascertain electors.[279]

Vice President Pence used the same phrasing for each of the 50 States counted.

The Vice President's attention to this issue was warranted. Trump's allies pushed the fake electors scheme until the very end. Although the Trump Campaign had taken pains to direct the fake electors to send their documents to the appropriate authorities immediately after voting on December 14th, and though the Senate Parliamentarian's and Vice President's offices had been tracking the receipt by mail of both the legitimate and fake certificates, the Trump Campaign apparently became concerned that two States' documents had not been received before the joint session.[280]

On January 4th, the Trump campaign asked Republican Party officials in Wisconsin to fly their fake electors' documents to Washington, DC.[281] Shortly after, staffers for Representative Mike Kelly (R–PA) and Senator Ron Johnson (R–WI) reached out to Vice President Pence's Director of Legislative Affairs, apparently seeking to deliver the fake certificates.[282] A message from Senator Johnson's staffer was sent just minutes before the beginning of the joint session. This staffer stated that Senator Johnson wished to hand-deliver to the Vice President the fake electors' certificates from Michigan and Wisconsin. The Vice President's aide unambiguously turned him away.[283]

Vice President Pence made certain to call for objections as well, in compliance with the Electoral Count Act. After the tellers read off the votes cast for each State, he asked: "Are there any objections to counting the certificate of vote of the state...that the teller has verified, appears to be regular in form and authentic?"[284]

For most States, there were no objections. Republicans only rose to object to the States that President Trump contested. The first such state was Arizona. At approximately 1:46 p.m., Congressman Paul Gosar (R–AZ) announced his objection.[285] "I rise for myself and 60 of my colleagues to object to the counting of the electoral ballots from Arizona," Gosar said.[286]

Vice President Pence then asked: "Is the objection in writing and Signed by a senator?" It was. Senator Ted Cruz endorsed the unfounded challenge to Arizona's electoral votes.[287] Because the objections complied with the law, Vice President Pence directed the House and Senate to withdraw from the joint session so that the House and Senate could separately debate and vote on the objection.[288]

When the joint session finally resumed after the attack on the Capitol, the clerks announced the results of each chamber's vote. Just six U.S. Senators voted for the objection to the counting of Arizona's electoral college votes. The objection was also defeated in the House, though 121 Republican Members voted to reject Arizona's legitimate electors.[289] Pennsylvania was the only other State the chambers debated, after the House's objection was signed by Senator Josh Hawley (R–Mo.).[290]

5.4 PRESIDENT TRUMP ENDANGERS PENCE'S LIFE, CAUSING THE VICE PRESIDENT, HIS FAMILY, AND STAFF TO NARROWLY MISS THE RIOTERS AS THEY FLEE THE MOB ATTACKING THE CAPITOL.

As the debate over Arizona's legitimate electors took place on the Senate floor, the Vice President's staff could see trouble brewing outside.[291] From inside the Vice President's ceremonial office, staffers witnessed the crowds swelling on the east side of the Capitol. Then, the rioters broke through security barriers.[292] Jacob told young staffers that they should stand back from the windows, because the Vice President's office was not "the most popular office on the block right now."[293] •

The Vice President was presiding over the Senate debate on the Arizona objection when the noise from the rioters became audible and those in the Senate Chamber realized the rioters had entered the Capitol.[294] The Secret Service evacuated Vice President Pence from the Senate floor at 2:12 p.m.[295] Twelve minutes later, at 2:24 p.m., President Trump tweeted that Vice President Pence "didn't have the courage to do what should have been done to protect our country and our Constitution."[296] By that time, the Secret Service had moved the Vice President to his ceremonial office across the hall.[297] But the situation was spiraling out of control—and they wouldn't stay there long. As Sarah Matthews, the Deputy White House Press Secretary, later explained: President Trump's tweet was like "pouring gasoline on the fire."[298]

Thirty seconds after President Trump's tweet, rioters who were already inside the Capitol opened the East Rotunda door just down the hall. A mere thirty seconds later, rioters breached the crypt one floor below the Vice President.

Though the Vice President refused the Secret Service's first two attempts to evacuate him from his ceremonial office, the situation quickly became untenable and the Vice President was told that the Secret Service could no longer protect him in this office in the Capitol that was quickly being overrun.[299] Marc Short recalls Tim Giebels, the head of the Vice President's Secret Service protective detail, saying, "At this point, I can't protect you behind these glass doors, and so I need to move you." [300] This time, the third, the Secret Service was not asking the Vice President to move; they were stating the fact that the Vice President must be moved.[301] At 2:20 p.m., NSC staff monitoring radio communications reported that the second floor of the Capitol and the door to the Senate Chamber "ha[ve] now been breached." [302]

At 2:25 p.m., the Secret Service rushed the Vice President, his family, and his senior staff down a flight of stairs, through a series of hallways and tunnels to a secure location.[303] The Vice President and his team stayed in that same location for the next four and a half hours.

The angry mob had come within 40 feet of the Vice President as he was evacuated.[304] President Trump never called to check on Vice President Pence's safety, so Marc Short called Mark Meadows to tell him they were safe and secure.[305] Short himself became *persona non grata* with President Trump. The President directed staff to revoke Short's access to the White House after Vice President Pence refused to betray his oath to the Constitution.[306] Marc Short never spoke with President Trump again.[307]

After arriving at the secure location, the head of the Vice President's Secret Service detail wanted to move the Vice President away from the Capitol, and staff hurried into the waiting vehicles. But the Vice President refused to get in the car.[308] As Greg Jacob explained in his testimony to the Select Committee:

> The Vice President wouldn't get in his car.... [H]e was determined that unless there was imminent danger to bodily safety that he was not going to abandon the Capitol and let the rioters have a victory of having made the Vice President flee or made it difficult to restart the process later that day.[309]

It was an unprecedented scene in American history. The President of the United States had riled up a mob that hunted his own Vice President.

The Vice President's staff came to believe that the theory "pushed and sold" to the public that the Vice President had a role to play in the joint session was a cause of the attack on the Capitol. "The reason that the Capitol was assaulted was that the people who were breaching the Capitol believed that... the election [outcome] had not yet been determined, and, instead, there was some action that was supposed to take place in Washington, D.C., to determine it," Jacob said.[310] "I do think [the violence] was the result of that position being continuously pushed and sold to people who ended up believing that with all their hearts." [311] The people had been "told that the Vice President had the authority" to determine the outcome of the election during the joint session.[312]

Photo provided to the Select Committee by the National Archives and Records Administration.

Of course, that was President Trump's and John Eastman's plan all along—to convince people that the election had been stolen, and that Vice President Pence could take action to change the outcome during the joint session on January 6th.

Jacob was writing an email to Eastman when the Capitol was breached.[313] At 2:14 p.m., just before being evacuated, Jacob hurriedly hit send on his email, but not before adding the following: "thanks to your bullshit, we are now under siege."[314]

Eastman quickly replied to Jacob's email and, incredibly, blamed Vice President Pence and Jacob for the attack. "The 'siege' is because YOU and your boss did not do what was necessary to allow this to be aired in a public way so the American people can see for themselves what happened," Eastman wrote.[315] Naturally, Jacob was "somewhere between aghast and livid."[316] It was "ridiculous" to blame Vice President Pence for the attack, when he simply followed the law.[317]

THE JOINT SESSION RECONVENES: "LET'S GET BACK TO WORK."

The Senate reconvened at approximately 8:06 p.m.[318] Congressional leadership and the Vice President insisted on finishing the work of the people. "Today was a dark day in the history of the United States Capitol," Vice President Pence said. "But thanks to the swift efforts of U.S. Capitol Police,

Photo provided to the Select Committee by the National Archives and Records Administration.

federal, state and local law enforcement, the violence was quelled. The Capitol is secured, and the people's work continues." The Vice President addressed "those who wreaked havoc in our Capitol today," saying "you did not win." Vice President Pence continued:

> Violence never wins. Freedom wins. And this is still the people's house. And as we reconvene in this chamber, the world will again witness the resilience and strength of our democracy, for even in the wake of unprecedented violence and vandalism at this Capitol, the elected representatives of the people of the United States have assembled again on the very same day to support and defend the Constitution of the United States.

"Let's get back to work," Vice President Pence concluded.[319]

Despite the violence that had unfolded at the Capitol, Eastman kept agitating for further delay. At 11:44 p.m. on January 6th, Eastman sent yet another email to Greg Jacob.[320] In a shockingly tone-deaf manner, Eastman claimed that the Electoral Count Act had been violated already, by allowing debate beyond two hours, so—he argued—Vice President Pence should no longer be concerned that what President Trump and Eastman had pressured him to do also would violate it.[321] "Of course," as Jacob pointed out, the debate couldn't have been completed in two hours due to the "intervening riot of several hours."[322]

Eastman argued that Vice President Pence should "adjourn for 10 days to allow the legislatures to finish their investigations, as well as to allow a full forensic audit of the massive amount of illegal activity that has occurred here."[323] Eastman described this—a delay in the certification of the vote and the peaceful transfer of power with no legal or historical precedent or support, based on entirely specious and disproven allegations of election fraud, following on a violent attack on the seat of American democracy—as a "relatively minor violation."[324]

Vice President Pence later described Eastman's email as "rubber room stuff," meaning it was certifiably crazy.[325]

5.5 AFTERMATH OF THE ATTACK.

Eastman called Herschmann on January 7th to discuss litigation on behalf of the Trump Campaign in Georgia.[326] This gave Herschmann another opportunity to lay into Eastman. "[Are] you out of your F'ing mind?" Herschmann asked. "I only want to hear two words coming out of your mouth from now on: orderly transition." Herschmann said. After some berating, Eastman repeated after Herschmann: "Orderly transition." "Now I'm going to give you the best free legal advice you're ever getting in your life," Herschmann said. "Get a great F'ing criminal defense lawyer, you're going to need it."[327] Days afterward, Eastman sent an email to Giuliani, making a request that tacitly acknowledged just how much trouble he was in: "I've decided that I should be on the pardon list, if that is still in the works."[328]

Vice President Pence and his team never bowed to President Trump's relentless pressure. They began January 6, 2021, with a prayer. The attack on the U.S. Capitol delayed the peaceful transfer of power. The joint session did not end until early in the morning on January 7th.

At 3:50 a.m. that morning, Short texted Vice President Pence a passage from Second Timothy, chapter 4, verse 7: "I fought the good fight. I finished the race. I have kept the faith."[329]

ENDNOTES

1. Select Committee to Investigate the January 6th Attack on the United States Capitol, Deposition of Marc Short, (Jan. 26, 2022), pp. 10–11.

2. Select Committee to Investigate the January 6th Attack on the United States Capitol, Deposition of Marc Short, (Jan. 26, 2022), pp. 10–11.

3. *See, e.g.*, Ivan E. Raiklin (Former Green Beret Commander) (@Raiklin), Twitter, Dec. 22, 2020, available at https://web.archive.org/web/20201222232155/https://twitter.com/Raiklin/

status/1341520753984942081 (archived) ("America, @VP @Mike_Pence MUST do this, tomorrow!"); Donald J. Trump (@realDonaldTrump), Twitter, Dec. 23, 2020 7:40:30 p.m. ET, available at https://web.archive.org/web/20201224033528/http://twitter.com/realDonaldTrump (archived).

4. Select Committee to Investigate the January 6th Attack on the United States Capitol, Deposition of Greg Jacob, (Feb. 1, 2022), pp. 95, ("[T]he Vice President mostly asked a series of questions in that meeting of Mr. Eastman"), 130 (Q: "Did John Eastman ever admit, as far as you know, in front of the President that his proposal would violate the Electoral Count Act?" A: "I believe he did on the 4th." Q: "Okay. And can you tell us what the President's reaction was?" A: "A I can't."); Documents on file with the Select Committee to Investigate the January 6th Attack on the United States Capitol (National Archives Production), VP-R0000107 (Greg Jacob memo to Vice President Pence, titled "Analysis of Professor Eastman's Proposals").

5. Select Committee to Investigate the January 6th Attack on the United States Capitol, Deposition of Greg Jacob, (Feb. 1, 2022), p. 96 (Eastman acknowledging that the legal basis for his proposed paths was the same and, as recounted by Greg Jacob, "[y]ou couldn't get there either way unless you . . . set aside a number of the positions of the Electoral Count Act").

6. Select Committee to Investigate the January 6th Attack on the United States Capitol, Deposition of Marc Short, (Jan. 26, 2022), pp. 26–27 ("But just to pick up on that, Mr. Short, was it your impression that the Vice President had directly conveyed his position on these issues to the President, not just to the world through a Dear Colleague Letter, but directly to President Trump?" A: "Many times." Q: "And had been consistent in conveying his position to the President?" A: "Very consistent.").

7. Select Committee to Investigate the January 6th Attack on the United States Capitol, Deposition of Marc Short, (Jan. 26, 2022), pp. 18–20.

8. Documents on file with the Select Committee to Investigate the January 6th Attack on the United States Capitol (U.S. Secret Service Production), CTRL0000092958 (January 6, 2021, message at 10:39 a.m. ET).

9. Documents on file with the Select Committee to Investigate the January 6th Attack on the United States Capitol (US Secret Service Production), CTRL0000092978 (January 6, 2021, message at 10:43 a.m. ET).

10. "Transcript of Trump's Speech at Rally Before US Capitol Riot," Associated Press, (Jan. 13, 2021), available at https://apnews.com/article/election-2020-joe-biden-donald-trump-capitol-siege-media-e79eb5164613d6718e9f4502eb471f27.

11. "Transcript of Trump's Speech at Rally Before US Capitol Riot," Associated Press, (Jan. 13, 2021), available at https://apnews.com/article/election-2020-joe-biden-donald-trump-capitol-siege-media-e79eb5164613d6718e9f4502eb471f27.

12. "Transcript of Trump's Speech at Rally Before US Capitol Riot," Associated Press, (Jan. 13, 2021), available at https://apnews.com/article/election-2020-joe-biden-donald-trump-capitol-siege-media-e79eb5164613d6718e9f4502eb471f27.

13. Donald J. Trump (@realDonaldTrump), Twitter, Jan. 6, 2021 2:24 p.m. ET, available at https://web.archive.org/web/20210106192450/https://twitter.com/realdonaldtrump/status/1346900434540240897 (archived).

14. Select Committee to Investigate the January 6th Attack on the United States Capitol, Hearing on the January 6th Investigation, 117th Cong., 2d sess., (June 16, 2022), available at https://www.govinfo.gov/committee/house-january6th; Rebecca Shabad, "Noose Appears Near Capitol; Protesters Seen Carrying Confederate Flags," NBC News, (Jan. 6, 2021), available at https://www.nbcnews.com/politics/congress/live-blog/electoral-college-certification-updates-n1252864/ncrd1253129#blogHeader.

15. *See* Quint Forgey, " 'Almost No Idea More Un-American': Pence Breaks with Trump on Jan. 6," *Politico*, (June 25, 2021), available at https://www.politico.com/news/2021/06/25/pence-trump-jan-6-496237.

16. Statement by Donald J. Trump, 45th President of the United States of America, Jan. 30, 2022, available at https://web.archive.org/web/20220131171840/https://www.donaldjtrump.com/news/news-8nkdvatd7g1481 (archived) ("If the Vice President (Mike Pence) had 'absolutely no right' to change the Presidential Election results in the Senate, despite fraud and many other irregularities, how come the Democrats and RINO Republicans, like Wacky Susan Collins, are desperately trying to pass legislation that will not allow the Vice President to change the results of the election? Actually, what they are saying, is that Mike Pence did have the right to change the outcome, and they now want to take that right away. Unfortunately, he didn't exercise that power, he could have overturned the Election!") (emphasis added).

17. Mike Allen, "Exclusive Audio: Trump Defends Threats to 'Hang' Pence," *Axios*, (Nov. 12, 2021), available at available at https://www.axios.com/2021/11/12/trump-hang-mike-pence-january-6-audio ("Jonathan Karl: 'Were you worried about him during that siege? Were you worried about his safety?' Trump: 'No, I thought he was well-rotected, and I had heard that he was in good shape. No. Because I had heard he was in very good shape. But, but, no, I think—' Karl: 'Because you heard those chants—that was terrible. I mean—' Trump: 'He could have—well, the people were very angry.' Karl: *They were saying 'hang Mike Pence.'* Trump: *Because it's common sense,* Jon. It's common sense that you're supposed to protect. How can you—if you know a vote is fraudulent, right?—how can you pass on a fraudulent vote to Congress? How can you do that?') (emphasis added).

18. Order Re Privilege of Documents Dated January 4-7, 2021 at 44, *Eastman v. Thompson et al.*, 594 F. Supp. 3d 1156, (C.D. Cal. Mar. 28, 2022) (No. 8:22-cv-99-DOC-DFM).

19. Order Re Privilege of Documents Dated January 4-7, 2021 at 36, 40, 44, *Eastman v. Thompson et al.*, 594 F. Supp. 3d 1156, (C.D. Cal. Mar. 28, 2022) (No. 8:22-cv-99-DOC-DFM) ("Based on the evidence, the Court finds that it is more likely than not that President Trump and Eastman dishonestly conspired to obstruct the Joint Session of Congress on January 6, 2021.").

20. Order Re Privilege of Documents Dated January 4-7, 2021 at 44, *Eastman v. Thompson et al.*, 594 F. Supp. 3d 1156, (C.D. Cal. Mar. 28, 2022) (No. 8:22-cv-99-DOC-DFM).

21. Documents on file with the Select Committee to Investigate the January 6th Attack on the United States Capitol (Chapman University Production), Chapman004708. This document was ordered to be produced to the Select Committee by Judge Carter over Eastman's assertion of attorney-client privilege and upon a finding that the crime-fraud exception to the attorney-client privilege applied. Order Re Privilege of Documents Dated January 4-7, 2021 at 41-42, *Eastman v. Thompson et al.*, 594 F. Supp. 3d 1156, (C.D. Cal. Mar. 28, 2022) (No. 8:22-cv-99-DOC-DFM).

22. Documents on file with the Select Committee to Investigate the January 6th Attack on the United States Capitol (Chapman University Production), Chapman004708.

23. Documents on file with the Select Committee to Investigate the January 6th Attack on the United States Capitol (Chapman University Production), Chapman004708.

24. Neither Eastman nor Chesebro provided substantive answers in response to the Select Committee's questions about the development of this strategy. *See* Select Committee to Investigate the January 6th Attack on the United States Capitol, Deposition of John Eastman, (Dec. 9, 2021); Select Committee to Investigate the January 6th Attack on the United States Capitol, Deposition of Kenneth Chesebro, (Oct. 25, 2022). It is thus difficult to determine who first suggested this concept. Evidence obtained by the Select Committee suggests that key players like Eastman, Giuliani, and Epshteyn were starting to discuss the Vice President's role at the joint session in late November or early December. *See, e.g.,* Select Committee to Investigate the January 6th Attack on the United States Capitol, Transcribed Interview of Cassidy Hutchinson, (Feb. 23, 2022), pp. 71–73 (discussing conversations

involving Mark Meadows, Rudolph Giuliani's legal team, and Members of Congress in late November or early December); Documents on file with the Select Committee to Investigate the January 6th Attack on the United States Capitol (Chapman University Production), Chapman023534 (December 5, 2020 email from John Eastman remarking that "folks at the top of the chain of command on this . . . are now aware of the issues"). *See also* Michael Wolff, *Landslide: The Final Days of the Trump Presidency* (New York: Henry Holt and Company, 2021), p. 135 (describing post-Thanksgiving outreach from Boris Epshteyn to the White House regarding the Vice President theory).

25. Order Re Privilege of Documents Dated January 4-7, 2021 at 41-42, *Eastman v. Thompson et al.*, 594 F. Supp. 3d 1156, (C.D. Cal. Mar. 28, 2022) (No. 8:22-cv-99-DOC-DFM) ("Because the memo likely furthered the crimes of obstruction of an official proceeding and conspiracy to defraud the United States, it is subject to the crime-fraud exception and the Court ORDERS it to be disclosed.").

26. The Select Committee's investigation found that Eastman was communicating about the joint session with Kenneth Chesebro in December 2020. *See e.g.*, Documents on file with the Select Committee to Investigate the January 6th Attack on the United States Capitol (Chapman University Production), Chapman053460, Chapman053475 (December 23, 2020, emails between John Eastman, Kenneth Chesebro, and Boris Epshteyn regarding procedural proposals for joint session).

27. Documents on file with the Select Committee to Investigate the January 6th Attack on the United States Capitol (Chapman University Production), Chapman052976. This memo was originally obtained by the *Washington Post*'s Bob Woodward and Robert Costa and subsequently published by CNN. "READ: Trump Lawyer's Memo on Six-Step Plan for Pence to Overturn the Election," CNN, (Sept. 21, 2021), available at https://www.cnn.com/2021/09/21/politics/read-eastman-memo/index.html.

28. Under the Constitution, if no candidate receives a majority of electoral college votes, this triggers a process where the House of Representatives decides the president. When that happens, each State gets one vote for President, chosen by the Representatives from that state. The candidate who receives a majority of the 50 State votes becomes the president. At the time, there were more Republicans than Democrats in 26 of the 50 State House delegations, leading Eastman to predict that "President Trump [would be] re-elected" under that scenario. *See* Documents on file with the Select Committee to Investigate the January 6th Attack on the United States Capitol (Chapman University Production), Chapman052976.

29. Documents on file with the Select Committee to Investigate the January 6th Attack on the United States Capitol (Chapman University Production), Chapman052976. Note that Eastman has acknowledged the authenticity of a publicly disclosed version of this document, describing it as "a preliminary, incomplete draft" of "the legal memo [he] wrote in January." John C. Eastman, "Trying to Prevent Illegal Conduct from Deciding an Election Is Not Endorsing a 'Coup'," *American Greatness*, (Sept. 30, 2021), available at https://amgreatness.com/2021/09/30/trying-to-prevent-illegal-conduct-from-deciding-an-election-is-not-endorsing-a-coup/ (linking to two-page document titled "PRIVILEGED AND CONFIDENTIAL, January 6 scenario, available at http://cdn.cnn.com/cnn/2021/images/09/20/eastman.memo.pdf).

30. Documents on file with the Select Committee to Investigate the January 6th Attack on the United States Capitol (Chapman University Production), Chapman053561 (December 23, 2020, email from John Eastman to Molly Michael).

31. Documents on file with the Select Committee to Investigate the January 6th Attack on the United States Capitol, (Verizon Production, July 11, 2022) (Dec. 23, 2020 cellular data records from John Eastman). The morning that Eastman began preparing the memo, he received a call from Boris Epshteyn at 8:58 am. Eleven minutes later, Eastman called Chesebro, and the two spoke for over 41 minutes. Eastman continued to trade calls with Epshteyn and Chesebro throughout the day. *See* Documents on file with the Select Committee to Investigate the January 6th Attack on the United States Capitol, (Verizon Production, July 11, 2022) (December 23, 2020, phone records for John Eastman)

32. Documents on file with the Select Committee to Investigate the January 6th Attack on the United States Capitol (Chapman University Production), Chapman052976, p. 2 (Memo regarding January 6 scenario).

33. Documents on file with the Select Committee to Investigate the January 6th Attack on the United States Capitol (Chapman University Production), Chapman003226.

34. Documents on file with the Select Committee to Investigate the January 6th Attack on the United States Capitol (Chapman University Production), Chapman003228. Note that this letter refers to, and purports to supplement, the recommendations of what Eastman described in his correspondence with Mr. Colbert as "a major war game simulation" that he claimed—on October 24, 2020—was "already before the President and his team." Documents on file with the Select Committee to Investigate the January 6th Attack on the United States Capitol (Chapman University Production), Chapman031983. The war game exercise in which Eastman participated is reflected in a report issued by the Claremont Institute and the Texas Public Policy Foundation. "79 Days Report", (Oct. 20, 2020), available at https://www.texaspolicy.com/79-days-to-inauguration-taskforce-report/.

35. Documents on file with the Select Committee to Investigate the January 6th Attack on the United States Capitol (Chapman University Production), Chapman003228 (emphasis added).

36. Documents on file with the Select Committee to Investigate the January 6th Attack on the United States Capitol (Chapman University Production), Chapman031983.

37. Documents on file with the Select Committee to Investigate the January 6th Attack on the United States Capitol (Chapman University Production), Chapman023534.

38. Documents on file with the Select Committee to Investigate the January 6th Attack on the United States Capitol (Chapman University Production), Chapman031983.

39. Documents on file with the Select Committee to Investigate the January 6th Attack on the United States Capitol (Chapman University Production), Chapman052976 (memo regarding January 6 scenarios).

40. Documents on file with the Select Committee to Investigate the January 6th Attack on the United States Capitol (Chapman University Production), Chapman052976 (memo regarding January 6 scenarios).

41. Documents on file with the Select Committee to Investigate the January 6th Attack on the United States Capitol (Chapman University Production), Chapman052966 (December 23, 2020, email from Kenneth Chesebro).

42. Documents on file with the Select Committee to Investigate the January 6th Attack on the United States Capitol (Chapman University Production), Chapman052976 (memo regarding January 6 scenarios).

43. Documents on file with the Select Committee to Investigate the January 6th Attack on the United States Capitol (Chapman University Production), Chapman052976 (memo regarding January 6 scenarios).

44. Documents on file with the Select Committee to Investigate the January 6th Attack on the United States Capitol (Chapman University Production), Chapman052976 (memo regarding January 6).

45. Select Committee to Investigate the January 6th Attack on the United States Capitol, Transcribed Interview of Eric Herschmann, (Apr. 6, 2022), p. 26; see also id., at 36-377 (stating that he did not understand Eastman's statement to be suggesting that violence would be justified to keep President Trump in office).

46. Select Committee to Investigate the January 6th Attack on the United States Capitol, Transcribed Interview of Eric Herschmann, (Apr. 6, 2022), p. 28.

47. Select Committee to Investigate the January 6th Attack on the United States Capitol, Transcribed Interview of Eric Herschmann, (Apr. 6, 2022), pp. 26, 28-29.

48. Select Committee to Investigate the January 6th Attack on the United States Capitol, Transcribed Interview of Eric Herschmann, (Apr. 6, 2022), p. 29.

49. Select Committee to Investigate the January 6th Attack on the United States Capitol, Transcribed Interview of Eric Herschmann, (Apr. 6, 2022), p. 29.

50. Select Committee to Investigate the January 6th Attack on the United States Capitol, Transcribed Interview of Eric Herschmann, (Apr. 6, 2022), p. 29.

51. Select Committee to Investigate the January 6th Attack on the United States Capitol, Deposition of Jason Miller, (Feb. 3, 2022), p. 157.

52. Select Committee to Investigate the January 6th Attack on the United States Capitol, Deposition of Jason Miller, (Feb. 3, 2022), pp. 142, 152.

53. Documents on file with the Select Committee to Investigate the January 6th Attack on the United States Capitol (National Archives Production), 079P-R0000731. Neither this memo, nor a December 8, 2020, memo that followed, reflects the full advice that Greg Jacob ultimately gave to the Vice President regarding the joint session. *See* Select Committee to Investigate the January 6th Attack on the United States Capitol, Deposition of Greg Jacob, (Feb. 1, 2022), pp. 10–11, 32. The OVP Legal Staff memo, dated October 26, 2020, is titled "The Unconstitutionality of the Electoral Count Act." This memo adopts certain legal academics' criticism of the Electoral Count Act and introduces several concepts that would later be cited by proponents of the theory of an expansive view of the Vice President's power. Greg Jacob's legal memo to the Vice President, dated December 8, 2020, notes that the Electoral Count Act prescribes the process for counting electoral votes "to the extent it is constitutional" and seems to allow for the possibility of the Vice President "assert[ing] a constitutional privilege." Documents on file with the Select Committee to Investigate the January 6th Attack on the United States Capitol (National Archives Production), 079P-R0000785. Through his extensive research and analysis, Greg Jacob's understanding developed both as to the legal and historical precedent for the joint session and ultimately led him to the unavoidable conclusions that, one, the Electoral Count Act governed the joint session and, two, its procedures had never been deviated from since it was passed.

54. Select Committee to Investigate the January 6th Attack on the United States Capitol, Deposition of Greg Jacob Deposition, (Feb. 1, 2022), pp. 11–13, 25–26 (noting that Marc Short didn't "name names" of the people he was concerned would encourage the President to prematurely declare victory).

55. Documents on file with the Select Committee to Investigate the January 6th Attack on the United States Capitol (National Archives Production), 079VP-R000011579_0001, 079VP-R000011579_0002 (November 3, 2020, Greg Jacob memo to Marc Short, titled "Electoral Vote Count"). The Election Day memo identifies the 12th Amendment and the Electoral Count Act as the relevant legal framework, but leaves open "whether it is the Vice President, or Congress, that has ultimate constitutional authority to decide electoral vote disputes." It also represents an incomplete understanding of the factual precedents, describing then-Vice President Nixon's conduct in January 1961 as "single-handedly resolv[ing] a dispute over competing slates of electors that were submitted by the State of Hawaii." (In fact, after additional research Jacob concluded the opposite was true.) As addressed elsewhere in this chapter, this memo does not reflect Greg Jacob's full legal analysis or ultimate advice, nor the Vice President's conclusion, about the authority of the Vice President at the joint session.

56. Daniel Villarreal, "Lincoln Project Ad Tells Trump That Pence 'Will Put the Nail in Your Political Coffin'," *Newsweek*, (Dec. 8, 2020), available at https://www.newsweek.com/lincoln–project-ad-tells-trump-that-pence-will-put-nail-your-political-coffin-1553331.

57. Select Committee to Investigate the January 6th Attack on the United States Capitol, Deposition of Greg Jacob, (Feb. 1, 2022), p. 13; Select Committee to Investigate the January 6th Attack on the United States Capitol, *Hearing on the January 6th Investigation*, 117th Cong., 2d sess., (Jun. 16, 2022), available at https://www.govinfo.gov/committee/house-january6th; Select Committee to Investigate the January 6th Attack on the United States Capitol, Deposition of Marc Short, (Jan. 26, 2022), pp. 135–36 (noting the ad buy was limited to "D.C. and Palm Beach").

58. Documents on file with the Select Committee to Investigate the January 6th Attack on the United States Capitol (National Archives Production), 079P-R0000785_0001, 079P-R0000785_0002, 079P-R0000785_0003, 079P-R0000785_0004 (December 8, 2020, Greg Jacob memo to Vice President Pence, titled "January 6 Process for Electoral Vote Count"); *see also*, Select Committee to Investigate the January 6th Attack on the United States Capitol, Deposition of Greg Jacob, (Feb. 1, 2022), p. 32. This December 8, 2020, memo reflects Jacob's more detailed understanding of the mechanics of "modern practice" under the Electoral Count Act, including the process by which the House and Senate separate to debate a member of the House's objection if it is signed by a Senator, but not the full analysis of the precedent that Jacob would ultimately do before January 6, 2021.

59. Select Committee to Investigate the January 6th Attack on the United States Capitol, Deposition of Greg Jacob, (Feb. 1, 2022), p. 102.

60. Select Committee to Investigate the January 6th Attack on the United States Capitol, Deposition of Greg Jacob, (Feb. 1, 2022), pp. 33, 102.

61. U.S. Const. art. II, § 1, cl 3; U.S. Const., Amend. XII.

62. Select Committee to Investigate the January 6th Attack on the United States Capitol, *Hearing on the January 6th Investigation*, 117th Cong., 2d sess., (June 16, 2022), available at https://www.govinfo.gov/committee/house-january6th.

63. Select Committee to Investigate the January 6th Attack on the United States Capitol, Deposition of Greg Jacob, (Feb. 1, 2022), pp. 14–16.

64. Select Committee to Investigate the January 6th Attack on the United States Capitol, Deposition of Greg Jacob, (Feb. 1, 2022), pp. 14–16.

65. Select Committee to Investigate the January 6th Attack on the United States Capitol, *Hearing on the January 6th Investigation*, 117th Cong., 2d sess., (June 16, 2022), available at https://www.govinfo.gov/committee/house-january6th. In testimony given at a Select Committee hearing, Judge Luttig disagreed with Jacob's characterization of the sentence carried through from the Constitution to the 12th Amendment, describing it instead as "pristine[ly] clear," but the witnesses were in agreement that there was "no basis in the Constitution or laws of the United States at all for the theory espoused by Mr. Eastman." *Id.*; *see* Select Committee to Investigate the January 6th Attack on the United States Capitol, *Hearing on the January 6th Investigation*, 117th Cong., 2d sess., (June 16, 2022), available at https://www.govinfo.gov/committee/house-january6th. ("I am in complete agreement with Judge Luttig; it is unambiguous that the Vice President does not have the authority to reject electors."). Note that Vice President Pence apparently agreed with Jacob regarding the clarity of the Constitutional language, as Jacob testified that he joked, "I can't wait to go to heaven and meet the Framers and tell them, 'The work that you did in putting together our Constitution is a work of genius. Thank you. It was divinely inspired. There is one sentence that I would like to talk to you a little bit about.'" *Id.*

66. Select Committee to Investigate the January 6th Attack on the United States Capitol, *Hearing on the January 6th Investigation*, 117th Cong., 2d sess., (June 16, 2022), available at https://www.govinfo.gov/committee/house-january6th.

67. Complaint, *Gohmert et al. v. Pence*, 510 F. Supp. 3d 435, (No. 6:20-cv-0660), (E.D. Tex. Dec. 27, 2020), ECF No. 1.

68. Mike Pence, *So Help Me God* (New York: Simon & Schuster, 2022), p. 443.

69. Complaint, *Gohmert et al. v. Pence*, 510 F. Supp. 3d 435, (No. 6:20-cv-0660), (E.D. Tex. Dec. 27, 2020), ECF No. 1.

70. Complaint, *Gohmert et al. v. Pence*, 510 F. Supp. 3d 435, (No. 6:20-cv-0660), (E.D. Tex. Dec. 27, 2020), ECF No. 1.

71. Complaint, *Gohmert et al. v. Pence*, 510 F. Supp. 3d 435, (No. 6:20-cv-0660), (E.D. Tex. Dec. 27, 2020), ECF No. 1.

72. Documents on file with the Select Committee to Investigate the January 6th Attack on the United States Capitol (Chapman University Production), Chapman055337 (December 22, 2020, John Eastman email to William Olson, Larry Joseph, Mark Martin, Kurt Olson, Kris Kobach, Phillip Jauregui, Pat McSweeney, and Don Brown, titled "Re: Draft Complaint").

73. Order Re Privilege of Documents Dated January 4-7, 2021 at 6, *Eastman v. Thompson et al.*, 594 F. Supp. 3d 1156 (C.D. Cal. 2022) (No. 8:22-cv-99-DOC-DFM).

74. Documents on file with the Select Committee to Investigate the January 6th Attack on the United States Capitol (Chapman University Production), Chapman055337 (December 22, 2020, William Olson email to Larry Joseph, Mark Martin, Kurt Olson, Kris Kobach, John Eastman, Phillip Jauregui, Pat McSweeney, and Don Brown, titled "Re: Draft Complaint").

75. Select Committee to Investigate the January 6th Attack on the United States Capitol, Transcribed Interview of Russell "Rusty" Bowers, (June 19, 2022), pp. 42–45; Documents on file with the Select Committee to Investigate the January 6th Attack on the United States Capitol (Chapman University Production), Chapman003584, (January 4, 2021, emails between John Eastman and Andrew Pappas, coordinating the call between Eastman and Speaker Bowers). Eastman also asked Speaker Bowers to sign a letter drafted by Arizona Rep. Mark Finchem directed to Vice President Pence asking him not to certify the election on January 6th; Bowers refused. Select Committee to Investigate the January 6th Attack on the United States Capitol, Transcribed Interview of Russell "Rusty" Bowers, (June 19, 2022), at p. 45–46.

76. Select Committee to Investigate the January 6th Attack on the United States Capitol, Transcribed Interview of Russell "Rusty" Bowers, (June 19, 2022), at p. 46. Speaker Bowers had already addressed publicly both the pressure he was receiving to overturn the result of the election as well as his firm belief that doing so would violate his oath of office. Documents on file with the Select Committee to Investigate the January 6th Attack on the United States Capitol (Rusty Bowers Production), CTRL0000062389 (Nov. 18, 2020, Dear Colleague letter with attached "Post-Election Frequently Asked Questions"), Documents on file with the Select Committee to Investigate the January 6th Attack on the United States Capitol (Rusty Bowers Production), CTRL0000071098_00069 (December 4, 2020, Press Release titled "Speaker Bowers Addresses Calls for the Legislature to Overturn 2020 Certified Election Results).

77. Select Committee to Investigate the January 6th Attack on the United States Capitol, Transcribed Interview of Russell "Rusty" Bowers, (June 19, 2022), at p. 46. Speaker Bowers also received a call on the morning of January 6th from Representative Andy Biggs in which Rep. Biggs asked Speaker Bowers to sign a letter being sent by other Arizona legislators and/or to support decertification of Arizona's electors; Speaker Bowers again refused. Select Committee to Investigate the January 6th Attack on the United States Capitol, *Hearing on the January 6th Investigation*, 117th Cong., 2d sess., (June 21, 2022), available at https://www.govinfo.gov/committee/house-january6th.

78. *Gohmert et al. v. Pence*, 510 F. Supp. 3d 435, 443 (E.D. Tx. 2021).

79. *Gohmert et al. v. Pence*, 141 S. Ct. 972 (2021).

80. Select Committee to Investigate the January 6th Attack on the United States Capitol, Deposition of John McEntee, (Mar. 28, 2022), pp. 132–34.

81. Documents on file with the Select Committee to Investigate the January 6th Attack on the United States Capitol (John McEntee Production), McEntee0001 (document titled "JEFFERSON USED HIS POSITION AS VP TO WIN").

82. Documents on file with the Select Committee to Investigate the January 6th Attack on the United States Capitol (National Archives Production), P-R000236-000238 (John McEntee note and drafted analysis, titled "PENCE CAN LET THE STATES DECIDE"). Note that the Select Committee received both documents from the National Archives in a format consistent with the documents having been torn apart and taped back together.

83. Documents on file with the Select Committee to Investigate the January 6th Attack on the United States Capitol (National Archives Production), P-R000236-237 (John McEntee note and drafted analysis, titled "PENCE CAN LET THE STATES DECIDE").

84. Documents on file with the Select Committee to Investigate the January 6th Attack on the United States Capitol (National Archives Production), P-R000237; Select Committee to Investigate the January 6th Attack on the United States Capitol, Deposition of John McEntee, (Mar. 28, 2022), p. 147.

85. Select Committee to Investigate the January 6th Attack on the United States Capitol, Deposition of John McEntee, (Mar. 28, 2022), pp. 147-48.

86. Documents on file with the Select Committee to Investigate the January 6th Attack on the United States Capitol (Short production), J6C-TSM-0001, J6C-TSM-0002. Note that the file name of the document ("MEMO_POTUS_January6VPAction.pdf") is visible in an email in which Marc Short forwards to Greg Jacob the memo received from Mark Meadows. Documents on file with the Select Committee to Investigate the January 6th Attack on the United States Capitol (National Archives Production), VP-R0000033, VP-R0000034.

87. Documents on file with the Select Committee to Investigate the January 6th Attack on the United States Capitol (National Archives Production), VP-R0000034.

88. Documents on file with the Select Committee to Investigate the January 6th Attack on the United States Capitol (Jenna Ellis Production), J.007206Ellis.

89. Documents on file with the Select Committee to Investigate the January 6th Attack on the United States Capitol (Jenna Ellis Production), J.007472Ellis.

90. Documents on file with the Select Committee to Investigate the January 6th Attack on the United States Capitol (Jenna Ellis Production), CTRL0000916457_00002, (January 5, 2021, memo from Jenna Ellis to Jay Sekulow). This document was published by *Politico* on December 10, 2021. Betsy Woodruff Swan and Kyle Cheney, "Trump Campaign Lawyer Authored 2 Memos Claiming Pence Could Halt Biden's Victory," *Politico*, (Dec. 10, 2021), available at https://www.politico.com/news/2021/12/10/trump-lawyer-pence-biden-524088. In response to a Select Committee subpoena, Ellis produced a privilege log reflecting several communications from Ellis to Sekulow on January 5 and 6, 2021, each of which was described as "[e]mail discussion of internal legal strategy for possible pending litigation."

91. Documents on file with the Select Committee to Investigate the January 6th Attack on the United States Capitol (Jenna Ellis Production), CTRL0000916457_00002 (January 5, 2021, memo from Ellis to Jay Sekulow).

92. Politico (@politico), Twitter, Jan. 5, 2021 2:31 p.m. ET, available at https://twitter.com/politico/status/1346539955724681221 ("'I actually don't think that's what the Constitution has in mind,' Jay Sekulow, the chief counsel of the American Center for Law & Justice, says about the possibility of Pence rejecting the Electoral College results").

93. Politico (@politico), Twitter, Jan. 5, 2021 2:31 p.m. ET, available at https://twitter.com/politico/status/1346539955724681221.

94. Select Committee to Investigate the January 6th Attack on the United States Capitol, Transcribed Interview of Eric Herschmann, (Apr. 6, 2022), p. 208.

95. Select Committee to Investigate the January 6th Attack on the United States Capitol, Transcribed Interview of Eric Herschmann, (Apr. 6, 2022), p. 208.

96. Select Committee to Investigate the January 6th Attack on the United States Capitol, Deposition of Greg Jacob, (Feb. 1, 2022), p. 68; Select Committee to Investigate the January 6th Attack on the United States Capitol, Transcribed of Matt Morgan, (Apr. 25, 2022), pp. 19, 113. Matt Morgan was at the time a lawyer with Elections, LLC serving as General Counsel of the Trump Campaign and also acting as counsel to Vice President Pence's leadership PAC.

97. Select Committee to Investigate the January 6th Attack on the United States Capitol, Transcribed Interview of Matthew Morgan, (Apr. 25, 2022), pp. 117, 125 ("I had no question about what he was going to do on January 6th.").

98. Select Committee to Investigate the January 6th Attack on the United States Capitol, Deposition of Greg Jacob, (Feb. 1, 2022), p. 68. *See also* Select Committee to Investigate the January 6th Attack on the United States Capitol, Deposition of Chris Hodgson, (Mar. 30, 2022), p. 179 (stating that the reasons why Vice President Pence wanted to issue a public statement included the public discourse, letters from State legislators, and reporting about communications between the President and Vice President).

99. Select Committee to Investigate the January 6th Attack on the United States Capitol, Transcribed Interview of Matthew Morgan, (Apr. 25, 2022), pp. 114, 116.

100. Select Committee to Investigate the January 6th Attack on the United States Capitol, Deposition of Marc Short, (Jan. 26, 2022), pp. 166-68 ("I'm not aware of any evidence that the campaign had, and I'm not aware of any evidence the campaign shared with our office that would have again provided specific evidence of theft or fraud that would have had a material change in any of the States.").

101. Select Committee to Investigate the January 6th Attack on the United States Capitol, Transcribed Interview of Matt Morgan, (Apr. 25, 2022), pp. 99–00; Select Committee to Investigate the January 6th Attack on the United States Capitol, Deposition of Greg Jacob, (Feb. 1, 2022), pp. 36-37.

102. Documents on file with the Select Committee to Investigate the January 6th Attack on the United States Capitol (National Archives Production), 079P-R0000745; *see also* Select Committee to Investigate the January 6th Attack on the United States Capitol, Deposition of Greg Jacob, (Feb. 1, 2022), p. 38. Following the meeting on January 2, 2021, Greg Jacob shared the following memo with Matt Morgan. *See* Documents on file with the Select Committee to Investigate the January 6th Attack, (Matt Morgan Production), AGSC16-000103.

103. Select Committee to Investigate the January 6th Attack on the United States Capitol, Deposition of Greg Jacob, (Feb. 1, 2022), pp. 61-62.

104. Documents on file with the Select Committee to Investigate the January 6th Attack on the United States Capitol (Matt Morgan Production), AGSC16-000066; Select Committee to Investigate the January 6th Attack on the United States Capitol, Transcribed Interview of Matt Morgan, (Apr. 25, 2022), p. 74 ("My view, for an electoral count vote to count, you need a certificate of ascertainment and then the vote of the elector itself, that the vote of an elector without a certificate of ascertainment would not be validly submitted.").

105. Documents on file with the Select Committee to Investigate the January 6th Attack on the United States Capitol (National Archives Production), 079P-R0000698; *see also* Documents on file with the Select Committee to Investigate the January 6th Attack on the United States Capitol (Chris Hodgson Production),00131; Select Committee to Investigate the January 6th Attack on the United States Capitol, Deposition of Chris Hodgson, (Mar. 30, 2022), p. 128 (stating that as of the date of this memo, January 2, 2021, "there were no open questions at that point that I'm aware of.").

106. Select Committee to Investigate the January 6th Attack on the United States Capitol, Deposition of Greg Jacob, (Feb. 1, 2022), p. 52.

107. Select Committee to Investigate the January 6th Attack on the United States Capitol, Deposition of Greg Jacob, (Feb. 1, 2022), pp. 68-69. Jacob shared a draft version of the statement with Matt Morgan. *See* Select Committee to Investigate the January 6th Attack on the United States Capitol, Transcribed Interview of Matt Morgan, (Apr. 25, 2022), pp. 119-120. This draft version clearly set forth Vice President Pence's position, "I Preside, Congress Decides." The draft statement read: I cannot believe that the Framers, who above all else feared the concentrated power of a Caesar, intended to appoint a single individual, often directly interested in the outcome, to unilaterally determine the validity of electoral votes. In the wrong hands, such a power would be the undoing of the Republic." Documents on file with the Select Committee to Investigate the January 6th Attack on the United States Capitol (Matt Morgan Production), AGSC16-000149.

108. Philip Rucker, Josh Dawsey, "Growing Number of Trump Loyalists in the Senate Vow to Challenge Biden's Victory," *Washington Post*, (Jan. 2, 2021), available at https://www.washingtonpost.com/politics/senators-challenge-election/2021/01/02/81a4e5c4-4c7d-11eb-a9d9-1e3ec4a928b9_story.html.

109. Select Committee to Investigate the January 6th Attack on the United States Capitol, Deposition of Marc Short, (Jan. 26, 2022), pp. 166–68.

110. Select Committee to Investigate the January 6th Attack on the United States Capitol, Deposition of Marc Short, (Jan. 26, 2022), pp. 165-66.

111. Documents on file with the Select Committee to Investigate the January 6th Attack on the United States Capitol (Select Committee Transcription), CTRL0000082311, p. 7 (January 2, 2021, Steve Bannon War Room Transcript).

112. Documents on file with the Select Committee to Investigate the January 6th Attack on the United States Capitol (Select Committee Transcription), CTRL0000082311, p. 3 (January 2, 2021, Steve Bannon War Room Transcript).

113. Documents on file with the Select Committee to Investigate the January 6th Attack on the United States Capitol (Select Committee Transcription), CTRL0000082311, p. 6 (January 2, 2021, Steve Bannon War Room Transcript).

114. Documents on file with the Select Committee to Investigate the January 6th Attack on the United States Capitol (Select Committee Transcription), CTRL0000082311, p. 7 (January 2, 2021, Steve Bannon War Room Transcript).

115. Documents on file with the Select Committee to Investigate the January 6th Attack on the United States Capitol (Select Committee Transcription), CTRL0000082311, p. 7 (January 2, 2021, Steve Bannon War Room Transcript).

116. Documents on file with the Select Committee to Investigate the January 6th Attack on the United States Capitol (Select Committee Transcription), CTRL0000082311, p. 7 (January 2, 2021, Steve Bannon War Room Transcript).

117. Documents on file with the Select Committee to Investigate the January 6th Attack on the United States Capitol (Select Committee Transcription), CTRL0000082311, p. 8 (January 2, 2021, Steve Bannon War Room Transcript).

118. Documents on file with the Select Committee to Investigate the January 6th Attack on the United States Capitol (Select Committee Transcription), CTRL0000082311, p. 7 (January 2, 2021, Steve Bannon War Room Transcript).

119. Andrew Kaczynski, Em Steck, "Trump Lawyer John Eastman Said 'Courage and the Spine' Would Help Pence Send Election to the House in Comments before January 6," CNN, (Oct. 30, 2021), available at https://www.cnn.com/2021/10/30/politics/kfile-john-eastman-said-pence-could-throw-election-to-house/index.html.

120. Documents on file with the Select Committee to Investigate the January 6th Attack on the United States Capitol (Public Source), CTRL0000923171 (January 3, 2021, 6-page Eastman memo). Note that Eastman publicly disclosed this document, describing it as "the final version of [his] memo" and embedding it with a filename "Jan 3 Memo on Jan 6 Scenario." John C. Eastman, "Trying to Prevent Illegal Conduct From Deciding an Election Is Not Endorsing a 'Coup'," *American Greatness*, (Sept. 30, 2021), available at https://amgreatness.com/2021/09/30/trying-to-prevent-illegal-conduct-from-deciding-an-election-is-not-endorsing-a-coup/. Eastman has also tried to rewrite history with regard to this memo, arguing that it noted that Congress has the power to make the final determination regarding electoral votes, even though the memo concludes, "[t]he fact is that the Constitution assigns this power to the Vice President as the ultimate arbiter. We should take all of our actions with that in mind." *See* John McCormack, "John Eastman vs. the Eastman Memo," *National Review*, (Oct. 22, 2021), available at https://www.nationalreview.com/2021/10/john-eastman-vs-the-eastman-memo (emphasis added).

121. Documents on file with the Select Committee to Investigate the January 6th Attack on the United States Capitol (Public Source) CTRL0000923171, pp. 4-5 (January 3, 2021, 6-page Eastman memo).

122. Documents on file with the Select Committee to Investigate the January 6th Attack on the United States Capitol (Public Source) CTRL0000923171, (January 3, 2021, 6-page Eastman memo) (describing the majority of the "TRUMP WINS" scenarios as resulting from the Vice President unilaterally determining "which" electoral slate from a State is valid, after "asserting that the authority to make that determination under the 12th Amendment . . . is his alone (and anything in the Electoral Count Act to the contrary is therefore unconstitutional).").

123. Documents on file with the Select Committee to Investigate the January 6th Attack on the United States Capitol (Public Source) CTRL0000923171, (January 3, 2021, 6-page Eastman memo) p. 5.

124. Documents on file with the Select Committee to Investigate the January 6th Attack on the United States Capitol (Public Source) CTRL0000923171, (January 3, 2021, 6-page Eastman memo) p. 2; Documents on file with the Select Committee to Investigate the January 6th Attack on the United States Capitol (Chapman University Production), Chapman052976 (December 23, 2020, 2-page Eastman memo).

125. John C. Eastman, "Constitutional Statesmanship," Claremont Review of Books, (Fall 2021) available at https://claremontreviewofbooks.com/constitutional-statesmanship/.

126. Documents on file with the Select Committee to Investigate the January 6th Attack on the United States Capitol (Chapman University Production), Chapman043035 (December 19, 2020, email from John Eastman to Bruce Colbert, re: Latest draft). It is not clear what relationship or connection existed between John Eastman and Bruce Colbert before the election; documents produced to the Select Committee demonstrate that Eastman and Mr. Colbert exchanged dozens of emails during the time period covered by the Select Committee's subpoena to Chapman University (November 3, 2020, to January 20, 2021).

127. Select Committee to Investigate the January 6th Attack on the United States Capitol, *Hearing on the January 6th Investigation*, 117th Cong., 2d sess., (Jun. 16, 2022), available at [https://www.govinfo.gov/committee/house-january6th.] (Judge Luttig testifying, "[T]here was no support whatsoever in either the Constitution of the United States nor the laws of the United States for the Vice President, frankly, ever to count alternative electoral slates from the States that had not been officially certified by the designated State official in the Electoral Count Act of 1887.").

128. Documents on file with the Select Committee to Investigate the January 6th Attack on the United States Capitol (Chapman University Production), Chapman053475, (December 23, 2020, email from John Eastman to Boris Epshteyn and Kenneth Chesebro, "FW: Draft 2, with edits"); Documents on file with the Select Committee to Investigate the January 6th Attack on the United States Capitol (Chapman University Production), Chapman053476 (December 23, 2020, 2-page Eastman memo).

129. Documents on file with the Select Committee to Investigate the January 6th Attack on the United States Capitol (Chapman University Production), Chapman063984 (January 10, 2021, email from John Eastman to Valerie Moon, re: Tell us in layman's language, what the heck happened with the dual electors? Please?). This email appears to be a response by Eastman to an unsolicited email from a member of the public.

130. Documents on file with the Select Committee to Investigate the January 6th Attack on the United States Capitol (Chapman University Production), Chapman063984 (January 10, 2021, email from John Eastman to Valerie Moon, re: Tell us in layman's language, what the heck happened with the dual electors? Please?).

131. Documents on file with the Select Committee to Investigate the January 6th Attack on the United States Capitol (Public Source) CTRL0000923171, p. 5 (January 3, 2021, 6-page Eastman memo).

132. Documents on file with the Select Committee to Investigate the January 6th Attack on the United States Capitol (Public Source), CTRL0000923171, p. 5 (January 3, 2021, 6-page Eastman memo).

133. Documents on file with the Select Committee to Investigate the January 6th Attack on the United States Capitol (Public Source), CTRL0000923171, p. 5 (January 3, 2021, 6-page Eastman memo).

134. Documents on file with the Select Committee to Investigate the January 6th Attack on the United States Capitol (Public Source), CTRL0000923171, p. 5 (January 3, 2021, 6-page Eastman memo).

135. The pressure placed on the Vice President by the President was a "multiweek campaign" that reached a crescendo in the days before January 6th. Select Committee to Investigate the January 6th Attack on the United States Capitol, Deposition of Greg Jacob, (Feb. 1, 2022), p. 33. The Vice President's Chief of Staff, Marc Short, saw the separation between the President and the Vice President building for weeks. Select Committee to Investigate the January 6th Attack on the United States Capitol, Deposition of Marc Short, (Jan. 26, 2022), pp. 34–35, 216-17.

136. Select Committee to Investigate the January 6th Attack on the United States Capitol, Deposition of Marc Short, (Jan. 26, 2022), pp. 191, 204-05; Select Committee to Investigate the January 6th Attack on the United States Capitol, Deposition of Greg Jacob, (Feb. 1, 2022), p. 82; Select Committee to Investigate the January 6th Attack on the United States Capitol, *Hearing on the January 6th Investigation*, 117th Cong., 2d sess., (June 16, 2022), available at https://www.govinfo.gov/committee/house-january6th.

137. Select Committee to Investigate the January 6th Attack on the United States Capitol, Deposition of Marc Short, (Jan. 26, 2022), pp. 191, 204-05.

138. Select Committee to Investigate the January 6th Attack on the United States Capitol, Transcribed Interview of Pasquale Antony "Pat" Cipollone, (July 8, 2022), pp. 49 (regarding the declaration of martial law), 56 (regarding the appointment of Sidney Powell as special counsel), 58–59, 66 (regarding the seizure of voting machines), 110 (regarding the elevation of Jeff Clark to Acting Attorney General).

139. Select Committee to Investigate the January 6th Attack on the United States Capitol, Informal Interview of Patrick Philbin, (Apr. 13, 2022), p. 5. Philbin told the Select Committee that in the end he decided not to resign out of a sense of obligation: "All of the pilots can't jump off the plane because there's still a lot of passengers in the back and we need to land the plane."

140. Select Committee to Investigate the January 6th Attack on the United States Capitol, Informal Interview of Patrick Philbin, (Apr. 13, 2022).

141. Select Committee to Investigate the January 6th Attack on the United States Capitol, Transcribed Interview of Pasquale Antony "Pat" Cipollone, (July 8, 2022), pp. 79 ("My view was that the Vice President didn't have the legal authority to do anything except what he did."), 81 (testifying that his views on the role of the Vice President were "extremely aligned" with the Vice President's staff), 88 ("I thought that the Vice President did not have the authority to do what was being suggested under a proper reading of the law."); *See also* Select Committee to Investigate the January 6th Attack on the United States Capitol, Informal Interview of Patrick Philbin, (Apr. 13, 2022).

142. Select Committee to Investigate the January 6th Attack on the United States Capitol, Transcribed Interview of Pasquale Antony "Pat" Cipollone, (July 8, 2022), pp. 85–86.

143. Select Committee to Investigate the January 6th Attack on the United States Capitol, Transcribed Interview of Pasquale Antony "Pat" Cipollone, (July 8, 2022), p. 85.

144. Select Committee to Investigate the January 6th Attack on the United States Capitol, Transcribed Interview of Pasquale Antony "Pat" Cipollone, (July 8, 2022), p. 94 (testifying that

the privileged interaction that resulted in his exclusion from the meeting took place in the presence of Meadows and Eastman, but before the Vice President, Short, and Jacob arrived).

145. Select Committee to Investigate the January 6th Attack on the United States Capitol, Transcribed Interview of Pasquale Antony "Pat" Cipollone, (July 8, 2022), pp. 85–86 ("I did walk to that meeting and I did go into the Oval Office with the idea of attending that meeting, and then I ultimately did not attend the meeting.").

146. Select Committee to Investigate the January 6th Attack on the United States Capitol, Transcribed Interview of Pasquale Antony "Pat" Cipollone, (July 8, 2022), pp. 86, 94. Cipollone refused to describe further why he didn't attend the meeting—"[t]he reasons for that are privileged"—and would not tell the Select Committee whether he voluntarily decided not to attend or was told not to.

147. Select Committee to Investigate the January 6th Attack on the United States Capitol, Transcribed Interview of Pasquale Antony "Pat" Cipollone, (July 8, 2022), pp. 85, 88.

148. Select Committee to Investigate the January 6th Attack on the United States Capitol, Deposition of Greg Jacob, (Feb. 1, 2022), pp. 88–89 ("[A]t the meeting on the 4th, Eastman expressed the view that both paths were legally viable.").

149. Select Committee to Investigate the January 6th Attack on the United States Capitol, *Hearing on the January 6th Investigation*, 117th Cong., 2d sess., (June 16, 2022), available at https://www.govinfo.gov/committee/house-january6th.

150. Select Committee to Investigate the January 6th Attack on the United States Capitol, Deposition of Greg Jacob, (Feb. 1, 2022), p. 89. *See also* Select Committee to Investigate the January 6th Attack on the United States Capitol, Deposition of Greg Jacob, (Feb. 1, 2022), pp. 90 ("I think that was threaded throughout, that, again, both were legally viable but that the preferred course would be to send it back to the States."), 91 ("... he [Eastman] thought that the more prudent course was a procedural send it back to the States, rather than reject electors."), 93 ("On the 4th, I think that he said that both were legally viable options. But I do think that he said that he was not saying that that was the one that the Vice President should do.").

151. Select Committee to Investigate the January 6th Attack on the United States Capitol, Deposition of Greg Jacob, (Feb. 1, 2022), pp. 89, 91 ("[H]e thought that the more prudent course was a procedural send it back to the states, rather than reject electors"), 96 ("[M]y impression was he was thinking more acceptance [by] the country of the action taken"). *See also* Select Committee to Investigate the January 6th Attack on the United States Capitol, *Hearings on the January 6th Investigation*, 117th Cong., 2d sess., (June 16, 2022), available at https://www.govinfo.gov/committee/house-january6th.

152. Select Committee to Investigate the January 6th Attack on the United States Capitol, Deposition of Greg Jacob, (Feb. 1, 2022), p. 96; Select Committee to Investigate the January 6th Attack on the United States Capitol, *Hearing on the January 6th Investigation*, 117th Cong., 2d sess., (June 16, 2022), available at https://www.govinfo.gov/committee/house-january6th.

153. Select Committee to Investigate the January 6th Attack on the United States Capitol, Deposition of Greg Jacob, (Feb. 1, 2022), pp. 95, 130 (Q: "Did John Eastman ever admit, as far as you know, in front of the President that his proposal would violate the Electoral Count Act?" A: "I believe he did on the 4th." Q: "Okay. And can you tell us what the President's reaction was?" A: "A I can't."); Documents on file with the Select Committee to Investigate the January 6th Attack on the United States Capitol (National Archives Production), VP-R0000107 (Greg Jacob writing after the Oval Office meeting on January 4th, "Professor Eastman acknowledges that his proposal violates several provisions of statutory law.").

154. Select Committee to Investigate the January 6th Attack on the United States Capitol, Deposition of Marc Short, (Jan. 26, 2022), pp. 202–03.

155. Documents on file with the Select Committee to Investigate the January 6th Attack on the United States Capitol (National Archives Production), VP-R0000107. Select Committee to Investigate the January 6th Attack on the United States Capitol, Deposition of Greg Jacob, (Feb. 1, 2022), p. 127.

156. Documents on file with the Select Committee to Investigate the January 6th Attack on the United States Capitol (National Archives Production), VP-R0000107 ("Professor Eastman acknowledges that his proposal violates several provisions of statutory law"); Select Committee to Investigate the January 6th Attack on the United States Capitol, Deposition of Greg Jacob, (Feb. 1, 2022), pp. 127–28.

157. Documents on file with the Select Committee to Investigate the January 6th Attack on the United States Capitol (National Archives Production), VP-R0000107.

158. Documents on file with the Select Committee to Investigate the January 6th Attack on the United States Capitol, (National Archives Production), VP-R0000107. Jacob notes in his memo that Eastman's proposal also "contradicted the opinion authored by Republican Supreme Court Justice Joseph Bradley as the decided vote on the Electoral Commission of 1877." Whereas Eastman wanted the Vice President to refer the manufactured dispute over slates of electors back to the State legislatures, Justice Bradley wrote that the President of the Senate (the Vice President) "is not invested with any authority for making any investigation outside of the joint meeting of the two Houses."

159. Documents on file with the Select Committee to Investigate the January 6th Attack on the United States Capitol (National Archives Production), VP-R0000107 ("[Professor Eastman] stated that in his view, the imprimatur of approval by a State legislature is important to the legitimacy of counting any slate of electors other than the one initially certified by the State's executive.").

160. Documents on file with the Select Committee to Investigate the January 6th Attack on the United States Capitol (National Archives Production), VP-R0000107.

161. When pressed by Eric Herschmann on whether states really wanted to certify an alternate slate, and why they hadn't taken steps to do so on their own, Eastman had no explanation or response. Select Committee to Investigate the January 6th Attack on the United States Capitol, Transcribed Interview of Eric Herschmann, (Apr. 6, 2022), pp. 28–29.

162. Documents on file with the Select Committee to Investigate the January 6th Attack on the United States Capitol (National Archives Production), VP-R0000107 ("Professor Eastman does not recommend that the Vice President assert that he has the authority unilaterally to decide which of the competing slates of electors should be counted"); Select Committee to Investigate the January 6th Attack on the United States Capitol, Deposition of Greg Jacob, (Feb. 1, 2022), p. 127.

163. Documents on file with the Select Committee to Investigate the January 6th Attack on the United States Capitol (National Archives Production), VP-R0000107.

164. Documents on file with the Select Committee to Investigate the January 6th Attack on the United States Capitol (National Archives Production), VP-R0000085.

165. Documents on file with the Select Committee to Investigate the January 6th Attack on the United States Capitol (National Archives Production), VP-R0000182, VP-R0000183, VP-R0000180, VP-R0000181; Select Committee to Investigate the January 6th Attack on the United States Capitol, Deposition of Greg Jacob, (Feb. 1, 2022), pp. 102–03 ("[I]n fact, there were no materials, new materials that were actually presented to me by Mr. Eastman . . . I was open to receiving anything that anybody wanted to give me that might bear on that question . . . But I also correctly was of the view that I had already looked at everything and that we knew [ ] where we stood.").

166. Select Committee to Investigate the January 6th Attack on the United States Capitol, Deposition of Greg Jacob, (Feb. 1, 2022), p. 95.

167. "Donald Trump Rally Speech Transcript Dalton, Georgia: Senate Runoff Election," Rev, (Jan. 4, 2021), available at https://perma.cc/VAD2-TWVQ ("Hello, Georgia, by the way. There's no

way we lost Georgia. There's no way. That was a rigged election, but we're still fighting it and you'll see what's going to happen. We'll talk about it.").

168. "Donald Trump Rally Speech Transcript Dalton, Georgia: Senate Runoff Election," Rev, (Jan. 4, 2021), available at https://perma.cc/VAD2-TWVQ.

169. "Donald Trump Rally Speech Transcript Dalton, Georgia: Senate Runoff Election," Rev, (Jan. 4, 2021), available at https://perma.cc/VAD2-TWVQ.

170. Select Committee to Investigate the January 6th Attack on the United States Capitol, Deposition of Greg Jacob, (Feb. 1, 2022), pp. 96, 105; Select Committee to Investigate the January 6th Attack on the United States Capitol, Deposition of Marc Short, (Jan. 26, 2022), p. 201; Documents on file with the Select Committee to Investigate the January 6th Attack on the United States Capitol (National Archives Production), VP-R0000182.

171. Select Committee to Investigate the January 6th Attack on the United States Capitol, Deposition of Marc Short Deposition (Jan. 26, 2022) p. 201; see also, Select Committee to Investigate the January 6th Attack on the United States Capitol, Deposition of Greg Jacob (Feb. 1, 2022) pp. 92, 94, 106; Select Committee to Investigate the January 6th Attack on the United States Capitol, *Hearing on the January 6th Investigation*, 117th Cong., 2d sess., (Jun. 16, 2022), available at https://www.govinfo.gov/committee/house-january6th.

172. Documents on file with the Select Committee to Investigate the January 6th Attack on the United States Capitol (Greg Jacobs Production), CTRL0000070421, p. 1 (Jan. 5, 2021, Greg Jacob handwritten notes).

173. Select Committee to Investigate the January 6th Attack on the United States Capitol, *Hearing on the January 6th Investigation*, 117th Cong., 2d sess., (June 16, 2022), available at https://www.govinfo.gov/committee/house-january6th; *See also* Select Committee to Investigate the January 6th Attack on the United States Capitol, Deposition of Greg Jacob, (Feb. 1, 2022), pp. 92 ("He, again, came into the meeting saying, 'What I'm here to ask you to do is to reject the electors.'").

174. Select Committee to Investigate the January 6th Attack on the United States Capitol, Deposition of Greg Jacob, (Feb. 1, 2022), pp. 93–95. Eastman acknowledged to Jacob that the previous day's discussions had included the "send it back to the states" path, but he reaffirmed that the ask on the morning of January 5th was to reject electors outright. Select Committee to Investigate the January 6th Attack on the United States Capitol, Deposition of Greg Jacob, (Feb. 1, 2022), p. 105; Select Committee to Investigate the January 6th Attack on the United States Capitol, *Hearing on the January 6th Investigation*, 117th Cong., 2d sess., (June 16, 2022), available at https://www.govinfo.gov/committee/house-january6th ("So on the 4th, that had been the path that he had said, 'I am not recommending that you do that,' but on the 5th, he came in and expressly requested that.").

175. Select Committee to Investigate the January 6th Attack on the United States Capitol, Transcribed Interview of Eric Herschmann, (Apr. 6, 2022), pp. 24-25.

176. Select Committee to Investigate the January 6th Attack on the United States Capitol, Transcribed Interview of Eric Herschmann, (Apr. 6, 2022), pp. 26-27.

177. Select Committee to Investigate the January 6th Attack on the United States Capitol, Transcribed Interview of Eric Herschmann, (Apr. 6, 2022), p. 24.

178. Select Committee to Investigate the January 6th Attack on the United States Capitol, Transcribed Interview of Eric Herschmann, (Apr. 6, 2022), p. 24.

179. Select Committee to Investigate the January 6th Attack on the United States Capitol, Deposition of Greg Jacob, (Feb. 1, 2022), pp. 107, 117.

180. Select Committee to Investigate the January 6th Attack on the United States Capitol, Deposition of Greg Jacob, (Feb. 1, 2022), pp. 107–08. Jacob debated with Eastman all of the historical examples, concluding that in "the 130 years of practice" the Electoral Count Act had been followed "every single time"; Select Committee to Investigate the January 6th Attack on the United States Capitol, Deposition of Greg Jacob, (Feb. 1, 2022), pp. 109-10.

181. Select Committee to Investigate the January 6th Attack on the United States Capitol, Deposition of Greg Jacob, (Feb. 1, 2022), p. 108. What Jacob found when he looked into the Nixon example is that first, there were no competing slates of electors from Hawaii. In fact, a Republican slate was originally certified by the outgoing Governor, but after a judicially ordered recount, it was clear that the Democratic candidate had won, and the incoming Governor certified a new slate consistent with the outcome of the election after the recount. Then-Vice President Nixon, when he arrived at Hawaii in the joint session, "magnanimously" acknowledged that it was clear that Hawaii's votes for Kennedy were the correct votes and called for objections (of which there were none). This precedent was therefore an example of the Vice President complying with the Electoral Count Act's procedures regarding objections to electors. See Select Committee to Investigate the January 6th Attack on the United States Capitol, Deposition of Greg Jacob, (Feb. 1, 2022), pp. 15-16.

182. Select Committee to Investigate the January 6th Attack on the United States Capitol, Deposition of Greg Jacob, (Feb. 1, 2022), p. 110.

183. Select Committee to Investigate the January 6th Attack on the United States Capitol, Deposition of Greg Jacob, (Feb. 1, 2022), p. 110 ("[H]e ultimately acknowledged that none of [the Justices] would actually back this position when you took into account the fact that what you have is a mildly ambiguous [constitutional provision], a nonsensical result that has all kinds of terrible policy implications, and uniform historical practice against it").

184. Select Committee to Investigate the January 6th Attack on the United States Capitol, Deposition of Greg Jacob, (Feb. 1, 2022), p. 110.

185. Select Committee to Investigate the January 6th Attack on the United States Capitol, Deposition of Greg Jacob, (Feb. 1, 2022), p. 111. Jacob told the Select Committee he did not know to whom Eastman was referring when he indicated "they" would be disappointed that Vice President Pence had not been convinced it was appropriate to reject electors.

186. Select Committee to Investigate the January 6th Attack on the United States Capitol, Deposition of Marc Short, (Jan. 26, 2022), pp. 95–96, 210–11.

187. J. Michael Luttig (@judgeluttig), Twitter, Jan. 5, 2021 9:53 a.m. ET, et seq., available at https://twitter.com/judgeluttig/status/1346469787329646592 ("The only responsibility and power of the Vice President under the Constitution is to faithfully count the electoral college votes as they have been cast,").

188. Select Committee to Investigate the January 6th Attack on the United States Capitol, Deposition of Marc Short, (Jan. 26, 2022), pp. 151-52.

189. Select Committee to Investigate the January 6th Attack on the United States Capitol, Deposition of Marc Short, (Jan. 26, 2022), pp. 151-52.

190. Select Committee to Investigate the January 6th Attack on the United States Capitol, Deposition of Marc Short, (Jan. 26, 2022), pp. 152, 209; see also Tom Hamburger, Josh Dawsey, and Jacqueline Alemany, "Jan. 6 Panel Grapples with How to Secure Testimony from Lawmakers, Pence," Washington Post, (Jan. 15, 2022), available at https://www.washingtonpost.com/politics/2022/01/15/jan-6-subpoenas-committee ("'I did not notice any hesitation on his part,' Quayle said of his conversation with Pence. 'I interpreted his questions as looking for confirmation that what he was going to do was right and that he had no flexibility. That's the way I read it. Given the pressure he was under, I thought it was perfectly normal, very smart on his part to call me.'").

191. Select Committee to Investigate the January 6th Attack on the United States Capitol, Deposition of Greg Jacob, (Feb. 1, 2022), p. 157.

192. Select Committee to Investigate the January 6th Attack on the United States Capitol, Deposition of Greg Jacob, (Feb. 1, 2022), p. 158; Select Committee to Investigate the January 6th Attack on the United States Capitol, Deposition of Marc Short, (Jan. 26, 2022), pp. 215-17.

193. Select Committee to Investigate the January 6th Attack on the United States Capitol, Deposition of Greg Jacob, (Feb. 1, 2022), pp. 157-58.

194. Select Committee to Investigate the January 6th Attack on the United States Capitol, Deposition of Marc Short, (Jan. 26, 2022), p. 215.

195. Select Committee to Investigate the January 6th Attack on the United States Capitol, Deposition of Marc Short, (Jan. 26, 2022), p. 216.

196. Bob Woodward and Robert Costa, *Peril*, (New York: Simon & Schuster, 2021), p. 229; Select Committee to Investigate the January 6th Attack on the United States Capitol, Deposition of Marc Short, (Jan. 26, 2022), pp. 215-16.

197. Select Committee to Investigate the January 6th Attack on the United States Capitol, Deposition of Greg Jacob, (Feb. 1, 2022), p. 160.

198. Select Committee to Investigate the January 6th Attack on the United States Capitol, Deposition of Marc Short, (Jan. 26, 2022), pp. 220-22; Select Committee to Investigate the January 6th Attack on the United States Capitol, Deposition of Greg Jacob, (Feb. 1, 2022), pp. 116, 120. Note that Marc Short recalled that it was this afternoon phone call that led to the in-person meeting between Eastman and Jacob, however, documents received by the Select Committee and Jacob's more detailed recollection of his interactions with Eastman establishes that the in-person meeting occurred in the morning of January 5, 2021.

199. Select Committee to Investigate the January 6th Attack on the United States Capitol, *Hearing on the January 6th Investigation*, 117th Cong., 2d sess., (June 16, 2022), available at https://www.govinfo.gov/committee/house-january6th. (describing the message on this phone call between the Vice President and President Trump with Eastman's participation as, "Well, we hear you loud and clear, you are not going to reject. But remember last night, I said that there was this more prudent course where you could just send it back to the States? Would you be willing to do that[?]"); *see also* Select Committee to Investigate the January 6th Attack on the United States Capitol, Deposition of Greg Jacob, (Feb. 1, 2022), pp. 96-97, 120.

200. Select Committee to Investigate the January 6th Attack on the United States Capitol, Deposition of Greg Jacob, (Feb. 1, 2022), p. 121.

201. Select Committee to Investigate the January 6th Attack on the United States Capitol, Deposition of Greg Jacob, (Feb. 1, 2022), pp. 121-22 (describing calls from Eastman and at least one other lawyer (likely either Kurt Olsen or Bill Olson)).

202. Select Committee to Investigate the January 6th Attack on the United States Capitol, Deposition of Greg Jacob, (Feb. 1, 2022), pp. 122-23.

203. Select Committee to Investigate the January 6th Attack on the United States Capitol, Deposition of Greg Jacob, (Feb. 1, 2022), p. 123 (recounting Eastman's argument that election fraud was resulting in the Constitution being "shredded across all these different states" and comparing it to the Civil War).

204. Select Committee to Investigate the January 6th Attack on the United States Capitol, Deposition of Greg Jacob, (Feb. 1, 2022), pp. 122-24.

205. Maggie Haberman and Annie Karni, "Pence Said to Have Told Trump He Lacks Power to Change Election Result," *New York Times*, (Jan. 5, 2021), available at https://web.archive.org/web/20210106003845/https://www.nytimes.com/2021/01/05/us/politics/pence-trump-election-results.html. The same *Times* reporters had also published on January 4th an article again accurately reporting that President Trump "had directly pressed Mr. Pence to find an alternative to certifying Mr. Biden's win." Annie Karni and Maggie Haberman, "Pence's Choice: Side with the Constitution or His Boss," *New York Times*, (Jan. 4, 2021), available at https://www.nytimes.com/2021/01/04/us/politics/pence-trump.html.

206. Maggie Haberman and Annie Karni, "Pence Said to Have Told Trump He Lacks Power to Change Election Result," *New York Times*, (Jan. 5, 2021), available at https://www.nytimes.com/2021/01/05/us/politics/pence-trump-election-results.html.

207. Maggie Haberman and Anne Karni, "Pence Said to Have Told Trump He Lacks Power to Change Election Result," *New York Times*, (Jan. 5, 2021), available at https://

web.archive.org/web/20210106003845/https://www.nytimes.com/2021/01/05/us/politics/
pence-trump-election-results.html (archived version showing original publication date of
Jan. 5, 2021, at 7:36 p.m. ET).

208. Select Committee to Investigate the January 6th Attack on the United States Capitol, Deposition of Jason Miller, (Feb. 3, 2022), pp. 169-70.

209. Documents on file with the Select Committee to Investigate the January 6th Attack on the
United States Capitol (National Archives Production), 076P-R000007439, (CTRL0000082597)
(January 5, 2021, White House Presidential call log).

210. Documents on file with the Select Committee to Investigate the January 6th Attack on the
United States Capitol (National Archives Production), 076P-R000007439, (CTRL0000082597)
(January 5, 2021, White House Presidential call log).

211. Documents on file with the Select Committee to Investigate the January 6th Attack on the
United States Capitol (National Archives Production), 076P-R000007439, (CTRL0000082597)
(January 5, 2021, White House Presidential call log).

212. Meredith Lee (@meredithllee), Twitter, Jan. 5, 2021, 9:58 p.m. ET, available at https://
twitter.com/meredithllee/status/1346652403605647367?lang=en (emphasis added); Select
Committee to Investigate the January 6th Attack on the United States Capitol, Deposition
of Jason Miller, (Feb. 3, 2022), p. 175 ("[T]ypically on these, I might have a couple of wording
suggestions . . . ultimately the way this came out was the way he wanted [it] to."); see id at
174-76.

213. Select Committee to Investigate the January 6th Attack on the United States Capitol, Hearing on the January 6th Investigation, 117th Cong., 2d sess., (June 16, 2022), available at
https://www.govinfo.gov/committee/house-january6th; Select Committee to Investigate
the January 6th Attack on the United States Capitol, Deposition of Marc Short, (Jan. 26,
2022), p. 224; Select Committee to Investigate the January 6th Attack on the United States
Capitol, Deposition of Chris Hodgson, (Mar. 30, 2022), pp. 184-85.

214. Meredith Lee (@meredithllee), Twitter, Jan. 5, 2021, 9:58 p.m. ET, available at https://
twitter.com/meredithllee/status/1346652403605647367?lang=en.

215. Select Committee to Investigate the January 6th Attack on the United States Capitol, Deposition of Greg Jacob, (Feb. 1, 2022), p. 161 ("[W]hoever drafted the statement it was not
accurate.").

216. Select Committee to Investigate the January 6th Attack on the United States Capitol, Deposition of Greg Jacob, (Feb. 1, 2022), p. 161.

217. Select Committee to Investigate the January 6th Attack on the United States Capitol, Deposition of Marc Short, (Jan. 26, 2022), p. 224; Select Committee to Investigate the January 6th
Attack on the United States Capitol, Deposition of Greg Jacob, (Feb. 1, 2022), p. 163.

218. Select Committee to Investigate the January 6th Attack on the United States Capitol, Deposition of Marc Short, (Jan. 26, 2022), p. 223.

219. Select Committee to Investigate the January 6th Attack on the United States Capitol, Deposition of Marc Short, (Jan. 26, 2022), p. 223.

220. Documents on file with the Select Committee to Investigate the January 6th Attack on the
United States Capitol (National Archives Production), CTRL0000082597, (reflecting calls with
Mr. Stephen Bannon on Jan. 5, 2021, from 8:57 a.m. to 9:08 a.m. and from 9:46 p.m. to 9:52
p.m.).

221. Documents on file with the Select Committee to Investigate the January 6th Attack on the
United States Capitol (Select Committee Transcription), CTRL0000082317 (Jan. 5, 2021, Steve
Bannon War Room Transcript) (Bannon: "All hell is going to break loose tomorrow. Just
understand this: All hell is going to break loose tomorrow. It's going to be quick . . . It's the
fog of war." Bannon discussed putting Sen. Grassley's number on the screen, and suggested they encourage users at TheDonald.win to contact the Senator. (At the time, users
at TheDonald.win were openly planning for violence and to surround the U.S. Capitol on

January 6. *See* Chapter 6.) Bannon told his audience. "I'll tell you this, it's not going to happen like you think it's going to happen, Ok? It's going to be quite extraordinarily different. And all I can say is strap in.").

222. Documents on file with the Select Committee to Investigate the January 6th Attack on the United States Capitol (Select Committee Transcription) CTRL0000082317, (Jan. 5, 2021) (Steve Bannon War Room Transcript).

223. Documents on file with the Select Committee to Investigate the January 6th Attack on the United States Capitol (Select Committee Transcription) CTRL0000082317, (Jan. 5, 2021) (Steve Bannon War Room Transcript).

224. Peter Navarro, *In Trump Time: A Journal of America's Plague Year* (St. Petersburg, FL: All Seasons Press, 2021), p. 252.

225. Peter Navarro, *In Trump Time: A Journal of America's Plague Year* (St. Petersburg, FL: All Seasons Press, 2021), p. 263.

226. Peter Navarro, *In Trump Time: A Journal of America's Plague Year* (St. Petersburg, FL: All Seasons Press, 2021), p. 271.

227. Peter Navarro, *In Trump Time: A Journal of America's Plague Year* (St. Petersburg, FL: All Seasons Press, 2021), p. 252.

228. Peter Navarro, *In Trump Time: A Journal of America's Plague Year* (St. Petersburg, FL: All Seasons Press, 2021), p. 263.

229. *See e.g.*, Documents on file with the Select Committee to Investigate the January 6th Attack on the United States Capitol (Chapman University Production), Chapman052976.

230. Select Committee to Investigate the January 6th Attack on the United States Capitol, Deposition of Marc Short, (Jan. 26, 2022), pp. 26-27 ("But just to pick up on that, Mr. Short, was it your impression that the Vice President had directly conveyed his position on these issues to the President, not just to the world through a Dear Colleague Letter, but directly to President Trump?" A: "Many times." Q: "And had been consistent in conveying his position to the President?" A: "Very consistent."); *see also* Select Committee to Investigate the January 6th Attack on the United States Capitol, Deposition of Greg Jacob, (Feb. 1, 2022), p. 102 ("[T]hat's where the Vice President started. That's where he stayed the entire way."); Select Committee to Investigate the January 6th Attack on the United States Capitol, Deposition of Chris Hodgson, (Mar. 30, 2022), p. 181 ("I believe that the Vice President was consistent in his understanding of the law and the precedent and his belief as to what his authority was and was not on January 6th.").

231. Donald J. Trump (@realDonaldTrump), Twitter, Jan. 6, 2021 1:00 a.m. ET, available at https://web.archive.org/web/20210106072109/https://twitter.com/realdonaldtrump/status/1346698217304584192 (archived).

232. Donald J. Trump (@realDonaldTrump), Twitter, Jan. 6, 2021 8:17 a.m. ET, available at https://web.archive.org/web/20210106131747/https://twitter.com/realdonaldtrump/status/1346808075626426371 (archived).

233. Donald J. Trump (@realDonaldTrump), Twitter, Jan. 6, 2021 8:22 a.m. ET, available at https://web.archive.org/web/20210106132244/https://twitter.com/realdonaldtrump/status/1346809349214248962 (archived).

234. At 9:02 a.m., President Trump instructed the White House operator to call back with the Vice President; the operator instead informed the President at 9:15 a.m. that a message was left for the Vice President. Documents on file with the Select Committee to Investigate the January 6th Attack on the United States Capitol (National Archives Production), P-R000261 (Presidential Call Log, White House Switchboard), P-R000255 (Daily Diary).

235. Documents on file with the Select Committee to Investigate the January 6th Attack on the United States Capitol (National Archives Production), P-R000285 ("11:20 –c w/ VPOTUS"); Documents on file with the Select Committee to Investigate the January 6th Attack on the United States Capitol (National Archives Production), P-R000255 ("The President talked on

a phone call to an unidentified person"); *see also* Select Committee to Investigate the January 6th Attack on the United States Capitol, Deposition of Marc Short, (Jan. 26, 2022), p. 12 (stating that a military aide interrupted Pence's meeting with staff to inform the Vice President that the President was holding to speak with him).

236. Present in the Oval Office during the call with the Vice President were Melania Trump, Donald Trump, Jr., Ivanka Trump, Eric Trump, Kimberly Guilfoyle, and Lara Trump, as well as Mark Meadows, Stephen Miller, Eric Herschmann, and Gen. Keith Kellogg. *See* Select Committee to Investigate the January 6th Attack on the United States Capitol, Transcribed Interview of Ivanka Trump, (Apr. 5, 2022), pp. 30-32, 37.

237. Select Committee to Investigate the January 6th Attack on the United States Capitol, Transcribed Interview of Eric Herschmann, (Apr. 6, 2022), p. 47.

238. Select Committee to Investigate the January 6th Attack on the United States Capitol, Transcribed Interview of Ivanka Trump, (Apr. 5, 2022), p. 39.

239. Select Committee to Investigate the January 6th Attack on the United States Capitol, Transcribed Interview of Ivanka Trump, (Apr. 5, 2022), p. 41.

240. Select Committee to Investigate the January 6th Attack on the United States Capitol, Deposition of Julie Radford, (May 24, 2022), pp. 17-18.

241. Select Committee to Investigate the January 6th Attack on the United States Capitol, Deposition of Julie Radford, (May 24, 2022), p. 19 ("And the word that she relayed to you that the President called the Vice President—apologize for being impolite—but do you remember what she said her father called him?" "The 'P'word."). *See also* Peter Baker, Maggie Haberman, and Annie Karni, "Pence Reached His Limit with Trump. It Wasn't Pretty," *New York Times*, (Jan. 12, 2021), available at https://www.nytimes.com/2021/01/12/us/politics/mike-pence-trump.html; Jonathan Karl, *Betrayal: The Final Act of the Trump Show*, (New York: Dutton, 2021), at pp. 273–74 ("[Y]ou said, 'You can be a patriot or you can be a pussy.' Did you really say that or is that an incorrect report? "I wouldn't dispute it,' [President Trump] answered.").

242. Select Committee to Investigate the January 6th Attack on the United States Capitol, Transcribed Interview of Nicholas Luna, (Mar. 21, 2022), p. 127.

243. Select Committee to Investigate the January 6th Attack on the United States Capitol, Deposition of Keith Kellogg, (Dec. 14, 2021), p. 90; *see also* Select Committee to Investigate the January 6th Attack on the United States Capitol, Transcribed Interview of Donald J. Trump, Jr., (May 3, 2022), p. 84 ("I know the line of questioning was about sending it back to the States, but that's about the extent of my recollection.").

244. Select Committee to Investigate the January 6th Attack on the United States Capitol, Deposition of Keith Kellogg, (Dec. 14, 2021), p. 91 ("Q: [Y]ou said he told the Vice President that he has the legal authority to reject certain votes. Is that what you said? A: That he had the constitutional authority to do that, yes."); *see also* Select Committee to Investigate the January 6th Attack on the United States Capitol, Transcribed Interview of Eric Herschmann (Apr. 6, 2022), p. 48 (describing it as "a general discussion about the legal and constitutional authority of the VP").

245. Select Committee to Investigate the January 6th Attack on the United States Capitol, Deposition of Keith Kellogg, (Dec. 14, 2021), p. 92.

246. Select Committee to Investigate the January 6th Attack on the United States Capitol, Hearing on the January 6th Investigation, 117th Cong., 2d sess., (June 16, 2022), available at https://www.govinfo.gov/committee/house-january6th; Select Committee to Investigate the January 6th Attack on the United States Capitol, Deposition of Greg Jacob, (Feb. 1, 2022), p. 169.

247. Select Committee to Investigate the January 6th Attack on the United States Capitol, Transcribed Interview of Eric Herschmann, (Apr. 6, 2022), p. 40; Documents on file with the Select Committee to Investigate the January 6th Attack on the United States Capitol, (AT&T Production, Feb. 9, 2022).

248. Select Committee to Investigate the January 6th Attack on the United States Capitol, Transcribed Interview of Eric Herschmann, (Apr. 6, 2022), pp. 40–41.

249. Documents on file with the Select Committee to Investigate the January 6th Attack on the United States Capitol, (AT&T Production, Feb. 9, 2022).

250. "Rudy Giuliani Speech Transcript at Trump's Washington, D.C. Rally: Wants 'Trial by Combat,'" Rev, (Jan. 6, 2021), available at https://www.rev.com/blog/transcripts/rudy-giuliani-speech-transcript-at-trumps-washington-d-c-rally-wants-trial-by-combat.

251. "Rudy Giuliani Speech Transcript at Trump's Washington, D.C. Rally: Wants 'Trial by Combat,'" Rev, (Jan. 6, 2021), available at https://www.rev.com/blog/transcripts/rudy-giuliani-speech-transcript-at-trumps-washington-d-c-rally-wants-trial-by-combat.

252. "Rudy Giuliani Speech Transcript at Trump's Washington, D.C. Rally: Wants 'Trial by Combat,'" Rev, (Jan. 6, 2021), available at https://www.rev.com/blog/transcripts/rudy-giuliani-speech-transcript-at-trumps-washington-d-c-rally-wants-trial-by-combat ("We now have letters from five legislators begging us to do that. They're asking us. Georgia, Pennsylvania, Arizona, Wisconsin, and one other coming in.").

253. See, e.g., Documents on file with the Select Committee to Investigate the January 6th Attack on the United States Capitol (Marc Short Production), J6C-TSM-0003, J6C-TSM-0004, (January 6, 2021, email from Molly Michael to March Short containing subject line "2057Rayburn_20210106_002040.pdf" and an attached letter). The letter bore the signatures of 19 of the 60 members of the Arizona House and 4 of the 30 members of the Arizona Senate.

254. Documents on file with the Select Committee to Investigate the January 6th Attack on the United States Capitol (Chapman University Production), Chapman005235, Chapman005236, (January 5, 2021, email from John Eastman to Greg Jacob with an attached letter dated January 4, 2021). In an interview given after January 6th, Eastman argued that the Vice President still should have acted on the basis of the statement of a minority of the Pennsylvania legislature because "it was over Christmas, and they were having trouble getting ahold of people to sign the letter." John McCormack, "John Eastman vs. the Eastman Memo," National Review, (Oct. 22, 2021), available at https://www.nationalreview.com/2021/10/john-eastman-vs-the-eastman-memo/.

255. Documents on file with the Select Committee to Investigate the January 6th Attack on the United States Capitol (Chapman University Production), Chapman005235, Chapman005236.

256. Select Committee to Investigate the January 6th Attack on the United States Capitol, Informal Interview of Jake Corman, (Jan. 25, 2022).

257. Select Committee to Investigate the January 6th Attack on the United States Capitol, Informal Interview of Jake Corman, (Jan. 25, 2022). Corman told the Select Committee that he understood the Vice President's role at the joint session was not substantive.

258. Select Committee to Investigate the January 6th Attack on the United States Capitol, Deposition of Greg Jacob, (Feb. 1, 2022), pp. 167-68; see also Select Committee to Investigate the January 6th Attack on the United States Capitol, Deposition of Marc Short, (Jan. 26, 2022), p. 14; Select Committee to Investigate the January 6th Attack on the United States Capitol, Deposition of Chris Hodgson, (Mar. 30, 2022), pp. 166-67.

259. "Rudy Giuliani Speech Transcript at Trump's Washington, D.C. Rally: Wants 'Trial by Combat'," Rev, (Jan. 6, 2021), available at https://www.rev.com/blog/transcripts/rudy-giuliani-speech-transcript-at-trumps-washington-d-c-rally-wants-trial-by-combat.

260. "Rudy Giuliani Speech Transcript at Trump's Washington, D.C. Rally: Wants 'Trial by Combat'," Rev, (Jan. 6, 2021), available at https://www.rev.com/blog/transcripts/rudy-giuliani-speech-transcript-at-trumps-washington-d-c-rally-wants-trial-by-combat.

261. "Rudy Giuliani Speech Transcript at Trump's Washington, D.C. Rally: Wants 'Trial by Combat'," Rev, (Jan. 6, 2021), available at https://www.rev.com/blog/transcripts/rudy-giuliani-speech-transcript-at-trumps-washington-d-c-rally-wants-trial-by-combat.

262. "Rudy Giuliani Speech Transcript at Trump's Washington, D.C. Rally: Wants 'Trial by Combat'," Rev, (Jan. 6, 2021), available at https://www.rev.com/blog/transcripts/rudy-giuliani-speech-transcript-at-trumps-washington-d-c-rally-wants-trial-by-combat (emphasis added). Note in particular Eastman's assertions regarding voting machines, for example, "They put those ballots in a secret folder in the machines. Sitting there waiting until they know how many they need." Eastman would later describe what he was calling on the Vice President to do as merely "to pause the proceedings." John C. Eastman, "Setting the Record Straight on the POTUS 'Ask'," The American Mind, (Jan. 18, 2021), available at https://americanmind.org/memo/setting-the-record-straight-on-the-potus-ask/.

263. Brian Naylor, "Read Trump's Jan. 6 Speech, A Key Part of Impeachment Trial," NPR, (Feb. 10, 2021), available at https://www.npr.org/2021/02/10/966396848/read-trumps-jan-6-speech-a-key-part-of-impeachment-trial.

264. Brian Naylor, "Read Trump's Jan. 6 Speech, A Key Part of Impeachment Trial," NPR, (Feb. 10, 2021), available at https://www.npr.org/2021/02/10/966396848/read-trumps-jan-6-speech-a-key-part-of-impeachment-trial.

265. Brian Naylor, "Read Trump's Jan. 6 Speech, A Key Part of Impeachment Trial," NPR, (Feb. 10, 2021), available at https://www.npr.org/2021/02/10/966396848/read-trumps-jan-6-speech-a-key-part-of-impeachment-trial.

266. Brian Naylor, "Read Trump's Jan. 6 Speech, A Key Part of Impeachment Trial," NPR, (Feb. 10, 2021), available at https://www.npr.org/2021/02/10/966396848/read-trumps-jan-6-speech-a-key-part-of-impeachment-trial.

267. Brian Naylor, "Read Trump's Jan. 6 Speech, A Key Part of Impeachment Trial," NPR, (Feb. 10, 2021), available at https://www.npr.org/2021/02/10/966396848/read-trumps-jan-6-speech-a-key-part-of-impeachment-trial.

268. Brian Naylor, "Read Trump's Jan. 6 Speech, A Key Part of Impeachment Trial," NPR, (Feb. 10, 2021), available at https://www.npr.org/2021/02/10/966396848/read-trumps-jan-6-speech-a-key-part-of-impeachment-trial.

269. Brian Naylor, "Read Trump's Jan. 6 Speech, A Key Part of Impeachment Trial," NPR, (Feb. 10, 2021), available at https://www.npr.org/2021/02/10/966396848/read-trumps-jan-6-speech-a-key-part-of-impeachment-trial.

270. Mike Pence (@Mike_Pence), Twitter, Jan. 6, 2021 1:02 p.m. ET, available at https://twitter.com/Mike_Pence/status/1346879811151605762. Between 12:45 and 1:00 p.m., Vice President Pence processed with the Senate to the House Chamber. See Select Committee to Investigate the January 6th Attack on the United States Capitol, Deposition of Chris Hodgson, (Mar. 30, 2022), pp. 202-03. The Vice President's statement was issued publicly and distributed on the House floor before the Vice President convened the joint session at approximately 1:05 p.m. See Select Committee to Investigate the January 6th Attack on the United States Capitol, Deposition of Greg Jacob, (Feb. 1, 2022), p. 173; see also Donna Cassata and Felicia Sonmez, "Congress Meets in Joint Session to Confirm Biden's Win, Over the Objections of Dozens of Republicans," Washington Post, (Jan. 6, 2021), available at https://www.washingtonpost.com/politics/2021/01/06/congress-electoral-college-vote-live-updates/#link-DUX3QUF3TVDNZDEGO7KIK2JSYE.

271. Select Committee to Investigate the January 6th Attack on the United States Capitol, Deposition of Greg Jacob, (Feb. 1, 2022), p. 164.

272. Mike Pence (@Mike_Pence), Twitter, Jan. 6, 2021 1:02 p.m. ET, available at https://twitter.com/Mike_Pence/status/1346879811151605762; see also Documents on file with the Select Committee to Investigate the January 6th Attack on the United States Capitol (National Archives Production), VP-R0000121, (January 6, 2021, Dear Colleague letter issued by Vice President Pence).

273. Select Committee to Investigate the January 6th Attack on the United States Capitol, Deposition of Marc Short, (Jan. 26, 2022), pp. 27-28 (testifying that, in consultation with the Senate Parliamentarian, the Vice President purposefully revised the standard language used by previous vice presidents at the joint session of Congress because of efforts by the

Trump Campaign and allies to create the public perception that there were "other slates of electors that were being considered or [ ] being put forward.").

274. Select Committee to Investigate the January 6th Attack on the United States Capitol, Deposition of Marc Short, (Jan. 26, 2022), pp. 186-88; Select Committee to Investigate the January 6th Attack on the United States Capitol, Deposition of Greg Jacob, (Feb. 1, 2022), pp. 53-54; Select Committee to Investigate the January 6th Attack on the United States Capitol, Deposition of Chris Hodgson, (Mar. 30, 2022), pp. 50-51. The Senate Parliamentarian offers advice and guidance on compliance with the Senate's rules. *See* CRS Report, The Office of the Parliamentarian in the House and Senate, (Nov. 28, 2018) RS20544. The Office of the Secretary of the Senate, on behalf of the Senate Parliamentarian and her staff, declined requests for information about this topic, as well as other January 6-related topics, from the Select Committee citing the independent relationship of the Senate and House as well as "historical congressional norms."

275. Select Committee to Investigate the January 6th Attack on the United States Capitol, Deposition of Greg Jacob, (Feb. 1, 2022), p. 64; Select Committee to Investigate the January 6th Attack on the United States Capitol, Deposition of Chris Hodgson, (Mar. 30, 2022), pp. 54-56 (testifying that the Vice President's understanding of his role as explained in the Dear Colleague letter he released on January 6th was set as of his meeting with the Parliamentarian on January 3rd).

276. Select Committee to Investigate the January 6th Attack on the United States Capitol, Deposition of Greg Jacob, (Feb. 1, 2022), pp. 68-70; Select Committee to Investigate the January 6th Attack on the United States Capitol, Deposition of Marc Short, (Jan. 26, 2022), pp. 2728; Documents on file with the Select Committee to Investigate the January 6th Attack on the United States Capitol (Chris Hodgson Production), 00163, (Vice President Superscript for Joint Session to Count Electoral Ballots January 6, 2021), 00181, (Response to Submissions NOT Certified by a State); Documents on file with the Select Committee to Investigate the January 6th Attack on the United States Capitol (National Archives Production), VP-R0000103_0001 (Pence joint session scripted responses).

277. Select Committee to Investigate the January 6th Attack on the United States Capitol, Deposition of Marc Short, (Jan. 26, 2022), p. 42. Jacob learned through the media that Trump electors had met and purported to cast electoral votes but, seeing no indication that any of the groups that met had "an imprimatur of State authority," he concluded that they would not qualify as competing slates under the Electoral Count Act. *See* Select Committee to Investigate the January 6th Attack on the United States Capitol, Deposition of Greg Jacob, (Feb. 1, 2022), p. 51; *see also* Select Committee to Investigate the January 6th Attack on the United States Capitol, Deposition of Greg Jacob, (Feb. 1, 2022), p. 54 ("I'm sure I, either in my oral conversation with Elizabeth [MacDonough] or in looking at this spreadsheet, confirmed my conclusion that none of these had the requisite State authority.").

278. The Senate Parliamentarian and her staff tracked the receipt of legitimate electoral votes from the states as well as the private citizen submissions (including the fake slates submitted by Trump electors) and identified the many deficiencies of the fake documents. Documents on file with the Select Committee to Investigate the January 6th Attack on the United States Capitol (National Archives Production), VP R0000323_0001 (Jan. 3, 2021 email exchange with Senate Parliamentarian), VP R0000417_0001 (Jan. 2 and 3, 2021 email exchange with Senate Parliamentarian), VP R0000418_0001 (list of deficiencies in alternate elector slates); Documents on file with the Select Committee to Investigate the January 6th Attack on the United States Capitol (Chris Hodgson Production), 00094, (list of deficiencies in alternate elector slates). The Senate Parliamentarian reviewed each purported slate of electoral votes to separate those in regular form and authorized by a State from those submitted by private citizens—the Trump Campaign's fake electors fell into this latter category. *See* Select Committee to Investigate the January 6th Attack on the United States Capitol, Deposition of Greg Jacob, (Feb. 1, 2022), pp. 53—54; *see also* Select Committee to Investigate the January 6th Attack on the United States Capitol, Deposition of Chris Hodgson, (Mar. 30, 2022), pp. 44-45.

279. "House Chamber During Joint Session," C-SPAN, at 11:07–11:37, Jan. 6, 2021, available at https://www.c-span.org/video/?507748-1/house-chamber-joint-session (emphasis added).

280. Select Committee to Investigate the January 6th Attack on the United States Capitol, Deposition of Andrew Hitt, (Feb. 28, 2022), pp. 94-95. *See also* Documents on file with the Select Committee to Investigate the January 6th Attack on the United States Capitol (National Archives Production), VP-R0000076, VP-R0000417, VP-R0000418, (January 3, 2021, emails and spreadsheet showing OVP staff tracking the arrival of fake electors' certificates).

281. Documents on file with the Select Committee to Investigate the January 6th Attack on the United States Capitol (Andrew Hitt Production), Hitt000090 (text messages exchanged between Republican officials in Wisconsin, including statement that "[f]reaking trump idiots want someone to fly original elector papers to the Senate President.").

282. Documents on file with the Select Committee to Investigate the January 6th Attack on the United States Capitol (Chris Hodgson Production), 00012, (message from Rep. Kelly's Chief of Staff, Matt Stroia, to Chris Hodgson on Jan. 6, 2021, at 8:41 am), 00058, (messages from Senator Johnson's Chief of Staff, Sean Riley, to Chris Hodgson on Jan. 6, 2021, around 12:37 pm).

283. Documents on file with the Select Committee to Investigate the January 6th Attack on the United States Capitol (Chris Hodgson Production), 00058 (Chris Hodgson responding to Sean Riley, "Do not give that to him. He's about to walk over to preside over the joint session, those were supposed to come in through the mail[.]" And, "The VP absolutely should not receive any mail that hasn't been screened.").

284. *See, e.g.,* "House Chamber During Joint Session," C-SPAN, at 15:33–15:59, Jan. 6, 2021, available at https://www.c-span.org/video/?507748-1/house-chamber-joint-session.

285. Karoun Demirjian, "GOP Members Object to Arizona's Electoral Votes for Biden," *Washington Post*, (Jan. 6, 2021), available at https://www.washingtonpost.com/politics/2021/01/06/congress-electoral-college-vote-live-updates/#link-TSWL74F2SVHBHET7GQR5IEP6FI .

286. "House Chamber During Joint Session," C-SPAN, at 15:59–17:16, Jan. 6, 2021, available at https://www.c-span.org/video/?507748-1/house-chamber-joint-session.

287. "House Chamber During Joint Session," C-SPAN, at 17:16–18:01, Jan. 6, 2021, available at https://www.c-span.org/video/?507748-1/house-chamber-joint-session.

288. Select Committee to Investigate the January 6th Attack on the United States Capitol, Deposition of Marc Short, (Jan. 26, 2022), p. 29.

289. House vote on Arizona (Roll No. 10): 167 Cong. Rec. H93 (daily ed. Jan. 6, 2021): 121-303; House vote on PA (Roll No. 11): 167 Cong. Rec. H112 (daily ed. Jan. 6, 2021): 138-282; Senate vote on Arizona (Rollcall Vote No. 1 Leg.): 167 Cong. Rec. S31-32 (daily ed. Jan. 6, 2021): 6-93; Senate vote on PA (Rollcall Vote. No. 2 Leg.): 167 Cong. Rec. S38 (daily ed. Jan. 6, 2021): 7-92.

290. Katie Meyer, "Congress Certifies Pa. Results, Biden's Victory After Chaotic Day of Violent Insurrection," WHYY, (Jan. 6, 2021), available at https://whyy.org/articles/casey-fitzpatrick-condemn-violent-insurrection-as-congress-moves-toward-certifying-biden/.

291. Select Committee to Investigate the January 6th Attack on the United States Capitol, Deposition of Greg Jacob, (Feb. 1, 2022), pp. 173-74.

292. Select Committee to Investigate the January 6th Attack on the United States Capitol, Deposition of Greg Jacob, (Feb. 1, 2022), pp. 173-75.

293. Select Committee to Investigate the January 6th Attack on the United States Capitol, Deposition of Greg Jacob, (Feb. 1, 2022), p. 193.

294. Select Committee to Investigate the January 6th Attack on the United States Capitol, Deposition of Chris Hodgson, (Mar. 30, 2022), pp. 208-09.

295. Select Committee to Investigate the January 6th Attack on the United States Capitol, Deposition of Chris Hodgson, (Mar. 30, 2022), pp. 208-10; Documents on file with the Select Committee to Investigate the January 6th Attack on the United States Capitol (National Archives Production), P-R001019–P-R001020 (Jan. 6, 2021, NSC Chat Log).

296. Donald J. Trump (@realDonaldTrump), Twitter, Jan. 6, 2021 2:24 p.m. ET, available at https://web.archive.org/web/20210106192450/https://twitter.com/realdonaldtrump/status/1346900434540240897.

297. Documents on file with the Select Committee to Investigate the January 6th Attack on the United States Capitol (National Archives Production), P-R001019–P-R001020 (NSC Chat Log).

298. Select Committee to Investigate the January 6th Attack on the United States Capitol, Transcribed Interview of Sarah Matthews, (Feb. 8, 2022), pp. 37-38.

299. Select Committee to Investigate the January 6th Attack on the United States Capitol, Deposition of Marc Short, (Jan. 26, 2022), pp. 30-31.

300. Select Committee to Investigate the January 6th Attack on the United States Capitol, Deposition of Marc Short, (Jan. 26, 2022), pp. 30-31.

301. Select Committee to Investigate the January 6th Attack on the United States Capitol, Deposition of Marc Short, (Jan. 26, 2022), pp. 30-31.

302. Documents on file with the Select Committee to Investigate the January 6th Attack on the United States Capitol (National Archives Production), P-R001019–P-R001020 (NSC Chat Log).

303. See Chapter 8; see also Select Committee to Investigate the January 6th Attack on the United States Capitol, Deposition of Marc Short, (Jan. 26, 2022), pp. 31-32.

304. Select Committee to Investigate the January 6th Attack on the United States Capitol, Hearing on the January 6th Investigation, 117th Cong., 2d sess., (June 16, 2022), available at https://www.govinfo.gov/committee/house-january6th.

305. Select Committee to Investigate the January 6th Attack on the United States Capitol, Deposition of Marc Short, (Jan. 26, 2022), pp. 63-65.

306. On the evening of January 6, 2021, the President's Military Aide told the Vice President's Military Aide (who relayed it to the Secret Service) that Marc Short's access to the White House complex had been cancelled. Documents on file with the Select Committee to Investigate the January 6th Attack on the United States Capitol (Secret Service Production), CTRL0000513149 (January 6-7, 2021), CTRL0000673145 (January 6, 2021). Several people relayed to Marc Short that "some who instigated the President"—possibly Peter Navarro—suggested to the President that "Marc was responsible for leading the Vice President on the path he took," which resulted in the President exclaiming that Mr. Short should be locked out of the White House. Select Committee to Investigate the January 6th Attack on the United States Capitol, Deposition of Marc Short, (Jan. 26, 2022), pp. 236-37; see also Biba Adams, "Pence's Chief of Staff Denied Entry into WH: Trump 'Blaming Me'," Yahoo News, (Jan. 7, 2021), available at https://www.yahoo.com/video/pence-chief-staff-denied-entry-173848235.html.

307. Select Committee to Investigate the January 6th Attack on the United States Capitol, Deposition of Marc Short, (Jan. 26, 2022), p. 238.

308. Select Committee to Investigate the January 6th Attack on the United States Capitol, Deposition of Marc Short, (Jan. 26, 2022), p. 31, 45 ("The reason was he felt like, for the world's greatest democracy, to see a motorcade, a 15-car motorcade fleeing the Capitol would send all the wrong signals. So he was adamant to say: I want to stay here in the Capitol."); see also Select Committee to Investigate the January 6th Attack on the United States Capitol, Hearing on the January 6th Investigation, 117th Cong., 2d sess., (June 16, 2022), available at https://www.govinfo.gov/committee/house-january6th.

309. Select Committee to Investigate the January 6th Attack on the United States Capitol, Deposition of Marc Short, (Jan. 26, 2022), pp. 29-31, 44-45; Select Committee to Investigate the January 6th Attack on the United States Capitol, Deposition of Greg Jacob, (Feb. 1, 2022), pp. 176-77; Select Committee to Investigate the January 6th Attack on the United States Capitol, Hearing on the January 6th Investigation, 117th Cong., 2d sess., (June 16, 2022), available at https://www.govinfo.gov/committee/house-january6th.

310. Select Committee to Investigate the January 6th Attack on the United States Capitol, Deposition of Greg Jacob, (Feb. 1, 2022), p. 198.

311. Select Committee to Investigate the January 6th Attack on the United States Capitol, Deposition of Greg Jacob, (Feb. 1, 2022), pp. 198-99.

312. Select Committee to Investigate the January 6th Attack on the United States Capitol, Deposition of Greg Jacob, (Feb. 1, 2022), pp. 198-99.

313. Jacob told the Select Committee that he recognized that January 6 was going to be "an historically important day" and he wanted to memorialize exactly what he thought of the arguments made by Eastman on January 5th, to supplement the memo he wrote to Vice President Pence reflecting the arguments Eastman made on January 4th. Select Committee to Investigate the January 6th Attack on the United States Capitol, Deposition of Greg Jacob, (Feb. 1, 2022), pp. 200-01.

314. Documents on file with the Select Committee to Investigate the January 6th Attack on the United States Capitol (Chapman University Production), Chapman005370 (January 6, 2021, emails between Greg Jacob and John Eastman).

315. Documents on file with the Select Committee to Investigate the January 6th Attack on the United States Capitol (Chapman University Production), Chapman005379 (January 6, 2021, emails between Greg Jacob and John Eastman).

316. Select Committee to Investigate the January 6th Attack on the United States Capitol, Deposition of Greg Jacob, (Feb. 1, 2022), p. 200.

317. Select Committee to Investigate the January 6th Attack on the United States Capitol, Deposition of Greg Jacob, (Feb. 1, 2022), p. 200.

318. Select Committee to Investigate the January 6th Attack on the United States Capitol, Deposition of Chris Hodgson, (Mar. 30, 2022), pp. 246-47.

319. "READ: Mike Pence's Statement to the Senate on the Storming of the Capitol," *U.S. News*, (Jan. 6, 2021), available at https://www.usnews.com/news/elections/articles/2021-01-06/read-mike-pences-statement-to-the-senate-on-the-storming-of-the-capitol; *see also* Select Committee to Investigate the January 6th Attack on the United States Capitol, Deposition of Chris Hodgson, (Mar. 30, 2022), p. 246 (testifying that the Vice President wrote his remarks himself in his ceremonial office after the Capitol was cleared).

320. Documents on file with the Select Committee to Investigate the January 6th Attack on the United States Capitol (National Archives Production), VP-R0000155, (January 6, 2021, emails between Greg Jacob and John Eastman).

321. Documents on file with the Select Committee to Investigate the January 6th Attack on the United States Capitol, (National Archives Production), VP-R0000155, p. 1, (January 6, 2021, emails between Greg Jacob and John Eastman).

322. Select Committee to Investigate the January 6th Attack on the United States Capitol, Hearing on the January 6th Investigation, 117th Cong., 2d sess., (June 16, 2022), available at https://www.govinfo.gov/committee/house-january6th.

323. Documents on file with the Select Committee to Investigate the January 6th Attack on the United States Capitol (National Archives Production), VP-R0000155, (January 6, 2021, emails between Greg Jacob and John Eastman). Note that Greg Jacob's testimony establishes that this email was likely received on January 6, 2021, at 11:44 p.m., not at 4:44 a.m. the following morning as shown on the face of this document as produced. Select Committee to Investigate the January 6th Attack on the United States Capitol, Deposition of Greg Jacob, (Feb. 1, 2022), p. 205. As noted in the Executive Summary, the Select Committee also received certain documents in UTC time, which is five hours ahead of EST.

324. Documents on file with the Select Committee to Investigate the January 6th Attack on the United States Capitol (Chapman University Production), Chapman005479 (January 6, 2021, emails between Greg Jacob and John Eastman). This email represents John Eastman again encouraging, in writing and just after the violent attack on the Capitol had been quelled,

that the Vice President use this as a justification for a further and much more serious violation of the law—delaying the certification. Select Committee to Investigate the January 6th Attack on the United States Capitol, *Hearing on the January 6th Investigation*, 117th Cong., 2d sess., (June 16, 2022), available at https://www.govinfo.gov/committee/house-january6th. Eastman attempted to minimize what he was doing by calling the Electoral Count Act a "minor procedural statute." Select Committee to Investigate the January 6th Attack on the United States Capitol, Deposition of Greg Jacob, (Feb. 1, 2022), p. 133. In an email sent at 1:33 p.m., just before the Capitol was breached, Eastman wrote, "I'm sorry Greg, but this is small minded. You're sticking with minor procedural statutes while the Constitution is being shredded." Documents on file with the Select Committee to Investigate the January 6th Attack on the United States Capitol (National Archives Production), VP-R0000166.

325. Select Committee to Investigate the January 6th Attack on the United States Capitol, *Hearing on the January 6th Investigation*, 117th Cong., 2d sess., (June 16, 2022), available at https://www.govinfo.gov/committee/house-january6th.

326. Select Committee to Investigate the January 6th Attack on the United States Capitol, Transcribed Interview of Eric Herschmann, (Apr. 6, 2022), pp. 43-44.

327. Select Committee to Investigate the January 6th Attack on the United States Capitol, Transcribed Interview of Eric Herschmann, (Apr. 6, 2022), pp. 43-44.

328. Documents on file with the Select Committee to Investigate the January 6th Attack on the United States Capitol (Chapman University Production), Chapman0064047, (January 11, 2021, email from John Eastman to Rudy Giuliani).

329. Select Committee to Investigate the January 6th Attack on the United States Capitol, Deposition of Marc Short, (Jan. 26, 2022), pp. 35-36.

Donald J. Trump ✓
@realDonaldTrump

Peter Navarro releases 36-page report alleging election fraud 'more than sufficient' to swing victory to Trump washex.am/3nwaBCe. A great report by Peter. Statistically impossible to have lost the 2020 Election. Big protest in D.C. on January 6th. Be there, will be wild!

⚠ This claim about election fraud is disputed

Peter Navarro releases 36-page report alleging election fraud 'more than sufficie...
Director of the Office of Trade and Manufacturing Policy Peter Navarro published a lengthy report Thursday outlining several examples of voting irregularities that a...
🔗 washingtonexaminer.com

1:42 AM · Dec 19, 2020 · Twitter for iPhone

6

"BE THERE, WILL BE WILD!"

On December 14, 2020, electors around the country met to cast their Electoral College votes. Their vote ensured former Vice President Joe Biden's victory and cemented President Donald J. Trump's defeat. The people, and the States, had spoken. Members of President Trump's own Cabinet knew the election was over. Attorney General William Barr viewed it as "the end of the matter."[1] Secretary of State Mike Pompeo and Secretary of Labor Eugene Scalia concurred.[2] That same day, Scalia told President Trump directly that he should concede defeat.[3]

President Trump had no intention of conceding. As he plotted ways to stay in power, the President summoned a mob for help.

At 1:42 a.m., on December 19th, President Trump tweeted: "Big protest in D.C. on January 6th. Be there, will be wild!"[4]

The President's tweet galvanized tens of thousands of his supporters around the country. President Trump had been lying to them since election day, claiming he won, and that the Democrats had stolen victory from him. Now, with a single tweet, the President focused his supporters' anger on the joint session of Congress in Washington, DC on January 6th.

Anika Navaroli, the longest-tenured member of Twitter's Trust and Safety Policy team, monitored the reaction to President Trump's "be wild" tweet. She told the Select Committee that the President was "essentially staking a flag in DC ... for his supporters to come and rally."[5] The tweet created a "fire hose" of calls to overthrow the U.S. Government. President Trump's supporters had a new sense of urgency because they felt "as if their Commander in Chief" had summoned them.[6]

For many extremists and conspiracy theorists, the President's announcement was a call to arms.[7]

For the Proud Boys—described in more detail below—and their leader, Henry "Enrique" Tarrio, President Trump's tweet set in motion a chain of events that led directly to the attack on the U.S. Capitol. In the days that followed, the Proud Boys reorganized their hierarchy, imposed a stricter

Tarrio's video appears on a screen during a Select Committee hearing on June 09, 2022.
Photo by Drew Angerer/Getty Images

chain-of-command, and instructed followers to go "incognito" on January 6th.[8] The Proud Boys had made their presence known at previous pro-Trump events, including "Stop the Steal" rallies, where they brandished their black and yellow apparel and engaged in street brawls.[9] Suddenly, they did not want to stand out from the crowd. They wanted to blend in. They were planning something big.[10]

Tarrio allegedly used encrypted messages to plot the January 6, 2021, attack. On January 4, 2021, Tarrio told his men that they should "storm the Capitol."[11] While the attack was underway, Tarrio claimed credit in a private chat, writing: "We did this."[12] And on the evening of January 6th, Tarrio released a video of a man, presumably Tarrio himself, dressed in an odd costume standing in front of the U.S. Capitol. The eerie production had been recorded prior to the events of that day. Tarrio—who was not in Washington, DC on January 6th[13]—titled it, "Premonition."[14]

The Oath Keepers, a far-right, anti-government militia movement—also described in more detail below—began planning for January 6th after the President's tweet as well. Stewart Rhodes, the group's leader, had agitated against the U.S. Government for years.[15] Immediately following the 2020 presidential election, Rhodes and others schemed to stop the peaceful transfer of power. They stored weapons outside of Washington, DC,[16] hoping that President Trump would deputize them as his own militia.[17] An Oath Keeper leader, Kelly Meggs, read President Trump's December 19th tweet and commented in a Facebook message: "He called us all to the Capitol and wants us to make it wild!!! Sir Yes Sir!!!"[18] The Oath Keepers formed two military "stacks" and marched up the steps of the U.S. Capitol on January 6th. Meggs led one of them.[19]

Members of both the Proud Boys and Oath Keepers have been charged with "seditious conspiracy" and other serious crimes, including conspiracy to interfere with a Federal proceeding; some, including Stewart Rhodes, have been convicted.[20] U.S. law defines seditious conspiracy as plotting "to overthrow," or "to oppose by force," or to use "force to prevent, hinder, or delay the execution of any law of the United States."[21] Some of the two groups' members have already admitted that this is what they intended to do.[22]

Other extremists and conspiracy theorists mobilized after President Trump's tweet as well. These movements are described in more detail in subsequent sections. Three Percenter militias—another far-right, anti-government movement—shared "#OccupyCongress" memes[23] and planned for violence at the U.S. Capitol.[24] Nick Fuentes, leader of the white nationalist "Groypers," rallied his followers for January 6th.[25] Fuentes bragged afterwards that the "Capitol siege was fucking awesome."[26] Users on TheDonald.win, a website populated by some of President Trump's most ardent fans, openly discussed surrounding and occupying the U.S. Capitol.[27]

Adherents of QAnon, a bizarre and dangerous conspiracy cult, believed January 6th would bring the prophesied "Storm"—a violent purge of Democrats and government officials promised by the mysterious online personality known only as "Q."[28] QAnon's devotees flocked to Washington, DC because of the President's tweet and subsequent rhetoric. They shared a digital banner, "Operation Occupy the Capitol," which depicted the U.S. Capitol being torn in two.[29]

One especially notorious conspiracy theorist, Alex Jones, repeatedly told his *InfoWars*' viewers that January 6th would be a day of reckoning.[30] Jones is known for his outlandish conspiracy-mongering, including his baseless claim that the massacre of school children at Sandy Hook Elementary School was really a "false flag" operation staged by the U.S. Government. Of course, his vicious lie was disproven in court, but Jones is obsessed with "deep state" conspiracy theories and often propagates them.[31] After the 2020 presidential election, Jones argued that President Trump should use the power of the Government to impose martial law on American citizens.[32] Along with his *InfoWars* co-hosts, Jones amplified President Trump's "Big

Lie" and relentlessly promoted President Trump's "wild" protest. One of Jones' co-hosts floated the idea of "storming right into the Capitol."[33] Jones himself marched to the Capitol January 6th.[34]

Jones's influence helped shape the planning for January 6th behind the scenes as well. The Select Committee investigated how event organizers and the White House staff planned President Trump's rally at the Ellipse, a park south of the White House. This event was intended to rile up the President's supporters just prior to the joint session of Congress. A wealthy heiress paid for the event after listening to Jones' *InfoWars* rant about the importance of President Trump's tweet. She spent $3 million with the goal to "get as many people there as possible."[35] It worked—Americans who believed the election was stolen flocked to the Nation's capital.

By January 5th, President Trump's supporters—a large, angry crowd ready for instructions—had assembled in Washington. That evening, he could hear his raucous supporters at a rally not far from the White House. The President knew his supporters were "angry,"[36] and he planned to call on them to march on the U.S. Capitol.[37] He even wanted to join them on the march.[38] It was all part of President Trump's plan to intimidate officials and obstruct the joint session of Congress.

"We fight like hell," President Trump told the crowd assembled at the Ellipse on January 6, 2021. "And if you don't fight like hell, you're not going to have a country anymore."[39] Some of those in attendance, as well as elsewhere in Washington that day, were already prepared to fight. They had begun preparing two and a half weeks earlier—when President Trump told them it would "be wild!"

6.1 HOW FAR-RIGHT EXTREMISTS AND CONSPIRACY THEORISTS PLANNED FOR JANUARY 6TH

THE "STOP THE STEAL" COALITION

President Trump's "be wild" tweet immediately mobilized extremists and conspiracy theorists in the "Stop the Steal" coalition. The phrase "Stop the Steal" was originally coined in early 2016 by President Trump's longtime political advisor, Roger Stone.[40] At the time, Stone alleged first that Candidate Trump's Republican rivals were attempting to steal Candidate Trump's nomination.[41] After Trump became the nominee, Stone repurposed the saying to claim that former Secretary of State Hillary Clinton would steal the presidency.[42] When President Trump won the 2016 election, "Stop the Steal" was rendered moot—and did not become a significant political movement until President Trump's defeat on election night in 2020.[43] As early as November 5, 2020, Stone advised associates that he intended to reconstitute "Stop the Steal" by building an army of lawyers and suing "like there's no tomorrow."[44]

Ali Alexander, a rightwing provocateur who has worked closely with Stone,[45] quickly organized a new "Stop the Steal" campaign. On November 10, 2020, Alexander established "Stop the Steal" as an entity incorporated in Alabama.[46] Alexander added a bank account and various websites.[47]

One of Alexander's key allies in the "Stop the Steal" movement was Alex Jones. Prior to January 6th, Jones riled up crowds both in-person and online with incendiary rhetoric about the election. Jones' *InfoWars* was also a platform for others in the election-denial coalition. For instance, both Enrique Tarrio and Stewart Rhodes made multiple appearances on *InfoWars*, including between election day 2020 and January 6, 2021.[48]

Another frequent guest on *InfoWars* was Roger Stone—a nexus character in the "Stop the Steal" coalition.[49] Stone recommended that then Presidential Candidate Donald Trump appear on Jones's show in December 2015.[50] Trump accepted the invitation and praised Jones at length during his appearance.[51] The significance of Trump's interview with Jones should not be underestimated. Donald Trump was a leading presidential contender at the time and would go on to win the election. His appearance with Jones normalized *InfoWars*, welcoming its conspiracy-minded audience into Trump's base.[52] Trump did not appear on *InfoWars* again. However, Stone continued to make regular guest appearances.[53]

After election day 2020, Alexander Jones, and other "Stop the Steal" organizers, held rallies around the country to protest fictional claims of voter fraud. These events provided an opportunity for radicals and extremists to coalesce. The Proud Boys, Oath Keepers, and Three Percenters were all attendees. QAnon adherents were well-represented. So, too, were the white nationalist Groypers and their leader, Nick Fuentes.

"Stop the Steal" events and other protests throughout 2020 helped build the momentum for January 6th. The Select Committee collected data on 85 right-wing events between January 1, 2020, and January 20, 2021, which were inspired by opposition to COVID-19 lockdown measures, racial justice protests, and, later, the perceived theft of President Trump's victory.[54] Far-right extremists protested at or inside State capitols, or at other government buildings, in at least 68 instances.[55] Of those, 49 occurred during the period after the election through January 6th.[56] In the year leading up to January 6th, there were at least nine events at which far-right actors entered State capitols.[57] At least four of these capitol incursions—in Michigan,[58] Idaho,[59] Arizona,[60] and Oregon[61]—involved identifiable individuals who later participated in the attack on the U.S. Capitol.

Alex Jones and Ali Alexander inside the Georgia State Capitol during a "Stop the Steal" rally on November 18, 2020 in Atlanta, Georgia.

Photo by Elijah Nouvelage/Getty Images

Consider, for example, the protests held in Atlanta between November 18 and 21, 2020. Leaders and rank-and-file members of the Proud Boys, Oath Keepers, and Groypers, gathered outside the State capitol and the governor's mansion for nonstop events, including armed protests. Enrique Tarrio[62] and Stewart Rhodes[63] personally led contingents of the Proud Boys and Oath Keepers, respectively.

Jones first announced the Atlanta events on InfoWars on November 16th. In his announcement, Jones teased that he would be joined by Roger Stone and also called on listeners to "surround the governor's mansion" in order to prevent the election results from being certified.[64] Fuentes advertised that he would be speaking at the capitol every day at noon.[65] In fiery speeches across Atlanta, Fuentes spread election lies as well as wink-and-nod hints at intimidation and violence.[66]

Alexander, standing alongside Jones and Fuentes outside the State capitol on November 18th, exhorted the crowd to "storm the capitol" with them.[67] The three men led a crowd into the State capitol building. On November 20th, Roger Stone gave a speech outside the Georgia capitol. Speaking through a telephone held up by Alexander, Stone advanced election lies, and finished with a provocative rallying cry: "Victory or death!"[68]

That same day, Fuentes told the crowd, "Look, we've been in front of the State capitol, maybe we've been trying the wrong approach." [69] Days earlier, at a nighttime event outside the governor's mansion, Alexander, again flanked by Jones and Fuentes, goaded the crowd: "We'll light the whole shit on fire." [70]

While the crowd did not turn violent, the "Stop the Steal" protests in Atlanta, Georgia, prefigured January 6th in important respects. "Stop the Steal" organizers tried to use the mob they had assembled—including extremists from the Proud Boys, Oath Keepers, Three Percenters and Groypers—to intimidate lawmakers and overturn the election results in Georgia, which was required to certify former Vice President Biden's victory in the State by the end of that week. [71] They implored their followers to "storm the capitol." [72] As discussed in Chapter 8, this same coalition of radicals did just that on January 6, 2021.

Other "Stop the Steal" events helped pave the way for the events of January 6th. Two rallies in Washington D.C.—on November 14 and December 12, 2020—were critically important. Alexander's "Stop the Steal" was not the only protest organization present at these events. Both were called "Million MAGA Marches" and drew in other rally organizers. One of these other protests was called the "Jericho March" prayer rally. [73] Regardless, the same constellation of actors that appeared in Atlanta also incited Trump supporters in Washington.

For instance, during the Jericho March rally on December 12th, Stewart Rhodes called on President Trump to invoke the Insurrection Act as part of a desperate gambit to remain in power. In Rhodes' vision, he would lead militiamen on behalf of President Trump when others tried to remove him from office. [74] If President Trump did not invoke the Insurrection Act, Rhodes warned the crowd, then they would be forced to wage a "much more desperate [and] much more bloody war." Alex Jones also gave an incendiary speech at the Jericho March event, declaring: "I don't know who is going to the White House in 38 days, but I sure know this, Joe Biden is a globalist, and Joe Biden will be removed, one way or another!" [75]

As the crowds gathered in Washington on December 12th, President Trump was publicly lobbying the Supreme Court to hear his fictious claims of election fraud. The President assailed the Supreme Court on Twitter throughout the day. [76] The "Stop the Steal" coalition was eager to help. After the Jericho March event ended, Jones, his InfoWars co-host Owen Shroyer, and Ali Alexander led a march on the Supreme Court. Once there, the crowd chanted slogans such as "Stop the Steal!"; "1776!!"; "Our revolution!"; and "The fight has just begun!!" [77]

"Million MAGA March" protest on November 14, 2020 in Washington, DC.
Photo by Tasos Katopodis/Getty Images

President Trump made sure to let the protestors in Washington know that he personally approved of their mission. During the November rally, President Trump waved to the crowd from his presidential motorcade.[78] Then, on the morning of December 12th, President Trump tweeted: "Wow! Thousands of people forming in Washington (D.C.) for Stop the Steal. Didn't know about this, but I'll be seeing them! #MAGA."[79] Later that day, President Trump flew over the protestors in Marine One.[80]

When President Trump tweeted one week later that there would be a "wild" protest in Washington on January 6th, the "Stop the Steal" coalition immediately began to mobilize. Jones posted an article on the *InfoWars* website asking readers if they would "answer President Trump's call to defend the Republic?"[81] The next day, December 20th, Jones devoted much of his *InfoWars* show to the President's announcement. Jones told his audience several times that if 10 million Americans came to Washington, DC on January 6th, Congress would have to listen to them.[82] He repeated this idea over the course of the episode, saying things such as, "He's calling *you*, he needs your help, we need your help, we need 10 million people there," "[w]e need martial law and have to prevent the police state of foreigners from taking over." Jones added: "It's literally in our hands. It's literally up to us."[83]

Other *InfoWars* hosts promoted the "wild" protest as well. In late December, Matt Bracken told InfoWars viewers that it may be necessary to storm the U.S. Capitol. "We're going to only be saved by millions of Americans moving to Washington, occupying the entire area, if—if necessary storming right into the Capitol," Bracken said. "You know, they're—we know the rules of engagement. If you have enough people, you can push down any kind of a fence or a wall." [84]

Far-right extremists planned to do just that.

6.2 THE PROUD BOYS: "[Y]OU WANT TO STORM THE CAPITOL"

From the Proud Boys' founding in 2016, violence was intrinsic to their mission. "We will kill you. That's the Proud Boys in a nutshell," their founder said.[85] New recruits pledge an oath, established in the group's bylaws, identifying themselves as unapologetic "Western chauvinists," [86] promoting an exclusionary, hyper-masculine interpretation of Western culture.[87] They find common ground in an embrace of misogyny and hate for their perceived enemies.[88] The group is somewhat ethnically diverse, but their public and private messages fester with toxic white supremacist, xenophobic, and anti-Semitic slurs.[89]

The Proud Boys have participated in, or instigated, protests since their founding.[90] They've long been known as street brawlers looking for a fight.[91] But 2020 was a watershed year for the group. As protests spread around the country, the Proud Boys deputized themselves as agents of law and order—vigilantes against perceived threats.[92] More often, they played the role of instigators.[93] They portrayed themselves as counter-protestors and identified their targets as Black Lives Matter and Antifa—though they were hard-pressed to define their organizational enemies.[94]

During the presidential debate on September 29, 2020, President Trump was asked to disavow far-right extremists, including the Proud Boys. The President did not explicitly condemn the group. Instead, he seemingly endorsed their mission. "Stand back and stand by," President Trump told the Proud Boys, before adding, "but I'll tell you what … somebody's got to do something about Antifa and the left." [95] The President's words electrified the group, injecting new life into their recruitment and activities. According to Nick Quested, a filmmaker who spent significant time with the group and testified before the Select Committee, the Proud Boys had found their "savior" in President Trump.[96]

Joseph Biggs, a senior Proud Boy, immediately trumpeted President Trump's debate statement on Parler,[97] a fringe social media platform. Biggs made it clear that the Proud Boys were ready to fight Antifa.[98] The group's

A Proud Boy during a "Stop the Steal" rally on November 7, 2020 in Salem, Oregon.
Photo by Nathan Howard/Getty Images

size "tripled" in response to President Trump's apparent endorsement, according to Jeremy Bertino, a Proud Boys leader who has pleaded guilty to seditious conspiracy in relation to January 6th.[99] Similarly, Enrique Tarrio and another Proud Boys member, George Meza, testified to the Select Committee that the President's comment was a pivotal, energizing moment.[100] The group started selling merchandise with their new "stand back and stand by" slogan the very same night.[101]

As the presidential votes were tallied, the Proud Boys became agitated at the prospect that President Trump would lose. On November 5, 2020, Biggs posted on social media, "It's time for fucking war if they steal this shit."[102] As former Vice President Joe Biden's victory became apparent, Proud Boys leaders directed their ire toward others in the Government. Biggs, speaking on a Proud Boys livestream show with Tarrio and others, warned that government officials are "evil scum, and they all deserve to die a traitor's death." Ethan Nordean—another Proud Boys leader who allegedly helped lead the attack at the Capitol—responded, "Yup, Day of the Rope,"[103] referring to a day of mass lynching of "race traitors" in the white supremacist novel *The Turner Diaries*.[104]

THE PROUD BOYS IN WASHINGTON PRIOR TO JANUARY 6TH

Within days of the election, dozens of "Stop the Steal" protests were organized around the country.[105] The Proud Boys participated alongside other right-wing extremist groups in some of them, including a November 7, 2020, protest outside of the Pennsylvania State capitol in Harrisburg.[106] The two events in Washington, DC—on November 14, 2020, and the other on December 12, 2020—proved to be especially important for the group's evolution.

The daytime events on both dates passed by without violence or major unrest, but as the sun set, bouts of violence erupted,[107] driven by clashes between far-right extremist groups—chiefly the Proud Boys—and counterprotestors.[108] Among far-right extremists, the Proud Boys had the largest showing in both November and December,[109] with roughly 200 to 300 Proud Boys at the November 14th rally, and the same number or more in December.[110] As discussed in Chapter 8, they mustered about the same contingent for the attack on the U.S. Capitol.

The gathering on November 14th provided a chance for Tarrio to socialize with rally leaders and far-right celebrities. In fact, his travel to DC by private jet appears to have been paid for by Patrick Byrne, a businessman who had President Trump's ear in the last weeks of his presidency and encouraged the President to authorize the seizure of voting machines in a December 18th meeting.[111] Tarrio's testimony and photographs from the day show that he met with "Stop the Steal" organizer Ali Alexander that evening, and the pair toasted each other.[112] Tarrio described the event as a "historic" meeting of Trump supporters and celebrated the opportunity to share that platform with Alexander, Jones, and Jones' *InfoWars* co-host, Owen Shroyer.[113] Shroyer would later be charged with crimes committed during the January 6th attack.[114]

A month later, the Proud Boys returned to the Nation's capital. On the evening of December 11th, hundreds of Proud Boys and friends gathered in downtown Washington, DC to listen to an impromptu bullhorn speech by Tarrio and Nordean, along with Roger Stone and Shroyer.[115] Stone implored the crowd to "fight to the bitter end." [116]

The next day, as the Proud Boys marched in force on the streets, Tarrio teased in a social media post that he had a meeting in the White House.[117] The visit, which was only a public White House tour, appears to have been facilitated by a friend, Bianca Gracia, the head of Latinos for Trump.[118] As the rallies concluded the next day, the Proud Boys took to the streets again. Two key events occurred that evening.

First, members of the Proud Boys tore down a Black Lives Matter banner from a historically Black church in downtown Washington, DC.[119] They filmed themselves burning it.[120] Tarrio was eventually charged with destruction of property.[121] He was arrested on January 4, 2021, and banned from Washington, DC, barring him from joining the group at the Capitol.[122] As explained in Chapter 8, however, Tarrio's arrest did not stop him from conspiring with his men on January 6th.

Minutes after the flag burning, a man wearing black clothes walked into a crowd of Proud Boys.[123] Assuming he was associated with Antifa, they began pushing and harassing him, and he drew a knife in response.[124] In the ensuing melee, four Proud Boys suffered stab wounds, including Bertino, a confidant to Tarrio.[125] Bertino's wounds were severe and life-threatening, preventing him from joining the group on January 6th.[126]

STORMING THE WINTER PALACE

The Proud Boys began to reorient and formalize their operations to focus on January 6th after President Trump's December 19th tweet. Inspired, in part, by Bertino's stabbing, the Proud Boys centered their new hierarchy in group chats that used terms such as "Ministry of Self Defense" (MOSD).[127] However, the words "Self Defense" were misleading: Enrique Tarrio and others would soon go on the offense. And the MOSD served as their organizational scaffolding for the January 6, 2021, attack.

On December 20, 2020, Tarrio established a "national rally planning committee" and created an encrypted MOSD chat to organize their activities.[128] Tarrio added Proud Boys leaders from across the country, including several who played lead roles in the violence on January 6th.[129] In the ensuing weeks, the Proud Boys traded equipment recommendations, shared maps marked with law enforcement positions, and established command and control structures.[130] A separate encrypted chat, named "Boots on the Ground," was established for foot soldiers who would be in Washington, DC on January 6th.[131]

The Proud Boys' planning for January 6th was a significant step in the group's evolution. Previously, they were loosely organized. The MOSD was created to enforce a "top down structure" with a defined leadership.[132] Tarrio stressed the command structure by telling members that they needed to "[f]it in [] or fuck off." [133]

From the start, it was clear that MOSD chat members were intensely interested in disrupting the electoral count on January 6th. On December 20, 2020, one MOSD leader stated, "I assume most of the protest will be at the capital [sic] building given what's going on inside." [134] On December 29, 2020, in a group message to the MOSD, a member wrote, "I know most of the events will be centered around freedom plaza...." Tarrio responded, "Negative. They're centered around the Capitol." [135]

On December 30, 2020, Tarrio received an intriguing document titled, "1776 Returns."[136] The document was apparently sent to him by cryptocurrency investors in South Florida.[137] The file's author(s) divided their plan into five parts, "Infiltrate, Execution, Distract, Occupy and Sit-In," with the goal of overrunning several Federal buildings around the U.S. Capitol. The plan specifically mentioned House and Senate office buildings, setting forth steps for occupying them. The author(s) called for "the masses to rush the building[s]," distract law enforcement in the area by pulling fire alarms around the city, target specific Senators' offices, and disguise participants' identities with COVID masks.[138]

One proposal mentioned in the document is titled, "Storm the Winter Palace."[139] This is a reference to a dramatic reenactment of the 1917 Bolshevik Revolution, during which Vladimir Lenin ordered his forces to take over the Romanovs' residence in Petrograd. The "Winter Palace" was the seat of the provisional government, which had held out against the Bolshevik revolutionaries. The Proud Boys would frame their actions on January 6th as part of the American Revolution. But the "1776 Returns" document shows their inspiration came at least in part from the Communist Revolution, which led to 70-plus years of totalitarian rule. No historical event has been less American.

The Proud Boys did not adopt the "1776 Returns" plan in full. Several Proud Boys testified that they were unaware of the document before it became public.[140] But the document does appear to have been significantly edited while in the Proud Boys' hands.[141] The person who sent it to Tarrio— his ex-girlfriend, Eryka Gemma Flores—commented, "The revolution is [more] important than anything." To which Tarrio responded: "That's what every waking moment consists of … I'm not playing games."[142]

On January 3rd, Tarrio posted a conspicuous question on Telegram: "What if we invade it?" The first response to his post read: "January 6th is D day [sic] in America."[143] In private, on the Proud Boys' leadership group message, planning continued. One MOSD leader, John Stewart, floated a plan that centered around "the front entrance to the Capitol building."[144] At 7:10 p.m. on January 3rd, Stewart wrote to the MOSD leaders:

> I mean the main operating theater should be out in front of the house of representatives. It should be out in front of the Capitol building. That's where the vote is taking place and all of the objections. So, we can ignore the rest of these stages and all that shit and plan the operations based around the front entrance to the Capitol building. I strongly recommend you use the national mall and not Pennsylvania avenue though. It's wide-open space, you can see everything coming from all angles.[145]

Early the next morning, on January 4th, Tarrio sent a voice memo to the same group of MOSD leaders stating, "I didn't hear this voice until now, you want to storm the Capitol." [146]

One of Tarrio's comrades in the Proud Boys' leadership, Charles Donohoe—who pleaded guilty to conspiracy to obstruct an official proceeding and assaulting, resisting, or impeding certain officers[147]—later told authorities that by January 4th he "was aware that members of MOSD leadership were discussing the possibility of storming the Capitol." [148] Donohoe "believed that storming the Capitol would achieve the group's goal of stopping the government from carrying out the transfer of presidential power" and "understood that storming the Capitol would be illegal." [149] By the following evening, January 5th, Tarrio was discussing with other Proud Boy leaders a "tactical plan" for the following day. Their "objective" was "to obstruct, impede, or interfere with the certification of the Electoral College vote." [150] Moreover, Donohoe understood that the Proud Boys "would pursue this through the use of force and violence, in order to show Congress that 'we the people' were in charge." [151] On January 6th, Charles Donohoe understood that two of his fellow Proud Boys' leaders—Ethan Nordean and Joe Biggs—"were searching for an opportunity to storm the Capitol." [152]

Jeremy Bertino, the Proud Boys leader who was stabbed on the night of December 12th, later told authorities that his fellow extremists plotted to stop the peaceful transfer of power. In October 2022, Bertino pleaded guilty to "seditious conspiracy" and other crimes.[153] Bertino admitted that the Proud Boys traveled to Washington, DC on January 6, 2021, "to stop the certification of the Electoral College Vote." They "were willing to do whatever it would take, including using force against police and others, to achieve that objective." [154]

In testimony before the Select Committee, Bertino recalled a telling text exchange with Tarrio on the evening of January 6th. "I was like, 'holy shit,' or something like that I said to him," Bertino recalled. "And I was like, 'I can't believe this is happening,' or something like that, and '1776.' " [155]

Tarrio replied to Bertino: "Winter Palace." [156]

6.3 THE OATH KEEPERS: "HE CALLED US ALL TO THE CAPITOL AND WANTS US TO MAKE IT WILD!!!"

The Oath Keepers, founded in 2009 by Elmer Stewart Rhodes, is a far-right anti-government organization. The group targets former and current military and law enforcement for recruitment. Their name refers to the oath taken by public servants to support and defend the U.S. Constitution. The Oath Keepers' claimed fealty to the U.S. Constitution is belied by their obsession with conspiracy theories about alleged evil-intentioned elites in the Government.[157] Rhodes has often spouted these conspiracy theories on *InfoWars*.[158]

Over the summer of 2020, the Oath Keepers organized armed groups, ostensibly to serve as volunteer, self-appointed security at protests around the country. The Oath Keepers used the protests to draw in new recruits.[159] They also built muscle memory by coordinating for these events. For example, the Oath Keepers hired Michael Greene, who later coordinated Oath Keepers' activities on January 5th and 6th, to lead security operations in multiple cities around the country.[160] In the early part of 2020, protests against COVID-related lockdowns served as additional growth and networking opportunities. Kellye SoRelle, a lawyer for the Oath Keepers, met the Oath Keepers at a lockdown protest in Austin, Texas in early 2020. SoRelle saw these COVID events as a "coalescing moment" for different far-right groups.[161]

The "Stop the Steal" movement created another opportunity for the Oath Keepers to grow their influence. Rhodes repeatedly amplified the stolen election conspiracy theory. On November 10, 2020, he posted a "Call to Action!" on the Oath Keepers website, alleging the election was "stolen" and exhorting his followers to "refuse to EVER recognize this as a legitimate election, and refuse to recognize Biden as a legitimate winner."[162] Under a section entitled "What We the People Must Do," Rhodes quoted a "patriot from Serbia, who also loves America." The Serbian author described how his fellow countrymen fomented a political revolution. Parts of the statement presaged the attack on the U.S. Capitol:

> ... Millions gathered in our capital [*sic*]. There were no barricades strong enough to stop them, nor the police determined enough to stop them. Police and Military aligned with the people after few hours of fist-fight [*sic*]. We stormed the Parliament. And burned down fake state Television! WE WON![163]

The Oath Keepers were obsessed with the Insurrection Act—seeing it as a way for President Trump to cling to power. Rhodes believed that the President could empower militias like the Oath Keepers to enforce law and order after other Americans refused to accept President Trump's rule.[164] Indeed, President Trump had been intensely interested in the Insurrection Act as a potential tool to quell the protests in summer 2020.[165] Rhodes wished the Act had been invoked then, but he did not give up on the fantasy.[166] As mentioned above, Rhodes called for President Trump to invoke the Insurrection Act during his speech in Washington on December 12, 2020.[167]

That day, Rhodes also coordinated with Jericho March organizers to provide security.[168] He coordinated with a paramilitary group known as 1st

Amendment Praetorian (1AP), to guard VIPs, including retired Lieutenant General Michael Flynn and Patrick Byrne.[169] Rhodes indicated that the Oath Keepers would be "working closely" with them for the event.[170]

The Oath Keepers continued to call for President Trump to invoke the Insurrection Act throughout December 2020, arguing that the President needed to do so to "Stop the Steal."[171] This fantasy reflected a warped sense of reality. Rhodes testified that President Trump could have mobilized "unorganized militia," including the Oath Keepers, to suppress an insurrection if he attempted to stay in power after losing the election.[172] But the Oath Keepers themselves were the ones contemplating insurrection. On December 10, 2020, Rhodes messaged others: "Either Trump gets off his ass and uses the Insurrection Act to defeat the Chicom puppet coup or we will have to rise up in insurrection (rebellion) against the ChiCom puppet Biden. Take your pick."[173] Rhodes was blunt in other messages to the Oath Keepers, writing: "We need to push Tump [sic] to do his duty. If he doesn't, we will do ours. Declare Independence. Defy[,] Resist[,] Defend[,] Conquer or Die. This needs to be our attitude."[174]

6.4 "TRUMP SAID IT'S GONNA BE WILD!!!!!!! IT'S GONNA BE WILD!!!!!!!"

As the Proud Boys began their plans for January 6th, Kelly Meggs, the leader of the Florida chapter of the Oath Keepers, reached out. In the past, the Proud Boys and the Oath Keepers had their differences, deriding each other's tactics and ethos during the summer 2020 protests.[175] But President Trump's tweet on December 19th conveyed a sense of urgency which provided the two extremist rivals the opportunity to work together for a common goal.

After President Trump's tweet, Meggs called Enrique Tarrio. They spoke for 3 minutes and 26 seconds.[176] Meggs also sent a message on Facebook, bragging about an alliance he had formed among the Oath Keepers, the Florida Three Percenters, and the Proud Boys: "We have decided to work together and shut this shit down."[177] The Oath Keepers were making plans of their own, too.

"Oath Keepers president [Rhodes] is pretty disheartened," Roberto Minuta, one of Rhodes' men, messaged someone on December 19th. "He feels like it's go time, the time for peaceful protest is over in his eyes. I was talking with him last night."[178] Minuta has been charged with "seditious conspiracy" and other crimes.[179]

In the days that followed, the Oath Keepers planned for violence. They used encrypted chats on Signal to discuss travel plans, trade tips on tactical equipment to bring, and develop their plans for once they were on the ground in the DC area.[180] On December 21st, 2020, Joshua James messaged the group, stating, "SE region is creating a NATIONAL CALL TO ACTION FOR DC JAN 6TH. ... 4 states are mobilizing[.]"[181] Meggs, Rhodes, and others created several different chat groups to coordinate for January 6th.[182]

On December 22nd, Meggs echoed President Trump's tweet in a Facebook message to someone else:

> Trump said It's gonna be wild!!!!!!! It's gonna be wild!!!!!!! He wants us to make it WILD that's what he's saying. He called us all to the Capitol and wants us to make it wild!!! Sir Yes Sir!!! Gentlemen we are heading to DC pack your shit!!"[183]

Meggs also wrote that the Oath Keepers would have 50–100 members in Washington, DC on January 6th.[184]

The Oath Keepers hosted periodic group video meetings to discuss plans for January 6th. Richard Dockery, a former Oath Keepers member, testified to the Select Committee about a video call that took place around December 31st, and related specifically to planning for January 6th.[185] During the call, Oath Keepers' leadership announced plans to provide security for far-right celebrities like Roger Stone.[186] If there were any problems while they were providing security, "there was a quick reaction force in Virginia that would come help them out ... and that they would have firearms."[187]

Rhodes announced during an episode of *InfoWars* in November 2020 that the Oath Keepers had established a "Quick Reaction Force" (QRF) outside of Washington, DC.[188] After President Trump announced the "wild" protest, the group's advanced coordination largely focused on planning related to their QRF, as well as the various security details for VIPs and stage areas on January 5th and 6th.[189] Oath Keepers from North Carolina, Florida, South Carolina, and Arizona converged on the Comfort Inn in Ballston, Virginia, and used the location to store their cache of weapons for January 6th.[190] Oath Keepers leaders communicated actively about the QRF for January 6th.[191] Rhodes and another contingent of Oath Keepers stayed at the Hilton Garden Inn in Vienna, Virginia, and stored weapons there as well.[192]

Rhodes amassed an arsenal of military-grade assault weapons and equipment in the days leading up to January 6th. On December 30th, Rhodes spent approximately $7,000 on two night-vision devices and a weapon sight and shipped them to Marsha Lessard, a rally organizer who lived near Washington, DC and who had previously been in contact with the organizers of the Ellipse rally.[193] On January 1st and 2nd, Rhodes purchased additional weapons and accessories at a cost of approximately $5,000.[194] The following day, January 3rd, Rhodes and Kellye SoRelle departed Texas for Washington, DC. While traveling, Rhodes spent an additional $6,000 on an AR-style rifle and firearms attachments.[195] Making one final shopping trip in Mississippi, Rhodes purchased $4,500 of firearms equipment including more sights, magazines, and weapons parts on January 4th.[196]

On the morning of January 6th, with weapons stockpiled, Rhodes messaged the Signal group of Oath Keepers leaders:

> We have several well equipped [sic] QRFs outside DC. And there are many, many others, from other groups, who will be watching and waiting on the outside in case of worst case [sic] scenarios.[197]

6.5 "READY TO STEP IN AND DO WHAT IS NEEDED"

Stewart Rhodes's and Oath Keepers' lawyer Kellye SoRelle arrived in Washington on the afternoon of January 5th.[198] They immediately went to Freedom Plaza, where President Trump had instructed rally organizers to give some of his most extreme supporters time to speak.[199] As a small group of Oath Keepers patrolled Freedom Plaza, they were able to see the results of President Trump's call to mobilize.[200] SoRelle testified that there were Oath Keepers, Proud Boys, and "Alex Jones people" mingling together in the crowd, with "just a small distinction between them." [201]

The Oath Keepers later found themselves at the Phoenix Park Hotel,[202] where they ate and drank with a motley coalition of far-right political activists who were united in their shared belief in President Trump's Big Lie.[203] Among them were: Proud Boys-linked Bianca Gracia of Latinos for Trump; Joshua Macias, leader of Vets for Trump;[204] and Amanda Chase, a Virginia State senator.[205] In a livestream discussion moderated by Chase, they promoted false election fraud claims. Macias and Rhodes encouraged President Trump to invoke the Insurrection Act and call up combat veterans who are "ready to step in and do what is needed." [206]

SoRelle later told the Select Committee that there was discussion of going to "storm the Capitol," although she claimed that this was "normal" discussion and supposedly did not indicate violence or "any of that type of stuff." [207]

That same evening, Gracia asked SoRelle and Rhodes to follow her to a garage where she was supposed to meet Proud Boys leader Enrique Tarrio,[208] who had just been released from custody and ordered to leave the DC area.[209] Instead of immediately leaving Washington, DC, Tarrio instead made his way to a garage near the hotel where the others gathered.[210] Portions of the ensuing meeting were captured on video by documentary filmmaker Nick Quested and his camera crew. SoRelle claims that she was asked to attend to discuss Tarrio's legal woes,[211] but there is evidence indicating that the conversation turned tactical.

Tarrio discussed the court's order, informing the group he was going north to Maryland, so he could "stay close just to make sure my guys are ok."[212] Tarrio discussed his confiscated phone with Gracia. He told her that "they couldn't get in there," apparently referencing the two-factor authentication enabled on his phone.[213] Tarrio also appeared familiar with another attendee, Vets for Trump leader Macias, who rested his hand on Tarrio's shoulder at various points.[214] Rhodes and Tarrio shook hands.[215]

Much of the substantive conversation between Rhodes, Tarrio, and the others cannot be heard because Tarrio asked Quested's camera crew to stop recording.[216] However, some of the conversation is audible from afar and Rhodes can be heard telling Tarrio that he "has three groups in Tyson's Corner,"[217] a reference to the QRFs that he had mustered in the event that President Trump called the Oath Keepers into service.

Tarrio later expressed appreciation for Rhodes's presence at the garage meeting and underscored that their two organizations needed to stand together on January 6th. Tarrio explained that the Proud Boys and Oath Keepers are "just two different groups" and that he and Rhodes "don't get along," but said that "for situations like this where there is a need to unite regardless of our differences … what he did today was commendable."[218] Tarrio added that Rhodes's presence at the garage meeting was "thoughtful" because Rhodes had "quickly provided security" for the meeting and "seemed concerned" about Tarrio's legal situation.[219] In a likely nod to prior coordination between Proud Boys and Oath Keepers at other post-election events, Tarrio further explained that "my guys have helped him [Rhodes] out in the past," and that he and Rhodes have "mutual respect" for one another.[220] Tarrio then traveled north to a hotel near Baltimore, Maryland, where he stayed through the events of the next day.[221]

6.6 "FRIENDS OF STONE"

As explained above, a constellation of far-right characters came together in late 2020 as part of the "Stop the Steal" cause. Among them was Roger Stone, a right-wing political operative whose career as a self-trumpeted dirty trickster stretched back decades. Stone is arguably President Trump's oldest political advisor.[222] For example, he worked for Donald Trump's independent presidential bid during the 2000 campaign.[223] In addition to his political connections, Stone cultivated relationships with far-right extremists, including the two groups charged with seditious conspiracy: the Oath Keepers and the Proud Boys.

The Select Committee found that at least seven members of the Oath Keepers provided security for Stone, or were seen with him, in the weeks

Roger Stone in front of the Supreme Court on January 5, 2021 in Washington, DC.
Photo by Tasos Katopodis/Getty Images

immediately preceding the attack on the U.S. Capitol.[224] Text messages released by Edward Vallejo, an Oath Keeper charged with seditious conspiracy and other crimes, show that Stewart Rhodes and Kelly Meggs discussed providing security for Stone.[225] Some of these Oath Keepers guarded Stone during an event at Freedom Plaza in Washington, DC on the night of January 5th.[226] Stone was also flanked by Oath Keepers outside of the Willard Hotel on the morning of January 6th.[227] One of the Oath Keepers who provided security for Stone was Joshua James, who pleaded guilty to seditious conspiracy, obstruction of Congress and other charges in March 2022.[228] James was also reportedly seen in Stone's hotel room at the Willard hours before the attack on the U.S. Capitol.[229]

Stone has a longstanding, close relationship with the Proud Boys. Stone has taken the Proud Boys oath[230] and repeatedly defended the group.[231] Danish documentarians filmed him working with Proud Boys for years.[232] In one scene, filmed in 2019, Stone warmly greets Joe Biggs, a Proud Boys leader central to the Capitol violence. Stone says of Biggs: "My guy, right here."[233] In a 2019 court case, Stone identified Enrique Tarrio as one of his volunteers, explaining that Tarrio had access to his phone and could post to Stone's Instagram account from it.[234]

As mentioned above, Stone, Tarrio and another Proud Boy leader, Ethan Nordean, addressed an impromptu rally in Washington, DC on the night of December 11, 2020. Owen Shroyer, an *InfoWars* host, was also with them.[235] "We will fight to the bitter end for an honest count of the 2020 election," Stone told the crowd. "Never give up, never quit, never surrender, and fight for America!"[236] A few weeks later, on January 2, 2021, Tarrio led a Proud Boys protest outside of Senator Marco Rubio's home in Florida. The Proud Boys wanted to convince Rubio to vote against certification of the vote on January 6th.[237] Stone reportedly called into the event to speak to Tarrio's crowd.[238]

One way in which Stone maintained these contacts was through a Signal chat group named "F.O.S."—or Friends of Stone.[239] Two days after the election, Stone sent a text: "We provide information several times a day. So please monitor the F.O.S. feed so you can act in a timely fashion."[240] Ali Alexander and Stone continued to coordinate about Stop the Steal strategy and events between the election and January 6th.[241] In addition to Alexander, Stone's "Friends" on the Signal chat included Rhodes and Tarrio.[242]

In July 2020, President Trump granted Stone clemency after he was convicted of lying to Congress and other charges.[243] Then, on December 23rd, President Trump pardoned Stone.[244] Several days later, at a dinner on the evening of December 27th, Stone thanked President Trump. In a post on Parler, Stone wrote that he "thanked President Trump in person tonight for pardoning me" and also recommended to the President that he "appoint a special counsel" to stop "those who are attempting to steal the 2020 election through voter fraud." Stone also wrote that he wanted "to ensure that Donald Trump continues as our president."[245] Finally, he added: "#StopTheSteal" and "#rogerstonedidnothingwrong."[246] The Select Committee has learned that Stone discussed the January 6th event with the President, likely at this same dinner on December 27th.[247] The President told Stone he "was thinking of speaking."[248]

The Select Committee sought to question Roger Stone about his relationships with President Trump and far-right extremists, as well as other issues. During his deposition, Stone invoked his Fifth Amendment right nearly 90 times.[249] Stone has publicly stated that he committed no wrongdoing and that he encouraged a peaceful protest.[250]

6.7 WHITE NATIONALISTS: "THE CAPITOL SIEGE WAS FUCKING AWESOME..."

Nick Fuentes is an online provocateur who leads a white nationalist movement known as "America First," or the "Groypers." Fuentes immediately responded to President Trump's "be wild" tweet. On December 19, 2020,

Fuentes wrote on Twitter: "I will return to Washington DC to rally for President Trump on January 6th!"[251] Fuentes and his Groypers did return to Washington, DC for the joint session. As the attack was underway, Fuentes incited followers from his perch immediately outside of the U.S. Capitol. Some of his followers joined the attack inside, with one even sitting in Vice President Pence's seat on the Senate dais.[252]

Fuentes and a fellow Groyper leader, Patrick Casey, rose to prominence in 2017 after rallying at the Charlottesville "Unite the Right" event.[253] For years, the Groypers have repeatedly promoted white supremacist and Christian nationalist beliefs, often cloaked in wink-and-nod humor, puns, or religion, and they regularly gin up public opposition to other right-wing organizations or politicians whom they deem insufficiently conservative.[254]

Fuentes was a key voice for "Stop the Steal" conspiracy theories leading up to January 6th. He spent 2 months leading rallies in State capitals across the country,[255] spreading the Big Lie and livestreaming coded calls to violence.[256] He also used his livestream to raise significant funds between November 2020 and January 2021.[257]

On November 9, 2020, Fuentes promised, "GROYPERS ARE GOING TO STOP THIS COUP!"[258] Two days later, Fuentes organized a "Stop the Steal" rally at the Michigan State Capitol. He told the crowd that they should be "more feral" in their tactics to overturn the election, suggesting that they target lawmakers in their homes.[259] On November 14th, Fuentes rallied a crowd of his followers at the Million MAGA March in Washington, DC, pushing "Stop the Steal" conspiracies, calling for President Trump to rule for life, and exhorting his followers to "storm every State capitol until January 20, 2021, until President Trump is inaugurated for 4 more years."[260]

As discussed above, Fuentes was a prominent figure at the "Stop the Steal" rally in Atlanta, Georgia, in November 2020.[261] He promoted election conspiracies, criticized the Republican Party, joked about the Holocaust, and denounced former Vice President Biden as illegitimate.[262] Fuentes also suggested his followers intimidate politicians in their homes.[263]

On December 12th, Fuentes again rallied a crowd of supporters at the "Stop the Steal" events in Washington, DC, calling for the destruction of the Republican Party because it had failed to overturn the election.[264] As others spoke at the Jericho March rally, Fuentes headlined a "Stop the Steal" protest just a few blocks away.[265]

On January 4th, Fuentes suggested that his followers kill State legislators who don't support efforts to overturn the 2020 election. As discussed in Chapter 2, President Trump and his surrogates were pressuring State legislators at the time to do just that. Fuentes complained that his side "had no leverage." Fuentes then asked: "What can you and I do to a state legislator, besides kill them?" He then quickly added: "Although we should not do that. I am not advising that, but I mean, what else can you do, right?[266]

On January 5th, Casey advertised the marches in Washington, DC on his Telegram channel and provided repeated updates on the logistics of getting into the city. Casey also spoke to his followers about the next day's rally on a livestream on DLive.[267] As discussed in Chapter 8, the Groypers clearly played a role in the January 6th attack. They even planted their flag in the inner chambers of the U.S. Capitol.[268] Fuentes crowed about the attack the day after, tweeting: "The Capitol Siege was fucking awesome and I'm not going to pretend it wasn't."[269] In another tweet on January 7th, Fuentes wrote: "For a brief time yesterday the US Capital [sic] was once again occupied by The American People, before the regime wrested back control."[270]

Despite his boasts on Twitter, Fuentes exercised his Fifth Amendment privilege against self-incrimination and refused to provide information about his organizing activities to the Select Committee.[271]

6.8   THE THREE (III%) PERCENTERS: "#OCCUPYCONGRESS"

The Oath Keepers were not the only anti-government extremists who viewed President Trump's December 19th, tweet as a call to arms. Militias around the country were similarly inspired to act. "People were retweeting it right and left. … I saw people retweeting it, talking about, yeah, it's going to be crazy, going to be a huge crowd," Michael Lee Wells, a militia leader in North Carolina, told the Select Committee.[272] Members of militias known as the "Three Percenters" were electrified.

The Three Percenters believe that three percent of American colonists successfully overthrew the British during the American Revolution.[273] This is not true. Far more than a tiny fraction of the colonial population fought in or supported the Revolutionary War.[274] Regardless, this ahistorical belief has become an organizing myth for militias around modern-day America.

As with the Oath Keepers, many Three Percenters have turned against the U.S. Government, such that they equate it with the British monarchy and believe it should be overthrown.[275] The movement does not have one, centralized hierarchy. Instead, semi-autonomous branches organize and run themselves.[276] The Three Percenter cause was growing prior to the attack on the U.S. Capitol. Jeremy Liggett, a militia leader in Florida, told the Select Committee it was "trendy" in far-right circles to identify with the Three Percenter movement in the months leading up to January 6th.[277]

President Trump tapped into this well of anti-government extremism. The President's repeated insistence that the election had been stolen resonated with militia members who were already inclined to believe in shady political conspiracies. The President's December 19th tweet mobilized Three Percenters around the country. Suddenly, they had a focal point for their anti-government beliefs: the joint session of Congress on January 6th. Court filings and other evidence reveal that Three Percenters immediately began planning for violence after President Trump's "be wild" announcement.

For example, Lucas Denney and Donald Hazard led a militia affiliated with the Three Percenter movement called the "Patriot Boys of North Texas." Both Denney and Hazard were charged with assaulting officers on January 6th.[278] Denney pleaded guilty and has been sentenced to 52 months in prison.[279] After President Trump's tweet, they discussed travel plans, as well as the need to procure body armor, helmets, knuckle gloves and pepper spray.[280] But they did not plan to act alone. Instead, they saw themselves as part of a coalition. In multiple messages, both Denney and Hazard claimed they were also affiliated with Proud Boys and intended to work with them on or before January 6th.[281]

Denney repeatedly cited President Trump's tweet. "Trump himself is calling for a big protest in DC on January 6th. I'm not going to miss this one," Denney told Hazard on December 21st.[282] On December 30th, Denney wrote in a Facebook message:

> Trump has called this himself. For everyone to come. It's the day the electoral college is suppose to be certified by congress to officially elect Biden. But, Pence is in charge of this and he's going to throw out all the votes from States that were proved to have fraud. There's so much more going on behind the scenes though. That's why he's called this rally for support. ... Trump will stay President ... [283]

As this message indicates, Denney was well-aware of President Trump's multi-part plan to disrupt the transfer of power. He thought that Vice President Pence had the power to "throw out" electoral votes, just as the President demanded. In other messages, Denney claimed that President Trump wanted militias to descend on Washington, DC so they could serve as a security force against a perceived threat from Antifa and Black Lives Matter on January 6th.[284]

Additional messages between the two reveal their intent to march on the U.S. Capitol. For instance, Denney attempted to post two banners on Facebook that advertised events on January 6th.[285] Both banners contained the hashtag "#OccupyCongress." The pictures contained images of the U.S. Capitol and referenced "The Great Betrayal." One of them read "If They Won't Hear Us" and "They Will Fear Us." In another post, Denney wrote: "I can't wait to be in the middle of it on the front line on the 6th." [286]

Curiously, Denney had also heard a "rumor" that President Trump would march with them. On January 4, 2021, he stated in a Facebook message:

> Things are going to be happening here. Trump is going to be speaking to everyone Wed [January 6] before everyone marches to the capital [sic]. Rumour [sic] has it that he may march with us. I'll tell you more when you get here on where to be wed and what time so you have the best seats.[287]

On or about January 6th, Denney sent another message via Facebook, writing: "Trump speaking to us around 11 am then we march to the capital and after that we have special plans that I can't say right now over Facebook. But keep an eye out for live feed tomorrow from me. Tomorrow will be historic." [288] Later on January 6th, during the attack, Hazard was captured on video bragging: "We have stormed our nation's capitol." [289]

The Patriot Boys of North Texas were not the only Three Percenter group that mobilized after President Trump's tweet. The Department of Justice has alleged that multiple other cadres of Three Percenter militiamen prepared for violence on January 6th and then took part in the attack on the U.S. Capitol.

In Florida, a Three Percenter organization known as the "Guardians of Freedom" established a "B-squad" for January 6th because they allegedly wanted to avoid being called a "militia." [290] These men were led by Jeremy Liggett, mentioned above.[291]

On December 24, 2020, the B-squad sent out a flyer, "CALLING ALL PATRIOTS!" to Washington, D.C.[292] The flyer read: "The Guardians of Freedom III% are responding to the call from President Donald J. Trump to assist in the security, protection, and support of the people as we all protest the fraudulent election and re-establish liberty for our nation. JOIN US & Thousands of other Patriots!" [293] The B-Squad claimed it was the "right & duty of the people to alter or to abolish" the Government.[294] Its members discussed bringing tactical gear to Washington, DC.[295]

On December 30th, Liggett posted a meme to Facebook stating that "3% Will Show In Record Numbers In DC." [296] When the Select Committee asked about this post, Liggett downplayed its significance or disclaimed any knowledge about other Three Percenter groups that might "show in record numbers." [297] However, on January 3, 2021, Liggett posted a "safety video" on Facebook in which he and others dressed in military gear. Liggett instructed listeners about self-defense and the tools they (like him) could bring to Washington, DC, including "an expandable metal baton, a walking cane and a folding knife." [298] He advised "all of you Patriots going to

Washington, D.C. ... to support Trump," and to "keep up the fight." [299] Several "B-squad" members have been charged with civil disorder and disorderly and disruptive conduct, which took place while rioters nearby were assaulting officers in the tunnel area of the Capitol's Lower West Terrace on January 6th.[300]

In California, another group of men associated with the Three Percenter movement quickly began plotting their next moves after President Trump's tweet. Alan Hostetter and Russell Taylor ran a non-profit known as the American Phoenix Project, which protested COVID-19 lockdowns and the 2020 election results, while also promoting violence ahead of January 6th.[301] Ahead of the joint session, Hostetter and Taylor organized a small group in an encrypted chat they named "The California Patriots—DC Brigade." [302]

On December 19th, Taylor linked to President Trump's "will be wild" tweet and asked members of the chat "Who is going?" [303] The same day, Hostetter posted a message to his Instagram account, explaining he was traveling to Washington, DC on January 6th because President Trump "tweeted that all patriots should descend on Washington DC" and that day "is the date of the Joint Session of Congress in which they will either accept or reject the fake/phony/stolen electoral college votes." [304] The next day, Taylor renamed the Telegram chat as "The California Patriots-Answer the Call Jan 6." [305] On December 29th, Taylor posted to that chat: "I personally want to be on the front steps and be one of the first ones to breach the doors!" [306]

Between December 19th and January 6th, Hostetter, Taylor and their alleged co-conspirators exchanged messages about bringing weapons, such as hatchets, bats, or large metal flashlights, as well as possibly firearms, with them to Washington, DC.[307] They were "ready and willing to fight." [308] In one message, Hostetter predicted that January 6th would be similar to the "War of Independence" because "[t]here will likely be 3% of us again that will commit fully to this battle, but just as in 1776 patriots will prevail." [309]

There are additional examples of how President Trump's "be wild" tweet led Three Percenters to descend on the U.S. Capitol. One Three Percenter group issued an open letter on December 16, 2020, announcing that they "stand ready and are standing by to answer the call from our President should the need arise that We The People are needed to take back our country from the pure evil that is conspiring to steal our country away from the American people....We will not act unless we are told to." [310] In late December, after the President's tweet, The Three Percenters Original (TTPO) issued a letter to its members announcing that "this organization will be answering that call!" [311]

There is also additional evidence showing that militia groups like the Three Percenters coordinated with other groups both before and on January 6th. Josh Ellis, the owner of the MyMilitia website, testified that he used Zello (a walkie-talkie app) when he was in Washington, DC on January 6th. The Proud Boys, Oath Keepers, other militia members, and "regular patriots" all used these Zello channels in the leadup to January 6th and in response to President Trump's December 19th tweet. They used these channels to share intelligence.[312]

6.9 QANON: "OPERATION OCCUPY THE CAPITOL"

Shortly after the January 6th attack, a video of a bearded man in a "Q" shirt chasing U.S. Capitol Police Officer Ryan Goodman through the halls of the U.S. Capitol went viral.[313] That man was Doug Jensen, a QAnon believer.[314] After Jensen's arrest, FBI agents asked him why he traveled from Iowa to Washington, DC in the first place. "Trump posted make sure you're there, January 6 for the rally in Washington, D.C.," Jensen responded.[315]

Jensen was not the only QAnon believer to attack the U.S. Capitol on January 6th. The letter "Q" and related slogans, such as "Where We Go One, We Go All," were ubiquitous among the rioters. They were visible on shirts, signs, and flags throughout the crowd. What was once a marginal digital movement had become a bricks-and-mortar force powerful enough to help obstruct a joint session of Congress.

QAnon is a bizarre and dangerous cult that gained popularity in 2017, when a person known only as "Q" began posting on 4chan, an anonymous message board.[316] The poster supposedly held a "Q" security clearance at the Department of Energy. QAnon adherents believe that President Trump is a messianic figure battling the forces of the "deep state" and a Satanic pedophile ring operated by leading Democrats and the American elite.[317] Q's first post in October 2017 predicted that former Secretary of State Hillary Clinton would be arrested in short order.[318] Although that prophecy did not come to pass, the conspiracy theory evolved and grew over time, spreading across social media platforms and eventually finding a home in 8kun, another anonymous message board known for trafficking in conspiracy theories and hate.[319]

President Trump was given multiple opportunities to disavow QAnon. Instead, he essentially endorsed its core tenets. During an August 19, 2020, press briefing, President Trump was asked what he thought about the QAnon belief that he was fighting a Satanic cabal. "I mean, you know, if I can help save the world from problems, I'm willing to do it. I'm willing to put myself out there," he replied.[320] During a townhall on NBC News two weeks prior to the election, President Trump first claimed he "knew nothing" about QAnon, but he then praised its believers for being "very strongly against pedophilia." The President emphasized: "And I agree with that. I mean, I do agree with that." [321]

In 2020, QAnon played a significant role in spreading various election conspiracy theories. After the election, QAnon accounts amplified the claim that Dominion Voting System's software had altered votes. [322] On November 19th, President Trump tweeted and retweeted a link to a segment on One America News Network (OAN) that was captioned, "Dominion-izing the Vote." [323] The segment claimed that Dominion had switched votes from President Trump to former Vice President Biden. OAN featured a supposed cyber expert, Ron Watkins, a key figure in the QAnon conspiracy movement. [324] Watkins's father, Jim, owned the 8kun site that "Q" called home, and Ron helped oversee its message boards. [325]

After promoting the OAN segment, President Trump retweeted Ron Watkins's account on several other occasions. On December 15, 2020, President Trump retweeted a post in which Watkins spread false claims of foreign influence in the election. [326] Then, on January 3rd, President Trump retweeted Ron Watkins's account four more times. [327]

QAnon's adherents were clearly paying attention to President Trump's words—and tweets. The President's "be wild" tweet was widely heard as a clarion call. Jim Watkins told the Select Committee that "thousands and thousands of people probably" agreed that the President's December 19th tweet was a call for them to come to Washington, DC. [328] Jim Watkins himself marched in Washington, DC on January 6th because of the President's call, but he has not been charged with any crime. [329]

Other QAnon adherents flocked to Washington, DC in response to the President's call to action. "POTUS HAS REQUESTED YOUR ATTENDANCE Washington DC JANUARY 6TH 2021," Thomas Munn, a QAnon believer, posted on Facebook. Munn added: "Our President has only asked two things from us, so far...#1 Vote #2 January 6, 2021." [330] Jacob Chansley, better known as the QAnon Shaman, told the FBI that he traveled from Arizona because President Trump had requested that all "patriots" come to Washington, DC on January 6th. [331]

During the investigation, the Select Committee learned that the QAnon conspiracy theory often overlaps with other extremist beliefs. Stewart Rhodes of the Oath Keepers testified to the Select Committee that he's "not a Q-tard" and "not a follower of Q at all." [332] However, Rhodes cynically exploited QAnon for his own purposes. The Oath Keepers' website and text messages were littered with QAnon phrases. [333] Nick Quested, a filmmaker who shadowed the Proud Boys, often heard QAnon themes in the Proud Boys' private discussions. [334]

As January 6th drew closer, multiple posts on the QAnon-linked website 8kun indicated that violence was imminent. "You can go to Washington on Jan 6 and help storm the Capitol," one user wrote. This same user continued: "As many Patriots as can be. We will storm the government buildings, kill cops, kill security guards, kill federal employees and agents, and demand a recount." [335] Other posts on 8kun debated the politicians that users should target once they got inside the Capitol. [336]

A QAnon-inspired banner was also widely shared by groups planning events for January 5th and 6th. The top of the image read: "Operation Occupy the Capitol." The central image showed the U.S. Capitol being torn in two. In the lower left corner, there appeared a QAnon phrase: "#WeAreTheStorm." [337]

6.10 THEDONALD.WIN: "OCCUPY THE CAPITOL"

Within three minutes of President Trump's tweet, a user on TheDonald.win message board posted: "Trump Tweet. Daddy Says Be In DC on Jan. 6th." [338] Moderators pinned the post to the top of the board from December 19th until January 6th. It garnered nearly 6,000 comments and more than 24,000 upvotes during that time. [339] Many of the site's users quickly interpreted President Trump's tweet as a call for violence. For example, one user wrote, "[Trump] can't exactly openly tell you to revolt. This is the closest he'll ever get." [340] Jody Williams, the site's then-owner, testified that while users had been talking about traveling to Washington, DC since the election, after the tweet "anything else was kind of shut out, and it just was going to be the 6th." [341]

In the days that followed, users on TheDonald.win discussed: surrounding and occupying the U.S. Capitol; cutting off access tunnels used by Members of Congress; the types of weapons they should bring; and even how to build a hangman's gallows. [342] The parallels to what transpired on January 6th are obvious.

TheDonald.win and its predecessor site was a website for some of its namesake's most ardent fans. Even before President Trump was elected, his social media team monitored and interacted with the site's users. In the summer of 2016, then-candidate Trump himself engaged in a written question and answer session on TheDonald, which at the time was a forum on Reddit. [343] This online community, which had upwards of 790,000 users, was banned by Reddit in mid-2020. [344] However, the site's users migrated to another online location, becoming TheDonald.win. [345]

Dan Scavino, the President's social media guru, amplified content from this website. During the 2016 presidential campaign, "a team in the war

White House social media director Dan Scavino Jr.

Photo by Chip Somodevilla/Getty Images

room at Trump Tower was monitoring social media trends, including TheDonald subreddit ... and privately communicating with the most active users to seed new trends." [346] "Campaign staffers monitored Twitter and TheDonald subreddit, and pushed any promising trends up to social media director Dan Scavino, who might give them a boost with a tweet." [347] In 2017, President Trump tweeted a video of himself attacking CNN.[348] The video had appeared on The Donald four days earlier.[349] In 2019, *Politico* reported that Scavino "regularly monitors Reddit, with a particular focus on the pro-Trump /r/The_Donald channel." [350]

The Select Committee sought to question Scavino about how he and others on President Trump's social media team interacted with The Donald subreddit and then TheDonald.win. But Scavino refused to cooperate with the committee's subpoena.[351]

After President Trump's December 19th tweet, users on the site posted simple maps of the U.S. Capitol and telegraphed their intent to invade the building.[352] "If we occupy the capitol building, there will be no vote," one user wrote.[353] "The media will call us evil if we have to occupy the Capitol Building on January 6th. Let them," another post read.[354] One user argued the goal should be to "surround the enemy" and "create [a] perimeter" around the Capitol on January 6th, such that no one was allowed to leave until President Trump was "re-admitted for another 4 years."[355] This same user posted a diagram of the U.S. Capitol's perimeter with arrows indicating where the "Capitol Access Tunnels" were located.

On January 5th, another user on TheDonald.win encouraged President Trump's supporters to "be prepared to secure the capitol building," claiming that "there will be plenty of ex military to guide you."[356] Multiple other posts made it clear that the U.S. Capitol was the target on January 6th, with one poster writing that people should bring "handcuffs and zip ties to DC," so they could enact "citizen's arrests" of those officials who certified the election's results.[357] Another post highlighted the "most important map for January 6th. Form a TRUE LINE around the Capitol and the tunnels."[358] That "post included a detailed schematic of Capitol Hill with the tunnels surrounding the complex highlighted."[359]

Other posts on TheDonald.win included specific plans to build gallows outside the U.S. Capitol. "Gallows are simpler and more cost effective, plus they're an American old west tradition too," one user wrote on December 22, 2020.[360] A week later, another wrote: "Let's construct a Gallows outside the Capitol building next Wednesday so the Congressmen watching from their office windows shit their pants."[361] Another said that "building a hanging platform in front of Congress on the 6 should send a strong message."[362] The site hosted a diagram showing how to tie a hangman's knot,[363] with one site member writing that they should build gallows "so the traitors know the stakes."[364] On January 5, 2021, hours before the attack began, a user posted an image of gallows and titled it, "Election Fraud Repair Kit."[365]

Text messages between Trump Campaign Senior Advisor Jason Miller and White House Chief of Staff Mark Meadows show that these kinds of posts reached deep into the President's inner circle. Miller sent Meadows a text on December 30th, declaring, "I got the base FIRED UP."[366] The thread contained a link to a TheDonald.win comment thread filled with reactions to a post by Miller promoting January 6th.[367] Users in the thread made comments such as "gallows don't require electricity," and that millions will "bust in through the doors if they try to stop Pence from declaring Trump the winner," all in response to Miller.[368]

On December 19, 2020, the same day President Trump posted his inflammatory "be wild" tweet, he also tweeted a noteworthy video. The short clip was titled, "FIGHT FOR TRUMP!—SAVE AMERICA—SAVE THE WORLD."[369] The video reportedly appeared on TheDonald.win two days earlier.[370] As with so much else on TheDonald.win, this refrain featured prominently on the day of the attack on the Capitol. During his speech at the Ellipse south of the White House on January 6th, the crowd broke out into a chant of "Fight for Trump! Fight for Trump!" President Trump thanked those in attendance.[371]

In the two and a half weeks since he first announced the January 6th "protest," extremists and conspiracy theorists plotted to make the unprecedented, presidentially announced protest against the peaceful transfer of power "wild" indeed. Meanwhile, event organizers and White House staffers prepared for the final rally of President Trump's term.

6.11 HOW THE WHITE HOUSE AND RALLY ORGANIZERS PREPARED FOR JANUARY 6TH

In the days following President Trump's tweet, rally organizers secured permits for about one dozen events in Washington, DC on January 5th and 6th.[372] At 7:12 a.m., not even 6 hours after President Trump's tweet, Cindy Chafian, an executive at Women for America First (WFAF), emailed the National Park Service (NPS) about an event that had been planned to coincide with President-elect Biden's inauguration on January 20, 2021.[373] Chafian's ask was simple: "Can I change the date to January 6th?"[374]

WFAF was founded in 2019 by Amy and Kylie Kremer, a mother-daughter pair who were longtime supporters of the President.[375] WFAF became a significant player in the "Stop the Steal" movement.[376] The Kremers started a "Stop the Steal" Facebook group that gathered some 365,000 members in less than 24 hours.[377] Their online organizing coincided with their on-the-ground mobilization activities. The Kremers organized a bus tour to promote the Big Lie, in addition to events in Washington, DC on November 14, 2020, and December 12, 2020.[378] After President Trump's December 19th tweet, the Kremers focused on January 6th. Kylie Kremer proudly declared their support on Twitter: "The calvary [sic] is coming, President! JANUARY 6th | Washington, DC TrumpMarch.com #MarchForTrump #StopTheSteal."[379] After the date of their permit was revised, WFAF ultimately provided President Trump the stage on the Ellipse where he would direct the crowd to march on the Capitol.[380]

The Kremers were not alone in responding quickly to the President's tweet. Ali Alexander, the founder of Stop the Steal, LLC,[381] was eager to get ahead of other organizers. On the morning of December 19th, Alexander told his event planner, "Everyone is trying to get the jump on us so I'd like to get the court side of the capitol (lawn) and I'd like to get capitol steps and court."[382] Alexander told his event planner to "grab whatever we can. All of it."[383] Alexander's team did just that: they registered and launched a new website, WildProtest.com,[384] which advertised planned events for January 6th under a banner that read: "President Trump Wants You in DC January 6."[385]

Still other organizers were quick to seize on the President's tweet. Arina Grossu and Robert Weaver, co-founders of the self-proclaimed "Judeo-Christian" Jericho March organization,[386] held a rally in Washington, DC on

December 12, 2020. Oath Keepers leader Stewart Rhodes, Flynn, Jones, Alexander, and others shared a stage at that event.[387] Grossu and Weaver exchanged emails just a few hours after President Trump's first mention of January 6th. In an email on the morning of December 19th, Weaver told Grossu to "enjoy the peace before the storm" and said, "Trump has called for a protest on 1/6, FYI."[388] The Jericho March's website used President Trump's "Be there, will be wild!" language to advertise additional events between January 2nd and January 6, 2021.[389]

Marsha Lessard, the leader of a vaccine-skeptic group, Virginia Freedom Keepers, worked to stage an event with Bianca Gracia, the leader of Latinos for Trump on January 6th.[390] The women had ties to the Oath Keepers[391] and Proud Boys,[392] respectively—two groups central to the violence on January 6. Latinos for Trump reportedly advertised their January 6th event with the same QAnon-inspired banner, "Operation Occupy the Capitol."[393] Another conservative group, Moms for America, worked with Alexander before securing a permit for an event on January 5th.[394]

6.12 "HE'S CALLING ON *YOU*, HE NEEDS YOUR HELP"

As discussed above, Alex Jones was one of the loudest supporters of the "Stop the Steal" movement. Jones dedicated much of the December 20th episode of his *InfoWars* show to President Trump's "be wild" tweet, telling his listeners that nothing less than the fate of the American Republic was at stake. "He's calling *you*, he needs your help, we need your help," Jones told his audience.[395] The Select Committee has learned that, between the time of the President's tweet and Jones's December 20th show, Jones's staff had several calls with Chafian, who had just procured a new permit for WFAF's event on the Ellipse.[396] The two parties apparently discussed whether this newly hatched January 6th event was an opportunity to work together.[397]

Jones's broadcast also led to an influx of funds for the January 6th event at the Ellipse. Julie Fancelli is the billionaire heiress to the Publix supermarket fortune and a longtime supporter of President Trump.[398] Fancelli had recently become a donor to Jones's *InfoWars* site.[399] She listened to Jones's December 20th show,[400] and decided she wanted to back the cause.

Inspired by Jones and the fervor that continued to surround the President's tweet, Fancelli called Caroline Wren, a Republican fundraiser linked to the Trump Campaign, the next day.[401] According to Wren, Fancelli said that "she wanted to see a lot of people there in DC, so how much would that cost?"[402] Fancelli spoke with Jones's staff and they recommended that she connect with Chafian, who was organizing the Ellipse rally.[403] In the waning days of 2020, Fancelli and Jones spoke several times.[404]

Fancelli worked with Wren to create a multimillion-dollar budget to convene as many supporters of President Trump as possible.[405] To ensure that Fancelli's dollars made maximum impact, Wren contacted some of the major players who were rallying supporters for January 6th. Wren emailed Kylie Kremer[406] and exchanged texts with Jones[407] and Chafian.[408] Fancelli's goal was clear: she wanted to spend $3 million to "get as many people there as possible."[409] The resulting budget allocated $500,000 to a busing program and a centralized ad campaign by the Tea Party Express to promote the event.[410] Another $500,000 went to assisting WFAF and Jones in their organizational efforts.[411]

Caroline Wren also connected with Ali Alexander. On December 29th, Wren told the Stop the Steal leader, "I can pay for the buses and I have my team looking for available companies, so let me know what cities you need them in!"[412] Wren's offer came in response to a tweet from Alexander earlier that day: "Coalition of us working on 25 new charter buses to bring people FOR FREE to #JAN6 #STOPTHESTEAL for President Trump. If you have money for more buses or have a company, let me know. We will list our buses sometime in the next 72 hours. STAND BACK & STAND BY!"[413]

The final words of Alexander's tweet directly echoed President Trump's command to the Proud Boys during the September 29, 2020, presidential debate.[414] Alexander's word choice was apt. The Proud Boys were already planning to show up in force, and to ensure that the crowd would be "wild."

6.13 "TRUMP IS SUPPOSED TO ORDER US TO THE CAPITOL"

On the evening of December 27th, President Trump boosted the upcoming event on Twitter: "See you in Washington, DC, on January 6th. Don't miss it. Information to follow!"[415] The Select Committee learned that this tweet came after the White House spoke with a former Trump staffer, Justin Caporale, who was asked to help produce the Ellipse rally.[416] That same evening, the President had dinner with Donald Trump, Jr., and his girlfriend Kimberly Guilfoyle,[417] who spoke with rally organizer Caroline Wren during the meal.[418] Wren also texted Guilfoyle talking points that described her ambitions for the event, saying that "buses of people are coming in from all over the country to support you. It's going to be huge, we are also adding in programming the night of January 5th."[419]

After Guilfoyle's call with Wren, there was a series of calls among the senior White House staff,[420] likely underscoring the seriousness of the White House's interest in the event.

Within a few days, the White House began to take a more direct role in coordinating the rally at the Ellipse.[421] In a December 29th text to Wren, Caporale wrote that after the President's planned speech there "maybe [sic] a call to action to march to the [C]apitol and make noise."[422]

This is the earliest indication uncovered by the Select Committee that the President planned to call on his supporters to march on the U.S. Capitol. But it wasn't the last. On January 2nd, rally organizer Katrina Pierson informed Wren that President Trump's Chief of Staff, Mark Meadows, had said the President was going to "call on everyone to march to the [C]apitol."[423]

Inside the White House, the President's intent was well-known. Cassidy Hutchinson, an aide to Meadows, recalled in her testimony that she overheard discussions to this effect toward the end of December or early January. One such discussion included an exchange between Meadows and Rudolph Giuliani that occurred on January 2nd.[424] Hutchinson understood that President Trump wanted to have a crowd at the Capitol in connection with what was happening inside—the certification of the electoral count.[425] Hutchinson also recalled that President Trump's allies in Congress were aware of the plan. During a call with members of the House Freedom Caucus, the idea of telling people to go to the Capitol was discussed as a way to encourage Congress to delay the electoral college certification and send it back to the States.[426]

On January 4th, WFAF's Kylie Kremer informed Mike Lindell, the CEO of MyPillow and an ally of President Trump, that "POTUS is going to have us march there [the Supreme Court]/the Capitol" but emphasized that the plan "stays only between us."[427]

The "Stop the Steal" coalition was aware of the President's intent. On January 5th, Ali Alexander sent a text to a journalist saying: "Ellipse then US capitol [sic]. Trump is supposed to order us to the capitol [sic] at the end of his speech but we will see."[428]

6.14 "WELL, I SHOULD WALK WITH THE PEOPLE."

President Trump wanted to personally accompany his supporters on the march from the Ellipse to the U.S. Capitol. During a January 4th meeting with staffers and event organizer Katrina Pierson, President Trump emphasized his desire to march with his supporters.[429] "Well, I should walk with the people," Pierson recalled President Trump saying.[430] Though Pierson said that she did not take him "seriously," she knew that "he would absolutely want to be with the people."[431] Pierson pointed out that President Trump "did the drive-by the first time and the flyover the second time"—a reference to the November and December 2020 protests in Washington, DC.[432] During these previous events, President Trump made cameo appearances to fire up his supporters. Now, as January 6th approached, the President again wanted to be there, on the ground, as his supporters marched on the U.S. Capitol.

The President's advisors tried to talk him out of it. White House Senior Advisor Max Miller "shot it down immediately" because of concerns about the President's safety.[433] Pierson agreed.[434] But President Trump was persistent, and he floated the idea of having 10,000 National Guardsmen deployed to protect him and his supporters from any supposed threats by leftwing counter-protestors.[435] Miller again rejected the President's idea, saying that the National Guard was not necessary for the event. Miller testified that there was no further conversation on the matter.[436] After the meeting, Miller texted Pierson, "Just glad we killed the national guard and a procession."[437] That is, President Trump briefly considered having the National Guard oversee his procession to the U.S. Capitol. The President did not order the National Guard to protect the U.S. Capitol, or to secure the joint session proceedings.

Although his advisors tried to talk the President out of personally going, they understood that his supporters would be marching.[438] Pierson's agenda for the meeting reflected the President's plan for protestors to go to the U.S. Capitol after the rally.[439] But President Trump did not give up on the idea of personally joining his supporters on their march, as discussed further in Chapter 7.

6.15 "POTUS...LIKES THE CRAZIES."

As Katrina Pierson helped plan the Ellipse rally, she faced another complication. The "Stop the Steal" movement played an outsized role in promoting January 6th. And now, as the day approached, its leading voices wanted prime speaking gigs—perhaps even on the same stage as President Trump. Roger Stone, Alex Jones and Ali Alexander were all angling for significant stage time. Pierson knew they were trouble.

In her testimony before the Select Committee, Pierson cited several concerns, including that Jones and Alexander had played a prominent role in the November 2020 protest in Atlanta, Georgia. This was no ordinary protest. Jones and Alexander "had gone into the Georgia Capitol with some inflammatory rhetoric," Pierson explained.[440] When Pierson was asked if Jones and Alexander "surrounding the governor's mansion" and "going into the Capitol" were the "kind of thing" that gave her pause, she responded: "Absolutely."[441] After the Georgia protest, Pierson explained,

Photos of Roger Stone, Alex Jones and Ali Alexander appear on a screen during a Select Committee hearing on July 12, 2022.

Photo by Anna Moneymaker/Getty Images

the Kremers—who had helped organize "Stop the Steal" activities—distanced themselves from Jones and Alexander.[442]

But there was an additional problem. President Trump wanted to include the "Stop the Steal" leaders in the January 6th event. As Pierson put it in a text message to Kylie Kremer: "POTUS ... likes the crazies."[443] Pierson said that she believed this was the case because President Trump "loved people who viciously defended him in public."[444] But their "vicious" defenses of the President clearly troubled Pierson.

Pierson tried to trim the speaker lineup—which still included the "Stop the Steal" trio of Stone, Jones, and Alexander. She was initially vetoed by the White House after Deputy Chief of Staff for Communications Dan Scavino,[445] who had approved the "original psycho list."[446] At one point, she texted Scavino's boss, Mark Meadows, saying: "Things have gotten crazy and I desperately need some direction."[447] She was concerned by the possibility of "crazy people" being included in the event, their incendiary role in Georgia, and the fact that people coming to Washington, DC were planning to protest at the U.S. Capitol.[448]

Meadows told Pierson that she should take control of the situation and remove the possibility of controversial speakers.[449] Pierson agreed to do so.[450] But the President remained an obstacle. During their January 4th meeting, Pierson tried to convince President Trump to minimize the role of these potentially explosive figures at the Ellipse. She offered to place them at a planned event the night before in Freedom Plaza or on other stages in DC on January 6th. She told the President to "[k]eep the fringe on the fringe"[451] and advised him to "[e]liminate convicted felons that could damage other speakers."[452]

President Trump was still unwilling to remove them from the lineup entirely. The President instructed Pierson to give Stone a speaking slot on January 5th and asked for more information about Ali Alexander.[453] After discussing the matter with Scavino, President Trump also requested that Alexander be given a speaking slot. President Trump "brought up Ali [Alexander] ... just keep him on stage not associated with POTUS or main event," Scavino wrote.[454]

In the end, the "Stop the Steal" leaders—Stone, Jones and Alexander — did not appear on the stage at the Ellipse on January 6th, although they did speak at other planned events, consistent with the President's request about Alexander. "POTUS expectations are [to have something] intimate and then send everyone over to the Capitol," Pierson explained in a text message to Justin Caporale and Taylor Budowich.[455] Caporale redacted this text and others in his early production of documents to the Select Committee, and he only revealed them after they had already been produced by other witnesses.[456]

However, other incendiary voices—in addition to President Trump's — were given time on the Ellipse stage. The Select Committee learned that President Trump's aides warned him against the inclusion of figures like John Eastman[457] and Rudolph Giuliani,[458] given their false claims about election fraud.[459] Both men, of course, ended up sharing a stage with him on January 6th.[460] Meadows himself directed that they be allowed to speak.[461]

6.16 JANUARY 5, 2021: "FORT TRUMP"

While the "Stop the Steal" coalition was not given speaking slots on the Ellipse stage on January 6th, its leaders had plenty of opportunities to speak the day before. And they used their platforms to rile up the crowd in Washington, DC in advance of the joint session.

Ali Alexander spoke at an event sponsored by Moms for America in front of the U.S. Capitol. Alexander claimed that he was honored to be sharing the same stage with President Trump the following day, even though behind the scenes his appearance had been nixed.[462]

"We must rebel," Alexander told rallygoers. "I'm not even sure if I'm going to leave D.C. We might make this 'Fort Trump,' right?" Alexander said, while standing in front of the U.S. Capitol. "We're going to keep fighting for you, Mr. President." [463] On his Twitter account, Alexander also spread the idea that President Trump's supporters should occupy areas of Washington, DC, using the phrases and hashtags such as "Fort Trump" and "#OccupyDC". [464]

Alex Jones and Roger Stone spoke at a separate event hosted by Virginia Women for Trump in front of the Supreme Court. [465] The event, named the "One Nation Under God" prayer rally, was cohosted by the American Phoenix Project—the Three Percenter-linked group run by Alan Hostetter and Russel Taylor, discussed above, which is charged with conspiracy to obstruct an official proceeding. [466]

Jones repeated his claims about the election being stolen, claiming that those in attendance stood against a "Satanic world government." [467] Stone led a "Stop the Steal" chant, claiming the "evidence of election fraud is not only growing, it is overwhelming, and it is compelling." President Trump "won the majority of the legal votes cast" and President Trump "won this election," Stone said. Nothing less than the fate of Western Civilization was at stake, according to Stone:

Let's be very clear. This is not fight between Republicans and Democrats. This is not a fight between liberals and conservatives. This is a fight for the future the United States of America. It is a fight for the future of Western Civilization as we know it. It's a fight between dark and light. It's a fight between the godly and the godless. It's a fight between good and evil. And we dare not fail, or we will step out into one thousand years of darkness. [468]

Stone claimed that they "renounce violence" and those on "the left ... are the violent ones." But he insisted that "nothing is over until we say it is," and "Victory will be ours." [469]

Both Taylor and Hostetter spoke as well. Hostetter told the crowd, "We are at war." [470] Taylor promised to "fight" and "bleed," vowing that "Patriot[s]" would "not return to our peaceful way of life until this election is made right." [471]

A long rally was also hosted at Freedom Plaza, an open-air space on Pennsylvania Avenue in Washington, DC. It is a symbolic protest site, standing in the direct line between the White House and the U.S. Capitol. Stone, Jones and Alexander all appeared at Freedom Plaza on the evening of January 5th. Their remarks were incendiary.

Stone repeated his apocalyptic language from earlier in the day, claiming that rallygoers were embroiled in "an epic struggle for the future of this country between dark and light." [472] "I want them to know that 1776 is always an option," Ali Alexander said. "These degenerates in the deep state are going to give us what we want, or we are going to shut this country down."[473] When Alex Jones took to the stage, he screamed at the crowd: "*It's 1776!*"[474]

Another speaker that evening was Lt. Gen. Michael Flynn (ret.). "Tomorrow, tomorrow, trust me, the American people that are standing on the soil that we are standing on tonight, and they're going to be standing on this soil tomorrow, this is soil that we have fought over, fought for, and we will fight for in the future," Flynn also told the crowd. Flynn addressed Members of Congress, saying "those of you who are feeling weak tonight, those of you that don't have the moral fiber in your body, get some tonight because tomorrow, we the people are going to be here, and we want you to know that we will not stand for a lie. We will not stand for a lie."[475]

6.17 "TOGETHER, WE WILL STOP THE STEAL."

On the evening of January 5th, the President edited the speech he would deliver the next day at the Ellipse. The President's speechwriting team had only started working on his remarks the day before.[476] Despite concerns from the speechwriting team, unfounded claims coming from Giuliani and others made their way into the draft.[477]

The initial draft circulated on January 5th emphasized that the crowd would march to the U.S. Capitol.[478] Based on what they had heard from others in the White House, the speechwriting team expected President Trump to use his address to tell people to go to the Capitol.[479]

That evening, President Trump convened an impromptu gathering in the Oval Office with members of his staff, primarily his press team[480] and White House Deputy Chief of Staff Dan Scavino, who was in charge of President Trump's personal Twitter account.[481] Despite the bitter cold, the President ordered his staff to keep the door to the Rose Garden open so he could hear the music and cheering from his supporters at Freedom Plaza.[482] The music playing at Freedom Plaza was so loud "you could feel it shaking in the Oval."[483]

As President Trump listened, he was tweeting, at one point telling his supporters he could hear them from the Oval Office.[484] His speechwriters incorporated those tweets into a second draft of the speech that was circulated later that evening.[485] The following appeared in both tweet form[486] and was adapted into the speech:

> "All of us here today do not want to see our election victory stolen
> by emboldened Radical Left Democrats. Our Country has had
> enough, they won't take it anymore! Together, we will STOP THE
> STEAL."[487]

President Trump and members of his staff in the Oval Office on the evening of January 5, 2021.
Photo provided to the Select Committee by the National Archives and Records Administration.

In speaking with staff, he still seemed optimistic that "Congress would take some sort of action in his favor."[488] The White House photographer, who was also in attendance, recalled that President Trump again remarked that he should go to the Capitol the next day, and even asked about the best route to get there.[489] The President peppered staff for ideas concerning how "we could make the RINOs do the right thing" and make the next day "big."[490] Deputy Press Secretary Sarah Matthews, who was present in the Oval Office that evening, understood that President Trump wanted to get Republican Members of Congress to send the electoral votes back to the States, rather than certify the election.[491] Matthews recalled that initially no one spoke up in response, since they were trying to "process" what he had said.[492]

Eventually, Deere suggested that President Trump should focus his speech on his administration's accomplishments, rather than on his claim that the election had been stolen.[493] But the President told Deere that while they had accomplished a lot, the crowd was going to be "fired up" and "angry" the next day because they believed the election had been stolen and was rigged.[494] President Trump knew the crowd was angry because he could hear them.[495] Of course, President Trump was responsible, more than any other party, for ginning up their anger.

President Trump ended the evening by asking an aide how many people were going to be at the rally. The aide responded that he was not sure but told President Trump that he saw videos on Twitter of "pro-trump people chanting on planes heading to DC," which he asked to be shared with Scavino.[496]

"We will not let them silence your voices," the President told the crowd from the podium at the Ellipse. "We're not going to let it happen, I'm not going to let it happen."[497] His supporters started chanting, "fight for Trump!" The President thanked them.[498]

President Trump knew not only that his supporters were angry, but also that some of them were armed.[499] At times, he ad-libbed, deliberately stoking their rage even more. At one point he said: "And we fight. We fight like hell. And if you don't fight like hell, you're not going to have a country anymore."[500] The word "fight," or a variation thereof, appeared only twice in the prepared text.[501] President Trump would go on to utter the word twenty times during his speech at the Ellipse.[502]

President Trump had summoned a mob, including armed extremists and conspiracy theorists, to Washington, DC on the day the joint session of Congress was to meet. He then told that same mob to march on the U.S. Capitol and "fight." They clearly got the message.

ENDNOTES

1. Select Committee to Investigate the January 6th Attack on the United States Capitol, Transcribed Interview of William Barr, (June 2, 2022), p. 62.

2. Select Committee to Investigate the January 6th Attack on the United States Capitol, Transcribed Interview of William Barr, (June 2, 2022), pp. 27,62; Select Committee to Investigate the January 6th Attack on the United States Capitol, Transcribed Interview of Michael Pompeo, (Aug. 9, 2022), p. 30; Select Committee to Investigate the January 6th Attack on the United States Capitol, Transcribed Interview of Eugene Scalia, (June 30, 2022), p. 11.

3. Select Committee to Investigate the January 6th Attack on the United States Capitol, Transcribed Interview of Eugene Scalia, (June 30, 2022), p. 11. Others throughout the White House similarly recognized that December 14 was a milestone in America's constitutional process, and it was time for the President to move on. But it was not just members of President Trump's Cabinet who viewed that the election was over, and that President Trump had lost by December 14—President Trump's top advisors at the White House came to similar conclusions. For example, White House Counsel Pat Cipollone agreed with Senator McConnell's December 15th comments on the Senate floor and viewed the process for challenging the election as "done." See Select Committee to Investigate the January 6th Attack on the United States Capitol, Transcribed Interview of Pasquale Anthony "Pat" Cipollone, (July 8, 2022), p. 73. White House Deputy Press Secretary and Deputy Assistant to the President Judd Deere also recognized the significance of the electoral college vote in determining the president and vice president and conveyed this to President Trump. He also advised him to concede. See Select Committee to Investigate the January 6th Attack on the United States Capitol, Deposition of Judson P. Deere, (Mar. 3, 2022), pp. 23-25. White House Advisor Ivanka Trump viewed the electoral college vote as important and had already started planning for leaving the administration prior to then. See Select Committee to Investigate the January 6th Attack on the United States Capitol, Transcribed Interview of Ivanka Trump, (Apr. 5, 2022), p. 193. White House Advisor Jared Kushner similarly viewed that day as "significant." Select Committee to Investigate the January 6th Attack on the United States Capitol, Transcribed Interview of Jared Kushner, (Mar. 31, 2022), p. 107.

4. President Trump's full tweet read: "Peter Navarro releases 36-page report alleging election fraud 'more than sufficient' to swing victory to Trump https://t.co/D8KrMHnFdK. A great report by Peter. Statistically impossible to have lost the 2020 Election. Big protest in D.C. on January 6th. Be there, will be wild!" President Donald J. Trump: Tweets of December 19, 2020, The American Presidency Project, available at https://www.presidency.ucsb.edu/documents/tweets-december-19-2020.

5. Select Committee to Investigate the January 6th Attack on the United States Capitol, Deposition of J. Smith, (May 9, 2022), p. 79. Navaroli appeared for two deposition session with the Select Committee, the first of which was conducted anonymously to protect her identity. In this deposition session, she was called "J. Smith." She later agreed to put her name in the record and sat for another round of questioning. Testimony from that second session is referred to as "Deposition of Anika Navaroli."

6. Select Committee to Investigate the January 6th Attack on the United States Capitol, Deposition of Anika Navaroli, (Sept. 1, 2022), pp. 66-67. She went on to characterize the tweet as an "RSVP card" that became a "rallying point" for the President's supporters, one that prompted violent responses from users that were highly suggestive of the coming violence targeting DC on January 6th. *Id.*, at p. 64. Another former Twitter employee, whose deposition was also conducted anonymously, testified that the tweet "in many ways kind of crystallized the plans" for violence and that, after that point, supporters of President Trump began tweeting about movements to D.C. Select Committee to Investigate the January 6th Attack on the United States Capitol, Deposition of J. Johnson, (Sept. 7, 2022), p. 55.

7. The President's call to action quickly reverberated beyond Twitter and spread across the internet. On one social networking site, Discord, a forum called "DonaldsArmy.US" erupted in the hours after the tweet, with users seeing it as a "call to action" and beginning to organize travel plans to D.C., including by discussing how and whether to evade DC gun restrictions and bring firearms into the city. *See* Summary Memorandum from Select Committee to Investigate the January 6th Attack on the United States Capitol. Briefing with Discord, (July 29, 2022); *see also* Documents on file with the Select Committee to Investigate the January 6th Attack on the United States Capitol (Discord Production), JAN6C_DIS_000269 (Memo from Discord titled "DonaldsArmy.US and BASEDMedia.").

8. Second Superseding Indictment at ¶ 28, *United States v. Nordean et al.*, No. 1:1:21-cr-175 (D.D.C. Mar. 7, 2022), ECF No. 305.

9. *See, e.g.*, Ian Ward, "How a D.C. Bar Became the 'Haven' for the Proud Boys," *Politico*, (Dec. 14, 2020), available at https://www.politico.com/news/magazine/2020/12/14/harrys-bar-proud-boys-washington-dc-445015.

10. Second Superseding Indictment at ¶37, *United States v. Nordean et al.*, No. 1:21-cr-175 (D.D.C. Mar. 7, 2022), ECF No. 305 (citing Tarrio's message to the Proud Boys on December 29, 2020, that they would "not be wearing our traditional Black and Yellow" on January 6th; they would "be incognito.").

11. Second Superseding Indictment at ¶ 50, *United States v. Nordean et al.*, No. 1:1:21-cr-175 (D.D.C. Mar. 7, 2022), ECF No. 305.

12. Second Superseding Indictment at ¶ 100, *United States v. Nordean et al.*, No. 1:1:21-cr-175 (D.D.C. Mar. 7, 2022), ECF No. 305.

13. Select Committee to Investigate the January 6th Attack on the United States Capitol, Deposition of Henry Tarrio, (Feb. 4, 2022), pp. 83-84.

14. Second Superseding Indictment at ¶ 107, *United States v. Nordean et al.*, No. 1:21-cr-175 (D.D.C. Mar. 7, 2022), ECF No. 305.

15. *See, e.g.*, Mike Levine, "How A Standoff in Nevada Years Ago Set The Militia Movement on A Crash Course with The US Capitol," ABC News, (Jan. 5, 2022), available at https://abcnews.go.com/US/standoff-nevada-years-ago-set-militia-movement-crash/story?id=82051940.

16. Indictment at ¶¶ 67, 68, *United States v. Rhodes, III, et al.*, No. 22-cr-15 (D.D.C. June 22, 2022), ECF No. 167.

17. *See* Select Committee to Investigate the January 6th Attack on the United States Capitol, Deposition of Elmer Stewart Rhodes, (Feb. 22, 2022), pp. 132,134; Stewart Rhodes and Kellye SoRelle, "Open Letter to President Trump: You Must Use the Insurrection Act to 'Stop the Steal' and Defeat the Coup," Oathkeepers.org, (Dec. 14, 2020), available at https://web.archive.org/web/20210123133022/https:/oathkeepers.org/2020/12/open-letter-to-president-trump-you-must-use-insurrection-act-to-stop-the-steal-and-defeat-the-coup/ (archived). Jason Van Tatenhove, the former spokesman of the Oath Keepers described how he suspected that Rhodes saw the Insurrection Act as a blank check: "He could pretty much do whatever he wanted, and [President Trump] could install Stewart and the Oath Keepers as some sort of security force that would bring them real legitimacy and political power." Select Committee to Investigate the January 6th Attack on the United States Capitol, Transcribed Interview of Jason Van Tatenhove, (Mar. 9, 2022), p. 73.

18. Third Superseding Indictment at ¶ 37, *United States v. Crowl et al.*, No. 1:21-cr-28 (D.D.C., Mar. 31, 2021), ECF No. 127.

19. Third Superseding Indictment at ¶ 95-99, *United States v. Crowl et al.*, No. 1:21-cr-28 (D.D.C., Mar. 31, 2021), ECF No. 127.

20. Trial Transcript at 10502-508, *United States v. Rhodes et al.*, No. 1:22-cr-15 (D.D.C. Nov. 29, 2022); Alan Feuer and Zach Montague, "Oath Keepers Leader Convicted of Sedition in Landmark Jan. 6 Case," *New York Times*, (Nov. 29, 2022), available at https://www.nytimes.com/2022/11/29/us/politics/oath-keepers-trial-verdict-jan-6.html.

21. 18 U.S.C. § 2384.

22. For example, one Proud Boy, Jeremy Bertino, pleaded guilty to "seditious conspiracy" and other crimes in October 2022. Bertino admitted to authorities that the Proud Boys traveled to Washington on January 6, 2021, "to stop the certification of the Electoral College Vote." They "were willing to do whatever it would take, including using force against police and others, to achieve that objective." *See* "Former Leader of Proud Boys Pleads Guilty to Seditious Conspiracy for Efforts to Stop Transfer of Power Following 2020 Presidential Election," Department of Justice, (Oct. 6, 2022), available at https://www.justice.gov/opa/pr/former-leader-proud-boys-pleads-guilty-seditious-conspiracy-efforts-stop-transfer-power.

23. Criminal Complaint at 10-11, *United States v. Hazard*, No. 1:21-mj-868 (D.D.C. Dec. 7, 2021), ECF No. 1.

24. *See, e.g.*, Indictment at ¶¶ 34-37, *United States v. Hostetter et al.*, No. 1:21-cr-392 (D.D.C. June 9, 2021), ECF No. 1.

25. Malachi Barrett, "Far-Right Activist Who Encouraged U.S. Capitol Occupation Also Organized 'Stop the Steal' Rally in Michigan," *Mlive*, (Jan. 7, 2021), available at https://www.mlive.com/politics/2021/01/far-right-activist-who-encouraged-us-capitol-occupation-also-organized-stop-the-steal-rally-in-michigan.html.

26. Nicholas J. Fuentes (@NickJFuentes), Twitter, Jan. 7, 2021 10:56 p.m. ET, available at https://web.archive.org/web/20210107185745/https:/twitter.com/NickJFuentes/status/1347255833516765185 (archived).

27. Ken Dilanian and Ben Collins, "There Are Hundreds of Posts About Plans to Attack the Capitol. Why Hasn't This Evidence Been Used in Court?," NBC News, (Apr. 20, 2021), available at https://www.nbcnews.com/politics/justice-department/we-found-hundreds-posts-about-plans-attack-capitol-why-aren-n1264291.

28. Statement of Mike Rothschild, (Mar. 23, 2022), at pp. 3-6.

29. *See*, "NCRI Assessment of The Capitol Riots," Rutgers Miller Center for Community Protection and Resilience," Network Contagion Research Institute, (Jan. 9, 2021) available at https://millercenter.rutgers.edu/wp-content/uploads/2021/01/NCRI-Assessment-of-the-Capitol-Riots-1.pdf.

30. "Breaking: Trump Calls for Americans to March on DC January 6 to Stop Foreign Takeover," InfoWars, (Dec. 19, 2020), (archived) available at https://web.archive.org/web/20201219175757/https://www.infowars.com/posts/breaking-trump-calls-for-americans-to-march-on-dc-january-6-to-stop-foreign-takeover/.

31. Jacob Knutson, "Jury Orders Alex Jones to Pay Nearly $1 Billion in Sandy Hook Defamation Trial," Axios, (Oct. 12, 2022), available at https://www.axios.com/2022/10/12/alex-jones-sandy-hook-defamation-trial.

32. "The Alex Jones Show," Prison Planet TV, at 21:53, Dec. 20, 2020, available at http://tv.infowars.com/index/display/id/11151.

33. Jones's promotion of the January 6th event began almost immediately after the President's tweet. See The Alex Jones Show, "January 6th Will Be a Turning Point in American History," Banned.Video, at 16:29, Dec. 31, 2020, available at https://banned.video/watch?id=5fee715284a7b6210e12a2f7.

34. See, Lena V. Groeger, Jeff Kao, Al Shaw, Moiz Syed, and Maya Eliahou, "What Parler Saw During the Attack on the Capitol," Pro Publica, (Jan. 17, 2021), available at https://projects.propublica.org/parler-capitol-videos/?id=5OCkdwJRD0a3 (showing Alex Jones marching down Pennsylvania Avenue at 1:10 p.m.).

35. Select Committee to Investigate the January 6th Attack on the United States Capitol, Deposition of Caroline Wren, (Dec. 17, 2021), pp. 50, 70-71.

36. Select Committee to Investigate the January 6th Attack on the United States Capitol, Deposition of Judson P. Deere, (Mar. 3, 2022), p. 86.

37. Select Committee to Investigate the January 6th Attack on the United States Capitol, Transcribed Interview of Cassidy Hutchinson, (Feb. 23, 2022), pp. 32-33, 41; Select Committee to Investigate the January 6th Attack on the United States Capitol, Continued Interview of Cassidy Hutchinson, (June 20, 2022), pp. 107-108, 135.

38. Select Committee to Investigate the January 6th Attack on the United States Capitol, Deposition of Judson P. Deere, (Mar. 3, 2022), pp. 70-71.

39. Senate Committee on Homeland Security and Governmental Affairs and Committee on Rules and Administration, 117th Congress, "Examining the U.S. Capitol Attack: A Review of the Security, Planning, and Response Failures on January 6" (Staff Report), (June 8, 2021), p. B-22.

40. Rob Kuznia, Curt Devine, Nelli Black, and Drew Grin, "Stop the Steal's Massive Disinformation Campaign Connected to Roger Stone and Steve Bannon," CNN Business, (Nov. 14, 2020), available at https://www.cnn.com/2020/11/13/business/stop-the-steal-disinformation-campaign-invs/index.html.

41. Charles Homans, "How 'Stop the Steal' Captured the American Right," New York Times, (July 19, 2022), available at https://www.nytimes.com/2022/07/19/magazine/stop-the-steal.html. ("During his time as a Trump campaign adviser, Stone urged the candidate to run on immigration, and now he linked these views to the plots that he claimed were afoot to deny Trump the nomination. In the Republican primaries, Trump was 'a nationalist in a field of globalists,' Stone said in an interview that April with Stefan Molyneux, a Canadian alt-right podcaster. If the globalists failed to steal the primaries outright, there would be a 'naked attempt to steal this from Donald Trump' at the Republican National Convention in Cleveland, Stone declared. 'The fix is in.'")

42. Rob Kuznia, Curt Devine, Nelli Black, and Drew Grin, "Stop the Steal's Massive Disinformation Campaign Connected to Roger Stone and Steve Bannon," CNN Business, (Nov. 14, 2020), available at https://www.cnn.com/2020/11/13/business/stop-the-steal-disinformation-campaign-invs/index.html.

43. Rob Kuznia, Curt Devine, Nelli Black, and Drew Grin, "Stop the Steal's Massive Disinformation Campaign Connected to Roger Stone and Steve Bannon," CNN Business, (Nov. 14,

2020), available at https://www.cnn.com/2020/11/13/business/stop-the-steal-disinformation-campaign-invs/index.html.

44. Documents on file with the Select Committee to Investigate the January 6th Attack on the United States Capitol (Christoffer Guldbrandsen Production), Video file 201105.

45. *See*, Hugo Lowell, "Film Offers Inside Look at Roger Stone's 'Stop the Steal' Efforts before January 6," *The Guardian*, (July 8, 2022), available at https://www.theguardian.com/us-news/2022/jul/07/roger-stone-ali-alexander-film-jan-6-stop-the-steal.

46. Select Committee to Investigate the January 6th Attack on the United States Capitol, Deposition of Ali Alexander, (Jan. 9, 2021), p. 18.

47. Select Committee to Investigate the January 6th Attack on the United States Capitol, Deposition of Ali Alexander, (Dec. 9, 2021), pp. 199-200.

48. *See, e.g.*, WillfulWarrior, "Hispanic Proud Boys Leader: 'We Fought Off Antifa Terrorists for 12 Hrs'," BitChute, Nov. 19, 2020, available at https://www.bitchute.com/video/if5u7EuD7NU3/; Infowars: War Room, "Enrique Tarrio Spat on While Flying to Austin Texas," BitChute, Dec. 2, 2020, available at https://www.bitchute.com/video/yKijHk6m25RL/; BNN, "Full Show: Witnesses Testify on Michigan Voter Fraud; Thousands of Illegal Votes Counted for Biden," BitChute, Dec. 2, 2020, available at https://www.bitchute.com/video/74N0WNHOjiRy/; Jan 6th Protest and Save America March (2020-2H), "Patriots Plot Their Recapture of America in D.C. This Weekend," Banned.Video, Nov. 9, 2020, available at https://archive.org/details/banned.video_-_jan_6th_protest_and_save_america_march_2020-2h/2020-11-11T02%3A07.148Z+-+Patriots+Plot+Their+Recapture+Of+America+In+D.C.+This+Weekend/2020-11-11T02%3A19%3A07.148Z+-+%20Patriots+Plot+Their+Recapture+Of+America+In+D.C.+This+Weekend.mp4 (archived); The Alex Jones Show, "Oathkeepers Founder: Americans Need to Overcome Their Fears And Join The March on DC," Banned.Video, Nov. 10, 2020, available at https://freeworldnews.tv/watch?id=5fab1b880ad7422090a8242f.

49. Kellye SoRelle, a lawyer for the Oath Keepers, described Stone (along with Alexander) as among the key players who were the "midpoint," "the ones who tr[ied] to orchestrate" joint efforts in the post-election period. *See* Select Committee to Investigate the January 6th Attack on the United States Capitol, Deposition of Kellye SoRelle, (Apr. 13, 2022), pp. 60-66.

50. Frontline, "Alex Jones and Donald Trump: How the Candidate Echoed the Conspiracy Theorist on the Campaign Trail," PBS, (July 28, 2020), available at https://www.pbs.org/wgbh/frontline/article/alex-jones-and-donald-trump-how-the-candidate-echoed-the-conspiracy-theorist-on-the-campaign-trail/.

51. Eric Bradner, "Trump Praises 9/11 Truther's 'Amazing' Reputation," CNN, (Dec. 2, 2015), available at https://www.cnn.com/2015/12/02/politics/donald-trump-praises-9-11-truther-alex-jones.

52. *See* Elizabeth Williamson, "Alex Jones and Donald Trump: A Fateful Alliance Draws Scrutiny," *New York Times*, (Mar. 7, 2022), available at https://www.nytimes.com/2022/03/07/us/politics/alex-jones-jan-6-trump.html ("Infowars grossed more than $50 million annually during the Trump presidency by selling diet supplements, body armor, and other products on its website.").

53. *See, e.g.*, Joshua Zitser, "Roger Stone Makes Donation Plea for Alex Jones After Verdict Says He Must Pay $49m for Sandy Hook 'Hoax' Claims," *Business Insider*, (Aug. 7, 2022), available at https://www.businessinsider.com/video-roger-stone-asks-donations-infowars-alex-jones-sandy-hook-2022-8.

54. *See* AirTable Collection from Select Committee to Investigate the January 6th Attack on the United States Capitol, "Images of State Protests before January 6, 2021."

55. *See* AirTable Collection from Select Committee to Investigate the January 6th Attack on the United States Capitol, "Images of State Protests before January 6, 2021."

56. *See* AirTable Collection from Select Committee to Investigate the January 6th Attack on the United States Capitol, "Images of State Protests before January 6, 2021."

57. See AirTable Collection from Select Committee to Investigate the January 6th Attack on the United States Capitol, "Images of State Protests before January 6, 2021."

58. Jonathan Oosting, "FBI arrests Ryan Kelley, Michigan GOP Governor Candidate, over Capitol Riots," *Bridge Michigan*, (June 9, 2022), available at https://www.bridgemi.com/michigan-government/fbi-arrests-ryan-kelley-michigan-gop-governor-candidate-over-capitol-riots.

59. James Dawson, "Unmasked Protesters Push Past Police into Idaho Lawmakers' Session," NPR, (Apr. 25, 2022), available at https://www.npr.org/2020/08/25/905785548/unmasked-protesters-push-past-police-into-idaho-lawmakers-session; Jeremy Stiles, "Boise Woman Sentenced for Role in U.S. Capitol Riot," KTVB, (May 24, 2022), available at https://www.ktvb.com/article/news/crime/boise-woman-sentenced-for-role-in-us-capitol-riot-pamela-hemphill-january-6-2021/277-3aa12194-5a54-4abe-88a2-d644cf5043aa.

60. Documents on file with the Select Committee to Investigate the January 6th Attack on the United States Capitol (Sergeant at Arms for the Arizona House of Representatives Production), CTRL0000930907, CTRL0000930908 (December 4, 2020, surveillance footage from the Arizona House of Representatives). available at https://house.app.box.com/folder/183317506767.

61. Sergio Olmos and Conrad Wilson, "At Least 3 Men from Oregon Protest Appear to Have Joined Insurrection at U.S. Capitol," Oregon Public Broadcasting, (Jan. 10, 2021), available at https://www.opb.org/article/2021/01/10/oregon-washington-protest-insurrection-david-anthony-medina-tim-davis/.

62. Brendan Guttenschwager (@BGOnTheScene), Twitter, Nov. 19, 2020 1:03 p.m. ET, available at https://twitter.com/BGOnTheScene/status/1329485442165706752.

63. Justwanna Grill, "Oathkeepers leader GROYPED in Atlanta," YouTube, Nov. 4, 2020, available at https://www.youtube.com/watch?v=V_rDOm5oKu0.

64. Timothy Johnson, "Alex Jones Calls on Supporters to 'Surround' the Georgia Governor's Mansion to Prevent Election Results from Being Certified," Media Matters, (Nov. 17, 2020), available at https://www.mediamatters.org/alex-jones/alex-jones-calls-supporters-surround-georgia-governors-mansion-prevent-election-results.

65. Nicholas J. Fuentes (@NickJFuentes), Twitter, Nov. 17, 2020, available at https://web.archive.org/web/20201120061341/https://twitter.com/NickJFuentes (archived).

66. *See, e.g.*, Aquarium Groyper, "Nick Fuentes Georgia State Capitol 11/20/2020," YouTube, Nov. 20, 2020, available at https://www.youtube.com/watch?v=OS1f—Tkn1M.

67. Jacqueline Alemany et al., "Red Flags," *Washington Post*, (Oct. 31, 2021), https://www.washingtonpost.com/politics/interactive/2021/warnings-jan-6-insurrection/.

68. Derrick Mullins, "'Stop the Steal' Connected 2 Roger Stone-Roger Stone Calls Ali Anderson in Front of Atlanta GA Crowd," YouTube Nov. 24, 2020, available at https://perma.cc/MWS3-HNGD.

69. Brendan Gutenschwager (@BGOnTheScene), Twitter, Nov. 20, 2022 12:38 p.m. ET, available at https://twitter.com/BGOnTheScene/status/1329841457377800198.

70. Zach D. Roberts (@zdroberts), Twitter, Jan. 14, 2022 11:38 p.m. ET, available at https://twitter.com/zdroberts/status/1482210446769807360.

71. Alexandra Hurtzler, "Alex Jones Leads 'Stop the Steal' Rally at Georgia's Capitol to Protest Election Results," *Newsweek*, (Nov. 18, 2020), available at https://www.newsweek.com/alex-jones-leads-stop-steal-rally-georgias-capitol-protest-election-results-1548533.

72. Jacqueline Alemany et al., "Red Flags," *Washington Post*, (Oct. 31, 2021), https://www.washingtonpost.com/politics/interactive/2021/warnings-jan-6-insurrection/.

73. Statement of Andrew Seidel, (Mar. 18, 2022), at p. 9.

74. Mike Giglio, "The Oath Keepers' Radical Legal Defense of January 6th," *New Yorker*, (Oct. 1, 2022), available at https://www.newyorker.com/news/news-desk/the-oath-keepers-radical-legal-defense-of-january-6th.

75. "Pro-Trump Rallies in DC Attract Extremists & Erupt into Violence," Anti-Defamation League, (Dec. 13, 2020), available at https://www.adl.org/blog/pro-trump-rallies-in-dc-attract-extremists-erupt-into-violence. Despite this, one of the organizers of the Jericho March maintained that the "tone" of the rally was supposed to be "prayerful, spirit-filled, peaceful, joyful, and vibrant, a unified celebration." *See* Select Committee to Investigate the January 6th Attack on the United States Capitol, Transcribed Interview of Arina Grossu, (Apr. 29, 2022), p. 40.

76. *See* President Donald J. Trump: Tweets of December 12, 2020, The American Presidency Project, available at https://www.presidency.ucsb.edu/documents/tweets-december-19-2020.

77. "Pro-Trump Rallies in DC Attract Extremists & Erupt into Violence," Anti-Defamation League, (Dec. 13, 2020), available at http://www.adl.org/blog/pro-trump-rallies-in-DC-attract-extremists-erupt-into-violence.

78. Grace Segers, "Trump's Motorcade Passes Supporters Gathered for 'Million MAGA March'," CBS News, (Nov. 14, 2020), available at https://www.cbsnews.com/news/million-maga-march-washington-dc-trumps-motorcade-passes-supporters/.

79. Donald J. Trump (@realdonaldtrump), Twitter, Dec. 12, 2020 9:59 a.m. ET, available at https://www.thetrumparchive.com/?searchbox=%22Wow%21+Thousands+of+people+forming%22 (archived).

80. Ashraf Khalil, "Marine One Buzzes Trump Supporters Rallying for President's Bid to Stay in Office in Washington," *Chicago Tribune*, (Dec. 12, 2020), available at https://www.chicagotribune.com/election-2020/ct-trump-election-20201212-z4zwtovupzhspphzrlfhj3i3a-story.html.

81. "Breaking: Trump Calls for Americans to March on DC January 6 to Stop Foreign Takeover," InfoWars, (Dec. 19, 2020), available at https://web.archive.org/web/20201219175757/https://www.infowars.com/posts/breaking-trump-calls-for-americans-to-march-on-dc-january-6-to-stop-foreign-takeover/ (archived).

82. "The Alex Jones Show," Prison Planet TV, Dec. 20, 2020, available at http://tv.infowars.com/index/display/id/11151.

83. "The Alex Jones Show," Prison Planet TV, Dec. 20, 2020, at 1:27:13, available at http://tv.infowars.com/index/display/id/11151.

84. The Alex Jones Show, "January 6th Will Be a Turning Point in American History," Banned.Video, at 16:29, Dec. 31, 2020, available at https://banned.video/watch?id=5fee715284a7b6210e12a2f7.

85. "Proud Boys," Anti-Defamation League, (Jan. 23, 2020), available at https://www.adl.org/proudboys.

86. Documents on file with the Select Committee to Investigate the January 6th Attack on the United States Capitol (Proud Boys International Production), PBI 12 (The Constitution and Bylaws of Proud Boys International L.L.C., revised November 24, 2018).

87. "Proud Boys," Stanford University Center for International Security and Cooperation, (January 2022), available at https://cisac.fsi.stanford.edu/mappingmilitants/profiles/proud-boys.

88. "Proud Boys," Stanford University Center for International Security and Cooperation, (January 2022), available at https://cisac.fsi.stanford.edu/mappingmilitants/profiles/proud-boys.

89. *See, e.g.,* Documents on file with the Select Committee to Investigate the January 6th Attack on the United States Capitol (Jay Thaxton Production), CTRL0000055644, (December 27-28, 2020, "Ministry of Self Defense," Telegram messages from 7:43 p.m.-1:53 a.m.); "Proud

Boys," Stanford University Center for International Security and Cooperation, (January 2022), available at https://cisac.fsi.stanford.edu/mappingmilitants/profiles/proud-boys.

90. See, e.g., Jason Wilson, "Portland Rally: Proud Boys Vow to March Each Month after Biggest Protest of Trump Era," *The Guardian*, (Aug. 17, 2019), available at https://www.theguardian.com/us-news/2019/aug/17/portland-oregon-far-right-rally-proud-boys-antifa.

91. See Statement of Heidi L. Beirich, Ph.D., (Mar. 22, 2022), at p.1.

92. See, e.g., Select Committee to Investigate the January 6th Attack on the United States Capitol, Deposition of George Meza, (Mar. 16, 2022), p. 155.

93. See, e.g., Cleve R. Wootson Jr., "Thousands of Proud Boys Plan to Rally in Portland, Setting Up Another Clash in a Combustible City," *Washington Post*, (Sept. 25, 2020), available at https://www.washingtonpost.com/nation/2020/09/25/portland-oregon-proud-boys-rally/; *see also*, Aaron Wolfson and Hampton Stall, "Actor Profile: Proud Boys," Armed Conflict Location & Event Data Project, (Apr. 22, 2021), available at https://acleddata.com/2021/04/22/actor-profile-proud-boys/ (noting the "percentage of events with counter-demonstrators in which Proud Boys members participated was more than 10 times the rate at which others engaged with counter-demonstrators.").

94. Nick Quested, a filmmaker who followed the Proud Boys through January 6th, described how Proud Boys couldn't define Black Lives Matter or Antifa—and that, in person, Proud Boys simply identified them as "people of color and people with progressive values." Select Committee to Investigate the January 6th Attack on the United States Capitol, Transcribed Interview of Nick Quested, (Apr. 5, 2022), p. 78.

95. Kathleen Ronayne and Michael Kunzelman, "Trump to Far-Right Extremists: 'Stand Back and Stand By'," *Associated Press*, (Sept. 30, 2020), available at https://apnews.com/article/election-2020-joe-biden-race-and-ethnicity-donald-trump-chris-wallace-0b32339da25fbc9e8b7c7c7066a1db0f.

96. Select Committee to Investigate the January 6th Attack on the United States Capitol, Transcribed Interview of Nick Quested, (Apr. 5, 2022), p. 117.

97. Emails obtained by the Select Committee show that Parler featured alarmingly violent and specific posts that in some cases advocated for civil war. *See, e.g.*, Documents on file with the Select Committee to Investigate the January 6th Attack on the United States Capitol (Parler Production), PARLER_00000006 (December 24, 2020, email forwarded to the FBI, "We need to mass an armed force of American Patriots 150,000 on the Virginia side of the Potomac prepared to react to the congressional events of January 6th"). In a January 2, 2021, email, a Parler employee wrote that they were "concerned about Wednesday," which would be January 6th. *See* Documents on file with the Select Committee to Investigate the January 6th Attack on the United States Capitol (Parler Production), PARLER_00000009 (January 2, 2021, email forwarded to the FBI, "One more from same account. More where came from. Concerned about Wednesday...").

98. Atlantic Council's DFRLab, "#StopTheSteal: Timeline of Social Media and Extremist Activities Leading to 1/6 Insurrection," Just Security, (Feb. 10, 2021), available at https://www.justsecurity.org/74622/stopthesteal-timeline-of-social-media-and-extremist-activities-leading-to-1-6-insurrection/.

99. Select Committee to Investigate the January 6th Attack on the United States Capitol, Deposition of Jeremy Bertino, (Apr. 26, 2022), p. 38; *see also* "Former Leader of Proud Boys Pleads Guilty to Seditious Conspiracy for Efforts to Stop Transfer of Power Following 2020 Presidential Election," Department of Justice, (Oct. 6, 2022), available at https://www.justice.gov/opa/pr/former-leader-proud-boys-pleads-guilty-seditious-conspiracy-efforts-stop-transfer-power.mer-leader-proud-boys-pleads-guilty-seditious-conspiracy-efforts-stop-transfer-power.

100. Select Committee to Investigate the January 6th Attack on the United States Capitol, Deposition of Henry Tarrio, (Feb. 4, 2022), pp. 50-51, 221-22; Select Committee to Investigate the January 6th Attack on the United States Capitol, Deposition of George Meza, (Mar. 16, 2022), pp. 21-22.

101. Select Committee to Investigate the January 6th Attack on the United States Capitol, Deposition of Henry Tarrio, (Feb. 4, 2022), p. 221.

102. Tom Dreisbach, "Conspiracy Charges Bring Proud Boys' History Of Violence into Spotlight," NPR, (Apr. 9, 2021), available at https://www.npr.org/2021/04/09/985104612/conspiracy-charges-bring-proud-boys-history-of-violence-into-spotlight.

103. Tom Dreisbach, "Conspiracy Charges Bring Proud Boys' History Of Violence into Spotlight," NPR, (Apr. 9, 2021), available at https://www.npr.org/2021/04/09/985104612/conspiracy-charges-bring-proud-boys-history-of-violence-into-spotlight.

104. "Day of the Rope," Anti-Defamation League, available at https://www.adl.org/resources/hate-symbol/day-rope.

105. "Contested States," #StopTheSteal, (Nov. 7, 2020), available at http://archive.ph/C9lwN (archived).

106. Christopher Mathias, "After Trump's Defeat, His Supporters Held a Heavily Armed Pity Party," Huff Post, (Nov. 7, 2020), available at https://www.huffpost.com/entry/harrisburg-trump-rally-defeat-extremists-proud-boys-armed-militias_n_5fa756ddc5b67c3259afbc42.

107. Select Committee to Investigate the January 6th Attack on the United States Capitol, Transcribed Interview of Robert Glover, (May 2, 2022), p. 10.

108. Select Committee to Investigate the January 6th Attack on the United States Capitol, Transcribed Interview of Robert Glover, (May 2, 2022), p. 10.

109. Select Committee to Investigate the January 6th Attack on the United States Capitol, Deposition of Michael Simmons, (Feb. 10, 2022), p. 71; Select Committee to Investigate the January 6th Attack on the United States Capitol, Deposition of George Douglas Smith, Jr., (Apr. 28, 2022), p. 47.

110. Select Committee to Investigate the January 6th Attack on the United States Capitol, Deposition of Jeremy Bertino, (Apr. 26, 2022), pp. 81-82; Select Committee to Investigate the January 6th Attack on the United States Capitol, Transcribed Interview of Robert Glover, (May 2, 2022), p. 19; Select Committee to Investigate the January 6th Attack on the United States Capitol, Transcribed Interview of Nick Quested, (Apr. 5, 2022), p. 26.

111. Select Committee to Investigate the January 6th Attack on the United States Capitol, Transcribed Interview of Patrick Byrne, (July 15, 2022), pp. 151-52.

112. Select Committee to Investigate the January 6th Attack on the United States Capitol, Deposition of Henry Tarrio, (Feb. 4, 2022), pp. 107-09; Luke O'Brien, "How Republican Politics (And Twitter) Created Ali Alexander, The Man Behind 'Stop the Steal'," Huff Post, (Mar. 7, 2021), available at https://www.huffpost.com/entry/republicans-twitter-ali-alexander-stop-the-steal_n_6026fb26c5b6f88289fbab57.

113. Select Committee to Investigate the January 6th Attack on the United States Capitol, Deposition of Henry Tarrio, (Feb. 4, 2022), pp. 107-09.

114. Criminal Complaint, United States v. Shroyer, No. 1:21-mj-572 (D.D.C. Aug. 19, 2021), ECF No. 1, available at https://www.justice.gov/usao-dc/case-multi-defendant/file/1428181/download.

115. Select Committee to Investigate the January 6th Attack on the United States Capitol, Transcribed Interview of Nick Quested, (Apr. 5, 2022), pp. 17-19; Ryan Goodman, Justin Hendrix, Just Security, "Exclusive: New Video of Roger Stone with Proud Boys Leaders Who May Have Planned for Capitol Attack," (Feb. 6, 2021), available at https://www.justsecurity.org/74579/exclusive-new-video-of-roger-stone-with-proud-boys-leaders-who-may-have-planned-for-capitol-attack/.

116. Ryan Goodman & Justin Hendrix, "EXCLUSIVE: New Video of Roger Stone with Proud Boys Leaders Who May Have Planned for Capitol Attack," Just Security, (Feb. 6, 2021), available at https://www.justsecurity.org/74579/exclusive-new-video-of-roger-stone-with-proud-boys-leaders-who-may-have-planned-for-capitol-attack/.

117. Will Carless, "How a Trump Booster Group Helped the Head of Extremist Proud Boys Gain Access to the White House," USA Today, (Dec. 19, 2020), available at https://www.usatoday.com/story/news/nation/2020/12/19/latinos-trump-group-tied-proud-boys-leader-enrique-tarrio/3931868001/.

118. Select Committee to Investigate the January 6th Attack on the United States Capitol, Deposition of Henry Tarrio, (Feb. 4, 2022), p. 117.

119. Select Committee to Investigate the January 6th Attack on the United States Capitol, Deposition of Jeremy Bertino, (Apr. 26, 2022), pp. 125-27; Affidavit in Support of Arrest Warrant, United States v. Tarrio, No. 2020 CRWSLD 5553, (D.C. Super. Ct. Dec. 30, 2020).

120. Select Committee to Investigate the January 6th Attack on the United States Capitol, Deposition of Jeremy Bertino, (Apr. 26, 2022), p. 127.

121. Affidavit in Support of Arrest Warrant, United States v. Tarrio, No. 2020 CRWSLD 5553, (D.C. Super. Ct. Dec. 30, 2020).

122. Peter Herman and Martin Weil, "Proud Boys Leader Arrested in the Burning of Church's Black Lives Matter Banner, D.C. Police Say," Washington Post, (Jan. 4, 2021), available at https://www.washingtonpost.com/local/public-safety/proud-boys-enrique-tarrio-arrest/2021/01/04/8642a76a-4edf-11eb-b96e-0e54447b23a1_story.html; Laura Wamsley, "Proud Boys Leader Released from Police Custody and Ordered to Leave D.C.," NPR, (Jan. 5, 2021), available at https://www.npr.org/2021/01/05/953685035/proud-boys-leader-released-from-police-custody-and-ordered-to-leave-d-c.

123. Select Committee to Investigate the January 6th Attack on the United States Capitol, Transcribed Interview of Robert Glover, (May 2, 2022), p. 16.

124. Elizabeth Elizalde, "Proud Boys Surround Man with Knife at Violent DC Trump Rally," New York Post, (Dec. 13, 2020), available at https://nypost.com/2020/12/13/one-person-stabbed-during-massive-proud-boys-brawl-in-dc/.

125. Select Committee to Investigate the January 6th Attack on the United States Capitol, Deposition of Jeremy Bertino, (Apr. 26, 2022), pp. 128-29.

126. Select Committee to Investigate the January 6th Attack on the United States Capitol, Deposition of Jeremy Bertino, (Apr. 26, 2022), p. 129.

127. Select Committee to Investigate the January 6th Attack on the United States Capitol, Deposition of Jeremy Bertino, (Apr. 26, 2022), pp. 130-131.

128. Second Superseding Indictment at ¶ 30, United States v. Nordean, et al., No. 1:21-cr-175 (D.D.C. Mar. 7, 2022), ECF No. 305.

129. Second Superseding Indictment at ¶ 32, United States v. Nordean, et al., No. 1:21-cr-175 (D.D.C. Mar. 7, 2022), ECF No. 305; see also Documents on file with the Select Committee to Investigate the January 6th Attack on the United States Capitol (Jay Thaxton Production), CTRL0000055644, (December 27-28, 2020, "Ministry of Self Defense," Telegram messages from 7:43 p.m.-1:53 a.m.).

130. See, Documents on file with the Select Committee to Investigate the January 6th Attack on the United States Capitol (Jay Thaxton Production), CTRL0000055644, (December 27-28, 2020, "Ministry of Self Defense," Telegram messages from 7:43 p.m.-1:53 a.m.).

131. Second Superseding Indictment at ¶ 55, United States v. Nordean, et al., No. 1:21-cr-175 (D.D.C. Mar. 7, 2022), ECF No. 305.

132. Third Superseding Indictment at ¶ 38, United States v. Nordean, et al., No. 1:21-cr-175 (D.D.C. June 6, 2022), ECF No. 380; Documents on file with the Select Committee to Investigate the January 6th Attack on the United States Capitol (Jay Thaxton Production),

CTRL0000055644, (December 27-28, 2020, "Ministry of Self Defense," Telegram messages from 7:43 p.m.-1:53 a.m.).

133. Second Superseding Indictment at ¶ 33, *United States v. Nordean, et al.*, No. 1:21-cr-175 (D.D.C. Mar. 7, 2022), ECF No. 305.

134. Second Superseding Indictment at ¶ 31, *United States v. Nordean, et al.*, No. 1:21-cr-175 (D.D.C Mar. 7, 2022), ECF No. 305; *see also* Carter Walker, "Carlisle Proud Boy Member Targeted in Search Warrant Tied to Jan. 6 Plot," *Lancaster Online* (Mar. 12, 2022), available at https://lancasteronline.com/news/politics/carlisle-proud-boy-member-targeted-in-search-warrant-tied-to-jan-6-plot/article_c2596928-a258-11ec-a6bb-c79ff2e0e8a7.html (identifying John Stewart as Person-3 in Second Superseding Indictment).

135. Documents on file with the Select Committee to Investigate the January 6th Attack on the United States Capitol, (Jay Thaxton Production), CTRL0000055644, (December 29, 2020, "Ministry of Self Defense," Telegram message at 11:09 a.m.).

136. Second Superseding Indictment at ¶ 41, *United States v. Nordean, et al.*, No. 1:21-cr-175 (D.D.C. Mar. 7, 2022) ECF No. 305.

137. Select Committee to Investigate the January 6th Attack on the United States Capitol, Transcribed Interview of Samuel Armes, (July 18, 2022), p. 10-14 (describing Armes' role in drafting a prior version of the document, which he then shared with Eryka Gemma Flores, another cryptocurrency investor who shared the document with Tarrio); Select Committee to Investigate the January 6th Attack on the United States Capitol, Informal Interview of Eryka Gemma Flores, (July 1, 2022).

138. Zachary Rehl's Motion to Reopen Detention Hearing and Request for a Hearing, Exhibit 1: "1776 Returns," *United States v. Nordean, et al.*, No. 1:21-cr-175 (D.D.C. June 15, 2022) ECF No. 401-1, available at https://s3.documentcloud.org/documents/22060615/1776-returns.pdf.

139. Zachary Rehl's Motion to Reopen Detention Hearing and Request for a Hearing, Exhibit 1: "1776 Returns," *United States v. Nordean, et al.*, No. 1:21-cr-175 (D.D.C. June 15, 2022) ECF No. 401-1, available at https://s3.documentcloud.org/documents/22060615/1776-returns.pdf.

140. Select Committee to Investigate the January 6th Attack on the United States Capitol, Deposition of Matthew Thomas Walter, (Mar. 9, 2022), pp. 70-71; Select Committee to Investigate the January 6th Attack on the United States Capitol, Deposition of Christopher Barcenas, (Mar. 10, 2022), p. 98; Select Committee to Investigate the January 6th Attack on the United States Capitol, Deposition of George Meza, (Mar. 16, 2022), p. 118; Select Committee to Investigate the January 6th Attack on the United States Capitol, Deposition of Jeremy Bertino, (Apr. 26, 2022), p. 23.

141. Select Committee to Investigate the January 6th Attack on the United States Capitol, Transcribed Interview of Samuel Armes, (July 18, 2022), p. 14.

142. Second Superseding Indictment at ¶ 41, *United States v. Nordean, et al.*, No. 1:21-cr-175 (D.D.C. Mar. 7, 2022), ECF No. 305.

143. Georgia Wells, Rebecca Ballhaus, and Keach Hagey, "Proud Boys, Seizing Trump's Call to Washington, Helped Lead Capitol Attack," *Wall Street Journal*, (Jan. 17, 2021), available at https://www.wsj.com/articles/proud-boys-seizing-trumps-call-to-washington-helped-lead-capitol-attack-11610911596.

144. Second Superseding Indictment at ¶ 49, *United States v. Nordean, et al.*, No. 1:21-cr-175 (D.D.C. Mar. 7, 2022), ECF No. 305; Carter Walker, "Carlisle Proud Boy Member Targeted in Search Warrant Tied to Jan. 6 Plot," *Lancaster Online* (Mar. 12, 2022), available at https://lancasteronline.com/news/politics/carlisle-proud-boy-member-targeted-in-search-warrant-tied-to-jan-6-plot/article_c2596928-a258-11ec-a6bb-c79ff2e0e8a7.html (identifying John Stewart as Person-3 in Second Superseding Indictment).

145. Second Superseding Indictment at ¶ 49, *United States v. Nordean, et al.*, No. 1:21-cr-175 (D.D.C. Mar. 7, 2022), ECF No. 305; Carter Walker, "Carlisle Proud Boy Member Targeted in Search Warrant Tied to Jan. 6 Plot," *Lancaster Online* (Mar. 12, 2022), available at https://lancasteronline.com/news/politics/carlisle-proud-boy-member-targeted-in-search-

warrant-tied-to-jan-6-plot/article_c2596928-a258-11ec-a6bb-c79ff2e0e8a7.html (identifying John Stewart as Person-3 in Second Superseding Indictment).

146. Second Superseding Indictment at ¶ 50, *United States v. Nordean et al.*, No. 1:21-cr-175 (D.D.C. Mar. 7, 2022) ECF No. 305.

147. Plea Agreement at 1, *United States v. Donohoe*, No. 1:21-cr-175 (D.D.C. Apr. 8, 2022), ECF No. 335.

148. Statement of Offense at 4, *United States v. Donohoe*, No. 1:21-cr-00175-4-TJK (D.D.C. Apr. 8, 2022).

149. Statement of Offense at 4, *United States v. Donohoe*, No. 1:21-cr-00175-4-TJK (D.D.C. Apr. 8, 2022).

150. Statement of Offense at 6, *United States v. Donohoe*, No. 1:21-cr-00175-4-TJK (D.D.C. Apr. 8, 2022).

151. Statement of Offense at 6, *United States v. Donohoe*, No. 1:21-cr-00175-4-TJK (D.D.C. Apr. 8, 2022).

152. Statement of Offense at 8, *United States v. Donohoe*, No. 1:21-cr-00175-4-TJK (D.D.C. Apr. 8, 2022).

153. "Former Leader of Proud Boys Pleads Guilty to Seditious Conspiracy for Efforts to Stop Transfer of Power Following 2020 Presidential Election," Department of Justice, (Oct. 6, 2022), available at http://www.justice.gov/opa/pr/former-leader-proud-boys-pleads-guilty-seditious-conspiracy-efforts-stop-transfer-power.

154. "Former Leader of Proud Boys Pleads Guilty to Seditious Conspiracy for Efforts to Stop Transfer of Power Following 2020 Presidential Election," Department of Justice, (Oct. 22, 2022), available at https://www.justice.gov/opa/pr/former-leader-proud-boys-pleads-guilty-seditious-conspiracy-efforts-stop-transfer-power.

155. Select Committee to Investigate the January 6th Attack on the United States Capitol, Deposition of Jeremy Bertino, (Apr. 26, 2022), p. 156.

156. Select Committee to Investigate the January 6th Attack on the United States Capitol, Deposition of Jeremy Bertino, (Apr. 26, 2022), p. 156.

157. *Statement of Sam Jackson, Ph.D., (Mar. 30, 2022), at p. 2.*

158. Zachary Cohen, "Oath Keepers Leader Spewed Anti-government Hate for More than a Decade. Alex Jones Gave Him the Audience," CNN, (Jan. 14, 2022), available at https://www.cnn.com/2022/01/14/politics/oath-keepers-stewart-rhodes-alex-jones-invs/index.html.

159. The Select Committee found that the idea that violence loomed from the left was a powerful draw for people to join the Oath Keepers. Richard Dockery, a former Oath Keepers member from Florida, decried "all the riots and stuff I was seeing on the news all over the country" and expressed concern about Antifa and Black Lives Matter activity in his area of Florida, a prospect that he called "nerve-wracking." Select Committee to Investigate the January 6th Attack on the United States Capitol, Deposition of Richard Dockery, (Feb. 2, 2022), pp. 10, 31. Because of this, he said that the Oath Keepers "seemed like a really good organization to support" in order to keep communities safe. *Id.*, at p. 9. Similarly, Jeff Morelock told the Select Committee that joining the Oath Keepers "would give me a chance to do something to help instead of just sitting on the couch," referring to watching protests on television. Select Committee to Investigate the January 6th Attack on the United States Capitol, Deposition of Jeffrey Lawrence Morelock, (Jan. 26, 2022), pp. 87-88. Jason Van Tatenhove, a former spokesman for the Oath Keepers and confidant to Rhodes who has since publicly denounced the group, described how the Oath Keepers tried to deliberately leverage this dynamic to increase their clout. Select Committee to Investigate the January 6th Attack on the United States Capitol, Transcribed Interview of Jason Van Tatenhove, (Mar. 9, 2022), pp. 54-55.

160. Select Committee to Investigate the January 6th Attack on the United States Capitol, Deposition of Elmer Stewart Rhodes, (Feb. 2, 2022), pp. 103-104.

161. Select Committee to Investigate the January 6th Attack on the United States Capitol, Deposition of Kellye SoRelle, (Apr. 13, 2022), pp. 9-10.

162. Stewart Rhodes, "Call to Action! March on DC, Stop the Steal, Defend the President, & Defeat the Deep State," Oath Keepers, (Nov. 10, 2020), available at https://oathkeepers.org/2020/11/call-to-action-march-on-dc-stop-the-steal-defend-the-president-defeat-the-deep-state/.

163. Stewart Rhodes, "Call to Action! March on DC, Stop the Steal, Defend the President, & Defeat the Deep State," Oath Keepers, (Nov. 10, 2020), available at https://oathkeepers.org/2020/11/call-to-action-march-on-dc-stop-the-steal-defend-the-president-defeat-the-deep-state/.

164. Stewart Rhodes and Kellye SoRelle, "Open Letter to President Trump: You Must Use the Insurrection Act to 'Stop the Steal' and Defeat the Coup," Oath Keepers, (Dec. 14, 2020), available at https://web.archive.org/web/20210123133022/https:/oathkeepers.org/2020/12/open-letter-to-president-trump-you-must-use-insurrection-act-to-stop-the-steal-and-defeat-the-coup/.

165. Michael S. Schmidt and Maggie Haberman, "Trump Aides Prepared Insurrection Act Order During Debate Over Protests," New York Times, (June 25, 2021), available at https://www.nytimes.com/2021/06/25/us/politics/trump-insurrection-act-protests.html.

166. Select Committee to Investigate the January 6th Attack on the United States Capitol, Deposition of Elmer Stewart Rhodes, (Feb. 2, 2022), p. 131.

167. "Pro-Trump Rallies in DC Attract Extremists & Erupt into Violence," Anti-Defamation League, (Dec. 13, 2020), available at https://www.adl.org/blog/pro-trump-rallies-in-dc-attract-extremists-erupt-into-violence.

168. In texts between Rhodes and Rob Weaver, one of the organizers of the Jericho March, Weaver instructed his associate to work with Rhodes "on extra security." Documents on file with the Select Committee to Investigate the January 6th Attack on the United States Capitol (Robert Weaver Production), Weaver J6 Prod. (S. Rhodes)0001 (December 11, 2020, text from Rob Weaver at 1:39 p.m.).

169. Documents on file with the Select Committee to Investigate the January 6th Attack on the United States Capitol, (Thomas Speciale Production), CTRL0000050180, pp. 1-6, 26-28 (Signal Chat Titled Dec 12 DC Security/Leadership); Documents on file with the Select Committee to Investigate the January 6th Attack on the United States Capitol (Robert Weaver Production), Weaver J6 Production) Prod. (S. Rhodes)0039 (Signal Chat Titled Dec 12 DC Security/Leadership).; Superseding Indictment at 12, United States v. Rhodes et al., No. 1:22-cr-15 (D.D.C. June 22, 2022), ECF No. 167 (noting that on December 11, 2020, Rhodes "sent a message to an invitation-only Signal group chat titled, 'Dec 12 DC Security/Leadership,' which included James, MINUTA, and others. RHODES stated that if President-Elect Biden were to assume the presidency, 'It will be a bloody and desperate fight. We are going to have a fight. That can't be avoided.' ").

170. Documents on file with the Select Committee to Investigate the January 6th Attack on the United States Capitol (Robert Weaver Production), Weaver J6 Prod. (S. Rhodes) 0045 (December 10, 2020, Stewart Rhodes chat with Dec. 12 DC Security/Leadership at 10:17p.m.).

171. Stewart Rhodes and Kellye SoRelle, "Open Letter to President Trump: You Must Use the Insurrection Act to 'Stop the Steal' and Defeat the Coup," Oath Keepers, (Dec. 14, 2020), available at https://web.archive.org/web/20210123133022/https:/oathkeepers.org/2020/12/open-letter-to-president-trump-you-must-use-insurrection-act-to-stop-the-steal-and-defeat-the-coup/.

172. Select Committee to Investigate the January 6th Attack on the United States Capitol, Deposition of Elmer Stewart Rhodes, (Feb. 2, 2022), pp. 132, 134.

173. Trial Exhibit 6748, *United States v. Rhodes et al.*, No. 1:22-cr-15 (D.D.C. Oct. 20, 2022); Kyle Cheney, "Prosecutors Detail Oath Keepers' Mounting Frustration with Trump as Jan. 6 Approached," *Politico*, (Oct. 20, 2022), available at https://www.politico.com/news/2022/10/20/oath-keepers-trump-jan-6-00062779.

174. Documents on file with the Select Committee to Investigate the January 6th Attack on the United States Capitol (Alondra Propes Production), CTRL0000029585, p.1 (Stewart Rhodes writing in 'OKFL Hangout' chat).

175. Stewart Rhodes and Alondra Propes characterized the Proud Boys as street brawlers in contrast to the Oath Keepers' discipline. *See* Select Committee to Investigate the January 6th Attack on the United States Capitol, Deposition of Elmer Stewart Rhodes, (Feb. 22, 2022), pp. 40, 43; Select Committee to Investigate the January 6th Attack on the United States Capitol, Transcribed Interview of Alondra Propes, (Jan. 31, 2022), pp. 42-43, 136. Kellye SoRelle described the Proud Boys as extreme white supremacists. *See* Select Committee to Investigate the January 6th Attack on the United States Capitol, Deposition of Kellye SoRelle, (Apr. 13, 2022), p. 63-64. Enrique Tarrio characterized the Oath Keepers as "oath breakers" and embarrassing. *See* Select Committee to Investigate the January 6th Attack on the United States Capitol, Deposition of Henry Tarrio, (Feb. 4, 2022), pp. 77, 193-94.

176. Documents on file with the Select Committee to Investigate the January 6th Attack on the United States Capitol (Google Voice Production, Feb. 25, 2022).

177. Government's Opposition to Defendant's Renewed Request for Pretrial Release at 7, *United States v. Meggs*, No. 1:21-cr-28 (D.D.C. Mar. 23, 2021). Select Committee to Investigate the January 6th Attack on the United States Capitol, Deposition of Henry Tarrio, (Feb. 4, 2022), p. 125.

178. Superseding Indictment at ¶ 28, *United States v. Rhodes et al.*, No. 1:22-cr-25 (D.D.C. June 22, 2022), ECF No. 167.

179. "Leader of Oath Keepers and 10 Other Individuals Indicted in Federal Court for Seditious Conspiracy and Other Offenses Related to U.S. Capitol Breach," Department of Justice, (Jan. 13, 2022), available at https://www.justice.gov/usao-dc/pr/leader-oath-keepers-and-10-other-individuals-indicted-federal-court-seditious-conspiracy.

180. *See* Superseding Indictment at ¶ 17, *United States v. Rhodes et al.*, No. 1:22-cr-25 (D.D.C. June 22, 2022), ECF No. 167; Select Committee to Investigate the January 6th Attack on the United States Capitol, Transcribed Interview of Landon Bentley, (May 12, 2022), p. 11 (discussing use of Signal as an encrypted chat).

181. Superseding Indictment at ¶ 29, *United States v. Rhodes, et al.*, No. 1:22-cr-15 (D.D.C. June 22, 2022), ECF No. 167.

182. Superseding Indictment at ¶¶ 38, 39, *United States v. Rhodes et al.*, No. 1:22-cr-15 (D.D.C. June 22, 2022), ECF No. 167.

183. Third Superseding Indictment at ¶ 37, *United States v. Crowl et al.*, No. 1:21-cr-28 (D.D.C., Mar. 31, 2021), ECF No. 127.

184. Third Superseding Indictment at ¶ 37, *United States v. Crowl et al.*, No. 1:21-cr-28 (D.D.C., Mar. 31, 2021), ECF No. 127.

185. Select Committee to Investigate the January 6th Attack on the United States Capitol, Deposition of Richard Dockery, (Feb. 2, 2022), pp. 48-52.

186. Select Committee to Investigate the January 6th Attack on the United States Capitol, Deposition of Richard Dockery, (Feb. 2, 2022), p. 49.

187. Select Committee to Investigate the January 6th Attack on the United States Capitol, Deposition of Richard Dockery, (Feb. 2, 2022), p. 51.

188. Infowars Army, "Alex Jones Show—DOJ Launches National Probe of Election Fraud," BitChute, Nov. 10, 2020, available at https://www.bitchute.com/video/NoELuXs06RzX/.

189. *See, e.g.,* Documents on file with the Select Committee to Investigate the January 6th Attack on the United States Capitol, (Robert Weaver Production), Weaver J6 Prod. (S. Rhodes) 0011 (January 1, 2021, Stewart Rhodes chat with Jan 5/6 DC OK Security/VIP Chat at 7:58-8:00 pm).

190. Superseding Indictment at ¶ 45, *United States v. Rhodes et al.,* No. 1:22-cr-15 (D.D.C. June 22, 2022), ECF No. 167; Select Committee to Investigate the January 6th Attack on the United States Capitol, Transcribed Interview of Frank Marchisella, (Apr. 29, 2022), p. 34.

191. Superseding Indictment at ¶ 44, *United States v. Rhodes et al.,* No. 1:22-cr-15 (D.D.C. June 22, 2022), ECF No. 167.

192. Superseding Indictment at ¶ 68, *United States v. Rhodes et al.,* No. 1:22-cr-15 (D.D.C. June 22, 2022), ECF No. 167. Documents filed with the Select Committee to Investigate the January 6th Attack on the United States Capitol (Hilton Garden Inn Production), MHG000049-103 (January 2-8, 2021, Hilton Garden Inn invoices).

193. Superseding Indictment at ¶ 37, *United States v. Rhodes et al.,* No. 1:22-cr-15 (D.D.C. June 22, 2022), ECF No. 167; Select Committee to Investigate the January 6th Attack on the United States Capitol, Deposition of Kellye SoRelle, (Apr. 13, 2022), p. 180.

194. Superseding Indictment at ¶ 47, *United States v. Rhodes et al.,* No. 1:22-cr-15 (D.D.C. June 22, 2022) ECF No. 167.

195. Superseding Indictment at ¶ 57, *United States v. Rhodes et al.,* No. 1:22-cr-15 (D.D.C. June 22, 2022), ECF No. 167.

196. Superseding Indictment at ¶ 61, *United States v. Rhodes, et al.,* No. 1:22-cr-15 (D.D.C. June 22, 2022), ECF No. 167.

197. Superseding Indictment at ¶ 70, *United States v. Rhodes et al.,* No. 1:22-cr-15 (D.D.C. June 22, 2022), ECF No. 167.

198. Select Committee to Investigate the January 6th Attack on the United States Capitol, Transcribed Interview of Frank Marchisella, (Apr. 29, 2022), p. 39.

199. Select Committee to Investigate the January 6th Attack on the United States Capitol, Deposition of Kellye SoRelle, (Apr. 13, 2022), p. 196.

200. Select Committee to Investigate the January 6th Attack on the United States Capitol, Transcribed Interview of Frank Marchisella, (Apr. 29, 2022), p. 40.

201. Select Committee to Investigate the January 6th Attack on the United States Capitol, Deposition of Kellye SoRelle, (Apr. 13, 2022), p. 196.

202. Select Comittee to Investigate the January 6th Attack on the United States Capitol, Transcribed Interview of Frank Marchisella, (Apr. 29, 2022), pp. 40-42.

203. Select Committee to Investigate the January 6th Attack on the United States Capitol, Transcribed Interview of Frank Marchisella, (Apr. 29, 2022), pp. 45-47.

204. Macias had traveled to DC after his arrest for bringing weapons to a vote-counting center in Philadelphia while votes were being counted in November 2020. Claudia Lauer, "Philly DA Seeks Contempt Charge for Vets for Trump Cofounder," *AP News,* (June 13, 2022), available at https://apnews.com/article/capitol-siege-pennsylvania-riots-philadelphia-virginia-d74b05c01aebde1ca26a9c080a5022d8.

205. Documents on file with the Select Committee to Investigate the January 6th Attack on the United States Capitol (Frank Marchisealla Production), CTRL0000040442 (January 5, 2021, Frank Marchisella video of Facebook live stream).

206. Documents on file with the Select Committee to Investigate the January 6th Attack on the United States Capitol (Frank Marchisealla Production), CTRL0000040442, (January 5, 2021, Frank Marchisella video of Facebook live stream) at 0:36.

207. Select Committee to Investigate the January 6th Attack on the United States Capitol, Deposition of Kellye SoRelle, (Apr. 13, 2022), pp. 207-08.

208. Select Committee to Investigate the January 6th Attack on the United States Capitol, Deposition of Kellye SoRelle, (Apr. 13, 2022), p. 197.

209. Select Committee to Investigate the January 6th Attack on the United States Capitol, Deposition of Kellye SoRelle, (Apr. 13, 2022), p. 197.

210. Second Superseding Indictment at ¶ 23, *United States v. Nordean, et al.*, No. 1:21-cr-175 (D.D.C. Mar. 7, 2022), ECF No. 305.

211. Select Committee to Investigate the January 6th Attack on the United States Capitol, Deposition of Kellye SoRelle, (Apr. 13, 2022), p. 197.

212. Documents on file with the Select Committee to Investigate the January 6th Attack on the United States Capitol, (Nick Quested Production), Video file ML_DC_20210105_Sony_FS7-GC_1859.mov, at 0:50 (Jan. 5, 2021).

213. Documents on file with the Select Committee to Investigate the January 6th Attack on the United States Capitol, (Nick Quested Production), Video file ML_DC_20210105_Sony_FS7-GC_1859.mov, at 1:31 (Jan. 5, 2021).

214. Documents on file with the Select Committee to Investigate the January 6th Attack on the United States Capitol, (Nick Quested Production), Video file ML_DC_20210105_Sony_FS7-GC_1859.mov, at 1:00 (Jan. 5, 2021).

215. Select Committee to Investigate the January 6th Attack on the United States Capitol, Deposition of Kellye SoRelle, (Apr. 13, 2022), p. 202.

216. Spencer S. Hsu, "Video Released of Garage Meeting of Proud Boys, Oath Keepers Leaders," *Washington Post*, embedded video at 3:20, (May 24, 2022), available at https://www.washingtonpost.com/dc-md-va/2022/05/24/tarrio-rhodes-video/.

217. Documents on file with the Select Committee to Investigate the January 6th Attack on the United States Capitol (Nick Quested Production), Video file ML_DC_20210105_Sony_FS7-GC_1864.mov, at 0:14 (Jan. 5, 2021).

218. Documents on file with the Select Committee to Investigate the January 6th Attack on the United States Capitol (Nick Quested Production), Video file ML_DC_20210105_Sony_FS5_Clip0042.mov, at 2:32-3:38 (Jan. 5, 2021).

219. Documents on file with the Select Committee to Investigate the January 6th Attack on the United States Capitol (Nick Quested Production), Video file ML_DC_20210105_Sony_FS5_Clip0042.mov, at 2:32-3:38 (Jan. 5, 2021).

220. Documents on file with the Select Committee to Investigate the January 6th Attack on the United States Capitol (Nick Quested Production), Video file ML_DC_20210105_Sony_FS5_Clip0042.mov, at 2:32-3:38 (Jan. 5, 2021).

221. Select Committee to Investigate the January 6th Attack on the United States Capitol, Deposition of Henry Tarrio, (Feb. 4, 2022), pp. 83-84.

222. See *In re Stone*, 940 F.3d 1332, 1334 (D.C. Cir. 2019); *United States v. Stone*, 394 F. Supp. 3d 1, 7-8 (D.D.C. 2019).

223. David Freedlander, "An Oral History of Donald Trump's Almost-Run for President in 2000," *Intelligencer*, (Oct. 11, 2018), available at https://nymag.com/intelligencer/2018/10/trumps-almost-run-for-president-in-2000-an-oral-history.html.

224. See Trial Transcript at 3806, *United States v. Rhodes et al.*, No. 1:22-cr-15 (D.D.C. Oct. 17, 2022) (testimony and exhibits showing Kelly Meggs and Jessica Watkins discussed providing security for Roger Stone); Dalton Bennett and Jon Swaine, "The Roger Stone Tapes," *Washington Post*, available at https://www.washingtonpost.com/investigations/interactive/2022/roger-stone-documentary-capitol-riot-trump-election/; Matthew Mosk, Olivia Rubin, Ali Dukakis, and Fergal Gallagher, "Video Surfaces Showing Trump Ally Roger Stone Flanked by Oath Keepers on Morning of Jan. 6," ABC News, (Feb. 5, 2021), available at https://abcnews.go.com/US/video-surfaces-showing-trump-ally-roger-stone-flanked/story?id=75706765; Christiaan Triebert (@trbrtc), Twitter, Feb. 19, 2021 4:35 p.m., available at https://twitter.com/trbrtc/status/1362878609334165505 (Kelly Meggs with Roger Stone); Spencer S.

Hsu, Manuel Roig-Franzia, and Devlin Barrett, "Roger Stone Keeps Appearing in Capitol Breach Investigation Court Filings," *Washington Post*, (Mar. 22, 2021), available at https://www.washingtonpost.com/local/public-safety/roger-stone-court-filings-capitol-riot/2021/03/22/c689a77c-87f8-11eb-82bc-e58213caa38e_story.html (Mark Grods with Roger Stone); Andrew Smrecek (@combat_art_training), Instagram, Dec. 15, 2020, available at https://www.instagram.com/p/Cl0g8dlhEyG/ (Connie Meggs and Jason Dolan with Roger Stone) (last accessed Dec. 11, 2022).

225. Motion for Bond, Exhibit 1 at 76, 90, 96, 98, *United States v. Rhodes et al.*, No. 1:22-cr-15 (D.D.C. Jan. 12, 2022), ECF No. 102-1.

226. Christiaan Triebert, Ben Decker, Derek Watkins, Arielle Ray, and Stella Cooper, "First They Guarded Roger Stone. Then They Joined the Capitol Attack," *New York Times*, (Feb. 14, 2021), available at https://www.nytimes.com/interactive/2021/02/14/us/roger-stone-capitol-riot.html.

227. Matthew Mosk, Olivia Rubin, Ali Dukakis, and Fergal Gallagher, "Video Surfaces Showing Trump Ally Roger Stone Flanked by Oath Keepers on Morning of Jan. 6," ABC News, (Feb. 5, 2021), available at https://abcnews.go.com/US/video-surfaces-showing-trump-ally-roger-stone-flanked/story?id=75706765.

228. "Leader of Alabama Chapter of Oath Keepers Pleads Guilty to Seditious Conspiracy and Obstruction of Congress for Efforts to Stop Transfer of Power Following 2020 Presidential Election," Department of Justice Office of Public Affairs, (Mar. 2, 2022), available at https://www.justice.gov/opa/pr/leader-alabama-chapter-oath-keepers-pleads-guilty-seditious-conspiracy-and-obstruction.

229. Dalton Bennett and Jon Swaine, "The Roger Stone Tapes," *Washington Post*, (Mar. 4, 2022), available at https://www.washingtonpost.com/investigations/interactive/2022/roger-stone-documentary-capitol-riot-trump-election/.

230. Kelly Weill, "How the Proud Boys Became Roger Stone's Personal Army," *Daily Beast*, (Jan. 29, 2019), available at https://www.thedailybeast.com/how-the-proud-boys-became-roger-stones-personal-army-6.

231. *See, e.g.*, Andy Campbell, "EXCLUSIVE: Roger Stone Admits He's Been Advising The Proud Boys For Years," *Huff Post*, (Sept. 22, 2022), available at https://www.huffpost.com/entry/roger-stone-we-are-proud-boys_n_632c57ebe4b09d8701bd02e2.

232. *See, e.g.*, Documents on file with the Select Committee to Investigate the January 6th Attack on the United States Capitol (Christoffer Guldbrandsen Production), Video files 190926 I bil + fondraiser, 191003 Stone dag 3 backstage fundraiser 2 onstage, 200220.

233. Documents on file with the Select Committee to Investigate the January 6th Attack on the United States Capitol (Christoffer Guldbrandsen Production), Video file 190926 i bil + fondraiser.

234. Ryan Goodman and Justin Hendrix, "EXCLUSIVE: New Video of Roger Stone with Proud Boys Leaders Who May Have Planned for Capitol Attack," Just Security, (Feb. 6, 2021), available at https://www.justsecurity.org/74579/exclusive-new-video-of-roger-stone-with-proud-boys-leaders-who-may-have-planned-for-capitol-attack/.

235. Ryan Goodman and Justin Hendrix, "EXCLUSIVE: New Video of Roger Stone with Proud Boys Leaders Who May Have Planned for Capitol Attack," Just Security, (Feb. 6, 2021), available at https://www.justsecurity.org/74579/exclusive-new-video-of-roger-stone-with-proud-boys-leaders-who-may-have-planned-for-capitol-attack/.

236. Ryan Goodman and Justin Hendrix, "EXCLUSIVE: New Video of Roger Stone with Proud Boys Leaders Who May Have Planned for Capitol Attack," Just Security, (Feb. 6, 2021), available at https://www.justsecurity.org/74579/exclusive-new-video-of-roger-stone-with-proud-boys-leaders-who-may-have-planned-for-capitol-attack/.

237. Georgia Wells, Rebecca Ballhaus, and Keach Hagey, " Proud Boys, Seizing Trump's Call to Washington, Helped Lead Capitol Attack," *Wall Street Journal*, (Jan. 17, 2021), available at https://www.wsj.com/articles/proud-boys-seizing-trumps-call-to-washington-helped-lead-capitol-attack-11610911596.

238. Georgia Wells, Rebecca Ballhaus, and Keach Hagey, " Proud Boys, Seizing Trump's Call to Washington, Helped Lead Capitol Attack," *Wall Street Journal*, (Jan. 17, 2021), available at https://www.wsj.com/articles/proud-boys-seizing-trumps-call-to-washington-helped-lead-capitol-attack-11610911596.

239. Documents on file with the Select Committee to Investigate the January 6th Attack on the United States Capitol (Kellye SoRelle Production), CTRL0000060762 - CTRL0000060858 (screenshotting messages in the Friends of Stone chat); Dalton Bennett and Jon Swaine, "The Roger Stone Tapes," *Washington Post*, available at https://www.washingtonpost.com/investigations/interactive/2022/roger-stone-documentary-capitol-riot-trump-election/; Documents on file with the Select Committee to Investigate the January 6th Attack on the United States Capitol (Christoffer Guldbrandsen Production), Video file 200705.

240. Documents on file with the Select Committee to Investigate the January 6th Attack on the United States Capitol (Christoffer Guldbrandsen Production), Video file 201105.

241. Hugo Lowell, "Film Offers Inside Look at Roger Stone's 'Stop the Steal' Efforts Before January 6," *The Guardian*, (July 8, 2022), available at https://www.theguardian.com/us-news/2022/jul/07/roger-stone-ali-alexander-film-jan-6-stop-the-steal.

242. Document on file with the Select Committee to Investigate the January 6th Attack on the United States Capitol (Kellye SoRelle Production), CTRL0000060802, CTRL0000060798 (screenshots from the Friends of Stone chat).

243. "Executive Grant of Clemency for Roger Jason Stone, Jr.," Department of Justice, (July 10, 2020), available at https://www.justice.gov/pardon/page/file/1293796/download.

244. Amita Kelly, Ryan Lucas, and Vanessa Romo, "Trump Pardons Roger Stone, Paul Manafort And Charles Kushner," NPR, (Dec. 23, 2020), available at https://www.npr.org/2020/12/23/949820820/trump-pardons-roger-stone-paul-manafort-and-charles-kushner.

245. PatriotTakes[American flag] (@PatriotTakes), Twitter, Dec. 28, 2020 3:50 a.m. ET, available at https://twitter.com/patriottakes/status/1343479434376974336.

246. PatriotTakes[American flag] (@PatriotTakes), Twitter, Dec. 28, 2020 3:50 a.m. ET, available at https://twitter.com/patriottakes/status/1343479434376974336; *See also* Ali Dukakis, "Roger Stone Thanks President Trump for Pardon in Person," ABC News, (Dec. 28, 2020), available at https://abcnews.go.com/Politics/roger-stone-president-trump-pardon-person/story?id=74940512.

247. Select Committee to Investigate the January 6th Attack on the United States Capitol, Transcribed Interview of Kristin Davis, (August 2, 2022), p. 41; Documents on file with Select Committee to Investigate the January 6th Attack on the United States Capitol, (Kristin Davis Production), CTRL0000928609, p. 7 (December 30, 2020, text message from Kristin Davis to Chris Lippe at 6:05 p.m.).

248. Documents on file with Select Committee to Investigate the January 6th Attack on the United States Capitol (Kristin Davis Production), CTRL0000928609, p. 7 (December 30, 2020, text message from Kristin Davis to Chris Lippe at 6:05 p.m.).

249. Select Committee to Investigate the January 6th Attack on the United States Capitol, Deposition of Roger Stone, (Dec. 17, 2021).

250. Will Steakin, Matthew Mosk, James Gordon Meek, and Ali Dukakis, "Longtime Trump Advisers Connected to Groups Behind Rally that Led to Capitol Attack," ABC News, (Jan. 15, 2021), available at https://abcnews.go.com/US/longtime-trump-advisers-connected-groups-rally-led-capitol/story?id=75261028.

251. "Nicholas J. Fuentes: Five Things to Know," Anti-Defamation League, (July 9, 2021, updated Nov. 30, 2022), available at https://www.adl.org/resources/blog/nicholas-j-fuentes-five-things-know?gclid=EAIaIQobChMI4ITXgYH6-wIVaUpyCh08sgxaEAAYASAAEgLGNPD_BwE; Nicholas J. Fuentes (@NickJFuentes), Twitter, Dec. 18, 2020 11:26 p.m. ET, available at https://web.archive.org/web/20201219072617/https:/twitter.com/NickJFuentes/status/1340196694571540490 (archived). As noted in the Executive Summary, this tweet, like others, was likely sent from or archived in a separate time zone, which explains why it shows a sent date of December 18, 2020, while President Trump issued his tweet at 1:42 a.m. on December 19, 2020.

252. "California Man Sentenced to 42 Months in Prison for Actions During Jan. 6 Capitol Breach," Department of Justice, (Oct. 19, 2022), available at https://www.justice.gov/usao-dc/pr/california-man-sentenced-prison-actions-during-jan-6-capitol-breach; Tom Dreisbach, Allison Mollenkamp, "A Former UCLA Student Was Sentenced to over Three Years in Prison for Capitol Riot," NPR, (Oct. 19, 2022), available at https://www.npr.org/2022/10/19/1129912913/a-former-ucla-student-was-sentenced-to-over-three-years-in-prison-for-capitol-ri.

253. "Student Who Attended Charlottesville White Supremacist Rally Leaves Boston University After Backlash," Time, (Aug. 17, 2017), https://time.com/4905939/nicholas-fuentes-white-supremacist-rally-charlottesville/; "Neo-Nazi Hipsters Identity Evropa Exposed In Discord Chat Leak," Unicorn Riot, (Mar. 6, 2019), https://unicornriot.ninja/2019/neo-nazi-hipsters-identity-evropa-exposed-in-discord-chat-leak/.

254. See Statement of Oren Segal, Marilyn Mayo and Morgan Moon, (Mar. 31, 2022); "Groypers Army and 'America First'," Anti-Defamation League, (Mar. 17, 2020), available at https://www.adl.org/reources/backgrounders/groyper-army-and-america-first.

255. See, e.g., Malachi Barrett, "Far-right Activist Who Encouraged U.S. Capitol Occupation also Organized 'Stop the Steal' Rally in Michigan," MLive, (Jan. 7, 2021), available at https://www.mlive.com/politics/2021/01/far-right-activist-who-encouraged-us-capitol-occupation-also-organized-stop-the-steal-rally-in-michigan.html; Studio IKN, "Nick Fuentes at Stop the Steal Phoenix," YouTube, Nov. 29, 2020, available at https://www.youtube.com/watch?v=U_vjzjMDenk.

256. Megan Squire (@MeganSquire0), Twitter, Jan. 5, 2021 10:27 a.m. ET, available at https://twitter.com/MeganSquire0/status/1346478478523125767?s=20.

257. Fuentes personally earned $50,000 from his livestreams between November 3, 2020, and January 19, 2021. He raised his highest-ever total the day after the 2020 election, and he raised similarly high figures on January 5, 2021. Some of Fuentes' proceeds were refunded to customers following Fuentes' ban from DLive. See Statement of Michael Edison Hayden, Megan Squire, Ph.D., Hannah Gais, and Susan Corke, (Apr. 7, 2022), at 6-7.

258. See, Statement of Oren Segal, Marilyn Mayo, and Morgan Moon, (Mar. 31, 2022), at 12.

259. Malachi Barrett, "Far-Right Activist Who Encouraged U.S. Capitol Occupation Also Organized 'Stop the Steal' Rally in Michigan," MLive, (Jan. 7, 2021), available at https://www.mlive.com/politics/2021/01/far-right-activist-who-encouraged-us-capitol-occupation-also-organized-stop-the-steal-rally-in-michigan.html.

260. Chuck Tanner, "Deciphering Nick Fuentes' 'Stop the Steal' Speeches," Institute for Research and Education on Human Rights, (Nov. 24, 2020), available at https://www.justsecurity.org/74622/stopthesteal-timeline-of-social-media-and-extremist-activities-leading-to-1-6-insurrection/.

261. "#StopTheSteal: Timeline of Social Media and Extremist Activities Leading to 1/6 Insurrection," Just Security (Feb. 10, 2021), available at https://www.justsecurity.org/74622/stopthesteal-timeline-of-social-media-and-extremist-activities-leading-to-1-6-insurrection/.

262. Chuck Tanner, "White Nationalists Prominent at 'Stop the Steal' Mobilization in Georgia," Institute for Research and Education on Human Rights," (Nov. 24, 2020), available at

https://www.irehr.org/2020/11/24/white-nationalists-prominent-at-stop-the-steal-mobilization-in-georgia/.

263. Aquarium Groyper, "Nick Fuentes Georgia State Capitol 11/20/2020," YouTube, at 1:38, Nov. 20, 2020, available at https://www.youtube.com/watch?v=OS1f--Tkn1M.

264. Peter White, "MAGA Protestors Chant 'Destroy the GOP' at Pro-Trump Rally," *Rolling Stone*, (Dec. 12, 2020), available at https://www.rollingstone.com/politics/politics-news/protesters-chant-destroy-the-gop-at-pro-trump-rally-1102967/.

265. "Pro-Trump Rallies in DC Attract Extremists & Erupt into Violence," Anti-Defamation League, (Dec. 13, 2020), available at https://www.adl.org/blog/pro-trump-rallies-in-dc-attract-extremists-erupt-into-violence.

266. Megan Squire (@MeganSquire0), Twitter, Jan. 5, 2021 10:27 a.m. ET, available at https://twitter.com/MeganSquire0/status/1346478478523125767?s=20.

267. Patrick Casey (@Patrickcaseyusa), Telegram, Jan. 5, 2021 6:20 p.m.; Documents on file with the Select Committee to Investigate the January 6th Attack on the United States Capitol (Public Source), CTRL0000930909 - CTRL0000930912 (collection of Patrick Casey telegram posts).

268. Mallory Simon and Sara Sidner, "Decoding the Extremist Symbols and Groups at the Capitol Hill Insurrection," CNN, (Jan. 11, 2021), available at https://www.cnn.com/2021/01/09/us/capitol-hill-insurrection-extremist-flags-soh/index.html.

269. Nicholas J. Fuentes (@NickJFuentes), Twitter, Jan. 7, 2021 10:56 a.m. ET, available at https://web.archive.org/web/20210107185745/https://twitter.com/NickJFuentes/status/1347255833516765185 (archived).

270. Nicholas J. Fuentes (@NickJFuentes), Twitter, Jan. 7, 2021 1:03 p.m. ET, available at https://web.archive.org/web/20210107210736/https://twitter.com/NickJFuentes/status/1347287851629764610 (archived).

271. *See* Select Committee to Investigate the January 6th Attack on the United States Capitol, Deposition of Nicholas J. Fuentes, (Feb. 16, 2022).

272. Select Committee to Investigate the January 6th Attack on the United States Capitol, Deposition of Michael Lee Wells, (Apr. 14, 2022), p. 72.

273. Alejandro J. Beutel, Daryl Johnson, "The Three Percenters: A Look Inside an Anti-Government Militia," Newlines Institute for Strategy and Policy, (Feb. 2021), at 8, available at https://newlinesinstitute.org/wp-content/uploads/20210225-Three-Percenter-PR-NISAP-rev051021.pdf; "Three Percenters," Southern Poverty Law Center, available at https://www.splcenter.org/fighting-hate/extremist-files/group/three-percenters.

274. Statement of Oren Segal, Marilyn Mayo, and Morgan Moon, (Mar. 31, 2022), at 12-13.

275. Statement of Oren Segal, Marilyn Mayo, and Morgan Moon, (Mar. 31, 2022), at 13.

276. Statement of Oren Segal, Marilyn Mayo, and Morgan Moon, (Mar. 31, 2022), at 13.

277. Select Committee to Investigate the January 6th Attack on the United States Capitol, Deposition of Jeremy Liggett, (May 17, 2022), pp. 6-7.

278. "Two Texas Men Charged with Assault on Law Enforcement During Jan. 6 Capitol Breach," Department of Justice, (Dec. 14, 2021), available at https://www.justice.gov/usao-dc/pr/two-texas-men-charged-assault-law-enforcement-during-jan-6-capitol-breach.

279. "Texas Man Sentenced to 52 Months in Prison For Assaulting Law Enforcement Officers During Jan. 6 Capitol Breach," Department of Justice, (Sept. 28, 2022), available at https://www.justice.gov/usao-dc/pr/texas-man-sentenced-prison-assaulting-law-enforcement-officers-during-jan-6-capitol.

280. Criminal Complaint at 9, 13, *United States v. Hazard*, No. 1:21-mj-868 (D.D.C. Dec. 7, 2021), ECF No. 1.

281. Criminal Complaint at 8-12, *United States. v. Hazard*, No. 1:21-mj-868 (D.D.C. Dec. 7, 2021), ECF No. 1. For example, Denney told Hazard that they "will need linking up with the proud

boys." *Id.*, at 8. Denney described the hotel he booked as "the same place everyone else is getting in the Proud Boys crew and other militia's until it gets full." *Id.*, at 9. In a separate post on Facebook, Denney stated that the Patriot Boys of North Texas were "allied with the Patriot Prayer and the Proud Boys." *Id.*, at 9. In another Facebook message on December 29, Denney wrote: "We are linking up with thousands of Proud Boys and other militia that will be there. This is going to be huge. And it's going to be a fight." *Id.*, at 10. Similarly, Hazard wrote on Facebook: "I belong to a militia group that's affiliated with the proud boys" and "We're affiliated with the proud boys which have folks of all races as there's several thousand members." *Id.*, at 12.

282. Criminal Complaint at 8, *United States. v. Hazard*, No. 1:21-mj-868 (D.D.C. Dec. 7, 2021), ECF No. 1.

283. Criminal Complaint at 10, *United States. v. Hazard*, No. 1:21-mj-868 (D.D.C. Dec. 7, 2021), ECF No. 1.

284. Criminal Complaint at 11, *United States. v. Hazard*, No. 1:21-mj-868 (D.D.C. Dec. 7, 2021), ECF No. 1. Hazard also echoed this idea. *Id.*, at 14.

285. Criminal Complaint at 10-11, *United States. v. Hazard*, No. 1:21-mj-868 (D.D.C. Dec. 7, 2021), ECF No. 1.

286. Criminal Complaint at 10, *United States. v. Hazard*, No. 1:21-mj-868 (D.D.C. Dec. 7, 2021), ECF No. 1.

287. Criminal Complaint at 12, *United States. v. Hazard*, No. 1:21-mj-868 (D.D.C. Dec. 7, 2021), ECF No. 1.

288. Criminal Complaint at 12, *United States. v. Hazard*, No. 1:21-mj-868 (D.D.C. Dec. 7, 2021), ECF No. 1.

289. Criminal Complaint at 16, *United States. v. Hazard*, No. 1:21-mj-868 (D.D.C. Dec. 7, 2021), ECF No. 1.

290. Statement of Facts at 2, *United States v. Cole et al.*, No. 1:22-mj-184-RMM (D.D.C. Aug, 29, 2022), ECF No. 5-1

291. Statement of Facts at 2, *United States v. Cole et al.*, No. 1:22-mj-184, (D.D.C. Aug. 29, 2022), ECF No. 5-1.

292. Statement of Facts at 4, *United States v. Cole et al.*, No. 1:22-mj-184, (D.D.C. Aug. 29, 2022), ECF No. 5-1.

293. Statement of Facts at 4, *United States v. Cole et al.*, No. 1:22-mj-184, (D.D.C. Aug. 29, 2022), ECF No. 5-1.

294. Statement of Facts at 4, *United States v. Cole et al.*, No. 1:22-mj-184, (D.D.C. Aug. 29, 2022), ECF No. 5-1.

295. Statement of Facts at 28, *United States v. Cole et al.*, No. 1:22-mj-184, (D.D.C. Aug. 29, 2022), ECF No. 5-1.

296. Statement of Facts at 5, *United States v. Cole et al.*, No. 1:22-mj-184, (D.D.C. Aug. 29, 2022), ECF No. 5-1.

297. Select Committee to Investigate the January 6th Attack on the United States Capitol, Deposition of Jeremy Liggett, (May 17, 2022), pp. 50-51.

298. Statement of Facts at 28, *United States v. Cole et al.*, No. 1:22-mj-184, (D.D.C. Aug. 29, 2022), ECF No. 5-1; #SeditionHunters (@SeditionHunters), Twitter, June 7, 2021 2:11 p.m. ET, available at https://twitter.com/SeditionHunters/status/1401965056980627458.

299. Statement of Facts at 5-6, *United States v. Cole et al.*, No. 1:22-mj-184, (D.D.C. Aug. 29, 2022), ECF No. 5-1; #SeditionHunters (@SeditionHunters), Twitter, June 7, 2021 2:11 p.m. ET, available at https://twitter.com/SeditionHunters/status/1401965056980627458.

300. "Five Florida Men Arrested on Charges for Actions During Jan. 6 Capitol Breach," United States Department of Justice, (Aug. 24, 2022) available at https://www.justice.gov/usao-dc/pr/five-florida-men-arrested-charges-actions-during-jan-6-capitol-breach.

301. Indictment Dated June 9, 2021 at 1, *United States v. Hostetter et. al.*, No. 1:1:21-cr-392 (D.D.C. June 9, 2021); Michael Kunzelman, "Capitol Rioter Used Charity to Promote Violence, Feds Say," *Associated Press*, (June 16, 2021), available at https://apnews.com/article/donald-trump-joe-biden-riots-health-coronavirus-pandemic-71a7b8121b6f70016f7cab601021a989.

302. Indictment at ¶ 38, *United States v. Hostetter et al.*, No. 1:21-cr-392 (D.D.C. June 9, 2021), ECF No. 1.

303. *Indictment at 7, United States v. Hostetter et al.*, No. 1:21-cr-392 (D.D.C. June 9, 2021), ECF No. 1.

304. Indictment at 7, *United States v. Hostetter et al.*, No. 1:21-cr-392 (D.D.C. June 9, 2021), ECF No. 1.

305. Indictment at 8, *United States v. Hostetter et al.*, No. 1:21-cr-392 (D.D.C. June 9, 2021), ECF No. 1.

306. Indictment at 9, *United States v. Hostetter et al.*, No. 1:21-cr-392 (D.D.C. June 9, 2021), ECF No. 1.

307. Indictment at 8-11, *United States v. Hostetter et al.*, No. 1:21-cr-392 (D.D.C. June 9, 2021), ECF No. 1.

308. Indictment at 8-11, *United States v. Hostetter et al.*, No. 1:21-cr-392 (D.D.C. June 9, 2021), ECF No. 1.

309. Indictment at 12, *United States v. Hostetter et al.*, No. 1:21-cr-392 (D.D.C. June 9, 2021), ECF No. 1.

310. The National Council and The Three Percenters - Original, "TTPO Stance on Election Fraud," Dec. 16, 2020, available at http://archive.ph/YemCC (archived).

311. *See* post by username @hatdonuts2, patriots.win, December 29, 2020, 7:56 p.m. ET, available at https://patriots.win/p/11RO2hdyR2/x/c/4DrwV8RcV1s; Statement of Facts at 7-8, *United States v. Buxton*, No. 1:21-cr-739 (D.D.C. Dec. 8, 2021), ECF No. 1-1.

312. Select Committee to Investigate the January 6th Attack on the United States Capitol, Deposition of Josh Ellis, (May 19, 2022), p. 38.

313. "Lone Capitol Police Officer Eugene Goodman Diverts Capitol Rioters," *Washington Post*, (Jan. 11, 2021). available at https://www.washingtonpost.com/video/national/lone-capitol-police-officer-eugene-goodman-diverts-capitol-rioters/2021/01/11/ba67a5e8-5f9b-4a9a-a7b7-93549f6a81b3_video.html

314. Scott MacFarlane and Gillian Morley, "QAnon Follower Doug Jensen Convicted on All Jan. 6 Charges," CBS News, (Sept. 23, 2022), available at https://www.cbsnews.com/news/qanon-follower-doug-jensen-convicted-on-all-jan-6-charges/.

315. Interview of: Douglas Austin Jensen Dated Jan. 8, 2021 at 19, *United States v. Jensen*, No. 1:21-cr-6 (D.D.C., Apr. 8, 2022), ECF No. 69-1.

316. Statement of Mike Rothschild, (Mar. 23, 2022), at 12.

317. Statement of Mike Rothschild, (Mar. 23, 2022), at 2-3.

318. "QAnon," Anti-Defamation League, (May 4, 2020), available at https://www.adl.org/resources/backgrounder/qanon.

319. Kelly Weill, "QAnon's Home 8kun is Imploding - and Q Has Gone Silent," *Daily Beast*, (Nov. 13, 2020), available at https://www.thedailybeast.com/qanons-home-8kun-is-implodingand-q-has-gone-silent?ref=scroll.

320. "Remarks by President Trump in Press Briefing," White House, (Aug. 19, 2020), available at https://trumpwhitehouse.archives.gov/briefings-statements/remarks-president-trump-press-briefing-august-19-2020/.

321. NBC News, "Trump Denounces White Supremacy, Sidesteps Question on QAnon," YouTube, at 1:32, 2:34, Oct. 15, 2020, available at https://youtu.be/3hybkzCWb_w.

322. Ben Collins, "QAnon's Dominion Voter Fraud Conspiracy Theory Reaches the President," NBC News, (Nov. 13, 2020), available at https://www.nbcnews.com/tech/tech-news/q-fades-qanon-s-dominion-voter-fraud-conspiracy-theory-reaches-n1247780; National Contagion Research Institute, "The QAnon Conspiracy: Destroying Families, Dividing Communities, Undermining Democracy," p. 20, available at https://networkcontagion.us/wp-content/uploads/NCRI-%E2%80%93-The-QAnon-Conspiracy-FINAL.pdf.

323. Donald J. Trump (@realdonaldtrump), Twitter, Nov. 19, 2020 12:41 a.m. ET and 3:47 p.m. ET, available at https://www.thetrumparchive.com/?searchbox=%22Dominion-izing+the+Vote%22 (archived).

324. One America News Network, "Cyber Analyst on Dominion Voting: Shocking Vulnerabilities," YouTube, at 0:45, Nov. 15, 2020, available at https://youtu.be/eKcPoCNW8AA.

325. Select Committee to Investigate the January 6th Attack on the United States Capitol, Deposition of James Watkins, (June 6, 2022), p. 11. Watkins denied under oath that either he or his son Ron are "Q." Id., at 38, 122.

326. Donald J. Trump (@realdonaldtrump), Twitter, Dec. 15, 2020 12:32 a.m. ET, available at https://www.thetrumparchive.com/?searchbox=%22Soon-to-be+AG+Rosen+recently+wrote+an+essay+on+foreign+influence+in+US+elections.+foreign+actors+are+covertly+trying+to%22 (archived).

327. President Donald J. Trump, "Tweets of January 3, 2021," The American Presidency Project, available at, available at https://www.presidency.ucsb.edu/documents/tweets-january-3-2021 (archived).

328. Select Committee to Investigate the January 6th Attack on the United States Capitol, Deposition of James Watkins, (June 6, 2022), p. 77; Select Committee to Investigate the January 6th Attack on the United States Capitol, Deposition of Jody Williams, (June 7, 2022), p. 67 (noting, as the then-owner of TheDonald.win, that President Trump's December 19th tweet was "everywhere," including with "Q people.").

329. Select Committee to Investigate the January 6th Attack on the United States Capitol, Deposition of James Watkins, (June 6, 2022), pp. 74, 76.

330. Statement of Offense at 3, United States v. Munn, No. 1:21-cr-474 (D.D.C. May 13, 2022), ECF No. 78.

331. Statement of Facts at 3, United States v. Chansley, No. 1:21-cr-3 (D.D.C. Jan. 8, 2021), ECF No. 1-1.

332. Select Committee to Investigate the January 6th Attack on the United States Capitol, Deposition of Elmer Stewart Rhodes, (Feb. 2, 2022), p. 162.

333. See, e.g., Trial Exhibit 6860 (1.S.656.9257), United States v. Rhodes et al., No. 1:22-cr-15 (D.D.C. Oct. 13, 2022) (Rhodes messaging an Oath Keepers chat that "Let's adopt the Q slogan of WWG1WGA. Where We Go One, We Go All. We nullify TOGETHER We defy TOGETHER. We resist TOGETHER We defend TOGETHER. They come for one of us, they come for all of us. When they come for us, we go for them. When they strike at our leaders, we strike at their leaders. This is the path of the Founders. It's what they did."); Trial Exhibit 4064, United States v. Rhodes et al., No. 1:22-cr-15 (D.D.C. Oct. 6, 2022) (printout of December 23, 2020, open letter to President Trump posted by Stewart Rhodes on the Oath Keeper website, imploring the President to invoke the Insurrection Act to prevent a communist takeover of the United States through the inauguration of Joe Biden).

334. Select Committee to Investigate the January 6th Attack on the United States Capitol, Transcribed Interview of Nick Quested, (Apr. 5, 2022), p. 53.

335. Ben Collins and Brandy Zadrozny, "Extremists Made Little Secret of Ambitions to 'Occupy' Capitol in Weeks Before Attack," NBC News, (Jan. 8, 2021), available at https://www.nbcnews.com/tech/internet/extremists-made-little-secret-ambitions-occupy-capital-weeks-attack-n1253499.

336. Kari Paul, Luke Harding and Severin Carrell, "Far-Right Website 8kun Again Loses Internet Service Protection Following Capitol Attack," *The Guardian*, (Jan. 15, 2021), available at https://www.theguardian.com/technology/2021/jan/15/8kun-8chan-capitol-breach-violence-isp.

337. Ben Collins and Brandy Zadrozny, "Extremists Made Little Secret of Ambitions to 'Occupy' Capitol in Weeks Before Attack," NBC News, (Jan. 8, 2021), available at https://www.nbcnews.com/tech/internet/extremists-made-little-secret-ambitions-occupy-capital-weeks-attack-n1253499.

338. Post by username r3deleven, "Trump Tweet. Daddy Says Be In DC On Jan. 6th," Patriots.Win, Dec. 19, 2020, available at https://web.archive.org/web/20210105024826/https://thedonald.win/p/11R4q2aptJ/trump-tweet-daddy-says-be-in-dc-/c/ (archived).

339. "How a Trump Tweet Sparked Plots, Strategizing to 'Storm and Occupy' Capitol with 'Hand-cuffs and Zip Ties'," SITE Intelligence Group, (Jan. 9, 2021), available at https://ent.siteintelgroup.com/Far-Right-/-Far-Left-Threat/how-a-trump-tweet-sparked-plots-strategizing-to-storm-and-occupy-capitol-with-handcuffs-and-zip-ties.html.

340. "How a Trump Tweet Sparked Plots, Strategizing to 'Storm and Occupy' Capitol with 'Hand-cuffs and Zip Ties'," SITE Intelligence Group, (Jan. 9, 2021), available at https://ent.siteintelgroup.com/Far-Right-/-Far-Left-Threat/how-a-trump-tweet-sparked-plots-strategizing-to-storm-and-occupy-capitol-with-handcuffs-and-zip-ties.html.

341. Select Committee to Investigate the January 6th Attack on the United States Capitol, Deposition of Jody Williams, (June 7, 2022), p. 72.

342. Ryan Goodman and Justin Hendrix, "The Absence of 'The Donald'," Just Security, (Dec. 6, 2021), available at https://www.justsecurity.org/79446/the-absence-of-the-donald/.

343. Amrita Khalid, "Donald Trump Participated in a Reddit AMA, but not Much of Anything was Revealed," *Daily Dot*, (July 27, 2016), available at https://www.dailydot.com/debug/donald-trump-reddit-ama-fail/.

344. Memorandum from Select Committee to Investigate the January 6th Attack on the United States Capitol, Briefing with Reddit, (May 19, 2022); Mike Isaac, "Reddit, Acting Against Hate Speech, Bans 'The_Donald' Subreddit," *New York Times*, (Jan. 29, 2020, Updated Jan. 27, 2021), available at https://www.nytimes.com/2020/06/29/technology/reddit-hate-speech.html.

345. Select Committee to Investigate the January 6th Attack on the United States Capitol, Deposition of Jody Williams, (June 7, 2022), pp. 31-32. In fact, Williams testified that he and other moderators had the opportunity to advertise the new website on Reddit for months. *See id.*, at 32-33. This gave TheDonald.win "immediate" access to "hundreds of thousands of people" who used the Reddit forum. *See id.*, at 33.

346. Ben Schreckinger, "World War Meme: How a Group of Anonymous Keyboard Commandos Conquered the Internet for Donald Trump and Plans to Deliver Europe to the Far Right," *Politico Magazine*, (Mar./Apr. 2017), available at https://www.politico.com/magazine/story/2017/03/memes-4chan-trump-supporters-trolls-internet-214856/.

347. Ben Schreckinger, "World War Meme: How a Group of Anonymous Keyboard Commandos Conquered the Internet for Donald Trump and Plans to Deliver Europe to the Far Right," *Politico Magazine*, (Mar./Apr. 2017), available at https://www.politico.com/magazine/story/2017/03/memes-4chan-trump-supporters-trolls-internet-214856/.

348. Daniella Silva, "President Trump Tweets Wrestling Video of Himself Attacking 'CNN'," NBC News, (July 2, 2017), available at https://www.nbcnews.com/politics/donald-trump/president-trump-tweets-wwe-video-himself-attacking-cnn-n779031.

349. Justin Hendrix, "TheDonald.win and President Trump's Foreknowledge of the Attack on the Capitol," Just Security, (Jan. 12, 2021), available at https://www.justsecurity.org/79813/thedonald-win-and-president-trumps-foreknowledge-of-the-attack-on-the-capitol/.

350. Andrew Restuccia, Daniel Lippman, and Eliana Johnson, "'Get Scavino in Here': Trump's Twitter Guru is the Ultimate Insider," *Politico*, (May 16, 2019), available at https://www.politico.com/story/2019/05/16/trump-scavino-1327921.

351. H. Rept. 117-284, Resolution Recommending that the House of Representatives Find Peter K. Navarro and Daniel Scavino, Jr., in Contempt of Congress for Refusal to Comply with a Subpoena Duly Issued by the Select Committee to Investigate the January 6th Attack on the United States Capitol, 117th Cong., 2d Sess. (2022), available at https://www.congress.gov/117/crpt/hrpt284/CRPT-117hrpt284.pdf.

352. Justin Hendrix, "TheDonald.win and President Trump's Foreknowledge of the Attack on the Capitol," Just Security, (Jan. 12, 2021), available at https://www.justsecurity.org/79813/thedonald-win-and-president-trumps-foreknowledge-of-the-attack-on-the-capitol/.

353. Post, "If we occupy the capitol building, there will be no vote," Patriots.Win, available at https://patriots.win/p/11Rh1RiP9l/if-we-occupy-the-capitol-buildin/.

354. Post by username REDMARAUDER, "The media will call us evil if we have to occupy the Capitol Building on January 6th. Let them," Patriots.Win, Jan. 2, 2021, available at https://patriots.win/p/11ROC9U7EM/the-media-will-call-us-evil-if-w/.

355. Post by username Sharker, "THIS IS NOT A RALLY OR PROTEST. We are all here for the sole purpose of correcting this ILLEGAL election. Surround the enemy and do NOT LET THEM LEAVE until this mess is cleaned up with Trump being re-admitted for 4 more years. SACK UP PATRIOTS." Patriots.Win, Jan. 5, 2021, available at https://patriots.win/p/11Rh1WGo3K/this-is-not-a-rally-or-protest-w/c/.

356. Ben Schreckinger, "World War Meme: How a Group of Anonymous Keyboard Commandos Conquered the Internet for Donald Trump—and Plans to Deliver Europe to the Far Right," *Politico Magazine*, (March/April 2017) available at https://www.politico.com/magazine/story/2017/03/memes-4chan-trump-supporters-trolls-internet-214856.

357. "How a Trump Tweet Sparked Plots, Strategizing to 'Storm and Occupy' Capitol with 'Handcuffs and Zip Ties'," SITE Intelligence Group, (Jan. 9, 2021), available at https://ent.siteintelgroup.com/Far-Right-/-Far-Left-Threat/how-a-trump-tweet-sparked-plots-strategizing-to-storm-and-occupy-capitol-with-handcuffs-and-zip-ties.html.

358. Alex Thomas, "Team Trump Was in Bed With Online Insurrectionists before He Was Even Elected," *Daily Dot*, (Jan. 15, 2021), available at https://www.dailydot.com/debug/dan-scavino-reddit-donald-trump-disinformation/.

359. Alex Jones, "Team Trump Was in Bed With Online Insurrectionists before He Was Even Elected," *Daily Dot*, (Jan. 15, 2021), available at https://www.dailydot.com/debug/dan-scavino-reddit-donald-trump-disinformation/.

360. Post by username wartooth6, "Gallows are simpler and more cost effective, plus they're an American old west tradition too," Patriots.Win, Dec. 22, 2020, available at https://patriots.win/p/11RNfN5v3p/gallows-are-simpler-and-more-cos/c/.

361. Post by username psybrnaut, "Builder Pedes…Let's construct a Gallows outside the Capitol Building next Wednesday so the Congressmen watching from their office windows shit their Pants…," Patriots.Win, Dec. 30, 2020, available at https://patriots.win/p/11RO2pYG2P/builder-pedes-lets-construct-a-g/c/.

362. Post by username TacticalGeorge, "Building a hanging platform in front of Congress on the 6 should send a strong message," Patriots.Win, Dec. 30, 2020, available at https://patriots.win/p/11RO2oQy77/building-a-hanging-platform-in-f/.

363. Post by username Krunchi, "The One Thing You Must Know Before Going To DC on The 6th…," Patriots.Win, Jan. 3, 2021, available at https://web.archive.org/web/20210105080829/https://thedonald.win/p/11ROGmlHG5/the-one-thing-you-must-know-befo/ (archived).

364. Post by username Badradness, "We will be building a gallows right in front of the Capitol so the traitors know the stakes. I'm driving up in a sedan but if a patriot with a pickup will assist I'm down to spend from my credit line at Home Depot for all of the supplies needed

for this. Driving up Monday night or early Tuesday.," Patriots.Win, Jan. 3, 2021, available at https://patriots.win/p/11ROGrJPVQ/we-will-be-building-a-gallows-ri/c/.

365. Post by username AFLP, "Gallows on the Capitol Lawn," Patriots.Win, Jan. 5, 2021, available at https://patriots.win/p/11RhArKEQ3/gallows-on-the-capitol-lawn/.

366. Documents on File with the Select Committee to Investigate the January 6th Attack on the United States Capitol, (Mark Meadows Production), MM014441; Select Committee to Investigate the January 6th Attack on the United States Capitol, Deposition of Jason Miller, (Feb. 3, 2022), pp. 209.

367. *See* Select Committee to Investigate the January 6th Attack on the United States Capitol, Deposition of Jason Miller, (Feb. 3, 2022), Exhibit 45, pp. 4, 13. In his testimony to the Select Committee, Miller denied reading such comments and claimed not to recall whether Meadows had followed up with him about the thread. However, Miller did say that "sometimes" he would "click and see what people are saying" on sites like TheDonald.win, if he received a Google alert about himself. Select Committee to Investigate the January 6th Attack on the United States Capitol, Deposition of Jason Miller, (Feb. 3, 2022), pp. 209, 212, 214.

368. Select Committee to Investigate the January 6th Attack on the United States Attack on the United States Capitol, Deposition of Jason Miller, (Feb. 3, 2022), p. 209, Exhibit 47.

369. Donald J. Trump (@realDonaldTrump), Twitter, Dec. 19, 2020 1:24 p.m. ET, available at https://twitter.com/realDonaldTrump/status/1340362336390004737.

370. Justin Hendrix, "TheDonald.win and President Trumps Foreknowledge of the Attack on the Capitol," Just Security, (Jan. 12, 2021), available at https://www.justsecurity.org/79813/thedonald-win-and-president-trumps-foreknowledge-of-the-attack-on-the-capitol/.

371. Lena V. Groeger, Jeff Kao, Al Shaw, Moiz Syed, and Maya Eliahou, "What Parler Saw During the Attack on the Capitol," *Pro Publica*, at 12:05 p.m. ET at 0:30, Jan. 17, 2021, available, https://projects.propublica.org/parler-capitol-videos/; Statement of Catherine A. Sanderson, Ph.D., (June 3, 2022), at 5.

372. Through review of public records, the Select Committee identified organizers for about a dozen events scheduled for January 5th or 6th secured permits from either the U.S. Capitol Police (USCP) or National Park Service (NPS). Except for two events—one unrelated to January 6th and the other put on by a group that regularly held demonstrations around D.C.—all of the applications were submitted after President Trump's December 19th tweet. The three most important events were: Cindy Chafian's January 5th event at Freedom Plaza (using the group name "The Eighty Percent Coalition"); WFAF's January 6th event at the Ellipse; and Ali Alexander's January 6th event on the Capitol grounds (under the "One Nation Under God" moniker). In addition to the permits issued to WFAF, Cindy Chafian, and Ali Alexander (under the "One Nation Under God" moniker), at least nine additional permits were issued by USCP or NPS for events in Washington, D.C., on January 5, 2021 or January 6, 2021.

373. Documents on file with the Select Committee to Investigate the January 6th Attack on the United States Capitol (Department of the Interior Production), DOI_46000428_00005162 (Dec. 19, 2020, Cindy Chafian email Re: Status of application - Women for America First at 7:12 AM).

374. Documents on file with the Select Committee to Investigate the January 6th Attack on the United States Capitol (Department of the Interior Production), DOI_46000428_00005162 (Dec. 19, 2020, Cindy Chafian email Re: Status of application - Women for America First at 7:12 AM).

375. Select Committee to Investigate the January 6th Attack on the United States Capitol, Transcribed Interview of Kylie Kremer, (Jan. 12, 2022), p. 5.

376. Select Committee to Investigate the January 6th Attack on the United States Capitol, Transcribed Interview of Amy Kremer, (Feb. 18, 2022), pp. 8-10.

377. Select Committee to Investigate the January 6th Attack on the United States Capitol, Transcribed Interview of Amy Kremer, (Feb. 18, 2022), pp. 8-10.

378. Women for America First, "March for Trump Bus Tour," trumpmarch.com, available at https://web.archive.org/web/20201226001527/https://trumpmarch.com/..

379. Kylie Jane Kremer (@KylieJaneKremer), Twitter, Dec. 19, 2020 3:50 p.m. ET, available at https://twitter.com/kyliejanekremer/status/1340399063875895296?lang=en.

380. Women For America First Ellipse Public Gathering Permit, National Park Service, available at https://www.nps.gov/aboutus/foia/upload/21-0278-Women-for-America-First-Ellispse-permit_REDACTED.pdf.

381. Select Committee to Investigate the January 6th Attack on the United States Capitol, Deposition of Ali Alexander, (Dec. 9, 2021), p. 15.

382. Documents on file with the Select Committee to Investigate the January 6th Attack on the United States Capitol (Resource Group Production), CTRL0000010113 (Dec. 19, 2020, Ali Alexandra text message to Stephen Brown at 10:49 a.m.).

383. Documents on file with the Select Committee to Investigate the January 6th Attack on the United States Capitol (Resource Group Production), CTRL0000010113 (Dec. 19, 2020, Ali Alexandra text message to Stephen Brown at 10:49 a.m.).

384. "Valuation and Analysis," WildProtest.com, (Jan. 14, 2021 (last updated)), available at https://wildprotest.com.siteindices.com/.

385. "President Trump Wants You in DC January 6," WildProtest.com, (Dec 19.2020), available at https://web.archive.org/web/20201223062953/http://wildprotest.com/ (archived).

386. Select Committee to Investigate the January 6th Attack on the United States Capitol, Transcribed Interview of Arina Grossu, (Apr. 29, 2022), p. 40.

387. Statement of Andrew J. Seidel, (Mar. 18, 2022), at 11, 13.

388. Documents on file with the Select Committee to Investigate the January 6th Attack on the United States Capitol (Arina Grossu Production), Grossu_01_002721 (Dec. 19, 2020, Rob Weaver email message to Arina Grossu at 8:20 a.m. CT).

389. Documents on file with the Select Committee to Investigate the January 6th Attack on the United States Capitol, (Arina Grossu Production), Arina Grossu Exhibit 20 (Jericho March Rally registration page).

390. Select Committee to Investigate the January 6th Attack on the United States Capitol, Informal Interview of Marsha Lessard, (Dec. 10, 2021); see also Documents on file with the Select Committee to Investigate the January 6th Attack on the United States Capitol (Capitol Police Production), CTRL0000001834 (Permit Relating to Demonstration Activities on United States Capitol Grounds for Virginia Freedom Keepers, No. 20-12-25).

391. . See Superseding Indictment at ¶ 37, United States v. Rhodes et al., No. 1:22-cr-15 (D.D.C. June 22, 2022) (noting that Stewart Rhodes, President of the Oath Keepers, shipped weapons to Lessard's home in Virginia before his arrival in DC for January 6th); Select Committee to Investigate the January 6th Attack on the United States Capitol, Deposition of Kellye SoRelle, (Apr. 13, 2022), p. 180.

392. See Select Committee to Investigate the January 6th Attack on the United States Capitol, Deposition of Henry Tarrio, (Feb. 4, 2021), p. 117 (testifying that Gracia arranged a White House tour for him in December 2020).

393. Latinos for Trump (@Officiallft2021), Twitter, Dec. 27, 2020 7:58 p.m., available at https://twitter.com/i/web/status/1343360740313321474.

394. Documents on file with the Select Committee to Investigate the January 6th Attack on the United States Capitol, (Nathan Martin Production), NMartin0318 (December 30, 2020, email from Kimberly Fletcher of Moms for America to Ali Alexander and Nathan Martin re: MFA VIP list for White House); Documents on file with the Select Committee to Investigate the January 6th Attack on the United States Capitol (Resource Group Production),

CTRL0000010100 (December 27, 2020, text messages between Nathan Martin, Stephen Martin, Kimberly Fletcher, and Ali Alexander discussing permitting); Documents on file with the Select Committee to Investigate the January 6th Attack on the United States Capitol (Capitol Police Production), CTRL0000000086, CTRL0000000086.0001 (December 23, 2020, Special Event Assessment identifying Fletcher as a speaker at the "Wild Protest" event during the same time as MFA's permitted event in a different area).

395. "The Alex Jones Show," Prison Planet TV, at 10:07, Dec. 20, 2020, available at http://tv.infowars.com/index/display/id/11151.

396. Documents on file with the Select Committee to Investigate the January 6th Attack on the United States Capitol, (T-Mobile Production, Nov. 19, 2021).

397. Select Committee to Investigate the January 6th Attack on the United States Capitol, Informal Interview of Cynthia "Cindy" Chafian (Nov. 1-2, 2021).

398. *See,* Beth Reinhard, Jaqueline Alemany, and Josh Dawsey, "Low-Profile Heiress Who 'Played a Strong Role' in Financing Jan. 6 Rally is Thrust Into Spotlight," *Washington Post,* (Dec. 8, 2021), available at https://www.washingtonpost.com/investigations/publix-heiress-capitol-insurrection-fancelli/2021/12/08/5144fe1c-5219-11ec-8ad5-b5c50c1fb4d9_story.html.

399. Documents on File with the Select Committee to Investigate the January 6th Attack on the United States Capitol (Julia Fancelli Production), REL0000000994, (Bank Statements for Julia Fancelli at the Bank of Central Florida from December 10, 2020, to January 10, 2021).

400. Select Committee to Investigate the January 6th Attack on the United States Capitol, Deposition of Caroline Wren, (Dec. 17, 2021), p. 58.

401. Documents on file with the Select Committee to Investigate the January 6th Attack on the United States Capitol, (Verizon Production, Feb. 9, 2022).

402. Select Committee to Investigate the January 6th Attack on the United States Capitol, Deposition of Caroline Wren, (Dec. 17, 2021), pp. 45-46.

403. Select Committee to Investigate the January 6th Attack on the United States Capitol, Deposition of Caroline Wren, (Dec. 17, 2021), p. 71.

404. Documents on file with the Select Committee to Investigate the January 6th Attack on the United States Capitol, (Verizon Production, Feb. 9, 2022).

405. Documents on file with the Select Committee to Investigate the January 6th Attack on the United States Capitol (Caroline Wren Production), REVU_000014 (January 4 - 6, 2021, Fancelli Budget & Trip Plan).

406. Documents on file with the Select Committee to Investigate the January 6th Attack on the United States Capitol (Caroline Wren Production), REVU_000005 (December 27, 2020, Kylie Kremer e-mail to Caroline Wren at 11:25 am).

407. Documents on file with the Select Committee to Investigate the January 6th Attack on the United States Capitol (Caroline Wren Production), REVU_000468 (December 27, 2020, Caroline Wren text message thread with Alex Jones).

408. Documents on file with the Select Committee to Investigate the January 6th Attack on the United States Capitol (Caroline Wren Production), REVU_000550 (Dec. 27, 2020, Caroline Wren text messages with Cindy Chafian).

409. Select Committee to Investigate the January 6th Attack on the United States Capitol, Deposition of Caroline Wren, (Dec. 17, 2021), pp. 50, 70-71.

410. Documents on file with the Select Committee to Investigate the January 6th Attack on the United States Capitol (Caroline Wren Production), REVU_000014 (January 4 - 6, 2021, Fancelli Budget & Trip Plan

411. Documents on file with the Select Committee to Investigate the January 6th Attack on the United States Capitol (Caroline Wren Production), REVU_000014 (January 4 - 6, 2021, Fancelli Budget & Trip Plan

412. Documents on file with the Select Committee to Investigate the January 6th Attack on the United States Capitol (Caroline Wren Production), REVU_000482 (December 29, 2020, Caroline Wren text message to Ali Alexander at 4:19 p.m.).

413. Documents on file with the Select Committee to Investigate the January 6th Attack on the United States Capitol (Caroline Wren Production), REVU_000482 (December 29, 2020, Caroline Wren text message to Ali Alexander at 4:19 pm).

414. Kathleen Ronayne and Michael Kunzelman, "Trump to Far-Right Extremists: 'Stand Back and Stand By,'" *Associated Press*, (Sept. 30, 2020), available at https://apnews.com/article/election-2020-joe-biden-race-and-ethnicity-donald-trump-chris-wallace-0b32339da25fbc9e8b7c7c7066a1db0f.

415. Donald J. Trump (@realDonaldTrump), Twitter, Dec. 27, 2020 5:51 p.m. ET, available at https://www.thetrumparchive.com (archived).

416. Select Committee to Investigate the January 6th Attack on the United States Capitol, Deposition of Justin Caporale, (Mar. 1, 2022), pp. 20-21.

417. *See* Select Committee to Investigate the January 6th Attack on the United States Capitol, Transcribed Interview of Donald Trump, Jr., (May 3, 2022), p.30; Anthony Man, "At Trump Golf Club in West Palm Beach, Roger Stone Thanks President for Pardon," *Orlando Sun Sentinel*, (Dec. 28, 2020), available at https://www.sun-sentinel.com/news/politics/elections/fl-ne-roger-stone-thanks-trump-pardon-20201228-2ejqzv6e7vhyvf26cxz6e6jysa-story.html.

418. Documents on file with the Select Committee to Investigate the January 6th Attack on the United States Capitol, (AT&T Production, Dec. 17, 2021).

419. Documents on file with the Select Committee to Investigate the January 6th Attack on the United States Capitol (Caroline Wren Production), REVU_000444, pp. 1-3 (December 27, 2020, text message from Caroline Wren to Kimberly Guilfoyle at 7:10 p.m.).

420. As revealed in the phone records for the personal cell phones of Max Miller and Anthony Ornato. *See* Documents on file with the Select Committee to Investigate the January 6th Attack on the United States Capitol, (Verizon Production, Dec. 17, 2021); Documents on file with the Select Committee to Investigate the January 6th Attack on the United States Capitol (Verizon Production, Sep. 23, 2022). The Select Committee also subpoenaed the phone records for the personal cell phones of Robert Peede, Mark Meadows, Dan Scavino, and Justin Caporale. They each filed lawsuits to block the respective phone companies' production of the phone records, which were still pending at the time of writing. Thus, there may have been additional relevant phone calls among or involving these four of which the Select Committee is not aware.

421. Select Committee to Investigate the January 6th Attack on the United States Capitol, Deposition of Max Miller, (Jan. 20, 2022), pp. 36-37.

422. Select Committee to Investigate the January 6th Attack on the United States Capitol, Deposition of Justin Caporale, (Mar. 1, 2020), p. 44; Documents on file with the Select Committee to Investigate the January 6th Attack on the United States Capitol (Caroline Wren Production), REVU_0644 (December 29, 2020, text messages with Justin Caporale).

423. Select Committee to Investigate the January 6th Attack on the United States Capitol, Transcribed Interview of Katrina Pierson, (Mar. 25, 2022), pp. 79-82; Documents on file with the Select Committee to Investigate the January 6th Attack on the United States Capitol (Caroline Wren Production), REVU_0181 (January 2nd email from Katrina Pierson to Caroline Wren and Taylor Budowich).

424. Select Committee to Investigate the January 6th Attack on the United States Capitol, Transcribed Interview of Cassidy Hutchinson, (Feb. 23, 2022), pp. 32-33, 41; Select Committee to Investigate the January 6th Attack on the United States Capitol, Continued Interview of Cassidy Hutchinson, (June 20, 2022), pp. 107-08, 135.

425. Select Committee to Investigate the January 6th Attack on the United States Capitol, Transcribed Interview of Cassidy Hutchinson, (Feb. 23, 2022), p. 42.

426. Select Committee to Investigate the January 6th Attack on the United States Capitol, Transcribed Interview of Cassidy Hutchinson, (Feb. 23, 2022), pp. 44-45, 47, 52-54; Select Committee to Investigate the January 6th Attack on the United States Capitol, Continued Interview of Cassidy Hutchinson, (June 20, 2022), p. 87.

427. Documents on file with the Select Committee to Investigate the January 6th Attack on the United States Capitol (Kylie Kremer Production), KKremer5447, p. 3 (January 4, 2021, text message from Kylie Kremer to Mike Lindell at 9:32 a.m.).

428. Documents on file with the Select Committee to Investigate the January 6th Attack on the United States Capitol (Ali Alexander Production), CTRL0000017718, p. 41 (January 5, 2021 text message with Liz Willis at 7:19 a.m.).

429. See Select Committee to Investigate the January 6th Attack on the United States Capitol, Transcribed Interview of Katrina Pierson, (Mar. 25, 2022), pp. 120-21.

430. Select Committee to Investigate the January 6th Attack on the United States Capitol, Transcribed Interview of Katrina Pierson, (Mar. 25, 2022), p. 121.

431. Select Committee to Investigate the January 6th Attack on the United States Capitol, Transcribed Interview of Katrina Pierson, (Mar. 25, 2022), p. 121.

432. Select Committee to Investigate the January 6th Attack on the United States Capitol, Transcribed Interview of Katrina Pierson, (Mar. 25, 2022), p. 121.

433. Select Committee to Investigate the January 6th Attack on the United States Capitol, Deposition of Max Miller, (Jan. 20, 2022), pp. 91-92.

434. Select Committee to Investigate the January 6th Attack on the United States Capitol, Transcribed Interview of Katrina Pierson, (Mar. 25, 2022), p. 123.

435. Select Committee to Investigate the January 6th Attack on the United States Capitol, Transcribed Interview of Katrina Pierson, (Mar. 25, 2022), pp. 121-26.

436. Select Committee to Investigate the January 6th Attack on the United States Capitol, Deposition of Max Miller, (Jan. 20, 2022), pp. 98-99.

437. Documents on file with the Select Committee to Investigate the January 6th Attack on the United States Capitol, (Max Miller Production) Miller Production 0001, p. 1 (January 4, 2021, text message from Max Miller to Katrina Pierson).

438. Select Committee to Investigate the January 6th Attack on the United States Capitol, Transcribed Interview of Katrina Pierson, (Mar. 25, 2022), p. 121.

439. Select Committee to Investigate the January 6th Attack on the United States Capitol, Transcribed Interview of Katrina Pierson, (Mar. 25, 2022), p. 95; Documents on file with the Select Committee to Investigate the January 6th Attack on the United States Capitol (Katrina Pierson Production), KPierson0180, at 180, 196-97 (January 4, 2021, President Trump Meeting Agenda).

440. Select Committee to Investigate the January 6th Attack on the United States Capitol, Transcribed Interview of Katrina Pierson, (Mar. 25, 2022), p. 41.

441. Select Committee to Investigate the January 6th Attack on the United States Capitol, Transcribed Interview of Katrina Pierson, (Mar. 25, 2022), p. 42.

442. Select Committee to Investigate the January 6th Attack on the United States Capitol, Transcribed Interview of Katrina Pierson, (Mar. 25, 2022), pp. 42-43.

443. Documents on file with the Select Committee to Investigate the January 6th Attack on the United States Capitol (Katrina Pierson Production), KPierson0374 (December 30, 2020, Katrina Pierson text message to Kylie Kremer); Select Committee to Investigate the January 6th Attack on the United States Capitol, Transcribed Interview of Katrina Pierson, (Mar. 25, 2022), p. 4.

444. Select Committee to Investigate the January 6th Attack on the United States Capitol, Transcribed Interview of Katrina Pierson, (Mar. 25, 2022), p. 86.

445.   Select Committee to Investigate the January 6th Attack on the United States Capitol, Transcribed Interview of Katrina Pierson, (Mar. 25, 2022), pp. 62-63.

446.   Select Committee to Investigate the January 6th Attack on the United States Capitol, Transcribed Interview of Katrina Pierson, (Mar. 25, 2022), p. 84; Documents on file with the Select Committee to Investigate the January 6th Attack on the United States Capitol, (Katrina Pierson Production), KPierson0924 (January 2, 2021, Katrina Pierson text message to Mark Meadows at 1:39 p.m. and 1:40 p.m.)

447.   Select Committee to Investigate the January 6th Attack on the United States Capitol, Transcribed Interview of Katrina Pierson, (March 25, 2022), p. 74; Documents on file with the Select Committee to Investigate the January 6th Attack on the United States Capitol (Katrina Pierson Production), KPierson0921, (January 2, 2021, Katrina Pierson text message to Mark Meadows at 5:16 p.m.).

448.   Select Committee to Investigate the January 6th Attack on the United States Capitol, Transcribed Interview of Katrina Pierson, (Mar. 25, 2022), pp. 76-77, 80-81.

449.   Select Committee to Investigate the January 6th Attack on the United States Capitol, Transcribed Interview of Katrina Pierson, (Mar. 25, 2022), pp. 75-77.

450.   Documents on file with the Select Committee to Investigate the January 6th Attack on the United States Capitol (Katrina Pierson Production), KPierson0924 (January 2, 2021 Katrina Pierson text message to Mark Meadows at 5:49 p.m.).

451.   Select Committee to Investigate the January 6th Attack on the United States Capitol, Transcribed Interview of Katrina Pierson, (Mar. 25, 2022), p. 108; Documents on file with the Select Committee to Investigate the January 6th Attack on the United States Capitol, (Katrina Pierson Production), KPierson180 (January 4, 2021, agenda for meeting with President Trump at 1:21 p.m.).

452.   Select Committee to Investigate the January 6th Attack on the United States Capitol, Transcribed Interview of Katrina Pierson, (Mar. 25, 2022), pp. 107-08; Documents on file with the Select Committee to Investigate the January 6th Attack on the United States Capitol, (Katrina Pierson Production), KPierson0196 (Document titled: "Meeting w/ POTUS - January 4th 2021 at 3:30pm ET").

453.   Select Committee to Investigate the January 6th Attack on the United States Capitol, Transcribed Interview of Katrina Pierson, (Mar. 25, 2022), pp. 116-18.

454.   Documents on file with the Select Committee to Investigate the January 6th Attack on the United States Capitol, (Katrina Pierson Production), KPierson0906 (January 5, 2021, text message from Dan Scavino to Katrina Pierson at 4:23 a.m.).

455.   Documents on file with the Select Committee to Investigate the January 6th Attack on the United States Capitol (Justin Caporale Production), Caporale_05_003987, (Jan. 3, 2021, Katrina Pierson text message to Justin Caporale and Taylor Budowich); see also Select Committee to Investigate the January 6th Attack on the United States Capitol, Transcribed Interview of Katrina Pierson, (Mar. 25, 2022), p. 79; Documents on file with the Select Committee to Investigate the January 6th Attack on the United States Capitol (Taylor Budowich Production), Budo-00714 (January 2, 2021, Katrina Pierson email to Caroline Wren and Taylor Budowich at 10:49 p.m.).

456.   Documents on file with the Select Committee to Investigate the January 6th Attack on the United States Capitol (Justin Caporale Production), Caporale_02_000673-88, (Jan. 3, 2021, Justin Caporale text message to Katrina Pierson, redacted).

457.   Select Committee to Investigate the January 6th Attack on the United States Capitol, Deposition of Max Miller, (Jan. 20, 2022), pp. 81-83. Miller testified that he had not been involved in or paying attention to the conversation until the President directly addressed him about Giuliani. Miller's testimony was not credible on this point. Miller said he did not take notes, yet in communications with people after the fact he recounted details about the President's decision regarding speakers other than Giuliani, Eastman, Powell, Wood, and Flynn. See Select Committee to Investigate the January 6th Attack on the United States

Capitol, Deposition of Max Miller, (Jan. 20, 2022), p. 85 (stating that neither he nor Peede took notes); *id.* at p. 107 (confirming that he told Megan Powers on January 5th that President Trump cut Paxton from the list).

458. In the January 4 meeting with Pierson and Miller, President Trump initially indicated that Giuliani would not be able to speak at the Ellipse because he needed to be working on lobbying Members of Congress to block certification of the electoral college vote, yet another sign that the President intended January 6th to be a full-fledged effort to stay in power. Select Committee to Investigate the January 6th Attack on the United States Capitol, Transcribed Interview of Katrina Pierson, (Mar. 25, 2022), p. 117.

459. Select Committee to Investigate the January 6th Attack on the United States Capitol, Deposition of Max Miller, (Jan. 20, 2022), pp. 81-83, 129-30.

460. User-Generated Clip, "John Eastman at January 6 Rally," CSPAN, Mar. 24, 2021, available at https://www.c-span.org/video/?c4953961/user-clip-john-eastman-january-6-rally.

461. Select Committee to Investigate the January 6th Attack on the United States Capitol, Deposition of Max Miller, (Jan. 20, 2022), pp. 115-116.

462. It appears that Alexander was given front row seating for the Ellipse rally. He tweeted a picture in front of the Ellipse stage, writing: "Nice seats! Thank you @realdonaldtrump!" Ali [Orange Square] #StopTheSteal (@Ali), Twitter, Jan. 6, 2021, available at https://web.archive.org/web/20210107094927/https:/twitter.com/ali (archived)

463. Moms for America, "Save the Republic: Ali Alexander," Rumble, at 2:24, Jan. 29, 2021, available at https://rumble.com/vdepmx-save-the-republic-ali-alexander.html.

464. Ali [Orange Square] #StopTheSteal (@Ali), Twitter, Jan. 5, 2021, available at https://web.archive.org/web/20210107094927/https:/twitter.com/ali (archived).

465. NTD Television, "'Virginia Women for Trump' Rally at Supreme Court," Facebook Live, Jan. 5, 2021, available at https://www.facebook.com/NTDTelevision/videos/220171109588984.

466. Radley Balko, "Meet the Police Chief Turned Yoga Instructor Prodding Wealthy Suburbanites to Civil War," *Washington Post*, (Jan. 27, 2021), available at https://www.washingtonpost.com/opinions/2021/01/27/alan-hostetter-capitol-riot-police-chief-yoga-instructor/.

467. NTD Television, "'Virginia Women for Trump' Rally at Supreme Court," Facebook Live, at 20:10, Jan. 5, 2021, available at https://www.facebook.com/NTDTelevision/videos/220171109588984.

468. NTD Television, "'Virginia Women for Trump' Rally at Supreme Court," Facebook Live, at 1:44:14 -1:45:54, Jan. 5, 2021, available at https://www.facebook.com/NTDTelevision/videos/220171109588984.

469. NTD Television, "'Virginia Women for Trump' Rally at Supreme Court," Facebook Live, at1:46:04 – 1:49:40, Jan. 5, 2021, available at https://www.facebook.com/NTDTelevision/videos/220171109588984.

470. Radley Balko, "Meet the Police Chief Turned Yoga Instructor Prodding Wealthy Suburbanites to Civil War," *Washington Post*, (Jan. 27, 2021), available at https://www.washingtonpost.com/opinions/2021/01/27/alan-hostetter-capitol-riot-police-chief-yoga-instructor/.

471. Indictment at ¶ 56, *United States v. Hostetter et al.*, No. 1:21-cr-392 (D.D.C., June 9, 2021), ECF No. 1.

472: EpiqEpoch, "Roger Stone January 5, 2021 Freedom Plaza," Rumble, at 8:09, Jan. 6, 2021, available at https://rumble.com/vchgtl-roger-stone-january-5-2021-freedom-plaza.html.

473. Project Truth Beam, "Jan 5th Freedom Plaza: Ali Alexander," Rumble, at 1:58-2:21, Jan.16, 2021, available at https://rumble.com/vcx1mt-jan-5th-freedom-plaza-ali-alexander.html.

474. EpiqEpoch, "Alex Jones January 5, 2021 Freedom Plaza," Rumble, at 1:24, Jan. 6, 2021, available at https://rumble.com/vchguz-alex-jones-january-5-2021-freedom-plaza.html.

475. EpiqEpoch, "Gen. Michael Flynn, January 5, 2021 Freedom Plaza," Rumble, at 5:28, Jan. 6, 2021, available at https://rumble.com/vchisz-gen.-michael-flynn-january-5-2021-freedom-plaza.html.

476. Select Committee to Investigate the January 6th Attack on the United States Capitol, Deposition of Ross Worthington, (Feb. 15, 2022), p. 112.

477. Select Committee to Investigate the January 6th Attack on the United States Capitol, Transcribed Interview of William Bock IV, (Apr. 15, 2022), pp. 23, 32; Documents on file with the Select Committee to Investigate the January 6th Attacks on the United States Capitol (National Archives Production), 076P-R000002884_00001, (January 5, 2021, email from Worthington to Staff Secretary at 7:46 p.m., attaching a draft speech). In the final hours before the speech, White House lawyers would insist that the speech needed fact-checking and were most worried about the claims about Dominion Voting. *See* Documents on file with the Select Committee to Investigate the January 6th Attack on the United States Capitol, (National Archives Production) 076P-R000007308_0001 (January 5, 2021, email from Worthington to Staff Secretary at 7:46 p.m.). But President Trump would deliver the speech with the allegations intact. *See* Senate Committee on Homeland Security and Governmental Affairs and Committee on Rules and Administration, 117th Congress, "Examining the U.S. Capitol Attack: A Review of the Security, Planning, and Response Failures on January 6" (Staff Report), p. B-18, (June 8, 2021).

478. Documents on file with the Select Committee to Investigate the January 6th Attack on the United States Capitol, (Vincent Haley Production), VMH-00002701-02 (Draft Speech, "Stop the Steal Rally").

479. Select Committee to Investigate the January 6th Attack on the United States Capitol, Deposition of Stephen Miller (Apr. 14, 2022), p. 125-26; Select Committee to Investigate the January 6th Attack on the United States Capitol, Transcribed Interview of Ross Worthington (Feb. 15, 2022), p. 124.

480. Select Committee to Investigate the January 6th Attack on the United States Capitol, Transcribed Interview of Sarah Matthews, (Feb. 8, 2022), pp. 15-16.

481. Select Committee to Investigate the January 6th Attack on the United States Capitol, Transcribed Interview of Sarah Matthews, (Feb. 8, 2022), p. 16; *see also* Documents on file with the Select Committee to Investigate the January 6th Attack on the United States Capitol, (National Archives Production), Photo files 69c1_x032_555c_7, 0d9d_x039_557d_7 (January 5, 2021, photos of the meeting).

482. Select Committee to Investigate the January 6th Attack on the United States Capitol, Deposition of Nicholas Luna, (Mar. 21, 2022), pp. 76-77; Select Committee to Investigate the January 6th Attack on the United States Capitol, Transcribed Interview of Sarah Matthews, (Feb. 8, 2022), pp. 17, 19-20; Select Committee to Investigate the January 6th Attack on the United States Capitol, Deposition of Judson P. Deere, (Mar. 3, 2022), p. 84; Select Committee to Investigate the January 6th Attack on the United States Capitol, Transcribed Interview of Madison Fox Porter, (May 5, 2022), p. 19.

483. Select Committee to Investigate the January 6th Attack on the United States Capitol, Transcribed Interview of Sarah Matthews, (Feb. 8, 2022), pp. 16-17; Select Committee to Investigate the January 6th Attack on the United States Capitol, Deposition of Judson Deere, (Mar. 3, 2022), pp. 83-84.

484. Donald J. Trump (@RealDonaldTrump), Twitter, Jan. 5, 2021 5:05 p.m. ET, available at https://www.thetrumparchive.com/?searchbox=%22Washington+is+being+inundated%22 (archived). ("Washington is being inundated with people who don't want to see an election victory stolen by emboldened Radical Left Democrats. Our Country has had enough, they won't take it anymore! We hear you (and love you) from the Oval Office. MAKE AMERICA GREAT AGAIN!").

485. The Select Committee has obtained two drafts of the speech from January 5th, one of which was circulated at approximately 3:30 p.m. and another at 7:40 p.m. *See* Documents on file with the Select Committee to Investigate the January 6th Attack on the United

States Capitol (Vincent Haley Production), VMH-00002700, VMH-00002708 (January 5, 2021, email from Ross Worthington to Stephen Miller circulating draft speech at 3:30 p.m.); Documents on file with the Select Committee to Investigate the January 6th Attack on the United States Capitol, (National Archives Production), 076P-R000002878_00001, 076P-R000002879_00001, (January 5, 2021, email from Ross Worthington to Stephen Miller circulating draft speech at 7:40 p.m.).

486. Donald J. Trump (@RealDonaldTrump), Twitter, Jan. 5, 2021 5:05 p.m. ET, available at https://www.thetrumparchive.com (archived). ("Washington is being inundated with people who don't want to see an election victory stolen by emboldened Radical Left Democrats. Our Country has had enough, they won't take it anymore! We hear you (and love you) from the Oval Office. MAKE AMERICA GREAT AGAIN!").

487. Documents on file with the Select Committee to Investigate the January 6th Attack on the United States Capitol, (National Archives Production), 076P-R000002879_00001 (Draft of Jan. 6, 2021 speech by President Donald Trump).

488. Select Committee to Investigate the January 6th Attack on the United States Capitol, Deposition of Judson P. Deere, (Mar. 3, 2022), pp. 91-92.

489. Select Committee to Investigate the January 6th Attack on the United States Capitol, Deposition of Shealah Craighead, (June 8, 2022), pp. 32-33. Craighead believed that she later shared this with Ornato. See id., at 33.

490. Select Committee to Investigate the January 6th Attack on the United States Capitol, Transcribed Interview of Sarah Matthews, (Feb. 8, 2022), p. 17; Select Committee to Investigate the January 6th Attack on the United States Capitol, Deposition of Judson P. Deere, (Mar. 3, 2022), p. 99.

491. Select Committee to Investigate the January 6th Attack on the United States Capitol, Transcribed Interview of Sarah Matthews, (Feb. 8, 2022), p. 17. Deere did not recall this specific question nor responding to it, but did remember advising President Trump that he should focus on his administration's accomplishments during his January 6th Ellipse rally speech rather than his stolen election claims. Deere recalled President Trump asking about which Members of Congress would be with him the next day and vote against certifying the election. Select Committee to Investigate the January 6th Attack on the United States Capitol, Deposition of Judson Deere, (Mar. 3, 2022), pp. 88-90, 92, 99-100.

492. Select Committee to Investigate the January 6th Attack on the United States Capitol, Transcribed Interview of Sarah Matthews, (Feb. 8, 2022), p. 17.

493. Select Committee to Investigate the January 6th Attack on the United States Capitol, Transcribed Interview of Sarah Matthews, (Feb. 8, 2022), p. 17; Select Committee to Investigate the January 6th Attack on the United States Capitol, Deposition of Judson Deere, (Mar. 3, 2022), pp. 85-86.

494. Select Committee to Investigate the January 6th Attack on the United States Capitol, Deposition of Judson P. Deere, (Mar. 3, 2022), pp. 86-87, 99.

495. Select Committee to Investigate the January 6th Attack on the United States Capitol, Deposition of Judson P. Deere, (Mar. 3, 2022), p. 86.

496. Documents on file with the Select Committee to Investigate the January 6th Attack on the United States Capitol, 076P-R000007361_0001 (January 5, 2021, email from Austin Ferrer to Dan Scavino at 10:16 p.m.).

497. Senate Committee on Homeland Security and Governmental Affairs and Committee on Rules and Administration, 117th Congress, "Examining the U.S. Capitol Attack: A Review of the Security, Planning, and Response Failures on January 6" (Staff Report), p. B-2, (June 8, 2021); Statement of Catherine A. Sanderson, Ph.D., (June 3, 2022), at 5.

498. Lena V. Groeger, Jeff Kao, Al Shaw, Moiz Syed, and Maya Eliahou, "What Parler Saw During the Attack on the Capitol," Pro Publica, at 12:05 p.m. ET at 0:30, Jan. 17, 2021, available, https://projects.propublica.org/parler-capitol-videos/; Statement of Catherine A. Sanderson, Ph.D., (June 3, 2022), at 5.

499.   Select Committee to Investigate the January 6th Attack on the United States Capitol, Continued Interview of Cassidy Hutchinson, (June 20, 2022), pp. 11-19.

500.   Senate Committee on Homeland Security and Governmental Affairs and Committee on Rules and Administration, 117th Congress, "Examining the U.S. Capitol Attack: A Review of the Security, Planning, and Response Failures on January 6" (Staff Report), pp. B-22, 23, (June 8, 2021).

501.   Documents on file with the Select Committee to Investigate the January 6th Attack on the United States Capitol (National Archives Production), 076P-R000002911_00001, 076P-R000002912_00001 (January 6, 2021, email from Robert Gabriel Jr. to Dan Scavino at 1:25 p.m. re: Final draft attached with attachment '210106 Save America March.doc'); Statement of Jennifer Mercieca, (Mar. 31, 2022), at 18.

502.   Statement of Jennifer Mercieca, (Mar. 31, 2022), at 18.

President Trump speaks at the January 6th Ellipse rally.

Photo by Tasos Katopodis/Getty Images

7

187 MINUTES OF DERELICTION

At 1:10 p.m. on January 6th, President Trump concluded his speech at the Ellipse. By that time, the attack on the U.S. Capitol had already begun. But it was about to get much worse. The President told thousands of people in attendance to march down Pennsylvania Avenue to the Capitol. He told them to "fight like hell" because if they didn't, they were "not going to have a country anymore." Not everyone who left the Ellipse did as the Commander-in-Chief ordered, but many of them did. The fighting intensified during the hours that followed.[1]

By 1:21 p.m., President Trump was informed that the Capitol was under attack. He could have interceded immediately. But the President chose not to do so. It was not until 4:17 p.m. that President Trump finally tweeted a video in which he told the rioters to go home.

The 187 minutes between the end of President Trump's speech and when he finally told the mob to leave the U.S. Capitol was a dereliction of duty. In the U.S. military, a service member is deemed to be "derelict in the performance of duties when that person willfully or negligently fails to perform that person's duties or when that person performs them in a culpably inefficient manner."[2] As Commander-in-Chief, President Trump had the power—more than any other American—to muster the U.S. Government's resources and end the attack on the U.S. Capitol. He willfully remained idle even as others, including his own Vice President, acted.

President Trump could have called top officials at the Department of Justice, the Department of Homeland Security, the Department of Defense, the F.B.I., the Capitol Police Department, or the DC Mayor's Office to ensure that they quelled the violence. He made no such calls. Instead, President Trump reached out to Rudolph Giuliani and friendly Members of Congress, seeking their assistance in delaying the joint session of Congress. And the President tweeted at 2:24 p.m., at the height of the violence, that his own Vice President lacked the "courage" to act—a statement that could only further enrage the mob. Meanwhile, Vice President Michael Pence assumed

577

the duties of the President, requesting the assistance of top officials, even though he was not in the chain of command and had no constitutional power to issue orders.

In testimony before the Select Committee, Chairman of the Joint Chiefs of Staff General Mark Milley explained that President Trump did "[n]othing," "[z]ero" to marshal the Government's resources during the assault on the U.S. Capitol.[3] In contrast, Vice President Pence had "two or three calls" with General Milley and other military officials—even as the mob hunted him. During those calls, Vice President Pence was "very animated" and "issued very explicit, very direct, unambiguous orders." The Vice President told Acting Secretary of Defense Chris Miller to "get the military down here, get the [National] [G]uard down here," and "put down this situation."[4] President Trump could have made those same demands. He chose not to do so—a damning fact that President Trump's own Chief of Staff, Mark Meadows, quickly tried to cover up.

"We have to kill the narrative that the Vice President is making all the decisions," General Milley recalled Meadows as saying. "We need to establish the narrative, you know, that the President is still in charge and that things are steady or stable," Meadows said, which General Milley described as a "[r]ed flag."[5] In his testimony, General Milley also reflected on what it meant for a President not to be taking action in a time of crisis:

> You know, you're the Commander in Chief. You've got an assault going on on the Capitol of the United States of America, and there's nothing? No call? Nothing? Zero? And it's not my place to, you know, pass judgment or—I'm the, you know—but no attempt to call the Secretary of Defense? No attempt to call the Vice President of the United States of America, who's down on the scene? To my knowledge, it wasn't—I just noted it.[6]

President Trump's closest advisors—both inside and out of the White House—implored him to act sooner. Earlier in the week, two of the President's most trusted aides, Eric Herschmann and Hope Hicks, both wanted President Trump to emphasize that January 6th would be a peaceful protest. President Trump refused.[7]

On the 6th, as the riot began to escalate, a colleague texted Hicks and wrote, "Hey, I know you're seeing this. But he really should tweet something about Being NON-violent."[8] "I'm not there," Hicks replied. "I suggested it several times Monday and Tuesday and he refused."[9]

Once the attack was underway, President Trump initially ignored the counsel of his own family, members of his administration, Republican elected officials, and friendly Fox News personalities. Both Ivanka Trump and Donald Trump, Jr. wanted their father to tell the rioters to go home sooner. The President delayed. At 2:38 p.m., President Trump sent this tweet: "Please support our Capitol Police and Law Enforcement. They are truly on the side of our Country. Stay peaceful!" [10] Sarah Matthews, the White House Deputy Press Secretary, told the Select Committee that President Trump resisted using the word "peaceful." The President added the words "Stay peaceful!" only after Ivanka Trump suggested the phrase. [11] Trump, Jr. quickly recognized that his father's tweet was insufficient. "He's got to condem [sic] this shit. Asap. The captiol [sic] police tweet is not enough," Trump, Jr. wrote in a text to White House Chief of Staff Mark Meadows. [12] President Trump did not tell the rioters to disperse in either his 2:38 p.m. tweet, or another tweet at 3:13 p.m. [13]

Multiple witnesses told the Select Committee that Minority Leader Kevin McCarthy contacted the President and others around him, desperately trying to get him to act. McCarthy's entreaties led nowhere. "I guess they're just more upset about the election theft than you are," President Trump told McCarthy. [14] Top lawyers in the White House Counsel's Office attempted to intercede. Two Fox News primetime personalities, always so obsequious, begged those around the President to get him to do more. But President Trump was unmoved.

There's no question that President Trump had the power to end the insurrection. He was not only the Commander-in-Chief of the U.S. military, but also of the rioters.

One member of the mob, Stephen Ayres, told the Select Committee that he and others quickly complied as soon as President Trump finally told them to go home. "[W]e literally left right after [President Trump's 4:17 p.m. video] come out. You know, to me if he would have done that earlier in the day, 1:30 [p.m.] . . . maybe we wouldn't be in this bad of a situation or something," Ayres said. [15] Another rioter, Jacob Chansley, commonly referred to as the "QAnon Shaman," was one of the first 30 rioters to enter the U.S. Capitol. Chansley told a reporter that he left the building because "Trump asked everybody to go home." [16] At 4:25 p.m., just eight minutes after President Trump tweeted his video, an Oath Keeper named Ed Vallejo messaged other members of his group, a fair number of whom were at the Capitol: "Gentleman [sic], Our Commander-in-Chief has just ordered us to go home. Comments?" [17]

Even then, President Trump did not disavow the rioters. He endorsed their cause, openly sympathized with them, and repeated his Big Lie once again. "I know your pain, I know you're hurt. We had an election that was stolen from us," President Trump said at the beginning of his 4:17 p.m. video. "It was a landslide election, and everyone knows it, especially the other side. But you have to go home now. We have to have peace. We have

President Trump appears on a monitor in the White House briefing room depicting a video he released instructing rioters to go home.

(Photo by Joshua Roberts/Getty Images)

to have law and order. We have to respect our great people in law and order. We don't want anybody hurt." The President portrayed the violence as something his political foes would use against him, saying: "This was a fraudulent election, but we can't play into the hands of these people." [18]

The President concluded his short video by again praising the men and women who had overrun the U.S. Capitol. "We have to have peace. So go home. We love you. You're very special," President Trump said. "You've seen what happens. You see the way others are treated that are so bad and so evil. I know how you feel, but go home, and go home in peace." [19]

Just after 6:00 p.m. on January 6th, President Trump issued his final tweet of the day, again lauding the rioters and justifying their cause. President Trump made excuses for the riot, saying this is what happens "when a sacred landslide election victory is so unceremoniously & viciously stripped away from great patriots who have been badly & unfairly treated for so long." The President added: "Go home with love & in peace. Remember this day forever!" [20]

The following day, President Trump's advisors encouraged him to deliver a short speech denouncing the attack on the U.S. Capitol. The President struggled to deliver his prepared remarks. According to Cassidy

Hutchinson, President Trump wanted to say that he would pardon the rioters. Lawyers in the White House Counsel's Office objected, so this language
was not included.[21] John McEntee, the Director of the White House Presidential Personnel Office, also testified that in the days following the attack,
he heard President Trump mention the possibility of a "blanket pardon" for
all those involved in the events of January 6th.[22]

President Trump never did give up on the prospect. Since leaving office,
the now former President has said he would consider "full pardons with an
apology to many" of the January 6th defendants if he is reelected.[23]

7.1 "REINSERT THE MIKE PENCE LINES"

President Trump tweeted three times on the morning of January 6th,
repeating a false claim of election fraud at 8:06 a.m.,[24] pressuring Vice
President Pence to delay the electoral count at 8:17 a.m.,[25] and urging
Republican party officials to do the same at 8:22 a.m.[26] He made calls to his
Republican allies in Congress, many of whom were already committed to
objecting to the electoral count.[27] And he dialed his lawyers and advisors—
including Steve Bannon and Rudolph Giuliani (twice), both of whom had
been counseling the President on how to stay in power.[28]

There was one person—critical to his plan—whom President Trump
tried to reach but couldn't. At 9:02 a.m., he asked the switchboard operator
to call his Vice President. Vice President Pence did not answer the call.[29]

Instead, between 9:52 a.m. and 10:18 a.m., the President spoke with his
speechwriter, Stephen Miller, about the words he would deliver at the Save
America Rally just hours later.[30] The former President's speech had come
together over the course of 36 hours, going from a screed aimed at encouraging congressional objections to one that would ultimately incite mob violence.[31]

Only four minutes after the call concluded, at 10:22 a.m., Miller emailed
revisions to the speechwriters, instructing them to "[s]tart inputting these
changes asap" that included "red highlights marking POTUS edits."[32] The
President had made some cosmetic additions, like peppering in the word
"corrupt" throughout,[33] but there was one substantive edit—a new
target—that would focus the crowd's anger on one man.

None of the preceding drafts mentioned Vice President Pence whatsoever. But now, at the very last minute, President Trump slipped in the following sentences calling the Vice President out by name:

> Today, we will see whether Republicans stand strong for the integ-
> rity of our elections. And we will see whether Mike Pence enters
> history as a truly great and courageous leader. All he has to do is

President Trump speaks with speechwriter Stephen Miller about his Ellipse speech in the Oval Office on the morning of January 6, 2021.
(Photo provided to the Select Committee by the National Archives and Records Administration)

refer the illegally-submitted electoral votes back to the states that were given false and fraudulent information where they want to recertify. With only 3 of the 7 states in question we win and become President and have the power of the veto.[34]

No one on the speechwriting team could explain why President Trump added these lines just 30 minutes before he was originally scheduled to speak at 11:00 a.m.[35] But by 10:49 a.m., Vincent Haley, a speechwriter who was helping load the teleprompter at the Ellipse, was told to hold off and delete the mention of the Vice President—for now.[36] Miller said that Eric Herschmann, a lawyer who was one of the President's senior advisors, asked him in a "brief sidebar" that morning to omit reference to the Vice President and his role in the certification process because he "didn't concur with the legal analysis" and that it "wouldn't advance the ball" but would be "counterproductive" instead.[37] As detailed in Chapter 5, Herschmann and others in the White House were vocal critics of Dr. John Eastman's theory, which claimed that the Vice President had the unilateral power to reject electors during the joint session of Congress. President Trump repeatedly pressured Pence to either reject certified electors, or delay the

President Trump on a phone call with Vice President Mike Pence in the Oval Office on the morning of January 6, 2021.
(Photo provided to the Select Committee by the National Archives and Records Administration)

electoral count based on Eastman's unconstitutional and illegal theory. Vice President Pence would not budge. The Vice President consistently rejected President Trump's demands.

After tweeting four more times that morning—all of them spreading lies about the election[38]—the President apparently thought he had one last chance to convince his number two to overrule the will of the American people.

As recounted in Chapter 5, President Trump called Vice President Pence at 11:17 a.m.[39] The call between the two men—during which the President soon grew "frustrat[ed] or heated,"[40] visibly upset,[41] and "angry"[42]—lasted nearly 20 minutes.[43] And President Trump insulted Vice President Pence when he refused to obstruct or delay the joint session.

After that call, General Keith Kellogg said that the people in the room immediately went back to editing the Ellipse speech.[44] At 11:30 a.m., Miller emailed his assistant, Robert Gabriel, with no text in the body but the subject line: "insert—stand by for phone call."[45] At 11:33 a.m., Gabriel emailed the speechwriting team: "REINSERT THE MIKE PENCE LINES. Confirm receipt."[46] One minute later, speechwriter Ross Worthington confirmed

President Trump looks backstage at the crowd gathered at the Ellipse.
(Photo provided to the Select Committee by the National Archives and Records Administration)

that he had reached Vincent Haley by phone.[47] Haley corroborated that he added one "tough sentence about the Vice President" while he was at the teleprompter.[48]

The final written draft had the following Pence reference: "And we will see whether Mike Pence enters history as a truly great and courageous leader."[49] Haley wasn't confident that line was what he reinserted, but email traffic and teleprompter drafts produced by the National Archives and Records Administration (NARA) indicate that he was mistaken.[50]

After defying President Trump's pressure, Vice President Pence—and the ire of the President he inspired—was back in the speech.

After the heated call, President Trump's personal assistant Nicholas Luna handed him a message on White House card stock and the President departed for the Ellipse to give his speech.[51] Preserved by NARA, the message read: "THEY ARE READY FOR YOU WHEN YOU ARE."[52] When it finally came time for him to speak, President Trump repeatedly directed his anger at Vice President Pence—often ad-libbing lines that were not included in the draft text.

7.2 "I'LL BE THERE WITH YOU"

From a tent backstage at the Ellipse, President Trump looked out at the crowd of approximately 53,000 supporters and became enraged. Just under half of those gathered—a sizeable stretch of about 25,000 people[53]— refused to walk through the magnetometers and be screened for weapons,[54] leaving the venue looking half-empty to the television audience at home.

According to testimony received by the Committee, earlier that morning at the White House, the President was told that the onlookers were unwilling to pass through the magnetometers because they were armed. "We have enough space, sir. They don't want to come in right now," Deputy Chief of Staff Tony Ornato reportedly told President Trump. "They have weapons that they don't want confiscated by the Secret Service." [55]

So, when President Trump got to the rally site and could see the crowd for himself, "[h]e was fucking furious," as Cassidy Hutchinson later texted Ornato.[56] Hutchinson testified that just minutes before addressing the crowd, President Trump shouted to his advance team: "I don't [fucking] care that they have weapons. They're not here to hurt *me*. Take the [fucking] mags away. Let my people in. They can march to the Capitol from here. Take the [fucking] mags away." [57]

By noon, President Trump took to the stage at the Ellipse.[58] The President wanted all of those in attendance, including those who hadn't passed through the magnetometers, to come closer to the stage. "And I'd love to have if those tens of thousands of people would be allowed," President Trump said. "But I'd love it if they could be allowed to come up here with us. Is that possible? Can you just let [them] come up, please?" [59]

President Trump repeatedly made it clear to those around him in the days before January 6th that he wanted to march to the Capitol alongside his supporters. That is, President Trump wanted to join his supporters in what the Secret Service refers to as an "off-the-record" movement (OTR).

While the President spoke, Hutchinson texted Ornato, "He also kept mentioning OTR to Capitol before he took the stage." [60] Minutes before the President stepped out, Chief of Staff Mark Meadows assured the President he was working on it.[61]

President Trump's plan to march appeared once in an early draft of the script, then a later revision was made to add the word "building" after "Capitol," making it clear exactly where the crowd should go.[62] And the President repeatedly told the crowd that he would join them.

"[A]fter this, we're going to walk down, and I'll be there with you, we're going to walk down, we're going to walk down," he said to the crowd. "[W]e're going to walk down to the Capitol, and we're going to cheer on

CHAPTER 7

our brave senators and congressmen and women, and we're probably not going to be cheering so much for some of them." [63]

President Trump used the phrase scripted for him by his White House speechwriters, "peacefully and patriotically" once, about 20 minutes into his speech.[64] Then he spent the next 50-or-so minutes amping up his crowd with lies about the election, attacking his own Vice President and Republican Members of Congress, and exhorting the crowd to fight. "And we fight. We fight like hell" the President said to a crowd that had already spent the day chanting, "Fight for Trump! Fight for Trump!," and that would keep up the chorus when storming the Capitol.[65]

Finally, he told the crowd where to go to "take back our country": "So we're going to, we're going to walk down Pennsylvania Avenue. I love Pennsylvania Avenue. And we're going to the Capitol, and we're going to try and give . . . we're going to try and give our Republicans, the weak ones because the strong ones don't need any of our help. We're going to try and give them the kind of pride and boldness that they need to take back our country. So let's walk down Pennsylvania Avenue." [66]

When the President announced his intentions from the microphone, people listened.

House Republican Leader Representative. Kevin McCarthy called Hutchinson mid-speech: [67]

"Do you guys think you're coming to my office[?]" he asked her.[68]
She assured him that they weren't coming at all.[69]

"Figure it out. Don't come up here," he replied.[70]

The announcement from the stage put the Secret Service on alert, prompting agents to designate over email a last-minute response team "to filter in with the crowds" on the President's "walk/motorcade over" to the Capitol and establish an emergency plan "if things go south." [71] White House security officials were monitoring the situation in real time, remarking that President Trump was "going to the Capitol" and that "they are finding the best route now." [72] Nonetheless, these staffers were in "a state of shock," [73] because they knew—particularly if the President joined—this would "no longer [be] a rally." [74]

"[W]e all knew . . . that this was going to move to something else if he physically walked to the Capitol," an employee said. "I don't know if you want to use the word 'insurrection,' 'coup,' whatever. We all knew that this would move from a normal democratic . . . public event into something else." [75]

But the logistics made the move all but impossible.

It was complicated for the Secret Service to coordinate a presidential movement even on a normal day. But today was not a normal day. Tens of thousands of President Trump's supporters had flooded into downtown DC in the days before the rally, and the Secret Service would have to account for that unpredictability. By the end of the President's speech, it was clear that the crowd at the Capitol was growing violent.

At 1:19 p.m., a Secret Service agent wrote to Bobby Engel, the head of President Trump's Secret Service detail: "FYSA . . . [Capitol Police] having serious challenges securing [the Capitol]. Nine priority breach attempts at this time. OTR to anywhere near there is not advisable. Give me a call when free. Front Office concerned about OTR to [the Capitol]."[76]

7.3 THE PRESIDENT'S ANGER WHEN HE COULD NOT MARCH TO THE CAPITOL

President Trump concluded his remarks at 1:10 p.m. Luna heard the President mention his intention to join the march to the Capitol "after he finished his remarks."[77] Just before the President got into his vehicle, Meadows told him, "We're going to work on it, sir."[78] President Trump was seated in his motorcade vehicle by 1:17 p.m.[79]

The Committee received information informally from current and former members of the Secret Service and former White House staff relevant to what happened next—what a number of witnesses have described as an "angry," "irate," or "furious" interaction in the Presidential vehicle between the President and the Secret Service.[80] That initial information, received informally, shaped the Committee's questioning of witnesses. The Committee's principal concern was that the President *actually intended* to participate personally in the January 6th efforts at the Capitol, leading the effort to overturn the election either from inside the Chamber or from a stage outside the Capitol. The Committee regarded those facts as important because they are relevant to President Trump's intent on January 6th. But a book published by Mark Meadows in November 2021 made the categorical claim that the President *never* intended to travel to the Capitol that day.[81] Because the Meadows book conflicted sharply with information that was being received by the Committee, the Committee became increasingly wary that witnesses might intentionally conceal what happened.

In our initial informal discussion with the lead of the President's detail, Robert Engel confirmed that President Trump did wish to travel to the Capitol from the Ellipse, but stated that he did not recall many other details.[82] But the Committee also received information from Kayleigh McEnany and Cassidy Hutchinson that also directly contradicted Mark Meadows's book and provided considerably more detail. McEnany testified that

President Trump did indeed wish to travel to the Capitol on January 6th, and continued to have that goal even after returning from the Ellipse to the White House.[83] McEnany, who spoke with President Trump shortly after he returned to the White House, recalls him expressing a desire to go to the Capitol: "I recall him . . . saying that he wanted to physically walk and be a part of the march and then saying that he would ride the Beast if he needed to, ride in the Presidential limo."[84] When asked, McEnany confirmed that "yes, he did seem sincere about wanting to do that."[85] Hutchinson's testimony was generally consistent with the information the Select Committee was receiving informally. Like McEnany, Hutchinson confirmed that the President did ask to be transported to Capitol Hill.[86] Many other White House witnesses would ultimately confirm that President Trump wished to travel to the Capitol on January 6th, comprehensively rebutting the false statements in Meadows's book.[87]

Part of Hutchinson's account was a second-hand description of what occurred in the Presidential vehicle, which built upon and was consistent with information the Committee has received informally.

Hutchinson testified that, when she returned from the Ellipse, Ornato was standing outside his office door when he "waved me down," Hutchinson said. The two of them walked into Ornato's office, and he shut the door behind them.[88] Engel was already there, sitting in a chair "looking down, kind of looking a little lost and kind of discombobulated."[89]

According to Hutchinson, Ornato then recounted a struggle in the President's car.[90] At no point during Ornato's telling—or at any point thereafter—did Engel indicate that what Ornato relayed was untrue.[91]

Another witness, a White House employee with national security responsibilities, provided the Committee with a similar description: Ornato related the "irate" interaction in the presidential vehicle to this individual in Ornato's White House office with Engel present.[92] And just as Hutchinson testified, this employee told the Select Committee that Engel listened to Ornato's retelling of the episode and did not dispute it: "I don't remember his specific body language, but . . . [h]e did not deny the fact that the President was irate."[93] Engel testified that he does not recall either the conversation with Hutchinson or the similar conversation with the White House employee with national security responsibilities.[94]

The Committee regarded both Hutchinson and the corroborating testimony by the White House employee with national security responsibilities national security official as earnest and has no reason to conclude that either had a reason to invent their accounts. A different Secret Service

Cassidy Hutchinson describes a story relayed to her by Tony Ornato about President Trump's desire to go to the Capitol after the Ellipse speech on January 6th during a January 6th Select Committee hearing.

(Photo by Brandon Bell/Getty Images)

agent, who served on a protective detail at the White House and was present in the presidential motorcade at the Ellipse, provided this view:

> Committee Staff: Just a couple of additional questions. Ms. Hutchinson has suggested to the Committee that you sympathized with her after her testimony, and believed her account. Is that accurate?
>
> Witness: I have no—yeah, that's accurate. I have no reason—I mean, we—we became friends. We worked—I worked every day with her for 6 months. Yeah, she became a friend of mine. We had a good working relationship. I have no reason—she's never done me wrong. She's never lied that I know of. I don't have any reason—I don't—I don't distrust Ms. Hutchinson.[95]

Also, the White House employee with national security responsibilities indicated that knowledge of the angry altercation in the Presidential vehicle was known within the White House—and was "[water] cooler talk."[96] In addition, Hutchinson has provided testimony to the Committee about efforts by her prior counsel, who was apparently paid by a Trump-funded organization, to suggest that Hutchinson did not need to testify about the issue in the presidential vehicle, could suggest that she "did not recall" it, or should downplay it.[97]

To further corroborate the accounts received of President Trump's intent to travel to the Capitol, the Committee interviewed a member of the Metropolitan Police who was also present in the motorcade, Officer Mark Robinson. Officer Robinson confirmed that he was aware contemporaneously of the "heated discussion" that took place in the Presidential vehicle:

> Committee Staff: And was there any description of what was occurring in the car?
>
> Mr. Robinson: No. Only that—the only description I received was that the President was upset and that he was adamant about going to the Capitol, and there was a heated discussion about that.
>
> Committee Staff: When you say "heated," is that your word, or is that the word that was described by the TS agent?
>
> Mr. Robinson: No. The word described by the TS agent meaning that the President was upset, and he was saying there was a heated argument or discussion about going to the Capitol.
>
> . . . .
>
> Mr. Schiff: So about how many times would you say you've been part of that motorcade with the President?
>
> Mr. Robinson: Probably over a hundred times.
>
> Mr. Schiff: And, in that hundred times, have you ever witnessed another discussion of an argument or a heated discussion with the President where the President was contradicting where he was supposed to go or what the Secret Service believed was safe?
>
> Mr. Robinson: No.[98]

The Committee also interviewed the Secret Service agent who was in the same car as Officer Robinson. That person shared a similar account, and confirmed that he did not take issue with Officer Robinson's testimony: "[The driver of the Presidential car] said something to the effect of, 'The President is pretty adamant that he wants to go to the Capitol,'" the agent said, recalling what he had heard on the 6th.[99]

In addition, the Committee interviewed the USSS Press Secretary, who communicated with both Engel and with the driver in the presidential vehicle after Hutchinson appeared publicly. That witness indicated that Engel's account of the events confirmed that the President was indeed angry, or furious.[100] In fact, when asked about a reporter's tweet indicating that sources within the Secret Service confirmed that "Trump was furious about not being [able] to go to [the] Capitol with his supporters," the Press Secretary said he "certainly corroborated it" with the reporter because "that's what I had been told, you know, that [the President] was upset, he was agitated, about not being able to go[.]" [101]

In addition to the testimony above, the Committee has reviewed hundreds of thousands of new Secret Service documents, including many demonstrating that the Secret Service had been informed of potential violence at the Capitol before the Ellipse rally on January 6th. (These documents were critical to our understanding of what the Secret Service and White House knew about the threat to the Capitol on January 6th.) The Committee has also more recently conducted additional interviews with Engel and Ornato, and has also interviewed the driver of the Presidential vehicle.

Both Engel and the driver [102] testified that, within 30 seconds of getting into the vehicle, the President asked if he could travel to the Capitol.[103] This again is directly inconsistent with the account of events in Meadows's book. According to Engel, he told the President immediately that the move wasn't happening.[104] The President was unhappy with Engel's response and began "pushing pretty hard to go." [105] The President repeatedly asked why he could not go to the Capitol.[106] Engel replied that the Secret Service "didn't have any people at the Capitol" to provide the President with appropriate security.[107] The President responded angrily, telling Engel and the driver "I'm the President and I'll decide where I get to go." [108] He reassured Engel that "it would essentially be fine and that the people there [meaning the people who were marching from the Ellipse to the Capitol at President Trump's instruction] were [Trump] supporters or something to that effect," [109] According to the Secret Service agent driving the vehicle, the President was "animated and irritated" about not going to the Capitol.[110]

According to Mr. Engel, he ultimately told the President that they would "assess what our options were and wait until we can get a plan in place before we went down there." [111] We note that the driver's account acknowledged President Trump's anger to a greater degree than either Engel's initial account in Spring 2022, or his more recent account in November 2022. Engel did not characterize the exchange in the vehicle the way Hutchinson described the account she heard from Ornato, and indicated that he did not recall President Trump gesturing toward him.[112] Engel did not recall being present when Ornato gave either Hutchinson or the White House employee with national security responsibilities an accounting of the events.[113] The driver testified that he did not recall seeing what President Trump was doing and did not recall whether there was movement.[114]

The Select Committee has great respect for the men and women of the Secret Service. That said, it is difficult to fully reconcile the accounts of several of the witnesses who provided information with what we heard from Engel and Ornato.[115] But the principal factual point here is clear and undisputed: President Trump specifically and repeatedly requested to be taken to the Capitol. He was insistent and angry, and continued to push to travel to the Capitol even after returning to the White House.

The motorcade didn't disband upon arriving to the White House, as they usually do. Instead, they were instructed to stand by in case the President's move to the Capitol did indeed happen.[116] The Select Committee received a document from the Secret Service that reflects that at 1:25 p.m., "PPD IS ADVISING THAT [THE PRESIDENT] IS PLANNING ON HOLDING AT THE WHITE HOUSE FOR THE NEXT APPROXIMATE TWO HOURS, THEN MOVING TO THE CAPITOL."[117] "They had not made a decision whether or not we were going to transport the President to the Capitol," Robinson was told.[118]

Engel testified that he went to Ornato's office when he returned to the West Wing in order to discuss a possible move to the Capitol by President Trump.[119] Given the deteriorating security conditions at the Capitol, it was quickly determined that they could not safely transport the President there.[120] The motorcade waited on West Executive Drive approximately 40 minutes before finally receiving word from the Secret Service that the move had been officially nixed. Internal Secret Service communications bear this out: Not until 1:55 p.m. did Engel notify other agents via email that "[w]e are not doing an OTR to [the Capitol]."[121]

7.4 "WE'RE GOING TO TRY TO GET THE PRESIDENT TO PUT OUT A STATEMENT"

Minutes after arriving back at the White House, the President ran into a member of the White House staff and asked whether he or she watched his speech on television.[122]

"Sir, they cut it off because they're rioting down at the Capitol," the employee said.

The President asked what he or she meant by that.

"[T]hey're rioting down there at the Capitol," the employee repeated.

"Oh really?" the President asked. "All right, let's go see."[123]

A photograph taken by the White House photographer—the last one permitted until later in the day—captures the moment the President heard the news from the employee at 1:21 p.m.[124] By that time, if not sooner, he had been made aware of the violent riot at the Capitol.

President Trump walked through the corridor from the Oval Office into the Presidential Dining Room and sat down at the table with the television remote and a Diet Coke close at hand.[125] For the rest of the afternoon—as his country faced an hours-long attack—he hunkered down in or around the dining room, watching television.[126] He left only for a few minutes—from 4:03 p.m. to 4:07 p.m.—to film a video in the Rose Garden, only a few steps away, after hours of arm-twisting.[127] But otherwise, the President remained in the dining room until 6:27 p.m., when he returned to his private residence.[128]

What happened during the 187 minutes from 1:10 p.m. to 4:17 p.m., when President Trump finally told the rioters to go home, is—from an official standpoint—undocumented.

For instance, the Presidential Daily Diary—the schedule that tracks every meeting and phone call in which the President partakes—is inexplicably blank between 1:21 p.m. and 4:03 p.m.[129] When asked to explain the gap in record-keeping on and around January 6th, White House officials in charge of its maintenance provided no credible explanation, including: "I don't recall a specific reason." [130]

The men who spent most of the afternoon in that room with the President, Mark Meadows and Dan Scavino, both refused to comply with lawful subpoenas from the Select Committee.[131] Others in the dining room appeared before the Select Committee but cited executive privilege to avoid answering questions about their direct communications with President Trump.[132] Others who worked just outside of the Oval Office, like the President's personal secretaries Molly Michael and Austin Ferrer Piran Basauldo, claimed not to remember nearly anything from one of the most memorable days in recent American history.[133]

The White House photographer, Shealah Craighead, had been granted access to photograph the President during his January 6th speech, but once she got to the White House—and it became clear that an attack was unfolding on the Capitol's steps—she was turned away.[134]

"The President [didn't] want any photos," she was told.[135]

Here's what President Trump did during the 187 minutes between the end of his speech and when he finally told rioters to go home: For hours, he watched the attack from his TV screen.[136] His channel of choice was Fox News.[137] He issued a few tweets, some on his own inclination and some only at the repeated behest of his daughter and other trusted advisors.[138] He made several phone calls, some to his personal lawyer Rudolph Giuliani, some to Members of Congress about continuing their objections to the electoral certification, even though the attack was well underway.[139]

Here's what President Trump did not do: He did not call any relevant law enforcement agency to ensure they were working to quell the violence. He did not call the Secretary of Defense; he did not call the Attorney General; he did not call the Secretary of Homeland Security.[140] And for hours on end, he refused the repeated requests—from nearly everyone who talked to him—to simply tell the mob to go home.[141]

Throughout the afternoon, senior staff regularly entered the room to give him updates on what was happening at the Capitol.[142] And, of course, President Trump used Twitter, where information is shared on an instantaneous basis.

Shortly after President Trump entered the dining room, White House Press Secretary Kayleigh McEnany swung by to "check in with him" about the letter Vice President Pence released around 1:00 p.m. announcing that he would not, in fact, overturn the will of the voters.

The President, once again, brought up going to the Capitol.[143] McEnany recorded what he said in her notes, certain of which she later produced to the Select Committee: "POTUS wanted to walk to [sic] capital. Physically walk. He said fine ride beast," referring to the nickname for the presidential vehicle. "Meadows said not safe enough[.]"[144]

Meadows told Hutchinson at some point in the day that "the President wasn't happy that Bobby [Engel] didn't pull it off for him," meaning the trip to the Capitol, "and that Mark didn't work hard enough to get the movement on the books."[145]

Despite the turmoil just outside its walls, the proceedings in the joint session—which had begun at 1:00 p.m.—were still ongoing, and the President was watching them on the television.[146] He was eager to know which senators were lodging objections on his behalf.[147] "Back there and he wants list of senators," McEnany's notes read. "Who [sic] objecting to what. He's calling them one by one."[148]

The Select Committee subpoenaed several Members of Congress who reportedly spoke with President Trump during the afternoon.[149] None of them complied.[150]

Cellular records obtained by the Select Committee suggest that President Trump was on the phone with his lawyer Rudolph Giuliani at least twice during this period. Giuliani's phone connected with the White House switchboard for 3 minutes and 53 seconds at 1:39 p.m. and again for more than 8 minutes at 2:03 p.m.[151] Between the two calls, at 1:49 p.m., President Trump tweeted a link to a video of his speech from the Ellipse.[152]

Before 1:57 p.m., Herschmann phoned Senior Advisor to the President Jared Kushner—who was on a plane travelling home from overseas—advising him that "people are trying to break into the Capitol" and that "this is getting pretty ugly."[153]

"We're going to see what we can do here," Herschmann said. "We're going to try to get the President to put out a statement."[154]

7.5 "HE DOESN'T WANT TO DO ANYTHING"

Throughout the afternoon, the President's advisors tried to get him to tell the mob to leave the Capitol, but to no avail.

Ben Williamson, the White House Acting Director of Communications, watched on the news as officers and rioters pepper sprayed each other and crowds used bicycle barricades to push against officers holding the line.[155] He and Sarah Matthews, the Deputy Press Secretary, devised a plan: He would go to Meadows and she would go to McEnany to urge that the President issue a statement.[156] Williamson first texted Meadows:

"Would recommend POTUS put out a tweet about respecting the police over at the Capitol."[157]

Minutes later, around 2:05 p.m., Hutchinson found Meadows seated in his office on the couch, absorbed by his cell phone screen.[158]

"Are you watching the TV, chief?" she asked. He indicated he was.

"Have you talked to the President?" she asked.

"No," he replied. "He wants to be alone right now."[159]

Rioters broke into the west side of the Capitol building around 2:13 p.m.[160] Just a few minutes later, Hutchinson saw Cipollone "barreling down the hallway" and—after looking at Hutchinson and shaking his head—opened the door to Meadows's office unannounced.[161] Meadows was right where she left him, "still sitting on his phone."[162]

"The rioters have gotten to the Capitol, Mark. We need to go down and see the President now," she heard Cipollone say.[163] Cipollone would not confirm or deny any of this exchange, citing executive privilege.[164]

"He doesn't want to do anything, Pat," Meadows said, peering up from his phone.[165]

"Mark something needs to be done, or people are going to die and the blood's gonna be on your [fucking] hands," Cipollone said. "This is getting out of control. I'm going down there."[166]

Meadows finally stood up from the couch and walked with Cipollone toward the dining room to meet with the President.[167]

7.6 "HE THINKS MIKE DESERVES IT"

At exactly 2:24 p.m., President Trump made his first public statement during the attack on the Capitol by tweet. It read nothing like the statement his advisors had envisioned. It read:

> Mike Pence didn't have the courage to do what should have been done to protect our Country and our Constitution, giving States a chance to certify a corrected set of facts, not the fraudulent or inaccurate ones which they were asked to previously certify. USA demands the truth! [168]

Minutes later, Meadows and Cipollone returned from their talk with the President.[169] No statement was forthcoming.

"Mark, we need to do something more. They're literally calling for the Vice President to be [fucking] hung," Hutchinson heard Cipollone say.[170]

"You heard him, Pat," Meadows replied. "He thinks Mike deserves it. He doesn't think they're doing anything wrong." [171]

"This is [fucking] crazy. We need to be doing something more," Cipollone said.[172]

Cipollone told the Select Committee that "there needed to be an immediate and forceful response, statement, public statement, that people need to leave the Capitol now." [173] He said he was "pretty clear" about his view in the White House that day, and he made that view known as soon as he became aware of the unrest.[174] He would not comment on how the President responded, or on this conversation with Meadows, citing executive privilege.[175] He did indicate that everyone in the White House—except President Trump—agreed that people needed to leave the Capitol:

> Vice Chair Cheney: And who on the staff did not want people to leave the Capitol?
>
> Mr. Cipollone: On the staff?
>
> Vice Chair Cheney: In the White House.
>
> Mr. Cipollone: I can't think of anybody on that day who didn't want people to get out of the Capitol once the—particularly once the violence started. No. I mean—
>
> Mr. Schiff: What about the President?
>
> Vice Chair Cheney: Yeah.
>
> Mr. Cipollone: Well, she said the staff. So I answered.
>
> Vice Chair Cheney: No. I said in the White House.

Noose set up outside of the Capitol on January 6, 2021.

(Photo by Drew Angerer/Getty Images)

Mr. Cipollone: Oh, I'm sorry. I apologize. I thought you said who else on the staff. [*Pauses to confer with counsel*] Yeah. I can't reveal communications. But obviously I think, you know—yeah.[176]

What the President *did* tweet—a broadside at his Vice President—enlarged the target on Vice President Pence's back. A Secret Service agent in the Protective Intelligence Division, tasked with monitoring threats against protectees in part by scouring social media, told his colleagues the tweet was "probably not going to be good for Pence."[177]

A second agent in reply noted that it had garnered "[o]ver 24K likes in under 2 mins."[178]

7.7 "I GUESS THEY'RE JUST MORE UPSET ABOUT THE ELECTION THEFT THAN YOU ARE"

Minutes after drawing increased attention to his besieged Vice President, the President called newly elected Senator Tommy Tuberville of Alabama at 2:26 p.m.[179] He misdialed, calling Senator Mike Lee of Utah instead, but one passed the phone to the other in short order.[180]

President Trump wanted to talk objections to the electoral count. But Senator Tuberville—along with every other elected official trapped and surrounded in the building—had other things on his mind.[181]

"I said, 'Mr. President, they've taken the Vice President out. They want me to get off the phone, I gotta go,'" Senator Tuberville told reporters.[182] " '[W]e're not doing much work here right now.' "[183]

In the next half hour, between 2:26 p.m. and 3:06 p.m., President Trump spoke with House Leader Kevin McCarthy.[184]

Leader McCarthy told the public in a live interview with CBS News, while he and his colleagues were sheltering at a secure location,[185] that he was "very clear" in telling President Trump "to talk to the nation to tell them to stop this."[186]

Leader McCarthy later recounted his conversation to a number of people, including Representative Jaime Herrera Beutler, a Republican congresswoman from Washington State.[187] "You have got to get on TV, you've got to get on Twitter, you've got to call these people off," he said he told the President.[188]

"[These] aren't my people, you know, these are—these are Antifa," President Trump insisted, against all evidence.[189] "They're your people. They literally just came through my office windows, and my staff are running for cover. I mean, they're running for their lives. You need to call them off," Leader McCarthy told him.[190]

What President Trump said next was "chilling," in Representative Herrera Beutler's words.[191]

"Well, Kevin, I guess they're just more upset about the election theft than you are," the President said.[192]

The call then devolved into a swearing match.[193]

Mick Mulvaney, former Chief of Staff to President Trump, had a similar call with Leader McCarthy in the days after the attack. McCarthy told Mulvaney that he urged the President to get the rioters to stop, and the President replied, "Kevin, maybe these people are just more angry about this than you are."[194]

Marc Short, the Vice President's Chief of Staff, spoke with Leader McCarthy later that afternoon.[195] Leader McCarthy told Short that he had spoken with President Trump and that he was "frustrat[ed]" that the White House was "not taking the circumstance as seriously as they should at that moment."[196] The administration was demonstrating a "lack of response or lack of responsibility," Leader McCarthy told Short.[197]

At 2:49 p.m.—as the violence escalated—President Trump's speechwriter Gabriel Robert texted someone: "Potus im sure is loving this."[198]

7.8 "STAY PEACEFUL!"

No one was getting through to the President.

So Herschmann went to Ivanka Trump's office, hoping she would come to the dining room and be "a calming influence" on her father.[199] Herschmann "just sort of barged in" and told her to turn on the television.[200] After taking in a few of the violent scenes together, Herschmann and Ivanka Trump left the room and walked to the dining room, where her father was holed up.[201]

At 2:38 p.m., the President issued a tweet:[202]

> Please support our Capitol Police and Law Enforcement. They are truly on the side of our Country. Stay peaceful![203]

Ivanka Trump told the Select Committee that the President "did not push back on [her] suggestion" to issue the tweet, and that it was either she or President Trump himself who suggested the last line, "Stay peaceful!"[204] She confirmed there may have been some tweaking of the wording.[205] McEnany, who was in the room at the time, wrote in her notes that "I say add 'we support PEACEFUL protest.' Ivanka add stay peaceful! Instead."[206] To the Select Committee, McEnany echoed Ivanka Trump that the President wasn't resistant in any way to putting out the message.[207]

But in private, McEnany told a different story to her deputy Sarah Matthews.

Back in the White House press office, Matthews told McEnany that the tweet did not go far enough in condemning the violence.[208] McEnany— noting that other staffers in the room were distracted—said "in a hushed tone . . . that the President did not want to include any sort of mention of peace in that tweet."[209]

That took "some convincing on their part," McEnany said, and "it wasn't until Ivanka Trump suggested the phrase 'Stay peaceful!' that he finally agreed to include it."[210]

Ivanka Trump repeatedly returned to the dining room to counsel her father throughout the day. It has been reported that each time Ivanka Trump "thought she had made headway" with her father, Meadows would call her "to say the [P]resident still needed more persuading"—a cycle that repeated itself over "several hours" that afternoon.[211] After one such trip, Ivanka Trump told the Select Committee she went to her husband's office next door because she needed to "regroup" and collect herself.[212]

Several witnesses corroborated pieces of this account. General Kellogg said he saw Ivanka Trump coming and going from the dining room at least twice that afternoon.[213] Hutchinson said that it was "several times."[214] Once, Ivanka Trump reportedly left her father with a look on her face as if

Sarah Matthews testifies at a January 6th Select Committee hearing.
(Photo by House Creative Services)

"[s]he had just had a tough conversation." [215] Radford, Ivanka Trump's Chief of Staff, saw that she was "[v]isibly upset" but continued going "down there when people were asking her to be down there and trying to get action taken." [216]

Radford told the Select Committee that Ivanka Trump believed that "[s]omething should be said or put out that was even stronger." [217]

Hutchinson, too, recalled Ivanka Trump dropping by Meadows's office alongside Cipollone and talking about trying to convince her father to say something "more direct than he had wanted to at that time and throughout the afternoon." [218]

"I remember her saying at various points," Hutchinson said, "she wanted her dad to send them home. She wanted her dad to tell them to go home peacefully, and she wanted to include language that he necessarily wasn't on board with at the time." [219]

7.9 "THE PRESIDENT NEEDS TO STOP THIS ASAP"

President Trump's 2:38 p.m. tweet did not condemn the violence at the Capitol. It did not tell rioters to leave the building.

Testimony footage of former White House Press Secretary Kayleigh McEnany is played during a January 6th Select Committee hearing.

(Photo by Pool/Getty Images)

In the minutes before the tweet, Fox News—on the President's screen—relayed that the Capitol was on lockdown; [220] that Capitol police officers were injured; that rioters were in the building and "just feet from the House chamber." [221] In the minutes afterward, networks would report there was tear gas in the Capitol, forcing Members of Congress to evacuate in protective masks. [222] At 2:39 p.m., Secret Service agents reported that "[m]ore just got in." [223]

"I don't know how they're gonna retake the Capitol building back at this point," one agent wrote to others two minutes later. [224]

At 2:44 p.m., a Capitol police officer shot a rioter named Ashli Babbitt. [225] A handwritten note—dashed off onto a White House pocket card and preserved by the National Archives—read: "1x civilian gunshot wound to chest @ door of House cha[m]ber." [226] One White House employee saw the note on the dining table in front of President Trump. [227]

A barrage of text messages inundated Meadows's phone with a consistent plea. [228] Everyone from conservative media personalities to Republican allies in Congress—and even the President's own family—urged the President to do more:

Representative Marjorie Taylor Greene, 2:28 p.m.: "Mark I was just told there is an active shooter on the first floor of the Capitol Please tell the President to calm people[.] This isn't the way to solve anything." [229]

Laura Ingraham, 2:32 p.m.: "Hey Mark, The [sic] president needs to tell people in the Capitol to go home." "This is hurting all of us." "He is destroying his legacy and playing into every stereotype . . . we lose all credibility against the BLM/Antifa crowd if things go South." "You can tell him I said this." [230]

Mick Mulvaney, 2:35 p.m.: "Mark: he needs to stop this, now. Can I do anything to help?" [231]

Representative Barry Loudermilk, 2:44 p.m.: "It's really bad up here on the hill." "They have breached the Capitol." [232] At 2:48 p.m., Meadows responded: "POTUS is engaging." [233] At 2:49 p.m., Loudermilk responded: "Thanks. This doesn't help our cause." [234]

Representative William Timmons, 2:46 p.m.: "The president needs to stop this ASAP." [235] At 2:49 p.m., Meadows responded: "We are doing it." [236]

Donald Trump, Jr., 2:53 p.m.: "He's got to condem [sic] this shit. Asap. The captiol [sic] police tweet is not enough." [237] Meadows responded: "I am pushing it hard. I agree." [238] Later, Trump, Jr., continued: "This his [sic] one you go to the mattresses on. They will try to fuck his entire legacy on this if it gets worse." [239]

White House staff discussed issuing yet another, stronger statement to address the ongoing—and escalating—violence. Around 3:00 p.m., one proposal was written in block capital letters on a pocket card from the chief of staff's office:

ANYONE WHO ENTERED THE CAPITOL ILLEGALLY WITHOUT PROPER AUTHORITY SHOULD LEAVE IMMEDIATELY[.] [240]

The handwriting appears to have been scrawled quickly and somewhat messily. Hutchinson recalled Meadows returning from the dining room with the note in hand and placing it on her desk. [241] The word "illegally" had been newly crossed out. [242]

But there would be no further action, Meadows told her. [243]

At 3:13 p.m., 35 minutes after his last tweet, the President issued another tweet. Rather than coming out with a stronger statement, the 3:13 p.m. tweet largely parroted the one preceding it:

Guns are drawn in the House Chamber on January 6th as rioters attempt to break in.
(Photo by Drew Angerer/Getty Images)

I am asking for everyone at the U.S. Capitol to remain peaceful. No violence! Remember, WE are the Party of Law & Order—respect the Law and our great men and women in Blue. Thank you![244]

Ivanka Trump—who was in the room when her father published the message—told the Select Committee that "the gravity of the situation" made her feel "that it would be helpful to tweet again."[245] "The [earlier] tweet didn't stop the violence," Herschmann said.[246]

This tweet—like the last one—didn't tell the rioters to go home. It suggested that they "remain" at the Capitol, albeit peacefully.

7.10 "WE LOVE YOU. YOU'RE VERY SPECIAL"

The President's tweets were not tamping down on the violence, and White House staff knew it.[247] By 3:17 p.m., Fox News was reporting gunshots on Capitol Hill. Law enforcement officers could be seen in the House chamber, pointing guns over the barricaded door: The chyron blared "Guns Drawn on House Floor."[248] Between 3:29 p.m. and 3:42 p.m., the network was flashing images of a protestor in the presiding officer's chair, right where Vice

President Pence had been sitting 90 minutes earlier.[249] Other images showed Members of Congress trapped in the House gallery, crouching below the balcony for cover.[250]

Allies continued to text Meadows, begging the President to order the mob to go home and indicating that it was time the American people hear from the President directly:

Unknown, 3:04 p.m.: "Are you with potus right now? Hearing he is in the dining room watching this on TV . . ." "Is he going to say anything to de-escalate apart from that Tweet?"[251]

Reince Priebus, 3:09 p.m.: "TELL THEM TO GO HOME !!!"[252]

Unknown, 3:13 p.m.: "POTUS should go on air and defuse this. Extremely important."[253]

Alyssa Farah, 3:13 p.m.: "Potus has to come out firmly and tell protestors to dissipate. Someone is going to get killed . . ."[254]

Representative Chip Roy, 3:25 p.m.: "Fix this now."[255] Meadows responded: "We are."[256]

Sean Hannity (Fox News), 3:31 p.m.: "Can he make a statement. I saw the tweet. Ask people to peacefully leave the capital [sic]."[257] Meadows responded: "On it."[258]

Katrina Pierson, 3:40 p.m.: "Note: I was able to keep the crazies off the stage. I stripped all branding of those nutty groups and removed videos of all of the psychos. Glad it [sic] fought it."[259]

Unknown, 3:42 p.m.: "Pls have POTUS call this off at the Capitol. Urge rioters to disperse. I pray to you."[260]

Unknown, 3:57 p.m.: "Is he coming out?" "He has to right?"[261]

Brian Kilmeade, 3:58 p.m. (Fox News): "Please get him on tv. Destroying every thing you guys have accomplished."[262]

Donald Trump, Jr., 4:05 p.m.: "We need an oval address. He has to lead now. It's gone too far and gotten out of hand."[263]

At any moment in the afternoon, it would have been easy for President Trump to get before cameras and call off the attack. The White House Press Briefing Room is just down the hallway from the Oval Office, past the Cabinet Room and around the corner to the right. It would have taken less than 60 seconds for the President to get there.[264] The space, moreover, is outfitted with cameras that are constantly "hot," meaning that they are on and ready to go live at a moment's notice.[265] The White House press corps is

also situated in the West Wing, right by the briefing room.[266] The whole affair could have been assembled in minutes.[267]

However, it was not until nearly 3 hours after the violence began that President Trump finally agreed to tell the mob to go home.[268]

The Presidential Daily Diary notes that President Trump left the dining room to shoot the video at 4:03 p.m.[269] By this point—per Fox News coverage playing continually in the dining room—more law enforcement officers had arrived at the Capitol to resist the violent mob.[270]

The video shoot took place in the Rose Garden, the outdoor space that borders the Oval Office and the West Wing.[271] The setup was not ornate, just a camera and a microphone. Luna made sure that the background and lighting looked good, and that President Trump's hair and tie were in place.[272] President Trump delivered his remarks in one take, more or less, although he stopped and restarted at one point.[273] In all, the video took less than 4 minutes to shoot, and the President was back in the dining room by 4:07 p.m.[274]

"I would stick to this script . . . ," McEnany told President Trump before he stepped out to film.[275]

He didn't.

Kushner and others had drafted a statement, but President Trump spoke entirely off the cuff.[276] Here's what he said:

> I know your pain. I know you're hurt. We had an election that was stolen from us. It was a landslide election and everyone knows it, especially the other side. But you have to go home now. We have to have peace. We have to have law and order. We have to respect our great people in law and order. We don't want anybody hurt. It's a very tough period of time. There's never been a time like this where such a thing happened where they could take it away from all of us, from me, from you, from our country. This was a fraudulent election. But we can't play into the hands of these people. We have to have peace. So go home, we love you. You're very special. You've seen what happens. You see the way others are treated that are so bad and so evil. I know how you feel, but go home and go home in peace.[277]

A photo obtained from the National Archives shows President Trump and Herschmann huddled next to each other, watching a completed take through the monitor on the video camera.[278]

"There needs to be a more direct statement" telling the rioters to leave the Capitol, Luna heard Herschmann—yet again—tell the President.[279] Herschmann testified that he did not recall this exchange.[280]

But according to Luna, President Trump rejected the note.

"These people are in pain," he said in reply.[281]

Down at the Capitol, the video began streaming onto rioters' phones, and by all accounts including video footage taken by other rioters, they listened to President Trump's command.

"Donald Trump has asked everybody to go home," one rioter shouted as he "deliver[ed] the President's message." "That's our order," another rioter responded. Others watching the video responded: "He says, go home."[282]

The crowd afterward began to disperse.[283] The video made clear what had been evident to many, including those closest to him: The President could have called off the rioters far earlier and at any point that day.[284] But he chose not to do so.[285]

It was not until it was obvious that the riot would fail to stop the certification of the vote that the President finally relented and released a video statement made public at 4:17 p.m.[286]

President Trump huddles with aides, watching a completed take of a video through the monitor of the video camera.
(Photo provided to the Select Committee by the National Archives and Records Administration)

7.11 "REMEMBER THIS DAY FOREVER!"

After leaving the Rose Garden, the President returned to the dining room. At 6:01 p.m., he issued another tweet, the last of the day:

These are the things and events that happen when a sacred landslide election victory is so unceremoniously & viciously stripped away from great patriots who have been badly & unfairly treated for so long. Go home with love & in peace. Remember this day forever![287]

He retired to his residence for the evening at 6:27 p.m.[288] A White House photographer captured the President walking back to the residence with an employee in tow, carrying personal items President Trump wished to bring home with him for the night.[289] In the employee's hands are the gloves the President was wearing while addressing the crowd at the Ellipse.[290]

The President had one parting comment to the employee—the thing that was evidently occupying his mind even after an afternoon of violence—before he retired to his home.

"Mike Pence let me down," the President concluded.[291]

7.12 PRESIDENT TRUMP STILL SOUGHT TO DELAY THE JOINT SESSION

Even after President Trump finally told the rioters to go home, he and his lead attorney, Rudolph Giuliani, continued to seek to delay the joint session of Congress.

Giuliani began frantically calling the White House line the very minute that the President's video went up on Twitter.[292] Failing to get through, he called back, once every minute—4:17 p.m., 4:18 p.m., 4:19 p.m., 4:20 p.m.[293] He managed to get through, briefly, to Mark Meadows at 4:21 p.m., and then kept calling the White House line: at 4:22 p.m., three times on two different phones at 4:23 p.m., 4:24 p.m., and once more at 5:05 p.m.[294] He finally managed to speak with President Trump at 5:07 p.m., and the two spoke for almost 12 minutes.[295]

After he spoke with President Trump, Giuliani's phone calls went nearly without fail to Members of Congress: Senator Marsha Blackburn, and then Senator Mike Lee.[296] He made three calls to Senator Bill Hagerty, then two to Representative Jim Jordan.[297] He called Senator Lindsey Graham,[298] Senator Josh Hawley,[299] and Senator Ted Cruz.[300] Giuliani had two calls with Senator Dan Sullivan over the course of the evening.[301] There were another three calls to Representative Jordan, none of which connected.[302] After 8:06 p.m., when the joint session resumed, the calls to Members of Congress finally stopped.[303] Shortly afterward, at 8:39 p.m., Giuliani had one final call of 9 minutes with the President.[304]

When asked about these calls during his deposition before the Select Committee, Giuliani initially refused to answer. Giuliani insisted his calls to Members of Congress—none of whom were his client—were all attorney-client privileged.[305] But Giuliani eventually relented.

"I was probably calling to see any—if anything could be done," he said. "About the vote—the vote." [306]

We know definitively what Giuliani was up to because he left a voice message for Senator Tuberville—inadvertently on Senator Lee's phone—recording his request.[307] He wanted for "you, our Republican friends to try to just slow it down," referring to the electoral count, and delay the joint session.[308] Here are his own words:

> The only strategy we can follow is to object to numerous States and raise issues so that we get ourselves into tomorrow—ideally until the end of tomorrow. So if you could object to every State and, along with a congressman, get a hearing for every State, I know we would delay you a lot, but it would give us the opportunity to get the legislators who are very, very close to pulling their vote.[309]

Mike Pence reopens the joint session of Congress and resumes counting electoral votes.
(Photo by Will McNamee/Getty Images)

The President, too, was at home, but he remained focused on his goal. Between 6:54 p.m. and 11:23 p.m., he spoke with 13 people, some more than once.[310] Of the 13, six ignored or expressly refused to comply with Select Committee requests for their testimony.[311] Two agreed to appear but refused to answer questions about their phone calls with the President, citing executive privilege.[312] Two more refused to answer questions, claiming attorney-client privilege.[313]

Of the 13, five were President Trump's attorneys or lawyers who worked with him on efforts to reverse the outcome of the election. With one exception, each of these calls took place before 8:06 p.m., when Vice President Pence reopened the joint session of Congress and resumed counting the electoral votes.[314] The President spoke with White House Counsel Pat Cipollone for 7 minutes at 7:01 p.m.[315] He spoke with Kurt Olsen and Mark Martin, lawyers who both advised him on the Vice President's role in the joint session:[316] He spoke with Martin for 9 minutes at 7:30 p.m., and Olsen twice, for 11 minutes at 7:17 p.m. and for another 10 minutes at 7:40 p.m.[317] He spoke with Cleta Mitchell, the lawyer leading his election challenges in Georgia, for 2 minutes at 7:53 p.m.[318] The President spoke with Herschmann for 5 minutes at 10:50 p.m.[319]

Another five of the people who spoke with President Trump that night were employees or outside advisors who counseled him on communications issues. These calls, by contrast, predominantly took place after the joint session resumed.[320] He spoke with his communications director, Scavino, twice: for 7 minutes at 7:08 p.m. and for 15 minutes at 9:55 p.m.[321] He spoke with McEnany for 11 minutes at 9:42 p.m.[322] He took calls from Steve Bannon, for 7 minutes at 10:19 p.m., and Sean Hannity, for 8 minutes at 11:08 p.m.[323]

At 9:23 p.m., President Trump spoke with Jason Miller, his Campaign Communications Director, for 18 minutes.[324]

Of his own initiative, Miller had drafted a statement for the President assuring the nation that the transfer of power—despite the day's events— would, indeed, take place.[325] On their call, the President pushed back on the phrasing.

The President wanted the statement to promise a "peaceful transition" of power, rather than just an "orderly" one.[326]

Miller rejected the change and told him why rather bluntly.

"[T]hat ship's kind of already sailed," he said, "so we're going to say 'orderly transition.' "[327]

7.13 HE "JUST DIDN'T WANT TO TALK ABOUT IT ANYMORE"

The President did not, by any account, express grief or regret for what happened at the Capitol. Neither did he appear to grasp the gravity of what he had set in motion.

In his last phone call of the night, the President spoke with Johnny McEntee, his Director of Personnel.[328]

"[T]his is a crazy day," the President told him. McEntee said his tone was one of "[l]ike, wow, can you believe this shit . . .?"[329]

Did he express sadness over the violence visited upon the Capitol?

"No," McEntee said. "I mean, I think he was shocked by, you know, it getting a little out of control, but I don't remember sadness, specifically."[330]

President Trump didn't make any other phone calls for the rest of the night.[331] The President didn't call Vice President Pence. In fact, President Trump never called to check on his Vice President's safety that day. He didn't call the heads of any of the Federal law enforcement agencies. He didn't call the leadership—neither Republican nor Democrat—of the legislative branch of government that had just been overrun by a mob.[332]

Only two days after the riot, by January 8th, the President was over the whole thing.

He "just didn't want to talk about it anymore," he told his press aides. "[H]e was tired of talking about it." [333]

Ivanka Trump claimed to the Select Committee that her father was "disappointed and surprised" by the attack, but she could not name a specific instance of him expressly saying it.

"He—I just felt that," she said. "I know him really well." [334]

Here's what she could definitively say:

Committee Staff: Has he ever expressed to you any sentiment that he did or did not do the right thing in how he responded on the day of the 6th?

Ms. Trump: No.

Committee Staff: Has he ever expressed any sentiment about something that he wished he had done on the day of the 6th?

Ms. Trump: No.

Committee Staff: Has he ever said anything to you about the people who were injured or who died that day?

Ms. Trump: No.

Committee Staff: Has he ever said anything to you about whether he should or should not continue to talk about the 2020 Presidential election after the events on the 6th?

Ms. Trump: No.[335]

7.14 PRESIDENT TRUMP'S "RHETORIC KILLED SOMEONE"

The President may not have expressed regret over his behavior, but some of his most loyal supporters made the connection between his words and the violence.

A member of the speechwriting team, Patrick MacDonnell, conceded the next day in a text that "maybe the rhetoric could have been better." [336] As the riot was in full throttle, even steadfast supporter Ali Alexander of "Stop the Steal" texted, "POTUS is not ignorant of what his words will do." [337]

"We all look like domestic terrorists now," Hope Hicks texted Julie Radford.[338]

Separately, Hicks texted Herschmann, "So predictable and so sad."

"I know," he replied. "Tragic."

"I'm so upset. Everything we worked for wiped away," she continued.

"I agree. Totally self-inflicted," he wrote.[339]

Brad Parscale, Trump's Former Campaign Manager, texted Katrina Pierson at 7:21 p.m. on January 6th, saying the day's events were the result of a "sitting president asking for civil war." [340]

"This week I feel guilty for helping him win . . . a woman is dead," Parscale added.

"You do realize this was going to happen," Pierson answered.

"Yeah. If I was trump [sic] and knew my rhetoric killed someone," he said.

"It wasn't the rhetoric," she said.

Parscale's reply: "Yes it was." [341]

ENDNOTES

1. As explained in Chapter 8, the Proud Boys and other extremists initiated the attack shortly before the joint session of Congress was set to begin at 1:00 p.m. The rioters who streamed down Pennsylvania to the U.S. Capitol from the Ellipse then provided crucial momentum for the attack.

2. "Manual for Courts-Martial United States," Department of Defense, (2019), at 334, available at https://jsc.defense.gov/Portals/99/Documents/2019%20MCM%20(Final)%20(20190108).pdf?ver=2019-01-11-115724-610.

3. Select Committee to Investigate the January 6th Attack on the United States Capitol, Transcribed Interview of General Mark. A. Milley, (Nov. 17, 2021), p. 268.

4. Select Committee to Investigate the January 6th Attack on the United States Capitol, Transcribed Interview of General Mark. A. Milley, (Nov. 17, 2021), p. 83.

5. Select Committee to Investigate the January 6th Attack on the United States Capitol, Transcribed Interview of General Mark. A. Milley, (Nov. 17, 2021), p. 296.

6. Select Committee to Investigate the January 6th Attack on the United States Capitol, Transcribed Interview of General Mark. A. Milley, (Nov. 17, 2021), p. 268.

7. Select Committee to Investigate the January 6th Attack on the United States Capitol, Transcribed Interview of Hope Hicks, (October 25, 2022), pp. 108-110; Documents on file with the Select Committee to Investigate the January 6th Attack on the United States Capitol (Hope Hicks Production), SC_HH_033 (Jan. 6, 2021, Hogan Gidley text message to Hope Hicks at 2:19 p.m. EST).

8. Documents on file with the Select Committee to Investigate the January 6th Attack on the United States Capitol (Hope Hicks Production), SC_HH_033 (Jan. 6, 2021, Hogan Gidley text message to Hope Hicks at 2:19 p.m. EST).

9. Documents on file with the Select Committee to Investigate the January 6th Attack on the United States Capitol (Hope Hicks Production), SC_HH_033 (Jan. 6, 2021, Hogan Gidley text message to Hope Hicks at 2:19 p.m. EST).

10. Donald J. Trump (@realDonaldTrump), Twitter, Jan. 6, 2021 2:38 p.m. ET, available at https://media-cdn.factba.se/realdonaldtrump-twitter/1346904110969315332.jpg (archived).

11. Select Committee to Investigate the January 6th Attack on the United States Capitol, Transcribed Interview of Sarah Matthews (Feb. 8, 2022), pp. 39–41.

12. Documents on file with the Select Committee to Investigate the January 6th Attack on the United States Capitol (Mark Meadows Production), MM014925 (January 6, 2021, Donald Trump Jr. text message to Mark Meadows at 2:53 p.m. ET).

13. At 3:13 p.m., President Trump tweeted: "I am asking for everyone at the U.S. Capitol to remain peaceful. No violence! Remember, WE are the Party of Law & Order—respect the Law and our great men and women in Blue. Thank you!" Donald J. Trump (@realDonaldTrump), Twitter, Jan. 6, 2021 3:13 p.m. ET, available at https://media-cdn.factba.se/realdonaldtrump-twitter/1346912780700577792.jpg (archived).

14. Tommy Christopher, "WATCH: GOP Rep Reveals Details of Trump's Bombshell Call with McCarthy Refusing to Call off Capitol Rioters," Mediaite, (Feb. 13, 2021), available at https://www.mediaite.com/news/watch-gop-rep-reveals-details-of-trumps-bombshell-call-with-mccarthy-refusing-to-call-off-capitol-rioters/.

15. Select Committee to Investigate the January 6th Attack on the United States Capitol, Hearing on the January 6th Investigation, 117th Cong., 2d sess., (July 12, 2022), available at https://www.govinfo.gov/committee/house-january6th.

16. "New Video of Capitol Rioter: 'Trump is Still Our President,'" CNN Business, at 0:37, Feb. 6, 2021, available at https://www.cnn.com/videos/media/2021/02/06/qanon-capitol-rioter-video-trump-still-president-sot-nr-vpx.cnn.

17. Trial Exhibit 6732 (1.S.159.1165-67, 84), United States v. Rhodes et al., No. 1:22-cr-15 (D.D.C Nov. 1, 2022). Vallejo was manning the quick reaction force at a hotel in Arlington, Virginia, awaiting word to bring in a cache of weaponry; he was not at the Capitol on January 6th. Trial Exhibit 6731, United States v. Rhodes et al., No. 1:22-cr-15 (D.D.C. Oct. 20, 2022) (Vallejo messaged his group in the afternoon "QRF standing by at hotel. Just say the word"); Trial Transcript at 2728, United States v. Rhodes et al., No. 1:22-cr-15 (D.D.C. Oct. 12, 2022) (Oath Keeper Terry Cummings testified that "I had not seen that many weapons in one location since I was in the military" when he arrived at the Arlington hotel).

18. "Trump Video Telling Protesters at Capitol Building to Go Home: Transcript," Rev, (Jan. 6, 2021), available at https://www.rev.com/blog/transcripts/trump-video-telling-protesters-at-capitol-building-to-go-home-transcript.

19. "Trump Video Telling Protesters at Capitol Building to Go Home: Transcript," Rev, (Jan. 6, 2021), available at https://www.rev.com/blog/transcripts/trump-video-telling-protesters-at-capitol-building-to-go-home-transcript.

20. Donald J. Trump (@realdonaldtrump), Twitter, Jan. 6, 2021 6:01 ET, available at https://www.presidency.ucsb.edu/documents/tweets-january-6-2021 (archived).

21. Select Committee to Investigate the January 6th Attack on the United States Capitol, Hearing on the January 6th Investigation, 117th Cong., 2d sess., (June 28, 2022), available at https://www.govinfo.gov/committee/house-january6th; Select Committee to Investigate the January 6th Attack on the United States Capitol, Continued Interview of Cassidy Hutchinson, (June 20, 2022), p. 125.

22. Select Committee to Investigate the January 6th Attack on the United States Capitol, Deposition of John McEntee, (Mar. 28, 2022), p. 157.

23. Mariana Alfaro, "Trump Vows Pardon, Government Apology to Capitol Rioters if Elected," Washington Post, (Sept. 1, 2022), available at https://www.washingtonpost.com/national-security/2022/09/01/trump-jan-6-rioters-pardon/.

24. Donald J. Trump (@realdonaldtrump), Twitter, Jan. 6, 2021 8:06 a.m. ET, available at https://www.thetrumparchive.com/?searchbox=%22Sleepy+Eyes+Chuck+Todd+is+so+happy%22 (archived).

25. Donald J. Trump (@realdonaldtrump), Twitter, Jan. 6, 2021 8:17 a.m. ET, available at https://www.thetrumparchive.com/?searchbox=%22All+Mike+Pence+has+to+do+is%22 (archived).

26. Donald J. Trump (@realdonaldtrump), Twitter, Jan. 6, 2021 8:22 a.m. ET, available at https://www.thetrumparchive.com/?results=1 (archived).

27. Documents with file with the Select Committee to Investigate the January 6th Attack on the United States Capitol (National Archives Production), P-R000255 (January 6, 2021, The Daily Diary of President Donald J. Trump at 8:23 a.m. ET).

28. Documents on file with the Select Committee to Investigate the January 6th Attack on the United States Capitol (National Archives Production), P-R000255 (January 6, 2021, The Daily Diary of President Donald J. Trump at 8:23 a.m. ET). The Select Committee issued subpoenas to Bannon, Olson, and Giuliani in order to learn more about these telephone conversations, among other things. Bannon refused to comply with his subpoena, leading to his referral and ultimate conviction for criminal contempt of Congress. Olson sued to block the Select Committee from enforcing his subpoena. Giuliani spoke with the Select Committee but asserted attorney-client privilege with respect to all of his telephone conversations with President Trump on January 6th. Select Committee to Investigate the January 6th Attack on the United States Capitol, Deposition of Rudolph Giuliani, (May 20, 2022), p. 198.

29. Documents on file with the Select Committee to Investigate the January 6th Attack on the United States Capitol (National Archives Production), P-R000255 (January 6, 2021, The Daily Diary of President Donald J. Trump at 9:02 a.m. ET); Select Committee to Investigate the January 6th Attack on the United States Capitol, Deposition of Marc Short, (Jan. 26, 2022), p. 12.

30. Select Committee to Investigate the January 6th Attack on the United States Capitol, Deposition of Stephen Miller, (Apr. 14, 2022), p. 145.

31. Select Committee to Investigate the January 6th Attack on the United States Capitol, Deposition of Ross Worthington, (Feb. 15, 2022), p. 112; Documents on file with the Select Committee to Investigate the January 6th Attack on the United States Capitol (Ross Worthington Production), RW_0002633 (Jan. 4, 2021, email at 10:00 p.m. from Ross Worthington to Patrick MacDonnell asking for research related to the January 6th speech).

32. Documents on file with the Select Committee to Investigate the January 6th Attack on the United States Capitol (Ross Worthington Production), RW_0002341–RW_0002351 (Jan. 6, 2021, Stephen Miller emails to Ross Worthington, Vincent Haley and Robert Gabriel, Jr. at 10:22 and 10:23 a.m. ET, attaching draft speech).

33. Documents on file with the Select Committee to Investigate the January 6th Attacks on the United States Capitol (Ross Worthington Production), RW_0002341–2344 (Jan. 6, 2021, email from Stephen Miller to Ross Worthington, Vincent Haley, and Robert Gabriel, re: EDITS, attaching draft Save America March speech with edits and comments).

34. Documents on file with the Select Committee to Investigate the January 6th Attacks on the United States Capitol (Ross Worthington Production), RW_0002341–2343 (Jan. 6, 2021, email from Stephen Miller to Ross Worthington, Vincent Haley, and Robert Gabriel, re: EDITS, attaching draft Save America March speech with edits and comments).

35. Select Committee to Investigate the January 6th Attack on the United States Capitol, Deposition of Ross Worthington, (Feb. 15, 2022), p. 164. Select Committee to Investigate the January 6th Attack on the United States Capitol, Deposition of Vincent Haley, (April 12, 2022), pp. 88–89; Select Committee to Investigate the January 6th Attack on the United States Capitol, Transcribed Interview of Sarah Miller, (April 14, 2022), p. 148.

36. Documents on file with the Select Committee to Investigate the January 6th Attack on the United States Capitol (National Archives Production), 076P-R000007430_0001 (Jan. 6, 2021, Ross Worthington email to Vincent M. Haley at 10:49 a.m. ET).

37. Select Committee to Investigate the January 6th Attack on the United States Capitol, Deposition of Stephen Miller, (Apr. 14, 2022), p. 154.

38. Donald Trump (@realDonaldTrump), Twitter, Jan. 6, 2021 9:00 a.m. ET, available at https://www.thetrumparchive.com/?results=1&searchbox=%22they+just+happened+to+find%22 (archived); Donald Trump (@realDonaldTrump), Twitter, Jan. 6, 2021 9:15 a.m. ET, available at https://www.thetrumparchive.com/?results=1&searchbox=%22they+states+want+to+redo%22 (archived); Donald Trump (@realDonaldTrump), Twitter, Jan. 6, 2021 9:16 a.m. ET, available at https://www.thetrumparchive.com/?results=1&searchbox=%22even+Mexico%22 (archived); Donald Trump (@realDonaldTrump), Twitter, Jan. 6, 2021 10:44 a.m. ET, available at https://www.thetrumparchive.com/?results=1&searchbox=%22these+scoundrels+are+only+toying%22 (archived).

39. Documents on file with the Select Committee to Investigate the January 6th Attack on the Capitol, (National Archives Production), P-R000285 (January 6, 2021, Schedule marked private with handwritten notes at 11:22 a.m. ET); Select Committee to Investigate the January 6th Attack on the United States Capitol, Deposition of Keith Kellogg, Jr., (Dec. 14, 2021) pp. 90–93; Select Committee to Investigate the January 6th Attack on the United States Capitol, Deposition of Nicholas Luna, (Mar. 21, 2021), p. 126.

40. Select Committee to Investigate the January 6th Attack on the United States Capitol, Transcribed Interview of Eric Herschmann, (Apr. 6, 2022), pp. 48–49; *see also* Select Committee to Investigate the January 6th Attack on the United States Capitol, Transcribed Interview of White House Employee, (June 10, 2022), p. 22 ("I could just tell in his voice when he was talking to the Vice President that he was disappointed and frustrated.").

41. Select Committee to Investigate the January 6th Attack on the United States Capitol, Transcribed Interview of Eric Herschmann, (Apr. 6, 2022), p. 4.

42. Select Committee to Investigate the January 6th Attack on the United States Capitol, Deposition of Julie Radford, (May 24, 2020), p. 18.

43. *Compare* Documents on file with the Select Committee to Investigate the January 6th Attack on the United States Capitol (National Archives Production), P-R000285 (January 6, 2021, schedule with handwritten notes about the meeting); *with* Documents on file with the Select Committee to Investigate the January 6th Attack on the United States Capitol (Secret Service Production), CTRL0000100198 (communication noting "Mogul" en route to the Ellipse at 11:39 a.m.).

44. Select Committee to Investigate the January 6th Attack on the United States Capitol, Deposition of Keith Kellogg, Jr., (Dec. 14, 2021), p. 93.

45. Documents on file with the Select Committee to Investigate the January 6th Attack on the United States Capitol (National Archives Production), 076P_R000007558_0001 (Jan. 6, 2021, Stephen Miller email to Robert Gabriel Jr.).

46. Documents on file with the Select Committee to Investigate the January 6th Attack on the United States Capitol (National Archives Production), 076P-R000007531_0001 (Jan. 6, 2021, Robert Gabriel Jr. email to Ross Worthington at 11:33 a.m. ET).

47. Documents on file with the Select Committee to Investigate the January 6th Attack on the United States Capitol (National Archives Production), 076P_R000007531_0001 (Jan. 6, 2021, Ross Worthington email to Robert Gabriel Jr. at 11:34 a.m. ET).

48. Select Committee to Investigate the January 6th Attack on the United States Capitol, Deposition of Vincent Haley, (Apr. 12, 2022), p. 95.

49. Documents on file with the Select Committee to Investigate the January 6th Attacks on the United States Capitol (Ross Worthington Production), RW_0002341–2343 (January 6, 2021, email from Stephen Miller to Ross Worthington, Vincent Haley, and Robert Gabriel, re: EDITS, attaching draft Save America March speech with edits and comments).

50. *See* Select Committee to Investigate the January 6th Attack on the United States Capitol, Deposition of Vincent Haley, (Apr. 12, 2022), p. 95; Document on file with the Select Committee (National Archives Production), 076P-R000007557_0001, 076P-R000007557_0034, 076P-R000002896_00001, 076P-R000002896_00025, 076P-R000002984_0001, 076P-R000002984_00304 (various drafts, including teleprompter inputs, of the speech).

51. Select Committee to Investigate the January 6th Attack on the United States Capitol, Deposition of Nicholas Luna, (Mar. 21, 2022), p. 126.

52. Documents on file with the Select Committee to Investigate the January 6th Attack on the United States Capitol (National Archives Production), P-R000286 (January 6, 2021, note from Nicholas Luna to President Trump).

53. Documents on file with the Select Committee to Investigate the January 6th Attack on the United States Capitol (Secret Service Production), CTRL0000111236 (January. 6, 2021, Email Re: CSD Activity Log #2 at 2:49 p.m. ET).

54. Select Committee to Investigate the January 6th Attack on the United States Capitol, Transcribed Interview of Cassidy Hutchinson, (Feb. 23, 2022), pp. 87–88; Documents on file with the Select Committee to Investigate the January 6th Attack on the United States Capitol, (National Archives Production), 076P-R000005179_0001–0002 (January 6, 2021 email reporting on the status of people going through the magnetometers and noting "[s]everal thousand on the mall watching but not in line.").

55. Select Committee to Investigate the January 6th Attack on the United States Capitol, Continued Interview of Cassidy Hutchinson, (June 20, 2022), pp. 12–13.

56. Documents on file with the Select Committee to Investigate the January 6th Attack on the United States Capitol (Cassidy Hutchinson Production), CH-0000000069, (January 6, 2021, Cassidy Hutchinson text message to Tony Ornato at 12:45 p.m. ET).

57. Select Committee to Investigate the January 6th Attack on the United States Capitol, Continued Interview of Cassidy Hutchinson, (June 20, 2022), pp. 15–16; see also Select Committee to Investigate the January 6th Attack on the United States Capitol, Hearing on the January 6th Investigation, 117th Cong., 2d sess., (June 28, 2022), available at https://www.govinfo.gov/committee/house-january6th ("[W]e were standing towards the front of the tent with the TVs really close to where he would walk out to go on to the stage. The—these conversations happened two to three minutes before he took the stage that morning").

58. Documents on file with the Select Committee to Investigate the January 6th Attack on the United States Capitol (National Archives Production), P-R000255 (Jan. 6, 2021, Daily Diary of President Donald J. Trump at 11:55 a.m. ET).

59. "Donald Trump Speech 'Save America' Rally Transcript January 6," Rev, (Jan. 6, 2021), available at https://www.rev.com/blog/transcripts/donald-trump-speech-save-america-rally-transcript-january-6 (time-stamping the speech).

60. Documents on file with the Select Committee to Investigate the January 6th Attack on the United States Capitol (Cassidy Hutchinson Production), CH-0000000069 (January 6, 2021, Cassidy Hutchinson text message to Tony Ornato at 12:45 p.m. ET).

61. Select Committee to Investigate the January 6th Attack on the United States Capitol, Continued Interview of Cassidy Hutchinson, (June 20, 2022), p. 8.

62. Documents on file with the Select Committee to Investigate the January 6th Attack on the United States Capitol (National Archives Production), 076P-R000002879_00001 ("Save America March" speech early draft); Select Committee to Investigate the January 6th Attack on the United States Capitol, Deposition of Ross Worthington, (Feb. 15, 2022), p. 157.

63. Brian Naylor, "Read Trump's Jan. 6 Speech, A Key Part of Impeachment Trial," NPR, (Feb. 10, 2021), available at https://www.npr.org/2021/02/10/966396848/read-trumps-jan-6-speech-a-key-part-of-impeachment-trial.

64. "Donald Trump Speech 'Save America' Rally Transcript January 6," Rev, (Jan. 6, 2021), available at https://www.rev.com/blog/transcripts/donald-trump-speech-save-america-rally-transcript-january-6 (timestamping the speech).

65. "Donald Trump Speech 'Save America' Rally Transcript January 6," Rev, (Jan. 6, 2021), available at https://www.rev.com/blog/transcripts/donald-trump-speech-save-america-rally-transcript-january-6 (time-stamping the speech); Documents on file with the Select Committee to Investigate the January 6th Attack on the United States Capitol (Alex Holder Production) Video file Clip 45DAY32CAMB0050.mov at 3:10–3:40 (capturing "fight for Trump" chants during Donald Trump, Jr.'s speech); Lena V. Groeger, Jeff Kao, Al Shaw, Moiz Syed, and Maya Eliahou, "What Parler Saw During the Attack on the Capitol," ProPublica, at 12:01 pm at 3:33 and at 12:05 pm at 0:30 (Jan. 17, 2021), available at https://projects.propublica.org/parler-capitol-videos/ (capturing "fight for Trump" chants droning out the President after he told the crowd "we will not let them silence your voices"); FORMER WAGIE, "FULL FOOTAGE: Patriots STORM U.S. Capitol," YouTube, at 59:00, Jan. 6, 2021, posted Jan. 8, 2021, available at https://www.youtube.com/watch?v=iNFcdpZdkh0.

66. Brian Naylor, "Read Trump's Jan. 6 Speech, A Key Part of Impeachment Trial," *NPR*, (Feb. 10, 2021), available at https://www.npr.org/2021/02/10/966396848/read-trumps-jan-6-speech-a-key-part-of-impeachment-trial.

67. Select Committee to Investigate the January 6th Attack on the United States Capitol, *Hearing on the January 6th Investigation*, 117th Cong., 2d sess., (June 28, 2022), available at https://www.govinfo.gov/committee/house-january6th. *But see* Select Committee to Investigate the January 6th Attack on the United States Capitol, Transcribed Interview of Cassidy Hutchinson, (Feb. 23, 2022), p. 129 ("It wasn't—he didn't give me an impressions that he was frustrated or angry at the prospect of what the President had said on the stage. It was more of him trying to rush to get insight on what our plans were and wanted to have insight and be read in on that in case we had been planning to go up to the Capitol.").

68. Documents on file with the Select Committee to Investigate the January 6th Attack on the United States Capitol (Cassidy Hutchinson Production), CH-0000000069.

69. Select Committee to Investigate the January 6th Attack on the United States Capitol, Transcribed Interview of Cassidy Hutchinson, (Feb. 23, 2022), pp.128–29; Select Committee to Investigate the January 6th Attack on the United States Capitol, *Hearing on the January 6th Investigation*, 117th Cong., 2d sess., (June 28, 2022), available at https://www.govinfo.gov/committee/house-january6th.

70. Select Committee to Investigate the January 6th Attack on the United States Capitol, *Hearing on the January 6th Investigation*, 117th Cong., 2d sess., (June 28, 2022), available at https://www.govinfo.gov/committee/house-january6th.

71. Documents on file with the Select Committee to Investigate the January 6th Attack on the United States Capitol (Secret Service Production), USSS0000176702.

72. Documents on file with the Select Committee to Investigate the January 6th Attack on the United States Capitol (National Archives Production), P-R001005-1026 (January 6, 2021, National Security Council staff chat logs); *See* Select Committee to Investigate the January 6th Attack on the United States Capitol, Transcribed Interview White House Security Official, (July 11, 2022), p. 47 (discussing clearing a route to the Capitol for "Mogul").

73. Select Committee to Investigate the January 6th Attack on the United States Capitol, Transcribed Interview of White House Security Official, (July 11, 2022), p. 45.

74. Select Committee to Investigate the January 6th Attack on the United States Capitol, Transcribed Interview of White House Security Official, (July 11, 2022), p. 45.

75. Select Committee to Investigate the January 6th Attack on the United States Capitol, Transcribed Interview of White House Security Official , (July 11, 2022), p. 45.

76. Documents on file with the Select Committee to Investigate the January 6th Attack on the United States Capitol (Secret Service Production), CTRL0000208061 (January 6, 2021, email to Robert Engel at 1:19 p.m. ET). Despite the fact that the prospect of an OTR to the Capitol was raised at the highest levels within the Secret Service, some of its highest-ranking agents insisted to the Select Committee that they did not recall any such discussions on the day of January 6th. Select Committee to Investigate the January 6th Attack on the United States Capitol, Transcribed Interview of Robert Engel, (Mar. 4. 2022), p. 77. When presented with his text messages with Cassidy Hutchinson in which she referred to an "OTR to Capitol," Tony Ornato insisted that he didn't "recall ever talking about this with her." Select Committee to Investigate the January 6th Attack on the United States Capitol, Transcribed Interview of Anthony Ornato, (Mar. 29, 2022), p. 62.

77. Select Committee to Investigate the January 6th Attack on the United States Capitol, Deposition of Nicholas Luna, (Mar. 21, 2022), p. 117.

78. Select Committee to Investigate the January 6th Attack on the United States Capitol, Continued Interview of Cassidy Hutchinson, (June 20, 2022), p. 8.

79. Documents on file with the Select Committee to Investigate the January 6th Attack on the United States Capitol (National Archives Production), P-R000257 (January 6, 2021, Presidential Daily Diary).

80. *See, e.g.*, Select Committee to Investigate the January 6th Attack on the United States Capitol, Transcribed Interview of United States Secret Service Employee "Press Secretary," (October 31, 2022), pp. 49–51 (the word "furious" was "consistent with what was described to me that occurred—you know, agitated, furious, upset, angry, whatever adjective").

81. Mark Meadows, *The Chief's Chief*, (St. Petersburg: All Seasons Press, 2021), at p. 250 ("When he got offstage, President Trump let me know that he had been speaking metaphorically about the walk to the Capitol. . . . It was clear the whole time that he didn't actually intent to walk down Pennsylvania Avenue with the crowd.").

82. Select Committee to Investigate the January 6th Attack on the United States Capitol, Informal Interview of Robert Engel, (Mar. 4, 2022).

83. Select Committee to Investigate the January 6th Attack on the United States Capitol, Deposition of Kayleigh McEnany, (Jan. 12, 2022), pp. 158–62.

84. Select Committee to Investigate the January 6th Attack on the United States Capitol, Deposition of Kayleigh McEnany, (Jan. 12, 2022), p. 159.

85. Select Committee to Investigate the January 6th Attack on the United States Capitol, Deposition of Kayleigh McEnany, (Jan. 12, 2022), p. 160.

86. *See, e.g.*, Select Committee to Investigate the January 6th Attack on the United States Capitol, Continued Interview of Cassidy Hutchinson, (June 20, 2022), pp. 5–8.

87. *See, e.g.*, Select Committee to Investigate the January 6th Attack on the United States Capitol, Deposition of Max Miller, (Jan. 20, 2022), p. 90; Select Committee to Investigate the January 6th Attack on the United States Capitol, Deposition of Judson P. Deere, (Mar. 3, 2022), p. 71; Select Committee to Investigate the January 6th Attack on the United States Capitol, Deposition of Nicholas Luna, (Mar. 21, 2022) p. 118; Select Committee to Investigate the January 6th Attack on the United States Capitol, Transcribed Interview of White House Security Official, (July 11, 2022) pp. 35–36.

88. Select Committee to Investigate the January 6th Attack on the United States Capitol, Continued Interview of Cassidy Hutchinson, (June 20, 2022), p. 5.

89. Select Committee to Investigate the January 6th Attack on the United States Capitol, Continued Interview of Cassidy Hutchinson, (June 20, 2022), p. 5.

90. Select Committee to Investigate the January 6th Attack on the United States Capitol, *Hearing on the January 6th Investigation*, 117th Cong., 2d sess., (June 28, 2022), available at https://www.govinfo.gov/committee/house-january6th.

91. Select Committee to Investigate the January 6th Attack on the United States Capitol, Continued Interview of Cassidy Hutchinson, (June 20, 2022), pp. 6–7.

92. Select Committee to Investigate the January 6th Attack on the United States Capitol, Transcribed Interview of White House Employee with National Security Responsibilities, (July 19, 2022), pp. 69–71.

93. Select Committee to Investigate the January 6th Attack on the United States Capitol, Transcribed Interview of White House Employee with National Security Responsibilities, (July 19, 2022), p. 71.

94. Select Committee to Investigate the January 6th Attack on the United States Capitol, Continued Interview of Robert Engel, (Nov. 17, 2022), pp. 143–44, 147-48.

95. Select Committee to Investigate the January 6th Attack on the United States Capitol, Transcribed Interview of United States Secret Service Employee, (Nov. 21, 2022), pp. 92–93.

96. Select Committee to Investigate the January 6th Attack on the United States Capitol, Transcribed Interview of White House Employee with National Security Responsibilities (July 19, 2022), p. 73 ("In the days following that, I do remember, you know, again, hearing again how angry the President was when, you know, they were in the limo.")

97. Select Committee to Investigate the January 6th Attack on the United States Capitol, Continued Interview of Cassidy Hutchinson, (Sep. 14, 2022), pp. 34, 36, 37–38, 55.

98. Select Committee to Investigate the January 6th Attack on the United States Capitol, Transcribed Interview of Mark Robinson, (July 7, 2022), pp. 18, 23.

99. Select Committee to Investigate the January 6th Attack on the United States Capitol, Transcribed Interview of United States Secret Service Employee, (Nov. 4, 2022), pp. 99–100.

100. Select Committee to Investigate the January 6th Attack on the United States Capitol, Transcribed Interview of United States Secret Service Employee "Press Secretary," (Oct. 31, 2022), pp. 46, 50.

101. Select Committee to Investigate the January 6th Attack on the United States Capitol, Transcribed Interview of United States Secret Service Employee "Press Secretary," (Oct. 31, 2022), p. 50; see also Carol Leonnig (@CarolLeonnig), Twitter, June 28, 2022 7:46 p.m. ET, available at https://twitter.com/CarolLeonnig/status/1541931078184845312. The press secretary confirmed that he or she confirmed this information to the reporter because "that's what I had been told." "[Engel] did indicate—you know, kind of outlined . . . that the President did want to go to the Capitol, and Mr. Engel advised that we cannot go," the press secretary testified. "And you know, [President Trump] was agitated, but Mr. Engel advised that—you know, it was kind of a non-issue. It was agitated verbally, and they proceeded to the White House." Select Committee to Investigate the January 6th Attack on the United States Capitol, Transcribed Interview of United States Secret Service Employee "Press Secretary," (Oct. 31, 2022), pp. 46, 50.

102. The Select Committee has agreed not to name the Secret Service agent who was driving the vehicle to protect his privacy. We will refer to him in this report as "the driver."

103. See Select Committee to Investigate the January 6th Attack on the United States Capitol, Transcribed Interview of Secret Service Employee "Driver," (Nov. 7, 2022), p. 77; Select Committee to Investigate the January 6th Attack on the United States Capitol, Continued Interview of Robert Engel, (Nov. 17, 2022), pp. 100–01.

104. Select Committee to Investigate the January 6th Attack on the United States Capitol, Continued Interview of Robert Engel, (Nov. 17, 2022), pp. 100–01.

105. Select Committee to Investigate the January 6th Attack on the United States Capitol, Transcribed Interview of Secret Service Employee "Driver," (Nov. 7, 2022), p. 77.

106. Select Committee to Investigate the January 6th Attack on the United States Capitol, Transcribed Interview of Secret Service Employee "Driver," (Nov. 7, 2022), p. 77.

107. Select Committee to Investigate the January 6th Attack on the United States Capitol, Transcribed Interview of Secret Service Employee "Driver," (Nov. 7, 2022), p. 78.

108. Select Committee to Investigate the January 6th Attack on the United States Capitol, Transcribed Interview of Secret Service Employee "Driver," (Nov. 7, 2022), p. 79.

109. Select Committee to Investigate the January 6th Attack on the United States Capitol, Transcribed Interview of Secret Service Employee "Driver," (Nov. 7, 2022), p. 78. This recollection of the President's phrasing seems very similar to Hutchinson's testimony about President Trump's statement before he took the stage at the Ellipse: "I'm the President. Take the F'ing mags away. They're not here to hurt me." Select Committee to Investigate the January 6th Attack on the United States Capitol, Continued Interview of Cassidy Hutchinson, (June 20, 2022), pp. 11–12.

110. Select Committee to Investigate the January 6th Attack on the United States Capitol, Transcribed Interview of United States Secret Service Employee, (Nov. 7, 2022), pp. 78, 92.

111. Select Committee to Investigate the January 6th Attack on the United States Capitol, Transcribed Interview of United States Secret Service Employee, (Nov. 7, 2022), p. 78.

112. Select Committee to Investigate the January 6th Attack on the United States Capitol, Continued Interview of Robert Engel, (Nov. 17, 2022), p. 102. Mr. Engel also did not recall another occasion where testimony indicates that the incident in the presidential vehicle was mentioned. Mr. Engel's counsel has asked the Committee not to make certain evidence relating to that occasion public.

113. Select Committee to Investigate the January 6th Attack on the United States Capitol, Continued Interview of Robert Engel, (Nov. 17, 2022), pp. 143–44, 147–48.

114. Select Committee to Investigate the January 6th Attack on the United States Capitol, Transcribed Interview of Secret Service Employee "Driver," (Nov. 7, 2022), p. 80.

115. The Justice Department will have all of the relevant information and can make decisions about whether and how to proceed based upon this evidence.

116. Select Committee to Investigate the January 6th Attack on the United States Capitol, Continued Interview of Robert Engel, (Nov. 17, 2022), p. 121.

117. Documents on file with the Select Committee to Investigate the January 6th Attack on the United States Capitol (Secret Service Production), CTRL0000882478 at p. 4 (January 6, 2021, PID update at 1:25 p.m.).

118. Select Committee to Investigate the January 6th Attack on the United States Capitol, Transcribed Interview of Mark Robinson, (July 7, 2022), pp. 18–19.

119. Select Committee to Investigate the January 6th Attack on the United States Capitol, Continued Interview of Robert Engel, (Nov. 17, 2022), p. 121.

120. Select Committee to Investigate the January 6th Attack on the United States Capitol, Continued Interview of Robert Engel, (Nov. 17, 2022), p. 125.

121. Documents on file with the Select Committee to Investigate the January 6th Attack on the United States Capitol (Secret Service Production), CTRL0000208061 (January 6 2021, email from Robert Engel at 1:55 p.m.).

122. Select Committee to Investigate the January 6th Attack on the United States Capitol, Transcribed Interview of White House Employee, (June 10, 2022), p. 27.

123. Select Committee Interview Investigate the January 6th Attack on the United States Capitol, Transcribed Interview of White House Employee, (June 10, 2022), p. 27.

124. Documents on file with the Select Committee to Investigate the January 6th Attack on the United States Capitol (National Archives Production), Photo file 40a8_hi_j0087_0bea.

125. Select Committee Interview Investigate the January 6th Attack on the United States Capitol, Transcribed Interview of White House Employee, (June 10, 2022), pp. 27–28.

126. Documents on file with the Select Committee to Investigate the January 6th Attack on the United States Capitol (National Archives Production), P-R000255 (Jan. 6, 2021, Daily Diary of President Donald J. Trump).

127. Documents on file with the Select Committee to Investigate the January 6th Attack on the United States Capitol (National Archives Production), P-R000255 (Jan. 6, 2021, Daily Diary of President Donald J. Trump).

128. Documents on file with the Select Committee to Investigate the January 6th Attack on the United States Capitol (National Archives Production), P-R000255 (Jan. 6, 2021, Daily Diary of President Donald J. Trump).

129. Documents on file with the Select Committee to Investigate the January 6th Attack on the United States Capitol (National Archives Production), P-R000255 (Jan. 6, 2021, Daily Diary of President Donald J. Trump). See also Documents on file with the Select Committee to Investigate the January 6th Attack on the United States Capitol (National Archives Production), P-R000028 (Memorandum from White House Diarist confirming that "[t]he Oval Log for January 6, 2021 was not received").

130. Select Committee to Investigate the January 6th Attack on the United States Capitol, Deposition of Molly Michael, (Mar. 24, 2022), p 29 ("Why did that change, that you were not taking any records?" "I don't recall a specific reason."); Select Committee to Investigate the January 6th Attack on the United States Capitol, Transcribed Interview of Eric Herschmann, (Apr. 6, 2022), p. 111–12 (attributing the lack of recordkeeping to Michael's absence in the

White House, though she was present in the Outer Oval during the afternoon); Select Committee to Investigate the January 6th Attack on the United States Capitol, Deposition of Austin Ferrer Piran Basualdo, (Apr. 8, 2022), p. 86.

131. H. Rept. 117-216, Resolution Recommending that the House of Representatives Find Mark Randall Meadows in Contempt of Congress for Refusal to Comply with a Subpoena Duly Issued by the Select Committee to Investigate the January 6th Attack on the United States Capitol, 117th Cong., 1st Ssess. (2021), available at https://www.congress.gov/117/crpt/hrpt216/CRPT-117hrpt216.pdf; H. Rept. 117-284, Resolution Recommending that the House of Representatives Find Peter K. Navarro and Daniel Scavino, Jr., in Contempt of Congress for Refusal to Comply with a Subpoena Duly Issued by the Select Committee to Investigate the January 6th Attack on the United States Capitol, 117th Cong., 2d sess. (2022), available at https://www.congress.gov/117/crpt/hrpt284/CRPT-117hrpt284.pdf.

132. *See, e.g.*, Select Committee to Investigate the January 6th Attack on the United States Capitol, Transcribed Interview of Eric Herschmann, (Apr. 6, 2022), p. 118; Select Committee to Investigate the January 6th Attack on the United States Capitol, Transcribed Interview of Pasquale Anthony "Pat" Cipollone, (July 8, 2022), pp. 155–57.

133. *See, e.g.*, Select Committee to Investigate the January 6th Attack on the United States Capitol, Deposition of Molly Michael, (Mar. 24, 2022), p. 136 ("The phones were ringing. A lot was happening. I don't recall."); Select Committee to Investigate the January 6th Attack on the United States Capitol, Deposition of Austin Ferrer Piran Basualdo, (Apr. 8, 2022), pp. 109–10 ("I don't remember where I was that afternoon." "Do you remember being at the White House that afternoon, even if you don't remember where exactly you were in the White House?" "No, I do not." "Do you remember being home, wherever home is for you, on the afternoon of January 6th, as opposed to being at the White House?" "No, I don't." "So you don't remember whether you were at home or at the White House in the afternoon of January 6th, 2021?" "Again, that day was very blurry.").

134. Select Committee to Investigate the January 6th Attack on the United States Capitol, Deposition of Shealah Craighead, (June 8, 2022), p. 46.

135. Select Committee to Investigate the January 6th Attack on the United States Capitol, Deposition of Shealah Craighead, (June 8, 2022), p. 46. It is the standard practice of the White House photographers to cover the President from the moment he steps out of the residence until he returns there at the end of the day. *Id.* at 7. Craighead pushed back, telling Michael that the White House would want to document the day for historical purposes, but Michael did not relent. *Id.* at p. 28.

136. *See, e.g.*, Select Committee to Investigate the January 6th Attack on the United States Capitol, Deposition of Keith Kellogg, Jr., (Dec. 14, 2021), p. 115 ("Well, I saw the President watching TV.").

137. Select Committee Interview Investigate the January 6th Attack on the United States Capitol, Transcribed Interview of White House Employee, (June 10, 2022), p. 23.

138. *See, e.g.*, Select Committee to Investigate the January 6th Attack on the United States Capitol, Transcribed Interview of Ivanka Trump, (Apr. 5, 2022), p. 64 ("I recall walking in and saying, 'You have to put out a strong statement condemning violence and asking for peace to be restored.").

139. *See, e.g.*, Documents on file with the Select Committee to Investigate the January 6th Attack on the United States Capitol (AT&T Production, Feb. 9, 2022); *See also* Jonathan Karl, *Betrayal: The Final Act of the Trump* Show, (New York: Dutton, 2021), p. 287.

140. *See, e.g.*, Select Committee to Investigate the January 6th Attack on the United States Capitol, Transcribed Interview of Pasquale Anthony "Pat" Cipollone, (July 8, 2022), p. 174; Select Committee to Investigate the January 6th Attack on the United States Capitol, Deposition of Keith Kellogg, Jr., (Dec. 14, 2021), pp. 126–27.

141. Select Committee to Investigate the January 6th Attack on the United States Capitol, Continued Interview of Cassidy Hutchinson, (June 20, 2022), p. 129.

142. Select Committee to Investigate the January 6th Attack on the United States Capitol, Deposition of Kayleigh McEnany, (Jan. 12, 2022), pp. 169–70.

143. Select Committee to Investigate the January 6th Attack on the United States Capitol, Deposition of Kayleigh McEnany, (Jan. 12, 2022), pp. 159–60.

144. Documents on file with the Select Committee to Investigate the January 6th Attack on the United States Capitol (Kayleigh McEnany Production), KMC_000000724 (Jan. 6, 2021, Kayleigh McEnany notes).

145. Select Committee to Investigate the January 6th Attack on the United States Capitol, Continued Interview of Cassidy Hutchinson, (June 20, 2022), p. 8.

146. Select Committee to Investigate the January 6th Attack on the United States Capitol, Deposition of Kayleigh McEnany, (Jan. 12, 2022), p. 164.

147. Select Committee to Investigate the January 6th Attack on the United States Capitol, Deposition of Kayleigh McEnany, (Jan. 12, 2022), p. 164.

148. Documents on file with the Select Committee to Investigate the January 6th Attack on the United States Capitol (Kayleigh McEnany Production), KMC_000000724 (Jan. 6, 2021, Kayleigh McEnany notes).

149. *See, e.g.*, Select Committee to Investigate the January 6th Attack on the United States Capitol, Subpoena to Honorable Kevin McCarthy, (May 12, 2022), available at https://january6th.house.gov/sites/democrats.january6th.house.gov/files/2022-05-12-Subpoena-for%20OGC-McCarthy%20Kevin%20%28002%29.pdf; Select Committee to Investigate the January 6th Attack on the United States Capitol, Subpoena to Representative Jim Jordan, (May 12, 2022), available at https://january6th.house.gov/sites/democrats.january6th.house.gov/files/2022-05-12-Subpoena-for%20OGC-Jordan%20Jim%20%28002%29.pdf.

150. *See, e.g.*, Select Committee to Investigate the January 6th Attack on the United States Capitol, Subpoena to Honorable Kevin McCarthy, (May 12, 2022), available at https://january6th.house.gov/sites/democrats.january6th.house.gov/files/2022-05-12-Subpoena-for%20OGC-McCarthy%20Kevin%20%28002%29.pdf; Select Committee to Investigate the January 6th Attack on the United States Capitol, Subpoena to Representative Jim Jordan, (May 12, 2022), available at https://january6th.house.gov/sites/democrats.january6th.house.gov/files/2022-05-12-Subpoena-for%20OGC-Jordan%20Jim%20%28002%29.pdf.

151. Documents on file with the Select Committee to Investigate the January 6th Attack on the United States Capitol (AT&T Production, Feb. 9, 2022).

152. Donald J. Trump (@realDonaldTrump), Twitter, Jan. 6, 2020 1:49 p.m. ET, available at https://www.thetrumparchive.com/?searchbox=%22https%3A%2F%2Ft.co%2FizItBeFE6G%22 (archived).

153. Select Committee to Investigate the January 6th Attack on the United States Capitol, Transcribed Interview of Jared Kushner, (Mar. 31, 2022), p. 144.

154. Select Committee to Investigate the January 6th Attack on the United States Capitol, Transcribed Interview of Jared Kushner, (Mar. 31, 2022), p. 145.

155. Select Committee to Investigate the January 6th Attack on the United States Capitol, Deposition of Benjamin Williamson, (Jan. 25, 2022) p. 60. Live feeds of the Capitol began showing pepper spray exchanges between officers and rioters around 1:29 p.m. See Documents on file with the Select Committee to Investigate the January 6th Attack on the United States Capitol (Secret Service Production), CTRL0000094153; Documents on file with the Select Committee to Investigate the Attack on the United States Capitol (Secret Service Production), CTRL0000094192; Select Committee to Investigate the January 6th Attack on the United States Capitol, *Hearing on the January 6th Investigation*, 117th Cong., 2d sess., (July 21, 2022), at 40:00, available at https://www.govinfo.gov/committee/house-january6th.

156. Select Committee to Investigate the January 6th Attack on the United States Capitol, Transcribed Interview of Sarah Matthews, (Feb. 8, 2022), pp. 36–37.

157. Documents on file with the Select Committee to Investigate the January 6th Attack on the United States Capitol (Benjamin Williamson Production), CTRL0000034784 (Jan. 6, 2021, Benjamin Williamson text message to Mark Meadows at 2:02 p.m. EST); Select Committee to Investigate the January 6th Attack on the United States Capitol, Deposition of Benjamin Williamson (Jan. 25, 2022), p. 64.

158. Select Committee to Investigate the January 6th Attack on the United States Capitol, Continued Interview of Cassidy Hutchinson, (June 20, 2022), p. 24 ("I saw that he was sitting on his couch on his cell phone, same as the morning, where he was just kind of scrolling and typing.").

159. Select Committee to Investigate the January 6th Attack on the United States Capitol, Continued Interview of Cassidy Hutchinson, (June 20, 2022), p. 24.

160. The Select Committee's review of U.S. Capitol Police surveillance footage showed that Proud Boy Dominic Pezzola smashed a Senate Wing window at 2:13 p.m. and rioters entered through that window, as well as an adjacent door, shortly thereafter. See also Third Superseding Indictment at 21, United States v. Nordean et al., No. 1:21-cr-175 (D.D.C. June 6, 2022), ECF No. 380 (noting that Dominic Pezzola "used [a] riot shield . . . to break a window of the Capitol" at "2:13 p.m." and that "[t]he first members of the mob entered the Capitol through this broken window"); 167 Cong. Rec. S634 (daily ed. Feb. 10, 2021), available at https://www.congress.gov/117/crec/2021/02/10/CREC-2021-02-10-pt1-PgS615-4.pdf.

161. Select Committee to Investigate the January 6th Attack on the United States Capitol, Continued Interview of Cassidy Hutchinson, (June 20, 2022), p. 25. Cipollone confirmed that he first went to the dining room when he saw that "people had breached the Capitol, they had gotten into the Capitol." Select Committee to Investigate the January 6th Attack on the United States Capitol, Transcribed Interview of Pasquale Anthony "Pat" Cipollone, (July 8, 2022), p. 149.

162. Select Committee to Investigate the January 6th Attack on the United States Capitol, Continued Interview of Cassidy Hutchinson, (June 20, 2022), p. 26.

163. Select Committee to Investigate the January 6th Attack on the United States Capitol, Continued Interview of Cassidy Hutchinson, (June 20, 2022), p. 26.

164. Select Committee to Investigate the January 6th Attack on the United States Capitol, Transcribed Interview of Pasquale Anthony "Pat" Cipollone, (July 8, 2022), p. 150.

165. Select Committee to Investigate the January 6th Attack on the United States Capitol, Continued Interview of Cassidy Hutchinson, (June 20, 2022), p. 26.

166. Select Committee to Investigate the January 6th Attack on the United States Capitol, Continued Interview of Cassidy Hutchinson, (June 20, 2022), p. 26. Cipollone did not elaborate but testified generally that he was "very upset about what was happening" at the Capitol and wanted "action to be taken related to that." Select Committee to Investigate the January 6th Attack on the United States Capitol, Transcribed Interview of Pasquale Anthony "Pat" Cipollone, (July 8, 2022), p. 149.

167. Select Committee to Investigate the January 6th Attack on the United States Capitol, Continued Interview of Cassidy Hutchinson, (June 20, 2022), p. 26.

168. Donald J. Trump (@realDonaldTrump), Twitter, Jan. 6, 2021 2:24 p.m. ET, available at https://www.thetrumparchive.com/?searchbox=%22Mike+Pence+didn%E2%80%99t+have+%22 (archived).

169. Select Committee to Investigate the January 6th Attack on the United States Capitol, Continued Interview of Cassidy Hutchinson, (June 20, 2022), p. 27.

170. Select Committee to Investigate the January 6th Attack on the United States Capitol, Continued Interview of Cassidy Hutchinson, (June 20, 2022), p. 27.

171. Select Committee to Investigate the January 6th Attack on the United States Capitol, Continued Interview of Cassidy Hutchinson, (June 20, 2022), p. 27. President Trump himself has defended publicly the rioters who chanted "Hang Mike Pence!" In an interview, journalist Jonathan Karl asked President Trump about the chants. "Well, the people were very angry," he responded. The President continued: "Because it's common sense . . . . How can you—if you know a vote is fraudulent, how can you pass a fraudulent vote to Congress? How can you do it?" Jonathan Karl, *Betrayal: The Final Act of the Trump Show*, (New York: Dutton, 2021), p. 340.

172. Select Committee to Investigate the January 6th Attack on the United States Capitol, Continued Interview of Cassidy Hutchinson, (June 20, 2022), p. 27. Hutchinson recalled one other thing that Meadows said, referring to the tweet attacking Vice President Pence: "[T]his is the best we're going to get for now." Select Committee to Investigate the January 6th Attack on the United States Capitol, Continued Interview of Cassidy Hutchinson, (May 17, 2022), p. 17. Hutchinson believes that this conversation took place after the 2:24 p.m. tweet, but the context suggests that it may have taken place after the 2:38 p.m. or 3:13 p.m. tweets.

173. Select Committee to Investigate the January 6th Attack on the United States Capitol, Transcribed Interview of Pasquale Anthony "Pat" Cipollone, (July 8, 2022), p. 150.

174. Select Committee to Investigate the January 6th Attack on the United States Capitol, Transcribed Interview of Pasquale Anthony "Pat" Cipollone, (July 8, 2022), p. 150.

175. Select Committee to Investigate the January 6th Attack on the United States Capitol, Transcribed Interview of Pasquale Anthony "Pat" Cipollone, (July 8, 2022), p. 161.

176. Select Committee to Investigate the January 6th Attack on the United States Capitol, Transcribed Interview of Pasquale Anthony "Pat" Cipollone, (July 8, 2022), p. 161; Select Committee to Investigate the January 6th Attack on the United States Capitol, *Hearing on the January 6th Investigation*, 117th Cong., 2d sess., (July 21, 2022), at 1:29:45–1:31:50, available at https://www.youtube.com/watch?v=pbRVqWbHGuo.

177. Documents on file with the Select Committee to Investigate the January 6th Attack on the United States Capitol (Secret Service Production), CTRL0000095185.

178. Documents on file with the Select Committee to Investigate the January 6th Attack on the United States Capitol (Secret Service Production), CTRL0000095247.

179. Lauren Fox and Clare Foran, "GOP Sen. Mike Lee Hands Over Phone Records to House Impeachment Managers," CNN, (Feb. 13, 2021), available at https://www.cnn.com/2021/02/13/politics/mike-lee-phone-records-impeachment-trial/index.html.

180. Mike Lillis, "Tuberville Defends Account of Trump Call During Capitol Riot," *The Hill*, (Feb. 12, 2021), available at https://thehill.com/homenews/senate/538704-tuberville-defends-account-of-trump-call-during-capitol-riot/. Sen. Tuberville stated publicly that the originating number was identified as "White House" on Sen. Lee's phone, suggesting that the call came through the White House Switchboard. *Id.*

181. Jonathan Karl, *Betrayal: The Final Act of the Trump* Show, (New York: Dutton, 2021), at p. 287.

182. Jonathan Karl, *Betrayal: The Final Act of the Trump* Show, (New York: Dutton, 2021), at p. 287.

183. Eddie Burkhalter, "Tuberville Says He Attended Jan. 5 Fundraiser at Trump's Washington Hotel," *Alabama Political Reporter*, (Feb. 19, 2021), available at https://www.alreporter.com/2021/02/19/tuberville-says-he-attended-jan-5-fundraiser-at-trumps-washington-hotel/.

184. The call likely happened after the evacuation of the House chamber starting at approximately 2:38 p.m., and Rep. McCarthy spoke about it to CBS News's Norah O'Donnell by phone between approximately 3:00 to 3:15 p.m. CBS News, "House Minority Leader Kevin McCarthy: I Completely Condemn the Violence in the Capitol," YouTube, Jan. 6, 2021, available at https://www.youtube.com/watch?v=MpBbpqO5qgU. Molly Michael testified that she

recalls receiving the incoming call from Leader McCarthy on Dan Scavino's landline and transferring it to a landline in the dining room. She does not recall when the call took place, nor did she hear anything about what was discussed. Select Committee to Investigate the January 6th Attack on the United States Capitol, Deposition of Molly Michael, (Mar. 24, 2022), pp. 131–32.

185. "House Minority Leader Kevin McCarthy: 'I Completely Condemn the Violence in the Capitol,'" CBS News, (Jan. 6, 2021), available at https://www.cbsnews.com/video/house-minority-leader-kevin-mccarthy-condemn-the-violence/#x.

186. "House Minority Leader Kevin McCarthy: 'I Completely Condemn the Violence in the Capitol,'" CBS News, (Jan. 6, 2021), available at https://www.cbsnews.com/video/house-minority-leader-kevin-mccarthy-condemn-the-violence/#x.

187. Tommy Christopher, "WATCH: GOP Rep Reveals Details of Trump's Bombshell Call with McCarthy Refusing to Call off Capitol Rioters," Mediaite, (Feb. 13, 2021), available at https://www.mediaite.com/news/watch-gop-rep-reveals-details-of-trumps-bombshell-call-with-mccarthy-refusing-to-call-off-capitol-rioters/.

188. Tommy Christopher, "WATCH: GOP Rep Reveals Details of Trump's Bombshell Call with McCarthy Refusing to Call off Capitol Rioters," Mediaite, (Feb. 13, 2021), available at https://www.mediaite.com/news/watch-gop-rep-reveals-details-of-trumps-bombshell-call-with-mccarthy-refusing-to-call-off-capitol-rioters/.

189. Tommy Christopher, "WATCH: GOP Rep Reveals Details of Trump's Bombshell Call with McCarthy Refusing to Call off Capitol Rioters," Mediaite, (Feb. 13, 2021), available at https://www.mediaite.com/news/watch-gop-rep-reveals-details-of-trumps-bombshell-call-with-mccarthy-refusing-to-call-off-capitol-rioters/.

190. Tommy Christopher, "WATCH: GOP Rep Reveals Details of Trump's Bombshell Call with McCarthy Refusing to Call off Capitol Rioters," Mediaite, (Feb. 13, 2021), available at https://www.mediaite.com/news/watch-gop-rep-reveals-details-of-trumps-bombshell-call-with-mccarthy-refusing-to-call-off-capitol-rioters/.

191. Tommy Christopher, "WATCH: GOP Rep Reveals Details of Trump's Bombshell Call with McCarthy Refusing to Call off Capitol Rioters," Mediaite, (Feb. 13, 2021), available at https://www.mediaite.com/news/watch-gop-rep-reveals-details-of-trumps-bombshell-call-with-mccarthy-refusing-to-call-off-capitol-rioters/.

192. Tommy Christopher, "WATCH: GOP Rep Reveals Details of Trump's Bombshell Call with McCarthy Refusing to Call off Capitol Rioters," Mediaite, (Feb. 13, 2021), available at https://www.mediaite.com/news/watch-gop-rep-reveals-details-of-trumps-bombshell-call-with-mccarthy-refusing-to-call-off-capitol-rioters/.

193. Tommy Christopher, "WATCH: GOP Rep Reveals Details of Trump's Bombshell Call with McCarthy Refusing to Call off Capitol Rioters," Mediaite, (Feb. 13, 2021), available at https://www.mediaite.com/news/watch-gop-rep-reveals-details-of-trumps-bombshell-call-with-mccarthy-refusing-to-call-off-capitol-rioters/.

194. Select Committee to Investigate the January 6th Attack on the United States Capitol, Transcribed Interview of John Michael "Mick" Mulvaney, (July 28, 2022), p. 43.

195. Select Committee to Investigate the January 6th Attack on the United States Capitol, Deposition of Marc Short, (Jan. 26, 2022), p. 46.

196. Select Committee to Investigate the January 6th Attack on the United States Capitol, Deposition of Marc Short, (Jan. 26, 2022), p. 46.

197. Select Committee to Investigate the January 6th Attack on the United States Capitol, Deposition of Marc Short, (Jan. 26, 2022), p. 47.

198. Documents on file with the Select Committee to Investigate the January 6th Attack on the United States Capitol (Ross Worthington Production), RW_0002307 (Jan. 6, 2021, Gabriel Roberts text message at 2:49 p.m.).

199. Select Committee to Investigate the January 6th Attack on the United States Capitol, Transcribed Interview of Eric Herschmann, (Apr. 6, 2022), p. 72.

200. Select Committee to Investigate the January 6th Attack on the United States Capitol, Transcribed Interview of Ivanka Trump, (Apr. 5, 2022), p. 68; *see also* Select Committee to Investigate the January 6th Attack on the United States Capitol, Transcribed Interview of Eric Herschmann, (Apr. 6, 2022), pp. 68–69.

201. Select Committee to Investigate the January 6th Attack on the United States Capitol, Transcribed Interview of Ivanka Trump, (Apr. 5, 2022), p. 70.

202. Select Committee to Investigate the January 6th Attack on the United States Capitol, Transcribed Interview of Eric Herschmann, (Apr. 6, 2022), p. 69 ("And she was in there for a few minutes, and then came out and he had issued a tweet."); Select Committee to Investigate the January 6th Attack on the United States Capitol, Transcribed Interview of Ivanka Trump, (Apr. 5, 2022), p. 64 ("Within, I believe, a few minutes he had issued that—he put out that tweet, a version of that tweet.").

203. Donald J. Trump (@realDonaldTrump), Twitter, Jan. 6, 2021 2:38 p.m. ET, available at https://www.thetrumparchive.com/?searchbox=%22please+support+our%22 (archived).

204. Select Committee to Investigate the January 6th Attack on the United States Capitol, Transcribed Interview of Ivanka Trump, (Apr. 5, 2022), pp. 87–89.

205. Select Committee to Investigate the January 6th Attack on the United States Capitol, Transcribed Interview of Ivanka Trump, (Apr. 5, 2022), p. 88.

206. Documents on file with the Select Committee to Investigate the January 6th Attack on the United States Capitol (Kayleigh McEnany Production), KMC_000000724, (January 6, 2021, Kayleigh McEnany Notes); Select Committee to Investigate the January 6th Attack on the United States Capitol, Deposition of Kayleigh McEnany, (Jan. 12, 2022), p. 185.

207. Select Committee to Investigate the January 6th Attack on the United States Capitol, Transcribed Interview of Ivanka Trump, (Apr. 5, 2022), pp. 88–89; Select Committee to Investigate the January 6th Attack on the United States Capitol, Deposition of Kayleigh McEnany, (Jan. 12, 2022), p. 185.

208. Select Committee to Investigate the January 6th Attack on the United States Capitol, *Hearing on the January 6th Investigation*, 117th Cong., 2d sess., (July 21, 2022), available at https://www.govinfo.gov/committee/house-january6th.

209. Select Committee to Investigate the January 6th Attack on the United States Capitol, *Hearing on the January 6th Investigation*, 117th Cong., 2d sess., (July 21, 2022), available at https://www.govinfo.gov/committee/house-january6th.

210. Select Committee to Investigate the January 6th Attack on the United States Capitol, *Hearing on the January 6th Investigation*, 117th Cong., 2d sess., (July 21, 2022), available at https://www.govinfo.gov/committee/house-january6th.

211. Carol Leonnig and Philip Rucker, *I Alone Can Fix It: Donald J. Trump's Catastrophic Final Year* (New York: Penguin, 2021), p. 474.

212. Select Committee to Investigate the January 6th Attack on the United States Capitol, Transcribed Interview of Ivanka Trump, (Apr. 5, 2022), p. 91.

213. Select Committee to Investigate the January 6th Attack on the United States Capitol, Deposition of Keith Kellogg, Jr., (Dec. 14, 2021), p 141.

214. Select Committee to Investigate the January 6th Attack on the United States Capitol, Transcribed Interview of Cassidy Hutchinson, (Feb. 23, 2022), p. 170.

215. Bob Woodward and Robert Costa, *Peril*, (New York: Simon & Schuster, 2021), p. 248.

216. Select Committee to Investigate the January 6th Attack on the United States Capitol, Deposition of Julie Radford, (May 24, 2022), p. 32.

217. Select Committee to Investigate the January 6th Attack on the United States Capitol, Deposition of Julie Radford, (May 24, 2022), p. 30.

218. Select Committee to Investigate the January 6th Attack on the United States Capitol, Continued Interview of Cassidy Hutchinson, (June 20, 2022), p. 37; Hutchinson recalls that Meadows, Herschmann, Ivanka Trump, and others would come and go from the Chief of Staff's office at intervals throughout the afternoon. "I don't know if it was for a breather or to have a conversation away from the dining room," she said. *Id.*, at 31.

219. Select Committee to Investigate the January 6th Attack on the United States Capitol, Continued Interview of Cassidy Hutchinson, (June 20, 2022), p. 38.

220. Fox News, "U.S. Capitol on Lockdown as Protests Threaten Security," YouTube, Jan. 6, 2021, available at https://www.youtube.com/watch?v=oFWGBnJ0rQA.

221. Fox News, "Breaking News: Protestors Now inside U.S. Capitol," YouTube, at 2:40, Jan. 6, 2021, available at https://www.fox29.com/video/887421.

222. Fox News, "Pro-Trump Protestors Storm U.S. Capitol," YouTube, Jan. 6, 2021, available at https://www.youtube.com/watch?v=tVPSYr-xG6s.

223. Documents on file with the Select Committee to Investigate the January 6th Attack on the United States Capitol (Secret Service Production), CTRL0000095389.

224. Documents on file with the Select Committee to Investigate the January 6th Attack on the United States Capitol (Secret Service Production), CTRL0000095393 (Jan. 6, 2021, text between Secret Service agents at 2:41 p.m. EST).

225. Marshall Cohen and Avery Lotz, "The January 6 Insurrection: Minute-by-Minute," CNN, (July 29, 2022), available at https://www.cnn.com/2022/07/10/politics/jan-6-us-capitol-riot-timeline/index.html.

226. Documents on file with the Select Committee to Investigate the January 6th Attack on the United States Capitol (National Archives Production), P-R000241 (Jan. 6, 2021, Note to President Trump).

227. Select Committee Interview Investigate the January 6th Attack on the United States Capitol, Transcribed Interview of White House Employee, (June 10, 2022), pp. 46–47.

228. *See, e.g.*, Documents on file with the Select Committee to Investigate the January 6th Attack on the United States Capitol (Mark Meadows Production), MM014921, MM014923, MM014926.

229. Documents on file with the Select Committee to Investigate the January 6th Attack on the United States Capitol (Mark Meadows Production), MM014906. Recently, Representative Greene has qualified her stance on armed rioters at the Capitol. At a Young Republicans event in New York, she said: "I got to tell you something, if Steve Bannon and I had oganized [January 6th], we would have won. Not to mention, it would've been armed." She claims she was joking. Aaron Blake, "Analysis: Marjorie Taylor Greene's Jan. 6 'Joke' Has Been Building for a Long Time," *Washington Post*, (Dec. 12, 2022), available at https://www.washingtonpost.com/politics/2022/12/12/greene-january-6-punchline/.

230. Documents on file with the Select Committee to Investigate the January 6th Attack on the United States Capitol (Mark Meadows Production), MM014907, MM014908, MM014909, (Jan. 6, 2021, Laura Ingraham text message to Mark Meadows at 2:32 pm); Documents on file with the Select Committee to Investigate the Jan. 6th Attack on the United States Capitol (Mark Meadows Production), MM014911 (Jan. 6, 2021, Laura Ingraham text message to Mark Meadows at 2:32 p.m.).

231. Documents on file with the Select Committee to Investigate the January 6th Attack on the United States Capitol (Mark Meadows Production), MM014912.

232. Documents on File with the Select Committee to Investigate the January 6th Attack on the United States Capitol (Mark Meadows Production), MM014914, MM014915.

233. Documents on file with the Select Committee to Investigate the January 6th Attack on the United States Capitol (Mark Meadows Production), MM014921.

234. Documents on file with the Select Committee to Investigate the January 6th Attack on the United States Capitol (Mark Meadows Production), MM014922.

235. Documents on file with the Select Committee to Investigate the January 6th Attack on the United States Capitol (Mark Meadows Production), MM014919.

236. Documents on file with the Select Committee to Investigate the January 6th Attack on the United States Capitol (Mark Meadows Production), MM014923.

237. Documents on file with the Select Committee to Investigate the January 6th Attack on the United States Capitol (Mark Meadows Production), MM014925.

238. Documents on file with the Select Committee to Investigate the January 6th Attack on the United States Capitol (Mark Meadows Production), MM014926.

239. Documents on file with the Select Committee to Investigate the January 6th Attack on the United States Capitol (Mark Meadows Production), MM014928.

240. Documents on file with the Select Committee to Investigate the January 6th Attack on the United States Capitol (National Archives Production), P-R000240 (January 6, 2021 proposed statement).

241. Select Committee to Investigate the January 6th Attack on the United States Capitol, *Hearing on the January 6th Investigation*, 117th Cong., 2d sess., (June 28, 2022), available at https://www.govinfo.gov/committee/house-january6th.

242. Select Committee to Investigate the January 6th Attack on the United States Capitol, *Hearing on the January 6th Investigation*, 117th Cong., 2d sess., (June 28, 2022), available at https://www.govinfo.gov/committee/house-january6th.

243. Select Committee to Investigate the January 6th Attack on the United States Capitol, *Hearing on the January 6th Investigation*, 117th Cong., 2d sess., (June 28, 2022), available at https://www.govinfo.gov/committee/house-january6th.

244. Donald Trump (@realDonaldTrump), Twitter, Jan. 6, 2021 3:13 p.m. EST, available at https://www.thetrumparchive.com/?searchbox=%22remain+peaceful%22 (archived).

245. Select Committee to Investigate the January 6th Attack on the United States Capitol, Transcribed Interview of Ivanka Trump, (Apr. 5, 2022), p. 119.

246. Select Committee to Investigate the January 6th Attack at the United States Capitol, Transcribed Interview of Eric Herschmann, (Apr. 6, 2022), p. 88.

247. *See, e.g.*, Select Committee to Investigate the January 6th Attack on the United States Capitol, Transcribed Interview of Eric Herschmann, (Apr. 6, 2022), p. 88; Select Committee to Investigate the January 6th Attack on the United States Capitol, Deposition of Kayleigh McEnany, (Jan. 12, 2022), p. 172; Select Committee to Investigate the January 6th Attack on the United States Capitol, Transcribed Interview of Pasquale Anthony "Pat" Cipollone, (July 8, 2022), p. 155.

248. "Pergram: Most Significant Breach of Government Institution Since 1814," Fox News, Jan. 6, 2021, available at https://www.foxnews.com/video/6220760122001#sp=show-clips.

249. Fox News, "Individual Shot in U.S. Capitol," YouTube, at 1:59, Jan. 6, 2021, available at https://www.youtube.com/watch?v=oL-M0LuE3Hk.

250. "Andy McCarthy Blasts Pro-Trump Protesters after Breach at Capitol," Fox News, at 1:28, Jan. 6, 2021, available at https://www.foxnews.com/video/6220757649001#sp=show-clips.

251. Documents on File with the Select Committee to Investigate the January 6th Attack on the United States Capitol (Mark Meadows Production), MM014932, MM014934.

252. Documents on File with the Select Committee to Investigate the January 6th Attack on the United States Capitol (Mark Meadows Production), MM014935. This was sent from a phone number associated with Priebus's family member.

253. Documents on File with the Select Committee to Investigate the January 6th Attack on the United States Capitol (Mark Meadows Production), MM014936.

254. Documents on File with the Select Committee to Investigate the January 6th Attack on the United States Capitol (Mark Meadows Production), MM014937.

255. Documents on File with the Select Committee to Investigate the January 6th Attack on the United States Capitol (Mark Meadows Production), MM014939.

256. Documents on File with the Select Committee to Investigate the January 6th Attack on the United States Capitol (Mark Meadows Production), MM014943.

257. Documents on File with the Select Committee to Investigate the January 6th Attack on the United States Capitol (Mark Meadows Production), MM014944.

258. Documents on file with the Select Committee to Investigate the January 6th Attack on the United States Capitol (Mark Meadows Production), MM014947.

259. Documents on File with the Select Committee to Investigate the January 6th Attack on the United States Capitol (Mark Meadows Production), MM014948.

260. Document on File with the Select Committee to Investigate the January 6th Attack on the United States Capitol (Mark Meadows Production), MM014949.

261. Documents on file with the Select Committee to Investigate the January 6th Attack on the United States Capitol (Mark Meadows Production), MM014956, MM014957.

262. Document on File with the Select Committee to Investigate the January 6th Attack on the United States Capitol (Mark Meadows Production), MM014961.

263. Document on File with the Select Committee to Investigate the January 6th Attack on the United States Capitol (Mark Meadows Production), MM014964.

264. Select Committee to Investigate the January 6th Attack on the United States Capitol, *Hearing on the January 6th Investigation*, 117th Cong., 2d sess., (July 21, 2022), available at https://www.govinfo.gov/committee/house-january6th.

265. Select Committee to Investigate the January 6th Attack on the United States Capitol, *Hearing on the January 6th Investigation*, 117th Cong., 2d sess., (July 21, 2022), available at https://www.govinfo.gov/committee/house-january6th; *see also* CBS News, "House Minority Leader Kevin McCarthy: 'I completely condemn the violence in the Capitol,'" YouTube, Jan. 6, 2021, available at https://www.youtube.com/watch?v=MpBbpqO5qgU.

266. Select Committee to Investigate the January 6th Attack on the United States Capitol, *Hearing on the January 6th Investigation*, 117th Cong., 2d sess., (July 21, 2022), available at https://www.govinfo.gov/committee/house-january6th.

267. Select Committee to Investigate the January 6th Attack on the United States Capitol, *Hearing on the January 6th Investigation*, 117th Cong., 2d sess., (July 22, 2022), available at https://www.govinfo.gov/committee/house-january6th; Select Committee to Investigate the January 6th Attack on the United States Capitol, Transcribed Interview of Pasquale Anthony "Pat" Cipollone, (July 8, 2022), p. 163.

268. Donald Trump (@realDonaldTrump), Twitter, Jan. 6, 2021 4:17 p.m. ET, available at https://www.thetrumparchive.com/?searchbox=%22https%3A%2F%2Ft.co%2FPm2PKV0Fp3%22 (archived).

269. Documents on file with the Select Committee to Investigate the January 6th Attack on the United States Capitol (National Archives Production), P-R000255 (Jan. 6, 2021, Daily Diary of President Donald J. Trump).

270. "Bill Hemmer Reports," Fox News, at 3:56 p.m. ET, available at https://archive.org/details/FOXNEWSW_20210106_200000_Bill_Hemmer_Reports/start/3360/end/3420 (archived).

271. Select Committee to Investigate the January 6th Attack on the United States Capitol, Deposition of Nicholas Luna, (Mar. 21, 2022), pp. 162–63.

272. Select Committee to Investigate the January 6th Attack on the United States Capitol, Deposition of Nicholas Luna, (Mar. 21, 2022), p. 162.

273. Documents on file with the Select Committee to Investigate the January 6th Attack on the United States Capitol (National Archives Production), Video file 40983.

274. Documents on file with the Select Committee to Investigate the January 6th Attack on the United States Capitol (National Archives Production), P-R000255 (Jan. 6, 2021, Daily Diary of President Donald J. Trump).

275. Select Committee to Investigate the January 6th Attack on the United States Capitol, Deposition of Kayleigh McEnany, (Jan. 12, 2022), p. 234. President Trump did not react to her suggestion, McEnany said. *See id.*

276. Select Committee to Investigate the January 6th Attack on the United States Capitol, Deposition of Nicholas Luna, (Mar. 21, 2022), p. 161; Select Committee to Investigate the January 6th Attack on the United States Capitol, Transcribed Interview of Eric Herschmann, (Apr. 6, 2022), pp. 97–99.

277. Donald Trump (@realDonaldTrump), Twitter, Jan. 6, 2021 4:17 p.m. ET, available at https://www.thetrumparchive.com/?searchbox=%22https%3A%2F%2Ft.co%2FPm2PKV0Fp3%22 (archived).

278. Documents on file with the Select Committee to Investigate the January 6th Attack on the United States Capitol (National Archives Production), Photo file 4243_hi_j0233_61ae.

279. Select Committee to Investigate the January 6th Attack on the United States Capitol, Deposition of Nicholas Luna, (Mar. 21, 2022), p. 182. See Select Committee to Investigate the January 6th Attack on the United States Capitol, Interview of White House Employee, (June 10, 2022), pp. 49–50 (remembering that someone in the Rose Garden told the President something along the lines "that he needed to use stronger, more forceful" language in the video).

280. Select Committee to Investigate the January 6th Attack on the United States Capitol, Transcribed Interview of Eric Herschmann, (Apr. 6, 2022), p. 99.

281. Select Committee to Investigate the January 6th Attack on the United States Capitol, Deposition of Nicholas Luna, (Mar. 21, 2022), p. 181.

282. Select Committee to Investigate the January 6th Attack on the United States Capitol, *Hearing on the January 6th Investigation*, 117th Cong., 2d sess., (July 21, 2022), at 1:58:30, available at https://www.youtube.com/watch?v=pbRVqWbHGuo.

283. Select Committee to Investigate the January 6th Attack on the United States Capitol, *Hearing on the January 6th Investigation*, 117th Cong., 2d sess., (July 12, 2022), available at https://www.govinfo.gov/committee/house-january6th. ("[A]s soon as that come out, everybody started talking about it and that's—it seemed like it started to disperse.").

284. Select Committee to Investigate the January 6th Attack on the United States Capitol, *Hearing on the January 6h Investigation*, 117th Cong., 2d sess., (July 12, 2022), available at https://www.govinfo.gov/committee/house-january6th ("Basically, when President Trump put his tweet out. We literally left right after that [had] come out.").

285. Select Committee to Investigate the January 6th Attack on the United States Capitol, Hearing on the January 6th Investigation, 117th Cong., 2d sess., (July 12, 2022), available at https://www.govinfo.gov/committee/house-january6th. ("[I]f he would have done that earlier in the day, 1:30, I—you know, we wouldn't be in this—maybe we wouldn't be in this bad of a situation or something.").

286. "Bill Hemmer Reports," Fox News, Jan. 6, 2021, available at https://archive.org/details/FOXNEWSW_20210106_200000_Bill_Hemmer_Reports/start/780/end/840.

287. Donald J. Trump (@realDonaldTrump), Twitter, Jan. 6, 2020 6:01 p.m. ET, available at https://www.thetrumparchive.com/?searchbox=%22these+are+the+things+and+events%22 (archived).

288. T, available at https://www.thetrumparchive.com/?searchbox=%22these+are+the+things+and+events%22 (archived).

289. *See* Select Committee to Investigate the January 6th Attack on the United States Capitol, Interview of White House Employee, (June 10, 2022), p. 53.

290. Documents on file with the Select Committee to Investigate the January 6th Attack on the United States Capitol (National Archives production), Photo file 364c_hi_j0246_2fa8.

291. See Select Committee to Investigate the January 6th Attack on the United States Capitol, Interview of White House Employee, (June 10, 2022), p. 53.

292. Documents on file with the Select Committee to Investigate the January 6th Attack on the United States Capitol (AT&T Production, Feb. 9, 2022).

293. Documents on file with the Select Committee to Investigate the January 6th Attack on the United States Capitol (AT&T Production, Feb. 9, 2022).

294. Documents on file with the Select Committee to Investigate the January 6th Attack on the United States Capitol (AT&T Production, Feb. 9, 2022).

295. Documents on file with the Select Committee to Investigate the January 6th Attack on the United States Capitol (AT&T Production, Feb. 9, 2022).

296. Documents on file with the Select Committee to Investigate the January 6th Attack on the United States Capitol (Rudolph Giuliani Production, Mar. 11, 2022).

297. Documents on file with the Select Committee to Investigate the January 6th Attack on the United States Capitol (Rudolph Giuliani Production, Mar. 11, 2022); Documents on file with the Select Committee to Investigate the January 6th Attack on the United States Capitol (AT&T Production, Feb. 9, 2022).

298. Documents on file with the Select Committee to Investigate the January 6th Attack on the United States Capitol (AT&T Production, Feb. 9, 2022).

299. Documents on file with the Select Committee to Investigate the January 6th Attack on the United States Capitol (Rudolph Giuliani Production, Mar. 11, 2022).

300. Documents on file with the Select Committee to Investigate the January 6th Attack on the United States Capitol (Rudolph Giuliani Production, Mar. 11, 2022).

301. Documents on file with the Select Committee to Investigate the January 6th Attack on the United States Capitol (Rudolph Giuliani Production, Mar. 11, 2022).

302. Documents on file with the Select Committee to Investigate the January 6th Attack on the United States Capitol (AT&T Production, Feb. 9, 2022).

303. Documents on file with the Select Committee to Investigate the January 6th Attack on the United States Capitol (Rudolph Giuliani Production, Mar. 11, 2022); Documents on file with the Select Committee to Investigate the January 6th Attack on the United States Capitol (AT&T Production, Feb. 9, 2022).

304. Documents on file with the Select Committee to Investigate the January 6th Attack on the United States Capitol (National Archives Production), P-R000255 (Jan. 6, 2021, Daily Diary of President Donald J. Trump); Documents on file with the Select Committee to Investigate the January 6th Attack on the United States Capitol (AT&T Production, Feb. 9, 2022).

305. Select Committee to Investigate the January 6th Attack on the United States Capitol, Deposition of Rudolph Giuliani, (May 20, 2022), p. 206. ("You were leaving messages or having phone calls with United States Senators about the joint session of Congress. How could that possibly be [a] privileged conversation?" "Because the conversation is about the theory of the case, and my representation of the client.").

306. Select Committee to Investigate the January 6th Attack on the United States Capitol, Deposition of Rudolph Giuliani, (May 20, 2022), p. 207.

307. Select Committee to Investigate the January 6th Attack on the United States Capitol, Deposition of Rudolph Giuliani, (May 20, 2022), p. 206; Documents on file with the Select Committee to Investigate the January 6th Attack on the United States Capitol (Robert O'Brien Production), NSA 0040 (January 6, 2021, text message from Sen. Mike Lee to Robert O'Brien at 10:55 p.m. EST reading, "You can't make this up. I just got this voice message [from] Rudy Giuliani, who apparently thought he was calling Senator Tuberville." "You've got to listen to that message. Rudy is walking malpractice.").

308. Steve Hayes, "Giuliani to Senator: 'Try to Just Slow it Down,'" *The Dispatch*, (Jan. 6, 2021), available at https://thedispatch.com/p/giuliani-to-senator-try-to-just-slow.

309. Steve Hayes, "Giuliani to Senator: 'Try to Just Slow it Down,'" *The Dispatch*, (Jan. 6, 2021), available at https://thedispatch.com/p/giuliani-to-senator-try-to-just-slow.

310. Those 13 people are Pat Cipollone, Dan Scavino, Kurt Olsen, Mark Martin, Cleta Mitchell, Rudy Giuliani, Kayleigh McEnany, Jason Miller, Mark Meadows, Steve Bannon, Eric Herschmann, Sean Hannity, and John McEntee. *See* Documents on file with the Select Committee to Investigate the January 6th Attack on the United States Capitol (National Archives Production), P-R000255 (Jan. 6, 2021, Daily Diary of President Donald J. Trump); Documents on file with the Select Committee to Investigate the January 6th Attack on the United States Capitol (National Archives Production), P-R000261 (Jan. 6, 2021, the Presidential Call Log).

311. H. Rept. 117-152, Resolution Recommending that the House of Representatives Find Stephen K. Bannon in Contempt of Congress for Refusal to Comply with a Subpoena Duly Issued by the Select Committee to Investigate the January 6th Attack on the United States Capitol, 117th Cong., 1st sess. (2021), available at https://www.congress.gov/117/crpt/hrpt152/CRPT-117hrpt152.pdf; H. Rept. 117–216, Resolution Recommending that the House of Representatives Find Mark Randall Meadows in Contempt of Congress for Refusal to Comply with a Subpoena Duly Issued by the Select Committee to Investigate the January 6th Attack on the United States Capitol, 117th Cong., 1st sess. (2021), available at https://www.congress.gov/117/crpt/hrpt216/CRPT-117hrpt216.pdf; H. Rept. 117–284, Resolution Recommending that the House of Representatives Find Peter K. Navarro and Daniel Scavino, Jr., in Contempt of Congress for Refusal to Comply with a Subpoena Duly Issued by the Select Committee to Investigate the January 6th Attack on the United States Capitol, 117th Cong., 2d sess. (2022), available at https://www.congress.gov/117/crpt/hrpt284/CRPT-117hrpt284.pdf; Erik Larson, "Lawyer Who Talked to Trump on Day of Capitol Riot Sues over Subpoena," *Bloomberg*, (Mar. 25, 2022), available at https://www.bloomberg.com/news/articles/2022-03-25/lawyer-who-talked-to-trump-on-day-of-mob-riot-sues-over-subpoena (discussing Kurt Olsen); Caleb Ecarma, "Sean Hannity Wants the January 6 Committee to Believe He's a Journalist," *Vanity Fair*, (Jan. 5, 2022), available at https://www.vanityfair.com/news/2022/01/sean-hannity-january-6-committee-journalist.

312. Select Committee to Investigate the January 6th Attack on the United States Capitol, Transcribed Interview of Eric Herschmann, (Apr. 6, 2022), p. 118; Select Committee to Investigate the January 6th Attack on the United States Capitol, Transcribed Interview of Pasquale Anthony "Pat" Cipollone, (July 8, 2022), p. 195.

313. Select Committee to Investigate the January 6th Attack on the United States Capitol, Deposition of Cleta Mitchell, (May 18, 2022), p. 131; Select Committee to Investigate the January 6th Attack on the United States Capitol, Deposition of Rudolph Giuliani, (May 20, 2022), p. 211.

314. Documents on file with the Select Committee to Investigate the January 6th Attack on the United States Capitol (National Archives Production), P-R000255 (Jan. 6, 2021, Daily Diary of President Donald J. Trump); "WATCH: 'Let's Get Back to Work,' Pence Urges Senate," PBS, (Jan. 6, 2021), available at https://www.pbs.org/newshour/politics/watch-lets-get-back-to-work-pence-urges-senate.

315. Documents on file with the Select Committee to Investigate the January 6th Attack on the United States Capitol (National Archives Production), P-R000255 (Jan. 6, 2021, Daily Diary of President Donald J. Trump).

316. Olsen authored a memo urging Vice President Pence to adjourn the joint session of Congress without counting electoral votes. *See* Documents on file with the Select Committee on the January 6th Attack on the United States Capitol (Chapman University Production) Chapman004979 (Jan. 2, 2021, Kurt Olsen Draft Memorandum Entitled, "The Role of the Vice President in Receiving Votes from the Electoral College.") Martin advised President Trump that Vice President Pence possessed the constitutional authority to impede the electoral

count. *See* Nicholas Fandos, Peter Baker, and Maggie Haberman, "House Moves to Force Trump Out, Vowing Impeachment if Pence Won't Act," *New York Times*, (Jan. 10, 2021), available at https://www.nytimes.com/2021/01/10/us/politics/trump-impeachment.html. Both corresponded with John Eastman and others regarding plans to convene alternate electors in states won by Joe Biden. *See* Documents on file with the Select Committee to Investigate the January 6th Attack on the United States Capitol (Chapman University Production), Chapman023998 (Dec. 6, 2020, Michael Farris email forwarding an email concerning the "Importance of Republican Electors in AZ, GA, MI, NV, PA and WI Voting on Dec 14" at 1:54 p.m. ET). President Trump asked to speak with Mr. Olsen and Mr. Martin before he left the dining room. *See* Documents on file with the Select Committee to Investigate the January 6th Attack on the United States Capitol (National Archives Production), 076P-R000007401_00001 (Jan. 6, 2021, Molly Michael email to MBX WHO MA Joint White House Switchboard at 11:28 p.m. ET).

317. Documents on file with the Select Committee to Investigate the January 6th Attack on the United States Capitol (National Archives Production), P-R000255 (Jan. 6, 2021, Daily Diary of President Donald J. Trump).

318. Documents on file with the Select Committee to Investigate the January 6th Attack on the United States Capitol (National Archives Production), P-R000255 (Jan. 6, 2021, Daily Diary of President Donald J. Trump). Mitchell declined to discuss her conversations with President Trump on attorney-client privilege grounds. She did, however, acknowledge that following the phone call, she took steps to dismiss the President's pending election suit in Georgia. *See* Select Committee to Investigate the January 6th Attack on the United States Capitol, Deposition of Cleta Mitchell, (May 18, 2022), p. 131.

319. Documents on file with the Select Committee to Investigate the January 6th Attack on the United States Capitol (National Archives Production), P-R000259 (Jan. 6, 2021, Daily Diary of the President Donald J. Trump); Select Committee to Investigate the January 6th Attack on the United States Capitol, Transcribed Interview of Eric Herschmann, (Apr. 6, 2022), p. 118 (Herschmann refused to answer questions about the phone call, citing executive privilege).

320. Documents on file with the Select Committee to Investigate the January 6th Attack on the United States Capitol (National Archives Production), P-R000255–P-R000259 (Jan. 6, 2021, Daily Diary of President Donald J. Trump).

321. Documents on file with the Select Committee to Investigate the January 6th Attack on the United States Capitol (National Archives Production), P-R000255–P-R000259 (Jan. 6, 2021, Daily Diary of President Donald J. Trump).

322. Documents on file with the Select Committee to Investigate the January 6th Attack on the United States Capitol (National Archives Production), P-R000255–P-R000259 (Jan. 6, 2021, Daily Diary of President Donald J. Trump).

323. Documents on file with the Select Committee to Investigate the January 6th Attack on the United States Capitol (National Archives Production), P-R000255–P-R000259 (Jan. 6, 2021, Daily Diary of President Donald J. Trump).

324. Documents on file with the Select Committee to Investigate the January 6th Attack on the United States Capitol (National Archives Production), P-R000255–P-R000259 (Jan. 6, 2021, Daily Diary of President Donald J. Trump).

325. Select Committee to Investigate the January 6th Attack on the United States Capitol, Deposition of Jason Miller, (Feb. 3, 2022), pp. 258–59.

326. Select Committee to Investigate the January 6th Attack on the United States Capitol, Deposition of Jason Miller, (Feb. 3, 2022), p. 258.

327. Select Committee to Investigate the January 6th Attack on the United States Capitol, Deposition of Jason Miller, (Feb. 3, 2022), p. 258.

328. Select Committee to Investigate the January 6th Attack on the United States Capitol, Deposition of John McEntee (Mar. 28, 2022), pp. 160–61; Documents on file with the Select Committee to Investigate the January 6th Attack on the United States Capitol (National Archives Production), P-R000259 (Jan. 6, 2021, Daily Diary of the President Donald J. Trump).

329. Select Committee to Investigate the January 6th Attack on the United States Capitol, Deposition of John McEntee, (Mar. 28, 2022), p. 161.

330. Select Committee to Investigate the January 6th Attack on the United States Capitol, Deposition of John McEntee, (Mar. 28, 2022), p. 161.

331. Insert: Documents on file with the Select Committee (National Archives Production), P-R000259 (Jan. 6, 2021, Daily Diary of the President Donald J. Trump).

332. Documents with file with the Select Committee to Investigate the January 6th Attack on the United States Capitol (National Archives Production), P-R000255 (Jan. 6, 2021, The Daily Diary of President Donald J. Trump).

333. Select Committee to Investigate the January 6th Attack on the United States Capitol, Deposition of Judson P. Deere, (Mar. 3, 2022), pp. 42–43.

334. Select Committee to Investigate the January 6th Attack on the United States Capitol, Transcribed Interview of Ivanka Trump, (Apr. 5, 2022), pp. 179–80.

335. Select Committee to Investigate the January 6th Attack on the United States Capitol, Transcribed Interview of Ivanka Trump, (Apr. 5, 2022), p. 180.

336. Documents on file with the Select Committee to Investigate the January 6th Attack on the United States Capitol (Patrick MacDonnell Production), PM000158 (Jan. 7, 2021, Patrick MacDonnell text message to personal contact at 9:46 p.m. EST).

337. Documents on file with the Select Committee to Investigate the January 6th Attack on the United States Capitol (Ali Alexander Production), CTRL0000017719, p. 3; Select Committee to Investigate the January 6th Attack on the United States Capitol, Deposition of Ali Alexander, (Dec. 9, 2021), p. 57.

338. Documents on file with the Select Committee to Investigate the January 6th Attack on the United States Capitol (Hope Hicks Production), SC_HH_042.

339. Documents on file with the Select Committee to Investigate the January 6th Attack on the United States Capitol (Hope Hicks Production), SC_HH_040.

340. Documents on file with the Select Committee to Investigate the January 6th Attack on the United States Capitol (Katrina Pierson Production), KPierson0717 (Jan. 6, 2021, Brad Parscale text message to Katrina Pierson at 7:14 p.m. ET).

341. Documents on file with the Select Committee to Investigate the January 6th Attack on the United States Capitol (Katrina Pierson Production), KPierson0718– KPierson20 (Jan. 6, 2021, Brad Parscale text message to Katrina Pierson at 7:22 p.m. ET).

8

ANALYSIS OF THE ATTACK

Late in the evening on January 6, 2021, Henry "Enrique" Tarrio, the head of the Proud Boys, posted a video on his Parler account. The brief footage showed a masked man, wearing a black cape, standing in front of the U.S. Capitol Building. Tarrio titled the 18-second video, set to ominous music, "Premonition." He offered no further explanation. The clear implication of the brief footage, recorded sometime prior to January 6th, was that Tarrio had foreknowledge of the events that transpired earlier that same day.[1]

Indeed, Tarrio cheered on his fellow Proud Boys as they attacked the U.S. Capitol. He had been arrested and ordered to leave Washington, DC two days earlier. Although Tarrio was not physically present, he continued to monitor and communicate with his men via encrypted chats and social media. At 2:36 p.m. on January 6th, Tarrio wrote on Parler that he was "enjoying the show," adding: "Do what must be done" and "#WeThePeople."[2] Two minutes later, Tarrio wrote: "Don't fucking leave." Several minutes after that, Tarrio messaged his Proud Boys: "Make no mistake..." and "We did this..."[3]

Law enforcement officials subsequently uncovered significant evidence showing that Tarrio and his lieutenants planned to storm the U.S. Capitol. In June 2022, Tarrio and four other Proud Boys were charged with seditious conspiracy and other crimes related to their alleged responsibility for the assault.[4] The U.S. Department of Justice (DOJ) has alleged that they "conspired to prevent, hinder and delay the certification of the Electoral College vote, and to oppose by force the authority of the government of the United States."[5] On January 6, 2021, the Proud Boys "directed, mobilized and led members of the crowd onto the Capitol grounds and into the Capitol, leading to dismantling of metal barricades, destruction of property, breaching of the Capitol building, and assaults on law enforcement."[6]

The Select Committee's analysis corroborates the DOJ's findings and allegations. The Select Committee reviewed extensive footage of the attack, including that recorded by the U.S. Capitol Police's (USCP) surveillance cameras, the Metropolitan Police Department's (MPD) body-worn cameras, publicly available videos, as well as on-the-ground film produced by an embedded documentarian. The Select Committee interviewed rioters, law enforcement officers, and witnesses that were present on January 6th, while also consulting thousands of court filings. Using these sources of information, the Select Committee developed a timeline of events to understand how the unprecedented attack on the U.S. Capitol unfolded.

As explained below, the Proud Boys marched from the Washington Monument to the U.S. Capitol on the morning of January 6th. While tens of thousands of President Trump's supporters gathered at a rally at the Ellipse near the White House, the Proud Boys prepared to attack. Shortly before the joint session of Congress was set to begin at 1:00 p.m., the Proud Boys instigated an assault on outmanned law enforcement at the Peace Circle, a key location. They quickly overran security barriers and made their way onto the U.S. Capitol's restricted grounds. Throughout the next several hours, members of the Proud Boys led the attack at key breach points, preventing law enforcement from gaining crowd control and inciting others to press forward.

President Trump finished his speech at the Ellipse at approximately 1:10 p.m. Toward the end of his remarks, the President directed his supporters to march down Pennsylvania Avenue to the Capitol. Their natural path took them through the Peace Circle, which had already been cleared out by the Proud Boys and their associates. Thousands of rioters and protestors streamed onto the Capitol's restricted grounds in short order.

The Proud Boys were not solely responsible for attacking the U.S. Capitol. As explained in Chapter 6, other far-right extremists and conspiracy theorists prepared for violence after President Trump summoned them to Washington for a "wild" protest on January 6th. And they joined in the assault as well. Three Percenters, QAnon adherents, and other radicals were on the frontlines, pressing the charge. The Oath Keepers attacked the Capitol, forming two military-style "stacks" to push their way into the building. The white nationalist Groypers were present as their leader gave an inflammatory speech from the same Peace Circle where the attack was launched. Like members of the Proud Boys, Oath Keepers, and Three Percenters, some of the Groypers have been charged for their actions on January 6th.

Unaffiliated Americans enraged by President Trump's lies rioted as well. The January 6th, attack has often been described as a riot—and that is partly true. Some of those who trespassed on the Capitol's grounds or entered the building did not plan to do so beforehand. But it is also true that extremists, conspiracy theorists and others were prepared to fight. That is

Trump supporters from around the country gather at the Washington Monument on the morning of January 6, 2021.

Photo by Brent Stirton/Getty Images

an insurrection. They answered President Trump's call to action. Some, like the Proud Boys, deliberately harnessed the mob's anger to overrun the Capitol.

8.1 THE MOB ASSEMBLES IN WASHINGTON

During the early morning hours of January 6th, tens of thousands of Americans from around the country began to gather at the Ellipse and the Washington Monument. They had come to hear President Trump speak and, more importantly, for his "wild" protest.

Nick Quested, a documentary filmmaker, captured the mood that morning. Jacob Chansley (a.k.a. the QAnon Shaman) proclaimed "this is our 1776," vowing "Joe Biden is never getting in." [7] An unnamed woman from Georgia, who said she hosted a podcast dedicated to a new so-called Patriot Party, also proclaimed January 6th to be the new 1776. She added an ominous warning. "I'm not allowed to say what's going to happen today because everyone's just going to have to watch. Something's gonna happen, one way or the other." [8]

The Secret Service set up magnetometers to screen for weapons and other contraband, but many rally-goers chose to avoid the screening altogether.

At 6:29 a.m., Stewart Rhodes, the leader of the Oath Keepers, reminded his group's members that DC prohibited blades over "3 inches" and encouraged them to "[k]eep [the knives] low profile." [9] Others were thinking along the same lines. At 7:25 a.m., the National Park Service reported that a significant number of attendees ditched their bags in trees, rather than have them inspected. [10] Cassidy Hutchinson told the Select Committee she heard that thousands of people refused to walk through magnetometers to enter the Ellipse because they did not want to be screened for weapons. [11] According to Hutchinson, the Deputy Chief of Staff for Operations whose responsibilities included security-related issues, Tony Ornato, told the President that the onlookers "don't want to come in right now. They—they have weapons that they don't want confiscated by the Secret Service." [12] When he arrived at the Ellipse that morning, President Trump angrily said: "I don't [fucking] care that they have weapons. They're not here to hurt *me*. They can march to the Capitol from here." [13]

Approximately 28,000 rally-goers did pass through the magnetometers. The Secret Service confiscated a significant number of prohibited items from these people, including: 269 knives or blades, 242 cannisters of pepper spray, 18 brass knuckles, 18 tasers, 6 pieces of body armor, 3 gas masks, 30 batons or blunt instruments, and 17 miscellaneous items like scissors, needles, or screwdrivers. [14]

At 8:07 a.m., Secret Service countersurveillance agents reported that "members of the crowd are wearing ballistic helmets, body armor and carrying radio equipment and military grade backpacks." [15] By 9:45 a.m., the Secret Service noted people openly carrying pepper spray as they strolled the streets. [16]

President Trump's mob was itching for a fight. National Park Service officers arrested a man who had entered the restricted area around the Washington Monument. Immediately, about 100 people started forming a circle around the officer, "threaten[ing] law enforcement," as the officer later recounted. [17] The officer retreated into the Washington Monument with the man in custody. [18] The crowd responded angrily, punching the Monument's glass windows and continuing to threaten officers. [19] Law enforcement around the Washington Monument felt so unsafe that they "locked themselves in a security box by the mall." [20] Rioters nevertheless "scaled the sides of the security box and climbed on top of the structure." [21] It was a harbinger of things to come.

MPD monitored and responded to a stream of threats that morning. Three men in fatigues from Broward County, Florida brandished AR-15s in front of MPD officers on 14th Street and Independence Avenue.[22] MPD advised over the radio that one individual was possibly armed with a "Glock" at Fourteenth Street and Constitution Avenue, and another was possibly armed with a "rifle" at Fifteenth Street and Constitution Avenue around 11:23 a.m.[23] The National Park Service detained an individual with a rifle between 12:00 and 1:00 p.m.[24]

Far-right extremists brought guns into Washington or the surrounding area. Christopher Kuehne, a member of the Proud Boys, met up with friends on January 5th to discuss their plans for the following day. One person in attendance said he did not travel to Washington just to "march around" and asked, "do we have patriots here willing to take it by force?"[25] Kuehne told them he had guns, and he was ready to go.[26] During the attack, Kuehne helped prop open Capitol blast doors as besieged law enforcement retreated inside.[27] Guy Reffitt, a Three Percenter from Texas, attended the rally at the Ellipse, and then carried a loaded firearm onto Capitol grounds.[28] Jerod Thomas Bargar lost his gun—that he'd carried from the Ellipse in a 'We the People' holster[29]—while scuffling with police on the west side of the Capitol around 2:30 p.m.[30] Bargar wanted to be armed, he said, when he went into the "belly of the beast."[31]

Mark Andre Mazza drove from Indiana, bringing a Taurus revolver, a .45-caliber weapon that he loaded with both shotgun and hollow-point rounds.[32] After assaulting a police officer, he lost the weapon,[33] dropping it or losing it on the steps of the lower West Plaza leading to the Capitol's West Front Terrace.[34] The Select Committee reviewed Mazza's social media accounts before they were taken down, finding that he shared multiple conspiracy theories, including QAnon material.[35] Mazza later indicated that he intended to target House Speaker Nancy Pelosi, telling authorities that "you'd be here for another reason" if he had found the Speaker inside the Capitol.[36]

Lonnie Leroy Coffman from Falkville, Alabama, parked by the Capitol building before walking nearly 2 miles to the Ellipse to hear the President speak.[37] In his car, he had stocked a handgun, a rifle, a shotgun, hundreds of rounds of ammunition, large-capacity ammunition-feeding devices, machetes, camouflage smoke devices, a bow and arrow, and 11 Mason jars filled with gasoline and styrofoam, as well as rags and a lighter (tools needed to make Molotov cocktails).[38] Police found two more handguns on Coffman when he was arrested later that day.[39]

Many in attendance were aware of Washington's prohibition on carrying a concealed weapon and made plans accordingly. The Oath Keepers left their guns stowed away in their cars or across State lines for easy access should they be needed.[40] The group staged a "quick reaction force" across the river in Virginia, amassing an arsenal to come to DC "by land" or "by sea," as Florida State-chapter lead—and defendant convicted of seditious conspiracy—Kelly Meggs said.[41] Oath Keeper Jason Dolan testified at the seditious conspiracy trial that the "quick reaction force [was] ready to go get our firearms in order to stop the election from being certified within Congress."[42] Dolan further testified that the Oath Keepers came to Washington, DC "to stop the certification of the election.... [b]y any means necessary. That's why we brought our firearms."[43]

Garret Miller—a January 6th defendant who traveled from Richardson, Texas—posted on Facebook that "he was bringing guns with him but 'might just keep 1 hidden one and store the rest in Virginia'" after learning about the DC law.[44] He also threatened to assassinate Congresswoman Alexandria Ocasio-Cortez and predicted a "civil war could start."[45]

Many members of the crowd decided against bringing firearms into the nation's capital, and armed themselves in other ways. Alex Kirk Harkrider from Carthage, Texas, and his co-defendant, Ryan Nichols, left guns in a parked car just outside the district before attending the rally.[46] Harkrider still brought a tomahawk axe.[47] During the march to the Capitol, he yelled "[c]ut their fucking heads off!"[48] One rioter told the Select Committee he saw another carrying a "pitchfork."[49]

Members of the mob carried flags and turned the flagpoles into weapons. Michael Foy, from Wixom, Michigan, carried a hockey stick to the Ellipse—he draped a Trump flag over it.[50] Just hours later, Foy used that hockey stick to repeatedly beat police officers at the inaugural tunnel.[51] Former New York City police officer Thomas Webster carried a Marine flag, which he later used to attack an officer holding the rioters back at the lower West Plaza.[52] Another individual, Danny Hamilton, carried a flag with a sharpened tip, which he said was "for a certain person," to which Trevor Hallgren(who had traveled with Hamilton to Washington, DC) responded: "it has begun." Later, Hallgren commented that "[t]here's no escape Pelosi, Schumer, Nadler. We're coming for you.... Even you AOC. We're coming to take you out. To pull you out by your hairs." On January 5th, Hallgren took a tour of the Capitol with Representative Barry Loudermilk, during which he took pictures of hallways and staircases.[53]

The mob President Trump summoned to Washington, DC, on January 6th, was prepared to fight.

8.2 MARCH OF THE PROUD BOYS

While tens of thousands of President Trump's supporters attended the rally at the Ellipse, the Proud Boys had other plans. On the morning of January

6th, they gathered at the Washington Monument. At 10:30 a.m., the Proud Boys started their march down the National Mall towards the U.S. Capitol. In total, there were approximately 200–300 Proud Boys, as well as their associates, in the group.[54]

Enrique Tarrio, the chairman of the Proud Boys, was not in attendance. As explained in Chapter 6, Tarrio had been arrested two days earlier and ordered to leave Washington. However, Tarrio continued to monitor events remotely from Baltimore, communicating with his men throughout the day. With Tarrio offsite, the Proud Boys were led by three other senior members of the group: Ethan Nordean, Joseph Biggs, and Zachary Rehl.

Ethan Nordean (a.k.a. "Rufio Panman") was a member of the Proud Boys' Elders chapter and president of his local chapter in Seattle, Washington.[55] Nordean was regarded as the leader for January 6th after Tarrio was arrested.[56] In the days leading up to January 6th, Nordean made ominous comments on social media. In conversations with his fellow Proud Boys, he argued that the Presidential election was tainted by fraud and violence was a necessary remedy. For example, on January 4th, Nordean posted a video on social media with the title: "Let them remember the day they decided to make war with us."[57] In another social media post on January 5th, Nordean warned "we are coming for them."[58] He added a telling line: "You've chosen your side, black and yellow teamed with red, white and blue against everyone else."[59] The "black and yellow" is a reference to the Proud Boys. And when Nordean wrote the "red, white and blue," he likely meant the Trump supporters who would be in attendance for January 6th.

Joseph Biggs (a.k.a. "Sergeant Biggs") was a senior Proud Boys member and served as an event "organizer" for the group.[60] Biggs previously worked with Alex Jones and InfoWars.[61] In late December 2020, Biggs posted a message on Parler in which he explained that the Proud Boys "will not be attending DC in colors."[62] That is, unlike at previous events, the Proud Boys would not wear their branded, black and yellow clothing, but instead seek to be inconspicuous. Biggs continued:

> We will be blending in as one of you. You won't see us. You'll even think we are you…We are going to smell like you, move like you, and look like you. The only thing we'll do that's us is think like us! Jan 6th is gonna be epic.[63]

Tarrio posted a similar message, saying the Proud Boys would go "incognito" on January 6th.[64] Consistent with this decision, Biggs was dressed in a plaid shirt, glasses, and dark hat as he led the march from the Washington Monument.[65] Other Proud Boys dressed in a similar fashion.

Protestors, including a group of Proud Boys, gather at the Capitol on January 6, 2021.
Photo by Jon Cherry/Getty Images

Zachary Rehl (a.k.a. "Captain Trump") was president of the local Philadelphia, Pennsylvania Proud Boys chapter.[66] Like his comrades, Rehl believed President Trump's Big Lie about the 2020 Presidential election.[67] He raised more than $5,500 in funds for January 6th. Like Nordean, Biggs and others, Rehl was dressed "incognito" as he helped lead the group from the Washington Monument.[68]

Shortly after 11:00 a.m., the Proud Boys arrived at the west side of the Capitol, near a reflecting pool. From there, they marched to the east front of the Capitol. Surveillance footage shows the Proud Boys passing Garfield Circle on the southwest corner of the Capitol at 11:15 a.m.[69] They walked north towards the Peace Circle next, and surveillance cameras captured them on video there at approximately 11:21 a.m.[70] There was just one USCP officer standing guard at the Peace Circle fence at the time.[71]

As the Proud Boys paraded around the Capitol grounds, Nick Quested, a documentary filmmaker who spent time with the group, recalled them taunting USCP officers. One Proud Boy told the officers to "[r]emember your oath," "[c]hoose a side," and "[b]e on the right side of history."[72] By 11:41 a.m., the Proud Boys made their way around to the east side of the Capitol, crossing along Constitution Avenue.[73] While on the east front, they posed for pictures with members of their Arizona delegation, who were clearly identifiable by their orange caps.[74] They then walked back across the north side of the Capitol towards the National Mall, where they stopped to eat at food trucks.[75] The Proud Boys stayed by the food trucks until they returned to the Peace Circle at approximately 12:49 p.m.[76]

8.3 THE INITIAL ATTACK

Within minutes of arriving at the Peace Circle, the Proud Boys and their associates launched the attack on the U.S. Capitol. The circle is the site of the Peace Monument, a statue erected from 1877 to 1878 to commemorate naval deaths at sea during the Civil War with "two classically robed" women—one woman representing "grief," covering her face, and the other woman representing "history." The woman standing in for "history" holds a tablet that reads, "They died that their country might live." [77]

The Peace Circle's geographical location is crucially important for understanding how the January 6th, attack unfolded. It sits at the end of Pennsylvania Avenue, just in front of the U.S. Capitol. At the conclusion of his speech at the Ellipse, President Trump directed rally attendees to march down Pennsylvania Avenue to the U.S. Capitol. Their shortest natural path would lead them right to the Peace Circle and to the northwest side of the Capitol grounds, also known as the West Plaza. By the time rally-goers arrived, the Proud Boys and their allies had already removed the fencing that stood in the crowd's way. As a result, thousands of people streamed into the restricted Capitol grounds with relative ease.

When the Proud Boys arrived back at the Peace Circle at 12:49 p.m., they still had about 200 to 300 members and many other protestors had joined them.[78] Shortly after arriving, the Proud Boys incited the crowd with antagonistic chants such as "1776."[79] Officer Caroline Edwards, who was standing guard, explained to the Select Committee that the Proud Boys asked her and the other USCP officers if they could walk past the fencing and talk to the officers. "No," she replied. The Proud Boys and others immediately turned on Edwards and her fellow officers, referring to them as "Nancy Pelosi's dogs" and shouting.[80]

At approximately 12:51 p.m., Quested captured a rioter named Ryan Samsel with his arm around Proud Boys leader Joe Biggs, who led the chants.[81] Samsel subsequently claimed that Biggs encouraged him to push through the barricades and, when Samsel hesitated to follow through, Biggs "flashed a gun, questioned his manhood and repeated his demand" to move to the front and "challenge the police." [82] Biggs has contested Samsel's version of events.[83] After speaking with Biggs, Samsel breached the outer fencing of the Peace Circle at 12:53 p.m.[84] The first set of fencing at the

Peace Circle was staged on 1st Street Northwest, with the second set of fencing not far behind. Once Samsel breached the outer fencing, USCP officers, including Officer Edwards, moved from their posts to meet Samsel and other rioters.[85]

In less than a minute, at 12:54 p.m., the rioters pushed USCP officers to the ground, removed the fencing, and quickly stormed east towards the U.S. Capitol building.[86] Officer Edwards was thrown to the ground, causing her to hit her head on concrete steps.[87]

Two Proud Boys from New York, Dominic Pezzola and William Pepe, were among those leading the march to the next line of security barriers.[88] Pepe, an employee of the Metropolitan Transportation Authority in upstate New York, took sick leave to travel to Washington for the January 6th events.[89] Pepe dragged part of the fence away at the next security barrier, ensuring that USCP officers were left defenseless.[90] The Proud Boys' actions were not spontaneous. Jeffrey Finley, a Proud Boys leader from West Virginia, later admitted "there appeared to be a coordinated effort to pull the barricades apart." [91] Proud Boy Jeremy Bertino admitted to similar facts when pleading guilty to seditious conspiracy, stating stated that he "believed...that the purpose of traveling to Washington, DC, on January 6, 2021, was to stop the certification of the Electoral College Vote, and that the MOSD leaders were willing to do whatever it would take, including using force against police and others, to achieve that objective." Based on discussions he and other Proud Boys leaders had in the leadup to January 6th, he "believed that storming the Capitol would achieve the group's goal of stopping Congress from certifying the Electoral College Vote. Bertino understood that storming the Capitol or its grounds would be illegal and would require using force against police or other government officials." [92]

Parallel to the Peace Circle, at the Garfield Circle walkway located at the southeast corner of the Capitol grounds, rioters breached the fencing at 12:55 p.m. and began rushing the West Plaza where they would converge with others from the Peace Circle.[93]

By 12:58 p.m., the crowd filled the lower West Plaza of the Capitol just below the inauguration stage that had been built for the ceremony scheduled two weeks later. After the initial breaches, the USCP was able to deploy enough officers to stop the rioters from advancing past the base of the inauguration stage. More importantly, rioter momentum was further halted when the first group of MPD officers arrived on scene at 1:11 p.m.,[94] almost precisely as President Trump finished his Ellipse speech. The MPD officers initially pushed back the rioters on the West Plaza, slowing them down before they would later breach the Capitol.[95]

A stalemate ensued on the West Plaza before rioters were able to make any further progress. Rally-goers arriving from the Ellipse provided crucial momentum.

8.4 PRESIDENT TRUMP'S MOB DESCENDS ON THE U.S. CAPITOL

Toward the end of his speech at the Ellipse, President Trump made sure an already angry crowd of his supporters stayed enraged. "We fight like hell[,] and if you don't fight like hell, you're not going to have a country any-more," the President told the tens of thousands of people who had assembled at the Ellipse, or in the vicinity. About one minute later, President Trump directed those in attendance "to walk down Pennsylvania Avenue ... to the Capitol." The President told the people they were "going to try and give" Republicans, including his own Vice President, "the kind of pride and boldness that they need to take back our country." [96]

"There's enough people here to storm the Capitol," a member of the crowd said at 1:06 p.m., just as the President was concluding his remarks.[97] Ronald Sandlin, who pleaded guilty to and has been sentenced for felonies committed on January 6th, including telling officers in the Capitol that "[y]ou're going to die," watched the President's speech from a nearby restaurant and live-streamed a video in which he encouraged "other patriots" to "take the Capitol." [98] Sandlin repeated the phrase "freedom is paid for with blood" several times during his video.[99]

"We're getting ready to go march on Capitol Hill. We're gonna go fuck some shit up," Cody Mattice, another January 6th defendant who pleaded guilty and has been sentenced,[100] said while walking to the Capitol. Mattice later added: "We're getting up front, and we're taking this shit." [101] Ryan Nichols, who was charged with eight felonies, livestreamed a diatribe as he marched towards the Capitol at 1:40 p.m. Nichols echoed the President's unconstitutional claim that Vice President Pence had the power to decide the election himself. "I'm hearing that Pence just caved.... I'm telling you if Pence caved, we're gonna drag motherfuckers through the streets," Nichols said.[102] "Cut their heads off!" Nichols yelled with his codefendant Harkrider, before encouraging others to join "Republican protestors [who] are trying to enter the House right now." [103]

On the way to the Capitol, Oath Keeper Jessica Watkins chatted with others in a Zello group named "Stop the Steal J6." Watkins said that "100%" of the Ellipse crowd was "marching on the Capitol," because "it has spread like wildfire that Pence has betrayed us." [104] As she approached the Capitol with a contingent of Oath Keepers, Watkins said: "I'm probably gonna go silent when I get there 'cause I'm a be a little busy.[105] Donald

Hazard, a Three Percenter from Texas who claimed to be allied with Proud Boys on January 6th, told a *Washington Post* reporter that he wanted his face recorded on video as he marched to the Capitol. "I want the enemy to know exactly who is coming after them," Hazard explained.[106]

Leaders of the "Stop the Steal" movement continued to incite the crowd during the march as well. Alex Jones of InfoWars arrived at the Ellipse shortly before 9:00 a.m. on the morning of January 6th.[107] After some initial difficulty gaining access to the event area, Jones was seated in the VIP section.[108] While Jones stayed to listen to a portion of President Trump's speech, planning for the crowd's march to the Capitol was already under-way and Jones intended to leave the Ellipse early to lead the march. The origins of the plan to have Jones lead the march are unclear. Jones has pub-licly stated that "the White House told me three days before, we are going to have you lead the March."[109] Stop the Steal's Ali Alexander also believed "the White House" wanted him to lead a march to the Capitol.[110] It is likely that both got that idea from Caroline Wren, a Republican fundraiser who helped organize the Ellipse event.[111] Jones texted Wren at 12:27 p.m., asking when he should leave the Ellipse and begin the march.[112]

While Wren originally expected Jones, Roger Stone, and retired Lt. Gen. Michael Flynn to march to the Capitol, Stone did not attend the Ellipse rally and so he was not present to accompany Jones on the march as planned.[113] Additionally, while President Trump was delivering his speech, Wren asked Flynn if he was going to march with Jones. Flynn responded, "Hell, no. It's freezing."[114]

While Stone and Flynn did not march, Jones and Alexander led others to the Capitol, though it is not clear how many people followed them.[115] Jones and Alexander gathered with Jones's camera and security crew just outside the event perimeter, near Freedom Plaza, to discuss their plans.[116] The dis-cussion, recorded by Alex Jones's film crew, sheds some light on what Jones and Alexander knew about the President's plans and what they intended for the march. The group, which included InfoWars host Owen Shroyer, huddled outside the Ellipse security perimeter to discuss how best to pro-ceed. They tried to predict the Presidential motorcade's route to the Capitol. The video shows Alex Jones telling his crew, "I think the Wren lady, where's she at? She knows what they said they were going to do. Everything she's said has been accurate, so we need to call her real quick."[117] They then decided to walk down Pennsylvania Avenue, as the President had directed in his speech.

Shroyer recommended the group wait for President Trump to finish speaking, and they agreed to at least delay their departure from Freedom Plaza to allow Jones to gather a crowd.[118] Jones began speaking from his

Alex Jones uses a bullhorn to speak to crowd on January 6, 2021.
Photo by Jon Cherry/Getty Images

bullhorn, imploring people to gather and walk down Pennsylvania Avenue.[119] While using the bullhorn, Jones told the crowd that they were experiencing "the second American revolution,"[120] and stated, "[l]et's go take our country back. Trump is only minutes away. Let's start marching to the Capitol, peacefully."[121]

Proud Boys were among the crowd Jones gathered during his march. Matthew Walter, president of a Tennessee chapter of the organization,[122] was near the National Mall with two other Proud Boys from Tennessee and decided to join Jones.[123] Other, more prominent members of the Proud Boys appear to have been in contact with Jones and Shroyer about the events of January 6th and on that day. Records for Enrique Tarrio's phone show that while the attack on the Capitol was ongoing, he texted with Jones three times and Shroyer five times.[124] Ethan Nordean's phone records reflect that he exchanged 23 text messages with Shroyer between January 4th and 5th, and that he had one call with him on each of those days.[125] Records of Joseph Biggs's communications show that he texted with Shroyer eight times on January 4th and called him at approximately 11:15 a.m. on January 6th, while Biggs and his fellow Proud Boys were marching at and around the Capitol.[126]

Once they had marched the length of Pennsylvania Avenue and reached the west side of the Capitol, Jones and Alexander used a bullhorn to continue directing those around them to the east side, making further references to President Trump's alleged imminent arrival. A video recorded by a rallygoer at 1:51 p.m. shows Jones and Alexander standing together as Jones encourages the crowd to proceed to the east side of the Capitol. He tells those listening that "we've got a permit on the other side, it's great that this happened, but Trump's not going to come when we've taken this over. We are not Antifa, we are not BLM." [127]

Jones has repeatedly claimed that he tried to calm the crowd, but his actions also coincided with two police line breaches and one breach of the Capitol building itself. At 1:57 p.m., minutes after Jones encouraged rally goers to move east, newly arrived protestors breached the bike rack fencing used to keep the crowd away from the east side steps. [128] After the breach, police retreated to the base of the large set of steps behind them and the crowd moved forward to meet the newly established police line. [129]

Jones followed shortly behind the crowd that led the initial east fence breach, and his arrival coincided with the next breach up the east stairs. Publicly available video shows Jones already departed from the west side, rounding the north side of the Capitol on the way to the east side at 2:00 p.m. [130] As he was walking, Jones told his group, "those fucking cops need to fucking back off man." [131] He was then asked about Vice President Pence, to which Jones responded: "he floundered and was neutral, he passed the ball." [132] At the conclusion of the video, one of Jones's camera crew can be heard saying, "let's take a break here. Let me talk to this cop to see if I can get Alex up there to deescalate the situation." Other video released by Jones shows one of his camera crew interacting with USCP officers and asking how Jones can help deescalate the situation. [133] The Select Committee's review of the evidence showed that Jones simultaneously called on the crowd to "fight" and start a "revolution," while occasionally peppering his rhetoric with the word "peacefully."

Minutes after Jones's arrival on the scene, at approximately 2:06 p.m., rioters breached the new police line and stormed up the stairs towards the Columbus Doors (also known as the Rotunda Doors). [134] The crowd's cheers and celebration as they move up the steps can be heard while Jones's camera crew negotiates with USCP officers nearby. [135] As explained below, the rioters broke through another key breach point with Jones and Alexander on the scene just minutes later.

Rioters clash with police at the Capitol on January 6, 2021.

Photo by Brent Stirton/Getty Images

8.5 THE MOB SURGES

Far-right extremists continued to lead the charge as protestors streamed onto the U.S. Capitol's restricted grounds. On the north side of the West Plaza, there was a scaffold with stairs used by construction workers to build the inauguration stage. Law enforcement officers were stationed at the base of the stairs, preventing rioters from climbing to the upper West Plaza, where doors to the Capitol building itself were located. At 1:49 p.m., MPD declared a riot at the Capitol.[136]

Shortly before 1:50 p.m., rioters gathered in front of this scaffold on the northwest corner of the Capitol. The rioters included Proud Boys and other extremists. One rioter, Guy Reffitt, belonged to a Three Percenter group from Texas.[137] By approximately 1:50 p.m., he stood at the front of the pack near the scaffold, carrying a pistol and flexicuffs.[138] He wore body armor under a blue jacket and a helmet with a mounted body camera.[139]

Reffitt advanced on the police line, absorbing rubber bullets and pushing through chemical spray.[140] As he recounted shortly after the attack, Reffitt got "everything started moving forward."[141] He "started the fire" and the presence of law enforcement was not going to prevent Reffitt's advance.[142] According to Reffitt:

> [T]here was no reason for me to give up because I had come so far to do what I wanted, what we wanted and needed to do. And I had a mindset. I didn't mean to actually be the first guy up there. I didn't even mean to do that. I just, the adrenaline and knowing that I can't let my country fall.[143]

Reffitt had indeed planned for violence on January 6th, noting on December 28, 2020, that he would "be in full battle rattle." [144] While driving to Washington, DC on January 5th, Reffitt expressed his desire to "drag[ ] those people out of the Capitol by their ankles" and "install[ ] a new government." [145] On the morning of January 6th, Reffitt clarified the target, telling "other members of his militia group and those gathered around him" at the Ellipse that "I'm taking the Capitol with everybody fucking else"and that "[w]e're all going to drag them mother fuckers out kicking and screaming....I just want to see Pelosi's head hit every fucking stair on the way out...And Mitch McConnell too. Fuck' em all." [146] Reffitt was convicted and ultimately sentenced to 7 years in prison for his conduct.[147]

A member of the Proud Boys, Daniel Scott, helped lead the charge up the scaffolding stairs.[148] Scott, also known as Milkshake, had marched with the Proud Boys from the Washington Monument to the Capitol. During the march, Scott was recorded in a video yelling, "Let's take the fucking Capitol!" [149] Someone else responded, "Let's not fucking yell that, alright?" And then Nordean added: "It was Milkshake, man, you know...idiot." Scott had apparently blurted out the Proud Boys' plan. At the scaffolding, Scott then helped others "take" the U.S. Capitol. While wearing a blue cap with white lettering that read, "Gods, Guns & Trump," he pushed police officers backwards, clearing a path for the rioters. Another Proud Boy, Chris Worrell, was also nearby.[150] As rioters massed under the scaffold, Worrell sprayed officers with OC (or pepper) spray. [151] Other Proud Boys were present at the scaffold, including Micajah Jackson[152] and Matthew Greene.[153]

The attack at and in the vicinity of the scaffolding cleared a path for a wave of rioters who forced their way up the stairs and to the U.S. Capitol building itself.[154] As the rioters rushed up the stairs, another January 6th defendant, Ryan Kelley, climbed up the scaffolding around 1:51 p.m.[155] In the ensuing minutes he waved people on, encouraging them to follow.[156] Kelley—who ran in the Republican primary to be the governor of Michigan in 2022—denied to the Select Committee that he had climbed the scaffolding to wave people on.[157] The FBI arrested Kelley a few months after his deposition.[158]

By 2:00 p.m., rioters at the top of the scaffolding stairs were only feet away from Capitol building doors and windows.

8.6 THE UNITED STATES CAPITOL IS BREACHED

Incited by President Trump, over the course of the next hour, extremists, conspiracy theorists and others breached the U.S. Capitol building at several locations. They probed for weaknesses in the building's defenses, battling law enforcement personnel who stood in their way. Once again, the Proud Boys and other extremists played conspicuous roles.

THE SENATE WING IS BREACHED AT 2:13 P.M.

At 2:13 p.m., Dominic Pezzola, a Proud Boy from New York, smashed a window on the Senate wing.[159] This was the first breach of the Capitol building. Pezzola used a riot shield he stole from a law enforcement officer to break through the window. After climbing through, rioters were able to easily open a nearby Senate wing door from the inside—giving them unfettered passage into the building at 2:14 p.m. Two minutes later, at approximately 2:16 p.m., rioters pushed opened a second door, the Senate fire door, from the inside.[160] Just as the building was being breached, Vice President Pence and Speaker Pelosi were ushered off the Senate and House floors, respectively.[161]

The first person to enter the Capitol building was a Kentucky native named Michael Sparks. Sparks had expressed his desire to kill people after watching protests in the summer of 2020.[162] Following one of President Trump's calls to Washington, DC on December 30, 2020, Sparks answered that he would "be there."[163]

As Pezzola entered the building, he was joined by other noteworthy extremists and conspiracy theorists. Robert Gieswein, an individual from Colorado affiliated with Three Percenters who espoused conspiracy beliefs, climbed through the Senate wing window.[164] Doug Jensen, a QAnon adherent, was part of this first cadre of people to enter the Capitol as well.[165] Jensen wore a brazen "Q" shirt. Jensen later told authorities that he "intentionally positioned himself to be among the first people inside the United States Capitol because...he wanted to have his t-shirt seen on video so that 'Q' could 'get the credit.'"[166] Another prominent QAnon believer, Jacob Chansley (a.k.a. the "QAnon Shaman"), also entered through the Senate wing door at approximately 2:14 p.m.[167]

White supremacists and Confederate-sympathizers were among the first rioters to enter the U.S. Capitol. Kevin Seefried and his son, Hunter, entered the building at approximately 2:13 p.m. through the Senate wing window smashed by Proud Boy Dominic Pezzola.[168] Kevin Seefried carried a

Doug Jensen and rioters confront police after storming the Capitol.
(Photo by Win McNamee/Getty Images)

Confederate Battle Flag with him and unfurled it inside the building. According to some historians, while the Confederate Flag has appeared in the building before, it was the first time that an insurrectionist ever carried the banner inside the U.S. Capitol.[169] According to court filings, Hunter Seefried helped punch out the Senate wing window and then clear the broken glass before he, his father and others entered the Capitol.[170] Kevin Seefried was found guilty of obstructing an official proceeding, which is a felony offense, as well as four misdemeanors.[171] The Department of Justice has alleged that at 2:16 p.m., just 3 minutes after the Senate wing was first breached, five individuals associated with the Nick Fuentes's white nationalist "America First" movement entered the U.S. Capitol.[172] The five, all of whom are in their 20s, have been identified as: Joseph Brody, Thomas Carey, Gabriel Chase, Jon Lizak, and Paul Lovley.[173] Four of the five "initially met at an America First event and attended subsequent events together."[174] Nick Fuentes and other America First leaders espouse "a belief that they are defending against the demographic and cultural changes in America."[175] Online researchers say that Brody is the masked man seen in a photo wearing a MAGA hat and holding a rifle in front of a Nazi flag.[176] (The photo was not taken on January 6th.) As discussed in Chapter 6, members of the America First movement, commonly known as

"Groypers," were well-represented at "Stop the Steal" events in late 2020 and these rallies helped pave the road to January 6th. Indeed, at least three members of the group—Lovley, Lizak and Chase—attended the "Stop the Steal, March for Trump" rally in Washington, DC on November 14, 2020.[177]

On January 6th, Brody and his America First associates made their way to various points inside and outside of the Capitol after the initial breach, including House Speaker Nancy Pelosi's conference room and office, as well as the U.S. Senate Chamber.[178] After exiting the Capitol, the group went to the north side of the building. One of the five, Brody, and another rioter allegedly used a "metal barricade" to assault a law enforcement officer who was defending the North Door.[179] (The attack on the North Door is discussed below.) Brody and Chase also allegedly helped others destroy media equipment.[180] Still another America First associate, Riley Williams, directed rioters up a staircase to Speaker Pelosi's office and was accused of aiding and abetting the theft of a laptop found there.[181] Other white supremacists were among the first rioters to enter the U.S. Capitol. Timothy Hale-Cusanelli, an Army Reservist from New Jersey who was identified by a confidential source to law enforcement as an "an avowed white supremacist and Nazi sympathizer," entered through the Senate wing breach around 2:14 p.m.[182] Hale-Cusanelli "[u]sed tactical hand signals" to direct other members of the mob, and he commanded them to "'advance' on the Capitol."[183] Afterwards, he bragged to a friend that January 6th was "exhilarating," that he hoped "for a 'civil war,'" and that the 'tree of liberty must be refreshed with the blood of patriots and tyrants.'"[184] Robert Packer was also among the first rioters to enter the Capitol, and he made his way into the Crypt by 2:25 p.m.[185] Packer was wearing a "Camp Auschwitz" sweatshirt, a "symbol of Nazi hate ideology," at the time.[186]

After breaking in, some of the first rioters headed north toward the Senate chambers.[187] Officer Eugene Goodman, a USCP officer, intercepted them before they headed up the stairs leading to the chambers. Immediately after entering, a rioter asked Officer Goodman, "Where are the [M]embers at?" and "where are they counting the votes?"[188] Jensen, Gieswein, Sparks, and others stalked Officer Goodman through the halls of the Senate.[189] Jensen demanded that Officer Goodman and other USCP officers arrest Vice President Pence.[190] Sparks chanted, "This is our America!"[191] Other rioters who entered through the Senate wing door clashed with police offices at the Senate carriage door located on the northeast side of the Capitol.[192] When the rioters followed Officer Goodman up the stairs to the Senate Chamber, they were stopped by a line of USCP officers outside the Ohio Clock Tower.[193]

Joe Biggs of the Proud Boys entered the Capitol shortly after the first breach. At 2:14 p.m., Biggs walked through the senate wing door and moved north. Part of his route was captured in videos posted on Parler, a right-wing social media site.[194] Someone recorded the Proud Boys leader shortly after he entered the Capitol and asked him, "Hey Biggs what do you gotta say?"[195] Smiling, Biggs replied: "this is awesome!"[196] Other Proud Boys were seen with Biggs, or near him, as he entered the Capitol. One of them is Paul Rae, a Proud Boys member from Florida, who appears to have communicated directly with Biggs after they entered through the door.[197] Another Proud Boy from Florida, Arthur Jackman, was seen with his hand on Biggs's right shoulder. Jackman "became involved in the Proud Boys to support Donald Trump," was in Washington on January 6th "to support President Trump and to stop the steal" and "believe[d] the election was stolen." Still another, Joshua Pruitt, who was clad in a Punisher shirt, entered the Capitol through the Senate wing door around this time.[198] At approximately 2:17 p.m., 3 minutes after entering the U.S. Capitol for the first time, Biggs exited through another door.[199]

At 2:43 p.m., law enforcement was able to regain control of the Senate wing door, forcing all the rioters out. But their success lasted for only 5 minutes. At 2:48 p.m., rioters again breached the Senate wing door, pushing law enforcement out of the way.[200] The second breach was one of the more violent breaches of the day, with the mob forcefully pushing law enforcement backwards until the pathway was clear for them to enter.

THE COLUMBUS DOORS (EAST ROTUNDA DOORS) ARE BREACHED AT 2:24 P.M. AND 2:38 P.M.

While the Proud Boys and other extremists were overwhelming law enforcement at the West Plaza scaffolding, another group led the attack on security barriers on the East Plaza. At 2:06 p.m., a crowd broke through security barriers and charged a set of doors just outside the Rotunda.[201] The mob's surge occurred just minutes after Alex Jones arrived on the scene.[202] The crowd's cheers and celebration as they move up the steps can be heard while Jones's camera crew negotiates with USCP officers nearby.[203]

Once rioters had filled the Rotunda stairs, Jones and his team, along with the Proud Boy Walter, ascended the stairs. They moved into the thick of the crowd at the top of the stairs, where Jones began calling for peace but also revolution, leading the crowd in chants of "1776" and other bellicose rhetoric.[204] Publicly available video shows that Jones reached the top of the stairs at 2:18 p.m.[205] Walter told the Select Committee that he thought Jones was successful in getting some people down, "but I also think that may have created enough space for people to be able to move, whereas before you couldn't move."[206] Apparently, Jones's security team also realized he was not successfully controlling the crowd, as one of his security guards reportedly told him, "Alex, they're going to blame this all on you, we got to get out of here as fast as possible." [207] By approximately 2:21 p.m., Jones began descending the stairs.[208] Despite claiming to make attempts to calm the crowd, Jones further incited the mob as he departed, loudly proclaiming "we will never submit to the new world order" and then leading the crowd in the chant "fight for Trump." [209]

At 2:24 p.m., rioters gained entrance to the Capitol through the doors leading into the Rotunda,[210] an entrance that was only a few feet directly behind Jones as he was speaking. As the Rotunda was breached by rioters, Jones and Alexander left the area and decided to leave the Capitol complex area altogether.[211]

Law enforcement officials were able to thwart the initial breach of the doors leading into the Rotunda. By 2:28 p.m., they temporarily regained control and stopped rioters from entering.[212] But their success was short-lived. Within ten minutes, the doors were breached once again.[213] And two members of the Proud Boys—Ronald Loehrke and James Haffner—helped lead the attack.[214]

Loehrke was allegedly recruited by Nordean, the Proud Boys leader, for January 6th. In late December 2020, Nordean asked Loehrke via text message if he was coming to "DC." [215] After Loehrke indicated he was, Nordean said he wanted Loehrke "on the front line" with him.[216] Loehrke replied, "Sounds good man." [217] Loehrke and Haffner marched with the Proud Boys from the Washington Monument to the Capitol grounds and were present during the breach at the Peace Circle.[218] The pair made their way to the east side of the Capitol, where they began removing the security barriers and resisting USCP officers. [219] Other members of the crowd joined. Eventually, the rioters breached these barriers too, allowing them to reach the doors of the Rotunda.

When the rioters reached the Columbus Doors, they were again stopped by USCP officers. But as the officers explained to the Select Committee, the rioters pushed them against the doors and sprayed them with OC spray (commonly known as pepper spray), making it impossible to defend the Capitol.[220] James Haffner was one of the rioters who allegedly sprayed the officers.[221]

Shortly after Haffner and others assaulted the USCP officers, they were able to breach the Columbus Doors at approximately 2:38 p.m. A Proud Boys contingent—including Haffner, Loehrke, and Joe Biggs—then entered the Capitol.[222] It was the second time that Biggs entered the U.S. Capitol that day.

A military-style "stack" of Oath Keepers entered through the Columbus Doors as well. The Oath Keeper members attended the Ellipse rally, where they were provided personal security details for VIPs in attendance.[223] Afterwards, they marched to the Capitol, as directed by President Trump.

Stewart Rhodes, the leader of the Oath Keepers, monitored the attack on the Capitol from just outside, including during the assault on the Columbus Doors. At 2:28 p.m., Rhodes texted members of the F.O.S., or Friends of Stone, (FOS) Signal chat—which included Roger Stone, the Proud Boys' Enrique Tarrio, Ali Alexander, Alex Jones, and others[224]—that he was at the "Back door of the U.S. Capitol." [225] Rhodes followed up at 2:30 p.m. by texting members of another chat that there was "Pounding on the doors" of the Capitol.[226]

At 2:32 p.m., Rhodes held a three-way call with two other Oath Keepers, Kelly Meggs and Michael Green.[227] Three minutes later, Meggs's group ("Stack 1") started pushing through the rioters amassed on the East Plaza steps in a military-stack formation, with each person placing a hand on the shoulder of the person in front.[228] This stack entered the Capitol around 2:40 p.m.[229]

One minute later, Rhodes was caught on camera on the Upper West Terrace responding to a rioter who said the Members of Congress must be "shitting their pants inside." Rhodes replied: "Amen They need to shit their fucking pants. Sic semper tyrannis." [230]

Once inside, Stack 1 moved through the Rotunda. At 2:44 p.m., Stack 1 pushed into the Senate hallway, which was filled with officers blocking the way. "Push, push, push. Get in there. They can't hold us," Watkins implored the others. However, the officers repelled their attack, pushing them back into the Rotunda.[231]

Other Oath Keepers made their way to the Capitol as Stack 1 tried to advance. Joshua James and another group of Oath Keepers ("Stack 2") pushed through the Columbus Doors at approximately 3:15 p.m.[232] "This is my fucking Capitol. This is not yours. This is my building," James shouted at officers inside the Rotunda who were trying to push the rioters out of the Capitol.[233]

ADDITIONAL BREACH POINTS

In addition to the breaches discussed above, rioters opened other entry points into the U.S. Capitol. The Upper West Terrace door, which leads directly into the Rotunda, was breached at 2:33 p.m. when rioters opened it from the inside.[234]

Inside the Capitol, rioters broke through the police lines, such as in the Crypt, a space located directly underneath the Rotunda. The Crypt is anchored by a marble "compass stone," marking the center of the building, and is lined with 13 statues representing the original American colonies.[235] The rioters quickly moved towards the House Chambers and, by 2:40 p.m., started to crowd the main doors outside the Chambers, moving to the east side near the Speaker's lobby. As they moved to the east side, rioters opened the east House doors from the inside at 2:41 p.m., allowing rioters from the northeast side of the Capitol to enter.[236]

The north doors were the last Capitol doors breached. At 3:10 p.m., rioters entered through the north doors where they were quickly met by USCP.[237] Within a minute, the hallway just inside the doors was filled with rioters. At 3:12 p.m., a combination of USCP and MPD officers forcefully pushed the rioters out of the doors.[238] However, rioters continued to attack just outside the north doors throughout the afternoon and evening.

The north doors have an outer entranceway that is separated by a vestibule from a set of inner doors that lead directly into the Capitol. Rioters threw bricks at the doors and forcefully tried to stop police officers from clearing the area.[239] Law enforcement officers briefly opened the inner doors to spray a chemical irritant that was intended to disperse the mob.[240] But the rioters continued to fight. For instance, as the crowd held the outer doors open, John Thomas Gordon of West Virginia repeatedly threw a heavy projectile at the inner doors, while swearing at the officers.[241] Another rioter gave Gordon, who came to Washington to attend the "Stop the Steal" rally, a pair of goggles so he would withstand the chemical spray. Gordon kicked the inner doors as he and others desperately tried to enter the Capitol.[242] Law enforcement held the doors, withstanding the mob's best efforts to break in.

As law enforcement officers started to clear the building, rioters continued to fight police officers at the tunnel on the West Plaza. Rioters violently struck officers, including MPD Officer Daniel Hodges, and sprayed them with OC spray. Although rioters did not break through the police line at the tunnel, they were able to successfully break a window just north of it. There is no surveillance coverage for this area, so Select Committee staff was unable to determine the precise time of the breach. According to open-source videos, however, the breach appears to occur at approximately 4:15 p.m.[243]

8.7 PRESIDENT TRUMP POURS FUEL ON THE FIRE

After Dominic Pezzola and others breached the Capitol at 2:13 p.m., a mob quickly entered and headed towards the Senate and House Chambers, where Members were meeting.[244] As the crowd moved through the Capitol, they chanted "Fight for Trump" and "Stop the Steal!" They also chanted

"Nancy, Nancy" as they searched for Speaker Pelosi.[245] At 2:18 p.m., the House went into recess as hundreds of rioters confronted USCP officers inside the Crypt, which is a short distance from the first breach point.[246]

USCP officers formed a line across the Crypt in an attempt to stop the mob's advance.[247] By 2:21 p.m., the rioters had tried to break through police lines, but they were temporarily unsuccessful.[248]

As USCP officers held the line inside the Crypt, President Trump poured fuel on the fire, tweeting at 2:24 p.m.:

> "Mike Pence didn't have the courage to do what should have been done to protect our Country and our Constitution, giving states a chance to certify a corrected set of facts, not the fraudulent or inaccurate ones which they were asked to previously certify. USA demands the truth!" [249]

One minute later, the mob violently pushed through the USCP officers in the Crypt and continued moving south towards the House Chamber.[250] Joshua Pruitt, the Proud Boy dressed in a Punisher shirt, was at the front of the line as rioters broke through in the Crypt.[251] Officer David Millard told the Select Committee that rioters in the Crypt claimed they were in the Capitol because their "boss" told them to be there—meaning President Trump.[252] Officer Millard also recalled members of the mob telling him they were there to stop the steal.[253]

After breaking through the police line in the Crypt, the mob pursued USCP officers as they retreated to the U.S. Capitol Visitor's Center (CVC). Pruitt was among the rioters who advanced into the CVC, where he came close to Senator Chuck Schumer.[254] When the USCP officers attempted to lower metal barriers to halt the crowd's momentum, another small group of Proud Boys immediately interceded to prevent the barricades from coming down.[255] The Proud Boy contingent included three men from the Kansas City, Kansas area: William Chrestman,[256] Chris Kuehne,[257] and Louis Colon.[258] Felicia Konold and Cory Konold, two Proud Boy associates from Arizona, joined the Kansas City group while marching from the Washington Monument to the Capitol earlier in the day and were on the scene.[259] Two other Proud Boys, Nicholas Ochs and Nicholas DeCarlo, filmed the incident.[260]

Surveillance footage shows Chrestman using a wooden club, or modified axe handle, to prevent the barrier from being lowered to the floor.[261] Colon later admitted to authorities that he purchased and modified an axe handle "to be used as both a walking stick and an improvised weapon" on January 6th.[262] Colon also told authorities that he attended a meeting with Chrestman and others on the night of January 5th, during which someone

Rioters enter the Senate Chamber.

Photo by Win McNamee/Getty Images

asked, "do we have patriots here willing to take it by force?" Colon understood that the individual meant that they should use "force against the
government." This same individual commented that they should "go in
there and take over." [263]

At 2:36 p.m., the mob pushed through a line of USCP officers guarding
the House Chamber.[264] Rioters also entered the Senate Chamber.[265] Within
minutes, Jacob Chansley (a.k.a. the QAnon Shaman) entered the Senate
Chamber, making his way to the Senate dais, where Vice President Pence
had been presiding over the joint session. An officer asked Chansley to
vacate the dais, but instead he shouted, "Mike Pence is a fucking traitor."
Chansley also left a note that read: "It's Only a Matter of Time. Justice is
Coming!"[266] Surrounded by others, Chansley held a conspiracy-laden
prayer session, saying: "Thank you for allowing the United States of
America to be reborn. Thank you for allowing us to get rid of the commu-
nists, the globalists, and the traitors within our government."[267] Other
extremists, including at least one associate of the white nationalist
"America First" movement, also sat in the Vice President's seat.[268]

While law enforcement fought to contain the mob inside the Capitol,
the fighting raged outside as well. Key agitators continued to fire up the

crowd. Nick Fuentes, the leader of the "America'First" movement, amplified President Trump's rhetoric aimed at Vice President Pence, including
the President's 2:24 p.m. tweet.[269] Speaking through a bullhorn while
standing on the Peace Monument, Fuentes shouted:

> We just heard that Mike Pence is not going to reject any fraudulent
> elector votes! That's right, you heard it here first: Mike Pence has
> betrayed the United States of America. Mike Pence has betrayed the
> President and he has betrayed the people of the United States of
> America—and we will never ever forget![270]

As rioters flowed through the halls and offices inside the Capitol, others
broke through the defensive lines of USCP and MPD officers on the lower
West Plaza at 2:28 p.m., allowing them to take over the inauguration
stage.[271] According to MPD Officer Michael Fanone, MPD officers were then
forced to conduct the "first fighting withdrawal" in the history of the force,
with law enforcement seeking to "reestablish defensive lines" to prevent
the "crowd that had swelled to approximately 20,000 from storming the
U.S. Capitol."[272]

After surging through the West Plaza, rioters quickly headed towards
the West Plaza tunnel. The violence that escalated at 2:28 p.m. on the lower
West Plaza continued as rioters reached the tunnel. By 2:41 p.m., law
enforcement retreated inside the tunnel, allowing rioters to slowly fill in.[273]
Just ten minutes later, the mob jammed the tunnel, desperately trying to
break through the police lines.[274] The fighting in and immediately outside
of the tunnel raged for over two hours.[275]

Throughout the afternoon, members of the mob struck officers with
weapons, shot them with OC (or pepper) spray, and dragged officers from
the tunnel into the crowd. Lucas Denney, a Three Percenter from Texas who
carried a baton on January 6th, pushed a riot shield into and on top of
police officers at the tunnel. The crowd chanted "heave-ho!" as Denney did
so.[276] Jeffrey Scott Brown sprayed a chemical or pepper spray at officers
and pushed the front of the line in the tunnel.[277] Kyle Young, a January 6th
defendant with a long prior criminal history, participated in multiple
assaults and violence at the tunnel, including using a pole to jab at police
officers.

Young's 16-year-old son was present during the fighting.[278] Robert
Morss, a former Army Ranger who wore a military-style vest, participated
in a heave-ho effort in the tunnel where he and rioters had created a shield
wall.[279] Peter Schwartz and another rioter passed a large cannister of spray
back and forth before Schwartz's companion sprayed officers and then the
two joined in the heave-ho.[280]

Rioters assault police officers at a tunnel to the Capitol.

Photo by Brent Stirton/Getty Images

One of the most brutal attacks of the day occurred outside the tunnel when rioters dragged MPD Officer Michael Fanone into the crowd, and then tased, beat, and robbed him while a Blue Lives Matter flag fluttered above him. Albuquerque Head, a rioter from Tennessee, grabbed Officer Fanone around the neck and pulled him into the mob.[281] "I got one!" Head shouted.[282] Lucas Denney, the Three Percenter, "swung his arm and fist" at Officer Fanone, grabbed him, and pulled him down the stairs.[283] Daniel Rodriguez then tased him in the neck. Kyle Young lunged towards Officer Fanone, restraining the officer's wrist.[284] While Young held him, still another rioter, Thomas Sibick, reached towards him and forcibly removed his police badge and radio.[285] Officer Fanone feared they were after his gun. Members of the crowd yelled: "Kill him!," "Get his gun!" and "Kill him with his own gun!"[286]

In an interview with FBI agents, Daniel Rodriguez admitted his role in the attack on Officer Fanone.[287] During that same interview, Rodriguez discussed the influences that led him down the path to January 6th. Rodriguez was a fan of Alex Jones's InfoWars and told FBI agents that he became active at rallies after watching the conspiracy show.[288] Rodriguez was motivated by Jones's decision to support then candidate Trump in 2015.[289] He also began to affiliate himself with the Three Percenter movement, which he learned about by watching InfoWars.[290] And when President Trump called for a "wild" protest in Washington on January 6th, Rodriguez thought it was necessary to respond. "Trump called us. Trump called us to DC," Rodriguez told interviewing agents.[291] "If he's the commander in chief and the leader of our country, and he's calling for help—I thought he was calling for help," Rodriguez explained. "I thought he was—I thought we were doing the right thing."[292]

Rodriguez and another January 6th defendant, Edward Badalian, began preparing for violence after President Trump's December 19th tweet. They gathered weapons and tactical gear[293] and discussed their plans in a Signal chat named, "Patriots 45 MAGA Gang."

"Congress can hang. I'll do it," Rodriguez posted to the chat. Please let us get these people dear God."[294]

Badalian also posted a flyer titled "MAGA_CAVALRY," which showed rally points for "patriot caravans" to connect with the "Stop The Steal" movement in DC.[295] The same flyer was popular among Three Percenters and other self-described "patriot" groups. It also garnered the attention of law enforcement. The FBI's Norfolk, Virginia division noted in a January 5th intelligence assessment that the flyer was accompanied by another image, titled "Create Perimeter," which depicted the U.S. Capitol and other buildings being surrounded by the same caravans.[296]

8.8 THE EVACUATION

When rioters surrounded the perimeter of the Capitol, and reached the Senate and House Chambers, Members were forced to evacuate for safety. USCP officers responded to both Chambers and served as escorts. By the time the Capitol was breached, the Senate and House had split from the joint session, with Senators returning to their Chamber to debate the objection to Arizona's electoral vote. The House remained in its Chamber to debate the objection.[297]

Starting in the Senate, Vice President Pence was escorted off the floor at 2:12 p.m. and was taken to his Senate office. Between 2:12 p.m. and 2:25 p.m., Secret Service agents worked to identify potential threats and a route that could be used to transport Vice President Pence.[298] One of the issues for Vice President Pence's evacuation was that the rioters were outside the Ohio Clock Tower, which was just feet away from the staircase that Vice President Pence could descend to evacuate.[299] Eventually, after the mob started filling the entire Capitol, the Secret Service made the decision to move Vice President Pence, and he was escorted from the Senate at 2:25 p.m.[300] By 2:27 p.m., the Vice President can be seen moving toward a secure

Members of Congress are evacuated from the House Chamber.
(Photo by Drew Angerer/Getty Images)

location connected to the Capitol. The Vice President arrived at the secure location at 2:29 p.m.[301] Following the Vice President's evacuation, Senators were evacuated at 2:30 p.m.[302]

On the House side, Speaker Pelosi, House Majority Leader Steny Hoyer, and House Majority Whip James Clyburn were removed from the House floor at the same time as Vice President Pence. By 2:18 p.m., USCP surveillance showed Speaker Pelosi in the basement hallway headed towards the garage.[303] The surveillance footage also showed Leader Hoyer and Whip Clyburn in the same basement as Speaker Pelosi. At 2:23 p.m., Speaker Pelosi and Whip Clyburn were moved to an undisclosed location.[304]

Minority Leader Kevin McCarthy was evacuated just after Speaker Pelosi left the Capitol. At 2:25 p.m., as rioters were moving through the Crypt and breaking through the east Rotunda door, Leader McCarthy and his staff hurriedly evacuated his office.[305] At approximately 2:38 p.m., the Members of Congress on the House floor began their evacuation.[306] Members of Congress can be seen evacuating through the Speaker's Lobby when a USCP officer fatally shot Ashli Babbitt at 2:44 p.m.[307] Members and staffers were just feet away when Babbitt attempted to climb through a shattered glass door. USCP officers had barricaded the door with furniture to prevent the rioters from gaining direct access to elected officials.

The congressional Members in the House Gallery were evacuated after the Members on the House floor. Congressional Members in the Gallery had to wait to be evacuated because rioters were still roaming the hallways right outside the Chamber. At 2:49 p.m., as Members were trying to evacuate the House Gallery, the USCP emergency response team cleared the hallways with long rifles so that the Members could be escorted to safety.[308] USCP surveillance footage shows several rioters lying on the ground, with long rifles pointed at them, as Members evacuate in the background.[309] By 3:00 p.m., the area had been cleared and Members were evacuated from the House gallery to a secure location. [310]

8.9 CLEARING THE U.S. CAPITOL BUILDING AND RESTRICTED GROUNDS

Shortly after law enforcement officers evacuated the House and Senate Members, they started to clear rioters out of the Capitol and off the grounds. Starting before 3:00 p.m., law enforcement spent approximately three hours pushing rioters out of the Capitol building and off the East and West Plazas. In general, law enforcement cleared rioters out of the Capitol through three doors: (1) the House side door located on the northeast side of the Capitol; (2) the Columbus Doors (East Rotunda Doors); and (3) the Senate wing door, which was next to the first breach point. As discussed above, the Proud Boys and other extremists led the charge at the latter two locations during the early stages of the attack.

Outside the Capitol, law enforcement pushed the mob from the upper West Plaza towards the East Plaza, crossing the north doors. Eventually, these rioters were forced to exit the Capitol grounds on the east side. The last point where rioters were removed was the lower West Plaza—the scene of some of the most intense hand-to-hand fighting that day. After law enforcement cleared the tunnel, where violence had raged for hours, police officers corralled rioters to the west and away from the Capitol building.[311]

After rioters first breached the Senate wing door on the first floor, they immediately moved south towards the House Chamber. This route took them to the Crypt—with the mob filling this room by 2:24 p.m. This was also one of the first rooms that law enforcement cleared as they started to secure the building. By 2:49 p.m., law enforcement officers cleared the Crypt by pushing towards the Senate wing door and up the stairs to the Rotunda.[312]

Around the same time that police officers cleared the Crypt, they also removed rioters from hallways immediately adjacent to the House and Senate Chambers. On the House side, rioters were pushed out shortly before 3:00 p.m. The House hallway immediately in front of the House Chamber's door was cleared at 2:56 p.m.[313] The mob outside of the Speaker's lobby was pushed out of the House side door at 2:57 p.m.[314]

USCP officers were able to quickly clear out the Senate Chamber, which was initially breached at 2:42 p.m.[315] Rioters were cleared from the hallways outside the Senate by 3:09 p.m.[316] Surveillance shows officers checking the Senate Gallery and hallways for rioters; there are no people on camera by this time.[317]

The Rotunda served as a key point where the mob settled during the Capitol attack. For example, at 2:45 p.m., hundreds of people can be seen standing in the Rotunda.[318] It appears law enforcement officers funneled rioters from other parts of the Capitol into the Rotunda. Once they had President Trump's supporters herded there, law enforcement started to push them towards the east doors shortly after 3:00 p.m. At 3:25 p.m., law enforcement successfully pushed rioters out of the Rotunda and closed the doors so that the room could remain secure.[319] By 3:43 p.m., just 18 minutes after the Rotunda doors were closed, law enforcement successfully pushed the rioters out of east doors of the Capitol.[320]

The last rioters in the Capitol building were cleared out of the Senate wing door—the same location where rioters first breached the building at 2:13 p.m. Like the other locations inside the Capitol, law enforcement began forcing rioters out of the Senate wing door after 3:00 p.m. By 3:40 p.m., law enforcement had successfully pushed many of the rioters out of the door and onto the upper West Plaza.[321] However, officers were unable to close the doors because some rioters remained in the doorway and attempted to re-enter the building. At 4:23 p.m., a combination of USCP and MPD officers forced these people out of the doorway and successfully secured the door.[322]

After clearing the inside of the Capitol, law enforcement officers proceeded to sweep the perimeter adjacent to the building, starting with the upper West Plaza. After pushing the last rioter out of the Senate wing door, officers started to clear the upper West Plaza, which is located just outside this same doorway. Law enforcement officers in riot gear formed a line and marshalled the crowd north from the upper West Plaza. By 4:31 p.m., 8 minutes after closing the Senate wing door, rioters were cleared from the upper West Plaza.[323]

Many of these same officers started to secure the north side of the Capitol as they pushed rioters from the upper West Plaza towards the East Plaza. By approximately 4:32 p.m., law enforcement officers walked out of the North Doors, forming additional lines to push rioters eastward. As discussed earlier, the North Doors had been the location of violent fighting throughout much of the afternoon. By 4:46 p.m., law enforcement had

Police officers form line to push rioters away from the Capitol building.
(Photo by Spencer Platt/Getty Images)

successfully pushed the rioters from the north side of the Capitol to the East Plaza.[324]

Law enforcement cleared the East Plaza next. By 4:59 p.m., officers had swept all the remaining rioters from the east stairs of the Capitol.[325] At this point, the mob that had overrun the upper West Plaza, the north side of the Capitol, and the East Plaza had been moved off the grounds adjacent to the Capitol.

The last areas of the Capitol grounds to get cleared were the tunnel and the lower West Plaza. Thousands of rioters had packed into the West Plaza just after the initial invasion, led by the Proud Boys and their associates. The tunnel was the location of the day's most violent fighting and the conflict extended until late in the day.

After 5:00 p.m., it appears that law enforcement directed their attention to clearing the lower West Plaza, including the tunnel. At 5:04 p.m., police officers in the tunnel shot smoke bombs to get the remaining rioters to back away from the doors.[326] By 5:05 p.m., the rioters had all retreated and the police officers inside the tunnel moved out and started clearing out the area.[327]

At 5:13 p.m., on the opposite side of the lower West Plaza, officers pushed the mob down the scaffold stairs and to the lower West Plaza.[328]

Vice President Pence and Speaker Pelosi preside over the joint session of Congress.
Photo by Erin Schaff—Pool/Getty Images

These are the same stairs that rioters, led by the Proud Boys and other extremists, had previously climbed before reaching the Senate wing door.

Once the rioters from the tunnel and the scaffold were all situated on the lower West Plaza, officers formed another line and started walking the mob back towards the grass—which was away from the actual Capitol building. The line appears to have been fully formed at 5:19 p.m., and the officers started their sweep at 5:30 p.m.[329] By 5:37 p.m., police officers pushed rioters back to the grassy area away from the Capitol. It was at this time that in or around the Capitol building.[330] At 6:56 p.m., a little more than an hour after the Capitol grounds were cleared, Vice President Pence returned to the Capitol from the loading dock.[331] Vice President Pence walked up the stairs in the basement of the Capitol to his office in the Senate at 7:00 p.m.[332]

Shortly after 8:00 p.m., the joint session of Congress resumed, with Vice President Pence saying: "Let's get back to work."[333] At 3:32 a.m., the Congress completed the counting of the votes and certified the election of Joseph R. Biden, Jr. as the 46th President of the United States.

ENDNOTES

1. Enrique Tarrio (@NobleLead), Parler, Jan. 6, 2021 11:16 p.m. ET, available at https://twitter.com/ryanjreilly/status/1533921251743391745 (Ryan J. Reilly (@ryanjreilly), Twitter, June 6, 2022 5:18 p.m. ET (retweeting the Premonition video)).

2. Third Superseding Indictment at 22, *United States v. Nordean et al.*, No. 1:21-cr-175 (D.D.C. June 6, 2022), ECF No. 380.

3. Third Superseding Indictment at 22, *United States v. Nordean et al.*, No. 1:21-cr-175 (D.D.C. June 6, 2022), ECF No. 380.

4. "Leader of Proud Boys and Four Other Members Indicted in Federal Court for Seditious Conspiracy and Other Offenses Related to U.S. Capitol Breach," Department of Justice, (June 6, 2022), available at https://www.justice.gov/opa/pr/leader-proud-boys-and-four-other-members-indicted-federal-court-seditious-conspiracy-and.

5. "Leader of Proud Boys and Four Other Members Indicted in Federal Court for Seditious Conspiracy and Other Offenses Related to U.S. Capitol Breach," Department of Justice, (June 6, 2022), available at https://www.justice.gov/opa/pr/leader-proud-boys-and-four-other-members-indicted-federal-court-seditious-conspiracy-and.

6. "Leader of Proud Boys and Four Other Members Indicted in Federal Court for Seditious Conspiracy and Other Offenses Related to U.S. Capitol Breach," Department of Justice, (June 6, 2022), available at https://www.justice.gov/opa/pr/leader-proud-boys-and-four-other-members-indicted-federal-court-seditious-conspiracy-and.

7. Documents on file with the Select Committee to Investigate the January 6th Attack on the United States Capitol (Nick Quested Production), Video file ML_DC_20210106_Sony_FS5_Clip0065_1, at 0:04 and 1:14 (Jacob Chansley being interviewed the morning of the 6th).

8. Documents on file with the Select Committee to Investigate the January 6th Attack on the United States Capitol (Nick Quested Production), Video file ML_DC_20210106_Sony_FS5_Clip0067_1, at 11:43 (an unnamed woman being interviewed the morning of the 6th).

9. Trial Transcript at 4542 and Trial Exhibit No. 6370, *United States v. Rhodes et al.*, No. 1:22-cr-15 (D.D.C. Oct. 20, 2022).

10. Documents on file with the Select Committee to Investigate the January 6th Attack on the United States Capitol (Secret Service Production), CTRL0000882478, p. 1 (event summary of January 6th rally).

11. *See, e.g.,* Select Committee to Investigate the January 6th Attack on the United States Capitol, Transcribed Interview of Cassidy Hutchinson, (Feb. 23, 2022), pp. 87–88; Select Committee to Investigate the January 6th Attack on the United States Capitol, Continued Interview of Cassidy Hutchinson, (June 20, 2022), pp. 12–13.

12. Select Committee to Investigate the January 6th Attack on the United States Capitol, Continued Interview of Cassidy Hutchinson, (June 20, 2022), pp. 12–13.

13. Select Committee to Investigate the January 6th Attack on the United States Capitol, Continued Interview of Cassidy Hutchinson, (June 20, 2022), pp. 11–12.

14. Documents on file with the Select Committee to Investigate the January 6th Attack on the United States Capitol (Secret Service Production), CTRL0000086772, (Coordinated Response to a Request for Information from the Select Committee, Nov. 18, 2021).

15. Documents on file with the Select Committee to Investigate the January 6th Attack on the United States Capitol (Secret Service Production), CTRL0000882478 (event summary of January 6th rally).

16. Documents on file with the Select Committee to Investigate the January 6th Attack on the United States Capitol (Secret Service Production), CTRL0000882478 (event summary of January 6th rally).

17. Documents on file with the Select Committee to Investigate the January 6th Attack on the United States Capitol (Department of Interior Production), DOI_46003146_00005053, (general arrest report at the Washington Monument on the morning of January 6th).

18. Documents on file with the Select Committee to Investigate the January 6th Attack on the United States Capitol (Department of Interior Production), DOI_46003146_00005053, (general arrest report at the Washington Monument on the morning of January 6th).

19. Documents on file with the Select Committee to Investigate the January 6th Attack on the United States Capitol (Department of Interior Production), DOI_46003146_00005053, (general arrest report at the Washington Monument on the morning of January 6th).

20. Select Committee to Investigate the January 6th Attack on the United States Capitol, Informal Interview of National Parks Service Staff, (Oct. 27–28, 2021), p. 6.

21. Select Committee to Investigate the January 6th Attack on the United States Capitol, Informal Interview of National Parks Service Staff, (Oct. 27–28, 2021), p. 6.

22. Tom Jackman, Rachel Weiner, and Spencer S. Hsu, "Evidence of Firearms in Jan. 6 Crowd Grows as Arrests and Trials Mount," *Washington Post*, (July 8, 2022), available at https://www.washingtonpost.com/dc-md-va/2022/07/08/jan6-defendants-guns/.

23. Documents on file with the Select Committee to Investigate the January 6th Attack on the United States Capitol (Secret Service Production), CTRL0000882478 (event summary of Jan 6 rally).

24. Documents on file with the Select Committee to Investigate the January 6th Attack on the United States Capitol (District of Columbia Production), MPD 73–78 (District of Columbia, Metropolitan Police Department, Transcript of Radio Calls, January 6, 2021); Documents on file with the Select Committee to Investigate the January 6th Attack on the United States Capitol (District of Columbia Production), CTRL0000070375, at 3:40 (District of Columbia, Metropolitan Police Department, audio file of radio traffic from Jan. 6, 2021, from 12:00–13:00).

25. Statement of Offense at 4, *United States v. Colon*, No. 1:21-cr-160, (D.D.C. Apr. 27, 2022), ECF 143.

26. Statement of Offense at 4, *United States v. Colon*, No. 1:21-cr-160, (D.D.C. Apr. 27, 2022), ECF 143.

27. Affidavit in Support of Criminal Complaint and Arrest Warrant at 21–23, *United States v. Kuehne*, No. 1:21-cr-160, (D.D.C. Feb. 10, 2021), available at https://www.justice.gov/usao-dc/case-multi-defendant/file/1366446/download.

28. See Spencer S. Hsu and Tom Jackman, "First Jan. 6 Defendant Convicted at Trial Receives Longest Sentence of 7 Years," *Washington Post*, (Aug. 1, 2022), available at https://www.washingtonpost.com/dc-md-va/2022/08/01/reffitt-sentence-jan6/.

29. Statement of Facts at 3, 5, *United States v. Bargar*, No. 1:22-mj-169, (D.D.C. July 29, 2022), ECF No. 1-1. *See* Documents on file with the Select Committee to Investigate the January 6th Attack on the United States Capitol, (District of Columbia Production, Axon Body 3 X6039BLAL, at 14:30:03 (MPD body camera footage).

30. Statement of Facts at 5, *United States v. Bargar*, No. 1:22-mj-169, (D.D.C. July 29, 2022), ECF No. 1-1.

31. Statement of Facts at 5, *United States v. Bargar*, No. 1:22-mj-169, (D.D.C. July 29, 2022), ECF No. 1-1.

32. Statement of Offense at 3, *United States v. Mazza*, No. 1:21-cr-736, (D.D.C. June 17, 2022), ECF No. 25.

33. Statement of Offense at 3-4, *United States v. Mazza*, No. 1:21-cr-736, (D.D.C. June 17, 2022), ECF No. 25; Statement of Facts at 2, *United States v. Mazza*, No. 1:21-cr-736, (D.D.C. Nov. 12, 2021), ECF No. 1-1.

34. Government's Sentencing Memorandum at 9–10, *United States v. Mazza*, No. 1:21-cr-736 (D.D.C. Sept. 23, 2022), ECF No. 30.

35. For example, on November 13, 2020, Mazza (@MarkNunzios64) tweeted at President Trump: "Can you unseal obama's birth certificate and college transcripts?" On Facebook, Mazza shared a Q "drop" titled "The Armor of God," a 9/11 Truther video, and multiple posts dedicated to lies about the 2020 Presidential election. Screenshots on file with the Select Committee.

36. Hannah Rabinowitz and Holmes Lybrand, "Armed US Capitol Rioter Tells Investigators if He Had Found Pelosi, 'You'd be Here for Another Reason,'" CNN, (Nov. 23, 2021), available at https://www.cnn.com/2021/11/22/politics/loaded-firearm-january-6-charged-mark-mazza/index.html.

37. Government's Memorandum in Aid of Sentencing at 3, *United States v. Coffman*, No. 1:21-cr-4, (Mar. 2, 2022), ECF 28.

38. Government's Memorandum in Aid of Sentencing at 3, *United States v. Coffman*, No. 1:21-cr-4, (Mar. 2, 2022), ECF 28.

39. Government's Memorandum in Aid of Sentencing at 4, *United States v. Coffman*, No. 1:21-cr-4, (Mar. 2, 2022), ECF 28.

40. Select Committee to Investigate the January 6th Attack on the United States Capitol, Deposition of Jeffrey Lawrence Morelock, (Jan. 26, 2022), p. 81.

41. Trial Exhibit 1.S.159.524, *United States v. Rhodes et al.*, No. 1:22-cr-15, (D.D.C Oct. 4, 2022); Trial Transcript at 10502-08, *United States v. Rhodes et al.*, No. 1:22-cr-15 (D.D.C. Nov. 29, 2022)

42. Trial Transcript at 4109, *United States v. Rhodes et al.*, No. 1:22-cr-15, (D.D.C. Oct. 18, 2022).

43. Trial Transcript at 4106-08, *United States v. Rhodes et al.*, No. 1:22-cr-15 (D.D.C. Oct. 18, 2022)

44. Government's Opposition to Defendant's Motion to Revoke Magistrate Judge's Detention Order at 4, *United States v. Miller*, No. 1:21-cr-119, (D.D.C. Mar. 29, 2021), ECF No. 16.

45. Statement of Facts at 2, 9, *United States v. Miller*, No. 1:21-cr-119 (D.D.C. Jan. 19, 2021), ECF No. 1-1.

46. Government's Opposition to Defendant's Motion to Modify Release Conditions at 3, *United States v. Harkrider*, No. 1:21-cr-117, (D.D.C. July 8, 2021), ECF No. 40.

47. Government's Opposition to Defendant's Motion to Modify Release Conditions at 3, *United States v. Harkrider*, No. 1:21-cr-117, (D.D.C. July 8, 2021), ECF No. 40.

48. Dylan Stableford, "New Video Shows Alleged Jan. 6 Capitol Rioters Threatening Pence," Yahoo! News (Feb. 7, 2022), available at https://news.yahoo.com/new-video-jan-6-capitol-riot-pence-threat-drag-through-streets-195249884.html.

49. Select Committee to Investigate the January 6th Attack on the United States Capitol, Transcribed Interview of Eric Barber, (Mar. 16, 2022), p. 41.

50. Statement of Facts at 3–4, *United States v. Foy*, No. 1:21-cr-108 (D.D.C. Jan. 20, 2021), ECF No. 1-1.

51. Statement of Facts at 3–4, *United States v. Foy*, No. 1:21-cr-108 (D.D.C. Jan. 20, 2021), ECF No. 1-1; Government's Opposition to Defendant's Emergency Bond Review Motion at 5 n.3, *United States v. Foy*, No. 1:21-cr-108 (D.D.C. Mar. 12, 2021), ECF No. 11.

52. Statement of Facts at 2–4, *United States v. Webster*, No. 1:21-cr-208 (D.D.C. Feb. 19, 2021), ECF No. 1-1. *See also* Holmes Lybrand, "Former NYPD Officer Sentenced to 10 Years in Prison for Assaulting a Police Officer on January 6," CNN (Sept. 1, 2022), available at https://www.cnn.com/2022/09/01/politics/nypd-officer-january-6-sentencing/index.html.

53. January 6th Committee, "Loudermilk Footage," YouTube, June 5, 2022, available at https://www.youtube.com/watch?v=G9RNJ1tx4zw.

54. Select Committee to Investigate the January 6th Attack on the United States Capitol, Transcribed Interview of Nick Quested, (Apr. 5, 2022), pp. 123–25.

55. First Superseding Indictment at 3, *United States v. Nordean et al.*, No. 1:21-cr-175 (D.D.C. Mar. 10, 2021), ECF No. 26; "Auburn, Washington Member of Proud Boys Charged with Obstructing an Official Proceeding, Other Charges Related to the Jan. 6 Riots," Department of Justice, (Feb. 3, 2021), available at https://www.justice.gov/usao-wdwa/pr/auburn-washington-member-proud-boys-charged-obstructing-official-proceeding-other.

56. Third Superseding Indictment at 16, *United States v. Nordean et al.*, No. 21-cr-175 (TJK) (D.D.C. June 6, 2022), ECF No. 380, available at https://www.justice.gov/usao-dc/case-multi-defendant/file/1510971/download; Statement of Offense at 4, *United States v. Finley*, No. 1:21-cr-526 (D.D.C. March 8, 2022), available at https://www.justice.gov/usao-dc/case-multi-defendant/file/1492396/download.

57. "Auburn, Washington Member of Proud Boys Charged with Obstructing an Official Proceeding, Other Charges Related to the Jan. 6 Riots," Department of Justice, (Feb. 3, 2021), available at https://www.justice.gov/usao-wdwa/pr/auburn-washington-member-proud-boys-charged-obstructing-official-proceeding-other.

58. "Auburn, Washington Member of Proud Boys Charged with Obstructing an Official Proceeding, Other Charges Related to the Jan. 6 Riots," Department of Justice, (Feb. 3, 2021), available at https://www.justice.gov/usao-wdwa/pr/auburn-washington-member-proud-boys-charged-obstructing-official-proceeding-other.

59. "Auburn, Washington Member of Proud Boys Charged with Obstructing an Official Proceeding, Other Charges Related to the Jan. 6 Riots," Department of Justice, (Feb. 3, 2021), available at https://www.justice.gov/usao-wdwa/pr/auburn-washington-member-proud-boys-charged-obstructing-official-proceeding-other.

60. Third Superseding Indictment at 16, *United States v. Nordean et al.*, No. 1:21-cr-175 (D.D.C. June 6, 2022), ECF No. 380, available at https://www.justice.gov/usao-dc/case-multi-defendant/file/1510971/download.

61. *See* "War Room - 2019-AUG 09, Friday - Joe Biggs and Owen Shroyer Talk Internet Censorship and Democrat Party Terrorism," Spreaker.com, (Aug. 9, 2019), available at https://www.spreaker.com/user/realalexjones/08-09-19-warroom; Alexandra Garrett, "Joe Biggs, Proud Boys Leader and Former Infowars Staffer, Arrested Over Capitol Riot," *Newsweek*, (Jan. 20, 2021), available at https://www.newsweek.com/joe-biggs-proud-boys-leader-former-infowars-staffer-arrested-over-capitol-riot-1563181.

62. Affidavit in Support of Criminal Complaint at 4, *United States v. Biggs*, No. 1:21-cr-175 (D.D.C. Jan. 19, 2021), available at https://www.justice.gov/opa/page/file/1357251/download.

63. Affidavit in Support of Criminal Complaint at 4, *United States v. Biggs*, No. 1:21-cr-175 (D.D.C. Jan. 19, 2021), available at https://www.justice.gov/opa/page/file/1357251/download.

64. Affidavit in Support of Criminal Complaint at 4, *United States v. Biggs*, No. 1:21-cr-175 (D.D.C. Jan. 19, 2021), available at https://www.justice.gov/opa/page/file/1357251/download.

65. Affidavit in Support of Criminal Complaint at 4, *United States v. Biggs*, No. 1:21-cr-175 (D.D.C. Jan. 19, 2021), available at https://www.justice.gov/opa/page/file/1357251/download.

66. Statement of Offense at 4, *United States v. Finley*, No. 1:21-cr-526 (D.D.C. Apr. 6, 2022), ECF No. 38, available at https://www.justice.gov/usao-dc/case-multi-defendant/file/1492396/download; First Superseding Indictment at 3, *United States v. Nordean et al.*, No. 1:21-cr-175 (D.D.C. Mar. 10, 2021), ECF No. 26, available at https://www.justice.gov/usao-dc/case-multi-defendant/file/1377586/download.

67. First Superseding Indictment at 3, *United States v. Nordean et al.*, No. 1:21-cr-175 (D.D.C. Mar. 10, 2021), ECF No. 26, available at https://www.justice.gov/usao-dc/case-multi-defendant/file/1377586/download.

68. First Superseding Indictment at 8–9, 12, *United States v. Nordean et al.*, No. 1:21-cr-175 (D.D.C. Mar. 10, 2021), ECF No. 26, available at https://www.justice.gov/usao-dc/case-multi-defendant/file/1377586/download.

69. U.S. Capitol Police Camera U.S. Capitol Police Camera 9004.

70. U.S. Capitol Police Camera 3187.

71. Documents on file with the Select Committee to Investigate the January 6th Attack on the United States Capitol (Nick Quested Production), Video file Iphone_Nick_DC_20210106_IMG_1081_1_1.mov, at 0:14; Select Committee to Investigate the January 6th Attack on the United States Capitol, Transcribed Interview of Nick Quested, (Apr. 5, 2022), pp. 139–40.

72. Select Committee to Investigate the January 6th Attack on the United States Capitol, Transcribed Interview of Nick Quested, (Apr. 5, 2022), p. 138.

73. Select Committee to Investigate the January 6th Attack on the United States Capitol, Transcribed Interview of Nick Quested, (Apr. 5, 2022), pp. 130–31.

74. Select Committee to Investigate the January 6th Attack on the United States Capitol, Transcribed Interview of Nick Quested, (Apr. 5, 2022), p. 134; Documents on file with the Select Committee to Investigate the January 6th Attack on the United States Capitol (Nick Quested Production), Video file M_DC_20210106_Sony_GC280A_0486.mov.

75. Select Committee to Investigate the January 6th Attack on the United States Capitol, Transcribed Interview of Nick Quested, (Apr. 5, 2022), pp. 132, 143.

76. U.S. Capitol Police Camera 946.

77. "Peace Monument," Architect of the Capitol, available at https://www.aoc.gov/explore-capitol-campus/art/peace-monument.

78. U.S. Capitol Police Cameras 946, 3187.

79. Documents on file with the Select Committee to Investigate the January 6th Attack on the United States Capitol (Nick Quested Production), Video file ML_DC_20210106_Sony_GC280A_0498.mov, at 0:00–0:30.

80. Select Committee to Investigate the January 6th Attack on the United States Capitol, Transcribed Interview of Caroline Elizabeth Edwards, (Apr. 18, 2022), pp. 33–38; Documents on file with the Select Committee to Investigate the January 6th Attack on the United States Capitol (Nick Quested Production), Video file ML_DC_20210106_Sony_GC280A_0498 2022-05-15 15.00.38 at 1:15.

81. Documents on file with the Select Committee to Investigate the January 6th Attack on the United States Capitol (Nick Quested Production), Video file Iphone_Nick_DC_20210106_IMG_1116_1.mov.

82. Alan Feuer, "Dispute over Claim that Proud Boys Leader Urged Attack at Capitol," *New York Times*, (Oct. 7, 2021), available at https://www.nytimes.com/2021/10/07/us/politics/proud-boys-capitol-riot.html.

83. Alan Feuer, "Dispute over Claim that Proud Boys Leader Urged Attack at Capitol," *New York Times*, (Oct. 7, 2021), available at https://www.nytimes.com/2021/10/07/us/politics/proud-boys-capitol-riot.html.

84. U.S. Capitol Police Camera 946.

85. Select Committee to Investigate the January 6th Attack on the United States Capitol, Transcribed Interview of Caroline Elizabeth Edwards, (Apr. 18, 2022), pp. 41–42.

86. U.S. Capitol Police Cameras 945, 946, and 3187; Documents on file with the Select Committee to Investigate the January 6th Attack on the United States Capitol (Nick Quested Production), Video files Iphone_Nick_DC_20210106_IMG_1127_1.mov, Iphone_Nick_DC_20210106_IMG_1127 2_1.mov; Elijah Schaffer (@ElijahSchaffer), Twitter, Jan.

6, 2021 6:46 p.m. ET, available at https://twitter.com/ElijahSchaffer/status/1346966514990149639.

87. Select Committee to Investigate the January 6th Attack on the United States Capitol, Transcribed Interview of Caroline Elizabeth Edwards, (Apr. 18, 2022), pp. 44; Video files Iphone_Nick_DC_20210106_IMG_1127_1.mov, Iphone_Nick_DC_20210106_IMG_1127 2_1.mov; Elijah Schaffer (@ElijahSchaffer), Twitter, Jan. 6, 2021 6:46 p.m. ET, available at https://twitter.com/ElijahSchaffer/status/1346966514990149639.

88. Affidavit in Support of Criminal Complaint and Arrest Warrant at 6–8, *United States v. Jackman*, No. 1:21-cr-378 (D.D.C. Mar. 26, 2021), ECF No. 1-1.

89. Statement of Facts at 1–2, *United States v. Pepe*, No. 1:21-cr-52 (D.D.C. Jan. 11, 2021), ECF No. 1-1.

90. Affidavit in Support of Criminal Complaint and Arrest Warrant at 7, *United States v. Jackman*, No. 1:21-cr-378 (D.D.C. Mar. 26, 2021), ECF No. 1-1.

91. Statement of Offense at 5, *United States v. Finley*, No. 1:21-cr-526 (D.D.C. Apr. 6, 2022), ECF No. 38.

92. Statement of Offense at 2–5, *United States v. Bertino*, No. 1:22-cr-329 (D.D.C. Oct. 6, 2022), ECF No. 5.

93. U.S. Capitol Police Camera 908.

94. U.S. Capitol Police Camera 944.

95. U.S. Capitol Police Camera 944; Trial Exhibit 1515.1, *United States v. Rhodes et al.*, No. 1:22-cr-15 (D.D.C. Oct. 18, 2022); Trial Exhibit 6757, *United States v. Rhodes et al.*, No. 1:22-cr-15 (D.D.C. Nov. 1, 2022) (showing timelapse of security footage outside the Capitol).

96. "Donald Trump Speech 'Save America' Rally Transcript January 6," Rev, (Jan. 6, 2021), available at https://www.rev.com/blog/transcripts/donald-trump-speech-save-america-rally-transcript-january-6.

97. Documents on file with the Select Committee to Investigate the January 6th Attack on the United States Capitol (Alex Holder Production), Video file 45DAY32CAMB0059.mov, at 2:11 (using audio track 4 to hear the statement clearly from someone off camera).

98. "Tennessee Man Pleads Guilty to Felony Charges for Actions During Jan. 6 Capitol Breach," Department of Justice, (Sep. 30, 2022), available at https://www.justice.gov/usao-dc/pr/tennessee-man-pleads-guilty-felony-charges-actions-during-jan-6-capitol-breach.

99. "Tennessee Man Pleads Guilty to Felony Charges for Actions During Jan. 6 Capitol Breach," Department of Justice, (Sep. 30, 2022), available at https://www.justice.gov/usao-dc/pr/tennessee-man-pleads-guilty-felony-charges-actions-during-jan-6-capitol-breach.

100. "Two Men Sentenced to 44 Months in Prison for Assaulting Law Enforcement Officers During Jan. 6 Capitol Breach," Department of Justice, (July 15, 2022), available at https://www.justice.gov/usao-dc/pr/two-men-sentenced-prison-assaulting-law-enforcement-officers-during-jan-6-capitol-breach.

101. Statement of Offense at 4, *United States v. Mattice*, No. 1:21-cr-657 (D.D.C. Apr. 22, 2022), ECF No. 44.

102. Government's Opposition to Defendant's Motion for Release from Pretrial Detention at 10–11, *United States v. Nichols*, No. 1:21-cr-117 (D.D.C. Nov. 29, 2021), ECF No. 61; Tom Dreisbach (@TomDreisbach), Twitter, Feb. 4, 2022, 7:40 p.m. ET, available at https://twitter.com/TomDreisbach/status/1489763508459687937?ref_src=twsrc%5Etfw%7Ctwcamp%5Etweetembed%7Ctwterm%5E1489763508459687937%7Ctwgr%5E%7Ctwcon%5Es1_&ref_url=; Select Committee to Investigate the January 6th Attack on the United States Capitol, Public Hearing, (June 16, 2022), at 0:14:11–0:15:00, https://youtu.be/vBjUWVKuDj0?t=851; Hearing on Motion to Modify Conditions of Release, Exhibit 07 at 7:43–8:00, *United States v. Nichols*, No. 1:21-cr-117 (D.D.C. Dec. 20, 2021). Nichols had made similarly violent statements since the November 2020 election, with increasing references to fighting on January 6th following President Trump's December 19th tweet. *See* Government's Opposition to Defendant's

Motion for Release from Pretrial Detention at 4–8, *United States v. Nichols*, No. 1:21-cr-117 (D.D.C. Nov. 29, 2021), ECF No. 61 (documenting the many communications Nichols had with his codefendant planning for violence).

103. Government's Opposition to Defendant's Motion for Release from Pretrial Detention at 10–11, *United States v. Nichols*, No. 1:21-cr-117 (D.D.C. Nov. 29, 2021), ECF No. 61; Tom Dreisbach (@TomDreisbach), Twitter, Feb. 4, 2022, 7:40 p.m. ET, available at: https:// twitter.com/TomDreisbach/status/1489763508459687937?ref_src=twsrc%5Etfw%7Ctwcamp% 5Etweetembed%7Ctwterm%5E1489763508459687937%7Ctwgr%5E%7Ctwcon%5Es1_&ref_url=; Select Committee to Investigate the January 6th Attack on the United States Capitol, Public Hearing, (June 16, 2022), at 0:14:11–0:15:00, https://youtu.be/vBjUWVKuDj0?t=851; Hearing on Motion to Modify Conditions of Release, Exhibit 07 at 7:43–8:00, *United States v. Nichols*, No. 1:21-cr-117 (D.D.C. Dec. 20, 2021).

104. On the Media, "Jessica Watkins on 'Stop The Steal J6' Zello Channel (Unedited)," Sound-Cloud, at 4:00–4:12, Mar. 8, 2021, available at https://soundcloud.com/user-403747081/ jessica-watkins-on-stop-the-steal-j6-zello-channel-unedited.

105. On the Media, "Jessica Watkins on 'Stop The Steal J6' Zello Channel (Unedited)," Sound-Cloud, at 5:30–5:34, Mar. 8, 2021, available at https://soundcloud.com/user-403747081/ jessica-watkins-on-stop-the-steal-j6-zello-channel-unedited.

106. Statement of Facts at 13, *United States v. Hazard*, No. 1:22-cr-70 (D.D.C. Dec. 7, 2021), ECF No. 1-1; Joy Sharon Yi and Kate Woodsome, "How the Capitol Attack Unfolded, from Inside Trump's Rally to the Riot | Opinion," *The Washington Post*, at 1:32–1:42, (Jan. 12, 2021), available at https://www.washingtonpost.com/video/opinions/how-the-capitol-attack-unfolded-from-inside-trumps-rally-to-the-riot-opinion/2021/01/12/a7146251-b076-426e-a2e3-8b503692c89d_video.html.

107. Documents on file with the Select Committee to Investigate the January 6th Attack on the United States Capitol (Caroline Wren Production), REVU_000474 (Jan. 6, 2021, Alex Jones text message to Caroline Wren).

108. Documents on file with the Select Committee to Investigate the January 6th Attack on the United States Capitol (Caroline Wren Production), REVU_000474 (Jan. 6, 2021, Alex Jones text message to Caroline Wren).

109. Select Committee to Investigate the January 6th Attack on the United States Capitol, Deposition of Alexander Jones, (Jan. 24, 2022), Exhibit 13 at 0:29 (excerpt from The Alex Jones Show on Jan. 7, 2022).

110. Select Committee to Investigate the January 6th Attack on the United States Capitol, Deposition of Caroline Wren, (Dec. 17, 2021), pp. 260–61.

111. Select Committee to Investigate the January 6th Attack on the United States Capitol, Deposition of Caroline Wren, (Dec. 17, 2021), pp. 260–61; *See generally* The Alex Jones Show, "Humanity is Carrying Out its Own Great Reset Against Planet's Corrupt Elite - FULL SHOW 1/24/22," Banned.Video, at 37:00, Jan. 24, 2022, available at https://banned.video/ watch?id=61ef3e9d186875155e97ece8&list=5d81058ce2ea200013c01580.

112. Select Committee to Investigate the January 6th Attack on the United States Capitol, Deposition of Alexander Jones, (Jan. 24, 2022), Ex. 13 at 0:29 (Excerpt from The Alex Jones Show on Jan. 7, 2022); Documents on file with the Select Committee to Investigate the January 6th Attack on the United States Capitol (Caroline Wren Production), REVU_000475 (Jan. 6, 2021, Alex Jones text message to Caroline Wren); Documents on file with the Select Committee to Investigate the January 6th Attack on the United States Capitol (Caroline Wren Production), REVU_000484 (Jan. 5, 2021, Tim Enlow text message to Caroline Wren).

113. Select Committee to Investigate the January 6th Attack on the United States Capitol, Deposition of Caroline Wren, (Dec. 17, 2021), p. 244.

114. Select Committee to Investigate the January 6th Attack on the United States Capitol, Deposition of Caroline Wren, (Dec. 17, 2021), p. 244.

115. Select Committee to Investigate the January 6th Attack on the United States Capitol, Deposition of Caroline Wren, (Dec. 17, 2021), p. 244.

116. The Alex Jones Show, "Humanity is Carrying Out its Own Great Reset Against Planet's Corrupt Elite - FULL SHOW 1/24/22," Banned.Video, at 37:00, Jan. 24, 2022, available at https://banned.video/watch?id=61ef3e9d186875155e97ece8&list=5d81058ce2ea200013c01580.

117. The Alex Jones Show, "Humanity is Carrying Out its Own Great Reset Against Planet's Corrupt Elite - FULL SHOW 1/24/22," Banned.Video, at 37:44, Jan. 24, 2022, available at https://banned.video/watch?id=61ef3e9d186875155e97ece8&list=5d81058ce2ea200013c01580.

118. The Alex Jones Show, "Humanity is Carrying Out its Own Great Reset Against Planet's Corrupt Elite - FULL SHOW 1/24/22," Banned.Video, at 37:26, Jan. 24, 2022, available at https://banned.video/watch?id=61ef3e9d186875155e97ece8&list=5d81058ce2ea200013c01580.

119. The Alex Jones Show, "Humanity is Carrying Out its Own Great Reset Against Planet's Corrupt Elite - FULL SHOW 1/24/22," Banned.Video, at 37:58, Jan. 24, 2022, available at https://banned.video/watch?id=61ef3e9d186875155e97ece8&list=5d81058ce2ea200013c01580.

120. The Alex Jones Show, "Humanity is Carrying Out its Own Great Reset Against Planet's Corrupt Elite - FULL SHOW 1/24/22," Banned.Video, at 38:00, Jan. 24, 2022, available at https://banned.video/watch?id=61ef3e9d186875155e97ece8&list=5d81058ce2ea200013c01580.

121. The Alex Jones Show, "Humanity is Carrying Out its Own Great Reset Against Planet's Corrupt Elite - FULL SHOW 1/24/22," Banned.Video, at 38:16, Jan. 24, 2022, available at https://banned.video/watch?id=61ef3e9d186875155e97ece8&list=5d81058ce2ea200013c01580 .

122. Select Committee to Investigate the January 6th Attack on the United States Capitol, Deposition of Matthew Walter, (Mar. 9, 2022), p. 78.

123. Select Committee to Investigate the January 6th Attack on the United States Capitol, Deposition of Matthew Walter, (Mar. 9, 2022), p. 75.

124. Documents on file with the Select Committee to Investigate the January 6th Attack on the United States Capitol (Google Voice Production, Feb. 25, 2022).

125. Documents on file with the Select Committee to Investigate the January 6th Attack on the United States Capitol (Verizon Production, Nov. 19, 2021).

126. Documents on file with the Select Committee to Investigate the January 6th Attack on the United States Capitol (AT&T Production, Nov. 24, 2021).

127. Select Committee to Investigate the January 6th Attack on the United States Capitol, Deposition of Alexander Jones, (Jan. 24, 2022), Exhibit 12 at 0:20.

128. Lena Groeger, Jeff Kao, Al Shaw, Moiz Syed and Maya Eliahou, "What Parler Saw During the Attack on the Capitol," ProPublica, (Jan. 17, 2021), available at https://projects.propublica.org/parler-capitol-videos/?id=HS34fpbzqg2b.

129. Lena Groeger, Jeff Kao, Al Shaw, Moiz Syed and Maya Eliahou, "What Parler Saw During the Attack on the Capitol," ProPublica, (Jan. 17, 2021), available at https://projects.propublica.org/parler-capitol-videos/?id=Qo3hom0Qb1at.

130. Lena Groeger, Jeff Kao, Al Shaw, Moiz Syed and Maya Eliahou, "What Parler Saw During the Attack on the Capitol," ProPublica, (Jan. 17, 2021), available at https://projects.propublica.org/parler-capitol-videos/?id=QgPXUnbdhx3q.

131. Lena Groeger, Jeff Kao, Al Shaw, Moiz Syed and Maya Eliahou, "What Parler Saw During the Attack on the Capitol," ProPublica, (Jan. 17, 2021), available at https://projects.propublica.org/parler-capitol-videos/?id=QgPXUnbdhx3q.

132. Lena Groeger, Jeff Kao, Al Shaw, Moiz Syed and Maya Eliahou, "What Parler Saw During the Attack on the Capitol," ProPublica, (Jan. 17, 2021), available at https://projects.propublica.org/parler-capitol-videos/?id=QgPXUnbdhx3q.

133. Jan. 6th Protest and Save America March, "Raw BodyCam: Watch As Alex Jones Works With Capitol Police To Try And Quell The Riot," Banned.Video, at 8:45, Jan. 12, 2021, available at https://banned.video/watch?id=5ffe25bc0d763c3dca0c4da1.

134. Lena Groeger, Jeff Kao, Al Shaw, Moiz Syed and Maya Eliahou, "What Parler Saw During the Attack on the Capitol," ProPublica, (Jan. 17, 2021), available at https://projects.propublica.org/parler-capitol-videos/?id=a8lp9oooOT3m.

135. Jan. 6th Protest and Save America March, "Raw BodyCam: Watch as Alex Jones Works with Capitol Police To Try And Quell The Riot," Banned.Video, at 15:10, Jan. 12, 2021, available at https://Banned.Video/watch?id=5ffe25bc0d763c3dca0c4da1.

136. Documents on file with the Select Committee to Investigate the January 6th Attack on the United States Capitol (District of Columbia Production), MPD 125–MPD 126 (District of Columbia, Metropolitan Police Department, Transcript of Radio Calls, January 6, 2021)

137. Government's Memorandum in Support of Pretrial Detention of Defendant Guy Wesley Reffitt at 4, *United States v. Reffitt*, No. 1:21-cr-32 (D.D.C. Mar. 13, 2021), ECF No. 10.

138. *See* Government's Memorandum in Support of Pretrial Detention of Defendant Guy Wesley Reffitt at 4–5, *United States v. Reffitt*, No. 1:21-cr-00032 (D.D.C. Mar. 13, 2021), ECF No. 10.

139. *See* Government's Memorandum in Support of Pretrial Detention of Defendant Guy Wesley Reffitt at 4–5, *United States v. Reffitt*, No. 1:21-cr-00032 (D.D.C. Mar. 13, 2021), ECF No. 10.

140. *See* Government's Memorandum in Support of Pretrial Detention of Defendant Guy Wesley Reffitt at 5, *United States v. Reffitt*, No. 1:21-cr-00032 (D.D.C. Mar. 13, 2021), ECF No. 10.

141. *See* Government's Memorandum in Support of Pretrial Detention of Defendant Guy Wesley Reffitt at 5, *United States v. Reffitt*, No. 1:21-cr-00032 (D.D.C. Mar. 13, 2021), ECF No. 10.

142. *See* Government's Memorandum in Support of Pretrial Detention of Defendant Guy Wesley Reffitt at 5, *United States v. Reffitt*, No. 1:21-cr-00032 (D.D.C. Mar. 13, 2021), ECF No. 10.

143. *See* Government's Memorandum in Support of Pretrial Detention of Defendant Guy Wesley Reffitt at 6, *United States v. Reffitt*, No. 1:21-cr-00032 (D.D.C. Mar. 13, 2021), ECF No. 10.

144. *See* Government's Memorandum in Support of Pretrial Detention of Defendant Guy Wesley Reffitt at 12, *United States v. Reffitt*, No. 1:21-cr-00032 (D.D.C. Mar. 13, 2021), ECF No. 10.

145. *See* Government's Memorandum in Support of Pretrial Detention of Defendant Guy Wesley Reffitt at 4, *United States v. Reffitt*, No. 1:21-cr-32 (D.D.C. Mar. 13, 2021), ECF No. 10.

146. Government's Sentencing Memorandum, *United States v. Reffitt*, No. 1:21-cr-32 (D.D.C. July 15, 2022), ECF No. 158.

147. *See* Spencer S. Hsu and Tom Jackman, "First Jan. 6 Defendant Convicted at Trial Receives Longest Sentence of 7 Years," *Washington Post*, (Aug. 1, 2022), available at https://www.washingtonpost.com/dc-md-va/2022/08/01/reffitt-sentence-jan6/.

148. *See* Statement of Facts at ¶¶ 14, 20, *United States v. Scott*, No. 1:21-mj-411 (D.D.C. April 29, 2021), ECF No. 1-1, available at https://www.justice.gov/usao-dc/case-multi-defendant/file/1395876/download.

149. *See* Statement of Facts at ¶ 16, *United States v. Scott*, No. 1:21-mj-411 (D.D.C. April 29, 2021), ECF No. 1-1, available at https://www.justice.gov/usao-dc/case-multi-defendant/file/1395876/download.

150. Statement of Facts at 9, *United States v. Worrell*, No. 1:21-mj-296 (D.D.C. Mar. 10, 2021), ECF No. 1-1, available at https://www.justice.gov/usao-dc/case-multi-defendant/file/1379556/download.

151. Statement of Facts at 10–11, *United States v. Worrell*, No. 1:21-mj-296 (D.D.C. Mar. 10, 2021), ECF No. 1-1, available at https://www.justice.gov/usao-dc/case-multi-defendant/file/1379556/download.

152. Statement of Offense at ¶ 9, *United States v. Jackson*, No. 1:21-cr-484 (D.D.C. Nov. 22, 2021), ECF No. 19, available at https://www.justice.gov/usao-dc/case-multi-defendant/file/1452291/download.

153. Statement of Offense at ¶¶ 1, 25, *United States v. Greene*, No. 1:21-cr-52-33 (D.D.C. Dec. 22, 2021), ECF No. 105, available at https://www.justice.gov/usao-dc/press-release/file/1458266/download.

154. Lena Groeger, Jeff Kao, Al Shaw, Moiz Syed and Maya Eliahou, "What Parler Saw During the Attack on the Capitol," ProPublica, (Jan. 17, 2021), available at https://projects.propublica.org/parler-capitol-videos/?id=zOZ8CgfNU1SY.

155. Statement of Facts at 5, *United States v. Kelley*, No. 1:22-cr-222 (D.D.C. June 8, 2022), ECF No. 1.

156. Statement of Facts at 6, *United States v. Kelley*, No. 1:22-cr-222 (D.D.C. June 8, 2022), ECF No. 1.

157. *See* Select Committee to Investigate the January 6th Attack on the United States Capitol, Deposition of Ryan Kelley, (Apr. 21, 2022), pp. 7, 70–71, 79–80, and Exhibit 15.

158. Arrest Warrant at 1, *United States v. Kelley*, No. 1:22-cr-222 (D.D.C. June 9, 2022), ECF No. 5.

159. U.S. Capitol Police Camera 102; Third Superseding Indictment at 21, *United States v. Nordean et al.*, No. 1:21-cr-175 (D.D.C. June 6, 2022), ECF No. 380 (noting that Dominic Pezzola "used [a] riot shield . . . to break a window of the Capitol" at "2:13 p.m." and that "[t]he first members of the mob entered the Capitol through this broken window"); 167 Cong. Rec. S634 (daily ed. Feb. 10, 2021), available at https://www.congress.gov/117/crec/2021/02/10/CREC-2021-02-10-pt1-PgS615-4.pdf.

160. U.S. Capitol Police Camera 689; Third Superseding Indictment at 21, *United States v. Nordean et al.*, No. 1:21-cr-175 (D.D.C. June 6, 2022), ECF No. 380 (noting that Dominic Pezzola "used [a] riot shield . . . to break a window of the Capitol" at "2:13 p.m." and that "[t]he first members of the mob entered the Capitol through this broken window."); 167 Cong. Rec. S634 (daily ed. Feb. 10, 2021), available at https://www.congress.gov/117/crec/2021/02/10/CREC-2021-02-10-pt1-PgS615-4.pdf.

161. Third Superseding Indictment at 21, *United States v. Nordean et al.*, No. 1:21-cr-175 (D.D.C. June 6, 2022), ECF No. 380 (noting that Dominic Pezzola "used [a] riot shield . . . to break a window of the Capitol" at "2:13 p.m." and that "[t]he first members of the mob entered the Capitol through this broken window"); 167 Cong. Rec. S634 (daily ed. Feb. 10, 2021), available at https://www.congress.gov/117/crec/2021/02/10/CREC-2021-02-10-pt1-PgS615-4.pdf. *See also* Ashley Parker, Carol D. Leonnig, Paul Kane, and Emma Brown, "How the Rioters Who Stormed the Capitol Came Dangerously Close to Pence," *Washington Post*, (Jan. 15, 2021), available at https://www.washingtonpost.com/politics/pence-rioters-capitol-attack/2021/01/15/ab62e434-567c-11eb-a08b-f1381ef3d207_story.html; Kat Lonsdorf, Courtney Dorning, Amy Isackson, Mary Louise Kelly, and Aeilsa Chang, "A Timeline of How The Jan. 6 Attack Unfolded—Including Who Said What and When," NPR, (June 9, 2022), available at https://www.npr.org/2022/01/05/1069977469/a-timeline-of-how-the-jan-6-attack-unfolded-including-who-said-what-and-when.

162. Peter Manseau, "His Pastors Tried to Steer Him Away from Social Media Rage. He Stormed the Capitol Anyway," *Washington Post*, (Feb. 19, 2021), available at https://www.washingtonpost.com/religion/2021/02/19/michael-sparks-capitol-siege-jan-6-christian/.

163. Statement of Facts at 9, *United States v. Sparks*, No. 1:21-cr-87 (D.D.C. Jan. 19, 2021), ECF No. 1.

164. Complaint and Affidavit at 9–10, *United States v. Gieswein*, No. 1:21-cr-24 (D.D.C. Jan. 16, 2021), ECF No. 1. As an example of his conspiracy beliefs, Gieswein claimed that American politicians "have completely destroyed our country and sold them to the Rothschilds and Rockefellers." This is a standard anti-Semitic trope. *See* Complaint and Affidavit at 11, *United States v. Gieswein*, No. 1:21-cr-24 (D.D.C. Jan. 16, 2021), ECF No. 1. Gieswein also denied that he was a Three Percenter as of January 6, 2021, even though he affiliated with an apparent Three Percenter group at previous times. *See* Mr. Gieswein's Motion for Hearing & Revocation of Detention Order at 2–3, 18–19, 25, *United States v. Gieswein*, No. 1:21-cr-24 (D.D.C. June 8, 2021), ECF No. 18. When the FBI arrested Gieswein, the criminal complaint noted that he "appears to be affiliated with the radical militia group known as the Three Percenters." Criminal Complaint at 5, *United States v. Gieswein*, No. 1:21-cr-24 (D.D.C. Jan. 16, 2021), available at https://www.justice.gov/opa/page/file/1360831/

download. *See also* Adam Rawnsley (@arawnsley), Twitter, Jan. 17, 2021 9:13 p.m. ET, available at https://twitter.com/arawnsley/status/1350989535954530315 (highlighting photos of Gieswein flashing a Three Percenter symbol).

165. Statement of Facts at 1–2, *United States v. Jensen*, No. 1:21-cr-6 (D.D.C. Jan. 8, 2021), ECF No. 1.

166. Statement of Facts at 2, *United States v. Jensen*, No. 1:21-cr-6 (D.D.C. Jan. 8, 2021), ECF No. 1.

167. "Arizona Man Sentenced to 41 Months in Prison On Felony Charge in Jan. 6 Capitol Breach," Department of Justice, (Nov. 17, 2021), available at https://www.justice.gov/usao-dc/pr/ arizona-man-sentenced-41-months-prison-felony-charge-jan-6-capitol-breach.

168. Statement of Facts at 2, *United States v. Seefried*, No. 1:21-mj-46 (D.D.C. Jan. 13, 2021), available at: https://www.justice.gov/usao-dc/press-release/file/1354306/download.

169. Statement of Facts at 2, *United States v. Seefried*, No. 1:21-mj-46 (D.D.C. Jan. 13, 2021), available at https://www.justice.gov/usao-dc/press-release/file/1354306/download; Maria Cramer, "Confederate Flag an Unnerving Sight in the Capitol," *New York Times*, (Jan. 9, 2021), available at https://www.nytimes.com/2021/01/09/us/politics/confederate-flag-capitol.html.

170. Statement of Facts at 2, 5, *United States v. Seefried*, No. 1:21-mj-46 (D.D.C. Jan. 13, 2021), available at https://www.justice.gov/usao-dc/press-release/file/1354306/download.

171. "Delaware Man Sentenced to 24 Months in Prison for Actions Related to Capitol Breach," Department of Justice, (Oct. 24, 2022), available at https://www.justice.gov/usao-dc/pr/ delaware-man-sentenced-24-months-prison-actions-related-capitol-breach.

172. "Virginia Man Arrested on Felony and Misdemeanor Charges for Actions During Jan. 6 Capitol Breach," Department of Justice, (Sep. 20, 2022), available at https://www.justice.gov/ usao-dc/pr/virginia-man-arrested-felony-and-misdemeanor-charges-actions-during-jan-6-capitol-breach; Statement of Facts at 44, *United States v. Brody, et al.*, No. 1:22-mj-203 (D.D.C. Sep. 12, 2022), available at https://www.justice.gov/usao-dc/press-release/file/ 1536736/download.

173. "Virginia Man Arrested on Felony and Misdemeanor Charges for Actions During Jan. 6 Capitol Breach," Department of Justice, (Sep. 20, 2022), available at https://www.justice.gov/ usao-dc/pr/virginia-man-arrested-felony-and-misdemeanor-charges-actions-during-jan-6-capitol-breach.

174. Statement of Facts at 44, *United States v. Brody, et al.*, No. 1:22-mj-203 (D.D.C. Sep. 12, 2022), available at https://www.justice.gov/usao-dc/press-release/file/1536736/download.

175. Statement of Facts at 44, *United States v. Brody, et al.*, No. 1:22-mj-203 (D.D.C. Sep. 12, 2022), available at https://www.justice.gov/usao-dc/press-release/file/1536736/download.

176. Neil Vigdor and Alan Feuer, "A Jan. 6 Defendant Coordinated Volunteers to Help Youngkin's Campaign," *New York Times*, (Oct. 6, 2022), available at https://www.nytimes.com/2022/10/ 06/us/politics/joseph-brody-jan-6-youngkin.html.

177. Statement of Facts at 43, *United States v. Brody, et al.*, No. 1:22-mj-203 (D.D.C. Sept. 12, 2022), available at https://www.justice.gov/usao-dc/press-release/file/1536736/download.

178. "Virginia Man Arrested on Felony and Misdemeanor Charges for Actions During Jan. 6 Capitol Breach," Department of Justice, (Sep. 20, 2022), available at https://www.justice.gov/ usao-dc/pr/virginia-man-arrested-felony-and-misdemeanor-charges-actions-during-jan-6-capitol-breach.

179. "Virginia Man Arrested on Felony and Misdemeanor Charges for Actions During Jan. 6 Capitol Breach," Department of Justice, (Sep. 20, 2022), available at https://www.justice.gov/ usao-dc/pr/virginia-man-arrested-felony-and-misdemeanor-charges-actions-during-jan-6-capitol-breach.

180. "Virginia Man Arrested on Felony and Misdemeanor Charges for Actions During Jan. 6 Capitol Breach," Department of Justice (Sep. 20, 2022), available at https://www.justice.gov/

usao-dc/pr/virginia-man-arrested-felony-and-misdemeanor-charges-actions-during-jan-6-capitol-breach; Statement of Facts at 40–43, *United States v. Brody, et al.*, No. 1:22-mj-203 (D.D.C. Sep. 12, 2022), available at https://www.justice.gov/usao-dc/press-release/file/1536736/download.

181. Statement of Facts at 2–3, 6–7, *United States v. Williams*, No. 1:21-cr-618 (D.D.C. Jan. 17, 2021), available at https://www.justice.gov/opa/page/file/1357051/download. A jury found Williams guilty of certain felony and misdemeanor charges, but could not reach a verdict on other charges, including the aiding and abetting charge. *See* "Pennsylvania Woman Found Guilty of Felony and Misdemeanor Charges Related to Capitol Breach," Department of Justice, (Nov. 21, 2022), available at https://www.justice.gov/usao-dc/pr/pennsylvania-woman-found-guilty-felony-and-misdemeanor-charges-related-capitol-breach.

182. Government's Sentencing Memorandum at 12, *United States v. Hale-Cusanelli*, No. 1:21-cr-37 (D.D.C. Sep. 15, 2022), ECF No. 110; "New Jersey Man Sentenced to 48 Months in Prison for Actions Related to Capitol Breach," Department of Justice, (Sep. 22, 2022), available at https://www.justice.gov/usao-dc/pr/new-jersey-man-sentenced-prison-actions-related-capitol-breach; Statement of Facts at 2, *United States v. Hale-Cusanelli*, No. 1:21-cr-37, (D.D.C. Jan. 15, 2021), available at https://www.justice.gov/opa/page/file/1356066/download. Pictures available online depict Hale-Cusanelli with a Hitler-style mustache. *See* Holmes Lybrand and Andrew Millman, "U.S. Capitol Rioter and Alleged Nazi Sympathizer Sentenced to 4 Years in Prison," CNN, (Sep. 22, 2022), available at https://www.cnn.com/2022/09/22/politics/timothy-hale-cusanelli-stephen-ayres-capitol-riot/index.html.

183. "New Jersey Man Sentenced to 48 Months in Prison for Actions Related to Capitol Breach," Department of Justice, (Sep. 22, 2022), available at https://www.justice.gov/usao-dc/pr/new-jersey-man-sentenced-prison-actions-related-capitol-breach.

184. "New Jersey Man Sentenced to 48 Months in Prison for Actions Related to Capitol Breach," Department of Justice, (Sep. 22, 2022), available at https://www.justice.gov/usao-dc/pr/new-jersey-man-sentenced-prison-actions-related-capitol-breach.

185. Statement of Offense at 3, *United States v. Packer*, No. 1:21-cr-103 (D.D.C. Jan. 13, 2021), available at https://www.justice.gov/usao-dc/case-multi-defendant/file/1469561/download.

186. Affidavit in Support of Criminal Complaint and Arrest Warrant at 4–5, *United States v. Packer*, No. 1:21-cr-103, (D.D.C. Jan. 13, 2021), available at https://www.justice.gov/usao-dc/press-release/file/1353201/download.

187. U.S. Capitol Police Cameras 102, 123.

188. Igor Bobic (@igorbobic), Twitter, Jan. 6, 2021 3:09 p.m. ET, available at https://twitter.com/igorbobic/status/1346911809274478594; Spencer S. Hsu, "Officer Describes How Jan. 6 Rioters Pursued Him through Capitol," *Washington Post*, (June 15, 2022), available at https://www.washingtonpost.com/dc-md-va/2022/06/13/eugene-goodman-capitol-police-testimony/.

189. Igor Bobic (@igorbobic), Twitter, Jan. 6, 2021 3:09 p.m. ET, available at https://twitter.com/igorbobic/status/1346911809274478594; Peter Manseau, "His Pastors Tried to Steer Him Away from Social Media Rage. He Stormed the Capitol Anyway," *Washington Post*, (Feb. 19, 2021), available at https://www.washingtonpost.com/religion/2021/02/19/michael-sparks-capitol-siege-jan-6-christian/; Government's Opposition to Defendant's Motion for Hearing & Revocation of Detention Order at 8, *United States v. Robert Gieswein*, No. 1:21-cr-24 (EGS) (D.D.C. June 15, 2021), available at https://extremism.gwu.edu/sites/g/files/zaxdzs2191/f/Robert%20Gieswein%20Government%20Opposition%20to%20Motion%20for%20Hearing%20and%20Revocation%20of%20Detention%20Order.pdf.

190. "Iowa Man Found Guilty of Felony and Misdemeanor Charges Related to Capitol Breach," Department of Justice, (Sep. 23, 2022), https://www.justice.gov/usao-dc/pr/iowa-man-found-guilty-felony-and-misdemeanor-charges-related-capitol-breach.

191. Peter Manseau, "His Pastors Tried to Steer Him Away from Social Media Rage. He Stormed the Capitol Anyway," Washington Post, (Feb. 19, 2021), available at https://www.washingtonpost.com/religion/2021/02/19/michael-sparks-capitol-siege-jan-6-christian/.

192. U.S. Capitol Police Cameras 113, 114.

193. U.S. Capitol Police Camera 213; Igor Bobic (@igorbobic), Twitter, Jan. 6, 2021 3:09 p.m. ET, available at https://twitter.com/igorbobic/status/1346911809274478594.

194. Lena Groeger, Jeff Kao, Al Shaw, Moiz Syed and Maya Eliahou, "What Parler Saw During the Attack on the Capitol," ProPublica, (Jan. 17, 2021), available at https://projects.propublica.org/parler-capitol-videos/?id=s8XNlAskWNvi.

195. Lena Groeger, Jeff Kao, Al Shaw, Moiz Syed and Maya Eliahou, "What Parler Saw During the Attack on the Capitol," ProPublica, (Jan. 17, 2021), available at https://projects.propublica.org/parler-capitol-videos/?id=s8XNlAskWNvi.

196. Lena Groeger, Jeff Kao, Al Shaw, Moiz Syed and Maya Eliahou, "What Parler Saw During the Attack on the Capitol," ProPublica, (Jan. 17, 2021), available at https://projects.propublica.org/parler-capitol-videos/?id=s8XNlAskWNvi.

197. Affidavit in Support of Criminal Complaint and Arrest Warrant at 12, *United States v. Rae*, No. 1:21-cr-378 (D.D.C. Mar. 23, 2021), ECF No. 1.

198. Statement of Offense at 4, United States v. Pruitt, No. 1:21-cr-23 (D.D.C. June 3, 2022), ECF No. 61, available at https://www.justice.gov/usao-dc/case-multi-defendant/file/1510401/download.

199. U.S. Capitol Police Cameras 113, 114.

200. U.S. Capitol Police Camera 102.

201. U.S. Capitol Police Cameras 932, 933.

202. Lena Groeger, Jeff Kao, Al Shaw, Moiz Syed and Maya Eliahou, "What Parler Saw During the Attack on the Capitol," ProPublica, (Jan. 17, 2021), available at https://projects.propublica.org/parler-capitol-videos/?id=a8lp9oooOT3m.

203. Jan. 6th Protest and Save America March, "Raw BodyCam: Watch as Alex Jones Works with Capitol Police to Try and Quell the Riot," Banned.Video, at 15:10, posted Jan. 12, 2021, available at https://banned.video/watch?id=5ffe25bc0d763c3dca0c4da1

204. CNN Business, "Alex Jones' Influence on January 6," CNN, Feb. 26, 2022, available at https://www.cnn.com/videos/media/2022/02/26/alex-jones-influence-january-6-documentary.cnnbusiness.

205. Hunting Insurrectionists, "East Main 'Columbus' Doors 1:45-4:45pm - 56 video sync - Jan 6th Capitol Attack Footage," YouTube, at 31:53, Mar. 12, 2021, available at https://www.youtube.com/watch?v=z1gODZvbhqs&t=1901s.

206. Select Committee to Investigate the January 6th Attack on the United States Capitol, Deposition of Matthew Thomas Walter, (Mar. 9, 2022), p. 79.

207. Select Committee to Investigate the January 6th Attack on the United States Capitol, Deposition of Matthew Thomas Walter, (Mar. 9, 2022), p. 79.

208. Hunting Insurrectionists, "East Main 'Columbus' Doors 1:45-4:45pm - 56 video sync - Jan 6th Capitol Attack Footage," YouTube, at 36:15, Mar. 12, 2021, available at https://www.youtube.com/watch?v=z1gODZvbhqs&t=1901s

209. CNN Business, "Alex Jones' Influence on January 6," CNN, at 2:20–2:28, Feb. 26, 2022, available at https://www.cnn.com/videos/media/2022/02/26/alex-jones-influence-january-6-documentary.cnnbusiness.

210. Hunting Insurrectionists, "East Main 'Columbus' Doors 1:45-4:45pm - 56 video sync - Jan 6th Capitol Attack Footage," YouTube, at 39:19, Mar. 12, 2021, available at https://www.youtube.com/watch?v=z1gODZvbhqs&t=1901s.

211. Select Committee to Investigate the January 6th Attack on the United States Capitol, Deposition of Ali Alexander, (Dec. 9, 2021), pp. 64–66.

212. U.S. Capitol Police Cameras 7029, 7216.

213. U.S. Capitol Police Camera 7029.

214. Complaint with Arrest Warrant at 16–19, *United States v. Loehrke*, No. 1:21-mj-672 (D.D.C. Nov. 30, 2021), ECF No. 1, available at https://www.justice.gov/usao-dc/case-multi-defendant/file/1459171/download.

215. Complaint with Arrest Warrant at 12, *United States v. Loehrke*, No. 1:21-mj-672 (D.D.C. Nov. 30, 2021), ECF No. 1, available at https://www.justice.gov/usao-dc/case-multi-defendant/file/1459171/download.

216. Complaint with Arrest Warrant at 12, *United States v. Loehrke*, No. 1:21-mj-672 (D.D.C. Nov. 30, 2021), ECF No. 1, available at https://www.justice.gov/usao-dc/case-multi-defendant/file/1459171/download.

217. Complaint with Arrest Warrant at 12, *United States v. Loehrke*, No. 1:21-mj-672 (D.D.C. Nov. 30, 2021), ECF No. 1, available at https://www.justice.gov/usao-dc/case-multi-defendant/file/1459171/download.

218. Complaint with Arrest Warrant at 14–19, *United States v. Loehrke*, No. 1:21-mj-672 (D.D.C. Nov. 30, 2021), ECF No. 1, available at https://www.justice.gov/usao-dc/case-multi-defendant/file/1459171/download; "Two Men Charged with Obstructing Law Enforcement During Jan. 6 Capitol Breach," Department of Justice, (Dec. 3, 2021), available at https://www.justice.gov/usao-dc/pr/two-men-charged-obstructing-law-enforcement-during-jan-6-capitol-breach.

219. Complaint with Arrest Warrant at 24–29, *United States v. Loehrke*, No. 1:21-mj-672 (D.D.C. Nov. 30, 2021), ECF No. 1, available at https://www.justice.gov/usao-dc/case-multi-defendant/file/1459171/download.

220. Select Committee to Investigate the January 6th Attack on the United States Capitol, Informal Interview of Brian Adams and Marc Carrion, (Apr. 20, 2022).

221. "Two Men Charged with Obstructing Law Enforcement During Jan. 6 Capitol Breach," Department of Justice, (Dec. 3, 2021), available at https://www.justice.gov/usao-dc/pr/two-men-charged-obstructing-law-enforcement-during-jan-6-capitol-breach.

222. U.S. Capitol Police Camera 7029.

223. *See* Chapter 6.

224. Trial Transcript at 4532:20–4534:9, *United States v. Rhodes et al.*, No. 1:22-cr-15 (D.D.C. Oct. 20, 2022).

225. Trial Transcript at 4642:24–4643:6 and Trial Exhibit 6731, United States v. Rhodes et al., No. 1:22-cr-15 (D.D.C. Oct. 20, 2022).

226. Trial Transcript at 4643:22–4644:4 and Trial Exhibit 6731, United States v. Rhodes et al., No. 1:22-cr-15 (D.D.C. Oct. 20, 2022).

227. Trial Transcript at 4520:9–4521:5, 4744:20–4745:21, Trial Exhibits 1503, 6740, *United States v. Rhodes et al.*, No. 1:22-cr-15 (D.D.C. Oct. 20, 2022).

228. Seventh Superseding Indictment at 21–22, *United States v. Crowl et al.*, No. 21-cr-28 (D.D.C. Jan. 12, 2022), available at https://www.justice.gov/opa/press-release/file/1462476/download.

229. Seventh Superseding Indictment at 22, *United States v. Crowl et al.*, No. 21-cr-28 (D.D.C. Jan. 12, 2022), available at https://www.justice.gov/opa/press-release/file/1462476/download.

230. Trial Transcript at 4724:8–15 and Trial Exhibit 1500 at 13:02–13:25, *United States v. Rhodes et al.*, No. 1:22-cr-15 (D.D.C. Oct. 20, 2022).

231. Trial Transcript at 4779:1–4790:3 and Trial Exhibit 1505, *United States v. Rhodes et al.*, No. 1:22-cr-15 (D.D.C. Oct. 20, 2022).

232. U.S. Capitol Police Camera 7029; "Leader of Alabama Chapter of Oath Keepers Pleads Guilty to Seditious Conspiracy and Obstruction of Congress for Efforts to Stop Transfer of Power Following 2020 Presidential Election," Department of Justice, (Mar. 2, 2022), available at https://www.justice.gov/opa/pr/leader-alabama-chapter-oath-keepers-pleads-guilty-seditious-conspiracy-and-obstruction#:~:text=Joshua%20James%2C%2034%2C%20of%20Arab,with%20the%20government's%20ongoing%20investigation; Statement of Offense at 8, *United States v. James*, No. 1:22-cr-15 (D.D.C. Mar. 2, 2022), ECF No. 60, available at https://www.justice.gov/opa/press-release/file/1479551/download.

233. Trial Transcript at 4803:10–4804:23 and Trial Exhibit 1089.1, *United States v. Rhodes et al.*, No. 1:22-cr-15 (D.D.C. Oct. 20, 2022).

234. U.S. Capitol Police Camera 912.

235. "Crypt," Architect of the Capitol, available at https://www.aoc.gov/explore-capitol-campus/buildings-grounds/capitol-building/crypt.

236. U.S. Capitol Police Camera 267.

237. U.S. Capitol Police Cameras 123, 124.

238. U.S. Capitol Police Cameras 123, 124.

239. Watchers Guild, "Rioters Fight with Police at Capitol Building - Washington D.C. - JAN/6/2020," YouTube, Jan. 6, 2020, available at https://www.youtube.com/watch?v=U7DiLh2Pbl4; News2Share, "January 6 United States Capitol Attack," YouTube, June 4, 2021, available at https://www.youtube.com/watch?v=9TshRdxXi9c.

240. Statement of Offense at 4, *United States v. Gordon*, No. 1:22-cr-343 (D.D.C. Oct. 28, 2022), ECF No. 26, available at http://www.justice.gov/usao-dc/press-release/file/1547751/download.

241. Statement of Offense at 4, *United States v. Gordon*, No. 1:22-cr-343 (D.D.C. Oct. 28, 2022), ECF No. 26, available at http://www.justice.gov/usao-dc/press-release/file/1547751/download.

242. Statement of Offense at 4, *United States v. Gordon*, No. 1:22-cr-343 (D.D.C. Oct. 28, 2022), ECF No. 26, available at http://www.justice.gov/usao-dc/press-release/file/1547751/download.

243. Hunting Insurrectionists, "West Terrace 'Tunnel' - 3:50 - 4:21 pm - Jan 6th," YouTube, Mar. 12, 2021, available at https://www.youtube.com/watch?v=Yil1JemYMM0&t=1405s.

244. U.S. Capitol Police Camera 102.

245. Documents on file with the Select Committee to Investigate the January 6th Attack on the United States Capitol (Nick Quested Production), Video file Inside Capitol.mov at 23:01–23:35.

246. U.S. Capitol Police Cameras 178, 402.

247. Documents on file with the Select Committee to Investigate the January 6th Attack on the United States Capitol (Nick Quested Production), Video file Inside Capitol.mov at 13:10–15:47.

248. U.S. Capitol Police Cameras 178, 402.

249. Jake Tapper (@jaketapper), Twitter, Feb. 10, 2021 5:50 p.m. ET, available at https://twitter.com/jaketapper/status/1359635955389509638 (screenshotting Donald J. Trump (@realDonaldTrump), Twitter, Jan. 6, 2021 2:24 p.m. ET, available at https://www.thetrumparchive.com/?searchbox=%22usa+demands+the+truth%22).

250. U.S. Capitol Police Cameras 178, 402.

251. U.S. Capitol Police Cameras 178, 402.

252. *See* Select Committee to Investigate the January 6th Attack on the United States Capitol, Transcribed Interview of David Millard, (Apr. 18, 2022), p. 28.

253. *See* Select Committee to Investigate the January 6th Attack on the United States Capitol, Transcribed Interview of David Millard, (Apr. 18, 2022), p. 28.

254. Plea Agreement at 5, *United States v. Pruitt*, No. 1:21-cr-23 (D.D.C. June 3, 2022), ECF No. 61.

255. Complaint at 34–38, *United States v. Chrestman*, No. 1:21-cr-160 (D.D.C. Feb. 10, 2021), available at https://www.justice.gov/usao-dc/case-multi-defendant/file/1366441/download; Ryan J. Reilly (@ryanjreilly), Twitter, Nov. 26, 2022 1:00 p.m. ET, available at https://twitter.com/ryanjreilly/status/1596564571371749378 (showing video Proud Boy Nicholas DeCarlo filmed while inside the Capitol).

256. Complaint at 34–38, *United States v. Chrestman*, No. 1:21-cr-160, (D.D.C. Feb. 10, 2021), available at https://www.justice.gov/usao-dc/case-multi-defendant/file/1366441/download.

257. Indictment at 5, 8–9, *United States v. Kuehne et al.*, No. 1:21-cr-160 (D.D.C. Feb. 26, 2021), ECF No. 29.

258. Statement of Offense at 3, *United States v. Colon*, No. 1:21-cr-160 (D.D.C. Apr. 27, 2022), ECF No. 143.

259. Indictment at 5, 8–9, *United States v. Kuehne et al.*, No. 1:21-cr-160 (D.D.C. Feb. 26, 2021), ECF No. 29.

260. Complaint at 36, *United States v. Chrestman*, No. 1:21-cr-160, (D.D.C. Feb. 10, 2021), available at https://www.justice.gov/usao-dc/case-multi-defendant/file/1366441/download; Ryan J. Reilly (@ryanjreilly), Twitter, Nov. 26, 2022 1:00 p.m. ET, available at https://twitter.com/ryanjreilly/status/1596564571371749378 (showing video Proud Boy Nicholas DeCarlo filmed while inside the Capitol).

261. Complaint at 36, *United States v. Chrestman*, No. 1:21-cr-160, (D.D.C. Feb. 10, 2021), available at https://www.justice.gov/usao-dc/case-multi-defendant/file/1366441/download.

262. Statement of Offense at 4, *United States v. Colon*, No. 1:21-cr-160, (D.D.C. Apr. 27, 2022), ECF No. 143.

263. Statement of Offense at 4, *United States v. Colon*, No. 1:21-cr-160, (D.D.C. Apr. 27, 2022), ECF No. 143.

264. U.S. Capitol Police Camera 251.

265. Lena Groeger, Jeff Kao, Al Shaw, Moiz Syed and Maya Eliahou, "What Parler Saw During the Attack on the Capitol," ProPublica, (Jan. 17, 2021), available at https://projects.propublica.org/parler-capitol-videos/?id=sbGOy4rN0ue4.

266. Statement of Offense at 12–14, *United States v. Chansley*, No. 1:21-cr-3 (D.D.C. Sep. 3, 2021), ECF No. 70.

267. Statement of Offense at 15, *United States v. Chansley*, No. 1:21-cr-3 (D.D.C. Sep. 3, 2021), ECF No. 70.

268. Christian Secor, a young Groyper, sat in the Vice President's seat. *See* "California Man Sentenced to 42 Months in Prison for Actions During Jan. 6 Capitol Breach," Department of Justice, (Oct. 19, 2022), available at https://www.justice.gov/usao-dc/pr/california-man-sentenced-prison-actions-during-jan-6-capitol-breach; Complaint at 6, 14–15, *United States v. Secor*, No. 1:21-mj-232 (D.D.C. Feb 13, 2021), ECF No. 1.

269. Other agitators, such as Vets 4 Trump founder Joshua Macias (who was with Stewart Rhodes and Enrique Tarrio on January 5th), also attacked Vice President Pence outside the Capitol. *See* Select Committee to Investigate the January 6th Attack on the United States Capitol, Deposition of Joshua Macias, (May 2, 2022), pp. 27–28, and Exhibit 14; capitolhunters (@capitolhunters), Twitter, May 27, 2021 8:36 p.m. ET, available at https://twitter.com/capitolhunters/status/1398075750482337792 (video of Macias calling Vice President Pence a "Benedict Arnold" outside of the Capitol on January 6th).

270. Reagan Battalion (@ReaganBattalion), Twitter, Jan. 7, 2021 5:03 a.m. ET, available at https://twitter.com/ReaganBattalion/status/1347121703823044608.

271. U.S. Capitol Police Camera 944.

272. Sentencing Transcript at 19, *United States v. Young*, No. 1:21-cr-291 (D.D.C. Sep. 27, 2022), ECF No. 170.

273. U.S. Capitol Police Camera 74.

274. U.S. Capitol Police Camera 74.

275. Government's Sentencing Memorandum at 4–8, *United States v. Head*, No. 1:21-cr-291 (D.D.C. Oct. 19, 2022), ECF No. 159.

276. Statement of Facts at 5, 29–31, 39, *United States v. Denney*, No. 1:22-cr-70 (D.D.C. Dec. 7, 2021), ECF No. 1-1; Status Coup News, "UNBELIEVABLE Footage | Trump Supporters Battle Cops Inside the Capitol," YouTube, at 24:09, Jan. 7, 2021, available at https://www.youtube.com/watch?v=cJOgGsC0G9U.

277. Statement of Facts at 2, 6–7, *United States v. Brown*, No. 1:21-cr-178 (D.D.C. Aug. 16, 2021), ECF No. 1-1; Storyful Viral, "Scenes of Chaos Captures Inside US Capitol as Crowd Challenges Police," YouTube, at 20:05, 21:03, Jan. 7, 2021, available at https://www.youtube.com/watch?v=qc0U755-uiM.

278. Government's Sentencing Memorandum at 25–28, 55, *United States v. Young*, No. 1:21-cr-291 (D.D.C. Sep. 13, 2022), ECF No. 140; Status Coup News, "UNBELIEVABLE Footage | Trump Supporters Battle Cops Inside the Capitol," YouTube, at 9:45–9:56, Jan. 7, 2021, available at https://www.youtube.com/watch?v=cJOgGsC0G9U.

279. Statement of Facts for Stipulated Trial at 6–9, *United States v. Morss*, No. 1:21-cr-40 (D.D.C. Aug. 23, 2022), ECF No. 430; Torsten Ove, "Former Army Ranger Charged with Assaulting Cops during Capitol Riot Faces DC Bench Trial," *Pittsburgh Post-Gazette*, (Aug. 17, 2022), available at: https://www.post-gazette.com/news/crime-courts/2022/08/17/robert-morss-pittsburgh-glenshaw-army-ranger-charged-assaulting-police-capitol-riot-insurrection-january-6-bench-trial/stories/202208170094.

280. Government's Opposition to Defendant's Motion to Set Bond and Conditions of Release at 6–7, *United States v. Schwartz*, No. 1:21-cr-178 (D.D.C. June 15, 2021), ECF No. 26.

281. Statement of Offense at 4, *United States v. Head*, No. 1:21-cr-291 (D.D.C. May 6, 2022), ECF No. 124; Government's Sentencing Memorandum at 1–4, 18, 25, *United States v. Head*, No. 1:21-cr-291 (D.D.C. Oct. 19, 2022), ECF No. 159; Documents on file with the Select Committee to Investigate the January 6th Attack on the United States Capitol (District of Columbia Production), Axon Body 3 No. X6039B9N0, at 15:17–15:20 (MPD body camera footage); "Tennessee Man Sentenced to 90 Months in Prison for Assaulting Law Enforcement Officer During Capitol Breach," Department of Justice, (Oct. 27, 2022), available at https://www.justice.gov/usao-dc/pr/tennessee-man-sentenced-prison-assaulting-law-enforcement-officer-during-capitol-breach.

282. Government's Sentencing Memorandum at 1–4, 18, 25, *United States v. Head*, No. 1:21-cr-291 (D.D.C. Oct. 19, 2022).

283. Statement of Facts at 33–34, *United States v. Denney*, No. 1:22-cr-70 (D.D.C. Dec. 7, 2021), ECF No. 1-1.

284. Government's Sentencing Memorandum at 2, 30–31, *United States v. Young*, No. 1:21-cr-291 (D.D.C. Sept. 13, 2022), ECF No. 140.

285. Statement of Facts at 4–11, *United States v. Sibick*, No. 1:21-cr-291 (D.D.C. Mar. 10, 2021), ECF No. 1-1 (noting that Sibick told the FBI he was trying to help Officer Fanone while other rioters attempted to get the officer's gun).

286. Documents on file with the Select Committee to Investigate the January 6th Attack on the United States Capitol (District of Columbia Production), (Axon Body 3 No. X6039B9N0), at 15:18:51–15:21:12 (MPD body camera footage); Government's Sentencing Memorandum at 27-28, *United States v. Young*, No. 1:21-cr-291 (D.D.C. Sept. 13, 2022), ECF No. 140.

287. Motion to Suppress by Daniel Rodriguez, Exhibit A at 38–39, 43–45, 70–71, *United States v. Rodriguez*, No. 1:21-cr-246 (D.D.C. Oct. 25, 2021), ECF No. 38-1.

288. Motion to Suppress by Daniel Rodriguez, Exhibit A at 17–18, *United States v. Rodriguez*, No. 1:21-cr-246 (D.D.C. Oct. 25, 2021), ECF No. 38-1.

289. Motion to Suppress by Daniel Rodriguez, Exhibit A at 118, *United States v. Rodriguez*, No. 1:21-cr-246 (D.D.C. Oct. 25, 2021), ECF No. 38-1 (quoting Rodriguez saying: "And I was already—Trump was already, like—this is 2015, and I was already into InfoWars and Alex Jones, and he's backing up Trump. And I'm like, all right, man. This is it. I'm going to—this is—I'm going to fight for this. I'm going to do—I want to do this.").

290. Motion to Suppress by Daniel Rodriguez, Exhibit A at 131, *United States v. Rodriguez*, No. 1:21-cr-246 (D.D.C. Oct. 25, 2021), ECF No. 38-1.

291. Motion to Suppress by Daniel Rodriguez, Exhibit A at 34, *United States v. Rodriguez*, No. 1:21-cr-246 (D.D.C. Oct. 25, 2021), ECF No. 38-1.

292. Motion to Suppress by Daniel Rodriguez, Exhibit A at 34, *United States v. Rodriguez*, No. 1:21-cr-246 (D.D.C. Oct. 25, 2021), ECF No. 38-1.

293. Indictment at 2, 5–7, *United States v. Rodriguez et al.*, No. 1:21-cr-246 (D.D.C. Nov. 19, 2021), ECF No. 65.

294. Indictment at 2, 5–7, *United States v. Rodriguez et al.*, No. 1:21-cr-246 (D.D.C. Nov. 19, 2021), ECF No. 65.

295. Indictment at 2, 5–7, *United States v. Rodriguez et al.*, No. 1:21-cr-246 (D.D.C. Nov. 19, 2021), ECF No. 65.

296. Documents on file with the Select Committee to Investigate the January 6th Attack on the United States Capitol (Capitol Police Production), CTRL0000001532.0001 (Jan. 5, 2021, FBI Situational Information Report); *see also* Statement of Facts at 11, 39, *United States v. Denney*, No. 1:22-cr-70 (D.D.C. Dec. 7, 2021), ECF No. 1-1 (noting that Denney, a Three Percenter, posted similar messages about occupying Congress on Facebook).

297. *See* 167 Cong. Rec. S633-38 (daily ed. Feb. 10, 2021), available at https://www.congress.gov/117/crec/2021/02/10/CREC-2021-02-10-pt1-PgS615-4.pdf; Marshall Cohen and Avery Lotz, "The January 6 Insurrection: Minute-by-Minute," CNN, (July 29, 2022), available at https://www.cnn.com/2022/07/10/politics/jan-6-us-capitol-riot-timeline/index.html.

298. United States Secret Service Radio Tango Frequency at 14:14–14:25. Select Committee staff reviewed recordings of this radio frequency. *See also*, U.S. Capitol Police Camera 462.

299. U.S. Capitol Police Camera 961.

300. United States Secret Service Radio Tango Frequency at 14:14–14:25. Select Committee staff reviewed recordings of this radio frequency. *See also* U.S. Capitol Police Camera 462.

301. U.S. Capitol Police Camera 7023.

302. U.S. Capitol Police Camera 461.

303. U.S. Capitol Police Camera 077.

304. U.S. Capitol Police Cameras 3062, 6059, 6146.

305. U.S. Capitol Police Camera 269.

306. Select Committee staff analyzed thousands of hours of surveillance footage from the United States Capitol. There is no camera that captured the evacuation because CSPAN cameras focus on the dais (so they miss the activity on the floor), and there are no CCTV cameras around the floor. The staff first identified Members appearing in the basement of the Capitol at exactly 2:40 p.m. ET. Based on knowledge of the Capitol and judging the distance traveled, staff have estimated that it took Members approximately 2 minutes from leaving the floor to getting to the basement, which puts the evacuation at approximately 2:38 p.m. This time is consistent with informal contemporaneous accounts provided by Members and law enforcement officers who were there. *See* U.S. Capitol Police Camera 0077.

307. U.S. Capitol Police Camera 0077

308. U.S. Capitol Police Camera 360.

309. U.S. Capitol Police Camera 360.

310. U.S. Capitol Police Camera 360.

311. U.S. Capitol Police Camera 944.

312. U.S. Capitol Police Camera 403.

313. U.S. Capitol Police Camera 251.

314. U.S. Capitol Police Camera 267.

315. U.S. Capitol Police Camera 304.

316. U.S. Capitol Police Cameras 202, 303, 461, 462.

317. U.S. Capitol Police Cameras 202, 303, 461, 462.

318. U.S. Capitol Police Camera 960.

319. U.S. Capitol Police Camera 960.

320. U.S. Capitol Police Camera 7029.

321. U.S. Capitol Police Camera 102.

322. U.S. Capitol Police Camera 102.

323. U.S. Capitol Police Camera 926.

324. U.S. Capitol Police Cameras 927, 928, 929.

325. U.S. Capitol Police Camera 933.

326. U.S. Capitol Police Cameras 074, 944.

327. U.S. Capitol Police Camera 074.

328. U.S. Capitol Police Camera 924.

329. U.S. Capitol Police Camera 944.

330. U.S. Capitol Police Camera 944.

331. U.S. Capitol Police Camera 7032.

332. U.S. Capitol Police Camera 011.

333. "WATCH: 'Let's Get Back to Work,' Pence Urges Senate," PBS, (Jan. 6, 2021), available at https://www.pbs.org/newshour/politics/watch-lets-get-back-to-work-pence-urges-senate.

1. Electoral Count Act.

As our Report describes, Donald J. Trump, John Eastman, and others corruptly attempted to violate the Electoral Count Act of 1887 in an effort to overturn the 2020 Presidential Election. To deter other future attempts to overturn Presidential Elections, the House of Representatives has passed H.R. 8873, "The Presidential Election Reform Act," and the Senate should act promptly to send a bill with these principles to the President. H.R. 8873 reaffirms that a Vice President has no authority or discretion to reject an official electoral slate submitted by the Governor of a state. It also reforms Congress's counting rules to help ensure that objections in the joint session conform to Congress's narrow constitutional role under Article II and the Twelfth Amendment. It provides that presidential candidates may sue in federal court to ensure that Congress receives the state's lawful certification, and leaves no doubt that the manner for selecting presidential electors cannot be changed retroactively after the election is over.

2. Accountability.

The Select Committee has made criminal referrals to the Department of Justice, and both the Department of Justice and other prosecutorial authorities will now make their determinations on whether to prosecute individuals involved in the events resulting in an attack on the United States Congress on January 6, 2021. Additional steps may also be appropriate to ensure criminal or civil accountability for anyone engaging in misconduct described in this Report. Those courts and bar disciplinary bodies responsible for overseeing the legal profession in the states and the District of Columbia should continue to evaluate the conduct of attorneys described in this Report. Attorneys should not have the discretion to use their law licenses to undermine the constitutional and statutory process for peacefully transferring power in our government. The Department of Justice should also take appropriate action to prevent its attorneys from participating in campaign-related activities, or (as described in this report) activities aimed at subverting the rule of law and overturning a lawful election. This report also identifies specific attorney conflicts of interest for the Department to evaluate.

3. Violent Extremism.

Federal Agencies with intelligence and security missions, including the Secret Service, should (a) move forward on whole-of-government strategies to combat the threat of violent activity posed by all extremist groups, including white nationalist groups and violent anti-government groups while respecting the civil rights and First Amendment civil liberties of all citizens; and (b) review their intelligence sharing protocols to ensure that threat intelligence is properly prioritized and shared with other responsible intelligence and security agencies on a timely basis in order to combat the threat of violent activity targeting legislative institutions, government operations, and minority groups.

4. Fourteenth Amendment, Section 3.

Under Section 3 of the Constitution's Fourteenth Amendment, an individual who previously took an oath to support the Constitution of the United States, but who has "engaged in an insurrection" against the same, or given "aid or comfort to the enemies of the Constitution" can be disqualified from holding future federal or state office. The Select Committee has referred Donald Trump and others for possible prosecution under 18 U.S.C. 2383, including for assisting and providing aid and comfort to an insurrection. The Committee also notes that Donald J. Trump was impeached by a majority of the House of Representatives for Incitement of an Insurrection, and there were 57 votes in the Senate for his conviction. Congressional committees of jurisdiction should consider creating a formal mechanism for evaluating whether to bar those individuals identified in this Report under Section 3 of the 14th Amendment from holding future federal or state office. The Committee believes that those who took an oath to protect and defend the Constitution and then, on January 6th, engaged in insurrection can appropriately be disqualified and barred from holding government office—whether federal or state, civilian or military—absent at least two-thirds of Congress acting to remove the disability pursuant to Section 3 of the Fourteenth Amendment. The Committee notes that Ms. Wasserman Schultz and Mr. Raskin have introduced H. Con. Res. 93 to declare the January 6 assault an insurrection and H.R. 7906 to establish specific procedures and standards for disqualification under section 3 of the Fourteenth Amendment in the United States district court for the District of Columbia.

5. National Special Security Event.

Until January 6th, 2021, the joint session of Congress for counting electoral votes was not understood to pose the same types of security risks as other major events on Capitol Hill. Both the inaugural and the State of the Union have long been designated as National Special Security Events, requiring specific security measures and significant advance planning and preparation. Given what occurred in 2021, Congress and the Executive Branch should work together to designate the joint session of Congress occurring on January 6th as a National Special Security Event.

6. To the extent needed, consider reforming certain criminal statutes, including to add more severe penalties.

As indicated in the Report, the Committee believes that 18 U.S.C. § 1512(c)2 and other existing provisions of law can be applied to efforts to obstruct, influence, or impede the joint session on January 6th, including to related planning efforts to overturn the lawful election results on that date. To the extent that any court or any other prosecutorial authorities ultimately reach any differing conclusion, Congress should amend those statutes to cover such conduct. Congress should also consider whether the severity of penalties under those statutes is sufficient to deter unlawful conduct threatening the peaceful transfer of power.

7. House of Representatives Civil Subpoena Enforcement Authority.

The current authority of the House of Representatives to enforce its subpoenas through civil litigation is unclear. Congressional committees of jurisdiction should develop legislation to create a cause of action for the House of Representatives to enforce its subpoenas in federal court, either following the statutory authority that exists for the Senate in 2 U.S.C. § 288d and 28 U.S.C. § 1365 or adopting a broad approach to facilitate timely oversight of the executive branch.

8. Threats to Election Workers.

Congressional committees of jurisdiction should consider enhancing federal penalties for certain types of threats against persons involved in the election process and expanding protections for personally identifiable information of election workers.

9. Capitol Police Oversight.

Congressional committees of jurisdiction should continue regular and rigorous oversight of the United States Capitol Police as it improves its planning, training, equipping, and intelligence processes and practices its critical incident response protocols, both internally and with law enforcement partners. Joint hearings with testimony from the Capitol Police Board should take place. Full funding for critical security measures should be assured.[1]

10. Role of the Media.

The Committee's investigation has identified many individuals involved in January 6th who were provoked to act by false information about the 2020 election repeatedly reinforced by legacy and social media. The Committee agrees that individuals remain responsible for their own actions, including their own criminal actions. But congressional committees of jurisdiction should continue to evaluate policies of media companies that have had the effect of radicalizing their consumers, including by provoking people to attack their own country.

11. Discussion of the Insurrection Act.

The Committee has been troubled by evidence that President Trump's possible use of the Insurrection Act was discussed by individuals identified in this Report. Congressional Committees of jurisdiction should further evaluate all such evidence, and consider risks posed for future elections.

ENDNOTE

1. The Select Committee has shared concerns about two specific areas of security with the Committee on House Administration.

GOVERNMENT AGENCY PREPARATION FOR AND RESPONSE TO JANUARY 6TH

INTRODUCTION

The Select Committee investigated the facts relating to law enforcement entities' preparation for, and response to, the January 6th events at the Capitol, including the character of the intelligence prior to the insurrection. This appendix does not address the cause of the attack, which resulted from then President Trump's multi-pronged effort to overturn the 2020 presidential election.

Prior to January 6th, numerous government agencies received intelligence that those descending on The Mall for a rally organized by the President were armed and that their target may be the Capitol. The intelligence community and law enforcement agencies detected the planning for potential violence directed at the joint session of Congress.

That intelligence included information about specific planning by the Proud Boys and Oath Keepers militia groups who ultimately led the attack on the Capitol. By contrast, the intelligence did not support a conclusion that Antifa or other left-wing groups would likely engage in a violent counterdemonstration, or attack President Trump's supporters on January 6th. Indeed, intelligence from January 5th indicated that some left-wing groups were instructing their members to "stay at home" and not attend on January 6th.[1]

As January 6th approached, some of the intelligence about the potential for violence was shared within the executive branch, including the Secret Service and the President's National Security Council. That intelligence should have been sufficient for President Trump, or others at the White House, to cancel the Ellipse speech, and for President Trump to cancel plans to instruct his supporters to march to the Capitol. Few in law enforcement predicted the full extent of the violence at the Capitol, or that the President of the United States would incite a mob attack on the Capitol, that he would send them to stop the joint session knowing they were armed and dangerous, that he would further incite them against his own vice President while the attack was underway, or that he would do nothing to stop the assault for hours.

Nevertheless, as explained below, and in multiple hearings by the Committee on House Administration, there are additional steps that should have been taken to address the potential for violence on that day.

DISCUSSION

INTELLIGENCE RECEIVED BY GOVERNMENT AGENCIES

On December 19, 2020, President Trump tweeted: "Big protest in D.C. on January 6th. Be there, will be wild!"[2] Following President Trump's tweet, an analyst at the National Capital Region Threat Intelligence Consortium (NTIC) noticed a tenfold uptick in violent online rhetoric targeting Congress and law enforcement.[3] The analyst also noticed that violent right-wing groups that had not previously been aligned had begun coordinating their efforts.[4] These indications reached the head of the D.C. Homeland Security and Emergency Management Agency (HSEMA), Christopher Rodriguez, as well as incoming Chief of D.C. Metropolitan Police Department (MPD) Robert Contee.[5] Chief Contee remembered that the information prompted the DC Police to "change the way that we were going to deploy for January the 6th."[6]

Following President Trump's "be there, will be wild!" tweet, Director Rodriguez arranged a briefing to provide the DC Mayor Muriel Bowser the latest threat intelligence about January 6th, outline the potential for violence, and "make operational recommendations," including that the Mayor request assistance from the DC National Guard.[7] During the briefing, the Mayor was told that "there is greater negative sentiment motivating conversation than the last two events in November and December of 2020," and that "others are calling to 'peacefully' storm the Capitol and occupy the building to halt the vote."[8]

As early as December 30th, in its intelligence briefing entitled, "March for Trump," the U.S. Secret Service (USSS) highlighted the President's "will be wild!" tweet alongside hashtags #WeAreTheStorm, #1776Rebel, and #OccupyCapitols, and wrote, "President Trump supporters have proposed a movement to occupy Capitol Hill."[9] It added that promoters of the January 6th rally on social media had borrowed the President's phrase and were marketing the January 6th rally as the "WildProtest."[10]

Other law enforcement entities were receiving similar indications from both government and private entities. By December 21st, the U.S. Capitol Police (USCP) had learned of a surge in viewers of online maps of the Capitol complex's underground tunnels, which were attracting increased attention on www.thedonald.win, alongside violent rhetoric supporting the President.[11] By the late afternoon of January 5, 2021, Capitol Police Assistant Chief for Intelligence Yogananda Pittman urged Capitol Police Chief Steven Sund to convene a "brief call" to discuss "a significant uptick in groups wanting to block perimeter access to the Capitol tomorrow starting as early as 0600 hours."[12] Chief Sund remembered discussing those indications and the preparations Capitol Police already had "in place, and [that] everybody seemed fine with utilizing the resources we had."[13] Chief Sund added that, by that time, he had already deployed "all the available resources."[14]

The Federal Bureau of Intelligence (FBI) and the U.S. Department of Homeland Security's Office of Intelligence and Analysis (DHS I&A) were also aware of the increased online interest in the Capitol tunnels. The FBI's special agent in charge of the intelligence division at the Washington Field Office, Jennifer Moore, pointed out that there was nothing illegal about discussing the tunnels. Without a very specific discussion of violence, it was a matter of ensuring that the appropriate law enforcement partner agencies were aware of the uptick, ensuring that the Capitol Police were aware.[15] "People's First Amendment rights, obviously, are protected. We cannot troll—can['t] just troll the internet looking for things that's out there," Moore said.[16] "So it would have to be with such specificity and such planning and such detail that we would be able to open a case, immediately seek authority for an undercover, have enough probable cause for that undercover off of one tip would be tough."[17]

Other agencies were also surfacing indications and receiving tips. On December 26, 2020, the Secret Service received a tip about the Proud Boys detailing plans of having "a large enough group to march into DC armed and will outnumber the police so they can't be stopped."[18] It stressed, "Their plan is to literally kill people....Please please take this tip seriously and investigate further."[19] On December 24th, the Secret Service received a compilation of social media posts from "SITE," a private intelligence group. One of them urged that protesters "march into the chambers."[20] Another, referring to President Trump's December 19th "will be wild!" post, wrote that Trump "can't exactly openly tell you to revolt," so the December 19th post was "the closest he'll ever get."[21] Another understood the President's tweet to be urging his supporters to come to Washington "armed."[22] Others were to the same effect ("there is not enough cops in DC to stop what is coming,"[23] "make sure they know who to fear,"[24] and "waiting for Trump to say the word"[25]).

By December 28th, that compilation had reached the newly installed head of the Capitol Police intelligence unit, Jack Donohue.[26] The same day, a self-styled "internet expert" who had been "tracking online far right extremism for years" sent an email to the Capitol Police public information inbox warning of "countless tweets from Trump supporters saying they will be armed," and of tweets "from people organizing to 'storm the Capitol' on January 6th."[27] She added, "January 6th will be the day most of these people realize there's no chance left for Trump. They'll be pushed to what they feel is the edge," noting that many would be armed and that she was, for the first time, "truly worried."[28] Other senior Capitol Police officers do not recall seeing that email before the January 6th attack.[29] The next day,

Secret Service agents forwarded to Capitol Police warnings that pro-Trump demonstrators were being urged to "occupy federal building[s]," "march into the capital building [sic] and make them quake in their shoes by our mere presence." [30]

In addition, on January 1, 2021, a lieutenant in the intelligence branch of the MPD forwarded to the Capitol Police intelligence unit a tip—later forwarded to USCP Deputy Chief Sean Gallagher—that he had "found a website planning terroristic behavior on Jan 6th, during the rally." [31] The source included a link to www.thedonald.win site, describing a "detailed plan on [s]torming the capitol in DC on Jan 6th." [32] On January 2, 2021, the FBI saved in its system a social media post stating, "This is not a rally and it's no longer a protest. This is a final stand…many are ready to die to take back #USA….And don't be surprised if we take the #capital building [sic]." [33] On January 3rd, FBI and Capitol Police received a Parler post that "after weds we are going to need a new congress," and "Jan 6 may actually be their last day in Congress." [34]

On January 4th, Jack Donoghue, head of USCP's intelligence unit, and his assistant director, Julie Farnam, briefed Capitol Police leadership, including Chief Gallagher and Chief Pittman (but not Chief Sund), about the January 3rd Threat Assessment, which highlighted that Congress itself was the target of potential violence on January 6th. Assistant Director Farnam explicitly warned the group:

> Supporters see this as the last opportunity to overturn the election. There was disappointment and desperation amongst the protestors, and this could be an incentive to become violent, because they have nothing left to lose. The targets are not the counter protestors; the target is Congress. The protests are heavily publicized. Stop the Steal has a propensity for attracting White supremacists, militia groups, groups like the Proud Boys. There are multiple social media posts saying that people are going to be coming armed, and it's potentially a very dangerous situation. [35]

On January 5, 2021, at 12:19 p.m., the Architect of the Capitol head of security, Valerie Hasberry, forwarded an alert to Capitol Police incident command that an individual was calling on thousands to "go to Washington Jan 6 and help storm the Capital [sic]," adding "we will storm the government buildings, kill cops, kill security guards, kill federal employees and agents." [36] "There is now chatter on Parler about storming the Capitol," Ms. Hasberry wrote to her AOC employee working at the USCP. [37] "Please let me know if there are any updates to credible threats." [38] Within an hour, she was advised by her staff that "[t]here is no talk about any credible threats or storming the Capitol." That same day, representatives from DHS,

FBI, HSEMA, Secret Service, DC Police, and Capitol Police shared notice of a website, Red State Secession, that urged its visitors to post the home and work addresses of Democratic Members of Congress and "political enemies" under the title, "Why the Second American Revolution Starts Jan 6." [39] It asked for their routes to and from the January 6th congressional certification because "the crowd will be looking for enemies." [40]

The FBI was uploading to, and tagging in, its system incoming information from all FBI field offices about January 6th under the label, "CERTUNREST2021." While the incoming information was reviewed on a regular basis by the Washington Field Office, "unified monitoring" of the items in the aggregate didn't begin until January 5th.[41] That same day, the FBI captured a January 6th-related threat that warned a "Quick Reaction Force" of Trump supporters was preparing for January 6th in Virginia with weapons and prepared "to respond to 'calls for help'" in the event that "protesters believed the police were not doing their job," and a "Situation Incident Report" from FBI's Norfolk Field Office warned of a "war" on January 6th.[42] While Capitol Police leadership received neither warning until after the attack,[43] Assistant Director Farnam, USCP intelligence unit, warned that Congress would be the target on January 6th. She noted that a "sense of desperation and disappointment may lead to more of an incentive to become violent. Unlike previous post-election protests, Congress itself is the target on the 6th." [44] The Chairman of the Joint Chiefs of Staff, General Mark Milley, remembers Deputy Secretary of Defense David Norquist expressing a similar view based on the social media traffic in early January 2021: "Norquist says... [t]he greatest threat is a direct assault on the Capitol. I'll never forget it." [45]

DISCUSSION OF THE POTENTIAL FOR VIOLENCE
Federal and local agencies agreed that there was a potential for violence on January 6th. As noted above, the intelligence leading up to January 6th did not support a conclusion that Antifa or other left-wing groups would likely engage in a violent counter-demonstration, or attack President Trump's supporters on January 6th. In fact, none of these groups was involved to any material extent with the attack on the Capitol on January 6th.

That said, certain witnesses testified that they believed that there would be violence with Antifa or similar counter protest groups. President Trump's National Security Advisor, Robert O'Brien, said the White House saw a risk of violence from counter-protesters.[46] Then Acting DHS Secretary Chad Wolfe said that his "main concern [...] at the time was what we had seen throughout the summer and throughout the fall, which was you were going to have groups on either side, and so you were going to have counterprotests. And usually where those counterprotests interacted was where you had the violence." [47]

General Milley said the potential for violence was clear to all: "Everyone knew. I can't imagine anybody in those calls that didn't realize that on the 6th was going to be the certification of an intensely contested election, and there were large crowds coming into town, and they were coming into protest. And everybody knew there was a probability, more than a possibility, a probability of violence."[48] He expected "street fights when the sun went down," while [Deputy Secretary] Norquist said the most dangerous thing was assault on the Capitol.[49] Director of DHS Special Operations Christopher Tomney remembered, "[T]here was broad discussion/acknowledgment that folks were calling for bringing weapons into the city on that day, so there was no surprise, there was no—you know, no one disagreed that there was going to be the high likelihood that there could be some violence on January 6."[50]

Acting Deputy Attorney General Richard Donoghue described the discussion about the threat landscape as "generally about left-wing, right wing, or Pro-Trump, anti-Trump groups coming to the Capitol. It didn't really matter what they called themselves. It was a matter of they're upset, they're coming to the Capitol, and there's a potential for violence."[51] Donoghue added: "Everyone knew what everyone else was doing. Everyone knew that there was a danger of violence. Everyone knew that the Capitol and other facilities were potential targets. And I think we all felt comfortable that we were aware what the situation was, and we had the resources in place to address it."[52]

OPERATIONALIZATION OF JANUARY 6-RELATED INTELLIGENCE

Preparing for January 6th required coordination among the several local and Federal law enforcement agencies that have distinct authorities and jurisdiction over adjacent areas in the Washington, DC, area. These range from the MPD, United States Park Police (USPP), and USSS to the USCP.

DC GOVERNMENT PREPARATION

December 30, 2020, HSEMA briefing. Following the DC HSEMA's December 30th intelligence briefing, Mayor Bowser, anticipating that President Trump's December 19th "will be wild!" tweet would have a big effect on the number of people coming into the District,[53] agreed with HSEMA Director Rodriguez, who thought "the intelligence was showing that we needed to posture ourselves, we needed to brace ourselves, and we needed additional resources in the city particularly the DC National Guard."[54] MPD Chief Contee, who attended the December 30th briefing and was seeing similar intelligence, concurred with the request for the DC National Guard.[55]

In light of the upcoming holiday weekend, HSEMA Director Rodriguez wanted to expedite the DC request for National Guard assistance.[56] On December 31st, Mayor Bowser requested the assistance of the DC National

Guard to assist the MPD at traffic points within the city.[57] Mayor Bowser's request explicitly limited National Guard assistance to "non-law enforcement activities" so that the MPD could focus on the civil protests and specified that Guard troops should not be armed.[58]Army Secretary Ryan McCarthy approved Mayor Bowser's request.[59] By this time, DC HSEMA Director Rodriguez had fully activated HSEMA and coordinated with Federal, State and local partners, to deal with "consequence management."[60]

On January 4th, Mayor Bowser held a press conference and invited the MPD, USCP, and USPP.[61] Mayor Bowser announced that she had activated the DC Fire and Emergency Management Services (DC FEMS) in preparation of the January 6th event and that the DC National Guard would assist MPD at traffic points and with crowd control. Mayor Bowser urged DC residents to stay out of downtown on January 5th and 6th, acknowledging the possibility of violence. She stated that, while "[p]eople are allowed to come into our city to participate in First Amendment activities," DC officials would "not allow people to incite violence, intimidate our residents, or cause destruction in our city."[62]

The next day, Mayor Bowser sent a letter requesting that Federal agencies coordinate with the Mayor's office and the MPD in their response on January 6th.[63] The letter plainly stated that it was intended to ensure coordination among the agencies involved. DC HSEMA Director Rodriguez testified that there was a concern, in light of the Federal response to the previous summer's civil justice protests, "that in the event that activities on the street escalated, the city could once again become...militarized and that armed military and Federal law enforcement personnel could be brought into the District," perhaps intimidating residents.[64]

DC FEMS PREPARATION
Mayor Bowser also activated DC FEMS (Fire and Emergency Medical Service Department), several days before January 6th.[65] DC FEMS focused most of its attention on the event at the Ellipse since the permits indicated it would be the largest event of the day, with an estimated 5,000 people attending. Other DC and Federal agencies believed the number would likely be closer to 35,000. This led DC FEMS to establish an area command for the Ellipse, including a Mobile Command Unit, six ambulances, four engine companies, and a first aid tent staffed by George Washington University medical staff.[66]

MPD PREPARATION
After the DC HSEMA's December 30th intelligence briefing, MPD Chief Contee ordered full deployment of the Department, cancelling previously scheduled days off, fully deploying the Civil Disturbance Unit, and contacting police departments in Montgomery and Prince George's Counties in Maryland so that their forces would be pre-staged at certain locations.

Chief Contee also staged police at the White House and Lafayette Park. Chief Contee said that although the MPD "are normally not fully deployed for civil disturbance for counting votes at the U.S. Capitol,"[67] "obviously, as we got closer from the time of the initial [December 19th Trump] tweet leading up, *with all of the rhetoric that's out there on social media, you know, people were going to bring guns,* were going to do this and that and so forth, that caused us obviously to change the way that we were going to deploy for January the 6th."[68] Because of the numerous social media posts about guns, MPD also posted signs on the National Mall indicating that possession of firearms in Washington, D.C., was illegal and would be prosecuted.[69]

U.S. CAPITOL POLICE PREPARATION

On January 3rd, the same day Capitol Police's Intelligence and Interagency Coordination Division (IICD) issued a threat assessment indicating that "Congress itself is a target," Chief Sund called House Sergeant-at-Arms Paul D. Irving to discuss requesting the DC National Guard to assist in policing the Capitol's perimeter.[70] Chief Sund needed approval from the Capitol Police Board, which consisted of Irving, Senate Sergeant-at-Arms Michael C. Stenger, and the Architect of the Capitol J. Brett Blanton. Chief Sund remembers that Irving responded immediately that he did not "like the optics" and that the intelligence did not support the request.[71] Irving, however, remembers Chief Sund calling him to say the DC National Guard had offered 125 unarmed National Guardsmen to the USCP and MPD.[72] He also remembered that, during a conference call, Chief Sund told Stenger and him that the National Guard would be utilized in similar fashion to the assistance provided to the DC police, namely, staffing intersections, and for traffic control to free up officers, but then could be used for crowd control, although he acknowledged that the Capitol campus does not have many intersections in need of staffing.[73]

The Capitol Police Board, including Chief Sund, later agreed that a request for the DC National Guard would not be necessary, particularly if the USCP was in an "all hands on deck" posture.[74] Chief Sund agreed with Stenger and Irving that the intelligence did not support a request for DC National Guard assistance.[75] According to Irving, Chief Sund did not believe the National Guard would add much to the USCP security plan for January 6th.[76] Chief Sund briefed the Capitol Police Board on the USCP's enhanced security plan, and "all hands on deck posture"—including 1,200-plus officers, added Civil Disturbance Units (CDU), an enhanced Containment Emergency Response Team ("CERT"), and an expanded perimeter.[77] Chief Sund did not believe, based on the intelligence he had, that it was then necessary to cancel officers' days off.[78]

USCP leadership did not create a department-wide plan for the January 6th event.[79] In retrospect Chief Sund believed "there should have been a plan for the joint session of Congress inside the Capitol to reflect all the planning and all the coordination that goes on inside the Capitol."[80]

GOVERNMENT AGENCY PREPARATION

Interagency Coordination. In the appendix on Deployment of the National Guard, we describe certain reasons why the deployment of the National Guard was delayed, highlighting the activity of Secretary of the Army McCarthy and how he understood an order given by Acting Secretary of Defense Christopher Miller. In our interviews with Department of Defense (DoD) officials, they testified that they had asked the Department of Justice to serve the role of "lead Federal agency," meaning to lead the coordination and the response on January 6th. The Justice Department does not command National Guard units. Department of Defense, Department of Justice (DOJ), and Department of Homeland Security (DHS) officials testified from each agency's perspective about the discussions concerning which department would serve as a lead Federal agency. Notably, these discussions occurred at the same time President Trump was offering the Acting Attorney General position to Jeffrey Clark, replacing then Acting Attorney General Jeffrey Rosen. Had Clark ultimately been appointed, and had he been placed in charge of the Federal security response to the violence on January 6th, the situation could have been materially worse.

January 3rd Coordination Call. Realizing that there had not yet been a coordination call among the Federal agencies engaged in planning for the January 6th events and related contingencies, Acting Secretary Miller convened one for January 3rd, because "nobody else was doing it."[81] In addition to DoD officials including General Milley, DOJ, DHS, Department of the Interior (DOI) officials participated. Acting Secretary Miller's objectives were to ensure that "everyone had the same perception of the threat and then figure out how to synchronize, coordinate." He also wanted to make sure that DoD was prepared for any additional requests for support.[82]

Director of DHS Special Operations Tomney remembered that participants discussed the threat outlook and estimated crowd[83] of up to 30,000—not large for the District.[84] The consensus was that 8,000 to 10,000 police officers would be available on January 6th, a force regarded as appropriate for up to a million protesters. General Milley asked the police participants on the call whether they needed any other assistance from the Department of Defense.[85] General Milley and Secretary Miller expressed concern about the number of groups requesting permits and the attendance of groups like the Proud Boys and Oath Keepers who, as Secretary Miller explained, had "conducted acts of violence in the past."[86] General Milley asked whether requests for permits could be declined, canceled, or permits revoked.[87] Participants from the Department of the Interior responded that "that wasn't an option." [88]

According to Director Tomney, DHS felt confident in the United States Secret Service's ability to protect the White House and Vice President, the Federal Protective Service's (FPS) ability to protect potentially affected Federal buildings, as well as the Immigration and Customs Enforcement and Customs and Border Protection's ability to augment FPS, if needed.[89] General Milley and the other DoD participants left the call reassured that the law enforcement agencies involved were prepared for January 6th.[90]

During the January 3rd call, the DoD also raised the issue of a lead Federal agency. General Milley noted the desirability of a law enforcement lead for coordinating the interagency planning and response effort, given the "potpourri of jurisdictions" and diversity of agency authorities.[91] Secretary Miller testified that he believed he and Acting Attorney General Jeffrey Rosen were in agreement that the DOJ should lead interagency coordination for January 6th,[92] although when asked during the call, Rosen did not confirm that the DOJ would play that role.[93] The question of a lead Federal agency remained "an open, unanswered question" at the end of the January 3rd call.[94] The same day, Rosen was attempting to secure a White House meeting with President Trump regarding the imminent appointment of Clark in his stead.[95]

DELIBERATION ON AGENCY ROLES

On a January 4th inter-agency call with the same group, Acting Deputy Attorney General Donoghue made the DOJ's role clear: it would take the lead in *certain areas* of responsibility, although he stressed that the DOJ was never designated lead Federal agency and could not serve in that capacity.[96] On the evening of January 4th, the FBI established a Strategic Information Operations Center ("SIOC") at FBI headquarters, which became operational on January 5th.[97] Unlike the previous summer's civil protests, DoD did not have a representative at the SIOC. All the DoD officials who were interviewed by the Select Committee, however, believe that the DOJ agreed to take—and may have been assigned by the White House—the lead coordinating role.[98] Director Tomney, however, remembered that the DOJ participants neither agreed to, nor explicitly declined, the lead agency role.[99]

During the January 3rd and 4th calls, General Milley, according to Donoghue, noted that "[t]here should be plenty of police forces available without using Federal military troops," so he was adamant that no active-duty troops would be deployed on January 6th.[100] During this call, participants also discussed whether there was a need for a police-based quick reaction force and concluded that the size of the MPD and USCP police forces made that unnecessary.[101]

According to Donoghue, at the end of the January 4th call, "[i]t was clear that everyone understood what everyone else's responsibility was, and everyone understood what was available to them if they needed more resources to meet their responsibilities."[102] The calls had also given local and Federal law enforcement entities the chance to "voice any issues, concerns, or requests for Department of Defense support if they felt that they were incapable of handling at their level. So, institutionally, there was agreement on the threat assessment and the plan going forward."[103] The DoD's leading role during the January 3rd and 4th calls had, in fact, left Acting DHS Secretary Chad Wolf with the impression that DoD was the lead agency, as they were "coordinating phone calls, they were setting agendas for phone calls, and they were calling out different people, okay, what do you need...So they were quarterbacking the situation and the response."[104]

AGENCY ACTIONS ON PERMITTING

Three organizations in the National Capitol Region handle permits for organized activities depending on where the planned activity is to occur. The USSS issues permits for the Ellipse, while the DC MPD issues permits for the area around the Ellipse. The USCP handles permitting for activities on the Capitol campus. All three entities, as well as other law enforcement agencies, communicate about applications for permits and the expected number of attendees. They are reluctant to deny permits for what appears to be First Amendment-protected protests.[105] The USCP received, evaluated, and approved six group permit requests for January 5th and 6th activity on Capitol Grounds.[106]

On December 19th, the day of President Trump's "will be wild!" tweet, Cindy Chafian, spokesperson from the "Eighty Percent Coalition," applied to the MPD and USCP for a permit to hold a rally.[107] On December 29th, Chafian applied to USPP for a permit for a January 5th rally in Freedom Plaza.[108] The next day, Kylie Kremer filed for a permit for "Women for America First" to hold a rally for up to 5,000 people on the Ellipse.[109] On December 31st, the National Park Service (NPS) held two meetings with Chafian as well as the MPD and USCP.[110] Then, on January 1st, the USSS confirmed that President Trump would attend the January 6th rally at the Ellipse, prompting USPP to provide additional support for the rally.[111]

On January 4th, "Women for America First" requested that the NPS increase the authorized attendance at its rally to 20,000 from the 5,000 in the original application. The same day, reacting to the USPP briefing that 5,000 people were expected, Joseph Roth, the USSS site lead, commented that he found it "funny that this permit says 5,000 people when they have said 30k repeatedly."[112] On January 5th, the NPS issued a permit for 30,000 participants for the Ellipse event.[113] At no point was any permit granted for a march from the Ellipse to the Capitol. The President planned to announce that march "spontaneously."[114]

At the White House, the increased crowd estimate concerned Bobby Peede, Director of Presidential Advance, who emailed White House Deputy Chief of Operations Anthony Ornato, noting that the USSS was planning on using only 12 magnetometers. Peede added that "the mag issue is a pretty major problem if the expected crowd shows up." Secret Service documents reveal internal discussion of an initial USSS assessment that 17 magnetometers would be needed. On January 6th, only 10 magnetometers were initially assigned to the Ellipse.[115]

AGENCY PREPARATIONS FOR JANUARY 6TH

January 5th Congressional Briefing by Chief Sund and Paul Irving. On January 5th, Chief Sund briefed the Chairperson of the Committee on House Administration (CHA), Representative Zoe Lofgren, along with numerous staff, as well as House Sergeant-at-Arms Paul Irving. Given CHA's oversight of the Capitol Police, this was "an opportunity for the chair of the committee to hear from the security professionals on the security plan."[116] Chair Lofgren's staff director described it as a "topline" briefing that covered various aspects of the security plan, including Chief Sund's direction of "all hands on deck," his focus on the prospect of counter protesters, as well as Chair Lofgren's concern that Members of Congress speaking at the Ellipse that day could incite protesters.[117] After the briefing, the CHA staff director specifically asked about the availability of the National Guard in case it was needed. "Chief Sund said that the Guard could be activated with an emergency declaration from the [Capitol Police] board, but they are here. They are a phone call away, and if we need them, they are ready to go."[118]

Speaker Pelosi did not receive a similar briefing, but her chief of staff was given a readout of Chief Sund's briefing to Chairperson Lofgren. On that basis, as well as the assurances Chief Sund provided, the Speaker's chief of staff said, "So I believed and the Speaker believed the security professionals were in charge of the security and they were prepared. We were told that there was a plan."[119]

FEDERAL AGENCY RESPONSE ON JANUARY 6TH

Although intelligence was available suggesting potential violence at the Capitol, it was not apparent exactly what President Trump would do to provoke the crowd at the January 6th Ellipse rally. Chief Sund, for example, drove into work on January 6th believing that preparations for the day's events were sound and that there was no extraordinary risk or threat. "You know, on my way in, I called Inspector Glover with MPD just to get a read. He said he was actually parked over by the Ellipse. Asked him, Hey, how are things going over there? He said, there's big crowds, lots of people in line, but right now he wasn't seeing any concern with the folks that we had. So that was my initial take," Sund told the Select Committee.[120]

Throughout the morning, Robert Engel, the special agent in charge of the President's Secret Service detail, received updates from the event at the Ellipse. At 10:35 a.m., an update informed Engel that 20,000 attendees had been processed and outside of the magnetometers, but that there were "several thousand on the mall watching but not in line."[121] An hour later, Engel forwarded an update to White House Deputy Chief of Operations Ornato, informing him that 30,000 attendees had been processed.[122]

Acting Attorney General Rosen met with FBI leadership for a briefing that morning.[123] He remembered this briefing, unlike previous ones, as "more of a situational update," adding that the DOJ was "going to hope for the best, prepare for the worst."[124] At 10:43 a.m., Acting Deputy Attorney General Donoghue received an email from Matt Blue, Acting Chief of the Counterterrorism Section, stating "[t]here are no credible threats as of the 10:00 brief."[125] Twelve minutes later, Rosen spoke to White House Counsel Pat Cipollone via phone.[126] Acting Attorney General Rosen admits that "in hindsight" no one at the Department contemplated "how bad that afternoon turned out to be."[127] Nobody in the DOJ leadership could have predicted President Trump's actions that day.

The President's speech at the Ellipse began just before noon. David Torres,[128] head of the USSS's Protective Intelligence Division (PID), insisted that the Secret Service was not listening to the President's speech, however PID agents monitored the speech throughout.[129] At 12:20 p.m., Faron Paramore, assistant director of Strategic Intel & Information (SII), sent an email to USSS leadership that "POTUS just said that he is going up to the U.S. Capitol to 'watch' the vote" and asked whether this is true. Secret Service executive Kimberly Cheatle responded "[h]e said it, but not going, to our knowledge."[130] Minutes later, the USSS PIOC warned that "Mogul just mentioned in his speech that he would accompany the protesters to the Capitol," with a note that "DAD Torres requested this be sent for awareness."[131] At 1:14 p.m., the USSS Joint Operations Center (JOC) sent an email designating a response team to accompany the President in his march to the Capitol, "per [his] announcement" at the Ellipse. The JOC notes: "Multiple reports of armed individuals with various weapons and malicious intent. Be on your guard."[132]

At 12:24 p.m., while the President was speaking, the Vice President, with his USSS detail, departed the Vice President's Residence for the Capitol.[133] After being routed to the Senate side due to the protests, the Vice President's detail arrived at the Capitol at 12:38 p.m. and was inside the Senate Chamber at 12:54 p.m.[134]

Around 1 p.m., Chief Contee notified Mayor Bowser about the discovery of a pipe bomb at the Republican National Committee and of the Capitol perimeter breach.[135] Within minutes, Mayor Bowser was at the Joint Operations Center with Chief Contee.[136] They tried to contact Chief Sund and sent command officials to Capitol Police headquarters.[137] At approximately 12:59 p.m., once the violence had begun, Chief Sund first called Deputy Chief Jeff Carroll of the MPD, which provided almost immediate reinforcements.[138] Approximately 10 minutes later, MPD officers arrived at the West Front balcony to assist the USCP officers. Chief Sund's next call was to the House and Senate Sergeants-at-Arms to request National Guard resources.[139]

As the violence at the Capitol escalated, DC FEMS realized that they were facing an "expanding incident with the potential for mass casualties, fires, active shooter, and hazardous materials incidents that would exceed the resources at hand."[140] As violence escalated at the West Front, non-lethal grenadiers began launching chemical munitions at the crowd.[141] Around the same time, the USCP discovered a nearby truck containing firearms and Molotov cocktails,[142] as well as a second explosive device at the Democratic National Headquarters at 1:07 p.m., while Vice President-elect Kamala Harris was inside. Responding to these incidents required a commitment of significant USCP resources for mitigation and to evacuate nearby buildings, preventing their deployment to the Capitol to help secure the building.

Chief Gallagher recalled that "it started to really unfold into an investigative—heavy on the investigation of let's pull up the cameras. Let's try to get an image of the pipe bombs. Let's get the images to our law enforcement partners. Let's try to play back the cameras and see if we can identify anybody that placed these pipe bombs. Let's get the owner of the vehicle, run the vehicle information for that suspicious vehicle. So we were coordinating all of that type of response that was from our Investigations Division....We also had our IICD team trying to run down as much information, working with our Investigations Division as they could, on the suspicious vehicle, the tags of the vehicle, stuff of that nature."[143] Not including those in the command center, the incidents would require the response of 34 USCP personnel, with additional assistance provided by the FBI and ATF. USCP's senior leadership at the Command Center and in the intelligence division also divided their time between the escalating threat to their officers at the Capitol and the explosive devices elsewhere on campus.

The next update to the DOJ was at 1:17 p.m., after President Trump had finished speaking at the Ellipse. After several attempts, Acting Attorney General Rosen got in touch with Acting U.S. Attorney for the District of Columbia Michael Sherwin, who was at the Ellipse. Rosen admits he was not very concerned with the situation at the time, because "[i]t was early, but at least the initial report was: Crowd size doesn't appear to be unexpected, and the conduct so far is okay."[144] He had only watched the end of the President's speech.[145] It was early afternoon before the DOJ's senior leadership began to realize the extent of what was occurring. Acting Deputy Attorney General Donoghue remembered hearing protesters outside the Department of Justice "marching down Constitution, going from the Ellipse toward the Capitol" in the late morning, early afternoon, but wasn't specifically monitoring the protests as "there were a million things going on."[146]

At the same time, the President was pressing his request to go to the Capitol. According to Robert Engel, the head of his Secret Service detail, President Trump asked to go to the Capitol once they had gotten into the Presidential SUV.[147] Engel denied the President's request and returned to the White House.[148] The Committee has significant evidence regarding this period of time.[149]

President Trump, nevertheless, persisted in his request to go to the Capitol. A 1:35 p.m. entry in the USSS Civil Disturbance Unit's time log shows that the plan was to hold at the White House for the next 2 hours and then move the President to the Capitol.[150] Soon after, Engel emailed USSS leadership from the West Wing to say they were "discussing options and setting expectations."[151] Minutes later, after receiving an email from USSS leadership saying that it would not be advisable for the President to go "anywhere near" the Capitol, Engel responded, "[w]e are not doing an OTR to Punch Bowl."[152]

Mayor Bowser also spoke directly with Army Secretary Ryan McCarthy who informed her that they had not gotten a request for National Guard assistance from the USCP. Mayor Bowser informed Secretary McCarthy that she did not have the authority to re-direct the 340 DC National Guard troops at traffic points across the city, but that she had already deployed the DC MPD and FEMs to the Capitol. Because she and Chief Sund had not connected, Mayor Bowser concluded that the security of the Capitol was "now our responsibility" and requested National Guard assistance. At the end of this call, Mayor Bowser believed that Secretary McCarthy was "running [her request] up his chain of command."[153]

USCP Chief Sund was concerned when the explosive device was discovered near RNC Headquarters but did not then believe there was a need to change the USCP's operational posture. Minutes later, when a large group of rioters approached the outer west perimeter of the Capitol, Chief Sund raised the alarm and began to reposition his officers: "When we looked up, and I saw them approaching the officers that were standing, you know, right there on the barrier, I looked over to Chief Thomas and I said, Chad, where's our—where's CDU? Get CDU down there now."[154]

The USCP timeline shows that at 12:55 p.m. all available officers were directed to the West Front of the Capitol. Then, at approximately 1:25 p.m., FBI Deputy Director David Bowdich received a report about the pipe bombs at the RNC and DNC.[155] Bowdich testified that the FBI considered the possibility that the DNC and RNC bombs were possible distractions.[156] At 1:28 p.m., USCP requested the AOC deliver 400 additional bike racks to the East Front to serve as protective barriers, even though rioters were using bike racks as weapons. The pipe bomb discovery at the DNC prevented the AOC from delivering them.[157]

Chief Gallagher was surprised that the violence had escalated so fast. "The amount of violence that immediately took place when that crowd of 30,000, 35,000, whatever the number that was estimated to come was, that did catch, I think, caught Capitol Police and all of our partners a little off guard with how violent they were and how quick they were." [158] At 1:49 p.m., DC MPD Commander Glover declared a riot on the West Front of the Capitol. "Cruiser 50, we're going to give riot warnings. We're going to give riot warnings. Going to try to get compliance, but this is now effectively a riot," Commander Glover yelled into his radio. "1349 hours. Declaring it a riot," the dispatcher responded, which allowed a change in the type of equipment the MPD could use in responding to the violence.[159]

While the violence continued to escalate at the Capitol, the USCP leadership focused on three things: (1) requesting support from local and Federal law enforcement agencies nearby; (2) planning for and coordinating with arriving reinforcements; and (3) protecting congressional leadership and other Members of Congress. Chief Sund was "still making other calls to other agencies for support—ATF, FBI, you name it, Secret Service." [160]

Yogananda Pittman, Gallagher's direct supervisor, told the Select Committee that she took roles that day beyond her responsibility as Assistant Chief of Police for Protective and Intelligence Operations. "So we started—so I started to take Protective Services Bureau resources, as well as the chief's staff, to set up operations adjacent to headquarters building, specifically lot 16, so that we could have a check-in procedure for those units so they could stage vehicles," Pittman said.[161] "Because like we know now, there were breaches on both sides of the buildings and these folks are inside of the Capitol. So you have to deploy them with your officers. They don't know the layout of the land. We're telling them to respond to north barricade. They don't know the north from the south." [162]

Just after 2 p.m., when the Capitol was breached, Assistant Chief Pittman turned her full attention to the protection of congressional leadership.[163] Meanwhile, the USCP officers at the West Front were overwhelmed. Commander Glover praised the actions of his fellow law enforcement officers that day but also noted a lack of leadership.[164] He observed that the

USCP officers he encountered when walking toward the Capitol's West Front seemed to be "very hectic and scattered, with no clear direction, ... fighting for every inch on the line," capable, but "without a whole lot of command and control." [165]

When it became clear to him that securing the Capitol would require additional resources, Chief Sund requested the assistance of the DC National Guard. [166] During a 2:30 p.m. call set up by HSEMA Director Rodriguez, the USCP specified the support they needed from the Guard. [167] Mayor Bowser also made "two urgent requests of the President" that she communicated to Chief of Staff Mark Meadows. [168] One was for the National Guard's assistance. [169] The other was that the President make a statement asking "people to leave, to leave the building and to get out of the city, to stop." [170] At 2:56 p.m., Meadows told Mayor Bowser that the President "had approved the request" and was "going to make a statement." [171]

At the Justice Department, it had become clear by early afternoon that the situation was rapidly deteriorating. Donoghue first became aware of the Capitol breach when he walked into Rosen's office and saw on television that the rioters were in the Rotunda. [172] Rosen turned to him and said, "[D]o you see this, do you see what's going on, can you believe this?" [173]

At 2:14 p.m., the Vice President's detail had alerted Secret Service over their radio channel that the Capitol Building had been breached and that they were holding the Vice President in his Senate office. [174] About 5 minutes later, the detail reported that the rioters had gained access to the second floor and that they would need to relocate the Vice President, [175] despite the Vice President's objection. [176] Five to 7 minutes later, after confirming that the route was safe, the lead agent on the Vice President's Secret Service detail reasserted the need for the Vice President to leave his Senate office. [177] (At 2:24 p.m. President Trump tweeted, "Mike Pence didn't have the courage to do what should have been done.") At 2:25 p.m., the Vice President and his detail left for a secure location. [178] Vice President Pence refused to leave the Capitol for his residence and remained in the secure Capitol location until the Senate and House floors were cleared around 7 that evening. [179]

At 2:29 p.m., DC MPD Commander Glover transmitted an emergency radio message: "Cruiser 50. We lost the line. We've lost the line. All MPD, pull back. All MPD, pull back up to the upper deck ASAP. All MPD, pull back to the upper deck ASAP. All MPD, come back to the upper deck. Upper deck. Cruiser 50. We've been flanked. 10–33. I repeat, 10–33 West Front of the Capitol. We have been flanked, and we've lost the line." [180] Commander Glover later told the Select Committee that a "10–33" indicates an immediate need for "emergency assistance for any officer, life or death at that moment in time. That's when that line on the north side finally just broke and we just lost it, and we kind of got overrun behind us...[W]hen you hear that in general daily activity, it's like the radio stops and you're focused on getting to that officer, wherever they are, because you know it's that bad, that they're fighting for their life; something they're perceiving or seeing or realizing is that their life is in immediate danger." [181]

Donoghue left Rosen's office to go to the FBI's Strategic Information and Operations Center (SIOC) across the street at the FBI's Hoover Building.[182] Before he left, Donoghue remembers someone at SIOC telling him "Capitol Police say they don't need help at this point, they've got it covered." [183] When Donoghue arrived at the Washington Field Office, he found FBI Deputy Director Bowdich in a conference room by himself on the phone with a senior FBI official.[184] After a brief discussion, Donoghue and Bowdich agreed that they should both go to the Capitol to evaluate the situation firsthand.[185] Donoghue remembered that they arrived at the assembly area on D Street.[186] Donoghue called Rosen to say that he and Bowdich were going to the Capitol.[187]

Around this time, Bowdich says that he received a call from Senator Mark Warner, who said "[t]his is a mess, and we now have the vast majority of the Senate in one room." [188] Bowdich recalls the number being about 87 senators,[189] and that he directed the FBI's Baltimore team to "protect that room, recognizing you have almost the entire Senate in one room." [190] Bowdich also directed a SWAT team to Senator Mitch McConnell's office, in response to a call from McConnell's staff informing him that rioters were kicking in their door. On arriving, the SWAT team found that McConnell's staff had reached safety.[191]

At 3:25 p.m., Rosen spoke to Speaker Nancy Pelosi and Senator Chuck Schumer about the ongoing crisis. A video of the call shows Senator Schumer imploring Rosen, "get the President to tell them to leave the Capitol, Mr. Attorney General, in your law enforcement responsibility. A public statement that they should all leave." [192]

As the day's crisis unfolded, Mayor Bowser activated the DC mutual assistance compact with neighboring jurisdictions for law assistance support and spoke to the Governors of Maryland and Virginia to solicit additional National Guard support. At about 3:30 p.m., Mayor Bowser spoke to congressional leadership, including Speaker Pelosi and House Majority Leader Steny Hoyer.[193] Then, around 4 p.m., Mayor Bowser, MPD Chief Contee and Army Secretary McCarthy met in the Joint Operations Center at MPD headquarters.[194] At 4:30 p.m., Mayor Bowser held a press conference with DC HSEMA Director Rodriguez as well as Secretary McCarthy.[195] Mayor Bowser also declared a 6 p.m. curfew for the District.[196]

Vice President Pence, who remained inside the Capitol, called Acting Attorney General Rosen at 4:34 p.m. to ask what the DOJ was doing and what more the Department could do to help.[197] Vice President Pence told Rosen that the situation at the Capitol seemed then to be "improving."[198] The head of his USSS security detail recalls overhearing the Vice President asking USCP Chief Sund, over the phone, whether it would be possible to "go back to finish the business of the government this evening."[199] At 4:42 p.m., the head of the Vice President's detail emailed the USSS Office of Protective Operations that the Vice President was confirming with Chief Sund that it would "take days to sweep and reopen" the Capitol.[200]

Congressional leadership continued to push to return to the Capitol to continue certifying the electoral votes. Senior DOJ and FBI officials—including Rosen, Bowdich, and Donoghue—held two conference calls. Donoghue remembered that the first, at 6 p.m., was a "law enforcement-level call" with General Daniel R. Hokansen, chief of the National Guard Bureau, and focused on the role of the DC National Guard.[201] The second call, at approximately 7 p.m., included Speaker Pelosi, Leader McConnell, Leader Schumer, the Vice President, the Secretary of Defense, and General Milley, as well as other congressional leaders.[202] During that call, FBI and other law enforcement officials on the ground provided an updated timeline for clearing the Capitol to "hopefully get in an hour later."[203]

At 8:05 p.m., the U.S. Capitol Police announced that the Capitol Building was clear and that Congress could resume counting electoral votes.[204] Shortly after Members returned, Donoghue left the Capitol.[205]

DC FEMS statistics help describe the scope of the January 6th riot at the Capitol. Over the course of the day, DC FEMS reported 22 EMS responses, 14 EMS transports, including two cardiac arrests and two critical injury transports. There were an estimated 250 injured law enforcement officers from numerous agencies.[206] One hundred-fourteen USCP officers reported injuries.[207] Five police officers who were at the Capitol on January 6th died in the days following the riot.

Federal and local law enforcement authorities were in possession of multiple streams of intelligence predicting violence directed at the Capitol prior to January 6th. Although some of that intelligence was fragmentary, it should have been sufficient to warrant far more vigorous preparations for the security of the joint session. The failure to sufficiently share and act upon that intelligence jeopardized the lives of the police officers defending the Capitol and everyone in it.

While the danger to the Capitol posed by an armed and angry crowd was foreseeable, the fact that the President of the United States would be the catalyst of their fury and facilitate the attack was unprecedented in American history. If we lacked the imagination to suppose that a President would incite an attack on his own Government, urging his supporters to "fight like hell," we lack that insight no more. And the best defense against that danger will not come from law enforcement, but from an informed and active citizenry.

ENDNOTES

1. *See* Documents on file with the Select Committee to Investigate the January 6th Attack on the United States Capitol (Secret Service Production), CTRL0000091086 (United States Secret Service Protective Intelligence Division communication noting left-wing groups telling members to "stay at home" on January 6th).

2. Donald J. Trump (@realDonaldTrump), Twitter, Dec. 19, 2020 1:42 a.m. ET, available at https://www.thetrumparchive.com/?searchbox=%22Be+there+will+be+wild%22.

3. *See* Select Committee Interview of Donell Harvin on January 24, 2022 at p. 14:9–12 ("Harvin Interview (January 24, 2022)"); *see also* Select Committee Informal Interview of Donell Harvin on November 12, 2021.

4. *See* Select Committee to Investigate the January 6th Attack on the United States Capitol, Transcribed Interview of Donell Harvin, (Jan. 24, 2022), p. 12; Select Committee to Investigate the January 6th Attack on the United States Capitol, Informal Interview of Donell Harvin, (Nov. 12, 2021).

5. Select Committee to Investigate the January 6th Attack on the United States Capitol, Transcribed Interview of Robert J. Contee III, (Jan. 11, 2022), p. 22; *see also* Select Committee to Investigate the January 6th Attack on the United States Capitol, Transcribed Interview of Donell Harvin, (Jan. 24, 2022), p. 22; Select Committee to Investigate the January 6th Attack on the United States Capitol, Transcribed Interview of Dr. Christopher Rodriguez, (Jan. 25, 2022), p.16.

6. Select Committee to Investigate the January 6th Attack on the United States Capitol, Transcribed Interview of Robert J. Contee III, (Jan. 11, 2022), p. 22.

7. Select Committee to Investigate the January 6th Attack on the United States Capitol, Transcribed Interview of Christopher Rodriguez, (Jan. 25, 2022), p. 20.

8. Select Committee to Investigate the January 6th Attack on the United States Capitol, Transcribed Interview of Muriel Bowser, (Jan. 12, 2022), p. 44.

9. Documents on file with the Select Committee to Investigate the January 6th Attack on the United States Capitol (Secret Service Production), CTRL0000101135.0001 (December 30, 2020, Protective Intelligence Brief titled "March for Trump").

10. Documents on file with the Select Committee to Investigate the January 6th Attack on the United States Capitol (Capitol Police Production), CTRL0000001473 (December 29, 2020, email from PIOC-ONDUTY to THREAT ASSESSMENT re: FW: [EXTERNAL EMAIL] - Neo-Nazi Calls on D.C. Pro-Trump Protesters to Occupy Federal Building).

11. Documents on file with the Select Committee to Investigate the January 6th Attack on the United States Capitol (Capitol Police Production), CTRL0000000436, CTRL0000000436.0001, CTRL0000000436.0002, CTRL0000000436.0003. CTRL0000000436.0004, CTRL0000000436.0005 (December 21, 2020, email re: Part II: FYSA - thread in OSINT research, attaching Donald.Win screenshots).

12. See Documents on file with the Select Committee to Investigate the January 6th Attack on the United States Capitol (Capitol Police Production), CTRL0000000091, CTRL0000000091,0001, CTRL0000000091,0002, CTRL0000000091,0003, CTRL0000000091,0004, CTRL0000000091,0005, CTRL0000000091,0006, CTRL0000000091,0007, CTRL0000000091,0008, CTRL0000000091,0009 (January 5, 2021, Yogananda Pittman email to Steven Sund at 4:55 p.m. re: FW: Interest in Tunnels Leading to the US Capitol, attaching screenshots of theDonald.win posts).

13. Select Committee to Investigate the January 6th Attack on the United States Capitol, Transcribed Interview of Steven Sund, (Apr. 20, 2022), pp. 60–61.

14. Select Committee to Investigate the January 6th Attack on the United States Capitol, Transcribed Interview of Steven Sund, (Apr. 20, 2022), pp. 60–61.

15. Select Committee to Investigate the January 6th Attack on the United States Capitol, Transcribed Interview of Jennifer Moore, (July 26, 2022), pp. 55, 57, 62.

16. Select Committee to Investigate the January 6th Attack on the United States Capitol, Transcribed Interview of Jennifer Moore, (July 26, 2022), p. 95.

17. Select Committee to Investigate the January 6th Attack on the United States Capitol, Transcribed Interview of Jennifer Moore, (July 26, 2022), p. 24.

18. Documents on file with the Select Committee to Investigate the January 6th Attack on the United States Capitol (Secret Service Production), CTRL0000236995 (December 26, 2021, email to PIOC, PIOC-ONDUTY re: (U//FOUO) Disruptions to DC Metro Area 01/06/2021 (Online Tip)).

19. Documents on file with the Select Committee to Investigate the January 6th Attack on the United States Capitol (Secret Service Production), CTRL0000236995 (December 26, 2021, email to PIOC, PIOC-ONDUTY re: (U//FOUO) Disruptions to DC Metro Area 01/06/2021 (Online Tip)).

20. Documents on file with the Select Committee to Investigate the January 6th Attack on the United States Capitol (Capitol Police Production), CTRL0000001509 (December 25, 2020, email to John Donohue re: Fwd: "Armed and Ready, Mr. President": Demonstrators Urged to Bring Guns, Prepare for Violence at January 6 "Stop the Steal" Protest in DC, with attachments).

21. Documents on file with the Select Committee to Investigate the January 6th Attack on the United States Capitol (Capitol Police Production), CTRL0000001509 (December 25, 2020, email to John Donohue re: Fwd: "Armed and Ready, Mr. President": Demonstrators Urged to Bring Guns, Prepare for Violence at January 6 "Stop the Steal" Protest in DC, with attachments).

22. Documents on file with the Select Committee to Investigate the January 6th Attack on the United States Capitol (Capitol Police Production), CTRL0000001509 (December 25, 2020, email to John Donohue re: Fwd: "Armed and Ready, Mr. President": Demonstrators Urged to Bring Guns, Prepare for Violence at January 6 "Stop the Steal" Protest in DC, with attachments).

23. Documents on file with the Select Committee to Investigate the January 6th Attack on the United States Capitol (Capitol Police Production), CTRL0000001509 (December 25, 2020, email to John Donohue re: Fwd: "Armed and Ready, Mr. President": Demonstrators Urged to Bring Guns, Prepare for Violence at January 6 "Stop the Steal" Protest in DC, with attachments).

24. Documents on file with the Select Committee to Investigate the January 6th Attack on the United States Capitol (Capitol Police Production), CTRL0000001509 (December 25, 2020, email to John Donohue re: Fwd: "Armed and Ready, Mr. President": Demonstrators Urged to Bring Guns, Prepare for Violence at January 6 "Stop the Steal" Protest in DC, with attachments).

25. Documents on file with the Select Committee to Investigate the January 6th Attack on the United States Capitol (Capitol Police Production), CTRL0000001509 (December 25, 2020, email to John Donohue re: Fwd: "Armed and Ready, Mr. President": Demonstrators Urged to Bring Guns, Prepare for Violence at January 6 "Stop the Steal" Protest in DC, with attachments).

26. Documents on file with the Select Committee to Investigate the January 6th Attack on the United States Capitol (Capitol Police Production), CTRL0000001509 (December 25, 2020, email to John Donohue re: Fwd: "Armed and Ready, Mr. President": Demonstrators Urged to Bring Guns, Prepare for Violence at January 6 "Stop the Steal" Protest in DC, with attachments).

27. Documents on file with the Select Committee to Investigate the January 6th Attack on the United States Capitol (Capitol Police Production), CTRL0000000087 (December 28, 2020, email re: 1/6 warning.).

28. Documents on file with the Select Committee to Investigate the January 6th Attack on the United States Capitol (Capitol Police Production), CTRL0000000087 (December 28, 2020, email re: 1/6 warning.).

29. Select Committee to Investigate the January 6th Attack on the United States Capitol, Transcribed Interview of John K. Donohue, (Jan. 31, 2022), p. 54; Select Committee to Investigate the January 6th Attack on the United States Capitol, Transcribed Interview of Yogananda Pittman, (Jan. 13, 2022), p. 47; Select Committee to Investigate the January 6th Attack on the United States Capitol, Transcribed Interview of Julie Farnam, (Dec. 15, 2021), p. 42; Select Committee to Investigate the January 6th Attack on the United States Capitol, Transcribed Interview of Sean Gallagher (Jan. 11, 2022), pp. 37, 57.

30. Documents on file with the Select Committee to Investigate the January 6th Attack on the United States Capitol (Capitol Police Production), CTRL0000001473 (December 29, 2020, email from PIOC-ONDUTY to THREAT ASSESSMENT re: FW: [EXTERNAL EMAIL] - Neo-Nazi Calls on D.C. Pro-Trump Protesters to Occupy Federal Building.)

31. *See* Documents on file with the Select Committee to Investigate the January 6th Attack on the United States Capitol (Capitol Police Production), CTRL0000001527 (Email from Shane Lamond to Julie Farnam re: Fwd: MPD MMS Text Tip.).

32. *See* Documents on file with the Select Committee to Investigate the January 6th Attack on the United States Capitol (Capitol Police Production), CTRL0000001527 (Email from Shane Lamond to Julie Farnam re: Fwd: MPD MMS Text Tip.).

33. *See* Documents on file with the Select Committee to Investigate the January 6th Attack on the United States Capitol (FBI Production, Jan. 31, 2022). This document is not being released due to national security concerns.

34. *See* Documents on file with the Select Committee to Investigate the January 6th Attack on the United States Capitol (Parler Production), PARLER_00000011 - PARLER_00000013 (January 2, 2021 email from Parler to FBI re: Another to check out).

35. Select Committee to Investigate the January 6th Attack on the United States Capitol, Transcribed Interview of Julie Farnam, (Dec. 15, 2021), pp. 33–36.

36. Documents on file with the Select Committee to Investigate the January 6th Attack on the United States Capitol (Architect of the Capitol Production), CTRL0000000002, p. 2 (January 5, 2021, email from AOC Command Center re: Individual says "go to Washington Jan 6 and help storm the Capital" adds "we will storm the government buildings, kill cops, kill security guards, kill federal employees and agents": Blog via 8kun).

37. Documents on file with the Select Committee to Investigate the January 6th Attack on the United States Capitol (Architect of the Capitol Production), CTRL0000000002, p. 2 (January 5, 2021, email from AOC Command Center re: Individual says "go to Washington Jan 6 and help storm the Capital" adds "we will storm the government buildings, kill cops, kill security guards, kill federal employees and agents": Blog via 8kun).

38. Documents on file with the Select Committee to Investigate the January 6th Attack on the United States Capitol (Architect of the Capitol Production), CTRL0000000002, p. 2 (January 5, 2021, email from AOC Command Center re: Individual says "go to Washington Jan 6 and help storm the Capital" adds "we will storm the government buildings, kill cops, kill security guards, kill federal employees and agents": Blog via 8kun).

39. Documents on file with the Select Committee to Investigate the January 6th Attack on the United States Capitol (Capitol Police Production), CTRL0000000083 (January 5, 2021, email re: (U//FOUO//LES) OSINT Post of Concern).

40. Documents on file with the Select Committee to Investigate the January 6th Attack on the United States Capitol (Capitol Police Production), CTRL0000000083 (January 5, 2021, email re: (U//FOUO//LES) OSINT Post of Concern).

APPENDIX 1

41. *See* Select Committee to Investigate the January 6th Attack on the United States Capitol, Informal Briefing by Steve Jensen, (Nov. 18, 2021). In an email sent by the FBI to the Select Committee on November 8, 2021, the FBI stated that on December 27, the FBI created a system to collect threats related to the "election certification" on January 6 by using a tag, "CERTUNREST." Despite making multiple requests for the number of guardians that were tagged prior to January 6, the FBI did not provide a precise number. The FBI identified several dozen guardians opened in advance of January 6th that included a reference to January 6, Washington D.C., and either the U.S. Capitol or a specific threat of violence.

42. *See* Documents on file with the Select Committee to Investigate the January 6th Attack on the United States Capitol (FBI Production), CTRL0000930224 p. 23, (noting "Communication and Establishment of a Quick Reaction Force by USPERs Related to an Identified Protest in Washington, District of Columbia, on 6 January 2021").

43. Select Committee to Investigate the January 6th Attack on the United States Capitol, Informal Interview of Yogananda Pittman, (Nov. 12, 2021).

44. *See* Documents on file with the Select Committee to Investigate the January 6th Attack on the United States Capitol (Capitol Police Production), CTRL0000001766, CTRL0000001766.0001 (Document from January 3, 2021, titled: "Special Event Assessment: Joint Session of Congress—Electoral College Vote Certification"); *see also,* Select Committee to Investigate the January 6th Attack on the United States Capitol, Transcribed Interview of Julie Farnam, (Dec. 15, 2021), pp 51–52.

45. Select Committee to Investigate the January 6th Attack on the United States Capitol, Transcribed Interview of Mark Milley, (Nov. 17, 2021), p. 236.

46. Select Committee to Investigate the January 6th Attack on the United States Capitol, Transcribed Interview of Robert O'Brien, (Aug. 23, 2022), p. 19.

47. Select Committee to Investigate the January 6th Attack on the United States Capitol, Transcribed Interview of Chad Wolf, (Jan. 21, 2022), p. 31.

48. Select Committee to Investigate the January 6th Attack on the United States Capitol, Transcribed Interview of Mark Milley, (Nov. 17, 2021), p. 235.

49. Select Committee to Investigate the January 6th Attack on the United States Capitol, Transcribed Interview of Mark Milley, (Nov. 17, 2021), p. 236.

50. Select Committee to Investigate the January 6th Attack on the United States Capitol, Transcribed Interview of Christopher Tomney, (Apr. 14, 2022), p. 40.

51. Select Committee to Investigate the January 6th Attack on the United States Capitol, Transcribed Interview of Richard Peter Donoghue, (Oct. 1, 2022), pp. 169–70.

52. Select Committee to Investigate the January 6th Attack on the United States Capitol, Transcribed Interview of Richard Peter Donoghue, (Oct. 1, 2022), pp. 169–70.

53. Select Committee to Investigate the January 6th Attack on the United States Capitol, Transcribed Interview of Muriel Bowser, (Jan. 12, 2022), p. 45.

54. Select Committee to Investigate the January 6th Attack on the United States Capitol, Transcribed Interview of Christopher Rodriguez, (Jan. 25, 2022), p. 18.

55. Select Committee to Investigate the January 6th Attack on the United Capitol, Transcribed Interview of Robert J. Contee III, (Jan. 11, 2022), p. 26.

56. Select Committee to Investigate the January 6th Attack on the United States Capitol, Transcribed Interview of Christopher Rodriguez, (Jan. 25, 2022), p. 24.

57. Documents on file with the Select Committee to Investigate the January 6th Attack on the United States Capitol (District of Columbia Production), CTRL0000007104 (December 31, 2020, letter from Mayor Bowser to General William Walker).

58. Select Committee to Investigate the January 6th Attack on the United States Capitol, Transcribed Interview of Christopher Rodriguez, (Jan. 25, 2022), p. 30.

59. Select Committee to Investigate the January 6th Attack on the United States Capitol, Transcribed Interview of Ryan McCarthy, (Feb. 4, 2022), pp. 78-79.

60. Select Committee to Investigate the January 6th Attack on the United States Capitol, Transcribed Interview of Christopher Rodriguez, (Jan. 25, 2022), p. 63.

61. Select Committee to Investigate the January 6th Attack on the United States Capitol, Transcribed Interview of Muriel Bowser, (Jan. 12, 2022), p. 50.

62. *See* DC Mayor's Office, "Mayor Bowers Provides Situational Update, 1/4/21," YouTube, Jan. 4, 2021, available at https://www.youtube.com/watch?v=UbZ07wdnQ-s; Julie Zauzmer Weil, Marissa J. Lang, and Dan Lamothe, "National Guard Activated for D.C. Protests, with More Restraints than in June, Officials Say," *Washington Post*, (Jan. 4, 2021), available at https://www.washingtonpost.com/local/dc-national-guard-protests-bowser/2021/01/04/220ced16-4e8d-11eb-83e3-322644d82356_story.html.

63. Select Committee to Investigate the January 6th Attack on the United States Capitol, Transcribed Interview of Muriel Bowser, (Jan. 12, 2022), pp. 27–28.

64. Select Committee to Investigate the January 6th Attack on the United States Capitol, Transcribed Interview of Dr. Christopher Rodriguez, (Jan. 25, 2022), p. 28.

65. Select Committee to Investigate the January 6th Attack on the United States Capitol, Transcribed Interview of Dr. Christopher Rodriguez, (Jan. 25, 2022), p.66.

66. Documents on file with the Select Committee to Investigate the January 6th Attack on the United States Capitol (District of Columbia production), CTRL0000930981 (Memo: Final January 6th After Action Quick Look Report, Government of the District of Columbia Fire and Emergency Medical Services Department. May 19, 2022).

67. Select Committee to Investigate the January 6th Attack on the United States Capitol, Transcribed Interview of Robert J. Contee III, (Jan. 11, 2022), p. 14.

68. Select Committee to Investigate the January 6th Attack on the United States Capitol, Transcribed Interview of Robert J. Contee III, (Jan. 11, 2022), p. 15. (emphasis added)

69. Select Committee to Investigate the January 6th Attack on the United States Capitol, Transcribed Interview of Robert J. Contee III, (Jan. 11, 2022), pp. 14–15.

70. Select Committee to Investigate the January 6th Attack on the United States Capitol, Transcribed Interview of Steven Andrew Sund, (Apr. 20, 2022), p. 114.

71. Select Committee to Investigate the January 6th Attack on the United States Capitol, Transcribed Interview of Steven Andrew Sund, (Apr. 20, 2022), p. 116.

72. Select Committee to Investigate the January 6th Attack on the United States Capitol, Transcribed Interview of Paul Irving, (Mar. 4, 2022), pp. 9. 21–23.

73. Select Committee to Investigate the January 6th Attack on the United States Capitol, Transcribed Interview of Steven Andrew Sund, (Apr. 20, 2022), p. 116.

74. Select Committee to Investigate the January 6th Attack on the United States Capitol, Transcribed Interview of Paul Irving, (Mar. 4, 2022), p. 10.

75. Select Committee to Investigate the January 6th Attack on the United States Capitol, Transcribed Interview of Steven Andrew Sund, (Apr. 20, 2022), p.125.

76. Select Committee to Investigate the January 6th Attack on the United States Capitol, Transcribed Interview of Paul Irving, (Mar. 4, 2022), p.12.

77. Select Committee to Investigate the January 6th Attack on the United States Capitol, Transcribed Interview of Paul Irving, (Mar. 4, 2022), pp. 12–13. The result was an estimated 923 Capitol Police officers on the Capitol campus at 7 a.m. on January 6 (50% of strength), 1,214 officers at 2 p.m. (66%), and a total of 1,457 at some point during the day (79% of a total of 1,840 officers).

78. Select Committee to Investigate the January 6th Attack on the United States Capitol, Transcribed Interview of Steven Andrew Sund, (Apr. 20, 2022), p. 76.

79. Select Committee to Investigate the January 6th Attack on the United States Capitol, Transcribed Interview of Steven Andrew Sund, (Apr. 20, 2022), p. 138.

80. Select Committee to Investigate the January 6th Attack on the United States Capitol, Transcribed Interview of Steven Andrew Sund, (Apr. 20, 2022), p. 138.

81. Select Committee to Investigate the January 6th Attack on the United States Capitol, Transcribed Interview of Christopher Charles Miller, (Jan. 14, 2022), p. 86.

82. Select Committee to Investigate the January 6th Attack on the United States Capitol, Transcribed Interview of Christopher Charles Miller, (Jan. 14, 2022), p. 87.

83. Select Committee to Investigate the January 6th Attack on the United States Capitol, Transcribed Interview of Christopher Charles Miller, (Jan. 14, 2022), p. 90.

84. Select Committee to Investigate the January 6th Attack on the United States Capitol, Transcribed Interview of Christopher J. Tomney, (Apr. 14, 2022), pp. 39, 43–44.

85. Select Committee to Investigate the January 6th Attack on the United States Capitol, Transcribed Interview of Mark Milley, (Nov. 17, 2021), p. 237; Select Committee to Investigate the January 6th Attack on the United States Capitol, Transcribed Interview of Richard Peter Donoghue, (Oct. 1, 2021), Exhibit 38.

86. *See* Select Committee to Investigate the January 6th Attack on the United States Capitol, Transcribed Interview of Christopher Charles Miller, (Jan. 14, 2022), pp. 82–83; Select Committee to Investigate the January 6th Attack on the United States Capitol, Transcribed Interview of Mark Milley, (Nov. 17, 2021), pp. 194, 281.

87. Select Committee to Investigate the January 6th Attack on the United States Capitol, Transcribed Interview of Christopher Charles Miller, (Jan. 14, 2022), pp. 81-82; *See also* Select Committee to Investigate the January 6th Attack on the United States Capitol, Transcribed Interview of Mark Milley, (Nov. 17, 2021), pp. 236–37.

88. Select Committee to Investigate the January 6th Attack on the United States Capitol, Transcribed Interview of Christopher Charles Miller, (Jan. 14, 2022), pp. 81–82.

89. Select Committee to Investigate the January 6th Attack on the United States Capitol, Transcribed Interview of Christopher J. Tomney, (Apr. 14, 2022), pp. 39, 43–44.

90. Select Committee to Investigate the January 6th Attack on the United States Capitol, Transcribed Interview of Christopher Charles Miller, (Jan. 14, 2022), p. 90.

91. Select Committee to Investigate the January 6th Attack on the United States Capitol, Transcribed Interview of Mark Milley, (Nov. 17, 2021), pp. 202–04.

92. Select Committee to Investigate the January 6th Attack on the United States Capitol, Transcribed Interview of Christopher Charles Miller, (Jan. 14, 2022), p. 88.

93. Select Committee to Investigate the January 6th Attack on the United States Capitol, Transcribed Interview of Mark Milley, (Nov. 17, 2021), p. 206.

94. Select Committee to Investigate the January 6th Attack on the United States Capitol, Transcribed Interview of Christopher J. Tomney, (Apr. 14, 2022), pp. 41, 45–46.

95. *See* Chapter 4.

96. Select Committee to Investigate the January 6th Attack on the United States Capitol, Transcribed Interview of Richard Peter Donoghue, (Oct. 1, 2021), pp. 157, 165–67.

97. Select Committee to Investigate the January 6th Attack on the United States Capitol, Transcribed Interview of David Bowdich, (Dec. 16, 2021), pp. 97–98; Select Committee to Investigate the January 6th Attack on the United States Capitol, Transcribed Interview of Richard Donoghue, (Oct. 1, 2021), p. 162.

98. Documents on file with the Select Committee to Investigate the January 6th Attack on the United States Capitol (Department of Defense Production), PRODUCTION 1—000017 ("On January 3, 2021, during an interagency meeting hosted by the White House, the Department of Justice was designated as the lead Federal agency for the planned First Amendment demonstrations on January 5–6.").

99. Select Committee to Investigate the January 6th Attack on the United States Capitol, Transcribed Interview of Christopher Tomney, (April 14, 2022), p. 45; Select Committee to Investigate the January 6th Attack on the United States Capitol, Transcribed Interview of Christopher Tomney, (April 14, 2022), p. 46.

100. Select Committee to Investigate the January 6th Attack on the United States Capitol, Transcribed Interview of Richard Peter Donoghue, (Oct. 1, 2021), p. 168.

101. Select Committee to Investigate the January 6th Attack on the United States Capitol, Transcribed Interview of Richard Peter Donoghue, (Oct. 1, 2021), p. 169.

102. Select Committee to Investigate the January 6th Attack on the United States Capitol, Transcribed Interview of Richard Peter Donoghue, (Oct. 1, 2021), p. 169.

103. Select Committee to Investigate the January 6th Attack on the United States Capitol, Transcribed Interview of Christopher Charles Miller, (Jan. 14, 2022), p. 83.

104. Select Committee to Investigate the January 6th Attack on the United States Capitol, Transcribed Interview of Chad Wolfe, (Jan 29, 2022), pp. 48–49

105. Select Committee to Investigate the January 6th Attack on the United States Capitol, Transcribed Interview of Julie Farnam, (Dec. 15, 2021), pp. 58–59.

106. Select Committee to Investigate the January 6th Attack on the United States Capitol, Transcribed Interview of Julie Farnam, (Dec. 15, 2021), pp. 58–59.

107. Documents on file with the Select Committee to Investigate the January 6th Attack on the United States Capitol (Department of the Interior Production), DOI_46000428_00005162 (Dec. 19, 2020, Cindy Chafian email Re: Status of application - Women for America First at 7:12 AM).

108. Documents on file with the Select Committee to Investigate the January 6th Attack on the United States Capitol (Department of Interior), DOI_46000114_00000246.

109. Documents on file with the Select Committee to Investigate the January 6th Attack on the United States Capitol (Department of Interior), DOI_46000114_00000246.

110. Documents on file with the Select Committee to Investigate the January 6th Attack on the United States Capitol (Department of Interior Response to questions), DOI_46000114_00000246.

111. Documents on file with the Select Committee to Investigate the January 6th Attack on the United States Capitol (Department of Interior Response to questions), DOI_46000114_00000246.

112. Documents on file with the Select Committee to Investigate the January 6th Attack on the United States Capitol (Department of Interior Response to questions), DOI_46000114_00000246.

113. Documents on file with the Select Committee to Investigate the January 6th Attack on the United States Capitol (Department of Interior), DOI_46000114_00000246.

114. See Executive Summary and Chapter 7.

115. Documents on file with the Select Committee to Investigate the January 6th Attack on the United States Capitol (Secret Service Production), CTRL0000481288 (January 6, 2021 email at 8:17 AM referencing 2 magnetometers being surged); Documents on file with the Select Committee to Investigate the January 6th Attack on the United States Capitol (Secret Service Production), CTRL0000495699 (January 6, 2021, email at 10:46 a.m re: Mags Update referencing 12 magnetometers, which means there were 10 earlier in the day).

116. Select Committee to Investigate the January 6th Attack on the United States Capitol, Transcribed Interview of Jamie Fleet, (Mar. 10, 2022), p. 24.

117. Select Committee to Investigate the January 6th Attack on the United States Capitol, Transcribed Interview of Jamie Fleet, (Mar. 10, 2022), pp. 25–26, 30.

118. Select Committee to Investigate the January 6th Attack on the United States Capitol, Transcribed Interview of Jamie Fleet, (Mar. 10, 2022), p. 28.

119. Select Committee to Investigate the January 6th Attack on the United States Capitol, Informal Interview of Terri McCullough, (Apr. 18, 2022).

120. Select Committee to Investigate the January 6th Attack on the United States Capitol, Transcribed Interview of Steven Sund, (Apr. 20, 2022), p. 146.

121. Documents on file with the Select Committee to Investigate the January 6th Attack on the United States Capitol (Secret Service production), CTRL0000481790 (January 6, 2021, email to Robert Engel at 10:35 am).

122. Documents on file with the Select Committee to Investigate the January 6th Attack on the United States Capitol (Secret Service production), CTRL0000536285 (January 6, 2021, email forwarded by Robert Engel to Anthony Ornato at 11:32 am).

123. Select Committee to Investigate the January 6th Attack on the United States Capitol, Transcribed Interview of Jeffrey Rosen, (Oct. 13, 2021), p. 168.

124. Select Committee to Investigate the January 6th Attack on the United States Capitol, Transcribed Interview of Jeffrey Rosen, (Oct. 13, 2021), p. 169.

125. Documents on file with the Select Committee to Investigate the January 6th Attack on the United States Capitol (Department of Justice Production), HCOR-Jan6-07222021-000587 (January 6, 2021, email to Richard Donoghue at 10:43 am).

126. Documents on file with the Select Committee to Investigate the January 6th Attack on the United States Capitol (Department of Justice Production), HCOR-Jan6-07222021-000621 (January 6, 2021, Jeffrey Rosen call list).

127. Select Committee to Investigate the January 6th Attack on the United States Capitol, Transcribed Interview of Jeffrey Rosen, (Oct. 13, 2021), p. 169.

128. Select Committee to Investigate the January 6th Attack on the United States Capitol, Transcribed Interview of David Torres, (Mar. 2, 2020), p. 80.

129. Documents on file with the Select Committee to Investigate the January 6th Attack on the United States Capitol (Secret Service Production), CTRL0000093384 (January 6, 2021, message to PID agents at 12:00 p.m.).

130. Documents on file with the Select Committee to Investigate the January 6th Attack on the United States Capitol (Secret Service Production), CTRL0000152321 (January 6, 2021, emails at 12:20 p.m. and 1:34 p.m.).

131. Documents on file with the Select Committee to Investigate the January 6th Attack on the United States Capitol (Secret Service Production), CTRL0000542477 (January 6, 2021, internal email at 12:26 p.m.).

132. Documents on file with the Select Committee to Investigate the January 6th Attack on the United States Capitol (Secret Service Production), CTRL0000087742 (January 6, 2021, Joint Operations Center (JOC) email designating a response team at 1:14 pm).

133. United States Secret Service Radio Tango Channel, Jan. 6, 2021. Select Committee staff reviewed recordings of this radio frequency.

134. United States Secret Service Radio Tango Channel, Jan. 6, 2021. Select Committee staff reviewed recordings of this radio frequency.

135. Select Committee to Investigate the January 6th Attack on the United States Capitol, Transcribed Interview of Muriel Bowser, (Jan. 12, 2022), pp. 6–7.

136. Select Committee to Investigate the January 6th Attack on the United States Capitol, Transcribed Interview of Muriel Bowser, (Jan. 12, 2022), pp. 7–8.

137. Select Committee to Investigate the January 6th Attack on the United States Capitol, Transcribed Interview of Muriel Bowser, (Jan. 12, 2022), pp. 8–9.

138. Select Committee to Investigate the January 6th Attack on the United States Capitol, Transcribed Interview of Steven Andrew Sund, (Apr. 20, 2022), p. 147.

139. This call, and subsequent coordination for National Guard assistance between various entities is detailed in the National Guard appendix.

140. Documents on file with the Select Committee to Investigate the January 6th Attack on the United States Capitol (District of Columbia production), CTRL0000930981 (Memo: Final January 6th After Action Quick Look Report, Government of the District of Columbia Fire and Emergency Medical Services Department. May 19, 2022).

141. Documents on file with the Select Committee to Investigate the January 6th Attack on the United States Capitol (Capitol Police Production), CTRL0000000056 (noting the event at 1:06 p.m.).

142. Documents on file with the Select Committee to Investigate the January 6th Attack on the United States Capitol (Capitol Police Production), CTRL0000000056 (marking the event at 1:03 p.m.).

143. Select Committee to Investigate the January 6th Attack on the United States Capitol, Transcribed Interview of Sean Gallagher, (Jan. 11, 2022), p. 19.

144. Select Committee to Investigate the January 6th Attack on the United States Capitol, Transcribed Interview of Jeffrey Rosen, (Oct. 13, 2021), p. 171.

145. Select Committee to Investigate the January 6th Attack on the United States Capitol, Transcribed Interview of Jeffrey Rosen, (Oct. 13, 2021), p. 169.

146. Select Committee to Investigate the January 6th Attack on the United States Capitol, Transcribed Interview of Richard Peter Donoghue, (Oct. 1, 2021), p. 176.

147. Select Committee to Investigate the January 6th Attack on the United States Capitol, Informal Interview of Robert Engel, (Mar. 4, 2022).

148. For further details of the SUV incident, see Chapter 7.

149. See Executive Summary and Chapter 7.

150. Documents on file with the Select Committee to Investigate the January 6th Attack on the United States Capitol (Secret Service Production), CTRL0000882478.

151. Documents on file with the Select Committee to Investigate the January 6th Attack on the United States Capitol (Secret Service Production), CTRL0000496064.

152. Documents on file with the Select Committee to Investigate the January 6th Attack on the United States Capitol (Secret Service Production), CTRL0000208061.

153. Select Committee to Investigate the January 6th Attack on the United States Capitol, Transcribed Interview of Muriel Bowser, (Jan. 12, 2022), pp. 6–7.

154. Select Committee to Investigate the January 6th Attack on the United States Capitol, Transcribed Interview of Steven Andrew Sund, (Apr. 20, 2022), p. 147.

155. Select Committee to Investigate the January 6th Attack on the United States Capitol, Transcribed Interview of David Bowdich, (Dec. 16, 2021), pp. 111–12.

156. Select Committee to Investigate the January 6th Attack on the United States Capitol, Transcribed Interview of David Bowdich, (Dec. 16, 2021), pp. 111–12.

157. Select Committee to Investigate the January 6th Attack on the United States Capitol, Transcribed Interview of Valerie Hasberry, (Apr. 14, 2022), pp. 59–61.

158. Select Committee to Investigate the January 6th Attack on the United States Capitol, Transcribed Interview of Sean Gallagher, (Jan. 11, 2022), p. 15.

159. Select Committee to Investigate the January 6th Attack on the United States Capitol, Transcribed Interview of David Bowdich, (Dec. 16, 2021), pp. 8, 9, 22–25.

160. Select Committee to Investigate the January 6th Attack on the United States Capitol, Transcribed Interview of Steven Andrew Sund, (Apr. 20, 2022), p. 155.

161. Select Committee to Investigate the January 6th Attack on the United States Capitol, Transcribed Interview of Yogananda Pittman, (Jan. 13, 2022), p. 72.

162. Select Committee to Investigate the January 6th Attack on the United States Capitol, Transcribed Interview of Yogananda Pittman, (Jan. 13, 2022), pp. 73–74.

163. Select Committee to Investigate the January 6th Attack on the United States Capitol, Transcribed Interview of Yogananda Pittman, (Jan. 13, 2022), pp. 73–74.

164. Select Committee to Investigate the January 6th Attack on the United States Capitol, Transcribed Interview of Robert Glover, (May 2, 2022), p. 80.

165. Select Committee to Investigate the January 6th Attack on the United States Capitol, Transcribed Interview of Robert Glover, (May 2, 2022), p. 77.

166. Select Committee to Investigate the January 6th Attack on the United States Capitol, Transcribed Interview of Steven Andrew Sund, (Apr. 20, 2022), p. 154.

167. Select Committee to Investigate the January 6th Attack on the United States Capitol, Transcribed Interview of Christopher Rodriguez, (Jan. 25, 2022), p. 64.

168. Select Committee to Investigate the January 6th Attack on the United States Capitol, Transcribed Interview of Muriel Bowser, (Jan. 12, 2022), p. 17.

169. Select Committee to Investigate the January 6th Attack on the United States Capitol, Transcribed Interview of Muriel Bowser, (Jan. 12, 2022), p. 17.

170. Select Committee to Investigate the January 6th Attack on the United States Capitol, Transcribed Interview of Muriel Bowser, (Jan. 12, 2022), p. 17.

171. Select Committee to Investigate the January 6th Attack on the United States Capitol, Transcribed Interview of Muriel Bowser, (Jan. 12, 2022), pp. 16-17.

172. Select Committee to Investigate the January 6th Attack on the United States Capitol, Transcribed Interview of Richard Peter Donoghue, (Oct. 1, 2021), p. 176.

173. Select Committee to Investigate the January 6th Attack on the United States Capitol, Transcribed Interview of Richard Peter Donoghue, (Oct. 1, 2021), p. 176.

174. United States Secret Service Radio Tango Channel, Jan. 6, 2021. Select Committee staff reviewed recordings of this radio frequency.

175. United States Secret Service Radio Tango Channel, Jan. 6, 2021. Select Committee staff reviewed recordings of this radio frequency.

176. Select Committee to Investigate the January 6th Attack on the United States Capitol, Transcribed Interview of Timothy Giebels, (Apr. 8, 2022), p. 54.

177. Select Committee to Investigate the January 6th Attack on the United States Capitol, Transcribed Interview of Timothy Giebels, (Apr. 8, 2022), p. 54.

178. United States Secret Service Radio Tango Channel, Jan. 6, 2021. Select Committee staff reviewed recordings of this radio frequency.

179. Select Committee to Investigate the January 6th Attack on the United States Capitol, Transcribed Interview of Timothy Giebels, (Apr. 8, 2022), pp. 72–73.

180. Documents on file with the Select Committee to Investigate the January 6th Attack on the United States Capitol (District of Columbia Production), CTRL0000070377 (recording of Metropolitan Police Department, Radio Transmission, from 1400–1500 hours).

181. Select Committee to Investigate the January 6th Attack on the United States Capitol, Transcribed Interview of Robert Glover, (May 2, 2022), pp. 61–62.

182. Select Committee to Investigate the January 6th Attack on the United States Capitol, Transcribed Interview of Richard Peter Donoghue, (Oct. 1, 2021), pp. 179–80.

183. Select Committee to Investigate the January 6th Attack on the United States Capitol, Transcribed Interview of Richard Peter Donoghue, (Oct. 1, 2021), p. 180.

184. Select Committee to Investigate the January 6th Attack on the United States Capitol, Transcribed Interview of Richard Peter Donoghue, (Oct. 1, 2021), pp. 180–81.

185. Select Committee to Investigate the January 6th Attack on the United States Capitol, Transcribed Interview of David Bowdich, (Dec. 16, 2021), p. 111; Select Committee to Investigate the January 6th Attack on the United States Capitol, Transcribed Interview of Richard Donoghue, (Oct. 1, 2021), p. 181.

186. Select Committee to Investigate the January 6th Attack on the United States Capitol, Transcribed Interview of Richard Donoghue, (Oct. 1, 2021), p. 182.

187. Select Committee to Investigate the January 6th Attack on the United States Capitol, Transcribed Interview of Jeffrey A. Rosen, (Oct. 13, 2021), p. 176.

188. Select Committee to Investigate the January 6th Attack on the United States Capitol, Transcribed Interview of David Bowdich, (Dec. 16, 2021), pp. 113–14.

189. Select Committee to Investigate the January 6th Attack on the United States Capitol, Transcribed Interview of David Bowdich, (Dec. 16, 2021), pp. 113–14.

190. Select Committee to Investigate the January 6th Attack on the United States Capitol, Transcribed Interview of David Bowdich, (Dec. 16, 2021), p. 114.

191. Select Committee to Investigate the January 6th Attack on the United States Capitol, Transcribed Interview of David Bowdich, (Dec. 16, 2021), p. 114.

192. "Video Shows Pelosi Trying to Secure the Capitol," *New York Times*, (Oct. 13, 2022), available at https://www.nytimes.com/video/us/politics/100000008581029/jan-6-pelosi-video.html.

193. Select Committee to Investigate the January 6th Attack on the United States Capitol, Transcribed Interview of Muriel Bowser, (Jan. 12, 2022), p. 15.

194. Documents on file with the Select Committee to Investigate the January 6th Attack on the United States Capitol (Department of Defense Production), PRODUCTION 1—000017.

195. "D.C. Mayor Muriel Bowser Press Conference on Capitol Protests Transcript January 6," Rev, (Jan. 6, 2021), available at https://www.rev.com/blog/transcripts/d-c-mayor-muriel-bowser-press-conference-on-capitol-protests-transcript-january-6.

196. Select Committee to Investigate the January 6th Attack on the United States Capitol, Transcribed Interview of Muriel Bowser, (Jan. 12, 2022), p. 7.

197. Select Committee to Investigate the January 6th Attack on the United States Capitol, Transcribed Interview of Jeffrey Rosen, (Oct. 13, 2021), p. 182.

198. Select Committee to Investigate the January 6th Attack on the United States Capitol, Transcribed Interview of Jeffrey Rosen, (Oct. 13, 2021), pp. 182–83.

199. Select Committee to Investigate the January 6th Attack on the United States Capitol, Transcribed Interview of Timothy Giebels, (Apr. 8, 2022), p. 82.

200. Documents on file with the Select Committee to Investigate the January 6th Attack on the United States Capitol (Secret Service Production), CTRL0000512238 (January 6, 2021, email at 4:42 p.m. noting "Hoosier going to call chief of Capital [sic] Police").

201. Select Committee to Investigate the January 6th Attack on the United States Capitol, Transcribed Interview of Richard Peter Donoghue, (Oct. 1, 2021), p. 190. Donoghue memorialized this call in handwritten notes. *See* Documents on file with the Select Committee to Investigate the January 6th Attack on the United States Capitol (Department of Justice Production), HCOR-Jan6-07222021-000614 (January 6, 2021, handwritten notes by Richard Donoghue, 7:00 p.m.).

202. Documents on file with the Select Committee to Investigate the January 6th Attack on the United States Capitol (Department of Justice Production), HCOR-Jan6-07222021-000614 (January 6, 2021, handwritten notes by Richard Donoghue, 7:00 pm.).

203. Select Committee to Investigate the January 6th Attack on the United States Capitol, Transcribed Interview of David Bowdich, (Dec. 16, 2021), p. 116.

204. Documents on file with the Select Committee to Investigate the January 6th Attack on the United States Capitol (Department of Justice Production), HCOR-Jan6-07222021-000614 (January 6, 2021, handwritten notes by Richard Donoghue, 7:00 pm.)

205. Select Committee to Investigate the January 6th Attack on the United States Capitol, Transcribed Interview of Richard Peter Donoghue, (Oct. 1, 2021), p. 191.

206. Documents on file with the Select Committee to Investigate the January 6th Attack on the United States Capitol (District of Columbia production), CTRL0000930981 (Memo: Final January 6th After Action Quick Look Report, Government of the District of Columbia Fire and Emergency Medical Services Department. May 19, 2022).

207. United States Government Accountability Office, *CAPITOL ATTACK: Additional Actions Needed to Better Prepare Capitol Police Officers for Violent Demonstrations*, 117th Cong., 2d sess. (March 2022), available at https://www.gao.gov/assets/gao-22-104829.pdf.

APPENDIX 2

DC NATIONAL GUARD PREPARATION FOR AND RESPONSE TO JANUARY 6TH

INTRODUCTION

H. Res. 503 Section 4(a) directs the Select Committee to examine the "facts, circumstances, and causes relating to the domestic terrorist attack on the Capitol," including the "activities of intelligence agencies, law enforcement agencies, and the Armed Forces, including with respect to intelligence collection, analysis, and dissemination and information sharing among the branches and other instrumentalities of government." This appendix focuses on the activities of the DC National Guard in the days leading up to and on January 6, 2021.

In contrast to the National Guard units in 50 States and three territories, where deployment authority lies with the governor of those respective jurisdictions, the DC Guard falls directly under the command of the United States President. In the discussion section below, this appendix provides a narrative of the preparations for and eventual deployment of the DC Guard on January 6th, and the interaction between then-President Trump and the DC Guard in the relevant time period. It is based on the Select Committee's interviews of 24 witnesses and review of over 37,000 pages of documents.

DISCUSSION

A "GUT-WRENCHING" SUMMER

The approval process for the deployment of the DC National Guard is unique, unlike any of the 50 States or three territories across the country where ultimate authority rests in the hands of the governor.[1] In the nation's capital, where no governorship exists, the Guard is ultimately under the command of the President of the United States when acting in its militia capacity to support civil authorities.[2] By executive order, however, President Richard Nixon delegated the President's day-to-day control of the DC Guard to the Secretary of Defense and specified that its Commanding General should report to the Secretary of Defense or the Secretary's designee.[3] By memorandum, the Secretary of Defense, in turn, delegated day-to-day control of the DC Guard to the Secretary of the Army.[4] The commander of the DC Guard reported directly to the Secretary of the Army on January 6, 2021.[5]

During the 2020 summer protests in response to the murder of George Floyd,[6] the approval process for Guard deployment ran smoothly. "Very, very proactive," then-Commanding General of the DC Guard William

Walker said.[7] Secretary of the Army Ryan McCarthy "really wanted us out there."[8] Secretary McCarthy, with all his authorities, was physically beside Major General Walker throughout that summer. "[H]e was with me for all of it," Major General Walker said.[9] "He came to the [A]rmory every day. He brought his staff with him."[10] As has been widely reported, a number of President Trump's senior advisors, including Attorney General Bill Barr, resisted President Trump's requests to deploy the Guard or other troops in various states and cities where violence had occurred or was underway.[11]

In the summer of 2020, nothing was being written down; it "was just all verbal back and forth."[12] That approach sped up response times. But as the DC Guard footprint grew and controversies began plaguing the operation, Secretary McCarthy came away with the lesson that deliberative and by written order beat fast and by oral command.[13]

"What we learned in the process was we were not capturing a lot of the information in writing in the orders process, which is fundamental, foundational because of the stress of the situation and the speed of the situation," Secretary McCarthy said.[14]

While a concept of operations ("con-op") was developed at the lower level during the summer 2020 operations, it did not require approval or input at the secretary level.[15] That approach came to be seen as a mistake that should not be replicated the next time there was a civil disturbance crisis in the nation's capital. General Walter Piatt, director of the Army staff, explained: "That's where Secretary McCarthy put that restriction to say, I want a concept of the operation before we just send a force to do something."[16]

One of the most visible and highly criticized of the summer 2020 operations was the use of low-flying helicopters that appeared to be bearing down on protesters with the aim of dispersing them. On June 1st, as Guard presence tripled overnight, the use of helicopters meant for aerial surveillance[17] "somehow got translated to a very competent Army officer that 'I am to fly low and loud to deter looters,'" General Piatt said.[18] "[W]hat the investigation revealed was that we did not have good procedures in place to provide military support to a very serious civil disturbance ongoing. The—because—the pilot of that aircraft believed that was his mission."[19]

The "embarrass[ment]"[20] of the low-flying helicopter affected Secretary McCarthy. General Charles Flynn, then-deputy chief of staff for operations, plans, and training, told the Select Committee, "I know the Secretary was concerned."[21] He further explained: "I'm sure that affected his thinking."[22]

Secretary McCarthy became convinced that a concept of operations needed to be "explicit, tailored"[23] and—most importantly—that it needed to "come from [the] top down."[24] Secretary McCarthy told his staff,

"[W]hen we get a request next time, we have to be absolutely certain that we understand the mission clearly,"[25] and that "no other civil authority could re-mission off that support without the approval of either the Secretary of the Army or, in certain circumstances, the Secretary of Defense."[26]

In mid-June 2020, then-Secretary of Defense Mark Esper, Secretary McCarthy, Chairman of the Joint Chiefs of Staff General Mark Milley, and Major General Walker huddled to talk about what went wrong in the preceding weeks. Senior defense officials then decided they would take a "more active" role in directing the force.[27] "[A]s a result, we all took a more active interest in what was happening down to the tactical level to make sure that we were, again, abiding by kind of the core principles of civil-military relations," former Secretary Esper said.[28]

Major General Walker said he was not told about that shift in perspective: "[I]f the Army thought different of how we respond to civil unrest, civil disturbance, I would hope . . . they would communicate that with the guy—with the person who is going to execute that change."[29]

In the words of General Milley, the summer of 2020 had been "a pretty gut-wrenching experience."[30] The Department of Defense was still recovering when it was faced with the decision of the manner and degree to which the DC Guard should provide assistance to law enforcement authorities planning, just seven months later, for the events anticipated in connection with Congressional certification of the electoral votes on January 6, 2021.

A "Tailored" Request for Guard Resources. On December 19, 2020, President Trump tweeted, "Big protest in DC on January 6th. Be there! Will be wild!" From that day forward, a rookie DC intelligence analyst saw a tenfold uptick in violent rhetoric targeting Congress and law enforcement.[31] Right-wing groups were sharing histories of violence and some not traditionally aligned had begun coordinating their efforts.[32] The analyst's report reached more senior DC leadership, including, eleven days later, Mayor Bowser.[33] In the course of the Committee's investigation, it received and reviewed a significant number of documents indicating that certain intelligence and law enforcement agencies understood that violence was possible or even likely on January 6th. The Committee received many of those materials from the U.S. Secret Service, but also from other agencies as well.

On Thursday, December 31, 2020, the day after the briefing, Mayor Bowser sent a letter to Major General Walker requesting Guard assistance for January 5 and 6, 2021.[34] A second letter specified the District's request as limited to two forms of assistance: crowd management at Metro stations and blocking vehicles at traffic posts. It did not request help with potential civil disturbance.[35]

General Piatt viewed the "limited request" [36] as a "pretty good, tailored mission," that was "not vague." [37] General James McConville, chief of staff of the Army, called the request appropriately "restricted" [38] with "a very low military signature." [39]

According to testimony by Defense Department witnesses, after a summer of perceived overreach, military leadership was grateful for the delineated parameters set by the city itself.

The substance of the request—limited to traffic and crowd control "so they could have more police officers to do police functions" [40]—was not seen as narrow by District officials. "I would say it's a specific request," Chief of DC Police (Metropolitan Police Department ("MPD")) Robert Contee said. [41] "[L]eave the unlawful stuff, leave that to the police to deal with." [42] Mayor Bowser said: "I don't know any law enforcement person who would suggest that urban disturbances aren't best handled by the police." [43]

"Civil disturbance was not something we requested at that time. Mostly also because the vast majority of the, if not all, of the permitted protests were taking place on Federal lands," said Director of the DC Homeland Security and Emergency Management Agency Christopher Rodriguez. [44] The District had no jurisdiction. "Mayor Bowser cannot make a request on behalf of the White House or on behalf of the Capitol for U.S. Capitol—for . . . DC National Guardsmen to deploy to those two entities. She can't," Chief Contee said. [45] At this time, it was well known that President Trump had planned a speech and rally on "Federal lands"—on the Ellipse south of the White House. It was not widely known that President Trump intended to "spontaneously" instruct the tens of thousands of supporters at that Ellipse rally to march down Pennsylvania Avenue to the Capitol. [46]

Five Days of "Tremendous Resistance". At first, Secretary McCarthy was not sold on involving the Guard at all. Major General Walker called Secretary McCarthy "instantly when I got the letters" from the District on Thursday, December 31st, and "initially I felt I must have caught him at a bad time." [47] Secretary McCarthy recalls it being a short conversation. "I said, 'okay, got it. Thank you.' You want to immediately flip it so that Secretary of Defense knows that we alerted his office," he said. [48]

According to Major General Walker's account of this call, the Secretary initially stated "'We're not doing it,'" [49] and then left the door open for further discussion. Major General Walker explained: "'I said, 'Well, sir, I think you should look at it.' And then he told me, 'Well, we'll talk about it, but we don't really want to do this, because the look it would give, the military out there interfering.' . . . He says, 'Well, we'll discuss it on Monday.'" [50]

On Sunday, January 3rd, Secretary McCarthy called Chief Contee, who had formally assumed the role of acting head of MPD just the day before.[51]

"I thought initially that . . . he is just calling me basically as a rubber stamp to say, . . . 'You asked for it, you got it.' . . . It didn't go that way," Chief Contee said.[52] "[H]e had concerns about deploying National Guard for this event. He talked about the optics of the event, having boots on the ground. . . . And I pushed back on that."[53]

In his interview with the Select Committee, Secretary McCarthy described evaluating the request on the evening of January 3rd. "I sat at home. I chewed on it," he said.[54] "You know, I'm not particularly inclined to support it, because my concern was really we didn't have a command-and-control architecture in place. We didn't really have all of the mechanisms to be successful, you know. . . . So it was a very tough decision for me."[55]

Over five days, from December 31st to January 4th, District officials faced what Major General Walker called "tremendous resistance."[56]

Both Chief Contee and Director Rodriguez recalled that five-day period on January 6th, when Chief Steven Sund, of the U.S. Capitol Police, was pleading for reinforcements.[57] Acting Defense Secretary Christopher Miller, "heard through the grapevine that [Secretary McCarthy] was inclined—I don't want to say inclined to disapprove, but, you know, looking at it carefully or whatever. So—but that's fine. He can do whatever he wants. I knew that I was going to honor [the mayor's] request . . . ."[58]

How close those Guard assets could go to the Capitol became a sticking point. Colonel Craig Hunter, the highest-ranking commander on the ground on January 6th, said the Army "really want[ed] to go through the concept of operations to see, okay, exactly—basically Metro stop by Metro stop, intersection by intersection, to see where will Guardsmen be exactly, you know, how close are you to the Capitol . . . ."[59] He said an initial request by MPD to post Guard troops at the South Capitol Metro station—like all other Metro stations—was denied.[60] In conference calls that "went back and forth,"[61] Major General Walker was told, "There was a concern about being too close, military uniforms too close to the Capitol."[62]

Major General Walker had a different perspective. He saw his people as "citizen soldiers," "your neighbors that are going to come to your aid and rescue when you need us,"[63]—not traditional boots on the ground. "[T]hat's where, to me, the vest came in. This was the National Guard, not the Army," he said.[64]

Military authorities determined that a geographical boundary would have to be established as a condition of approving the Guard's deployment to assist MPD. No servicemember could go east of Ninth Street. It wasn't made explicit to District officials, but they all knew what lay east. "[T]he

Capitol is east," Chief Contee said.[65] "[I]f you move them anywhere east of Ninth Street, they will be close to the Capitol. That was certainly the way I understood it."[66]

Director Rodriguez worried "that it constrained our ability to react quickly if the situation got out of hand."[67] Without the limitation, the District fully intended to post its resources farther east: "[W]e couldn't get as close to the Capitol as could have been helpful," Mayor Bowser said.[68] "[W]e would have had a broader traffic box."[69]

Fears of Politicizing the Military in an Antidemocratic Manner. Both Acting Secretary Miller and Secretary McCarthy were sensitive to the sight of troops near the site of the Congressional certification of electoral votes, because of President Trump's previous expression of interest in using Federal troops in civilian situations. Again, Attorney General Barr and other members of the Trump Administration had resisted President Trump's desire to deploy such troops. Secretary Esper said it "tended to be the case . . . that the President was inclined to use the military," contrary to longstanding principles of reserving the armed forces as a last resort.[70]

According to his testimony, Acting Secretary Miller's express first priority—after being installed with just two months left in the Trump administration—was "to make every effort to return the Department of Defense to a nonpoliticized entity," because previously, "the Department was being showcased too much."[71] In testimony to the U.S. House Committee on Oversight and Reform on May 12, 2021, he cited "fears that the President would invoke the Insurrection Act to politicize the military in an antidemocratic manner" as shaping his thinking.[72] "No such thing was going to occur on my watch," he wrote,[73] later adding that "if I would have put troops on Capitol Hill" before the attack and without a request from civil authorities, "that would have been seen as extremely provocative, if not supporting this crazy narrative that the military was going to try to overturn the election."[74]

Secretary McCarthy felt similar pressure. He had been taken aback when—as he was walking down the Pentagon's hallways—"one of the most seasoned reporters" asked him whether the Army was planning to seize ballot boxes.[75] It was "an incredibly tense period," according to Secretary McCarthy.[76] As our investigation has demonstrated, President Trump had considered proposals from Lt. General (ret.) Michael Flynn, Sidney Powell, and others that troops be utilized to seize ballot boxes in certain parts of the country.

On December 18, 2020—the same day as the contentious White House meeting with Flynn and others,—Secretary McCarthy issued a statement, "mirror[ing] what General Milley said about a month before,"[77] reiterating that "There is no role for the U.S. military in determining the outcome of an

American election." [78] Given the heat of the rhetoric, he thought, "[I]f we don't say anything, it's going to scare people." [79] Secretary McCarthy told the Select Committee he thought he would be fired after publicly stating that the military would not assist in a coup.[80] General McConville, who signed the statement alongside Secretary McCarthy's signature,[81] linked their words directly to the Ninth Street limitation: "[T]here was no plan to put any military anywhere near the Capitol because of what we had said, the military has no role in determining the outcome of elections." [82]

On January 1st, Executive Officer to Secretary McCarthy Colonel John Lubas wrote in an internal email that the Secretary "wants to clearly communicate that this request is NOT from the White House." [83] The email noted that the Secretary wanted to "aggressively message" that the request had come from District officials, not the President.[84]

"We wanted everybody to know that, because it would create confusion and even more tension of having soldiers on the street without a request and that they be near the Capitol with certification of an election, a contested election," Secretary McCarthy said.[85]

On January 3, 2021, 10 former Secretaries of Defense, including the recently fired, former Secretary Esper, published a joint op-ed warning that "[i]nvolving the military in election disputes would cross into dangerous territory." [86] Secretary McCarthy had himself worked for five of the 10 secretaries.[87] "I know all these [men]," he said.[88] "[T]hey were—everyone was telling us, be very conscious of your actions and how you—you know, what you're going to do that day. So we wanted to know where every soldier was by street corner." [89]

Was Secretary McCarthy concerned that President Trump might use the military to cling to power? "There was a lot of talk in the lead-up about martial law . . . and the employment of forces, and you know, that was something that we were all, you know, conscious of." [90] Our investigation suggests that those civilian and military officials who had considerable experience working directly with President Trump had genuine concerns about whether he would attempt to use the military to change the election results. Again, at this time, there is no evidence the Department of Defense understood exactly what President Trump and his associates planned for January 6th.

"Very Strict on the Use of the Military" on January 6th. By Monday, January 4th, with Secretary McCarthy now backing the operation, Acting Secretary Miller was briefed. He told the Select Committee that he "made the decision right there to honor the request." [91] That approval came with strings attached. The role of the DC Guard would be spelled out and tightly circumscribed in a memorandum that, as characterized by General Milley, was "very strict on the use of the military." [92] It decreed that without the Acting Secretary's "subsequent, personal authorization," the Guard would not be issued batons, helmets, or body armor; could not interact physically with protestors, except in self-defense; and that the Quick Reaction Force (QRF)—40 servicemembers staged in case of an emergency at Joint Base Andrews in Prince George's County, Maryland—could be deployed only as a last resort.[93]

Above the tactical level, changes in the mission of the Guard had to be approved by the Secretary of the Army and, in some cases—in order to "interact physically with protestors" or be issued batons—required running further up the chain to the Secretary of Defense.[94]

To District officials, that seemed new—and unnecessary. "[The Secretary told us,] if you send them to any other kind of mission, that has to get approval from me. And I just think that those were unnecessary restrictions . . ." Chief Contee said.[95]

What the QRF would be called upon to do, even in the case of an emergency, is a matter of debate. The letter and memorandum do not expressly note whether the QRF could be used to support the original mission of the Guard—traffic and crowd control—or a new mission helping contain sudden and out-of-hand civil disturbance.[96] The DC Guard official put in charge of the QRF for January 5th and 6th, Lieutenant Colonel David Reinke, said he had not been given much guidance as to their role.[97]

The Army and the DC Guard appear to have had different understandings. "[T]he intent of the quick reaction force was really to send these troops over to help if they had a problem at one of the traffic command posts," General McConville said.[98] "There never was an intent for a quick reaction force to go to the Capitol . . . ." [99] According to Army officials, without a con-op and a formal change in mission, the QRF could do traffic control and no more.

That was not how others imagined an emergency unit would or should operate. According to Major General Walker, "a quick reaction force, something's happening; do I have time to find you and call you and ask you?" [100] He called the preapproval language "highly unusual," [101] particularly as their name "already implied that it's a last resort," [102] their intended purpose was if "[u]nexpectedly, you have a spontaneous unrest," [103] and if "I need to write a concept of operations for a quick reaction force? They're no longer quick. It's just a reaction force." [104]

Capitol Police Board "Prepared" without Guard Help. It wasn't clear to everyone involved in planning for the events anticipated on January 6th that all agencies, including the Capitol Police, were deploying all their resources ahead of that day. "We had had issues understanding, getting the full picture of U.S. Capitol Police's operational posture and what their planning was," Director Rodriguez said.[105]

Mayor Bowser was struck when—right before the press briefing that Monday, January 4th—the mayor asked the Capitol Police representative, "[W]here does your perimeter start? [And h]e gets up out of the room, calls somebody. And the next thing I know he can't participate in the conference."[106] She elaborated: "[T]hat should have been like a trigger to me. Like these people, they don't want to answer questions about their preparation."[107]

On the morning of January 3rd, Capitol Police Chief Steven Sund approached two of the members of the Capitol Police Board and purportedly requested—but concededly did not push for—Guard resources for the Capitol.[108] According to Chief Sund, in a minutes long meeting in the office of House Sergeant at Arms Paul Irving, Irving told Chief Sund he did not like the optics of asking for the Guard in advance and that the intelligence did not support it.[109] Chief Sund said he did not push back on either point.[110] In fact, he agreed that his reading of the intelligence—despite a forewarning put out by his own intelligence unit that "Congress was itself the target" on January 6th[111]—did not call for Guard support,[112] only that having more personnel on his perimeter would make him "more comfortable."[113] Irving suggested he talk to the Senate Sergeant at Arms, and then-chairman of the Capitol Police Board, Michael Stenger.[114] According to Irving, Stenger, in a meeting in his office, asked Chief Sund to reach out to the Guard and find out, if an emergency called for it, "how many people can [the commanding general] give us and how quickly can he give us those people?"[115] Chief Sund said he took their responses to mean "no," despite conceding that he was never told "you cannot have the National Guard" or anything to that effect.[116] "It was 100 percent a denial," he maintained.[117]

Irving recalled the matter coming up on a three-way phone conference during which "the consensus was that we didn't need" the Guard.[118] He did not consider it a request.[119] On the call, Chief Sund noted that the District planned to use the servicemembers to staff intersections, but the Capitol grounds had few of those, and it would not relieve many officers if they were used in a similar fashion.[120] "It was a combination of operationally the chief didn't feel that they would add much to his plan, and the intelligence really didn't speak for anything that we felt would justify the need for them," Irving said.[121] Irving doesn't recall taking the "optics" into consideration.[122] According to Irving, the conversation ended the same way Chief Sund said it had: "Why don't you just tell them to be on standby?" Stenger suggested.[123] It was never brought up again.[124]

The discussion about the use of the Guard remained within the Capitol Police Board and did not reach congressional leadership, including the Speaker of the House. That was normal. "[F]rom a tactical perspective, we would make decisions without the input from congressional leadership,"

Irving said.[125] "I always felt that I had full authority to implement security decisions as I deemed appropriate."[126] In fact, when the three men briefed congressional leaders on January 5th, Chief Sund conveyed the same optimistic outlook as he had with Major General Walker: "[We told them] we felt we were prepared based on the information we had, yes," he said.[127]

To keep these exchanges in perspective, we note again that we are aware of no evidence that these individuals were privy to President Trump's plans to instruct tens of thousands of his supporters to walk down Pennsylvania Avenue to the Capitol to help "take back" their country. Nor were they aware of how President Trump would suggest to his followers that Vice President Pence had the authority to change the outcome of the election, or how President Trump would behave in the hours that followed. Certain members of Congress, including those who met at the White House on December 21, 2020, may have had considerably more insight into President Trump's planning, but the Committee has no information suggesting that any of those members alerted the Capitol Police or other authorities of President Trump's plans.

Soldiers Prepare for the Worst in Secret. Guard reinforcements could draw from a pool of three groups already activated for the day: (1) the 40 members making up the QRF, staged in Maryland;[128] (2) the 90 members at the traffic control points, 24 at the Metro stations, and four as part of the command staff distributed throughout the city—but no farther east than Ninth Street—for a total of 118 representing the first shift;[129] and (3) the second shift of another 118 members,[130] preparing at the Armory in Southeast Washington, D.C, for a 3:00 p.m. shift takeover.[131] The Armory also housed a command-and-control squad that handled logistics at about 52 members strong, in addition to a Civil Support Team of about 20 members.[132] That gave Colonel Hunter a maximum limit of 348 activated servicemembers, eight more than the allotted 340—nearly all of whom reported directly to him on January 6th.[133]

The QRF was most prepared for responding to sudden and escalating civil unrest. At Joint Base Andrews, they were provisioned with full riot-control kits,[134] including a helmet with a face shield already attached, protective vest, shin guards, knee guards, shield, and baton.[135] The head of the QRF—himself provided little guidance on the contours of his mission—had his squad train for civil disturbance on January 5th and the morning of the 6th as they waited.[136] Not only had they trained, but they trained *together*, as a unit—a benefit military officials all agreed is ideal. Army leadership, all the way up to Secretary McCarthy,[137] had no idea that Lt. Col. Reinke had taken these initiatives. Secretary McCarthy agreed that had he known of their civil disturbance preparation, "it could have" affected the speed with which approval was ultimately given for their deployment.[138]

As to the second group of available resources—the servicemembers stationed at traffic control points since the early morning of January 6th—Army leadership held misconceptions about what equipment was available to them. Secretary McCarthy had agreed that some gear—expressly not batons—could remain stowed away in vehicle trunks.[139] Colonel Hunter had his troops put the gear into a white box truck instead and designated a rally point for the truck that would be central to all traffic control points.[140] On the night of January 5th, in anticipation of January 6th, Colonel Hunter had his troops move the civil disturbance gear—including the prohibited batons—into the individual vehicles themselves.[141] Captain Tarp, the head of the second shift, agreed that they were told to load the equipment into their vehicles "on the down low. Done so it wasn't visible, so it wouldn't look like we were escalating [our] role."[142]

The commanding general of the DC Guard was aware that the troops had all they needed in their trunks and—in the case of an emergency—would not need to return to the Armory to get it: "They already had it," Major General Walker said.[143]

But Army leadership did not know that. Although General Piatt said "We never asked, like, what was actually—I have no knowledge of what they [actually] had in" the vehicles,[144] the guidance from Secretary McCarthy's letter led him to believe that "weapons, ammunition, batons, shields, kneepads, other protection that we may be asked to do for civil disturbance, that was not [there]—because they were specifically told they would not participate in that mission . . . ."[145] Secretary McCarthy said, "The only thing I authorized General Walker to do was their ballistic helmets and body armor in the vehicle, not their shields or their riot batons."[146] He figured his orders had been followed.[147] When asked why he was not aware of the moves the Guard had made, Secretary McCarthy said, "I mean, I made a mistake. I think a local unit commander was anticipating more than what potentially we were prepared for."[148]

DC Guard leadership understood that loading this equipment flouted direct orders. "I wasn't going to have my soldiers unprepared," Major General Walker said.[149] The prohibition on batons, in particular, had been sent 54 minutes after the Guard had already begun their traffic control shifts on the morning of January 5th.[150]

The third group of available resources—the servicemembers awaiting at the Armory to take over as the second shift at the traffic control points—had equipment accessible to them at headquarters. Captain Tarp did note that it took time to ensure that the Armory equipment was in working order: repairing straps that were broken, wiping off dirt on the shields because "they were the same from the George Floyd protests," and affixing the helmet to the shields, which took upwards of 20 to 30 minutes.[151] In the three different locations where the Guard was stationed as the Capitol was being breached, all servicemembers had access to full civil disturbance gear right there with them.

Outside of the QRF, which had recently returned from two days of training together, there is debate as to how ready the rest of the Guard was to engage in civil disturbance response on January 6th. The notion that the military is not primed or naturally skilled to deal with civil disturbance appears to stand in tension with National Guard traditions, training, and doctrine. "They were not missioned, tasked, organized, equipped to do civil disturbance operations," General Flynn said.[152] Although General Piatt conceded that "[a]ll soldiers are trained in civil disturbance," he maintained that on "that day we were not postured to do civil disturbance operations."[153]

Major General Walker—who pointed out that the DC Guard shield, on Guard troop uniforms, features the Capitol building itself: "Protect the Capitol. That's why Thomas Jefferson created it"[154]—called civil disturbance "foundational" to what they do.[155]

DC Ground Commander Takes Initiative. On January 5th, as he led his forces in traffic control, Colonel Hunter did not observe activity that raised concerns.[156] But by the next morning—as thousands of out-of-towners invited by President Trump descended on the nation's capital—that all changed. "I could see like the Proud Boys," he said.[157] "I could see different people with Kevlars on, with bulletproof vests on. You know, they're all kitted up and they're wearing different patches and colors. And I said, 'Well, this crowd is definitely different . . . .' "[158] This, of course, was an indication of the potential for violence in the hours that followed.

Colonel Hunter, sitting at the intersection of 15th Street and Pennsylvania Avenue, saw crowds flowing past him and his soldiers toward the Capitol—walking as one, chanting as one. "Hey, is it that way to the Capitol? Where's the Capitol?" some asked.[159] Colonel Hunter got in his car and began writing an update report.[160]

He was interrupted by a soldier who had been watching CNN on his phone: "Hey, sir, I think there's been shots fired at the Capitol."[161] It was then that Colonel Hunter began to put a plan in place for the redeployment of the Guard. "So at that point in my mind I said, 'Okay, then they will be requesting the DC National Guard now, so we have to move."[162] The time was 2:12 p.m.[163]

The first thing he did was designate a rally point for DC Guard reinforcements.[164] Over the radio, he relayed the rally point to all 118 members currently spread across the city doing traffic control, and one by one, in order by their points, they called in to acknowledge where they would go once approval came down.[165] At 2:17 p.m., he called Lt. Col. Reinke, the head of the 40-strong QRF, and ordered his subordinate to "have all of your guys put their gear on and get on the bus."[166] "In my mind, this is about to happen really fast," he said.[167] "As soon as I make one call, I will get clearance to go and support. The United States Capitol was breached. I mean, this is unheard of."[168] Accordingly, he advised Lt. Col. Reinke that, "[W]e will be getting a call soon."[169]

He next tried to find the incident command post. He ran into the Assistant MPD Chief Jeffery Carroll, piled into a car and, sirens flipped on, sped off to U.S. Capitol Police headquarters.[170]

Once there, they got into the elevator, and "before the doors even closed," Assistant Chief Carroll asked him, "How many do you have coming right now?"[171] Colonel Hunter said, "I'm working on it. I need to make some calls, but we are—we're coming . . . . And I said, as soon as I start making these calls, I'm going to have so many National Guardsmen just flooding this way. I just need to have the location, have the plan set, be ready to receive them."[172]

No later than 2:50 p.m., Colonel Hunter had confirmed with Lt. Col. Reinke that the QRF was on the bus and ready.[173] The highest-ranking Guard official on the ground had sorted out all of the details and linked up with the law enforcement agencies that would lead them in support. At least 135 National Guard servicemembers—the 40 QRF members already in gear and on the bus and the 90 at traffic control posts awaiting word, with gear in their trunks to be donned at the rally point, along with four command staff plus Colonel Hunter himself—were ready to go. At 3:10 p.m., Colonel Hunter felt it was time to tell his superiors all that he had done and hopefully get fast approval.[174]

3 Hours and 19 Minutes At the Capitol, MPD Chief Contee was on the West Front, himself inhaling chemical agents—"you can smell it before you see it, felt it in my throat"[175]—as officers tried to resist rioters beating back the perimeter, having reached the stage built for the Inauguration set for two weeks later. "[T]he gas stuff and the spray, the mist that's in the air, I mean, it's real," he said.[176] "I'm trying to talk to the Mayor to give her a situational update, and the city administrator—I've got them both on the line. I'm coughing, trying to explain what's going on."[177] Chief Contee cut through the crowds of people around the Capitol to meet the mayor at MPD headquarters.[178]

Chief Sund said he reached out to House Sergeant at Arms Irving at 12:57 or 12:58 p.m., and told him, "We are getting overrun on the West Front by thousands. We need the National Guard now."[179] Irving recalled the call coming before a break in the electoral certification session just short of 1:30 p.m. and that the Chief said "that conditions were deteriorating outside and he *might* be making a request for the National Guard."[180]

Although Irving was firm in his stance that only the Capitol Police Board had the authority to request National Guard assistance, he nonetheless sought out the chief of staff to the Speaker to inform her of the impending request.[181] He did not need her to sign off, but "[a]ny change in security posture, given the time, I would give them a heads-up."[182]

The Speaker's chief of staff "immediately scribbled down a note" and went over to inform the Speaker—who was in the chair presiding over the floor debate on the Arizona objections—about the request for the National Guard.[183] "Absolutely. Go," Speaker Nancy Pelosi said.[184] Later, as they were evacuating the floor to an undisclosed location, the Speaker asked her, "Is the National Guard coming?"[185] The Speaker's chief of staff said, "Yes, we asked them."[186]

Irving said the formal request for Guard assistance came in a call after 2 p.m. from Chief Sund "and, of course, we said absolutely."[187] Chief Sund said he had made the request in that earlier 12:57 or 12:58 call and had been waiting for 71 minutes.[188] "I hung up the phone. I yelled across the command center, ['M]ark the time, 2:10, I finally got approval from the Capitol Police Board for the use of the National Guard,'" Chief Sund said.[189]

At around 2:30 p.m., Director Rodriguez patched Chief Contee—and a largely silent Mayor Bowser listening in[190]—into the conference call with Chief Sund and Major General Walker, who brought in General Piatt.[191] Major General Walker ordered his aide-de-camp on his second day on the job, Lt. Timothy Nick, to take handwritten notes of the call and the rest of the day.[192]

On the line at the Pentagon—gathered around the speaker of the Secretary of the Army's desk phone—were General Piatt, General McConville, and Secretary McCarthy.[193] According to Secretary McCarthy, it was during the call that he learned the Capitol had been breached,[194] watching it unfold in real time on television.[195] He didn't recall hearing Chief Sund's voice on the call, but said "we were trying to get . . . what we call the operational sight picture. What is going on? How big is the crowd? How violent is the crowd? . . . They started laying out really the—just how bad it was."[196] Secretary McCarthy resolved to run to the office of Acting Secretary of Defense Miller, leaving behind instructions to General Piatt to "find out the requirements," as he was "going to get the authority."[197] "[W]e go zipping down there," General McConville said.[198] As they were leaving, General Flynn showed up.[199]

General Flynn said, "when I came by the phone," he "heard voices screaming on the end."[200] He called the tones of their voices as "chaotic"[201] and that "[y]ou couldn't tell who was talking sometimes."[202] Chief Sund was pleading for help. "I want to say he even used the word, like, 'I am pleading,'" Chief Contee said.[203] Col. Matthews, listening in beside Major General Walker, said of Chief Sund: "His voice was cracking. He was almost crying." [204]

According to Chief Contee, the reaction to his pleas was "tepid." [205] "It was a very sluggish response," Chief Contee said.[206] "I remember just, you know, with all that was going on, not hearing a 'yes,' you know, just ... what I would in my mind qualify as, like, excuses and not decisive action ... I was hearing, like, all the reasons, you know, why we shouldn't be doing this." [207] Director Rodriguez called it a "kind of bureaucratic" response in the midst of "a rapidly evolving situation where literally the Capitol was being overrun." [208] He added: "I don't want to use the word disinterested, but more just, 'let's just hold on. Let's just wait. Let's just kind of calm down for a second while literally Rome is burning.'" [209]

For his part, General Flynn depicted General Piatt—the main interlocutor—as "the calming voice in an otherwise chaotic situation." [210] General McConville agreed: "I talked to some of my staff, and they said that General Piatt did an incredible job. He was like the—you know, in a very calm [voice], just saying, 'let's just settle ....'" [211]

But Major General Walker said he "just couldn't believe nobody was saying: 'Hey, go.'" [212] He asked the generals on the other line, "'Aren't you watching the news? Can't you see what's going on? We need to get there.' And [I was] cognizant of the fact that I'm talking to senior ... people, but I could see what was happening ...." [213] Chief Sund was "perplexed" and "dumbfounded." [214] "It wasn't what I expected of, yeah, the cavalry's coming. It was a bunch of, round-the-house, oh, hey, let's do this, let's do that," he said.[215] "I was borderline getting pretty pissed off." [216]

Many participants on the call say General Piatt's stated concern was the optics of sending troops to the site of a democratic process.

"[T]he infamous talk about optics. That came up again. There was talk about boots on the ground again. You know, that's not good optics, having boots on the ground," Chief Contee said.[217] He recalled how Secretary McCarthy had vocalized the same hesitance during the five-day deliberation preceding January 6th.[218]

Director Rodriguez believed General Piatt replied to the request by saying, "[W]e don't like the optics of having military personnel at the Capitol against peaceful protesters." [219]

He recalls Chief Contee replying bluntly, "[W]ell, they're not peaceful anymore." [220]

Major General Walker heard one of the Army generals say it "wouldn't be their best military advice or guidance to suggest to the Secretary that we have uniformed presence at the Capitol." [221] He added: "They were concerned about how it would look, the optics." [222] Chief Sund heard the general use the word twice.[223] "General Piatt said—and I will never forget this—'Yeah, I don't know. I'm concerned about the optics of the National Guard standing a line with the Capitol in the background,'" Chief Sund said.[224] "[M]y officers are getting beaten, and they're worried about the optics of the National Guard." [225]

Although General Piatt denies explicitly using the word "optics"—"I don't recall ever saying that word on that phone call, because at the time it just wasn't important" [226]—he agreed that he said use of the Guard was "not my best military judgment or my best military advice." [227] He said he "made a couple of suggestions that were not well-received," [228] including "if there was any other facility where we could go and relieve police . . . I think they took that as I was saying no, because they immediately came back and said, you're denying our request." [229]

General McConville—who wasn't present at the time—said he talked to people in the room about the use of the word "optics," and "some people said, 'No, it wasn't said.' And then some people said it was said." [230] Nonetheless, the sentiment behind it should not be a particularly controversial one, according to General McConville. "People like to use optics—I'm going to stay away because that's a political term in my eyes. But what type of signature do you want on the streets in Washington, DC? Do you want a police signature? Do you want a military signature? Do you want a Federal signature?" he said.[231] "[T]hat creates a reaction from the American people, and we need to think our way through that . . ." [232]

On the call, talk of needing a plan—the so-called con-op that had been a lesson learned from the summer—emerged. "[A]fter the optics, . . . then it was, you know, they wanted, like, specific information. There was something they were talking about, like, mission and . . . what exactly they're going to be doing when they get there," Chief Contee said.[233] Before running off, Secretary McCarthy had instructed General McConville to put together a plan: "My charter, my direction from him is to get a plan. We're gonna support; I just wanted to get something to support with." [234] But he acknowledged the impression nonetheless remained that he was "denying or pushing back." [235]

That impression was made explicit: "They said three times to me clearly, 'You're denying my request,'" General Piatt said.[236]

Chief Contee interrupted "Chief Sund mid-sentence" and said, "Wait a minute. Hold up. Let me make sure that I understand this correctly . . . [A]re you asking for support from the National Guard at the U.S. Capitol?" [237]

Chief Sund said, "Yes." [238]

Chief Contee then addressed the Army generals: "'Are you guys honoring his request?' I asked them that. And they didn't say 'no,' but they also didn't say 'yes.'"[239] Chief Sund recalled it the same way.[240]

General Piatt said he was "clear in my response, 'I don't have any authority to deny or approve. The Secretary is getting approval.'"[241]

"[T]he third time when they said, 'You're denying our request,' they also said, 'And we're going to go to the media,'" General Piatt said.[242] "[W]e were desperate. Everyone was desperate. So I'm not angry at that, but I just knew it wasn't helpful, so we told that to Secretary McCarthy."[243]

As for the threat to go public, Major General Walker said, "I remember that very clearly."[244] According to him, after the generals would not say yes or no, "Chief Contee says: 'I'm going to call the mayor and ask her to have a press conference saying that the Army is not going to allow the DC Guard to come and support.'"[245] General Piatt reportedly replied, "Please don't do that. I don't have the authority to authorize the National Guard to go. So please don't do that. Please don't hold the press conference."[246] Chief Contee doesn't recall saying that.[247] Mayor Bowser doesn't know if she was still on the line when the remark was made, but "it was certainly going to be something that I would do."[248]

In the end, "the call sort of ended very abruptly, ..."[249] The DC head of homeland security and emergency management left the call thinking "that help was not coming, and—at least [not] from the National Guard."[250] That was Chief Sund's belief, too. "[I]f a general says his troops are not coming, his troops aren't coming," he said.[251]

Before the call ended, General Flynn set up a video-conferencing bridge. General Piatt explained to the Select Committee that this was meant "to get the principals and the team together to start making a plan."[252] But Major General Walker—under whom "it was actually written . . . would maintain control of National Guard forces"[253]—said he was not privy to any planning while on the call.

"We were just told to hold," he said.[254]

How long did Major General Walker hold?

"Three hours and 19 minutes," he said.[255]

Major General Walker told the Select Committee regarding what occurred during this time. "[W]e all thought, it's in a minute, we're going to be told to go, in a minute. Then 5 minutes, then 10 minutes, then 15 minutes. We kept thinking, any minute now, somebody is going to say 'go,'" he said.[256] "And then an hour went by, then more time went by . . . . But we never thought it would take that long."[257] Col. Matthews confirmed that there were periods on the call when no one was talking.[258] At times, there was talk of securing buildings other than the Capitol.[259] He called the open channel essentially "a general officer chat line."[260]

What did Major General Walker think was happening in those 3 hours and 19 minutes?

"Delay." [261]

An Absent Commander-in-Chief. Vice President Mike Pence called several times to check in on the delayed response of the Guard. President Trump did not.

Vice President Pence called Acting Secretary Miller at least two times.[262] "He was very animated, and he issued very explicit, very direct, unambiguous orders. There was no question about that," General Milley said.[263] "And he said, 'Get the National Guard down here. Get them down here now, and clear the Capitol.' You know, and this is the Vice President of the United States. And there was other forceful language.'" [264]

Acting Secretary Miller clarified that "he did not order me," as "he's not in the chain of command," but he considered the talk with the Vice President "[h]yper professional" and "[v]ery focused," in which the secretary "highlighted that District of Columbia National Guard . . . was activated, and we were throwing every asset we could marshal to support law enforcement." [265]

In contrast, according to General Milley, Chief of Staff Meadows called and said, "'We have to kill the narrative that the Vice President is making all the decisions. We need to establish the narrative, you know, that the President is still in charge and that things are steady or stable,' or words to that effect. I immediately interpreted that as politics, politics, politics." [266]

President Trump himself did not call. As reports of Departments of Defense denials and delay were echoing in the media, no high-level Defense official—including Secretaries Miller [267] and McCarthy [268]—received a call from him that day.[269] At the time, General Milley thought that was "absolutely . . . highly unusual." [270]

"[Y]ou're the Commander in Chief. You've got an assault going on on the Capitol of the United States of America, and there's nothing? No call? Nothing? Zero?" he said.[271] "I grew up in an organization where commanders are responsible and take charge and they see situations unfolding and they issue orders and take charge." [272]

On January 3rd, at the end of a national security meeting concerning a foreign threat, the President asked "in passing" about January 6th preparations.[273] Acting Secretary Miller informed him they would be fulfilling Mayor Bowser's request for DC Guard support.[274] From then on, if not earlier, the secretary "felt like I had all the authorities I needed and did not need to discuss anything with the President regarding authorities." [275] The conversation lasted all of 30 seconds to a minute.[276] Secretary Miller testified that he never received any order at any time from President Trump to deploy the National Guard on January 6th. "There was no direct—there was no order from the President," he said.[277]

On January 5th, as demonstrators rallied in support of the President, Acting Secretary Miller received a call from the commander-in-chief.[278] The President asked him if he was watching the events on television.[279] The secretary told him he had caught some of the coverage.[280]

Unprompted, President Trump then said, "You're going to need 10,000 people" the following day, as in troops.[281] An email sent by Chief of Staff Meadows on January 5th explicitly noted that the DC Guard would be on hand to "protect pro Trump people."[282] The President and his staff appeared to be aware of the likelihood of violence on the day the election certification of his loss was slated to transpire. This communication from President Trump contemplated that the Guard could support and secure the safety of Trump supporters, not protect the Capitol. At that time, Secretary Miller apparently had no information on what President Trump planned for January 6th.

Acting Secretary Miller thought the 10,000 number was astronomical— "we expected 35,000 protesters . . . [and] even if there were more protesters than expected, [we thought] that local law enforcement could handle it"[283]—but, again, this was "no order from the President," just "President Trump banter that you all are familiar with."[284]

Parallel Plans in the Midst of Crisis. While the Army and the District engaged in the "heated"[285] 2:30 p.m. phone call, Secretary McCarthy was hurrying down the Pentagon hallways to Acting Secretary Miller's office. General Milley had been summoned there before Secretary McCarthy arrived with General McConville in tow,[286] "running down the hall, and he was actually winded when he showed up . . ."[287]

The next half hour was spent in "a quick, rapid fire meeting, [with] lots of quick questions."[288] Secretary McCarthy—out of breath—said he started by saying, "We've got to go. We've got to get something—we've got to put every capability we can up there."[289] The response he received was, "They were all kind of, like, 'Slow down. What's going on?' They wanted to get a sense of the situation."[290] Secretary McCarthy said it took about 15 to 20 minutes to "relay this," "laying out what I thought we needed to do."[291]

By 3:04 p.m., Acting Secretary Miller said he approved deployment of the DC Guard to assist law enforcement at the Capitol at that time.[292] Acting Secretary Miller did not understand why Major General Walker—if he felt the exigency demanded it—did not deploy troops as soon as his 3 p.m. order allowed it. "Why didn't he launch them? I'd love to know," he said.[293]

Secretary McCarthy agreed "*that's where we may have talked past each other in his office,*" because Secretary McCarthy thought he "had the authority as the Secretary of the Army" to conduct a mission analysis and send troops at *his* discretion, not that of Major General Walker.[294]

Major General Walker himself understood he had to wait for approval from Secretary McCarthy to deploy his forces. *But as he waited on that video call for hours, he did strongly consider sending them anyway.* He turned to his lawyer and said, "Hey, you know what? You know, we're going to go, and I'm just going to shoulder the responsibility."[295] According to Major General Walker, his lawyer responded, "What if you get sued?"[296] Colonel Mathews, that lawyer, "told him not to do that. Just hold on."[297] The Guard officials located with Major General Walker at the Armory all say he seriously contemplated aloud the possibility of breaking with the chain of command.

"Should we just deploy now and resign tomorrow?" was how Lieutenant Nick recalled Major General Walker bluntly putting it.[298]

"I would have done just that," Major General Walker said, "but not for those two letters"[299] from his superiors curtailing Guard redeployment.[300]

The man who signed one of the letters, however—himself a former member of the DC Guard[301]—now says Major General Walker should have moved forward regardless of whether he had proper authorization.

"I've launched QRF without approval more than once," Acting Secretary Miller said.[302] "If you're the person on the ground in the Army, and you realize that there's something that is unpredictable or unexpected and you have the ability to influence it, the culture, the training, the education, the expectation of you, the American people, is that you will execute and do what you can, even if it costs you your job."[303]

After authorization at 3:04 p.m., Secretary McCarthy said he gave Major General Walker a call. He told him to "[m]obilize the entire Guard, bring everybody in. . . . And I said, you know, move the QRF to the armory and get as many people as you can to the armory and configure them in a minimum of riot gear and batons. And then we're going to do a mission analysis of what we need to do with the police . . . ."[304] Major General Walker "categorically denies" that any such call took place.[305] In fact, Major General Walker said the two men did not talk at all until much later that night.[306] "Here's the bottom line. The Secretary was unavailable to me, and he never called me," Major General Walker said.[307]

Beginning around 3:00 p.m., 25 minutes of Secretary McCarthy's time was spent reassuring members of Congress that the Guard was indeed coming,[308] although he had not yet conveyed the order. That was time unspent on facilitating their actual coming. In addition to the alleged threat on the 2:30 p.m. call, a media tweet had gone out at 2:55 p.m. declaring that the Department of Defense had denied requests for Guard support.[309]

By 3:45 p.m., Secretary McCarthy was done with his calls and—after picking up some things from his office—headed down to the MPD headquarters to draft a con-op beside law enforcement.[310] Acting Secretary Miller arrived at 4:10 p.m.[311]

While he was waiting, Colonel Hunter decided he would keep the first shift handling traffic control out at their posts in case they were needed for re-mission by the MPD, relying instead only on the QRF and the second shift at the Armory to respond to the Capitol.[312] Those servicemembers ended up manning their traffic control posts up to 20 hours straight.[313] Army leadership never found out that the servicemembers at the traffic control posts didn't end up responding to the Capitol that night, incorrectly crediting some of the Guard's delay that day to their travel time.[314]

By 3:50 p.m., the QRF had arrived at the Armory, bringing their own equipment, given no new information upon making the extra pit stop there instead of the Capitol.[315] They were ready to go, steeped in "a lot of nerves." [316] The second shift of servicemembers originally missioned for traffic control had been told as early as 2:30 p.m. to expect a switch in mission to handling civil disturbance.[317] They rushed to gear up and prepare, but it was a lot of "hurry up and wait." [318] Not long afterward, "we're all ready. Now we're all donned. So go sit on the bleachers and wait . . . We were in a tight holding pattern until the time to deploy." [319]

At around the same time, at 3:49 p.m., Speaker Pelosi is heard in video footage from that day urging Acting Secretary Miller to hurry.

"Just pretend for a moment this was the Pentagon or the White House or some other entity that was under siege," she told him over the phone while she—and the rest of the Congressional leadership—were huddled in a secure location.[320] "Just get them there!" [321]

When Secretary McCarthy arrived at MPD headquarters, he joined Chief Contee, his Army Operations Director Brigadier General Chris LaNeve, and Assistant Chief Carroll by phone.[322]

In the next 20 minutes, Secretary McCarthy developed a con-op.

As Secretary McCarthy had decided after the summer, crafting a strategy was his job—"I was doing it with the Mayor, the police chief, and the deputy director of the FBI, my counterparts, and then ultimately wanted to understand what our role would be, the conditions"—and afterward, "we turned to [Major General Walker] to work the tactical details for that." [323]

But Major General Walker said, "If I need you to tell me how to execute a civil disturbance mission," he "[s]hould relieve me. Should fire me." [324]

It wasn't until later, post-January 6th, that Major General Walker said he found out that Secretary McCarthy, his boss, had been putting together a con-op—without him. "Then later they said they had to put together a plan for me to execute . . . which I found kind of disturbing," Major General Walker said.[325] "You're coming up with a plan without me being involved in the plan?"[326]

General McConville agreed that "usually[,] the Secretary of Army is not developing concepts for the employment, but because of the situation that wasn't done," so the secretary had to fill in the gap.[327] That, of course—given the preparations Colonel Hunter had laid out hours earlier—was not true. But Secretary McCarthy did not know that.[328]

He said Major General Walker never told him about how Colonel Hunter had prepared and that it was his responsibility to tell him.[329] "I don't talk to troop lead commanders, no," he said.[330]

Ultimately, no plan from Army leaders—strategic or tactical—made it to the troops.

"[I]f they came up with a plan, they never shared it with us," Major General Walker said.[331] *They claim they were putting a plan together. That's what took so long.* I never saw a plan from the Department of Defense or the Department of the Army."[332]

Colonel Hunter agreed that "[n]o one ever told me, because I already had the plan there, and no one ever informed me that there was a different plan or a different [con-op]."[333] He said to the extent a "hasty plan" was put into action on January 6th, it was his: "I created the concept of operation."[334] He added: "The [plan] that was actually used as far as which lot they would come into, who would meet them at the lot, and then who would lead them over to the Capitol. That was between myself and MPD and Capitol Police."[335]

After hours of wait, Major General Walker said, "The plan was executed just like we said it would be [from the start], get to the Capitol, take direction from the ranking police officers there . . . to help restore order."[336] Colonel Hunter passed the details of his hasty plan onto Lt. Col. Reinke—the highest ranking officer at the rally point—letting him know, "Hey, when you pull into this lot, they will meet you there. This is who is—you know, you're going with these personnel," exactly what Secretary McCarthy had just spent 20 minutes putting together.[337]

Although Lt. Col. Reinke said his QRF servicemembers were given rules of engagement before arriving at the rally point, he was not told more than report to Capitol Police and supplement and assist them.[338]

Captain Tarp, outranked by Lt. Col. Reinke but in charge of the second shift, was merely told by Brigadier General Ryan: "'You need to act like there's a fire now. You're going to [the] Capitol.' Those were his directions."[339]

After an hour and a half spent in calls, travel, and making plans, Secretary McCarthy was prepared to green light the deployment of the Guard at 4:35 p.m. But miscommunication led to another half-hour delay.

Secretary McCarthy relayed the "go" order to Major General Walker—with his subordinate Brigadier General LaNeve serving as the intermediary—in a conversation Major General Walker said never happened.

According to Secretary McCarthy, Brigadier General LaNeve "wasn't a junior aide."[340] In his role, "he can speak, once given the authority, delegated authority to speak as the Sec Army . . ."[341] He said that the first-star officer "was standing next to me,"[342] and General Piatt said that it was generally "not uncommon" for him to ask his staff to "transmit [the] communication from the Secretary to General Walker."[343]

For his part, Brigadier General LaNeve denies that he himself conveyed the "go" order.[344] He said he spoke with Major General Walker first at 4:25 p.m. to tell him that his forces should, "Get on the bus, do not leave."[345] On a second call at 4:35 p.m., Brigadier General LaNeve said he overheard Secretary McCarthy himself convey the "go" order to Major General Walker: He said something "to the effect of 'You're approved to provide support.'"[346] Secretary McCarthy, on his part, said he never spoke a word.[347]

Brigadier General LaNeve said the secretary then again handed him the phone to convey the details of "where to go and what officer to meet up with."[348] Those two details would be the full extent of the "con-op" allegedly communicated to Major General Walker.[349] He even recalled Major General Walker saying, "Roger," to acknowledge the plan.[350] But, Brigadier General LaNeve said, there was "mass confusion in that room," and he agreed that "[t]here were huge communications problems."[351]

Major General Walker said there was no such call, nor any like it.[352] He said he remained on the video conference line the whole time "with everybody else," he said.[353] He said he would not have taken an order from Brigadier General LaNeve anyhow. "[W]hy would I ever take directions from General LaNeve? Anybody? Brigadier General LaNeve, one-star," Major General Walker said.[354] "I mean, he's not a peer, it wouldn't be somebody that would convey that type of message to me. . . So my thinking wouldn't have been that he would have been speaking on behalf of the Secretary."[355]

Although his staff confirms they didn't see him field a call from Secretary McCarthy or Brigadier General LaNeve,[356] including never seeing him leave their conference room,[357] Major General Walker's own note taker appears to have jotted down at 4:37 p.m. the following: "advised to sent [sic] 150 to establish D st / 1st outer perimeter, General LaNeve," beside what appears to be his phone number.[358] That address is the rally point

Secretary McCarthy had asked General LaNeve to convey, the same one Colonel Hunter and law enforcement had already chosen earlier. Major General Walker said, "the only way [Lt. Nick] could have got it was listening to the VTC, which I was on." [359] He further said, "I never saw General LaNeve on the [video teleconference] . . . I didn't hear General LaNeve's voice." [360] Lt. Nick said he had it penned at much later—at 5:09 p.m.—"as the time they received the orders" to deploy. [361]

Major General Walker certainly did not *act* as if he had been given authority until, fortuitously, General McConville—who had heard about the 4:35 p.m. call—walked by the teleconference screen and was "surprised" to see the commanding general sitting idly at 5:09 p.m. [362]

Major General Walker agreed the first time he heard he had the authority was from the lips of the general: "General McConville came back into the call and said, Hey, you're a go." [363]

Lt. Col. Reinke's QRF and Captain Tarp's second shift got on the bus at 5:10 p.m. [364] They left at 5:15 p.m. [365] Lt. Col. Reinke said they didn't arrive at the Capitol Police parking lot until 5:55 p.m., [366] although official timing from the Army and Department of Defense put their arrival time at 5:40 p.m. and from the DC Guard at 5:20 p.m. [367] At the earliest, the troops arrived in the vicinity of the Capitol grounds at 5:29 p.m., when Lt. Col. Reinke texted Colonel Hunter: "Apparently we pulled into the wrong lot, trying to reroute to LOT 16 now." [368] He said they sat around for 20 minutes once they arrived, and then were sworn in, before relieving an entire line of officers. [369] Captain Tarp said they remained idle for 45 minutes waiting for Capitol Police to come "bus by bus to swear-in the officers. It was a long wait. Frustrating—we're sitting a mile from where we['re] going." [370]

Captain Tarp said, "By the time we got there, we were just holding back the people who remained past the curfew." [371] The height of the riot had passed.

Colonel Hunter estimated that—had his preparations been approved— the DC Guard could have arrived as early as an hour and a half earlier than they did.

"Within one hour, I'd say I could've had 135. So the [about 40] coming from Joint Base Andrews, if they would've headed directly to me at the Capitol, and then the 90 I had on the street and the 4 that were—including myself," he said. [372] "[S]o I arrived at the Capitol at 3:10. So, if I would've recalled everyone by 3:30, 3:40, we could've been—had gear on and walking towards the Capitol." [373]

He further stated: "I would give them another hour. So by 4:40 I should've had at least 250 coming from the Armory . . . That includes the second shift as well as full-timers." [374]

Presented with the plans Colonel Hunter had set in motion and the easy accessibility of their equipment, neither of which he had known about at the time, Secretary McCarthy conceded "you could have shaved minutes," [375] and the speed of deployment "could have" been pushed up, but "[i]t depends." [376]

When the Guard finally arrived at the Capitol, "pretty much all the other fighting, per se, had stopped on the Capitol complex," according to Robert Glover, head of the MPD Special Operations Division.[377] Then-Inspector Glover received the Guard troops when they arrived.[378] "[T]he bus just kind of showed up. It was my decision at that point, looking at their numbers and their capabilities at that moment in time and what was the most pressing activity—and that was to make the arrests," he said.[379] He had them create a secure "prisoner cordon" where they could stand guard as arrested individuals waited transport to jail.[380] "They were the freshest personnel that we had at that moment in time. And, again, they didn't have any significant numbers to really do much else at that moment in time either," he said.[381] "[T]heir orders were basically, support us in whatever we told them to do . . ." [382]

Secretary McCarthy said that it was possible that DOD and DC National Guard leaders had simply not been coordinating their planning.[383] He acknowledged that "a lot of things were probably missed. It was tremendously confusing," [384] and "that makes for a messy response." [385]

No one within the Department of Defense, Army, or Guard leveled accusations of an intentional delay. "I didn't see anybody trying to throw sand in the gearbox and slow things down," General Milley said.[386]

Major General Walker said the Army's reluctance to approve National Guard assistance to the Mayor during the planning for the anticipated January 6th events continued through January 6th itself.[387] "I don't know where the decision paralysis came from, but it was clearly there. The decision paralysis, decision avoidance," he said.[388]

CONCLUSION

Former President Trump's eagerness to engage the U.S. military to play a visible role in addressing domestic unrest during the late spring and summer of 2020 does appear to have prompted senior military leadership to take precautions, in preparing for the joint session, against the possibility that the DC Guard might be ordered to deploy for an improper purpose. Those precautions seem to have been prudential as much as legal in nature.

What that entailed in the unprecedented circumstances of the January 6th attack on the Capitol is, however, harder to accept: a 3 hour and 19 minute lag-time in making a relatively small, but riot-trained and highly capable military unit available to conduct one of its statutory support missions.

While the delay seems unnecessary and unacceptable, it was the byproduct of military processes, institutional caution, and a revised deployment approval process. We have no evidence that the delay was intentional. Likewise, it appears that none of the individuals involved understood what President Trump planned for January 6th, and how he would behave during the violence. Imperfect inter-government and intra-military communications as the January 6th rally morphed, with President Trump's active encouragement, into a full-blown riot at the Capitol also help explain the time it took to deploy Guard troops to the Capitol after their assistance there was requested and approved. Post-hoc evaluation of real-time communications during an unprecedented and evolving crisis and limited tactical intelligence, nevertheless, carries the risk of a precision that was unrealistic at the time. It is also clear from testimony provided to the Select Committee that DoD and DC National Guard leaders have differing perspectives that are not reconcilable regarding the timing of deployment authorization.

Where the DC Guard's deployment on January 6th is concerned, then, the "lessons learned" at this juncture include: careful evaluation on the basis of limited information may take time; statutorily constrained inter-governmental requests for assistance and multi-level approval processes are complex and may be time-consuming; any visible military presence in the domestic setting is circumscribed by law and triggers considerable, constitutionally-driven sensitivities; and crisis communications are often imperfect, especially in unforeseen and rapidly evolving situations.

ENDNOTES

1. Select Committee to Investigate the January 6th Attack on the United States Capitol, Transcribed Interview of General James Charles McConville, (Nov. 4, 2021), p. 8.

2. DC Code § 49-409, ("The President of the United States shall be the Commander-in-Chief of the militia of the District of Columbia."), available at https://code.dccouncil.gov/us/dc/council/code/sections/49-409 (The DC National Guard is the "organized militia" of the District of Columbia. DC Code § 49-406, available at https://code.dccouncil.gov/us/dc/council/code/sections/49-406). Subject to that top-level command distinction, the DC National Guard is, when acting in its civil support or militia capacity, comparable to the National Guard of the various States, which act as those States' militias. 32 U.S.C. §101(4) ("Army National Guard" statutorily defined as "that part of the organized militia of the several States . . . and the District of Columbia . . ."). The Department of Justice's Office of Legal Counsel has interpreted the DC Code provisions authorizing the DC National Guard's use as a militia in support of DC law enforcement activities as within the exemptions from the Posse Comitatus Act's prohibitions on use of the military for domestic law enforcement (18 U.S.C. § 1385 ("Whoever, except in cases and under conditions expressly authorized by the Constitution or Act of Congress, willfully uses any part of the Army or the Air

Force as a posse comitatus or otherwise to execute the laws shall be fined . . . or imprisoned . . . .")). *See* Memorandum Opinion, "Use of the National Guard to Support Drug Inter-
diction Efforts in the District of Columbia," 13 Op. O.L.C. 91, 92, 93, 97 (Apr. 4, 1989),
available at https://www.justice.gov/olc/opinions-volume (Posse Comitatus Act, 18 U.S.C. §
1385, does not prohibit use of DC National Guard as a militia in support of DC Metropolitan
Police Department). The President also has authority to mobilize the National Guard,
which is a reserve component of the U.S. armed forces, to active duty (10 U.S.C. §12301 et
seq.), and may "federalize" any National Guard unit to assist in addressing insurrection (10
U.S.C. §§251-253), invasion, or rebellion and to give effect to Federal law (10 U.S.C. §12406).
The President did not exercise those authorities on January 6, 2021. The DC National Guard
operated that day as the DC militia, in its civil support and law enforcement assistance
capacity under the separate authorities noted above. *See also*, Select Committee to Investigate the January 6th Attack on the United States Capitol, Transcribed Interview of General
James Charles McConville, (Nov. 4, 2021), p. 8.

3. Executive Order 11485, 34 F.R. 15411, § 1, (Oct. 1, 1969), available at https://
www.federalregister.gov/documents/search?conditions%5Bterm%5D=34+f.r.15411# ("The
Commanding General of the [DC] National Guard shall report to the Secretary of Defense
or to an official of the Department of Defense designated by the Secretary . . ."). The Secretary of Defense exercises command authority over the "military operations, including
training, parades and other duty" of the DC National Guard while in its non-federalized
militia status, through the Commanding General of the DC National Guard. *Id.* Executive
Order 11485 reserves appointment of the Commanding General of the DC National Guard to
the President (*i.e.*, does not delegate that authority to the Secretary of Defense or the Secretary's designee). *Id.*, at §§ 1, 3. That Executive Order also specifies that, "[s]ubject to the
direction of the President as Commander-in-Chief, the Secretary [of Defense] may order
out the [DC] National Guard . . . to aid the civil authorities . . . of the District of Columbia."
Id., at § 1. Under a longstanding Congressional authorization, the Mayor of the District of
Columbia may request that the Commander-in-Chief (now, by the President's delegation,
the Secretary of Defense), direct the National Guard to assist in suppressing "violence to
persons or property" or "force or violence to break and resist the laws," including when
"tumult, riot or mob is threatened." DC Code §49-103 ("Suppression of riots"), available at
https://code.dccouncil.gov/us/dc/council/code/sections/49-103. *See also*, Select Committee to Investigate the January 6th Attack on the United States Capitol, Transcribed Interview of William Walker, (Dec. 13, 2021), p. 104.

4. Memorandum, Secretary of Defense to Secretary of the Army and Secretary of the Air
Force, "Supervision and Control of the National Guard of the District of Columbia," (Oct. 10,
1969), ¶ 3. That memorandum is available as an attachment to the Secretary of Defense
Lloyd Austin's December 30, 2021 memorandum modifying that 1969 delegation: "Effective
immediately, the Secretary of Defense is the approval authority for DC Government
requests for the DCNG to provide law enforcement support" to the District of Columbia if
the support is to be provided within 48 hours of the request or if acceding to the request
would require the DC National Guard to engage directly in civilian law enforcement activities, including "crowd control, traffic control, search, seizure, arrest, or temporary detention." Memorandum, Secretary of Defense for Secretary of the Army, "Authority to Approve
District of Columbia Government Requests for District of Columbia National Guard Support
Assistance," (Dec. 30, 2021), available at https://www.airandspaceforces.com/austin-
streamlines-authority-to-deploy-dc-national-guard. *See also*, Select Committee to Investigate the January 6th Attack on the United States Capitol, Transcribed Interview of William
Walker, (Dec. 13, 2021), p. 104.

5. Select Committee to Investigate the January 6th Attack on the United States Capitol, Transcribed Interview of Ryan McCarthy, (Feb. 4, 2022), p. 10.

6. George Floyd was murdered on Monday, May 25, 2020. *See* Catherine Thorbecke, "Derek
Chauvin Had His Knee on George Floyd's Neck for Nearly 9 Minutes, Complaint Says," ABC
News, (May 29, 2020)), available at https://abcnews.go.com/US/derek-chauvin-knee-
george-floyds-neck-minutes-complaint/story?id=70961042. Over the ensuing days, weeks,
and months, Americans demonstrated in cities across the country. See Major Cities Chiefs

Association Intelligence Commanders Group, Report on the 2020 Protests & Civil Unrest (Oct. 2020) at p. 8, Fig. 6, https://majorcitieschiefs.com/wp-content/uploads/2021/01/MCCA-Report-on-the-2020-Protest-and-Civil-Unrest.pdf.

7. Select Committee to Investigate the January 6th Attack on the United States Capitol, Transcribed Interview of William Walker, (Apr. 21, 2022), p. 5.

8. Select Committee to Investigate the January 6th Attack on the United States Capitol, Transcribed Interview of William Walker, (Apr. 21, 2022), p. 8.

9. Select Committee to Investigate the January 6th Attack on the United States Capitol, Transcribed Interview of William Walker, (Dec. 13, 2021), p. 66.

10. Select Committee to Investigate the January 6th Attack on the United States Capitol, Transcribed Interview of William Walker, (Dec. 13, 2021), p. 66.

11. Select Committee to Investigate the January 6th Attack on the United States Capitol, Transcribed Interview of William Barr, (June 2, 2021), pp. 67-68 ("[Trump] was very upset at the news that had come out that he had been taken down to the bunker in the preceding days, you know, when some of the rioting right by the White House was at its worst. He was very upset by this, and, as I recall, he bellowed at everyone sitting in front of him in a semicircle and he waved his finger around the semicircle saying we were losers, we were losers, we were all fucking losers," Barr said. "[H]e then raised—you know, he talked about whether he should invoke the Insurrection Act . . . And, you know, my position was that the Insurrection Act should only be invoked when you really need to invoke it as a last resort, when you don't really have other assets that can deal with civil unrest.").

12. Select Committee to Investigate the January 6th Attack on the United States Capitol, Transcribed Interview of Ryan McCarthy, (Feb. 4, 2022), p. 86.

13. Select Committee to Investigate the January 6th Attack on the United States Capitol, Transcribed Interview of Ryan McCarthy, (Feb. 4, 2022), p. 20.

14. Select Committee to Investigate the January 6th Attack on the United States Capitol, Transcribed Interview of Ryan McCarthy, (Feb. 4, 2022), p. 20.

15. Select Committee to Investigate the January 6th Attack on the United States Capitol, Transcribed Interview of General Walter Piatt, (Nov. 3, 2021), pp. 47-48.

16. Select Committee to Investigate the January 6th Attack on the United States Capitol, Transcribed Interview of General Walter Piatt, (Nov. 3, 2021), p. 47.

17. Select Committee to Investigate the January 6th Attack on the United States Capitol, Transcribed Interview of General James Charles McConville, (Nov. 4, 2021), p. 38.

18. Select Committee to Investigate the January 6th Attack on the United States Capitol, Transcribed Interview of General Walter Piatt, (Nov. 3, 2021), p. 18.

19. Select Committee to Investigate the January 6th Attack on the United States Capitol, Transcribed Interview of General Walter Piatt, (Nov. 3, 2021), pp. 17-18. "Brigadier General Robert Kenneth Ryan was the joint task force commander [who] authorized the—the helicopters to fly over the crowd to observe and report, and the Secretary of the Army approved that," Major General Walker said. Select Committee to Investigate the January 6th Attack on the United States Capitol, Transcribed Interview of William Walker, (Dec. 13, 2021), p. 55. "Now, the pilots came a little too close to the civilians on the ground." Id., at 57.

20. Select Committee to Investigate the January 6th Attack on the United States Capitol, Transcribed Interview of Muriel Bowser, (Jan. 12, 2022), p. 27.

21. Select Committee to Investigate the January 6th Attack on the United States Capitol, Transcribed Interview of General Charles Anthony Flynn, (Oct. 28, 2022), p. 14.

22. Select Committee to Investigate the January 6th Attack on the United States Capitol, Transcribed Interview of General Charles Anthony Flynn, (Oct. 28, 2022), p. 14.

23. Select Committee to Investigate the January 6th Attack on the United States Capitol, Transcribed Interview of General Walter Piatt, (Nov. 3, 2021), p. 19.

24. Select Committee to Investigate the January 6th Attack on the United States Capitol, Transcribed Interview of General Walter Piatt, (Nov. 3, 2021), p. 18.

25. Select Committee to Investigate the January 6th Attack on the United States Capitol, Transcribed Interview of General Walter Piatt, (Nov. 3, 2021), p. 19.

26. Select Committee to Investigate the January 6th Attack on the United States Capitol, Transcribed Interview of General Walter Piatt, (Nov. 3, 2021), p. 19.

27. Select Committee to Investigate the January 6th Attack on the United States Capitol, Transcribed Interview of Mark Esper, (Apr. 1, 2022), pp. 47-48.

28. Select Committee to Investigate the January 6th Attack on the United States Capitol, Transcribed Interview of Mark Esper, (Apr. 1, 2022), pp. 47-48.

29. Select Committee to Investigate the January 6th Attack on the United States Capitol, Transcribed Interview of General William Walker, (Apr. 1, 2022), p. 25.

30. Select Committee to Investigate the January 6th Attack on the United States Capitol, Transcribed Interview of General Mark Milley, (Nov. 17, 2021), pp. 242–43.

31. Select Committee to Investigate the January 6th Attack on the United States Capitol, Transcribed Interview of Donell Harvin, (Jan. 24, 2022), p. 14; Select Committee to Investigate the January 6th Attack on the United States Capitol, Informal Interview of Donell Harvin, (Nov. 12, 2021).

32. Select Committee to Investigate the January 6th Attack on the United States Capitol, Transcribed Interview of Donell Harvin, (Jan. 24, 2022), pp. 22-23.

33. Select Committee to Investigate the January 6th Attack on the United States Capitol, Transcribed Interview of Christopher Rodriguez, (Jan. 25, 2022), p. 24; Select Committee to Investigate the January 6th Attack on the United States Capitol, Transcribed Interview of Donell Harvin, (Jan. 24, 2022), p. 24.

34. Documents on file with the Select Committee to Investigate the January 6th Attack on the United States Capitol (Department of Defense Production), DoD 00001680 (December 31, 2020, Letter from Mayor Bowser to Major General Walker re: DCNG).

35. Documents on file with the Select Committee to Investigate the January 6th Attack on the United States Capitol (Department of Defense Production), DoD 00001679 (December 31, 2020, Letter from Dr. Christopher Rodriguez to Major General Walker re: DCNG).

36. Select Committee to Investigate the January 6th Attack on the United States Capitol, Transcribed Interview of General Walter Piatt, (Nov. 3, 2021), p. 20.

37. Select Committee to Investigate the January 6th Attack on the United States Capitol, Transcribed Interview of General Walter Piatt, (Nov. 3, 2021), p. 26.

38. Select Committee to Investigate the January 6th Attack on the United States Capitol, Transcribed Interview of General James Charles McConville, (Nov. 4, 2021), p. 14.

39. Select Committee to Investigate the January 6th Attack on the United States Capitol, Transcribed Interview of General James Charles McConville, (Nov. 4, 2021), p. 38.

40. Select Committee to Investigate the January 6th Attack on the United States Capitol, Transcribed Interview of General William Walker, (Dec. 13, 2021), p. 75.

41. Select Committee to Investigate the January 6th Attack on the United States Capitol, Transcribed Interview of Robert J. Contee III, (Jan. 11, 2022), p. 47.

42. Select Committee to Investigate the January 6th Attack on the United States Capitol, Transcribed Interview of Robert J. Contee III, (Jan. 11, 2022), p. 44.

43. Select Committee to Investigate the January 6th Attack on the United States Capitol, Transcribed Interview of Muriel Bowser, (Jan. 12, 2022), p. 50.

44. Select Committee to Investigate the January 6th Attack on the United States Capitol, Transcribed Interview of Christopher Rodriguez, (Jan. 25, 2022), p. 47.

45. Select Committee to Investigate the January 6th Attack on the United States Capitol, Transcribed Interview of Robert J. Contee III, (Jan. 11, 2022), p. 49.

46. *See* Chapter 7.

47. Select Committee to Investigate the January 6th Attack on the United States Capitol, Transcribed Interview of General William Walker, (Dec. 13, 2021), pp. 79, 85.

48. Select Committee to Investigate the January 6th Attack on the United States Capitol, Transcribed Interview of Ryan McCarthy, (Feb. 4, 2022), p. 56.

49. Select Committee to Investigate the January 6th Attack on the United States Capitol, Transcribed Interview of General William Walker, (Dec. 13, 2021), pp. 78-79, 80.

50. Select Committee to Investigate the January 6th Attack on the United States Capitol, Transcribed Interview of General William Walker, (Dec. 13, 2021), pp. 78-79, 80.

51. Select Committee to Investigate the January 6th Attack on the United States Capitol, Transcribed Interview of Robert J. Contee III, (Jan. 11, 2022), p. 6.

52. Select Committee to Investigate the January 6th Attack on the United States Capitol, Transcribed Interview of Robert J. Contee III, (Jan. 11, 2022), p. 53-54.

53. Select Committee to Investigate the January 6th Attack on the United States Capitol, Transcribed Interview of Robert J. Contee III, (Jan. 11, 2022), p. 54.

54. Select Committee to Investigate the January 6th Attack on the United States Capitol, Transcribed Interview of Ryan McCarthy, (Feb. 4, 2022), p. 75.

55. Select Committee to Investigate the January 6th Attack on the United States Capitol, Transcribed Interview of Ryan McCarthy, (Feb. 4, 2022), pp. 75-76.

56. Select Committee to Investigate the January 6th Attack on the United States Capitol, Transcribed Interview of General William Walker, (Apr. 21, 2022), p. 10.

57. Select Committee to Investigate the January 6th Attack on the United States Capitol, Transcribed Interview of Robert J. Contee III, (Jan. 11, 2022), p. 63; Select Committee to Investigate the January 6th Attack on the United States Capitol, Transcribed Interview of Christopher Rodriguez, (Jan. 25, 2022), pp. 32-33.

58. Select Committee to Investigate the January 6th Attack on the United States Capitol, Transcribed Interview of Christopher Charles Miller, (Jan. 14, 2022), p. 84.

59. Select Committee to Investigate the January 6th Attack on the United States Capitol, Transcribed Interview of Craig Hunter, (Jan. 20, 2022), p. 11.

60. Select Committee to Investigate the January 6th Attack on the United States Capitol, Transcribed Interview of Craig Hunter, (Jan. 20, 2022), pp. 11-12.

61. Select Committee to Investigate the January 6th Attack on the United States Capitol, Transcribed Interview of General William Walker, (Dec. 13, 2021), p. 98.

62. Select Committee to Investigate the January 6th Attack on the United States Capitol, Transcribed Interview of General William Walker, (Dec. 13, 2021), p. 97.

63. Select Committee to Investigate the January 6th Attack on the United States Capitol, Transcribed Interview of General William Walker, (Dec. 13, 2021), p. 103.

64. Select Committee to Investigate the January 6th Attack on the United States Capitol, Transcribed Interview of General William Walker, (Dec. 13, 2021), p. 99.

65. Select Committee to Investigate the January 6th Attack on the United States Capitol, Transcribed Interview of Robert J. Contee III, (Jan. 11, 2022), p. 57.

66. Select Committee to Investigate the January 6th Attack on the United States Capitol, Transcribed Interview of Robert J. Contee III, (Jan. 11, 2022), p. 57.

67. Select Committee to Investigate the January 6th Attack on the United States Capitol, Transcribed Interview of Christopher Rodriguez, (Jan. 25, 2022), p. 49.

68. Select Committee to Investigate the January 6th Attack on the United States Capitol, Transcribed Interview of Muriel Bowser, (Jan. 12, 2022), p. 27.

69. Select Committee to Investigate the January 6th Attack on the United States Capitol, Transcribed Interview of Muriel Bowser, (Jan. 12, 2022), p. 27.

70. Select Committee to Investigate the January 6th Attack on the United States Capitol, Transcribed Interview of Mark Esper, (Apr. 14, 2022), pp. 22-23.

71. Select Committee to Investigate the January 6th Attack on the United States Capitol, Transcribed Interview of Christopher Miller, (Jan. 14, 2022), pp. 12-13, 15.

72. U.S. House Committee on Oversight and Reform, *Hearing on Unexplained Delays and Unanswered Questions*, 117th Cong., 1st sess., (May 12, 2021), Statement of Christopher C. Miller, p. 4.

73. U.S. House Committee on Oversight and Reform, *Hearing on Unexplained Delays and Unanswered Questions*, 117th Cong., 1st sess., (May 12, 2021), Statement of Christopher C. Miller, p. 4.

74. Select Committee to Investigate the January 6th Attack on the United States Capitol, Transcribed Interview of Christopher Miller, (Jan. 14, 2022), p. 133.

75. Select Committee to Investigate the January 6th Attack on the United States Capitol, Transcribed Interview of Ryan McCarthy, (Feb. 4, 2022), p. 73.

76. Select Committee to Investigate the January 6th Attack on the United States Capitol, Transcribed Interview of Ryan McCarthy, (Feb. 4, 2022), p. 73.

77. Select Committee to Investigate the January 6th Attack on the United States Capitol, Transcribed Interview of Ryan McCarthy, (Feb. 4, 2022), p. 51.

78. Documents on file with the Select Committee to Investigate the January 6th Attack on the United States Capitol (Department of Defense Production), DoD 00005855–DoD 00005886 (December 18, 2021, email from General James C. McConville to Curtis Kellogg re: HOT MEDIA FOX NEWS & POLITICO MEDIA QUERY: Response to MG (R) Flynn's remarks.).

79. Select Committee to Investigate the January 6th Attack on the United States Capitol, Transcribed Interview of Ryan McCarthy, (Feb. 4, 2022), p. 51.

80. Select Committee to Investigate the January 6th Attack on the United States Capitol, Transcribed Interview of Ryan McCarthy, (Feb. 4, 2022), pp. 54-55 ("Q: Were you ever told you would be fired if you ever made such a statement again? A: It was implied. It was implied that I was, you know, not to do that again, ...").

81. Lara Seligman (@laraseligman), Twitter, Dec. 18, 2021 11:27 a.m. ET, available at https://twitter.com/laraseligman/status/1339985580785086466.

82. Select Committee to Investigate the January 6th Attack on the United States Capitol, Transcribed Interview of General James Charles McConville, (Nov. 4, 2021), p. 68.

83. Documents on file with the Select Committee to Investigate the January 6th Attack on the United States Capitol (Department of Defense Production), DoD 00003488.

84. Documents on file with the Select Committee to Investigate the January 6th Attack on the United States Capitol (Department of Defense Production), DoD 00003488.

85. Select Committee to Investigate the January 6th Attack on the United States Capitol, Transcribed Interview of Ryan McCarthy, (Feb. 4, 2022), p. 73.

86. Ashton Carter, Dick Cheney, William Cohen, Mark Esper, Robert Gates, Chuck Hagel, James Mattis, Leon Panetta, William Perry, and Donald Rumsfeld, "All 10 living former defense secretaries: Involving the military in election disputes would cross into dangerous territory," *Washington Post*, (Jan. 3, 2021), available at https://www.washingtonpost.com/opinions/10-former-defense-secretaries-military-peaceful-transfer-of-power/2021/01/03/2a23d52e-4c4d-11eb-a9f4-0e668b9772ba_story.html.

87. Select Committee to Investigate the January 6th Attack on the United States Capitol, Transcribed Interview of Ryan McCarthy, (Feb. 4, 2022), p. 71.

88. Select Committee to Investigate the January 6th Attack on the United States Capitol, Transcribed Interview of Ryan McCarthy, (Feb. 4, 2022), p. 71.

89. Select Committee to Investigate the January 6th Attack on the United States Capitol, Transcribed Interview of Ryan McCarthy, (Feb. 4, 2022), p. 71.

90. Select Committee to Investigate the January 6th Attack on the United States Capitol, Transcribed Interview of Ryan McCarthy, (Feb. 4, 2022), p. 148.

91. Select Committee to Investigate the January 6th Attack on the United States Capitol, Transcribed Interview of Christopher Miller, (Jan. 14, 2022), p. 84.

92. Select Committee to Investigate the January 6th Attack on the United States Capitol, Transcribed Interview of General Mark Milley, (Nov. 17, 2021), p. 247.

93. *See* Documents on file with the Select Committee to Investigate the January 6th Attack on the United States Capitol (Department of Defense Production), DoD 00000006 (January 4, 2021, Memorandum from the Secretary of Defense Christopher Miller to the Secretary of the Army Ryan McCarthy).

94. *See* Documents on file with the Select Committee to Investigate the January 6th Attack on the United States Capitol (Department of Defense Production), DoD 00000006 (January 4, 2021, Memorandum from the Secretary of Defense Christopher Miller to the Secretary of the Army Ryan McCarthy); Select Committee to Investigate the January 6th Attack on the United States Capitol, Transcribed Interview of Robert J. Contee III, (Jan. 11, 2022), p. 56.

95. Select Committee to Investigate the January 6th Attack on the United States Capitol, Transcribed Interview of Robert J. Contee III, (Jan. 11, 2022), p. 56.

96. *See* Documents on file with the Select Committee to Investigate the January 6th Attack on the United States Capitol (Department of Defense Production), DoD 00000006 (January 4, 2021, Memorandum from the Secretary of Defense Christopher Miller to the Secretary of the Army Ryan McCarthy); Documents on file with the Select Committee to Investigate the January 6th Attack on the United States Capitol (Department of Defense Production), DoD #2/000633, (January 5, 2021, Colonel John Lubas email to Major General William Walker with the subject, "Final Signed Memo to DCNG," at 7:54 a.m. ET).

97. *See* Select Committee to Investigate the January 6th Attack on the United States Capitol, Informal Interview of Lt. Col. David Reinke, (Jan. 6, 2022).

98. Select Committee to Investigate the January 6th Attack on the United States Capitol, Transcribed Interview of General James Charles McConville, (Nov. 4, 2021), p. 68.

99. Select Committee to Investigate the January 6th Attack on the United States Capitol, Transcribed Interview of General James Charles McConville, (Nov. 4, 2021), p. 68.

100. Select Committee to Investigate the January 6th Attack on the United States Capitol, Transcribed Interview of General William Walker, (Dec. 13, 2021), p. 89.

101. Select Committee to Investigate the January 6th Attack on the United States Capitol, Transcribed Interview of General William Walker, (Dec. 13, 2021), p. 92.

102. Select Committee to Investigate the January 6th Attack on the United States Capitol, Transcribed Interview of General William Walker, (Dec. 13, 2021), p. 93.

103. Select Committee to Investigate the January 6th Attack on the United States Capitol, Transcribed Interview of General William Walker, (Dec. 13, 2021), p. 90.

104. Select Committee to Investigate the January 6th Attack on the United States Capitol, Transcribed Interview of General William Walker, (Dec. 13, 2021), pp. 93–94.

105. Select Committee to Investigate the January 6th Attack on the United States Capitol, Transcribed Interview of Christopher Rodriguez, (Jan. 25, 2022), p. 42.

106. Select Committee to Investigate the January 6th Attack on the United States Capitol, Transcribed Interview of Muriel Bowser, (Jan. 12, 2022), p. 50.

107. Select Committee to Investigate the January 6th Attack on the United States Capitol, Transcribed Interview of Muriel Bowser, (Jan. 12, 2022), p. 50.

108. Select Committee to Investigate the January 6th Attack on the United States Capitol, Transcribed Interview of Steven Andrew Sund, (Apr. 20, 2022), p. 133 ("Q: It doesn't sound to me, like, really, you're pushing for it when you raised the National Guard with Sergeant At Arms Irving or Stenger? It would have been nice, but not essential for you to be ready. Is that a fair characterization of your personal position on that? A: Yes.").

109. Select Committee to Investigate the January 6th Attack on the United States Capitol, Transcribed Interview of Steven Andrew Sund, (Apr. 20, 2022), pp. 116-17.

110. Select Committee to Investigate the January 6th Attack on the United States Capitol, Transcribed Interview of Steven Andrew Sund, (Apr. 20, 2022), p. 124.

111. Documents on file with the Select Committee to Investigate the January 6th Attack on the United States Capitol (Capitol Police Production), CTRL0000001766, CTRL0000001766.0001 (Document from January 3, 2021, titled: "Special Event Assessment: Joint Session of Congress—Electoral College Vote Certification"); see also, Select Committee to Investigate the January 6th Attack on the United States Capitol, Transcribed Interview of Julie Farnam, (Dec. 15, 2021), pp. 51-52.

112. Select Committee to Investigate the January 6th Attack on the United States Capitol, Transcribed Interview of Steven Andrew Sund, (Apr. 20, 2022), p. 125.

113. Select Committee to Investigate the January 6th Attack on the United States Capitol, Transcribed Interview of Steven Andrew Sund, (Apr. 20, 2022), p. 114.

114. Select Committee to Investigate the January 6th Attack on the United States Capitol, Transcribed Interview of Steven Andrew Sund, (Apr. 20, 2022), p. 116.

115. Select Committee to Investigate the January 6th Attack on the United States Capitol, Transcribed Interview of Steven Andrew Sund, (Apr. 20, 2022), p. 119.

116. Select Committee to Investigate the January 6th Attack on the United States Capitol, Transcribed Interview of Steven Andrew Sund, (Apr. 20, 2022), p. 128.

117. Select Committee to Investigate the January 6th Attack on the United States Capitol, Transcribed Interview of Steven Andrew Sund, (Apr. 20, 2022), p. 128.

118. Select Committee to Investigate the January 6th Attack on the United States Capitol, Transcribed Interview of Paul Irving, (Mar. 4, 2022), pp. 9-10.

119. Select Committee to Investigate the January 6th Attack on the United States Capitol, Transcribed Interview of Paul Irving, (Mar. 4, 2022), p. 35.

120. Select Committee to Investigate the January 6th Attack on the United States Capitol, Transcribed Interview of Paul Irving, (Mar. 4, 2022), p. 10.

121. Select Committee to Investigate the January 6th Attack on the United States Capitol, Transcribed Interview of Paul Irving, (Mar. 4, 2022), p. 12.

122. Select Committee to Investigate the January 6th Attack on the United States Capitol, Transcribed Interview of Paul Irving, (Mar. 4, 2022), p. 35.

123. Select Committee to Investigate the January 6th Attack on the United States Capitol, Transcribed Interview of Paul Irving, (Mar. 4, 2022), p. 10.

124. Select Committee to Investigate the January 6th Attack on the United States Capitol, Transcribed Interview of Paul Irving, (Mar. 4, 2022), p. 41.

125. Select Committee to Investigate the January 6th Attack on the United States Capitol, Transcribed Interview of Paul Irving, (Mar. 4, 2022), pp. 7-8, 45.

126. Select Committee to Investigate the January 6th Attack on the United States Capitol, Transcribed Interview of Paul Irving, (Mar. 4, 2022), pp. 52-53.

127. Select Committee to Investigate the January 6th Attack on the United States Capitol, Transcribed Interview of Steven Andrew Sund, (Apr. 20, 2022), pp. 131-32.

128. Select Committee to Investigate the January 6th Attack on the United States Capitol, Transcribed Interview of Craig Hunter, (Jan. 20, 2022), pp. 19, 26.

129. Select Committee to Investigate the January 6th Attack on the United States Capitol, Transcribed Interview of Craig Hunter, (Jan. 20, 2022), pp. 19, 26.

130. Select Committee to Investigate the January 6th Attack on the United States Capitol, Transcribed Interview of Craig Hunter, (Jan. 20, 2022), pp. 19, 26.

131. Select Committee to Investigate the January 6th Attack on the United States Capitol, Informal Interview of Stewart Tarp, (Jan. 6, 2022).

132. Select Committee to Investigate the January 6th Attack on the United States Capitol, Transcribed Interview of Craig Hunter, (Jan. 20, 2022), p. 26.

133. Select Committee to Investigate the January 6th Attack on the United States Capitol, Transcribed Interview of Craig Hunter, (Jan. 20, 2022), p. 26.

134. Select Committee to Investigate the January 6th Attack on the United States Capitol, Informal Interview of Robert Ryan, (Dec. 9, 2022).

135. Select Committee to Investigate the January 6th Attack on the United States Capitol, Informal Interview of David Reinke, (Dec. 9, 2022).

136. Select Committee to Investigate the January 6th Attack on the United States Capitol, Informal Interview of David Reinke, (Dec. 9, 2022).

137. Select Committee to Investigate the January 6th Attack on the United States Capitol, Transcribed Interview of Ryan McCarthy, (Feb. 4, 2022), p. 116.

138. Select Committee to Investigate the January 6th Attack on the United States Capitol, Transcribed Interview of Ryan McCarthy, (Feb. 4, 2022), p. 117.

139. Select Committee to Investigate the January 6th Attack on the United States Capitol, Transcribed Interview of General Charles Anthony Flynn, (Oct. 28, 2022), p. 31.

140. Select Committee to Investigate the January 6th Attack on the United States Capitol, Transcribed Interview of Craig Hunter, (Jan. 20, 2022), p. 23.

141. Select Committee to Investigate the January 6th Attack on the United States Capitol, Transcribed Interview of Craig Hunter, (Jan. 20, 2022), p. 25, 27-28.

142. Select Committee to Investigate the January 6th Attack on the United States Capitol, Informal Interview of Stewart Tarp, (Jan. 6, 2022).

143. Select Committee to Investigate the January 6th Attack on the United States Capitol, Transcribed Interview of General William Walker, (Dec. 13, 2021), p. 130.

144. Select Committee to Investigate the January 6th Attack on the United States Capitol, Transcribed Interview of General Walter Piatt, (Nov. 3, 2021), p. 26.

145. Select Committee to Investigate the January 6th Attack on the United States Capitol, Transcribed Interview of General Walter Piatt, (Nov. 3, 2021), p. 45.

146. Select Committee to Investigate the January 6th Attack on the United States Capitol, Transcribed Interview of Ryan McCarthy, (Feb. 4, 2022), p. 107.

147. Select Committee to Investigate the January 6th Attack on the United States Capitol, Transcribed Interview of Ryan McCarthy, (Feb. 4, 2022), p. 107.

148. Select Committee to Investigate the January 6th Attack on the United States Capitol, Transcribed Interview of Ryan McCarthy, (Feb. 4, 2022), p. 109.

149. Select Committee to Investigate the January 6th Attack on the United States Capitol, Transcribed Interview of General William Walker, (Apr. 21, 2022), p. 29.

150. Documents on file with the Select Committee to Investigate the January 6th Attack on the United States Capitol (Department of Defense Production), DoD 00003050 (January 5, 2021, email from John Lubas to William Walker and Earl Matthews re: Final Signed Memo to DCNG).

151. See Select Committee to Investigate the January 6th Attack on the United States Capitol, Informal Interview of Stewart Tarp, (Jan. 6, 2022).

152. Select Committee to Investigate the January 6th Attack on the United States Capitol, Transcribed Interview of General Charles Anthony Flynn, (Oct. 28, 2022), p. 33.

153. Select Committee to Investigate the January 6th Attack on the United States Capitol, Transcribed Interview of General Walter Piatt, (Nov. 3, 2021), p. 49.

154. Select Committee to Investigate the January 6th Attack on the United States Capitol, Transcribed Interview of General William Walker, (Dec. 13, 2021), p. 65.

155. Select Committee to Investigate the January 6th Attack on the United States Capitol, Transcribed Interview of General William Walker, (Dec. 13, 2021), p. 22.

156. Select Committee to Investigate the January 6th Attack on the United States Capitol, Transcribed Interview of Craig Hunter, (Jan. 20, 2022), p. 26.

157. Select Committee to Investigate the January 6th Attack on the United States Capitol, Transcribed Interview of Craig Hunter, (Jan. 20, 2022), p. 31.

158. Select Committee to Investigate the January 6th Attack on the United States Capitol, Transcribed Interview of Craig Hunter, (Jan. 20, 2022), p. 31.

159. Select Committee to Investigate the January 6th Attack on the United States Capitol, Transcribed Interview of Craig Hunter, (Jan. 20, 2022), pp. 31-32.

160. Select Committee to Investigate the January 6th Attack on the United States Capitol, Transcribed Interview of Craig Hunter, (Jan. 20, 2022), pp. 31-32.

161. Select Committee to Investigate the January 6th Attack on the United States Capitol, Transcribed Interview of Craig Hunter, (Jan. 20, 2022), p. 32.

162. Select Committee to Investigate the January 6th Attack on the United States Capitol, Transcribed Interview of Craig Hunter, (Jan. 20, 2022), p. 32.

163. Select Committee to Investigate the January 6th Attack on the United States Capitol, Transcribed Interview of Craig Hunter, (Jan. 20, 2022), p. 34.

164. Select Committee to Investigate the January 6th Attack on the United States Capitol, Transcribed Interview of Craig Hunter, (Jan. 20, 2022), p. 32.

165. Select Committee to Investigate the January 6th Attack on the United States Capitol, Transcribed Interview of Craig Hunter, (Jan. 20, 2022), p. 35.

166. Select Committee to Investigate the January 6th Attack on the United States Capitol, Transcribed Interview of Craig Hunter, (Jan. 20, 2022), p. 34.

167. Select Committee to Investigate the January 6th Attack on the United States Capitol, Transcribed Interview of Craig Hunter, (Jan. 20, 2022), p. 34.

168. Select Committee to Investigate the January 6th Attack on the United States Capitol, Transcribed Interview of Craig Hunter, (Jan. 20, 2022), p. 37.

169. Select Committee to Investigate the January 6th Attack on the United States Capitol, Transcribed Interview of Craig Hunter, (Jan. 20, 2022), p. 34.

170. Select Committee to Investigate the January 6th Attack on the United States Capitol, Transcribed Interview of Craig Hunter, (Jan. 20, 2022), p. 41.

171. Select Committee to Investigate the January 6th Attack on the United States Capitol, Transcribed Interview of Craig Hunter, (Jan. 20, 2022), p. 41.

172. Select Committee to Investigate the January 6th Attack on the United States Capitol, Transcribed Interview of Craig Hunter, (Jan. 20, 2022), pp. 41-42.

173. Select Committee to Investigate the January 6th Attack on the United States Capitol, Transcribed Interview of Craig Hunter, (Jan. 20, 2022), pp. 38-39. Text messages show that Lieutenant Colonel Reinke texted Colonel Hunter, "Loading buses now. Meeting police escort. Do you have destination. Contact info?" at 2:43 PM. See Documents on file with the Select Committee to Investigate the January 6th Attack on the United States Capitol (Davie Reinke Production), CTRL0000930918 (January 6, 2021, text messages).

174. Select Committee to Investigate the January 6th Attack on the United States Capitol, Transcribed Interview of Craig Hunter, (Jan. 20, 2022), pp. 44-45. (He called his direct supervisor, Brigadier General Robert Ryan: "The first conversation with him, I first informed him, hey, sir, this is where I am, this is who I've talked to, and they both asked for assistance. And I asked for release of the QRF now. And I asked for, basically send all the additional forces, you know, that you have now. And his response to me was, we are working on it. So he said he was going to coordinate with General Dean and Major General Walker, but they were working on it.").

175. See Select Committee to Investigate the January 6th Attack on the United States Capitol, Informal Interview of Robert J. Contee III, (Dec. 16, 2021).

176. Select Committee to Investigate the January 6th Attack on the United States Capitol, Transcribed Interview of Robert J. Contee III, (Jan. 11, 2022), p. 78.

177. Select Committee to Investigate the January 6th Attack on the United States Capitol, Transcribed Interview of Robert J. Contee III, (Jan. 11, 2022), p. 78.

178. Select Committee to Investigate the January 6th Attack on the United States Capitol, Transcribed Interview of Robert J. Contee III, (Jan. 11, 2022), pp. 75-76.

179. Select Committee to Investigate the January 6th Attack on the United States Capitol, Transcribed Interview of Steven Andrew Sund, (Apr. 20, 2022), p. 148.

180. See Select Committee to Investigate the January 6th Attack on the United States Capitol, Transcribed Interview of Paul Irving, (Mar. 4, 2022), p. 18.

181. Select Committee to Investigate the January 6th Attack on the United States Capitol, Transcribed Interview of Paul Irving, (Mar. 4, 2022), pp. 7-8, 19.

182. Select Committee to Investigate the January 6th Attack on the United States Capitol, Transcribed Interview of Paul Irving, (Mar. 4, 2022), pp. 19, 53 ("[Q: T]he Speaker's office isn't part of that process in terms of requesting the National Guard, correct? A[:] Correct. It would just be on the notification side.").

183. Select Committee to Investigate the January 6th Attack on the United States Capitol, Informal Interview of Terri McCullough, (Apr. 18, 2022).

184. Select Committee to Investigate the January 6th Attack on the United States Capitol, Informal Interview of Terri McCullough, (Apr. 18, 2022).

185. Select Committee to Investigate the January 6th Attack on the United States Capitol, Informal Interview of Terri McCullough, (Apr. 18, 2022).

186. Select Committee to Investigate the January 6th Attack on the United States Capitol, Informal Interview of Terri McCullough, (Apr. 18, 2022).

187. Select Committee to Investigate the January 6th Attack on the United States Capitol, Transcribed Interview of Paul Irving, (Mar. 4, 2022), p. 21.

188. Select Committee to Investigate the January 6th Attack on the United States Capitol, Transcribed Interview of Steven Andrew Sund, (Apr. 20, 2022), pp. 148-50.

189. Select Committee to Investigate the January 6th Attack on the United States Capitol, Transcribed Interview of Steven Andrew Sund, (Apr. 20, 2022), p. 152.

190. Select Committee to Investigate the January 6th Attack on the United States Capitol, Transcribed Interview of Muriel Bowser, (Jan. 12, 2022), p. 57 ("I wasn't speaking, but I was there.").

191. Select Committee to Investigate the January 6th Attack on the United States Capitol, Transcribed Interview of Christopher Rodriguez, (Jan. 25, 2022), p. 64.

192. Select Committee to Investigate the January 6th Attack on the United States Capitol, Informal Interview of Timothy Nick, (Dec. 8, 2021).

193. Select Committee to Investigate the January 6th Attack on the United States Capitol, Transcribed Interview of Ryan McCarthy, (Feb. 4, 2022), p. 99.

194. Select Committee to Investigate the January 6th Attack on the United States Capitol, Transcribed Interview of Ryan McCarthy, (Feb. 4, 2022), pp. 98-99.

195. Select Committee to Investigate the January 6th Attack on the United States Capitol, Transcribed Interview of General Walter Piatt, (Nov. 3, 2022), p. 54.

196. Select Committee to Investigate the January 6th Attack on the United States Capitol, Transcribed Interview of Ryan McCarthy, (Feb. 4, 2022), p. 99.

197. Select Committee to Investigate the January 6th Attack on the United States Capitol, Transcribed Interview of Ryan McCarthy, (Feb. 4, 2022), p. 99; Select Committee to Investigate the January 6th Attack on the United States Capitol, Transcribed Interview of General Walter Piatt, (Nov. 3, 2022), p. 56 ("And he immediately says, 'I'm going to get approval. Get me a plan,' is what he tells me").

198. Select Committee to Investigate the January 6th Attack on the United States Capitol, Transcribed Interview of General James Charles McConville, (Nov. 4, 2021), p. 84.

199. Select Committee to Investigate the January 6th Attack on the United States Capitol, Transcribed Interview of Ryan McCarthy, (Feb. 4, 2022), p. 99. The Army at first denied that General Flynn was present for the call at all. *See* Select Committee to Investigate the January 6th Attack on the United States Capitol, Transcribed Interview of General James Charles McConville, (Nov. 4, 2021), p. 98 ("I think there was just confusion—I know some people are trying, you know, to make it something else, but I think there was just confusion. There were a whole bunch of meetings going on because, you know, I didn't think he was there, because when I was there, he wasn't there."). General McConville said: "And there was no intent to deceive anybody, or there's no conspiracy because of who Charlie Flynn's brother is," General Michael Flynn. *Id.*, at 99. General Flynn said he did not speak on the call. *See* Select Committee to Investigate the January 6th Attack on the United States Capitol, Transcribed Interview of General Charles Anthony Flynn, (Oct. 28, 2021), p. 41 ("A [:] I did not speak on that call. Q [:] Did you identify yourself as being on the call? A [:] I did not. Now, if I said anything, if I—my recollection, if I said anything, I may have tugged on General Piatt's sleeve and asked and said, "What's going on here?" like, "What's the situation?" you know." But others, like Colonel Matthews listening in from the National Guard end of the call, said both Generals Piatt and Flynn were the main interlocuters. *See* Select Committee to Investigate the January 6th Attack on the United States Capitol, Informal Interview of Earl Matthews, (Dec. 20, 2021). On Lt. Nick's notes, at 2:35 p.m., General Flynn's title is written down. *See* Documents on file with the Select Committee to Investigate the January 6th Attack on the United States Capitol (Department of Defense Production), CTRL0000930917 (January 6, 2021, handwritten notes taken by Lt. Timothy Nick). Lt Nick said, "I was just trying to jot down who was on the call." *See* Select Committee to Investigate the January 6th Attack on the United States Capitol, Informal Interview of Timothy Nick, (Dec. 8, 2021). General Flynn ultimately said he was there for a short time. *See* Select Committee to Investigate the January 6th Attack on the United States Capitol, Transcribed Interview of General Charles Anthony Flynn, (Oct. 28, 2021), pp. 40, 42 ("It was—I was literally there—the total time that I'm talking about was about 4 to 5 minutes. I was really around that phone call, rough order of magnitude, for maybe a minute of that;" "it became clear to me that I was in the wrong place. And so I made the decision to leave because General Piatt had a handle on the situation.").

200. Select Committee to Investigate the January 6th Attack on the United States Capitol, Transcribed Interview of General Charles Anthony Flynn, (Oct. 28, 2021), p. 37.

201. Select Committee to Investigate the January 6th Attack on the United States Capitol, Transcribed Interview of General Charles Anthony Flynn, (Oct. 28, 2021), p. 37.

202. Select Committee to Investigate the January 6th Attack on the United States Capitol, Transcribed Interview of General Charles Anthony Flynn, (Oct. 28, 2021), p. 39.

203. Select Committee to Investigate the January 6th Attack on the United States Capitol, Transcribed Interview of Robert J. Contee, III, (Jan. 11, 2022), pp. 79-80.

204. Select Committee to Investigate the January 6th Attack on the United States Capitol, Informal Interview of Earl Matthews, (Dec. 20, 2021).

205. Select Committee to Investigate the January 6th Attack on the United States Capitol, Transcribed Interview of Robert J. Contee, III, (Jan. 11, 2022), p. 83.

206. Select Committee to Investigate the January 6th Attack on the United States Capitol, Transcribed Interview of Robert J. Contee, III, (Jan. 11, 2022), p. 81.

207. Select Committee to Investigate the January 6th Attack on the United States Capitol, Transcribed Interview of Robert J. Contee, III, (Jan. 11, 2022), p. 85.

208. Select Committee to Investigate the January 6th Attack on the United States Capitol, Transcribed Interview of Christopher Rodriguez, (Jan. 25, 2022), p. 70.

209. Select Committee to Investigate the January 6th Attack on the United States Capitol, Transcribed Interview of Christopher Rodriguez, (Jan. 25, 2022), p. 70.

210. Select Committee to Investigate the January 6th Attack on the United States Capitol, Transcribed Interview of General Charles Anthony Flynn, (Oct. 28, 2021), p. 40.

211. Select Committee to Investigate the January 6th Attack on the United States Capitol, Transcribed Interview of General James Charles McConville, (Nov. 4, 2021), pp. 81-82.

212. Select Committee to Investigate the January 6th Attack on the United States Capitol, Transcribed Interview of General William Walker, (Dec. 13, 2021), p. 113.

213. Select Committee to Investigate the January 6th Attack on the United States Capitol, Transcribed Interview of General William Walker, (Dec. 13, 2021), p. 115.

214. Select Committee to Investigate the January 6th Attack on the United States Capitol, Transcribed Interview of Steven Andrew Sund, (Apr. 20, 2022), p. 162.

215. Select Committee to Investigate the January 6th Attack on the United States Capitol, Transcribed Interview of Steven Andrew Sund, (Apr. 20, 2022), p. 161.

216. Select Committee to Investigate the January 6th Attack on the United States Capitol, Transcribed Interview of Steven Andrew Sund, (Apr. 20, 2022), p. 160.

217. Select Committee to Investigate the January 6th Attack on the United States Capitol, Transcribed Interview of Robert J. Contee, III, (Jan. 11, 2022), p. 80.

218. Select Committee to Investigate the January 6th Attack on the United States Capitol, Transcribed Interview of Robert J. Contee, III, (Jan. 11, 2022), p. 80.

219. Select Committee to Investigate the January 6th Attack on the United States Capitol, Transcribed Interview of Christopher Rodriguez, (Jan. 25, 2022), p. 65.

220. Select Committee to Investigate the January 6th Attack on the United States Capitol, Transcribed Interview of Christopher Rodriguez, (Jan. 25, 2022), p. 65.

221. Select Committee to Investigate the January 6th Attack on the United States Capitol, Transcribed Interview of General William Walker, (Dec. 13, 2021), p. 116.

222. Select Committee to Investigate the January 6th Attack on the United States Capitol, Transcribed Interview of General William Walker, (Dec. 13, 2021), p. 116.

223. Select Committee to Investigate the January 6th Attack on the United States Capitol, Transcribed Interview of Steven Andrew Sund, (Apr. 20, 2022), pp. 156-57.

224. Select Committee to Investigate the January 6th Attack on the United States Capitol, Transcribed Interview of Steven Andrew Sund, (Apr. 20, 2022), p. 156.

225. Select Committee to Investigate the January 6th Attack on the United States Capitol, Transcribed Interview of Steven Andrew Sund, (Apr. 20, 2022), p. 156.

226. Select Committee to Investigate the January 6th Attack on the United States Capitol, Transcribed Interview of General Walter Piatt, (Nov. 3, 2021), p. 61.

227. Select Committee to Investigate the January 6th Attack on the United States Capitol, Transcribed Interview of General Walter Piatt, (Nov. 3, 2021), p. 59.

228. Select Committee to Investigate the January 6th Attack on the United States Capitol, Transcribed Interview of General Walter Piatt, (Nov. 3, 2021), p. 57.

229. Select Committee to Investigate the January 6th Attack on the United States Capitol, Transcribed Interview of General Walter Piatt, (Nov. 3, 2021), p. 58.

230. Select Committee to Investigate the January 6th Attack on the United States Capitol, Transcribed Interview of General James Charles McConville, (Nov. 4, 2021), p. 99.

231. Select Committee to Investigate the January 6th Attack on the United States Capitol, Transcribed Interview of General James Charles McConville, (Nov. 4, 2021), p. 105.

232. Select Committee to Investigate the January 6th Attack on the United States Capitol, Transcribed Interview of General James Charles McConville, (Nov. 4, 2021), p. 105.

233. Select Committee to Investigate the January 6th Attack on the United States Capitol, Transcribed Interview of Robert J. Contee, III, (Jan. 11, 2022), pp. 81-82.

234. Select Committee to Investigate the January 6th Attack on the United States Capitol, Transcribed Interview of General Walter Piatt, (Nov. 3, 2021), p. 59.

235. Select Committee to Investigate the January 6th Attack on the United States Capitol, Transcribed Interview of General Walter Piatt, (Nov. 3, 2021), p. 61.

236. Select Committee to Investigate the January 6th Attack on the United States Capitol, Transcribed Interview of General Walter Piatt, (Nov. 3, 2021), p. 59.

237. Select Committee to Investigate the January 6th Attack on the United States Capitol, Transcribed Interview of Robert J. Contee, III, (Jan. 11, 2022), p. 82.

238. Select Committee to Investigate the January 6th Attack on the United States Capitol, Transcribed Interview of Robert J. Contee, III, (Jan. 11, 2022), p. 82.

239. Select Committee to Investigate the January 6th Attack on the United States Capitol, Transcribed Interview of Robert J. Contee, III, (Jan. 11, 2022), p. 82.

240. Select Committee to Investigate the January 6th Attack on the United States Capitol, Transcribed Interview of Steven Andrew Sund, (Apr. 20, 2022), p. 157.

241. Select Committee to Investigate the January 6th Attack on the United States Capitol, Transcribed Interview of General Walter Piatt, (Nov. 3, 2021), p. 59.

242. Select Committee to Investigate the January 6th Attack on the United States Capitol, Transcribed Interview of General Walter Piatt, (Nov. 3, 2021), p. 63.

243. Select Committee to Investigate the January 6th Attack on the United States Capitol, Transcribed Interview of General Walter Piatt, (Nov. 3, 2021), p. 63.

244. Select Committee to Investigate the January 6th Attack on the United States Capitol, Transcribed Interview of General William Walker, (Dec. 13, 2021), p. 116.

245. Select Committee to Investigate the January 6th Attack on the United States Capitol, Transcribed Interview of General William Walker, (Dec. 13, 2021), p. 116.

246. Select Committee to Investigate the January 6th Attack on the United States Capitol, Transcribed Interview of General William Walker, (Dec. 13, 2021), pp. 116-17.

247. Select Committee to Investigate the January 6th Attack on the United States Capitol, Transcribed Interview of Robert J. Contee, III, (Jan. 11, 2022), p. 85.

248. Select Committee to Investigate the January 6th Attack on the United States Capitol, Transcribed Interview of Muriel Bowser, (Jan. 12, 2022), p. 59.

249. Select Committee to Investigate the January 6th Attack on the United States Capitol, Transcribed Interview of Christopher Rodriguez, (Jan. 25, 2022), p. 65.

250. Select Committee to Investigate the January 6th Attack on the United States Capitol, Transcribed Interview of Christopher Rodriguez, (Jan. 25, 2022), p. 65.

251. Select Committee to Investigate the January 6th Attack on the United States Capitol, Transcribed Interview of Steven Andrew Sund, (Apr. 20, 2022), p. 160.

252. Select Committee to Investigate the January 6th Attack on the United States Capitol, Transcribed Interview of General Walter Piatt, (Nov. 3, 2021), p. 60.

253. Select Committee to Investigate the January 6th Attack on the United States Capitol, Transcribed Interview of General Walter Piatt, (Nov. 3, 2021), p. 39.

254. Select Committee to Investigate the January 6th Attack on the United States Capitol, Transcribed Interview of General William Walker, (Dec. 13, 2021), p. 118.

255. Select Committee to Investigate the January 6th Attack on the United States Capitol, Transcribed Interview of General William Walker, (Dec. 13, 2021), p. 118.

256. Select Committee to Investigate the January 6th Attack on the United States Capitol, Transcribed Interview of General William Walker, (Dec. 13, 2021), p. 141.

257. Select Committee to Investigate the January 6th Attack on the United States Capitol, Transcribed Interview of General William Walker, (Dec. 13, 2021), pp. 141-42.

258. Select Committee to Investigate the January 6th Attack on the United States Capitol, Informal Interview of Earl Matthews, (Dec. 20, 2021).

259. Select Committee to Investigate the January 6th Attack on the United States Capitol, Informal Interview of Earl Matthews, (Dec. 20, 2021).

260. Select Committee to Investigate the January 6th Attack on the United States Capitol, Informal Interview of Earl Matthews, (Dec. 20, 2021).

261. Select Committee to Investigate the January 6th Attack on the United States Capitol, Transcribed Interview of General William Walker, (Dec. 13, 2021), p. 141.

262. Select Committee to Investigate the January 6th Attack on the United States Capitol, Transcribed Interview of General Mark Milley, (Nov. 17, 2021), p. 83.

263. Select Committee to Investigate the January 6th Attack on the United States Capitol, Transcribed Interview of General Mark Milley, (Nov. 17, 2021), p. 83.

264. Select Committee to Investigate the January 6th Attack on the United States Capitol, Transcribed Interview of General Mark Milley, (Nov. 17, 2021), p. 288.

265. Select Committee to Investigate the January 6th Attack on the United States Capitol, Transcribed Interview of Christopher Miller, (Jan. 14, 2022), p. 125.

266. Select Committee to Investigate the January 6th Attack on the United States Capitol, Transcribed Interview of General Mark Milley, (Nov. 17, 2021), p. 296.

267. Select Committee to Investigate the January 6th Attack on the United States Capitol, Transcribed Interview of Christopher Miller, (Jan. 14, 2022), p. 124.

268. Select Committee to Investigate the January 6th Attack on the United States Capitol, Transcribed Interview of Ryan McCarthy, (Feb. 4, 2022), p. 143.

269. Select Committee to Investigate the January 6th Attack on the United States Capitol, Transcribed Interview of General Mark Milley, (Nov. 17, 2021), p. 82 ("So at no time did I and I am not aware of anyone in the Pentagon having a conversation with President Trump on the day of the 6th.").

270. Select Committee to Investigate the January 6th Attack on the United States Capitol, Transcribed Interview of General Mark Milley, (Nov. 17, 2021), p. 285.

271. Select Committee to Investigate the January 6th Attack on the United States Capitol, Transcribed Interview of General Mark Milley, (Nov. 17, 2021), p. 268.

272. Select Committee to Investigate the January 6th Attack on the United States Capitol, Transcribed Interview of General Mark Milley, (Nov. 17, 2021), p. 285.

273. Select Committee to Investigate the January 6th Attack on the United States Capitol, Transcribed Interview of Christopher Miller, (Jan. 14, 2022), pp. 95-96.

274. Select Committee to Investigate the January 6th Attack on the United States Capitol, Transcribed Interview of Christopher Miller, (Jan. 14, 2022), p. 96.

275. Select Committee to Investigate the January 6th Attack on the United States Capitol, Transcribed Interview of Christopher Miller, (Jan. 14, 2022), p. 96.

276. Select Committee to Investigate the January 6th Attack on the United States Capitol, Tran-
      scribed Interview of Christopher Miller, (Jan. 14, 2022), pp. 97-98.

277. Select Committee to Investigate the January 6th Attack on the United States Capitol, Tran-
      scribed Interview of Christopher Miller, (Jan. 14, 2022), pp. 100-01.

278. Select Committee to Investigate the January 6th Attack on the United States Capitol, Tran-
      scribed Interview of Christopher Miller, (Jan. 14, 2022), p. 98.

279. Select Committee to Investigate the January 6th Attack on the United States Capitol, Tran-
      scribed Interview of Christopher Miller, (Jan. 14, 2022), p. 98.

280. Select Committee to Investigate the January 6th Attack on the United States Capitol, Tran-
      scribed Interview of Christopher Miller, (Jan. 14, 2022), p. 98.

281. Select Committee to Investigate the January 6th Attack on the United States Capitol, Tran-
      scribed Interview of Christopher Miller, (Jan. 14, 2022), p. 102.

282. Documents on file with the Select Committee to Investigate the January 6th Attack on the
      United States Capitol (Mark Meadows Production), MM000789 (January 5, 2021, emails
      between Mark Meadows and John Aycoth, "Re: DC mayor activates National Guard ahead of
      pro-Trump demonstrations, The Hill").

283. Select Committee to Investigate the January 6th Attack on the United States Capitol, Tran-
      scribed Interview of Christopher Miller, (Jan. 14, 2022), pp. 99-100.

284. Select Committee to Investigate the January 6th Attack on the United States Capitol, Tran-
      scribed Interview of Christopher Miller, (Jan. 14, 2022), pp. 99-101. (Q: "[D]id you take that
      as a request for you or an order to you to deploy 10,000 troops? A[:] No, absolutely not. I
      interpreted it as a bit of presidential banter or President Trump banter that you all are
      familiar with, and in no way, shape, or form did I interpret that as an order or direction.");
      ("Q[:] So I want to be clear here that—since then, in February 2021, Mark Meadows said on
      Fox News that, quote: Even in January, that was a given as many as 10,000 National Guard
      troops were told to be on the ready by the Secretary of Defense. Is there any accuracy to
      that statement? A[:] I'm not—not from my perspective. I was never given any direction or
      order or knew of any plans of that nature."); (Q: "To be crystal clear, there was no direct
      order from President Trump to put 10,000 troops to be on the ready for January 6th, cor-
      rect? A[:] No. Yeah. That's correct. There was no direct—there was no order from the Presi-
      dent.").

285. Select Committee to Investigate the January 6th Attack on the United States Capitol, Tran-
      scribed Interview of Muriel Bowser, (Jan. 12, 2022), p. 13.

286. Select Committee to Investigate the January 6th Attack on the United States Capitol, Tran-
      scribed Interview of General Mark Milley, (Nov. 17, 2021), pp. 78-79.

287. Select Committee to Investigate the January 6th Attack on the United States Capitol, Tran-
      scribed Interview of General Mark Milley, (Nov. 17, 2021), pp. 252-53.

288. Select Committee to Investigate the January 6th Attack on the United States Capitol, Tran-
      scribed Interview of General Mark Milley, (Nov. 17, 2021), p. 253.

289. Select Committee to Investigate the January 6th Attack on the United States Capitol, Tran-
      scribed Interview of Ryan McCarthy, (Feb. 4, 2022), p. 102.

290. Select Committee to Investigate the January 6th Attack on the United States Capitol, Tran-
      scribed Interview of Ryan McCarthy, (Feb. 4, 2022), p. 102.

291. Select Committee to Investigate the January 6th Attack on the United States Capitol, Tran-
      scribed Interview of Ryan McCarthy, (Feb. 4, 2022), p. 102.

292. Select Committee to Investigate the January 6th Attack on the United States Capitol, Tran-
      scribed Interview of Christopher Miller, (Jan. 14, 2022), p. 113 ("So, at 3 o'clock, I gave the
      order to mobilize the entire District of Columbia National Guard, however, big they
      are . . . . everybody show up at the [Armory and], . . . move them to the Capitol immedi-
      ately to support local law enforcement.").

293. Select Committee to Investigate the January 6th Attack on the United States Capitol, Tran-
      scribed Interview of Christopher Miller, (Jan. 14, 2022), p. 122.

294. Select Committee to Investigate the January 6th Attack on the United States Capitol, Transcribed Interview of Ryan McCarthy, (Feb. 4, 2022), p. 124 (emphasis added).

295. Select Committee to Investigate the January 6th Attack on the United States Capitol, Transcribed Interview of William Walker, (Dec. 13, 2021), p. 120.

296. Select Committee to Investigate the January 6th Attack on the United States Capitol, Transcribed Interview of William Walker, (Dec. 13, 2021), p. 120.

297. Select Committee to Investigate the January 6th Attack on the United States Capitol, Informal Interview of Earl Matthews, (Dec. 20, 2021).

298. Select Committee to Investigate the January 6th Attack on the United States Capitol, Informal Interview of Timothy Nick, (Dec. 8, 2021).

299. The two letters referenced include Secretary Miller's January 4 memorandum setting restrictions on the Guard and a follow-up letter from Secretary McCarthy on January 5 expounding on those limitations. See Documents on file with the Select Committee to Investigate the January 6th Attack on the United States Capitol (Department of Defense Production), DoD 00000006 (January 4, 2021, memorandum), DoD Production DoD 00003493 (January 5, 2021 follow-up letter).

300. Select Committee to Investigate the January 6th Attack on the United States Capitol, Transcribed Interview of William Walker, (Apr. 21, 2022), p. 45.

301. Select Committee to Investigate the January 6th Attack on the United States Capitol, Transcribed Interview of William Walker, (Dec. 13, 2021), p. 104.

302. Select Committee to Investigate the January 6th Attack on the United States Capitol, Transcribed Interview of Christopher Miller, (Jan. 14, 2022), p. 122.

303. Select Committee to Investigate the January 6th Attack on the United States Capitol, Transcribed Interview of Christopher Miller, (Jan. 14, 2022), p. 123.

304. Select Committee to Investigate the January 6th Attack on the United States Capitol, Transcribed Interview of Ryan McCarthy, (Feb. 4, 2022), p. 104.

305. Select Committee to Investigate the January 6th Attack on the United States Capitol, Transcribed Interview of William Walker, (Apr. 21, 2022), p. 47; Earl Matthews, "The Harder Right: An Analysis of a Recent DoD Inspector General Investigation and Other Matters," (Dec. 1, 2021), available at https://www.justsecurity.org/wp-content/uploads/2021/12/january-6-clearinghouse-Colonel-Earl-G.-Matthews-An-Analysis-of-a-Recent-DoD-Inspector-General-Investigation-and-Other-Matters-December-1-2021.pdf.

306. Select Committee to Investigate the January 6th Attack on the United States Capitol, Transcribed Interview of William Walker, (Apr. 21, 2022), p. 55.

307. Select Committee to Investigate the January 6th Attack on the United States Capitol, Transcribed Interview of William Walker, (Apr. 21, 2022), p. 52.

308. Select Committee to Investigate the January 6th Attack on the United States Capitol, Transcribed Interview of Ryan McCarthy, (Feb. 4, 2022), p. 125.

309. Aaron C. Davis (@byaaroncdavis), Twitter, Jan. 6, 2021 2:55 p.m. ET, available at https://twitter.com/byaaroncdavis/status/1346908166030766080.

310. Select Committee to Investigate the January 6th Attack on the United States Capitol, Transcribed Interview of Ryan McCarthy, (Feb. 4 2022), p. 109, 127, 129.

311. Select Committee to Investigate the January 6th Attack on the United States Capitol, Transcribed Interview of Ryan McCarthy, (Feb. 4 2022), p. 130.

312. Select Committee to Investigate the January 6th Attack on the United States Capitol, Transcribed Interview of Craig Hunter, (Jan. 20, 2022), p. 49. ("I mentioned that to Chief Carroll. I said, hey, Chief, you know, I may just pull everyone back. And he told me, he said, well, right now I may need your Guardsmen who are on the traffic control points, because all of my officers are here at the Capitol, so I don't have officers out there in the city right now, so I may need to re-mission those guys for other things. Can you just send me the personnel from the Armory here? You know, so it was almost like we were talking about splitting.

We'll use that 90 to support MPD on anything they needed in the city, but I can still get, you know, another 200, 250 from the Armory to come to the Capitol now."). But Assistant Chief Carroll didn't recall such a conversation. Select Committee to Investigate the January 6th Attack on the United States Capitol, Informal Interview of Jeffrey Carroll, (Nov. 18, 2022) ("I don't think it happened. It doesn't sound like something that would've happened.") Sergeant Major Brooks said it was him who made the recommendation to hold the first shift at their posts. Select Committee to Investigate the January 6th Attack on the United States Capitol, Informal Interview of Michael F. Brooks, (Dec. 13, 2021).

313. *See* Select Committee to Investigate the January 6th Attack on the United States Capitol, Informal Interview of Stewart Tarp, (Jan. 6, 2022).

314. Select Committee to Investigate the January 6th Attack on the United States Capitol, Informal Interview of Ken Ryan, (Dec. 9, 2021) ("Those that were on the TCPs on the 6th did not go to the Capitol on the night of the 6th."); Select Committee to Investigate the January 6th Attack on the United States Capitol, Transcribed Interview of Craig Hunter, (Jan. 20, 2022), p. 81; Select Committee to Investigate the January 6th Attack on the United States Capitol, Transcribed Interview of James Charles McConville, (Nov. 4, 2021), pp.88-89 ("Well, what I would think was happening during that hour and a half is they're . . . leaving their check points, the traffic control points, the 30 traffic control points so that all of those vehicles, they're hopping in their cars and they're driving back in traffic through the [A]rmory and getting set."); Select Committee to Investigate the January 6th Attack on the United States Capitol, Transcribed Interview of General Walter Piatt, (Nov. 3, 2021), p. 50 ("They were out on traffic control points. They were doing another job. The QRF was across the river. We brought them over to the Armory. But they had to reconfigure, reorganize now to go into a civil disturbance operation.").

315. Select Committee to Investigate the January 6th Attack on the United States Capitol, Informal Interview of David Reinke, (Jan. 6, 2022).

316. Select Committee to Investigate the January 6th Attack on the United States Capitol, Informal Interview of David Reinke, (Jan. 6, 2022).

317. Select Committee to Investigate the January 6th Attack on the United States Capitol, Informal Interview of Stewart Tarp, (Jan. 6, 2022).

318. Select Committee to Investigate the January 6th Attack on the United States Capitol, Informal Interview of Stewart Tarp, (Jan. 6, 2022).

319. Select Committee to Investigate the January 6th Attack on the United States Capitol, Informal Interview of Stewart Tarp, (Jan. 6, 2022).

320. Select Committee to Investigate the January 6th Attack on the United States Capitol, *Business Meeting on the January 6th Investigation*, 117th Cong., 2d sess., (Oct. 13, 2022), available at https://www.govinfo.gov/committee/house-january6th.

321. Select Committee to Investigate the January 6th Attack on the United States Capitol, *Business Meeting on the January 6th Investigation*, 117th Cong., 2d sess., (Oct. 13, 2022), available at https://www.govinfo.gov/committee/house-january6th.

322. Select Committee to Investigate the January 6th Attack on the United States Capitol, Transcribed Interview of Ryan McCarthy, (Feb. 4, 2022), p. 109; Select Committee to Investigate the January 6th Attack on the United States Capitol, Transcribed Interview of Robert J. Contee III, (Jan. 11, 2022), p. 86.

323. Select Committee to Investigate the January 6th Attack on the United States Capitol, Transcribed Interview of Ryan McCarthy, (Feb. 4, 2022), p. 129.

324. Select Committee to Investigate the January 6th Attack on the United States Capitol, Transcribed Interview of William Walker, (Dec. 13, 2021), pp. 121-22.

325. Select Committee to Investigate the January 6th Attack on the United States Capitol, Transcribed Interview of William Walker, (Dec. 13, 2021), p. 108.

326. Select Committee to Investigate the January 6th Attack on the United States Capitol, Transcribed Interview of William Walker, (Dec. 13, 2021), p. 108.

327. Select Committee to Investigate the January 6th Attack on the United States Capitol, Transcribed Interview of James Charles McConville, (Nov. 4, 2021), pp. 91-92.

328. Select Committee to Investigate the January 6th Attack on the United States Capitol, Transcribed Interview of Ryan McCarthy, (Feb. 4, 2022), p. 107.

329. Select Committee to Investigate the January 6th Attack on the United States Capitol, Transcribed Interview of Ryan McCarthy, (Feb. 4, 2022), p. 123.

330. Select Committee to Investigate the January 6th Attack on the United States Capitol, Transcribed Interview of Ryan McCarthy, (Feb. 4, 2022), p. 141.

331. Select Committee to Investigate the January 6th Attack on the United States Capitol, Transcribed Interview of William Walker, (Dec. 13, 2021), p. 121.

332. Select Committee to Investigate the January 6th Attack on the United States Capitol, Transcribed Interview of William Walker, (Dec. 13, 2021), p. 122 (emphasis added).

333. Select Committee to Investigate the January 6th Attack on the United States Capitol, Transcribed Interview of Craig Hunter, (Jan. 20, 2022), p. 67.

334. Select Committee to Investigate the January 6th Attack on the United States Capitol, Transcribed Interview of Craig Hunter, (Jan. 20, 2022), pp. 65, 70.

335. Select Committee to Investigate the January 6th Attack on the United States Capitol, Transcribed Interview of Craig Hunter, (Jan. 20, 2022), p. 65.

336. Select Committee to Investigate the January 6th Attack on the United States Capitol, Transcribed Interview of William Walker, (Dec. 13, 2021), p. 121.

337. Select Committee to Investigate the January 6th Attack on the United States Capitol, Transcribed Interview of Craig Hunter, (Jan. 20, 2022), p. 66.

338. Select Committee to Investigate the January 6th Attack on the United States Capitol, Informal Interview of David Reinke, (Jan. 6, 2022).

339. Select Committee to Investigate the January 6th Attack on the United States Capitol, Informal Interview of Stewart Tarp, (Jan. 6, 2022); Select Committee to Investigate the January 6th Attack on the United States Capitol, Informal Interview of David Reinke, (Jan. 6, 2022).

340. Select Committee to Investigate the January 6th Attack on the United States Capitol, Transcribed Interview of Ryan McCarthy, (Feb. 4, 2022), p. 134.

341. Select Committee to Investigate the January 6th Attack on the United States Capitol, Transcribed Interview of Ryan McCarthy, (Feb. 4, 2022), p. 131.

342. Select Committee to Investigate the January 6th Attack on the United States Capitol, Transcribed Interview of Ryan McCarthy, (Feb. 4, 2022), p. 131.

343. Select Committee to Investigate the January 6th Attack on the United States Capitol, Transcribed Interview of General Walter Piatt, (Nov. 3, 2021), p. 15.

344. Select Committee to Investigate the January 6th Attack on the United States Capitol, Informal Interview of Chris LaNeve, (Feb. 25, 2022).

345. Select Committee to Investigate the January 6th Attack on the United States Capitol, Informal Interview of Chris LaNeve, (Feb. 25, 2022).

346. Select Committee to Investigate the January 6th Attack on the United States Capitol, Informal Interview of Chris LaNeve, (Feb. 25, 2022).

347. Select Committee to Investigate the January 6th Attack on the United States Capitol, Transcribed Interview of Ryan McCarthy, (Feb. 4, 2022), p. 133.

348. Select Committee to Investigate the January 6th Attack on the United States Capitol, Informal Interview of Chris LaNeve, (Feb. 25, 2022).

349. Select Committee to Investigate the January 6th Attack on the United States Capitol, Informal Interview of Chris LaNeve, (Feb. 25, 2022); Select Committee to Investigate the January 6th Attack on the United States Capitol, Transcribed Interview of General James Charles McConville, (Nov. 4, 2021), p. 91 ("General LaNeve provided the link up location and the lead.").

350. Select Committee to Investigate the January 6th Attack on the United States Capitol, Informal Interview of Chris LaNeve, (Feb. 25, 2022).

351. Select Committee to Investigate the January 6th Attack on the United States Capitol, Informal Interview of Chris LaNeve, (Feb. 25, 2022).

352. Earl Matthews, "The Harder Right: An Analysis of a Recent DoD Inspector General Investigation and Other Matters," (Dec. 1, 2021), available at https://www.justsecurity.org/wp-content/uploads/2021/12/january-6-clearinghouse-Colonel-Earl-G.-Matthews-An-Analysis-of-a-Recent-DoD-Inspector-General-Investigation-and-Other-Matters-December-1-2021.pdf ("MG Walker denies that LaNeve called him at 4:25PM, or that he spoke to LaNeve at anytime between the phone call from Chief Sund at 1:49PM and the eventual DCNG deployment to the Capitol at 5:08PM.").

353. Select Committee to Investigate the January 6th Attack on the United States Capitol, Transcribed Interview of William Walker, (Dec. 13, 2021), p. 139.

354. Select Committee to Investigate the January 6th Attack on the United States Capitol, Continued Interview of William Walker, (Apr. 21, 2022), p. 60.

355. Select Committee to Investigate the January 6th Attack on the United States Capitol, Continued Interview of William Walker, (Apr. 21, 2022), p. 65-66.

356. Select Committee to Investigate the January 6th Attack on the United States Capitol, Informal Interview of Earl Matthews, (Dec. 20, 2021) ("One reason I know that there is no 4:30 call—is that I was sitting next to Gen. Walker").

357. Select Committee to Investigate the January 6th Attack on the United States Capitol, Informal Interview of Michael F. Brooks, (Dec. 13, 2021).

358. Documents on file with the Select Committee to Investigate the January 6th Attack on the United States Capitol (Department of Defense Production), CTRL0000930917 (January 6, 2021, handwritten notes taken by Lt. Timothy Nick).

359. Select Committee to Investigate the January 6th Attack on the United States Capitol, Continued Interview of William Walker, (Apr. 21, 2022), p. 60.

360. Select Committee to Investigate the January 6th Attack on the United States Capitol, Continued Interview of William Walker, (Apr. 21, 2022), pp. 60-61.

361. Select Committee to Investigate the January 6th Attack on the United States Capitol, Informal Interview of Timothy Nick, (Dec. 8, 2021).

362. Select Committee to Investigate the January 6th Attack on the United States Capitol, Transcribed Interview of James Charles McConville, (Nov. 4, 2021), pp. 90-92.

363. Select Committee to Investigate the January 6th Attack on the United States Capitol, Transcribed Interview of William Walker, (Dec. 13, 2021), p. 140.

364. Select Committee to Investigate the January 6th Attack on the United States Capitol, Informal Interview of David Reinke, (Jan. 6, 2022).

365. Select Committee to Investigate the January 6th Attack on the United States Capitol, Informal Interview of David Reinke, (Jan. 6, 2022).

366. Select Committee to Investigate the January 6th Attack on the United States Capitol, Informal Interview of David Reinke, (Jan. 6, 2022).

367. Documents on file with the Select Committee to Investigate the January 6th Attack on the United States Capitol (Department of Defense Production), DoD 00001196 (January 8, 2021, Memorandum for Record from Office of the Secretary of Defense re: Timeline for December 31, 2020–January 6, 2021), DoD 00001090 (January 7, 2021, Memorandum for Record from the Secretary of the Army re: Timeline For 31 December–7 January 2021), 00000490 (January 7, 2021, Memorandum for Record from Joint Force Headquarters re: Timeline for Request for Assistance during Civil Unrest on 6 January 2021 and DC National Guard Authorization to Respond).

368. Text message from David Reinke to Colonel Hunter on January 6, 2021.

369. Select Committee to Investigate the January 6th Attack on the United States Capitol, Informal Interview of David Reinke, (Jan. 6, 2022).

370. Select Committee to Investigate the January 6th Attack on the United States Capitol, Informal Interview of Stewart Tarp, (Jan. 6, 2022).

371. Select Committee to Investigate the January 6th Attack on the United States Capitol, Informal Interview of Stewart Tarp, (Jan. 6, 2022).

372. Select Committee to Investigate the January 6th Attack on the United States Capitol, Transcribed Interview of Craig Hunter, (Jan. 20, 2022), pp. 50-51.

373. Select Committee to Investigate the January 6th Attack on the United States Capitol, Transcribed Interview of Craig Hunter, (Jan. 20, 2022), p. 51.

374. Select Committee to Investigate the January 6th Attack on the United States Capitol, Transcribed Interview of Craig Hunter, (Jan. 20, 2022), p. 53.

375. Select Committee to Investigate the January 6th Attack on the United States Capitol, Transcribed Interview of Ryan McCarthy, (Feb. 4, 2022), p. 120.

376. Select Committee to Investigate the January 6th Attack on the United States Capitol, Transcribed Interview of Ryan McCarthy, (Feb. 4, 2022), pp. 111-12.

377. Select Committee to Investigate the January 6th Attack on the United States Capitol, Transcribed Interview of Robert Glover, (May 2, 2022), p. 72.

378. Select Committee to Investigate the January 6th Attack on the United States Capitol, Transcribed Interview of Robert Glover, (May 2, 2022), p. 72.

379. Select Committee to Investigate the January 6th Attack on the United States Capitol, Transcribed Interview of Robert Glover, (May 2, 2022), p. 72.

380. Select Committee to Investigate the January 6th Attack on the United States Capitol, Transcribed Interview of Robert Glover, (May 2, 2022), pp. 67-68.

381. Select Committee to Investigate the January 6th Attack on the United States Capitol, Transcribed Interview of Robert Glover, (May 2, 2022), p. 72.

382. Select Committee to Investigate the January 6th Attack on the United States Capitol, Transcribed Interview of Robert Glover, (May 2, 2022), p. 73.

383. Select Committee to Investigate the January 6th Attack on the United States Capitol, Transcribed Interview of Ryan McCarthy, (Feb. 4, 2022), p. 144.

384. Select Committee to Investigate the January 6th Attack on the United States Capitol, Transcribed Interview of Ryan McCarthy, (Feb. 4, 2022), p. 111.

385. Select Committee to Investigate the January 6th Attack on the United States Capitol, Transcribed Interview of Ryan McCarthy, (Feb. 4, 2022), p. 130.

386. Select Committee to Investigate the January 6th Attack on the United States Capitol, Transcribed Interview of General Mark Milley, (Nov. 17, 2021), p. 83.

387. Select Committee to Investigate the January 6th Attack on the United States Capitol, Continued Interview of William Walker, (Apr. 21, 2022), p.71.

388. Select Committee to Investigate the January 6th Attack on the United States Capitol, Continued Interview of William Walker, (Apr. 21, 2022), p. 72.

APPENDIX 3

THE BIG RIP-OFF: FOLLOW THE MONEY

INTRODUCTION

This appendix will consider the extent to which President Trump's Campaign and related entities raised an unprecedented amount of political donations using inflammatory messaging alleging that the 2020 U.S. Presidential election was fraudulent or stolen. It will review what tools and methods were used to produce, transmit and optimize these fundraising solicitations; who drafted and approved the messaging and what they knew about the accuracy of the messaging; who ultimately benefitted from these donations; and the impact of these messages on their recipients.

The Select Committee's investigation demonstrates that President Trump's baseless claims of election fraud—the Big Lie—served a dual purpose, forming the foundation of his attempts to overturn the 2020 Presidential election and launching a fundraising effort to fund the former President's other endeavors and to enrich his associates—the Big Rip-off.

The false election fraud narrative embedded in fundraising emails and text messages amplified the Big Lie by perpetuating a belief that the 2020 election was stolen from President Trump and effectuated the Big Rip-off by misleading donors into thinking their donations could alter the election results.

At the same time, the Big Lie helped President Trump and the Republican National Committee (RNC) raise more than $250 million after the election, much of it from small-dollar donors who were promised their money would "Stop the Steal."

Despite what they told their supporters, however, most of their money was not used to stop any purported steal—it was diverted to accomplish the Big Rip-off. Millions of dollars that were raised ostensibly for "election defense" and "fighting voter fraud" were not spent that way at all.

Moreover, the Select Committee's investigation shows that the *RNC knew* that President Trump's claims about winning the election were baseless and that post-election donations would not help him secure an additional term in office. Yet, both the Trump Campaign and the RNC decided to continue fundraising after the election, *a decision that would have come from President Trump himself.*

In short, President Trump and his Campaign ripped off supporters by raising more than $250 million by claiming they wanted to fight fraud they knew did not exist and to challenge an election they knew he lost.

DISCUSSION

THE TRUMP CAMPAIGN FUNDRAISING TEAM

As detailed below, the Trump Campaign misled the American public and President Trump's donors on how they planned to use, and did use, the donated funds while bombarding supporters with hundreds of emails, as many as twenty-five emails per day, stating the election had been stolen. In those emails, they used inflammatory language accusing Democrats of trying to "steal the election," encouraged supporters to join the "Trump army"; "Defend" the election: and to "fight back" over, and over, and over again.[1] They sent these emails out because they knew they were effective at raising money.[2] This was made possible by the creation of a fundraising machine powered jointly by the Trump Campaign and the RNC.

A. The TMAGAC Fundraising Machine

During the 2020 election cycle, President Trump operated a structure under which the Trump reelection campaign and the RNC merged programs and raised money jointly through the Trump Make America Great Again Committee (internally referred to by its acronym TMAGAC, which RNC officials pronounced "T-Magic").[3] TMAGAC was focused on raising money online through small-dollar donations.[4] Tim Murtaugh, the Trump Campaign's communications director, described the TMAGAC fundraising operation as "an entity unto itself within the campaign."[5]

The individual charged with leading the digital operation in 2020 was Gary Coby.[6] Coby first started working with the RNC in 2016 even before President Trump became the nominee.[7] Coby explained that, as digital director, his role during the 2020 Presidential election cycle was to "oversee the digital operation."[8] Similarly, senior staffers at the Trump Campaign and the RNC all made clear that Coby was the individual in charge of the TMAGAC digital team.[9] Both high-level staffers at the Trump Campaign and at the RNC confirmed that Coby had the trust of Jared Kushner, the President's son-in-law.[10]

Coby explained that during the 2020 Presidential election cycle, the TMAGAC digital team was a "big team with multiple organizations and vendor teams all working together as one, that include[d] RNC staff, [Donald J. Trump for President] staff, [and] maybe a half dozen vendor teams."[11] The RNC digital team, a subset of the TMAGAC digital team, was led operationally by Kevin Zambrano, Chief Digital Officer at the RNC. In 2020, members of the digital staff of both the RNC and Trump Campaign merged in an office building in Arlington, Virginia, with some suites jointly hosting RNC and Trump Campaign staff on the digital team, and other suites hosting third-party companies, such as Opn Sesame and Direct Persuasion.[12] Thereafter, Zambrano assisted Coby in managing the TMAGAC digital team.[13] Zambrano explained, "The majority of the staff was at the RNC doing both RNC and TMAGAC work."[14] This work was focused squarely on fundraising.[15]

The RNC digital team included Austin Boedigheimer, who, starting in January 2019, was the RNC's digital deputy director[16] and technically served as Zambrano's deputy.[17] In reality, Boedigheimer reported to both Zambrano and Coby.[18] Boedigheimer also led the TMAGAC digital fundraising team, which was comprised of all online fundraising efforts, including fundraising emails and text messages.[19] At the end of the 2020 cycle, that team had 20 or 30 people within smaller teams, such as the copy team, the text message team, the data team, the advertising team, and the graphics team.[20]

The RNC digital team also included a team of copywriters, who were responsible for writing the fundraising emails and text messages to solicit small-dollar donations through TMAGAC.[21] These copywriters reported to Hanna Allred, the RNC's Chief Copywriter.[22] By mid-2020, there were three copywriters who reported to Allred: Alex Murglin,[23] Ethan Katz,[24] and Alex Blinkoff.[25] Blinkoff and Katz worked in that role from June 2020 until they were fired approximately three weeks after the 2020 election, while Murglin remains a copywriter at the RNC.

Although the TMAGAC team consisted of both Trump Campaign and RNC staffers, TMAGAC operated as one entity working towards one goal—raising as much money as possible.[26]

B. The Fundraising Assembly Line

The copywriting process worked like an assembly line, where different individuals performed a task and passed on the work product to someone else, including for internal approval.[27] To generate content for fundraising communications, Allred explained, the copywriting fundraising team was "watching the messaging coming out of the committee [RNC] and the campaign and from the President himself and what his family was talking about."[28] For example, in a November 2020 email, Boedigheimer stated to Allred, "Good to include lines like [']we need the resources to make sure they don't try to steal this election. We saw what happened on election night, we can't let them take the senate too.[']"[29]

It was evident that the copywriters "would draft a lot of the content based on...what the President was saying."[30] And there was no mistaking it, President Trump "was providing us [the copywriters] with a lot of content online."[31] Allred said Boedigheimer was encouraging her to use this language because it would cause President Trump's supporters to donate by "giving a purpose to their donation"[32] and that they used this repeatedly because it worked.[33] Boedigheimer did not dispute this, and reaffirmed that such language had been successful at fundraising.[34]

Further, the emails that were signed by President Trump or "Team Trump" were intentionally drafted to capture President Trump's voice, tone and messaging.[35] Boedigheimer explained, "[President Trump] obviously has a very aggressive[,] excitable tone, and we would try to incorporate that in our messaging as well."[36] The goal was to make the millions of recipients of aggressive, hyperbolic fundraising emails believe that the emails were coming from President Trump himself. In Zambrano's words, the purpose was to give recipients "red meat."[37]

C. The Approvals Process

The Structure. Draft emails were submitted for approval to a designated group that handled approvals of all TMAGAC fundraising copy (the "Approvals Group").[38] Boedigheimer retained responsibility for ensuring that TMAGAC's fundraising copy was approved before being sent to the public.[39]

The Approvals Group consisted of three sets of stakeholders from the RNC and the Trump Campaign,[40] and included a variety of other interested staffers, including Zambrano, Boedigheimer, and Allred.[41] TMAGAC's fundraising copy could not be sent without approval from the legal, communications and research departments.[42]

Perceived Responsibilities. After election day, a small group of staffers in the Approvals Group actively reviewed and approved the numerous fundraising emails and text messages that spread false election fraud claims. These staffers included:

- **RNC Legal:** Justin Reimer, RNC Chief Counsel[43] and Jenna Kirsch, RNC Associate Counsel[44]
- **RNC Communications:** Cassie Docksey, Deputy Communications Director[45]
- **RNC Research:** Michael Reed, Deputy Chief of Staff for Communications[46]
- **Trump Campaign Legal:** Alex Cannon, Deputy General Counsel[47]
- **Trump Campaign Communications and Research:** Zach Parkinson, Deputy Director of Communications and Director of Research[48]

Boedigheimer, as head of the fundraising team handling the drafting and propagation of fundraising messaging, told the Select Committee his understanding of the role the three components of the Approvals Group (legal, communications, and research) performed when reviewing emails and text messages.

Regarding legal, Boedigheimer explained that he understood Alex Cannon's role, as the Trump Campaign's Deputy General Counsel, was to review the emails from a "legal perspective" by "essentially making sure that there's no legal issues with the content."[49]

Regarding communications, Boedigheimer stated that the communications staffers in the Approvals Group were reviewing the content and "[m]aking sure that it's on message and good from a comms perspective."[50]

Lastly, Boedigheimer explained that the research team was "looking for . . . things that are inaccurate."[51]

Although Boedigheimer provided only a vague explanation of the role of the Approvals Group, he emphasized that he had to "trust that the research, the comms, and the legal team are going to do their processes to make sure it's [the TMAGAC fundraising copy was] accurate."[52] He further noted, "[I]t was the approval chain's job to see what the accuracy of the email is and whether it's true or not. . . . We were sending information and then leaning on our approval chain to make sure that it's accurate."[53]

The Select Committee's investigation revealed that the Approvals Group did not operate that way, however. The Select Committee interviewed members of the Approvals Group handling the communications, research, and legal functions and confirmed that members of the Approvals Group typically engaged only in cursory reviews of the fundraising messages and did not review substantive claims of election fraud for accuracy.

Zach Parkinson, the Trump Campaign's Deputy Director of Communications and Research Director, represented the Trump Campaign's communications and research functions in the Approvals Group. Parkinson made clear, "Generally, our role when it came to fundraising emails and texts was to approve them for the communications team."[54] Parkinson noted that that he was typically the person who weighed in on behalf of the Trump Campaign's communications and research team.[55] He added, "we would review them for messaging consistency, sometimes we would review them for factual accuracy, and then we would provide the communications approval for those."[56]

Parkinson clarified that the scope of review for "factual accuracy" was limited. Specifically, his review of fundraising emails and text messages for accuracy was limited to questions concerning items such as time and location.[57]

Critically, Parkinson did not review statements regarding election fraud in the fundraising copy for accuracy because "most political text messages and fundraising emails are political rhetoric, and so a lot of them don't necessarily require fact checking."[58] He added that "political rhetoric," such as "Democrats are trying to steal the election," was not something he and his team were "necessarily tasked to say no to."[59] Parkinson made clear that he thought the legal department, namely Alex Cannon, would handle reviewing for accuracy, noting "I deferred to the legal team on the legitimacy and the ability to substantiate claims that were made that were put through these approvals and whether or not we could, again, substantiate them or they were in line with our legal efforts."[60] Parkinson, as the head of the research team, the very campaign team meant to fact-check and ensure accuracy in the Trump Campaign's statements, said he was "simply looking for messaging consistency."[61] Whether Democrats were engaged in fraud to steal the election was a "political argument" to Parkinson, which he did not review for accuracy.[62]

Like Parkinson, Michael Reed, then the RNC's Deputy Chief of Staff for Communications, was not reviewing the TMAGAC emails about election fraud for broader accuracy. Notably, Reed could not recall a single email that he researched to do a fact-check or follow up on to see if claims contained in the email were, in fact, true.[63]

Boedigheimer and the copywriters believed the research staffers were looking for messages that they believed were inaccurate, but they were doing no such thing.

Alex Cannon, the Trump Campaign's legal representative in the Approvals Group, was no different—the TMAGAC fundraisers thought he was doing far more than he was in fact doing. The Select Committee received a November 4, 2020, email from Nathan Groth, counsel for the Trump Campaign, to Alex Cannon. This email reflected that Cannon was not tasked with substantively reviewing fundraising emails like Boedigheimer thought. Groth wrote to Cannon, "Matt [Morgan, Trump Campaign's General Counsel] has instructed me to hand off all compliance matters, including approvals, to you."[64] Cannon confirmed, "I saw myself as doing exactly what I was instructed to do here, which is do what Nathan had previously been doing. So it's this. It's compliance issues like disclaimers and typos."[65] Therefore, when Cannon received emails that included claims such as "the Democrats are trying to steal the election," he viewed reviewing the veracity of this statement as "outside the purview of what [he] was tasked."[66] When asked, Cannon stated that he did not know who was tasked with ensuring that fundraising emails were true and accurate.[67]

Boedigheimer, and other members of the digital fundraising team he led, claimed to see the Approvals Group as a guardrail of sorts in the fundraising effort to protect from the dissemination of false messaging about the election, but the Approvals Group served no such role. The very staffers in the Approvals Group repeatedly told the Select Committee that they did not review the claims about election fraud to confirm whether they were even true.

When all was said and done, no one in the Trump Campaign claimed to be responsible for confirming the accuracy of President Trump's words, or other allegations of election fraud, before they were blasted to millions of Americans.[68]

Thus, after the election, the TMAGAC team drafted emails filled with inflammatory and unfounded claims, and the members of the Approvals Group tasked with fact checking these claims did no such thing—effectively, President Trump's claims were treated as true and blasted to millions of people with little to no scrutiny by those tasked with ensuring accuracy. This process was a fertile ground for the Big Lie to spread through hundreds of emails and text messages.

D. Focus on Fundraising Metrics

Boedigheimer spoke with Coby and Zambrano often about how much money TMAGAC was raising, and they provided feedback regarding fundraising goals.[69] Trump Campaign leadership was fully aware of post-election fundraising totals. According to Coby, President Trump's son-in-law and senior advisor Jared Kushner "had the most interest in the digital program" and "would just check in on [fundraising] results," and routinely received updates regarding fundraising from Coby.[70] Coby also made clear that Kushner was heavily involved in the Campaign's budget process[71] and that he updated Kushner on TMAGAC's post-election fundraising totals.[72]

The Select Committee received documents confirming Kushner's involvement. For example, on November 8, 2020, Kushner requested that a daily tracker be created showing the Trump Campaign's financial position from election day forward.[73] In an email, Kushner noted that the tracker would allow the Campaign to consider its cash flow ahead of the creation of "a new entity for POTUS['s] other political activities."[74] Just days after the election, and after the Campaign had three of its four best fundraising days ever on November 4th, 5th, and 6th,[75] Kushner was preparing for the launch of President Trump's new leadership PAC, Save America. Kushner stated that he needed this new daily tracker because the Trump Campaign was going to continue fundraising post-election.[76] Kushner continued to receive these detailed daily trackers, which included Save America's fundraising hauls, through at least December 2020.[77]

2020 ELECTION: THE ROLE OF ELECTION FRAUD MESSAGING

A. The Decision to Continue Fundraising after Election Day

Heading into election night of the 2020 Presidential race, as Americans across the country waited in line to vote on election day, the Trump Campaign and the RNC were planning what they would tell the American public about the results in the upcoming days. On election day, Boedigheimer and

Darren Centinello, a Trump Campaign staffer, discussed the three message options that the Trump Campaign had on the table.[78]

The first option was to send out copy claiming President Trump had won the 2020 election. But the Campaign knew this message was false, and Boedigheimer told Centinello that he could not get this messaging approved yet.[79] The Trump Campaign's second option was an email stating they were still waiting on the election results. This message would have been *the truth*. The Campaign rejected this option.

Instead, the Trump Campaign chose a third option. Boedigheimer confirmed that TMAGAC fundraisers had received approval for copy claiming that the Democrats are going to "try to steal the election" *before* election night.[80]

Zambrano confirmed that it would not surprise him that TMAGAC was immediately claiming that Democrats were trying to steal the election, because President Trump has been pushing that message.[81] Zambrano added, "That was the President's phrasing in the messaging that the team was sourcing from."[82] Importantly, Boedigheimer confirmed that the TMAGAC copywriting team did *not* base its use of the "trying to steal" language on any awareness of actual fraud.[83]

B. Post-Election Fundraising Off the Big Lie

Both the Trump Campaign and the RNC directed TMAGAC to continue fundraising after the election.[84] Justin Clark, the deputy campaign manager, explained that the decision to continue fundraising after the election would have come from President Trump himself.[85]

Starting after the election and until January 6th, the Trump Campaign, along with the RNC, sent millions of emails to their supporters, with messaging such as claiming that the election was "RIGGED."[86] The Trump Campaign viewed the TMAGAC emails as another avenue to get out President Trump's post-election messaging about the alleged fraud.[87] These emails used false claims of voter fraud to create a sense of urgency that the election was being stolen. The Trump Campaign and the RNC told their supporters that their donations could stop Democrats from "trying to steal the election." They consistently encouraged donors to give money to continue "uncovering" fraud that had not occurred. These emails were sent out after being reviewed and approved by the Approvals Group.[88]

The TMAGAC fundraisers used inflammatory language and false election fraud claims after the election because it was both effective at fundraising and accurately captured President Trump's ongoing tone and messaging.[89] When the digital fundraising team drafted emails claiming, for example, that "Democrats are trying to steal the election," they did not bother to confirm whether or not those inflammatory statements were true, and instead they merely took President Trump's words and made an effective fundraising email.[90] As Zambrano stated, "the President issuing statements or tweets would be the genesis of the copy that would then go into the approval process for edits, for checks. That is why the approval process worked."[91] President Trump was the source of the lies. Not only was President Trump's fundraising driven by his daily deluge of lies about the election, but these lies were also able to go unchallenged before being spread because TMAGAC had an ineffective process when it came to scrutinizing and correcting those lies.

The TMAGAC fundraising machine continued to churn out hundreds of fundraising emails and text messages regardless of external developments. For example, Zambrano said that, after former Vice President Biden was widely declared the winner of the election, TMAGAC's fundraising efforts moved ahead the same way they had previously,[92] even though he "would say it wasn't looking good" as soon as one week after the election.[93]

ALARMS RAISED ABOUT TMAGAC FUNDRAISING CONTENT

A number of individuals and entities associated with the TMAGAC fundraising campaign raised concerns about the dangerous and inflammatory language used in the emails issued for this campaign.

Concerns Raised in Internal RNC Review

Evidence obtained by the Select Committee shows that the RNC knew that President Trump's claims about winning the election were baseless and that additional donations would not help him secure an additional term in office. They walked as close to the line as they dared—making several changes to fundraising copy that seemingly protected the RNC from legal exposure while still spreading and relying on President Trump's known lies and misrepresentations.

The Select Committee did not interview a member of the RNC legal team due to concerns surrounding attorney-client privilege, but the Select Committee nonetheless got insight into their role from documents produced by Campaign and RNC staff, as well as interviews with staffers. As detailed below, the RNC lawyers were the only individuals who even attempted to walk back the fundraising emails.

Allred and Katz both received direction from the RNC's lawyers shortly after the election to not say "steal the election" and instead were told to use "try to steal the election."[94] Allred also recalled that, at some point, the RNC legal team directed the copywriters not to use the term "rigged."[95]

After the media called the election for former Vice President Joe Biden on Saturday, November 7, 2020, the RNC began to quietly pull back from definitive language about President Trump having won the election and instead used language of insinuation. For example, on November 10, 2020, Justin Reimer, RNC's then-chief counsel, revised a fundraising email sent to the Approvals Group to remove the sentence that "Joe Biden should not wrongfully claim the office of the President."[96] Instead, Reimer indicated the email should read, "Joe Biden does not get to decide when this election ends. Only LEGAL ballots must be counted and verified."[97] Both Alex Cannon and Zach Parkinson signed off on Reimer's edits.[98]

On November 11, 2020, Reimer again revised a fundraising email sent to the Approvals Group. This time, he revised a claim that "President Trump won this election by a lot" to instead state that "President Trump got 71 MILLION LEGAL votes."[99] Once again Cannon and Parkinson signed off on Reimer's edits.[100]

Also on November 11, 2020, Jenna Kirsch, associate counsel at the RNC, revised a fundraising email sent to the Approvals Group to, among other things, remove the request "to step up and contribute to our critical **Election Defense Fund** so that we can DEFEND the Election and secure FOUR MORE YEARS."[101] Instead of "secure FOUR MORE YEARS," Kirsch's revised version stated a contribution would "finish the fight."[102] Once again Cannon and Parkinson signed off on these edits for the Trump Campaign.[103] Regarding the change to finish the fight, Zambrano conceded, "I would say this a substantive change from the legal department."[104] Kirsch made numerous edits like this, in which she removed assertions about "four more years."[105] Such edits continued into late November 2020.

Further, Boedigheimer stated that he took questions to RNC legal in the post-election period about TMAGAC fundraisers using the "steal the election" language.[106] The RNC was clearly aware that President Trump's claims regarding the election were not true and tried to have it both ways.

The private split between the RNC and the Trump Campaign became even more pronounced when President Trump decided to double down on his false election fraud claims and chose Rudolph Giuliani to lead his legal efforts to overturn the election.[107] On November 19, 2020, Giuliani held a press conference at the RNC's headquarters in which he falsely suggested that the Biden Campaign orchestrated an elaborate nationwide voter-fraud scheme.[108] Cassie Docksey, a senior RNC staffer at the time, recalled that she spoke that day with Michael Ahrens, then the RNC's communications director, about the diverging from the Trump Campaign.[109] Ahrens told her that the RNC would no longer automatically amplify or replicate statements from the Trump Campaign or President Trump's legal team.[110] Docksey understood Ahrens to be relaying a decision made at the most senior levels of the RNC.[111]

Ahrens asserted that the RNC was unwilling to adopt the wide-ranging, baseless assertions President Trump's legal team was making and quietly decided to focus its communication strategy elsewhere.[112] Distancing the RNC from President Trump's false statements was a "regular course of the job before the election," and it "carried through after the election" in relation to President Trump's false claims about the election.[113] Starting at or before the November 19, 2020, press conference, the RNC senior leadership was in agreement that they would not claim that President Trump had won the election,[114] although the RNC "frequently" had to have internal discussions about President Trump's false statements about the election.[115]

According to Michael Reed, then the RNC's deputy chief of staff for communications, "there were conversations amongst [RNC] legal and comms and digital to ensure that anything that was being written by the digital team based off of something President Trump or the Campaign said was something we all were more comfortable with."[116] RNC Chairwoman McDaniel was a part of these conversations.[117]

RNC leadership knew that President Trump was lying to the American people. Yet, they did nothing to publicly distance themselves from his efforts to overturn the election. The RNC's response was merely to tinker around the edges of the fundraising copy but never to fundamentally challenge the one message that remained present in TMAGAC's post-election fundraising copy—President Trump's Big Lie.

In the end, multiple senior RNC staffers approved fundraising emails raising questions about the election results even though they did not know of any evidence about fraud impacting the winner of the 2020 Presidential election. For example, Cassie Docksey stated that she was not aware of any fraud that impacted the results of the Presidential election.[118] Ahrens conceded that "there was not evidence that we [the RNC] had seen that he [President Trump] won the election, that Biden had not won the election."[119]

Similarly, Justin Clark was "not aware of [fraudulent activity . . . to like defraud voters] by an individual or an entity that would have [changed the outcome of an election]."[120] Alex Cannon "did not find or see, in [his] limited ability as one individual…evidence that would be sufficient within the time period to change any sort of election results in any of the States."[121]

Nonetheless, the RNC and the Trump Campaign continued to send out hundreds of emails, spreading the Big Lie to and fundraising off of millions of supporters. Even though the RNC had closely held reservations about repeating the most extreme and unsupportable claims of fraud, the RNC stayed the course with a coordinated, single fundraising plan with the Trump Campaign. The RNC privately and quietly softened the most blatantly egregious claims written by its own copywriters but publicly stood shoulder to shoulder with President Trump and his Big Lie.

This is clearly evidenced by multiple TMAGAC emails in late December 2020 that asserted that former Vice President Joe Biden would be an "illegitimate President" when he took office.[122] These emails came after December 14, 2020, the day electors from each State met to cast their votes for President and Vice President. These emails came after Senate Majority Leader Mitch McConnell made it clear that he accepted the electoral college's certification of Biden's victory. These emails came after President Trump and his allies had lost all but one lawsuit challenging the election.[123] None of this made a difference to TMAGAC. When asked why TMAGAC would repeatedly send these emails stating that former Vice President Biden would be an illegitimate President, Hanna Allred, the chief copywriter, stated that it would be because the emails were "effective" for fundraising.[124]

Trump Campaign Discussions

Alex Cannon was so bothered by the emails he was reviewing as a member of the Approvals Group that he took his concerns to Justin Clark, the campaign's deputy campaign manager. Cannon explained that he had discussions with Clark about the problematic tone of the post-election TMAGAC emails and noted to Clark that the emails "seemed a little over the top to [him]."[125] Cannon raised those concerns because, after spending weeks researching which fraud claims were verifiable and which were not, Cannon saw that the TMAGAC emails were inconsistent with the fact that systemic fraud did not exist.[126] Cannon also recalled that he may have expressed concern to Matt Morgan, the campaign's general counsel, regarding the difference between claims of election fraud made in the TMAGAC fundraising emails and his conclusion that there was not fraud that impacted the election results.[127] Cannon was not aware of any actions taken to address the concerns he had with this inconsistency.[128]

Justin Clark could not recall whether he looked at any fundraising emails after Cannon raised these concerns or whether Cannon spoke to Gary Coby about the substance of the fundraising emails.[129]

Challenges From Within the Digital Team

In the days after the election, one junior copywriter presented senior Campaign staffers with a template for a more honest approach. Shortly after election night, Coby led a meeting of the entire Trump digital team, which included individuals from the Campaign, the RNC, Opn Sesame, Direct Persuasion, and others. In that meeting, as Coby addressed the staff and expressed that the digital team would continue to work, Ethan Katz, an RNC staffer in his early twenties, rose to ask a question:[130] How were staffers supposed to tell voters that the Trump Campaign wanted to keep counting votes in Arizona but stop counting votes in other States (like Pennsylvania, Georgia, and Michigan)?[131]

Katz said that Coby provided an answer without substance, which caused Katz to reiterate his question. His question made clear that the Campaign's position was wildly inconsistent.[132] Allred and Boedigheimer corroborated that Katz confronted leadership.[133]

Katz also recalled that, shortly after the election, Allred directed him to write an email declaring that President Trump had won the State of Pennsylvania before anyone had called Pennsylvania for either party.[134] Katz believed the Trump Campaign wanted to send this email out to preempt a potential call that was likely to be in former Vice President Biden's favor.[135] He refused to write the email. Allred was stunned, and instead assigned it to another copywriter.[136] Allred confirmed that Katz expressed discomfort at writing such an email and that she relied on another copywriter.[137] On November 4, 2020, the Trump Campaign sent out an email preemptively and falsely declaring that President Trump won Pennsylvania.[138]

Katz was fired approximately three weeks after the election.[139] In an interview with the Select Committee, when Allred was asked why Katz, her direct report, was fired, she explained that she was not sure why because TMAGAC was raising more money than ever after the election, but that the decision was not hers to make.[140]

Concerns Raised by Trump Campaign Vendor Iterable

The Trump Campaign knew that emails that the Approvals Group had blessed were being rejected by another email service provider. After the election, the Trump Campaign attempted to expand the reach of their false voter fraud emails. The Trump Campaign formed a company named Data-Pier, owned by Cannon and Sean Dollman.[141] DataPier hired an outside company named Iterable to deliver its emails.[142] Cannon tried to send "toned-down RNC emails," through Iterable, but they still had to be "further toned [] down through [an] iterative process[.]"[143] For example, on November 7, 2020, Seth Charles, who was then Iterable's principal email deliverability and industry relations manager, said that there was an issue with the TMAGAC copy and offered line edits.[144] Two days later, Charles recommended to the Trump Campaign staffers that they look for "modified copy there [from TMAGAC emails] to be a little less threatening."[145] Charles claimed that some TMAGAC copy "obviously insinuates the so far unsubstantiated theory of voter fraud, as well as contributions and legal actions will result in some sort of different outcome."[146]

But Salesforce, TMAGAC's original email service provider, continued sending millions of Trump Campaign emails up until January 6th.

Internal Complaints at Salesforce

The Trump Campaign knew that emails that the Approvals Group had blessed were being rejected by Iterable. However, the RNC continued to send millions of Trump Campaign emails through Salesforce, TMAGAC's original email service provider, up until January 6th. Evidence uncovered by the Select Committee shows that there were internal concerns at Salesforce regarding the content of the TMAGAC emails.

The Select Committee interviewed an individual ("J. Doe") who worked at Salesforce during the post-election period during which TMAGAC was sending out the fundraising emails concerning false election fraud claims.[147] Doe worked for Salesforce's privacy and abuse management team, colloquially known as the abuse desk.[148] An abuse desk is responsible for preventing fraud and abuse emanating from the provider's user or subscriber network.

Doe indicated to the Select Committee that, as soon as early 2020, they recalled issues arising with the RNC's use of Salesforce's services and that a "deluge of abuse would've started in June-ish."[149] Doe noted that Salesforce received a high number of complaints regarding the RNC's actions, which would have been primarily the fundraising efforts of TMAGAC.[150] In the latter half of 2020, Doe noticed that the emails coming from the RNC's account included more and more violent and inflammatory rhetoric in violation of Salesforce's Master Service Agreement ("MSA") with the RNC, which prohibited the use of violent content.[151] Doe stated that, near the time of the election, they contacted senior individuals at Salesforce to highlight the "increasingly concerning" emails coming from the RNC's account.[152] Doe explained that senior individuals at Salesforce effectively ignored their emails about TMAGAC's inflammatory emails[153] and Salesforce ignored the terms of the MSA and permitted the RNC to continue to use its account in this problematic manner.[154] Doe said, "Salesforce very obviously didn't care about anti-abuse."[155]

Ultimately, the Trump Campaign and the RNC let the Big Lie spread because they were making hundreds of millions of dollars from President Trump's supporters who believed that lie. The Big Rip-off needed the Big Lie to motivate unsuspecting individuals to donate their money to a lost cause, and it worked.

WHERE DID THE MONEY GO?

The Trump Campaign and the RNC had three of their largest fundraising days of the 2020 election cycle immediately after the election.[156] Together, the Trump Campaign and the RNC raised more than one hundred million dollars in three days, telling people they were raising the money for the "Official Election Defense Fund." According to the TMAGAC fundraising pitches, the Trump Campaign and RNC team had created a so-called "Official Election Defense Fund" to help pay for legal challenges to the election results.[157] But there was no "Official Election Defense Fund"—it was simply "a marketing tactic."[158] The TMAGAC fundraisers did not know where the donated money was actually going.[159] The TMAGAC copywriting team simply took the lies that President Trump told them about the need to raise money to overturn the election results and put them into emails to his supporters.

The false claims of election fraud and the "Official Election Defense Fund" were so successful President Trump and his allies raised more than $250 million *after* the election.[160] However, the Trump Campaign was raising too much money to spend solely on their legal efforts to overturn the results of the 2020 election. The Trump Campaign continued to publicly state the election had been stolen by "the Left," while behind closed doors they prepared a new plan to spend their supporters' money.

A. The Creation of the Save America PAC

On November 9, 2020, President Trump created a separate leadership PAC called Save America that allowed him to keep millions of dollars raised after the election and spend it with very few restrictions in the future. Jared Kushner worked with Alex Cannon, Deputy General Counsel for the Trump Campaign, in creating the entity.[161] Prior to the formation of Save America, any money raised by the Trump Campaign could effectively only be spent on recount and election-contest related expenses, and to pay off campaign debt.[162] But now the money raised into Save America could allow President Trump to pay for his personal expenses, such as travel or hotel stays. After Save America was formed, it was added to the TMAGAC joint fundraising agreement with the RNC, and the percentage of the proceeds allocated to the Trump Campaign began to flow to Save America.[163]

Importantly, Save America, as a leadership PAC, was not even legally permitted to pay for recount and election-contest related expenses in excess of the Federal Election Campaign Act ("FECA") limit of $5,000.[164] Save America never hit that limit in 2020, as it spent no money on recount and election-contest related expenses.[165]

Several reporters noticed the switch and contacted the Campaign asking about the "bait and switch" and the "misleading" nature of the emails. One reporter said directly: "it's misleading to raise money for a committee marked on the website as an 'election defense fund' if it's going to a leadership PAC."[166] Another reporter asked, "Why is the campaign telling its supporters they are contributing toward an 'Election Defense Fund' if only a small percentage of those funds are actually going toward funding legal efforts?" and "How can the campaign justify directing 75% of contributions intended for a 2020 legal fund toward the President's political action committee?"[167]

The Trump Campaign came up with a messaging plan about this tactic, which President Trump personally approved.[168] Tim Murtaugh, the Trump Campaign's communications director, repeatedly asked Justin Clark, the deputy campaign manager, whether they should respond to the reporters.[169] When Murtaugh flagged that the communications team was not responding to the reporters, Justin Clark said, "Good. Don't."[170]

B. Outlays to Trump-Associated Individuals and Companies

The Trump Campaign spent the money on President Trump, giving donations to his associates, and keeping it for himself in Save America. Hundreds of millions of dollars that were raised to go towards "election defense" and "fighting voter fraud" were not spent that way at all. To the contrary, most of the funds remain unspent, and millions have been paid to companies that are known affiliates of President Trump, or payments to entities associated with former Trump administration officials. Since the election, former Trump officials who are still working for President Trump's PACs, and are publicly receiving salaries as FEC-reported "payroll," are also associated with these companies.

For example, from July 2021 to the present, Save America has been paying approximately $9,700 per month to Dan Scavino,[171] a political adviser who served in the Trump administration as White House Deputy Chief of Staff.[172] Save America was also paying $20,000 per month to an entity called Hudson Digital LLC. Hudson Digital LLC was registered in Delaware twenty days after the attack on the Capitol, on January 26, 2021,[173] and began receiving payments from Save America on the day it was registered.[174] Hudson Digital LLC has received payments totaling over $420,000, all described as "Digital consulting."[175] No website or any other information or mention of Hudson Digital LLC could be found online.[176] Though Hudson Digital LLC is registered as a Delaware company, the FEC Schedule B listing traces back to an address belonging to Dan and Catherine Scavino.[177]

Nick Luna, President Trump's former personal assistant and "body man," was being paid from April 2021 to December 2021 approximately $12,000 per month by Save America for "payroll."[178] The Make America Great Again PAC (MAGA PAC)—formerly the authorized committee of President Trump's reelection campaign, Donald J. Trump for President—paid $20,000 per month to a limited liability corporation called Red State Partners LLC from April 2021 through October 2021, and Save America paid Red State Partners LLC $20,000 in February 2022.[179] The company was registered in Delaware on March 11, 2021[180] and has received a total of $170,000.[181] Though it is registered in Delaware, disclosures filed with the

Federal Election Committee (FEC) list Red State Partners at an address in Miami, Florida, that is an address for Nick Luna and his wife, Cassidy Dumbauld.[182]

Further, Vince Haley, Taylor Swindle, and Ross Worthington are corporate officers of a company known as Pericles LLC.[183] Haley is a former policy advisor to President Trump,[184] Swindle is the Chief Financial Officer for Gingrich 360,[185] and Ross Worthington is the former White House speechwriter[186] who wrote the speech President Trump delivered on the Ellipse on January 6th.[187] Pericles LLC was registered on January 27, 2021,[188] the day after Scavino's Hudson Digital LLC, and, since then, has received payments from Save America totaling at least $352,700.[189]

Another former speechwriter for President Trump, Robert Gabriel, Jr., has also been receiving payments from Save America. Gabriel was involved in writing the speech President Trump delivered on the White House Ellipse on January 6th, and specifically told the speechwriters, including Worthington, to reinsert previously removed incendiary lines about Vice President Pence into the speech.[190] This direction came after Vice President Pence told President Trump that he would not try to change the outcome of the election.[191] In September 2021, Gabriel formed called Gabriel Strategies LLC,[192] which began receiving payments from Save America the following month.[193] Since October 2021, Save America has paid Gabriel Strategies LLC at least $167,674.00.[194] For both Pericles and Gabriel Strategies, the description of the payments is always for "consulting" in political strategy or communications, and some payments are purported to include travel expenses.

Through October 2022, Save America has paid nearly $100,000 in "strategy consulting" payments to Herve Pierre Braillard,[195] a fashion designer who has been dressing Melania Trump for years.[196]

From January 2021 to June 2022, Save America has also reported over $2.1 million in "legal consulting." Many firms perform different kinds of practice, but more than 67% of those funds went to law firms that are representing witnesses involved in the Select Committee's investigation who were subpoenaed or invited to testify.

Additionally, Save America has reported other expenditures, like:

- $1,000,000 donation to America First Policy Institute, home to several former Trump officials and witnesses subpoenaed to testify before the Committee.[197]
- $1,000,000 donation to Conservative Partnership Institute, a conservative nonprofit organization where Mark Meadows is a senior partner.[198]
- More than $10.6 million to Event Strategies, Inc., the preferred staging company for President Trump that staged the January 6th rally.[199]

- More than $327,000 in payments to the Trump Hotel Collection and Mar-A-Lago Club since the 2020 election.[200]
- An "event sponsorship fee" of $165,937.50 to American Conservative Union,[201] the Chairman of which is Matt Schlapp. Schlapp and his wife have offered to pay the legal fees of witnesses called to testify before the January 6th Committee and have extensive ties with former President Trump.
- A little over $140,000 to National Public Affairs, LLC,[202] a consulting company started by former Trump Campaign Manager Bill Stepien and Deputy Campaign Manager Justin Clark.[203] Stepien testified that he knew the claims of voter fraud were false, that he didn't think what was happening was necessarily honest, and that he was stepping away from the Trump Campaign.[204] However, he continues to work and receive hundreds of thousands of dollars consulting for President Trump and several other congressional candidates who continue to spread false voter fraud claims related to the 2020 election.[205]

C. Payments to 2M Management LLC

As described above, the Trump Campaign, after paying off its general election debt, raised millions of dollars that flowed into a segregated recount account ("Recount Account") by encouraging donors to help pay for legal challenges to the election results. Pursuant to the FECA, the Trump Campaign could only spend these funds on a few limited purposes (e.g., for actual recounts and election-contest expenses or, in the case of surplus funds, donations to charitable organizations or transferring the funds to a national party committee's separate, segregated account for election recounts).[206]

Justin Clark told the Select Committee that he understood that, "[a]fter election day, ... you can raise money for a recount and to pay off debt,"[207] and that "[t]he money going into the campaign, principal campaign committee, at that point, [after the election] was dead money. It couldn't be spent on things."[208] Alex Cannon agreed.[209] That's why, after the election, the Trump Campaign set up the Recount Account—"a segregated restricted account [held] by the campaign"[210]—and raised money for the Recount Account through TMAGAC.[211]

In February 2021, the Trump Campaign was converted into MAGA PAC.[212] In March 2021, MAGA PAC began disclosing on required FEC forms that it was paying millions of dollars to an eDiscovery vendor called 2M Document Management & Imaging LLC ("2M Management") for what MAGA PAC described as "recount" and "Recount: Research Consulting."[213]

Although the MAGA PAC reported that 2M Management was being paid for recount-related expenses, 2M Management was primarily processing and reviewing documents slated to be produced by the National Archives and Records Administration in response to subpoenas from (1) the House Select Subcommittee on the Coronavirus Crisis ("Covid Subcommittee") and (2) the Select Committee to Investigate the January 6th Attack.[214]

From just March 2021 to May 2021, MAGA PAC paid 2M Management almost $1 million from the Recount Account to review documents related solely to the Covid Subcommittee.[215] Alex Cannon confirmed that he understood these payments to 2M Management came from the Recount Account.[216] Federal campaign finance law requires committees to accurately report information related to expenditures, including the purpose of payments. FEC regulations provide that the "purpose" be described in relevant reports through a brief statement of why the disbursement was made and must be sufficiently specific to make the purpose of the disbursement clear.[217]

IMPACT OF THE TRUMP CAMPAIGN'S FALSE CLAIMS

Between the election and January 6th, the Trump Campaign sent out hundreds of emails urging President Trump's supporters to "fight the Liberal MOB" and "join the Trump army." Users on the same extreme social media platforms used to plan the attack on the Capitol repeatedly shared the "Official Election Defense Fund" donation links in the week following election day.[218] Links to donate were often accompanied by mentions of voter fraud and calls to save the country, mirroring the language of the fundraising emails and the countless discussions being held by the President's supporters of coming to Washington, DC, on January 6th to "Stop the steal."[219]

On January 6th, while President Trump was speaking at the Ellipse rally and directing his supporters to march to the Capitol, his Campaign was also sending fundraising emails inflaming people to "fight back." One email stated, "100 Members of Congress. . . . Join them in the FIGHT to DEFEND the Election. . . . *This is our last line of defense.*"[220] Another email stated, "TODAY will be a historic day in our Nation's history. Congress will either certify, or object to, the Election results. Every single Patriot from across the Country must step up RIGHT NOW if we're going to successfully DEFEND the integrity of this Election."[221] A third email stated, "TODAY. This is our LAST CHANCE . . . The stakes have NEVER been higher. President Trump needs YOU to make a statement and publicly stand with him and FIGHT BACK."[222]

Thirty minutes after the last fundraising email was sent, the Capitol was breached. It was then and only then that TMAGAC fundraisers decided to stop sending emails containing baseless claims of election fraud.[223] Boedigheimer explained, "And at some point during that time, I don't know if it was right then, if it was a little after, maybe a little before, but either

Gary or Kevin kind of directed us to stop sending fundraising messages out."[224] Cannon stated, "[O]n January 6th, Gary called me and said, [']are you seeing what's happening? I'm obviously turning everything off.[']"[225]

After raising $250 million dollars on false voter fraud claims, mostly from small-dollar donors, President Trump did not spend it on fighting an election he knew he lost. Instead, a significant portion of the money was deposited into the Save America account and not used for the purposes the Campaign claimed it would be. President Trump got a war chest with millions of dollars, and the American people were left with the U.S. Capitol under attack.

There is evidence suggesting that numerous defendants charged with violations related to the January 6th attack on the U.S. Capitol and others present on the Capitol grounds that day were motivated by false claims about the election.[226]

Further, J. Doe, the Salesforce employee interviewed by the Select Committee, provided insight into the action that Salesforce took after the attack. Doe explained that after they became aware of the ongoing attack, they (Doe) took unilateral action to block the RNC's ability to send emails through Salesforce's platform.[227] Doe noted that the shutdown lasted until January 11, 2021, when senior Salesforce leadership directed Doe to remove the block from RNC's Salesforce account.[228] Doe stated that Salesforce leadership told Doe that Salesforce would now begin reviewing RNC's email campaigns to "make sure this doesn't happen again."[229]

CONCLUSION

In the weeks after the 2020 election leading up to January 6, 2021, President Trump's Campaign and his allies sent his supporters a barrage of emails and text messages pushing lies about a stolen election and asking for contributions to challenge the outcome of the election. In reality, the funds raised went primarily towards paying down the Trump Campaign's outstanding 2020 debt, financing President Trump's newly created Save America PAC, and raising money for the RNC.

Overall, only a small amount of the contributions ever went to President Trump's recount account or were otherwise obviously used in connection with post-election recounts or litigation. As President Trump used the Big Lie as a weapon to attack the legitimacy of the 2020 election, his Campaign used that same Big Lie to raise millions of dollars based on false claims and unkept promises.

Not only did President Trump lie to his supporters about the election, but he also ripped them off.

ENDNOTES

1. Trump Fundraising Emails (@TrumpEmail), Twitter, Nov. 21, 2020, 5:30 a.m. ET, available at https://twitter.com/TrumpEmail/status/1330277503160741888 ("Democrats are attempting to STEAL this Election and the White House. This Election is far from over as long as we have YOU on our team to FIGHT BACK."); Trump Fundraising Emails (@TrumpEmail), Twitter, Nov. 21, 2020, 7:16 a.m. ET, available at https://twitter.com/TrumpEmail/status/1330122927958859777 ("With your help, we will DEFEND the Election and keep America America.").

2. Select Committee to Investigate the January 6th Attack on the United States Capitol, Transcribed Interview of Hanna Allred, (Mar. 30, 2022), p. 104 ("I do think those words are effective, because people were upset and they wanted their donation to go towards an effort to—the legal effort.").

3. Select Committee to Investigate the January 6th Attack on the United States Capitol, Transcribed Interview of Richard Walters, (May 25, 2022), pp. 15-16; Select Committee to Investigate the January 6th Attack on the United States Capitol, Transcribed Interview of Austin Boedigheimer, (Apr. 20, 2022), p. 9.

4. Select Committee to Investigate the January 6th Attack on the United States Capitol, Transcribed Interview of Gary Coby, (Feb. 23, 2022), p. 28; Select Committee to Investigate the January 6th Attack on the United States Capitol, Transcribed Interview of Hanna Allred, (Mar. 30, 2022), p. 13.

5. Select Committee to Investigate the January 6th Attack on the United States Capitol, Transcribed Interview of Timothy Murtaugh, (May 19, 2022), p. 95.

6. Select Committee to Investigate the January 6th Attack on the United States Capitol, Transcribed Interview of Gary Coby, (Feb. 23, 2022), p. 10. (noting that as digital director he oversaw the digital operation).

7. Select Committee to Investigate the January 6th Attack on the United States Capitol, Transcribed Interview of Gary Coby, (Feb. 23, 2022), pp. 6-7; Select Committee to Investigate the January 6th Attack on the United States Capitol, Transcribed Interview of Kevin Zambrano, (Apr. 27, 2022), p. 11.

8. Select Committee to Investigate the January 6th Attack on the United States Capitol, Transcribed Interview of Gary Coby, (Feb. 23, 2022), p. 10.

9. Select Committee to Investigate the January 6th Attack on the United States Capitol, Transcribed Interview of William Stepien, (Feb. 10, 2022), p. 187 (naming Coby as person controlling fundraising operation); Select Committee to Investigate the January 6th Attack on the United States Capitol, Transcribed Interview of Austin Boedigheimer, (Apr. 20, 2022), p. 9 ("And then Gary Colby would have been the kind of the lead of the entire digital team for the Joint Fundraising Committee"); Select Committee to Investigate the January 6th Attack on the United States Capitol, Transcribed Interview of A. Zachary Parkinson, (May 18, 2022), p. 81 ("Gary ran the campaign's digital team").

10. Select Committee to Investigate the January 6th Attack on the United States Capitol, Informal Interview of Kevin Zambrano, (Dec. 16, 2021), p. 3 (Zambrano stated that Coby expressed that he spoke with "the family," meaning the Trumps, and Zambrano believed that Kushner was the family member to whom Coby spoke most frequently.); Select Committee to Investigate the January 6th Attack on the United States Capitol, Transcribed Interview of William Stepien, (Feb. 10, 2022), p. 190; Select Committee to Investigate the January 6th Attack on the United States Capitol, Informal Interview of Cole Blocker, (Dec. 29, 2021), p. 2 (Blocker stated that he knew Coby talked to Jared Kushner a lot, and that their relationship was common knowledge.).

11. Select Committee to Investigate the January 6th Attack on the United States Capitol, Transcribed Interview of Gary Coby, (Feb. 23, 2022), p. 13.

12. Select Committee to Investigate the January 6th Attack on the United States Capitol, Transcribed Interview of Kevin Zambrano, (Apr. 27, 2022), p. 11; Select Committee to Investigate

the January 6th Attack on the United States Capitol, Transcribed Interview of Hanna Allred, (Mar. 30, 2022), p. 12; Select Committee to Investigate the January 6th Attack on the United States Capitol, Transcribed Interview of Austin Boedigheimer, (Apr. 20, 2022), p. 9.

13. Select Committee to Investigate the January 6th Attack on the United States Capitol, Transcribed Interview of Kevin Zambrano, (Apr. 27, 2022), pp. 11-13.

14. Select Committee to Investigate the January 6th Attack on the United States Capitol, Transcribed Interview of Kevin Zambrano, (Apr. 27, 2022), p. 11.

15. Select Committee to Investigate the January 6th Attack on the United States Capitol, Transcribed Interview of Kevin Zambrano, (Apr. 27, 2022), p. 15.

16. Select Committee to Investigate the January 6th Attack on the United States Capitol, Transcribed Interview of Austin Boedigheimer, (Apr. 20, 2022), p. 7.

17. Select Committee to Investigate the January 6th Attack on the United States Capitol, Transcribed Interview of Austin Boedigheimer, (Apr. 20, 2022), p. 10 ("I think that's fair to say. I think my direct report was Kevin but then we also viewed Gary as a leader of kind of the digital JFC team"); Select Committee to Investigate the January 6th Attack on the United States Capitol, Informal Interview of Ethan Katz, (Nov. 3, 2021), p. 2 (indicating Boedigheimer reported to Coby but that there may have been additional people between Boedigheimer and Coby).

18. Select Committee to Investigate the January 6th Attack on the United States Capitol, Transcribed Interview of Austin Boedigheimer, (Apr. 20, 2022), p. 10.

19. Select Committee to Investigate the January 6th Attack on the United States Capitol, Transcribed Interview of Austin Boedigheimer, (Apr. 20, 2022), p. 7; Select Committee to Investigate the January 6th Attack on the United States Capitol, Transcribed Interview of Hanna Allred, (Mar. 30, 2022), p. 9; Select Committee to Investigate the January 6th Attack on the United States Capitol, Transcribed Interview of Gary Coby, (Feb. 23, 2022), pp. 16-17 ("Austin led the fundraising team . . . [and] [o]versaw the variety of fundraising channels and led that team.").

20. Select Committee to Investigate the January 6th Attack on the United States Capitol, Transcribed Interview of Hanna Allred, (Mar. 30, 2022), pp. 9-10.

21. Select Committee to Investigate the January 6th Attack on the United States Capitol, Transcribed Interview of Kevin Zambrano, (Apr. 27, 2022), p. 14 (Committee Staff: "Now, the emails that Austin and Hannah and folks were working on, those are primarily drafting emails for TMAGAC, correct?" Zambrano: "Yes, I believe so.").

22. Select Committee to Investigate the January 6th Attack on the United States Capitol, Transcribed Interview of Hanna Allred, (Mar. 30, 2022), p. 12; Select Committee to Investigate the January 6th Attack on the United States Capitol, Informal Interview of Ethan Katz, (Nov. 3, 2021); Select Committee to Investigate the January 6th Attack on the United States Capitol, Informal Interview of Ethan Katz, (Jan. 21, 2022), p. 2; Select Committee to Investigate the January 6th Attack on the United States Capitol, Informal Interview of Alex Murglin, (Mar. 17, 2022), p. 2; Select Committee to Investigate the January 6th Attack on the United States Capitol, Informal Interview of Alex Blinkoff, (Feb. 7, 2022), p. 2; Select Committee to Investigate the January 6th Attack on the United States Capitol, Transcribed Interview of Austin Boedigheimer, (Apr. 20, 2022), p. 10.

23. Select Committee to Investigate the January 6th Attack on the United States Capitol, Transcribed Interview of Hanna Allred, (Mar. 30, 2022), p. 11 ("Alex Murglin joined I believe in March of 2020 . . . That summer, Ethan Katz and Alex Blinkoff both joined."); Select Committee to Investigate the January 6th Attack on the United States Capitol, Informal Interview of Alex Murglin (Mar. 17, 2022), p. 2.

24. Select Committee to Investigate the January 6th Attack on the United States Capitol, Informal Interview of Ethan Katz, (Nov. 3, 2021), p. 2.

25. Select Committee to Investigate the January 6th Attack on the United States Capitol, Transcribed Interview of Kevin Zambrano, (Apr. 27, 2022), p. 12.

26. Select Committee to Investigate the January 6th Attack on the United States Capitol, Transcribed Interview of Austin Boedigheimer, (Apr. 20, 2022), p. 9 ("So, we, as in the RNC digital employees and then campaign employees and vendors as well, came to work together on the JFC. And the general structure was all working together on that goal."); Select Committee to Investigate the January 6th Attack on the United States Capitol, Informal Interview of Hanna Allred, (Dec. 1, 2021), p. 3 ("ALLRED said that on the 5th floor, the RNC and Campaign employees all worked together for joint fundraising committee, and exactly who worked for which entity kind of didn't matter. . . . Rather, everyone just referred to everything as TMAGAC.").

27. Select Committee to Investigate the January 6th Attack on the United States Capitol, Informal Interview of Ethan Katz, (Nov. 3, 2021), p. 2 ("He explained that the copywriting process worked like a Henry Ford style assembly line, where different individuals performed a task and passed on the work product to someone else.").

28. Select Committee to Investigate the January 6th Attack on the United States Capitol, Transcribed Interview of Hanna Allred, (Mar. 30, 2022), pp. 15-16.

29. Documents on file with the Select Committee to Investigate the January 6th Attack on the United States Capitol (Austin Boedigheimer Production), BA-0003821, (Nov. 30, 2020 email from Austin Boedigheimer to Hanna Allred, "Fwd: It's happening again, Austin.").

30. Select Committee to Investigate the January 6th Attack on the United States Capitol, Transcribed Interview of Kevin Zambrano, (Apr. 27, 2022), p. 20.

31. Select Committee to Investigate the January 6th Attack on the United States Capitol, Transcribed Interview of Hanna Allred, (Mar. 30, 2022), p. 30.

32. Select Committee to Investigate the January 6th Attack on the United States Capitol, Transcribed Interview of Hanna Allred, (Mar. 30, 2022), pp. 103-104.

33. Select Committee to Investigate the January 6th Attack on the United States Capitol, Transcribed Interview of Hanna Allred, (Mar. 30, 2022), pp. 112-113 ("On average, yes, you repeat things that do well."); Select Committee to Investigate the January 6th Attack on the United States Capitol, Transcribed Interview of Austin Boedigheimer, (Apr. 20, 2022), p. 21 ("[I]f you were sending it repeatedly[,] it's the understanding that it's doing well so you want to keep sending e-mails like that.").

34. Select Committee to Investigate the January 6th Attack on the United States Capitol, Transcribed Interview of Austin Boedigheimer, (Apr. 20, 2022), pp. 107-108 ("President Trump's saying it, surrogates are saying it, everybody's saying it. So my, you know, I don't remember exactly this but it seems like it was, you know, we should do something like that since it's been working.").

35. Select Committee to Investigate the January 6th Attack on the United States Capitol, Transcribed Interview of Kevin Zambrano, (Apr. 27, 2022), p. 23; Select Committee to Investigate the January 6th Attack on the United States Capitol, Transcribed Interview of Hanna Allred, (Mar. 30, 2022), p. 28; Select Committee to Investigate the January 6th Attack on the United States Capitol, Transcribed Interview of Michael Reed, (July 20, 2022), p. 8 (agreeing that copywriters sought to capture the voice and tone of President Trump in its messaging); Select Committee to Investigate the January 6th Attack on the United States Capitol, Transcribed Interview of Michael Reed, (July 20, 2022), p. 9 (agreeing that President Trump was focused on a particular issue, copywriters they would also tend to focus on similar issues).

36. Select Committee to Investigate the January 6th Attack on the United States Capitol, Transcribed Interview of Austin Boedigheimer, (Apr. 20, 2022), p. 12; Select Committee to Investigate the January 6th Attack on the United States Capitol, Transcribed Interview of Austin Boedigheimer, (Apr. 20, 2022), p. 45 ("I think we've determined that it's aggressive language. We would want to use that for this.").

37. Select Committee to Investigate the January 6th Attack on the United States Capitol, Transcribed Interview of Kevin Zambrano, (Apr. 27, 2022), pp. 25-29.

38. Select Committee to Investigate the January 6th Attack on the United States Capitol, Transcribed Interview of Austin Boedigheimer, (Apr. 20, 2022), pp. 23-24.

39. Select Committee to Investigate the January 6th Attack on the United States Capitol, Transcribed Interview of Kevin Zambrano, (Apr. 27, 2022), pp. 14, 49 ("Austin would have reviewed all the content before it would go up to the approval chains or Hannah."). Zambrano stated that, on a day-to-day basis, he was not very involved in overseeing Boedigheimer's handling of the copywriting process. Select Committee to Investigate the January 6th Attack on the United States Capitol, Transcribed Interview of Kevin Zambrano, (Apr. 27, 2022), p. 16.

40. Select Committee to Investigate the January 6th Attack on the United States Capitol, Transcribed Interview of Kevin Zambrano, (Apr. 27, 2022), p. 43.

41. Select Committee to Investigate the January 6th Attack on the United States Capitol, Transcribed Interview of Hanna Allred, (Mar. 30, 2022), p. 44.

42. Select Committee to Investigate the January 6th Attack on the United States Capitol, Transcribed Interview of Kevin Zambrano, (Apr. 27, 2022), pp. 63-64.

43. Select Committee to Investigate the January 6th Attack on the United States Capitol, Transcribed Interview of Cassie Docksey, (Aug. 25, 2022), p. 10; Select Committee to Investigate the January 6th Attack on the United States Capitol, Transcribed Interview of Michael Ahrens, (Sep. 1, 2022), pp. 9-10.

44. Select Committee to Investigate the January 6th Attack on the United States Capitol, Transcribed Interview of Cassie Docksey, (Aug. 25, 2022), p. 10.

45. Select Committee to Investigate the January 6th Attack on the United States Capitol, Transcribed Interview of Cassie Docksey, (Aug. 25, 2022), p. 6 ("And then that's also where I started doing some of the approval for the fundraising emails, the small-dollar fundraising emails."); Select Committee to Investigate the January 6th Attack on the United States Capitol, Transcribed Interview of Michael Ahrens, (Sep. 1, 2022), p. 8 ("To the best of my recollection, that was primarily Cassie Docksey, Mike Reed, who handled approvals on that content.").

46. Select Committee to Investigate the January 6th Attack on the United States Capitol, Transcribed Interview of Michael Reed, (July 20, 2022), p. 7 ("I had a role in approv[ing] them [the TMAGAC fundraising emails], yes.").

47. Select Committee to Investigate the January 6th Attack on the United States Capitol, Transcribed Interview of Alexander Cannon, (Apr. 13, 2022), p. 138.

48. Select Committee to Investigate the January 6th Attack on the United States Capitol, Transcribed Interview of A. Zachary Parkinson, (May 18, 2022), p. 80 ("There would be—I don't know if my team members were routinely getting those emails as well or if they were just being directed to me, but we were participants in them."); Select Committee to Investigate the January 6th Attack on the United States Capitol, Transcribed Interview of Hanna Allred, (Mar. 30, 2022), pp. 45-46 ("I know from the Trump Campaign, I remember Zach Parkinson was someone who responded. I was never sure if he was from research or comms, or maybe he did both, I'm not entirely sure, but he would typically, if something was wrong, like, inaccurate, he would flag it.").

49. Select Committee to Investigate the January 6th Attack on the United States Capitol, Transcribed Interview of Austin Boedigheimer, (Apr. 20, 2022), p. 51.

50. Select Committee to Investigate the January 6th Attack on the United States Capitol, Transcribed Interview of Austin Boedigheimer, (Apr. 20, 2022), p. 51.

51. Select Committee to Investigate the January 6th Attack on the United States Capitol, Transcribed Interview of Austin Boedigheimer, (Apr. 20, 2022), p. 51.

52. Select Committee to Investigate the January 6th Attack on the United States Capitol, Transcribed Interview of Austin Boedigheimer, (Apr. 20, 2022), p. 58.

53. Select Committee to Investigate the January 6th Attack on the United States Capitol, Transcribed Interview of Austin Boedigheimer, (Apr. 20, 2022), pp. 60, 75-76 ("I think what I said earlier was, at the time the election wasn't over, President Trump was saying those things. I didn't have a reason to believe it was false. So as far as the accuracy of that in the approval chain, that was up to them to decide.").

54. Select Committee to Investigate the January 6th Attack on the United States Capitol, Transcribed Interview of A. Zachary Parkinson, (May 18, 2022), p. 77.

55. Select Committee to Investigate the January 6th Attack on the United States Capitol, Transcribed Interview of A. Zachary Parkinson, (May 18, 2022), p. 78.

56. Select Committee to Investigate the January 6th Attack on the United States Capitol, Transcribed Interview of A. Zachary Parkinson, (May 18, 2022), p. 77.

57. Select Committee to Investigate the January 6th Attack on the United States Capitol, Transcribed Interview of A. Zachary Parkinson, (May 18, 2022), pp. 77-78.

58. Select Committee to Investigate the January 6th Attack on the United States Capitol, Transcribed Interview of A. Zachary Parkinson, (May 18, 2022), p. 77.

59. Select Committee to Investigate the January 6th Attack on the United States Capitol, Transcribed Interview of A. Zachary Parkinson, (May 18, 2022), pp. 86-87.

60. Select Committee to Investigate the January 6th Attack on the United States Capitol, Transcribed Interview of A. Zachary Parkinson, (May 18, 2022), pp. 88-89 ("I, as best I recall, that is who I assumed would be doing that type of review [about whether it was true that Democrats were trying to steal the election].").

61. Select Committee to Investigate the January 6th Attack on the United States Capitol, Transcribed Interview of A. Zachary Parkinson, (May 18, 2022), p. 91.

62. Select Committee to Investigate the January 6th Attack on the United States Capitol, Transcribed Interview of A. Zachary Parkinson, (May 18, 2022), p. 96.

63. Select Committee to Investigate the January 6th Attack on the United States Capitol, Transcribed Interview of Michael Reed, (July 20, 2022), pp. 54-55.

64. Documents on file with the Select Committee to Investigate the January 6th Attack on the United States Capitol, (Alexander Cannon production), AC-0001631, (Nov. 4, 2020, "Re: Hand-off on Compliance Review").

65. Select Committee to Investigate the January 6th Attack on the United States Capitol, Transcribed Interview of Alexander Cannon, (Apr. 13, 2022), p. 138.

66. Select Committee to Investigate the January 6th Attack on the United States Capitol, Transcribed Interview of Alexander Cannon, (Apr. 13, 2022), p. 140.

67. Select Committee to Investigate the January 6th Attack on the United States Capitol, Transcribed Interview of Alexander Cannon, (Apr. 13, 2022), p. 140.

68. Select Committee to Investigate the January 6th Attack on the United States Capitol, Transcribed Interview of A. Zachary Parkinson, (May 18, 2022), p. 89.

69. Select Committee to Investigate the January 6th Attack on the United States Capitol, Transcribed Interview of Austin Boedigheimer, (Apr. 20, 2022), p. 17.

70. Select Committee to Investigate the January 6th Attack on the United States Capitol, Transcribed Interview of Gary Coby, (Feb. 23, 2022), pp. 19-20.

71. Select Committee to Investigate the January 6th Attack on the United States Capitol, Transcribed Interview of Gary Coby, (Feb. 23, 2022), p. 26.

72. Select Committee to Investigate the January 6th Attack on the United States Capitol, Transcribed Interview of Gary Coby, (Feb. 23, 2022), p. 116.

73. Documents on file with the Select Committee to Investigate the January 6th Attack on the United States Capitol (Jared Kushner Production), JK_00367, (Nov. 8, 2020, email from Jared Kushner to Sean Dollman, Gary Coby, Bill Stepien, Justin Clark, and Eric Trump, at 5:51 pm, and Nov. 7, 2020 email from Sean Dollman to Jared Kushner at 2:54 pm).

74. Documents on file with the Select Committee to Investigate the January 6th Attack on the United States Capitol (Jared Kushner Production), JK_00367, (Nov. 8, 2020, email from Jared Kushner to Sean Dollman, Gary Coby, Bill Stepien, Justin Clark, and Eric Trump, at 5:51 pm, and Nov. 7, 2020 email from Sean Dollman to Jared Kushner at 2:54 pm).

75. Documents on file with the Select Committee to Investigate the January 6th Attack on the United States Capitol (Jared Kushner Production), JK_00416, (Nov. 7, 2020, text messages between Jared Kushner and Gary Coby).

76. Select Committee to Investigate the January 6th Attack on the United States Capitol, Transcribed Interview of Jared Kushner, (Mar. 31, 2022), p. 200.

77. Documents on file with the Select Committee to Investigate the January 6th Attack on the United States Capitol (Sean Dollman Production), DOLLMAN-0003821, (Dec. 23. 2020, emails between Jared Kushner, Sean Dolman, Gary Coby, Justin Clark, and Cassie Dumbauld "Re: [EXTERNAL]Re: 12/22/20 Cash Position Update"). Despite email communications showing his involvement in the Campaign's finances through late December 2020, Kushner claimed that, from around November 13 onward, he was only "nominally involved" with the Campaign's budgeting and fundraising. Select Committee to Investigate the January 6th Attack on the United States Capitol, Transcribed Interview of Jared Kushner, (Mar. 31, 2022), p. 205.

78. Documents on file with the Select Committee to Investigate the January 6th Attack on the United States Capitol (Austin Boedigheimer Production), BA-0006823, (Nov. 3, 2020, Signal chat between Austin Boedigheimer and Darren Centinello); Select Committee to Investigate the January 6th Attack on the United States Capitol, Transcribed Interview of Kevin Zambrano, (Apr. 27, 2022), p. 54 ("Austin could have. I'm not sure if people on the campaign instructed anyone else on the campaign or anything, but I wouldn't be surprised if there were a couple different scenarios floating around most people's heads on that."); Select Committee to Investigate the January 6th Attack on the United States Capitol, Transcribed Interview of Kevin Zambrano, (Apr. 27, 2022), p. 54 ("I don't recall specific—I don't recall conversations around it, other than there may have just been general [']we need to be ready for whatever may come['].").

79. Documents on file with the Select Committee to Investigate the January 6th Attack on the United States Capitol (Austin Boedigheimer Production), BA-0006823, (Nov. 3, 2020, Signal chat between Austin Boedigheimer and Darren Centinello).

80. Documents on file with the Select Committee to Investigate the January 6th Attack on the United States Capitol (Austin Boedigheimer Production), BA-0006823 (Nov. 3, 2020, Signal chat between Austin Boedigheimer and Darren Centinello); Select Committee to Investigate the January 6th Attack on the United States Capitol, Transcribed Interview of Austin Boedigheimer, (Apr. 20, 2022), p. 39 ("I'm basically saying on the victory topic, which is the first one that he covered. We're waiting until closer to election results are coming in to be able to get that approved and then I'm giving him some copy about how they are trying to steal the election that has already been approved.").

81. Select Committee to Investigate the January 6th Attack on the United States Capitol, Transcribed Interview of Kevin Zambrano, (Apr. 27, 2022), p. 55.

82. Select Committee to Investigate the January 6th Attack on the United States Capitol, Transcribed Interview of Kevin Zambrano, (Apr. 27, 2022), p. 55; Select Committee to Investigate the January 6th Attack on the United States Capitol, Transcribed Interview of Kevin Zambrano, (Apr. 27, 2022), p. 56 ("But, again, this was the President's messaging and his phrasing").

83. Select Committee to Investigate the January 6th Attack on the United States Capitol, Transcribed Interview of Austin Boedigheimer, (Apr. 20, 2022), p. 44 ("I didn't have a great understanding of what was going to happen or what happened on the ground. I wouldn't have really any knowledge into that.").

84. Select Committee to Investigate the January 6th Attack on the United States Capitol, Transcribed Interview of Kevin Zambrano, (Apr. 27, 2022), pp. 52-53; Select Committee to Investigate the January 6th Attack on the United States Capitol, Transcribed Interview of Hanna Allred, (Mar. 30, 2022), p. 55; Select Committee to Investigate the January 6th Attack on the United States Capitol, Transcribed Interview of Hanna Allred, (Mar. 30, 2022), p. 66 ("... reported to Austin, so I would've received direction from him"); Select Committee to Investigate the January 6th Attack on the United States Capitol, Transcribed Interview of Gary Coby, (Feb. 23, 2022), pp. 52-54.

85. Select Committee to Investigate the January 6th Attack on the United States Capitol, Transcribed Interview of Justin Clark, (May. 17, 2022), p. 146 ("Well, it would have been approval by the principal. So Mr. Trump would have had to do that.").

86. Trump Fundraising Emails (@TrumpEmail), Twitter, Nov. 20, 2020 7:24 a.m. ET, available at https://twitter.com/TrumpEmail/status/1329762574494298112.

87. Select Committee to Investigate the January 6th Attack on the United States Capitol, Transcribed Interview of Gary Coby, (Feb. 23, 2022), p. 104 ("Yeah, I think they [the Trump Campaign] viewed that as helping to get the message out, especially, you know, that's the base, right?").

88. Select Committee to Investigate the January 6th Attack on the United States Capitol, Transcribed Interview of Hanna Allred, (Mar. 30, 2022), p. 57.

89. Select Committee to Investigate the January 6th Attack on the United States Capitol, Transcribed Interview of Kevin Zambrano, (Apr. 27, 2022), pp. 56-57.

90. Select Committee to Investigate the January 6th Attack on the United States Capitol, Transcribed Interview of Kevin Zambrano, (Apr. 27, 2022), p. 57.

91. Select Committee to Investigate the January 6th Attack on the United States Capitol, Transcribed Interview of Kevin Zambrano, (Apr. 27, 2022), p. 67.

92. Select Committee to Investigate the January 6th Attack on the United States Capitol, Transcribed Interview of Kevin Zambrano, (Apr. 27, 2022), p. 86.

93. Select Committee to Investigate the January 6th Attack on the United States Capitol, Transcribed Interview of Kevin Zambrano, (Apr. 27, 2022), pp. 86-87.

94. Select Committee to Investigate the January 6th Attack on the United States Capitol, Informal Interview of Hanna Allred, (Dec. 1, 2021), p. 4 ("Similarly, they could say the Democrats were trying or tried to steal the election, but not state that they were or had."); Select Committee to Investigate the January 6th Attack on the United States Capitol, Informal Interview of Ethan Katz, (Nov. 3, 2021), p. 2 ("KATZ recalled that Allred told him to say the Democrats were "trying to" steal the elections. He added that he did not have any discussions about why "trying to" was important, but his impression was that it was used to give some legal wiggle room and make the statement about stealing the election to be 'less false.'").

95. Select Committee to Investigate the January 6th Attack on the United States Capitol, Transcribed Interview of Hanna Allred, (Mar. 30, 2022), p. 75, ("I do remember at some point we were told we could no longer use the word 'rigged.'").

96. Documents on file with the Select Committee to Investigate the January 6th Attack on the United States Capitol (Alexander Cannon Production), AC-0013714, (Nov. 3, 2020, Fundraising email approval chain, "Re: FOR APPROVAL: Pennsylvania & Election Poll").

97. Documents on file with the Select Committee to Investigate the January 6th Attack on the United States Capitol (Alexander Cannon Production), AC-0013714 (Nov. 3, 2020, Fundraising email approval chain, "Re: FOR APPROVAL: Pennsylvania & Election Poll").

98. Documents on file with the Select Committee to Investigate the January 6th Attack on the United States Capitol (Alexander Cannon Production), AC-0013714 (Nov. 3, 2020, Fundraising email approval chain, "Re: FOR APPROVAL: Pennsylvania & Election Poll").

99. Documents on file with the Select Committee to Investigate the January 6th Attack on the United States Capitol (Alexander Cannon Production), AC-0013757 (Nov. 10, 2020, Fundraising email approval chain, "Re: [External]Re: FOR APPROVAL: Defend the Election & Vaccine"); Select Committee to Investigate the January 6th Attack on the United States Capitol, Transcribed Interview of Kevin Zambrano, (Apr. 27, 2022), p. 106 (Zambrano concedes that the revision "creates a new sentence" that means something different.); Select Committee to Investigate the January 6th Attack on the United States Capitol, Transcribed Interview of A. Zachary Parkinson, (May 18, 2022), p. 109 (In response to whether fair to say that that this was a substantive change, Parkinson states, "You could characterize it as that, I guess, yeah.").

100. Documents on file with the Select Committee to Investigate the January 6th Attack on the United States Capitol (Alexander Cannon Production), AC-0013757 (Nov. 10, 2020, Fundraising email approval chain, "Re: [External]Re: FOR APPROVAL: Defend the Election & Vaccine").

101. Documents on file with the Select Committee to Investigate the January 6th Attack on the United States Capitol (Alexander Cannon Production), AC-0013863 (Nov. 11, 2020, Fundraising email approval chain, "Re: [External]Re: FOR APPROVAL: Alaska & Election Defense") (emphasis in original).

102. Documents on file with the Select Committee to Investigate the January 6th Attack on the United States Capitol (Alexander Cannon Production), AC-0013863 (Nov. 11, 2020, Fundraising email approval chain, "Re: [External]Re: FOR APPROVAL: Alaska & Election Defense").

103. Documents on file with the Select Committee to Investigate the January 6th Attack on the United States Capitol (Alexander Cannon Production), AC-0013863 (Nov. 11, 2020, Fundraising email approval chain, "Re: [External]Re: FOR APPROVAL: Alaska & Election Defense").

104. Select Committee to Investigate the January 6th Attack on the United States Capitol, Transcribed Interview of Kevin Zambrano, (Apr. 27, 2022), p. 101.

105. Documents on file with the Select Committee to Investigate the January 6th Attack on the United States Capitol (Alexander Cannon Production), AC-0013891 (Nov. 12, 2020, Fundraising email approval chain, "Re: FOR APPROVAL: NC, GA Election Defense" at 3:08 a.m.); Documents on file with the Select Committee to Investigate the January 6th Attack on the United States Capitol (Alexander Cannon Production), AC-0013928 (Nov. 12, 2020, Fundraising email approval chain, "Re: FOR APPROVAL: NC, GA Election Defense" at 4:49 a.m.); Documents on file with the Select Committee to Investigate the January 6th Attack on the United States Capitol (Alexander Cannon Production), AC-0014006 (Nov. 13, 2020, Fundraising email approval chain, "Re: [External]Re: FOR APPROVAL: Defense Fund & GA/NC Victory").

106. Select Committee to Investigate the January 6th Attack on the United States Capitol, Transcribed Interview of Austin Boedigheimer, (Apr. 20, 2022), pp. 84, 137.

107. Select Committee to Investigate the January 6th Attack on the United States Capitol, Transcribed Interview of Michael Ahrens, (Sep. 1, 2022), pp. 14-15.

108. Jane C. Timm, "Rudy Giuliani baselessly alleges 'centralized' voter fraud at free-wheeling news conference," NBC News (Nov. 19, 2020), available at https://www.nbcnews.com/politics/donald-trump/rudy-giuliani-baselessly-alleges-centralized-voter-fraud-free-wheeling-news-n1248273.

109. Select Committee to Investigate the January 6th Attack on the United States Capitol, Transcribed Interview of Cassie Docksey, (Aug. 25, 2022), p. 37.

110. Select Committee to Investigate the January 6th Attack on the United States Capitol, Transcribed Interview of Cassie Docksey, (Aug. 25, 2022), p. 37 ("So on that press conference day, which I think is November 19th, Michael and I talked after that where he was generally telling me, 'Hey, we don't need to be out there. It's not automatic that we're just going to go out there and parallel or mimic what the campaign or what Rudy Giuliani or that legal team might be saying. Don't feel the need to put that through on the GOP social channels.'").

111. Select Committee to Investigate the January 6th Attack on the United States Capitol, Transcribed Interview of Cassie Docksey, (Aug. 25, 2022), p. 38.

112. Select Committee to Investigate the January 6th Attack on the United States Capitol, Transcribed Interview of Michael Ahrens, (Sep. 1, 2022), pp. 15-16. Ahrens thought this press conference was "embarrassing" and that other members of the RNC leadership team shared his view. Select Committee to Investigate the January 6th Attack on the United States Capitol, Transcribed Interview of Michael Ahrens, (Sep. 1, 2022), pp. 28-29.

113. Select Committee to Investigate the January 6th Attack on the United States Capitol, Transcribed Interview of Michael Ahrens, (Sep. 1, 2022), pp. 19-20.

114. Select Committee to Investigate the January 6th Attack on the United States Capitol, Transcribed Interview of Michael Ahrens, (Sep. 1, 2022), pp. 21-22.

115. Select Committee to Investigate the January 6th Attack on the United States Capitol, Transcribed Interview of Michael Ahrens, (Sep. 1, 2022), pp. 25-27.

116. Select Committee to Investigate the January 6th Attack on the United States Capitol, Transcribed Interview of Michael Reed, (July 20, 2022), pp. 56, 58 ("[T]here was a conversation at some point in November, December with either colleagues of mine or the legal team at the RNC" about the messaging that was coming out of TMAGAC."); Select Committee to Investigate the January 6th Attack on the United States Capitol, Transcribed Interview of Michael Reed, (July 20, 2022), p. 65, Select Committee to Investigate the January 6th Attack on the United States Capitol, Transcribed Interview of Michael Reed, (July 20, 2022), p. 66 (recalling "that there were conversations at some point that the RNC was more comfortable with more toned-down emails").

117. Select Committee to Investigate the January 6th Attack on the United States Capitol, Transcribed Interview of Michael Reed, (July 20, 2022), pp. 85, 86 ("I generally remember in regards to these emails in the post-election period conversations to make sure that the legal team and the chairman's office or whatever else was comfortable with the language that was going out of the JFC.").

118. Select Committee to Investigate the January 6th Attack on the United States Capitol, Transcribed Interview of Cassie Docksey, (Aug. 25, 2022), p. 45.

119. Select Committee to Investigate the January 6th Attack on the United States Capitol, Transcribed Interview of Michael Ahrens, (Sep. 1, 2022), p. 22.

120. Select Committee to Investigate the January 6th Attack on the United States Capitol, Transcribed Interview of Justin Clark, (May 17, 2022), p. 202.

121. Select Committee to Investigate the January 6th Attack on the United States Capitol, Transcribed Interview of Alexander Cannon, (Apr. 13, 2022), p. 183.

122. Trump Fundraising Emails (@TrumpEmail), Twitter, Dec. 20, 2020 12:20 p.m. ET, available at https://twitter.com/TrumpEmail/status/1341433522331017217; Trump Fundraising Emails (@TrumpEmail), Twitter, Dec. 27, 2020 3:23 p.m. ET, available at https://twitter.com/TrumpEmail/status/1343291529943781378.

123. William Cummings, Joey Garrison and Jim Sergent, "By the numbers: President Donald Trump's failed efforts to overturn the election," *USA Today*, (Jan. 6, 2021), available at https://www.usatoday.com/in-depth/news/politics/elections/2021/01/06/trumps-failed-efforts-overturn-election-numbers/4130307001/.

124. Select Committee to Investigate the January 6th Attack on the United States Capitol, Transcribed Interview of Hanna Allred, (Mar. 30, 2022), pp. 117-118.

125. Select Committee to Investigate the January 6th Attack on the United States Capitol, Transcribed Interview of Alexander Cannon, (Apr. 13, 2022), p. 144; Select Committee to Investigate the January 6th Attack on the United States Capitol, Transcribed Interview of Justin Clark, (May. 17, 2022), pp. 177-178 ("[I]n terms of people raising concerns about it, Alexander Cannon, at one point, came into my office and said something to the effect—and he was just doing legal reviews. It was like, I can't believe we're sending this stuff out, or something to that effect. I said—I told him he should go talk to Gary and speak to him about it, and I told him you don't need to do legal reviews on these anymore. . . . It was just about information that he knew wasn't correct.").

126. Select Committee to Investigate the January 6th Attack on the United States Capitol, Transcribed Interview of Alexander Cannon, (Apr. 13, 2022), p. 178.

127. Select Committee to Investigate the January 6th Attack on the United States Capitol, Transcribed Interview of Alexander Cannon, (Apr. 13, 2022), p. 180.

128. Select Committee to Investigate the January 6th Attack on the United States Capitol, Transcribed Interview of Alexander Cannon, (Apr. 13, 2022), p. 180.

129. Select Committee to Investigate the January 6th Attack on the United States Capitol, Transcribed Interview of Justin Clark, (May. 17, 2022), p. 178.

130. Select Committee to Investigate the January 6th Attack on the United States Capitol, Informal Interview of Ethan Katz, (Nov. 3, 2021), p. 2; Select Committee to Investigate the January 6th Attack on the United States Capitol, Informal Interview of Ethan Katz, (Jan. 21, 2022), p. 1.

131. Select Committee to Investigate the January 6th Attack on the United States Capitol, Informal Interview of Ethan Katz, (Nov. 3, 2021), p. 2; Select Committee to Investigate the January 6th Attack on the United States Capitol, Informal Interview of Ethan Katz, (Jan. 21, 2022), p. 1.

132. Select Committee to Investigate the January 6th Attack on the United States Capitol, Informal Interview of Ethan Katz, (Nov. 3, 2021), p. 2; Select Committee to Investigate the January 6th Attack on the United States Capitol, Informal Interview of Ethan Katz, (Jan. 21, 2022), p. 1.

133. Select Committee to Investigate the January 6th Attack on the United States Capitol, Transcribed Interview of Hanna Allred, (Mar. 30, 2022), p. 69; Select Committee to Investigate the January 6th Attack on the United States Capitol, Transcribed Interview of Austin Boedigheimer, (Apr. 20, 2022), p. 89.

134. Select Committee to Investigate the January 6th Attack on the United States Capitol, Informal Interview of Ethan Katz, (Nov. 3, 2021), p. 2; Select Committee to Investigate the January 6th Attack on the United States Capitol, Informal Interview of Ethan Katz, (Jan. 21, 2022), p. 1.

135. Select Committee to Investigate the January 6th Attack on the United States Capitol, Informal Interview of Ethan Katz, (Nov. 3, 2021), p. 2; Select Committee to Investigate the January 6th Attack on the United States Capitol, Informal Interview of Ethan Katz, (Jan. 21, 2022), p. 1.

136. Select Committee to Investigate the January 6th Attack on the United States Capitol, Informal Interview of Ethan Katz, (Nov. 3, 2021).

137. Select Committee to Investigate the January 6th Attack on the United States Capitol, Transcribed Interview of Hanna Allred, (Mar. 30, 2022), pp. 83-86. (Allred confirmed that Boedigheimer would have given the directive to draft this email); Select Committee to Investigate the January 6th Attack on the United States Capitol, Transcribed Interview of Hanna Allred, (Mar. 30, 2022), p. 86.

138. Trump Fundraising Emails (@TrumpEmail), Twitter, Nov. 4, 2020, 9:42 a.m. available at https://twitter.com/TrumpEmail/status/1324180321676546050.

139. Select Committee to Investigate the January 6th Attack on the United States Capitol, Informal Interview of Ethan Katz, (Nov. 3, 2021), p. 3.

140. Select Committee to Investigate the January 6th Attack on the United States Capitol, Informal Interview of Hanna Allred, (Dec. 1, 2021), p. 7.

141. Select Committee to Investigate the January 6th Attack on the United States Capitol, Transcribed Interview of Alexander Cannon, (Apr. 13, 2022), p. 176.

142. Select Committee to Investigate the January 6th Attack on the United States Capitol, Transcribed Interview of Alexander Cannon, (Apr. 13, 2022), pp. 116-117.

143. Select Committee to Investigate the January 6th Attack on the United States Capitol, Transcribed Interview of Alexander Cannon, (Apr. 13, 2022), p. 137. Similarly, on January 6th, DataPier stopped sending emails, and the list went cold, and, therefore, DataPier is now defunct; see Select Committee to Investigate the January 6th Attack on the United States Capitol, Transcribed Interview of Alexander Cannon, (Apr. 13, 2022), p. 122.

144. Documents on file with the Select Committee to Investigate the January 6th Attack on the United States Capitol (Alexander Cannon Production), AC-0002048 (Nov. 7, 2020, email from Seth Charles to Darren Centinello, Alexander Cannon, Sean Dollman, and Sarah Grounder,

"FW: [PROOF] Michael – increase your impact NOW"). ("Again this comes in chorus with less inflammatory language that could be misleading as accusatory or assuming intent upon a particular population.").

145. Documents on file with the Select Committee to Investigate the January 6th Attack on the United States Capitol (Alexander Cannon Production), AC-0004724 (Nov. 9, 2020, email from Seth Charles to Darren Centinello, Alexander Cannon, Sean Dollman, and Sarah Grounder, "Re: FW: [PROOF] Hanna—I need you.").

146. Documents on file with the Select Committee to Investigate the January 6th Attack on the United States Capitol (Alexander Cannon Production), AC-0013741 (Nov. 11, 2020, email from Seth Charles to Darren Centinello, Alexander Cannon, Sean Dollman, and Sarah Grounder, "Re: FW: [PROOF] BIG NEWS").

147. J. Doe expressed safety concerns and a fear of retaliation for cooperating with the Select Committee. Accordingly, the Select Committee has not revealed their identity.

148. Select Committee to Investigate the January 6th Attack on the United States Capitol, Deposition of J. Doe, (May 20, 2022), pp. 7-8.

149. Select Committee to Investigate the January 6th Attack on the United States Capitol, Deposition of J. Doe, (May 20, 2022), p. 30.

150. Select Committee to Investigate the January 6th Attack on the United States Capitol, Deposition of J. Doe, (May 20, 2022), pp. 30-31.

151. Select Committee to Investigate the January 6th Attack on the United States Capitol, Deposition of J. Doe, (May 20, 2022), pp. 42-43.

152. Select Committee to Investigate the January 6th Attack on the United States Capitol, Deposition of J. Doe, (May 20, 2022), p. 46.

153. Select Committee to Investigate the January 6th Attack on the United States Capitol, Deposition of J. Doe, (May 20, 2022), p. 47.

154. Select Committee to Investigate the January 6th Attack on the United States Capitol, Deposition of J. Doe, (May 20, 2022), pp. 49-50.

155. Select Committee to Investigate the January 6th Attack on the United States Capitol, Deposition of J. Doe, (May 20, 2022), p. 25.

156. Select Committee to Investigate the January 6th Attack on the United States Capitol, Transcribed Interview of Gary Coby, (Feb. 23, 2022), p. 49 (noting that the Trump Campaign had "three of our best four fundraising days occur immediately after the election").

157. Select Committee to Investigate the January 6th Attack on the United States Capitol, Transcribed Interview of Hanna Allred, (Mar. 30, 2022), p. 86.

158. Select Committee to Investigate the January 6th Attack on the United States Capitol, Transcribed Interview of Hanna Allred, (Mar. 30, 2022), p. 86 ("We frequently use funds as a marketing tactic. . . So I don't believe there is actually a fund called the 'Election Defense Fund,' not that I'm aware of."); Select Committee to Investigate the January 6th Attack on the United States Capitol, Transcribed Interview of Austin Boedigheimer, (Apr. 20, 2022), pp. 91-92.

159. Select Committee to Investigate the January 6th Attack on the United States Capitol, Transcribed Interview of Hanna Allred, (Mar. 30, 2022), p. 87; Select Committee to Investigate the January 6th Attack on the United States Capitol, Transcribed Interview of Hanna Allred, (Mar. 30, 2022), pp. 96-97 (Allred noting that she only became aware of Save America in February 2021); Select Committee to Investigate the January 6th Attack on the United States Capitol, Transcribed Interview of Austin Boedigheimer, (Apr. 20, 2022), p. 92 ("From my understanding, the money was going towards, I believe this is a TMAGAC e-mail. So it was going to TMAGAC. And then how the money was spent from there, you know, that's not something that I would do or have knowledge to."); Select Committee to Investigate the January 6th Attack on the United States Capitol, Transcribed Interview of Austin Boedigheimer, (Apr. 20, 2022), p. 94 ("I'm not sure how the funds went or how they were allocated. I don't know precisely.").

160. Shane Goldmacher and Rachel Shorey, "Trump Raised $255.4 Million in 8 Weeks as He Sought to overturn Election Result," *New York Times*, (Jan. 31, 2021), available at https://www.nytimes.com/2021/01/31/us/politics/trump-voter-fraud-fundraising.html ("President Donald J. Trump and the Republican Party raised $255.4 million in the eight-plus weeks following the Nov. 3 election, new federal filings show, as he sought to undermine and overturn the results with unfounded accusations of fraud.").

161. Select Committee to Investigate the January 6th Attack on the United States Capitol, Transcribed Interview of Alexander Cannon, (Apr. 13, 2022), p. 153.

162. Select Committee to Investigate the January 6th Attack on the United States Capitol, Transcribed Interview of Justin Clark, (May. 17, 2022), p. 143 ("After election day . . . you can raise money for a recount and to pay off debt.").

163. Select Committee to Investigate the January 6th Attack on the United States Capitol, Transcribed Interview of Gary Coby, (Feb. 23, 2022), p. 125; Jarrett Renshaw and Joseph Tanfani, "Donations under $8K to Trump 'election defense' instead go to president, RNC," Reuters, (Nov. 11, 2020), available at https://www.reuters.com/article/us-usa-election-trump-fundraising-insigh/donations-under-8k-to-trump-election-defense-instead-go-to-president-rnc-idUSKBN27R309 ("The emailed solicitations send supporters to an 'Official Election Defense Fund' website that asks them to sign up for recurring donations to 'protect the results and keep fighting even after Election Day.' The fine print makes clear most of the money will go to other priorities. A large portion of the money goes to 'Save America,' a Trump leadership PAC, or political action committee, set up on Monday, and the Republican National Committee (RNC).").

164. Federal Election Commission, Advisory Opinion 2006-24, (Oct. 5, 2006), p. 6, available at https://www.fec.gov/files/legal/aos/2006-24/2006-24.pdf (The Act "prohibits Federal officeholders and candidates, their agents, and entities directly or indirectly established, financed, maintained or controlled by or acting on behalf of one or more Federal officeholders or candidates, from soliciting, receiving, directing, transferring, or spending funds for expenses related to a recount of the votes cast in a Federal election, including the recount activities described above, unless those funds are subject to the limitations, prohibitions, and reporting requirements of the Act. . . . [A] Federal candidate's recount fund must not receive or solicit donations in excess of the Act's amount limitations. . . . [A]ny recount fund established by a Federal candidate may not receive donations that in the aggregate exceed . . . $5,000 per multicandidate political committee.").

165. FEC Reported Disbursements in 2020 by Save America, (last accessed on Nov. 18, 2022), available at https://www.fec.gov/data/disbursements/?committee_id=C00762591&two_year_transaction_period=2020&data_type=processed.

166. Documents on file with the Select Committee to Investigate the January 6th Attack on the United States Capitol (Timothy Murtaugh Production), XXM-0011244, (Nov. 11, 2020, emails between Timothy Murtaugh and Justin Clark, "Re: [EXTERNAL]Trump legal defense and leadership PAC").

167. Documents on file with the Select Committee to Investigate the January 6th Attack on the United States Capitol (Timothy Murtaugh Production), XXM-0013276, (Nov. 24, 2020, emails between Timothy Murtaugh and Justin Clark, "Re: [EXTERNAL]Re: Fundraising questions").

168. When the Trump Campaign learned that reporters were going to write about their misleading fundraising, Murtaugh advised further comment from the Campaign would "serve to highlight the argument that the fundraising pitch is misleading." Documents on file with the Select Committee to Investigate the January 6th Attack on the United States Capitol (Timothy Murtaugh Production), XXM-0018627, (Dec. 1, 2020, emails between Timothy Murtaugh, Jason Miller, Sean Dollman, Justin Clark, and Bill Stepien, "Re: [EXTERNAL]$$$$$$"). Murtaugh further noted that "POTUS is on board with how it will be described." Documents on file with the Select Committee to Investigate the January 6th Attack on the United States Capitol (Timothy Murtaugh Production), XXM-0018627, (Dec. 1, 2020, emails between Timothy Murtaugh, Jason Miller, Sean Dollman, Justin Clark, and Bill Stepien, "Re: [EXTERNAL]$$$$$$").

169. Documents on file with the Select Committee to Investigate the January 6th Attack on the United States Capitol (Timothy Murtaugh Production), XXM-0011244, (Nov. 11, 2020, emails between Timothy Murtaugh and Justin Clark, "Re: [EXTERNAL]Trump legal defense and leadership PAC"), (Murtaugh asking Justin Clark, "Still ignoring?"); Documents on file with the Select Committee to Investigate the January 6th Attack on the United States Capitol (Timothy Murtaugh Production), XXM-0013276, (Nov. 24, 2020, emails between Timothy Murtaugh and Justin Clark, "Re: [EXTERNAL]Re: Fundraising questions"), (Murtaugh telling Justin Clark, "FYI – Still not answering.").

170. Documents on file with the Select Committee to Investigate the January 6th Attack on the United States Capitol (Timothy Murtaugh Production), XXM-0013276, (Nov. 24, 2020, emails between Timothy Murtaugh and Justin Clark, "Re: [EXTERNAL]Re: Fundraising questions").

171. FEC Reported Disbursements to Daniel Scavino by Save America, (last accessed on Nov. 10, 2022), available at https://www.fec.gov/data/disbursements/?data_type=processed&committee_id=C00762591&recipient_name=scavino%2C+dan.

172. Katelyn Polantz and Ryan Nobles, "Trump's former deputy chief of staff, Dan Scavino, not ready to cooperate with January 6 committee, attorney says," CNN, (Oct. 21, 2021), available at https://www.cnn.com/2021/10/20/politics/dan-scavino-january-6-committee/index.html.

173. "Hudson Digital LLC," State of Delaware Division of Corporations, (last accessed on Dec. 9, 2022), available at https://icis.corp.delaware.gov/Ecorp/EntitySearch/NameSearch.aspx (search "Hudson Digital LLC" in the "Entity Name" field).

174. Schedule B (FEC Form 3x) Itemized Disbursements by Save America, (July 31, 2021), available at https://docquery.fec.gov/cgi-bin/fecimg/?202107319465699743.

175. FEC Reported Disbursements to Hudson Digital LLC, (last accessed on Nov. 10, 2022) available at https://www.fec.gov/data/disbursements/?data_type=processed&recipient_name=hudson+digital+llc.

176. An unrelated company, Hudson Digital, has operated for approximately 10 years in Hudson, NY, over 80 miles from the addresses associated with Hudson Digital LLC.

177. Schedule B (FEC Form 3x) Itemized Disbursements by Save America, (July 31, 2021), available at https://docquery.fec.gov/cgi-bin/fecimg/?202107319465699743.

178. FEC Reported Disbursements to Nicholas Luna by Save America, (last accessed on Nov. 10, 2022), available at https://www.fec.gov/data/disbursements/?data_type=processed&committee_id=C00762591&recipient_name=luna%2C+nicholas.

179. FEC Reported Disbursements to Red State Partners LLC, (last accessed on Nov. 10, 2022) available at https://www.fec.gov/data/disbursements/?data_type=processed&recipient_name=red+state+partners.

180. "Red State Partners LLC," State of Delaware Division of Corporations, (last accessed on Dec. 9, 2022), available at https://icis.corp.delaware.gov/Ecorp/EntitySearch/NameSearch.aspx (search "Red State Partners LLC" in the "Entity Name" field).

181. FEC Reported Disbursements to Red State Partners LLC, (last accessed on Nov. 10, 2022) available at https://www.fec.gov/data/disbursements/?data_type=processed&recipient_name=red+state+partners.

182. Schedule B (FEC Form 3x) Itemized Disbursements by Make America Great Again PAC, (Dec. 2, 2021), available at https://docquery.fec.gov/cgi-bin/fecimg/?202112029469645374.

183. "Pericles, LLC," District of Columbia Department of Business Licensing Division, (last accessed on Dec. 9, 2022), available at https://corponline.dcra.dc.gov/BizEntity.aspx/ViewEntityData?entityId=4292880.

184. "Vincent M. Haley," ProPublica: Trump Town, (last accessed on Nov. 10, 2022), available at https://projects.propublica.org/trump-town/staffers/vincent-m-haley.

185. "Taylor Swindle," Gingrich360, (last accessed on Nov. 10, 2022), available at https://www.gingrich360.com/about/gingrich-360-team/taylor-swindle/.

186. "Ross Worthington," ProPublica: Trump Town, (last accessed on Nov. 10, 2022), available at https://projects.propublica.org/trump-town/staffers/ross-worthington.

187. Documents on file with the Select Committee to Investigate the January 6th Attack on the United States Capitol, (National Archives Production), 076P-R000007531_0001, (January 6, 2021, emails between Ross Worthington, Robert Gabriel, Jr., Vincent Haley, and others).

188. "Pericles, LLC," District of Columbia Department of Business Licensing Division, (last accessed on Dec. 9, 2022), available at https://corponline.dcra.dc.gov/BizEntity.aspx/ViewEntityData?entityId=4292880.

189. FEC Reported Disbursements to Pericles LLC by Save America, (last accessed on Nov. 10, 2022) available at https://www.fec.gov/data/disbursements/?data_type=processed&committee_id=C00762591&recipient_name=pericles+llc.

190. Documents on file with the Select Committee to Investigate the January 6th Attack on the United States Capitol, (National Archives Production), 076P-R000007531_0001, (January 6, 2021, emails between Ross Worthington, Robert Gabriel, Jr., Vincent Haley, and others).

191. Documents on file with the Select Committee to Investigate the January 6th Attack on the United States Capitol, (National Archives Production), 076P-R000007531_0001, (January 6, 2021, emails between Ross Worthington, Robert Gabriel, Jr., Vincent Haley, and others).

192. The organization was originally formed as Believe in America LLC, then changed its name the following day to Gabriel Strategies LLC. See "Gabriel Strategies LLC", State of New Jersey Division of Revenue and Enterprise Search, (last accessed on Dec. 9, 2022), available at https://www.njportal.com/DOR/BusinessNameSearch/Search/BusinessName (search "Gabriel Strategies LLC" in the "Business Name" field).

193. Schedule B (FEC Form 3x) Itemized Disbursements by Save America, (May 5, 2022), available at https://docquery.fec.gov/cgi-bin/fecimg/?202205059502664518.

194. FEC Reported Disbursements to Red State Partners LLC by Save America, (last accessed on Nov. 10, 2022) available at https://www.fec.gov/data/disbursements/?data_type=processed&committee_id=C00762591&recipient_name=gabriel+strategies.

195. FEC Reported Disbursements to Herve Pierre Braillard by Save America, (last accessed on Nov. 10, 2022) available at https://www.fec.gov/data/disbursements/?data_type=processed&committee_id=C00762591&recipient_name=Herve+Pierre+Braillard.

196. Suzy Menkes, "Herve Pierre: Dressing the First Lady," *Vogue*, (Apr. 12, 2017), available at https://www.vogue.pt/herve-pierre-dressing-the-first-lady; Rosemary Feitelberg, "Melania Trump's Former Stylist Addresses $60,000 Save America Payment," Women's Wear Daily, (Aug. 8. 2022), available at https://wwd.com/fashion-news/designer-luxury/melania-trump-herve-pierre-60000-save-america-payment-1235294733/.

197. Schedule B (FEC Form 3x) Itemized Disbursements by Save America, (July 31, 2021), available at https://docquery.fec.gov/cgi-bin/fecimg/?202107319465699856.

198. Schedule B (FEC Form 3x) Itemized Disbursements by Save America, (May 5, 2022), available at https://docquery.fec.gov/cgi-bin/fecimg/?202205059502664847.

199. FEC Reported Disbursements to Event Strategies Inc by Save America, (last accessed on Nov. 10, 2022) available at https://www.fec.gov/data/disbursements/?data_type=processed&committee_id=C00762591&recipient_name=event+strategies+inc.

200. FEC Reported Disbursements to Trump Hotel and Mar-A-Lago by Save America, (last accessed on Nov. 10, 2022) available at https://www.fec.gov/data/disbursements/?data_type=processed&committee_id=C00762591&recipient_name=mar-a-lago&recipient_name=trump+hotel.

201. Schedule B (FEC Form 3x) Itemized Disbursements by Save America, (June 15, 2022), available at https://docquery.fec.gov/cgi-bin/fecimg/?202206159514906341.

202. FEC Reported Disbursements to National Public Affairs by Save America, (last accessed on Nov. 10, 2022) available at https://www.fec.gov/data/disbursements/?data_type=processed&committee_id=C00762591&recipient_name=National+Public+Affairs.

203. "Meet Our Team," National Public Affairs, (last accessed on Nov. 10, 2022), available at https://natpublicaffairs.com/.

204. Select Committee to Investigate the January 6th Attack on the United States Capitol, Transcribed Interview of William Stepien, (Feb. 10, 2022), p. 174.

205. FEC disclosures show that other than Save America, National Public Affairs LLC received payments from only three other organizations since 2021. All three are campaigns for election deniers, Kelly Tshibaka (AK-Senate), Jason Smith (MO-08), and Harriet Hageman (WY-AL). See FEC Reported Disbursements to National Public Affairs LLC since 2021, (last accessed on Nov. 10, 2022), available at https://www.fec.gov/data/disbursements/?data_type=processed&recipient_name=national+public+affairs+llc&min_date=01%2F01%2F2021.

206. Federal Election Commission, Advisory Opinion 2019-02, (Mar. 28, 2019), available at https://www.fec.gov/files/legal/aos/2019-02/2019-02.pdf.

207. Select Committee to Investigate the January 6th Attack on the United States Capitol, Transcribed Interview of Justin Clark, (May. 17, 2022), p. 143.

208. Select Committee to Investigate the January 6th Attack on the United States Capitol, Transcribed Interview of Justin Clark, (May. 17, 2022), p. 145.

209. Select Committee to Investigate the January 6th Attack on the United States Capitol, Transcribed Interview of Alexander Cannon, (Apr. 13, 2022), p. 156 ("[G]enerally after an election, you can raise money for debt retirement, and you can raise money for recount.").

210. Documents on file with the Select Committee to Investigate the January 6th Attack on the United States Capitol (Alexander Cannon Production), AC-0013889 (Nov. 12, 2020, emails between Alexander Cannon and Cleta Mitchell, "Re: [External]Legal defense fund").

211. Documents on file with the Select Committee to Investigate the January 6th Attack on the United States Capitol (Alexander Cannon Production), AC-0013889 (Nov. 12, 2020, emails between Alexander Cannon and Cleta Mitchell, "Re: [External]Legal defense fund").

212. Statement of Organization FEC Form 1, filed by Make America Great Again PAC, (Feb. 27, 2021), available at https://docquery.fec.gov/pdf/093/202102279429078093/202102279429078093.pdf#navpanes=0.

213. FEC Reported Disbursements to 2M Document Management and Imaging, LLC by Make America Great Again PAC, (last accessed on Nov. 10, 2022) available at https://www.fec.gov/data/disbursements/?data_type=processed&committee_id=C00580100&recipient_name=2m+document&two_year_transaction_period=2022.

214. Select Committee to Investigate the January 6th Attack on the United States Capitol, Transcribed Interview of Matthew Clarke (Aug. 4, 2022), p. 28 (agreeing that "the vast majority of the work that 2M has done to date that has been paid for by MAGA PAC relates to January 6th documents or COVID-related documents coming from NARA"); Select Committee to Investigate the January 6th Attack on the United States Capitol, Transcribed Interview of Alexander Cannon, (Aug. 18, 2022), p. 31 ("There was a House Oversight investigation into the administration's COVID response, and there were a large number of documents that were coming through that needed to be processed.").

215. Select Committee to Investigate the January 6th Attack on the United States Capitol, Transcribed Interview of Matthew Clarke, (Aug. 4, 2022), pp. 31-32 ("During that time, I believe all we were doing was work related to the White House—the Trump administration's response to COVID.").

216. Select Committee to Investigate the January 6th Attack on the United States Capitol, Transcribed Interview of Alexander Cannon, (Aug. 18, 2022), pp. 15-16 (noting his understanding that "if the funds were raised to DJTFP and they were not spent on debt retirement, any remaining funds that were not spent on debt retirement would have gone to this segregated, restricted account for recounts for MAGA PA?"); Select Committee to Investigate the January 6th Attack on the United States Capitol, Transcribed Interview of Alexander Cannon, (Aug. 18, 2022), p. 16; Select Committee to Investigate the January 6th Attack on the

United States Capitol, Transcribed Interview of Alexander Cannon, (Aug. 18, 2022), pp. 37-38 (agreeing that if funds paid to 2M are labeled recount then he would assume they came from Recount Account).

217. *See* Statement of Policy: "Purpose of Disbursement" Entries for Filings with the Commission, 72 Fed. Reg. 887 (Jan. 9, 2007) (citing 11 C.F.R. § § 104.3(b)(3)(i)(b), (4)(i)(A)).

218. Documents on file with the Select Committee to Investigate the January 6th Attack on the United States Capitol (Aug. 21, 2022, Memorandum regarding Fundraising communication rhetoric's influence on social media).

219. Documents on file with the Select Committee to Investigate the January 6th Attack on the United States Capitol (Aug. 21, 2022, Memorandum regarding Fundraising communication rhetoric's influence on social media).

220. Trump Fundraising Emails (@TrumpEmail), Twitter, Jan. 6, 2021, 12:20 p.m. ET, available at https://twitter.com/TrumpEmail/status/1346794824591093763.

221. Trump Fundraising Emails, (@TrumpEmail), Twitter, Jan. 6, 2021, 1:31 p.m. ET, available at https://twitter.com/TrumpEmail/status/1346887173438636032.

222. Trump Fundraising Emails (@TrumpEmail), Twitter, Jan. 6, 2021, 11:29 a.m. ET, available at https://twitter.com/TrumpEmail/status/1346856536338030601.

223. Select Committee to Investigate the January 6th Attack on the United States Capitol, Transcribed Interview of Austin Boedigheimer, (Apr. 20, 2022), p. 42 (noting "yes, we stopped sending emails on January 6"); Select Committee to Investigate the January 6th Attack on the United States Capitol, Transcribed Interview of Hanna Allred, (Mar. 30, 2022), p. 128 ("I believe we got some sort of message, either on Microsoft Teams or Signal from Austin, saying pause everything.").

224. Select Committee to Investigate the January 6th Attack on the United States Capitol, Transcribed Interview of Austin Boedigheimer, (Apr. 20, 2022), p. 140.

225. Select Committee to Investigate the January 6th Attack on the United States Capitol, Transcribed Interview of Alexander Cannon, (Apr. 13, 2022), p. 124.

226. See Criminal Complaint, *United States v. Grayson*, No. 1:21-mj-00163 (D.D.C. Jan. 25, 2021); Criminal Complaint, *United States v. Fitzsimmons*, No. 1:21-cr-00158-RC (D.D.C. Feb. 1, 2021); (noting that the defendant in that case "believed voter fraud occurred" and that "[c]onvinced that the election results had been fraudulently reported, he was moved by the words of then-President Trump to travel to the District of Columbia for the 'Save America Rally.'").

227. Select Committee to Investigate the January 6th Attack on the United States Capitol, Deposition of J. Doe, (May 20, 2022), pp. 64-65.

228. Select Committee to Investigate the January 6th Attack on the United States Capitol, Deposition of J. Doe, (May 20, 2022), pp. 68-69.

229. Select Committee to Investigate the January 6th Attack on the United States Capitol, Deposition of J. Doe, (May 20, 2022), p. 72.

APPENDIX 4

MALIGN FOREIGN INFLUENCE

INTRODUCTION

In the wake of the 2020 U.S. Presidential election, President Donald J. Trump and his apologists attempted to blame his loss on foreign interference. They falsely claimed that foreign-manufactured voting machines had been manipulated so that votes cast for Trump were instead recorded as votes for Joseph R. Biden, Jr.[1] No one has ever, either at the time or since, offered any evidence to support Trump's assertion. On the contrary, ample evidence collected by the Intelligence Community (IC) and reviewed by the Select Committee disproves those claims.

That is not to say foreign actors made no attempt to influence the American political climate during and after the 2020 Presidential election. This appendix evaluates the role foreign influence played in the circumstances surrounding the insurrection.[2]

DISCUSSION

ELECTION MEDDLING IN 2020:
FOREIGN INTERFERENCE? NO. FOREIGN INFLUENCE? YES.

In its postmortem assessment of the 2020 U.S. Presidential election, the Intelligence Community comprehensively examined two types of foreign meddling: interference and influence. The distinction between the two is critical in evaluating President Trump's repeated public assertions that there had been massive and widespread "fraud" that had the effect of "stealing" the election for then-candidate Biden.

For its analytic purposes, the Intelligence Community defines election *interference* as "a subset of election influence activities targeted at the technical aspects of the election, including voter registration, casting and counting ballots, or reporting results."[3] That definition notes that election interference is a subset of election *influence*, which the Intelligence Community defines to include "overt and covert efforts by foreign governments or actors acting as agents of, or on behalf of, foreign governments intended to affect directly or indirectly a US election—including candidates, political parties, voters or their preferences, or political processes."[4]

The Intelligence Community's Assessment (ICA) found no factual basis for any allegation of technical interference with the 2020 U.S. election: "We have no indications that any foreign actor attempted to interfere in the 2020 US elections by altering any technical aspect of the voting process, including voter registration, ballot casting, vote tabulation, or reporting results."[5] Put simply, allegations that foreign powers rigged voting machines and swapped ballots were false and unsupported.

Although there is no evidence of foreign technical interference in the 2020 election, there is evidence of foreign influence. Specifically, the Intelligence Community's Assessment concluded that "Russian President Putin authorized, and a range of Russian government organizations conducted, influence operations aimed at denigrating President Biden's candidacy and the Democratic Party, supporting former President Trump, undermining public confidence in the electoral process, and exacerbating sociopolitical divisions in the US."[6] The two Intelligence Community analytic conclusions about the 2020 U.S. Presidential election—that there was evidence of foreign influence, but not foreign interference—are completely consistent.

MALIGN FOREIGN EFFORTS TO INFLUENCE THE 2020 U.S. ELECTIONS

The 2020 U.S. elections saw an increase in the number of foreign state and non-state entities that attempted to influence the U.S. electorate. The U.S. Intelligence Community suggests, as a possible explanation, that more such foreign entities "may view influence operations as important tools for projecting power abroad."[7] More ascertainably, "[t]he growth of internet and social media use means foreign actors are more able to reach US audiences directly, while the tools for doing so are becoming more accessible."[8]

The United States' principal foreign adversaries—Russia, China, and Iran—all of them autocracies, engage, to varying degrees, in disguised efforts to influence U.S. public opinion.[9] In the context of these overarching efforts,[10] U.S. elections offer special opportunities.

For Russia, "[e]lections...often serve as an opportune target. But attacks on elections are typically just one part of ongoing, multi-pronged operations."[11] The U.S. Intelligence Community's definitive post-election assessment of foreign influence activities during the 2020 Presidential election concluded that Russia was deeply engaged in disinformation activities intended to influence the outcome by supporting President Trump while disparaging then-candidate Biden; Iran also engaged in efforts to influence the election's outcome, but unlike Russia, did not actively promote any candidate; and that China considered opportunities to influence the election's outcome, but ultimately decided that potential costs outweighed any foreseeable benefits.[12] Both Russia and Iran worked to undermine the American public's confidence in U.S. democratic processes and to deepen socio-political divisions in the United States.[13]

RUSSIA'S MALIGN INFLUENCE EFFORTS TARGETING THE UNITED STATES

Russian malign disinformation efforts are both strategic in scope and opportunistic in nature. They aim to corrode the power and appeal of the U.S. democratic processes, worsen U.S. domestic divisions, and weaken America at home and abroad. The Intelligence Community's February 2022 unclassified "Annual Threat Assessment" puts this sustained Russian threat in a nutshell:

> Russia presents one of the most serious foreign influence threats to the United States, using its intelligence services, proxies, and wide-ranging influence tools to try to divide Western alliances, and increase its sway around the world, while attempting to undermine U.S. global standing, amplify discord inside the United States, and influence U.S. voters and decisionmaking.[14]

RUSSIAN DISINFORMATION AND THE 2020 PRESIDENTIAL ELECTION

Foreign adversaries' influence campaigns routinely push disinformation to U.S. audiences. Elections offer an important forum for Russia and other U.S. adversaries to seek to deepen divisions within American society through disinformation campaigns.[15] The Intelligence Community projects that both Russia and China will, for the foreseeable future, continue to press their disinformation campaigns attempting to undermine the U.S. population's confidence in their government and society.[16] Russia certainly did so in the period following the election and preceding the January 6th attack.

The disinformation spread by Russia and its messengers during that time was not, however, entirely original. The Intelligence Community Assessment found that Russia's disinformation engine borrowed President Trump's own words to achieve its goals:

> Russian online influence actors generally promoted former President Trump and his commentary, including repeating his political messaging on the election results; the presidential campaign; debates; the impeachment inquiry; and, as the election neared, US domestic crises.[17]

Indeed, President Trump's messaging during and after the 2020 election was reflected in Russian influence efforts at the time. In September of 2020, the Department of Homeland Security's Office of Intelligence and Analysis warned that Russia was engaged in pre-election activity targeting the U.S. democratic process.[18] The bulletin advised that "Russia is likely to continue amplifying criticisms of vote-by-mail and shifting voting processes amidst the COVID−19 pandemic to undermine public trust in the electoral process."[19]

Deliberately spreading disinformation to discredit a U.S. election was not new to Russia's influence arsenal. In the judgment of the U.S. Intelligence Community, it is a tactic Russia was prepared to deploy after the 2016 U.S. Presidential election:

Even after the [2020] election, Russian online influence actors continued to promote narratives questioning the election results and disparaging President Biden and the Democratic Party. These efforts parallel plans Moscow had in place in 2016 to discredit a potential incoming Clinton administration, but which it scrapped after former President Trump's victory.[20]

Russian influence efforts in the 2016 and 2020 elections, while distinct in their particulars, shared some similarities. Historically, Russia has engaged in near-industrial scale online influence efforts.[21] The Intelligence Community Assessment states that in 2020, Russia again relied on internet trolls to amplify divisive content aimed at American audiences:

> The Kremlin-linked influence organization Project Lakhta and its Lakhta Internet Research (LIR) troll farm—commonly referred to by its former moniker Internet Research Agency (IRA)—amplified controversial domestic issues. LIR used social media personas, news websites, and US persons to deliver tailored content to subsets of the US population. LIR established short-lived troll farms that used unwitting third-country nationals in Ghana, Mexico, and Nigeria to propagate these US-focused narratives....[22]

The threats posed by Russia's influence efforts are not new, nor are they diminishing. The latest unclassified Intelligence Community Annual Threat Assessment throws this into sharp relief:

> Moscow has conducted influence operations against U.S. elections for decades, including as recently as the 2020 presidential election. We assess that it probably will try to strengthen ties to U.S. persons in the media and politics in hopes of developing vectors for future influence operations.[23]

PROXIES AMONG US: MALIGN FOREIGN INFLUENCE AND U.S. AUDIENCES

Tech-enabled or not, if ever there was a "people business," foreign influence is it. People working on behalf of a foreign government—foreign government officials, their agents, and proxies—work to influence, directly or indirectly, a target audience in another country—its officials and citizens at large. Most who are engaged in those efforts act overtly: ambassadors, consuls general, government delegations and so forth. Their foreign influence efforts are not, however, focused on philanthropy or foreign aid. Moreover, the perspectives they seek to embed in their target audiences may be intentionally and materially inaccurate, propagandistic, or driven by unstated motives. In such instances, foreign influence may amount to injecting foreign disinformation into the U.S. media ecosystem for re-branding and onward transmission to an American audience.[24]

Foreign state adversaries of the United States generally disguise their efforts to influence U.S. audiences, particularly when they seek to influence U.S. voters' views in the run-up to an election. Among the many ways of concealing the foreign-state origin or sponsorship of such a message is to use unattributable proxies—"cut-outs"—or fully independent ideological allies in the United States as messaging organs. A cooperative American messenger—a proxy for the foreign government itself—may be needed to make the foreign-origin message congenial to the target American audience.

Malign foreign influencers, including foreign governments, used an additional such masking tool during the Trump administration: amplifying U.S.-originated messages so that they reached a broader audience. These influencers often took advantage of the algorithms by which social media platforms bring congenial messages and other information to users whose views are likely to be similar or compatible.

Shortly after the January 6th attack, the National Intelligence Council summarized the scope and significance of Russia's use of proxies in the 2020 U.S. Presidential election:

> A key element of Moscow's strategy this election cycle was its use of proxies linked to Russian intelligence to push influence narratives—including misleading or unsubstantiated allegations against President Biden—to US media organizations, US officials, and prominent US individuals, including some close to former President Trump and his administration.[25]

The success of the proxy depends on shielding its foreign sponsorship. For that reason, it can be difficult or impossible to determine conclusively whether someone parroting a foreign government adversary's point of view to a U.S. audience is that government's controlled proxy or a volunteer taking full advantage of U.S. First Amendment freedoms.

ANTI-U.S. FOREIGN STATE PROPAGANDA AND THE JANUARY 6TH ATTACK

U.S. adversaries use anti-American propaganda and disinformation to advance their strategic foreign policy objectives. They aim to corrode U.S. influence abroad while diluting U.S. citizens' trust in their democratic institutions and processes. They hope to deepen and sharpen the sociopolitical divisions in American society.[26] In doing so, foreign adversaries hope not only to limit U.S. ability to influence the policy choices of other foreign states, but also to help immunize their own populations against the attractions of American-style democracy.

That matters, as Russia and other adversaries of the United States well know. If the United States has long demonstrated such a globally effective cultural power to attract, its corrosion must be a primary strategic objective of Russia or any other of the United States' principal adversaries. Accordingly, over the next 20 years, the Intelligence Community expects that "China and Russia probably will try to continue targeting domestic audiences in the United States and Europe, promoting narratives about Western decline and overreach."[27] The January 6th attack played into their hands.

PRESIDENT TRUMP AND THE 2020 ELECTION AS AN OPPORTUNITY FOR FOREIGN INFLUENCE

With President Trump in the White House, Russia benefited from a powerful American messenger creating and spreading damaging disinformation it could amplify. The Intelligence Community's comprehensive March 2021 assessment noted that throughout the 2020 Federal election cycle, "Russian online influence actors generally promoted former President Trump and his commentary...."[28]

President Trump's relentless propagation of the Big Lie damaged American democracy from within and made it more vulnerable to attack from abroad. His actions did not go unnoticed by America's adversaries, who seized on the opportunity to damage the United States. According to the Intelligence Community's March 2021 assessment, "[e]ven after the election, Russian online influence actors continued to promote narratives questioning the election results...."[29] What President Trump was saying was, in sum, exactly what the Russian government wanted said—but he was doing it on his own initiative and from the trappings of the Oval Office.

ENDNOTES

1. Taking the Trump conspiracy theory of manipulated Venezuelan voting machines head-on in an overarching assessment, the Intelligence Community's definitive post-election assessment stated: "We have no information suggesting that the current or former Venezuelan regimes were involved in attempts to compromise US election infrastructure." National Intelligence Council, "Intelligence Community Assessment: Foreign Threats to the 2020 US Federal Elections," ICA 2020–00078D, (Mar. 10, 2021), p. 8, available at https://www.dni.gov/files/ODNI/documents/assessments/ICA-declass-16MAR21.pdf (archived).

2. For case studies illustrating how such efforts may have manifested at the Capitol on January 6th, see Staff Memo, "Case Studies on Malign Foreign Influence," (Dec. 19, 2022).

3. National Intelligence Council, "Intelligence Community Assessment: Foreign Threats to the 2020 US Federal Elections," ICA 2020–00078D, (Mar. 10, 2021), Definitions, available at https://www.dni.gov/files/ODNI/documents/assessments/ICA-declass-16MAR21.pdf (archived).

4. National Intelligence Council, "Intelligence Community Assessment: Foreign Threats to the 2020 US Federal Elections," ICA 2020–00078D, (Mar. 10, 2021), Definitions, available at https://www.dni.gov/files/ODNI/documents/assessments/ICA-declass-16MAR21.pdf (archived).

5. National Intelligence Council, "Intelligence Community Assessment: Foreign Threats to the 2020 US Federal Elections," ICA 2020–00078D, (Mar. 10, 2021), pp. i, 1, available at https://www.dni.gov/files/ODNI/documents/assessments/ICA-declass-16MAR21.pdf (archived) (emphasis removed).

6.   National Intelligence Council, "Intelligence Community Assessment: Foreign Threats to the 2020 US Federal Elections," ICA 2020–00078D, (Mar. 10, 2021), p. i, available at https://www.dni.gov/files/ODNI/documents/assessments/ICA-declass-16MAR21.pdf (archived) (emphasis removed).

7.   National Intelligence Council, "Intelligence Community Assessment: Foreign Threats to the 2020 US Federal Elections," ICA 2020–00078D, (Mar. 10, 2021), p. 1, available at https://www.dni.gov/files/ODNI/documents/assessments/ICA-declass-16MAR21.pdf (archived).

8.   National Intelligence Council, "Intelligence Community Assessment: Foreign Threats to the 2020 US Federal Elections," ICA 2020–00078D, (Mar. 10, 2021), p. 1, available at https://www.dni.gov/files/ODNI/documents/assessments/ICA-declass-16MAR21.pdf (archived).

9.   The U.S. Intelligence Community is well aware of these foreign influence campaigns, including in the context of elections. See, e.g., National Intelligence Council, "Intelligence Community Assessment: Foreign Threats to the 2020 US Federal Elections," ICA 2020–00078D, (Mar. 10, 2021), pp. 4–5, 7, available at https://www.dni.gov/files/ODNI/documents/assessments/ICA-declass-16MAR21.pdf (archived) ("Russian state media, trolls, and online proxies, including those directed by Russian intelligence, published disparaging content about President Biden, his family, and the Democratic Party, and heavily amplified related content circulating in US media ...", p. 4; "Iran's election influence efforts were primarily focused on sowing discord in the United States and exacerbating societal tensions ...", p. 5; "China has long sought to influence US policies by shaping political and social environments to press US officials to support China's positions and perspectives." p. 7). Over the next 20 years, the Intelligence Community assesses that "China and Russia probably will try to continue targeting domestic audiences in the United States and Europe, promoting narratives about Western decline and overreach." National Intelligence Council, "Global Trends 2040: A More Contested World," (March 2021), p. 94, available at https://www.dni.gov/files/images/globalTrends/GT2040/GlobalTrends_2040_for_web1.pdf (archived).

10.   The National Intelligence Council notes that "some foreign actors may perceive influence activities around US elections as continuations of broad, ongoing efforts rather than specially demarcated campaigns." National Intelligence Council, "Intelligence Community Assessment: Foreign Threats to the 2020 US Federal Elections," ICA 2020–00078D, (Mar. 10, 2021), p. 1, available at https://www.dni.gov/files/ODNI/documents/assessments/ICA-declass-16MAR21.pdf (archived).

11.   House Committee on Foreign Affairs, Subcommittee on Europe, Eurasia, Energy and the Environment, Hearing on Undermining Democracy: Kremlin Tools of Malign Political Influence, Testimony of Laura Rosenberger, 116th Cong., 1st sess., (May 21, 2019), p. 1, available at https://docs.house.gov/meetings/FA/FA14/20190521/109537/HHRG-116-FA14-Wstate-RosenbergerL-20190521.pdf. Ms. Rosenberger was, at the time, Director of the Alliance for Securing Democracy and Senior Fellow at the German Marshall Fund of the United States. In an August 2018 briefing for the Senate Select Committee on Intelligence, Dr. John Kelly, the chief executive officer of Graphika, an analytics firm that studies online information flows, stated: "The data now available make it clear that Russian efforts are not directed against one election, one party, or even one country. We are facing a sustained campaign of organized manipulation, a coordinated attack on the trust we place in our institutions and in our media—both social and traditional." Senate Select Committee on Intelligence, Open Hearing on Foreign Influence Operations' Use of Social Media Platforms, Statement of Dr. John W. Kelly, 115th Cong., 2d sess., (Aug. 1, 2018), p. 1, available at https://nsarchive.gwu.edu/document/17963-john-w-kelly-chief-executive-officer-graphika.

12.   National Intelligence Council, "Intelligence Community Assessment: Foreign Threats to the 2020 US Federal Elections," ICA 2020–00078D, (Mar. 10, 2021), p. i, available at https://www.dni.gov/files/ODNI/documents/assessments/ICA-declass-16MAR21.pdf (archived). But see, John Ratcliffe, Director of National Intelligence, "Views on Intelligence Community Election Security Analysis," (Jan. 7, 2021), available at https://context-cdn.washingtonpost.com/notes/prod/default/documents/6d274110-a84b-4694-96cd-6a902207d2bd/note/733364cf-0afb-412d-a5b4-ab797a8ba154 (archived). In this

memorandum, DNI Ratcliffe, who had been in office seven months and lacked any prior intelligence experience, said he felt the need to "lead by example and offer my analytic assessment." He argued that the ICA majority's "high confidence" view that "China considered but did not deploy influence efforts intended to change the outcome of the US presidential election" did not "fully and accurately reflect[ ] the scope of the Chinese government's efforts to influence the 2020 U.S. federal elections." Aside from the DNI's very willingness to conclude, in conformity with then-President Trump's contention but without reference to any supporting data, that the IC's combined analytic judgment on China was wrong, this seems a very odd document for the DNI to have chosen to issue the day after the January 6th attack on the U.S. Capitol.

13. National Intelligence Council, "Intelligence Community Assessment: Foreign Threats to the 2020 US Federal Elections," ICA 2020–00078D, (Mar. 10, 2021), p. i, available at https://www.dni.gov/files/ODNI/documents/assessments/ICA-declass-16MAR21.pdf (archived).

14. Office of the Director of Central Intelligence, "Annual Threat Assessment of the U.S. Intelligence Community," (Feb. 2022), at p. 12, available at https://www.dni.gov/files/ODNI/documents/assessments/ATA-2022-Unclassified-Report.pdf (emphasis removed).

15. The National Intelligence Council's comprehensive post-election assessment covers the spectrum, including not only Russia, but also China, Iran, and others, as well as certain non-state actors. *See generally*, National Intelligence Council, "Intelligence Community Assessment: Foreign Threats to the 2020 US Federal Elections," ICA 2020–00078D, (Mar. 10, 2021), available at https://www.dni.gov/files/ODNI/documents/assessments/ICA-declass-16MAR21.pdf (archived). *See also*, "Dual U.S. / Russian National Charged With Acting Illegally As A Russian Agent In The United States," Department of Justice, U.S. Attorney's Office, S. Dist. N.Y., (Mar. 8, 2022), available at https://www.justice.gov/usao-sdny/pr/dual-us-russian-national-charged-acting-illegally-russian-agent-united-states (archived); "Russian National Charged with Conspiring to Have U.S. Citizens Act as Illegal Agents of the Russian Government," Department of Justice, Office of Public Affairs, (July 29, 2022), available at https://www.justice.gov/opa/pr/russian-national-charged-conspiring-have-us-citizens-act-illegal-agents-russian-government (archived).

16. National Intelligence Council, "Intelligence Community Assessment: Foreign Threats to the 2020 US Federal Elections," ICA 2020–00078D, (Mar. 10, 2021), p. i, available at https://www.dni.gov/files/ODNI/documents/assessments/ICA-declass-16MAR21.pdf.

17. National Intelligence Council, "Intelligence Community Assessment: Foreign Threats to the 2020 US Federal Elections," ICA 2020–00078D, (Mar. 10, 2021), p. 4, available at https://www.dni.gov/files/ODNI/documents/assessments/ICA-declass-16MAR21.pdf.

18. Department of Homeland Security, "Russia Likely to Continue to Undermine Faith in U.S. Electoral Process," Intelligence in Focus, (Sept. 3, 2020), at p. 1, available at https://publicintelligence.net/dhs-russia-undermining-election/.

19. Department of Homeland Security, "Russia Likely to Continue to Undermine Faith in U.S. Electoral Process," Intelligence in Focus, (Sept. 3, 2020), at p. 1, available at https://publicintelligence.net/dhs-russia-undermining-election/ (emphasis removed).

20. National Intelligence Council, "Intelligence Community Assessment: Foreign Threats to the 2020 US Federal Elections," ICA 2020–00078D, (Mar. 10, 2021), pp. 4–5, available at https://www.dni.gov/files/ODNI/documents/assessments/ICA-declass-16MAR21.pdf.

21. Senate Select Committee on Intelligence, "Russian Active Measures Campaigns And Interference In The 2016 U.S. Election," Volume 2, (Nov. 10, 2020), pp. 18–19, available at https://www.intelligence.senate.gov/publications/report-select-committee-intelligence-united-states-senate-russian-active-measures.

22. National Intelligence Council, "Intelligence Community Assessment: Foreign Threats to the 2020 US Federal Elections," ICA 2020–00078D, (Mar. 10, 2021), p. 4, available at https://www.dni.gov/files/ODNI/documents/assessments/ICA-declass-16MAR21.pdf.

23. Office of the Director of Central Intelligence, "Annual Threat Assessment of the U.S. Intelligence Community," p. 12, (Feb. 7, 2022), available at https://www.dni.gov/files/ODNI/documents/assessments/ATA-2022-Unclassified-Report.pdf.

24. National Intelligence Council, "Intelligence Community Assessment: Foreign Threats to the 2020 US Federal Elections," ICA 2020–00078D, (Mar. 10, 2021), at p. 1, available at https://www.dni.gov/files/ODNI/documents/assessments/ICA-declass-16MAR21.pdf.

25. National Intelligence Council, "Intelligence Community Assessment: Foreign Threats to the 2020 US Federal Elections," ICA 2020–00078D, (Mar. 10, 2021), at p. i, Key Judgment 2, available at https://www.dni.gov/files/ODNI/documents/assessments/ICA-declass-16MAR21.pdf (emphasis removed).

26. National Intelligence Council, "Emerging Dynamics – International: More Contested, Uncertain, and Conflict Prone – Contested and Transforming International Order – Increasing Ideological Competition," Global Trends 2040, 7th ed., (Mar. 2021), p. 95, available at https://www.dni.gov/files/images/globalTrends/GT2040/GlobalTrends_2040_for_web1.pdf.

27. National Intelligence Council, "Emerging Dynamics – International: More Contested, Uncertain, and Conflict Prone – Contested and Transforming International Order – Increasing Ideological Competition," Global Trends 2040, 7th ed., (Mar. 2021), p. 94, available at https://www.dni.gov/files/images/globalTrends/GT2040/GlobalTrends_2040_for_web1.pdf.

28. National Intelligence Council, "Intelligence Community Assessment: Foreign Threats to the 2020 US Federal Elections," ICA 2020-00078D, (Mar. 10, 2021), p. 4, available at https://www.dni.gov/files/ODNI/documents/assessments/ICA-declass-16MAR21.pdf.

29. National Intelligence Council, "Intelligence Community Assessment: Foreign Threats to the 2020 US Federal Elections," ICA 2020-00078D, (Mar. 10, 2021), p. 4, available at https://www.dni.gov/files/ODNI/documents/assessments/ICA-declass-16MAR21.pdf.

Rubens *and his Age*
Treasures from the Hermitage Museum, Russia

Edited by Christina Corsiglia
CURATOR, EUROPEAN ART, ART GALLERY OF ONTARIO

RUBENS *and his Age*

TREASURES FROM THE
HERMITAGE MUSEUM, RUSSIA

MERRELL

in association with

ART GALLERY OF ONTARIO

This book has been produced to accompany the exhibition

RUBENS *and his Age:*
TREASURES FROM THE HERMITAGE MUSEUM, RUSSIA

at

ART GALLERY OF ONTARIO
317 Dundas Street West
Toronto
Ontario
Canada M5T 1G4

First published in 2001 by
MERRELL PUBLISHERS LIMITED

Distributed in the USA and Canada by Rizzoli International Publications, Inc.
through St. Martin's Press, 175 Fifth Avenue, New York, New York 10010

Produced by
MERRELL PUBLISHERS LIMITED
42 Southwark Street
London SE1 1UN
www.merrellpublishers.com

Designed by studioGossett
Edited by Christina Corsiglia (Curator, European Art, Art Gallery of Ontario), Julian Honer, Iain Ross and Sarah Kane (Merrell Publishers)
Russian texts translated by Catherine Phillips

Printed and bound in Italy

National Library of Canada Cataloguing-in-Publication Data:
Main entry under title:
Rubens and his age : Treasures from the Hermitage Museum, Russia
Catalogue of an exhibition held at the Art Gallery of Ontario, May 5–Aug. 12, 2001.
Includes bibliographical references.
ISBN 1 85894 127 X (hardback)
ISBN 1 85894 162 8 (paperback)
1. Art, Flemish – Exhibitions. 2. Art, Modern – 17th–18th centuries – Belgium – Flanders – Exhibitions. 3. Art – Russia (Federation) – Saint Petersburg – Exhibitions. 4. Gosudarstvennyi Ermitazh (Russia) – Exhibitions. Corsiglia, Christina. II. Art Gallery of Ontario. III. Gosudarstvennyi Ermitazh (Russia).
N6936.T73 2001   709′ 493′ 1074713541
C00-933265-0

British Library Cataloguing-in-Publication Data:
Rubens and his age : treasures from the Hermitage Museum, Russia
1.Rubens, Peter Paul, 1577–1640 – Exhibitions
2.Painting, Flemish 3.Painting, Modern – 17th–18th Centuries – Belgium
I.Corsiglia, Christina
759.9′493

Front jacket/cover and frontispiece:
PETER PAUL RUBENS, *The Union of Earth and Water* (details; see cat. 4), *c.* 1618

Back jacket/cover (left to right):
Cupid Pendant (cat. 166), *c.* 1580
Swan Pendant (cat. 171), *c.* 1590
Mermaid Pendant (cat. 167), *c.* 1610–20

CONTENTS

Sponsor's Foreword

Goldman Sachs Canada is pleased and proud to assist the Art Gallery of Ontario with the presentation of *Rubens and his Age: Treasures from the Hermitage Museum, Russia*, an extraordinary exhibition of seventeenth-century masterworks.

During her reign in the eighteenth century, Catherine the Great assembled one of the world's greatest art collections, now housed in the State Hermitage Museum. For the first time ever, the Art Gallery of Ontario has joined with the State Hermitage Museum to present some of its finest works by such renowned artists as Peter Paul Rubens and Anthony van Dyck. Many of these masterpieces have not left the Hermitage since the eighteenth century.

Around the world, Goldman Sachs strives to support excellence and achievement in the communities in which we operate. We celebrate the Art Gallery of Ontario's success in securing these treasures from the Hermitage Museum. We are honoured to sponsor this unique opportunity for audiences to view these remarkable works of art.

GEORGE C. ESTEY
Chairman and Managing Director
Goldman Sachs Canada

DIRECTOR'S FOREWORD

State Hermitage Museum

In recent years the museum world has witnessed a renewed fascination with the Flemish Baroque, an artistic epoch defined by the contribution of its greatest genius, Peter Paul Rubens. The State Hermitage Museum, which possesses one of the world's richest collections of Flemish art, has played an essential role in the revival of interest in Rubens and his contemporaries, and in the presentation of their works before an ever-growing public.

A belief in the strength of human endeavour and in the power of nature was a central quality of seventeenth-century Flemish art and life. It is these characteristics that such artists as Rubens, Frans Snyders and Jacob Jordaens instilled in their works of extraordinary force and exultant splendour, the elegant refinement of van Dyck's portraits providing a striking contrast. With this exhibition the Hermitage not only presents major paintings by these renowned artists, but also depictions of the artists themselves. This special loan to the Art Gallery of Ontario in Toronto includes a portrait of Rubens, and self-portraits of van Dyck and Jordaens, and an image of David Teniers the Younger, who is thought to have represented himself as a falconer in his famous painting *The Kitchen* (cat. 84).

The intimacy of these artists' portraits is echoed in other works in the exhibition. A group of cameos from Rubens's own collection allows us a rare glimpse into this artist's private world. He, like the founder of the Hermitage, Catherine the Great, was fascinated by these miniature masterpieces. The wonderful selection of drawings by the Flemish masters on view in this exhibition equally reflect the inner worlds of these artists and engage the spectator in direct and intimate dialogue with both the reality and imagination of their age.

Never before has the Hermitage shown such a comprehensive selection of its Flemish collection abroad. This is the first time in two hundred years that Rubens's great painting *The Union of Earth of Water* (cat. 4) – the centerpiece of this exhibition – has left Russian soil. Here, Rubens has transformed the Classical heritage, imbuing it with the splendour and symbolism of the Flemish style as an eloquent expression of the political realities of his time – events in which Rubens himself played a significant diplomatic rôle. The *Union of Earth and Water* epitomizes Rubens and his age, and it alone would suffice to make this an important event. Yet this unprecedented loan exhibition from the Hermitage collection includes nearly two hundred masterpieces of painting, drawing and the decorative arts. Toronto viewers, I am sure, will immerse themselves with pleasure into the exuberant character of Rubens's time.

This occasion inaugurates a new chapter in the long-standing friendship between the Hermitage and Canada. We are grateful to the State Hermitage Museum Foundation of Canada and to our numerous friends for the support of many of the Hermitage's projects, including the exchange of exhibitions such as this one. We are pleased to collaborate with our colleagues at the Art Gallery of Ontario, knowing that the Hermitage's treasures are in good hands, and are displayed with sensitivity in a beautiful setting.

I am happy to welcome all visitors to this exhibition and extend an invitation to each of them to come to the Hermitage itself, to the shores of the mighty Neva, where the similar climate will make them feel very much at home.

DR. M.B. PIOTROVSKY
Director, State Hermitage Museum

DIRECTOR'S FOREWORD

Art Gallery of Ontario

The royal collections of Russia epitomize the ambitions and achievements of generations of collectors, whose legacy, the State Hermitage Museum, has long been a symbol of bold aspiration and grand realization. The Hermitage ranks among the world's foremost museums, and the great breadth of its holdings testifies, in a fashion scarcely paralleled, to the entire history of artistic achievement.

The opening of *Rubens and his Age: Treasures from the Hermitage Museum* is a deeply rewarding occasion. In this exclusive exhibition, audiences have the opportunity to see a display of one of the Hermitage Museum's greatest strengths: Flemish paintings and drawings of the seventeenth century. *Rubens and his Age* assembles masterworks from eight departments of the Hermitage Museum in order to bring to life this remarkable era in the history of art and culture. The accompanying catalogue and its essays set these works of art within both the visual culture of their time and the grand tradition of Russian collecting inaugurated by Catherine the Great.

The exhibition is doubly rewarding as a project developed by the Art Gallery of Ontario in direct consultation with the Hermitage. We are most grateful to Dr. Mikhail Piotrovsky, Director of the Hermitage, whose enlightened leadership has played a central role in the exhibition's conception and realization.

In selecting the works for the exhibition, Art Gallery of Ontario curators Martha Kelleher and Christina Corsiglia, together with their Russian counterparts Natalya Gritsay, Natalya Babina, Alexey Larionov, Tatyana Kossourova, Elena Anisimova, Yulia Kagan, Olga Kostiuk, Marina Lopato, Yurij Miller, and Elena Shlikevich, have striven to evoke the great age of seventeenth century Antwerp in all its artistic breadth and splendour. On exhibition are major paintings by Rubens, van Dyck, and their contemporaries, outstanding drawings by the great masters of the Flemish Baroque, and a remarkable selection of the decorative arts installed in the manner of a seventeenth-century "cabinet of curiosities."

We are fortunate to welcome as our partners in presenting this exhibition the investment banking and securities firm of Goldman Sachs Canada Inc. They have worked with us before, in 1995, in the presentation of three exhibitions of the work of the great English artists Constable, Gainsborough and Turner. Goldman Sachs Canada's commitment, then as now, is rooted in the belief that great art should be presented internationally to the largest public possible. It is a sentiment we heartily share.

Rubens and his Age: Treasures from the Hermitage Museum is the first of four projects planned between the Art Gallery of Ontario and the Hermitage Museum. Our international collaboration will extend through 2005, and will continue to bring to Toronto exhibitions of the greatest interest and works of art of the highest quality.

MATTHEW TEITELBAUM
Director, Art Gallery of Ontario

ART AND VISUAL CULTURE IN SEVENTEENTH-CENTURY FLANDERS

CHRISTINE GÖTTLER

FIG. 1: WILLEM VAN
EHRENBERG, *Interior of the Jesuit
Church*, mid-17th century,
oil on marble, 97.5 × 103 cm,
Antwerp, Rubenshuis

In July 1641, an Italian ambassador and an English man of letters, both at that time in their early twenties and living in England, embarked for the Netherlands where they would travel for several weeks. While the two gentlemen certainly had common acquaintances at the English court and would remain faithful to the royal cause in the years to come, there is no evidence that they ever met. Moreover, the purposes of their sojourns were very different: Cardinal Carlo Rossetti (born 1615), nuncio of Pope Urban VIII to the English queen Henrietta Marietta (the wife of Charles I), travelled on a diplomatic mission,[1] and the writer John Evelyn (1620–1706) departed as a volunteer to help the Dutch troops in besieging the fortress at Gennep. However, soon discovering his distaste for camp life, Evelyn took leave in order to visit the major cities of the Northern and Southern Netherlands as an art tourist.[2]

Interestingly, both travellers visited Antwerp during the same week. Rossetti arrived in the city on Monday evening, September 30. The following morning he attended a ceremony at the church of the Jesuits (fig. 1), celebrated in honour of the blessed Francisco de Borja (1510–1570). Rossetti was very impressed by the lavish decoration of the church, which, in his view, "truly surpasses the wonders of every other church in every other style," although the city had "remarkable ones such as the Cathedral of Our Lady."[3] He especially mentions the "rich apparatuses, the superb sacred ornaments and

FIG. 2: PIETER NEEFFS THE
ELDER AND BONAVENTURA
PEETERS, *Interior of Antwerp
Cathedral*, before 1659, oil on
panel, 50 × 70 cm, Vienna,
Kunsthistorisches Museum

the copious relics" that the Jesuits kept in their church and sacristy. On his tour through the library, he admired the abundance of books written in all languages and covering all branches of knowledge, as well as the great skill by which they were preserved. Shown some flower paintings by the Jesuit lay brother and painter Daniel Seghers (1590–1661), Rossetti referred to an old topos used in acclaiming the mimetic and deceptive quality of art: according to his description, they "really surpass art and deceive nature itself" (cat. 63).[4]

Rossetti next walked to the wharf, where he enjoyed looking at the numerous ships and vessels. He noticed the "continuous traffic" on one of the bridges, "not only of foreigners but also of citizens" who would gather there toward evening. Visiting the citadel (see cat. 75) he was struck by its similarity to the one in Ferrara.[5] In his journal, he further comments on the cleanliness of the slaughterhouses and the local custom of training dogs to pull small carts filled with various commodities, especially barrels of beer, the most popular beverage in Antwerp. On October 3, the day Rossetti departed by boat for Brussels, he observed, together with hundreds of other citizens assembled at the wharf, a Spanish garrison file by, apparently sent out to fight the enemy from Holland.[6]

On the following day (Friday, October 4), John Evelyn arrived, providing us with a much more detailed report than that written by Rossetti. Evelyn, too, began

his visit by "seeing divers Churches, Coledges, Monasteries." Like Rossetti, he "exceedingly admired that sumptuous and most magnificent Church of the Jesuites, being a very glorious fabrique without; and within wholy incrusted with marble inlayd and polished into divers representations of histories, Landskips, Flowers etc."[7] Evelyn was especially captivated by Hans van Mildert's elaborate stone frame of the high altar, which was crowned with a statue of the Virgin and the Christ Child; he was also intrigued by the votive figures hung up in the church, "containing the Pictures or Emblemes of severall dissasters, and recoveries," and the beautifully carved pulpit. He further mentions some "rare Pictures wrought by the hand of Rubens now newly deceased."[8]

Visiting the cathedral, Evelyn first climbed the stairs of the tower to enjoy the view of "both the Land and Water" around the city. The peculiar pattern of sun-dappled areas stimulated Evelyn's thought concerning lunar phenomena, which was most probably derived from the recently published book *The Discovery of a World in the Moone* (1638), by the English clergyman and scientist John Wilkins:[9] a book he would have been wise not to mention in Jesuit circles, in which the Copernican world system was banned as heretical as late as 1691.[10]

In the church he was stunned by the number of privileged altars, of which he counted thirty (fig. 2 and

FIG. 3: Unknown Antwerp Master, *Market Scene on the Meirbrug in Antwerp*, c. 1600, oil on panel, 90 × 140 cm, Brussels, Koninklijke Musea voor Schone Kunsten van België

FIG. 4: Lucas van Uden, *View of the Hansa House in Antwerp*, 17th century, oil on panel, 41 × 71 cm, Antwerp, Koninklijk Museum voor Schone Kunsten

[...] a very faire and noble Street; cleane, and sweete to admiration,"[13] his attention was held by the the over-life-size marble crucifix erected at the intersection of the Meir and the Huidevettersstraat, close to the church of the convent of the Discalced Carmelites (fig. 3).[14] Walking north towards the Nieuwstad, Evelyn visited the Hansa or Eastern House, a Renaissance building that served as the office of the North German merchants (fig. 4).[15] From the Hansa House, he crossed the entire city, arriving at the southern citadel, which he described as "doubtlesse the most matchlesse piece of modern Fortification in the World [...] the Graffs [moats], ramparts, and Platformes are stupendious." At the Plantin Press, still run at that time by Balthasar Moretus the Elder (1574–1641), the son of Jan Moretus the Elder (1543–1610), he "bought some bookes for the namesake onely of that famous Printer."[16] In the evening he strolled among numerous other citizens along the quay and felt "ravished" by the "delicious shades" of the "stately trees, which render the incomparably fortified Workes of the Towne one of the Sweetest places in Europe."[17]

Evelyn decided to spend another day in "this magnificent and famous Citty of Antwerp," during which he again visited churches, convents, palaces and gates until the evening, when he was invited by "Signor Duerts, a Portuguese by nation, an exceedingly rich Merchant, whose Palace I found to be furnish'd like a Princes."[18] Built at the Meir, the palace of the wealthy Portuguese merchant and art collector Gaspar Rodrigues Duarte (1588–1653) was indeed one of the largest and most splendid residences in this affluent area where – because of its proximity to the exchange – many foreign merchants had settled. Humanists, erudite merchants, musicians and artists gathered in Duarte's home, often to share a musical evening with his family, some of whom were renowned for their instrumental and vocal accomplishments. Among others, the Dutch poets Constantijn Huygens (1596–1687) and Anna Roemers Visscher (1583–1621) frequented Duarte's palace. With his interests in music and literature, Gaspar Duarte also collected art, joining the St. Luke's Guild in 1623 as a *liefhebber*, a designation that referred to a collector as an "amateur" or "lover of art." Additionally, he belonged to the Chamber of Rhetoric known as De Violieren (The Gilly Flowers), the most important Chamber of Rhetoric in Antwerp.

cat. 48). While Evelyn does not comment on the renowned altarpieces created by Rubens, he was particularly intrigued by the "rarely painted" altar of St. Sebastian. Representing the *Martyrdom of St. Sebastian* (1575), this altarpiece was created by the ageing Michel Coxcie (1499–1592) for the triptych of the Oude Handboog, one of Antwerp's influential militia guilds.[11]

After attending a forty-hour devotion in a nunnery,[12] Evelyn next visited the town hall on the Grote Markt (see cat. 76) and the Jesuits' school. Strolling on the Meir, "the great Street which is built after a more Italian mode,

Perhaps the most interesting aspect of Duarte's social life, however, was his membership of a circle of friends around Balthasar Moretus the Elder, the head of the Plantin Press, and his successor Balthasar Moretus the Younger. This group of humanists included Moretus's childhood friend Peter Paul Rubens, the humanist and municipal registrar Jan Caspar Gevaerts (Gevartius), the antiquarian and burgomaster Nicolaes Rockox (cat. 24), and the Catholic polemicist Richard Verstegen. Also among the members of this group involved in the flowering of Catholic Humanism were the canon, writer and numismatist Jan Hemelaers (Joannes Hemelarius), the lawyer Jacob Edelheer, the Portuguese physician and antiquarian Ludovicus Núnez (Nonnius), and Jan Mantels (Joannes Mantelius), the well-known preacher at the convent of the Augustinians.[19] In Duarte's circle and in other groups of wealthy merchants, moral and philosophical tendencies closely related to Neo-Stoicism developed, and the latest editions of Classical texts and studies in such diverse fields as optics, anatomy, astronomy, cartography and botany were discussed and exchanged.

In Rossetti's and Evelyn's journals as well as in other travellers' accounts, the physical space of the city is envisioned through the visual experience of its material culture. Be it religious, political or social, Antwerp society valorized display. While leisurely walking through the streets of the city, the eyes of our visitors were caught by different kinds of objects, images and representations. These included: the cult statue of the Virgin above the high altar in the Jesuit church (Evelyn especially notices that her girdle was adorned with jewels); an altarpiece depicting the martyrdom of a saint who was in demand during the frequent outbreaks of plague;[20] and a painting of flower garlands, a pictorial genre particularly associated with Antwerp. Both Rossetti and Evelyn comment upon the imposing grandeur of the citadel and the marble decorations of the Jesuit church. While Rossetti mentions the pomp of religious festival decorations and the powerful image of a marching militia, Evelyn remarks on votive gifts, written promises of indulgences, and books and prints produced by Antwerp's most renowned publishing firm. Finally, Evelyn discusses the view he observed from the cathedral's tall north tower, partially flooded in light, partially obscured by dark shadows.

The Changing Face of a City

Interestingly, neither Rossetti nor Evelyn mentions the Bourse. Constructed by order of the city itself in 1531, Antwerp's stock exchange served the rapidly growing maritime trade, visited daily by several hundred merchants, brokers and insurers. The Florentine businessman Lodovico Guicciardini, in his account of the Low Countries first published in Antwerp in 1567, describes Antwerp's Bourse as one of the "most noble places" in this ideal city. He adds that local residents and foreigners communicated amicably in a broad variety of languages.[21] Located in close proximity to the Meir, the street along which the handsome palaces for the patricians and the wealthy merchants were built, the new exchange served as the model for the exchanges both in London and Amsterdam.

Soon after Guicciardini completed his praise of Antwerp, however, the prospering cultural metropolis was hit by a series of religious and political crises. In 1566, under the governor Margaret of Parma, growing tensions between the nobility and the Spanish Crown, as well as the open-air preaching by Calvinist leaders, which attracted up to 25,000 listeners, finally resulted in iconoclastic riots during August and September. This outbreak saw the most extensive image-breaking that had taken place in the sixteenth century, during which hundreds of churches and monasteries were "cleansed" of altarpieces, statues, epitaphs and holy vessels that had served the Catholic Church for generations. The rigorous policy of the Duke of Alva, sent out by Philip II to suppress heresy and revolt, and the climate of uncertainty that followed these events led to a mass exodus, especially of foreign merchants.[22] Although the Calvinists again gained power in the mid-1570s, their control of the city was shortlived, and Antwerp fell once more to Spain in 1585. With the subsequent closing of the Scheldt, many remaining foreign merchants' families fled to other cities, both out of religious concerns and economic motivations. Artists also left in search of better opportunities offered in more prosperous regions. The population decreased by more than half, from about 105,000 in 1568 to about 42,000 in 1589.[23] While approximately 1,600 merchants resided in Antwerp in the middle of the sixteenth century (of whom about 1,000 were foreigners), their numbers dropped to around 500 in 1625. Only 100 of these

FIG. 5: ABEL GRIMMER AND
HENDRIK VAN BALEN, *View of
the Port of Antwerp*, 1600, oil on
panel, 37.7 × 44.4 cm,
Antwerp, Koninklijk Museum
voor Schone Kunsten

remaining merchants were foreigners, mostly from the
southern nations of Spain, Portugal and Italy.[24]

After his triumphant entry into the city, the newly
appointed governor Alexander Farnese, Duke of Parma,
undertook everything in his power to restore Catholic
traditions. Protestants in Antwerp were given four years
either to reconcile with the Catholic Church or to leave
the city. The deans of the guilds were instructed to
rebuild and redecorate their chapels and altars, an
expensive and time-consuming task that in some cases
was not accomplished until the beginning of the
seventeenth century. In the course of these events
Antwerp was gradually transformed from a commercial
metropolis that favoured a tolerant attitude toward
Protestantism, an attitude widespread among merchants
and traders,[25] to a most pious city that has often been
described as a bulwark of the Counter-Reformation.[26]

After 1585, Farnese also rebuilt the citadel in the
south of the city, praised by Scribanius, Rossetti, Evelyn
and other visitors for its excellence in military
engineering. The southern citadel, begun by the Duke of
Alva in 1567 as a device to control the rebellious city, and

demolished in 1577 at the beginning of the Calvinist
Republic (1577–1585), symbolized the sinister side of the
Spanish authorities who dominated the city.
Representing Catholic and Spanish Habsburg rule, the
fortifications formed a counter-monument to the almost
contemporaneous new town hall (1566), which has been
interpreted as an "expression of Antwerp's struggle for
freedom."[27] The ambivalent meanings associated with
the principal sites of the city are reflected in seventeenth-
century paintings. In a view of Antwerp by Abel Grimmer
(1570–*c.* 1619) and Hendrik van Balen (1574/45–1632),
dated 1600, Christ and the Virgin intercede for Antwerp's
Catholic population before God, who gives his blessing to
the city (fig. 5).[28] While the distinct profile of Antwerp
Cathedral marks the central axis of the composition, the
pentagonal shape of the citadel appears under a visibly
darker and cloudier sky to the right. It stands as a
menacing gesture against those who have not yet
returned to the Catholic faith. The protective function of
the citadel is, however, emphasized in David Teniers's
Guardroom (cat. 75). The painting was executed in 1642,
the year in which the Portuguese Francisco de Melo,

FIG. 6: ABRAHAM JANSSEN, *Scaldis and Antverpia*, 1608–09, oil on panel, 172 × 208 cm, Antwerp, Koninklijk Museum voor Schone Kunsten

acting governor after the death of the Cardinal Infante Ferdinand (November 9, 1641), succeeded against the French army at Honnecourt. The sunlit fortifications are further glorified by the half-raised curtain of the portal, while the military trophies displayed in the foreground accentuate notions of power and strength.

By the beginning of the seventeenth century, Antwerp had lost to Amsterdam its dominant position as an international trading place. However, a new phase began in 1598 when Isabella Clara Eugenia (1566–1633), Philip II's favourite daughter, and her husband Albert (1559–1621) were appointed archdukes to govern the Low Countries. With their own patronage they initiated a Catholic renewal on a large scale: they promoted the new religious orders of the Counter-Reformation, founded churches and monasteries and restored traditional places of pilgrimage, the most important of which was the pilgrimage to the Blessed Virgin of Scherpenheuvel. The patronage of the Brussels court was imitated by wealthy élites, especially the foreign merchant-bankers to whom the archdukes granted titles of nobility, securing their loyalty and financial services. While the Discalced Carmelites, for example, received permission to settle in Antwerp only on the intervention of Archduchess Isabella, their church and monastery were more or less entirely financed by a small group of wealthy Portuguese merchant-bankers. Their donations may have been further motivated by the fact that most of them, shortly before, were suspected of secretly practising Jewish rites.

On April 9, 1609, the signing of the Twelve Years' Truce induced hope of renewed prosperity. The

optimism is expressed in Abraham Janssen's representation of *Scaldis and Antverpia* (fig. 6), a large painting commissioned by the city council to decorate the *Statenkamer* in the town hall, the very same room in which the treaty was signed.[29] Here, an athletic river god, crowned with reeds and foliage, comfortably reclining on his flowing urn, exchanges gifts with the goddess of Antwerp. Identifiable by her mural crown, the young Flemish maiden receives a horn of plenty filled with the fruits of the earth and points with her index finger toward the source of such wealth: the flowing water of the Scheldt. The mutual affection expressed by their gestures also illustrates the benefits achieved by production and trade.[30] The visual vocabulary of gift-giving and exchange plays a powerful rôle in Antwerp's political and mercantile iconography, as also shown, for instance, in Rubens's *Union of Earth and Water* (cat. 4). Peace, the necessary prerequisite for trade, however, was equally hoped for in 1609. A drawing by Hendrik de Clerck (before 1570?–1630), painter to the archducal court, celebrates the negotiations for the 1609 truce and ties these hopes to the virtues of the archdukes (cat. 107).[31] Here, the city of Antwerp is depicted as an imploring woman seated on a stony bench in front of a battle scene: ten warrior maidens shielding themselves with the emblems of the Catholic provinces fight against the female warriors from the ten northern provinces disloyal to the Spanish Crown. On a cloud in the background, sent by God, the archdukes appear as heavenly messengers of peace, commanding both water and land.

FIG. 7: PETER PAUL RUBENS, *Mercury Leaving Antwerp*, 1634, oil sketch, cradled panel, 77 × 79 cm, St Petersburg, State Hermitage Museum

While hopes for the free passage of the Scheldt proved to be in vain, Antwerp's economy nonetheless slowly recovered. Consequently, the population grew: when Rossetti and Evelyn sojourned in Antwerp, there were about 57,000 residents.[32] Antwerp had become a distribution place for luxury goods, and had regained and even expanded its position as a centre for the arts. Our young travellers visited Antwerp at a crucial date indeed. As remarked by John Evelyn, Peter Paul Rubens had died in May of the previous year. Anthony van Dyck was also in the city in October 1641, considering a return to the Southern Netherlands and the eventual supervision of Rubens's workshop. He died, however, on December 9, at the age of 42, shortly after arriving back in London.[33] Rossetti, describing the court residence on the Coudenberg in Brussels, mentions that the Cardinal Infante Ferdinand was dying (he died on November 9, 1641). The brother of Philip IV and successor of Isabella as governor of the Southern Netherlands, Ferdinand had made his entry into Antwerp in 1635, a politically crucial event for which Rubens designed the festive decorations (see cat. 9).

With Ferdinand's successor, Archduke Leopold Wilhelm, a new generation of artists became active. Among them, David Teniers was appointed court painter and also curator of the archduke's famous art collection; Leopold Wilhelm's superb collection of Italian masters, which was painted by Teniers on several occasions, may have served as a model for wealthy Antwerp collectors such as Diego Duarte, whose father, Gaspar Rodrigues Duarte, had invited Evelyn to his palace-like home. Under the reign of Archduke Leopold Wilhelm, the Treaty of Münster was signed and proclaimed on the Grote Markt in Antwerp before a theatrical stage designed by Erasmus II Quellinus (1607–1678), who, because of his broad humanist erudition, was sometimes considered as Rubens's greatest successor.[34]

The year 1648 marked the beginning of a new era that finally brought the long-desired peace and political stability; but it also reinforced and precipitated the decline of Antwerp both as an economic and as an artistic centre. On the occasion of the "joyous entry" of Don Juan of Austria (another brother of Philip IV) into Antwerp on May 6, 1657, Erasmus Quellinus the Younger, in his function as official painter of the city, was again engaged in designing the festive decorations (cat. 110). As was traditionally the case in Antwerp's spectacles and public events, Mercury, the god of free commerce, held an important position among the mythological figures welcoming the new governor. In Rubens's famous sketch for the royal entry of Cardinal Infante Ferdinand in 1635, Mercury departs from the city leaving behind a chained Scheldt, lethargically leaning on his dry urn, and a desperate Antwerp appealing to the viewer and new ruler to change the city's calamitous condition (fig. 7).[35] Erasmus Quellinus, however, portrays Mercury and other deities and personifications as sculpted monuments supporting the structure on which a mounted Don Juan appears, victorious over Discord, which is trampled underfoot, thus concealing the fact that at that time prosperity belonged to the city's past.

THE DECORUM OF PLACE

It was in the (former) centre of international trade, rather than at the residence of the archdukes on the Coudenberg in Brussels, that the important art market developed. The vast majority of seventeenth-century Flemish art was therefore produced by Dutch-speaking artists living in Antwerp.[36] Major art patrons belonged to the political élite (such as the patrician and humanist Nicolaes Rockox; cat. 24),[37] the high-ranking clergy (such as Antonius Triest, Bishop of Ghent and influential patron of David Teniers the Younger; cat. 35), and, most importantly, the rich merchant class. Both the spice merchant Cornelis van der Geest, whose gallery of predominantly Flemish works is celebrated in a painting by Willem van Haecht (1593–1637), the keeper of his collection,[38] and Diego Duarte, whose collection is documented by an inventory,[39] epitomize the new merchant who surrounds himself with the very best of Antwerp's society, displaying luxury as well as exquisite taste.

Much has been written about the aristocratization of wealthy merchant families in seventeenth-century Antwerp. Hugo Soly explained how rich merchants increasingly withdrew from business and aligned themselves with the old nobility by buying country estates and cultivating a leisurely lifestyle.[40] As luxury commodities, art works were an essential part of this new culture of consumption, and further demonstrated their owner's Classical humanist erudition, a refinement that was equally associated with noble status.

We should, however, keep in mind that art collecting was not an activity solely reserved for wealthy merchants. From 1643 to 1652 there were roughly 9,900 paintings listed in inventories and other legal documents issued in Antwerp, which have been published by Erik Duverger.[41] Seventeenth-century documents give evidence that men and women with moderate incomes also cherished pictures and often decorated the walls of their homes with inexpensive copies of works of art created by major artists. Of particular interest, in this respect, is an entry in the inventory of the mason Joris Mochaerts, who died in Lier in 1624. He possessed seven pictures, all of which hung in his kitchen.[42] Among them was a representation of Cimon and Pero, a subject from ancient history that showed a young woman secretly suckling her imprisoned father to save him from starvation. The

mason's predilection for this erotic and erudite subject may have been influenced by Rubens's well-known version of the theme, most probably painted for Carel van den Bosch, who later became Bishop of Bruges and Chancellor of Flanders (cat. 3).[43]

But where were the 10,000 pictures in Antwerp in the 1640s to be found? And what functions did they serve? Both Rossetti and Evelyn discuss the principal sites in which visual culture in Antwerp at the beginning of the 1640s was on display. These were first and foremost the numerous churches and monasteries that defined the sacred space of the city. Secondly, the urban space itself was shaped and transformed by theatrical performances, religious processions, *ommegangs* (annual civic and religious processions), military parades and "joyous entries" in which visiting monarchs were ceremonially received (cat. 8, 9). These celebrations, designed and produced by local artists, were multimedia events featuring floats, banners and images paraded through the streets. Moreover, victories and other important political events were generally commemorated by water festivities on the Scheldt. Artists' studios, publishers' firms and the palaces of patricians and prosperous merchants formed a third arena in which art was viewed, evaluated and judged.

Both Rossetti and Evelyn refer to a broad range of media and genres used in seventeenth-century Flemish art, as well as to the various public and more private occasions on which such imagery was displayed. Skilled in diplomacy, our travellers must have been able to read the different meanings and codes of decorum required by these distinct spaces. A closer look at a few of the exemplary works from the Flemish Collection of the Hermitage, now on exhibit in the Art Gallery of Ontario, will enable me briefly to comment on some of the functions and communicative qualities of the locations these works once occupied. Which visual devices did the Flemish painters use to instruct, inform, move and delight the spectator, or to negotiate an ethically or intellectually inspired response?

SACRED SPACE

It is telling that Evelyn's eyes, when entering the Jesuit church, were drawn toward the open choir, which he called "a most glorious piece;" conversely, on his tour of Antwerp Cathedral, the young Englishman walked from altar to altar, noticing those indulgenced ones at which special masses for the souls of the deceased were said.[44] The cathedral of Our Lady, the largest Gothic church in Flanders, and the Jesuit church, the first religious building in Antwerp to incorporate elements of the Italian Baroque, were the principal monuments of the city. Praised by foreign visitors, these sacred centres provided the subject-matter for numerous paintings of Flemish church interiors. While most interior views of the Jesuit church emphasize the high altar as the new focal point of a post-Tridentine church (fig. 1), paintings of Antwerp Cathedral direct the gaze toward the corporate altars erected against the huge piers. In contrast to the spacious, uninterrupted naves of most Jesuit churches, the view of the high altar in a Gothic cathedral is restricted by the rood screen that marks the entrance to the distant choir (fig. 2; cat. 48).

Religious imagery, either to receive public veneration in churches and chapels or to serve individual needs for private devotion, formed by far the greatest part of Antwerp's artistic production. The patronage of the archdukes and especially the signing of the Twelve Years' Truce in 1609 initiated a boom in church construction. In a number of churches and monasteries, the decorations that had been destroyed during the religious and political troubles of the previous century had yet to be replaced. Moreover, the new monastic foundations that were established within the first two decades of the seventeenth century changed Antwerp's religious landscape dramatically. In March 1613, Bishop Joannes Malderus (1611–1633) laid the foundation stone for the church of the Capuchins.[45] Three cornerstone ceremonies took place in 1615, when the first stones for the new churches of the orders of the Augustinians, Annunciate sisters and Spanish Carmelites were laid by the archdukes themselves.[46] The Jesuit church, so admired by all visitors, was begun in 1615 and consecrated in 1621, again by Bishop Malderus.[47] The Minims officially settled in Antwerp in 1614; although they enjoyed the special protection of the powerful Genoese merchant family Balbi, they were unable to

build their church until 1636.[48] The Discalced Carmelites, upon the intervention of the archdukes, were introduced in Antwerp in 1618. Following the primitive Carmelite rule, the Discalced monks were bitterly opposed by the Old Carmelites, and waited until 1626 to see their church finally consecrated.[49]

In 1645, Bishop Nemius listed thirteen men's foundations and fourteen nunneries; in total, about 1,000 monks and nuns were attached to one of the many monastic houses of the city.[50] The multiplication of churches and monasteries in the first decades of the seventeenth century increased the competition between the religious institutions, which struggled against one another for wealthy patrons and space. Altarpieces, cult images, relics and indulgences proved to be effective means of attracting devotional gifts.

Rubens, who had returned from Italy at the end of 1608, was particularly innovative in his response to the renewal of Habsburg Catholicism as promoted by the archdukes and the secular and clerical élites. As David Freedberg states, it would take "one's breath away" to list the numerous altarpieces Rubens painted for churches in Antwerp, Brussels, Lille, Ghent, Mechelen, Tournay and other towns and villages of the Catholic Low Countries.[51] Moreover, Rubens and his studio provided the monumental decorations for the high altars of the most important churches in Antwerp, particularly the *Raising of the Cross* for the parish church of St. Walburgis (1610–11),[52] the *Adoration of the Magi* for St. Michael's Abbey, the church of the influential Premonstratensian order (1624),[53] and the *Mystic Marriage of St. Catherine* for the Sint-Augustinuskerk (1628). Innovative both in iconography and style, these large-scale works demonstrate Rubens's astonishing ability to employ a broad range of visual means in the service of these religious institutions, winning diverse audiences for their specific educational and pastoral goals. Completing most altarpieces *in situ*, Rubens always considered the actual architectural space, often interfering in the construction of the altar and its crowning sculpture, and suggesting various methods to improve the illumination.

It is hard to believe that Rossetti and Evelyn, while visiting the Gothic cathedral, could have overlooked two of the most glorious altarpieces created by this master's famous brush. Both were, perhaps, more interested in what may be called Catholic popular culture. In 1611, the

FIG. 8: PETER PAUL RUBENS, *The Assumption of the Virgin*, 1626, oil on panel, 490 × 325 cm, Antwerp, Antwerp Cathedral

other reasons, Rubens's commission was repeatedly delayed, and his altarpiece placed above the high altar only in 1626. The dynamic movement of the ascending Virgin, surrounded by winged putti, the expressive gesture of one of the Apostles, the foreshortenings and the light tonality form part of an illusionistic visual strategy especially effective when seen from afar (fig. 8).

While Rubens's *Assumption* reinstalled the Virgin as Queen of Heaven and patron of the Spanish Habsburg crown, honouring her victory over iconoclasts and heretics, his monumental paintings for the Jesuit church served to promote the cults of Ignatius of Loyola, the founder and spiritual leader of the Society of Jesus, and Francis Xavier, his closest disciple, who would later become the first Jesuit missionary to India and Japan. Ironically, Francis Xavier died peacefully in Macao in 1552; but thousands of European and Japanese Jesuits working as missionaries in Japan in the late sixteenth and seventeenth centuries died a gruesome death by fire or crucifixion, as, for example, represented in Abraham van Diepenbeek's drawing (cat. 111).[55]

Although not entirely uncommon, it conflicted, strictly speaking, with the policy of the church to place above altars the images of men and women who were in the odour of sanctity but not yet officially recognized as saints. Originally, Rubens's paintings of the *Miracles of St. Ignatius* (fig. 9) and the *Miracles of Francis Xavier* were exhibited above the high altar in alternation.[56] About six years later, a representation of the *Raising of the Cross* by Gerhard Seghers (1591–1651) was added. Finally, Cornelis Schut (1597–1655) was commissioned to paint a *Virgin and Child*, most probably in 1639–40. If we believe an eighteenth-century source, Schut received the prestigious commission on the intervention of his friend and collaborator Daniel Seghers.[57] At the time Rossetti and Evelyn visited the church, the Jesuits had four pictures that rotated according to the feast days of the liturgical year.

Interior views of the Antwerp Jesuit church generally depict the high altar with Rubens's *Miracles of St. Ignatius* (fig. 1); Rubens portrays the saint in liturgical vestments before an altar, freeing a young man and young woman from demons. The sufferers, separated from the saint by the altar railing, are dramatically displayed in the foreground, screaming, contorted,

lawyer and burgomaster Nicolaes Rockox secured for Rubens one of the most prestigious commissions: the altarpiece of the *Descent from the Cross* (1612–14) in Antwerp Cathedral for the guild of the Arquebusiers, over which Rockox presided as dean. Additionally, in 1611 Rubens won a competition, which his teacher Otto van Veen (1556–1629) had also entered, for a high altarpiece representing the *Assumption and Coronation of the Virgin* (see cat. 2).[54] The history of this commission is revealing. The new altarpiece was meant to replace an *Adoration of the Shepherds* by Frans Floris (1519/20–1570), temporarily placed over the high altar in 1585 when Farnese ordered the restoration of the damaged altars – a temporary arrangement that would, however, last for more than forty years. Floris's *Adoration* took the place of his earlier *Assumption*, which had been removed in the so-called "Quiet Iconoclasm" of 1581. For financial or

FIG. 9: PETER PAUL RUBENS, *The Miracles of St Ignatius of Loyola*, 1617–18, oil on canvas, 535 × 395 cm, Vienna, Kunsthistorisches Museum

tearing off their clothes and throwing themselves on the ground. In later works, Rubens adjusted the iconography to advertise the intercessory power of other saints.[58] In his altarpiece (1623–26) for the brotherhood of St. Roch, founded in St. Martin's Church in Alost, victims of the plague appeal to the saint, who appears on a stage-like platform. In portraying St. Roch experiencing a vision of Christ, Rubens brings to life the saint's intercessory power (see cat. 96).[59] Shortly after Rubens completed this painting, Paulus Pontius made an engraving of it. The print must have been a response to an intensified devotion to this special patron during times of plague: not only of Alost, for many towns and villages in seventeenth-century Flanders were regularly afflicted by outbreaks of plague.

THE OPEN SPACE OF THE STREETS[60]

The reordering of public and religious life in Antwerp after 1585 was also marked by the erection (and, in some cases, destruction) of statues, especially in the visual centres of the city. In December 1585, on Alexander Farnese's order, the burgomaster Edwaerd van der Dilft encouraged the erection of images of the Virgin Mary in the streets and squares of the city, to atone for the destruction of sacred objects during the iconoclastic riots. Evoking past destruction, the pictures would serve as an incentive to bring lapsed Catholics back to the Church.[61]

Two years later, again on the initiative of the Spanish regent, the statue of Silvius Brabo, the mythical founder of Antwerp, located in the top niche of the façade of the town hall (fig. 10), was replaced by a statue of the Virgin. The figure of Brabo, positioned between fighting sea centaurs, served as a communicative public statue, alluding to the municipal and provincial powers guaranteed by ancient privileges.[62] Its replacement by a statue of the Virgin was accompanied by a series of rituals, which included the consecration of the stone from which the figure was carved, and blessings on the occasions of the completion of the sculpture and its installation. The unveiling of the new image of the Virgin on the feast of the Annunciation (April 7) was celebrated with a mass and a festive procession. The new image was also crowned and provided with a sceptre, thus enhancing the royal authority it represented.[63] Public sculptures on streets, squares and on the façades of churches and civic buildings therefore functioned within a complex interrelationship, contributing to the ways citizens experienced the city, often regulating and directing their behaviour.[64] Regulations concerning the huge crucifix on the Meir suggest that this public image, admired by Evelyn, was equally understood as a holy object whose power would benefit the business activities that took place in its surroundings.[65]

During the time Rossetti and Evelyn visited the city, an elaborate publication was feverishly prepared to commemorate one of the greatest spectacles that had taken place in the previous years: the joyous entry of the Cardinal Infante Ferdinand who now, in his palace in Brussels, was approaching death and therefore would not see the completion of the project. The text of the *Pompa Triumphalis Introitus Ferdinandi*, published in 1642, was written by Caspar Gevaerts, who had, together with

FIG. 10: MELCHISEDECH VAN HOOREN, *The New Town Hall of Antwerp*, coloured etching, published by Maarten Peters, 1565, Vienna, Graphische Sammlung Albertina

Nicolaes Rockox, assisted Rubens in devising the programme. It contained etchings by Theodoor van Thulden (1609–1669) reproducing the four stages and five arches set up at key locations along the processional route to welcome the new ruler. Interestingly, these festive decorations were Rubens's largest and, at the same time, most ephemeral project (cat. 8, 9): in a letter addressed to Peiresc, the artist complained of the burden the magistrate had placed on his shoulders.[66] While Rubens had much experience in devising panegyrical cycles for rulers (see cat. 7), in this case, the elaborate praise dedicated to Ferdinand is juxtaposed with themes that would remind the prince of Antwerp's economic concerns, as the programme for the stage of Mercury illustrates (fig. 7). By far the most lavish of all "joyous entries" into the city, the event involved all the major painters of Antwerp specializing in history painting, with one important exception: although Anthony van Dyck had returned to Antwerp the previous year, there is no evidence that the city approached him, perhaps fearing that the high prices demanded by the English court painter could not be met by their restricted funds. Originally planned for January 1635, the spectacle was postponed several times. Finally staged in the afternoon of April 17, it lasted but two short hours.

THE PRIVATE SPACE OF THE DOMESTIC INTERIOR

Paintings of art galleries, a pictorial genre intimately associated with the culture of Antwerp's leading merchants, reflect the various ways in which pictures and other objects representing knowledge, value and wealth were viewed, savoured and judged.[67] Originating in the second decade of the seventeenth century, the genre was most probably introduced by the shrewdest member of the Francken family, Frans Francken the Younger (1581–1642). A cabinet depicted by an anonymous Flemish master in the National Gallery, London (fig. 11), displays a particularly varied and rich collection, thus challenging the represented (and real) art connoisseurs to demonstrate their competence in judgements about works of art.[68]

As has been remarked in scholarly literature, the arrangement of these painted collections is strikingly similar. Opening up into a large representative room (usually the back room of a prosperous merchant's palace or house), diverse groups of gentlemen are examining and discussing the objects on display. In the National Gallery work, for example, paintings representing the wealth of the Flemish school are arrayed across the back and side walls of a palatial room. A wide range of different genres are included: an *Interior*

FIG. 11: FLEMISH SCHOOL, *Cognoscenti in a Room Hung with Pictures, c.* 1620, oil on oak, 95.5 × 123.5 cm, London, National Gallery

of a Church by Hendrick van Steenwijk the Younger (*c.* 1580 – before 1649), a *Vase with Flowers* and a *Forest Landscape* by Jan Brueghel the Elder (1568–1625), a *Mountain Landscape* by Joos de Momper (1564–1635), ships by Andries van Ertvelt (1590–1652), a *Herd of Cows* by Jan Wildens (1586–1653), a religious history by Frans Francken the Younger, a mythological scene by Hendrik van Balen (1574/75–1632), a *Burning Landscape* by a follower of Bosch, and a cavalry picture by Sebastiaen Vrancx (1573–1647).

Some pictures are especially accentuated by their position or the attention they receive, as is the case with the painting of the *Four Elements* (perhaps by Jan Brueghel or Hendrik van Balen), displayed on the chair. Above the buffet on the side wall, Rubens's *Union of Earth and Water* (see cat. 4) occupies a prominent position and appears to converse with the statues of Minerva and Mercury on the porch opposite. The gentleman at the far left holds up for our inspection a small painting of insects, from which he has just drawn the protective cover. Conversely, on the far wall, in the right-hand corner, a picture is shown with its face to the wall, while above it, a sixteenth-century portrait in a roundel looks out at us, as does the gentleman behind the connoisseur who examines the Brueghel or Balen.

The range of knowledge is enriched by copies of Classical sculpture, shells, prints, drawings, cameos or coins, and some instruments, such as a planispheric astrolabe and a sundial, used in navigation and perhaps produced in Antwerp by Michael Coignet.[69]

The genre has been interpreted in many ways: as the ostentatious display of luxury and wealth, as a visual theoretical discourse about the mimetic properties of the arts, and, perhaps most importantly, as an encouragement for the development of artistic criteria and judgement. In a playful manner it also celebrates the flowering of the arts during peacetime, admonishing the viewer to take advantage of the fortunate occasion. But this, too, is a subject invented by Frans Francken the Younger and represents a challenge that the viewer of this exhibition is invited to take (see cat. 15).

NOTES

1. Carlo Rossetti embarked on July 12, 1641, and stayed mainly in Ghent until the end of September; he then travelled *via* Antwerp, Brussels, Namur and Liège to Cologne. The report of his voyage was compiled by his travel companion Domenico Parma in 1644: *Il diario de' viaggi fatti dal signore dottore Domenico Parma, Ferrarese, servendo all'Eminentissimo religiosissimo signore Cardinale Rossetti, in Italia, Francia, Inghilterra, Fiandra, Colonia e Germania, regnante la Santità di Papa Urbano VIII l'anno 1644, con la descrittione de' paesi e cose più notabili spettanti alle corti de' principi.* See the edition by Joseph Cuvelier, "Un récit de voyage inédit du XVIIe siècle," *Bulletin de l'Institut historique belge de Rome*, 6 (1926), pp. 121–44. I would like to thank my students at the University of Washington, Seattle, for sharing my interest in art and visual culture in early modern Antwerp; I am particularly grateful to Barbara Budnick for her detailed comments on several versions of this essay.
2. John Evelyn left England on July 21, 1641; after a short stay at Gennep he visited, among other places, Rotterdam, The Hague, Amsterdam, Haarlem, Leyden, 's-Hertogenbosch, Dordrecht, Lille, Antwerp, Brussels and Ghent. See *The Diary of John Evelyn*, ed. E.S. de Beer, vol. II, Oxford, 1855, pp. 29–75.
3. Cuvelier 1926, p. 133: "Chiesa veramente che trapassa le meraviglie d'ogn'altra in ogni genere; e pur in detta città ve ne sono di segnalatissime, come la cathedrale detta di Nostra Dama."
4. Cuvelier 1926, p. 134: "Volsero che fosse veduto alcuni quadri che di fiorami ne faceva professione un suo padre, che realmente superano l'arte e la natura medesima ingannarebbero."
5. *Ibid.* For the southern citadel of Antwerp, which was rebuilt after the fall of Antwerp in 1585, see *Antwerp, Story of a Metropolis 16th–17th Century*, ed. J. Van der Stock, exh. cat., Antwerp, Hessenhuis, 1993, p. 264 (Piet Lombaerde).
6. Cuvelier 1926, p. 135.
7. De Beer 1855, p. 63. In the seventeenth century, other writers eulogized the "marble temple" of the Jesuits with similar words: Peter Sutton, "The Spanish Netherlands in the Age of Rubens," in Peter Sutton, ed., *The Age of Rubens*, exh. cat., Boston, Museum of Fine Arts, 1993, pp. 118f.; *Antwerp, Story* 1993, p. 328, cat. 178 (Véronique van Passel).
8. De Beer 1855, p. 64.
9. On the English writer John Wilkins, see Eileen Reeves, *Painting the Heavens: Art and Science in the Age of Galileo*, Princeton, 1997, pp. 165, 231–32, note 3.
10. Sutton 1993, p. 122. John Wilkins, in *That the World May be a Planet*, also commented on the Jesuits' opposition to Copernican ideas: "the Jesuits, who are otherwise the greatest affectors of those opinions which seem to be new and subtle, do yet forbear to say anything in defence of [Copernicanism]; but rather take all occasions to inveigh against it." Cited by Reeves 1997, p. 219.
11. Panel, 267 × 235 cm, Koninklijk Museum voor Schone Kunsten, Antwerp. See David Freedberg, "The Representation of Martyrdoms During the Early Counter-Reformation in Antwerp," *The Burlington Magazine*, CXVIII (1976), p. 128; Carl Van de Velde, "De Coxcies uit de Onze-Lieve-Vrouwekerk van Antwerpen," in *Michel Coxcie, pictor regis (1499–1592)*. International colloquium, Mechelen 1992, *Handelingen van de Koninklijke Kring voor Oudheidkunde, Letteren en Kunst van Mechelen*, Mechelen, 1993, pp. 193–214.
12. De Beer 1855, p. 65: "[...] we heard a Dutch sermon at a Quarantia, or Exposure of the Sacrament as they tearme it."
13. De Beer 1855, p. 66.
14. *Antwerp, Story* 1993, p. 319, cat. 171 (Véronique Van Passel).
15. For the Hansa House, see, for example, *Antwerp, Story* 1993, p. 238, cat. 87 (Frank Huygens).
16. De Beer 1855, p. 67. For the history of the *Officina Plantiniana* under Balthasar Moretus the Younger, see *The Illustration of Books Published by the Moretuses*, exh. cat., Antwerp, Plantin-Moretus Museum of Antwerp, 1996–97, pp. 23–24, and 153ff. The Jesuit Carolus Scribanius (1561–1629), in his book on Antwerp (*Antverpia*, 1610), also lists the major sightseeing attractions of the city: the cathedral, the town hall, the new exchange, a house serving for the sale of tapestries, the Hansa House and the southern citadel. As a humanist well-versed in Classical literature, Scribanius also mentions the Plantin Press, where his own books were printed,

calling this notable publishing house in the Southern Netherlands the "sun of printing," around which the other publishers revolved. At the beginning of the seventeenth century, the Officina Plantiniana was, indeed, one of the largest printing–publishing houses in the world, as well as perhaps the leading humanist centre in the Southern Netherlands. See Julius S. Held, "Carolus Scribanius's Observations on Art in Antwerp," *Journal of the Warburg and Courtauld Institutes*, 59 (1996), p. 197.
17. For other comments on the social life on Antwerp's quay, see Sutton 1993, p. 126, citing Jan Albert Goris, *Lof van Antwerpen: Hoe reizigers Antwerpen zagen, van de XVe tot de XXe Eeuw*, Brussels, 1940, pp. 103–04.
18. De Beer 1855, p. 67.
19. On Gaspar Duarte, see Hans Pohl, *Die Portugiesen in Antwerpen (1567–1648). Zur Geschichte einer Minderheit*. Vierteljahrschrift für Sozial– und Wirtschaftsgeschichte, Beihefte, vol. LXIII, Wiesbaden, 1977, pp. 319–21, citing Maurits Sabbe, "De Antwerpsche vriendenkring van Anna Roemers Visscher," in *De Moretussen en hun kring: Verspreide Opstellen*, Antwerp, 1928, pp. 53–77. On Duarte's palace, see Pohl 1977, p. 282. For Rubens's portrait of Ludovicus Nonnius, see Hans Vlieghe, *Rubens: Portraits of Identified Sitters Painted in Antwerp*, Corpus Rubenianum Ludwig Burchard, part 19/2, London, 1987, pp. 137–39.
20. Evelyn's description of Michel Coxcie's painting for the altar of the Oude Handboog in Antwerp Cathedral was most probably influenced by Carolus Scribanius's remarks on Antwerp's art. See Held 1996, pp. 200, 204.
21. On Guicciardini's description of Antwerp's new exchange, see Jan Materné, "Schoon ende bequaem tot versamelinghe der cooplieden: De Antwerpse beurs tijdens de gouden 16de eeuw," in G. De Clercq, ed., *Ter Beurze: Geschiedenis van de aandelenhandel in België, 1300–1990*, Antwerp, Bruges, 1992; Ludovico Guicciardini, *Descrittione di tutti i Paesi Bassi, altrimenti detti Germania Inferiore*, Anversa (Guglielmo Silvio) 1568, p. 116. See also *Antwerp, Story* 1993, pp. 234–35.
22. The most thorough account of the events that occurred during the years 1566 to 1567 is by Guido Marnef, *Antwerp in the Age of Reformation: Underground Protestantism in a Commercial Metropolis, 1550–1577*, trans. J.C. Grayson, Baltimore and London, 1996, pp. 88–105.
23. Sutton 1993, p. 108.
24. Herman Van der Wee and Jan Materné, "Antwerp as a World Market in the Sixteenth and Seventeenth Centuries," in *Antwerp, Story* 1993, p. 25.
25. Marnef 1996, p. 180.
26. Alfons K.L. Thijs, *Van Geuzenstad tot Katholiek bolwerk: Maatschappelijke betekenis van de Kerk in contrareformatorisch Antwerpen*, Turnhout, 1990.
27. Marnef 1996, p. 22. See also Holm Bevers, *Das Rathaus von Antwerpen (1561–1565): Architektur und Figurenprogramm*, Hildesheim, Zürich and New York, 1985.
28. *Antwerp, Story* 1993, p. 285, cat. 140.
29. *Antwerp, Story* 1993, pp. 146–47, cat. 1 (Jan C. Van Dam).
30. For a stimulating study on gift practices, see Natalie Zemon Davis, *The Gift in Sixteenth-Century France*, Oxford and New York, 2000.
31. *Dessins flamands et hollandais du dix-septième siècle. Collections de l'Ermitage, Leningrad et du Musée Pouchkine, Moscou*, exh. cat., Brussels, Bibliothèque Royale Albert Ier; Rotterdam, Musée Boymans–van Beuningen; Paris, Institut Néerlandais, 1972, pp. 13–14, cat. 18. On Hendrick de Clerck, see Hans Vlieghe, *Flemish Art and Architecture, 1585–1700*, New Haven CT and London, 1998, pp. 109–11.
32. According to Thijs 1990, p. 66, Antwerp had 56,948 inhabitants in 1645.
33. Christopher Brown, "Introduction," in Christopher Brown and Hans Vlieghe, eds., *Van Dyck 1599–1641*, exh. cat., Antwerp, Koninklijk Museum voor Schone Kunsten; London, Royal Academy of Arts, 1999, pp. 31–32.
34. On Erasmus Quellinus the Younger, see Vlieghe 1998, p. 83; Sutton 1993, p. 378. For his stage on the occasion of the proclamation of the peace of Münster, see *Antwerp, Story* 1993,

p. 317, cat. 169 (Inge Wouters).

35. On Rubens's sketch for the stage of *Mercury's Departure*, see Julius Held, *The Oil Sketches of Peter Paul Rubens*, vol. I, Princeton NJ, 1980, pp. 240–43.

36. Vlieghe 1998, p. 1.

37. On Rockox, see Sutton 1993, pp. 158–59, cat. 16 (Marjorie E. Wieseman).

38. The most recent contributions on Willem van Haecht's gallery paintings are: Elizabeth Alice Honig, *Painting and the Market in Early Modern Antwerp*, New Haven CT and London, 1998; Vlieghe 1998, pp. 204–05; and Barbara Welzel, "Galerien und Kunstkabinette als Orte des Gesprächs," in W. Adam, ed., *Geselligkeit und Gesellschaft im Barockzeitalter*, Wiesbaden, 1997, pp. 179–92.

39. G. Dogaer, "De inventaris der schilderijen van Diego Duarte," *Jaarboek van het Koninklijk Museum voor Schone Kunsten, Antwerpen* (1971), pp. 195–221.

40. Hugo Solis, "Social Relations in Antwerp in the Sixteenth and Seventeenth Centuries," in *Antwerp, Story* 1993, p. 43.

41. The statistics from Duverger have been compiled by Jeffrey Muller, "Private Collections in the Spanish Netherlands: Ownership and Display of Paintings in Domestic Interiors," in Sutton 1993, pp. 196–97.

42. Muller, "Private Collections," in Sutton 1993, p. 198.

43. On Rubens's painting in St. Petersburg, see Elizabeth McGrath, *Rubens: Subjects from History*, ed. Arnout Balis, Corpus Rubenianum Ludwig Burchard, part 13/2, London, 1997, pp. 97–103.

44. On privileged altars, see Christine Göttler, *Die Kunst des Fegefeuers nach der Reformation: Kirchliche Schenkungen, Ablass und Almosen in Antwerpen und Bologna um 1600*, Berliner Schriften zur Kunst, vol. VII, Mainz, 1996, pp. 54–126; Pierroberto Scaramella, *Le Madonne del Purgatorio: iconografia e religione in Campania tra rinascimento e controriforma*, Genoa, 1991, p. 268.

45. Floris Prims, *Geschiedenis van Antwerpen*, vol. VI/B, Brussels, 1982, p. 567.

46. Prims 1982, pp. 557, 570–71 (Augustinians); 580 (Annunciate sisters); 581 (Spanish Carmelites).

47. On the Jesuit church, see John Rupert Martin, *The Ceiling Paintings for the Jesuit Church in Antwerp*, Corpus Rubenianum Ludwig Burchard, part 1, London and New York, 1968, pp. 21–43.

48. Prims 1982, pp. 571–75.

49. Göttler 1996, pp. 213–25.

50. Thijs 1990, p. 66; Sutton 1993, p. 117.

51. David Freedberg, "Painting and the Counter Reformation in the Age of Rubens," in Sutton 1993, p. 134.

52. Cynthia Lawrence, "Before *The Raising of the Cross*: The Origins of Rubens's Earliest Antwerp Altarpieces," *Art Bulletin* 81 (1999), pp. 267–96.

53. Barbara Haeger, "Rubens's *Adoration of the Magi* and the program for the high altar of St. Michael's Abbey in Antwerp," *Simiolus* 25 (1997), pp. 45–71.

54. For the following I rely on David Freedberg, *The Life of Christ after the Passion*, Corpus Rubenianum Ludwig Burchard, part 7, London and Oxford, 1984, pp. 172–78, cat. 43.

55. On the martyrdom of missionaries in Japan, see R. Po-Chia Hsia, *The World of Catholic Renewal 1540–1770*, Cambridge, 1998, pp. 125, 184–86.

56. Hans Vlieghe, *Saints*, Corpus Rubenianum Ludwig Burchard, part 8/2, Brussels, 1973, pp. 73–74, cat. 115; Christine Göttler, "'Actio' in Peter Paul Rubens' Hochaltarbildern für die Jesuitenkirche in Antwerpen," in *Barocke Inszenierung*, ed. Joseph Imorde, Fritz Neumeyer and Tristan Weddigen, Emsdetten/Zürich, 1999, pp. 10–31.

57. Gertrude Wilmers, *Cornelis Schut (1597–1655): A Flemish Painter of the High Baroque*, Pictura Nova, vol. I, Turnhout, 1996, pp. 20, 101–03.

58. Göttler 1996, pp. 27–30.

59. Vlieghe 1973, vol. II, pp. 142–44, cat. 140.

60. I borrow this term from Peter Burke, "Cities, Spaces and Rituals in the Early Modern World," in *Urban Rituals in Italy and the Netherlands: Historical Contrasts in the Use of Public Space, Architecture and the Urban Environment*, ed. Heidi de Mare and Anna Vos, Assen, 1993, p. 29.

61. Roland A.E. De Beeck, *The gilde van Onze-Lieve-Vrouwe-Lof in de Kathedraal van Antwerpen: Vijfhonderd Jaar Maria verering te Antwerpen*, Antwerp, 1978, p. 35; L. Wuyts, "Het St.-Jorisretabel van de Oude Voetboog door Maarten De Vos: Een ikonologisch onderzoek," *Jaarboek van het Koninklijk Museum voor Schone Kunsten Antwerpen* (1971), p. 128. On the "conversational mode" of public statues, see John Shearman, *Only Connect ... Art and the Spectator in the Italian Renaissance*. The A.W. Mellon Lectures in the Fine Arts, 1988; Bollingen series, XXXV, 37, Washington, D.C., 1992, pp. 46–47.

62. De Beeck 1973, p. 37; Wuyts 1971, p. 128; A.K.L. Thijs, "De Contrareformatie en het economisch transformatieproces te Antwerpen voor en na 1585," in *Religieuze stromingen te Antwerpen voor en na 1585, Bijdragen tot de Geschiedenis*, 70 (1987), p. 107; Bevers 1985, pp. 55–58.

63. Augustin Thijssen, Antwerpen Vermaerd door den Eeredienst van Maria: Geschiedkundige aanmerkingen over de 500 Mariabeelden in de Straten der Stad, Antwerp, 1922, pp. 147–54. I am grateful to Nancy J. Kay for bringing this reference to my attention and discussing her research project with me. Nancy Kay is preparing a Ph.D. thesis on the sacred sculptures of Counter-Reformation Antwerp.

64. For a discussion of the mutual dependency of social order and the physical structure of the city in early modern Italy, see Edward Muir and Ronald F.E. Weissmann, "Social and symbolic places in Renaissance Venice and Florence," in J. Agnew and J. Duncan, eds., *The Power of Place*, Boston et al., 1989, pp. 81–103.

65. Thijssen 1922, p. 114.

66. See, among others, Held 1980, I, p. 221.

67. For literature on painted picture galleries, see Zirka Zaremba Filipczak, *Picturing Art in Antwerp 1550–1700*, Princeton, 1987, pp. 58–72; Victor I. Stoichita, *The Self-Aware Image: An Insight into Early Modern Meta-Painting*, Cambridge, 1997, pp. 114–47; see also above, note 38.

68. Gregory Martin, *The Flemish School, circa 1600 – circa 1900*, National Gallery Catalogues, London, 1986, pp. 68–73, cat. 1287.

69. See *Antwerp, Story* 1993, pp. 300–01, cat. 154; p. 304, cat. 157.

FLEMISH PAINTINGS FROM THE AGE OF RUBENS IN THE HERMITAGE MUSEUM

NATALYA GRITSAY

The more one looks at this painting, the more one admires it.
This is not to be confused with one of those detached portraits,
where the sole interest for the spectator lies in the sitter
himself: here we have life, here we have passion.

Such is Count Alexander Sergeevich Stroganov's
impassioned description of one of the most interesting
pictures he owned, *Portrait of Rubens with his Son Albert*
(cat. 22), in the catalogue of 1793 of his gallery of
paintings.[1] Then attributed to Rubens himself, this
portrait by the "Raphael of Flanders" (as Stroganov called
him, in the tradition of eighteenth-century scholars[2]) was
the first work in the catalogue's Netherlandish painting
section. This publication, essentially a catalogue
raisonné, first appeared in St. Petersburg in French, and
made accessible to the broader public one of Russia's
most famous private collections of Western European
painting from the sixteenth century onward.[3]

Alexander Stroganov (1733–1811) came from a
wealthy Russian family renowned for its patronage and
charitable works. The first member of his family to hold
the title of count, he was put in charge of St. Petersburg's
Imperial Public Library, was elected an honorary member
of the Academy of Arts, and then became its president in
1801. He was a man of great erudition, and a renowned
connoisseur of the arts, who assembled his own picture
gallery and compiled its catalogue.

Many other Russian aristocratic collections were also

SCHOOL OF PETER PAUL RUBENS,
Portrait of Rubens with his Son Albert
(detail; see cat. 22), *c.* 1620

27

formed during the second half of the eighteenth century, when the fashion was set by Catherine the Great. Acting through Russian diplomatic representatives and special agents abroad, she assembled one of the finest picture galleries in Europe during the two decades from 1760 to 1780. It grew rapidly, since the Russian empress generally purchased entire collections rather than individual items. In all of the great European collections acquired by Catherine, seventeenth-century Flemish paintings occupied a notable place. It was thus Catherine who assembled what is today the nucleus of the Hermitage's Flemish collection, with paintings by such leading masters as Rubens, van Dyck, Jordaens, Snyders and Teniers. These artists' works still dominate the Hermitage, even though the museum's extensive collection has grown to include pictures by over 140 Flemish artists of the seventeenth and eighteenth centuries. With only a few exceptions, the paintings by these artists arrived during the eighteenth century, and thus the core of the Flemish section owes much to the taste of collectors of that time.

In the mid-eighteenth century, seventeenth-century Flemish paintings were actively collected throughout Western Europe, and demand was particularly great in Paris. They were a prominent feature there in galleries and "cabinets," private collections in which paintings, sculpture, drawings and decorative arts were grouped with objects as varied as natural specimens and ancient coins. The Paris art market was glutted with these extremely fashionable paintings, and the taste remained prevalent almost to the end of the century. During his stay there from 1771 to 1778, Count Alexander Stroganov acquired his finest Flemish paintings, including van Dyck's *Portrait of Nicolaes Rockox* (cat. 24).[4] According to Pierre-Jean Mariette (1694–1774), the renowned engraver, publisher, collector and patron, this picture formerly belonged to Claude Henri Watelet (1718–1786), a government official, writer, collector and connoisseur residing in Paris.[5] Watelet was the author of *L'Art de peindre* (1760), a long didactic poem on the principles and techniques of painting that served as the basis for his election to the Académie Française.

The Paris art market between the 1760s and the 1780s was also the source for many of Catherine the Great's acquisitions of seventeenth-century Flemish paintings still on display at the Hermitage. Most

significant in this respect was the collection of Baron Crozat de Thiers purchased by Catherine in 1772, which included works by Rubens, van Dyck, Jordaens, Snyders and Teniers. Through a Paris auction, she also obtained the collection of Jean de Jullienne (1686–1767), a leading industrialist, patron, and friend of Antoine Watteau. This brought, among other works essential to the Flemish section of her picture gallery, an early study by Snyders (cat. 66).[6] The collection of Etienne-François, duc de Choiseul (1719–1785), Minister of Foreign Affairs under Louis XV, was purchased in April 1772[7] and provided David Teniers the Younger's *Village Festival* (cat. 81) and *Kermess* (cat. 82). The Hermitage's most important painting by Teniers's teacher, Adriaen Brouwer, is *Tavern Scene* (cat. 86), bought in Paris in 1770 from the collection of François Tronchin (1704–1798).[8]

Other renowned European collections purchased by the Russian empress also added major paintings to the Flemish portion of the Old Master collection. Of greatest importance were her purchases of the renowned collections of Count Cobenzl (Brussels, 1768), Count Brühl (Dresden, 1769) and Sir Robert Walpole (Houghton Hall, England, 1779). All three of these added major paintings by Rubens: one (Walpole), brought works by van Dyck and Snyders; two (Walpole and Brühl), paintings by Jordaens; and all three included works by Teniers.

Six works attributed to Rubens arrived with the collection of Johann Ernst Gotzkowsky (1710–1775), a Berlin merchant, and their acquisition in 1764 laid the foundation for the Imperial Picture Gallery, although it was later ascertained that none of these works was actually by Rubens.[9] Such, for instance, was the case with *Cook at a Kitchen Table with Dead Game* (cat. 68), which was attributed to Rubens and Snyders while it was in Gotzkowsky's possession.

The first authentic works by Rubens arrived at the Hermitage, and indeed in Russia, with the collection of Count Carl Cobenzl (1712–1770), Plenipotentiary Minister to Empress Maria-Theresa in the Southern Netherlands. Cobenzl lived in Brussels from 1753, taking advantage of the opportunity and of his status to add to his collection. This relatively small group of just forty-six paintings brought to St. Petersburg important works by Rubens, the best of which was *Roman Charity, or Cimon and Pero* (cat. 3). In the mid-seventeenth century this painting had belonged to Karel van den Bosch (1597–1665),[10] Bishop of Bruges and a great connoisseur of paintings, prints and books.

The entire collection of Count Heinrich Brühl (1700–1763), Plenipotentiary Minister to Frederick Augustus II, Elector of Saxony (Augustus III, King of Poland), was acquired from his heirs, and enriched the Hermitage with a whole series of masterpieces, more than forty of them seventeenth-century Flemish paintings.[11] Many are of outstanding quality, including an early sketch by Rubens for *The Adoration of the Shepherds* (cat. 1),[12] and such mature works as *Perseus and Andromeda* and *Pastoral Landscape with Rainbow* (cat. 40); the marvellous *Wooded Landscape* (*The Rest on the Flight into Egypt*) by Jan Brueghel the Elder (cat. 58); and a number of works by less well-known Flemish artists (cat. 19, 51, 87, 88, 93).

Many paintings from the Brühl collection had already passed through the hands of Paris collectors. During the second half of the seventeenth century, Rubens's *Pastoral Landscape with Rainbow* belonged to the duc de Richelieu (1629–1715),[13] great-nephew of the famous Cardinal Richelieu, and a great admirer of Flemish art. This landscape figured in the Paris auction of property belonging to the famous banker and collector Everhard Jabach, whose portrait by van Dyck appears in the exhibition (cat. 28). The picture had been presented to Brühl by the Duke and Elector of Bavaria, Maximilian III Joseph (1727–1777).[14]

The most important additions to the Hermitage's Flemish collection came with Catherine's purchase in Paris of the renowned paintings of the French financier Pierre Crozat (1665–1740) and his nephew Louis-Antoine Crozat, baron de Thiers (1699–1770).[15] Some fifty Flemish works came from this collection, representing all the genres: religious, allegorical and mythological scenes, landscapes, portraits, scenes of everyday life, church interiors and still lifes, as well as sporting and hunting compositions. Most prized were the paintings by Rubens and van Dyck. By Rubens were such masterpieces as the *Portrait of a Lady-in-Waiting to the Infanta Isabella*, and *Bacchus*, one of the artist's last works, mentioned in the posthumous inventory of his property[16] and acquired by Pierre Crozat at the sale of the duc de Richelieu's collection;[17] by van Dyck, *The Apparition of Christ to His Disciples* (*The Incredulity of St. Thomas*; cat. 11), and a

FIG. 12: ANTHONY VAN DYCK,
Self-portrait (see cat. 23), 1622–23

series of superb portraits, including *Portrait of a Man* (Virginio Cesarini?; cat. 25), *Self-portrait* (cat. 23) and *Portrait of Everhard Jabach* (cat. 28). The collection of paintings by van Dyck assembled by Crozat was of unrivalled quality in eighteenth-century Paris, and formed the basis of Pierre-Jean Mariette's writings about the artist's work.

Crozat's nephew, Louis-Antoine, baron de Thiers, Lieutenant-General to Louis XV, was no less a passionate collector than his uncle. His collection brought to St. Petersburg three sketches by Rubens for the painted cycle of *The Life of Marie de' Medici*, one of which is included in the exhibition (cat. 5). These were probably acquired from the collection of Claude Maugis, Abbot of Saint-Ambroise (?–1658) and chaplain to Marie de' Medici. Maugis was an admirer of Rubens, and had acted as an intermediary between the artist and the Queen

Mother. A noted connoisseur, he was clearly appreciative of the skill and finesse of Rubens's works, especially the lightness and freedom of his brush strokes, qualities most clearly manifest in his oil sketches. Such discerning connoisseurship, however, was rare in the seventeenth century, as most of his contemporaries placed more value on the concept and structure of a painting than on the skill of its execution.

Connoisseur collectors of the following century, by contrast, placed greater value on the painter's technical virtuosity, and Cobenzl, Brühl and Pierre Crozat clearly prized the small oil sketches and "cabinet" paintings by Rubens that so brilliantly revealed the artist's mastery of colour. Their pronounced interest in Rubens's sketches and painted "kitchens," as well as those by other Old Masters, was also rooted in their passionate collecting of drawings, a vast number of which came from the Cobenzl and Brühl collections and enriched the Hermitage's holdings.[18]

Catherine's last major acquisition in Paris, made in 1783, was the collection of Silvan Raphaël Baudouin (1715–1797), a brigadier in the French royal army and an amateur engraver and collector.[19] It brought her significant works by David Teniers the Younger, including *Landscape with Peasants Bowling* (cat. 79), *Landscape with a Maid at a Well* (cat. 78) and *Landscape with Peasants Before an Inn* (cat. 77).

Notably different from the Continental collections, especially in the manner in which it was assembled, was the picture gallery of Sir Robert Walpole (1676–1745), 1st Earl of Orford, and England's first Prime Minister under George I and George II. It added to Catherine's collection a considerable number of large seventeenth-century Flemish paintings, both monumental and decorative in character, irrevocably linked to the very nature of this school.[20] One of Britain's greatest eighteenth-century collections of paintings, the Walpole gallery was acquired from Sir Robert's grandson, George, 3rd Earl of Orford (1730–1791), and enriched the Hermitage with forty-nine seventeenth-century Flemish works. While it was not comparable in quantity to the Crozat collection, it contributed significantly to the overall quality of the museum's selection of paintings from the Flemish school. That the majority, nearly two thirds, was by Rubens and van Dyck, and over a third was large-scale, says much about Walpole's taste and his concentrated efforts as a collector. It is well known that Sir Robert sent special agents to the Austrian Netherlands and the United Northern Provinces to buy large paintings,[21] and eventually he acquired major works such as Rubens's *Christ in the House of Simon the Pharisee*; van Dyck's *Holy Family with Partridges*, as well as the portraits of *Philadelphia and Elizabeth Wharton* (cat. 32) and *Henry Danvers, Earl of Danby* (cat. 30); Jordaens's *Self-portrait with Parents, Brothers and Sisters* (cat. 33); Snyders's *Bird Concert* (cat. 67), as well as four of his vast *Markets*. Even a "cabinet" painter such as David Teniers the Younger was represented by one of his few large paintings, *The Kitchen* (cat. 84). There were also several excellent oil sketches by Rubens, including *The Apotheosis of James I* (cat. 7), and a series of designs for arches and porticoes for the triumphal entrance into Antwerp of the new Spanish governor, Cardinal Infante Ferdinand on April 17, 1635 (cat. 8, 9). These had come from the collections of two English artists: *The Apotheosis of James I* had once belonged to Sir Godfrey Kneller (1646–1723), and the arch designs to Prosper Henricus Lankrink (1628–1692).

While the oil sketches allowed connoisseurs fully to appreciate one distinctive aspect of Rubens's style, larger works revealed other characteristics. In 1621, the artist himself noted in a letter that "the large size of a picture gives one much more courage to express one's ideas clearly and realistically," admitting further that "by natural instinct" he was "better fitted to execute very large works than small curiosities."[22] For the English painter Joshua Reynolds (1723–1792), seventeenth-century Flemish painting would always be associated with large-scale pictures. He was inclined to associate small Flemish paintings showing little figures with the Dutch school, since Flemish painters "generally painted figures large as life." Thus, for Reynolds, it followed that one should then "distinguish those two schools rather by their style and manner, than by the place where the artists happened to be born."[23]

A typically English feature of the Walpole collection was its inclusion of family portraits by van Dyck, such as those from the Wharton portrait gallery at Winchendon (cat. 26, 32). Sir Robert purchased them around 1725 from Philip, 4th Lord Wharton (1613–1696), who commissioned them during the late 1630s. With the exception of the *Portrait of Everhard Jabach*, all of the

Hermitage's English portraits by van Dyck come from the Walpole collection, where, as in the case of the Crozat gallery, the artist's portraits considerably outnumbered his history paintings. Indeed, throughout the eighteenth century, van Dyck was far more highly prized as a painter of portraits than of historical subjects.

The purchases that Catherine made on the Russian market were of considerably less importance to the growth of the Flemish section during the eighteenth century. One notable exception was the acquisition in 1792 of the St. Petersburg picture gallery belonging to the empress's secret husband, Prince Grigory Potemkin of Tauride (1739–1791), which included some interesting Flemish paintings (see cat. 71).[24]

The last significant addition to the museum's Flemish paintings during the eighteenth century was that of Rubens's magnificent *Union of Earth and Water* (cat. 4), acquired in Rome between 1798 and 1800. It was purchased by Catherine's son Paul I for his new St. Petersburg residence, the Mikhail Castle, built between 1797 and 1800 to a design by the architect Vincenzo Brenna (1745–1820), but was in fact never displayed there.[25]

During the nineteenth century, the Hermitage collection of works from the Flemish school continued to grow, but at a considerably slower rate. The most important additions were the paintings acquired in 1814 by Alexander I from Napoleon Bonaparte's first wife, Josephine Beauharnais (1763–1814), whose collection was kept at Malmaison, near Paris. These were a monumental canvas by Rubens, *The Descent from the Cross*,[26] and three superb works by David Teniers the Younger, *The Guardroom* (cat. 75), *Portrait of the Members of the Oude Voetboog Guild in Antwerp* (cat. 76) and *Monkeys in a Kitchen* (cat. 83). Such acquisitions of important seventeenth-century Flemish paintings had become rare events, and more often what was obtained were pictures by artists whose work had not previously been represented in the Hermitage. The collection of Dmitry Tatischev (1767–1845), for example, Russian envoy to Naples, Madrid, The Hague and Vienna, which was bequeathed to Nicholas I, included Jan Fyt's *Fruit and Parrot* (cat. 62). There were also several notable acquisitions during the 1890s, among them *Allegory of Time Revealing Truth* by Theodoor van Thulden (cat. 18) and *David with the Head of Goliath* by Jacob van Oost the Elder (cat. 12).

Further additions were made to the collection in the twentieth century. In 1915 the paintings owned by Pyotr Semenov-Tyan-Shanksy (1827–1914) came to the museum. Beginning in the 1850s, this famous Russian scholar, geographer and traveller amassed many works, mainly by less prominent Dutch and Flemish artists, most of whom had been only poorly represented, if at all, in the Hermitage. Semenov's collection enriched the museum with some one hundred seventeenth- and eighteenth-century Flemish paintings, including works by major artists such as David Teniers the Younger (cat. 80), as well as those by less well-known masters (cat. 43, 59). The main value of the collection was the opportunity it provided for a broader vision of Dutch and Flemish seventeenth- and eighteenth-century painting.

The nationalization of private collections after the October Revolution of 1917 brought to the Hermitage works of art from the imperial summer palaces and the museum of the Academy of Arts. Among them were some outstanding pictures, now part of the Hermitage's permanent exhibition. These include portraits from the Stroganov collection, as well as an early painting by Adriaen Brouwer, *The Village Charlatan* (*Operation for Stone in the Head*; cat. 85) from the Gatchina Palace, and such significant works as *Christ Crowned by Thorns* (*Ecce Homo*) by Rubens, and *The King Drinks* by Jordaens, both of which had been acquired at the end of the eighteenth century by Alexander Bezborodko (1747–1799). Throughout the 1920s and 1930s, still more interesting seventeenth-century Flemish paintings came to the museum, including works by less well-known artists such as Frans Denys (cat. 38) and Peter Franchoys (cat. 39), and by major artists such as Jordaens (cat. 13), Frans Pourbus the Younger (cat. 36), Jan Wildens (cat. 54) and Jan Siberechts (cat. 56). A special purchasing commission was established at the Hermitage in 1935, and in 1939 the museum acquired *Still Life with a Skull* (*Wall in the Artist's Studio*; cat. 65) by Sebastiaen Bonnecroy, a painter whose works are rarely seen.

NOTES

1. Cat. Stroganoff 1793, p. 29.

2. The text reproduced in Cat. Stroganoff 1793 in smaller typeface is a quotation from *Abrégé de la vie des plus fameux peintres, avec leurs portraits gravés en taille-douce, les indications de leur principaux ouvrages, quelques réflexions sur leur caractères, et la manière de connoître les desseins et les tableaux des grands maîtres. Par M*** [Dezallier d'Argenville]*, vol. 2, Paris, 1745, p. 142.

3. The first publication of the catalogue compiled by Count Stroganov included eighty-seven paintings; the second edition of 1800 had 115.

4. J.A. Schmidt: "Bürgermeister Rockox und seine Nichte," unpublished MS, Hermitage Archive [1931].

5. Mariette, *Abecedario* 1853–59, vol. II, p. 207.

6. *Catalogue raisonné des tableaux, desseins, estampes, et autres effets curieux, après le décès de M. de Jullienne ... par Pierre Remy*, Paris, 1767, p. 45, no. 111.

7. *Catalogue des tableaux qui composent le cabinet de Monseigneur le Duc de Choiseul, dont la vente se fera le lundi 6 avril 1772 en son Hôtel, rue de Richelieu*, ed. J.F. Boileau, Paris, 1772.

8. The list of paintings sold by Tronchin in 1770 was published by V.F. Levinson-Lessing in "Sobranie kartin Fransua Tronshena. Iz istorii kollektsiy Ermitazha" [François Tronchin's Collection of Paintings. From the History of the Hermitage Collections], *Soobshchenie Gosudarstvennogo Ermitazha* [Bulletin of the State Hermitage], XXXI (1970), pp. 3–13.

9. Thus, for instance, the sketch *The Martyrdom of St. Lieven*, listed by Gotzkowsky as an original by Rubens (Malinovsky 1990, vol. II, p. 100) was already described by Labensky in the Hermitage's manuscript catalogue of 1797 (under no. 1243) as school of Rubens.

10. According to the dedication on a print after this composition by Cornelis van Caukercken (*c.* 1625–*c.* 1680). The print may have been produced between 1651 and 1660, when van den Bosch was Bishop of Bruges.

11. The best paintings from Brühl's gallery were reproduced in a richly engraved publication, *Recueil d'estampes gravées d'après les tableaux de la Galerie et du Cabinet de S.E. Mr. Le Comte de Brühl ... à Dresde ...*, 1754. A second volume was in preparation but remained unpublished on the owner's death.

12. While in the Brühl collection this sketch was thought to be the work of Cornelis Schut.

13. Roger de Piles: *Le Cabinet de Monseigneur le duc de Richelieu* (Paris, 1677), pp. 146–49.

14. Somoff 1901, no. 595.

15. *Catalogue des tableaux de cabinet de M. Crozat, baron de Thiers* (Paris, 1755); H. Tronchin: *Le conceillier François Tronchin et ses amis* (Paris, 1895), pp. 307–31; M. Stuffmann: "Les Tableaux de la collection de Pierre Crozat. Historique et destinée d'un ensemble célèbre, établis en parlant d'un inventaire après décès inédits (1740)", *Gazette des Beaux-Arts* (July–September 1968), pp. 5–144.

16. Denucé 1932, p. 60; B. Teyssèdre: "Une collection française de Rubens au XVIIe siècle: Le Cabinet du duc de Richelieu décrit par Roger de Piles (1676–1681)", *Gazette des Beaux-Arts* (November 1963), pp. 291, 292.

17. De Piles 1677, pp. 139–41.

18. Pierre Crozat also owned a unique collection of Old Master drawings by the most renowned European artists – over 19,000 sheets in all – but by his will these, along with his prints and engraved gems, were sold at auction.

19. The manuscript catalogue of this collection, compiled in 1780, "Description des tableaux du Cabinet de M. Le Comte de Baudouin," is in the Hermitage Archive.

20. For the history of the collection see *Houghton Hall: The Prime Minister, the Empress and the Hermitage*, ed. Andrew Moore (London, 1996); further detailed information on the sale and fate of the collection in Russia will be given in the forthcoming publication *The Aedes Walpolianae* by Larisa Dukelskaya and Andrew Moore (New Haven CT and London, 2001).

21. We know, for instance, that John Ellis, Sir Robert's agent, acquired at auction in Rotterdam in 1733 van Dyck's *Holy Family with Partridges* (see *Houghton Hall: The Prime Minister ...* 1996, pp. 88–89); his secret agent John Macky bought the Snyders series of four *Markets* in Brussels (Koslow 1995, pp. 112–16).

22. Letter from Rubens to William Trumbell of September 13, 1621; translated in Magurn 1971, p. 77.

23. Sir Joshua Reynolds, *A Journey to Flanders and Holland*, ed. H. Mount, Cambridge, 1996, p. 110.

24. The most important Flemish painting in this collection, *Self-portrait with his Wife Susanna Cock and their Children Magdalena, Jan-Baptist, Susanna, Cornelis the Younger and Elisabeth*, by Cornelis de Vos (then attributed to van Dyck), was presented to Potemkin by Catherine II before 1774, *i.e.* during the first decade of the Hermitage Picture Gallery's existence.

25. Kalnitskaya 1995, pp. 80–81.

26. N.I. Gritsay, "Kompozycje Rubensa na temat Zdjęcia z krzyża' w galerii malarstwa w Ermitażu" [Rubens's Compositions on the Subject 'The Descent from the Cross' in the Painting Gallery of the Hermitage], *Arcydzieło Petera Paula Rubensa 'Zdjęcie z krzyża' z zbiorów panstwowego Ermitażu w Sankt Peterburgu* [Masterpieces by Peter Paul Rubens: "The Descent from the Cross" from the Collection of the Imperial Hermitage in St. Petersburg], Warsaw, 2000, pp. 16–22.

ANTHONY VAN DYCK AND WORKSHOP,
Portrait of Philadelphia and Elizabeth Wharton
(detail; see cat. 32), 1640

iladelphia Wharton and Elizabeth
haron y onely daughters of Philip
m Lord Wharton by Elizabeth his
rst wife, 1640 about y age of 4 &3

PAINTINGS IN THE EXHIBITION

RUBENS AND HIS FOLLOWERS

NATALYA GRITSAY

The exhibition includes paintings by forty artists, works produced in different styles and representing various genres. In accordance with their importance to the history of Flemish art and their predominance in the Hermitage collection, the paintings of Peter Paul Rubens and his close followers – Anthony van Dyck, Jacob Jordaens and Frans Snyders – form the centrepiece of this selection, with pride of place given to Rubens, the acknowledged leader of the Flemish school, who was known by his contemporaries as "the Apelles of our time."[1]

The Hermitage's collection of works by Rubens is famous for both its high quality and its great variety. While this exhibition includes only slightly more than a third of the master's works owned by the Hermitage, these nonetheless demonstrate both the wealth of the collection and the all-encompassing nature of Rubens's œuvre. The exhibition allows us to judge the breadth of his accomplishments as it presents examples from nearly all the genres in which he worked, including history paintings, religious works, allegorical pictures, portraits and landscapes. These varied examples convincingly justify the artist's assertion that: "My talent is such that no undertaking, however vast in size, or diversified in subject, has ever surpassed my courage."[2]

The *Portrait of Rubens with his Son Albert* (cat. 22), possibly a contemporary copy of a lost original by Rubens, shows the artist in his private world, surrounded by objects from his own collection. Rubens was an avid collector of antiquities, a passion he shared with many of his contemporaries, such as Nicolaes Rockox. His encyclopedic knowledge of antiquity – both its literature and arts – provided the basis for his allegorical artistic language. In both his history paintings and his prints, such as his designs for title pages of books issued by Antwerp's renowned Plantin Press, Rubens made extensive use of this language, one that allowed him not only to embody abstract concepts, but also to draw apt parallels with contemporary events. Allegory was for him an extremely vital means of expression, offering a symbolic language that could easily be deciphered by educated men and women of his own day.

This is confirmed by what is undoubtedly the central work in the exhibition, *The Union of Earth and Water* (cat. 4). In this painting, the traditional depiction of the elements, a very popular theme among Flemish artists at the turn of the sixteenth and seventeenth centuries, has not only lost its former abstraction but has become imbued with an incisive topicality. Here Rubens has employed his favourite images from ancient mythology to convey his meaning, and has rendered them with motifs borrowed from antique art.[3] The basic compositional device employed for the main figures' contrasting poses, one seen from the front, the other from the back, was nevertheless drawn from northern sources;[4] Rubens's innovation lies in the presumption of the viewer's active collaboration and collusion with the world of images he had created.

Painted oil sketches form an extremely important part of the Hermitage collection of works by Rubens, reflected by the eight examples included in the exhibition. With their rapid brush strokes, which seem to suggest the flight of the artist's fantasy, and their transparent, almost melting colours, they allow us to recognize Rubens's absolute mastery of this medium. Both the patron and purpose for the commission of each of these sketches is well known. They represent various types: a *bozzetto* recording a first idea (*The Arrival in Lyons*; cat. 5), or finished *modelli* intended for clients' approval (*The Adoration of the Shepherds*, cat. 1; *The Assumption and Coronation of the Virgin*, cat. 2). The diverse genres are also represented: a study for a religious altarpiece (cat. 1); complex allegories (cat. 4, 5); a sketch for a ceiling (*The Apotheosis of James I*; cat. 7); and designs for elaborate architectural structures

includes some magnificent portraits by Anthony van Dyck, whom Rubens described in one of his letters as "the best of my pupils."[6] Like that of his great teacher, van Dyck's talent knew no bounds, and he was master of a variety of genres. Despite his considerable accomplishments as a history painter, reflected in the exhibition by his unusual and interesting *The Apparition of Christ to His Disciples* (*The Incredulity of St. Thomas*; cat. 11), he is best known for his portraits. Of all the portrait types van Dyck perfected, the Hermitage lacks only an example of the large, full-length portrait commissions he completed in Italy. Just under half of his portraits from the Hermitage, nearly all the best examples in the museum's collection, are included in the exhibition and demonstrate van Dyck's skill in this genre. Even in those cases where he seemed to be using similar compositional schemes, such as in the *Self-portrait* (cat. 23) and the *Portrait of Everhard Jabach* (cat. 28), one can recognize the various expressive techniques and devices he employed to introduce the idiosyncrasies of character required by each portrait commission.

The œuvre of Jacob Jordaens, the third of the leading seventeenth-century Flemish masters, is reflected in the Hermitage collection to a lesser degree. There are several key works, among them *Self-portrait with Parents, Brothers and Sisters* (cat. 33), presented in the guise of a monumental genre scene, which was painted the year the artist became a master of Antwerp's Guild of St. Luke. Jordaens, unlike van Dyck, never studied with Rubens, nor did he work in his studio, yet the art of Rubens provided the central stimulus to his artistic formation. Jordaens, too, practised in a variety of genres, and the paintings displayed exemplify his work both as a history painter (cat. 13) and as a portraitist.

The Hermitage collection of eleven works by Frans Snyders is relatively small, but outstanding, and demonstrates the artist at his very best. Snyders worked actively with Rubens for many years, becoming one of his closest collaborators. The four paintings chosen for the exhibition present him as an astute painter of animals and a brilliant master of still life (cat. 60, 66, 67, 68). These works reveal how Snyders succeeded in transforming the intimate scale and character so fundamental to both genres at the beginning of the seventeenth century into truly monumental art forms, full of dynamism and life.

prepared to celebrate the arrival of the new Spanish governor, Cardinal Infante Ferdinand, into Antwerp (cat. 8, 9). The exhibition encompasses all phases of Rubens's career, including one of his earliest works, created "on the eve of his great fame" (cat. 1),[5] as well as several of his last paintings, the commissions of which attest to his international recognition, such as *The Arrival in Lyons* for the French queen, Marie de' Medici, or *The Apotheosis of James I*, for England's Charles I.

Also included is a series of those less-than-monumental-scale works that were intended for the private collections or "cabinets" of connoisseurs, such as the marvellous early *Roman Charity, or Cimon and Pero* (cat. 3), from Rubens's "classical" period, and two landscapes, *The Carters* (cat. 41) and *Pastoral Landscape with Rainbow* (cat. 40).

Rubens's career as a portraitist is reflected to a considerably lesser degree (cat. 21, 22), but the exhibition

FLEMISH MASTERS OUTSIDE THE CIRCLE OF RUBENS

NATALYA BABINA

Alongside paintings by Rubens and his closest followers, this exhibition includes works by lesser-known Flemish artists, some of them, such as Adriaen Brouwer and David Teniers the Younger, no less distinguished than the members of Rubens's circle.

Brouwer, a superb master of genre scenes, is represented by two paintings. While still young, the artist acquired a taste for the grotesque treatment of different character types from his predecessors Hieronymus Bosch and Pieter Bruegel the Elder. In his early *The Village Charlatan* (*Operation for Stone in the Head*; cat. 85), for example, this is manifest in the figures depicted as laughing idiots. Brouwer's subject was taken from the commonly held notion that there was a stone of stupidity inside one's head that could be removed, thus liberating man from his vices and negative characteristics. Despite the appearance of his characters, Brouwer's genre scenes, such as this example, are not so much monstrous as comical, and, ultimately, laughter is the hero of his works. While the painting is filled with distorted figures, seemingly leaving no place for the beauties of nature, closer study reveals the artist's sense of beauty in his engagement with landscape motifs and in the subtly elegant colouring of luminous yellow and pink tones. *Tavern Scene* (*The Village Fiddler*; cat. 86), dates from later in Brouwer's career, and is imbued with a slightly muted greyish-brown colour occasionally broken by areas of brighter colour, which was

characteristic of the tonal manner of painting during this period. Rubens's personal collection included seventeen works by Brouwer, and among the many paintings depicted in Corneille de Baellier's *The Cabinet of Rubens* (Palazzo Pitti, Florence) is a larger version of the Hermitage picture.

David Teniers the Younger, an outstanding Flemish master, produced a wide variety of works, including landscapes (*Landscape with Peasants before an Inn*; *Landscape with a Maid at a Well*; *Landscape with Peasants Bowling*; *Reaping*; cat. 77, 78, 79, 80); religious paintings (*The Temptation of St. Anthony*; cat. 74); genre scenes (*The Guardroom*; *The Kitchen*; cat. 75, 84); animal paintings (*Monkeys in a Kitchen*; cat. 83); and portraits (*Portrait of Antonius Triest, Bishop of Ghent, and his Brother Eugene, a Capuchin Monk*; cat. 35). Teniers was a highly skilled painter, not only of such intimate individual portraits, but also of official formal group portraits, one of which, *Portrait of Members of the Oude Voetboog Guild* (cat. 76), is considered among his masterpieces. An important feature of this work is the urban setting, and the dominance of its architectural forms sets the painting apart from similar group portraits by earlier Dutch artists, such as Hals and Rembrandt, in whose works the figures were given clear priority over any such specificity of setting.[7] The group portrait had gained renown during this period and occupies a special place among Flemish architectural views of the first half of the seventeenth century. Although Teniers did not specialize in painting architecture, his skill in its depiction was such that he was certainly the equal of Hendrick van Steenwijk the Younger (cat. 45) and Peeter Neeffs the Elder, both of whom specialized in this genre. Teniers set the *Members of the Oude Voetboog Guild* in Antwerp's main square, the Grote Markt, with the town hall as the background. The severity and simplicity of the building's left wing contrasts with the elaborately decorated projecting central section of the façade, whose massive pediment, paired columns, and niches decorated with statues of *The Virgin and Child on a Crescent Moon* (*The Immaculate Conception*), *Justice* and *Wisdom*, all convey the splendour and richness of its architectural forms. Painting even the tiniest details with incredible precision, Teniers seems to have been determined to evoke a forceful impression of this monument to Antwerp's power and prestige.

Also from the Antwerp period of the artist's career are two works, *Village Festival* and *Kermess* (cat. 81, 82), in which Teniers, like Rubens (*e.g. Kermess*, Musée du Louvre, Paris), continues a genre tradition deriving from the work of Pieter Bruegel the Elder. Echoes of Bruegel and Rubens are also found in works by less well-known Flemish artists, notably Frans Francken the Younger, three of whose works are included here.[8]

While Francken's *Seven Acts of Charity* (cat. 14) follows the Netherlandish adoption of seventeenth-century Roman classicism, his *Allegory of Opportunity* (cat. 15) reveals Baroque tendencies and the influence of Rubens. In the latter, the female figure under the canopy who personifies Good Government recalls, in her pose and the bend of her head, the enthroned Marie de' Medici beneath her baldachin in the sketch for Rubens's *Death of Henri IV and the Proclamation of the Regency* (Alte Pinakothek, Munich). Rubens's influence is also found in Francken's *David's Entry into Jerusalem* (cat. 16). There is an analogous but smaller painting of this subject in the Mittelrheinisches Museum in Mainz.[9] On the right side of the Hermitage composition is a turbaned rider holding a banner, missing from the picture in Mainz. His horse, depicted in a free, painterly manner, seems to have been borrowed from Rubens's *Perseus and Andromeda* (State Hermitage Museum, St. Petersburg). Nonetheless, Francken has reworked it, turning the winged Pegasus into an ordinary horse mounted by a soldier.

These two late works of the 1630s in Mainz and St. Petersburg are distinguished in that they borrow motifs from different sources. The painting in Mainz displays an indebtedness to the work of Pieter Bruegel the Elder,[10] and appears monotonous and archaic compared to the Hermitage work, where both iconography and composition seem considerably freer. One picture (Mainz) looks back to the past, to the traditions of the sixteenth century, and the other (that in the Hermitage), looks ahead to new trends associated with Rubens. Frans Francken the Younger was indeed interested in Rubens, and the characteristically Baroque features of his works. It was Rubens's influence that led Francken to adopt a similarly free approach to the representation of the human figure, a greater ease in conveying movement, and the ability to create lively groups and better describe them convincingly in their settings. Thus, despite their conservatism, Francken and other lesser-known Flemish artists revealed considerable flexibility as they reacted to the new tendencies emerging in Flemish painting during the seventeenth century.

NOTES

1. One contemporary who described Rubens thus was Constantijn Huygens, the Dutch writer and statesman, secretary to Stadthalter Frederik Hendrik, Prince of Orange; see J.A. Worp, "Fragment eener Autobiographie van Constantijn Huygens," *Bijdragen en mededeelingen van het Historisch Genootschap te Utrecht*, XVIII (1897), pp. 71–73.

2. Letter from Rubens to William Trumbell, September 13, 1621; translated in Magurn 1971, p. 77.

3. Cybele's pose recalls the figure of Peitho in *The Aldobrandini Wedding* (*c.* 325 BC), a fresco discovered in 1604 (now Pinacoteca Vaticana), and well known to Rubens.

4. A reference to Jacob de Backer's *Justitia et Pax* (Koninklijk Museum voor Schone Kunsten, Antwerp), which once hung in the Great Hall of the building belonging to the St. Lucasgilde [Guild of St. Luke] in Antwerp.

5. Jaffé 1963, pp. 232–34.

6. Letter from Rubens to Sir Dudley Carleton, April 28, 1618; translated in Magurn 1971, p. 61.

7. Teniers's group portrait in the Hermitage can be compared with the paintings *Officers of the Militia Company of St. Hadrian* by Hals (*c.* 1633; Frans Hals Museum, Haarlem) and *The Night Watch* by Rembrandt (1642; Rijksmuseum, Amsterdam).

8. Hermitage paintings by Frans Francken the Younger are virtually unknown to Western scholars. The only scholar to have made a monographic study of the work of Francken, Ursula Härting, in both a dissertation (Härting 1983) and monograph (Härting 1989), had not actually seen the Hermitage paintings; she relied exclusively on the Hermitage catalogue of 1958, which included no reproductions. At present, of the eight paintings published in the 1958 catalogue, only three signed works are in our opinion undoubted authentic works by Frans Francken the Younger: *Allegory of Opportunity* (listed in Cat. 1958 as *Allegory of Happiness*), *The Seven Acts of Charity* and *David's Entry into Jerusalem*.

9. Härting, without citing the Hermitage work, mentions only one known painting on this subject (Härting 1989, no. 11), that in Mainz. Hence the need for comparison of both works, revealing that despite an apparent likeness, the paintings differ not only in dimension (Hermitage painting 69.5 × 111.5 cm; Mainz painting 37 × 64.5 cm) but in a whole series of elements.

10. Closer study reveals that a boy in a tree on the left side of the Mainz picture recalls the birdnester in Pieter Bruegel the Elder's *The Peasant and the Birdnester* (Kunsthistorisches Museum, Vienna).

1
PETER PAUL RUBENS
1577 Siegen – 1640 Antwerp
The Adoration of the Shepherds,
1608
Oil on canvas, transferred from
panel in 1868. 63.5 × 47 cm
Provenance: Acquired in 1769
from the Brühl collection,
Dresden
Inv. no. GE 492
Selected literature: Somoff
1901, no. 659; Cat. 1958, p. 79;
Varshavskaya 1975, no. 1 (ed.
1989, pls. 1–2); Held 1980,
vol. I, no. 321; Cat. 1981, p. 60;
Jaffé 1989, no. 78; Bodart 1990,
no. 20; D. Jaffé 1992, no. 22.

The Hermitage sketch is a
modello, a preparatory, usually
small, image setting out a
future composition for
approval. As documents from
the archiepiscopal archive in
Fermo (published in Jaffé
1963) demonstrate, in February
1608 Flaminio Ricci, rector of
the congregation of Oratorians
in Rome, commissioned an
altarpiece of the Nativity from
Rubens for the Oratorian
church of Santo Spirito (San
Filippo Neri) in Fermo. While
this was only the artist's second
major commission in Italy,
together with the altarpiece for
Santa Maria in Vallicella in
Rome, it displays all of the
characteristic features that
mark the works of Rubens's
Italian period. It was the
success of these two
commissions that led the
young Flemish painter to be
accepted as one of the leading
artists in Rome.

As his prototype for the
composition of the Fermo
altarpiece, Rubens used
Correggio's famous *Adoration
of the Shepherds* (*La Notte*),
which he would have seen in
the church of San Prospero in
Reggio (now Gemäldegalerie,
Dresden). This painting
provided Rubens with the
overall two-tier arrangement of
the composition, the upper half
filled by a group of hovering
angels and the lower by Mary
and the shepherds grouped
about the Child in the manger.
The general principles of
arrangement along the
diagonal and into depth are
also based on Correggio's
painting, as are the particulars
of the scene: the shepherd
shown full length on the left,
partially cut off by the frame,
the young man turned towards
him and the shepherdess with
tightly clasped hands, and,
above all, the dramatic

illumination of all the figures
by a bright stream of light that
radiates from the body of the
Christ Child. In this sketch,
however, Rubens includes not
three shepherds, as in
Correggio's painting, but four.
Their emphatically plain and
simple appearance sets them
apart from Correggio's rather
prettified figures, and is
evidence of the influence on
Rubens of another Italian
artist, the great reformer of
Italian painting, Michelangelo
da Caravaggio. In particular,
the image of the old woman
beside the young shepherd,
with hands raised in awe, her
gaze turned reverentially
towards the Virgin, is a direct
reworking of a similar figure
from Caravaggio's *Madonna di
Loreto* in the church of
Sant'Agostino, in Rome
(Longhi 1927, pp. 191–97).
The impression made by
Caravaggio on Rubens is also
clear in the sharp contrasts of
light and shade. The influence
of Venetian painting is equally
evident, above all that of Titian.
Rubens's deep admiration for
Titian can be seen in the
sketch's impasto surface, the
free brush strokes and the
profoundly rich red tonality of
the painting that sets this work
apart from the light-filled
paintings of Rubens's later
period. To effect this imitation
of Venetian colour, Rubens
employed the red bole or clay
ground that contributed to the
painterly effect of works from
the Venetian school, rather
than the white chalk ground
conventionally used by Flemish
artists.

Rubens worked extremely
quickly on this commission.
On May 17, 1608, Ricci wrote
to Fermo that work was well
advanced, and less than two
months later, on July 7, he noted
that the painting was complete.
The Hermitage sketch was thus
probably produced no later than
May 1608.

A preparatory drawing, *Two
Shepherds and a Man in a
Turban*, is in the Fodor
collection of the Amsterdams
Historisches Museum, and the
finished painting is in the
Pinacoteca Civica, Fermo
(formerly the Constantini
Chapel, Santo Spirito/San
Filippo Neri). A slightly altered
version of the painting, by
Rubens and his workshop, is in
the Sint-Pauluskerk, Antwerp.
N.G.

KEY TO CONTRIBUTORS

E.A.   Elena Anisimova, Curator, Glass, State Hermitage Museum
N.B.   Natalya Babina, Curator, Flemish Paintings, State Hermitage Museum
N.G.   Natalya Gritsay, Curator, Flemish Paintings, State Hermitage Museum
O.K.   Olga Kostiuk, Curator, Jewellery, State Hermitage Museum
T.K.   Tatyana Kossourova, Curator, Western European Decorative Arts, State Hermitage Museum
Y.K.   Yulia Kagan, Curator, Gems, State Hermitage Museum
A.L.   Alexey Larionov, Curator, Northern European Drawings, State Hermitage Museum
M.L.   Marina Lopato, Curator, Metalwork, State Hermitage Museum
Y.M.   Yurij Miller, Curator, Arms and Armour, State Hermitage Museum
E.S.   Elena Shlikevich, Curator, Western European Ivories, State Hermitage Museum

2

PETER PAUL RUBENS
1577 Siegen – 1640 Antwerp
*The Assumption and Coronation
of the Virgin*, 1611
Oil on canvas, transferred from
panel in 1868. 106 × 78 cm
Provenance: Acquired in 1770
at the sale of François Ignace
de Dufresne, Amsterdam,
August 22, 1770 (lot 134)
Inv. no. GE 1703
Selected literature: Somoff
1901, no. 547; Cat. 1958, p. 94;
Varshavskaya 1975, no. 3 (ed.
1989, pls. 4–7); Held 1980,
vol. I, no. 374; Cat. 1981, p. 61;
Freedberg 1984, no. 46; Jaffé
1989, no. 149; Gritsay 1990,
no. 12; D. Jaffé 1992, no. 23

Baudouin (1968, pp. 11–13)
suggested that this sketch was
one of two *modelli* presented by
Rubens in April 1611 to the
Chapter of Antwerp Cathedral
for an intended altarpiece to
stand upon the main altar, for
which the subject was to be
"Our Lord Inviting His Bride
from Lebanon to Her
Coronation" (a reference to The
Song of Solomon 4:8; see Held
1980). As Baudouin noted, the
modello presented in March
1611 by Rubens's teacher, Otto
Vaenius, and rejected by the
Chapter, was of the same
subject.
    The iconography of the
Hermitage *modello* is unusual,
uniting two events in a single
composition, the Assumption
and the Coronation of the
Virgin, subjects to which
Rubens turned separately on
numerous occasions. In the
lower half is "the miracle with
the roses," in which the
Apostles and the Three Maries
(the Virgin Mary, Mary
Magdalene and Mary the wife
of Cleophas) gather at the
entrance to the Virgin's tomb
and find only flowers in the
empty grave, as her body had
been raised up to the heavens.
(A further discussion of the
iconography can be found in
Réau 1957, pp. 602–26.)
    The upper half of the
composition contains the
Coronation, an unusual image
in that Rubens has portrayed
Christ alone, rather than as
part of the Trinity according to
accepted Netherlandish
practice from the fifteenth
century onward. Freedberg
(1978, pp. 432–33) considered
the point of departure for such
a treatment probably to have
been Geronimo Nadal's
Counter-Reformatory books,
Adnotationes et meditationes in

Evangelia, published in 1595,
with engravings by Jerome
Wierix (1553–1619). Four of the
engravings concern the Death,
Burial, Assumption and
Coronation of the Virgin
(pls. 150–53). The third print
(pl. 152), bearing the heading
"Suscitatur Virgo Mater a Filio,"
served according to Freedberg as
the source for the composition
in the Hermitage *modello*, or at
least for its upper portion.
    The Hermitage *modello* is
Rubens's earliest depiction of
the Assumption of the Virgin.
As was first indicated by Rooses
(1886–92, vol. II, p. 189), the
lower portion was repeated
with minor changes in a later
painting by Rubens of 1614–15,
the monumental *Assumption of
the Virgin* from the Jesuit
church in Antwerp, now in the
Kunsthistorisches Museum in
Vienna. During restoration of
the Vienna painting, an
original version of the
composition was discovered
beneath the upper layers of
paint, a composition in some
details identical to the
Hermitage *modello*. The
foreground space, for example,
was originally enclosed by a
group of Apostles and Holy
Women, and there were
cypress trees in the foreground
(Prohaska 1977, pp. 69–70), as
in the Hermitage *modello*.
N.G.

3

PETER PAUL RUBENS
1577 Siegen – 1640 Antwerp
*Roman Charity, or Cimon and
Pero*, 1610–12
Oil on canvas, transferred from
panel in 1846. 140.5 × 180.3 cm
Provenance: Carel van den
Bosch, Bishop of Bruges, in
mid-17th century; acquired in
1768, with the collection of
Count Cobenzl, Brussels
Inv. no. GE 470
Selected literature: Somoff
1901, no. 1785; Cat. 1958, p. 79;
Varshavskaya 1975, no. 5 (ed.
1989, pls. 8–9); Cat. 1981,
p. 61; Jaffé 1989, no. 192;
McGrath 1997, no. 18

The subject of this painting is
taken from a book by the first-
century Roman writer Valerius
Maximus, *Factorum
dictorumque memorabilium*
(Great Deeds and Speeches;
book 5, chapter IV). Pero, a
young Greek woman, mother
of a newborn infant, sought to
save her father Cimon, who
had been imprisoned and
sentenced to death by
starvation, by feeding him at
her breast, since she was
unable to bring food past his
guards.

This Classical image of self-
effacing filial loyalty is treated
by Rubens within the context of
Christian charity. Charity is
considered one of the greatest
Christian virtues, expressed in
good deeds toward the healing
of both physical and spiritual
wounds. The good Christian
must feed the hungry, give
drink to the thirsty, clothe the
naked, visit the sick and those
in prison, receive the weary
traveller and bury the poor. A
subtext of this work is the
liberation of a man who has set
out on the path of true
Christian faith, rejecting the
ways of the devil and sin. In the
top left part of the composition,

on the window grille that lets a
feeble light into the dungeon,
is a spider and its web, an
element of some significance
as the spider was a symbol of
the devil, seeking to catch man
at every turn, tempting weak
human souls into the web of
sin. Mixed in with the straw
on which Cimon lies chained
to the wall, are ears of wheat,
symbolizing the bread of the
Eucharist and thus Communion,
one of the central mysteries of
the Christian Church.

Rubens turned to the legend
of Cimon and Pero – a very
popular subject in seventeenth-

century Western European art
– on a number of occasions,
but the Hermitage painting is
his earliest treatment of it. The
canvas is also one of the best
works from Rubens's
"classical" period, with its
marked clarity of construction
and the rich and beautiful
plasticity of the figures, while
the nature of the painting and
the use of bright local colours
clearly reveal the Netherlandish
tradition's propensity for rich,
"open" colours.
N.G.

4

PETER PAUL RUBENS
1577 Siegen – 1640 Antwerp
The Union of Earth and Water,
c. 1618
Oil on canvas. 222.5 × 180.5 cm
Provenance: Chigi collection,
Rome; possibly from the
collection of Fabio Chigi (Pope
Alexander VII, 1655–1667);
acquired between 1798 and
1800 by Paul I, for his newly
built Mikhail Castle in
St. Petersburg (Kalnitskaya
1995, pp. 80–81).
Inv. no. GE 464
Selected literature: Michel 1771,
pp. 315–16; Somoff 1901,
no. 554; Cat. 1958, p. 80;
Varshavskaya 1975, no. 16 (ed.
1989, pls. 33–36); Held 1980,
vol. I, p. 325–26; Cat. 1981, p. 61;
Jaffé 1989, p. 206, note 304;
Gritsay 1993a, pp. 49–56.

Personifications of Water and Earth are seen here in the act of forming a union. The allegorical character of the picture has long been recognized (Michel 1771), but a detailed interpretation of the painting as an allegorical union between the god of the River Scheldt (Scaldanus), and the goddess of Antwerp (Antverpia), was not proposed for another two hundred years (Varshavskaya 1975). Varshavskaya related its creation to a subject that formed a constant element of the decorations erected from 1594 onward for the numerous ceremonial entrances into Antwerp of new rulers of the Southern Netherlands. This recurrent theme was the liberation of the Scheldt, the river on which Antwerp stands, and the restoration of the city's former glory as a naval port. This allegorical representation of the interrelationship between Antwerp's prosperity and the newly revitalized river became particularly relevant after the conclusion in 1609 of the Twelve Years' Truce with the Republic of the United Provinces, which revived hopes for a removal of the Dutch blockade of the Scheldt's mouth. Varshavskaya connected this painting with an iconographically similar allegory by Abraham Janssens, *Scaldis and Antverpia* (Koninklijk Museum voor Schone Kunsten, Antwerp), commissioned from the artist to decorate Antwerp Town Hall in 1609 – *i.e.* the year the Twelve Years' Truce was concluded.

Evidence for such an interpretation is to be found above all in the attributes of the main figures. Although the trident is an emblem of Neptune, ruler of the seas, and thus a customary symbol of the seas and oceans, the urn with cascading water was also traditionally employed as a symbol of rivers, as are the god's short beard and his garland of water lilies. That Rubens specifically intended a river god was suggested in an eighteenth-century reading of the painting as an allegory of the River Tiber (Michel 1771, pp. 35, 315–16). The putti in the foreground, one of whom holds a fish in his hand, personify the watery elements, and as part of the river god's suite they would seem also to symbolize fertility. Another symbol of fertility is the cornucopia that the personification of Earth holds in her right hand. An overflowing cornucopia is the traditional attribute both of the goddess of the Earth, "the great Mother Cybele," and a city's personified "Fortune" or Tyche. It is also the constant attribute of the personification of *Abundantia* and the regular companion of *Pax* – symbol of prosperity, peace and happiness. Another symbol of peace and happiness is probably to be found in the garland of myrtle with which the female figure with eagle's wings (*Victoria*) crowns Cybele. Overall the composition can be seen as embodying an accepted formula established in the emblematical literature from the sixteenth century (Baumstark 1974, p. 148): "Ex pace ubertas" – Abundance comes from Peace (see cat. 9, *The Arch of Ferdinand*). The two divinities conclude a peace, uniting their hands in a gesture of agreement; the triton blows on his conch, calming the waves, in which children play. Even the wild tiger has been tamed: he approaches the cornucopia's fruits, as if recalling that legendary "golden age" in the history of mankind when people and all the creatures of the earth lived with each other in peace and harmony and the world knew no beasts of prey (Genesis 1:30; Ovid, *Metamorphoses*, I:89–112).

Rubens has depicted several kinds of shells and other marine life that were regular features of contemporary *Kunst und Wunderkammers*. For instance, a key attribute of the Triton is a conch (Ovid, *Metamorphoses*, I:330), here represented by a polished shell of the so-called "Charonia tritonis," one of the largest molluscs of the group of "Triton trumpets," used for alarm and military trumpets even in antiquity. It is possible that this example of the highly prized Charonia shell was from the artist's own collection. Among the shells scattered at the feet of Cybele and Neptune, serving as a further symbol of the watery elements, can be identified, in the left foreground, a shell of the large tropical Achatina snail.

It appears that, with the exception of the cornucopia, the tiger, and perhaps the putti in the foreground (those elements having been executed by the master's assistants), the painting is the work of Rubens himself (Varshavskaya 1975). Although the image of the cornucopia and its fruits (apples, grapes, pumpkin, figs, pomegranates, apricots, redcurrants and mulberries) recalls the works of Snyders, its execution and surface texture are very different from his work. These passages show none of the sheen and the brilliance, or indeed the transparent surfaces familiar from Snyder's autograph paintings.

A preparatory sketch (without the putti and tiger, the latter being replaced by a satyr with fruits of the earth and with a flying Cupid in place of the winged female figure crowning Cybele) is in the Fitzwilliam Museum, Cambridge (inv. no. 267; oil on panel, 34.5 × 30 cm; Held 1980, vol. I, no. 238).

The painting was copied and engraved on numerous occasions. The central group (without the winged female figure crowning Cybele, and with Cybele wearing a mural crown) was used in a painting by the Dutch artist Isaak Isaacz (1599–1688), *Allegory of Sound* (Statens Museum for Kunst, Copenhagen; inv. no. 343), painted in 1622. This was commissioned by King Christian IV of Denmark for his palace at Rosenborg (see F. Becket: *Kristien IV og Malerkunsten*, Copenhagen, 1937, p. 98, pl. 134). A similar image, also of horizontal format, was in a private collection in the seventeenth century in Antwerp and figures in a painting by an unknown Flemish artist of *c.* 1620, *Cognoscenti in a Room Hung with Pictures* (National Gallery, London; inv. no. 1287), where it can be seen on the right wall in the second row from the top.
N.G.

45

5

PETER PAUL RUBENS
1577 Siegen – 1640 Antwerp
The Arrival in Lyons, 1622
Oil on canvas, transferred from
panel in 1893. 33.5 × 24.2 cm
Provenance: Probably in the
collection of Claude de Maugis,
Abbé de Saint-Ambroise, Paris,
in the 17th century; acquired in
1772 with the Crozat collection,
Paris
Inv. no. GE 505
Selected literature: Cat. Crozat
1755, p. 8; Somoff 1901,
no. 567; Cat. 1958, p. 82;
Varshavskaya 1975, no. 24
(ed. 1989, pl. 53); Cat. 1981,
pp. 62–63; Held 1980, vol. I,
no. 64; Jaffé 1989, no. 724;
Gritsay 1993, no. 24; Renger
1997, no. 13, p. 35; Gritsay
1998, no. 8

This sketch, in lightly coloured
grisaille, presents an allegorical
depiction of the marriage of
Marie de' Medici and Henri IV
at Lyons. The king first met his
bride at Lyons on December 9,
1600, and the official wedding
ceremony took place in the
cathedral there eight days later.
This is a rough outline, or
bozzetto, for the tenth
composition in the cycle of
twenty-four pictures
representing *The Life of Marie
de' Medici* that was
commissioned from Rubens in
1622 by the French queen (now
in the Louvre). The cycle was
conceived to decorate the
gallery in the west wing of her
new Luxembourg Palace in
Paris. This sketch is the only
surviving preparatory work for
the entire cycle.
    Following the traditions of
court art (von Simson 1936,
p. 312), Rubens presented the
king and queen as Olympian
gods enthroned in the clouds.
They are easily identified as
Jupiter and Juno by their
attributes, he by his eagle and
she by her peacock, with
Hymenaeus, the god of
marriage, presiding over their
union. In the lower part of the
composition the
personification of the city of
Lyons, wearing a mural crown,
with a shield bearing the city's
arms in her hand, rides in a
chariot drawn by her
eponymous lions. A surviving
manuscript setting out the
programme for the cycle
explains that "le chariot est
tresné par deux lyons pour
représenter tout ce qui fust fait
à l'entrée du Roy et de la Royne
à Lyon" (the chariot is drawn by
two lions to represent all that

has been done for the entry of
the king and queen at Lyons;
Thuillier 1969, p. 57). This
same motif has also been seen
as a symbolic depiction of the
expression "Etiam ferocissimos
domari" (I tame even the most
ferocious), which derives from
one of the emblems of Andrea
Alciati, included in the book
Emblematum Liber, issued in
Augsburg in 1531 (von Simson
1936, p. 312; Held 1980, vol. I,
pp. 106–07). Thus, in the final
version of the scene (Musée du
Louvre, Paris), the cupids
seated on the lions, holding
burning torches in their hands,
should be understood as
indicating that Henri IV is
overcome by the force of love,
which can tame even the most
ferocious lion. The depiction of
the chariot itself is reminiscent
of a sixteenth-century Italian
cameo, *The Triumph of Semele*
(Hermitage, inv. no. K 601),
that was owned by Rubens, and
which he believed to be
ancient.
    Painted in 1622, this sketch
differs little from the final
version. In the Louvre painting,
beyond the addition of the
cupids' torches, there is a
chariot with two peacocks
alongside Juno; the winged
genius at the feet of the divine
couple is missing; Juno wears a
diadem upon her head; in the
depth of the composition we
see the city of Lyons; and at the
top is a rainbow and a six-
pointed star.
N.G.

6

PETER PAUL RUBENS
1577 Siegen – 1640 Antwerp
The Vision of St. Ildefonso,
1630–31
Oil on canvas. 52 × 83 cm
Provenance: Clemens August,
Duke of Bavaria, Prince-Elector
and Archbishop of Cologne;
sale of Clemens August,
December 10, 1764, Paris
(lot 28); belonged to the Paris
auctioneer Boileau *père*, and
while in his possession was
seen by the collector Lalive de
Jully (Castan 1885, pp. 5–6);

acquired before 1774
Inv. no. GE 520
Selected literature: Somoff
1901, no. 557; Cat. 1958, p. 93;
Vlieghe 1972–73, vol. II,
no. 117b; Varshavskaya 1975,
no. 31 (ed. 1989, pls. 61–63);
Held 1980, vol. I, no. 412; Jaffé
1989, no. 996; Gritsay 1993,
no. 26; Duerloo 1998, no. 393;
Duerloo 1999, no. 97

According to medieval legend,
the Virgin appeared in a church
to St. Ildefonso (606–667),
Bishop of Toledo from 657, and

presented him with a rich
chasuble as a reward for his
upholding of the dogma of the
Immaculate Conception. In
this sketch the Virgin is seated
on a throne and surrounded by
saints: to the left – St. Rosalia,
to the right – Saints Agnes,
Catherine and Barbara (Rooses
1886–92, vol. II, no. 456). In
the foreground to either side of
the central group are the
painter's donors: the Infanta
Isabella (1566–1633) and
Archduke Albert (1559–1621),
who kneel and observe the

miraculous event. They are
accompanied by the standing
figures of St. Elizabeth of
Hungary and St. Albert of Liège,
who wears cardinal's robes.

   The Hermitage composition
is a preparatory sketch for a
triptych now in the
Kunsthistorisches Museum in
Vienna. This was commis-
sioned from Rubens by the
Infanta Isabella, ruler of the
Southern Netherlands, for the
Brotherhood of St. Ildefonso in
the church of Sint-Jacob op de
Coudenberg in Brussels, in

memory of her late husband,
Archduke Albert, the founder
of the Brotherhood. The main
difference between the sketch
and the final version is that the
altarpiece consists of three
independent parts, each with
its own frame, while the sketch
displays a single unified
composition.

   Since Rubens's triptych was
installed in the church and
consecrated in 1632, the sketch
should be dated to *c.* 1630–31.
N.G.

7
PETER PAUL RUBENS
1577 Siegen – 1640 Antwerp
The Apotheosis of James I,
c. 1632–1633
Oil on canvas. 89.7 × 55.3 cm
Provenance: 1639 collection of
Charles I; collection of Godfrey
Kneller, London; collection of
Sir Robert Walpole, London,
then Houghton Hall, Norfolk;
acquired in 1779 with the
Walpole collection, Norfolk
Inv. no. GE 507
Selected literature: *Aedes* 1/52,
pp. 69–70; Somoff 1901, no.
573; Cat. 1958, p. 93;
Varshavskaya 1975, no. 33
(ed. 1989, pls. 67–8); Held
1980, vol. I, no. 135; Cat. 1981,
p. 63; Jaffé 1989, no. 1004;
Gritsay 1991, p. 130; Gritsay
1993, no. 25

This is a sketch for the central
medallion of the ceiling of the
Banqueting House at Whitehall
(London), Rubens's only
decorative ensemble to survive
in its original location.
Designed by Inigo Jones and
built between 1619 and 1622,
the Banqueting House was
intended for court ceremonies
and theatrical presentations.
The idea of inviting Rubens to
paint the ceiling would seem to
have arisen in 1621, but it was
only in the winter of 1629–30,
when he was in London on a
diplomatic mission concerning
preliminary negotiations for the
conclusion of a peace between
Spain and England, that these
plans were finalized. Rubens
was officially commissioned to
paint the work by Charles I
(r. 1600–1649) with the
intention that it glorify the
deeds of his father James I
(r. 1603–1625), who united the
disparate parts of the kingdom
and who brought peace and
prosperity.

The composition adapts the
conventional scheme for the
apotheosis of Roman emperors.
James I, sceptre in hand, sits on
a globe borne by an eagle with
Jupiter's thunderbolts in its
talons, surrounded by
allegorical personages. To the
right is Justice with her scales
and sword, to the left Religion
before an altar and Faith with a
book; a winged Victory with a
caduceus and Minerva with her
sword and shield jointly crown
James with a laurel wreath,
while fluttering cupids bear the
royal crown and orb, palm and
olive branches, and herald the
event with trumpets.

There are only slight
differences between the sketch,
produced *c.* 1632–33, and the
finished work, which is set
within an oval frame that
underscores the structure of
Rubens's composition. In the
final painting Justice holds
forked lightning, and Minerva
bears only a sword; in the
sketch the figures are arranged
more freely with more
pronounced foreshortening,
particularly the figure of James.

The original sketch for the
ceiling (Mrs. Humphrey Brand
Collection, Glynde Place, East
Sussex) includes seven of the
nine compositions – the central
oval and the side friezes and
ovals. A sketch for the figures of
Faith and Victory is in the
Louvre.
N.G.

8
PETER PAUL RUBENS
1577 Siegen – 1640 Antwerp
The Arch of Hercules (front face),
1634–35
Oil on canvas, transferred from
panel in 1871. 103 × 72 cm
Provenance: Antwerp Town
Hall (property of the
magistrature); sale of the
collection of Prosper Henricus
Lankrink, London, May 23,
1693; collection of Sir Robert
Walpole, Houghton Hall,
Norfolk; acquired in 1779 with
the Walpole collection, Norfolk
Inv. no. GE 503
Selected literature: *Aedes* 1752,
p. 70; Somoff 1901, no. 563;
Cat. 1958, p. 94; Martin 1972,
no. 52a; Varshavskaya 1975,
no. 40 (ed. 1989, pl. 89); Cat.
1981, p. 65; Jaffé 1989, no. 1162;
Held 1980, vol. I, no. 165

Another of the series of oil
sketches for the *Pompa Introitus
Ferdinandi* (ceremonial entrance
of Ferdinand) on April 17, 1635
(see cat. 9), this sketch presents
the design for the front of the
arch near the entrance to the
abbey of St. Michael.

Installed above the arch is
a framed picture showing
*Hercules at the Crossroads
between Virtue and Vice*. Vice is
represented by Venus with
Bacchus and Cupid, and Virtue
by Minerva, who summons the
hero, intended to represent
Ferdinand, to the Temple of
Glory. The subject is taken from
a story told by the ancient
Sophist, the philosopher
Prodicus. Rubens would have
known the story from either
Xenophon, *Memoirs of Socrates*
(II, 1:21–34) or Hesiod, *Works
and Days* (287–91).

The arch is crowned with a
palm tree, symbol of virtue,
justice and moral victory; the
palm is winged, which indicates
that it should be understood as
victory, glory, peace and reason.
To the sides of the palm are
banners and two Victories
holding the monograms of King
Philip IV and Ferdinand. On
the cornice is a sphinx, symbol
of firmness, agility and
prudence.

It is possible that the sketch
was executed between
December 1634 and January
1635 (Held 1980), when the
Fugger family bank provided
funds for this third arch.
N.G.

9
PETER PAUL RUBENS
1577 Siegen – 1640 Antwerp
The Arch of Ferdinand (*rear face*),
1634
Oil on canvas, transferred from
panel in 1867. 104 × 72.5 cm
Provenance: Antwerp Town
Hall (property of the
magistrature); sale of the
collection of Prosper Henricus
Lankrink, London, May 23,
1693; collection of Sir Robert
Walpole, Houghton Hall,
Norfolk; acquired in 1779 with
the Walpole collection, Norfolk
Inv. no. GE 502
Selected literature: *Aedes* 1752,
p. 70; Somoff 1901, no. 564;
Cat. 1958, p. 94; Martin 1972,
no. 40a; Varshavskaya 1975,
no. 37 (ed. 1989, pls. 82–83);
Held 1980, vol. I, no. 160; Cat.
1981, p. 64; Jaffé 1989, no. 1116

This is one of a series of oil
sketches for the ceremonial
decoration of Antwerp on the
occasion of the *Pompa Introitus
Ferdinandi* (ceremonial entrance
of Ferdinand) on April 17, 1635.
This sketch represents a design
for the rear of the arch erected
at the entrance on to Lange
Nieuw-straat, and was intended
as an allegorical representation
of the joint victory over the
Swedes at Nördlingen in
Germany on September 4–5,
1634 by Cardinal Infante
Ferdinand and Ferdinand, King
of Hungary (future Emperor
Ferdinand III).
    Displayed over the central
span of the arch is a gold-
framed painting representing
The Triumph of Ferdinand.
Ferdinand, in a chariot, is being
crowned by Victory; over his
head flies another Victory with a
palm, the symbol of peace, and
the figure of Hope with a
trophy. A half-length sculpted
portrait of the genius of
Nördlingen and a *labarum* or
imperial standard with the letter
F are being carried in front of
the chariot, the latter
surrounded by prisoners of war
led by a soldier carrying
trophies and a standard-bearer.
Above the painting is the
Spanish king's coat of arms,
protected by two lions; to the
sides are statues of Honour
(left), with a sceptre and
cornucopia, and Virtue (right),
who bears the club and lion
skin of Hercules and carries a
sword. In the left niche is a
figure of the king's Liberality
pouring coins from a
cornucopia; in the right niche is
Providence with a globe and
helm. Medallions show Nobility

(left) and Ferdinand's Youth
(right). At top left and right are
trumpeting Glories, trophies
and fettered prisoners, with
Victories holding shields. The
arch is crowned with a winged
horse and the barely discernible
figure of the Morning Star
(Lucifer) or Aurora.
    The sketch was clearly
painted before November 24,
1634 (Varshavskaya 1975;
Held 1980), when the wooden
framework for the arch was
ordered.
N.G.

10

PETER PAUL RUBENS
1577 Siegen – 1640 Antwerp
The Temple of Janus, 1634
Oil on panel. 70 × 65.5 cm
Provenance: Antwerp Town
Hall (property of the
magistrature); sale of the
collection of Prosper Henricus
Lankrink, London, May 23,
1693; collection of Sir Robert
Walpole, Houghton Hall,
Norfolk; acquired in 1779 with
the Walpole collection, Norfolk
Inv. no. GE 500
Selected literature: *Aedes* 1752,
p. 70; Somoff 1901, no. 566;
Cat. 1958, p. 94; Martin 1972,
no. 44a; Varshavskaya 1975,
no. 38 (ed. 1989, pls. 84–85);
Held 1980, vol. I, no. 161; Jaffé
1989, no. 1151; Thomas 1998,
no. 406; Thomas 1999, no. 114

This is one of a series of
sketches commissioned for the
decoration of Antwerp on the
occasion of the *Pompa Introitus
Ferdinandi* (ceremonial
entrance of Ferdinand) on
April 17, 1635. This design was
for the portico of the Dairy
Market (Melkmarket).

According to legend, as
related by Plutarch and
Macrobius, the Temple of
Janus, the ancient Roman god
of time and beginnings, was
erected by Numa Pompilius,
who introduced the custom of
keeping the temple gates closed
in times of peace and open
upon declaration of war.

In Rubens's sketch, the
doors of the temple are pried
open by personifications of
Discord, symbolized by her
hair of snakes, and one of the
ancient furies, Tisiphone, who
overturns an urn of blood, as a
bloodthirsty Harpy flies
overhead. The blindfolded
personification of Fury bursts
through the open doors
brandishing a sword and
holding aloft a flaming torch.
To the right, the goddess of
Peace with a caduceus, symbol
of peaceful activity, overturns a
cornucopia in her frantic
attempt to reclose the door.
Behind her is Piety with a
patera who gestures towards a
burning altar. In the background is the Infanta Isabella,
attired as a widowed nun.

Under the portico on the left
Rubens depicted the horrors of
war: a soldier drags a woman
by her hair as she tries in vain
to protect her infant child;
above her is Death with a
scythe and torch, and the flying
figure of Famine. On the right,
in contrast, are the benefits of

peace: Security with hand on
heart, and Tranquillity, with
sheaves of grain and poppies in
one hand and a palm in the
other; between them is a stone
pillar symbolizing Permanence.
Above the figures of Security
and Tranquillity is a medallion
with paired profiles of Honour
and Virtue set within a wreath
formed of a lyre, brushes, a
palette, compass and ruler. To
the left, above the scene
showing the horrors of war, is a
double profile of Pallor and Fear
set within a wreath of thorns,

whips and chains. Over the
portico to the left are Poverty
and Grief; they lean toward an
empty candlestick on which
stands a pedestal emblazoned
with lowered funerary torches.
Above the portico to the right is
Abundance with wheat sheaves
and a cornucopia, and Fertility
scattering gifts from her
cornucopia. Between them
stands a burning candle atop a
pedestal on which are depicted
two intertwined cornucopias
with children's heads,
symbolizing Happiness.

The motif of the Temple of
Janus with closed doors was
used for many years in the
decoration of "secular
apotheoses" and "triumphal
entries" to symbolize the idea of
the peace a ruler could bring his
subjects. Varshavskaya (1967
and 1975) stressed that in the
Hermitage sketch the open
doors represent an urgent call
to decisive action aimed directly
at the governor; Ferdinand was
here called upon to follow the
example of his predecessor, the
Infanta Isabella, who sought

peace, and to "close the doors of
Janus" (*Janum cludere*).

The sketch must have been
produced before December 7,
1634 when the wooden
structure was ordered
(Varshavskaya 1975; Held 1980).
N.G.

II

ANTHONY VAN DYCK
1599 Antwerp – 1641 London
The Apparition of Christ to His Disciples (*The Incredulity of St. Thomas*), early 1620s
Oil on canvas. 147 × 110.3 cm
Provenance: Acquired in 1772 with the Crozat collection, Paris
Inv. no. GE 542
Selected literature: Cat. Crozat 1755, p. 15; Somoff 1901, no. 607; Cat. 1958, p. 52; Varshavskaya 1963, no. 8; Cat. 1981, p. 39; Larsen 1988, no. 284.

In the eighteenth century, while in the Crozat collection, this painting was identified as "The Incredulity of St. Thomas" (John 20:26–29), an identification that was retained until 1981. In that year, M. Varshavskaya listed the painting as *The Apparition of Christ to His Disciples* (John 20:19–23), even though it is difficult to identify Christ's disciples precisely. It is possible that the Hermitage work, like the central part of Rubens's *Rockox Triptych* (Koninklijk Museum voor Schone Kunsten, Antwerp), the composition of which it recalls very closely (Rosenberg 1921, p. 74), is in fact a doctrinal work illustrating the subject "Christum videre" (The Apparition of Christ), in which the resurrected Christ appears to three of his disciples, two of whom (Peter and Paul?) look upon him with reverential amazement, while the third (Thomas?) kneels so that he might better see the wounds made by the nails in Christ's palms. The identification of Rubens's Antwerp panel as "Christum videre" seems very likely, since we know the purpose of the *Rockox Triptych* to which it belonged. (Monballieu 1970, pp. 133–55; von Simson 1996, p. 131.) Rubens painted it in 1613–15 as an epitaph, commissioned by the Antwerp burgomaster Nicolaes Rockox (cat. 24) to be placed on his tomb in the church of the Minorite Recollets in Antwerp. But of van Dyck's painting, the early history of which remains unknown, such an interpretation must remain speculative.

The Hermitage painting is usually dated to the early 1620s, the artist's years in Italy (Glück 1931, fig. 136; Varshavskaya 1963); the exception is Larsen (1988), who regards it as earlier, *c.* 1618–20. Although the composition is close to Rubens's Antwerp panel in the tight grouping of the figures and in their gesticulations, it differs considerably in style. It has none of the tangible three-dimensionality of the figures found in the paintings of Rubens, nor the intense drama of the action. The image of Christ is the very embodiment of restraint and vulnerability. His character, like the moderated colouring and the lighting, in which bright areas of colour alternate with transparent, soft half-shadow, bring the Hermitage canvas close to van Dyck's *Ecce Homo* of 1625–26 (Barber Institute of Fine Arts, Birmingham).
N.G.

12
JACOB VAN OOST THE ELDER
1601 Bruges – 1671 Bruges
David with the Head of Goliath,
1643
Oil on canvas. 102 × 81 cm
Signed and dated right, on the
sword: *Ja.v. Oost F. 1643*
Provenance: Van Praet sale of
the collection of Charles-Jozef
de Schryvere in Bruges, June 1,
1763 (lot 49); acquired in 1895
from V.P. Kostromitinova
Inv. no. GE 676
Selected literature: Somoff
1901, no. 1840; Cat. 1958, p. 76;
Cat. 1981, p. 57; Meulemeester
1984, no. A 21

As the Israelites and the
Philistines stood facing each
other on the field of battle, the
giant Goliath emerged from the
ranks of the Philistines and
challenged his opponents to
send a single champion to fight
him. The young David, who had
left his father's flock to visit his
elder brothers, decided to try his
strength against him. Taking up
his sling and several stones, he
launched a stone that hit
Goliath in the forehead. The
giant was struck dead and the
Philistines fled.

Here the Bruges painter
Jacob van Oost depicts the
triumphant young David
carrying the head and sword of
the defeated Goliath. Although
Dutch and Flemish masters
repeatedly depicted the biblical
story, the graphic image of
David with his terrifying trophy
was rare in seventeenth-century
Flemish art. Van Oost's models
were Italian, most probably
Caravaggio's famous painting in
the Galleria Borghese, Rome.
The two works are related not
so much by their style as by
their iconography, derived from
the Catholic Church's
traditional interpretation of
David's victory over Goliath as a
prefiguration of Christ's victory
over Satan.

Van Oost's painting comes
from the artist's mature period
and is notable for its pale
colours and its delicate
brushwork. David's figure and
pose in the Hermitage canvas
are precisely repeated in a work
showing a young painter with a
folder of drawings (Christie's,
New York, on January 18, 1983,
lot 54), possibly the work of the
artist's son, Jacob van Oost the
Younger (1639–1713).
N.G.

13

Jacob Jordaens
1593 Antwerp – 1678 Antwerp
Cleopatra's Banquet, 1653
Oil on canvas. 156.4 × 149.3 cm
Signed and dated top centre: *J Jor. 1653*
Provenance: Transferred in 1937 *via* the State Museums Fund, Leningrad
Inv. no. GE 8536
Selected literature: Gritsay 1979, no. 9; Cat. 1981, p. 49 (as workshop of Jordaens); d'Hulst 1993, no. A 87

Jordaens here turned to a subject popular in European art of the sixteenth and

seventeenth centuries, an episode from the story of Anthony and Cleopatra. Pliny, the first-century encyclopedist, records in his *Natural History* (Book IX, 58) how the Egyptian ruler Cleopatra (68–30 BC) made a bet with the Roman commander Mark Anthony (82–30 BC) that she could spend more than ten million *sestertii* on a single feast. Cleopatra won the bet by drinking a cup of vinegar in which she had dissolved a large and priceless pearl removed from her earring.

In Jordaens's painting we see the oft-depicted moment at which the Egyptian queen drops

the pearl into the goblet. This festive episode allowed artists to depict a rich and colourful scene of court life and was thus especially prized in the decorative arts, often being used as the subject for tapestries. Indeed, Jordaens's painting shares certain formal characteristics with the textile arts. It is similar to tapestries in its decorative richness and has an affinity with the all-over patterning of carpets in its filling of the surface with imagery. Jordaens also introduced a moralizing tone, clearly echoing the interpretation of the subject in

the work of the Dutch poet Jacob Cats (1577–1660). In Cats's interpretation, Mark Anthony, by breaking his connubial vows and surrendering himself up to his fateful passion for Cleopatra, was also untrue to his own duty as ruler and military commander and thus brought about his own death (d'Hulst 1974, pp. 377–79). Jordaens's introduction of a laughing jester pointing at Cleopatra joins a series of related symbolic references, such as the parrot on the jester's right hand, perhaps alluding to eroticism, and the two dogs in the

foreground – traditional symbols of fidelity – which may represent an ironic commentary on the queen's lack of restraint.

This painting dates from Jordaens's late period and has all the features to be found in his more decorative works of that time. It is perhaps a mate to *The Death of Cleopatra* in the Staatliche Museen, Kassel; both paintings are usually identified as being from a series of *The History of Cleopatra*, mentioned in the will of Giacomo Antonio Carenna of March 9, 1669 (Denucé 1932, pp. 259–60). N.G.

14
FRANS FRANCKEN THE YOUNGER
1581 Antwerp – 1642 Antwerp
The Seven Acts of Charity, c. 1617
Oil on canvas, transferred from
panel in 1818. 68.5 × 110.5 cm
Signed bottom left: *D Ffranck in
et F*
Provenance: Acquired before
1859
Inv. no. GE 395
Selected literature: Somoff
1901, no. 503; Cat. 1958, p. 111;
Cat. 1981, p. 78; Babina 1999b,
p. 11

In the foreground bread is
being distributed; to the left on
a covered terrace a rich man
shares his clothes with the poor;
to the right the other terrace
shows a scene of visiting the
sick. The architectural
background is composed of
fantastical pseudo-Renaissance
buildings (in the foreground
and middle ground) and Gothic
structures (the cathedral in the
far background). Thus the artist
creates the effect of stage wings
or sets, framing individual
scenes that illustrate each of the
different acts of Charity. It is
interesting that the artist found
unusual architectural niches in

which to set nearly all the seven
acts: the prisoner being visited
to right in the middle ground,
with the figure of the prisoner
himself visible in the window of
a tower; the hospitable
householder taking pilgrims
into his house in the
background, beneath the
overhanging architecture to left.
Two scenes are exceptions:
giving drink to the thirsty (right,
middle ground) and burying the
dead (in the background), which
are placed in the more open
space before the cathedral,
although they are still enclosed
by the architectural forms to
right and left.

The closest analogy for this
work is a signed and dated
painting of 1617, bearing the
same title, by Frans Francken
the Younger (Kunstmuseum,
Basle, inv. no. 1142), and the
Hermitage painting should thus
probably be put at the same date.
N.B.

15
FRANS FRANCKEN THE YOUNGER
1581 Antwerp – 1642 Antwerp
Allegory of Opportunity, 1627
Oil on canvas. 151 × 181 cm
Dated left on the edge of the top
book: *ANNO 1627*; signed on
the edge of the lower book: *Do F
ffranck in f*
Inscription bottom on the
cartouche: *OCCASIO/ REM
TIBI QUAM/ NOSCES APTA/
DIMITTERE NOLI/ FRONTE
CAPIL/ LATA EST/ SED POST/
OCCASIO CALVA* [Do not
dismiss a thing that you know
to be appropriate to you;
Opportunity has hair in front
but is bald behind]
Provenance: Collection of the
painter Nicolas Roerich, St.
Petersburg; transferred in 1921
from the State Museum Reserve
Inv. no. GE 6144
Selected literature: Cat. 1958,
p. 111; Cat. 1981, p. 78; Babina
1999b, pp. 11, 12

Another version of this
painting, almost identical in
size (149 × 182.5 cm) and
composition, is in the Wavel
Museum, Cracow. The Cracow
painting, which has no
signature but bears the date
1627, has been considered by
scholars a political allegory, and
its interpretation has a direct
bearing on that of the related
Hermitage picture.

Panofsky (1966, pp. 319–20,
326) proposed that the Cracow
painting shows events linked
either with the battle for the
Mantuan succession (1627–31)
or the battle between England
and France for the La Rochelle
Fortress (1627–29). Since both
these events commenced in
1627, each accords with the date
on the Polish painting. This led
Panofsky to see their reflection
in this allegory, identifying the
man in the costume decorated
with lilies to right of the Cracow
painting as Louis XIII and the
man nearby as Cardinal
Richelieu.

De Mirimonde (1966,
pp. 129–44; 1967, p. 118)
suggested that the Cracow
painting was conceived in
honour of the First False
Dmitry, a patron of the arts who
sought to spread Catholicism
through the Russian state
during his brief period on the
Russian throne (1605–06). It is
difficult to concur with this
opinion, and Panofsky also took a
negative view of the suggestion.

While the evidence for a
topical interpretation of the
Cracow painting is weak, the
basic suggestion that the image

is allegorical is surely correct
and is wholly relevant to the
Hermitage composition. Both
paintings represent an *Allegory
of Opportunity*, and following
the interpretations of Panofsky
and de Mirimonde, the
Hermitage version may be
interpreted as follows:

Winged Fame, sounding her
trumpet, leads the main hero to
a tent where he is to be crowned
by a seated woman who, with
her cornucopia, probably
personifies Good Government,
under whom, in times of peace,
the arts and sciences flourish.
These are represented in the
foreground and to the left by the

personifications of Dialectic (the
gesticulating man), Geometry
(the man with compasses),
Astronomy (the bearded man
with the Earth at his feet),
Scholarship (the man seated at
a desk) and Painting (the artist
with his easel). In the bottom
right corner lie sheet music and
instruments, the attributes of
Music.

In the lower left corner is a
dog that, according to de
Mirimonde, should be
understood as a symbol of Faith.
Panofsky notes that the
depiction of the dog refers
rather to intellectual activity
and, in the context of this

particular painting, the latter
interpretation is more
convincing, since the dog is
shown near the scholar's books.

The statue of a naked female
figure balanced on a sphere,
hair flowing, a razor in her right
hand and wings on her heels,
dominates the painting, and is
probably an allegory of
Opportunity rather than
Fortune (a point on which both
Panofsky and de Mirimonde
agree). The hero, who stands
just to the right of the sculpture,
should thus be understood as
having taken advantage of good
fortune and achieved success,
while the lazy figure reclining to

the left of the statue has allowed
all proffered opportunities to
pass him by. De Mirimonde
unpersuasively suggested the
identification of the "homo
fortunatus" with the First False
Dmitry, although the possibility
that the artist had some
particular historic individual in
mind cannot definitely be
excluded, especially since the
figures standing to the left of
Fame are also quite
individualized. The painting
may simply be a political
allegory in which the artist's
dreams of peace and prosperity
in Europe are realized.
N.B.

16
FRANS FRANCKEN THE YOUNGER
1581 Antwerp – 1642 Antwerp
David's Entry into Jerusalem,
1630s
Oil on canvas, transferred from
panel in 1818. 69.5 × 111.5 cm
Signed centre bottom: *D ffranck.*
in f
Provenance: Acquired before
1797
Inv. no. GE 438

17
PEETER VAN LINT
1609 Antwerp – 1690 Antwerp
Jephthah and his Daughter,
1640–50
Oil on canvas. 48 × 64 cm
Initials bottom right: *P.V.L. f*
Provenance: Acquired in 1717 in
Antwerp by Yury Kologrivov,
agent to Peter the Great
(Malinovsky 1990, vol. II, p. 71,
note 240); Imperial Picture
Gallery, Monplaisir, Peterhof,
near St. Petersburg; acquired
before 1797 (kept in store until
1887)
Inv. no. GE 2055

18

THEODOOR VAN THULDEN
1606 's-Hertogenbosch – 1669
's-Hertogenbosch
Allegory of Time Revealing Truth,
1657
Oil on canvas. 141.2 × 173 cm
Signed and dated bottom right:
T.van Thulden fecit A 1657
Provenance: Collection of
Prince Wilhelm of
Mecklenburg-Schwerin;
possibly at auction in
Amsterdam, May 6, 1716 (lot 9);
acquired in 1892 from the
collection of F. Moritz,

St. Petersburg
Inv. no. GE 563
Selected literature: Somoff
1901, no. 1790; Cat. 1958,
p. 110; Cat. 1981, pp. 76–77;
Roy 1992, p. 221 (under no. 56)

Van Thulden's painting
illustrates a popular
seventeenth-century allegorical
theme, *Veritas Filia Temporis*,
"Truth is the daughter of Time,"
an epigram found in the works
of the second-century Roman
writer Aulus Gellius. The
artist's inscriptions on his

preparatory drawing for this
painting (Victoria and Albert
Museum, London) clarify its
meaning.

Naked Truth ("Naakte
Waerheid"), depicted here as a
young woman, is rescued by a
winged figure of Old Father
Time as she emerges from the
profound darkness of the cave
in which she has been confined.
In the foreground, a snake-
haired Envy appears at the left
with a burning torch in her
hand, and at the centre,
Stupidity, both seeking to

prevent Truth's progress.
Floating above the figure of
Envy are two chimeras, female
figures with snake's tails in
place of legs. On the ground,
beneath the feet of Father Time,
is the fallen figure of Hypocrisy
whose conventional mask lies
in his hands.

It is possible that this is the
painting sold in Amsterdam in
1716 ("Daer de Tyd de Waerheid
ontdekt, van Theodoor van
Thulden"; Hoet, Terwesten
1752–70, I, p. 194).
N.G.

19
Nicolaes van Verendael
1640 Antwerp – 1691 Antwerp
and Gaspard Jacob van Opstal
the Elder
c. 1610 Antwerp (?) – after 1661
Allegory of Transience, early
1660s
Oil on canvas. 93 × 102 cm (at
the top an addition of
approximately 5 cm along the
full width of the painting)
Provenance: Possibly in the
collection of Jan van Weerden,
Antwerp, in 1686; (Hairs 1965,
p. 420); acquired in 1769 with
the collection of Count Brühl,
Dresden
Inv. no. GE 558

20

JAN VAN KESSEL THE ELDER
1626 Antwerp – 1679 Antwerp
Venus at the Forge of Vulcan
(*Allegory of Fire*), 1662
Oil on canvas. 59.5 × 84 cm
Signed and dated bottom
centre: *J.V.Kessel fecit 1662*
Provenance: Collection of A.G.
Teplov, St. Petersburg; acquired
before 1797
Inv. no. GE 1709
Selected literature: Somoff
1901, no. 1741; Cat. 1958, p. 70;
Cat. 1981, p. 50; Gritsay 1986,
no. 5

In his *Aeneid* (VIII:370–86),
Virgil tells of Venus's visit to the
forge of her husband, Vulcan, to
request that he make weapons
for her son Aeneas, who was
about to depart for war with the
Rutuli. As it is presented here,
the mythological subject has
been elaborated as an allegory
of Fire. Van Kessel depicts the
element's different states. It is
embodied by the fire-breathing
mountain in the background, by
the furnace in Vulcan's forge, as
well as by the pair of spotted
salamanders on the ground by
Vulcan, which, according to the

medieval bestiary, are a symbol
of fire, since they would not
burn and even had the power to
extinguish flames. Yet the most
important place in the
composition is allocated to a
large array of military
equipment, all of it made at the
forge: weapons (spears, rapiers,
pistols, muskets and cannon),
armour (helmets, breastplates,
gloves, parade shields,
mannequins wearing armour)
and attributes of military music
(side drums, horn and
kettledrum). The composition
also includes a large flag on a

pole, and a metal-trimmed
saddle with its trappings (saddle
and horse cloths). Further
symbolic significance attaches
to a number of everyday objects
made with the aid of fire –
silver, glass and ceramics –
grouped together in a silver
wine cooler in the centre
foreground. The theme is
completed with the still-life
"Vanitas" displayed on the table
by the painting's right edge.
The emptiness and vanity of
earthly passions are evoked by
the open mechanical clock, the
burning candle and the pipes

and tobacco, while the salt
cellar, the tumbler and the glass
of wine are motifs that recall the
Eucharist.
    Although as a depiction of
Fire the painting echoes similar
compositions by Velvet
Brueghel, such as *Allegory of
Fire* in the Galleria Doria
Pamphili, Rome, the display of
military equipment and musical
instruments was clearly
borrowed from works by David
Teniers the Younger that
represent guardrooms.
N.G.

21
PETER PAUL RUBENS
1577 Siegen – 1640 Antwerp
Head of a Franciscan Monk,
c. 1615
Oil on canvas, transferred from
panel in 1842. 52 × 44 cm
Provenance: Collection of Sir
Robert Walpole, Houghton Hall,
Norfolk; acquired in 1779 with
the Walpole Collection, Norfolk
Inv. no. GE 472
Selected literature: *Aedes* 1752,
p. 47; Somoff 1901, no. 584;
Cat. 1958, p. 80; Varshavskaya
1975, no. 12 (ed. 1989 pl. 26);
Cat. 1981, p. 61; Jaffé 1989,
no. 325; Gritsay 1992, no. 33

On account of its markedly
individual nature, this painting
should be understood as a
portrait study. In style it recalls
the profile head in Rubens's
Two Satyrs (Alte Pinakothek,
Munich, inv. no. 873), and it is
possible that it depicts the same
sitter. The Hermitage study was
probably produced at the same
time as *Two Satyrs, c.* 1615.
N.G.

22
SCHOOL OF PETER PAUL
RUBENS
*Portrait of Rubens with his Son
Albert, c. 1620*
Oil on canvas. 133.5 × 112.2 cm
Provenance: By 1793 in the
collection of Count Alexander
Stroganov, St. Petersburg (Cat.
Stroganoff 1793, no. 30); 1864
collection of Count Sergey
Stroganov, St. Petersburg;
collection of the Counts
Stroganov, St. Petersburg;
transferred in 1932 from the
Stroganov Palace Museum,
Leningrad
Inv. no. GE 7728
Selected literature: Cat. 1958,
p. 52 (as van Dyck); Cat. 1981,
p. 55 (as unknown seventeenth-
century Flemish artist); Gritsay
1986, no. 6; Vlieghe 1987,
p. 158 (under no. 136: Copies
[1]); Gritsay 1992, no. 36;
Hunter-Stiebel 2000, no. 121

This portrait shows Rubens
with his elder son Albert
(1614–1657), later a lawyer and
secretary to the Privy Council
in Brussels and author of a
number of antiquarian works,
most famously his *Dissertatio de
gemma Augustea* and *De re
vestiaria veterum*, which were
published in 1665.
    Both catalogues of the
collection of Alexander
Sergeyevich Stroganov (Cat.
Stroganoff 1793, no. 30; Cat.
Stroganoff 1800, no. 40)
ascribe this portrait to Rubens,
an attribution that it retained
until the twentieth century.
Critical reassessments have
struck the painting from
Rubens's œuvre, and attributed
it instead to the artist's
followers, either to Anthony
van Dyck (Yaremich 1949) or
Jan Cossiers (1600–1671; D.
Jaffé 1988, p. 27, fig. 20). The
portrait is most probably an old
copy of a lost self-portrait by
Rubens, produced by an artist
of Rubens's school.
    The figure of the artist is
based on a self-portrait drawing
(Graphische Sammlung
Albertina, Vienna, inv. no.
8202; possibly a copy: Mitsch
1977, no. 67), which also
served as a model for a painted
self-portrait at the Rubenshuis,
Antwerp. The main elements
of the composition confirm
Rubens's concept of portraiture
in general, and the artist is
shown surrounded by objects
reflecting his interests as an
antiquarian and a humanist.
An antique statue of the
goddess Hecate (Hecate
Triformis), once in the artist's

own collection, stands in a
niche to the right (now
Rijksmuseum van Oudheden,
Leiden; Bastet 1981; sold in 1626
to the Duke of Buckingham:
Muller 1989, p. 152, no. 9). The
lit antique lamp that crowns the
statue, probably intended to
signify the lamp of knowledge,
is found in many of Rubens's
works. Finally, the touching
gesture of the child embracing
Rubens's hand, employed to
signal the son's devotion to his
father, recalls how a similar
gesture symbolized the
closeness of the sitters in
*Rubens and Isabella Brant in a
Honeysuckle Bower* (Alte
Pinakothek, Munich). Bastet
(1981) considers that in the
Stroganov painting Rubens is
presented as teacher and
educator of his son, whom he is
introducing to the world of the
arts and sciences under the
protection of the Three Graces
(thus, according to Bastet,
should we interpret the statue
of Hecate).
    The child's age suggests that
the original composition should
be dated to the late 1610s, but
execution of this version must
be dated later, although not after
the middle of the seventeenth
century.
N.G.

23
ANTHONY VAN DYCK
1599 Antwerp – 1641 London
Self-portrait, 1622–23
Oil on canvas. 116.5 × 93.5 cm
Provenance: Acquired in 1772
with the Crozat collection, Paris
Inv. no. GE 548
Selected literature: Cat. Crozat
1755, p. 7; Somoff 1901, no. 628;
Cat. 1958, p. 56; Varshavskaya
1963, pp. 110–12; Cat. 1981, p. 39;
Larsen 1988, no. 43; Barnes
1990, no. 33; Gritsay 1994b,
no. 72; Brown 1999, no. 31

Van Dyck painted many self-portraits during his lifetime, perhaps less than Rembrandt but far more than either Rubens or Jordaens. Each of these paintings reflects his personal ideal of the elegant and noble individual. As a group they present the image of a man of innately aristocratic refinement and display a broad range of van Dyck's inner emotions. The Hermitage self-portrait is a perfect example of this ideal. Here the young van Dyck

portrays himself as a slender and elegantly attired cavalier leaning nonchalantly against the pedestal of a broken column, gazing slightly mysteriously out towards the viewer. The carefree elegance of the pose, the fine and sensitive aristocratic hands with their long fingers, and the magnificent black silk attire all confirm the impression the Flemish painter made on his fellow artists when he arrived in Rome. There he was known as

"il pittore cavalieresco." In his *Le vite de 'pittori, scultori et architetti moderni* (Lives of the Modern Painters, Sculptors, and Architects; 1672), Gian Pietro Bellori justifiably remarked that van Dyck's manner was more in keeping with that of an aristocrat than of an ordinary man. The richness of his clothing, the fine fabrics, feathered hats and ribbons, all revealed the young Flemish artist's desire to be associated with the titled nobility, to whom

he became portraitist within the first few months of his arrival in Italy.

This aristocratic idea of man's spiritual and intellectual superiority, so vividly expressed in the Hermitage self-portrait, has its closest analogies in Italian Renaissance art. The young artist's pose, his proud bearing, the free turn of his figure and the complex silhouette of his costume with its rich sleeves, as was perceptively noted by Barnes (1990, p. 163), were probably suggested by Raphael's *Portrait of a Young Man* (formerly Czartoryski Museum, Cracow), of which van Dyck made a sketch in his *Italian Sketchbook* (fol. 109v; British Museum, London). The type of portrait itself, showing the model leaning against a pedestal, derives from Venetian paintings, above all the works of Titian (e.g. *Portrait of Benedetto Varchi*, Kunsthistorisches Museum, Vienna, inv. no. 91), copies of whose portraits fill whole pages of that same *Italian Sketchbook*.

Barnes's observation conerning the portrait's models indicates that the possible dating of the Hermitage self-portrait should be limited to van Dyck's Italian years. This is confirmed by the manner in which the canvas was painted: a finely applied layer of paint covers but does not conceal the texture of the canvas, over which individual parts are picked out and painted in more impasto fashion, primarily those that capture the light. These characteristics link the self-portrait with van Dyck's works during his first years in Italy (*Portrait of Filippo Cattaneo*, 1623, National Gallery of Art, Washington, D.C.). The half-destroyed column should probably be understood as a hint at the ancient ruins of Rome, where van Dyck spent several months in 1622 and 1623.

Earlier versions of the Hermitage self-portrait are in the Alte Pinakothek, Munich (bust-length, inv. no. 405) and the Metropolitan Museum, New York (three-quarter length).
N.G.

24

Anthony van Dyck
1599 Antwerp – 1641 London
Portrait of Nicolaes Rockox, 1621
Oil on canvas. 122.5 × 117 cm
Provenance: Collection of
Nicolaes Rockox, Antwerp
(no. 4 in the posthumous
inventory of his property,
compiled December 19–20,
1640); sale of the collection of
Anna Theresia van Halen,
Antwerp, August 19, 1749
(lot 2); sale of the collection of
Frederik Graaf van Thoms,
Leiden, April 7, 1750 (lot 1);
collection of Claude Henri
Watelet, Paris (according to
Mariette, *Abecedario* 1853–59,
p. 207); acquired by Count
Alexander Stroganov in Paris
between 1771 and 1779;
collection of Count Alexander
Stroganov, St. Petersburg; 1864
collection of Count Sergey
Stroganov, St. Petersburg;
transferred in 1932 from the
Stroganov Palace Museum
Inv. no. GE 6922
Selected literature: Cat.
Stroganoff 1793, no. 34; Cat.
Stroganoff 1800, no. 45; Cat.
1958, p. 52; Varshavskaya 1963,
no. 6; Cat. 1981, p. 39; Larsen
1988, no. 55; Baudouin 1999,
no. 1; Hunter-Stiebel 2000,
no. 122, p, 221

Nicolaes Rockox (1560–1640),
a lawyer by education, was
burgomaster of Antwerp, a post
to which he was elected nine
times between 1603 and 1636.
He was also a notable scholar
of numismatics, an active
collector and patron of the arts,
and well known for his
charitable activities. A friend –
and frequent patron – of
Rubens, he is shown in this
portrait with some favourite
objects from his collection
including books and sculpture.
On the table at which he sits
are two antique sculptures, a
marble head of Jupiter, which
later entered the collection of
Christina of Sweden (now
Nationalmuseum, Stockholm)
and a small bronze head of
Hercules (Scheller 1978,
pp. 20, 28, 34, fig. 16). In the
engraving by Lucas Vorsterman
that reproduces this
composition, another bust is
shown (thought in the
seventeenth century to show
the Athenian orator and
politician Demosthenes), which
Rockox acquired in late 1621 or
early 1622.
    Visible in the far ground
through the billowing drapery
is the tower of the Hansa or
Eastern House in Antwerp

(destroyed by fire in 1893), clearly
another reference to the multiple
and varied activities of the sitter,
symbolizing his trading links
with the Hanseatic League.
    The portrait was painted in
1621, shortly before the artist
departed for Italy. It represents
an unusual combination of the
calm, representative portrait
common to the Flemish
tradition with the additional
influence of Titian. This became
particularly noticeable in van
Dyck's work after he became

acquainted with the rich royal
collections found in London,
where he spent some time in
1620–21. A preparatory drawing
for the portrait is in the Print
Room of the British Museum
(Vey 1962, no. 168; brown ink
and black chalk, 19.2 × 16.3 cm).
    Count Alexander Sergeyevich
Stroganov (1733–1811), who
acquired the portrait of the
Antwerp burgomaster during
his stay in Paris, was
particularly fond of the
painting, describing it in his

catalogue of 1793 as one of van
Dyck's masterpieces. Desirous
that the portrait should serve
as a model to students in the
painting classes at St.
Petersburg's Imperial Academy
of Arts, of which he was
president, Stroganov entrusted
the Russian painter Orest
Kiprensky (1782–1836) with the
painting of a copy (Russian
Museum, St. Petersburg) in 1807.
    In May 1931 the painting was
offered for sale with many other
items from the Stroganov

collection, at an auction held at
R. Lepke in Berlin, but it was
not sold and was returned to
Russia.
N.G.

25
ANTHONY VAN DYCK
1599 Antwerp – 1641 London
Portrait of a Man (Virginio
Cesarini?), *c.* 1622–1623
Oil on canvas. 104.8 × 86.5 cm
Provenance: By 1709 in the
collection of Boyer d'Aiguilles,
Aix; collection of Pierre Crozat,
Paris; acquired in 1772 with the
Crozat collection, Paris
Inv. no. GE 552
Selected literature: Cat. Crozat
1755, p. 5; Somoff 1901, no. 632;
Cat. 1958, p. 56; Varshavskaya
1963, no. 9; Cat. 1981, p. 39;
Larsen 1988, no. 550; Barnes
1990, no. 32; Gritsay 1996,
p. 66

On the basis of an inscription
on the print by Sebastien Barras
(1653–1703), found in some
copies of the anthology *Recueil
des plus beaux tableaux du
cabinet de M. Boyer, seigneur
d'Aiguilles* (Aix, 1709), this
portrait was long considered to
depict the Antwerp doctor
Lazarus Maharkyzus
(1571–1647). In accordance with
such an identification, the
portrait was placed in van
Dyck's second Antwerp period,
between 1628 and 1632. The
dynamism of the image and its
obvious strong Venetian
colouring, however (particularly
recalling the works of Titian,
such as his *Concert* of *c.* 1510–12

in the Palazzo Pitti, Florence),
suggest the portrait was painted
during the artist's stay in Italy.
A more precise dating was
made possible with the help of
X-ray analysis undertaken in
1955 in the Hermitage
laboratories (Panfilova 1955,
pp. 36–37). This revealed that
beneath the upper paint layer
was a sketch for the famous
portrait of Cardinal Guido
Bentivoglio (Palazzo Pitti,
Florence), which van Dyck
painted in Rome in 1622 or
1623.
    The sitter for the Hermitage
portrait has been variously
identified as the Lotharingian
painter Jean Leclerc (Smith

1829–42, vol. III, no. 535, p. 151;
no. 818, p. 229) and as an
"Unknown Roman Clergyman"
from the circle of Cardinal
Bentivoglio (Barnes 1990).
Recently, however, the highly
plausible suggestion was put
forward that the model was
Virginio Cesarini (1595–1624),
favourite, protégé and
chamberlain to Maffeo
Barberini (from June 1623 Pope
Urban VIII; Freedberg 1994,
pp. 153–56). Author of elegant
verses in Italian and Latin,
member of the Accademia dei
Lincei from 1618, publisher and
defender of Galileo, Cesarini
was a central figure in Roman
cultural and intellectual life

during the late 1610s and early
1620s. Several factors support
such an identification: the
similarity between the subject
and the tomb sculpture of
Cesarini in the Sala dei Capitani
(Museo Capitolino, Rome); his
attire, which reveals him to be a
member of the clergy, and, last
but not least, his pale, sickly
face with its feverish flush,
which suggests Cesarini's ill
health at this time – he died,
perhaps of consumption, in
April 1624. In all likelihood the
portrait was painted by van
Dyck during his stay in Rome
in 1622 or 1623.
N.G.

26
ANTHONY VAN DYCK
1599 Antwerp – 1641 London
Portrait of Lady Jane Goodwin,
1639
Oil on canvas. 132.5 × 106 cm
Inscriptions (from the time of
the first owner) at bottom right:
P.Sr. Ant. Vandike; and five lines
at bottom left: *Jane Daughter of
Richard Lord ˜/ Viscount
Wenman mother of Jane/
Goodwin wife of Philip now/ Lord
Wharton/ 1639 about ye age of 36*
Provenance: Collection of Philip,
4th Lord Wharton, Winchendon,
near Aylesbury,
Buckinghamshire; acquired by
Sir Robert Walpole from the
heirs of Lord Wharton in 1725;
collection of Sir Robert Walpole,
London (?), then Houghton Hall,
Norfolk; acquired in 1779 with
the Walpole collection, Norfolk
Inv. no. GE 549
Selected literature: *Aedes* 1752,
p. 52; Somoff 1901, no. 619;
Cat. 1958, p. 63; Varshavskaya
1963, no. 21; Cat. 1981, p. 40;
Larsen 1988, no. 850; Millar
1994, no. 13; Lurie 1995, no. 28;
Egerton 1999, p. 330, fig. 1

Lady Jane Goodwin, née
Wenman (*c.* 1603 – after 1639),
was the wife of Arthur Goodwin
(1593/4–1643), a wealthy
Buckinghamshire landowner
and the mother of their daughter
and sole heir, Jane Goodwin
(1618–58), who married Lord
Philip Wharton in 1637.

Lady Jane is shown holding a
large, streaked, pink-and-white
tulip of a kind then extremely
fashionable and expensive. This
is the sole representation of such
a flower in any of van Dyck's
portraits, though it is unlikely to
have been of symbolic
significance, serving simply to
complement her rich attire.

One of a group of portraits
commissioned from van Dyck
by Lord Philip Wharton in the
years 1637–39, this painting was
executed by van Dyck himself,
the participation of assistants
seeming likely only in the
background. The date of 1639,
inscribed at the lower left of the
portrait, is supported by the
picture's manner of execution
and the smooth, enamel-like
surface, as well as the style of
Lady Jane's dress, which
accords with fashions of the late
1630s (Varshavskaya 1963,
p. 126). Further, this type of
portrait with the sitter shown
three-quarter length against a
rocky background was typical of
van Dyck's work during the
second half of the 1630s.
N.G.

27
ANTHONY VAN DYCK
1599 Antwerp – 1641 London
Portrait of Inigo Jones, 1632–35
Oil on canvas. 64.5 × 53.2 cm
(oval in a profiled frame set into
a rectangle)
Provenance: Collection of Inigo
Jones (Vertue III, 1933–34,
p. 112); given by Jones to his
nephew, the architect John
Webb (Vertue I, 1929–30,
p. 135); acquired by Sir Robert
Walpole in or shortly after 1736;
collection of Sir Robert Walpole,
Houghton Hall, Norfolk;
acquired in 1779 with the
Walpole collection, Norfolk
Inv. no. GE 557
Selected literature: *Aedes* 1752,
p. 48; Somoff 1901, no. 626;
Cat. 1958, p. 60; Varshavskaya
1963, no. 13; Cat. 1981, p. 40;
Larsen 1988, no. 885

Inigo Jones (1573–1652), the
illustrious English architect
known as "the English
Vitruvius," designed the
Banqueting Hall of Whitehall
Palace in London for which
Rubens produced the ceiling
paintings (a sketch for one part
of which is included in this
exhibition; cat. 7). Jones was
also an accomplished painter
and theatrical designer.

Van Dyck may have begun
work on the portrait as part of
his *Iconography*, intended as an
anthology of engraved portraits
of the artist's notable
contemporaries. Jones could
only have posed for van Dyck
during the latter's stay in
England between 1632 and
March 1634, or in the spring of
1635 when van Dyck returned to
London from Flanders. The
portrait was certainly completed
before the death of Robert van
der Voerst (1597–1636) who
engraved the same image for
the *Iconography* in October
1636. Such a dating in the first
half of the 1630s, between 1632
and 1636, would be in keeping
with the style of the painting
and the generally dark tonality,
which relate it to works of van
Dyck's "second Antwerp
period." Compositionally the
image is related to the oval
Portrait of Jan Brueghel the Elder
(collection of Lord Methuen,
Corshem Court), which Larsen
(1980, no. 615) dates to the
same period, between 1628 and
1632.

In the Devonshire Collection
at Chatsworth (inv. no. 1002 A)
is a portrait drawing by van
Dyck depicting Jones from the
same angle as in the Hermitage
portrait (Vey 1962, no. 271).

There is disagreement about the
chronology and relationship
between the painting, the
drawing and the engraving. The
drawing is believed by some to
have been the model for the
Hermitage portrait (d'Hulst,
Vey 1960; Varshavskaya 1963),
and by others the basis for the
engraving (Mauquoy-Hendrickx
1956, no. 72). Alternatively, the
drawing was based on the
Hermitage portrait or another
drawing from life, now lost
(Brown 1991, no. 72). What is
remarkable is how the painted
portrait creates the impression
of having been taken from life,
so very strikingly has van Dyck
captured Jones's upward gaze, a
quality visibly lacking in the
drawing.
N.G.

28
ANTHONY VAN DYCK
1599 Antwerp – 1641 London
Portrait of Everhard Jabach,
1636–37
Oil on canvas. 113 × 91.5 cm
Provenance: Collection of
Everhard Jabach, Paris; acquired
in 1772 with the Crozat
collection, Paris
Inv. no. GE 555
Selected literature: Cat. Crozat
1755, pp. 9–10; Somoff 1901,
no. 631; Cat. 1958, p. 60;
Varshavskaya 1963, no. 15; Cat.
1981, p. 40; Larsen 1988,
no. 883; Gritsay 1993, no. 9

Everhard Jabach (1610–1695), a
well-known banker and
collector, was born in Cologne,
and moved to Paris in 1638.
Jabach's collections entered the
Louvre when they were acquired
by Louis XIV in 1671. The
landscape visible in the distance
behind the sitter has been
associated with an event in
Jabach's life. It shows a view of
Ypres tower, a twelfth-century
Romanesque citadel in the
English port of Rye in East
Sussex, from the sea. Rye was
one of the so-called "cinque
ports" and was an active centre
of communications with France
during the seventeenth century.
On his way to settle in France
Jabach visited England in
1636–37, and this image of the
port of Rye may have served as a
remembrance of that time
(d'Hulst, Vey 1960, pp. 138–39).
The view of Rye and Ypres
tower was drawn by van Dyck
on numerous occasions (Vey
1962, nos. 288, 289) and he
probably used these sketches
when he met Jabach during the
latter's stay in England.
    The posthumous inventory of
Jabach's property, compiled by
his son on June 17, 1696, lists
under no. 338: "Portrait de mon
père de Vandeck demy figure,
400 L" (Grossmann 1951,
pp. 17, 19).
N.G.

29
ANTHONY VAN DYCK
1599 Antwerp – 1641 London
*Portrait of Sir Thomas Chaloner,
c.* 1637
Oil on canvas. 104 × 81.5 cm
Provenance: Collection of Sir
Robert Walpole, Houghton Hall,
Norfolk; acquired in 1779 with
the Walpole collection, Norfolk
Inv. no. GE 551
Selected literature: *Aedes* 1752,
p. 46; Somoff 1901, no. 620;
Cat. 1958, p. 60; Varshavskaya
1963, no. 23; Cat. 1981, p. 40;
Larsen 1988, no. 784; Wheelock
1990, no. 80

Sir Thomas Chaloner
(1595–1661) was one of the
judges who sentenced Charles I
to be executed in 1648. Upon
the restoration of the House of
Stuart, Chaloner was exiled
from Britain and died at
Middelburg in Holland. In the
Walpole (*Aedes* 1752) and
Hermitage inventories and
catalogues up to 1893, the sitter
was confused with his father,
also Thomas Chaloner, who
died in 1615.
    This is one of the latest
works entirely by van Dyck of
the late 1630s (*c.* 1637), and
undoubtedly one of his best.
Without any attempt at
idealization, the artist depicts
Chaloner's ageing face with its
flaccid skin and reddened
cheeks. The energetic, powerful
turn of the head, the flaring
nostrils, the tightly pressed lips,
and particularly the bright,
piercing eyes, convey the
dynamic character of the sitter.
The whole portrait is suffused
with an intense sense of passion
and is executed with such
freedom that it seems likely to
have been painted in one
sitting. Van Dyck applied the
paint on the face and hand with
tiny, delicate strokes, in contrast
to the sketch-like freedom he
employed for the sitter's long
wavy hair, and the elegant and
vibrant strokes used to convey
the rippling sheen of the black
silk and the play of light over its
broken folds. The almost
monochromatic palette
emphasizes the extreme
elegance of the image.
N.G.

30
ANTHONY VAN DYCK
1599 Antwerp – 1641 London
Henry Danvers, Earl of Danby, in Garter Robes, late 1630s
Oil on canvas. 223 × 130.6 cm
Provenance: Collection of
Henry Danvers, Earl of Danby;
inherited by his nephew John
Danvers; presented by the
latter's son, Joseph Danvers, to
Sir Robert Walpole; collection of
Sir Robert Walpole, Houghton
Hall, Norfolk; acquired in 1779
with the Walpole collection,
Norfolk
Inv. no. GE 545
Selected literature: *Aedes* 1752,
p. 72; Somoff 1901, no. 615; Cat.
1958, p. 56; Varshavskaya 1963,
no. 24; Cat. 1981, p. 40; Millar
1982, no. 20; Larsen 1988,
no. 819; Gritsay 1996–97, no. 3;
Egerton 1999, no. 73

Henry Danvers, Earl of Danby
(1573–1644), took part in
military campaigns in the
Southern Netherlands under
the Stadthalter of the
Netherlands, Maurice of
Orange, fighting also in Ireland
and France as part of the army
of Henri IV of France. It was
apparently during one such
campaign that he received a
head wound, which he covered
with a patch worn near his left
eye. Danvers was the founder of
the first botanical garden in
England, bequeathing land and
funds for this purpose to Oxford
University. He was renowned at
the court of James I for his love
of art and was also one of
Rubens's patrons. In November
1633 he was made a Knight of
the Order of the Garter.
    Danvers is shown full length,
wearing the red and white attire
of the Order, with a blue velvet
cloak lined with white satin. On
the table on which he rests his
hand lies the hat of the Order.
In its skilful composition and
fine execution, this should
certainly be considered one of
van Dyck's best works from his
English period. This is the only
full-length depiction of a Knight
of the Order of the Garter by
van Dyck, and the flowing,
almost sketchy manner in
which it is painted suggests a
date at the very end of the
1630s. A preparatory drawing
(knee-length) is in the British
Museum (Vey 1962, no. 212).
N.G.

31
Anthony van Dyck
1599 Antwerp – 1641 London
Ladies-in-Waiting to Queen
Henrietta Maria (Anne Killigrew
with an Unidentified Lady),
c. 1638
Oil on canvas. 131.5 × 150.6 cm
Provenance: Acquired between
1763 and 1774
Inv. no. GE 540
Selected literature: Somoff
1901, no. 633; Cat. 1958, p. 63;
Varshavskaya 1963, no. 25; Cat.
1981, p. 40; Larsen 1988,
no. 894; Lurie 1995, no. 26;
Gritsay 1996, p. 128; Egerton
1999, no. 99

This painting came to the
Hermitage as a portrait of the
English queen Henrietta Maria
and Elizabeth of Bohemia,
sister of Charles I. Smith
(1829–42, vol. III, no. 532,
p. 150) identified the sitters as
Anne Dalkeith, Countess
Morton, and Anne Kirke, both
ladies of the court, and this
interpretation was followed in
Hermitage catalogues from
1901 (Somoff). Varshavskaya
(1963) and the catalogue of 1981
concurred that the woman
seated to the right is Anne
Killigrew, Mrs. Kirke
(1607–1641), dresser to Queen
Henrietta Maria, but was
unsure of the identify of her
companion. The same sitter, in
the same pose and wearing the
same white satin dress, but with
a silvery-grey shawl, is portrayed
alone in a work by van Dyck in
the Museo Nacional of Cuba,
where it is catalogued as a
portrait of Lady Mayo (oil on
canvas, 126 × 100 cm).

Clearly produced on
commission, the portrait is
remarkable for its harmony of
colour in the striking, yet
restrained and elegant,
combination used in the sitters'
clothing of silvery-white and
soft lilac tones with deep cherry-
red, black and white. Their
sumptuous costumes are set off
by the black and gold drapery, as
well as the twilit landscape in
the distance. In its vivid sense
of nature, this view recalls the
landscape drawings and
watercolours that van Dyck
produced in the 1630s, although
no direct prototype can be
found among them.
N.G.

32

Antwerp 1599 – London 1641
Portrait of Philadelphia and Elizabeth Wharton, 1640
Oil on canvas. 162 × 130 cm
Inscriptions (from the time of the first owner) at bottom right: *P. Sr Ant. Vandike*; and four lines at bottom left: *Philadelphia Wharton and Elizabeth/ Wharton ye only daughters of Philip/ now Lord Wharton by Elizabeth his/ first wife, 1640 about ye age of 4 and 5*
Provenance: Collection of Philip, 4th Lord Wharton, Winchendon, near Aylesbury, Buckinghamshire; 1725 acquired by Sir Robert Walpole from the heirs of Lord Wharton; collection of Sir Robert Walpole, London, then Houghton Hall, Norfolk; acquired in 1779 with the Walpole collection, Norfolk
Inv. no. GE 533
Selected literature: *Aedes* 1752, p. 51; Somoff 1901, no. 618; Cat. 1958, p. 60; Varshavskaya 1963, no. 19; Cat. 1981, p. 40; Larsen 1988, no. 1032; Millar 1994, no. 14; Gritsay 1997, no. 2; Egerton 1999, no. 103

The two girls portrayed here by van Dyck were the daughters of Philip, 4th Lord Wharton, by his first wife Elizabeth, daughter of Sir Rowland Wandesford, whom he married in 1632. The eldest sister, Elizabeth, married Robert Bertie in 1659, later 3rd Earl of Lindsey, and died ten years later in 1669. Nothing is known of the younger sister, Philadelphia, and it seems likely that she died in childhood.

Despite the inscription on both the painting and the engraving taken from it, doubts have arisen regarding the identity of the sitters. Citing official sources that Philip Wharton's first marriage produced only one daughter, Elizabeth, Cust (1900) suggested that the portrait shows Wharton's cousins, daughters of his mother's brother Thomas Carey – Philadelphia, born 1631, and Elizabeth, born 1632. This identification was accepted in Hermitage catalogues published between 1902 and 1958. Varshavskaya (1963) rightly noted, however, that there is no reason to doubt the inscription, added during the lifetime of Lord Philip Wharton himself. Inscriptions similar in

content and form of lettering are found only on paintings from the Wharton collection. Philip Wharton is known to have been married three times and had as many as fifteen children, six of whom died in childhood. The Wharton family tree states that Philip's second marriage produced four children "with other issue" (Varshavskaya 1963, p. 125). The last daughter from the second marriage was also named

Philadelphia, perhaps in honour of the deceased elder child.

One of a group of works commissioned from van Dyck between 1637 and 1639 by Lord Philip Wharton, this double portrait is one of the artist's most touching images of children. The artist undoubtedly painted the figures of the girls himself, without workshop assistance, as the *pentimenti* in the outlines of the dresses suggest. The dry and somewhat

schematic execution of the background, however, particularly in the landscape, is evidence of workshop participation.
N.G.

33
JACOB JORDAENS
1593 Antwerp – 1678 Antwerp
*Self-portrait with Parents,
Brothers and Sisters, c.* 1615
Oil on canvas. 175 × 137.5 cm
Provenance. Probably Het
Paradijs (home of Jordaens's
parents) in Antwerp, now 13
Hoogstraat, which Jordaens
purchased in 1634 at the sale of
his deceased parents' property;
collection of Henry Bentinck,
Duke of Portland; 1722 acquired
from him by Sir Robert Walpole
and kept first in London, then at
Houghton Hall, Norfolk;
acquired in 1779 with the
Walpole collection, Norfolk
Inv. no. GE 484
Selected literature: *Aedes* 1752,
p. 65; Held 1940, pp. 70–82;
Cat. 1958, p. 65; Jaffé 1968,
no. 3; Gritsay 1977, pp. 83–87;
Cat. 1981, p. 49; d'Hulst 1993,
no. A 5

Julius Held (1940) recognized
this painting as a Jordaens
family portrait, an identification
confirmed by George Vertue,
who saw the painting in 1722
when it was already in the
Walpole collection, and
described it in his *Note Books*
(III, 1933–34) as a portrait of
Jordaens, his parents and his
family. It depicts the artist's
parents, Jacob Jordaens the
Elder, an Antwerp linen
merchant, together with his
wife, Barbara van Wolschaten,
the artist himself (holding a
lute), and seven of his brothers
and sisters. In the foreground
are the twins Abraham and
Isaac (born 1606); on her
mother's knee, Elizabeth (born
1613); to left of the mother is
Maria (born 1596), and gazing
upward behind her is Anne
(born 1597); the girl looking
over the mother's shoulder is
Catherine (born 1600), and the
child to the right of the father is
Madeleine (born 1608).
Jordaens's parents are known to
have had three more children,
Anne (born 1595), Elizabeth
(born 1605) and Susanne (born
1610), who seem to have died in
early childhood. The three putti
holding sprigs of laurel (?) who
hover above the whole group
should be seen as personifying
the souls of the deceased. The
identification of the sitters
suggests a date for the work in
the early period of Jordaens's
career, around 1615.
Jaffé (1968) believed that the
portrait depicted celebrations in
honour of Jordaens's acceptance
as a master in the Antwerp
Guild of St. Luke in 1615, and

that it was painted specially for
this event. This is debatable,
since several details of the
composition are common to
family portraits and bear a
specific symbolic meaning in
accordance with existing
traditions. The lute
conventionally symbolizes
harmony (*concordia*), and in the
context of a family portrait
indicates harmony within the
marriage and the family. The
dog in the foreground embodies
conjugal faithfulness, and in
this case the same meaning
should probably be read in the
vine growing over the bower
framing the group, which often
served as a symbol of
permanence in love. Wine and
bread are associated with the
Eucharist, or more broadly with
religious faith, which unites the
parents and children. The fruits
on the platter carried aloft by
the maid at the upper right can
be understood as *pace frui*
("enjoyment of peace;" d'Hulst
1993). Overall, the painting's
content reflects traditional
ideals of Christian morality. In
this context, the father's gesture
of raising a glass of wine in his
right hand should be
understood as a precaution
against excessive loyalty to vain
earthly pleasures and as a
reminder of the need for
moderation, one of the most
important Christian virtues
(compare J. Bruyn, M. Thierry
de Bye Dolleman, "Maerten van
Heemskercks 'Familiengroep' te
Kassel: Pieter Jan Foppesz. en
zijn gezin," *Oud Holland*,
vol. 97 [1983], no. 1, pp. 20, 24).
The identification of the
sitters suggests a date for the
work in the early period of
Jordaens's career, around 1615.
The composition was
undoubtedly inspired by an
altarpiece, *The Circumcision*,
painted by Rubens around 1605
(church of Sant'Ambrogio,
Genoa), most likely known to
Jordaens from the sketch
Rubens brought back with him
from Italy (Gemäldegalerie der
Akademie der bildenden
Künste, Vienna).
N.G.

34
JACOB JORDAENS
1593 Antwerp – 1678 Antwerp
Portrait of an Old Man, c. 1637
Oil on canvas. 154 × 118.5 cm
Inscription bottom left corner,
on the base of the column:
Aetatis 73
Provenance: Acquired in 1772
with the Crozat collection, Paris
Inv. no. GE 486
Selected literature: Somoff
1901, no. 653; Cat. 1958, p. 65;
Gritsay 1979, no. 6; Cat. 1981,
p. 49; Gritsay 1993, no. 17.

This painting is an example of the numerous commissions Jordaens received during the 1630s and 1640s, in which he made use of the full repertoire of compositions and motifs traditionally employed for the ceremonial portrait. These characteristic features had been brilliantly developed in the art of Rubens and van Dyck and include the elaborate architectural background, the striking repoussoir drapery, the rich costume and the low point of view that allowed the artist to elevate the sitter, both literally and figuratively. But while van Dyck always sought to emphasize some innate nobility and to express the force of the sitter's character, Jordaens reveals a clear desire to portray a specific portrait type, that of a successful member of the bourgeoisie. In the Hermitage portrait, Jordaens seems to render his subject without flattery, an interpretation based on the elderly sitter's bloated facial features, his puffy, dim eyes, and his corpulent figure that is barely contained by his armchair. Yet the rich architectural setting and the scale of the figure, whose large form looms in the foreground, lend the image an undoubted sense of majesty and pretension.

The portrait was produced *c.* 1637 (Gritsay 1993) and forms a pair with *Portrait of a Lady in an Armchair* (Buscot Park, The Faringdon Collection Trust, Berkshire). There is a preparatory drawing in the Louvre (inv. no. 20.200).
N.G.

35

DAVID TENIERS THE YOUNGER
1610 Antwerp – 1690 Brussels
*Portrait of Antonius Triest, Bishop
of Ghent, and his Brother Eugene,
a Capuchin Monk,* 1652
Oil on canvas. 97.2 × 130.5 cm
To right on the column base the
arms of Antonius Triest,
composed of two hunting horns
and dogs with the Latin
inscription *CONFIDENTER.* In
the upper part of the arms the
inscription *AET 76* (indicating
the bishop's age). Also a barely
decipherable date: *A 1652*
Provenance: Acquired in 1768
with the collection of Count
Cobenzl, Brussels
Inv. no. GE 589

36
FRANS POURBUS THE YOUNGER
1569 Antwerp – 1622 Paris
*Portrait of Margaret of Savoy,
Duchess of Mantua*, 1608
Oil on canvas. 206.5 × 116.3 cm
Provenance: Transferred 1931
via Antikvariat (state trading
organization responsible for
selling art treasures)
Inv. no. GE 6957
Selected literature: Cat. 1981,
p. 58; Gritsay 1989, p. 29

Pourbus here portrays Margaret
of Savoy (1589–1655), daughter
of Carlo Emmanuele I, Duke of
Savoy, and Catherine of Spain,
who married Francesco IV
Gonzaga, Duke of Mantua, in
1608. She is shown standing,
full length, turned slightly to
her left, set against billowing
brown and blue drapery,
wearing her wedding dress, the
skirt of which is richly
embroidered with ducal crowns
and the monogram *FGMA*
(Francesco Gonzaga,
Margherita).

This painting is typical of the
official portraiture that
developed at the Spanish court
during the second half of the
sixteenth century and which
had spread across Europe by the
early seventeenth century.
Characteristic of such portraits
are the fixed pose and gestures,
the obligatory background
drapery and the close attention
to the smallest details of the
costume (as attire was indicative
of the sitter's status) – all
attributes determined by the
strict demands of court
etiquette. The Hermitage
portrait, in common with the
majority of such works, displays
a striking contrast between the
vivid, animated movements of
the facial features and hands,
and the flat lifelessness of the
figure, encumbered by its stiff,
heavily embroidered costume,
which appears as a series of flat,
geometrical masses. Yet
Pourbus cannot be accused of
any lack of refined taste or skill,
as it is these that allow him to
smooth over the contradictions
imposed by the genre and to
create an overall impression of
harmony.

The portrait was clearly
painted in 1608, the year of the
marriage of Margaret of Savoy
and Francesco IV Gonzaga, as
the sitter is shown in her
wedding dress. The picture was
possibly intended for the
"Gallery of Beauties" in the
palace of the Duke of Mantua,
since its composition does not
suggest that it had a pendant
male portrait. A slightly earlier
version of the portrait (*c.* 1606),
in which the sitter wears a
different dress, is in San Carlo
al Corso, Rome.
N.G.

37
CORNELIS DE VOS
1584 Hulst – 1651 Antwerp
Portrait of an Elderly Woman,
1630s
Oil on canvas, transferred from
panel in 1846. 124.5 × 93.5 cm
Top left corner (dimensions
57 × 37 cm) is a later addition
Provenance: Collection de
Scawen, England; collection of
Sir Robert Walpole, Houghton
Hall, Norfolk; acquired in 1779
with the Walpole collection,
Norfolk
Inv. no. GE 483
Selected literature: *Aedes* 1752,
p. 85; Rooses 1886–92, vol. IV,
no. 1113; Somoff 1901, no. 578;
Cat. 1958, p. 63; Cat. 1981, p. 43;
Gritsay 1993, no. 37

The painting's composition
suggests that it would originally
have had a pendant male
portrait. The family's coat of
arms was probably included in
the upper left corner, but seems
to have been lost even before
the painting was transferred
from panel to canvas.

While in the Walpole
collection, and then for many
years once it had come to the
Hermitage, the painting was
attributed to Rubens. Glück
(1931) believed it to be by van
Dyck, but the authorship of
Cornelis de Vos was established
by M. Varshavskaya (oral
communication) and accepted,
with some hesitation, in the
museum's 1981 catalogue. Of
other known works by de Vos,
the closest in style to the
Hermitage painting is a *Portrait
of a Woman* in the Museum
voor Schone Kunsten in Ghent
(reproduced in *Les Amis du
Musée de Gand, 65 ans d'activité*,
exh. cat., Ghent, 1963, no. 91,
p. 30). Both portraits show a
similar treatment of the eyes,
nose and lips, and the oval
outline of the face. There are
also parallels between the
clothing and headgear in the
two paintings.

A reduced, half-length
version of this portrait (oil on
canvas, 50 × 39 cm) was
included in an auction of the
property of Heinrich Hahn in
Frankfurt, May 14, 1911 (lot 152).
N.G.

38
Frans Denys
c. 1610 Antwerp – 1670 Mantua
Portrait of the Architect Leo van Heil, 1647
Oil on canvas. 119 × 87 cm
Inscription top right on the background: *AETATIS 42*
Signed bottom left: *F.Denys fecit*
Provenance: Collection of P.V. Delarov, Pavlovsk, near St. Petersburg; transferred from Antikvariat (state trading organization responsible for selling art treasures) in 1933
Inv. no. GE 7692

39
PEETER FRANCHOYS
1606 Mechelen – 1654
Mechelen
Self-portrait, c. 1637
Oil on canvas. 73 × 50.5 cm
Provenance: Possibly in the
collection of M.I. Knebel,
St. Petersburg; transferred from
the Museums Fund at the State
Hermitage Museum in 1939
Inv. no. GE 8495

40

PETER PAUL RUBENS
1577 Siegen – 1640 Antwerp
*Pastoral Landscape with
Rainbow*, c. 1632–35
Oil on canvas, transferred from
panel in 1869. 86 × 130 cm
Provenance: 1677 duc de
Richelieu, Paris; June 17, 1696,
sale of Everhard Jabach, Paris
(lot 150); presented to Count
Brühl by the Elector of Bavaria,
son of the Emperor Charles VII
(Somoff 1901); acquired in 1769
with the Brühl collection,
Dresden
Inv. no. GE 482
Selected literature: De Piles
1677, pp. 146–49; Somoff 1901,

no. 595; Cat. 1958, p. 93;
Varshavskaya 1975, no. 34
(ed. 1989, pls. 69–71); Cat.
1981, p. 64; Adler 1982, no. 39;
Jaffé 1989, no. 1218; Brown
1996, no. 48

The idyllic mood of this
painting differs decisively from
the tense dynamism of
Rubens's "heroic" landscapes of
the late 1610s (see cat. 41). The
artist's vision is revealed in the
formal equilibrium of the
picture's structure and in the
harmony of its motifs, as the
pastoral idyll in the foreground
echoes the calm and stability of
nature, manifest, above all, in

the rainbow that dominates the
sky. Many of this composition's
elements are borrowed from
Italian masters, notably from a
drawing by the Venetian artist
Domenico Campagnola (Kieser
1931, pp. 281–91; Vergara 1982,
pp. 57, 59). The flautist's pose
recalls that of the shepherd in
Titian's *Pastoral* (*Paris and
Oenone*; Vergara 1982, p. 57),
while the upper part of the
figure derives from a drawing of
a model by Annibale Carracci
(Hodge 1977, p. 268). Such
Italian reminiscences notably
set *Pastoral Landscape with
Rainbow* apart from the so-
called "Flemish landscapes" that

Rubens produced in the second
half of the 1630s. On these
grounds, the Hermitage
painting is usually dated to the
period between 1632 and 1635.

A preparatory drawing for
the painting, *Shepherd and
Shepherdess*, a study of the
seated shepherd to left, is in the
Institut Néerlandais, Fondation
Custodia, Paris (inv. no. 2535;
Adler 1982, no. 39b). A larger
version of the composition,
painted c. 1635, is in the Louvre
(inv. no. 2118; Adler 1982,
no. 40).
N.G.

41

PETER PAUL RUBENS
1577 Siegen – 1640 Antwerp
The Carters, c. 1615–20
Oil on canvas, transferred from
panel in 1823. 86 × 126.5 cm
Provenance: Probably in
collection of Cardinal Mazarin
(inv. no. 1286) in 1661; sale of
the collection of D. Potter, The
Hague, May 19, 1723 (lot 44):
collection of the 1st Earl of
Cadogan; collection of Sir
Robert Walpole, London, then
Houghton Hall, Norfolk;
acquired in 1779 with the
Walpole collection, Norfolk
Inv. no. GE 480
Selected literature: *Aedes* 1752,
p. 87; Somoff 1901, no. 594;
Cat. 1958, p. 82; Varshavskaya
1975, no. 19 (ed. 1989,
pls. 40–43); Cat. 1981, p. 62;
Adler 1982, no. 19; Jaffé 1989,
no. 402; Sutton 1993, no. 89,
pp. 480–82; Brown 1996,
no. 20, pp. 48–51

The painting depicts two carters
as they guide a wagon heavily
laden with stone across a ford,
an action set against a steep,
overgrown landscape that rises
up between two twisted oaks.
The rocky crag, which
dominates the middle of the
composition, divides two
landscape motifs. To the right, a
panorama opens to a sunlit hilly
landscape that disappears into
the distance, and, to the left, the
darkened woods and river are lit
by a full moon. The
simultaneous presence of night
and day within the picture has
led a number of scholars to
suggest a relationship with the
conventions of Late Medieval
cycles of the day, the months
and the seasons, and hence with
the symbolism of the cycle of
life and death (Evers 1942;
Vergara 1982). An alternative
explanation of the unusual
lighting effects in this work
(Smith 1829–42) suggests that
the artist was attempting to
capture the precise moment
before the sun disappears over
the horizon when the moon has
already risen in the sky. It is
also possible that the painting
illustrates the verse from Psalm
104 (19): "He appointed the
moon for seasons: the sun
knoweth his going down."
    Stylistically, *The Carters*
clearly belongs with Rubens's
early landscapes. The majority
of contemporary scholars date it
between 1615 and 1620 (*c.* 1617:
d'Hulst 1977, Adler 1982;
c. 1620: Varshavskaya 1975,
Brown 1996). The wooden cart
in the painting's foreground is
recorded in a drawing of
c. 1615–16, *A Man Thrashing
beside a Wagon, Farm Buildings
Beside,* formerly at Chatsworth
and now in the J. Paul Getty
Museum, Los Angeles. The
landscape on the left, showing
the moon reflected in water,
echoes the work of Adam
Elsheimer (1578–1610), such as
his *Flight into Egypt* of 1609
(Alte Pinakothek, Munich).
There are numerous copies of
this painting by contemporary
and later artists.
N.G.

42
BONAVENTURA PEETERS
1614 Antwerp – 1652 Hoboken
Sea Harbour, 1640s
Oil on canvas, transferred from
panel in 1869. 46.5 × 63.5 cm
Initials bottom right: *BP*
Provenance: Acquired in 1834
from the collection of Páez de la
Cadena, Spanish ambassador to
the imperial court, St. Petersburg
Inv. no. GE 2153

43
PEETER VAN DEN VELDE
1634 Antwerp – 1687 (?1707)
Antwerp
Castle on a River Bank, 1670s
Oil on canvas. 61.5 × 93.5 cm
Signed bottom left: *Peeter van den Velde*
Provenance: Acquired in 1915 with the collection of P.P. Semenov-Tyan-Shansky, Petrograd
Inv. no. GE 2906

44
WILHELM SCHUBERT VON
EHRENBERG
1630 Germany – c. 1676
Antwerp
Interior of a Church, 1665
Oil on canvas. 104.5 × 116.5 cm
Signed and dated bottom right
corner: *van Ehrenberg 1665*
Provenance: Acquired before
1859; during the second half
of the nineteenth century
at Gatchina Palace, near

St. Petersburg; 1920 returned to
the Hermitage
Inv. no. GE 1441
Selected literature: Cat. 1958,
p. 112; Cat. 1981, p. 81; Babina
1995, p. 12

Von Ehrenberg depicted the
interiors of Italian churches on
several occasions, despite the
fact that he never visited Italy.
He based his fantastical
perspectives on prints (such as

those by Giovanni Battista
Falda, 1643–76), from which he
borrowed individual
architectural elements. Such
was the case with this *Interior of
a Church*, whose architectural
structure and decorative
elements, notably the powerful
pillars supporting the arches
and the baldacchino, recall
those of St. Peter's in Rome.
Several years later, in 1671, von
Ehrenberg painted an *Interior of*

St. Peter's in Rome (Museum
voor Schone Kunsten, Ghent),
which presents a relatively
authentic view of the inside of
the basilica, including that
famous monument of the
Baroque style, Bernini's
Baldacchino of 1624–33. In the
Hermitage canvas, by contrast,
the baldacchino is almost
unrecognizable and appears as
a pseudo-Classical rotunda.
N.B.

45
HENDRICK VAN STEENWIJK THE
YOUNGER
c. 1580 Antwerp (?) – *c.* 1649
The Netherlands (?)
Interior of a Gothic Church,
c. 1610
Oil on panel. 94 × 125 cm
Provenance: Transferred in
1919 from the museum of the
Academy of Arts, Petrograd
Inv. no. GE 4360

46
HENDRICK VAN STEENWIJK THE
YOUNGER
c. 1580 Antwerp (?) – c. 1649
The Netherlands (?)
St. Jerome in his Study, 1634
Oil on panel. 28.5 × 22.9 cm
Signed and dated bottom left: *H
V STEIN 1634*
Provenance: Acquired between
1763 and 1773
Inv. no. GE 1894

47
PEETER NEEFFS THE YOUNGER
1620 Antwerp – after 1675
Antwerp
and Frans Francken the
Younger I
1603 Antwerp – after 1667
Antwerp
*Interior of the Church of
St. Charles Borromeo, Antwerp,*
late 1630s
Oil on canvas. 50 × 72 cm
Inscription left, on the column
base: *F.ffranck Fecit*
Provenance: Acquired before
1859
Inv. no. GE 2731

48
Peeter Neeffs the Younger
1620 Antwerp – after 1675
Antwerp
Interior of Antwerp Cathedral,
c. 1655
Oil on panel, transferred from
panel in 1843. 49 × 64.5 cm
Signed right on the pillar: *peeter*
neffs
Provenance: Acquired in 1781
from the collection of Count
Baudouin, Paris
Inv. no. GE 1892

49
Andries van Eertvelt
1590 Antwerp – 1652 Antwerp
Battle Between the Spanish Fleet and Dutch Ships in May 1573 during the Siege of Haarlem,
c. 1625–27
Oil on canvas. 134 × 165.5 cm
Monogram centre bottom: *AVE*
Spanish inscription on the sail of Neptune's trident:
VICTORIA QUE ARMADA/ REAL DE QUE ES GENERAL DON/ FADRIQUE DE

TOLEDOTUVO EN/ EL ESTRECHO CON NUEVE NAOS/ SU ESQUADRA CONTRAVENT [...]/ *Y S* [...] *DE OLANDES ES QUE VENIAN DE/ LEVANTE* [Victory in the gulf by the royal armada, brought by nine ships from the Levant, under the command of Don Fadrique of Toledo over the squadron of insurgents and [...] Dutch]
Provenance: Collection of S.N. Plautin, St. Petersburg;

transferred in 1924 *via* the State Museum Reserve
Inv. no. GE 6416
Selected literature: Cat. 1958, p. 112; Linnik 1980, p. 59; Cat. 1981, p. 81

The subject of this painting was identified by a comparison of the somewhat illegible inscription with documented historical events. It is clear that the Hermitage canvas shows a sea battle between the Spanish

and Dutch ships in the gulf near Haarlem: such a battle took place on May 26, 1573, and concluded in a Spanish victory. The Spanish squadron was commanded by Don Fadrique of Toledo, son of the Duke of Alba. Despite heroic resistance by the Dutch, Haarlem fell on July 12, 1573.

Here the Dutch ships, identified by tricolour flags, are much smaller than the Spanish. Several fill the background of

the main action, while others are shown sinking in the foreground. To the right are two Spanish ships, and, in the centre, the crew of a Spanish flagship is shown boarding a Dutch vessel. On the largest sail of the Spanish flagship a depiction of a religious scene is partially visible, possibly the Assumption of the Virgin. In the lower left corner Neptune charges through the waves on his chariot, drawn by a

hippocamp. The sea god appears as protector of the Spanish fleet, demonstrated by the inscription declaring the victory on the pendant that flies from his trident.

When the painting entered the Hermitage it was catalogued simply as a *Sea Battle* and was attributed to the Dutch artist Hendrick Cornelisz. Vroom, probably on the basis of Vroom's painting of the 1630s of the same battle,

now in the Rijksmuseum, Amsterdam (*Battle Between Dutch and Spanish Ships on the Haarlemmermeer 26 May 1573*). While Vroom depicted the battle objectively, the sympathies of the Flemish Eertvelt were clearly with the Spanish.

A monogram revealed on the Hermitage canvas after restoration led to the identification of Eertvelt as the painter. Linnik (1980) placed

the canvas among the artist's early works; it was probably completed in Antwerp during the late 1620s, before the artist's departure for Genoa in 1627.
N.B.

50
ANDRIES VAN EERTVELT
1590 Antwerp – 1652 Antwerp
Two Ships at Anchor, 1640s
Oil on canvas, transferred from panel in 1854. 64 × 98 cm
Monogram left, on a floating piece of wood: *AVE*
Provenance: Collection of I.P. Balashov, St. Petersburg; acquired in 1919
Inv. no. GE 5596

51
PAUL BRILL
1554 Antwerp – 1626 Rome
Mountainous Landscape, 1626
Oil on canvas. 75 × 103 cm
Signed and dated bottom left:
PAVOLO BRILLI 1626
Provenance: Acquired in 1769
with the collection of Count
Brühl, Dresden
Inv. no. GE 1955

52
JOOS MOMPER THE YOUNGER
1564 Antwerp – 1635 Antwerp
and Jan Brueghel the Elder
1568 Brussels – 1625 Antwerp
*Mountainous Landscape with a
Fallen Donkey, c.* 1610
Oil on canvas, transferred from
panel. 46 × 74.5 cm
Provenance: Collection of
Prince D.M. Golitsyn, Vienna;
after his death in 1793 passed to
A.M. Golitsyn, Moscow; 1817–18
sold as part of the museum of
the Golitsyn Hospital, Moscow;
Prince S.M. Golitsyn, Moscow;
collection of the latter's great-
nephew, also S.M. Golitsyn;
1865–86, Golitsyn Museum,
Moscow; transferred in 1886
from the Golitsyn Museum,
Moscow
Inv. no. GE 448

53

54
JAN WILDENS
1585–86 Antwerp – 1653
Antwerp
and Hans Jordaens III
c. 1595 Antwerp – *c.* 1643
Antwerp
*Landscape with Christ and His
Disciples on the Road to Emmaus,
c.* 1640
Oil on canvas. 123 × 168 cm
Provenance: Collection of A.V.
Krivosheyn, St. Petersburg;
transferred in 1924 *via* the State
Museums Fund from the Lvova
collection, Petrograd
Inv. no. GE 6319
Selected literature: Cat. 1958,
p. 46 (as Wildens?); Adler 1980,
no. G 65; Cat. 1981, p. 43

This panoramic landscape, like
many others by Wildens, is
divided into clear spatial planes
constructed in the manner of
stage scenery. The artist also
makes use of aerial perspective
to indicate distance, the thick
brownish-green tone of the
foreground gradually
weakening into a lighter and
more transparent bluish-grey in
the distance. The landscape is
calm and sedate, in Wildens's
usual manner, which sets his
work so clearly apart from that
of Rubens. Its main motif is the
broad road leading off into the
hilly distance, framed on both
sides by tall trees, at the centre
of which Christ stands talking

to two of his disciples (Luke
24:13–28). In the left
foreground is a pond, on the far
bank of which, visible in a
clearing between the trees, is a
house with a well; on the near
side of the pond, at the edge of
the road, a man sits fishing. The
figures were painted by
Antwerp artist Hans Jordaens
III (*c.* 1595 – *c.* 1643). The
importance of vertical elements
in the composition and the
nature of the colour harmonies
indicate that the canvas was
painted *c.* 1640.
N.G.

55
Jacques d'Arthois
1613 Brussels – 1686 Brussels
Wooded Landscape with Men Driving Cows on the Road, c. 1635
Oil on canvas. 115 × 146 cm
Provenance: Acquired before 1859; in the 19th century kept at Gatchina Palace, near St. Petersburg; returned to the Hermitage in 1932
Inv. no. GE 8678

56
Jan Siberechts
1627 Antwerp – c. 1703 London
Shepherdess, late 1660s
Oil on canvas. 103.5 × 77.5 cm
Provenance: Collection of Grand Duchess Maria Nikolayevna, St. Petersburg; collection S.V. Sheremetev, St. Petersburg; transferred in 1920 *via* the State Museums fund, from the collection of S.V. Sheremetev, Petrograd
Inv. no. GE 6240
Selected literature: Waagen 1853, vol. I, p. 139; Fokker 1931, pp. 31–32, 94; Cat. 1958, p. 97; Cat. 1981, p. 68; Gritsay 1983, no. 20; Thiery 1987, p. 84

This picture was painted while Siberechts was resident in Antwerp, between 1661 and 1672, after his return from Italy and before his departure for England, during which time he is thought to have completed his finest work. It is one of a group of paintings in which the artist achieved a synthesis of landscape and genre types, showing the peaceful quiet and calm of a summer's midday, when time almost seems to come to a halt, and man and nature meld into harmonious unity. Not immediately apparent is the peasant girl beneath the trees, who is occupied in that

most prosaic of tasks, picking lice from her clothing. The local tones of her dress – the blue skirt, white apron and red blouse with its white collar – stand out as bright spots against the overall background of green grass and leaves, without disrupting the dominant and restrained silvery-green harmony. As in his other works from the second half of the 1660s, the artist achieves an almost stereometric effect in the depiction of figures and objects in the foreground. Siberechts creates a strong sense of illusion in the round water vessels, one of his favourite

motifs, which he employed in endless variations for compositions of this period. He also repeated the basic motif in several works produced at this time: *La Vachère et sa fille* (dated 1667; collection del Monte, Brussels), *La Toilette au bord de l'eau* (Louvre, Paris, inv. no. 2140 A) and *Pastoral Scene* (North Carolina Museum of Art, Raleigh, inv. no. Kress GL 60.17.70).
N.G.

57
Cornelis Huysmans
1648 Antwerp – 1727 Mechelen
Wooded Landscape, n.d.
Oil on canvas. 81 × 116.5 cm
Provenance: Received before
1797
Inv. no. GE 656

58
JAN BRUEGHEL THE ELDER
(VELVET BRUEGHEL)
1568 Brussels – 1625 Antwerp
*Wooded Landscape (The Rest on
the Flight into Egypt)*, 1607
Oil on panel. 51.5 × 91.5 cm
Signed and dated bottom left:
BRUEGHEL 1607
Provenance: Collection of
Clemens August, Duke of
Bavaria, Prince-Elector and
Archbishop of Cologne
(according to Cat. 1773–85);
acquired in 1769 with the
Count Brühl collection,
Dresden
Inv. no. GE 424
Selected literature: Somoff
1901, no. 513; Cat. 1958, p. 39;
Ertz 1979, no. 154; Cat. 1981,
p. 34

In its composition, achieved by
the dominant diagonals, this
painting is close to works by Jan
Brueghel's older contemporary
(and possible teacher), Gillis
van Coninxloo (1544–1607),
such as *Wooded Landscape with
a River* (Staatliches Museum,
Schwerin). Yet, in its evocative,
peaceful dreaminess, it is
readily distinguished from the
romantic, often gloomy mood
that so marks the work of
Coninxloo. Moreover, nothing
draws the beholder into the
depths, into the tempting cool
of the forest, which to
Coninxloo is always magical
and mysterious. Instead, the
viewer's gaze is arrested by the
small area in the foreground,
resting on each detail: the tiny

figures in their variegated
clothes, the dried twigs and
colourful grasses all around, the
birds hiding in thick
undergrowth, the whimsical
pattern of the vegetation and
leaves, all rendered with
incredible precision.

The Virgin Mary with the
Child in her lap (The Pseudo-
Eyangeliary of Matthew, 20–21;
Matthew 2:13–15), seated by the
roots of a large tree in the centre
foreground, is set amid
peasants and woodcutters going
about their everyday labours,
and seems at first glance to be
engaged in some simple everyday episode, observed from life.
N.G.

59
PEETER SNEYERS
1681 Antwerp – 1752 Antwerp
Flowers, Fruits and a Hedgehog,
c. 1725
Oil on canvas. 101.3 × 77 cm
Signed bottom right: *P.Snyers*
Provenance: Acquired with the
collection of P.P. Semenov-
Tyan-Shansky in 1915
Inv. no. GE 3448

60
FRANS SNYDERS
1579 Antwerp – 1657 Antwerp
Bowl of Fruit on a Red Tablecloth,
1640s
Oil on canvas, transferred from
panel in 1867. 59.8 × 90.8 cm
Provenance: Acquired before
1797
Inv. no. GE 612

61
ADRIAEN VAN UTRECHT
1599 Antwerp – 1652 Antwerp
Still Life with Grapes, 1640s
Oil on canvas. 119 × 99 cm
Signed bottom left on the edge
of the table: *A. van Uytrecht f.*
Provenance: Acquired before
1859
Inv. no. GE 660
Selected literature: Somoff
1901, no. 1350; Cat. 1958, p. 113;
Kuznetsov 1966, no. 16; Cat.
1981, p. 77; Gritsay 1986, no. 15;
Gritsay 1993, no. 33

This canvas is an example of the
"luxurious still life," or
pronkstilleven, which appeared
in Flemish painting under the
influence of Jan Davidsz. de
Heem, a native of Utrecht who
lived in Antwerp from 1636. On
a table appear objects of obvious
luxury: exotic fruits that ripen in
the southern sun, a large,
precious, Chinese porcelain
bowl, an elaborately wrought
silver platter and a tall, green,
glass *roemer*. All seem pregnant
with symbolism: the glass of
wine and the grapes may refer

to the Eucharist, while the
damaged stone wall may
suggest the traditional theme of
vanitas.

Adriaen van Utrecht was
strongly influenced by Frans
Snyders as well as Jan Davidsz.
de Heem, whose works instilled
in the artist a more profound
taste for the luxurious and
decorative. The majority of
Utrecht's paintings show
overloaded, rather static
compositions with somewhat
muted colouring. This painting
is no exception, although it

displays an attractive plasticity
of form and is finely drawn. In
composition, this still life is
particularly close to de Heem's
works of the 1640s (such as his
*Still Life with Fruit with Precious
Casket*, Mauritshuis, The
Hague, inv. no. 48; *Still Life with
Herring* and *Still Life with
Faience Ewer*, both Schloss
Vaduz, Sammlung des Fürsten
von Liechtenstein, inv. nos. 777,
778) and was probably painted
during the same period.
N.G.

62
JAN FYT
1611 Antwerp – 1661 Antwerp
Fruit and Parrot, 1645
Oil on canvas, transferred from
panel in 1894. 58.3 × 90.7 cm
Signed right on the table edge:
Joannes. Fyt
Provenance: Acquired in 1846,
by bequest of D.P. Tatishchev,
St. Petersburg
Inv. no. GE 613

63

DANIEL SEGHERS
1590 Antwerp – 1661 Antwerp
and Thomas Willeboirts
Bosschaert
1613/14 Bergen-op-Zoom – 1654
Antwerp
Flower Garland with Jesus and St.
John the Baptist as Children, 1651
Oil on canvas. 129 × 97.4 cm
Signed bottom right: *Daniel*
Seghers Soctis Jesu
Provenance: Acquired in 1915,
by bequest of V.P. Zurov,
Tsarskoye Selo (near St.
Petersburg)
Inv. no. GE 3468
Selected literature: Schmidt
1916, p. 30; Cat. 1958, p. 97;
Kuznetsov 1966, no. 17; Hairs
1985, p. 155; Wilmers 1996,
no. D 26

Seghers's choice of plants for
the flower garland that
dominates the image was
determined by the central scene,
which shows a playful Christ
Child and John. John the Baptist
places a floral crown on Christ's
head, which includes roses that
echo those of the surrounding
garland. The garland decorating
the cartouche, however, also
includes a variety of thorns,
thistles, sprigs of holly, thorn-
apples and brambles – all of
which evoke the crown of
thorns, one of the traditional
symbols of Christ's Passion. In
compositional type, the painting
is close to Seghers's *Flower*
Garland Pietà of 1651 (Schloss
Mosigkau, Dessau) and can be
assigned the same date.

The composition within the
cartouche repeats *Two Children*
Playing (Rijksmuseum,
Amsterdam, inv. no. A 622),
which Larsen (1988) believed to
be the work of an assistant to
van Dyck. The composition was
engraved by Hendrik Bary
(1640–1707) under the name
van Dyck, and the subject
identified as an allegorical
depiction of Spring and
Autumn (Hollstein 1949–81,
vol. I, no. 7).

Stylistically, the depiction of
the children within the
cartouche is closest to paintings
by Thomas Willeboirts
Bosschaert (compare, for
instance, the image of the Child
in his *Vision of St. Francis of*
Assisi, Noordbrabants Museum,
's-Hertogenbosch). A painting
attributed to Willeboirts
Bosschaert, similar to the
Amsterdam painting, *Two Putti*,
was sold at auction in 1991
(Phillips, London, April 16,
1991, lot 95).
N.G.

64

NICOLAES VAN VERENDAEL
1640 Antwerp – 1691 Antwerp
Garland with a Bust of the Virgin,
1680s
Oil on canvas. 117 × 86.5 cm
Inscription on the pedestal of
the bust (in two lines): *Hortvs*
Conclusus
Provenance: Acquired between
1733 and 1783
Inv. no. GE 560

65

Sebastiaen Bonnecroy
1618 – 1676; worked in
Antwerp and The Hague
Still Life with a Skull (*Wall in the
Artist's Studio*), 1668
Oil on canvas. 111 × 88 cm
Signed bottom left: *Sebastiaen
Bonnecroy*; dated bottom right:
Fecit anno 1668
Provenance: Acquired in 1939
through the Leningrad State
Purchasing Commission from a
private collection in Leningrad
Inv. no. GE 9229
Selected literature: Cat. 1958,
p. 38; Kuznetsov 1966, no. 20;
Cat. 1981, p. 32

This composition unites motifs
from two different types of still
life, the trompe l'œil and the
vanitas. Attributes of an artist's
studio are presented in the
trompe l'œil technique: in the
centre of the composition is a
canvas with a still life on a
stretcher; to the left on a nail
hangs a palette with paints; and
above this is a miniature oval
portrait of a man in armour.
A maulstick leaning against
the wall cuts across the lower
part of the stretcher, and a
bottle of varnish hangs on a
nail, while at the bottom on a
ledge, beside a metal box, lie

brushes and a knife.
   The centre of the
composition, however, is
dominated by a painting of a
vanitas still-life painting, to
which the content of the whole
picture is subordinated. The
vanity and brevity of earthly life
and pleasures, an idea drawn
from the Bible ("*Vanitas
vanitatum, omnia vanitas*"
(Vanity of vanities; all is vanity),
Ecclesiastes 1:2), is symbolized
by the skull, the soap bubble,
the hourglass, smoke (by means
of the pipe and wick to light it)
and the large seashell and the
hunting horn. The concept of

vanitas, as was noted by Marks
(1986), is also emphasized by
*The Death of the Children of
Niobe* (Ovid: *Metamorphoses*,
VI:204–312), the subject of the
grisaille relief depicted in the
painting. Yet there is a note of
hope: the ivy wreath on the
skull hints at resurrection to
eternal life in another world.
   This work was probably
painted under the influence of
similar paintings by Cornelis
Norbertus Gijsbrechts (? – after
1678), who in 1668 painted a
slightly different version
(Statens Museum for Kunst,
Copenhagen, inv. no. 242).

Another version of the same
composition, signed by the
French artist Jean-François
Lemotte (de Le Motte, Delmotte;
fl. second half of the
seventeenth century) is in the
Musée des Beaux-Arts, Dijon.
N.G.

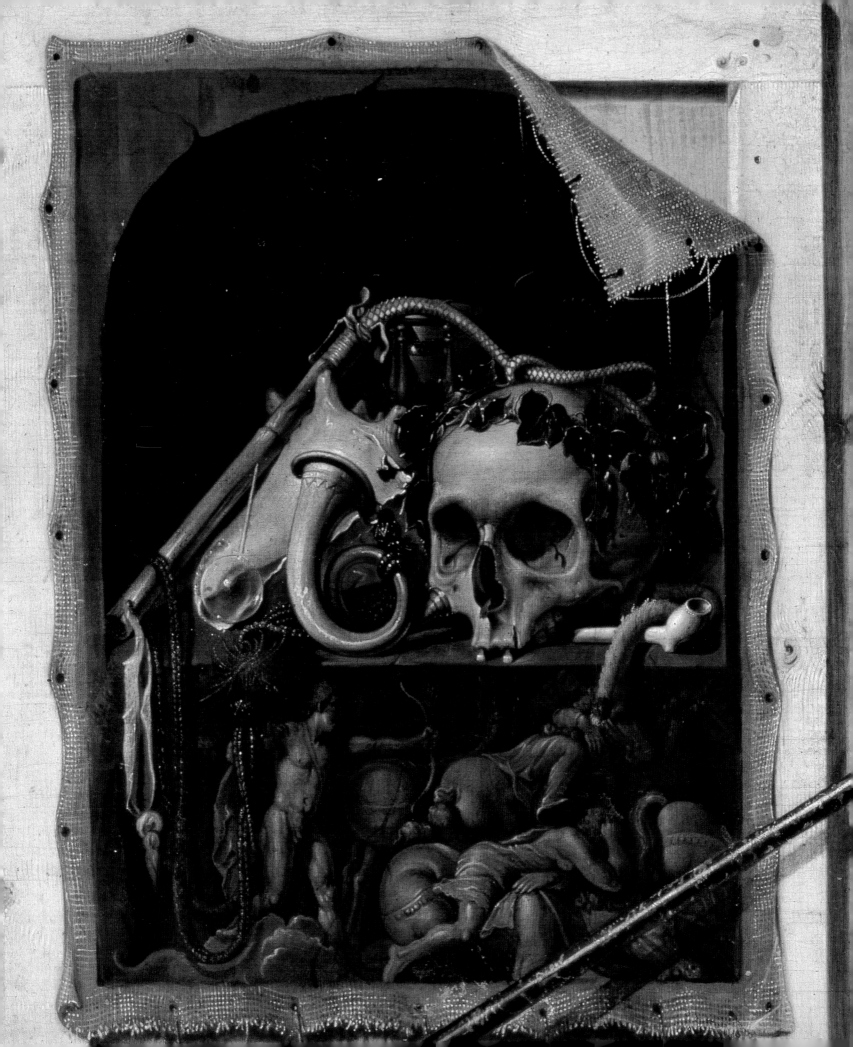

66
FRANS SNYDERS
1579 Antwerp – 1657 Antwerp
Sketches of a Cat's Head, 1609
Oil on canvas, transferred from
old canvas in 1850.
42.5 × 32.5 cm
Signed and dated bottom left:
F.Snyders 1609
Provenance: Acquired from the
collection of Jean de Jullienne,
Paris, in 1767
Inv. no. GE 609

67
FRANS SNYDERS
1579 Antwerp – 1657 Antwerp
A Concert of Birds, 1630–40
Oil on canvas. 136.5 × 240 cm
Provenance: Collection of
Grinling Gibbons, London;
November 1722 acquired by Sir
Robert Walpole at the sale of the
Gibbons collection; collection of
Sir Robert Walpole, London,
then Houghton Hall, Norfolk;
acquired in 1779 with the
Walpole collection, Norfolk

Inv. no. GE 607
Selected literature: *Aedes* 1752,
p. 38; Somoff 1901, no. 1324;
Cat. 1958, p. 89; Cat. 1981,
p. 69; Robels 1989, no. A 205;
Koslow 1995, pp. 291, 296, 297

This concert of birds is
composed of a colourful
assembly of winged creatures
gathered around an owl seated
on a branch above an open
musical score. The theme,
which was to become

widespread in seventeenth-
century Flemish art under the
influence of Snyders, seems to
derive from one of Aesop's
fables ("The Owl and the Birds")
that is known from two
speeches attributed to the Greek
orator and philosopher Dio
Cocceianus Chrysostomus
(*c.* 40–120). The fable was recast
as a religious allegory in the
medieval period (Vandenbroeck
1985, pp. 26–30), yet Snyders's
presentation of the subject is

purely secular, the artist using it
as a pretext to demonstrate the
wide variety of feathered beasts
in creation. In the Hermitage
picture, as in the paintings of
Jan Brueghel the Elder (Velvet
Brueghel), who often turned to
this subject, depictions of
different birds commonly found
in European woods, fields and
waterways are imaginatively
united with more decorative,
cultivated European breeds,
such as peacocks and puffer

pigeons, as well as such exotic
imports from the New World as
toucans, Amazonian parrots
and red aras.

Judging by its dimensions
and format, the picture may
have been intended to hang
over a door; many versions and
copies of the painting are
known (Robels 1989).
N.G.

68

FRANS SNYDERS
1579 Antwerp – 1657 Antwerp
and Jan Boeckhorst (?)
1604 Münster – 1668 Antwerp
*Cook at a Kitchen Table with
Dead Game*, 1636–38
Oil on canvas. 171 × 173 cm
Provenance: Acquired in 1764
with the collection of Johann
Ernst Gotzkowsky, Berlin
Inv. no. GE 608
Selected literature: Somoff
1901, no. 1319; Cat. 1958,
p. 100; Cat. 1981, p. 69; Robels
1989, no. 286

This still life displays Snyders's
virtuosity in his characteristic
depiction of dead game –
hunting trophies – and
household birds. On the table
are a grey heron, several
partridges and a bundle of small
songbirds, while a tall woven
basket holds snipe, pheasant
and a woodgrouse, and a bittern
hangs on the wall. A cook
stands over the low table and
threatens the household cat that
attempts to drag off the grey
heron that hangs over the side
of the table.

The figure of the cook is

possibly the work of Jan
Boeckhorst. The flaccid and
somewhat uncertain manner of
execution of this figure argues
against Jaffé's attribution of it to
Rubens (1971; 1989). A pendant
to the Hermitage painting,
*Serving Woman with a Boy in a
Fruit Store*, is in the collection of
Lady Bute, Dumfries House,
Cumnock, Ayrshire. Linnik
(1965) first established that both
paintings derive from a sketch
(Christie's, London, July 6,
1990, lot 108) published by
Greindl (1956), which is
generally considered to be by

Rubens. The basis for the dating
of both paintings lies in the
similarity between the boy in
Lady Bute's painting and
portraits of Rubens's son from
his second marriage to Helène
Fourment, Frans, who was born
in 1633. Slight differences of
scholarly opinion result mainly
from the age assigned to the boy
in Lady Bute's painting. Linnik
(1965) dated both works to
c. 1636, Robels (1989) to
c. 1636–37; Jaffé (1971; 1989)
put them at roughly 1637–38
and Koslow (1995) at *c.* 1635.
N.G.

69
JAN FYT
1611 Antwerp – 1661 Antwerp
Dead Game and a Dog, c. 1655
Oil on canvas. 93.5 × 120 cm
Signed by the left edge, slightly
below centre: *Joannes. Fyt*
Provenance: Acquired before
1797
Inv. no. GE 657

70
JAN FYT
1611 Antwerp – 1661 Antwerp
Hunting Trophy, c. 1645
Oil on canvas. 82 × 114 cm
Provenance: Collection of S.M.
Golitsyn, Moscow; collection of
M.K. Gorchakov, Petrograd;
transferred *via* the State
Museums Fund, Leningrad, in
1923
Inv. no. GE 6241

71
ALEXANDER ADRIAENSSEN
1587 Antwerp – 1661 Antwerp
Fish and Dead Game, 1643
Oil on canvas. 57.5 × 86.5 cm
Signed and dated left on the
table leg: *Alex Adriaenssen f A*
1643
Provenance: Acquired from the
collection of Prince Grigory
Potemkin of Tauris in 1792;
transferred to Pavlovsk Palace,
near St. Petersburg in the
nineteenth century; returned to
the Hermitage in 1933
Inv. no. GE 7282, pendant to
inv. no. GE 7281

72
ALEXANDER ADRIAENSSEN
1587 Antwerp – 1661 Antwerp
Fish, 1643
Oil on canvas. 59.5 × 85 cm
Signed left on the table leg: *Alex
Adriaenssen fecit*
Provenance: See cat. 71
Inv. no. GE 7281, pendant to
inv. no. GE 7282

54.

73

PETER PAUL RUBENS
1577 Siegen – 1640 Antwerp
Pastoral Scene, c. 1635
Oil on canvas. 114.5 × 91 cm
Provenance: Probably sale of
Domburg collection,
Amsterdam, May 7, 1770 (lot 6);
acquired before 1774.
Inv. no. GE 493
Selected literature: Hoet,
Terwesten 1752–70, vol. I,
p. 137; Somoff 1901, no. 591;
Cat. 1958, p. 94; Varshavskaya
1975, no. 42 (ed. 1989, pl. 94);
Cat. 1981, p. 65; Jaffé 1989,
p. 370.

The Hermitage canvas is
Rubens's autograph, reduced-
scale replica of a painting (now
Alte Pinakothek, Munich) listed
in the posthumous inventory
(1640) of the artist's property as
"Un Berger caressant sa
bergère" (A Shepherd
embracing his Shepherdess,
Denucé 1932, no. 94, p. 60).
Here, the only details that recall
such a rural theme are the
bagpipes slung across the man's
back, and the ivy wreath he
wears, for the young woman's
costume is clearly both sylish
and contemporary.

During the first half of the
seventeenth century, the
depiction of shepherds and
shepherdesses was extremely
popular in the Netherlands,
especially in Holland. Peter
Corneliszoon Hooft's pastoral
drama *Granida*, which appeared
in 1605, played a significant rôle
in establishing the theme's
currency, especially among
artists. In common with the
majority of such theatrical
works of the age, it was a
variation on motifs borrowed
from Torquato Tasso's more
famous pastoral drama, *Aminta*.
Like Hooft's heroes, Rubens has
blurred the distinction between
antiquity's Arcadia and the
contemporary world. The
Hermitage painting reflects his
interest in ancient pastorals,
such as the poems of
Theocritus, and their Arcadian
vision of idyllic landscape and
imagination.

Rubens turned frequently to
such pastoral themes during the
last decade of his life (see
*Pastoral Landscape with a
Rainbow*; cat. 40), when he had
ceased his diplomatic activities
and was able to devote himself
completely to art. *Pastoral Scene*
presents all the main
characteristics of the master's
late works, especially his soft
painterly manner, his warmth of
tone, and the incorporation of
form and colour into a single
harmonious environment.
Numerous versions of this
composition are known.
N.G.

74

DAVID TENIERS THE YOUNGER
1610 Antwerp – 1690 Brussels
The Temptation of St. Anthony,
1650s
Jacopo da Voragine: *The Golden
Legend* XXI, 1
Oil on canvas. 99 × 132 cm
Signed centre bottom on the
stone: *D TENIERS*
Provenance: 1862 bequeathed
to Academy of Arts, St.
Petersburg; transferred in 1922
from the museum of the
Academy of Arts, Petrograd.
Formerly: collection of Count
Nikolay Kushelev-Bezborodko,
St. Petersburg
Inv. no. GE 3780

75
David Teniers the Younger
1610 Antwerp – 1690 Brussels
The Guardroom, 1642
Oil on canvas. 69 × 103 cm
Signed and dated bottom left:
DAVID, TENIERS AN 1642
Provenance: Before 1806 in the
collection of the Landgrave of
Hesse, Kassel; acquired in 1814
from the collection of Empress
Josephine at the Château de
Malmaison, near Paris
Inv. no. GE 583
Selected literature: Somoff
1901, no. 673; Cat. 1958, p. 103;
Cat. 1981, p. 73; Babina 1989a,
p. 3; Klinge 1991, no. 25

Klinge (1991) regarded the
Hermitage painting's three
main elements – the military
still life in the foreground, the
figures grouped in the second
plane that comprise the interior
scene, and the landscape view
beyond – as the expression of a
single idea of military might,
protection of the realm and
defence of the River Scheldt.
Babina (1989a), by contrast, saw
here a theatrical
characterization of the
traditional guardroom theme.
The "stage front" is filled with a
rich still life of military armour,
flags and weapons. The centre
of the composition is occupied

by the head of the watch, who is
further distinguished by his
brilliant costume and his
striking pose. His placement
unites the figures of the second
plane at left and right, and
draws the beholder's eye toward
the open archway. The curtain
further accentuates the
theatrical note as it rises to open
on a new landscape view, vastly
increasing the artist's "stage."
In the distance is depicted a
besieged fortress.
    In the treatment of the
riflemen, the weapons, banners
and military costumes, this
painting anticipates to a certain
degree the *Portrait of the*

*Members of the Oude Voetboog
Guild in Antwerp* (cat. 76),
which Teniers painted the
following year. Teniers is known
to have depicted objects from
the Brussels royal collection, to
which he had access as court
painter and keeper of the
Picture Gallery.
    The closest version to the
Hermitage *Guardroom* is in the
Walters Art Gallery, Baltimore
(inv. no. 37).
N.B.

76
DAVID TENIERS THE YOUNGER
1610 Antwerp – 1690 Brussels
*Portrait of the Members of the
Oude Voetboog Guild in Antwerp,*
1643
Oil on canvas. 135 × 183 cm
Signed and dated bottom left:
DAVID. TENIERS AN 1643
Provenance: Before 1806
collection of the Landgrave of
Hesse, Kassel; acquired in 1814
from the collection of Empress
Josephine at the Château de
Malmaison, near Paris
Inv. no. GE 572
Selected literature: van den
Branden 1883, p. 991; Somoff
1901, no. 672; Delen 1930,

p. 48, no. 272; Cat. 1958, p. 103;
Cat. 1981, p. 73; Babina 1989a,
p. 4; Klinge 1991, no. 26

This group portrait is set in
Antwerp's Grote Markt square.
To the left stands Antwerp
Town Hall (1561–65; Cornelis
Floris, architect) and to the right
of that the Zilversmidstraat
lined with sixteenth-century
buildings. On the extreme right
is the "Huys van Spanien"
(House of the Spaniards), the
home of the Oude Voetboog
Guild (the Crossbow Archers'
Guild), its façade decorated
with a red cloth bearing coats
of arms.

Various suggestions
regarding the event commemorated by the picture have been
proposed. Van den Branden
(1883) saw here a parade on the
occasion of the anniversary of
the guild's deacon, Godevaart
Snijders, in 1643. This was
rejected by Klinge (1991), owing
to the lack of documentary
evidence. Like Delen (1930), she
rightly noted that the event
taking place in the square is a
parade by the oldest of
Antwerp's guilds, the Oude
Voetboog, of which the deacon
was usually the city
burgomaster. Members of the
guild are shown in black

costume with red sashes tied
around their midriffs, with the
exception of three elderly men
to the right, probably the leaders
of the guild, whose red sashes
are worn across their shoulders.
In order to introduce variety
into the potentially monotonous
repetition of black costumes,
and to add lighter tones into the
painting, Teniers depicted some
members of the guild in yellow
attire, notably the drummer and
standard-bearer.
    The Hermitage painting was
Teniers's first large-scale
commission and was intended
to hang in the guild's assembly
hall. Comparatively recently,

archival documents uncovered
by de Poorter (1988, p. 207)
revealed that Teniers was
himself a member of the Oude
Voetboog Guild. On this basis,
Klinge (1991) has suggested
that the artist may have been
freed from the military service
obligatory for all members of
the guild in return for
producing the painting. The
picture remained in place until
1749 when, owing to the guild's
financial difficulties, it was sold
along with Rubens's *Coronation
of the Victor* (now Gemäldegalerie,
Kassel) to the Dutch artist
Gerard Hoet.
N.B.

77
DAVID TENIERS THE YOUNGER
1610 Antwerp – 1690 Brussels
*Landscape with Peasants before
an Inn, c.* 1635
Oil on canvas. 104.5 × 201.5 cm
Signed centre bottom on the
stone: *D T F*
Provenance: Acquired in 1781
from the collection of Count
Baudouin, Paris
Inv. no. GE 629, pendant to
inv. no. GE 628

78
DAVID TENIERS THE YOUNGER
1610 Antwerp – 1690 Brussels
Landscape with a Maid at a Well,
c. 1635
Oil on canvas, transferred from
panel. 104.5 × 202 cm
Signed centre bottom: *D.*
TENIERS F
Provenance: Acquired in 1781
from the collection of Count
Baudouin, Paris
Inv. no. GE 628, pendant to
inv. no. GE 629

79
DAVID TENIERS THE YOUNGER
1610 Antwerp – 1690 Brussels
Landscape with Peasants Bowling.
1640s
Oil on canvas. 61.5 × 89.5 cm
Signed centre bottom: *D.*
TENIERS F
Provenance: Acquired in 1781
from the collection of Count
Baudouin, Paris
Inv. no. GE 578

80
DAVID TENIERS THE YOUNGER
1610 Antwerp – 1690 Brussels
Reaping, c. 1645
Oil on canvas, transferred from
panel. 49.5 × 69.5 cm
Signed centre bottom: *D.*
TENIERS F
Provenance: Acquired in 1915
with the collection of P.P.
Semenov-Tyan-Shansky,
Petrograd
Inv. no. GE 2778

81

DAVID TENIERS THE YOUNGER
1610 Antwerp – 1690 Brussels
Village Festival, 1648
Oil on canvas. 97 × 129 cm
(published in error in Cat. 1958
and Cat. 1981 as 97 × 138 cm)
Signed and dated centre
bottom: *DAVID TENIERS F
1648*
Provenance: Collection of the
comtesse de Verrue, Paris;
collection of the marquis
d'Argenson, Paris; acquired in
1772 from the collection of the
duc de Choiseul, Paris
Inv. no. GE 593
Selected literature: Somoff
1901, no. 675; Cat. 1958, p. 103;
Cat. 1981, p. 73; Babina 1989a,
p. 5; Klinge 1991, no. 58

On the left of this scene of rural
festivity, far from the
merrymaking and dancing
peasants, the artist depicted a
group of noblemen who have
come to witness the village
celebration. J.Ph. Le Bas, in the
dedication on a 1736 print after
this painting, then in the
collection of the comtesse de
Verrue, noted that the group of
noble figures includes Teniers
and his family. A similar
opinion was expressed in old
Hermitage catalogues, but
Klinge (1991) points out that it
is impossible to identify the
figures with any certainty as
being Teniers and members of
his family.
N.B.

82

DAVID TENIERS THE YOUNGER
1610 Antwerp – 1690 Brussels
Kermess, 1646
Oil on canvas, transferred from
old canvas in 1868.
97.2 × 130.5 cm
Signed bottom left: *DAVID
TENIERS FEC*. On the flag of
St. George the date: *1646*
Provenance: Collection of the
comtesse de Verrue, Paris;
collection of the marquis
d'Argenson, Paris; acquired in
1772 from the collection of the
duc de Choiseul, Paris
Inv. no. GE 594
Selected literature: Somoff
1901, no. 674; Cat. 1958, p. 103;
Cat. 1981, p. 73; Babina 1989a,
p. 5; Klinge 1991, no. 50

Teniers turned frequently to the
subject of rural festivals and the
Hermitage has two examples,
this picture dating from 1646
and cat. 81 from 1648. They
were mistakenly regarded as
pendants in the eighteenth
century.

Though the theme of the
rural feast had a long tradition,
Teniers introduced his own
interpretation, above all through
his inventive construction of a
setting for simultaneous action
by many figures. Although
seemingly so very much alike in
his different renditions of this
theme, Teniers's stock figures
each have their own character
and their own small rôle to play.
In this painting of 1646, for

instance, a young page holds a
jug and a tray with food to serve
a nobleman, while in the
picture of 1648 (cat. 81) the
same figure is otherwise
occupied, holding a horse by its
bridle; each thus takes part in
its own "episode." Such
vignettes are usually comical,
sometimes with a moralizing
subtext, and as one looks closer,
one cannot help but be
impressed with Teniers's skill in
"directing" events. On the left of
the 1646 painting, for example,
alongside the pigsty, a wife seeks
to help her drunken husband to
his feet, which Klinge (1991)
sees as an illustration of an old
saying: "Whosoever be a pig
belongs in the pigsty."

Klinge suggested that, twenty
years after painting *Kermess*,
Teniers repainted three of the
figures in the foreground to the
right of the page (the seated
nobleman and the young
peasant girl whom he embraces
and the older woman in red
nearby). Klinge believed that the
artist, while retaining the poses,
changed only their costumes,
which she thought were not
only painted in a different style,
but reflected the later fashion of
the 1660s. The flirtatious
couple does indeed differ
slightly from the other
participants, but this might be
explained partly by the fact that
Teniers has given them a central
place in the composition, a rôle

reinforced by the attention they
attract from several other
figures (such as the man who
points his finger at them and
the drunken man being
expelled through the gates who
looks at them curiously). Infra-
red analysis of the painting,
however, has revealed no
significant changes to any of the
three figures discussed by
Klinge. On the contrary, it
confirms that the page and the
three standing figures are
painted in the same manner as
the three seated figures in the
foreground.
N.B.

83
David Teniers the Younger
1610 Antwerp – 1690 Brussels
Monkeys in a Kitchen, c. 1645
Oil on canvas, transferred from
panel in 1842. 36 × 50 cm
Signed bottom left:
D TENIERS F
Provenance: Before 1806
collection of the Landgrave of
Hesse, Kassel; acquired in 1814
from the collection of Empress
Josephine, Château de
Malmaison, near Paris
Inv. no. GE 568

84

DAVID TENIERS THE YOUNGER
1610 Antwerp – 1690 Brussels
The Kitchen, 1646
Oil on canvas. 171 × 237 cm
Signed and dated left on the
step: *DAVID TENIERS 1646*;
date repeated over the fireplace
on the drawing: *AN 1646*
Provenance: Collection of Sir
Robert Walpole, London, then
Houghton Hall, Norfolk;
acquired in 1779 with the
Walpole Collection, Norfolk
Inv. no. GE 586
Selected literature: *Aedes* 1752,
p. 45; Livret 1838, p. 100;
Somoff 1901, no. 698; Cat.
1958, p. 103; Bazin 1958, p. 118;
Cat. 1981, p. 73; Babina 1989a,
p. 4; Klinge 1991, no. 49

Scholars have seen here either
the interior of Teniers's own
kitchen at his country house,
Dry Toren (Somoff 1901), or a
depiction of the kitchen in the
palace of Archduke Leopold
Wilhelm (Bazin 1958). The
painting's inscribed date, 1646,
would seem to contradict both
suggestions. Teniers became
court artist to Leopold Wilhelm
and left for Brussels only in
1651, and did not acquire Dry
Toren, his house in the
neighbouring village of Perk,
until even later, in 1662 or 1663.
Thus, the painting is probably
an invented composition.

Our earliest source, *Aedes*
1752, indicates that Teniers
included a self-portrait in the
work, depicting himself as the
falconer, on the far left, an
identification questioned only

by Klinge (1991). Labensky
(Livret 1838) proposed that
Teniers employed his father as
the model for the blind man at
the centre, which led Bazin
(1958) mistakenly to suggest
that the Hermitage painting in
fact illustrated the biblical story
of Tobit.

Babina (1989a), and after her
Klinge (1991) have interpreted
Teniers's *Kitchen* as an allegory
of the Four Elements. In the
Hermitage scene, as in an
engraving by Jacques de Gheyn
the Younger (Hollstein
1949–81, vol. VII, no. 1, p. 119),
the falconer's bird is used to
personify Air, and to draw
attention to this Teniers placed
him beneath a window through
which stream both air and light.
Fire is symbolized by the
brazier, the hearth, and the

figure of the cook; and Water by
the two fishermen. In Teniers's
interpretation, however, the
falconer himself represents
Earth, for he is a hunter, and
thus he is shown surrounded by
dogs, dead game and an array of
fruits of the earth such as
cabbage and apples at his feet.
Teniers's sources for such an
allegorical representation of
Earth, in addition to the works
of Jacques de Gheyn the
Younger (who used a hunter to
symbolize Earth; Hollstein
1949–81, vol. VII, no. 3, p. 119),
included an engraving, *Earth*, by
Nicolaes de Bruyn (Hollstein
1949–81, vol. IV, no. 3, p. 22),
which also shows an abundance
of Earth's attributes, similar to
those in the left foreground of
Teniers's *Kitchen*.

The kitchen scene provided

Teniers with a single, unusual
setting in which to unite these
symbols of the Four Elements,
affording greater possibilities
than was customary for this
subject. Snyders, for instance,
in his famous paintings of
market stalls (State Hermitage
Museum, St. Petersburg),
addressed each element in a
separate painting.

A close analogy to the
Hermitage picture can be seen
in a signed *Kitchen* by David
Teniers the Younger (Christie's,
London, July 6, 1990, lot 107).
A copy of the Hermitage
painting was exhibited in
London in 1969 (reproduced in
*Dennis Vanderkar Gallery.
Exhibition of Dutch and Flemish
Old Masters*, London, April 1 –
May 31, 1969, no. 28).
N.B.

85

Adriaen Brouwer
1605/06 Oudenaerde – 1638
Antwerp
The Village Charlatan (Operation for Stone in the Head), 1620s
Oil on panel. 28.2 × 25 cm
Provenance: Acquired before 1859
Inv. no. GE 668
Selected literature: Cat. 1958, p. 42; Cat. 1981, p. 33; Babina 1985, pp. 7–8

In this early painting of the 1620s, Brouwer seems merely to reproduce a subject traditional in Netherlandish painting: a quack doctor performing surgery. Its iconography is actually more specific, and derives from sixteenth-century Netherlandish paintings that represent an *Operation for Stone in the Head* (*Removing the Stone of Stupidity*), by Hieronymus Bosch (Museo del Prado, Madrid) and Pieter Bruegel the Elder (engraving 1557; Hollstein 1949–81, vol. III, no. 192, p. 293). While Bosch and Bruegel depicted an apparently real operation, Brouwer's picture represents a fraud: the "doctor" will make an incision in the forehead of his patient, and will then produce the bloody stone concealed between his fingers and reveal it to the public.

In the Hermitage painting, two stones, apparently already "removed" by the quack from the heads of other patients, lie in the foreground, and two patients already operated on are shown behind the "doctor." One has a bandaged head and sits on the ground, while the other stands with his back to the viewer, his gesture indicating that he is asking for a drink. A man leaning out of a tavern window pours him some wine from a ewer.

The quack, who is distinguished both by his brightly coloured clothing and his central position, nevertheless seems to belong to this "tavern of fools" who are ruled by stupidity and foolish entertainments. These peasants pour wine over each other, laugh at one another's pain, and their offspring seem more like strange dwarfs than children. The merry child wearing a hood in the foreground or the laughing little head rising above the table, which seems to be attached to a stick held by the peasant on the left, both share with the adult figures Brouwer's grotesque characterization. Brouwer has produced an unusual treatment of his subject and given it a very specific meaning: human stupidity is incurable by surgical means.
N.B.

86

Adriaen Brouwer
1605/06 Oudenaerde – 1638
Antwerp
Tavern Scene (The Village Fiddler), c. 1634
Oil on panel. 25 × 33.5 cm
Provenance: Acquired in 1770 with the collection of François Tronchin, Geneva
Inv. no. GE 643

87
DAVID RYCKAERT III
1612 Antwerp – 1661 Antwerp
Peasant Woman with a Cat,
1640s
Oil on canvas, transferred from
panel in 1842. 28 × 34.8 cm
Provenance: Acquired in 1769
with the collection of Count
Brühl, Dresden
Inv. no. GE 653, pendant to
inv. no. GE 654

88
David Ryckaert III
1612 Antwerp – 1661 Antwerp
Peasant with a Dog, 1640s
Oil on canvas. 26.5 × 37 cm
Provenance: Acquired in 1769
with the collection of Count
Brühl, Dresden
Inv. no. GE 654, pendant to
inv. no. GE 653

89
BALTHASAR VAN DEN BOSSCHE
1681 Antwerp – 1715 Antwerp
A Sculptor's Studio, 1712
Oil on canvas. 66 × 86 cm
Half-erased signature and date
bottom left: *BVB ... F.1712*
Provenance: Transferred in 1918
from the Anichkov Palace,
Petrograd
Inv. no. GE 5718, pendant to
inv. no. GE 5719

90
BALTHASAR VAN DEN BOSSCHE
1681 Antwerp – 1715 Antwerp
A Painter's Studio, 1709
Oil on canvas. 66 × 84 cm
Signed and dated bottom left:
B.V. Bosche f.1709
Provenance: Acquired in 1918
from the collection of Prince
A.S. Dolgorukov, Petrograd
Inv. no. GE 5719, pendant to
inv. no. GE 5718

91
JAN MIEL
1599 Beveren-Waes (Antwerp) –
1664 Turin
The Charlatan, c. 1645
Oil on canvas. 60 × 74 cm
Inscription on the sign to right:
Vero secret/ cont .../ [True Means
Against ...]
Provenance: Acquired in 1802
from the collection of the Count
de Narp, St. Petersburg
Inv. no. GE 646

93
PEETER SNEYERS
1681 Antwerp – 1752 Antwerp
Winter, 1727
Oil on canvas. 82 × 68 cm
Half-erased signature bottom
left: *P [...] Snijers f.*
Provenance: Acquired in 1769
with the collection of Count
Brühl, Dresden; from after 1797
to 1920 kept at Gatchina Palace,
near St. Petersburg; returned to
the Hermitage in 1920
Inv. no. GE 672

92
PEETER SNEYERS
1681 Antwerp – 1752 Antwerp
Autumn, 1727
Oil on canvas. 84.5 × 69 cm
Signed bottom right on the
pedestal: *P.Snijers*
Inv. no. GE 674

SEVENTEENTH-CENTURY FLEMISH DRAWINGS IN THE HERMITAGE: EIGHTEENTH-CENTURY TASTE AND COLLECTING

Alexey Larionov

The Hermitage department of Old Master drawings, like many others, owes its foundation and a vast proportion of its riches to the all-embracing passion for collecting of Catherine the Great, a passion for which she was justly famous. During the nearly three and a half decades of her reign (1762–1796), Catherine II acquired works of art with unflagging energy and on a truly imperial scale, procuring nearly everything on the European art market that caught her eye. Her purchases covered a vast array, from ancient statues to Baroque paintings, and included jewellery, rare books, cameos, prints, medieval manuscripts, works by fashionable contemporary artists, and Western European drawings. The several large collections of graphic works acquired at the beginning of Catherine's reign established the basis for the museum's Cabinet of Drawings and formed the nucleus of the collection for all the European schools, including Flemish.

It seems unlikely that the empress had a particular interest in drawings, since her acquisitions were considerably more than the expression of her own personal tastes: Catherine's collecting was no mere pastime but a vital component of official Russian policy. Her sensational, nearly annual purchases were intended to demonstrate Russia's wealth and prosperity to the world. Indeed, they succeeded in reinforcing the established opinion of Catherine abroad as "the Minerva of the North," the most enlightened ruler in all of Europe.

PETER PAUL RUBENS,
Head of a Youth looking up
(detail; see cat. 113), 1615–16

Nor did her collecting lack that didactic and proselytizing spirit that marked so much of Catherine's activity. Driven by a desire to make Russia more European, she was constantly seeking ways to imbue educated Russian society with an appreciation for Western European art. By her own example, Catherine instilled in her courtiers a taste for collecting, as she strove to give St. Petersburg the brilliance of a truly European capital.

For the Russian capital to accumulate the artistic riches that would rank it alongside Europe's traditional cultural centres seemed at first impossible and too ambitious a task even for Catherine's closest advisers to envisage.[1] Only extreme and energetic measures could bring about this fulfilment of her aims, and thus she adopted the policy of acquiring large art collections en masse when they became available. Such was the method by which works were accumulated for both the Hermitage Picture Gallery and the Cabinet of Drawings.

Catherine was first presented with the opportunity to acquire a large body of drawings in 1768, when Prince Dmitry Golitsyn, the Russian envoy in Paris, informed her of the availability of the entire Brussels art collection of Count Cobenzl. 1768 is thus considered to be the official date for the foundation of the Cabinet of Drawings. Count Carl Cobenzl (1712–1770), a leading Austrian diplomat and statesman, resided in Brussels from 1753 to 1768, during which time he was in charge of the administration of the Austrian Netherlands and held the rank of Plenipotentiary Minister to Empress Maria-Theresa. Cobenzl's collection was assembled during this period, and included a small but well-chosen picture gallery and some 4,000 drawings from all the European schools. Such a collection was ideally suited to Catherine's purpose, as it provided her with a ready-made museum of Western European drawings that had already been fully organized. Each drawing had been glued on to a dark lilac mount in one of five standard formats, was classified by artist and school, and then arranged alphabetically in richly decorated folders and wooden boxes, some of which are still used to store the drawings today. A suggested attribution was written within a specially engraved cartouche[2] on the mount of each drawing, and the entire collection was accompanied by a bound, handwritten catalogue.

Neither Cobenzl nor his artistic advisers had a profound understanding of drawings, and the collection was somewhat uneven in quality, with insignificant works alongside true masterpieces. Nor could the catalogue be described as a model of scholarship. Its author was Johann-Philipp Cobenzl, the count's nephew, who later became a renowned diplomat. His memoirs provide an interesting description of the task he had been set:

"From the very start my role was one of keeper of his collection of original drawings by illustrious Old Master painters. Given my talent for drawings, he found me well-suited to the task. I arranged the drawings by artist and by school, I glued them onto paper, I framed them, I organized them in portfolios, and I catalogued them. This task gave me a knowledge of the fine arts, for which I have had an enduring appreciation ever since."[3]

Cataloguing this vast collection in such an amateur manner, without the consultation of specialists or connoisseurs, could only result in a text that reflected the author's personal opinions, with all the mistakes and exaggerations that might be expected. Although some traditional attributions of specific drawings were fully justified, others were flights of fantasy and imagination. Without any foundation, many lesser drawings were attributed to Michelangelo, Raphael, Titian, van Eyck, Dürer, Veronese and Rembrandt. Had the collection been placed on the open market, such uninformed attributions would undoubtedly have been questioned; but in Russia, where no tradition of connoisseurship of European drawings existed, these attributions aroused no questions. They were subsequently reprinted without reservation a century later in the first printed catalogues of the Hermitage drawings. Despite its uneven quality and unjustified claims to universality, Cobenzl's collection was an extremely fortunate and significant acquisition, one that enriched the Hermitage with a great number of excellent drawings from all the European schools, although its main attractions were the Flemish, French and Italian drawings.

During the fifteen years he was based in Brussels, as the *de facto* ruler of the Southern Netherlands, Cobenzl took advantage of the privileges of his position to acquire works by the finest Flemish masters. He seems to have been little interested in the works of the fifteenth and sixteenth centuries, as he owned only a few significant pieces from the early Netherlandish school. By contrast, his collection reflected the history of Flemish drawing from around 1600 until the mid-eighteenth century without any significant omissions.

Of the many sheets from Cobenzl's collection attributed to Rubens, at least twenty have proved to be originals by the master, and many others are linked to his workshop. The portrait studies by van Dyck, a large gouache (*Kermess*) by Roelant Savery, as well as watercolours and gouaches by Jacob Jordaens and Jan Fyt, are among these artists' best and most typical works. Particularly worthy of attention are the drawings of Jan Brueghel (Velvet Brueghel), Sebastiaen Vrancx, Frans Francken the Younger, Lucas van Uden and David Teniers the Younger, along with numerous sheets by Abraham van Diepenbeeck and Jan Erasmus Quellinus. Count Cobenzl was also a keen collector of contemporary Flemish drawings, and consequently the Hermitage holdings of Flemish graphic art from the beginning to the mid-eighteenth century are virtually unequalled outside Belgium.

In 1769, almost immediately after the purchase of the Cobenzl paintings and drawings, Catherine obtained another large collection, that of Count Heinrich Brühl, Prime Minister to Augustus III, Elector of Saxony and King of Poland. Brühl was for many years entrusted with purchasing works of art for the Dresden Gallery, and took advantage of the opportunity to amass a private collection at the same time. On his death, Catherine acquired it in its entirety from his heirs, and thus added to her Hermitage some 600 paintings, many books of engravings, and 14 folio albums containing 1,020 drawings of various dates and schools.

Count Brühl had benefited from the advice of Heinrich von Heinecken, a noted connoisseur, which contributed greatly to the generally high quality of his collection. Drawings were not, however, the main object of Brühl's collecting activities, and they seem to have been acquired almost by chance. Thus, his collection was markedly different from Cobenzl's. Brühl's albums seem to have been compiled at random, probably in the order in which the works were acquired. Furthermore, there was no attempt to be comprehensive or to acquire works from different periods so as to produce a more balanced collection. While it contained fewer outstanding masterpieces than the Cobenzl collection, and also lacked rigorous principles of selection, the more modest attributions, written in pencil at the bottom of each

sheet, tend to be more credible. Among the relatively few seventeenth-century Flemish drawings that the Brühl collection brought to the Hermitage is a fine selection of drawings by Jordaens, as well as other interesting works by seventeenth-century landscape artists, including some large sheets by Jan Frans van Bloemen.

Another major collection of European drawings was being formed in St. Petersburg at the same time as the Imperial Cabinet of Drawings at the Hermitage. This was also under the direct patronage of Catherine II, and was based at the Imperial Academy of Arts. In the twentieth century, much of this collection was transferred to the Hermitage. The basis of the Academy's collection was the 6,979 drawings "brought from foreign lands" by the president of the Academy, Ivan Ivanovich Betskoy, and "donated by Her Imperial Majesty to this Academy" in 1767 according to archival documents.[4] Many of the circumstances surrounding this acquisition remain unclear, but the collection itself is so noteworthy that its history deserves examination.

Ivan Betskoy (1703–1795) occupied a series of important state posts at Catherine's court and was one of the few who enjoyed her unwavering trust and favour. Unlike many of the empress's courtiers, he seems to have exhibited no personal passion for collecting, despite the fact that his activities fell very much within the sphere of the arts. From 1762 Betskoy was in charge of all educational institutions in Russia, including the Academy of Arts, of which he was the director for over thirty years. He enlarged the academic library and the museum of plaster casts, and was also responsible for official correspondence relating to artistic commissions for the court and acquisitions for the Hermitage.

Betskoy was half Swedish, and was the illegitimate son of a Swedish baroness and Peter the Great's Fieldmarshal, Prince Trubetskoy, who spent eighteen years as a prisoner of war in Sweden during the Northern War. He grew up in Stockholm, and, when his father returned to Russia, Betskoy was sent to study in Copenhagen. Later in life he spent many years at different European courts during his service in the Collegium of Foreign Affairs. Exiled from the court of Elizabeth (1741–1761/62) during the last years of her reign, he spent five years (1756–61) in Paris, where he had long-standing official and personal connections in both literary and artistic circles. It is thought that his collection may have been formed during this time.

This extremely large collection was most unusual and varied greatly in composition, with no attempt made to attribute any of the drawings or even to identify them with a particular school or period. Works of excellent quality were combined with modest and anonymous sheets, copies, working studies and sketches, as well as drawings by students and dilettantes. No particular principle seems to have been applied to their selection, and this vast body of unsorted drawings suggests the simultaneous mass acquisition of everything from the shelves of some antiquarian's storehouse, or perhaps even several. We cannot say whether Betskoy acquired the drawings for himself or, as seems more likely, if they were always intended for the Academy of Arts. It is also unclear whether he was acting on his own initiative or at the behest of the empress, who must have paid for the purchases.

On their arrival in St. Petersburg, the drawings, most of them stamped with a special collector's mark,[5] were given similar mounts and put into thirty-one albums, without any indication of authorship or school, even when works were signed. The collection was forgotten for the next 150 years and eventually thought to be lost. It was only by chance, during sorting work at the Academy of Arts library in the autumn of 1923, that it was rediscovered. Vladimir Levinson-Lessing and Mikhail Dobroklonsky, both scholars from the Hermitage, selected some 2,000 of the best works and in January 1924 these were transferred to the museum in exchange for duplicate printed publications.

Only Russia's post-revolutionary isolation can explain why the discovery of the Betskoy collection was not a worldwide sensation. Although three-quarters of it was composed of "utter rubbish," to quote Levinson-Lessing, hundreds of excellent works previously unknown to scholars were scattered throughout the albums. The drawings selected for the Hermitage came from all the European schools and include now-famous works by Ercole Roberti, Dürer, Bellange, Goltzius, Poussin, Claude Lorrain and many other renowned artists. Of particular interest to the museum was a marvellous group of sixteenth-century Netherlandish drawings, but the seventeenth-century holdings also gained considerably.

Among the latter, special mention should be made of several works by Jordaens, a large series of composition sketches and life studies by Jan Fyt (cat. 123, 124), a masterpiece by Hendrick de Clerk, *Allegory of the Truce of 1609* (cat. 107), and numerous landscapes and genre drawings by such artists as Roelant Savery, Sebastian Vranx, Lucas van Uden, Gillis Neyts, Jacques Foucquier and Adrian van Aertvelt.

The Academy of Arts was also the Hermitage's source for a large number of other valuable sheets that had arrived in Russia during Catherine's reign. Few were by Flemish masters, but several superb drawings once in the famous Paris collection of Jean de Jullienne should be noted, despite the fact that the precise date and origin of these acquisitions remains a mystery. Among these drawings was a compositional sketch by van Dyck included in the exhibition, *Pentecost* (cat. 101).

Catherine's interest in the museum of the Academy of Arts often prompted her to transfer works of art there that had originally been acquired for the Hermitage. These were mainly paintings, but a number of important graphic works were also included. For example, no place could be found in the Picture Gallery or the Cabinet of Drawings for several monumental cartoons. Some of them, including those by Anton Raphael Mengs, perished in 1906 during a fire in the Academy Museum, but a number were returned to the Hermitage in the 1920s, including eight vast works in gouache on paper, preparatory cartoons for tapestries produced jointly by Abraham van Diepenbeeck and Peter Boel, now on display in the Hermitage's Knights' Hall. These rare cartoons, notable for their large size and their excellent state of preservation, are thought to have arrived in Russia in 1777 with the English adventurer the Duchess of Kingston, but the precise date of their acquisition by Catherine II remains unknown.

Catherine's death in 1796 brought an end to the active acquisition of Western European drawings for the imperial collections. While her successors on the Russian throne did much to enlarge the Picture Gallery and other parts of the Hermitage, they showed no particular interest in the Cabinet of Drawings. Despite this lack of new acquisitions for the Hermitage, the flow of Western European drawings into Russia did not cease, and throughout the nineteenth and early twentieth centuries many drawings continued to arrive in

St. Petersburg, thanks to the activities of private collectors. By the middle of the nineteenth century, private collections of prints and drawings, which had been extremely rare in eighteenth-century Russia, were increasingly widespread, and by 1900 both St. Petersburg and Moscow had thriving markets for old prints and drawings. Collectors in both cities enjoyed regular contact with antiquarians in Paris and other European capitals, as well as established circles of connoisseurs who served as experts. New collections now appeared, some of them quite small and modestly assembled, but well chosen and imbued with the tastes and personality of the collector. Unfortunately this golden age of Russian private collecting proved to be very short, and in just a few decades its development was halted by the Revolution. Nevertheless, by 1917 various St. Petersburg collections contained a great number of Western European drawings, which provided material for the museums and ensured the success of an antiquarian market in Russia throughout the next century.

Various fates awaited St. Petersburg's private collections of prints and drawings after the Revolution. Some were taken abroad by their owners, others were dispersed, and still others were confiscated and sold on the international market. A large number, however, remained in the country and were transferred to state museums, above all to the Hermitage, where they considerably enriched the Cabinet of Drawings. Among them were some significant additions to the collection of works by Flemish Old Masters.

Other collections brought additional Flemish drawings to the Hermitage. From the collection of Nikolay Vorobyov, bequeathed in 1924, the museum acquired five superb drawings by Jordaens, two by Sebastiaen Vrancx, works by David Teniers the Younger, Jacques Foucquier, Jan Miel and Caspar-Jacob Opstal. The nationalized collection of the Princes Yusupov brought works by Marten de Vos, Teniers and Diepenbeeck. From the outstanding collection of Prince Vladimir Argutinsky-Dolgoruky, the greater part of which was taken abroad, the Hermitage gained sheets by Godfried Maes, Willem Pannels, Gillis Neyts and Foucquier. The collection of E. Shvarts (Schwarz) brought some fifteen Flemish drawings, the best of which is Jordaens's *Study of a Young Woman's Head* (cat. 117).

The most important and the largest of all post-

revolutionary accessions (apart from those transferred from the Academy of Arts in 1924) was the vast collection of prints and drawings from the library of the Central School for Technical Drawing of Baron Stieglitz. Founded and financed in 1876 by the famous industrialist Alexander Stieglitz, it was not only the largest museum of applied and decorative arts in Russia but also had an extensive collection of prints and drawings. At its core were the Paris collections of Alfred Beurdeley, Michel Carré and André-Denis Bérard, all of which were acquired between 1888 and 1891 on the initiative of Alexander Polovtsov, the Russian statesman and patron who was for many years an honorary trustee and chairman of the school's council. The collection was regularly supplemented with purchases from the Russian and European markets, and through the addition of the personal collections of Polovtsov and of Grand Duchess Ekaterina Mikhaylovna. By 1917 the Stieglitz School had over 9,000 drawings, mainly designs for the decorative and applied arts, architectural drawings and sketches for theatrical sets, but also a considerable number of sheets without any direct relation to the decorative arts. After the Revolution, the Stieglitz School became a branch of the Hermitage, and, during the 1920s and early 1930s, the main body of drawings was transferred to the Hermitage.

Although most of the works were French, they also included a number of excellent sheets that enriched other sections of the Hermitage's Cabinet of Drawings. A highly significant acquisition for the museum was the group of some fifty Flemish seventeenth-century drawings by Jordaens (*Decorative Frieze*, cat. 105, and two others), Jan Brueghel the Elder, Theodoor van Thulden, Jan Erasmus Quellinus, François Duquesnoy and Cornelis Schut.

The steady flow of acquisitions during the 1920s and 1930s was offset by a number of transfers. Many drawings, including Flemish ones, were, in accordance with state plans for the establishment of a network of provincial museums, transferred to the State Museum of Fine Arts in Moscow, to museums in Krasnodar and Khabarovsk, and to those in the Ukraine, Armenia and Georgia. The drawings selected for dispersal were generally not of the highest quality, with the exception of a few sheets that went to Moscow, among them several Flemish drawings from the Cobenzl collection, notably some superb works by Rubens.

On balance, the acquisitions for and losses from the Hermitage's collection of Flemish drawings during the two decades immediately after the Revolution were in the museum's favour. The collection grew considerably, not only in quantity but in the range of artists included, and by the mid-1930s it had taken on those features that characterize it today. Occasional acquisitions of individual sheets in subsequent years were of no great significance.

Today the Hermitage has some 1,000 works by seventeenth-century Flemish masters, which occupy an important place within the context of other collections of Netherlandish works around the world. The most significant part of the collection consists of drawings by Rubens and Jordaens, and by those artists working later in the century who had developed under their influence. The debt to Rubens is especially clear in the works of Abraham van Diepenbeeck, Theodoor van Thulden and Jan Erasmus Quellinus. There are also numerous sheets that reflect the styles of landscape artists working in the middle of the century, notably Lucas van Uden, Gillis Neyts, Jacques Foucquier and Bonaventura Peeters. Conversely, artists of the early sixteenth century whose work was tied to the tradition of late Mannerism, such as Jan Brueghel the Elder, Hendrick van Balen, Adam van Noort and Otto van Veen, are represented sparingly in the collection.

The Hermitage collection does not comprise a balanced selection of drawings of different types and functions. A characteristic feature of the dilettante collections of the eighteenth century, such as those acquired by Catherine II, was the predominant taste for highly finished drawings. The Hermitage is extremely rich in these works, such as carefully worked-out *modelli* for paintings and prints, life studies, copies after the antique, landscapes intended for sale, as well as designs for book illustrations, and it is the scope of such works that determine the character of the collection. Conversely, working sketches, spontaneous improvizations, and rapid drawings from life of the kind valued today for the direct information they provide about the artistic process, were of interest in the eighteenth century only to a narrow circle of select connoisseurs; thus they are represented in the Hermitage by only a few examples. This disproportion of types was determined by historical factors and is both the defining feature and the sole defect of the Hermitage collection of Flemish drawings, which otherwise provides an almost exhaustive coverage of the genre.

Some of the most famous sheets from the Hermitage have been selected for this exhibition. They represent the work of the leading seventeenth-century Flemish masters and provide a broad picture of the development of a national school. Eight works by Rubens, beginning with examples from his early years in Italy to those of the mid-1630s, demonstrate the full variety of graphic means employed by him and the different types of drawings he produced. Anthony van Dyck is presented by almost as full a selection, with five drawings in a variety of genres. The evolution of the Baroque "grand style" in mid-seventeenth-century graphic art is clearly reflected in the large decorative sheets of Jacob Jordaens and Jan Fyt, and in the works of Rubens's pupils and followers Abraham van Diepenbeeck, Erasmus Quellinus, Caspar de Crayer and Jan Boeckhorst. Another aspect of Flemish drawing, not linked directly with Rubens and his school, is manifest in the works of artists who were active into the 1630s, although within the traditions of the previous century. The watercolour-tinted pen drawings executed with miniature-like precision by Hendrick de Clerk, Frans Francken the Younger, Tobias Verhaegt, Geysbrecht Leytens and Jan Brueghel the Elder characterize this conservative tendency in Flemish seventeenth-century art.

The history that lies behind the formation of the Hermitage Museum's rich collection of Flemish drawings differs greatly from that of other similar large European and American collections. The specific nature of Russian history as a whole, and of the development of the Hermitage Museum in particular, has left a profound mark on its holdings. Many of the Flemish drawings were acquired by Catherine II, and the tastes of the eighteenth century are still clearly preserved today in the way the collection reflects those early preferences for the work of particular artists and trends in Flemish drawing.

Notes

1. In 1767 Diderot suggested that Catherine purchase a large collection of engraved reproductions of works of art, since it seemed to him impossible for her to accumulate in St. Petersburg a sufficient quantity of original paintings that would allow a sophisticated taste for the fine arts to develop there. See V.V. Levinson-Lessing, *Istoriya kartinnoy galerei Ermitazha (1784–1917)* [The History of the Hermitage Picture Gallery (1784–1917)], 2nd edn, Leningrad, 1986.

2. F. Lugt: *Les Marques de collection de dessins et d'estampes, Supplément*, The Hague, 1956, no. 2858b.

3. A.R. Von Arneth: *Graf Philipp Cobenzl und seine Memoiren*, Vienna, 1885, p. 79.

4. S. Yaremich: *Russkaya akademicheskaya khudozhestvennaya schkola v XVIII v.* [Russian Academic Art in the Eighteenth Century], Moscow and Leningrad, 1934, note 52, pp. 88–89.

5. Lugt 1956, no. 2878a.

94
PETER PAUL RUBENS
1577 Siegen – 1640 Antwerp
The Descent from the Cross,
c. 1612
Pen and brown ink, brown
wash, over black chalk. Laid
down. 43.5 × 38 cm
Top left corner, author's
inscription in pen and brown
ink: *Videntur ex Daniele*
Volterano/ Unis qui quasi tenes
tamen relinguit/ Item alius qui
diligentissime/ descendit ut laterus
opem.
Bottom right, inscription in pen
and brown ink, crossed out, of
which only the last word is
legible: *Rubens*
Provenance: Acquired in 1768
(mark L. 2061) from the
collection of Count Carl
Cobenzl, Brussels (mark L.
2858b)
Inv. no. 5496
Selected literature:
Dobroklonsky 1930–31a, p. 32;
Dobroklonsky 1940, no. 8;
Evers 1943, p. 144; Robels 1950,
pp. 24–25; Dobroklonsky 1955,

no. 633; Held 1959, no. 3;
Müller Hofstede 1962,
pp. 279–80; Burchard, d'Hulst
1963, no. 37; Friedländer 1964,
p. 80; Bialostocki 1964,
pp. 512–13; Müller Hofstede
1965, pp. 259–60; Burchard,
d'Hulst 1956, no. 31a;
Kuznetsov 1972–73, no. 88;
Kuznetsov 1974, no. 22;
Hofstede 1977, no. 26a; Jaffé
1977, pp. 29, 30, 51, 62, 75, 82,
fig. 148; Kuznetsov 1978,
no. 107; Held 1986, no. 15,
fig. 14; Brown 1982, p. 19, fig. 8;
Bottacin, Limentani Virdis
1990, no. 56; Larionov 1998,
no. 64, p. 132

Among the many versions of
The Descent from the Cross by
Rubens, this expressive drawing
occupies a special place. It bears
traces of numerous corrections
and reworkings, and was clearly
produced by the artist for his
own use, predating all of the
painted versions, and
containing the germ of many of
his later artistic ideas. This

drawing has the greatest
similarity with his monumental
painting of the subject from
1612, made as the altarpiece for
Antwerp Cathedral. The
placement of the figures, their
gestures, facial expressions and
features, are strikingly similar
and demonstrate a fundamental
relationship between the two
works, even if the drawing's
specific rôle in the execution of
the famous painting has given
rise to much discussion.

Mikhail Dobroklonsky, who
first published the drawing as
an autograph work, linked its
creation to the period when
Rubens received the
commission for the Antwerp
altarpiece, thus dating it to the
second half of 1611, an opinion
supported by Hans Gerhard
Evers, Hella Robels, Ludwig
Burchard and Roger d'Hulst.
In 1959, however, Julius Held
suggested that the drawing,
although used by Rubens as the
starting point for the Antwerp
painting, was actually executed

much earlier and should be
placed in the early years of the
artist's career (1598–1602).
Since that time, Held's
arguments have been accepted
by the majority of authors, with
the exception of Walter
Friedländer, who also noted the
drawing's independence from
the painting, but suggested a
slightly later date of *c.* 1604–07.
He further emphasized the
compositional link between the
drawing and a painting by
Ludovico Cigoli (Palazzo Pitti,
Florence), dated to the sixteenth
century. The drawing's
dependence on Cigoli's
composition was also stressed
by Michael Jaffé, who was
undecided about the dating of
the Hermitage sheet but
eventually arrived at a date close
to Held's, of *c.* 1603 (?). Jan
Bialostocki, who analyzed the
place of this drawing in the
context of all Rubens's works on
the subject, similarly hesitated to
offer a specific date, but also
favoured an early dating. It
should be noted that the
characterization of the drawing
as a direct sketch for the Antwerp
painting has never completely
disappeared from modern
scholarship (see Brown 1982).

Resolution of the problem of
this drawing's date is
complicated by a lack of clarity
in the chronology of Rubens's
early graphic works. Those
drawings closest in style to the
Hermitage *Descent from the*
Cross, such as *Washing the Body*
of Christ (Museum Boymans–
van Beuningen, Rotterdam) and
sketches for *The Last Supper* (J.
Paul Getty Museum, Los
Angeles; Duke of Devonshire
Collection), likewise have no
firm date and different scholars
have placed them variously
between 1600–02 and 1611–12.
Nor does analysis of the
composition of the Hermitage
drawing provide a firm answer.
Held spoke of the "mistakes
and shortcomings" of a young
artist, and saw a relationship
with the traditions of sixteenth-
century Mannerism in the lack
of a central place of action and
the disconnected nature of the
figures. Such an assessment
seems open to question, since
many of the specific features
that Held noted in the drawing
possibly resulted from Rubens's
reworking of the sheet, during
which the original composition
was altered.

The seemingly illogical
placing of the cross and Christ's
body at the edge of the
composition, as well as traces of

a pencil sketch originally
extending beyond the right
edge, suggest that the format of
the sheet was initially more
horizontal, and that Rubens had
intended to place other figures,
of which only the hands are
now visible, to the right of
Christ's body. The composition
was later decisively re-oriented
to the left, and the placement of
the figures on this part of the
sheet underwent considerable
alteration. The head of Mary
Cleophas was clearly a later
addition, as it appears to be
suspended in the air, her body
only barely indicated as there is
no place for it. The figure of
Mary Magdalene, probably as a
consequence of the reworking,
now projects too far forward
towards the viewer, so that there
is no room for her feet within
the borders of the sheet.
Obvious spatial distortions have
also arisen; for example, Mary is
placed at such a distance from
the base of the cross that,
although this too has been
displaced towards the left, her
hands could not possibly reach
to Christ's shroud and feet.
Christ's left leg, which was
formerly caught up in the
shroud, has been made
disproportionately longer, with
his foot projecting sharply out
of the plane and now touching
Mary Magdalene's shoulder.

This last feature, like many
others arrived at in the process
of work on the drawing, was
actually taken up by Rubens in
his Antwerp painting. Similarly,
the lowering of Christ's body
down along the diagonal into
the arms of his relatives and
followers was brilliantly
developed in the painting as a
single smooth movement.

The drawing's connection
with the altarpiece in Antwerp
Cathedral was first established
by Dobroklonsky through the
inscription Rubens placed in
the top left corner of the sheet.
This contains a reference to the
sixteenth-century Roman artist
Daniele da Volterra and
describes two figures from his
fresco of *The Descent from the*
Cross in the church of Santa
Trinità dei Monti. The figures
described do not appear in the
drawing, although they do
feature in Rubens's Antwerp
painting, where one of them is a
close quotation of the Roman
fresco. The many similarities
between the sketch and the
Antwerp Cathedral altarpiece
strongly suggest that they are
indeed close in date.
A.L.

95

PETER PAUL RUBENS
1577 Siegen – 1640 Antwerp
*Sheet of Studies with the
"Caritas," c.* 1625
Black and red chalk, brown
wash. 33.9 × 45.5 cm
Provenance: Acquired in 1768
(mark L. 2061) from the
collection of Count Carl
Cobenzl, Brussels (mark L.
2858b)
Inv. no. 5513
Selected literature:
Dobroklonsky 1930–31a,
pp. 35–36; Dobroklonsky 1955,
no. 635; Burchard, d'Hulst
1963, no. 142; Martin 1968,
vol. II, p. 124–26, no. 19a;
Kuznetsov 1972–73, no. 86;
Kuznetsov 1978, no. 114

These studies of female figures
and children are an extremely
rare example in Rubens's œuvre
of a drawing that cannot be
linked with work on a specific
composition. Several of the
studies on this sheet do,
however, appear in his
paintings. When the work was
first published, Dobroklonsky
(1930–31a) noted that the
woman with a child in her
arms, labelled by Rubens as
"Caritas," appears in *The
Triumph of Divine Love* (Museo
del Prado, Madrid), painted
c. 1627–28. Burchard and
d'Hulst (1963) pointed out other
apparent uses that Rubens
made of these sketches: the
naked female figure walking to

the right, repeated four times
on this sheet, is very close to the
figure of Venus in his painting
The Judgement of Paris (*c.* 1633;
National Gallery, London); the
seated naked female figure,
which derives from Diana in
Titian's *Diana and Acteon* (The
National Gallery, London),
recalls the figure of a nymph in
Rubens's early composition
(*c.* 1614–15), *Gathering Fruits*
(Evers 1943, fig. 240), and the
standing naked figure facing
left finds parallels in *The
Education of Marie de' Medici*
(Musée du Louvre, Paris),
Contento (Courtauld Institute,
London) and *The Three Graces*
(Galleria degli Uffizi, Florence).
The images in the upper part of

the sheet are cut off, and
demonstrate that the sheet was
originally vertical in format.
The highly finished black
chalk drawing on the back is
a sketch for Rubens's
*St. Athanasius Defeating
Arianism*, painted for the ceiling
of the Jesuit Church in
Antwerp. Numerous differences
in detail between this drawing
and both the painted *modello*
(Castle Museum, Gotha) and
the finished composition (which
perished in 1718 and is known
from prints) indicate that it
was produced before the
composition was resolved,
probably soon after Rubens
received the commission in
1620.

We cannot, however, give a
similar date to the sketches on
the obverse. The soft, painterly
manner of *Sheet of Studies with
the "Caritas"* and its similarity to
the painting in the Prado, the
most direct and incontrovertible
of all the cited analogies,
suggested to Dobroklonsky a
date no earlier than the second
half of the 1620s, a date that has
been accepted by all later
scholars.
A.L.

96
RUBENS AND AN ASSISTANT
1577 Siegen – 1640 Antwerp
St. Roch, Patron of the Plague-
stricken, 1626
Black chalk, pen and brown and
black wash, heightened with
white. Laid down.
52.6 × 35.8 cm
Provenance: Acquired in 1768
(mark L. 2061) from the
collection of Count Carl
Cobenzl, Brussels (mark L.
2858b)
Inv. no. 5522

97
PETER PAUL RUBENS
1577 Siegen – 1640 Antwerp
Rubens Vase, 1622–26
Pen and brown ink. Laid down.
20.1 × 14.8 cm
Provenance: Acquired in 1768
(mark L. 2061) from the
collection of Count Carl
Cobenzl, Brussels (mark L.
2858b)
Inv. no. 5430
Selected literature: Kuznetsov
1978, no. 117; Kuznetsov
1976–78, pp. 100–03, figs. 3–4;
D. Jaffe 1988, p. 38, fig. 33a;
Larionov 1991, p. 138; van der
Meulen 1995, no. 184

Identified as an original Rubens
drawing by Kuznetsov (1978),
this work had previously been
seen as a copy. The drawing
offers a side view of a late
Classical carved agate vase
known as the "Rubens Vase"
(Walters Art Gallery, Baltimore),
which once formed part of the
artist's collection of antiquities.
It was acquired by Rubens in
Paris in 1619 and was
subsequently discussed in his
correspondence with Nicolas-
Claude Fabri de Peiresc of 1635,
in which he stated that it had
been sent to the East Indies on
board a vessel belonging to the
Dutch East India Company. The
ship was destroyed and the vase
confiscated by the Company, as
it had been dispatched

clandestinely. A drawing of the
vase remained in the artist's
possession, possibly that now in
the Hermitage.
  Certainly this drawing
formed the basis for a mirror
image engraving by Paulus
Pontius included in a book of
Rubens's engraved drawings,
Livre a dessiner, published after
the artist's death. Both the
drawing and the Pontius
engraving, however, may have
been produced in connection
with an earlier project. During a
meeting in 1622, Rubens and
Peiresc conceived a plan to
publish an illustrated work with
commentaries, showing the
most famous engraved gems
and hardstones, as well as other
antique objects, the vase

probably among them.
Although the volume was never
realized, Rubens did produce
several drawings for the book,
from which engravings were
made. If the drawing and the
Pontius engraving do indeed
relate to this project, they
should be dated between
1622 and 1626, a dating
commensurate with the style
of the drawing.
  The engraving also shows a
frontal view of the vase, which
suggests that Rubens had also
produced such a drawing. This
drawing has not, however,
survived.
A.L.

98

PETER PAUL RUBENS
1577 Siegen – 1640 Antwerp
*Design for the Printer's Mark of
Jan van Meers, c.* 1630
Pen and black ink, grey wash
over black chalk. Laid down.
13 × 15 cm
Provenance: Acquired in 1768
(mark L. 2061) from the
collection of Count Carl
Cobenzl, Brussels (mark L.
2858b)
Inv. no. 5418
Selected literature:
Dobroklonsky 1926, no. 111;
Dobroklonsky 1940, no. 27;
Dobroklonsky 1955, no. 663;
Kuznetsov 1965–66, no. 27;
Kuznetsov 1974, no. 98; Held
1980, pp. 422–23

Jan van Meers (1583–1652) was
an Antwerp printer, who from
1618 to 1629 was a partner with
Balthasar Moretus in the
Plantin Press, the humanist
publishing house with which
Rubens enjoyed a close
association. In 1629 van Meers
founded his own printing house
in the building known as "De
Vette Hinne" (The Fat Hen),
adopting as his motto "*Noctu
incubando diuque*" (Brooding by
night and day). Rubens
produced the Hermitage
drawing as the *modello* for van
Meers's printer's mark, which
was in turn engraved by
Cornelius Galle the Younger
and regularly appeared on the
title pages of books published by
van Meers from 1631 onwards.

The Hermitage drawing was
preceded by a painted oil sketch
(Plantin-Moretus Museum,
Antwerp). Rubens then
produced this intermediate
version, which reversed the
composition, and its contours
were incised to facilitate
transfer on to the plate in
preparation for the engraving.

The allegorical language of
Rubens's composition was most
clearly explained by Held (1980,
no. 307, pp. 422–23). In the
centre is a hen sitting on her
eggs, an illustration of the
printer's Latin motto, which is
inscribed above on a banderole.
This central image is surrounded
by several emblematic elements:
two palm fronds form a frame
and support a burning oil lamp,

a symbol of learning; flanking
the device are profile images of
Minerva and Mercury,
personifying the union of
Wisdom and Eloquence. Perched
above on the palm fronds are
Minerva's night owl, beside the
word "*Noctu*" (night), and the
cockerel often associated with
Mercury, alongside the word
"*Diu*" (day). Tied together, the
caduceus of Mercury and the
horn of Eloquence or Glory
conclude the composition.

Some doubt has been
expressed regarding the
attribution of the drawing to
Rubens. It had been given to
Cornelius Galle the Elder, on the
presumption that Rubens may
have entrusted the purely
technical task of producing a

reverse drawing of his painted
sketch to the engraver. Yet the
high quality of the pen drawing
unmistakably reveals the hand of
Rubens himself. More
convincingly, Held suggested
that the preparatory sketch in
black chalk "reversing" the
original composition may have
been produced by an assistant,
but that the final work in pen
and brush was carried out by
Rubens himself. He further
noted that the drawing provides
further confirmation of how,
during the process of
transferring his designs to
engravings, "Rubens remained
very much in control of the
material until the end" (Held
1980, p. 423).
A.L.

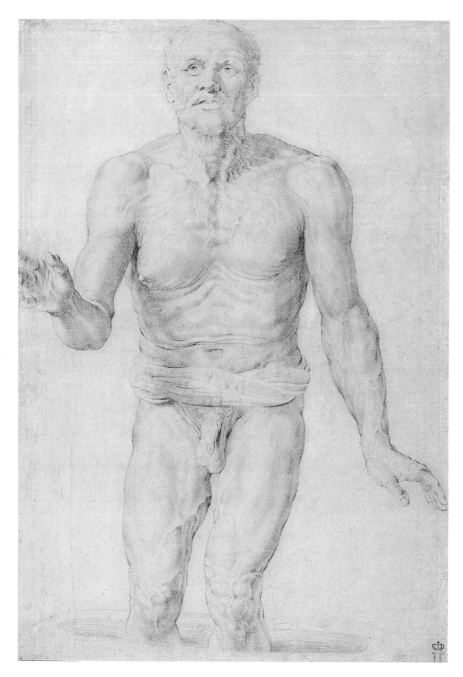

99
PETER PAUL RUBENS
1577 Siegen – 1640 Antwerp
Classical Figure ("Seneca"),
c. 1600–05
Black chalk. Laid down.
46 × 32 cm
Provenance: Acquired in 1768
(mark L. 2061) from the
collection of Count Carl
Cobenzl, Brussels (mark L.
2858b)
Inv. no. 5499
Selected literature: Rooses
1886–92, vol. IV, p. 201; Glück,
Haberditzl 1928, no. 26;
Dobroklonsky 1935, no. 143;
Dobroklonsky 1955, no. 644;
Miesel 1963, no. 4, p. 315, fig. 1
(as Rubens); Fubini, Held 1964,
no. 21, p. 134 (as Rubens); Pérez
Sanchez, p. 9, pl. III; Müller-
Hofstede 1968, no. 51, p. 233;
Stechow 1968, p. 29; Judson,
van de Velde 1977, no. 2, p. 163;
Held 1982, no. 21, pp. 99, 104;
Larionov 1991, p.134; van der
Meulen 1995, no. 8

This drawing depicts an antique
statue, the so-called "African
Fisherman" (in the Louvre since
the early nineteenth century), a
Roman copy in black marble
after a lost Hellenistic original.
Found during excavations in
Rome during the second half of
the sixteenth century, the statue
formed part of the collection of
Cardinal Scipione Borghese in
the early 1600s. It was seen
there by Rubens, who made a
close study of the ancient works
in this famous collection during
his stay in Italy from 1600 to
1608. At this time (and up until
the appearance of Johann
Winckelmann's works in the
mid-eighteenth century) the
statue was thought to depict the
death of the Roman philosopher
Seneca, who, according to
Tacitus, committed suicide by
severing the veins in his feet in
a bath of hot water in order to
pre-empt the murderers
dispatched by Nero to kill him.
The basis for such an
identification was probably
provided by the pronounced
naturalistic depiction of the
swollen veins and by the loss of
the statue's legs below the
knees, allowing for the
hypothetical reconstruction of
its original appearance. Soon
after it was discovered, the
sculpture was restored and the
figure was set on a pedestal in
the form of a marble bath,
tinted red at the top to indicate
blood flowing from the
philosopher's veins. Part of this
pedestal (later removed) is
visible in the drawing, and

several strokes of red chalk
recall the somewhat unusual
colouring.
    Seneca was among the
ancient authors most admired
by Rubens; his Stoic philosophy
was extremely influential in the
Netherlandish humanist
intellectual circle to which the
artist belonged from his youth.
In Rubens's time, it was
believed that this was a
surviving ancient representation
of Seneca, and not surprisingly
it drew his attention. Rubens
produced at least six careful
drawings of the statue,
capturing it from different
viewpoints, four of which
survive (Ambrosiana, Milan;
priv. coll., USA; two in the
Hermitage), and two of which
are known from copies by
Rubens's pupils (Kgl.
Kobberstiksamling,
Copenhagen).
    Another drawing in the
Hermitage (inv. no. 5500) is
almost identical in size,
technique and detail to this one,
but some changes are evident in
the facial features and colour;
both drawings are considered in
the literature to be original
works by Rubens. While in the
case of inv. no. 5500 such an
attribution may well be open to
dispute (it might be a copy
produced within the artist's own
circle), the exhibited drawing is
without doubt an authentic
work. It reveals a greater sense
of space and breadth, the plastic
nature of the depiction is more
convincing and the sculpture's
features closely resemble the
model.
    It is generally thought that
the drawing under discussion
was produced during Rubens's
early years in Italy, a theory
supported by its meticulous
technique, which differs
markedly from the more freely
executed studies produced
between 1606 and 1608.
    Cornelis Galle of Antwerp
engraved the drawing after
Rubens's return from Italy, and
Rubens himself used the figure
in the drawing as his model for
Seneca in his painting *Dying
Seneca* (*c.* 1611, Alte Pinakothek,
Munich).
A.L.

100
ANTHONY VAN DYCK
1599 Antwerp – 1641 London
(Formerly attributed to Rubens)
Mars and Venus, c. 1621
Black chalk. Laid down.
45.8 × 31.4 cm
Provenance: Acquired in 1768
(mark L. 2061) from the
collection of Count Carl
Cobenzl, Brussels (mark L.
2858b)
Inv. no. 5498
Selected literature:
Dobroklonsky 1930–31a, no. 7,
p. 15, pl. VII; Dobroklonsky
1955, no. 642, p. 132; Burchard,
d'Hulst 1963, no. 13, pp. 29–30;
Miesel 1963,no. 12, p. 319, fig.
12; Fubini, Held 1964,no. 36,
p. 138; Müller-Hofstede 1965,
p. 270; Kuznetsov 1972–73,
no. 80; Jaffé 1977, no. 45, p. 82;
Held 1982, no. 36, p. 102; van
der Meulen 1995, no. 99,
pp. 108–10; Balis 1999

This magnificent drawing of the
antique sculptural group *A
Roman Couple in the Guise of
Mars and Venus* (Musée du
Louvre, Paris) has traditionally
been attributed to Rubens. The
only cause for controversy has
surrounded its dating. While
the majority of authors have
placed the drawing in the
artist's second Roman period,
between 1606 and 1608, Fubini
and Held (1964) suggested an
earlier dating of *c.* 1602–03. In
1999, however, Arnout Balis
expressed the opinion, fully
shared by the present author,
that the drawing, like several
other studies of antiquities
executed in a similar style,
should be removed from
Rubens's œuvre and given to
Anthony van Dyck. The
drawings mentioned by Balis do
indeed differ in their graphic
manner and in the character of
their imagery. In the case of the
Hermitage *Mars and Venus*,
there is also documentary
evidence that supports this
reassessment of its attribution.
    Archival records published by
Marjon van der Meulen (1995,
pp. 109–10), prove incontro-
vertibly that the sculptural group
depicted in the drawing,
believed in the seventeenth
century to represent *Faustina
and the Gladiator*, became widely
known only around 1620, when
Scipione Borghese acquired it
for his collection. It was at this
time that the group was
restored; the helmet plumage,
the nose, the left hand resting
on the sword hilt, three fingers
of the right hand, the toes and
other lost elements were

replaced on the male figure, as
well as both hands and part of
the head on the female figure.
Since the drawing shows the
sculpture in its restored state, it
could not have been produced
by Rubens, who left Rome in
1608. Van Dyck, however, spent
several months there in 1622
and again in 1623, by which
time the newly discovered and
restored statue had been on
public view and was
undoubtedly attracting
attention.
    Many specific features of the
drawing also suggest the
authorship of van Dyck. His
personal style is revealed by the
manner in which he altered the
model: the poses and gestures
are more elegant and refined
than those of the original
figures, both more slender and
finely proportioned. Van Dyck's
hand is also recognizable in the
treatment of many individual
details such as the drawing of
the faces and hands.
    Van Dyck paid little attention
to the study of antiquities
during his stay in Italy, and,
unlike Rubens, was not
particularly interested in
producing detailed copies,
limiting himself instead to
rapid sketches of works that
took his fancy. As such, this
drawing stands apart from
others of his Italian period and
may have been produced at the
request of Rubens. Balis
compared it with two other
drawings by van Dyck, *Study of
Classical Sculpture* (Institut
Néerlandais, Paris) and *Greek
Philosopher* (Kupferstichkabinet,
Berlin), both of statues in the
London collection of Lord
Arundel during the seventeenth
century. Balis suggested that
both were sketched by van Dyck
while he was in London in 1620
specifically for Rubens, who
throughout his life made a
systematic collection of a variety
of images for subsequent use in
his work. Thanks to his
voluminous correspondence, we
know that Rubens was
informed of all the latest artistic
developments in Italy, and we
also learn from which of his
fellow artists he commissioned
drawings of newly discovered
works. The appearance of a
previously unknown antique
sculpture of this importance
would surely not have gone
unnoticed. The sculpture was
placed on display in the Villa
Borghese in the spring of 1621,
and van Dyck, who set off for
Italy in October of that year,
may have been asked by Rubens

to draw it. If this drawing was
indeed sent by van Dyck to
Rubens, it would naturally have
been kept together with his
copies from the antique. Thus
we should not be surprised that
the sheet lost the name of its
original author and was
subsequently seen as the work
of Rubens himself.
A.L.

IOI

ANTHONY VAN DYCK
1599 Antwerp – 1640 London
Pentecost, n.d.
Pen and brown ink, brown,
grey and green wash, heightened
with white. 25.8 × 21.7 cm
(irregular shape)
Provenance: Sold in 1741 from
the collection of Pierre Crozat,
Paris; sold in 1767 from the
collection of Jean de Jullienne,
Paris; library of the Academy of
Arts, St. Petersburg; transferred
in 1924 from the library of the
Academy of Arts, St. Petersburg
Inv. no. 14537
Selected literature: Mariette
1741, p. 99, no. 854;
Remy 1767, no. 535;
Dobroklonsky 1930–31b, p. 237;
Dobroklonsky 1955, no. 107;
Vey 1962, no. 68; Kuznetsov
1972–73, no. 29; *Western
European Drawing* 1981, no. 145;
Larionov 1998, no. 69

A distinctive feature of van
Dyck's creative method during
his early years as an
independent artist was the
careful working out of each
significant painted composition
in a series of preliminary
graphic sketches. Numerous
surviving drawings from these
years confirm the young artist's
imaginative experimentation.
For each of his subjects, van
Dyck created several variations
on the theme, and the original
idea often went through
considerable changes during his
working process. The
preparatory work for his large
painting *Pentecost* (c. 1620;
Sans-Souci, Potsdam), to which
the Hermitage drawing is
related, exemplifies these
methods. Eight drawings
survive that record the progress
of this painting's composition
or that show separate groups of
its figures (Vey 1962, nos.
63–70). Closest to the final
resolution is a sheet in the
Albertina (Vienna), which may
be regarded as the *modello* that
directly preceded production of
the painting. The sequence of
execution for the other
drawings and sketches cannot
be established with certainty,
but it seems likely that the
Hermitage sheet, which differs
significantly from the painted
version, relates to an early stage
of the process.

As with many other works
from these early years, van Dyck
took as his starting point a print
of *Pentecost* by his teacher,
Rubens, produced as an
illustration for the 1614
publication, *Breviarium*

Romanum. The classicizing
scheme realized so brilliantly by
Rubens is repeated in van
Dyck's Hermitage sketch
without significant alteration.
The figure of Mary, seated in
prayer, is surrounded by the
Apostles arranged in a semicircle, thus forming a single,
evenly distributed group. The
composition was rooted in
sixteenth-century artistic
tradition. Rubens had relied on
Italian Renaissance precedents,
above all Titian's 1540 painting
for the church of Santa Maria
della Salute in Venice. The
leading sixteenth-century
Antwerp artist, Martin de Vos,
had also rendered this subject
in similar compositions, and
prints after his designs were
probably known to van Dyck
(Vey 1962, p. 136).

For *Pentecost*, van Dyck made
considerable changes to his
initial composition. As he
worked out his ideas in
subsequent stages, the artist
rejected the frontal and
symmetrical placing of the
Apostles; gave greater variety to
their poses; moved the figure of
the Virgin to the right, turning

her subtly toward the viewer,
and introduced a striking
architectural background. As a
result, the finished painting has
little in common with the
Hermitage sketch and is an
outstanding example of a
mature Baroque treatment of
this subject.

Van Dyck's graphic style in
his compositional sketches was
shaped by the influence of
Rubens, but acquired an
independent character quite
early on. His elegant and
expressive style is marked by
the use of a variety of technical
devices: the artist touches the
figures with the brush, defining
the facial features and gestures
of the hands with the pen, and
broad areas of wash in the
shadows give the composition
spatial depth and a sense of
light. Van Dyck achieves a series
of refined colouristic effects
with different shades of bistre
combined with a grey wash, by
the softening of some of the
contours with white, and by
introducing delicate colour
accents, such as the green that
marks the Virgin's robes.
A.L.

IO2

ANTHONY VAN DYCK
1599 Antwerp – 1641 London
Rest on the Flight into Egypt,
1629–30
Pen and brown ink, brown
wash. Laid down. 12.2 × 17.2 cm
Provenance: Acquired in 1768
(mark L. 2061) from the
collection of Count Carl
Cobenzl, Brussels (mark L.
2858b)
Inv. no. 5870

103
JACOB JORDAENS
1593 Antwerp – 1678 Antwerp
The Crucifixion, 1658
Black and red chalk,
watercolour and white
highlights. The sheet composed
of several pieces of paper,
rounded at the top. Lined.
59 × 36.8 cm
Bottom right, author's
inscription in pen and brown
ink: *27 martii 1658 Hage.*
Bottom centre: *Overmidst de
Joden Teeckens begeeren En de
Griecken Wysheyd soecken, doch
wy Predicken Christum den
gekruysten, den Joden Een
Ergenisse en der griecken een
dwaesheydt maer beyde de Joden
En griecken die predicken wy de
wysheydt Godts en de Cracht
Godts, I, cor.2* [sic].*22.23.24.*
Beneath the drawing in a
cartouche on the mount (dating
from the Cobenzl collection),
an old inscription in pen and
brown ink: *Jordaens*
Provenance: Acquired in 1768
(mark L. 2061) from the
collection of Count Carl
Cobenzl, Brussels (mark L.
2858b)
Inv. no. 4203
Selected literature: Rooses 1903,
p. 154; Kamenskaya 1934–36,
p. 203; Dobroklonsky 1955,
no. 195; d'Hulst 1956, no. 169,
pp. 287, 390; *Western European
Drawing* 1981, no. 140; d'Hulst
1974, no. A 327; Kuznetsov
1972–73, no. 55; Kuznetsov
1979, no. 26; Larionov 1998,
no. 68, p. 142

Despite its conventional title, this drawing is not so much a direct illustration of the New Testament story of the death of Christ as it is a didactic religious allegory. As was first suggested by Roger d'Hulst (1956, p. 287), Jordaens illustrated a fragment from The First Epistle of Paul the Apostle to the Corinthians, and the artist included a quotation from it in a cartouche at the bottom of the sheet: "For the Jews require a sign, and the Greeks seek after wisdom: But we preach Christ crucified, unto the Jews a stumbling block, and unto the Greeks foolishness; but unto them which are called, both Jews and Greeks, Christ the power of God, and the wisdom of God" (I Corinthians, 1:22–24). To the left, at the foot of the cross, the Jews "require a sign," which is supplied by Moses striking the rock and bringing forth water. In the foreground are the Greeks who seek the answer in books and learned treatises. For them the idea of a crucified Christ is "foolishness" and one laughing figure shakes a jester's rattle at the Crucifixion. To the right of the cross are those who have recognized that Christ is the sole source of wisdom. Allegorical female figures among the angels on clouds personify "the power of God" and "the wisdom of God," while the rising sun embodies the light of Christian truth that pours forth over all humanity.

Y. Kuznetsov (1972–73, no. 55) noted that this allegory, in addition to a direct illustration of the epistle in the cartouche, contains a parallel deriving from medieval typology, that of Moses striking water from the rock as a prefiguration of Christ. The spring that quenches the thirst of the believers finds its source not in the rock, but in Christ's body ("for they drank of that spiritual Rock that followed them: and that Rock was Christ" wrote Paul in the same Epistle, I Corinthians 10:4). The parallel between the water that Moses struck from the rock and the blood that sprang from Christ's wounds is found in the ninth-century texts of Walafrid Strabo; it was later incorporated into the *Biblia Pauperum* (the Pauper's Bible) and came to be generally accepted. Jordaens also used it in his painting *Moses Striking Water from the Rock* (Staatliche Kunstsammlungen, Kassel).

The drawing is a sketch for a work either unexecuted or now lost. It may have been a design for a tapestry, as is suggested by the rounded top with the frame and text set in a cartouche below. This large sheet is composed of several pieces of paper glued entirely or partly on top of each other, which is typical of Jordaens's working method as he often enlarged an original drawing with additional sheets. He also introduced corrections into his compositions by reworking certain aspects on new pieces of paper pasted down over the original sheet. In this case, the figures at the foot of the cross were redrawn on a separate piece of paper and glued over an original version that apparently displeased the artist.

The abstract theological subject is treated by the artist with a narrative quality and expressiveness that are unusual in his work. The figures are drawn energetically, and the artist's use of line simplifies form and produces a vivid, genre-like realism. In this drawing Jordaens employs the most simple of artistic techniques: he combines, for instance, the black and red chalk drawing with reddish-brown wash and, by introducing separate colour accents in pale-blue and greenish watercolour, he creates an impression of rich and decorative abundance.
A.L.

104
JACOB JORDAENS
1593 Antwerp – 1678 Antwerp
The Infant Jupiter Suckled by the Goat Amalthea, c. 1640
Black chalk, pen and brush and brown ink, heightened with white-blue and white-rose body-colour. 37.0 × 46.0 cm
Provenance: acquired in 1768 (mark L. 2061) from the collection of Count Carl Cobenzl, Brussels (mark L. 2858b).
Inv. no. 4200

105
Jacob Jordaens
1593 Antwerp – 1678 Antwerp
Decorative Frieze, 1630s
Red chalk with brown wash, body-colour heightened with white. 11.0 × 135.5 cm
Provenance: transferred in 1923 from the Library of the former Stieglitz School of Technical Drawing.
Inv. no. 33446

106

Frans Francken the Younger
1581 Antwerp – 1642 Antwerp
The Feast of Herod, c. 1620
Pen and brown ink, brown, blue
and red wash, over black chalk.
24 × 14 cm
Provenance: Acquired in 1768
(mark L. 2061) from the
collection of Count Carl
Cobenzl, Brussels (mark L.
2858b)
Inv. no. 3109
Selected literature:
Dobroklonsky 1961, no. 27
(as Frans Francken I); *Western
European Drawing* 1981, no. 134;
Kuznetsov 1972–73, no. 36;
Larionov 1998, no. 67, p. 140

This drawing was for many
years attributed to Frans
Francken the Elder and was
considered to be an illustration
to the parable of the marriage
feast at Galilee (Matthew
22:1–4). The attribution to
Frans Francken the Younger
was made by Yury Kuznetsov
(1972–73), who was also the
first to provide a correct
interpretation of the subject.
Three episodes appear: in the
background to the left is
Herod's feast, to the right the
beheading of John the Baptist,
while in the foreground is
Salome who, on her mother's
advice, begs Herod for the
Baptist's head as a reward for
her dancing (Mark 6:21–28).
The central place given to the
conversation between Herod
and Salome, with the main
episodes described in the
Gospel relegated to the
background, is somewhat
unusual, as the famous subject
had a long iconographic
tradition. Their dialogue,
expressively conveyed in
gestures and facial expressions,
emphasizes Herod's physical
attraction to the young dancer,
and Francken's unique
interpretation of the story
implies that it was this
attraction that led to the
Baptist's murder. Thus
Francken accentuates the story's
erotic appeal, which lends the
drawing its pronounced
moralizing and didactic
character.

The two central figures on
the Hermitage sheet were
employed by Francken again, in
the identical poses and
costumes, for a drawing in a
private collection in Brussels,
Richly Attired Couple (pen and
ink, brown wash, blue wash,
white highlights; 26 × 12 cm;
signed bottom centre with the
monogram *F*). In the Brussels

drawing, however, both figures
are less carefully worked in
detail, the man appears to be
younger, and above the heads is
a cartouche with a shield and
emblem, a heart pierced by an
arrow. This drawing was
reproduced in reverse, with
some insignificant alterations,
in a print signed with the
monogram *ML* and bearing the
legends *F. Franck. Inven.* and *Le
Blond excud avec privelege.*

Kuznetsov, who was not
aware of either the Brussels
drawing or the related print,
based his attribution on a
number of correspondences
with other works known to be
by Francken the Younger
(Kuznetsov 1972–73, p. 62). The
Hermitage drawing's scene of
the beheading of John the
Baptist is almost precisely
reproduced in his painting of
Herod's Feast (Musée des Beaux-
Arts, Dunkirk); a bearded man
in almost the same rich attire is
found in the painting
Connoisseur's Study/Cabinet
(Galleria Borghese, Rome); and
a girl similar in appearance is
shown on the right-hand side of
the painting *Allegory on Charles
V's Abdication* (Rijksmuseum,
Amsterdam).

Kuznetsov noted that the
Hermitage sheet stands
somewhat apart from the body
of graphic works by Francken
the Younger, and that the
characteristic mark of his
drawings is seen only in the
treatment of the scenes in the
background. The detailed pen
work and delicate use of
watercolour are unusual devices
in his work. This suggests that
the sheet, unlike the known
sketches by the artist for
paintings and prints, was
conceived as an independent
finished work, intended for sale
or as a gift. The taste for elegant
calligraphy in the pen drawing,
seen in the plasticity of the
graceful, elegant figures with
their elongated proportions and
affected gesticulation, set this
work within the traditions of
Netherlandish Mannerism and
suggest a relatively early date,
no later than 1620.
A.L.

107

HENDRICK DE CLERK
c. 1570 Brussels – 1630 Brussels
Allegory of the Truce of 1609, n.d.
Pen and brown ink, brown
wash, gouache, gold (in the coat
of arms). 25.4 × 33.6 cm
Bottom right corner, an old
inscription in pen and brown
ink: *Hen: de Clerck. Bruxel: F.*
Below in pen and red ink: *N 6*
Provenance: Collection of
Prosper Henricus Lankrink,
London (mark L. 2090);
collection of Count Ivan
Betskoy, St. Petersburg (mark
L. 2878a); from 1767 in
the Academy of Arts,
St. Petersburg; transferred in
1924 from the Academy of Arts
Inv. no. 15123
Selected literature: Kuznetsov
1972–73, no. 18; *Western
European Drawing* 1981, no. 126;
Larionov 1998, no. 61, p. 126

Allegorical works presenting
events from contemporary
political life were extremely
widespread in European art
from the second half of the
sixteenth century. A
characteristic example of this
genre is the Hermitage
drawing, which reflects one of
the turning points in the history
of the Netherlands, the Truce of
1609. The truce lasted for
twelve years and put an end to
the long civil war between
Flanders and Holland that had
impoverished Flanders for
decades. In effect, the truce
represented recognition by the
Spanish of the independence of
the Protestant Northern
Provinces and was perceived by
the Dutch as a national
triumph. For Catholic Flanders,
which remained a protectorate
of the Spanish Crown, peace
brought about hopes for the
restoration of trade and a return
to economic prosperity. In this
drawing, Brussels court artist
Hendrick de Clerk depicts the
event from the perspective of
the rulers of the Southern

Netherlands, as a victory of the
forces of peace over the furies of
discord.

The female figure in the
centre foreground personifies a
country torn apart by war.
Behind her are seventeen young
women each of whom
symbolize a Netherlandish
province identified by shields
emblazoned with their
respective coats-of-arms, all
shown in warlike poses with
raised swords. The ten figures
to the left personify the Catholic
Southern Provinces opposed by
the seven Northern Provinces.
Descending from the heavens
by divine command are the
rulers of Flanders, the
Archduke Ferdinand and the
Infanta Isabella, with myrtle
branches in their hands,
bringing news of peace. The
landscape background contains
a topical political subtext as
well; behind the figures
representing the south of the
country is a seaside town, while
behind their enemies are the
sea and ships guarding the
mouth of a river. This is an

allusion to the ruinous Dutch
naval blockade of the mouth of
the River Scheldt, the lifting of
which was one of the most
desired results of the truce.

Kuznetsov (1972–73)
established that the main
elements of the allegorical
language used in this drawing
were borrowed from works by
the artist's predecessors. A
triumphal arch of 1599
designed by Otto Vaenius in
honour of the arrival in
Antwerp of Albert and Isabella
(Roeder-Baumbach 1943, p. 60,
fig. 39), for example, depicts
messengers of the gods
descending from the heavens to
present branches of peace to
despairing Belgium. Seventeen
women with heraldic shields
embodying the Netherlandish
provinces are also present in a
painting by Pieter Claessins the
Younger, *The Doorninck Truce of
1584* (Groeningemuseum,
Bruges).

The traditional attribution of
this sheet to Hendrick de Clerk
is based on an old inscription in
the lower right corner and is

confirmed by comparison with
signed works by the artist, such
as *St. Sebastian Before the
Emperor Diocletian* (Musées
Royaux des Beaux-Arts de
Belgique, Brussels) and *Moses
Striking the Rock* (Musée du
Louvre, Paris). The same
unmistakable graphic hand is
discernible in all three works:
the fine, nervous pen lines
outlining the whimsical
contours of the elegantly
elongated figures, the
characteristic "sharp" folds of
the drapery and the elegant
details of the hairstyles and
costumes.

The Hermitage sheet stands
somewhat apart from de Clerk's
other graphic works in its
particularly fine execution. The
careful working of the smallest
details and the use of gouache
and gold bring it closer to the
art of miniature painting, a
tradition widespread in
northern Europe at the end of
the sixteenth century.
A.L.

109
CASPAR DE CRAYER
1584 Antwerp – 1669 Ghent
The Martyrdom of St. Peter,
c. 1650
Oil on paper. Laid down.
34.5 × 28 cm
Provenance: Acquired in 1768
(mark L. 2061) from the
collection of Count Carl
Cobenz, Brussels (mark L.
2858b)
Inv. no. 2061

108
ABRAHAM VAN DIEPENBEECK
bapt. 1596 's-Hertogenbosch –
1675 Antwerp
and Peter Paul Rubens
1577 Siegen – 1640 Antwerp
The Marriage of the Virgin, n.d.
Black chalk, grey wash and
white highlights, corrections in
pen and brown ink.
57.0 × 43.5 cm
Provenance: acquired in 1768
(mark L. 2061) from the
collection of Count Carl
Cobenzl. Formerly collection of
Pierre Crozat, Paris; collection
of Count Carl Cobenzl, Brussels
(mark L. 2858b).
Inv. no. 5523

III

ABRAHAM VAN DIEPENBEEK
bapt. 1596 's-Hertogenbosch –
1675 Antwerp
*The Martyrdom of Jesuits in
Japan*
Pen and brown ink, blue wash,
heightened with white.
29.5 × 22.0 cm
Provenance: acquired in 1768
(mark L. 2061) from the
collection of Count Carl
Cobenzl, Brussels (mark L.
2858b).
Inv. no. 2782

110
ERASMUS QUELLINUS THE
YOUNGER
1607 Antwerp – 1678 Antwerp
Design for a Triumphal Arch,
c. 1657
Pen and brown ink, grey wash,
heightened with white on green
paper. 50 × 63.5 cm
Signed bottom left corner:
Erasmus Quellinus F.
In the centre on the pediment:
Don juan.
Beneath the right trophy: *o
valenc : lib : res gerere et caj...
ostendere civibus caj...*
On the socle beneath the image
of Heracles defeating the
Nemean lion: *Acheloum Lictâ
vine* (in pen and brown ink)
On the reverse: *n° 48 12
teeckeninge* (in pen and black
ink)
Provenance: Collection of A.
Beurdeley, Paris (mark L. 421);
library of the Stieglitz School of
Technical Drawing; transferred
in 1923 from the library of the
former Stieglitz School
Inv. no. 40794
Selected literature:
Dobroklonsky 1955, no. 223;
Kuznetsov 1972–73, no. 71

Throughout his long career,
Erasmus Quellinus was
frequently commissioned by the
magistrate of the city of
Antwerp to produce official city
decorations for ceremonial
occasions. This drawing is a
design for a temporary structure
to mark the entry of the new
governor of the Spanish
Netherlands, Don Juan of
Austria, son of King Charles IV,
into Antwerp on May 6, 1657.
The traditional title for this
drawing, *Design for a Triumphal
Arch*, is not entirely accurate, as
it is a design for a decorative
portico or loggia to be erected
before the façade of a building
along the route travelled by the
ceremonial cortege. A very
similar temporary structure,
known from a print by
Wenceslas Hollar, was erected
by Quellinus some twenty years
earlier on the Grote Markt
before the town hall in
Antwerp, when the city
celebrated the Peace of Münster.
It is possible that the edifice
depicted in the Hermitage
drawing was intended for the
same location.

Yury Kuznetsov was the first
to interpret the allegorical
programme of the decorations.
The central portico is crowned
with an equestrian statue of
Don Juan holding a marshal's
baton in his hand, while putti
hovering above crown him with
a victor's wreath. The rearing
horse tramples a female figure
with the head of the Gorgon
Medusa, entwined with snakes,
the image thus serving as an
allegory of the quelling of
Dissent. To the sides are the
personification of Justice with
her attributes, scales and a
sword, as well as the figure of
Good Government with her
rudder and sceptre. Decorating
the balustrade atop the portal
are triumphal standards held
aloft by putti, military trophies
with bound prisoners, as well as
heraldic images of a rampant
lion and an eagle with Jupiter's
thunderbolts in its talons. The
paired caryatids on the
colonnade represent Mercury
and Minerva, Apollo and Diana
(?), an allegorical figure of
Justice and Ceres, as well as
Neptune and Hercules. Below
on the socle are eight reliefs
illustrating the seven labours of
Hercules. The overall purpose
of the allegory was thus to
glorify Don Juan's military feats
and liken him to the invincible
Hercules. The image was also
an expression of hope for the
growth of trade and navigation,
the prosperity of the land, and
the flourishing of the arts and
sciences, all of which would be
under the new governor's
benevolent rule.

In its composition, imagery
and the very nature of its
allegorical language, this design
reveals Quellinus's dependence
on the similar project that
Rubens created for the
ceremonial entrance into
Antwerp of Cardinal Infante
Ferdinand on April 17, 1635
(cat. 8, 9), in which Quellinus
played a central rôle as
Rubens's assistant. The
decoration of the portal's upper
tier in this drawing is especially
closely related to Rubens's oil
sketch of the *Arch of Ferdinand*
(cat. 9).
A.L.

112
Peter Paul Rubens
1577 Siegen – 1640
Antwerp
Sheet of Studies: Head of a Man Looking Up, Hand, and Lower Part of a Head in Profile, 1618–19
Black and white chalk on yellow-grey paper. Laid down. 32 × 22 cm
Beneath the drawing in a cartouche on the mount (dating from the Cobenzl collection) is an old inscription in pen and brown ink: *Rubens*
Provenance: Acquired in 1768 (mark L. 2061) from the collection of Count Carl Cobenzl, Brussels (mark L. 2858b)
Inv. no. 5454

113
Peter Paul Rubens
1577 Siegen – 1640
Antwerp
Head of a Youth looking up, 1615–16
Charcoal and white chalk on grey paper. Laid down. 34 × 27 cm
Provenance: Acquired in 1768 (mark L. 2061) from the collection of Count Carl Cobenzl, Brussels (mark L. 2858b)
Inv. no. 5888

114

ANTHONY VAN DYCK
1599 Antwerp – 1641 London
Portrait of Cornelis Schut,
c. 1628–36
Black chalk, brown wash,
contours traced for transfer.
Laid down. 23 × 19 cm
Provenance: Acquired in 1768
(mark L. 2061) from the
collection of Count Carl
Cobenzl, Brussels (mark L.
2858b)
Inv. no. 5907
Selected literature: Spicer
1985–86, p. 34; Larionov 1998,
no. 71, p. 148

Van Dyck produced this
drawing for an engraving by
Lucas Vorsterman, which was to
form part of his *Iconography*, a
collection of engraved portraits
of the artist's famous
contemporaries. Van Dyck
conceived the idea for this
extensive series of portraits after
his return from Italy in late
1627. He engaged leading
engravers of the time to work
on the project, including
Vorsterman, Paulus Pontius,
Schelte à Bolswert and Pieter de
Jode. The portraits were
engraved from drawings by the
master, and were to be divided
into three large groups
consisting of monarchs and
military commanders,
statesmen and philosophers, as
well as artists and collectors.
During van Dyck's lifetime,
eighty sheets were issued by the
Antwerp printing house of
Martin van Emden, but no
complete set was ever
assembled. Later issues of full
sets, published posthumously,
included portrait etchings by
van Dyck himself, together with
reproductions of some of his
paintings, increasing the total
number of sheets to 124.

A large number of
preparatory sketches for the
prints in the *Iconography*
survive. In manner and
technique they can be divided
into several groups that clearly
relate to different stages of
work. It seems that van Dyck
produced from life only a first,
quick sketch in black chalk,
which would have captured the
sitter's features. Several such
drawings survive, in which only
the sitter's head is carefully
worked out, while the pose and
costume are barely indicated by
a few quick strokes. The
original sketch was then revised
by the artist in his studio, when
he determined the position of
the body, the placement of
hands, and details of the

costume and accessories. At this
stage the image acquired the
careful arrangement typical of
the artist, and a life study was
transformed into a formal
Baroque portrait.

The majority of van Dyck's
known drawings for the
Iconography reflect this last
stage, when the full conception
of the portrait was realized. On
the basis of such drawings, van
Dyck and his assistants
produced several painted
sketches on panel in grisaille,
which then served as models for
the prints. In some cases,
however, the artist simplified
the procedure, and the need for
a painted sketch would be
rendered superfluous as the
necessary details for the
printmaker were finalized
directly on the drawing. This
was always done by van Dyck
himself, who retouched such
sketches with brown wash to
render the details, to determine
the distribution of light and
shade, and to establish the
setting. This portrait of the
Flemish painter Cornelis Schut
(1599–1655) is one such *modello*.

Although it displays all the
features and skill typical of van
Dyck's graphic works, this
drawing was ignored until
relatively recently. It was
thought to be a copy of a
drawing in the Louvre, identical
in composition and technique,
which was recorded in the
literature as the original (Vey
1962, no. 280). In 1986,
Joaneath Spicer noted the
artistic superiority of the
Hermitage version of the
portrait, and observed that,
unlike the Louvre drawing, it is
incised along its contours for
transfer, thus demonstrating
that it was used in the process
of making the print.

The drawing could not have
been produced before 1628,
when work began on the
Iconography, and no later than
1636, when van Dyck moved to
England.
A.L.

115

ANTHONY VAN DYCK
1599 Antwerp – 1641 London
Portrait of Pieter Brueghel the Younger, c. 1628–32
Black chalk. Laid down.
23 × 19 cm
Provenance: Acquired in 1768 (mark L. 2061) from the collection of Count Carl Cobenzl, Brussels (mark L. 2858b)
Inv. no. 5908
Selected literature: Spicer 1985–86, p. 34; Larionov 1998, no. 70, p. 146; Depauw, Ger Lijten 1999, no. 7

This drawing, another preparatory study for van Dyck's *Iconography*, depicts Pieter Brueghel the Younger (1564–1636), the successful Antwerp painter and son of the renowned Pieter Bruegel the Elder, whose style and compositions he often imitated. As in van Dyck's other surviving sketches for his etchings, this sheet is somewhat larger than the final print. The black chalk drawing is freely executed, and the fact that this is one of the portraits with ink wash for which van Dyck produced the etching himself probably explains why it has not been retouched.

The portrait of Pieter Bruegel the Younger is the only print in the *Iconography* for which two autograph sketches survive. In addition to the Hermitage drawing there is a study, similar in technique and style, in the collection of the Duke of Devonshire, in which the same figure is shown in a somewhat different pose, turned three-quarters to the left. The relationship between these two drawings remains unclear. It is possible that the Devonshire sheet was produced first, but that the angle of the pose did not satisfy van Dyck, who later reworked the composition to show the sitter *en face*, which offered a more penetrating analysis of Brueghel's personality. It is possible that both drawings were begun together from life, but that the Hermitage version was chosen by the artist as the basis for the final print.

The etching that forms part of the *Iconography* follows the drawing in all details, reproducing it in reverse. Van Dyck squared the sketch in order to simplify the precise transfer of the image on to the etching plate. The same scaled grid is found on other drawings that were etched by the artist himself for the *Iconography*, and its presence on the Hermitage sheet constitutes an argument for its autograph status. Cited in nineteenth-century publications as an original by van Dyck, the drawing was later considered a copy from a lost original and was not subsequently included in the scholarly literature. It was only in 1986 that Joaneath Spicer drew attention to it once more.

Doubts regarding van Dyck's authorship can partly be explained by signs of later retouching. It is possible that the column sketched behind the figure is not by the artist; the untidy pencil lines in the background are probably of much later date; and the face and costume have been retouched in a different shade of black chalk from that on the original drawing, in a manner that is unlikely to have been the work of van Dyck. While such intrusions inhibit our perception of the original drawing, even in its present state this is an outstanding example of the artist's portrait style.

This image of the aged artist, who must have seemed to van Dyck a messenger from another time and the embodiment of Flemish artistic tradition, is an insightful study of the sitter's inner tension. The lack of attention to the setting and the penetrating psychological portrayal of the sitter were unusual in van Dyck's portraits, and set this drawing apart from other sheets connected with the *Iconography*. The drawing may be dated to between 1628 and 1632.
A.L.

116
Jan Boeckhorst
1605 Münster – 1668 Antwerp
Young Lady in a Beret, n.d.
Black and red chalk, black wash, watercolour. 175 × 150 mm
Provenance: Acquired in 1768 (mark L. 2061) from the collection of Count Carl Cobenzl, Brussels (mark L. 2858b)
Inv. no. 4330
Selected literature:
Dobroklonsky 1955, no. 22;
Kuznetsov 1972–73, no. 11;
Western European Drawing 1981, no. 148; Foulon 1971–72, no. T15; Lahrkamp 1982, no. 77; Held 1985, p. 22, fig. 16; Luckhardt 1990, no. 36, p. 212

Boeckhorst's position as one of the most talented and interesting draughtsmen of the school of Rubens has become apparent only in recent years. This has been established by several publications and a 1990 exhibition devoted to the artist that assembled all of the attributed drawings alongside his known paintings. The Hermitage drawing of *Young Lady in a Beret* occupies a place somewhat apart from the artist's other drawings in its combination of black and red chalk, its delicate tinting, and its careful finish of details. All of these features would seem to be atypical of Boeckhorst's graphic works, which were usually executed in a temperamental, sketchy manner. At the same time, the facial type and the pronounced elegance of the sitter's pose in this drawing have close analogies in Boeckhorst's paintings, leading the majority of scholars to accept the traditional attribution to this artist that dates back to the middle of the eighteenth century.

The sheet was probably produced as a *modello* for a painting that appeared on the art market several years ago under the name of Justus van Egmonts, and that was acquired by the Stadtmuseum, Münster, and attributed to Boeckhorst by comparison with the Hermitage drawing. The only differences between the painted version of the portrait and the drawing are that in the painting the woman holds a branch of flowering roses instead of a fan in her outstretched hand, and the landscape background is treated slightly differently. In style and overall conception, this portrait, to a greater degree than the drawing, reveals the strong influence of van Dyck, which is also true of other works by Boeckhorst.

It has not been possible to learn the woman's identity. Kuznetsov (1972–73) suggested that she might be the artist's mistress, Menzia Montoia, yet this remains merely a romantic supposition. A reduced replica of the Münster painting in a European private collection during the early 1930s (Foulon 1972, no. P4) was entitled *Portrait of Charlotte de Tremouille, Countess of Derby*, but there is no convincing evidence for such an identification.
A.L.

117
JACOB JORDAENS
1593 Antwerp – 1678 Antwerp
Study of a Young Woman's Head,
1630s
Black and red chalk.
16.0 × 14.1 cm
Provenance: acquired by the Hermitage in 1923. Formerly Suchtelen collection,
St. Petersburg (mark L. 2332);
E. Schwarz collection,
St. Petersburg.
Inv. no. 27328

118
PETER PAUL RUBENS
1577 Siegen – 1640 Antwerp
Landscape with a Dam, 1635–40
Gouache, tempera and black
chalk over a sketch in black
chalk. 43.5 × 59.0 cm
Provenance: acquired in 1768
(mark L. 2061) from the
collection of Count Carl
Cobenzl, Brussels (mark L.
2858b).
Inv. no. 5518

119
GIJSBRECHTS LEYTENS (MASTER
OF WINTER LANDSCAPES)
1586 (?) Antwerp – 1643/56
Winter Scene, n.d.
Pen and brown and blue ink.
18.6 × 29.0 cm
Provenance: acquired in 1768
(mark L. 2061) from the
collection of Count Carl
Cobenzl, Brussels (mark L.
2858b).
Inv. no. 459

120
TOBIAS VERHAECHT
1561 Antwerp – 1631 Antwerp
Landscape with Tobias and Angel,
n.d.
Pen and brown ink, blue wash.
17.9 × 27.1 cm
Provenance: Collection of Count
Ivan Betskoy, St. Petersburg
(mark L. 2878a); from 1767
in the Academy of Arts,
St. Petersburg; transferred in
1924 from the Academy of Arts.
Inv. no. 15090

121
LUCAS VAN UDEN
1595 Antwerp – 1672 Antwerp
Landscape with a Hut by a River,
c. 1645
Pen and brown ink, brown, grey
and blue wash. 22.5 × 38 cm
Bottom edge on the stone,
signed and dated in pen and
brown ink: *Lucas Van Uden*
164[5?]
Provenance: Acquired in 1768
(mark L. 2061) from the
collection of Count Carl
Cobenzl, Brussels (mark L.
2858b)
Inv. no. 6234

122
Jan Brueghel I (Velvet Brueghel)
1568 Brussels –1625 Antwerp
Winter Landscape, 1611
Pen and brown ink, grey and
blue wash. 19.2 × 27.0 cm
Provenance: acquired in 1768
(mark L. 2061) from the
collection of Count Carl
Cobenzl, Brussels (mark L.
2858b).
Inv. no. 470

123
Jan Fyt
1611 Antwerp – 1661 Antwerp
Fox Hunt, n.d.
Gouache over black chalk on
yellowish-grey paper; squared in
white chalk. 51 × 51.8 cm
Provenance: Acquired in 1768
(mark L. 2061) from the
collection of Count Carl
Cobenzl, Brussels (mark L.
2858b)
Inv. no. 3083
Selected literature: Waagen
1864, p. 319; Dobroklonsky
1926, no. 98; Delen 1938,
nos. 422, 423; Dobroklonsky
1955, no. 737; Kuznetsov 1970,
p. 16; Western European
Drawings 1981, no. 147;
Depauw 1988, no. 40, p. 195

This striking gouache must be
considered one of the
masterpieces of the Hermitage
collection of Flemish drawings.
While in the possession of
Cobenzl it was ascribed to Jan
Fyt, but a century after its
acquisition by the Hermitage it
was attributed to the eighteenth-
century French painter Jean-
Baptiste Oudry (Waagen 1864),
who was much influenced by
Flemish artists of the previous
century. In 1924 the Hermitage
acquired another gouache (*Dog
Barking at Swans*, inv. no. 15278),
clearly by the same hand, and,
judging by its similar technique
and dimensions, conceived as a
pendant to the *Fox Hunt*. A
large group of studies for
individual animals linked with
both compositions was acquired
simultaneously. Dobroklonsky
(1926) attributed the entire
group to Fyt, thus returning to
the original attribution of the
Fox Hunt. Since that time Fyt's
authorship has never been
questioned, although it is based
on purely stylistic grounds such
as its emphatically decorative
nature and the dynamism of its
composition, its extremely vivid
depiction of animals and its fine
sense of colour. The white chalk
grid applied over the drawing
provides evidence that it was a
sketch for a large work, perhaps
an easel painting or a tapestry
cartoon. This is confirmed by
the group of seven life studies
for individual details of the *Fox
Hunt*, five of which are in the
Hermitage, and two in the
Stedelijk Prentenkabinet,
Antwerp.
A.L.

124
JAN FYT
1611 Antwerp – 1661 Antwerp
Study of a Dog, n.d.
Black chalk, body-colour.
50.1 × 39 cm
Provenance: Collection of Count
Ivan Betskoy, St. Petersburg
(mark L.2878a); from 1767
in the Academy of Arts,
St. Petersburg; transferred in
1924 from the Academy of Arts.
Inv. no. 15279

125
Jacob Jordaens
1593 Antwerp – 1678 Antwerp
*The Light Once Loved by Me, I
Give, Dear Child, to Thee*, n.d.
Pen and brown ink, brown and
blue wash over black chalk.
13.0 × 20.1 cm
Provenance: donated to the
Hermitage in 1924. Formerly
collection of Nikolay Vorobyov,
St. Petersburg.
Inv. no. 14233

126
SEBASTIAEN VRANCX
1573 Antwerp – 1647 Antwerp
*A Village Plundered by
Marauders*, n.d.
Pen and brown ink.
16.0 × 31.0 cm
Provenance: transferred in
1924 from the Academy of Arts,
St. Petersburg. Formerly
collection of Count Ivan Betskoy,
St. Petersburg (mark L. 2878a);
from 1767 in the Academy of
Arts, St. Petersburg.
Inv. no. 14237

Seventeenth-Century Decorative Arts in Flanders and Russia

Tatyana Kossourova

Adoration of the Magi
(detail; see cat. 165),
Germany, 17th century

FIG. 14: RAPHAEL DE LA
PLANCHE MANUFACTORY,
Paris, France, *fl.* 1633–1668,
The Coronation of Constantine,
from The History of Emperor
Constantine series, designed
by Peter Paul Rubens

(1577 Siegen – 1640 Antwerp)
for the manufactory of Marc de
Comans and François de La
Planche, *c.* 1623–25, wool and
silk, State Hermitage Museum,
St. Petersburg, inv. no. 15601

RUBENS'S INFLUENCE ON THE DECORATIVE ARTS

A survey of seventeenth-century Flemish art would be
incomplete without a discussion of Rubens's
considerable impact on the decorative arts. His interest in
monumental decorative ensembles seems almost
inevitable, given what we know of his unrestrained
creativity, technical virtuosity and decorative feel for
colour. He was able to conceptualize and realize
grandiose projects that transformed majestic suites of
rooms in palaces, vaults of churches and open spaces of
the city into complex and powerful works of art. This
exhibition includes examples of Rubens's direct
involvement in such projects as well as numerous objects
clearly indebted to his artistic supremacy. In examining
his influence, it might indeed be said that Rubens
determined the appearance of Western European
decorative arts during his lifetime.

TAPESTRIES

Rubens's designs for tapestries, a traditional Flemish art
form, fully reflect his distinctive artistic practice. Heroic
battle and triumph formed the leitmotif in the four
tapestry series he designed: *The History of Decius Mus,
The History of Constantine, The Story of Achilles* and *The
Triumph of the Eucharist*. In these he introduced radical
innovations, altering accepted colour schemes and
introducing resonant local areas of colour, filling scenes
with monumental figures and lending compositions a

totally new dynamism. Rubens's innovative manner is most obvious in *The Triumph of the Eucharist*, the most important Netherlandish tapestry series on a religious theme produced during the first half of the seventeenth century. In this series he employed the original compositional conceit of a "tapestry within a tapestry," with flanking architectural columns serving simultaneously as both the setting and as an outer frame. This device was adopted by Rubens's contemporaries and became fashionable for a time, although weavers subsequently returned to the more traditional treatment of borders dominated by vegetable motifs.

The hanging of these tapestries within a church interior was unusual. Since the subjects were placed opposite each other, their full narrative could not be "read" in an uninterrupted sequence, and their arrangement forced viewers to slow their pace and alternate their attention between the two facing walls. This reinforced the effect of one's participation in the events unfolding before one, in a manner consonant with Rubens's work as a whole. He had used this device somewhat earlier in his painting cycle *The Life of Marie de' Medici* (1622–25) for the Luxembourg Palace in Paris. In both cases, measured rhythmic movement created a specific and appropriate engagement – in the Luxembourg Palace that of a majestic royal procession, in the church, of religious ritual.

The History of Constantine series differed from other works by Rubens, and was the only one woven in France rather than at the famous workshops in Brussels or Antwerp. Many scholars believe the series to have been commissioned by the French king Louis XIII, but it has also been suggested that the patron was the manufactory at Saint-Marcel itself.[1] Van Tichelen believes this to be the most "classical" of Rubens's four tapestry series, reflecting the French tendency towards rational treatment of Baroque forms, and has suggested that the severe borders were made by local French cartoon makers.[3]

Rubens made extensive use of architectural elements both in his paintings and in his decorative designs, which he composed himself from several favourite motifs rather than relying on known buildings. Generalized details might simply form part of a background, but were also included as independent elements, often as part of the central composition, used to frame the figurative scenes. One of the artist's most

frequently employed conceits was a portal with its corners cut off, bordered by two rusticated Doric columns. *The Triumph of the Eucharist* tapestries included both twisted, Solomonic columns and rusticated Doric columns, while in *The Story of Achilles* the frame is composed of herms and caryatids with baskets on their heads. This latter kind of frame may have derived from the title page of a work on optics by Franciscus Aguilonius that Rubens illustrated in 1611.

Rubens also had an indirect effect on the production of Flemish tapestries, many of which repeat compositions from his painted work, particularly the hunting scenes. The borders of these tapestries, however, were conceived independently by the weavers who transferred his compositions into thread, adapting them to current tastes or to accord with the patron's desires. Thus they are usually composed of abundant festoons of fruits and flowers hanging in swags or falling in bunches, reflecting purely Flemish tastes. The entire repertoire of sixteenth-century Netherlandish ornamental borders might be employed (Harpies, masks, dolphins, shells, cornucopias), although these were subjected to purely Baroque treatment of form, as in *The History of Decius Mus*.

Compositions by Rubens, such as *The Supper at Emmaus,* were also used for the woven tapestry table coverings that were so common in the Northern Netherlands. Set against a black ground in central medallions, these compositions were framed with luxuriant garlands of fruits and flowers, the remainder of the space scattered with tulips, roses, lilies and irises, recalling French *millefleurs* tapestries.

Embroidery

The seventeenth century was also a golden age of Flemish embroidery, particularly in Antwerp. The triumph of the Catholic Church during the first half of the century led to a demand for a large quantity of new liturgical robes, and the art of embroidery thus flourished. These garments were characterized by such Baroque techniques as "needle painting," or satin stitch, and relief embroidery.

As with tapestries, many of Rubens's painted designs were repeated in silk threads on these luxurious Catholic robes. His altarpiece compositions for various Antwerp churches – *The Descent of the Holy Ghost*, the

Assumption, St. Barbara and *St. Catherine of Alexandria,* for example – were embroidered in medallions on robes and chalice veils.[4] Executed in satin stitch with additional gilded threads, they faithfully reflected the painted originals, conveying the figure modelling and fine nuances of colour. Such figurative medallions were usually framed with relief ornament in gilded threads, employed to recall, illusionistically, sculptural forms in their play of light and shade. Their brilliant sheen served to reinforce the sense of luxury and the ceremony of Catholic ritual. This interest in the play of light and colour was very much in the spirit of Rubens's painted œuvre, and it manifested itself in both religious and purely decorative embroidery throughout Europe during the seventeenth century. "Needle painting" was particularly suited to the Baroque age as it was able fully to convey ideas of abundance and fertility, as well as to represent the sensual world of nature and its imagery.

Standing somewhat apart are the Lenten veils produced in Flanders during the first quarter of the seventeenth century: long narrow panels embroidered with white linen threads showing scenes from the life of St. Ignatius. These monochrome, graphic subject compositions derive from engravings in the book *Vita Beati P. Ignatii*, some scenes of which are related to drawings by Rubens.[5]

IVORY

Rubens's influence on ivory carving was so profound and varied that it spread far beyond the borders of Flanders itself, being felt by nearly all practising craftsmen. The artist himself had a deep personal interest in this art form and assembled his own collection of ivory sculpture. A new attitude to the material itself transformed ivory carving in the seventeenth century: as it was now seen to have the potential to express specific ideas, like painting, sculptors rejected the use of gilding and paint in favour of the more natural warm tone of the material itself, which emphasized its innate qualities and the image's emotional content. Both works in the round and reliefs were affected, as the soft material was equally able to convey light and shade, and to create the illusion of multi-plane construction in relief and the soft plasticity of large volumes in the round. Ivory's capacity for fine modelling allowed the unsurpassed expression of painterly effects in sculpture, emphasized by the smooth

sheen of the surface and by the soft yellowish tone of the material, which recalled the natural colour of the naked human form. No other material was better suited to convey fully the ideal of female beauty as presented in the canvases of Rubens. Ivory figures, naked and sensual, whose unflawed smooth surfaces so readily reflected real light (cat. 158), could easily compete, with their pearly skin, with his painted images of women.

Rubens took direct charge of the sculptors in his workshop, seeking to endow them with a sense of the commonality of painting and sculpture. The most famous of his pupils were the German sculptor Georg Petel (?1601/02–c. 1634) and the Flemish sculptor Lucas Fayd'herbe (1617–1697). Although Petel worked in Augsburg, the influence of Rubens was apparent in both his secular and religious works. Fayd'herbe was greatly influenced by Rubens himself and regularly made use of his compositions in bacchanalian scenes and depictions of nereids and tritons.

Favoured subjects taken up by carvers included Rubens's *Adoration of the Magi* (cat. 165), of which numerous sculptural versions were produced. These skilfully combine individual borrowed motifs in a single relief, yet still preserve a unity of composition. Rubens's beloved hunting scenes also appeared frequently, his *Boar Hunt* serving as a model for the carved hunt scenes of Diana and Acteon on a display platter by German sculptor Johann Michael Maucher (cat. 164). In turning to Rubens's *The Judgement of Solomon*, Flemish masters reproduced the work more precisely in both composition and style. A German carver who used the same image on the body of a tankard, however, borrowed only the figures while excluding the impressive architectural background, and rejected the artist's complex foreshortenings and movements in favour of simplified and frontal images.

Putti and cupids are intrinsic to the work of Rubens, the artist being well acquainted with them from the work of his teacher, Otto van Veen (Vaenius), in his famous *Emblems.* These pudgy winged figures enliven even the serious scholarly work on optics by Aguilonius that Rubens illustrated.[6] As Liskenkov has noted, cupids "here clearly embody the Platonic idea of Eros, source of all creative work – an idea that was of course well known in the circle of Rubens's scholarly friends."[7] Putti were frequently the subject of ivory carvings, notably in the work of François Duquesnoy, who may have modelled the two small figures in the round included in this exhibition (cat. 161, 163). They sometimes appear in high relief, as in a sleeping putto in the Hermitage (cat. 162), in scenes of bacchanalia on tankards and vases, and they also crown the lids of cups and tankards, particularly on seventeenth-century German examples reflecting Flemish influence, notably those by Ignaz Elhafen (1685–1715), one of the most outstanding Baroque ivory carvers.

Silver

Beginning in the second quarter of the seventeenth century, the Baroque was firmly established as the dominant style in German gold and silver work. The influence of Rubens on silver was manifest in the overall development of Baroque ornamental forms and the choice of subject-matter rather than in specific objects or models. Augsburg and Nuremberg, the largest and most important centres of production since the late sixteenth century, acquired ever greater authority; nevertheless, the art of Rubens played a rôle in changing the appearance of works produced there. His influence can be seen in the introduction of a painterly approach to form, greater plastic expression, an enlarged sense of scale and the use of colour. This was the age when the full potential of silver's malleable qualities and its sculptural possibilities were recognized. A variety of surface treatments were realized through different techniques such as chasing and embossing, which created distinctions between sculptural masses; high relief reinforced the tendency toward dynamic compositions and created multiple layers of form; polish gave the objects a lustrous surface and partial gilding introduced colour highlights to the monochrome silver. Objects were thus permeated with a sense of movement that was reinforced by a painterly play of light and shade.

The choice of subjects for works in silver reveals a taste for ancient mythology, for bacchanalian scenes, the seasons and allegories, all of which also echo Flemish art. Artists continued to reflect maritime themes, taken from sixteenth-century Netherlandish art, with numerous images of naiads, Neptune and shells. As in ivory carving of the period, cupids and putti, probably inspired by Rubens's paintings, appear in reliefs on tankards, as finials on lids, and intertwining into ornamental borders. New forms also appeared, such as

the broad-edged display platters, which were embellished with large flowers, fruits and berries (cat. 129, 130, 138, 143, 144, 164). In common with the borders of Flemish tapestries, the collars of these large chargers play a significant rôle in the overall composition, the rhythmic alternation of their ornamental forms contrasting with the massive forms of the central compositions.

Collecting Seventeenth-Century European Decorative Arts in Russia

In the sixteenth and seventeenth centuries diplomatic relations between Russia and Europe flourished. In the sixteenth century a special body was set up in Moscow, the Embassy Office, which was in charge of Russia's contacts with other nations. Numerous exchanges of envoys took place, the most important being the great embassies that concluded alliances and marriages between members of ruling houses. Foreign envoys from both West and East flooded into Russia bearing gifts of silver, arms and armour, precious garments, even rich horse trappings. Such valuable gifts from foreign states were intended to express profound respect for Muscovite Russia, which, by the middle of the seventeenth century, had become a viable and serious partner in European politics. Some donors stunned the court with the immense quantity of their gifts; for example, over 1,000 objects were presented by the Danish king Waldemar in 1644 upon his engagement to Irina, daughter of Tsar Mikhail Fyodorovich. Others offered gifts notable for their strangeness and rarity, such as exotic birds and beasts. Luxurious and rare objects became part of the state treasury, known as the Armoury, where everything was carefully described and valued. The Armoury of the Moscow Kremlin is still extant and now functions as a museum.[8] These diplomatic gifts of the sixteenth and seventeenth centuries form the major part of its collection, one without parallel in its variety and value. Such works helped to introduce Russia to foreign tastes and interests, as well as to the traditions of collecting that had been established in other countries.

The riches collected in the Armoury made a lasting impression on contemporary visitors. Nicolai Varkoch, envoy of the German emperor Rudolf II, described a dinner at which he was present on October 9, 1593: "… they led us through a room in which around the walls stood broad tables rising up in three steps. These were set with an untold abundance of silver and gold vessels such that it was impossible to count them. And truly in Germany no one would believe such a wealth of precious objects."[9] Such a display of treasures acted as a declaration of both the authority of the ruling powers and the luxury of the Russian court. Particular objects might, at times, be employed for their symbolism, as for instance when Tsar Boris Godunov, during a farewell reception given in 1598 in honour of Varkoch, ordered that he be brought a cup in the form of a ship and said: "Thou shalt travel by ship, and thus from a ship shall I drink thy health and beseech God to give thee a happy journey."[10]

A visible place among the ambassadorial gifts was occupied by cups of all sizes (the largest over two metres high), mainly the work of Nuremberg and Gdansk masters. Some reveal the influence of Flemish art in their decoration, as for instance a Gdansk cup of 1621–25 by Bartel Preis, whose reliefs depicting Summer and Autumn are derived from Flemish prototypes.[11]

A sumptuous still life of berries and fruits on the lid of a Hamburg tankard from the 1630s calls to mind paintings by Flemish masters of the circle of Rubens.[12] An unusual tankard in the form of a melon on a plate with fruits and berries, and the figure of the goddess Ceres forms an unusual still life, seeming to proclaim the wonders of nature's fertility.[13] Among the gifts presented by Christian IV of Denmark to Mikhail Fyodorovich in 1644 were nautilus cups by Nuremberg and Hamburg masters, the carved openwork shells of which are exceedingly fine.[14] Gifts were also made of clocks, which were, at that time, perceived as somewhat fantastical. Other objects imitated globes of the earthly and heavenly spheres and were used as wine bowls or candlesticks.[15]

Amid all of these these gifts, works by Flemish artists were extremely rare, one of the few examples being a unique Mannerist basin from Antwerp (1567–68) presented to Alexey Mikhaylovich in 1651 by the King of Poland, Jan II.[16] The basin is inlaid with large mother-of-pearl shells set into a mount covered with fantastical grotesques and strapwork in the spirit of prints by the Antwerp artist Cornelis Floris the Younger (c. 1513/14–1575).

The acquisition of decorative arts changed radically with the accession to the throne of Alexey Mikhaylovich's heir, Peter I. It is only with Peter's reign that we can truly speak of conscious collecting in Russia. From his youth Peter had been familiar with the rarities in the Moscow Kremlin, and his first journey abroad (1696–98) served only to increase his interest. When the Russian capital moved from Moscow to St. Petersburg, Peter's private collections – the "Sovereign's Cabinet" – were moved to the Summer Palace, completed in 1714. That same year is thought to have been the date of the foundation of Russia's first public museum, the Kunstkammer. By 1728 the collections, greatly enriched as a result of Peter the Great's second great "embassy" of 1716–17, were housed in a new building on Vasilevsky Island. The legend of the building is curious: Peter I was evidently impressed by an unusually shaped pine tree, and "as he came by chance upon this place, he saw a tree curious in the manner of its growth, ordered it to be cut down and said: 'Where I found this curious tree, there shall with time be built my Kunstkammer.'" This log was the first object "of curiosity" to enter the Kunstkammer collection.[17]

Exhibited there, so "that people should see and learn," were beasts and fish acquired from the collection of the apothecary A. Seba and by Peter in Amsterdam; anatomical preparations of the anatomist Frederik Ruysch; minerals, shells, precious stones and jasper enclosing trapped insects once belonging to the Danzig (Gdansk) physician H. Gotwald; and a collection of carved shells and gems from N. Chevalier of Utrecht. There were rarities from expeditions to Siberia undertaken by D. Messerschmidt, who was sent on Peter's orders, and the famous "Siberian collection" of Scythian gold, the gift of Nikolay Demidov, owner of the Tagil factories. After the death of the tsar in 1725, the Kunstkammer also acquired a large number of commemorative objects, among them the Cabinet of Peter the Great, which included a life-size wax figure of the tsar himself by Carlo Rastrelli (c. 1765–1744), his clothing, and a group of ivory and wood objects turned and carved by the tsar. It also included his favourite horse Lisetta, Peter's mount during the famous Battle of Poltava against the Swedes, and his two favourite dogs – all stuffed and mounted – as well as a tin cup and steel spurs from the Swedish king Charles XII. There were also other remarkable objects, such as the red silk kerchief embroidered on both sides not with silver thread but with the skin of a single fish known as Stremling, presented to the Kunstkammer from the Duke of Holstein in 1724.

It was the reign of Catherine II that opened a new period in the history of Russian collecting, during which acquisitions were made on a grand scale. In many ways, her interests were formed by the Enlightenment and extended far beyond the bounds of mere collecting. As was the case with Peter I, her collecting activities were closely tied to state politics, but, unlike her great predecessor, Catherine assembled a personal collection, paying little attention to the creation of a public museum. Her acquisitions in Europe of entire collections astounded everyone and were perceived as Russian imperial victories on a par with the military victories of the Russian army. The encyclopedic character of the Kunstkammer collections in private hands came to be seen as archaic and did not appeal to the empress, who concentrated instead on paintings, gems and medals.

Research in recent years has enabled us to establish that the collections that laid the foundation for the future Hermitage were housed in the Winter Palace in the second half of the 1760s–80s.[18] In addition to storage areas, where a vast quantity of ancient silver objects were housed, the greater part of the collection of engraved gems, miniatures, coins and medals that formed the first "imperial museum" were kept in the private rooms of Catherine II in the attic of the second floor of the south-eastern block.

It was here, in the empress's favourite attic rooms, that her collections of decorative arts gradually took shape. It was to these rooms that Catherine referred when she wrote that "only the mice and I enjoy it all," and not to the Hermitage itself.[19] By 1785 the whole collection from the "imperial museum" of the Winter Palace had been moved into the newly built Large Hermitage and, much later, in the 1850s, many things were placed on view in the Gallery of *Objets de Vertu* of the Small Hermitage.

From 1786, the "Natural Cabinet of Her Imperial Majesty," an unusual collection of rarities – where Siberian marbles and jasper stood alongside objects from America, where various rare and precious woods were displayed with corals and magnificent shells – was housed alongside the Raphael Loggias. Catherine's largesse extended also to the Cabinet of the Imperial Academy of Sciences. In the words of Russian ethnologist Johann Georgi (1729–1802), it became "one of the richest and most worthy of note in Europe."[20] The Academy acquired a vast quantity of minerals from

scientific expeditions around Russia, and, on the order of the director of the Academy, Princess Catherine Dashkova, this material was put into systematic order, with Russian minerals separated from others. By 1793 the collection included 12,000 examples of different ores, among them some presented by Dashkova herself. The princess, drawn to collecting from the age of seventeen, had her own rich cabinet composed largely of gifts from members of imperial families, such as the Holy Roman Emperors Joseph II and Leopold II and the Queen of Naples, who gave her a unique collection of Sicilian jasper.[21] Of the numerous collections of minerals, from 1772 that of the Mineral Cabinet of the Mining Cadet Corps was particularly notable. In addition to the collection of Russian minerals, it also included the collections of Casanova, Leibe, Laksman, Renovants and others, and by 1793 it had over 30,000 examples of ores. They included great rarities, such as a giant piece of malachite weighing 3,896 pounds, and a smoky topaz with naturally inset beryl.

During Catherine's reign the Kunstkammer also acquired rare and interesting objects, including collections of fish and insects, shells and corals, and curiosities from the Americas, Japan, Brazil and Chukotka, which formed the basis of today's rich ethnographical collections. Johann Georgi, noting that "Petersburg has varied and rich and at times precious private collections or cabinets of works of the natural sciences and art, antiquities etc., which may be visited by specialists and foreigners," regretted that many of them were dispersed upon the death of the owners.[22]

In their collecting habits the Russian aristocracy – and Catherine the Great's circle – followed fashion, but they also pursued more personal interests, often adhering to the old "universal" principles of the *Kunst- und Wunderkammer* tradition. Their collections contained not only paintings and sculptures but coins, sea charts, anatomical preparations and books. Ivan Shuvalov and Nikolay Yusupov, for example, preferred gems and "other precious items." The interest in collecting that seized the wealthier and more educated sectors of Russian society in the eighteenth century did not cease during the nineteenth century, when increasing numbers of the working class began to collect. Long-established private collections of both fine art and decorative arts continued to grow: that of Prince

B. Orlov was dominated by works in ivory and seventeenth-century German silver tankards and drinking cups, while Count A. Sheremetev acquired seventeenth-century nautilus cups and German silver.[23]

It was during the nineteenth century that interest in Flemish decorative arts became more firmly established. The collection of Grand Duke Alexander Alexandrovich included seventeenth-century ceramics, notably grey clay ewers with blue enamel painting and sixteenth-century wood reliefs and Flemish embroidery.[24] Count Pyotr Stroganov owned seventeenth-century Flemish wood reliefs, and the Naryshkin family collection included Flemish sculpture and reliefs, wooden knife handles, ceramics and ivory carving.[25] Several palaces were hung with tapestries, such as Gatchina Palace, near St. Petersburg, where thirty-two of the forty-two tapestries were Flemish.[26]

In the middle of the nineteenth century the movement towards the reorganization of the arts and industry was born in England, and soon spread to encompass the whole of Europe, as well as Russia. This marked a new and serious stage in the collecting of the decorative arts, as museums were aligned with research institutions for the training of artist-designers. The first such museum in Russia was that attached to the Stroganov School for Technical Drawing in Moscow in the 1860s, and during the following decade in St. Petersburg a whole network of study museums was established, the largest and most famous of which was that attached to the Central School of Technical Drawing, which opened in 1878. Funded by a leading Russian financier, Baron Stieglitz, it had almost unlimited resources for acquisitions, particularly during the 1880s and 1890s, when whole collections were acquired in Europe, at auctions in Frankfurt, Vienna and Paris. These included the Riani Spanish glass, the textiles of J. Kraut, and the extensive decorative arts collection of L. Ricard-Abenheimer. The Stieglitz Museum, widely famous among European collectors, antiquarians and connoisseurs, was a magnificent phenomenon in St. Petersburg's cultural life. After the 1917 Revolution, when all private museums were nationalized, many of these objects passed to the Hermitage, where they now occupy a central place in the decorative arts holdings. Among these are many Flemish objects, including furniture, glass, tapestries and stamped leather, some of which are included in this exhibition (cat. 132, 134, 159, 161, 163).

NOTES

1. *Rubenstextiel. Rubens's Textiles*, G. Delmarcel, ed., exh. cat., Antwerp, Hessenhuis, 1997, p. 66.
2. *Rubenstextiel* 1997, p. 32
3. The question of identification and systematization of the architectural motifs found in Rubens's paintings is the subject of an article by G.G. Grimm: "Arkhitektura v kartinakh Rubensa [Architecture in Rubens's Pictures]," *Trudy Gosudarstvennogo Ermitazha* [Papers of the State Hermitage], III, Leningrad, 1949, pp. 61–71.
4. *Rubenstextiel* 1997, nos. 27a, 28a, 29a, 29b, 30a, 30b.
5. *Rubenstextiel* 1997, pp. 168–72.
6. Ye. G. Lisenkov, "Illustratsii Rubensa k knige Agviloniusa ob optike [Rubens's Illustrations to Aguilonius's Book on Optics], *Trudy Gosudarstvennogo Ermitazha* [Papers of the State Hermitage], III, Leningrad, 1949, pp. 49–60.
7. Lisenkov 1949, p. 57
8. *Sokrovishcha Oruzheynoy Palaty. Posolskiye dary* [The Treasury of the Armoury. Ambassadorial Gifts], State Historical and Cultural Reserve, Moscow, Kremlin, 1996.
9. *Sokrovishcha Oruzheynoy Palaty* 1996, p. 9.
10. *Sokrovishcha Oruzheynoy Palaty* 1996, p. 62.
11. *Sokrovishcha Oruzheynoy Palaty* 1996, p. 83, nos. 73–77.
12. *Sokrovishcha Oruzheynoy Palaty* 1996, no. 62.
13. *Sokrovishcha Oruzheynoy Palaty* 1996, no. 61.
14. *Sokrovishcha Oruzheynoy Palaty* 1996, nos. 58–60.
15. *Sokrovishcha Oruzheynoy Palaty* 1996, p. 79.
16. *Sokrovishcha Oruzheynoy Palaty* 1996, nos. 26–28.
17. O. Beliacv, *Cabinet Petra Velikogo* [Cabinet of Peter the Great], St. Petersburg, 1800.
18. "Imperatorskyy muzeum v Zimnem dvortse [The Imperial Museum in the Winter Palace]," *Zimnyy dovrets* [Winter Palace], St. Petersburg, 1793, p. 392.
19. "Imperatorskyy muzeum v Zimnem dvortse," 1793, p. 110.
20. I. Georgi, *Opisanie rossiysko – imperatorskogo stolichnogo goroda S. Petersburga I dostopamiatnostey v okrestnosniach onogo. s planom* [The description of the Russian Imperial captial St. Petersburg, with the plan], St. Petersburg, 1793, p. 392
21. Georgi 1793, p. 405.
22. Georgi 1793, p. 404.
23. *Ukazatel vystavki starinykh khudozhestvennykh predmetov i kartin v polzu uchrezhdeniy, sostoyashchikh pod pokrovitelstvom Ye. I. Vysochestva Velikoy knyaginy Marii Pavlovny* [Index to the Exhibition of Ancient Artistic Objects and Paintings for the Benefit of Organizations Under the Patronage of H[er] I[mperial] Highness Grand Duchess Maria Pavlovna], St. Petersburg, 1897.
24. *Ukazatel predmetov iskusstva I redkostey, sostavlyayushchikh sobraniye Ye. I. Vysochestva gosudarya Velikogo Knyazya naslednika tsesarevicha Aleksandra Aleksandrovicha* [Index of Artistic Objects and Rarities Forming the Collection of H[is] I[mperial] Highness Grand Duke Crown Prince Alexander Alexandrovich], St. Petersburg, 1870, pp. 20–21, 45, no. 407.
25. *Ukazatel sobraniyu khudozhestvennykh proizvedeniy, pozhalovannomu gosudarem imperatororum muzeyu OPKh I podnesennomu gosudaryu B.L. Naryshkinym* [Index of the Collection of Works of Art Donated by the Imperial Sovereign to the Museum of the Society for the Encouragement of the Arts and Presented to the Sovereign by N.L. Naryshkin], St. Petersburg, 1871.
26. *Opis predmetam, imeyushchim presimushchestvenno khudozhestvennoe znacheniye* [Inventory of Objects Mainly of Artistic Significance], St. Petersburg, 1885.

127
Nef
Cast, chased and partially gilded silver
Flanders, Bruges, 1596
Marks: Bruges with the year 1595–1596 (half chipped)
Height 31 cm
Provenance: Acquired in 1987 *via* the Hermitage Purchasing Commission
Inv. no. E 17345

The tradition of making objects in the form of ships dates to the medieval period when they were seen as symbols of life. They had a variety of uses – as votive objects, as wine vessels at princely feasts, as salt cellars and spice containers or simply as table decorations placed before the host or highly respected guests. Because of the sacred significance attached to them, such vessels were thought to preserve any spices they might contain from poison, or if used as a relic to protect the owner from danger in the sea of life or from potential shipwreck on ocean voyages. By the seventeenth century, nefs had largely lost their traditional significance and were used as decorative centrepieces or drinking cups.
M.L.

128

Aquamanile
Cast, chased and partially gilded
silver
Christian Hornung the Elder
(Heppigen ? – Augsburg 1680)
Germany, Augsburg, *c.* 1665
Marks: Augsburg, Hornung
Height 32.6 cm
Provenance: Transferred to the
Hermitage in 1925 from the
State Valuables Store
Inv. no. E 7411

Aquamaniles, literally meaning
water on the hands, were water
ewers used for washing one's
hands at table. They were in
common use during the Middle
Ages, often being of
zoomorphic form. By the
Renaissance the form had
become more decorative than
functional, though the hinged
lid forming the top of the
horse's head on this example
suggests it may have been
intended for ceremonial use.
The object, one of two such
figures by silversmith Christian
Hornung, is in the form of a
classicizing equestrian warrior
in armour. The horse and rider
are mounted on a base
enlivened by chased and cast
ornament in the auricular, or
lobate, style characterized by
undulating, curving forms
similar to those found on the
interior of shells or ear lobes.
Engraved on the horse's
stomach is a ducal crown with
the monogram *LZ*.

The maker of the Hermitage
aquamanile was clearly
influenced by a whole series of
such objects by the Augsburg
silversmith and draughtsman
David Schwestermüller the
Elder (1596–1678). The riders
portrayed by Schwestermüller
depicted specific historical
figures, which in turn were
based on bronze statuettes of
archdukes of the house of
Habsburg, made around
1620–30 by Caspar Gras in
Innsbruck and quickly adopted
by Augsburg craftsmen as
models.
M.L.

129

Display Platter with Solomon and the Queen of Sheba
Wrought, chased and partially gilded silver
Central relief made in Augsburg, Germany, 1630s–40s
Platter made by Johan Nutzel, Stockholm, Sweden, 1680s–90s
Marks on the dish: Stockholm, Nutzel
77.5 × 92.5 cm
Provenance: Presented to Peter I by Charles XII of Sweden; Winter Palace
Inv. no. E 8766

The quality of the relief at the centre of this display platter suggests that it was made by an Augsburg silversmith, possibly one working in the circle of Elias Drentwett, a well-established master. The composition of the figures and overall style of the relief show a clear dependence on the school of Rubens. The relief differs markedly in style and date from the charger on which it was later mounted, the extremely dense florid decoration of which includes six cast and applied

birds of gilded silver, in flight amid bunches of fruit bordered by acanthus leaves. This object is one of a number of gifts that Charles II of Sweden had his ambassador present to Peter the Great on the eve of the Northern War.
M.L.

130
Dish with a Bacchanalian Scene
Wrought, chased and gilded
silver
Abraham Warnberger the
Younger (? 1632 – Augsburg
1704)
Germany, Augsburg, 1670–75
Marks: Augsburg (unclear),
Warnberger, St. Petersburg
control with the year 17 ... (half
chipped), assay master N.N.,
fineness 78
64.5 × 56 cm
Provenance: Presented to Peter
I by Charles XII of Sweden;

transferred in 1762 from
Oranienbaum Palace, near
St. Petersburg, to the Winter
Palace; in 1904 moved from
the Hofmarshal's Office to the
"Museum" in the Winter Palace
Inv. no. E 8713

Abraham Warnberger the
Younger was a member of an
extensive family of Augsburg
silversmiths and became a well-
known artist during the second
half of the seventeenth century.
The Hermitage owns six display
platters by him, all of which are

in a highly developed Baroque
style characterized by the
festoons of fruits around the
rim and the exuberant handling
of the family bacchanal on the
central relief.
M.L.

131
Rhyton
Wrought, cast, chased, etched
and gilded silver
Christoph Erhart (? – Augsburg
1604)
Germany, Augsburg, 1570–75
Marks: Augsburg, Erhart
Height 22 cm; diameter 12.1 cm
Provenance: Acquired in 1908
from the collection of Grand
Duke Alexey Alexandrovich
Inv. no. E 476

The rhyton is a form of
drinking cup derived from
ancient examples made of
pottery, metal and stone that
had to be drained of their
contents before they could be
put down. Like their ancient
antecedents, they were often
given zoomorphic form, such
as this example, based on an
eagle's head. The silversmith
Christoph Erhart seems to have
specialized in such pieces, as a
number of animal rhytons by
him are known.
M.L.

132

Drinking Cup in the form of an Owl

Chased and gilded silver
Flanders, early 17th century
Height 17 cm; diameter of base 7.8 cm
Provenance: Collection of A. Ricard-Abelheimer until 1886; purchased for the museum of the Stieglitz School of Technical Drawing in 1886; transferred to the Hermitage from the museum of the former Stieglitz School in 1925
Inv. no. E 11922

In the sixteenth and seventeenth centuries drinking vessels in the form of various beasts and birds were very common. As a rule, such animals had specific connotations, indicating, for instance, the client's occupation. The guild of butchers might thus commission cups in the form of bulls, while hunters chose cups shaped as stags or boars. The vessels might also have allegorical meanings, as in the case of the owl, which symbolizes wisdom.
M.L.

133
Tankard with The Judgement of Paris
Wrought, cast, chased and
partially gilded silver
Germany, Augsburg (?), 1650s
Mark: Paris import of the 19th
century
Height 26.6 cm; diameter of
top 14 cm; diameter of base
17 cm
Provenance: Collection of the
Princes Yusupov; transferred
to the Hermitage in 1923
Inv. no. E 11050

The sleeve of this skilfully made
tankard is decorated with a
relief depicting the story of the
Judgement of Paris. Its high
quality suggests it was probably
made in Augsburg, an important
centre of metalworking during
the seventeenth century. The
Swedish inscription on its base,
probably added during the
eighteenth century, reads: *Kung
FRIEDRICHS milda Hanbor jag
paminna mig, Nar Denna Qafwa
mig bland Wanner Skall fornoija:
Mitt trogna/ uerta dai Wordnad
boijer ig, Min Store Konungs
Nadoch Ynnetit atuphoija.
Qudlate Kung FRIEDRICH fler
Sallheter finna. An droppar af
drufwor Har Kunna utrinna!!!
Stockholm 30 Iunii 1747.* [The
generous hand of King
Friedrich I must recall when I
shall admire this gift in the
circle of my friends. My faithful
heart shall then beat with
excitement, [ex]tolling the
generosity and kindness of my
king. May the Lord send King
Friedrich more blessings than
there are drops in the grapes
which will run from hence!!!
Stockholm June 30, 1747.]
M.L.

134
Tankard with Hercules and Omphale
Wrought, cast, chased and
partially gilded silver
Klaus Schmidt (? – before 1694)
Germany, Lübeck, 1680s
Marks: Lübeck, Schmidt
Height 18.1 cm
Provenance: Collection of the
Princes Yusupov; transferred to
the Hermitage in 1922
Inv. no. E 12773

The tankard's sleeve is chased
with compositions from the
story of Hercules and Omphale.
Hercules is shown with his club

embracing the naked Omphale;
Hercules holds a spindle while
Omphale, who wears the skin of
the Nemean lion, stands near
an old woman with yarn;
flanking the figures are Cupid
and a putto. On the tankard's
lid, which bears the signature of
Albert Reimers, is an applied
relief with a kneeling youth in
Roman armour offering his
heart to a seated woman. The
treatment of the ornament and
the figural compositions is
characteristic of the 1680s and
1690s and clearly derives from
a printed source.
M.L.

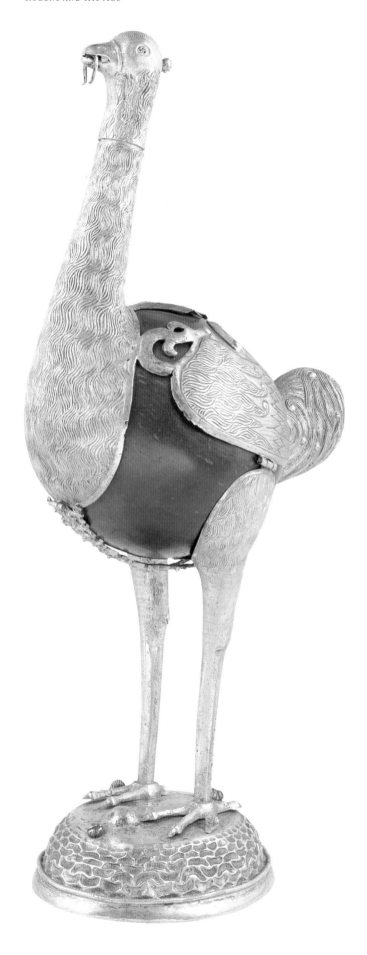

135
Ostrich Cup
Coconut mounted with cast,
chased and gilded silver
Germany, early 17th century
Unmarked
Height 31.6 cm
Provenance: Transferred to the
Hermitage from the Winter
Palace
Inv. no. E 2509

136
Coconut Cup
Carved coconut and walnut with cast, chased and gilded silver mounts
Czechoslovakia, Olomutz (?), maker SG (GS),
mid-17th century (1655?)
Engraved on lid: *MG – OB anno 1655*, a cross and *DM JC*
Marks: Olomutz (?), maker, fineness 14
Height 30.5 cm; diameter of base 10.5 cm
Provenance: Winter Palace; transferred to the Hermitage in 1925 from the Cottage Palace, Peterhof, near St. Petersburg
Inv. no. E 7935

Nearly all the minutely carved images on the surface of these drinking cups were taken from the Old Testament, as is the case with two of those on this example, *The Judgement of Solomon* and *Susanna and the Elders*. The third scene is a depiction of the *Ecce Homo*. The cup is of extremely skilful execution, and the finely carved scenes on the coconut are almost certainly based on prints.
M.L.

137
Basin with Gigantomachy (Battle of the Giants)
Wrought, chased, punched and gilded silver
Elias Drentwett the Elder
(c. 1588 – Augsburg 1643)
Germany, Augsburg, 1630s
Marks: Augsburg, Drentwett
Diameter 72 cm
Provenance: Collection of Peter I, kept in the Winter Palace and, in the 19th century, in the Gallery of *Objets de Vertu*;

transferred to the Hermitage from the Winter Palace
Inv. no. E 8767

This monumental basin would almost certainly have been made *en suite* with a tall ewer that would have fit over the central umbo of the basin; it would have been displayed on a sideboard when not being used for the ceremonial washing of hands before, during and after a meal. Its iconography, known as

a Gigantomachy, refers to the battle between the gods and the giants, among whom can be identified Hercules, Prometheus with a torch and Jupiter astride his eagle in the sky. In the centre of the dish is a barely decipherable inscription in Polish, applied with a punch: *IEREMI MICHAL KORIBUTH XIAZE NA WISNIOWIV y LUBNIACH* [Jeremiah Michael Koributh Prince of Vishnevets and Lubny].

An outstanding example of the great skill of Augsburg craftsmen, the imagery used on this basin reveals associations with prints by engravers from the circle of the de Passe family, Dutch artists active as printmakers and publishers during the sixteenth and seventeenth centuries. The inscription provides evidence that the dish belonged to the renowned Ukrainian landowner, Prince Jeremiah

Vishnevets (1612–1651) of the Koributh family, whose arms are shown in the centre. The prince's vast estates in the Ukraine included a residence at Lubny and a magnificent family castle at Vishnevets that was burned in 1672 by the Turks but later restored by Jan Sobieszki.
M.L.

138
Display Platter with Allegory of Learning
Wrought, chased and gilded silver
Marx Weinold (? – Augsburg 1700)
Germany, Augsburg, 1680s
Marks: Augsburg (half chipped off), Weinold
71 × 63 cm
Provenance: Collection of the Princes Yusupov, St. Petersburg; transferred to the Hermitage in 1923
Inv. no. E 13211

The extremely finely chased scene on the oval relief mounted at the centre of this charger is perhaps an allegory of learning. Seated at the centre of a wooded landscape is the figure of Selene (identifiable by the crescent moon on her forehead), in conversation with a bearded man who points to an open book on the table between them. To her right a putto holds open another book, while others are scattered on the ground between them. In the background is a statue of a bearded man, draped in robes and holding a scroll, possibly meant to suggest a philosopher and serving as an allegory of wisdom. The collar of the platter is decorated with four large flowers surrounded with foliage; between these are centred four round medallions with inscribed profiles of the Roman emperors Magnus Constantinus, Maxentius, Probus Caesar and Valentenianus.

This charger is a magnificent example of the high quality of metalwork produced by Augsburg masters during the Baroque era. The complex allegorical composition in the centre is chased in graduated relief; at its lowest point the imagery appears to be drawn rather than sculpted, almost melting into the background and demonstrating the full extent of Weinold's considerable skill as a silversmith.
M.L.

139
Shell Cup with Neptune as a Naiad
Bullmouth helmet shell mounted with cast, chased and gilded silver
Germany, maker MW, 1640s–60s
Marks: maker
Height 50 cm
Provenance: Transferred to the Hermitage in 1934 *via* Antikvariat (state trading organization responsible for selling art treasures).
Inv. no. E 13568

140
Tulip Cup
Cast, wrought, chased and partially gilded silver
Germany, Nuremberg, maker CWM, 1660s–70s
Marks: Nuremberg, maker, control mark for St. Petersburg with the year 1753, fineness 77
Height 36 cm
Provenance: In the Gallery of *Objets de Vertu* during the 19th century; transferred to the Hermitage from the Winter Palace
Inv. no. E 8713

Tulip cups were extremely fashionable in the mid-seventeenth century. This example is in the style of the Nuremberg silversmith Samuel Birfreund, who is known to have specialised in tulip cups. The cup's stem, in the form of a tree trunk, includes a figure with a net attempting to capture a bird mounted on the spiralled silver wire around the tree's circumference.
M.L.

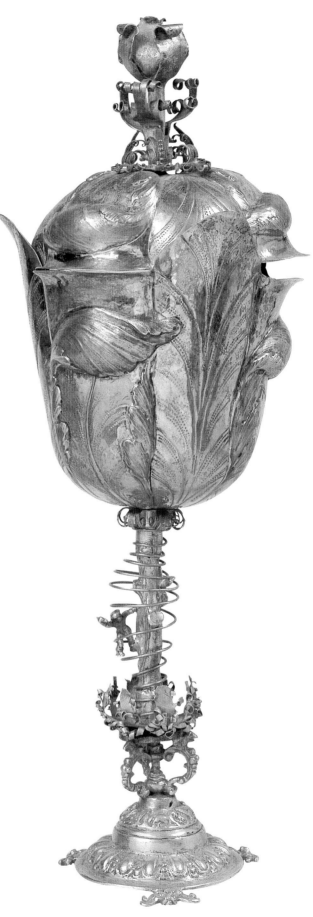

141
Standing Cup and Cover
Cast, chased and gilded silver
Adam van Vianen (Utrecht
1569–1627)
Holland, Utrecht, 1594
Marks: Utrecht, year, maker
Height 59.5 cm
Provenance: Transferred to the
Hermitage in 1925 from the
museum of the former Stieglitz
School
Inv. no. E 13312

On the body of the cup, which
is the earliest known example of
the work of Adam van Vianen,
is a depiction of the *Rape of
Europa* based on plaques by the
silversmith's brother Paul van
Vianen. Engraved inside the lid
is an enamelled lion with a
shield and two keys, and the
inscription: *v Adelbrecht van
Duvenvoorde en Woude,
Wenschen, H.H. Burgermeesteren
Regierders der Stadt Leyden, des
H. Van Warmondts, uus vaders
naegebuyrde vrunden, en getuygen
dat gy deur den doop Christo
Jhesu syt innegelyft, veel:gelux, en
henls. 1599. Sept: 5.* [Adelbrecht
van Duvenvoorde and his wife,
wish the burgomaster and ruler
of the city of Leiden, Mr. Van
Warmondts, joy as father of a
newborn child and evidence
that the newborn child has
through baptism come close to
Jesus Christ, much happiness
and prosperity. 1599 Sept. 5.]
M.L.

142
Standing Cup and Cover
Cast, chased, engraved and
gilded silver
Holland, Haarlem, 1604 (?)
Marks: The Netherlands,
Haarlem, unknown maker
Height 28.5 cm; diameter of
base 10 cm
Provenance: In the collection of
A. Ricard-Abenheimer,
Frankfurt am Main until 1886;
purchased for the museum of
the Stieglitz School of Technical
Drawing in 1886; transferred to
the Hermitage in 1925 from the
museum of the former Stieglitz
School in 1925
Inv. no. E 13467

143
Display Platter with Diana and Actaeon
Chased and gilded silver
Holland (?), *c.* 1662
48.5 × 39.3 cm
Provenance: Collection of the Princes Yusupov; transferred to the Hermitage in 1922
Inv. no. E 13150

144
Display Platter with Vertumnus and Pomona
Chased and gilded silver
Jan Bogaert (*fl.* 1600s)
Holland, Amsterdam, 1665
Marks: Amsterdam, year, control for 1689, maker
Diameter 52 cm
Provenance: Collection of the Princes Yusupov; transferred to the Hermitage in 1922
Inv. no. E 13848

145
Wager Cup
Cast, wrought, chased and
gilded silver
Wolf Eispinger (?–1606)
Germany, Nuremberg, 1580s
Marks: Nuremberg, Eispinger
Height 26 cm
Provenance: Collection of
Countess E.V. Shuvalova;
transferred to the Hermitage in
1925 from the Shuvalov House
Museum
Inv. no. E 13753

This cup is one of a large
number of reversible drinking
cups known in Germany as
Jungfraubecher and elsewhere as
marriage or wager cups. The
form originated in Germany
during the last quarter of the
sixteenth century, and derives
from ornamental engravings in
costume books, illustrating the
direct link between the graphic
and the decorative arts. The
woman's skirt as well as the
smaller pivoting cup raised over
her head were simultaneously
filled with wine and offered to
guests who competed in
emptying both without spilling.
When used at wedding
celebrations, the groom drank
from the larger cup and the
bride from the smaller cup.
Eispinger made skilful use of
flat chasing to imitate Italian
velvet on the woman's skirt,
revealing himself to be a
talented ornamentalist.
M.L.

146
Bratina
Chased, engraved and gilded silver
Holland, Amsterdam, 1664
Marks: Amsterdam control for the 17th century, year
Height 16.8 cm; diameter 13.4 cm
Provenance: Collection of the Counts Stroganov; transferred to the Hermitage in 1922
Inv. no. E 9022

A bratina is a common form of Russian drinking cup passed between guests during feasts, the name of which derives from the Russian word *brataniye* or brotherhood. Northern European silversmiths often made traditional vessels such as bratina and kovsh (ladles) for Russian clients. The upper edge of this cup is inscribed: "Of the Noble Lord Grigory Dmitriyevich Stroganov."
M.L.

147
Ewer
Cast and gilded bronze inlaid
with carved coral
Sicily, Trapani, 1630–50
Height 27 cm; width of base
17.3 cm
Provenance: Transferred to the
Hermitage from the Winter
Palace
Inv. no. E 2708

This highly colourful ewer is
made of double bronze plaques
into which are set pieces of
coral. The high bronze handle
is cast with typically Baroque
foliate ornament and crowned
with the head of a cherub.
During the second half of the
sixteenth and seventeenth
centuries the Sicilian town of
Trapani was famed for its coral
wares. Combining this
attractive material with gilded

bronze and brass, metalsmiths
created a variety of religious
objects, including icons and
holy water fonts, paxes and
chalices, as well as secular
sculptural compositions.
Trapani craftsmen also
incorporated other materials
into their wares, including
mother-of-pearl, ivory,
polychrome enamel and
additional pieces of ornamental
silver.
M.L

148
Clock
Cast, chased and gilded silver
with bronze, metal alloys and
glass
Spain, 1660–70
Height 27.8 cm; diameter of
base 16 cm
Provenance: Collection of
Countess E.V. Shuvalova;
transferred to the Hermitage in
1925 from the Shuvalov House
Museum
Inv. no. E 14103

149
Reliquary
Cast, chased, enamelled and
gilded silver
Spain, Valencia, mid-17th
century
Marks: Valencia, unknown (half
chipped)
Height 56 cm; base 22 × 25.5 cm
Provenance: Transferred to the
Hermitage in 1925 from the
museum of the former Stieglitz
School
Inv. no. E 15341

This reliquary represents a
rather unusual marriage of
elements. Its central portion is
in the form of a medieval casket
atop which is a round
architectural form covered by a
dome, surmounted by a cast
figure of St. Christopher.
Chased on the long sides of the
casket are reliefs of the Last
Supper and the Washing of the
Feet. In the niches of the cupola
are figures of saints, while other
saints and the four Evangelists
adorn the stem bosses and the
quatrefoil base. This superb
object demonstrates the high
level of craftsmanship achieved
by Spanish silversmiths,
displaying a remarkable
originality of form and
decoration.
M.L.

150
Chalice
Cast, chased, engraved,
enamelled and gilded silver
with bronze and copper
Spain, mid-17th century
Height 30.7 cm; diameter of
bowl 9.2 cm
Provenance: Transferred to the
Hermitage in 1925 from the
museum of the former Stieglitz
School
Inv. no. E 15045

151
Cameo with Joseph and his Brothers
Sardonyx with gold mount
Southern Italy, c. 1240
Inscribed in Hebrew at top right: "Get you up in peace unto your father" (Genesis 44:17)
6.4 × 7.5 cm
Provenance: Property of Charles V in 14th century, Château de Vincennes, Paris; collection of Peter Paul Rubens, Antwerp; bequeathed to Albert Rubens in 1640; in the 18th century owned by Jacopo Nani, Venice, A. Pelle and Dazincours, Paris and William Hamilton, Naples; acquired in 1805 from the collection of N. Khitrovo, St. Petersburg
Inv. no. K 690

"I have never in my life seen anything that gives me more pleasure than the gems you have sent me," wrote Peter Paul Rubens in 1623 to his friend the famous French antiquarian and scholar Nicolas-Claude Fabri de Peiresc (1580–1637; Rooses-Ruelens 1887–1909, vol. III, p. 215). Rubens had collaborated with Peiresc on a project to publish engravings of the best examples from his own gem collection, pieces that he had acquired mainly in Italy and France. Rubens made the preparatory drawings himself and there are separate surviving engravings by his pupil Lucas Vorsterman, but the publication of the full series as intended by Rubens and Peiresc was never completed.

In 1626, after the death of his first wife, the artist sold part of his collection of engraved gems, together with his painting and sculpture collections, to the Duke of Buckingham, but he wrote to Peiresc that "the most excellent and rare gems I have kept for myself" (Rooses-Ruelens 1887–1909, vol. V, p. 292). Rubens ultimately bequeathed these objects to his son Albert, who inherited his father's passionate interest in gems. Historical circumstances led to the further division of both parts of Rubens's gem collection, his dactylotheque, before the end of the seventeenth century. In 1649 the Duke of Buckingham was executed and his collections were auctioned, while the same fate awaited the works bequeathed to Albert Rubens when he died in 1657.

In recent decades the work of a number of scholars, in particular M. van der Meulen and Oleg Neverov, has led to the reconstruction of the collection of carved gems assembled by Rubens, now scattered among various museums throughout the world. Oleg Neverov identified a large group of engraved gems now in the Hermitage collections of ancient and Western European glyptics as having once belonged to Rubens, and these were presented in a 1978 Hermitage exhibition dedicated to the 400th anniversary of Rubens's birth.

A central place in this group is occupied by *Joseph and his Brothers* (Leningrad 1978, no. 273), which was identified by its correspondence with a description in the list of gems belonging to Albert Rubens, compiled in 1658 by Abbé Jean Chiflet: "Joseph, sold by his brothers, with Hebrew inscription, carved in relief on large agate" (van der Meulen 1975, p. 224).

The story of Joseph, son of Jacob and Rachel, relates how he was sold by his half-brothers into slavery as a child. Later in life, after much adversity and many unfortunate adventures, success brought him a post at the Pharaoh's court. It was there, many years later, that Joseph recognized his brothers when they came to Egypt to buy corn. Without revealing himself, Joseph decided to subject his brothers to a trial. To accuse them of theft, he ordered his servant to throw a silver cup into the sack of the youngest, Benjamin, the only one of his siblings with whom he shared both parents.

Despite the claim of the renowned medievalist Hans Wentzel (1956) that the gem is a direct illustration of one episode from this story, it in fact conflates several sequential events. On the Hermitage gem, Joseph, wearing the attire of an Egyptian ruler, sits with sceptre in hand, enthroned before his brothers, who do not recognize him. The servant, identified by his lack of a beard, stands between Benjamin and Joseph, to whom he presents the "stolen" cup. With a hand on Benjamin's shoulder, Joseph indicates that he is taking him into slavery and letting the others go, as explained in the inscription. The brothers, in a demonstration of their innocence, tear their robes, while Judah steps forward and desperately beseeches Joseph to take him instead, for he cannot return to his father without the beloved Benjamin.

The multi-figure composition is arranged horizontally on a single large sardonyx oval, which is carved in three layers. The lowest dark brown layer forms the background, the middle white layer was employed for the figural group, Joseph's throne, the inscription and the raised white border framing the composition, while the uppermost layer of pale, semi-translucent brown, distinguishes the areas in highest relief, including the pedestal beneath Joseph's throne, his lower robes, his toes and the straps of his sandals, and the robes of the figures at the centre and the far left.

The unusually large size of this cameo, the extremely high quality of its carving and the Hebrew inscription have all attracted the attention of scholars for many years. A number of contradictory conclusions regarding its date and place of production have resulted, however, owing to the complex stylistic influences that appear to have had an effect on the gem's design. Antique motifs sit side by side with Byzantine compositional structure, in which figures reduce significantly in size as they are presumed to retreat into the distance (full-length figures in the foreground, half figures in the middle layer, mere busts and heads in the background). In a device Wentzel describes as "montage," the engraver borrowed many figures and even whole groups from Byzantine objects – ivory plaques of the tenth to eleventh centuries showing the Forty Martyrs standing in the icy waters of the lake of Sebaste, in the Berlin Museums (Goldschmidt, Weitzmann 1979, no. 10, pl. 3) and the Hermitage (Bank 1977, p. 294, nos. 123–27) – which clearly have an earlier source. At the same time, these figures have all acquired a new volume and freedom of movement, recalling Early Renaissance Florentine sculpture.

This led early scholars, who saw the sources of the cameo in the work of Giovanni Pisano, to associate the piece with the Italo-Tuscan circle and to date it to the early fifteenth century (Wirenius-Matzoulevitch 1928, pp. 111–13; Kris 1929, p. 26). A Venetian provenance and an earlier dating were suggested by the Byzantine influences – which were particularly strong in Venice during the thirteenth and fourteenth centuries. The last word came from Wentzel, who saw all cameos with Hebrew inscriptions (including this one) as the outstanding products of a court workshop that he believed flourished during the second half of the thirteenth century at the Sicilian court of Friedrich II Hohenstaufen, a uniquely distinguished centre of medieval culture. (Wentzel 1943, pp. 6–8; Wentzel 1956, pp. 85–105)

A reduced replica of the same composition with fewer figures, and without the inscription, carved in two-layer sardonyx, is in the Royal Collection at Windsor Castle (Tonnochy 1935, p. 275). Previously thought to be Byzantine, it is now recognized as a simplified copy of the Hermitage cameo.

On compositional and stylistic grounds, the cameo closest to that in the Hermitage, but lacking a biblical inscription, is from the collection of Lorenzo de' Medici, *Noah's Ark* (British Museum, London), although an exhibition in 1977 devoted to the Hohenstaufen era did not recognize the two cameos (Stuttgart 1977, nos. 879, 881) as coming from the same workshop (Kahsnitz 1979, pp. 510–14).

Friedrich Hohenstaufen the Younger amassed a large collection of engraved gems, as is confirmed by documents in the Genoese archives (Byrne 1935), and cameos such as *Joseph and his Brothers* would have been very much in accord with his refined and informed taste. Wentzel also suggested that such cameos should be seen as marks of honour presented to the emperor by the Jewish community in recognition of his religious tolerance and the freedom that that community enjoyed at Friedrich's court in Palermo (Wentzel 1956). In the recent exhibition catalogue *Friedrich II and Italy*, it was emphasized that the motivation behind the use of iconography so unusual in a cameo remains unclear (Rome 1995, p. 256, N. V. 25). The catalogue mistakenly indicates that the cameo came to the Hermitage from the collection of the Duc d'Orléans.
Y.K.

152
Cameo with Allegory of Constancy and Valour (?)
Sardonyx with gold mount
Italy, 16th century
3.7 × 3.3 cm
Provenance: Owned by Peter Paul Rubens, Antwerp, during the seventeenth century; acquired in the late 18th century
Inv. no. K 4844

Oleg Neverov identified this cameo as having belonged to Rubens (Neverov 1979, p. 431, fig. 21; Neverov 1981, p. 67) on the basis of a description of it by Nicolas-Claude Fabri de Peiresc (van der Meulen 1975, p. 204). Peiresc saw the female figure as a personification of Constancy and the male figure as the personification of Valour or *Virtus*, remarking that they were like Castor and Pollux but without helmets and spears. In the eighteenth century, Hermitage sources identified the cameo as representing Venus and Aeneas.
Y.K.

153
Cameo with Temple of Venus
Sardonyx with gold mount
Italy, late 16th – early 17th century
Greek inscription on statue base: *XAPITOY*
5.8 × 7 cm
Provenance: Owned by Peter Paul Rubens, Antwerp, during the 17th century; acquired in 1792 from the collection of Jean-Baptiste Casanova, Dresden
Inv. no. 1979

In his description of Rubens's gems, the antiquarian and gem collector Nicolas-Claude Fabri de Peiresc noted that this cameo "is particularly notable for the inscription on the base of the statue of Venus, with whose cult the figures carved around should be identified" (Rooses-Ruelens, vol. IV, p. 417). In the nineteenth century the cameo was thought to be ancient (*Compte-rendu* 1874, p. 223, table VI), yet the Mannerist style of the five-figure group suggests a Late Renaissance date. The visual source for this group and the true meaning of the inscription remain unknown despite many attempts to identify them.
Y.K.

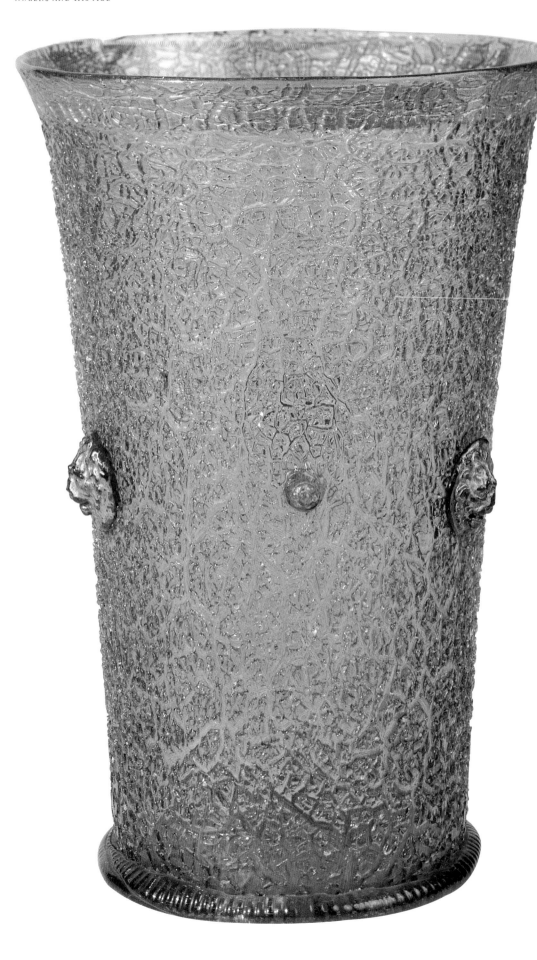

154
Beaker
Slightly smoky colourless glass gilded and blown in ice-glass technique
Antwerp (?), late 16th – early 17th century
Height 25.4 cm, diameter 16.9 cm
Provenance: Acquired in 1885 with the collection of A.P. Basilewski, Paris.
Inv. no. F 487

The technique of "ice glass" originated in Venice in the sixteenth century. In order to obtain the craquelured surface the glass master plunged the bubble of molten glass into cold water, causing the outer surface to crack from the sudden temperature change; the object was then blown into its final form.

Production of glass "*à la façon de Venise*" began in the Netherlands during the second half of the sixteenth century. In form and decoration such objects imitated famous Venetian vessels, and the elegant "ice" pattern was often used to adorn traditional Dutch cylindrical vessels used for beer. The Hermitage beaker is further decorated with gilded glass prunts moulded in the form of lion masks and a gilded band along the upper edge. A similarly decorated bowl is depicted in a still life with a jug and pipes by Pieter van Auraedt in the Mauritshuis, The Hague.
E.A.

155
Roemer
Blown and gilded green
transparent glass
The Netherlands, mid-17th
century
Height 25 cm; diameter 11 cm
Provenance: Collection of A.
Ricard-Abenheimer, Frankfurt
am Main until 1886; transferred
in 1933 from the museum of the
former Baron Stieglitz School,
Leningrad
Inv. no. K 2346

The name *roemer* is first used in
mid-fifteenth-century German
documents, but the form
derives from small cylindrical
vessels decorated with applied
"prunts" or glass drops, which
were in circulation in the Holy
Roman Empire from the
thirteenth century. A
characteristic feature of the
roemer is its tripartite form,
consisting of a large round or
oval bowl supported by a hollow
cylindrical stem decorated with
prunts on a low, conical foot. In
the seventeenth century the
roemer was one of the most
popular vessel forms in
Germany and Holland, and
was used mainly for wine.
This example represents the
commonest form of *roemer*,
although the type continued to
evolve into the eighteenth
century.
   In Holland the largest glass
manufactories producing
various *roemer* forms were those
in Laubach and Amsterdam,
and the scale of production can
be judged from the fact that in
just over thirty-one weeks in
1607 alone, 55,349 *roemers* were
made at Laubach (Theuerkauff-
Liederwald 1968, p. 123).
Roemers are often depicted in
Dutch still-life paintings, and
when filled with wine were a
common element in the
popular mid-seventeenth-
century *bancketje* or "breakfast
pieces" – still lifes depicting the
makings of a small meal by
such artists as Willem Claes.,
Heda, Pieter Claesz., Paulus van
den Bos, Willem Kalf, Jasper
Gerards and Willem van Alst.
E.A.

156
Serpent Goblet
Slightly smoky colourless glass
with turquoise glass threads
and diamond engraving
Venice or The Netherlands,
first half 17th century
Height 16 cm, diameter 7.2 cm
Provenance: Acquired in 1960
via the Hermitage Purchasing
Commission
Inv. no. 26666

In Venice in 1549, Vincenzo di
Angelo dal Gallo received a
patent for diamond point
engraving on glass, a technique
he had developed in 1534 that
involved scratching or stippling
directly on to the glass surface,
allowing for the creation of very
finely detailed imagery. The
technique was employed by
Venetian glass masters for
subject-matter such as vegetable
patterns, which echoed lace in
their complexity and intricacy.
In the late sixteenth and early
seventeenth centuries diamond
engraving came into use in the
Netherlands, mainly for the
decoration of objects in the
Venetian style, known as *"façon
de Venise"* glass.
    Goblets with serpentine
stems such as the present
example were referred to as
snake glasses in seventeenth-
century documents and were
produced in Venice and by
various Netherlandish
manufactories.
E.A.

157
Bottle
Mould-blown blue transparent glass with brass mount
The Netherlands, second half of the 17th century
Height 25 cm
Provenance: Collection of A. Ricard-Abenheimer, Frankfurt am Main until 1886; transferred 1933 from the museum of the former Baron Stieglitz School, Leningrad
Inv. no. K 2087

Bottles of this type, with a spherical body and high narrow neck, were common in the Netherlands during the seventeenth century, and were made of colourless, green or blue glass. Examples such as this were generally known as pumpkin bottles, a name suggested by the vertically applied ribbing around the bottle's circumference.
E.A.

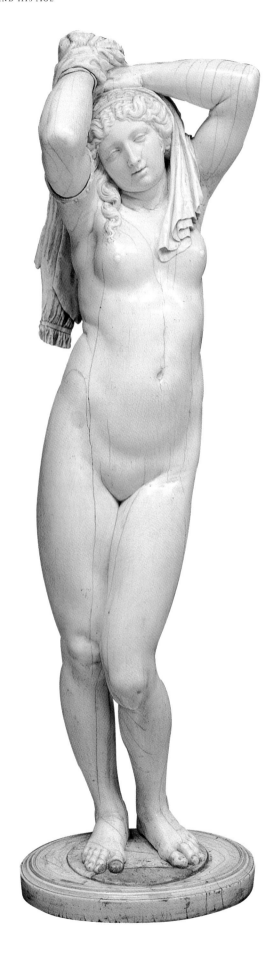

158
Figure of Venus
Ivory
Flanders, Antwerp, workshop of
Peter Paul Rubens, *c.* 1639
Height 55 cm
Provenance: Collection of the
Princes Yusupov; transferred in
1923
Inv. no. E 12261

This figure of Venus is first
mentioned in the posthumous
inventory made of the property
remaining in the home of Peter
Paul Rubens upon his death in
1640. In 1652 the sculpture was
acquired by Queen Christina of
Sweden, through Michel Le
Blon (1587–1656), a German
goldsmith and engraver who
served as an agent of the
Swedish court while living in
England. An inventory
compiled in Antwerp in 1656 of
the objects Christina took with
her into voluntary exile included
the figure of Venus (Denucé
1932, vol. II, p. 70). The object
was later acquired by Prince
Nikolay Yusupov (1751–1831)
and in 1822 was kept at his
Arkhangel'skoye country estate
near Moscow, in the so-called
Cupid Room (Archive of
Ancient Acts 1822). In 1837,
six years after the prince's
death, this sculpture, along with
other works of art from the
Yusupov collection, was
transferred to the family palace
in St. Petersburg and was first
published in a catalogue of the
Yusupov collection in 1839
(Youssoupoff 1839, p. 39).
Specialists have found
attribution of this piece
extremely difficult, partly
because the aforementioned
history of the sculpture was
unknown. Prakhov believed it to
be by the German sculptor
Simon Troger (1683–1768;
Prakhov 1907, p. 13; Yusupov
Gallery 1920, p. 14), while a
different opinion was expressed
by Kube, who dated the figure to
the late seventeenth century and
attributed it to a circle of
German sculptors (Kube 1925,
no. 209). Refuting this
suggestion, Lapkovskaya
ascribed the work to Georg Petel
(1601/02–*c.* 1634; Lapkovskaya
1971, pp. 23–27), on the basis of
a drawing in the Louvre,
Woman Removing her Clothes,
which Lapkovskaya also
attributed to Petel. Other
scholars, however, have seen the
Louvre drawing as the work of
Rubens himself, which allowed
Schädler to doubt the
correctness of Lapkovskaya's
conclusion. Since Glück and

Haberditzl date the drawing to
1635–40 (Glück, Haberditzl
1928, fig. 28; compare the
opinion of Burchard, who dated
it to 1638–40), and Georg Petel
died in *c.* 1634, Schädler
attributed the figure of Venus to
Flemish sculptor Artus
Quellinus the Elder
(1609–1688; Schädler 1973,
p. 180). In an article in 1987,
the present author suggested
that in style the sculpture recalls
the work of Lucas Fayd'herbe
(1617–1697; Shlikevich 1987,
pp. 10–13). While the question
of authorship remains open,
there is no doubt that it was
once part of Rubens's personal
collection and was made by one
of his closest pupils, whom he
strongly influenced.
The Hermitage also owns a
figure of Mercury that has
traditionally been considered a
pair to the Venus. It too came
from Rubens's collection and
entered the museum from the
Yusupov collection with the
Venus. Leaving aside the
attribution of the Mercury, it is
extremely likely that the two
sculptures in fact formed part of
a group illustrating the
Judgement of Paris.
Y.S.

159
The Crucifixion
Ivory and ebony
Gabriel Grupello (?; Grammont
1644 – Ehrenstein 1730)
Flanders, before 1695
Height 58 cm
Provenance: Transferred in 1925
from the State Museums Fund
Inv. no. E 12264

V.K. Shtegman-Gayeva
attributed this work to the
renowned German sculptor
Georg Petel (Bavaria ?1601/02 –
Augsburg *c.* 1634), who had
studied under Rubens
(Shtegman-Gayeva 1949,
pp. 104–06). Other historians,
however, including Theuerkauff
(1964, p. 282), believe this
Crucifixion to be of later date.
In his book on Petel, Alfred
Schädler (1973, no. 150)
supported an attribution put
forward by H.P. Higler, who
believed the sculpture to have
been made by Flemish sculptor
Gabriel Grupello during his
residence in Brussels.
Beginning in 1658, Grupello
received his training in Antwerp
under Artus Quellinus the Elder
(1609–1668), after which he
became municipal sculptor in
Brussels. In 1688, he was
appointed court sculptor to
Charles II of Spain, a position
he held until moving to
Düsseldorf in 1695 as court
sculptor to Johan Wilhelm,
Elector Palatine.
Y.S.

160
Tankard with Allegorical Figures
Ivory with silver gilt mounts
and glass finial
Lucas Fayd'herbe (?; Mechelen
1617–1697)
Flanders, first half 17th century
Height 38.5 cm
Marked on mounts: Augsburg
and AW (Andreas Wickert,
1660–1661; see Rosenberg
1922, nos. 540f.).
Provenance: Acquired before
1859
Inv. no. E 7285

Felkersam attributed the
carving of the tankard's ivory
sleeve to Christoph Angermair
(c. 1580–1633; Felkersam 1915a,
p. 134). In an exhibition
catalogue (Leningrad 1973),
Lapkovskaya, noting the
Baroque features in the
treatment of the allegorical
figures and their likeness to
figures in Rubens's
Bacchanalia, attributed the
carving to works associated with
German sculptor Georg Petel
(?1601/02–c. 1634). In ascribing
the silver gilt mounts she
mistakenly indicated that the
mark was that of "Georg"
Wickert the Elder, who is known
to have mounted Petel's works
(Leningrad 1973, no. 28). In our
opinion, the relief figures on the
sleeve are close to the circle of
Flemish sculptor Lucas
Fayd'herbe (1617–1697), a
friend and pupil of Rubens.
Y.S.

162
Figure of a Sleeping Putto
Ivory
Artus Quellinus (?; 1609–1668)
Flanders, mid-17th century
Length 12 cm
Provenance: Transferred in
1886 from the Golitsyn
Museum, Moscow (Golitsyn
Guide 1882, no. 290).
Inv. no. E 7282

161
*Figure of a Putto Seated on a
Skull*
Ivory on wood base
Flanders, 17th century
Height 14.1 cm
Provenance: Transferred in 1925
from the Shuvalov House
Museum; formerly collection of
Countess E.V. Shuvalova
Inv. no. E 11310

163
*Figure of a Putto Astride a
Tortoise*
Ivory with wood base
Flanders, 17th century
Height 15.5 cm
Provenance: Transferred in
1930 from the museum of the
Society for the Encouragement
of the Arts, Leningrad (Museum
Catalogue 1904, p. 445)
Inv. no. E 15020

164
*Display Platter with Hunting
Scenes and Diana and Acteon*
Ivory and reindeer horn
Johann Michael Maucher
(Schwäbisch Gmünd 1645 –
Würzburg 1701)
Germany, second half 17th
century
59 × 73 cm
Provenance:
Acquired before 1811
Inv. no. E 7267

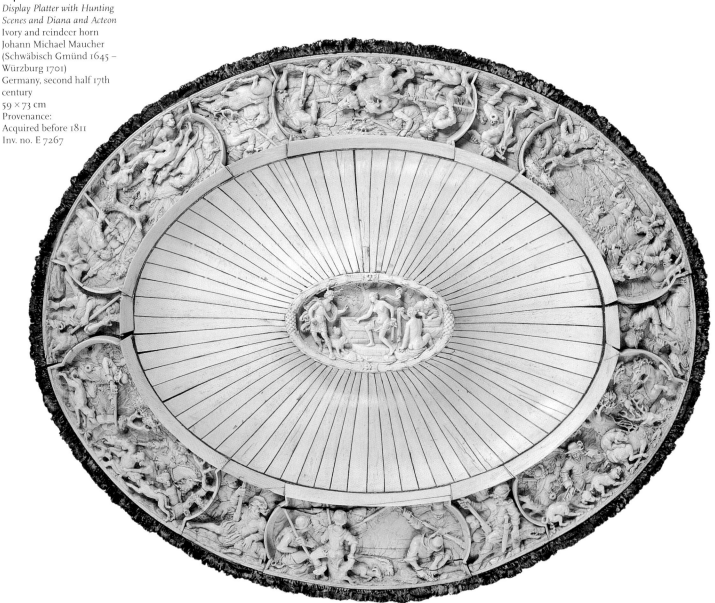

This display platter is recorded in the 1811 Hermitage inventory of turned and carved ivory objects (Lukin 1811, no. 109). The central relief depicts Diana and Acteon, while the collar contains six medallions of hunting scenes between which are individual figures of hunters. All the scenes are sculpted in extremely high relief, the modelling undoubtedly reflecting the influence of silver- and goldsmiths' work.

Kube, referring to a nineteenth-century description of works in the Gallery of *Objets de Vertu* (Inventory 1859, vol. IV, no. 3411), presumed that the ivory strips radiating from the central medallion might

originally have been gilded. (Kube 1925, no. 182). In 1940 Shtegman attributed the charger to the celebrated German sculptor Johann Michael Maucher, who worked in Gmünde until moving to Würzburg in 1688 (Shtegman 1940, pp. 141–51). Convincing analogies to other known works by Maucher and a detailed iconographic analysis provided by Shtegman leave little room for doubting the correctness of the attribution.

The scenes around the collar and the figures between them are closely tied to contemporary Flemish art, as they are based on compositions and individual figures by such well-known artists as Rubens, Joannes

Stradanus (Jan van der Straet), Frans Floris the Elder and Antonio Tempesta. The boar hunt at the lower left reproduces a composition by Rubens widely available in numerous engraved versions; in this case Maucher based his carving on a print by Pieter Soutman. The falcon hunt on the upper right is only partially related to the work of Rubens: in style it echoes a print after Rubens by Soutman, but the actual composition is derived from a print by Tempesta with which Rubens was clearly familiar. In the medallion with figures hunting mountain goats just below the central medallion, Maucher precisely reproduced two different groups

of figures from works by Stradanus, based on a print by Philipp Galle. In the bear hunt just above the central medallion Maucher used a slightly altered composition by Stradanus, and for the wolf hunt, as was suggested by Shtegman, the figures were borrowed from canvases by Rubens in Marseilles and Dresden. For the sixth medallion, a stag hunt at the lower right, Shtegman could find no iconographic source; this allowed her to see this relief, which is rather weak in terms of its composition, as an original work by Maucher (Shtegman 1940, p. 146). The figures between the medallions are all in a similar style and also derive from those in works by

Rubens, with the exception of the half-reclining hunter with the long beard, resting on a dead hare at the lower left, which Shtegman suggested was stylistically derived from figures by Stradanus.

The central medallion with Diana and Acteon differs markedly from the images on the collar of the charger. In Shtegman's opinion, its style has much in common with German sixteenth-century classicism; it has iconographic parallels with prints by Georg Pencz, (*c.* 1500–1550); and may be based on a print by Floris showing a similar subject (Shtegman 1940, pp. 148–49).
Y.S.

165
Adoration of the Magi
Ivory
Germany, 17th century
49 × 30 cm
Provenance: Acquired in 1923
from the collection of F.I.
Paskevich (Paskevich Collection
1885, no. 1476)
Inv. no. 14900

This relief is loosely based on
Rubens's paintings of the
Adoration, of which he
produced several versions.
Y.S.

166

Cupid Pendant
Chased and enamelled gold
with diamonds, rubies and
pearls
The Netherlands, c. 1580
11 × 6.1 cm
Provenance: Transferred 1882
from the Kremlin Armoury,
Moscow
Inv. no. E 4791

The pendant consists of a figure
of Cupid releasing an arrow
from his bow, above which are a
pair of kissing doves and
clasped hands, all made of
enamelled gold. Cupid's wings
and bow and the links of the
suspension chain are mounted
with rubies and diamonds,
while drilled baroque pearls are
suspended from above and
below.

Depictions of Cupid and the
use of related love symbolism
were common in Europe during
the sixteenth and seventeenth
centuries. Such pendants, like
other items made of precious
stones and metals, were not
intended for everyday use but
generally formed part of
ceremonial attire. They were
usually kept in *Kunstkammern*
or cabinets of curiosities,
housed in specially designed
cupboards or chests. We do not
know how this particular
pendant came to be in the
Moscow Armoury, but as early
as the sixteenth century the
Armoury (attached to the
Kremlin, the official residence
of the Russian tsars) was used
as a storage area for precious
objects, gifts of state, and the
contents of the imperial
treasury.

This is one of two such
pendants owned by the
Hermitage, the other being
from Catherine II's personal
jewellery collection. Upon
entering the Hermitage, this
Cupid pendant was thought to
have been made in a German
workshop of the sixteenth
century, an attribution in
accordance with the leading rôle
played by South German
jewellers working mainly in
Nuremberg and Augsburg. To
this day many such pendants
with a figure of Cupid have still
not been precisely attributed,
and are generally described as
the work of Netherlandish or
South German masters, as with
an example in the
Württembergisches
Landesmuseum in Stuttgart.

In the early twentieth
century, however, this pendant
was re-attributed and identified
as the work of Netherlandish
masters, an opinion supported
by Hackenbroch, who dated it to
c. 1580 and published several
related prints by contemporary
Antwerp masters (Hackenbroch
1979, p. 253). The printed
designs for such pendants,
however, are often characterized
by a greater dynamism and
careful attention to details.

Several pendants of similar
type and decoration are known,
the closest example being one
in the Rijksmuseum,
Amsterdam, which is dated to
around 1590. The subject of the
pendant, Cupid shooting an
arrow, was common not only in
the Netherlands but also in
Spain. A portrait of the Spanish
Infanta Isabella, daughter of
Philip II, in the Royal
Collection, London, shows her
wearing just such a pendant
(Hackenbroch 1979, p. 254).

The jeweller who set the gold
and precious stones on the
Hermitage pendant combined
the different materials with
great skill. Coloured enamel
rosettes in the chain and wings
sit alongside rubies and
diamonds in deep gold settings.
Most of the stones are used in
flat, faceted form, only the
suspended pearls preserving
their natural shape.
O.K.

167

Mermaid Pendant
Polished baroque pearl, chased,
engraved and enamelled gold,
diamonds and sapphires
The Netherlands, *c.* 1610–20
7.7 × 3.6 cm
Provenance: Acquired before
1839
Inv. no. E 2650

The body of the mermaid or
siren is made of a large baroque
pearl, the arms, hands, head
and hair of enamelled gold. The
mermaid's collar, mirror and
head and the upper cartouche
are mounted with diamonds,
while the suspension chains
and the lower openwork
cartouche are decorated with
pale blue sapphires. This
pendant was initially thought to
have been made in the sixteenth
century, but Hackenbroch
believed it to be Netherlandish
and dated it between 1610 and
1620 (Hackenbroch 1979,
fig. 718).
O.K.

168
Ship Pendant
Baroque pearl, rubies,
emeralds, glass, and chased,
engraved and enamelled gold
Italy (?), 1590–1600
4 × 3.8 cm
Provenance: Acquired before
1859
Inv. no. E 2651

169

Ship Pendant
Emeralds and chased, engraved
and enamelled gold
Spain, 1580s–90s
9.3 × 6 cm
Provenance: Entered the Winter
Palace before 1789
Inv. no. E 2944

Justly considered one of the
finest pieces of jewellery in the
Hermitage collection, this
pendant incorporates a large,
transparent deep green
Colombian emerald. Five
additional emeralds form a
cross, which serves as the
pendant's fastener. The mast of
the ship and details of its
rigging are made of emeralds
and gold, partially chased and
covered with enamel.

Such pendants were worn on
chains by both men and
women. In the sixteenth and
seventeenth centuries the ship
motif, associated with
geographical exploration and
the discovery of new lands,
became increasingly widespread
and descriptions of the Russian
imperial collections in various
Kunstkammern made repeated
mention of cups and decorative
chalices in the form of ships.

It is difficult to state precisely
when and how this particular
pendant entered the Hermitage.
The earliest documentary
source is a manuscript
inventory of the *objets de vertu* in
the "Armitazh" (Hermitage) of
Empress Catherine II, compiled
in 1789. Later, in the middle of
the nineteenth century, a special
Gallery of *Objets de Vertu* was
opened to the public. This was
housed in the Small Hermitage,
which was built alongside the
Winter Palace between 1764
and 1775.

A later inventory of the
collection ascribed this pendant
to sixteenth-century Italian
masters, an attribution with
which many scholars have
concurred. In the middle of the
20th century, however, Pavel
Derviz (1941, pp. 86–88)
suggested the authorship of late
sixteenth-century Spanish
masters; this has not
subsequently been refuted,
though Hackenbroch assigned a
more precise dating of 1580–90
(Hackenbroch 1979, p. 342).

In Spain, such pendants
served not only as decoration
inspired by the country's great
naval prowess and its national
identity as "victor of the seas,"
but were also designed as
memorial gifts, talismans or
charms. A number of such

pieces survive in museum and
private collections, differing in
decoration and materials, but
often including precisely
detailed replicas of ships,
complete with rigging and other
equipment. In each case
jewellers would have been
guided by the potential inherent
within the specific materials
used and the manner in which
they might be combined. The
Hermitage pendant is
remarkable both for the
jeweller's skill in cutting and
mounting the emeralds, but
also for the exceedingly fine
chasing of the gold. The gold
details that encompass the main
part of the ship play a secondary
rôle and serve to enhance the
large emerald, while the white
enamel borders and sails and
the black enamelled gold rudder
emphasize the severity and
rather graphic quality of the
whole object. The lower edge of
the ship would originally have
included suspended pearls,
although such an important
object may alternatively have
incorporated drilled emeralds.
O.K.

170
Parrot Pendant
Chased and enamelled gold,
pearls, rubies, emeralds and
diamonds
Germany or Spain, late 16th
century
9 × 4.3 cm
Provenance: Entered the Winter
Palace before 1789
Inv. no. E 2941

It is thought that this pendant
was brought to Russia by Peter
the Great and presented to his
wife, Catherine (later Catherine
I). In 1727 it was listed in the
inventory recording the division
of Catherine's property between
her daughters, Princesses Anna
and Elizabeth. The object is a
superb example of sixteenth-
century craftsmanship,
characteristic features of which
are the setting of precious
stones in deep claws and the
combination of minerals that
vary in colour and faceting.
O.K.

171
Swan Pendant
Baroque pearls, chased and
enamelled gold, rubies and
diamonds
The Netherlands, *c.* 1590
9.2 × 5.9 cm
Provenance: From the mid-19th
century in the Gallery of *Objets
de Vertu*
Inv. no. E 2652

The swan's body is formed of a
large baroque pearl, its head,
neck, wings and tail of chased
and enamelled gold, mounted
with diamonds in deep settings.
The two suspension chains are
joined above the swan's body by
an enamelled rosette,
surmounted with a ruby in a
gold setting, below which hangs
a pearl. The lower part of the
pendant consists of an
openwork gold cartouche with
polychrome enamel, set with a
cabochon ruby in the centre and
a drilled pearl below.

Jewellery made of pearls,
particularly large pearls of
excellent quality, has always
been highly prized. In ancient
Russia, many objects were
decorated with pearls, and
during the sixteenth and
seventeenth centuries jewellery
was frequently decorated with
strands of large or small drilled
pearls, mainly those from
northern Russian rivers. Pearls
from the Varzugi River became
particularly sought after in
Russia, and all the pearls
obtained there entered the
patriarch's treasury, for use in
the decoration of church
utensils and robes. Individual
pearls were also imported, the
most prized being "Gurmyzh"
pearls, found in the Gulf of
Persia, the so-called Gurmyzh
Sea. At this time such pearls
were brought into Russia *via*
Kaffa (the old name for
Feodosia in Crimea) and
Kholmogory, and sold
individually.

An inventory of the collection
of *objets de vertu* compiled in the
middle of the nineteenth
century listed the pendant as
the work of French sixteenth-
century jewellers, while an early
twentieth-century inventory
attributed it to late sixteenth-
century Italian masters. More
recently, Hackenbroch cited a
group of analogous pieces and
ascribed the pendant to a
Netherlandish master, dating it
around 1590 (Hackenbroch
1979, p. 252).

It seems likely that the
pendant was not acquired by the
imperial Russian court for

personal adornment, but as a
work of art in its own right and
a superb example of jewellery
from a period when baroque
pearls were highly sought after
and much in use for pendants.
The pearl in the Hermitage
example is not only extremely
large, but of striking colour and
form, which clearly suggested
the object's ultimate subject.
The pearl's natural defects are
masked by careful mounting,
and the jeweller's technical
virtuosity is further revealed in
the skilful setting of the
precious stones.
O.K.

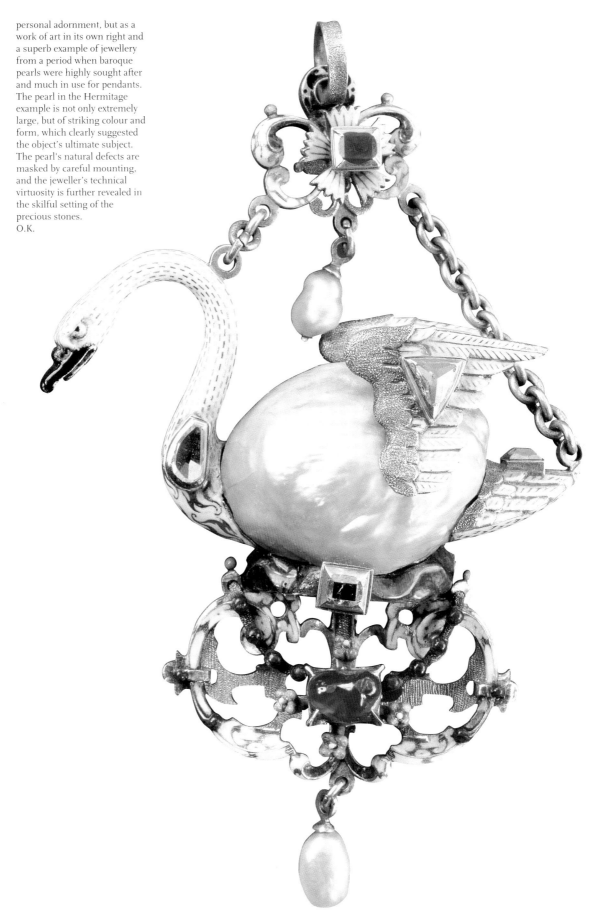

172

Footed Cup with Lid
Carved and polished bloodstone
mounted with enamelled gold
Ottavio Miseroni (Milan 1567 –
Prague 1624) *and* Hans
Vermeyen (before 1559–1608)
Prague, *c.* 1605
10.1 × 6.1 cm
Provenance: Acquired before
1859
Inv. no. E. 1867

This small round cup, carved
from bloodstone, or heliotrope,
has a removable lid decorated
with a profiled crown, both of
which are set in gold mounts
further embellished with
polychrome enamel. Such
objects were made for state
interiors and for exhibition in
palace treasuries, and the
inventories of many
Kunstkammern at the courts of
sixteenth- and seventeenth-
century monarchs record
numerous bowls, vases and cups

such as this, made of decorative
hardstones and displayed in
specially designed cases or on
individual tables with other
curiosities.

By the late sixteenth century
a workshop producing elaborate
carved and mounted objects
from semi-precious stones had
been established at the court of
Emperor Rudolf II in Prague.
Among the most well-known
artists working there was
Ottavio Miseroni, who moved to
Prague from Milan (where he
had previously worked in his
father's studio), entering the
service of Rudolf on January 22,
1588. His workshop, which
included his brothers Giovanni
and Alessandro (Distelberger
1997, p. 190), produced
numerous objects incorporating
bloodstone, the most famous of
which is undoubtedly the
monumental bowl of 1608 now
in the Louvre, made to
commemorate twenty years of

work for the emperor and
Ottavio's elevation to noble
rank.

During this period Miseroni
actively collaborated with Hans
Vermeyen (before 1559–1608),
a Flemish jeweller and
goldsmith; their work together
is exemplified by several well-
known objects in the Vienna
Kunsthistorisches Museum.
The Hermitage cup is probably
another example of their
collaboration: the bloodstone is
extremely carefully worked, its
polished surface leaving no
traces of the chisel, while the
profile curves emphasize the
mineral's natural beauty. In the
bowl of the cup the stone is
worked so finely that some parts
of the surface appear to be
translucent. The hardstone
itself was usually the dominant
component of such objects, the
decoration serving primarily
to enhance its natural qualities.
In this case the jeweller

embellished the bloodstone
cup and lid with stepped gold
rims decorated with polychrome
enamel images of fantastic
animals, birds, swags, arabesques
and coloured roundels imitating
precious stones. The cup is a
consummate example of the
collaboration between carver and
goldsmith, each of whom was
extremely skilled in his own
sphere.

The top of the lid has lost
some of its decorative details,
still partly extant when the cup
was recorded in eighteenth-
century inventories. Comparison
with a similar work of *c.* 1600
in the Württembergisches
Landesmuseum in Stuttgart
suggests that the lid was
originally mounted with a small
enamelled gold vase. A mid-
nineteenth-century inventory of
the Imperial Hermitage
collection listed this object as
sixteenth-century Italian, an
attribution typical of its time,

since the majority of carved
hardstone items were then
thought to have been made in
Italy. The attribution of the cup
to Ottavio Miseroni, however, is
assured by its close similarity to
the aforementioned objects
from the Kunsthistorisches
Museum in Vienna, which were
originally part of Rudolf II's
Kunstkammer, as well as pieces
from the Museo degli Argenti in
Florence. The nearly identical
facture of various details
between those objects and the
Hermitage cup allow us to date
it to *c.* 1605. So harmonious is
this work in composition and
decoration – the working of the
stone, the quality of the gold
mounts and the elegance of the
enamel ornament – that it can
justly be considered one of the
masterpieces of Rudolf's
treasury.
O.K.

173

Footed vessel
Carved and ground smoky
quartz mounted with chased,
engraved and gilded silver
Workshop of Dionisio Miseroni
(1607? – Prague 1661)
Prague, mid-seventeenth
century
9.6 × 19.3 × 7.5 cm
Provenance: Acquired before
1859
Inv. no. E 2371

This footed vessel, carved of
smoky quartz, is supported by
hinged silver gilt mounts in the
form of engraved and chased
leaves. The entire surface of the
quartz is carved with acanthus
leaves, wave-shaped relief
ornaments and volutes and, on
one side, a carved mask with
two openings. On the lateral
sides are hinged silver gilt
garlands set in the centre
with a pearl, which serve as
supplementary reinforcement

for so large a piece of stone. The
quartz foot has an ornamental
band where it is joined to the
cup and a chased silver gilt rim.
    The earliest mention of this
work is found in the mid-
nineteenth-century inventory of
the Hermitage collection of
objets de vertu, where it was
listed as the work of Russian
masters, an obvious error as
there was no developed
tradition of hardstone carving in
seventeenth-century Russia.
Nonetheless, the relatively large
number of such works in the
Hermitage attests to the great
interest they aroused in Russia.
They were found in both court
and private collections, although
the pieces considered to be
artistically superior were taken
for the imperial family. In an
inventory compiled in the early
twentieth century, this cup was
listed as seventeenth-century
German, and was then published
as such (Felkersam 1915b, p. 9).

    In fact, the artist responsible
for this vessel was Dionisio
Miseroni, son of Ottavio
Miseroni, maker of the
bloodstone cup also included in
the exhibition. Dionisio further
developed the tradition of
hardstone carving practised by
his father and became one of
the most famous carvers of the
period, serving Ferdinand III,
Holy Roman Emperor, as
official hardstone carver. He
was also appointed keeper of
the Prague imperial treasury,
which he saved during the
Swedish occupation of Prague
during the Thirty Years' War by
moving it to Vienna. Most
carved hardstone works in the
"Rudolfine" style are thus today
in the Kunsthistorisches
Museum.
    Owing to his masterful
carving technique, Miseroni
was able to take advantage of a
mineral's natural qualities, with
results so assured that works

such as this vessel seem to have
been made of wax rather than
stone. As exemplified by the
surface of this quartz cup, the
artist made repeated use of leaf
ornament, also found on some
vases from about 1650 in the
Kunsthistorisches Museum of
Vienna. Like the Hermitage
vessel, these were made of
different shades of quartz,
citrine and smoky topaz; other
minerals employed by the
Prague workshop were agate,
jasper and bloodstone, as well
as Bohemian garnet and
different shades of rock crystal
from the Alps. The physical
qualities and natural forms of
these hardstones often dictated
the final shape of an object, and
their rare natural colours
contributed significantly to the
expressive effect of the finished
works.
    Vessels such as this were
highly valued by contemporary
European collectors and

connoisseurs, and we know
from documentary evidence
that Miseroni was well paid
for them (Distelberger 1997,
p. 539). It seems likely that
the lapidary and goldsmith
responsible for the Hermitage
cup collaborated from an early
stage to achieve such harmony
between the masterfully carved
hardstone and the silver gilt
mounts.
O.K.

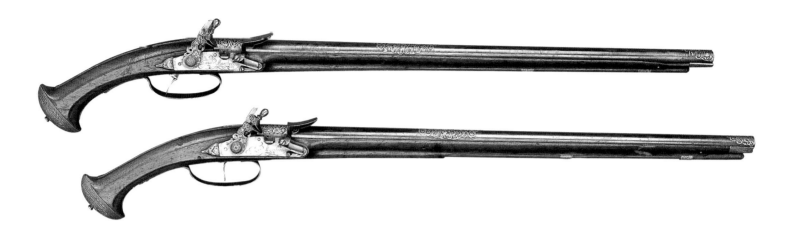

174
Pair of Pistols
Wood, steel damascened with gold, engraved and gilded bronze
The Netherlands, Maastricht, c. 1640
Overall length 75.6 cm; length of barrel 55.8 cm; calibre 14 mm
Provenance: Transferred in 1885 from the Arsenal of the imperial summer palace at Tsarskoye Selo
Inv. no. ZO 302 (a,b)
Selected literature: Tarassuk 1972, nos. 123, 124, p. 166; Soldatenko 1996, HSP 12–13, pp. 388–89

These pistols are typical of the work of Dutch seventeenth-century gunsmiths. The barrels and trigger guards of burnished steel have been treated with bluing (a method by which the metal is heated in fire until it assumes a blue colour) and are damascened with gold. One barrel is stamped with the maker's mark *MLC*, while the locks are engraved and the lock-plates inscribed *Facit Masestrecht* (made in Maastricht); the bronze mounts are gilded and engraved with floral ornament. This pair of pistols, as well as several other objects in the exhibition, was originally housed at Tsarskoye Selo, one of several imperial summer residences in the environs of St. Petersburg. In the 1830s, Nicholas I established a museum of ancient arms and armour there, known as the Arsenal, which was transferred to the Hermitage Museum in 1855.
Y.M.

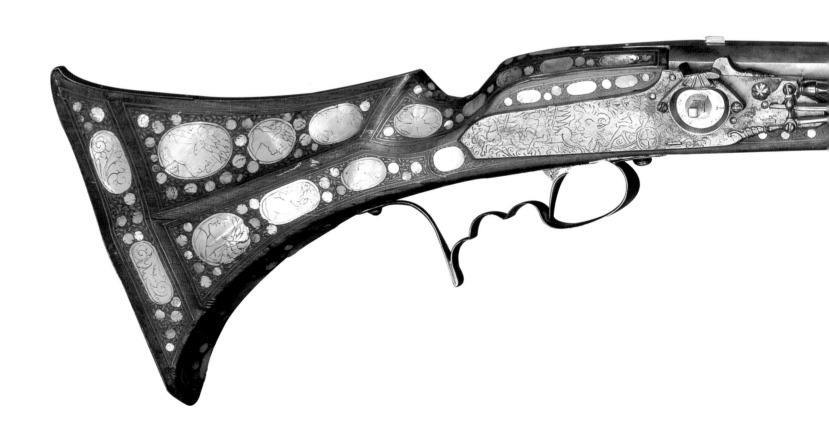

175
Flintlock Gun
Wood with welded and carved
copper and steel
The Netherlands, *c.* 1630–40
Overall length 124.1 cm; length
of barrel 85.4 cm; calibre
44.5 mm
Provenance: Transferred in
1903 from the collection of
Count S.D. Sheremetev,
St. Petersburg
Inv. no. ZO 5346
Selected literature: Lenz 1895,
no. 876; Tarassuk 1972, no. 127,
p. 166

This gun belongs to the well-
known category of firearms with
an early form of Anglo-Dutch
flintlock used in the sixteenth
and seventeenth centuries
known as a snaphance. The
absence of decoration indicates
that the gun was designed solely
as a utilitarian weapon, in
contrast to the other examples
in the exhibition.
Y.M.

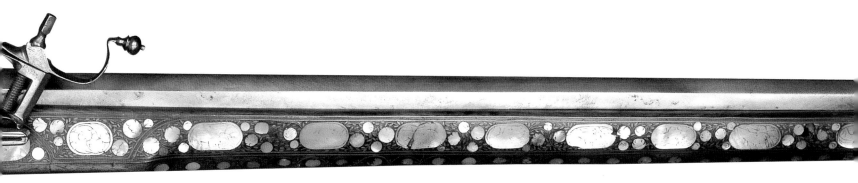

176
Wheel-lock Gun
Wood inlaid with engraved
mother-of-pearl, etched steel,
iron and brass
The Netherlands, *c.* 1610–20
Overall length 158 cm; length of
barrel 119.9 cm; calibre
18.5 mm
Provenance: Transferred in 1885
from the Arsenal of the
imperial summer palace at
Tsarskoye Selo
Inv. no. ZO 5827
Selected literature: Sayger 1840,
vol. I, no. 165, p. 121; Tarassuk
1972, no. 84, p. 162; Soldatenko
1996, HSP 2, pp. 370–71

This gun's octagonal barrel is
typical of this period. The lock
and steel trigger guard are
engraved with mythological
subjects, the floral ornament on
the gun's stock is made of inlaid
brass wire, and the inlaid
roundels of mother-of-pearl are
engraved with male heads
garlanded with laurel. The
elaborate inlaid decoration
indicates the gun was made for
a collector rather than for use.
The barrel is stamped with the
mark *RS* beneath a crown,
probably indicating the
gunsmith's name.
Y.M.

177
Morion
Etched and chased steel
Germany, c. 1605–10
Height 34 cm
Provenance: Transferred in 1885
from the Arsenal of the
imperial summer palace at
Tsarskoye Selo
Inv. no. ZO 3962
Unpublished; not previously
exhibited

This helmet is a typical example
of European head armour of the
mid-sixteenth to seventeenth
centuries. A morion is a form of
helmet common during this
period without visor or beaver
(the lower portion of the face
guard). The skilfully chased and
etched floral ornamentation
suggests a German origin for
this example.
Y.M.

178
Burgonet
Forged steel
Germany, late 16th century
Height 25 cm
Provenance: Transferred in 1885
from the Arsenal of the
imperial summer palace at
Tsarskoye Selo
Inv. no. ZO 6042
Unpublished; not previously
exhibited

This helmet's pointed crown
and faceted form were intended
to deflect an adversary's blows
while the long cheek guards and
the prominent visor offered
additional protection. Burgonets
were intended primarily for the
use of the infantry, especially
pikemen, and were traditionally
fitted to the neck-piece or
gorget, so that the wearer's head
could be turned without
exposing the neck. The absence
of surface decoration suggests
that this helmet was intended
only for battle.
Y.M.

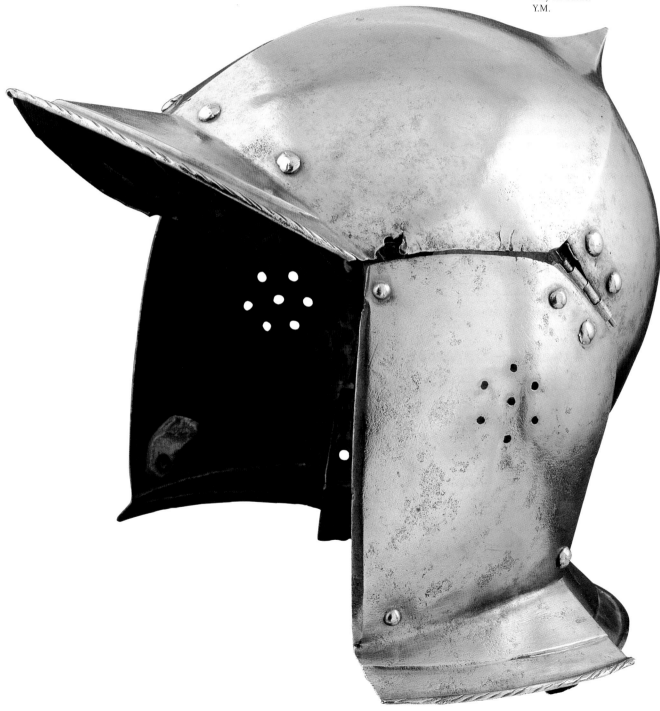

179
Morion
Forged and patinated steel and copper
Germany, *c*. 1600
Height 31 cm
Provenance: Transferred from the Museums Fund (government body set up after the Revolution to control and reallocate nationalized art objects) in the 1920s or 1930s
Inv. no. ZO 3204
Unpublished; not previously exhibited

This helmet is of a well-known European type, its notable features being the high comb and wide flaps, which were both designed to provide a high degree of protection. Such helmets were often used by the nobility and their personal bodyguards, in which case both sides were decorated with the family's crest or emblem, such as this example's fleurs-de-lis.
Y.M.

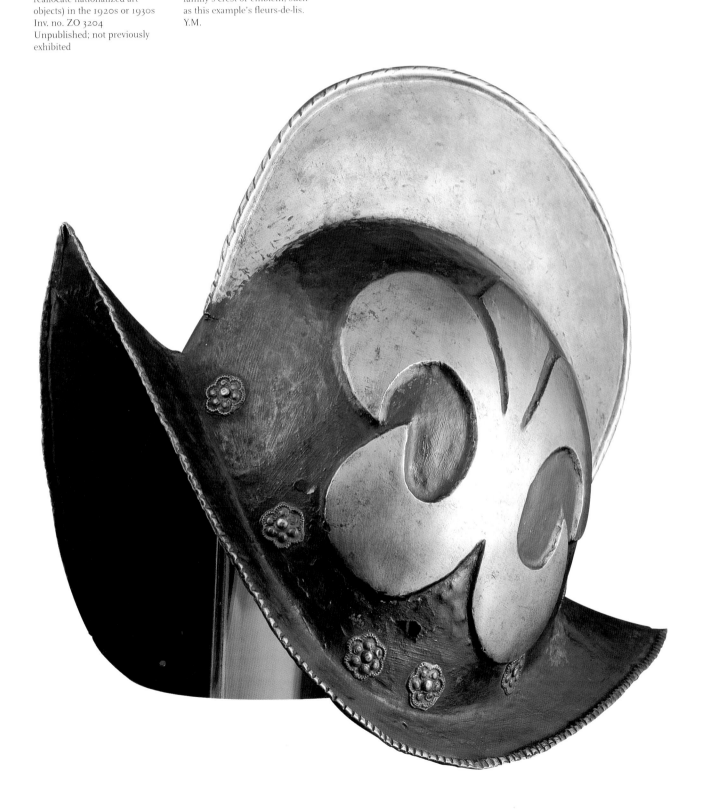

180
Half-armour
Forged and engraved steel and copper
Germany or Switzerland (?),
c. 1600
Provenance: Transferred in 1885 from the Arsenal of the imperial summer palace at Tsarskoye Selo
Inv. no. ZO 3340
Unpublished; not previously exhibited

Such half-armour is typical of the early seventeenth century, by which time the need for heavy full harness armour had passed. Nonetheless, this less cumbersome armour provided quite effective protection. In keeping with contemporary fashion, the armour has only limited decoration, in this case limited to its surface patination and the finely tooled linear borders edging the individual pieces.
Y.M.

181
Small sword
Chased and carved steel and iron
Germany, late 17th century
Provenance: Transferred in 1885 from the Arsenal of the imperial summer palace at Tsarskoye Selo.
Inv. no. ZP 1010
Unpublished; not previously exhibited

This rapier belongs to a standard category of European side arms. The blade bears the engraved inscription *fidi sed cuiuidi* [trust only what I see], and the grip is delicately chiselled with floral ornament.
Y.M.

182
Small sword
Chased and carved steel and iron
Germany, Solingen, 17th century
Provenance: Transferred in 1885 from the Arsenal of the imperial summer palace at Tsarskoye Selo
Inv. no. ZO 4523
Unpublished; not previously exhibited

The blade is stamped with the mark of an unknown bladesmith from Solingen, a city in southern Germany well known for its production of blades, knives and scissors since the Middle Ages, and with that of another bladesmith, the well-known Spanish master Sebastien Hernandez.
Y.M.

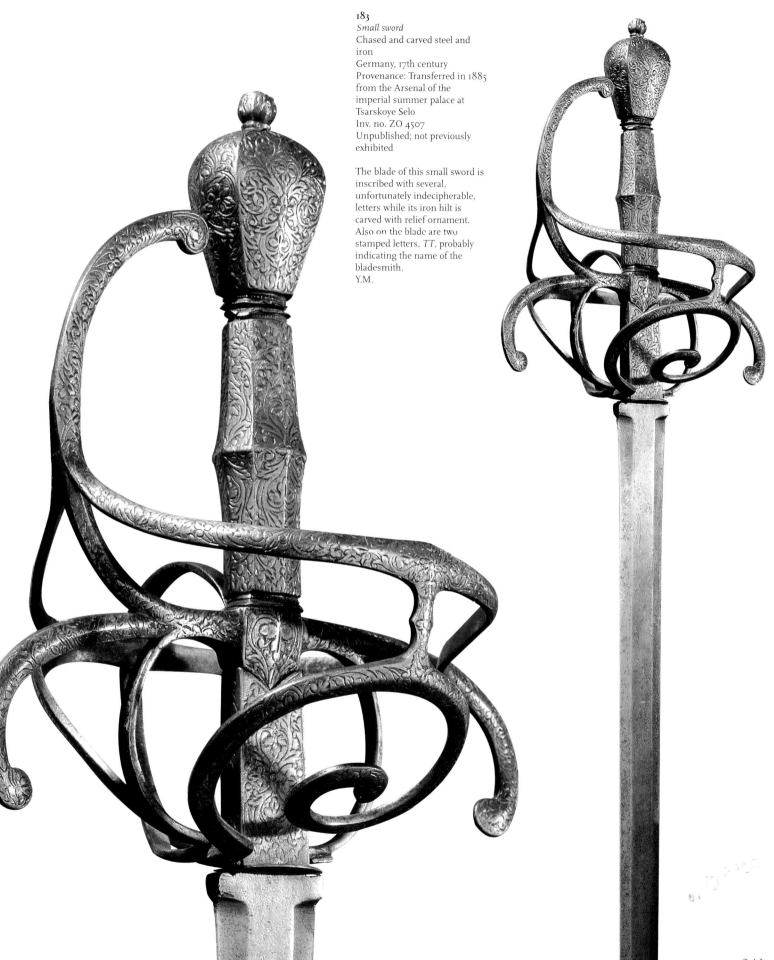

183
Small sword
Chased and carved steel and
iron
Germany, 17th century
Provenance: Transferred in 1885
from the Arsenal of the
imperial summer palace at
Tsarskoye Selo
Inv. no. ZO 4507
Unpublished; not previously
exhibited

The blade of this small sword is
inscribed with several,
unfortunately indecipherable,
letters while its iron hilt is
carved with relief ornament.
Also on the blade are two
stamped letters, *TT*, probably
indicating the name of the
bladesmith.
Y.M.

WORKS IN THE EXHIBITION

1
PETER PAUL RUBENS
1577 Siegen – 1640 Antwerp
The Adoration of the Shepherds,
1608
Oil on canvas, transferred from
panel in 1868. 63.5 × 47 cm
Provenance: Acquired in 1769
from the Brühl collection,
Dresden
Inv. no. GE 492

2
PETER PAUL RUBENS
1577 Siegen – 1640 Antwerp
*The Assumption and Coronation
of the Virgin,* 1611
Oil on canvas, transferred from
panel in 1868. 106 × 78 cm
Provenance: Acquired in 1770 at
the sale of François Ignace de
Dufresne, Amsterdam, August
22, 1770 (lot 134)
Inv. no. GE 1703

3
PETER PAUL RUBENS
1577 Siegen – 1640 Antwerp
*Roman Charity, or Cimon and
Pero,* 1610–12
Oil on canvas, transferred from
panel in 1846. 140.5 × 180.3 cm
Provenance: Carel van den
Bosch, Bishop of Bruges, in
mid-17th century; acquired in
1768, with the collection of
Count Cobenzl, Brussels
Inv. no. GE 470

4
PETER PAUL RUBENS
1577 Siegen – 1640 Antwerp
The Union of Earth and Water,
c. 1618
Oil on canvas. 222.5 × 180.5 cm
Provenance: Chigi collection,
Rome; possibly from the
collection of Fabio Chigi (Pope
Alexander VII, 1655–1667);
acquired between 1798 and
1800 by Paul I, for his newly
built Mikhail Castle in
St. Petersburg (Kalnitskaya
1995, pp. 80–81).
Inv. no. GE 464

5
PETER PAUL RUBENS
1577 Siegen – 1640 Antwerp
The Arrival in Lyons, 1622
Oil on canvas, transferred from
panel in 1893. 33.5 × 24.2 cm
Provenance: Probably in the
collection of Claude de Maugis,
Abbé de Saint-Ambroise, Paris,
in the 17th century; acquired in
1772 with the Crozat collection,
Paris
Inv. no. GE 505

6
PETER PAUL RUBENS
1577 Siegen – 1640 Antwerp
The Vision of St. Ildefonso,
1630–31
Oil on canvas. 52 × 83 cm
Provenance:Clemens August,
Duke of Bavaria, Prince-Elector
and Archbishop of Cologne;
sale of Clemens August,
December 10, 1764, Paris
(lot 28); belonged to the Paris
auctioneer Boileau *père,* and
while in his possession was
seen by the collector Lalive de
Jully (Castan 1885, pp. 5–6);
acquired before 1774
Inv. no. GE 520

7
PETER PAUL RUBENS
1577 Siegen – 1640 Antwerp
The Apotheosis of James I,
c. 1632–1633
Oil on canvas. 89.7 × 55.3 cm
Provenance: 1639 collection of
Charles I; collection of Godfrey
Kneller, London; collection of
Sir Robert Walpole, London,
then Houghton Hall, Norfolk;
acquired in 1779 with the
Walpole collection, Norfolk
Inv. no. GE 507

8
PETER PAUL RUBENS
1577 Siegen – 1640 Antwerp
The Arch of Hercules (front face),
1634–35
Oil on canvas, transferred from
panel in 1871. 103 × 72 cm
Provenance: Antwerp Town
Hall (property of the
magistrature); sale of the
collection of Prosper Henricus
Lankrink, London, May 23,
1693; collection of Sir Robert
Walpole, Houghton Hall,
Norfolk; acquired in 1779 with
the Walpole collection, Norfolk
Inv. no. GE 503

9
PETER PAUL RUBENS
1577 Siegen – 1640 Antwerp
The Arch of Ferdinand (rear face),
1634
Oil on canvas, transferred from
panel in 1867. 104 × 72.5 cm
Provenance: Antwerp Town
Hall (property of the
magistrature); sale of the
collection of Prosper Henricus
Lankrink, London, May 23,
1693; collection of Sir Robert
Walpole, Houghton Hall,
Norfolk; acquired in 1779 with
the Walpole collection, Norfolk
Inv. no. GE 502

10
PETER PAUL RUBENS
1577 Siegen – 1640 Antwerp
The Temple of Janus, 1634
Oil on panel. 70 × 65.5 cm
Provenance: Antwerp Town
Hall (property of the
magistrature); sale of the
collection of Prosper Henricus
Lankrink, London, May 23,
1693; collection of Sir Robert
Walpole, Houghton Hall,
Norfolk; acquired in 1779 with
the Walpole collection, Norfolk
Inv. no. GE 500

11
ANTHONY VAN DYCK
1599 Antwerp – 1641 London
*The Apparition of Christ to His
Disciples (The Incredulity of
St. Thomas),* early 1620s
Oil on canvas. 147 × 110.3 cm
Provenance: Acquired in 1772
with the Crozat collection, Paris
Inv. no. GE 542

12
JACOB VAN OOST THE ELDER
1601 Bruges – 1671 Bruges
David with the Head of Goliath,
1643
Oil on canvas. 102 × 81 cm
Signed and dated right, on the
sword: *Ja.v. Oost F. 1643*
Provenance: Van Praet sale of
the collection of Charles-Jozef
de Schryvere in Bruges, June 1,
1763 (lot 49); acquired in 1895
from V.P. Kostromitinova
Inv. no. GE 676

13

JACOB JORDAENS
1593 Antwerp – 1678 Antwerp
Cleopatra's Banquet, 1653
Oil on canvas. 156.4 × 149.3 cm
Signed and dated top centre: *J Jor. 1653*
Provenance: Transferred in 1937 *via* the State Museums Fund, Leningrad
Inv. no. GE 8536

14

FRANS FRANCKEN THE YOUNGER
1581 Antwerp – 1642 Antwerp
The Seven Acts of Charity, c. 1617
Oil on canvas, transferred from panel in 1818. 68.5 × 110.5 cm
Signed bottom left: *D Ffranck in et F*
Provenance: Acquired before 1859
Inv. no. GE 395

15

FRANS FRANCKEN THE YOUNGER
1581 Antwerp – 1642 Antwerp
Allegory of Opportunity, 1627
Oil on canvas. 151 × 181 cm
Dated left on the edge of the top book: *ANNO 1627*; signed on the edge of the lower book: *Do F ffranck in f*
Inscription bottom on the cartouche: *OCCASIO/ REM TIBI QUAM/ NOSCES APTAM/ DIMITTERE NOLI/ FRONTE CAPIL/ LATA EST/ SED POST/ OCCASIO CALVA*
[Do not dismiss a thing that you know to be appropriate to you; Opportunity has hair in front but is bald behind]
Provenance: Collection of the painter Nicolas Roerich, St. Petersburg; transferred in 1921 from the State Museum Reserve
Inv. no. GE 6144

16

FRANS FRANCKEN THE YOUNGER
1581 Antwerp – 1642 Antwerp
David's Entry into Jerusalem, 1630s
Oil on canvas, transferred from panel in 1818. 69.5 × 111.5 cm
Signed centre bottom: *D ffranck. in f*
Provenance: Acquired before 1797
Inv. no. GE 438

17

PEETER VAN LINT
1609 Antwerp – 1690 Antwerp
Jephthah and his Daughter, 1640–50
Oil on canvas. 48 × 64 cm
Initials bottom right: *P.V.L. f*
Provenance: Acquired in 1717 in Antwerp by Yury Kologrivov, agent to Peter the Great (Malinovsky 1990, vol. II, p. 71, note 240); Imperial Picture Gallery, Monplaisir, Peterhof, near St. Petersburg; acquired before 1797 (kept in store until 1887)
Inv. no. GE 2055

18

THEODOOR VAN THULDEN
1606 's-Hertogenbosch – 1669 's-Hertogenbosch
Allegory of Time Revealing Truth, 1657
Oil on canvas. 141.2 × 173 cm
Signed and dated bottom right: *T.van Thulden fecit A 1657*
Provenance: Collection of Prince Wilhelm of Mecklenburg-Schwerin; possibly at auction in Amsterdam, May 6, 1716 (lot 9); acquired in 1892 from the collection of F. Moritz, St. Petersburg
Inv. no. GE 563

19

NICOLAES VAN VERENDAEL
1640 Antwerp – 1691 Antwerp
and Gaspard Jacob van Opstal the Elder
c. 1610 Antwerp (?) – after 1661
Allegory of Transience, early 1660s
Oil on canvas. 93 × 102 cm (at the top an addition of approximately 5 cm along the full width of the painting)
Provenance: Possibly in the collection of Jan van Weerden, Antwerp, in 1686; (Hairs 1965, p. 420); acquired in 1769 with the collection of Count Brühl, Dresden
Inv. no. GE 558

20

JAN VAN KESSEL THE ELDER
1626 Antwerp – 1679 Antwerp
Venus at the Forge of Vulcan (Allegory of Fire), 1662
Oil on canvas. 59.5 × 84 cm
Signed and dated bottom centre: *J.V.Kessel fecit 1662*
Provenance: Collection of A.G. Teplov, St. Petersburg; acquired before 1797
Inv. no. GE 1709

21

PETER PAUL RUBENS
1577 Siegen – 1640 Antwerp
Head of a Franciscan Monk, c. 1615
Oil on canvas, transferred from panel in 1842. 52 × 44 cm
Provenance: Collection of Sir Robert Walpole, Houghton Hall, Norfolk; acquired in 1779 with the Walpole Collection, Norfolk
Inv. no. GE 472

22

SCHOOL OF PETER PAUL RUBENS
Portrait of Rubens with his Son Albert, c. 1620
Oil on canvas. 133.5 × 112.2 cm
Provenance: By 1793 in the collection of Count Alexander Stroganov, St. Petersburg (Cat. Stroganoff 1793, no. 30); 1864 collection of Count Sergey Stroganov, St. Petersburg; collection of the Counts Stroganov, St. Petersburg; transferred in 1932 from the Stroganov Palace Museum, Leningrad
Inv. no. GE 7728

23

ANTHONY VAN DYCK
1599 Antwerp – 1641 London
Self-portrait, 1622–23
Oil on canvas. 116.5 × 93.5 cm
Provenance: Acquired in 1772 with the Crozat collection, Paris
Inv. no. GE 548

24

ANTHONY VAN DYCK
1599 Antwerp – 1641 London
Portrait of Nicolaes Rockox, 1621
Oil on canvas. 122.5 × 117 cm
Provenance: Collection of Nicolaes Rockox, Antwerp (no. 4 in the posthumous inventory of his property, compiled December 19–20, 1640); sale of the collection of Anna Theresia van Halen, Antwerp, August 19, 1749 (lot 2); sale of the collection of Frederik Graaf van Thoms, Leiden, April 7, 1750 (lot 1); collection of Claude Henri Watelet, Paris (according to Mariette, *Abecedario* 1853–59, p. 207); acquired by Count Alexander Stroganov in Paris between 1771 and 1779; collection of Count Alexander Stroganov, St. Petersburg; 1864 collection of Count Sergey Stroganov, St. Petersburg; transferred in 1932 from the Stroganov Palace Museum
Inv. no. GE 6922

25

ANTHONY VAN DYCK
1599 Antwerp – 1641 London
Portrait of a Man (Virginio Cesarini?), c. 1622–1623
Oil on canvas. 104.8 × 86.5 cm
Provenance: By 1709 in the collection of Boyer d'Aiguilles, Aix; collection of Pierre Crozat, Paris; acquired in 1772 with the Crozat collection, Paris
Inv. no. GE 552

26

ANTHONY VAN DYCK
1599 Antwerp – 1641 London
Portrait of Lady Jane Goodwin, 1639
Oil on canvas. 132.5 × 106 cm
Inscriptions (from the time of the first owner) at bottom right: *P.Sr. Ant. Vandike*; and five lines at bottom left: *Jane Daughter of Richard Lord ~/ Viscount Wenman mother of Jane/ Goodwin wife of Philip now/ Lord Wharton/ 1639 about ye age of 36*
Provenance: Collection of Philip, 4th Lord Wharton, Winchendon, near Aylesbury, Buckinghamshire; acquired by Sir Robert Walpole from the heirs of Lord Wharton in 1725; collection of Sir Robert Walpole, London (?), then Houghton Hall, Norfolk; acquired in 1779 with the Walpole collection, Norfolk
Inv. no. GE 549

27

ANTHONY VAN DYCK
1599 Antwerp – 1641 London
Portrait of Inigo Jones, 1632–35
Oil on canvas. 64.5 × 53.2 cm (oval in a profiled frame set into a rectangle)
Provenance: Collection of Inigo Jones (Vertue III, 1933–34, p. 112); given by Jones to his nephew, the architect John Webb (Vertue I, 1929–30, p. 135); acquired by Sir Robert Walpole in or shortly after 1736; collection of Sir Robert Walpole, Houghton Hall, Norfolk; acquired in 1779 with the Walpole collection, Norfolk
Inv. no. GE 557

28

ANTHONY VAN DYCK
1599 Antwerp – 1641 London
Portrait of Everhard Jabach, 1636–37
Oil on canvas. 113 × 91.5 cm
Provenance: Collection of Everhard Jabach, Paris; acquired in 1772 with the Crozat collection, Paris
Inv. no. GE 555

29

ANTHONY VAN DYCK
1599 Antwerp – London 1641
Portrait of Sir Thomas Chaloner, c. 1637
Oil on canvas. 104 × 81.5 cm
Provenance: Collection of Sir Robert Walpole, Houghton Hall, Norfolk; acquired in 1779 with the Walpole collection, Norfolk
Inv. no. GE 551

30

ANTHONY VAN DYCK
1599 Antwerp – 1641 London
Henry Danvers, Earl of Danby, in Garter Robes, late 1630s
Oil on canvas. 223 × 130.6 cm
Provenance: Collection of Henry Danvers, Earl of Danby; inherited by his nephew John Danvers; presented by the latter's son, Joseph Danvers, to Sir Robert Walpole; collection of Sir Robert Walpole, Houghton Hall, Norfolk; acquired in 1779 with the Walpole collection, Norfolk
Inv. no. GE 545

31

ANTHONY VAN DYCK
1599 Antwerp – 1641 London
Ladies-in-Waiting to Queen Henrietta Maria (Anne Killigrew with an Unidentified Lady), c. 1638
Oil on canvas. 131.5 × 150.6 cm
Provenance: Acquired between 1763 and 1774
Inv. no. GE 540

32

ANTHONY VAN DYCK AND WORKSHOP
1599 Antwerp – 1641 London
Portrait of Philadelphia and Elizabeth Wharton, 1640
Oil on canvas. 162 × 130 cm
Inscriptions (from the time of the first owner) at bottom right: *P. Sr Ant. Vandike*; and four lines at bottom left: *Philadelphia Wharton and Elizabeth/ Wharton ye only daughters of Philip/ now Lord Wharton by Elizabeth his/ first wife, 1640 about ye age of 4 and 5*
Provenance: Collection of Philip, 4th Lord Wharton, Winchendon, near Aylesbury, Buckinghamshire; 1725 acquired by Sir Robert Walpole from the heirs of Lord Wharton; collection of Sir Robert Walpole, London, then Houghton Hall, Norfolk; acquired in 1779 with the Walpole collection, Norfolk
Inv. no. GE 533

33
JACOB JORDAENS
1593 Antwerp – 1678 Antwerp
Self-portrait with Parents,
Brothers and Sisters, c. 1615
Oil on canvas. 175 × 137.5 cm
Provenance: Probably Het
Paradijs (home of Jordaens's
parents) in Antwerp, now 13
Hoogstraat, which Jordaens
purchased in 1634 at the sale of
his deceased parents' property;
collection of Henry Bentinck,
Duke of Portland; 1722 acquired
from him by Sir Robert Walpole
and kept first in London, then at
Houghton Hall, Norfolk;
acquired in 1779 with the
Walpole collection, Norfolk
Inv. no. GE 484

34
JACOB JORDAENS
1593 Antwerp – 1678 Antwerp
Portrait of an Old Man, c. 1637
Oil on canvas. 154 × 118.5 cm
Inscription bottom left corner,
on the base of the column:
Aetatis 73
Provenance: Acquired in 1772
with the Crozat collection, Paris
Inv. no. GE 486

35
DAVID TENIERS THE YOUNGER
1610 Antwerp – 1690 Brussels
Portrait of Antonius Triest, Bishop
of Ghent, and his Brother Eugene,
a Capuchin Monk, 1652
Oil on canvas. 97.2 × 130.5 cm
To right on the column base the
arms of Antonius Triest,
composed of two hunting horns
and dogs with the Latin
inscription: *CONFIDENTER*. In
the upper part of the arms the
inscription: *AET 76* (indicating
the bishop's age). Also a barely
decipherable date: *A 1652*
Provenance: Acquired in 1768
with the collection of Count
Cobenzl, Brussels
Inv. no. GE 589

36
FRANS POURBUS THE YOUNGER
1569 Antwerp – 1622 Paris
Portrait of Margaret of Savoy,
Duchess of Mantua, 1608
Oil on canvas. 206.5 × 116.3 cm
Provenance: Transferred 1931
via Antikvariat (state trading
organization responsible for
selling art treasures)
Inv. no. GE 6957

37
CORNELIS DE VOS
1584 Hulst – 1651 Antwerp
Portrait of an Elderly Woman,
1630s
Oil on canvas, transferred from
panel in 1846. 124.5 × 93.5 cm
Top left corner (dimensions
57 × 37 cm) is a later addition
Provenance: Collection de
Scawen, England; collection of
Sir Robert Walpole, Houghton
Hall, Norfolk; acquired in 1779
with the Walpole collection,
Norfolk
Inv. no. GE 483

38
FRANS DENYS
c. 1610 Antwerp – 1670 Mantua
Portrait of the Architect Leo van
Heil, 1647
Oil on canvas. 119 × 87 cm
Inscription top right on the
background: *AETATIS 42*
Signed bottom left: *F.Denys fecit*
Provenance: Collection of
P.V. Delarov, Pavlovsk, near
St. Petersburg; transferred
from Antikvariat (state trading
organization responsible for
selling art treasures) in 1933
Inv. no. GE 7692

39
PEETER FRANCHOYS
1606 Mechelen – 1654
Mechelen
Self-portrait, c. 1637
Oil on canvas. 73 × 50.5 cm
Provenance: Possibly in the
collection of M.I. Knebel,
St. Petersburg; transferred from
the Museums Fund at the State
Hermitage Museum in 1939
Inv. no. GE 8495

40
PETER PAUL RUBENS
1577 Siegen – 1640 Antwerp
Pastoral Landscape with
Rainbow, c. 1632–35
Oil on canvas, transferred from
panel in 1869. 86 × 130 cm
Provenance: 1677 Duc de
Richelieu, Paris; June 17, 1696,
sale of Everhard Jabach, Paris
(lot 150); presented to Count
Brühl by the Elector of Bavaria,
son of the Emperor Charles VII
(Somoff 1901); acquired in 1769
with the Brühl collection,
Dresden
Inv. no. GE 482

41
PETER PAUL RUBENS
1577 Siegen – 1640 Antwerp
The Carters, c. 1615–20
Oil on canvas, transferred from
panel in 1823. 86 × 126.5 cm
Provenance: Probably in
collection of Cardinal Mazarin
(inv. no. 1286) in 1661; sale of
the collection of D. Potter, The
Hague, May 19, 1723 (lot 44);
collection of the 1st Earl of
Cadogan; collection of Sir
Robert Walpole, London, then
Houghton Hall, Norfolk;
acquired in 1779 with the
Walpole collection, Norfolk
Inv. no. GE 480

42
BONAVENTURA PEETERS
1614 Antwerp – 1652 Hoboken
Sea Harbour, 1640s
Oil on canvas, transferred from
panel in 1869. 46.5 × 63.5 cm
Initials bottom right: *BP*
Provenance: Acquired in 1834
from the collection of Páez de
la Cadena, Spanish ambassador
to the imperial court,
St. Petersburg
Inv. no. GE 2153

43
PEETER VAN DEN VELDE
1634 Antwerp – 1687 (?1707)
Antwerp
Castle on a River Bank, 1670s
Oil on canvas. 61.5 × 93.5 cm
Signed bottom left: *Peeter van*
den Velde
Provenance: Acquired in 1915
with the collection of P.P.
Semenov-Tyan-Shansky,
Petrograd
Inv. no. GE 2906

44
WILHELM SCHUBERT VON
EHRENBERG
1630 Germany – *c.* 1676
Antwerp
Interior of a Church, 1665
Oil on canvas. 104.5 × 116.5 cm
Signed and dated bottom right
corner: *van Ehrenberg 1665*
Provenance: Acquired before
1859; during the second half
of the nineteenth century
at Gatchina Palace, near
St. Petersburg; 1920 returned
to the Hermitage
Inv. no. GE 1441

45
HENDRICK VAN STEENWIJK THE
YOUNGER
c. 1580 Antwerp (?) – *c.* 1649
The Netherlands (?)
Interior of a Gothic Church,
c. 1610
Oil on panel. 94 × 125 cm
Provenance: Transferred in
1919 from the museum of the
Academy of Arts, Petrograd
Inv. no. GE 4360

46
HENDRICK VAN STEENWIJK THE
YOUNGER
c. 1580 Antwerp (?) – *c.* 1649
The Netherlands (?)
St. Jerome in his Study, 1634
Oil on panel. 28.5 × 22.9 cm
Signed and dated bottom left:
H V STEIN 1634
Provenance: Acquired between
1763 and 1773
Inv. no. GE 1894

47
PEETER NEEFFS THE YOUNGER
1620 Antwerp – after 1675
Antwerp
and Frans Francken the
Younger
1603 Antwerp – after 1667
Antwerp
Interior of the Church of St.
Charles Borromeo, Antwerp, late
1630s
Oil on canvas. 50 × 72 cm
Inscription left, on the column
base: *F.ffranck Fecit*
Provenance: Acquired before
1859
Inv. no. GE 2731

48
PEETER NEEFFS THE YOUNGER
1620 Antwerp – after 1675
Antwerp
Interior of Antwerp Cathedral,
c. 1655
Oil on panel, transferred from
panel in 1843. 49 × 64.5 cm
Signed right on the pillar: *peeter*
neffs
Provenance: Acquired in 1781
from the collection of Count
Baudouin, Paris
Inv. no. GE 1892

49
ANDRIES VAN EERTVELT
1590 Antwerp – 1652 Antwerp
Battle Between the Spanish Fleet
and Dutch Ships in May 1573
during the Siege of Haarlem,
c. 1625–27
Oil on canvas. 134 × 165.5 cm
Monogram centre bottom: *AVE*
Spanish inscription on the sail
of Neptune's trident:
VICTORIA QUE ARMADA/
REAL DE QUE ES GENERAL
DON/ FADRIQUE DE
TOLEDOTUVO EN/ EL
ESTRECHO CON NUEVE
NAOS/ SU ESQUADRA
CONTRAVENT [...]/ Y S [...] DE
OLANDES ES QUE VENIAN
DE/ LEVANTE [Victory in the
gulf by the royal armada,
brought by nine ships from the
Levant, under the command of
Don Fadrique of Toledo over the
squadron of insurgents and [...]
Dutch]
Provenance: Collection of S.N.
Plautin, St. Petersburg;
transferred in 1924 *via* the State
Museum Reserve
Inv. no. GE 6416

50
ANDRIES VAN EERTVELT
1590 Antwerp – 1652 Antwerp
Two Ships at Anchor, 1640s
Oil on canvas, transferred from
panel in 1854. 64 × 98 cm
Monogram left, on a floating
piece of wood: *AVE*
Provenance: Collection of I.P.
Balashov, St. Petersburg;
acquired in 1919
Inv. no. GE 5596

51
PAUL BRILL
1554 Antwerp – 1626 Rome
Mountainous Landscape, 1626
Oil on canvas. 75 × 103 cm
Signed and dated bottom left:
PAVOLO BRILLI 1626
Provenance: Acquired in 1769
with the collection of Count
Brühl, Dresden
Inv. no. GE 1955

52
JOOS MOMPER THE YOUNGER
1564 Antwerp – 1635 Antwerp
and Jan Brueghel the Elder
1568 Brussels – 1625 Antwerp
Mountainous Landscape with a Fallen Donkey, c. 1610
Oil on canvas, transferred from panel. 46 × 74.5 cm
Provenance: Collection of Prince D.M. Golitsyn, Vienna; after his death in 1793 passed to A.M. Golitsyn, Moscow; 1817–18 sold as part of the museum of the Golitsyn Hospital, Moscow; Prince S.M. Golitsyn, Moscow; collection of the latter's great-nephew, also S.M. Golitsyn; 1865–86, Golitsyn Museum, Moscow; transferred in 1886 from the Golitsyn Museum, Moscow
Inv. no. GE 448

53
LUCAS VAN UDEN
1595 Antwerp – 1672 Antwerp
and David Teniers the Younger
1610 Antwerp – 1672 Antwerp
Landscape with Hunters, 1640s
Oil on canvas. 87.5 × 147.0 cm
Provenance: Acquired in 1768 with the collection of Count Cobenzl, Brussels
Inv. no. GE 626

54
JAN WILDENS
1585–86 Antwerp – 1653 Antwerp
and Hans Jordaens III
c. 1595 Antwerp – *c.* 1643 Antwerp
Landscape with Christ and His Disciples on the Road to Emmaus, c. 1640
Oil on canvas. 123 × 168 cm
Provenance: Collection of A.V. Krivosheyn, St. Petersburg; transferred in 1924 *via* the State Museums Fund from the Lvova collection, Petrograd
Inv. no. GE 6319

55
JACQUES D'ARTHOIS
1613 Brussels – 1686 Brussels
Wooded Landscape with Men Driving Cows on the Road, c. 1635
Oil on canvas. 115 × 146 cm
Provenance: Acquired before 1859; in the 19th century kept at Gatchina Palace, near St. Petersburg; returned to the Hermitage in 1932
Inv. no. GE 8678

56
JAN SIBERECHTS
1627 Antwerp – *c.* 1703 London
Shepherdess, late 1660s
Oil on canvas. 103.5 × 77.5 cm
Provenance: Collection of Grand Duchess Maria Nikolayevna, St. Petersburg; collection S.V. Sheremetev, St. Petersburg; transferred in 1920 *via* the State Museums fund, from the collection of S.V. Sheremetev, Petrograd
Inv. no. GE 6240

57
CORNELIS HUYSMANS
1648 Antwerp – 1727 Mechelen
Wooded Landscape, n.d.
Oil on canvas. 81 × 116.5 cm
Provenance: Received before 1797
Inv. no. GE 656

58
JAN BRUEGHEL THE ELDER
(VELVET BRUEGHEL)
1568 Brussels – 1625 Antwerp
Wooded Landscape (The Rest on the Flight into Egypt), 1607
Oil on panel. 51.5 × 91.5 cm
Signed and dated bottom left: *BRUEGHEL 1607*
Provenance: Collection of Clemens August, Duke of Bavaria, Prince-Elector and Archbishop of Cologne (according to Cat. 1773–85); acquired in 1769 with the Count Brühl collection, Dresden
Inv. no. GE 424

59
PEETER SNEYERS
1681 Antwerp – 1752 Antwerp
Flowers, Fruits and a Hedgehog, c. 1725
Oil on canvas. 101.3 × 77 cm
Signed bottom right: *P.Snyers*
Provenance: Acquired with the collection of P.P. Semenov-Tyan-Shansky in 1915
Inv. no. GE 3448

60
FRANS SNYDERS
1579 Antwerp – 1657 Antwerp
Bowl of Fruit on a Red Tablecloth, 1640s
Oil on canvas, transferred from panel in 1867. 59.8 × 90.8 cm
Provenance: Acquired before 1797
Inv. no. GE 612

61
ADRIAEN VAN UTRECHT
1599 Antwerp – 1652 Antwerp
Still Life with Grapes, 1640s
Oil on canvas. 119 × 99 cm
Signed bottom left on the edge of the table: *A. van Uytrecht f.*
Provenance: Acquired before 1859
Inv. no. GE 660

62
JAN FYT
1611 Antwerp – 1661 Antwerp
Fruit and Parrot, 1645
Oil on canvas, transferred from panel in 1894. 58.3 × 90.7 cm
Signed right on the table edge: *Joannes. Fyt*
Provenance: Acquired in 1846, by bequest of D.P. Tatishchev, St. Petersburg
Inv. no. GE 613

63
DANIEL SEGHERS
1590 Antwerp – 1661 Antwerp
and Thomas Willeboirts Bosschaert
1613/14 Bergen-op-Zoom – 1654 Antwerp
Flower Garland with Jesus and St. John the Baptist as Children, 1651
Oil on canvas. 129 × 97.4 cm
Signed bottom right: *Daniel Seghers Soctis Jesu*
Provenance: Acquired in 1915, by bequest of V.P. Zurov, Tsarskoye Selo (near St. Petersburg)
Inv. no. GE 3468

64
NICOLAES VAN VERENDAEL
1640 Antwerp – 1691 Antwerp
Garland with a Bust of the Virgin, 1680s
Oil on canvas. 117 × 86.5 cm
Inscription on the pedestal of the bust (in two lines): *Hortvs Conclusus*
Provenance: Acquired between 1733 and 1783
Inv. no. GE 560

65
SEBASTIAEN BONNECROY
1618 – 1676; worked in Antwerp and The Hague
Still Life with a Skull (Wall in the Artist's Studio), 1668
Oil on canvas. 111 × 88 cm
Signed bottom left: *Sebastiaen Bonnecroy*; dated bottom right: *Fecit anno 1668*
Provenance: Acquired in 1939 through the Leningrad State Purchasing Commission from a private collection in Leningrad
Inv. no. GE 9229

66
FRANS SNYDERS
1579 Antwerp – 1657 Antwerp
Sketches of a Cat's Head, 1609
Oil on canvas, transferred from old canvas in 1850.
42.5 × 32.5 cm
Signed and dated bottom left: *F.Snyders 1609*
Provenance: Acquired from the collection of Jean de Jullienne, Paris, in 1767
Inv. no. GE 609

67
FRANS SNYDERS
Antwerp 1579 – Antwerp 1657
A Concert of Birds, 1630–40
Oil on canvas. 136.5 × 240 cm
Provenance: Collection of Grinling Gibbons, London; November 1722 acquired by Sir Robert Walpole at the sale of the Gibbons collection; collection of Sir Robert Walpole, London, then Houghton Hall, Norfolk; acquired in 1779 with the Walpole collection, Norfolk
Inv. no. GE 607

68
FRANS SNYDERS
1579 Antwerp – 1657 Antwerp
and Jan Boeckhorst (?)
1604 Münster – 1668 Antwerp
Cook at a Kitchen Table with Dead Game, 1636–38
Oil on canvas. 171 × 173 cm
Provenance: Acquired in 1764 with the collection of Johann Ernst Gotzkowsky, Berlin
Inv. no. GE 608

69
JAN FYT
1611 Antwerp – 1661 Antwerp
Dead Game and a Dog, c. 1655
Oil on canvas. 93.5 × 120 cm
Signed by the left edge, slightly below centre: *Joannes. Fyt*
Provenance: Acquired before 1797
Inv. no. GE 657

70
JAN FYT
1611 Antwerp – 1661 Antwerp
Hunting Trophy, c. 1645
Oil on canvas. 82 × 114 cm
Provenance: Collection of S.M. Golitsyn, Moscow; collection of M.K. Gorchakov, Petrograd; transferred *via* the State Museums Fund, Leningrad, in 1923
Inv. no. GE 6241

71
ALEXANDER ADRIAENSSEN
1587 Antwerp – 1661 Antwerp
Fish and Dead Game, 1643
Oil on canvas. 57.5 × 86.5 cm
Signed and dated left on the table leg: *Alex Adriaenssen f A 1643*
Provenance: Acquired from the collection of Prince Grigory Potemkin of Tauris in 1792; transferred to Pavlovsk Palace, near St. Petersburg in the 19th century; returned to the Hermitage in 1933
Inv. no. GE 7282, pendant to inv. no. GE 7281

72
ALEXANDER ADRIAENSSEN
1587 Antwerp – 1661 Antwerp
Fish, 1643
Oil on canvas. 59.5 × 85 cm
Signed left on the table leg: *Alex Adriaenssen fecit*
Provenance: See cat. 71
Inv. no. GE 7281, pendant to inv. no. GE 7282

73
PETER PAUL RUBENS
1577 Siegen – 1640 Antwerp
Pastoral Scene, c. 1635
Oil on canvas. 114.5 × 91 cm
Provenance: Probably sale of Domburg collection, Amsterdam, May 7, 1770 (lot 6); acquired before 1774.
Inv. no. GE 493

74
DAVID TENIERS THE YOUNGER
1610 Antwerp – 1690 Brussels
The Temptation of St. Anthony, 1650s
Jacopo da Voragine: *The Golden Legend XXI, 1*
Oil on canvas. 99 × 132 cm
Signed centre bottom on the stone: *D TENIERS*
Provenance: 1862 bequeathed to Academy of Arts, St. Petersburg; transferred in 1922 from the museum of the Academy of Arts, Petrograd. Formerly: collection of Count Nikolay Kushelev-Bezborodko, St. Petersburg
Inv. no. GE 3780

75
DAVID TENIERS THE YOUNGER
1610 Antwerp – 1690 Brussels
The Guardroom, 1642
Oil on canvas. 69 × 103 cm
Signed and dated bottom left:
DAVID, TENIERS AN 1642
Provenance: Before 1806 in the
collection of the Landgrave of
Hesse, Kassel; acquired in 1814
from the collection of Empress
Josephine at the Château de
Malmaison, near Paris
Inv. no. GE 583

76
DAVID TENIERS THE YOUNGER
1610 Antwerp – 1690 Brussels
*Portrait of the Members of the
Oude Voetboog Guild in Antwerp*,
1643
Oil on canvas. 135 × 183 cm
Signed and dated bottom left:
DAVID. TENIERS AN 1643
Provenance: Before 1806
collection of the Landgrave of
Hesse, Kassel; acquired in 1814
from the collection of Empress
Josephine at the Château de
Malmaison, near Paris
Inv. no. GE 572

77
DAVID TENIERS THE YOUNGER
1610 Antwerp – 1690 Brussels
*Landscape with Peasants before
an Inn, c.* 1635
Oil on canvas. 104.5 × 201.5 cm
Signed centre bottom on the
stone: *D T F*
Provenance: Acquired in 1781
from the collection of Count
Baudouin, Paris
Inv. no. GE 629, pendant to inv.
no. GE 628

78
DAVID TENIERS THE YOUNGER
1610 Antwerp – 1690 Brussels
*Landscape with a Maid at a Well,
c.* 1635
Oil on canvas, transferred from
panel. 104.5 × 202 cm
Signed centre bottom: *D.
TENIERS F*
Provenance: Acquired in 1781
from the collection of Count
Baudouin, Paris
Inv. no. GE 628, pendant to inv.
no. GE 629

79
DAVID TENIERS THE YOUNGER
1610 Antwerp – 1690 Brussels
Landscape with Peasants Bowling,
1640s
Oil on canvas. 61.5 × 89.5 cm
Signed centre bottom: *D.
TENIERS F*
Provenance: Acquired in 1781
from the collection of Count
Baudouin, Paris
Inv. no. GE 578

80
DAVID TENIERS THE YOUNGER
1610 Antwerp – 1690 Brussels
Reaping, c. 1645
Oil on canvas, transferred from
panel. 49.5 × 69.5 cm
Signed centre bottom: *D.
TENIERS F*
Provenance: Acquired in 1915
with the collection of P.P.
Semenov-Tyan-Shansky,
Petrograd
Inv. no. GE 2778

81
DAVID TENIERS THE YOUNGER
1610 Antwerp – 1690 Brussels
Village Festival, 1648
Oil on canvas. 97 × 129 cm
(published in error in Cat. 1958
and Cat. 1981 as 97 × 138 cm)
Signed and dated centre
bottom: *DAVID TENIERS F
1648*
Provenance: Collection of the
comtesse de Verrue, Paris;
collection of the marquis
d'Argenson, Paris; acquired in
1772 from the collection of the
duc de Choiseul, Paris
Inv. no. GE 593

82
DAVID TENIERS THE YOUNGER
1610 Antwerp – 1690 Brussels
Kermess, 1646
Oil on canvas, transferred from
old canvas in 1868.
97.2 × 130.5 cm
Signed bottom left: *DAVID
TENIERS FEC.* On the flag of
St. George the date: *1646*
Provenance: Collection of the
comtesse de Verrue, Paris;
collection of the marquis
d'Argenson, Paris; acquired in
1772 from the collection of the
duc de Choiseul, Paris
Inv. no. GE 594

83
DAVID TENIERS THE YOUNGER
1610 Antwerp – 1690 Brussels
Monkeys in a Kitchen, c. 1645
Oil on canvas, transferred from
panel in 1842. 36 × 50 cm
Signed bottom left:
D TENIERS F
Provenance: Before 1806
collection of the Landgrave of
Hesse, Kassel; acquired in 1814
from the collection of Empress
Josephine, Château de
Malmaison, near Paris
Inv. no. GE 568

84
DAVID TENIERS THE YOUNGER
1610 Antwerp – 1690 Brussels
The Kitchen, 1646
Oil on canvas. 171 × 237 cm
Signed and dated left on the
step: *DAVID TENIERS 1646*;
date repeated over the fireplace
on the drawing: *AN 1646*
Provenance: Collection of Sir
Robert Walpole, London, then
Houghton Hall, Norfolk;
acquired in 1779 with the
Walpole Collection, Norfolk
Inv. no. GE 586

85
ADRIAEN BROUWER
1605/06 Oudenaerde – 1638
Antwerp
*The Village Charlatan (Operation
for Stone in the Head), 1620s*
Oil on panel. 28.2 × 25 cm
Provenance: Acquired before
1859
Inv. no. GE 668

86
ADRIAEN BROUWER
1605/06 Oudenaerde – 1638
Antwerp
*Tavern Scene (The Village
Fiddler), c.* 1634
Oil on panel. 25 × 33.5 cm
Provenance: Acquired in 1770
with the collection of François
Tronchin, Geneva
Inv. no. GE 643

87
DAVID RYCKAERT III
1612 Antwerp – 1661 Antwerp
Peasant Woman with a Cat,
1640s
Oil on canvas, transferred from
panel in 1842. 28 × 34.8 cm
Provenance: Acquired in 1769
with the collection of Count
Brühl, Dresden
Inv. no. GE 653, pendant to
inv. no. GE 654

88
DAVID RYCKAERT III
1612 Antwerp – 1661 Antwerp
Peasant with a Dog, 1640s
Oil on canvas. 26.5 × 37 cm
Provenance: Acquired in 1769
with the collection of Count
Brühl, Dresden
Inv. no. GE 654, pendant to
inv. no. GE 653

89
BALTHASAR VAN DEN BOSSCHE
1681 Antwerp – 1715 Antwerp
A Sculptor's Studio, 1712
Oil on canvas. 66 × 86 cm
Half-erased signature and date
bottom left: *BVB ... F.1712*
Provenance: Transferred in 1918
from the Anichkov Palace,
Petrograd
Inv. no. GE 5718, pendant to
inv. no. GE 5719

90
BALTHASAR VAN DEN BOSSCHE
1681 Antwerp – 1715 Antwerp
A Painter's Studio, 1709
Oil on canvas. 66 × 84 cm
Signed and dated bottom left:
B.V. Bosche f.1709
Provenance: Acquired in 1918
from the collection of Prince
A.S. Dolgorukov, Petrograd
Inv. no. GE 5719, pendant to
inv. no. GE 5718

91
JAN MIEL
1599 Beveren-Waes (Antwerp) –
1664 Turin
The Charlatan, c. 1645
Oil on canvas. 60 × 74 cm
Inscription on the sign to right:
*Vero secret/ cont .../ [True Means
Against ...]*
Provenance: Acquired in 1802
from the collection of the Count
de Narp, St. Petersburg
Inv. no. GE 646

92
PEETER SNEYERS
1681 Antwerp – 1752 Antwerp
Autumn, 1727
Oil on canvas. 84.5 × 69 cm
Signed bottom right on the
pedestal: *P.Snijers*
Inv. no. GE 674

93
PEETER SNEYERS
1681 Antwerp – 1752 Antwerp
Winter, 1727
Oil on canvas. 82 × 68 cm
Half erased signature bottom
left: *P [...] Snijers f.*
Provenance: Acquired in 1769
with the collection of Count
Brühl, Dresden; from after 1797
to 1920 kept at Gatchina Palace,
near St. Petersburg; returned to
the Hermitage in 1920
Inv. no. GE 672

94
PETER PAUL RUBENS
1577 Siegen – 1640 Antwerp
*The Descent from the Cross,
c.* 1612
Pen and brown ink, brown
wash, over black chalk. Laid
down. 43.5 × 38 cm
Top left corner, author's
inscription in pen and brown
ink: *Videntur ex Daniele
Volterano/ Unis qui quasi tenes
tamen relinquit/ Item alius qui
diligentissime/ descendit ut laterus
opem.*
Bottom right, inscription in pen
and brown ink, crossed out, of
which only the last word is
legible: *Rubens*
Provenance: Acquired in 1768
(mark L. 2061) from the
collection of Count Carl
Cobenzl, Brussels (mark L.
2858b)
Inv. no. 5496

95
PETER PAUL RUBENS
1577 Siegen – 1640 Antwerp
*Sheet of Studies with the
"Caritas," c.* 1625
Black and red chalk, brown
wash. 33.9 × 45.5 cm
Provenance: Acquired in 1768
(mark L. 2061) from the
collection of Count Carl
Cobenzl, Brussels (mark L.
2858b)
Inv. no. 5513

96
RUBENS AND AN ASSISTANT
1577 Siegen – 1640 Antwerp
*St. Roch, Patron of the Plague-
stricken*, 1626
Black chalk, pen and brown and
black wash, heightened with
white. Laid down.
52.6 × 35.8 cm
Provenance: Acquired in 1768
(mark L. 2061) from the
collection of Count Carl
Cobenzl, Brussels (mark L.
2858b)
Inv. no. 5522

97
PETER PAUL RUBENS
1577 Siegen – 1640 Antwerp
Rubens Vase, 1622–26
Pen and brown ink. Laid down.
20.1 × 14.8 cm
Provenance: Acquired in 1768
(mark L. 2061) from the
collection of Count Carl
Cobenzl, Brussels (mark L.
2858b)
Inv. no. 5430

98
PETER PAUL RUBENS
1577 Siegen – 1640 Antwerp
*Design for the Printer's Mark of
Jan van Meers, c.* 1630
Pen and black ink, grey wash
over black chalk. Laid down.
13 × 15 cm
Provenance: Acquired in 1768
(mark L. 2061) from the
collection of Count Carl
Cobenzl, Brussels (mark L.
2858b)
Inv. no. 5418

99
PETER PAUL RUBENS
1577 Siegen – 1640 Antwerp
Classical Figure ("Seneca"),
c. 1600–05
Black chalk. Laid down.
46 × 32 cm
Provenance: Acquired in 1768
(mark L. 2061) from the
collection of Count Carl
Cobenzl, Brussels (mark L.
2858b)
Inv. no. 5499

100
ANTHONY VAN DYCK
1599 Antwerp – 1641 London
(Formerly attributed to Rubens)
Mars and Venus, c. 1621
Black chalk. Laid down.
45.8 × 31.4 cm
Provenance: Acquired in 1768
(mark L. 2061) from the
collection of Count Carl
Cobenzl, Brussels (mark L.
2858b)
Inv. no. 5498

101
ANTHONY VAN DYCK
1599 Antwerp – 1640 London
Pentecost, n.d.
Pen and brown ink, brown, grey
and green wash, heightened
with white. 25.8 × 21.7 cm
(irregular shape)
Provenance: Sold in 1741 from
the collection of Pierre Crozat,
Paris; sold in 1767 from the
collection of Jean de Jullienne,
Paris; library of the Academy of
Arts, St. Petersburg; transferred
in 1924 from the library of the
Academy of Arts, St. Petersburg
Inv. no. 14537

102
ANTHONY VAN DYCK
1599 Antwerp – 1641 London
Rest on the Flight into Egypt,
1629–30
Pen and brown ink, brown
wash. Laid down. 12.2 × 17.2 cm
Provenance: Acquired in 1768
(mark L. 2061) from the
collection of Count Carl
Cobenzl, Brussels (mark L.
2858b)
Inv. no. 5870

103
JACOB JORDAENS
1593 Antwerp – 1678 Antwerp
The Crucifixion, 1658
Black and red chalk,
watercolour and white
highlights. The sheet composed
of several pieces of paper,
rounded at the top. Lined. 59 ×
36.8 cm
Bottom right, author's
inscription in pen and brown
ink: *27 martii 1658 Hage.*
Bottom centre: *Overmidst de
Joden Teeckens begeeren En de
Griecken Wysheyd soecken, doch
wy Predicken Christum den
gekruysten, den Joden Een
Ergenisse en der griecken een
dwaesheydt maer beyde den Joden
En griecken die predicken wy de
wysheydt Godts en de Cracht
Godts, I, cor.2 [sic].22.23.24.*
Beneath the drawing in a
cartouche on the mount (dating
from the Cobenzl collection), an
old inscription in pen and
brown ink: *Jordaens*
Provenance: Acquired in 1768
(mark L. 2061) from the
collection of Count Carl
Cobenzl, Brussels (mark L.
2858b)
Inv. no. 4203

104
JACOB JORDAENS
1593 Antwerp – 1678 Antwerp
*The Infant Jupiter Suckled by the
Goat Amalthea, c.* 1640
Black chalk, pen and brush and
brown ink, heightened with
white-blue and white-rose body-
colour. 37.0 × 46.0 cm
Provenance: acquired in 1768
(mark L. 2061) from the
collection of Count Carl
Cobenzl, Brussels (mark L.
2858b).
Inv. no. 4200

105
JACOB JORDAENS
1593 Antwerp – 1678 Antwerp
Decorative Frieze, 1630s
Red chalk with brown wash,
body-colour heightened with
white. 11.0 × 135.5 cm
Provenance: transferred in 1923
from the Library of the former
Stieglitz School of Technical
Drawing.
Inv. no. 33446

106
FRANS FRANCKEN THE YOUNGER
1581 Antwerp – 1642 Antwerp
The Feast of Herod, c. 1620
Pen and brown ink, brown, blue
and red wash, over black chalk.
24 × 14 cm
Provenance: Acquired in 1768
(mark L. 2061) from the
collection of Count Carl
Cobenzl, Brussels (mark L.
2858b)
Inv. no. 3109

107
HENDRICK DE CLERK
c. 1570 Brussels – 1630 Brussels
Allegory of the Truce of 1609, n.d.
Pen and brown ink, brown
wash, gouache, gold (in the coat
of arms). 25.4 × 33.6 cm
Bottom right corner, an old
inscription in pen and brown
ink: *Hen: de Clerck. Bruxel: F.*
Below in pen and red ink: *N 6*
Provenance: Collection of
Prosper Henricus Lankrink,
London (mark L. 2090);
collection of Count Ivan
Betskoy, St. Petersburg
(mark L. 2878a); from 1767
in the Academy of Arts,
St. Petersburg; transferred in
1924 from the Academy of Arts
Inv. no. 15123

108
ABRAHAM VAN DIEPENBEECK
bapt. 1596 's-Hertogenbosch –
1675 Antwerp
and Peter Paul Rubens
1577 Siegen – 1640 Antwerp
The Marriage of the Virgin, n.d.
Black chalk, grey wash and
white highlights, corrections in
pen and brown ink.
57.0 × 43.5 cm
Provenance: acquired in 1768
(mark L. 2061) from the
collection of Count Carl
Cobenzl. Formerly collection of
Pierre Crozat, Paris; collection
of Count Carl Cobenzl, Brussels
(mark L. 2858b).
Inv. no. 5523

109
CASPAR DE CRAYER
1584 Antwerp – 1669 Ghent
The Martyrdom of St. Peter,
c. 1650
Oil on paper. Laid down.
34.5 × 28 cm
Provenance: Acquired in 1768
(mark L. 2061) from the
collection of Count Carl
Cobenz, Brussels (mark L.
2858b)
Inv. no. 2061

110
ERASMUS QUELLINUS THE
YOUNGER
1607 Antwerp – 1678 Antwerp
Design for a Triumphal Arch,
c. 1657
Pen and brown ink, grey wash,
heightened with white on green
paper. 50 × 63.5 cm
Signed bottom left corner:
Erasmus Quellinus F.
In the centre on the pediment:
Don juan.
Beneath the right trophy: *o
valenc : lib : res gerere et caj...
ostendere civibus caj...*
On the socle beneath the image
of Heracles defeating the
Nemean lion: *Acheloum Lictâ
vine* (in pen and brown ink)
On the reverse: *n° 48 12
teeckeninge* (in pen and black
ink)
Provenance: Collection of A.
Beurdeley, Paris (mark L. 421);
library of the Stieglitz School of
Technical Drawing; transferred
in 1923 from the library of the
former Stieglitz School
Inv. no. 40794

111
ABRAHAM VAN DIEPENBEEK
bapt. 1596 's-Hertogenbosch –
1675 Antwerp
*The Martyrdom of Jesuits in
Japan*
Pen and brown ink, blue wash,
heightened with white.
29.5 × 22.0 cm
Provenance: acquired in 1768
(mark L. 2061) from the
collection of Count Carl
Cobenzl, Brussels (mark L.
2858b).
Inv. no. 2782

112
PETER PAUL RUBENS
1577 Siegen – 1640 Antwerp
*Sheet of Studies: Head of a Man
Looking Up, Hand, and Lower
Part of a Head in Profile,*
1618–19
Black and white chalk on
yellow-grey paper. Laid down.
32 × 22 cm
Beneath the drawing in a
cartouche on the mount (dating
from the Cobenzl
collection) is an old inscription
in pen and brown ink: *Rubens*
Provenance: Acquired in 1768
(mark L. 2061) from the
collection of Count Carl
Cobenzl, Brussels (mark L.
2858b)
Inv. no. 5454

113
PETER PAUL RUBENS
1577 Siegen – 1640 Antwerp
Head of a Youth looking up,
1615–16
Charcoal and white chalk on
grey paper. Laid down.
34 × 27 cm
Provenance: Acquired in 1768
(mark L. 2061) from the
collection of Count Carl
Cobenzl, Brussels (mark L.
2858b)
Inv. no. 5888

114
ANTHONY VAN DYCK
1599 Antwerp – 1641 London
Portrait of Cornelis Schut,
c. 1628–36
Black chalk, brown wash,
contours traced for transfer.
Laid down. 23 × 19 cm
Provenance: Acquired in 1768
(mark L. 2061) from the
collection of Count Carl
Cobenzl, Brussels (mark L.
2858b)
Inv. no. 5907

115
Anthony van Dyck
1599 Antwerp – 1641 London
Portrait of Pieter Brueghel the Younger, c. 1628–32
Black chalk. Laid down.
23 × 19 cm
Provenance: Acquired in 1768 (mark L. 2061) from the collection of Count Carl Cobenzl, Brussels (mark L. 2858b)
Inv. no. 5908

116
Jan Boeckhorst
1605 Münster – 1668 Antwerp
Young Lady in a Beret, n.d.
Black and red chalk, black wash, watercolour. 175 × 150 mm
Provenance: Acquired in 1768 (mark L. 2061) from the collection of Count Carl Cobenzl, Brussels (mark L. 2858b)
Inv. no. 4330

117
Jacob Jordaens
1593 Antwerp – 1678 Antwerp
Study of a Young Woman's Head, 1630s
Black and red chalk.
16.0 × 14.1 cm
Provenance: acquired by the Hermitage in 1923. Formerly Suchtelen collection, St. Petersburg (mark L. 2332); E. Schwarz collection, St. Petersburg.
Inv. no. 27328

118
Peter Paul Rubens
1577 Siegen – 1640 Antwerp
Landscape with a Dam, 1635–40
Gouache, tempera and black chalk over a sketch in black chalk. 43.5 × 59.0 cm
Provenance: acquired in 1768 (mark L. 2061) from the collection of Count Carl Cobenzl, Brussels (mark L. 2858b).
Inv. no. 5518

119
Gijsbrechts Leytens (Master of Winter Landscapes)
1586 (?) Antwerp – 1643/56
Winter Scene, n.d.
Pen and brown and blue ink.
18.6 × 29.0 cm
Provenance: acquired in 1768 (mark L. 2061) from the collection of Count Carl Cobenzl, Brussels (mark L. 2858b).
Inv. no. 459

120
Tobias Verhaecht
1561 Antwerp – 1631 Antwerp
Landscape with Tobias and Angel, n.d.
Pen and brown ink, blue wash.
17.9 × 27.1 cm
Provenance: Collection of Count Ivan Betskoy, St. Petersburg (mark L. 2878a); from 1767 in the Academy of Arts, St. Petersburg; transferred in 1924 from the Academy of Arts.
Inv. no. 15090

121
Lucas van Uden
1595 Antwerp – 1672 Antwerp
Landscape with a Hut by a River, c. 1645
Pen and brown ink, brown, grey and blue wash. 22.5 × 38 cm
Bottom edge on the stone, signed and dated in pen and brown ink: *Lucas Van Uden 164[5?]*
Provenance: Acquired in 1768 (mark L. 2061) from the collection of Count Carl Cobenzl, Brussels (mark L. 2858b)
Inv. no. 6234

122
Jan Brueghel the Elder (Velvet Brueghel)
1568 Brussels –1625 Antwerp
Winter Landscape, 1611
Pen and brown ink, grey and blue wash. 19.2 × 27.0 cm
Provenance: acquired in 1768 (mark L. 2061) from the collection of Count Carl Cobenzl, Brussels (mark L. 2858b).
Inv. no. 470

123
Jan Fyt
1611 Antwerp – 1661 Antwerp
Fox Hunt, n.d.
Gouache over black chalk on yellowish-grey paper; squared in white chalk. 51 × 51.8 cm
Provenance: Acquired in 1768 (mark L. 2061) from the collection of Count Carl Cobenzl, Brussels (mark L. 2858b)
Inv. no. 3083

124
Jan Fyt
1611 Antwerp – 1661 Antwerp
Study of a Dog, n.d.
Black chalk, body-colour.
50.1 × 39 cm
Provenance: Collection of Count Ivan Betskoy, St. Petersburg (mark L.2878a); from 1767 in the Academy of Arts, St. Petersburg; transferred in 1924 from the Academy of Arts.
Inv. no. 15279

125
Jacob Jordaens
1593 Antwerp – 1678 Antwerp
The Light Once Loved by Me, I Give, Dear Child, to Thee, n.d.
Pen and brown ink, brown and blue wash over black chalk.
13.0 × 20.1 cm
Provenance: donated to the Hermitage in 1924. Formerly collection of Nikolay Vorobyov, St. Petersburg.
Inv. no. 14233

126
Sebastiaen Vrancx
1573 Antwerp – 1647 Antwerp
A Village Plundered by Marauders, n.d.
Pen and brown ink.
16.0 × 31.0 cm
Provenance: transferred in 1924 from the Academy of Arts, St. Petersburg. Formerly collection of Count Ivan Betskoy, St. Petersburg (mark L. 2878a); from 1767 in the Academy of Arts, St. Petersburg.
Inv. no. 14237

127
Nef
Cast, chased and partially gilded silver
Flanders, Bruges, 1596
Marks: Bruges with the year 1595–1596 (half chipped)
Height 31 cm
Provenance: Acquired in 1987 *via* the Hermitage Purchasing Commission
Inv. no. E 17345

128
Aquamanile
Cast, chased and partially gilded silver
Christian Hornung the Elder (Heppigen ? – Augsburg 1680)
Germany, Augsburg, *c.* 1665
Marks: Augsburg, Hornung
Height 32.6 cm
Provenance: Transferred to the Hermitage in 1925 from the State Valuables Store
Inv. no. E 7411

129
Display Platter with Solomon and the Queen of Sheba
Wrought, chased and partially gilded silver
Central relief made in Augsburg, Germany, 1630s–40s Platter made by Johan Nutzel, Stockholm, Sweden, 1680s–90s
Marks on the dish: Stockholm, Nutzel
77.5 × 92.5 cm
Provenance: Presented to Peter I by Charles XII of Sweden; Winter Palace
Inv. no. E 8766

130
Dish with a Bacchanalian Scene
Wrought, chased and gilded silver
Abraham Warnberger the Younger (? 1632 – Augsburg 1704)
Germany, Augsburg, 1670–75
Marks: Augsburg (unclear), Warnberger, St. Petersburg control with the year 17 ... (half chipped), assay master N.N., fineness 78
64.5 × 56 cm
Provenance: Presented to Peter I by Charles XII of Sweden; transferred in 1762 from Oranienbaum Palace, near St. Petersburg, to the Winter Palace; in 1904 moved from the Hofmarshal's Office to the "Museum" in the Winter Palace
Inv. no. E 8713

131
Rhyton
Wrought, cast, chased, etched and gilded silver
Christoph Erhart (? – Augsburg 1604)
Germany, Augsburg, 1570–75
Marks: Augsburg, Erhart
Height 22 cm; diameter 12.1 cm
Provenance: Acquired in 1908 from the collection of Grand Duke Alexey Alexandrovich
Inv. no. E 476

132
Drinking Cup in the form of an Owl
Chased and gilded silver
Flanders, early 17th century
Height 17 cm; diameter of base 7.8 cm
Provenance: Collection of A. Ricard-Abelheimer until 1886; purchased for the museum of the Stieglitz School of Technical Drawing in 1886; transferred to the Hermitage from the museum of the former Stieglitz School in 1925
Inv. no. E 11922

133
Tankard with The Judgement of Paris
Wrought, cast, chased and partially gilded silver
Germany, Augsburg (?), 1650s
Mark: Paris import of the 19th century
Height 26.6 cm; diameter of top 14 cm; diameter of base 17 cm
Provenance: Collection of the Princes Yusupov; transferred to the Hermitage in 1923
Inv. no. E 11050

134
Tankard with Hercules and Omphale
Wrought, cast, chased and partially gilded silver
Klaus Schmidt (? – before 1694)
Germany, Lübeck, 1680s
Marks: Lübeck, Schmidt
Height 18.1 cm
Provenance: Collection of the Princes Yusupov; transferred to the Hermitage in 1922
Inv. no. E 12773

135
Ostrich Cup
Coconut mounted with cast, chased and gilded silver
Germany, early 17th century
Unmarked
Height 31.6 cm
Provenance: Transferred to the Hermitage from the Winter Palace
Inv. no. E 2509

136
Coconut Cup
Carved coconut and walnut with cast, chased and gilded silver mounts
Czechoslovakia, Olomutz (?), maker SG (GS), mid-17th century (1655?)
Engraved on lid: *MG – OB anno 1655*, a cross and *DM JC*
Marks: Olomutz (?), maker, fineness 14
Height 30.5 cm; diameter of base 10.5 cm
Provenance: Winter Palace; transferred to the Hermitage in 1925 from the Cottage Palace, Peterhof, near St. Petersburg
Inv. no. E 7935

137
Basin with Gigantomachy (Battle of the Giants)
Wrought, chased, punched and gilded silver
Elias Drentwett the Elder (*c.* 1588 – Augsburg 1643)
Germany, Augsburg, 1630s
Marks: Augsburg, Drentwett
Diameter 72 cm
Provenance: Collection of Peter I, kept in the Winter Palace and, in the 19th century, in the Gallery of *Objets de Vertu*; transferred to the Hermitage from the Winter Palace
Inv. no. E 8767

138
Display Platter with Allegory of Learning
Wrought, chased and gilded silver
Marx Weinold (? – Augsburg 1700)
Germany, Augsburg, 1680s
Marks: Augsburg (half chipped off), Weinold
71 × 63 cm
Provenance: Collection of the Princes Yusupov, St. Petersburg; transferred to the Hermitage in 1923
Inv. no. E 13211

139
Shell Cup with Neptune as a Naiad
Bullmouth helmet shell mounted with cast, chased and gilded silver
Germany, maker MW, 1640s–60s
Marks: maker
Height 50 cm
Provenance: Transferred to the Hermitage in 1934 *via* Antikvariat (state trading organization responsible for selling art treasures).
Inv. no. E 13568

140
Tulip Cup
Cast, wrought, chased and partially gilded silver
Germany, Nuremberg, maker CWM, 1660s–70s
Marks: Nuremberg, maker, control mark for St. Petersburg with the year 1753, fineness 77
Height 36 cm
Provenance: In the Gallery of *Objets de Vertu* during the 19th century; transferred to the Hermitage from the Winter Palace
Inv. no. E 8713

141
Standing Cup and Cover
Cast, chased and gilded silver
Adam van Vianen (Utrecht 1569–1627)
Holland, Utrecht, 1594
Marks: Utrecht, year, maker
Height 59.5 cm
Provenance: Transferred to the Hermitage in 1925 from the museum of the former Stieglitz School
Inv. no. E 13312

142
Standing Cup and Cover
Cast, chased, engraved and gilded silver
Holland, Haarlem, 1604 (?)
Marks: The Netherlands, Haarlem, unknown maker
Height 28.5 cm; diameter of base 10 cm
Provenance: In the collection of A. Ricard-Abenheimer, Frankfurt am Main until 1886; purchased for the museum of the Stieglitz School of Technical Drawing in 1886; transferred to the Hermitage in 1925 from the museum of the former Stieglitz School in 1925
Inv. no. E 13467

143
Display Platter with Diana and Actaeon
Chased and gilded silver
Holland (?), *c.* 1662
48.5 × 39.3 cm
Provenance: Collection of the Princes Yusupov; transferred to the Hermitage in 1922
Inv. no. E 13150

144
Display Platter with Vertumnus and Pomona
Chased and gilded silver
Jan Bogaert (*fl.* 1600s)
Holland, Amsterdam, 1665
Marks: Amsterdam, year, control for 1689, maker
Diameter 52 cm
Provenance: Collection of the Princes Yusupov; transferred to the Hermitage in 1922
Inv. no. E 13848

145
Wager Cup
Cast, wrought, chased and gilded silver
Wolf Eispinger (?–1606)
Germany, Nuremberg, 1580s
Marks: Nuremberg, Eispinger
Height 26 cm
Provenance: Collection of Countess E.V. Shuvalova; transferred to the Hermitage in 1925 from the Shuvalov House Museum
Inv. no. E 13753

146
Bratina
Chased, engraved and gilded silver
Holland, Amsterdam, 1664
Marks: Amsterdam control for the 17th century, year
Height 16.8 cm; diameter 13.4 cm
Provenance: Collection of the Counts Stroganov; transferred to the Hermitage in 1922
Inv. no. E 9022

147
Ewer
Cast and gilded bronze inlaid with carved coral
Sicily, Trapani, 1630–50
Height 27 cm; width of base 17.3 cm
Provenance: Transferred to the Hermitage from the Winter Palace
Inv. no. E 2708

148
Clock
Cast, chased and gilded silver with bronze, metal alloys and glass
Spain, 1660–70
Height 27.8 cm; diameter of base 16 cm
Provenance: Collection of Countess E.V. Shuvalova; transferred to the Hermitage in 1925 from the Shuvalov House Museum
Inv. no. E 14103

149
Reliquary
Cast, chased, enamelled and gilded silver
Spain, Valencia, mid-17th century
Marks: Valencia, unknown (half chipped)
Height 56 cm; base 22 × 25.5 cm
Provenance: Transferred to the Hermitage in 1925 from the museum of the former Stieglitz School
Inv. no. E 15341

150
Chalice
Cast, chased, engraved, enamelled and gilded silver with bronze and copper
Spain, mid-17th century
Height 30.7 cm; diameter of bowl 9.2 cm
Provenance: Transferred to the Hermitage in 1925 from the museum of the former Stieglitz School
Inv. no. E 15045

151
Cameo with Joseph and his Brothers
Sardonyx with gold mount
Southern Italy, *c.* 1240
Inscribed in Hebrew at top right: "Get you up in peace unto your father" (Genesis 44:17)
6.4 × 7.5 cm
Provenance: Property of Charles V in 14th century, Château de Vincennes, Paris; collection of Peter Paul Rubens, Antwerp; bequeathed to Albert Rubens in 1640; in the 18th century owned by Jacopo Nani, Venice, A. Pelle and Dazincours, Paris and William Hamilton, Naples; acquired in 1805 from the collection of N. Khitrovo, St. Petersburg
Inv. no. K 690

152
Cameo with Allegory of Constancy and Valour (?)
Sardonyx with gold mount
Italy, 16th century
3.7 × 3.3 cm
Provenance: Owned by Peter Paul Rubens, Antwerp, during the 17th century; acquired in the late 18th century
Inv. no. K 4844

153
Cameo with Temple of Venus
Sardonyx with gold mount
Italy, late 16th – early 17th century
Greek inscription on statue base: *XAPITOY*
5.8 × 7 cm
Provenance: Owned by Peter Paul Rubens, Antwerp, during the 17th century; acquired in 1792 from the collection of Jean-Baptiste Casanova, Dresden
Inv. no. 1979

154
Beaker
Slightly smoky colourless glass gilded and blown in ice-glass technique
Antwerp (?), late 16th – early 17th century
Height 25.4 cm, diameter 16.9 cm
Provenance: Acquired in 1885 with the collection of A.P. Basilewski, Paris.
Inv. no. F 487

155
Roemer
Blown and gilded green transparent glass
The Netherlands, mid-17th century
Height 25 cm; diameter 11 cm
Provenance: Collection of A. Ricard-Abenheimer, Frankfurt am Main until 1886; transferred in 1933 from the museum of the former Baron Stieglitz School, Leningrad
Inv. no. K 2346

156
Serpent Goblet
Slightly smoky colourless glass with turquoise glass threads and diamond engraving
Venice or The Netherlands, first half 17th century
Height 16 cm, diameter 7.2 cm
Provenance: Acquired in 1960 *via* the Hermitage Purchasing Commission
Inv. no. 26666

157
Bottle
Mould-blown blue transparent glass with brass mount
The Netherlands, second half 17th century
Height 25 cm
Provenance: Collection of A. Ricard-Abenheimer, Frankfurt am Main until 1886; transferred 1933 from the museum of the former Baron Stieglitz School, Leningrad
Inv. no. K 2087

158
Figure of Venus
Ivory
Flanders, Antwerp, workshop
of Peter Paul Rubens, *c.* 1639
Height 55 cm
Provenance: Collection of the
Princes Yusupov; transferred
in 1923
Inv. no. E 12261

159
The Crucifixion
Ivory and ebony
Gabriel Grupello (?; Grammont
1644 – Ehrenstein 1730)
Flanders, before 1695
Height 58 cm
Provenance: Transferred in
1925 from the State Museums
Fund
Inv. no. E 12264

160
Tankard with Allegorical Figures
Ivory with silver gilt mounts
and glass finial
Lucas Fayd'herbe (?; Mechelen
1617–1697)
Flanders, first half 17th century
Height 38.5 cm
Marked on mounts: Augsburg
and AW (Andreas Wickert,
1660–1661; see Rosenberg
1922, nos. 540f.).
Provenance: Acquired before
1859
Inv. no. E 7285

161
*Figure of a Putto Seated on a
Skull*
Ivory on wood base
Flanders, 17th century
Height 14.1 cm
Provenance: Transferred in
1925 from the Shuvalov House
Museum; formerly collection of
Countess E.V. Shuvalova
Inv. no. E 11310

162
Figure of a Sleeping Putto
Ivory
Artus Quellinus (?;
1609–1668)
Flanders, mid-17th century
Length 12 cm
Provenance: Transferred in
1886 from the Golitsyn
Museum, Moscow (Golitsyn
Guide 1882, no. 290).
Inv. no. E 7282

163
*Figure of a Putto Astride a
Tortoise*
Ivory with wood base
Flanders, 17th century
Height 15.5 cm
Provenance: Transferred in
1930 from the museum of the
Society for the Encouragement
of the Arts, Leningrad (Museum
Catalogue 1904, p. 445)
Inv. no. E 15020

164
*Display Platter with Hunting
Scenes and Diana and Acteon*
Ivory and reindeer horn
Johann Michael Maucher
(Schwäbisch Gmünd 1645 –
Würzburg 1701)
Germany, second half 17th
century
59 × 73 cm
Provenance: Acquired before
1811
Inv. no. E 7267

165
Adoration of the Magi
Ivory
Germany, 17th century
49 × 30 cm
Provenance: Acquired in 1923
from the collection of F.I.
Paskevich (Paskevich Collection
1885, no. 1476)
Inv. no. 14900

166
Cupid Pendant
Chased and enamelled gold
with diamonds, rubies and
pearls
The Netherlands, *c.* 1580
11 × 6.1 cm
Provenance: Transferred 1882
from the Kremlin Armoury,
Moscow
Inv. no. E 4791

167
Mermaid Pendant
Polished baroque pearl, chased,
engraved and enamelled gold,
diamonds and sapphires
The Netherlands, *c.* 1610–20
7.7 × 3.6 cm
Provenance: Acquired before
1839
Inv. no. E 2650

168
Ship Pendant
Baroque pearl, rubies,
emeralds, glass, and chased,
engraved and enamelled gold
Italy (?), 1590–1600
4 × 3.8 cm
Provenance: Acquired before
1859
Inv. no. E 2651

169
Ship Pendant
Emeralds and chased, engraved
and enamelled gold
Spain, 1580s–90s
9.3 × 6 cm
Provenance: Entered the Winter
Palace before 1789
Inv. no. E 2944

170
Parrot Pendant
Chased and enamelled gold,
pearls, rubies, emeralds and
diamonds
Germany or Spain, late 16th
century
9 × 4.3 cm
Provenance: Entered the Winter
Palace before 1789
Inv. no. E 2941

171
Swan Pendant
Baroque pearls, chased and
enamelled gold, rubies and
diamonds
The Netherlands, *c.* 1590
9.2 × 5.9 cm
Provenance: From the mid-19th
century in the Gallery of *Objets
de Vertu*
Inv. no. E 2652

172
Footed Cup with Lid
Carved and polished bloodstone
mounted with enamelled gold
Ottavio Miseroni (Milan 1567 –
Prague 1624) *and* Hans
Vermeyen (?; before 1559–1608)
Prague, *c.* 1605
10.1 × 6.1 cm
Provenance: Acquired before
1859
Inv. no. E. 1867

173
Footed vessel
Carved and ground smoky
quartz mounted with chased,
engraved and gilded silver
Workshop of Dionisio Miseroni
(1607? – Prague 1661)
Prague, mid-seventeenth
century
9.6 × 19.3 × 7.5 cm
Provenance: Acquired before
1859
Inv. no. E 2371

174
Pair of Pistols
Wood, steel damascened with
gold, engraved and gilded
bronze
The Netherlands, Maastricht,
c. 1640
Overall length 75.6 cm; length
of barrel 55.8 cm; calibre 14 mm
Provenance: Transferred in 1885

from the Arsenal of the
imperial summer palace at
Tsarskoye Selo
Inv. no. ZO 302 (a,b)
Selected literature: Tarassuk
1972, nos. 123, 124, p. 166;
Soldatenko 1996, HSP 12–13,
pp. 388–89

175
Flintlock Gun
Wood with welded and carved
copper and steel
The Netherlands, *c.* 1630–40
Overall length 124.1 cm; length
of barrel 85.4 cm; calibre
44.5 mm
Provenance: Transferred in
1903 from the collection of
Count S.D. Sheremetev,
St. Petersburg
Inv. no. ZO 5346
Selected literature: Lenz 1895,
no. 876; Tarassuk 1972, no. 127,
p. 166

176
Wheel-lock Gun
Wood inlaid with engraved
mother-of-pearl, etched steel,
iron and brass
The Netherlands, *c.* 1610–20
Overall length 158 cm; length of
barrel 119.9 cm; calibre
18.5 mm
Provenance: Transferred in 1885
from the Arsenal of the
imperial summer palace at
Tsarskoye Selo
Inv. no. ZO 5827
Selected literature: Sayger 1840,
vol. I, no. 165, p. 121; Tarassuk
1972, no. 84, p. 162; Soldatenko
1996, HSP 2, pp. 370–71

177
Morion
Etched and chased steel
Germany, *c.* 1605–10
Height 34 cm
Provenance: Transferred in 1885
from the Arsenal of the
imperial summer palace at
Tsarskoye Selo
Inv. no. ZO 3962
Unpublished; not previously
exhibited

178
Burgonet
Forged steel
Germany, late 16th century
Height 25 cm
Provenance: Transferred in 1885
from the Arsenal of the
imperial summer palace at
Tsarskoye Selo
Inv. no. ZO 6042
Unpublished; not previously
exhibited

179
Morion
Forged and patinated steel and
copper
Germany, *c.* 1600
Height 31 cm
Provenance: Transferred from
the Museums Fund
(government body set up after
the Revolution to control and
reallocate nationalized art
objects) in the 1920s or 1930s
Inv. no. ZO 3204
Unpublished; not previously
exhibited

180
Half-armour
Forged and engraved steel and
copper
Germany or Switzerland (?),
c. 1600
Provenance: Transferred in 1885
from the Arsenal of the
imperial summer palace at
Tsarskoye Selo
Inv. no. ZO 3340
Unpublished; not previously
exhibited

181
Small sword
Chased and carved steel and
iron
Germany, late 17th century
Provenance: Transferred in 1885
from the Arsenal of the
imperial summer palace at
Tsarskoye Selo
Inv. no. ZP 1010
Unpublished; not previously
exhibited

182
Small sword
Chased and carved steel and
iron
Germany, 17th century
Provenance: Transferred in 1885
from the Arsenal of the
imperial summer palace at
Tsarskoye Selo
Inv. no. ZO 4507
Unpublished; not previously
exhibited

183
Small sword
Chased and carved steel and
iron
Germany, Solingen, 17th
century
Provenance: Transferred in 1885
from the Arsenal of the
imperial summer palace at
Tsarskoye Selo
Inv. no. ZO 4523
Unpublished; not previously
exhibited

BIBLIOGRAPHY

Adler 1980
W. Adler: *Jan Wildens. Der Landschaftsmitarbeiter des Rubens*, Fridingen, 1980

Adler 1982
W. Adler: *Landscapes and Hunting Scenes*, vol. I, *Landscapes*, in the series Corpus Rubenianum Ludwig Burchard, part XVIII, London, 1982

Aedes 1752
Aedes Walpolianae: or, A Description of the collection of Pictures at Houghton Hall in Norfolk, The Seat of the Rght Honourable Sir Robert Walpole, Earl of Orford, 1747; all references in this book are to the 2nd revised and more complete edition of 1752, reprinted unaltered in 1767

Archive of Ancient Acts 1822
Manuscript in the Archive of Ancient Acts, Moscow, for 1822, fund 1290, *opis* 3, *delo* 2415

Babina 1985
N.P. Babina: "O syuzhete A. Brauvera, izvestnoy pod nazvaniyem 'Derevenskiy sharlatan'" [On A. Brouwer's Subject Known Under the Title of 'The Village Charlatan'], *Soobshcheniya Gosudarstvennogo Ermitazha* [Reports of the State Hermitage], L (1985), pp. 7–8

Babina 1986a
N.P. Babina in *Antwerpse Meesters uit de Hermitage, Leningrad*, exh. cat., Antwerp, Rubenshuis, 1986, nos. 3, 8, 12, 13

Babina 1986b
N.P. Babina: "Vnov opredelyonnaya kartina Yana Petersa v sobranii Ermitazha"

[A Newly Identified Painting by Jan Peters in the Hermitage Collection], *Pamyatniki kultury. Novyye otkrytiya. Yezhegodnik 1984* [Cultural Monuments. New Discoveries. Annual for 1984], Leningrad, 1986, pp. 222–27, note 14

Babina 1989a
N.P. Babina: *David Teniers the Younger (Masters of World Painting)*, Leningrad, 1989

Babina 1989b
N.P. Babina: "K voprosu o sotrudnichestve khudozhnikov XVII veka: neizvestnyye peyzazhi Alessandro Saluchchi i Yana Milya" [On the Collaboration Between Artists in the seventeenth Century: Unknown Landscapes by Alessandro Salucci and Jan Miel], in *Issledovaniya, poiski, otkrytiya. Kratkiye tezisy dokladov nauchnoy konferentsii k 225–letiyu Ermitazha* [Research, Exploration, Discoveries. Brief Outlines of Papers from a Scholarly Conference on the 225th Anniversary of the Hermitage], Leningrad, 1989, pp. 12–14

Babina 1991
N.P. Babina in *The Masterpieces of European Paintings of the Hermitage*, Seoul, 1991

Babina 1993
N.P. Babina: "Kartiny Khendrika van Steynveka Mladshego v sobranii Ermitazha" [Pictures by Hendrick van Steenwyck the Younger in the Hermitage Collection], in *Problemy razvitiya zarubezhnogo iskusstva. Sbornik nauchnykh trudov, Chast I*

[Questions in the Development of Foreign Art. Anthology of Scholarly Papers, Part I], Repin Institute of Painting, Sculpture and Architecture, St. Petersburg, 1993, pp. 43–49

Babina 1995
N.P. Babina: *Arkhitecturnyy zhanr vo flamandskoy zhivopisi XVII veka (po materialam ermitazhnoy kollektsii)* [The Architectural Genre in Flemish Seventeenth-century Painting (From Material in the Hermitage Collection)], summary of a dissertation presented for the title of Candidate of Art History, St. Petersburg, 1995

Babina 1999a
N.P. Babina: "Kollektsiya kartin flamandskikh masterov arkhitekturnogo zhanra v sobranii Ermitazha" [Collection of Paintings by Flemish Masters in the Architectural Genre in the Hermitage Collection], *Pamyatniki kultury. Novyye otkrytiya. Yezhegodnik 1998* [Cultural Monuments. New Discoveries. Annual for 1998], Moscow, 1999, pp. 278–91

Babina 1999b
N.P. Babina: "Novoye o kartinakh Fransa Frankena II v sobranii Ermitazha" [New Information on Paintings by Frans Francken in the Hermitage Collection], in *Ermitazhnyye chteniya pamyati V.F. Levinsona-Lessinga 1972. Kratkoye soderzhaniye dokladov* [Hermitage Readings in Memory of V.F. Levinson-Lessing 1972. Brief Content of Papers], St. Petersburg, 1999, pp. 10–13

Balis 1999
A. Balis: "Van Dyck's Drawings after the Antique," *Colloquium Van Dyck, Antwerp, 19 May 1999*, to be published 2001

Bank 1977
A. Bank: *Byzantine Art in the Collections of Soviet Museums*, Leningrad, 1977

Barnes 1990
S. Barnes in *Anthony van Dyck*, exh. cat., Washington, D.C., National Gallery of Art, 1990

Bastet 1981
F.L. Bastet: "Oudheden uit Rubens' verzameling te Leiden," *Nederlands Kunsthistorisch Jaarboek*, 235 (1981)

Baudouin 1968
F. Baudouin: "Een Jeugwerk van Rubens 'Adam en Eva', en de relatie van Veen en Rubens," *Antwerpen (Tijdschrift der Stad Antwerpen)*, 2 (July 1968)

Baudouin 1999
F. Baudouin in *4 × Anthony van Dyck. 4 × Nicolas Rockox. A selection from the portrait collection of burgomaster Nicolas Rockox*, exh. cat., Antwerp, Rockoxhuis, Stichting Nicolas Rockox vzw, 1999

Baumstark 1974
R. Baumstark: "Ikonographische Studien zu Rubens' Kriegs- und Friedensallegorien," *Aachener Kunstblätter*, XLV (1974), pp. 125–234

Bazin 1958
G. Bazin: *Musée de l'Ermitage*, Paris, 1958

Bialostocki *et al.* 1964
J. Bialostocki *et al.*: *Galeria Malarstwa Obcego; przewodnik*, Warsaw, 1964

Bodart 1990
D. Bodart in *Pietro Paolo Rubens (1577–1640)*, exh. cat., Padua, Palazzo della ragione, 1990

Bode 1924
W. Bode: *Adriaen Brouwer*, Berlin, 1924

Bottacin, Limentani Virdis 1990
Pietro Paolo Rubens, exh. cat. by F. Bottacin and C. Limentani Virdis, Padua, Palazzo della Ragione; Rome, Palazzo delle Esposizioni; Milan, Società per le Belle Arti ed Esposizione Permanente, 1990

van den Branden 1883
F. Jos. van den Branden: *Geschiedenis der Antwerpsche Schilderschool*, Antwerp, 1883

Brown 1982
C. Brown: *Van Dyck*, Oxford, 1982

Brown 1991
C. Brown: *Van Dyck Drawings*, exh. cat., New York, Pierpont Morgan Library, 1991

Brown 1996
C. Brown: *Making and Meaning: Rubens's Landscapes*, exh. cat., London, National Gallery, 1996

Brown 1999
C. Brown in *Van Dyck. 1599–1641*, exh. cat., Antwerp, Koninklijk Museum voor Schone Kunsten; London, Royal Academy of Arts, 1999

Burchard, d'Hulst 1956
Tekeningen van P.P. Rubens, exh. cat. by L. Burchard and R.-A. d'Hulst, Antwerp, Rubenshuis, 1956

Burchard, d'Hulst 1963
L. Burchard and R.-A. d'Hulst: *Rubens Drawings*, 2 vols., Brussels, 1963

Byrne 1935
E.H. Byrne: "Some Medieval Gems and Relative Values," *Speculum*, 10 (1935), pp. 177–87

Carnavalet 1977
L'Art de l'estampe et la Révolution française, exh. cat., Paris, Musée Carnavalet, 27 June – 20 November 1977

Castan 1885
A. Castan: *Une visite au Saint Ildefonce de Rubens*, Besançon, 1885

Cat. 1773–85
[E. Munich:] "Catalogue raisonné des tableaux qui se trouvent dans les galeries, salons et cabinets du palais impérial de Pétersbourg," MS, 3 vols., I: 1773–1783, III: 1785; Hermitage Archives

Cat. 1958
Gosudarstvennyy Ermitazh. Otdel Zapadnoyevropeyskogo iskusstva. Katalog Zhivopis [The State Hermitage. Department of Western European Art. Catalogue of Painting], I: Italy, Spain, France, Switzerland; II: The Netherlands, Flanders, Belgium, Holland, Germany, Austria, England, Sweden, Denmark, Norway, Finland, Hungary, Czechoslovakia, Leningrad and Moscow, 1958

Cat. 1981
Gosudarstvennyy Ermitazh. Zapadnoyevropeyskaya zhivopis. Katalog 2. Niderlandyye, Flandriya, Belgiya, Gollandiya, Germaniya, Avstriya, Angliya, Daniya, Norvegiya, Finlyandiya, Shvetsiya, Vengriya, Polsha, Rumyniya, Chekhoslovakiya [The State Hermitage. Western European Painting. Catalogue 2. The Netherlands, Flanders, Belgium, Holland, Germany, Austria, England, Denmark, Norway, Finland, Sweden, Hungary, Poland, Romania, Czechoslovakia], Leningrad, 1981

Cat. Crozat 1755
Catalogue des tableaux du cabinet de M. Crozat, baron de Thiers, Paris, 1755

Cat. Stroganoff 1793
Catalogue raisonné des tableaux qui composent la collection du Comte A. de Stroganoff, St. Petersburg, 1793

Cat. Stroganoff 1800
Catalogue raisonné des tableaux qui composent la collection du Comte A. de Stroganoff, St. Petersburg, 1800

Coll. Paul Delaroff 1914
Collection Paul Delaroff. Catalogue des tableaux anciens des écoles allemande, anglaise, espagnole, flamande, française, hollandaise, italienne, suisse des XVe, XVIe, XVIIe, XVIIIe siècles, Paris, 1914

Compte-rendue 1874
Compte-rendu de la Commission Impériale archéologique, 1870–1871, St. Petersburg, 1874

Cust 1900
L. Cust: *Anthony van Dyck: A Historical Survey of his Life and Work*, London, 1900

Dalton 1915
O.M. Dalton: *Catalogue of the Engraved Gems of the Post-Classical Period in the Department of British Medieval Antiquities in the British Museum*, London, 1915

Delen 1930
A.J.J. Delen: *Iconographie van Antwerpen*, Brussels, 1930

Delen 1938
A.J.J. Delen: *Catalogue des dessins anciens. Ecole flamande et hollandaise du Cabinet d'Estampes de la Ville d'Anvers*, Brussels, 1938

Demus et al. 1977
Peter Paul Rubens, 1577–1640, exh. cat. by Klaus Demus et al., Vienna, Kunsthistorisches Museum, 1977

Denucé 1932
J. Denucé: *Antwerp Art Galleries. Inventories of the Art Collections in Antwerp in the Sixteenth and Seventeenth Centuries*, 's-Gravenhage, 1932, in the series *Historical Sources for the Study of Flemish Art*, vol. II

Depauw 1988
Meesterwerken uit het Stedelijk Prentenkabinet van Antwerpen. Tekeningen uit de XVIde en XVIIde eeuw, exh. cat. by C. Depauw, Antwerp, 1988

Depauw, Ger Luijten 1999
C. Depauw and Ger Luijten: *Anthony van Dyck as a Printmaker*, exh. cat., Antwerp, Museum Plantin-Moretus/ Stedelijk Prentenkabinet; Amsterdam, Antwerpen Open/Rijksmuseum, 1999

Derviz 1941
P.P. Derviz: "Neskolko pamyatnikov ispanskogo iskusstva 16–17 vekov v Ermitazhe" [Several Monuments of sixteenth and seventeenth-century Spanish Art in the Hermitage], in *Trudy Gosudarstvennogo Ermitazha* [Papers of the State Hermitage], Leningrad, 1941,

Distelberger 1997
R. Distelberger: "Thoughts on Rudolfine Art in the 'Court Workshop' in Prague," in *Rudolf II and Prague*, London, 1997

Dobroklonsky 1926
M.V. Dobroklonsky: *Dessins des maîtres anciens. Musée de l'Ermitage*, exh. cat., Leningrad, State Hermitage Museum, 1926

Dobroklonsky 1930–1931a
M.V. Dobroklonsky: "Einige Rubenszeichnungen in der Ermitage," *Zeitschrift für bildende Kunst*, 64 (1930–31), pp. 31–37

Dobroklonsky 1930–1931b
M.V. Dobroklonsky: "Van Dyck Zeichnungen in der Ermitage," *Zeitschrift für bildende Kunst*, 64 (1930–31), pp. 237–43

Dobroklonsky 1935
M.V. Dobroklonsky: "Graficheskoye naslediye Rubensa" [Rubens's Graphic Heritage], *Iskusstvo*, 5 (1935)

Dobroklonsky 1940
M.V. Dobroklonsky: *Risunki Rubensa* [Rubens Drawings], Moscow, 1940

Dobroklonsky 1949
M.V. Dobroklonsky: "Risunki Verkhagta" [Drawings by Verkhagt], in *Trudy otdela zapadnoyevropeyskogo iskusstva Gosudarstvennogo Ermitazha* [Papers of the Department of Western European Art of the State Hermitage], vol. II, 1949 [Gritsay had vol. III for 1949]

Dobroklonsky 1955
M.V. Dobroklonsky: *Gosudarstvennyy Ermitazh. Risunki flamandskoy shkoly 17–18 vekov* [State Hermitage: Drawings of the Flemish School, Seventeenth–Eighteenth Centuries], Moscow, 1955

Dobroklonsky 1961
M.V. Dobroklonsky: *Grafika*, State Hermitage Museum, Leningrad, 1961

Duerloo 1998
L. Duerloo in *Albert et Isabelle. 1598–1621*, exh. cat., Brussels, Musées Royaux d'Art et d'Histoire, 1998

Duerloo 1999
L. Duerloo in *El Arte en la carte de los archiduques Alberto de Austria e Isabel Clara Eugenia (1598–1633). Un Reino imaginado*, exh. cat., Madrid, Palacio Real, 1999

Durey 1977
Durey: *Le siècle de Rubens dans les collections publiques françaises*, 12, Paris, 1977

Egerton 1999
J. Egerton in *Van Dyck. 1599–1641*, exh. cat., Antwerp, Koninklijk Museum voor Schone Kunsten; London, Royal Academy of Arts, 1999

Ernst 1928
S. Ernst: "L'Exposition de la peinture française des XVIIe et XVIIIe siècles au Musée de l'Ermitage à Petrograd. 1922–1925," *Gazette des Beaux-Arts*, 17 (1928), pp. 246–47

Ertz 1979
K. Ertz: *Jan Brueghel der Altere (1568–1625). Die Gemälde. Mit kritischem Œuvrekatalog*, Cologne, 1979

Ertz 1986
K. Ertz: *Josse de Momper der Jüngere. Die Gemälde mit kritischem Œuvrekatalog*, Freren, 1986

Evers 1942
H.G. Evers: *Peter Paul Rubens*, Munich, 1942

Evers 1943
H.G. Evers: *Rubens und sein Werk*, Neue Forschungen, Brussels, 1943

Felkersam 1915a
A.Y. Felkersam: "Slonovaya kost i yeyo primeneniye v iskusstve" [Elephant Ivory and Its Use in Art], *Staryye gody* [Days of Yore], October 1915

Felkersam 1915b
A.Y. Felkersam: "Gornyy khrustal i yego primeneniye v iskusstve" [Rock Crystal and its Use in Art], *Staryye gody* [Days of Yore], December 1915

Fokker 1931
T.H. Fokker: *Jan Siberechts. Peintre de la paisanne flamande*, Brussels and Paris, 1931

Foulon 1971–72
N. Foulon: *Johan Boeckhorst 1605–1668. Zijn Leven en zijn Werk*, diss., University of Ghent, 1971–72

Freedberg 1978
D. Freedberg: "A Source for Rubens's Modello of the Assumption and Coronation of the Virgin: A Case Study in the Response to Images," *The Burlington Magazine*, CXX (1978), pp. 432–41

Freedberg 1984
D. Freedberg: *The Life of Christ After the Passion*, in the series Corpus Rubenianum Ludwig Burchard, part VII, London and New York, 1984

Freedberg 1994
D. Freedberg: "Van Dyck and Virginio Cesarini: A Contribution to the Study of Van Dyck's Roman Sojourns," in S.J. Barnes and A.K. Wheelock, Jr.: *Van Dyck 350*, exh. cat., Washington, D.C., National Gallery of Art, 1994, pp. 153–56

Friedländer 1964
W. Friedländer: "Early to Full Baroque. Cigoli and Rubens," in *Studien zur Toskanischen Kunst: Festschrift für Ludwig Heydenreich*, Munich, 1964

Fubini, Held 1964
G. Fubini and J.S. Held: "Padre Resta's Rubens Drawings after Ancient Sculpture," *Master Drawings*, II, 1964

Glück, Haberditzl 1928
G. Glück and F.M. Haberditzl: *Die Handzeichnungen von Peter Paul Rubens*, Berlin, 1928

Glück 1931
Van Dyck. Des Meisters Gemälde in 571 Abbildungen, ed. G. Glück, 2nd edn, vol. XIII in the series Klassiker der Kunst in Gesamtausgaben, Stuttgart and Berlin, 1931

Goldschmidt, Weitzmann 1979
A. Goldschmidt and K. Weitzmann: *Die bisantinischen Elfenbeinskulpturen des X–XIII Jahrhunderts*, II, no. 10, pl. 3

Golitsyn Guide 1882
Ykazatel Golitsynskogo muzeya [Guide to the Golitsyn Museum], Moscow, 1882

Greindl 1956
E. Greindl: *Les Peintres flamands de nature morte au XVIIe siècle*, Brussels, 1956

Greindl 1983
E. Greindl: *Les Peintres flamands de nature morte au XVIIe siècle*, Sterrebeek, 1983

Gritsay 1977
N.I. Gritsay: "Portrety Yakoba Iordansa v Ermitazhe" [Portraits by Jacob Jordaens in the Hermitage], in *Trudy Gosudarstvennogo Ermitazha* [Papers of the State Hermitage], XVIII, 1977, pp. 83–85

Gritsay 1979
N.I. Gritsay in *Yakob Iordans (1593–1678). Zhivopis. Risunok. Katalog vystavki k 300-letiyu so dnya smerti Ya. Iordansa* [Jacob Jordaens (1593–1678). Painting. Drawing. Catalogue of an Exhibition on the 300th Anniversary of the Death of J. Jordaens], exh. cat., Leningrad, State Hermitage Museum, 1979

Gritsay 1983
N.I. Gritsay in *Seventeenth-Century Dutch and Flemish Paintings and Drawings from the Hermitage*, Leningrad, exh. cat., Osaka, Museum of Art, 1983

Gritsay 1986
N.I. Gritsay: "O nekotorykh osobennostyakh ikonografii rannikh bol'shikh natyurmortov Fransa Sneydersa" [On Some Peculiarities of the Iconography in the Large Early Still Lifes of Frans Snyders], in: *Veshch' v iskusstve. GMII im. A. S.*

Pushkina. Materialy nauchnoy konferentsii [The Object in Art. Pushkin Museum of Fine Arts. Materials from a Scholarly Conference], 17 (1984), Moscow, 1986, pp. 65–73

Gritsay 1989
N.I. Gritsay: *Ermitazh. Flamandskaya zhivopis XVII veka. Ocherk-putevoditel* [The Hermitage. Flemish Seventeenth-century Painting. Essay Guide], Leningrad, 1989

Gritsay 1990
N.I. Gritsay in *Master Paintings from the Hermitage Museum*, exh. cat., Nara Prefectural Museum of Art, 1990

Gritsay 1991
N.I. Gritsay in *Rubens (1577–1640)*, exh. cat., Punkaharju, Finland, Retretti Art Center, 1991

Gritsay 1993a
N.I. Gritsay: " 'Soyuz Zemli i Vody' Rubensa. Ikonografiya" [Rubens's 'Union of Earth and Water.' Iconography], in the anthology *Problemy razvitiya zarubezhnogo iskusstva. Sbornik nauchnykh trudov, Chast I* [Questions in the Development of Foreign Art. Anthology of Scholarly Papers, Part I], Repin Institute of Painting, Sculpture and Architecture, St. Petersburg, 1993, pp. 49–56

Gritsay 1993b
N.I. Gritsay in *L'Age d'or flamand et hollandais. Collections de Catherine II. Musée de l'Ermitage, Saint-Pétersbourg*, exh. cat., Musée des Beaux-Arts de Dijon, 1993

Gritsay 1994a
N.I. Gritsay: "O tak nazyvayevym 'Portrete skulptora' Petera Franshua v sobranii Ermitazha" [On the so-called 'Portrait of a Sculptor' by Peeter Franchoys in the Hermitage Collection] in: *Ermitazhnyye chteniya pamyati V.F. Levinsona-Lessinga* [Hermitage Readings in Memory of V.F. Levinson-Lessing], St. Petersburg, 1994

Gritsay 1994b
N.I. Gritsay in *Treasures from the Hermitage, St. Petersburg*, The European Fine Art Fair, Maastricht, 1994, no. 28, p. 72

Gritsay 1996
N.I. Gritsay: *Anthony van Dyck*, Bournemouth and St. Petersburg, 1996

Gritsay 1996–97
N.I. Gritsay in *British Art Treasures from Russian Imperial Collections in the Hermitage*, ed. by B. Allen and L. Dukelskaya, Yale Center for British Art, New Haven CT; Toledo Museum of Art, Toledo OH; St. Louis Art Museum, St. Louis MI, 1996–97

Gritsay 1998
N.I. Gritsay: *Staatliche Eremitage. Die heroischen Apotheosen des Peter Paul Rubens. Rubensskizzen aus der staatlichen Eremitage, Sankt-Petersburg und der Alten Pinakothek, München*, exh. cat., St. Petersburg, State Hermitage Museum, 1998

Grossmann 1951
F. Grossmann: "Holbein, Flemish Painting and Everhard Jabach," *The Burlington Magazine*, XCIII (January 1951), pp. 16–25

Hackenbroch 1979
Y. Hackenbroch: *Renaissance Jewellery*, London, 1979

Hairs 1965
M.-L. Hairs: *Les Peintres flamands de fleurs au XVIIème siècle*, Brussels, 1965

Hairs 1985
M.-L. Hairs: *The Flemish Flower Painters in the Seventeenth Century*, Brussels, 1985

Härting 1983
U.A. Härting: *Studien zur Kabinettbildmalerei des Frans Francken II. 1581–1642*, Hildesheim, Zürich and New York, 1983

Härting 1989
U. Härting: *Frans Francken der Jüngere (1581–1642)*, Freren, 1989

Held 1940
J.S. Held: "Jordaens' Portraits of His Family," *The Art Bulletin*, 22 (1940), pp. 70–82

Held 1959
J.S. Held: *Rubens: Selected Drawings*, 2 vols., London, 1959

Held 1980
J.S. Held: *The Oil Sketches of Peter Paul Rubens: A Critical Catalogue*, 2 vols., Princeton NJ, 1980

Held 1982
J.S. Held: *Rubens and his Circle*, Princeton NJ, 1982

Held 1985
J.S. Held: "Nachträge zum Werk des Johann Bockhorst (alias Jan Boeckhorst)", *Westfalen*, 63 (1985), pp. 14–37

Held 1986
J.S. Held: *Rubens: Selected Drawings*, Mt Kisco, 1986

Hodge 1977
R. Hodge: "A Carracci Drawing in the Studio of Rubens," *Master Drawings*, 15, 1977

Hoet, Terwesten 1752–70
G. Hoet: *Catalogus of naamlyst van schildereyen, met derzelver pryzen, zedert een langen reeks van jaaren zoo in Holland als op andere plaatsen in het openbaar verkogt ...* vols. I–II, 's-Gravenhage, 1752; P. Terwesten: *Catalogus of naamlyst van schilderyen ... zedert den 22 aug. 1752 tot den 22 Nov. 1768 ... verkogt ...*, vol. III, 's-Gravenhage, 1770; reprint ed. Soest, 1976

Hollstein 1949–81
F.W.H. Hollstein: *Dutch and Flemish Etchings, Engravings and Woodcuts. 1450–1700*, 24 vols., Amsterdam, 1949–81

d'Hulst 1956
R.-A. d'Hulst: *De tekeningen van Jakob Jordaens. Bijdrage tot de geschiedenis van de XVIIe-eeuwse kunst in de Zuidelijke Nederlanden*, Brussels, 1956

d'Hulst 1974
R.-A. d'Hulst: *Jordaens Drawings*, Monographs of the National Centrum voor de Plastische Kunsten van de XVIde en XVIIde eeuw, 5, 4 vols., Brussels, 1974

d'Hulst 1977
R.-A. d'Hulst in *P.P. Rubens. Paintings – Oil Sketches – Drawings*, exh. cat., Antwerp, Koninklijk Museum voor Schone Kunsten, 1977

d'Hulst 1993
R.-A. d'Hulst in *Jacob Jordaens (1593–1678). Paintings and Tapestries. Drawings and Engravings*, exh. cat., Antwerp, Koninklijk Museum voor Schone Kunsten, 1993

d'Hulst, Vey 1960
Antoon van Dyck: Tekeningen en Olieverfschetsen, exh. cat. by R.-A. d'Hulst and H. Vey, Antwerp, Rubenshuis; Rotterdam, Boymans–van Beuningen Museum, 1960

Hunter-Stiebel 2000
Penelope Hunter-Stiebel, ed.: *Stroganoff: The Palace and Collections of a Russian Noble Family*, exh. cat., Portland OR, Portland Art Museum, 2000

Inventory 1859
"Opis predmetam, nakhodyashchimsya v Galereye dragotsennostey veshchey vedeniya II Otdeleniya Imperatorskogo Ermitazha" [Inventory of Objects in the Gallery of *Objets de Vertu* under the Control of the II Department of the Imperial Hermitage], MS, Hermitage Archive, St. Petersburg, 1859

D. Jaffé 1988
D. Jaffé: *Rubens' Self-portrait in Focus*, exh. cat., Canberra, Australian National Gallery, August 13 – October 30, 1988

D. Jaffé 1992
D. Jaffé in *Esso Presents Rubens and the Renaissance*, exh. cat., Canberra, Australian National Gallery, 1992

Jaffé 1963
M. Jaffé: "Peter Paul Rubens and the Oratorian Fathers," *Proporzioni*, IV (1963)

Jaffé 1968
Jacob Jordaens (1593–1678), exh. cat. by M. Jaffé, Ottawa, National Gallery of Canada, 1968

Jaffé 1971
M. Jaffé: "Rubens and Snyders, a Fruitful Partnership," *Apollo*, 93 (1971), pp. 184–96

Jaffé 1977
M. Jaffé: *Rubens and Italy*, Oxford, 1977

Jaffé 1989
M. Jaffé: *Rubens. Catalogo completo*, Milan, 1989

Judson, van de Velde 1977
J.R. Judson, C. van de Velde: *Book Illustrations and Title-pages*, 2 vols., in the series Corpus Rubenianum Ludwig Burchard, part XXI, London, 1982

Kahsnitz 1979
R. Kahsnitz: "Staufische Kameen. Zur Forschungsstand nach dem Tode von Hans Wentzel, zugleich ein Rückblick auf die Ausstellung," in *Die Zeit der Staufer*, V, Stuttgart, 1979, pp. 477–520

Kalnitskaya 1995
E.Y. Kalnitskaya: "Kollektsiya zhivopisi imperatora Pavla I v Mikhaylovskom zamke" [Emperor Paul I's Collection of Paintings in the Mikhail Castle], in the anthology *Chastnoye kollektsionerovaniye v Rossii* [Private Collecting in Russia], *Vipperovskiye chteniya 1994* [Wipper Readings 1994], XXVII, Moscow, 1995, pp. 76–85

Kamenskaya 1934–36
T. Kamenskaya: "Zeichnungen Jacob Jordaens' in der Ermitage," *Belvedere*, 1934–36, pp. 199–207

Kieser 1931
E. Kieser: "Tizians und Spaniens Einwirkungen auf die späteren Landschaften des Rubens," *Münchner Jahrbuch der bildenden Kunst*, VIII, no. 4, 1931

Klinge 1991
M. Klinge: *David Teniers the Younger*, exh. cat., Antwerp, Museum voor Schone Kunsten, 1991

Koslow 1995
S. Koslow: *Frans Snyders. The Noble Estate: Seventeenth-century Still-life and Animal Painting in the Southern Netherlands*, Antwerp, 1995

Kren 1978
T.J. Kren: *Jan Miel (1599–1664): A Flemish Painter in Rome*, PhD thesis, 2 vols., New Haven CT, 1978

Kris 1929
E. Kris: *Meister und Meisterwerke der Steinschneiderkunst in der italienischen Renaissance*, Vienna, 1929

Kube 1925
A.N. Kube: *Gosudarstvennyy Ermitazh. Reznaya kost. Katalog* [State Hermitage. Carved Ivory. Catalogue], Leningrad, 1925

Kuznetsov 1965–66
Risunki Rubensa v muzeyakh SSSR [Rubens Drawings in USSR Museums], exh. cat. by

Yu. Kuznetsov, Leningrad, State Hermitage Museum; Moscow, Pushkin Museum, 1965

Kuznetsov 1966
Yu. Kuznetsov: *Zapadnoyevropeyskiy natyurmort* [Western European Still Life], Leningrad and Moscow, 1966

Kuznetsov 1970
Yu. Kuznetsov: *Capolavori fiamminghi e ollandesi*, Milan, 1970

Kuznetsov 1972–73
Yu. Kuznetsov: *Hollandse en Vlaamse tekeningen uit de zeventiende eeuw: Verzameling van de Hermitage, Leningrad, en het Museum Poesjkin, Moskou*, exh. cat. by Yuri Kuznetsov and T. Tsezhkovskaya, Brussels, Koninklijke Bibliotheek Albert; Rotterdam, Boymans–van Beuningen Museum; Paris, Institut Néerlandais, 1972–73

Kuznetsov 1974
Yu. Kuznetsov: *Risunki Rubensa* [Rubens Drawings], Moscow, 1974

Kuznetsov 1976–78
Yu. Kuznetsov: "Neu bestimmte Zeichnungen von P.P. Rubens," *Gentse bijdragen tot de kunstgeschiednis*, XXIV (1976–78)

Kuznetsov 1978
Yu. Kuznetsov: *Rubens i flamandskoe barokko. Vystavka k 400-letiyu so dnya rozhdeniya P.P. Rubensa. 1577–1977* [Rubens and the Flemish Baroque. Exhibition on the 400th Anniversary of the Birth of P.P. Rubens. 1577–1977], Leningrad, State Hermitage Museum, 1978

Kuznetsov 1979
Yu. Kuznetsov: *Yakob Iordans (1593–1678). Zhivopis. Risunok. Katalog vystavki k 300-letiyu so dnya smerti Ya. Iordansa* [Jacob Jordaens (1593–1678). Painting. Drawing. Catalogue of an Exhibition on the 300th Anniversary of the Death of J. Jordaens], Leningrad, State Hermitage Museum, 1979

Lahrkamp 1982
H. Lahrkamp: "Der 'Lange Jan'. Leben und Werk des Barockmalers Johann Bockhorst aus Munster," *Westfalen*, 60 (1982), pp. 1–198

Lapkovskaya 1971
E.A. Lapkovskaya: "Dve figury slonovoy kosti po risunkam Georga Petelya" [Two Ivory Figures Designed by Georg Petel], *Soobshcheniya Gosudarstvennogo Ermitazha* [Bulletin of the State Hermitage], 33 (1971)

Larionov 1991
A. Larionov in *Rubens (1577–1640)*, exh. cat., Punkaharju, Finland, Retretti Art Center, 25 May – 1 September 1991

Larionov 1998
A. Larionov in *Master Drawings from the Hermitage and Pushkin Museums*, exh. cat., New York, Pierpont Morgan Library, 25 September 1998 – 10 January 1999

Larsen 1980
E. Larsen: *L'opera completa di Van Dyck*, 2 vols., Milan, 1980

Larsen 1988
E. Larsen: *The Paintings of Anthony van Dyck*, 2 vols., Freren, 1988

Leningrad 1973
M.Y. Kryzhanovskaya, E.A. Lapkovskaya, L.I. Faenson: *Zapadnoyevropeyskaya reznaya kost IX–XIV vv. iz sobraniya Ermitazha* [Western European Carved Ivory of the Ninth to Fourteenth Centuries], exh. cat., Leningrad, State Hermitage Museum, 1973

Leningrad 1978
Rubens i flamandskoye barokko [Rubens and Flemish Baroque Art], exh. cat., Leningrad, State Hermitage Museum, 1978

Levinson-Lessing 1926
V.F. Levinson-Lessing: *Sneyders i flamandskiy natyurmort* [Snyders and the Flemish Still Life], Leningrad, 1926

Lieven 1902
G.E. Lieven: *Putevoditel po Galereye Dragotsennostey i Kabinetu Petra Velikogo* [Guide to the Gallery of *Objets de Vertu* and the Cabinet of Peter the Great], St. Petersburg, 1902

Linnik 1965
I.V. Linnik: "Kartina Fransa Sneydersa po eskizu Rubensa" [A Painting by Frans Snyders from a Sketch by Rubens], in *Trudy Gosudarstvennogo*

Ermitazha [Papers of the State Hermitage], 1965, pp. 178–86

Linnik 1980
I. Linnik: *Gollandskaya zhivopis XVII veka i problemy atributsii kartin* [Dutch Seventeenth-century Painting and Questions in the Attribution of Paintings], Leningrad, 1980

Livret 1838
Livret de la Galerie Impériale de l'Hermitage de Saint-Pétersbourg. Contenant l'explication des tableaux qui la composent, avec de courtes notices sur les autres objects d'art ou de curiosité qui y sont exposés, St. Petersburg, 1838

Longhi 1927
R. Longhi: "La Notte del Rubens a Fermo," *Vita artistica*, September 1927, pp. 191–97

Luckhardt 1990
J. Luckhardt: *Jan Boeckhorst: 1604–68; Maler der Rubenszeit*, exh. cat., Antwerp, Rubenshuis; Münster, Westfälisches Landesmuseum für Kunst und Kulturgeschichte, 1990

Lukin 1811
I. Lukin: *Opisaniye imeyushchimsya v Ermitazhe tokarnym i reznym veshcham* [Description of the Turned and Carved Objects in the Hermitage], St. Petersburg, 1811

Lurie 1995
Van Dyck and his Age, exh. cat. by D.J. Lurie, Tel Aviv Museum of Art, 1995–96

Magurn 1971
R.S. Magurn: *The Letters of Peter Paul Rubens*, Cambridge MA, 1971

Malinovsky 1990
Jacob Stählin: *Zapiski Yakoba Stelina ob izyashchnykh iskusstvakh v Rossi* [Jacob Stählin's Notes on the Fine Arts in Russia], edited with commentaries by V. Malinovsky, 2 vols., Moscow, 1990

Mariette 1741
P.J. Mariette, *Description sommaire des desseins des grands maîtres d'Italie, des Pays-Bas et de France du Cabinet de feu M. Crozat*, Paris, 1741

Mariette, *Abecedario* 1853–59
Abecedario de P.-J. Mariette et autres notes inédites de cet auteur sur les arts et les artistes, 5 vols.,

Paris, 1853–59 (Archives de l'art français, IV)

Marks 1986
Kh. Marks: "'Trompe l'œil' i 'Cognitio.' O nekotorykh kartinakh drezdenskoy vystavki 'Natyurmort i yego predmet'" ['Trompe l'œil' and 'Cognitio.' On Several Paintings from the Dresden Exhibition 'Still Life and Its Object'], in *Veshch v iskusstve* [The Object in Art], Moscow, 1986, pp. 121–22

Martin 1968
J.R. Martin: *The Ceiling Painting for the Jesuit Church in Antwerp*, in the series Corpus Rubenianum Ludwig Burchard, part I, Brussels, 1968

Martin 1972
R. Martin: *The Decorations for the Pompa Introitus Ferdinandi*, in the series Corpus Rubenianum Ludwig Burchard, part XVI, Brussels, 1972

Mauquoy-Hendrickx 1956
Marie Mauquoy-Hendrickx: *L'Iconographie d'Antoine van Dyck. Catalogue raisonné*, 2 vols., Brussels, 1956

McGrath 1997
E. McGrath: *Subjects from History*, 2 vols., in the series Corpus Rubenianum Ludwig Burchard, part XIII (I), London, 1997

Meulemeester 1984
J.Z. Meulemeester: *Jacob van Oost en het Zeventiende-eeuwse Brugge*, Bruges, 1984

van der Meulen 1975
M. van der Meulen: *Petrus Paulus Rubens Antiquarius, Collector and Copyist of Antique Gems*, Alphen aan de Rijn, 1975

van der Meulen 1995
M. van der Meulen: *Copies after the Antique*, 3 vols., in the series Corpus Rubenianum Ludwig Burchard, part XXII, II: Catalogue, London, 1995

Michel 1771
J.F.M. Michel: *Histoire de la vie de P.P. Rubens*, Brussels, 1771

Miesel 1963
V.H. Miesel: "Rubens' Study Drawings after Ancient Sculpture," *Gazette des Beaux-Arts*, May–June 1963

Millar 1982
Van Dyck in England, exh. cat.
by O. Millar, London National
Portrait Gallery, 1982

Millar 1994
Oliver Millar: "Philip, Lord
Wharton, and his Collection of
Portraits," *The Burlington
Magazine*, XXXVI (August 1994),
pp. 517–30

de Mirimonde 1966
A.P. de Mirimonde: "Les
Allégories politiques de
'L'occasion' de Frans Francken
II," *Gazette des Beaux-Arts*,
March 1966, pp. 129–44, fig. 2

de Mirimonde 1967
A.P. de Mirimonde: "Frans
Francken II et Louis XIII:
L'Allégorie pour la prise de la
Rochelle," *Jaarboek van het
Koninklijk Museum voor Schone
Kunsten Antwerpen*, 1967,
pp. 117–30, fig. 1

Mitsch 1977
Mitsch in *Peter Paul Rubens.
1577–1640. Ausstellung zur 400
Wiederkehr seines Geburtstages*,
exh. cat., Vienna,
Kunsthistorisches Museum,
1977

Monballieu 1970
A. Monballieu: "Bij de
iconografie van Rubens'
Rockoxepitafium," *Jaarboek van
het Koninklijk Museum voor
Schone Kunsten*, Antwerp, 1970,
pp. 133–155

Muller 1989
J.M. Muller: *Rubens: The Artist
as Collector*, Princeton NJ, 1989

Müller-Hofstede 1962
J. Müller-Hofstede: "Zur
Antwerpener Frühzeit von P.P.
Rubens," *Münchener Jahrbuch
der bildenden Kunst*, series III, 13
(1962)

Müller-Hofstede 1965
J. Müller-Hofstede: "Beiträge
zum zeichnerischen Werk von
Rubens," *Wallraf-Richartz
Jahrbuch*, XXVII (1965),
pp. 259–356

Müller-Hofstede 1968
J. Müller-Hofstede: "Zur
Kopfstudie im Werk von
Rubens," *Wallraf-Richartz-
Jahrbuch*, XXX (1968)

Müller-Hofstede 1977
J. Müller-Hofstede: *Peter Paul
Rubens, 1577–1640, Katalog I:*

*Rubens in Italien: Gemälde,
Ölskizzen, Zeichnungen*, exh.
cat., Cologne, Kunsthaus, 1977

Museum Catalogue 1904
*Katalog Muzeya Imperatorskogo
Obshchestva pooshchreniya
khudozhestv* [Catalogue of the
Museum of the Imperial Society
for the Encouragement of the
Arts], St. Petersburg, 1904

Neverov 1979
O. Neverov: "Gems in the
Collection of Rubens," *The
Burlington Magazine*, CXXI (July
1979), pp. 424–32

Neverov 1981
O. Neverov: "Reznyye kamni v
sobranii Rubensa" [Carved
Gems in the Collection of
Rubens], *Zapadnoyevropeyskoye
iskusstvo XVII veka* [seventeenth-
century Western European Art],
Leningrad, 1981, pp. 63–77

Panfilova 1955
O.I. Panfilova: "Eskiz Van
Deyka k portretu kardinala
Bentivolyo" [Van Dyck's Sketch
for the Portrait of Cardinal
Bentivoglio], *Soobshcheniya
Gosudarstvennogo Ermitazha*
[Bulletin of the State
Hermitage], 7 (1955), pp. 36f.

Panofsky 1966
E. Panofsky: " 'Good
Government' or Fortune?",
Gazette des Beaux-Arts,
December 1966, pp. 319–20

Paskevich Collection 1885
*Katalog predmetam iskusstva,
sostavlyayushchim sobraniye
knyazya F. I. Paskevicha*
[Catalogue of Works of Art
Composing the Collection of
Prince F.I. Paskevich],
St. Petersburg, 1885

Pérez Sanchez 1964
A. Pérez Sanchez: "Dos
importantes pinturas del
Barroco – Una 'Muerte de
Seneca' de Rubens
reencontrada," *Archivo Español
de Arte*, CXLV (1964), pp. 7–12

de Piles 1677
R. de Piles: *Conversations sur la
connaissance de la peinture et sur
le jugement qu'on doit faire des
tableaux. Ou par occasion il est
parlé de la vie de Rubens et de
quelques-uns de ses plus beaux
ouvrages*, Paris, 1677

de Poorter 1988
N. de Poorter: "Rubens 'onder

de wapenen'. De Antwerpse
schilders als gildebroders van
de kolviers in de eerste helft van
de 17de eeuw," *Jaarboek van het
Koninklijk Museum voor Schone
Kunsten Antwerpen*, 1988, p. 207

Prakhov 1907
A. Prakhov:
"Khudozhestvennoye sobraniye
knyazey Yusupovykh.
Nemetskaya shkola. Troger,
Simon" [The Art Collection of
the Princes Yusupov. German
School. Troger, Simon],
*Khudozhestvennyye sokrovishcha
Rossii* [Art Treasures of Russia],
no. 1, St. Petersburg, 1907

Prohaska 1977
Prohaska in *Peter Paul Rubens.
1577–1640. Ausstellung zur 400
Wiederkehr seines Geburtstages*,
exh. cat., Vienna,
Kunsthistorisches Museum,
1977

Randall 1985
Richard H. Randall, Jr.:
Masterpieces of Ivory, New York,
1985

Raspe 1791
R.E. Raspe: *A Descriptive
Catalogue of a General Collection
of Ancient and Modern Engraved
Gems and Cameos as well as
Intaglios, Taken from the Most
Celebrated Cabinets in Europe;
and Cast in Coloured Pastes,
White Enamel, and Sulphur, by
James Tassie, Modeller*, London,
1791

Réau 1957
L. Réau: *Iconographie de l'art
chrètien*, vol. II, *Iconographie de
la Bible. II. Nouveau Testament*,
Paris, 1957

Remy 1767
P. Remy: *Catalogue raisonné des
tableaux, dessins ... dans le
Cabinet de feu M. de Julienne*,
Paris, 1767

Renger 1997
K. Renger: *Bayerische
Staatsgemäldesammlungen. Die
Pranke des Löwen. Rubens –
Skizzen aus St. Petersburg und
München*, exh. cat., Munich,
Neue Pinakothek, 1997–98

Robels 1950
H. Robels: *Die Niederländische
Tradition in der Kunst des
Rubens*, Cologne, 1950

Robels 1989
H. Robels: *Frans Snyders'*

*Stilleben und Tiermaler,
1579–1657*, Munich, 1989

Roeder-Baumbach 1943
Irmengard von Roeder-
Baumbach: *Versieringen bij blijde
inkomsten, gebruikt im de
zuidelijke Nederlanden gedurende
de 16e n 17e eeuw*, Antwerp, 1943

Rome 1995
*Federico II e l'Italia. Percorsi,
luoghi e strumenti*, exh. cat.,
Rome, Palazzo Venezia, 1995,
p. 256, no. V. 25

Rooses 1886–92
Max Rooses: *L'Œuvre de P.P.
Rubens: Histoire et description de
ses tableaux et dessins*, 5 vols.,
Antwerp, 1886–92

Rooses 1903
M. Rooses: "De Teekeningen
der Vlaamsche Meesters: P.P.
Rubens; De Leerlingen van
Rubens; Jordaens en andere
Historischilders der XVII
eeuw," *Onze Kunst*, 2 (1903),
pp. 1–9, 133–42, 151–61

Rooses, Ruelens 1887–1909
M. Rooses, C. Ruelens:
Correspondance de Rubens ...,
Anvers, 1887–1909

Rosenberg 1921
A. Rosenberg: *Peter Paul
Rubens, des Meisters Gemälde in
538 Abbildungen, herausgegeben
von Rudolf Oldenbourg*, Stuttgart,
1921, p. 7

Rosenberg 1922
M. Rosenberg: *Der Goldschmiede
Merkzeichen*, I, Frankfurt am
Main, 1922

Rosenberg 1925
M. Rosenberg: *Der Goldschmiede
Merkzeichen*, II, Frankfurt am
Main, 1925

Roy 1992
A. Roy in *Theodoor van Thulden.
Un peintre baroque du cercle
de Rubens*, exh. cat.,
's-Hertogenbosch,
Noordbrabants Museum;
Strasbourg, Musée des Beaux-
Arts, 1991–92

Schädler 1973
A. Schädler: *Georg Petel.
1601/2–1634*, Berlin, 1973

Scheller 1977
R.W. Scheller: *Nicolaas Rockox
als Oudheidkundige*, Antwerp,
1978

Schmidt 1916
J.A. Schmidt: "Dar V.P. Zurova
Imperatorksomu Ermitazhu" [A
Gift from V. P. Zurov to the
Imperial Hermitage], *Staryye
gody* [Days of Yore], March 1916

Semenov 1906
P.P. Semenov: *Catalogue de la
collection Semenov à Saint-
Pétersbourg*, St. Petersburg,
1906

Shlikevich 1987
Y.A. Shlikevich: "Gruppa
slonovoy kosti 'Amur i
Psikheya'" [The Ivory Group
'Cupid and Psyche'],
*Soobshcheniya Gosudarstvennogo
Ermitazha* [Bulletin of the State
Hermitage], 52 (1987)

Shtegman 1940
V.K. Shtegman: "Blyudo reznoy
slonovoy kosti raboty Mikhaelya
Maukhera v sobranii
Gosudarstvennogo Ermitazha"
[A Carved Ivory Dish by Michael
Maucher, in the Collection of
the State Hermitage], in *Trudy
Otdela zapadnoyevropeyskogo
iskusstva Gosudarstvennogo
Ermitazha* [Papers of the
Department of Western
European Art of the State
Hermitage], I, Leningrad, 1940

Shtegman-Gayeva 1949
V.K. Shtegman-Gayeva:
"Vlyaniye Rubensa na iskusstvo
rezby iz slonovoy kosti" [The
Influence of Rubens on the Art
of Ivory Carving], in *Trudy
Otdela zapadnoyevropeyskogo
iskusstva Gosudarstvennogo
Ermitazha* [Papers of the
Department of Western
European Art of the State
Hermitage],III, Leningrad,
1949

von Simson 1936
O.G. von Simson: *Zur
Genealogie der weltlichen
Apotheose im Barock, besonders
der Medicigalerie des P.P. Rubens*,
Strasbourg, 1936

von Simson 1996
O. von Simson: *Peter Paul
Rubens (1577–1640). Humanist,
Maler und Diplomat*, Mainz,
1996

Smith 1829–42
J. Smith: *A Catalogue Raisonné
of the Works of the Most Eminent
Dutch, Flemish and French
Painters ...*, 8 parts and
Supplement, London, 1829–42

Somoff 1901
A. Somoff: *Ermitage Impérial. Catalogue de la galerie des tableaux. Ecoles néerlandaises et école allemande*, St. Petersburg, 1901

Spicer 1985–86
Joaneath Spicer: "Unrecognized Studies for Van Dyck's Iconography in the Hermitage," *Master Drawings*, 2–24, no. 4 (1985–86), pp. 537–44

Spiessens 1990
G. Spiessens: *Leven en werk van de Antwerpse schilder Alexander Adriaenssen (1587–1661)*, Brussels, 1990

Stechow 1968
W. Stechow: *Rubens and the Classical Tradition*, Cambridge MA, 1968

Stuttgart 1977
Die Zeit der Staufer. Geschichte-Kunst-Kultur, exh. cat., Stuttgart, Württembergisches Landes-museum, 1977, vols. I–II

Sutton 1993
P.C. Sutton: "Introduction: Painting in the Age of Rubens," *The Age of Rubens*, exh. cat., Boston, Museum of Fine Arts, 1993

Theuerkauff 1964
C. Theuerkauff: *Studien zur Elfenbeinplastik des Barock*, diss., Freiburg, 1964

Theuerkauff-Liederwald 1968
A.E. Theuerkauff-Liederwald: "Der Römer, Studien zu einer Glasform," *Journal of Glass Studies. The Corning Museum of Glass, Corning, New York*, X, no. 8 (1968), pp. 114–55

Thiery 1987
Y. Thiery, M.K. de Meerendre: *Les Peintres flamands de paysage au XVIIe siècle. La baroque anversoise et l'école bruxelloise*, Brussels, 1987

Thomas 1998
W. Thomas in *Albert et Isabelle. 1598–1621*, exh. cat., Brussels, Musées Royaux d'Art et d'Histoire, 1998

Thomas 1999
W. Thomas in *El Arte en la carte de los archiduques Alberto de Austria e Isabel Clara Eugenia (1598–1633). Un Reino Imaginado*, exh. cat. Madrid, Palacio Real, 1999

Thuillier 1969
J. Thuillier: "La 'Galérie de Medicis' de Rubens et sa genèse: un document inédit," *Revue de l'Art*, 4 (1969), pp. 52–62

Tonnochy 1935
A.B. Tonnochy: "Jewels and Engraved Gems at Windsor Castle," *The Connoisseur*, May 1935, pp. 11–12

Trubnikov 1908
A. Trubnikov: "Gollandskiye peyzazhi" [Dutch Landscapes], *Staryye gody* [Days of Yore], November–December, 1908, p. 700

Vandenbroeck 1985
P. Vandenbroeck: "Bulbo Significans. Die Eule als Schlechtigheit und Torheit, vor allem in der niederlandischen und deutschen Bilddarstellung und bei Jheronimus Bosch", in *Jaarboek van het Koninklijk Museum voor Schone Kunsten*, Antwerp, 1985

Varshavskaya 1963
M.Ya. Varshavskaya: *Van Deyk. Kartiny v Ermitazhe* [Van Dyck. Paintings in the Hermitage], Leningrad, 1963

Varshavskaya 1967
M.Ya.Varchavskaya: "Certains traits particuliers de la decoration d'Anvers par Rubens pour l'Entrée triomphale de l'Infant-Cardinal Ferdinand en 1635," *Bulletin des Musées Royaux des Beaux-Arts de Belgique*, 1967

Varshavskaya 1975
M.Ya. Varshavskaya: *Kartiny Rubensa v Ermitazhe* [Paintings by Rubens in the Hermitage], Leningrad, 1975; English [*Rubens in Soviet Museums*] and French editions, updated and with additional commentaries by N. Gritsay, Leningrad, 1989

Vergara 1982
L. Vergara: *Rubens and the Poetics of Landscape*, New Haven CT and London, 1982

Vertue I
Vertue III
George Vertue: "Notebooks I–VI," Walpole Society, XVIII (1929–30) [I]; XXII (1933–34) [III]; all six vols. reprinted 1968

Vey 1962
H. Vey: *Die Zeichnungen Anton*

van Dyck, 2 vols., Brussels, 1962

Vlieghe 1972–73
H. Vlieghe: *Saints*, 2 vols., in the series Corpus Rubenianum Ludwig Burchard, part VIII, London, 1972–73

Vlieghe 1987
H. Vlieghe: *Portraits of Identified Sitters painted in Antwerp*, in the series Corpus Rubenianum Ludwig Burchard, part XIX(2), London, 1987

Waagen 1853
G.F. Waagen: *Kunstwerke und Künstler in Deutschland*, Leipzig, 1853, vol. I

Waagen 1864
G.F. Waagen: *Die Gemäldesammlung in der Kaiserlichen Ermitage zu St. Petersburg nebst Bemerkungen über andere dortige Kunstsammlungen*, Munich, 1864, 2nd edn, St. Petersburg, 1870

Wentzel 1943
H. Wentzel: "Eine Kamee aus Lothringen und andere Kunstkammer Gemmen," *Jahrbuch der Preussische Kunstsammlungen*, 64 (1943), pp. 1–6

Wentzel 1956
H. Wentzel: "Die Kamee mit dem Agyptischen Joseph in Leningrad (Zur Bildmontage und 'Protorenaissance' im Kameenschnitte des 13. Jh.)," *Kunstgeschichtliche Studien für Hans Kauffmann*, Berlin, 1956, pp. 85–105

Western European Drawing 1981
The State Hermitage Museum Drawings, Western European Drawings, Leningrad, 1981

Wheelock 1990
A.K. Wheelock in *Anthony van Dyck*, exh. cat., Washington, D.C., National Gallery of Art, 1990

Wilmers 1996
G. Wilmers: *Cornelis Schut (1597–1655): A Flemish Painter of the High Baroque* (Pictura Nova I), Turnhout, 1996

Wirenius-Matzoulevitch 1928
J. Wirenius-Matzoulevitch: "Quelques camées inédits du Musée de l'Ermitage," *Aréthuse*, no. 2, 3e trimestre (1928), pp. 100–16

Yaremich 1949
S.P. Yaremich: "K voprosu ob ikonografii Rubensa v svyazi s odnoy rannoy rabotoy van Deyka" [On the Iconography of Rubens in Connection with an Early Work by van Dyck], *Trudy otdela zapadnoyevropeyskogo iskusstva Gosudarstvennogo Ermitazha* [Papers of the Department of Western European Art of the State Hermitage], vol. III, 1949, pp. 3–15

Yegorova 1998
K. Yegorova: *Gosudarstvennyy muzey izobraziteľnykh iskusstv im. A.S. Pushkina. Niderlandy XV–XVI veka, Flandriya XVII–XVIII veka, Beľgiya XIX–XX veka. Sobraniye zhivopisi* [The Pushkin Museum of Fine Arts. The Netherlands Fifteenth–Sixteenth Century, Flanders Seventeenth–Eighteenth Century, Belgium Nineteenth–Twentieth Century. Collection of Paintings], Moscow, 1998

Youssoupoff 1839
Musée du prince Youssoupoff, St. Petersburg, 1839

Yusupov Gallery 1920
Gosudarstvennyy muzeynyy fond. Katalog khudozhestvennykh proizvedeniy byvshey Yusupovskoy galerei [State Museums Fund. Catalogue of Works of Art in the Former Yusupov Gallery], Petrograd, 1920